Saint-Julien

Léoville-Las-Cases

Langoa-Barton and Léoville-Barton

Talbot

D206

D101

Gloria

Ducru-Beaucaillou

Beychevelle

Lagrange

D2

Gruaud-Larose

Saint-Pierre

0   1 kilometre
0   1 mile

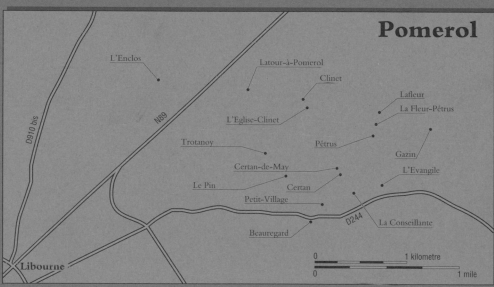

Pomerol

L'Enclos

Latour-à-Pomerol

Clinet

Lafleur

La Fleur-Pétrus

L'Eglise-Clinet

N89

D910 bis

Trotanoy

Pétrus

Gazin

Certan-de-May

L'Evangile

Le Pin

Certan

Petit-Village

D244

La Conseillante

Beauregard

Libourne

0   1 kilometre
0   1 mile

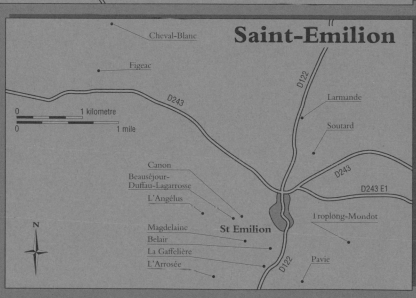

Saint-Emilion

Cheval-Blanc

Figeac

D243

D122

Larmande

Soutard

0   1 kilometre
0   1 mile

D243

D243 E1

Canon

Beauséjour-
Duffau-Lagarrosse

L'Angélus

Troplong-Mondot

Magdelaine

St Emilion

Belair

La Gaffelière

L'Arrosée

D122

Pavie

N

GARONNE

GRANDS
VINS

GRANDS VINS

THE FINEST CHÂTEAUX OF BORDEAUX AND THEIR WINES

CLIVE COATES MW

Weidenfeld and Nicolson

London

CONTENTS

PREFACE

In my book *Claret*, published in 1982, there were some 53 Château profiles and twenty years of Vintage Assessments. More than a decade on, *Grands Vins* is not so much a second edition as an entirely new work. Not only have the existing profiles been completely revised and updated, but the scope has been considerably extended. Here you will find articles on 100 different properties, including those producing white Graves and Sauternes as well as red wines, plus vintages which extend back from the present day to 1928.

As far as I am aware, with the exception of a few concentrating separately on the top growths, no books have been produced which have explored in depth the histories of the leading Bordeaux estates and described the personalities and techniques behind the wines of today, let alone with a full series of tasting notes on all, or most, of the wines which are likely to be in circulation. This is the object of this book. It is not intended as a guide to the region in general. It is simply a celebration of the top properties and their great wines.

There is today a great deal more documentary evidence available to the historian than there was a decade ago when I completed *Claret*, let alone the mid-1960s when I first started to write about the Bordeaux châteaux and their wines. Many châteaux have commissioned research into their archives. Scarce nineteenth-century books have been republished in facsimile edition. Other evidence has come to light. Simply by covering more ground I have been able to relate a piece of information unearthed on one property to illuminate a grey area in the history of another. In doing so, a few hoary items of legend, long since passed down from one writer to another, have been shown to be untrue. A shame that it spoils a good story; but at least what is left is closer to the truth.

A great deal has happened in the Bordeaux region in the last ten years. There has been a series of large, successful red wine harvests unparalleled in recent times. Perfectionistic policies such as a rigorous selection, the production of a second wine, a 'green harvest' - crop thinning in July - and ever greater control of the viticultural and wine-making processes are now commonplace not just at the top of the hierarchy but even at *cru bourgeois* level. All this, coupled with an increased average age of the *vignoble* as the plantations which followed the great February 1956 frost have reached full maturity, has helped to produce a degree of quality and consistency which the Bordeaux region has never hitherto enjoyed. Moreover, on the white wine front a welcome revival of the fortunes of Sauternes and a revolution in the techniques of dry white wine-making have led to a renaissance in the quality of these wines which now matches that of the reds.

Sadly, not all the developments of the last ten years have been as encouraging. High opening prices have produced profits for the château owners but have led to a lack of reward for the merchant or wholesaler who is sitting on the stock in the medium term. There is little incentive for them to finance the wine's maturity. The result has been an increasing reliance on the *en primeur* or 'futures' campaigns. Without this yearly injection of cash flow one suspects a lot of wine merchants would simply be unable to play the fine wine market. One dreads to speculate what would be the effect of three poor vintages in quick succession, as has happened, and might happen again. Indeed, though it is early to pronounce definitely on the 1993 vintage as this book goes to press, it looks as if this has happened.

Another effect of high prices at the château end of the pipeline has been to increase to astronomical levels the nominal value of these estates. When properties change hands they now do so at levels way beyond what even the wildest imagination might have predicted only a couple of decades ago. When Château Margaux changed hands in 1976 the price was said to have been 72 million French francs (about £8 million). When Allied-Lyons bought the Pearson's share of Latour thirteen years later this estate was valued at £100 million, almost fourteen times as much. High levels of inheritance and profits tax, plus a tax on inventory, have combined with these high prices to mean that only large institutions, or millionaires, can today afford to invest in these top properties. More and more are now owned by insurance companies or other conglomerations whose chief interests are not in wine. One consequence is the ready availability of the increasingly expensive investment necessary to make good wine. Another benefit is that these concerns are able to take a long-term view. But the risk is the eventual disappearance of the passionately committed owner and his replacement by someone who, however capable, is simply no more than a manager. However free the hired hand may feel himself to be there is always the temptation of targets and budgets to be achieved, and perhaps bonuses to be gained thereby. How is this going to affect the difficult choices which inevitably have to be made during the course of the creation of a *grand vin*? The decision to include a marginal vat in the top wine may only be noticed by a few at the outset. It may be put down to a temporary aberration in the way the young wine has presented itself. But ten years down the road, when the bottle is actually drunk and fails to live up to expectation, the customer may feel cheated, and reputations will suffer.

Grands Vins could not have been written without the help, generosity, hospitality, and most importantly, the encouragement of the proprietors themselves. At the outset of my career as a wine writer, I knocked on the door of a famous Médoc château, having previously written to the owner announcing my intention of making a vertical tasting of his wine. The warmth of the reception, the liberality with which he opened bottles spanning several decades and the kindness he proffered towards someone who was totally unknown, at a time when any sort of comparative tasting, either vertically (of one property) or horizontally (of one vintage) was very much rarer than it is today, were infinitely greater than I had any right to expect. This sort of welcome was often to be repeated in the years to come. Without it, my knowledge of the wines of Bordeaux would be infinitely the poorer.

Similarly, a huge vote of thanks must be extended to an unofficial tasting team comprised of friends in the wine trade in Britain. This group meets a number of times a year, each member making half a dozen or so bottles available so that all can profit from the pooled experience. The horizontal vintage tastings in this book would not have been nearly as comprehensive without the generosity of Simon Loftus and Alastair Marshall of Adams, Richard Wheeler and John Thorogood of Lay and Wheeler, Bill Baker of Reid Wines, John Avery of Avery's of Bristol, Richard Peat of Corney and Barrow, Simon Cock of Heyman Brothers, Nick Davies, late of the Hungerford Wine Company, Mark Savage of Windrush Wines, Jasper Morris of Morris and Verdin, Sebastian Payne of the Wine Society, Giles de Maré, Stephen Browett and Lindsay Hamilton of Farr Vintners, and Andrew Bruce of Andrew Bruce Wines.

Many other individuals or groups have been equally generous in inviting me to participate in other extensive horizontal or vertical tastings in England, in France, in the USA and elsewhere. I am particularly indebted to Liz and Mike Berry of La Vigneronne and Mark Reynier of La Réserve in London, to Clive Sharples of Coningsby, Lincolnshire, to Bob Feinn of Mount Carmel Wines, Connecticut, and the rest of the New Haven wine weekend group, to Jack and Thelma Hewitt of South Woodstock, Vermont, to Bipin Desai of Riverside, California, to Marvin Overton of Fort Worth, Texas, to Stephen Kaplan of Chicago, to John McNulty of Philadelphia, to Bob Paul and Robert Maliner of Miami, to George Sape and Daniel Oliveros of New York, to Murphy Clark of Medford, Oregon, to Jan Paulson of Paulson Fine Wines of Germany, to Hardy Rodenstock, and to Jean-Michel Arcaute and Michel Rolland in Bordeaux, who were kind enough to invite me to their fortieth birthday party, and a tasting of 1947s to celebrate, in December 1987. To all of these, and to the many others who have invited me to their tastings or asked me to speak to a range of wines, I offer my thanks.

Grands Vins was conceived and originally written as a series of separate articles, so a certain amount of inevitable repetition will therefore become apparent to those who read the book from cover to cover. My apologies in advance. But I did not want to destroy the unity and entirety of each article by the removal of these duplications. Most of the articles originally appeared in the pages of my monthly magazine, *The Vine*; others variously in *Decanter* of London, in the *Quarterly Review of Wines of Boston*, the *Wine Enthusiast*, and the *Friends of Wine Magazine*, all in the USA, in *Decanter Oy* of Finland or in *Falstaff* of Vienna. To the editors of all these journals I again offer my thanks for their encouragement and support.

A WORD ABOUT THE MARKING SYSTEM

In principle I am against the indiscriminate allocation of marks to every single wine that is ever tasted. For a start it tends to make people forget that the appreciation of wine is personal and temperamental. Wine-tasting is a sensual process, and nothing is more subjective and individual as personal taste. A specific mark allocated to a wine, often made well in advance of the wine's optimum drinking, is merely one man's view of that wine and its potential. If it is not made within the context of a reasonable collection of peer groups it becomes of even less value to outsiders.

Secondly I find it personally impossible to conceive of the idea of an absolute mark. In my view marks can only be contextual. If one is marking a minor vintage, or a series of wines of minor pretention, one must applaud or criticize within the possibilities of that aspiration. A generic Bordeaux Rouge can be equally as fine, or as poor, within its context, as a top classified growth within *its* objectives.

This makes the allocation of marks to a vertical tasting somewhat of a pointless exercise. What are you awarding marks for? The wine being better or worse than the wine above, or good or bad within the context of the vintage? For this reason I have refrained from marking the vertical tastings in this book. I hope the comments, adulatory or disapproving, speak for themselves. The value judgements expressed – fine, good, not bad, and so on – refer to the wine within the context of the vintage.

Naturally, however, when I make a comprehensive horizontal tasting of a vintage, I award my own marks and these are reproduced here. They are out of twenty, a system I have used all my life (I have no objection to those who mark out of 100, but I personally find it somewhat unwieldy). My marks out of twenty correspond to the value judgements expressed in the text.

19.0–20.0	Excellent, the best
16.5–18.5	Very good to very fine indeed
15.0–16.0	Good to very good
13.5–14.5	Quite good
12.0–13.0	Not bad, average
10.0–11.5	Disappointing if not poor
Less than 10	Somewhat disagreeable, if not faulty

Optimum drinking: irrespective of when the tastings took place, the comments refer to the state of maturity of the wines concerned in the autumn of 1994, when this book first went to press.

BORDEAUX AND ITS WINES

Bordeaux is by far the largest fine wine region in France. It is also, arguably, the greatest, and as such, again a matter for dispute, the finest in the world. Bordeaux produces all the three main types of wine – red, dry white and luscious sweet white wine. At the top levels these are the most aristocratic, the most profound and the most sumptuous of all wines. Here the word 'breed', used to describe wines of the highest finesse and elegance, can be applied in the greatest numbers and with the most consistent regularity.

It is the number and variety of its finest wines that, for me, makes Bordeaux the most fascinating wine area of all. Burgundy has as many quality wine-growers and top domaines, but production is on a very much smaller scale: a few casks rather than several dozen *tonneaux*. One single vineyard, itself much less extensive than a Bordeaux estate, may in Burgundy be divided among a couple of dozen owners. In Bordeaux the vineyard will be in single hands and the economies of scale will make it much easier for the top growers to be as rigorous as possible in their selection of which *cuvée* will go into the *grand vin* and which will be rejected.

There are some 175 classed growths in Bordeaux: 60 Médocs, 28 Sauternes, 75 Saint-Emilions and a dozen Graves. Add to this the top wines of Pomerol – which has never been classified – and the best of the *bourgeois* estates, many of whom produce wine of similar quality, and you have perhaps 250 single wine names producing at the highest level. Multiply that figure by the number of vintages drinkable or not yet mature that may be on the market, and you will have upwards of 5,000 different wines. Each will be constantly changing as it gradually ages, acquiring further profundity, complexity and uniqueness of character as it does so. Every year a new crop will unleash another substantial batch to be appreciated.

But this is only the tip of the iceberg, perhaps 5 per cent – but as much as 26 million bottles in total – of the annual harvest. Underneath that lies the unsung Bordeaux – good, if not fine, but still worthy of recognition. Not perhaps the sort of wines to which wine writers will devote pages of purple prose, nor drinkers any abject ceremony, but bottle after bottle of the most part solidly dependable wine at prices we can all afford to dispense regularly.

Bordeaux is both a city and the name of wine. The city, eighth largest in France, and until recently one of its major ports, lies on a bend of the river Garonne in south-west France. The Garonne flows north-westwards from the middle of the Pyrenees into the Atlantic Ocean. Some ten kilometres north of Bordeaux it is joined by the last of its great tributaries, the river Dordogne. Together these form the estuary of the Gironde, from which comes the name of the *département* of which Bordeaux is the capital.

The Gironde *département* (with the exception of the coastal area) corresponds with the wine-growing region of Bordeaux. Roughly 100,000 hectares of land are planted with vines, producing, during the last decade, an average of over 4 million hectolitres of *appellation contrôlée* or AC wine per annum, about 22 per cent of the total AC production of France. This is approximately twice as much as that of Burgundy (including Beaujolais) and half as much again as the Rhône Valley. For example, Château Brane-Cantenac, one of the largest of the classed growths, produces over 40,000 cases of wine, as much as the total production of Hermitage in the Rhône Valley.

Almost 75 per cent of the AC Gironde harvest is red wine. This makes the Bordeaux area by far the largest quality red wine area of France. The Gironde's production of almost 4 million hectolitres of AC red wine dwarfs that of Burgundy's mere one million hectolitres of red (Pinot Noir) AC wine.

Unlike Burgundy – indeed unlike much of the rest of France – Bordeaux is an area of largely proprietorial rather than peasant ownership, and hence is one of relatively large estates, often long-established, self-sufficient in wine terms and which market their wines under their own 'château' names. Cocks and Féret, the 'Bible of Bordeaux', lists some 4,200 single vineyards and the proprietors thereof, and this itself represents only the cream of around 21,000 growers who officially declare a crop each vintage.

A BRIEF HISTORY

In books devoted solely to the wines of Bordeaux, such as Edmund Penning-Rowsell's *The Wines of Bordeaux* and Pamela Vandyke Price's *The Wines of the Graves*, the history of the region and its produce has been covered with great depth and authority. I shall not attempt to emulate them. I refer readers to both these lucid accounts and acknowledge my debt to them in preparing the résumé which follows.

It seems likely, says Penning-Rowsell, that Bordeaux was a wine-trading centre before it was a vine-growing region. The western side of the region is very flat, and in early Roman times it would have been marshy, covered in forest and infested with mosquitoes. The soil was poor and the climate less propitious for the cultivation of the vine than the higher ground, the *Haut Pays*, further to the south and west. At the start Bordeaux was an *emporium*, important primarily as a port. It is therefore probable that it was not until the third century AD that the vine began to be widely planted in the locality. Ausonius, poet, consul and tutor to Roman emperors, owned vineyards in the area in the fourth century, though whether this was at Château Ausone is a matter for dispute. In one of his poems he refers not to the Dordogne but to the Garonne flowing gently at the bottom of his garden. Yet the most impressive Roman ruins outside Bordeaux are to be found in the grounds of Château La Gaffelière, at the foot of the Château Ausone escarpment.

Historical details during the next several hundred years, as elsewhere in the Europe of the Dark Ages, are sparse. There was an expansion of the vineyard in the eleventh century, but it was the arrival of the English after the marriage of the redoubtable Eleanor of Aquitaine to Henry Plantagenet in 1152 that had the profoundest effect. For three centuries the Bordeaux vineyards came under the jurisdiction of the English crown. England became the Gironde's most important export market, and each year, shortly after the harvest, before the winter had set in, a vast fleet would transport the cream of the crop, first chiefly to Bristol and Southampton, later to London. During the thirteenth, fourteenth and fifteenth centuries the vine gradually replaced all other forms of agriculture in the area, and though at first most of the wine shipped to England seems to have come from further north, from the Poitou and the Charente, Bordeaux soon became the major point of departure. For many hundreds of years, long after the English left in 1453, wine was France's leading export, Britain its most important customer, and Bordeaux the chief exporter.

Not all the wine exported was strictly 'Bordeaux', however; much was the produce of the *Haut Pays* – wine of the Dordogne, the Lot, the Tarn and the upper Garonne. These had to pay a tax, higher if from the French side of whatever was the border between the French and the English at the time, and faced other restrictions, such as being embargoed from shipment until after the Gironde harvest had left. Nevertheless, the whole of the South-West looked to England, and later to the Low Countries, Hamburg and the Baltic ports, for its market. Communications overland were cumbersome, hazardous and prolonged, and the French crown bought its wine from nearer at hand, from the upper Loire, Champagne and Burgundy.

Sensibly, even after the expulsion of the English after the battle of Castillon in 1453, the French kings took care not to disrupt the Bordeaux trade. The local inhabitants had never considered themselves anything other than Gascon, neither English nor French. The privileges the Bordeaux merchants had enjoyed under the English were confirmed, and after an initial bout of petty commercial warfare the French were forced to realize that they were now competing in their most important export market with wines from the Iberian peninsula and elsewhere.

The English remained customers for the finest Bordeaux wines even after the rise of the Dutch as an economic power in the seventeenth century, and the various economic treaties discriminating against the French and in favour of Portugal which culminated in the Methuen Treaty in 1703. The Dutch became Bordeaux's major customer, but their requirements were for cheap wines, largely white, much of which was re-exported to Scandinavia and the Hanseatic ports.

The last quarter of the seventeenth century and the first half of the eighteenth was the period of the establishment of most of the great estates, what were to become the *crus classés* in 1855. Prior to this period, the quality red wines had come from the upper Graves, surrounding the town of Bordeaux. Dutch engineers, with their experience in the Low Countries, drained the Médoc, formerly a land of marshes liable to widespread flooding at the time of neap tides, thus exposing the mounds of almost pure gravel, excellent for the vine, on which the great properties are centred to this day.

Château Haut-Brion in the Graves, then owned by the influential Pontac family, was the first of the Bordeaux estates to achieve renown and the first in English literature to be specifically named, Samuel Pepys enjoying the wine at the Royal Oak Tavern in 1663. Forty years later the *London Gazette* advertised the sale of Lafite, Margaux and Latour wines, as well as 'Pontac', looted from ships captured in the War of the Spanish Succession. These estates were all owned by a new aristocracy, the *noblesse de la robe*. As the seventeenth century had progressed, a new breed of moneyed classes had replaced the old *noblesse d'épée*. These families, of largely merchant origin, owed their power to their place in the Bordeaux *parlement*, their wealth to their land. Increasingly during the eighteenth century, suitable terrain in the Médoc was converted into monocultural vineyards, and after the French Revolution this expansion continued in Saint-Emilion, Pomerol and the Léognan part of the Graves.

The Revolution and the Napoleonic wars which followed, though serious for the wine trade, left the top growths relatively unscathed. A few proprietors were guillotined, others emigrated and had their estates sequestrated, as were those vineyards in ecclesiastical ownership. Though business suffered, there was little social upheaval. The great estates preserved their unity and remained the property of the moneyed classes. Bordeaux is a region of large domaines, vinously self-sufficient, *bourgeois* in ownership; Burgundy is a region of much-fragmented vineyards in largely peasant possession. It is this which has caused the great difference between Bordeaux and Burgundy which continues to this day.

The nineteenth century saw three major scourges in the vineyard, the arrival of a new generation of proprietors, industrialists or those who had made their money out of the wine trade itself, and the beginning of the adoption of modern mechanical and scientific methods of tilling the land and making the wine.

The first of the great natural disasters was the arrival of oidium in the early 1850s. Oidium, or powdery mildew, is a cryptogamic disease which affects both leaves and grapes. The leaves shrivel and drop off; the fruit is split and dries up. Though the solution, the application of sulphur, was soon discovered, production was decimated and prices rose steeply, never to return to their previous levels.

Though phylloxera, a member of the aphid family, was first discovered in France in 1863, it did not make its appearance in the Gironde until 1869, and did not really begin to cause serious damage in the Médoc until a decade later. Phylloxera is the greatest pest of them all for, unlike oidium and mildew which, like a spring frost attack, bad weather during the flowering or hail in late summer, only affect a single year's harvest; the phylloxera kills the plant itself. Potentially its ravages are catastrophic. It is not for nothing that its cognomen is *Vastastrix*. Phylloxera arrived in Europe from America, and it was in America that the imagination of the Bordeaux viticulturalist Leo Laliman found the solution to the problem, astonishingly as early as 1871. This was to graft the noble European varieties of the *vinifera* vine onto American non-*vinifera* rootstocks. Opposition to this radical proposal seemed solid until, despairing of finding an alternative solution, the growers had to face the inevitable. By 1882 97.5 per cent of the Gironde had been overrun by the louse, but it was only gradually, far more gradually in the top states than most people realize, that grafted vines began to be introduced. As late as the 1890s *vignes françaises* were still being planted. Château Latour did not begin to plant grafted vines seriously until 1901 and it took a couple of decades completely to replace the non-grafted old French vines.

Meanwhile Bordeaux had been hit by the third of its plagues. Downy mildew or peronospera arrived in the South of France in 1882, and seems to have spread rapidly west to the Gironde. Like oidium it is a cryptogamic disease, but affecting mainly the leaves. An antidote, copper sulphate solution, was soon discovered, and by 1888 the outbreak was under control.

As important as this succession of natural disasters were the economic consequences. Bordeaux, indeed the whole of France south of Paris, had many more hectares of land under vine in the 1850s than in 1900, even today. In hard-nosed financial terms the arrival of phylloxera could be termed salutary. Uneconomic vineyards were allowed to decay, and their owners and workers forced to seek alternative employment. The human corollary, compounded by the Franco-Prussian War and by a recession in wine prices which remained until the mid-1950s, is incalculable. This cloud of misery, which hung over the peasant *vigneron* for three successive generations, still continues as a folk memory.

It was not just the smallholder who was affected by this lack of prosperity. Though Bordeaux was not in general as badly off as elsewhere in France, owing to the reputation of its wines and the fact that the majority of its reds could be held to mature in bottle, nevertheless it was more dependent than other areas on its export markets. Demand from Germany, a major customer for the cheaper wines, collapsed after the First World War, the British market was moribund before the war and declined afterwards, and sales to pre-Prohibition America were negligible. The world recession of the 1930s, followed by the Second World War, almost forced even well-known classed growths out of business.

All this seems hardly credible today. Rising standards of living, appreciation of wine as part of a good living, a widening of the consumer base and the emergence of countries such as the United States as customers for the top growths have transformed the scene. At the bottom level of the pyramid a minor change in the ratio of the price of Bordeaux Rouge to Côtes du Rhône or Beaujolais, coupled with a plentiful harvest, can still cause problems. Prices of first growths and the best of the rest have been rising at an alarming rate alongside a succession of very good but also highly plentiful vintages. It is now apparent that even the 'second-best' Bordeaux are wines which most of us can only afford to drink rarely. And with prices of new wines almost as expensive as those now reaching maturity it hardly seems worthwhile to bother to buy them *en primeur*.

One benefit, though, has been that the whole of Bordeaux, from first growth to the regional co-operative, is making better wine. Scientific progress in vineyard and *chai*, the arrival of the trained oenologue (wine chemist), the financial means and the moral duty to make a rigorous selection of the *grand vin* have led to fewer poor vintages, more wine and a higher quality product. Some of those proprietors who price the best wines may believe they can get away with murder. At least those who market them are fully aware of the competition from elsewhere.

Red Wines

There are two quite separate wine-making districts in Bordeaux as far as the top red wines are concerned. West of the Garonne and Gironde, on a low-lying, gravel-covered peninsula, stretch the vineyards of the Graves and the Médoc, on either side of Bordeaux. The best wines of the Médoc come from six communes, each of which has its own particular character, four of which are described in detail in the following pages. The coastal parishes of Margaux, Saint-Julien, Pauillac and Saint-Estèphe contain the majority of the most respected growths. In the Graves, the best wines are found in Léognan, and closer to Bordeaux in Pessac and Talence.

Fifty kilometres away, north of the Dordogne river, lies a quite separate region covering the wines of Saint-Emilion and Pomerol which, in their own ways, are the equal of the Médoc and the Graves. Saint-Emilion itself is divided into an easterly section, known as the *Côtes*-Saint-Emilion, on the slopes around the town of Saint-Emilion itself, and the *Graves*-Saint-Emilion, four kilometres to the west on the border of Pomerol. Pomerol, north of the port of Libourne, has only recently received its due recognition for the quality of its wines.

Médoc and Graves wines, based on Cabernet Sauvignon, are full, firm and tannic when young, even austere. Saint-Emilion wines may be equally abundant and rich, but lack the muscle and backbone of their westerly neighbours. Based on the Merlot, their wines are fruit-cakey rather than blackcurrant in flavour, more aromatic in character. They mature faster and do not last as long. Pomerol wines, from a clay rather than limestone soil, are fuller than those of Saint-Emilion. They can be rich and fat, heavier than Graves or Margaux (the two lightest regions of the west bank) and as long-lasting.

Adjacent to Saint-Emilion and Pomerol are the Libournais satellites. Lalande de Pomerol, Néac, Fronsac and Côtes-Canon-Fronsac produce lesser wines in the style of Pomerol. Surrounding Saint-Emilion are Montagne-Saint-Emilion, which absorbed Saint-Georges-Saint-Emilion and Parsac-Saint-Emilion in 1972 (though they still exist as *appellations* in their own right), Lussac-Saint-Emilion and Puisseguin-Saint-Emilion. Some of these wines are as good as ordinary Saint-Emilions themselves, but in the main those with a simple Saint-Emilion AC are more consistently reliable.

North-west of the Libournais, on the right bank of the Gironde estuary, lie the districts of Bourg and Blaye. East of Saint-Emilion in the direction of Bergerac are the Côtes de Castillon and the Côtes de Francs. All these are now thriving areas, providing *petit château* wines of great interest at prices hardly far removed from that of Bordeaux Supérieur. These are wines which can be bought and drunk regularly, rather than being preserved for special occasions. Land in these areas is cheap compared with the astronomical prices now being paid for classed growths in the Médoc. Able young men and women, suitably trained, have moved in, or taken over from their less expert parents.

The remainder of the Gironde region, with the exception of the coastal area, is authorized for the production of Bordeaux Rouge and Bordeaux Supérieur. Entre-Deux-Mers is a white wine *appellation* only, and any red wines produced there will be simply Bordeaux or Bordeaux Supérieur.

White Wines

The Graves, stretching south from the suburbs of Bordeaux down the west side of the Garonne as far as Langon, produces the best dry white wines of Bordeaux as well as red wines; though to many people's surprise more red wine is made than white. For many years the dry white wines continued to be made by rustic, old-fashioned methods. Quite deservedly, they fell out of fashion. Recently there has been a dramatic improvement in the wine, and a revival of the region's fortunes.

Within the Graves, towards the southern end, is the enclave of Sauternes and Barsac, origin of the world's richest and most sumptuous sweet white wines. Lesser, medium-sweet white wines are made nearby at Cérons, and on the opposite bank of the Garonne at Sainte-Croix-du-Mont, Loupiac and the Premières Côtes de Bordeaux.

The peninsula between the Dordogne and Garonne rivers is known as the Entre-Deux-Mers. This generic *appellation*, like that of Graves Supérieures (Graves *tout court* can be red or white), is used solely for white wines. Yet this is another source of good *petit château* red wine. Within the Entre-Deux-Mers are four more districts: Graves-de-Vayres, opposite Fronsac and the town of Libourne; Sainte-Foy-Bordeaux, at the extreme east below Montravel in the *département* of Dordogne; Côtes-de-Bordeaux, Saint-Macaire in the south, taking over where the Premières Côtes de Bordeaux ends; and Haut-Benauge, a sub-division of the Entre-Deux-Mers. In all, in 1993 there were 50 *appellations* within the Gironde.

GRAPE VARIETIES

The grape variety – or mix of grape varieties – is the single most important contributor to both the flavour and the character of a wine. The soil is important, as is the expertise and techniques of vine-growing (viticulture) and wine-making (vinification). The weather is paramount in determining the quality of the vintage. But the grape variety contributes most to the style of the wine. The following are the main quality varieties planted in Bordeaux.

Red Varieties

Cabernet Sauvignon

Though not the most widely planted grape in the Gironde, Cabernet Sauvignon is accepted as the classic claret grape. It is a vigorous but small producer, which develops late in the season – thus an advantage against spring frosts – and ripens late. It flourishes on most types of soil, consistently showing its style and quality, as evidenced by the wide adoption of this grape outside the Bordeaux area, as a *cépage améliorateur* in the Midi, and in Australia and California. It is less susceptible to *coulure* (failure of the flower to set into fruit) or to *pourriture* (grey rot) than Merlot, but more so to powdery mildew. The grape cluster is cylindrical-conical, made up of small round berries, very black in colour. The variety is cane pruned.

This is the grape which gives claret its particular blackcurrant taste. It provides the firmness, the tannin and the backbone. It gives the colour and the acidity, whence come the longevity, the depth, the finesse and the complexity of top Bordeaux wine.

Cabernet Franc

This vine is the 'poor country cousin' of Cabernet Sauvignon, and shares many of its characteristics, though wine made from it is less positive and less distinctive. Though losing ground in the Médoc, it is widely preferred to Cabernet Sauvignon in Saint-Emilion and Pomerol (where it is called Bouchet), where it thrives better on the more limestone- and clay-based soils. Wine made from it is softer, more subtle, more aromatic than from Cabernet Sauvignon. It is for this reason, as well as its shorter growing cycle, that Cabernet Franc is the grape used for Chinon and Bourgueil in the Touraine. The bunch is looser, the grapes still small, but larger than Cabernet Sauvignon, and the resultant wine is more fragrant but less coloured, less full and less tannic. The variety is cane pruned.

Merlot

The Merlot is the leading grape of the Dordogne side of the Bordeaux region and the most widely planted across the area as a whole. It is a vigorous, productive vine, which buds early – thus rendering it liable to spring frost damage – and ripens earlier than both the Cabernets. It is susceptible to *coulure*, downy mildew and botrytis (rot) which can cause considerable damage if there is rain at the time of harvest. It is less adaptable to different soils. The grape cluster is cylindrical, but looser than the Cabernets, and the berries are round, less thick-skinned, but larger, and less intensely coloured. The variety is cane pruned. A Merlot wine is generally a degree or two higher in alcohol than the Cabernets, less acidic, less tannic and less muscular. It is softer, fatter and more aromatic in character, and it matures faster.

Malbec

This is the principal grape of Cahors, where it is called the Auxerrois, and is grown in the Loire, where it is known as the Cot. In Bordeaux it is also authorized but it is little grown in the top properties, particularly in the Médoc, though it can be found in small proportions in the top estates of Saint-Emilion and Pomerol where it is known as the Pressac. The berries are large and the cluster loose. Merlot is prone to *coulure*, downy mildew and rot. The variety is cane pruned. The quantity of wine which results is large, compared to other Bordeaux varieties. Malbec is quite rich in tannin and colour, but with less intensity of aroma and with much less finesse. In Bordeaux the wine is only medium in body, though in Cahors the grape makes wine that is rather more beefy.

Petit Verdot

This variety is of minor importance, but is inserted here in order that all the five Bordeaux red varieties are listed together. The Petit Verdot is a sort of super-concentrated Cabernet Sauvignon, which has all but disappeared except in some of the top Médoc estates. It is difficult to grow, prone to disease, and ripens last of all, often not completely successfully. The variety is cane pruned. Some growers swear by it, saying it brings finesse, acidity, alcoholic concentration and backbone. Others, like Monsieur Charmolüe at Château Montrose or Robert Dousson at Château de Pez, who have each carried out tests to discern the development of blends with or without wine from this grape, have decided it is not for them. As Peter Sichel of Château Palmer ruefully points out, in the good vintages when everything ripens successfully, Petit Verdot is superfluous; in the poor years, when you need it, it does not ripen at all. Nevertheless, he adds, a mixture of grape varieties, each budding, flowering and ripening at a different time, acts as a kind of insurance against sudden attacks of frost, hail and other climatic hazards.

White Varieties

Sauvignon Blanc

The Sauvignon Blanc, to differentiate it from other Sauvignons, is a vigorous variety which matures early, forming a compact, conical cluster of small round berries. According to leading ampelographers, or vine botanists, it is subject to *coulure*, but in my experience the size of the crop in Bordeaux does not seem to vary nearly as much as a result of poor flowering as does the Merlot, for example, and in the Loire crops suffer more as a result of frost, so no doubt more *coulure*-resistant strains have been developed. Oidium is more of a problem. It is also prone to botrytis, though not so much as Sémillon. The Sauvignon is cane pruned.

The Sauvignon grape produces a wine with a very individual flavour: steely, grassy, high in acidity, very flinty and aromatic. Words like gooseberry, blackcurrant leaf, even cat's urine are employed. As such the dry, stainless-steel-aged, youthfully bottled Sauvignon is a wine now widely seen, though the Bordeaux version is somewhat fuller and less racy than that of the Touraine and Central Loire, and in Bordeaux many seemingly pure Sauvignons have a little Sémillon in the blend to round the wine off. Strange as it may seem for a white wine, this variety produces a wine with a certain amount of tannin, and as a result of this, fermentation and *élevage* (initial maturing) of pure Sauvignon in new oak is a procedure which needs to be handled with care. Combined with Sémillon in various proportions and aged in oak, Sauvignon produces the great white Graves.

Sémillon

Sémillon is the base for all Bordeaux's great sweet wines, though its value for dry wine production is only just beginning to be appreciated once again. This is the most widely planted white grape in the Bordeaux area. Sémillon is a vigorous, productive variety. It is spur pruned; and pruned very hard in Sauternes to reduce the crop to a minimum. It produces a cylindrical bunch of round berries, noticeably larger than the Sauvignon Blanc. These tend to develop a pinkish shade at full maturity, turning to browny-purple with over-ripeness. It is a hardy variety but susceptible to rot, both *pourriture grise* and *pourriture noble*, as it has a thin skin.

Poorly vinified, dry Sémillon wines can lack freshness and bouquet, character, breed and acidity. The result is heavy, neutral and dull. Correctly vinified, as increasingly this variety is in the Graves, particularly at places such as Château Rahoul and in enterprising hands elsewhere in the region, the results are totally different. The wines, though dry, are rich, fat and aromatic, with almost tropical, nutty fruit flavours and quite sufficient acidity. Good dry Sémillon is very classy, a far more interesting wine in my view than dry Sauvignon, and it has been underrated in Bordeaux. It has taken the Australians, where for many years the variety has been grown in the Hunter Valley, to show the Bordeaux wine producers the potential for this grape.

Muscadelle

The Muscadelle has nothing in common, despite the similarity of spelling, with either the Muscadet of the Pays Nantais or the several varieties of Muscat. It is moderately vigorous but very productive, develops late, and produces a large, loose, conical cluster of sizeable round berries. It is susceptible to *coulure*, powdery mildew, *pourriture grise* and botrytis (*pourriture noble*) while being less prone to downy mildew. You will rarely come across the Muscadelle except in small proportions in the sweet white wine areas of Bordeaux. Even here it is frowned upon at the highest level, for it is considered to produce coarse wine, very perfumed, but lacking finesse. The variety is cane pruned.

A YEAR IN THE VINEYARD

Good wine is produced from ripe, healthy, concentrated grapes. The object of viticulture is to produce fruit in as optimal a condition as possible at the time of the harvest, to produce as much as is compatible with the highest quality – but not too much, for quality is inversely proportional to quantity – and to mitigate the vagaries of the climate and the depredations of pests and diseases.

The first element to consider is the soil. The vine will thrive on a wide range of geological structures and compositions, but some varieties do better on some soils than on others. Cabernet Sauvignon, for instance, while it has a tolerance for limestone and marl (limestone-clay mixtures), provided the soils are not too cool, performs to its most elegant capacity on well-drained gravel. Hence its preponderance in the Médoc and the Graves areas of Bordeaux. Here the soil is undulating but predominantly flat, the gravel mounds or *croupes* rising gently above the interlying marshy land, drained by *jalles* or ditches. The subsoil of the Médoc and the Graves is an iron-rich sandstone (*alios*), which rests on marl or limestone.

In the Libournais, the Saint-Emilion and Pomerol regions, the countryside is more hilly and the soil structure more varied. Round the town of Saint-Emilion itself the layer of surface soil is thin and marly, and lies on limestone rock; to the south the escarpment is steep, with more alluvial sandy soil on the valley floor. Adjacent to the Pomerol border there are three ridges of gravel over sand and clay, the 'Graves Saint-Emilion'. This soil is continued into Pomerol itself, where the soil is more clayey and is variously mixed with gravel and sand, on an iron-rich clay base known as *machefer*. Here the Merlot is the predominant grape, and the Cabernet Franc is preferred to the Cabernet Sauvignon.

The soil of Sauternes and Barsac is essentially limestone, mixed with gravels of various sizes, clay and siliceous elements. In Barsac the soil is richer in iron and deeper red in colour.

It is lighter further away from the River Garonne in the communes of Fargues, Bommes and Sauternes itself. There is less clay and more sand than further north or across in the Libournais, and consequently white grape varieties perform better than red. Moreover the microclimate encourages the formation of noble rot.

In general the soil needs to be poor in nitrogenous matter. Above all it must be well-drained, particularly where the rainfall is higher. Aspect is important. Though the main quality wine-growing areas of the Gironde are by no means hilly, an orientation towards the east or south-east is ideal. The first rays of the morning will warm up the ground, drive away the mist and ensure that maximum use is made of the heat of the sun.

In general the weather in Bordeaux is mild and even. Severe winter frosts are rare, as is severe summer heat, because the region's climatic extremes are cushioned by the effects of the Atlantic Ocean. It is both warmer in winter and more stable in summer than in Burgundy. Spring frost is less of a danger, as is hail. On the other hand, particularly in the Médoc and in the Graves where the drainage of the soil is super-efficient, drought can be a problem. In the driest of vintages, the more water-retentive subsoils of the Libournais can keep the roots of the vine refreshed. But also, of course, vice versa.

Having chosen his site and prepared his land, if necessary by manuring and adjusting the chemical composition and certainly by ensuring that it is free of disease, the grower's next task is the choice of grape variety and clone or strain of that particular variety, and the selection of a rootstock to go with it. The former choice will, of course, be determined by the local *appellation contrôlée* laws. A permanent result of the phylloxera epidemic is that all vine varieties in France (except in one or two isolated pockets, particularly where the soil is predominantly sandy, for the aphid cannot thrive here) are today grafted on to American, phylloxera-resistant rootstocks.

While it is fair to say that over the last 30 years the developments in viniculture have outstripped the evolution of viticulture, there has nevertheless been considerable research into the production of disease-resistant clones which can produce quantity without sacrificing quality, and the propagation of suitable rootstocks which are compatible, both with the clone and with the chemical and physical composition of the soil. Grafting normally takes place at the horticulturalist's greenhouse, not in the vineyard.

With considerations of mechanical tending of the vineyard, and, indeed, increasingly today, mechanical harvesting of the vintage, determining the space between the vines and the space between the rows, the vineyard is then planted. The amount of vines per given area varies greatly. Half as many vines can exploit the same amount of soil and produce as much wine as double the quantity. But in the better areas the density tends to be greater. The closer together, the more the vine is encouraged to develop a deeply penetrating root system. It will then extract the maximum complexity from soil and subsoil and be more resistant to temporary drought and floods.

Over the next few years, as the vine slowly develops into a mature plant, it is carefully pruned and trained into a particular shape. There are, in essence, two basic pruning methods – long or cane pruning, and short or spur pruning – and two basic shapes. Cane pruning lends itself to the ultimate formation of a hedge shape, the canes – one or two, with about six buds on each – being tied to a series of horizontal wires stretched along the row of the vines. This is known as the Guyot system. Spur pruning, or the Gobelet method, produces a free-standing bush shape. There are six or so short spurs, each with two or so buds. A compromise between the two, giving short spurs on horizontal branches which can be trained on wires, is the Cordon de Royat system. In the Bordeaux region the vine is almost invariably pruned to the Guyot system: in the Médoc a double Guyot is more common, in the Libournais, a single Guyot. Only in Sauternes, with the Sémillon, is short pruning adopted. Here the system is known as the Cot.

The vine flowers, and therefore will ultimately fruit, on the previous year's wood. The object of pruning is to select the best of this wood, and to reduce the eventual crop to a potential of six to a dozen bunches of grapes per vine.

The yearly cycle of the vine begins after the harvest. With the onset of the cold weather of winter the vine has become dormant, the sap has descended into the roots of the vine and the process of tidying up, cutting away the dead wood and preparing the vineyard for next year's harvest, can begin. The roots will be earthed up to protect them against frost, manure and other fertilizers can be ploughed in, and stakes and wires can be renewed if necessary. This is the time to rip up old vines which are dead or beyond their useful life, and to begin to prepare sections of the vineyard for replanting in the spring after a year or two's rest. It is also the time to replace soil which may have been washed down the slopes by the rain of the previous season. Throughout the winter pruning takes place. It must be finished before the warmer weather returns again in the spring and the sap of the vine begins to rise anew.

In March the vine begins to wake up from its winter dormancy. A further ploughing is undertaken, this time to weed and aerate the soil and to uncover the base of the vine. The buds begin to swell, and will eventually burst in late April to reveal a small cluster of tiny leaves. This is when the danger of frost is at its greatest. The vine itself can withstand winter temperatures as low as minus 20°C. The embryonic leaf-cluster is susceptible to just the slightest descent below zero.

After the emergence of the leaves the vineyard is regularly sprayed: with sulphur against oidium, with copper sulphate (Bordeaux mixture) against mildew, and with other chemicals against red spider, moths and other insects. Later on the fruit may be sprayed to harden its skin and prevent the emergence of rot. Increasingly nowadays, vineyards – and indeed the wine-making which follows – are run on organic and ecological principles.

In June the vine flowers, and this is one of the most critical times in the yearly cycle. Warm, dry weather is required to ensure that the fruit setting, which follows the flowering, takes place swiftly and successfully. If the weather is cold and humid the flowers may not set into fruit (coulure) or the fruit may remain as small, green, bullet-hard berries and not develop (millerandage). Moreover, should the flowering be prolonged the result will be bunches of uneven ripeness at the time of the harvest.

Throughout the summer spraying continues, particularly if the weather is inclement; the vineyard is ploughed to aerate the soil and eliminate weeds; the shoots are trained on to the wires, so that they do not break off in the wind, and the vegetation is trimmed back so that the vine can concentrate its resources into producing fruit. Increasingly in the best vineyards today there is a 'green harvest', an elimination of excess bunches before they develop and change colour, in order to reduce the final crop and so concentrate the eventual wine.

This colour change (véraison) takes place in August. Grapes as green as Granny Smith apples turn red and eventually black, or else soften into a greeny gold. From then it is seven weeks or so to the harvest (100 to 110 days after the flowering). Spraying must soon cease. The work in the vineyard is now over. All one can do is to pray for fine weather. Whatever might have happened earlier in the season the result will only have affected the quantity to be harvested. The weather from the véraison onwards is critical for the quality. What is required during these weeks is an abundance of sunshine, to ripen the fruit, an absence of excessive rain, which would only expand the grapes and dilute the wine, and an absence of humidity, which would encourage rot.

In about the third week of September the harvest starts. Preliminary tests to establish the sugar and acidity contents of the grapes will have taken place to ensure that ripeness and concentration are at their optimum at the time of collection. The weather forecast is anxiously studied. A preliminary passage through the vineyard to eliminate the diseased or otherwise inadequate bunches or part of bunches, and therefore make the life of the picker easier, is often undertaken. And when the time is ripe the vintage begins. The result of a year's hard labour is soon evident.

Today the majority of the Gironde vineyards, like the majority elsewhere, is harvested by machine. Only in the top estates of Bordeaux and Burgundy and elsewhere, or where the land is inappropriate – and of course in places which produce individual bunch-selected sweet wines such as Sauternes – does harvesting continue by hand. And even there, among the classed growths of the Haut-Médoc, mechanical harvesters are increasingly seen.

The advantage of mechanical harvesting is its convenience and its speed. One machine can do the work of 25 manual pickers and removes the stems from the bunches of grapes too. It can work 24 hours a day, if desired; and the new, second generation of machines, if correctly driven, does little harm to the vines. Mechanical harvesting can mean a later start to the harvest and a quicker conclusion, concentrating collection at the optimum state of the fruit's ripeness. This is the future.

HOW WINE IS MADE

Wine is produced by fermenting the juice of freshly gathered grapes. It sounds simple, but in fact it is not. Yeasts excrete enzymes which cause the sugar in the grape juice (or must) to turn into alcohol. The chemical process is very complicated. The reaction is exo-thermic, producing heat, so needs to be controlled. Carbon dioxide is also produced, and there is an additional 3 per cent of other chemical by-products.

It is this 3 per cent of 'other' which is crucial. Alcohol has no flavour, nor does water – and the grape juice and therefore the wine is 85 per cent or so water. It is in the 3 per cent of other that you will find the colour and the flavour. The reason the fermentation process needs to be controlled is not only that at too high temperatures the process will 'stick' and the danger of acetifaction (the production of vinegar) will arise, but that the flavour elements are very volatile. They need to be prevented from evaporating into the air. They need to be preserved in the wine. Moreover the extraction and fixing of colour, tannins and flavour from the skins and pulp of the grape varies not only with the temperature, pressure and availability of oxygen and with the length of maceration of these skins with the fermenting must, but with the increasing amount of alcohol as the must turns itself into wine.

There is a further problem. The effect of oxygen on wine will cause further chemical reactions to take place. Wine (alcohol) is only a halfway house between sugar and vinegar. While a little oxygenation is necessary for maturation, at all times in the vinification process, and during the time the wine is retained in bulk thereafter, evolving and undergoing the various treatments which take place before it is put in bottle, the wine-maker must ensure that the wine is uncontaminated by too much oxygen. He must not unduly expose the wine to air. Control, the equipment with which to control, as well as a thorough knowledge of the process, are crucial.

Making Red Wine

Vinification

On arrival at the *cuverie* or vinification centre, the grape bunches are dumped into a v-shaped trough and churned by means of a revolving vice through a *fouloir-égrappoir*. This pulls off the stalks and gently breaks the skin of the grape berry. Only rarely in Bordeaux – at Pétrus, for instance – is the must vinified with the stalks. There is enough tannin in the skins already.

The produce of different grapes, different sections of the vineyard, and, particularly, vines of different age, will be vinified separately. For red wines, there are two concurrent aspects to vinification: the fermentation itself – the grape sugar being converted to alcohol – and maceration, the length of time the must is in contact with the skins, extracting tannin, colour and extract from the pulp. The temperature is important, for the reasons outlined above.

Today the finer red wines are usually vinified at about 30°C, allowing the temperature to rise no higher than 33°C before cooling. Some estates, Léoville-Las-Cases, for instance, prefer to ferment between 26°C and 28°C. The need for control of temperature, as well as the ability fully to clean and sterilize the fermenting receptacle, has led to a movement away from the more traditional oak to the adoption of stainless-steel fermentation vats, which are easily cooled by running cold water down the outside, by a heat exchanger inside, or by means of an enveloping, thermostatically controlled 'cummerbund'.

Periodically during fermentation the juice is pumped over the floating mass of skins, pips and stalks (if any), or this cap, or *chapeau*, is pushed down into the must and broken up, a process called *bombage* or *pigeage*. (This process is rare in Bordeaux, but takes place, for example, at Domaine de Chevalier.) This is to combine the colour-releasing components with the must, equalize the temperature and assist the release of colour, tannin and extract from the skins. The current trend is to 'pump over' more frequently, but to macerate in total for a shorter time before running the liquid off the skins. The length of maceration (*cuvaison*) will vary from three or four days for a light red wine to as much as four weeks in the case of a top red Bordeaux.

When fermentation is over, the juice is then run off into a clean, empty vat or barrel. This juice is the *vin de goutte*. The residue of skins is then pressed. The *vin de presse* that results is important. It will be firmer, more tannic and more acidic than the free-run juice, and a proportion will normally be blended back in varying quantities, or added periodically when the wine is later racked. No addition of *vin de presse* may result in a rather weak, ephemeral wine, however enjoyable and supple it may be in its youth.

Chaptalization

Chaptalization is the addition of sugar to a fermenting must, and is a practice permitted in Bordeaux for white and rosé wines as well as for red. The process is not intended to make sweet wine but to make one with a higher level of alcohol. In vintages unblessed by a sunny autumn there is not enough natural sugar in the fruit to produce a wine with a sufficiently stable level of alcohol, say 12 degrees or so. It is now customary everywhere in France except in parts of the Midi to add sugar to the must, to the equivalent of a degree or two of alcohol, even in years when the grapes are fully ripe. It is said to knit the wine together. Moreover, if the sugar is added, not at the beginning of the fermentation but towards the end, it will extend the process, thus helping to extract more tannin (because the temperature will increase) and give both added density and added suppleness (eventually) to the wine.

Elevage

Once the fermentation process is complete the must is now wine and it must be looked after with meticulous care until it is ready for bottling, a process that must be done at the right time and with correct attention to detail. I am convinced that as much potentially good wine is ruined by incorrect or simply sloppy cellarwork or *élevage* as by poor vinification before or inferior storage afterwards.

After fermentation the first thing is to ensure that the wine is clean, in the sense of free of potential chemical or bacteriological contamination, and that it has completed its malolactic fermentation. This 'second' or malolactic fermentation, which also gives off carbon dioxide, often takes place immediately following the sugar-to-alcohol fermentation, and can be encouraged by warming the must or the surrounding environment to between 18° and 20°C, and the addition of an artificial malolactic bacterium to get the fermentation going. The result is to lower the apparent acidity by a degree or two, so rounding off the wine and softening it up.

The next step is the *égalisage*, or blending. This takes place normally during the winter a few months after the harvest. This is the moment of truth – the creation of the château wine, the blending together of the constituent parts from different grape varieties (if there is more than one), vine ages and sections of the vineyard. A large property might have as many as 30 vats-worth of wine to choose from, and not all of these may be suitable. If the weather has not been perfect, or if much of the vineyard consists of immature vines – less than ten or even fifteen years old in a top growth – many will not be of the required standard for the *grand vin* or top wine. Today a severe selection is increasingly common. Almost all the top properties now regularly produce commercial quantities of a second wine.

Having made the blend (and we are assuming wine of some pretension here: lesser wines are stored in bulk), the wine is transferred to oak barrels – in which it may well have been lying before the *égalisage* – and allowed to mature and settle out its sediment, or lees. The barrels will need constant topping up, to make up for evaporation, particularly in the first few months, and for this reason they are first stored with the bung-hole upright, loosely covered by a glass stopper or rubber bung. Later, a wooden, more permanent bung will be driven into this hole, and the casks moved over so the bung is on the side.

One of the questions continually asked of a proprietor or his cellar manager is the proportion of new oak hogsheads he uses each year. As a new cask now costs upwards of 3,000 francs or £350 (1993 price), the provision of a large proportion of new oak is a major financial undertaking. Nevertheless, the extra muscle and tannin, coupled with the flavour the oak gives to a wine, is an essential ingredient in the taste of a fine red wine. A few of the very top estates invariably put their top wine entirely into new oak. For most producers, a proportion of between a quarter and a half, depending on the quality and style of the vintage, is normal. More would impart too much of a *boisé* (woody) smell to the wine. Nevertheless, there has been a trend toward the use of more new wood. On the other hand, together with more new wood has come a reduction in the time the wine spends there. Ageing used to be for a minimum of two years. Today it is frequently as much as six months less before bottling, and the wine may well have been run off into older casks or into vat after only a year to avoid taking up too much taste of the oak. The major French oak forests lie in the centre of the country. Limousin imparts a very marked oak flavour and is not used for fine wine. Tronçais, Nevers and Allier are widely found, the latter being the most delicate and is largely used for white wines. The way in which the oak has been allowed to dry, and its 'toast' will equally influence the flavours the wood imparts to the wine.

During the first year of a wine's life, it will be racked to separate the wine from its lees, and also to transfer it from new to old oak and vice versa, so that all the wine spends an equal amount of time in wood of different ages. Big full wines such as Bordeaux throw more sediment than lighter wines such as Burgundy. In Bordeaux the wine will be racked every three months in the first year, every four months thereafter. In principle the less you move or manipulate the wine the better. During the first winter of the second year, the wine is 'fined', traditionally with beaten white of egg for fine wines, to coagulate and deposit further unstable elements. Lesser wines are fined with isinglass, casein (milk powder), bentonite and other natural or proprietary substances.

Bottling

The date of bottling is an important matter which has only received sufficient attention relatively recently. I still do not consider that it is flexible enough to allow for variations between one vintage and the next. A wine matures much quicker in cask than in bottle, and a variation of six or even three months in the date of bottling can hence have a decisive effect on the eventual date of maturity and on the balance of the wine.

A big, concentrated, tannic wine from a Bordeaux vintage such as 1982 or 1990 may need a full two years or even more in cask before it is ready for bottling, but equally a light vintage, particularly one that is feeble in acidity, such as 1987, needs early bottling. Currently, most top Bordeaux châteaux bottle during the spring and early summer of the second year, when the wine is between eighteen and twenty months old. Wine which is kept longer may dry out and become astringent, losing some of its fruit before it is ready for drinking.

When to Drink the Wine

Once a wine has been bottled, when will it be ready for drinking? And perhaps more important, how long will it be at peak after that? It has for long been the general rule that a wine such as a good second or third growth Médoc from a fine vintage like 1985, 1978 or 1970 requires ten years from the date of harvest to mature; a first growth fifteen or more; and lesser Médocs, Saint-Emilions and Pomerols from five to ten years. *Petits châteaux* are at their best between three and six years after the harvest. These figures would be less in a softer, less tannic vintage such as 1981, 1979 or 1976, and proportionately more in a big, hard vintage such as 1982 or 1975. Thereafter, a well-made, well-stored wine will last for at least as long as it has taken to mature. The proportion between the time a wine will live once mature and the time it has taken to reach maturity increases with the quality of the wine and the vintage, so that a top wine from an excellent claret vintage, 1961, ready in 1981, instead of having thereafter a 20-year life at peak, may have as much as 40, or twice the length of time it took to mature, before beginning to go downhill.

When you prefer to drink your wine is a matter of personal taste. While I personally incline more to the French taste – which to some in England and elsewhere seems a predilection for infanticide – I normally stick to the Bordeaux ten-year rule, and its equivalent elsewhere. Given the choice, however, I would prefer to drink a wine at the beginning of its 'at peak' plateau, rather than at the very end.

Making Dry White Wine

Vinification

The grapes which will produce dry white wine normally reach maturity a few days before the red varieties, and the precise date for top quality is even more crucial in order that the exact balance between sugar and acidity can be obtained.

With the trend in the 1960s towards drier, crisper wines came an unfortunate move in Bordeaux and elsewhere towards picking a few days in advance of the optimum moment in order to make wines with a good refreshing acidity. This was sadly carried a bit too far and the results, too often, were wines with a rasping, malic acidity and a consequent lack of ripe fruit. The wines were too green. As the grape ripens the malic acidity changes into tartaric acidity. Now, with the help of mechanical harvesting, the grower can wait longer without the risk of prolonging the collection of the crop beyond the desired period. It is now appreciated that once the correct maturity in the grapes has been reached, provided the climatic conditions are favourable, the acidity, now essentially tartaric rather than malic, will not continue to diminish and may even concentrate further to give a wine with both ripeness and balance.

White wines are vinified without their skins, and the first procedure is to press them as soon as possible after arrival from the vineyard, normally in some form of horizontal, cylindrical apparatus. The juice is then run off and allowed to settle (a process called *débourbage*) for 24 hours so that the solid matter falls to the bottom before being vinified. Except in the top estates where fermentation takes place in oak barrels, vinification takes place in vat or tank, often in anaerobic conditions and for white wines must proceed at a reduced temperature in order to prolong the process as long as possible, thus preventing loss of the volatile elements which impart flavour and aroma, and maximizing the intensity of the fruit. The common temperature for the controlled fermentation of most white wines is between 18 and 20°C. For a long time it has been accepted that the lower the temperature of fermentation the more the volatile, flavour-enhancing chemicals in the fruit are preserved in the resulting wine. It is not the lower temperature *per se*, however, but the prolongation of the fermentation which is important. The longer the fermentation, the more complex the flavour. Today artificial yeasts are widely employed, for they make the fermentation easier to control and produce wines of greater fruit definition and finesse.

Today, in order to maintain a crisper acidity in the finished wine, the second, malolactic fermentation is discouraged for many fine white wines in Bordeaux. Whether the wine is matured in cask or in tank, bottling takes place much earlier than for reds, often as early as the following spring. The object is to preserve the freshness and fruit and to minimize oxidation. Only the best, oak-vinified and oak-aged examples will develop in bottle.

Macération préfermentaire, or skin contact before fermentation, is a white-wine technique new to France. The principle which lies behind this idea of allowing white grape juice to remain in contact with the grape skins for a few hours before pressing is that most of the flavour-producing elements in the pulp of the grape lie near or within the skin. It is a process which needs to be handled with great care, for bruised or rotten berries will taint the whole wine. The results, though, are most rewarding, producing wines of greater complexity and depth of flavour, and it is a procedure which is spreading. So is the idea of leaving the new white wine on its fine lees (*sur lie*) for as long as possible before the first racking. The wine feeds off this sediment, mainly dead yeast cells, and becomes richer and fuller in flavour. In some of the top estates in the Graves the wine might be kept on its lees until midsummer. An additional technique is to stir these lees up periodically, once a week or fortnight. This process is known as *batonnage*.

The bane of white wine has been the over-use of sulphur. Sulphur is a necessary ingredient in the preservation of wine. It protects it against oxidation and bacterial infection, but too heavy a hand with it will kill the wine. The sulphur will bind in with the wine, destroying the freshness, the nuances of the fruit, and producing a sickly, heavy 'wet-wool' flavour. This used to be particularly prevalent in Bordeaux. Thankfully, after years of maltreating their white wines, the Bordeaux wine-makers are beginning to realize – as their counterparts in the Loire and southern Burgundy did years ago – that, when well-handled, dry and sweet white wines do not require as much sulphur to protect them as they thought. More careful wine-making, in anaerobic conditions and with a cleaner must, enables the wine-maker to reduce his recourse to sulphur dioxide during the fermentation. Healthy wine, correctly balanced, requires less sulphur thereafter. Modern equipment and sensitive *élevage* reduces its necessity even more. If the Loire and Burgundian wine-makers can do it, why can't the Bordelais? The penny is beginning to drop. Fewer and fewer dry white Graves – though there are still far too many depressing examples – taste of nothing but sulphur dioxide.

Elevage

The use of oak, new or newish, is another relatively recent development in white wine production. Prior to the 1960s, wood – old barrels for the most part – was the most common receptacle for *élevage* and transport. The fashion then swung to the tank, enamelled or stainless steel, and the concrete vat. All the old, bug-infected barrels were burned, and probably a good thing too. Only the very top wine estates persisted with oak for their dry white wines.

But oak, new oak, adds weight, complexity of flavour, depth and class. Happily today, not only across the board of the nine white Bordeaux classed growths but more widely elsewhere, a proportion of new oak is *de rigueur*. Wines are even being fermented in new wood. This is yet more preferable. The wood flavours derived thereby are more delicate and complex and exist in greater harmony with the rest of the flavour ingredients of the wine. Oak should be mandatory for any white wine aspiring to quality status.

Bottling

White wines are generally bottled much earlier than reds, the vast majority, those not matured in oak, within six months of vinification. Most of the rest of the fine dry wines are bottled the following autumn. Only the richest sweet wines such as those of Sauternes are given more than twelve months in cask.

When to Drink the Wine

When should you drink white wine? The lesser wines, like 'small' white wines all over the world, are essentially made one year for drinking the next. Within twelve months after bottling, i.e., eighteen months after the harvest, they will begin to lose their youthful, fruity freshness. This applies to most *petits* Graves and Entre-Deux-Mers.

Grander white wines — most of the *crus classés* Graves — those that have been fermented and matured in oak, can, and must, be kept. Often they enter a rather dumb phase after bottling, and for two or three years they will appear rather clumsy, particularly if they have been bottled with a little too much sulphur, as is still, sadly, often the case. Lesser vintages will be at their best between three and eight years after the harvest. The best white wines need longer before they are fully ready, and will keep for a decade or more after that.

Making Sweet White Wine

The world's greatest sweet wines are rare in number, highly prized, expensive to produce and infrequent in occurrence. That they appear at all is a tribute to the dedication and patience of the few wine-growers who make a speciality of them, and is a consequence of a particular microclimate acting on a small number of specific grape varieties, the result of an Indian summer of misty mornings and balmy afternoons continuing long after the rest of the *vignerons* have cleared their vines and are busy in the cellars nurturing the birth of their new vintage.

The great sweet wines are not merely sweet. If this were all, the addition of sugar syrup to a finished dry wine would be all that was necessary. Indeed, this is how cheap sweet wines are made. But these the consumer will soon find bland and cloying.

Noble Rot

The finest dessert wines are the result of a particular phenomenon, the attack on the ripe, late-harvested fruit by a fungus known as *Botrytis cinerea*. It produces what is known in France as *pourriture noble* and in Germany as *Edelfaüle*, both of which can be translated as 'noble rot'. Leave any fruit on the tree after it has ripened and eventually it will rot. This rot (*pourriture grise*), however, will not be 'noble'; the fruit will be ruined and the taste disgusting. In certain parts of the vineyard areas of the world, though, in the right climatic conditions, the noble rot will occur and this in Bordeaux will produce the great Sauternes and Barsacs, and occasionally similar wines in Cérons, Loupiac and Sainte-Croix-du-Mont.

What is required is a particular microclimate. The grapes are left on the vine after the normal harvesting time for the production of dry white wine. The conditions thereafter need to combine both warmth and humidity. It must continue fine and sunny long into the autumn but not be too dry. Most high-quality vineyard areas, however, are near the extremes of viable grape production; in poor years the fruit does not ripen sufficiently and the later the harvest the greater the risk that summer will have finished and autumn rains and chilly winter weather will have set in. This further complicates matters for the quality sweet wine producer. He needs not just a fine late summer but a prolonged and clement autumn. These occur rarely. Two years out of three, or even three out of four, are good years for red and dry white wines. For great sweet wines, the regularity is hardly one in three or even one in four. Sauternes has been exceptionally fortunate recently to have had three fine years in a row – 1988, 1989 and 1990.

When the noble rot attacks the ripe grapes, they will first darken; from golden, they will turn a burnished, almost purple brown. Then the surface will appear to get cloudy, the skin will begin to wither and get mouldy as the spores of the fungus multiply, feeding on the sugar and the berry. Finally, the grape will become shrivelled like a raisin and completely decomposed. The noble rot does not have a very prepossessing appearance!

Unfortunately, it does not strike with equal regularity and precision over the whole vineyard or even over the whole of a single bunch of grapes. This necessitates picking over the vineyard a number of times in order to select each bunch, part bunch or even, at Château d'Yquem, each individual berry, separately. A prolonged harvest is therefore implicit in the production of noble rot wines. In some cases it will continue not just into November but even into December.

The effect of this noble rot attack is to alter the chemical and physical composition of the grape and therefore, obviously, the taste of the wine. First, the water content of the berries is considerably reduced. Second, the acidities are changed and, third, the quantity of higher sugars such as glycerine is increased. The net effect is to create a very small quantity of juice with a sugar content equivalent to an alcohol level which in a top Sauternes will be well above 20 degrees. This produces a wine with an actual alcohol level of 14 or 15 degrees or so and 4 or 5 degrees (higher in the most successful vintages) of unfermented sugar. This is the sweetness. The other effect of the noble rot is to combine this sweetness with a luscious, spicy, complex, individual flavour and a high, naturally ripe acidity level.

There is much talk in Sauternes today of a new technique called 'cryo-extraction'. Briefly the principle is that juice heavy in sugars and glycerine freezes at a lower temperature than water. Thus, should you have a situation where it rains during the harvest, if you are able to freeze the grapes to a certain temperature and then press them carefully you should be able to capture the concentrated Sauternes-producing juice without it being diluted by the rain, for this rain will be frozen into ice-crystals and will not flow off during the pressing: a sort of artificial *Eiswein*, in fact.

Sauternes by its very nature is an aberration. Contrary to all normal agricultural principles and practices the grower deliberately allows his harvest to rot. He has to wait until he is at the mercy of the elements as autumn evolves into winter: 'We are playing poker with God,' as one grower once told me. All too often a state of rot which was incipiently noble can be turned by bad weather into ignoble. This is where cryo-extraction comes in. It is not intended to replace normal harvesting and pressing in fine weather, but it will enable a grower to rescue his harvest if the climatic conditions turn against him.

The fermentation of sweet white wine proceeds in general along the same lines as that for dry white wines. Crushing has to be slow, repeated and gentle – often, paradoxically, the best juice does not come from the first pressing – and the wine is often chilled or centrifuged to eliminate the gross lees rather than being allowed to settle of its own accord. This is in order to prevent oxidation. The fermentation is slow, often difficult. It is important to preserve the correct balance between alcohol and sugar. A Cérons or Sainte-Croix-du-Mont in most vintages with, say 12.5 degrees of alcohol can support only a maximum 35 grams of sugar per litre. This wine would be called *moelleux* (medium-sweet) but not *doux* (very sweet). A *doux* Sainte-Croix, Cérons or Loupiac, such as were produced in 1989, with say 50 grams of sugar per litre, will need to be more alcoholic. A Sauternes with 14 to 15 degrees of alcohol needs to be really luscious or it will appear oily and heavy.

Once the sweet wine has been made it will take longer than a dry one to settle down and stabilize. Moreover the wine will be susceptible to further fermentation as, by its very nature, it will have a large amount of unfermented sugar in it. It needs therefore to be carefully nurtured, its sulphur level maintained at a relatively high level to preserve it. Exposure to the air must be avoided at all costs.

Nevertheless maturation in (at least partially) new oak, and often for a year and a half or more, does wonders for the richest and most concentrated of these sweet wines. No classy Sauternes should be matured without oak.

Sweet white wines need maturing. Though often delicious young they mature so well and can reach such levels of complexity that it is a tragedy to pull the cork too soon. A medium-sweet Cérons wine may be mature at five years. Ten is the minimum for a good Sauternes. And they will last. A twenty-year-old Sauternes of a top vintage like 1988, 1986 or 1983 will still be a virile teenager.

BORDEAUX CLASSIFICATIONS OF THE RED WINES BEFORE 1855

A group of Frenchmen form an argument; a group of Englishmen form a queue. So goes the old joke. If so, then a group of Bordeaux châteaux will form themselves into a classification, betraying both their French location and ancient English heritage. What could be a better amalgam of a queue and an argument?

There seems to be an instinctive desire – sometimes, these days, carried to excess – to collate, tabulate, classify and place into some sort of pecking order any miscellaneous collection of similar things. It is part of man's attempt to impose his meagre sense of order on a creation which is greatly more complicated than he is capable of comprehending. We classify the animal and vegetal worlds. The mineral is analysed down to its constituent parts. We even attempt to impose some sort of grid onto religion, philosophy and politics. Ever since the first Bordeaux châteaux emerged as individual wine-producing estates, they have been assessed and compared with one another and, largely by the price the wine has been capable of fetching on the open market, its quality has been assumed and its relative worth established. It is interesting, but no coincidence, that the first four properties to emerge as wines in their own right, the first estates to take up wine-making on a large-scale, monocultural basis, the first individual château names to appear on the market, should be precisely those to be classified more than 150 years later as *premiers crus*: Haut-Brion, Lafite, Margaux and Latour.

The wine of Château Haut-Brion, also known as Pontac, after the name of the owners in the seventeenth century, was the earliest to become established. The famous reference in Pepys' diary in 1663 to 'Ho Bryen' is probably the first to a wine of a specific estate. At the time, wines were matured for longer in cask, shipped when ready for drinking – and the wines were then vinified for consumption much sooner after the vintage – and drunk straight from the wood or bottled for immediate use in the locality of the wholesale purchaser. The philosopher John Locke, who visited Haut-Brion in 1677, attests to the status and high prices of the wine, and this is substantiated by the diarist John Evelyn, who met the proprietor in London in 1683. The latter was responsible for 'the choicest of our Bordeaux wines'.

Margaux, Lafite and Latour emerge towards the turn of the century. During the War of the Spanish Succession, a number of merchant ships conveying French wine to destinations in northern Europe were captured by the English and the contents put up for sale in London. These 'new French Clarets', when specifically named, were Haut-Brion or Pontac, Lafite, Margaux and Latour, the same wines as were imported by John Harvey, first Earl of Bristol, also in the first decade of the eighteenth century.

Perhaps the first classification, as such, occurs in a letter written from Bordeaux in 1723 by a certain J. Bruneval to Henry Powell who was responsible for the cellar of the Prince of Wales. The same four wines are described as 'topping', i.e., the best. Bruneval also makes a favourable mention of Château d'Issan.

In his *Bottlescrew Days*, André Simon quotes from an anonymous French report dated 1730. 'The red wines [of the Graves and the Médoc] may be divided into three principal classes. The first comprises the growths of Pontac, Lafitte [*sic*] and Château de Margo [*sic*] which . . . sell for 1,200 to 1,500 *livres* per tun. It is the English who buy the greater part of this wine. The second class comprises a very large number of growths which . . . fetch from 300 to 500 *livres* per tun. They are shipped chiefly to England, Ireland, Scotland, Holland and Hamburg. The third class includes wines the usual price of which is only 100 to 200 *livres* per tun, the cheapest being shipped, as a rule, to Brittany, Normandy, Picardy and Dunkirk and the dearest to the north'.

It would be fascinating to have more specific information on the châteaux which were included in this second category. It would be instructive to see which, if any, of the other Graves estates were highly regarded at the time, for it seems unlikely that it was only Haut-Brion which made wines of renown; and it was the Graves area, in what are now the suburbs of the city, which was exploited for wine long before the marshy gravels of the Médoc were drained by the Dutch and became suitable for the vine. Moreover, it would give us concrete evidence of where in addition to the *premiers crus* there was large-scale wine production in the Médoc prior to the 1740s.

For it was not, in general, until the 1740s at the earliest that the vast majority of what are now the Médoc-classed growths outside the *premiers crus* were intensively planted and started to take the form we know today. One or two had begun their existence earlier and the first records of the broking firm Tastet and Lawton, established in 1740, give us an indication of which they were. Senior was Léoville which fetched 850 *livres* in 1744 (Lafite and Latour sold for 1,400).

Brane-Mouton, later Mouton-Rothschild, obtained 530; Pichon, then undivided, 500; Brassier (Beychevelle) 400; Giscours 380; Rozan (*sic*) and Malescot 285 *livres*, according to Edmund Penning-Rowsell in his masterly *Wines of Bordeaux*.

THE TASTET AND LAWTON ARCHIVES

Professor Pijassou, in his *Le Médoc*, delved further into the Tastet and Lawton archives and has established a classification based on the average prices in *livres tournois* per *tonneau en primeur* from 1741 to 1774. As I often refer to this *en passant* in my château profiles, I quote it here in full. It makes fascinating reading:

Haut-Brion	1458	Giscours	506
Lafite	1278	De Gasq (later Palmer)	494
Château Margaux	1275	La Chesnaye, Cussac	492
Latour	1215	(incorporating Lanessan?)	
Léoville	810	La Colonie, Margaux	488
Brane-Saint-Julien (Lagrange)	800	(eventually part of Malescot)	
Calon-Ségur	775	Bergeron	483
Lascombes	768	(Ducru-Beaucaillou)	
Marquis-de-Terme	766	Goudal, Cantenac (?)	459
Gruaud (Larose)	734	Beychevelle	440
Brane-Mouton	716	La Tour-de-Mons	430
(Mouton-Rothschild)		Citran	421
Gorse (Brane-Cantenac)	686	Lynch-Bages	400
Malescot	670	Duluc (Branaire)	394
Petit-Cazaux, Margaux (?)	665	Pontet-Canet	365
Pouget	654	Paveil (de Luze)	361
Pontac, Margaux (?)	605	Pontet-Saint-Julien (Langoa)	360
Rauzan	603	Pomies, Ludon	342
Desmirail	540	Lafon (Rochet)	332
Issan	537	(Fourcas) Hostein	310
Pichon-Longueville	534		

Whether Tastet and Lawton dealt in the wines of the Graves other than Haut-Brion (and I don't see why not), I do not know, but the absence of any other Graves is significant. The explanation is perhaps that the next three top estates after Haut-Brion which remain today were at the time all in ecclesiastical hands: La Mission-Haut-Brion, Pape-Clément and Carbonnieux. Today's main Léognan properties; Chevalier, Haut-Bailly, Malartic-Lagravière and De Fieuzal, were not constituted until the nineteenth century. However, if La Mission and Pape-Clément were reserved for local use, the wine of the larger Benedictine Carbonnieux belonging to the Abbey of Bordeaux certainly was exported, for Simon has shown us evidence of a sale in 1762. This, however, could have been a white wine.

What is also interesting in the above list is the dominance of the wines of the commune of Margaux. No fewer than 19 of the 37 wines listed come from here or elsewhere in the southern Médoc. Cos d'Estournel and Montrose were formed later but significant by their absence are Batailley and the Grand-Puys; Talbot, then owned by the Marquis d'Aux; and Saint-Pierre.

Moreover, there are no wines from the Libournais. The wines of Saint-Emilion, Pomerol and Fronsac had more humble proprietors than the landed gentry and *parlementaires* of the Médoc, fetched greatly reduced prices and were traded directly out of Libourne. It was not until Napoleonic times that a bridge was built over the Garonne at Bordeaux and not until the 1830s that Libournais wines begin to appear in the Tastet and Lawton records.

THOMAS JEFFERSON

Thomas Jefferson, Minister in France for the new United States of America prior to the French Revolution, was a keen amateur of wine. He made an extensive tour of the French vineyards and visited Bordeaux in 1787. Here is his list of top wines:

First Growths
1500 *livres* per *tonneau* 'new'.
Margaux
La Tour
Haut-Brion
Lafitte (*sic*)

Second Growths
1000 *livres*
Rauzan
Léoville
Gruaud-Larose

Kirwan (spelt Quirouen)
Durfort

Third Growths
800–900 *livres*
Calon-Ségur
Mouton (Rothschild)
Gorse (Brane-Cantenac)
Arboete (Lagrange)
Pontet-Canet
De Terme
Candale (Issan)

Kirwan, one assumes, appears in the Tastet and Lawton compilation under another name, perhaps as Petit-Cazaux or Pontac-Margaux and possibly one of these names hides Durfort, though Durfort had its origins in Lascombes. Otherwise, the list follows, very largely, that of the above, only showing that the second and third growth prices had begun to catch up those of the *premiers crus*.

ANDRÉ SIMON'S CLASSIFICATION OF 1800

Surprisingly, the French Revolution had little effect on the leading Bordeaux proprietors, their estates and the relative standing of their wines. Only a small number of château owners fell foul of the new authorities. One or two had to face the guillotine, and it was only when a handful of others decided to emigrate that large domaines like that of Léoville were split up. The ecclesiastical properties were, of course, sequestrated, and there were a number of changes of ownership, but as wine-making concerns the top growths emerged largely unscathed.

In *Bottlescrew Days*, André Simon gives the following classification of the Médoc as it stood at the close of the eighteenth century:

First Growths
(Opening price £24 per hogshead)
Margaux
Lafitte (sic)
Latour

Second Growths
(£20 per hogshead)
Brane-Mouton (Rothschild)
Rauzan
Lascombes
Durfort (Vivens)
Gorse (Brane-Cantenac)
Léoville
Gruaud-Larose

Third Growths
(£18 per hogshead)
Pichon-Longueville
Cos d'Estournel
Bergeron (Ducru-Beaucaillou)
Brane-Arbouet (Lagrange)

Pontet-Langlois (Langoa)
Kirwan
Château de Candale (Issan)
Malescot
De Loyac – Margaux (?)

Fourth Growths
(£12 per hogshead)
Giscours
Saint-Pierre
Mandavit (Duhart-Milon)
Pontet-Canet
Dinac (Grand-Puy-Lacoste)
La Colonie, Margaux (eventually part of
Malescot)
Ferrière
Tronquoy-Lalande
(Grand-Puy) Ducasse
Pouget
De Terme
Boyd (Cantenac)

There are several interesting omissions: Calon-Ségur, most importantly; de Gasq, later Château Palmer; the continuing absence of Talbot, Beychevelle and Branaire-Ducru. Lynch-Bages, despite the fact that the owner was a leading figure on the Bordeaux stage, also does not figure.

BORDEAUX AFTER THE RESTORATION

The 1820s saw the first comprehensive accounts of the wines of Bordeaux by Wilhelm Franck and the broker Paguierre and the first books on the wines of France, among them André Jullien's *Topographie de Tous les Vignobles Connus* and Alexander Henderson's *The History of Ancient and Modern Wines*. Jullien's first edition appeared in 1816 and his information on the hierarchy of the Bordeaux châteaux is reproduced in Henderson (1824). The first of many editions of Franck's *Traité sur les Vins du Médoc et les Autres Vins Rouges du Département de la Gironde* came out in the same year. Paguierre's *Classification et Description des Vins de Bordeaux* appeared in 1828.

At the same period, Tastet and Lawton produced a detailed classification, publishing an extensive list down to Fourth Growths, from *quatrièmes purs* to *quatrième et ⁷/₈*. Lawton was first in the field to produce his own classification. As a broker between the buyer and the seller, he was close to the action and a man in the know. He produced a list of the Médoc containing 52 *crus*: three firsts, six seconds, twenty thirds and twenty-three fourths. Thirteen were in Saint-Julien, twelve in Cantenac, nine in Margaux, eight in Pauillac, five in Saint-Estèphe and one each in Ludon, Labarde, Arsac and Saint-Laurent.

LAWTON'S CLASSIFICATION OF 1815

First Growths
Lafite
Latour
Margaux

Second Growths
Brane-Mouton (Rothschild)
Rausan
Léoville-Las-Cases

Léoville-d'Abbadie (later incorporated into
Las-Cases)
Léoville-Barton
Léoville-Poyferré as they would become
Gruaud-Larose
Rauzan
Lascombes

Third Growths
3 'Purs'
Calon-Ségur
Pichon-Longueville
Gorse (Brane-Cantenac)
Ducru-Beaucaillou
Kirwan
Brown
Castelnau (?)
Candale (Issan)
3 ⅛ Malescot
3 ³⁄₁₆ Lagrange
3 ¼ Loyac, Margaux
La Colonie (later part of Malescot)
Marquis d'Alesme
Ferrière
Cos d'Estournel
3 ½ La Tour-Carnet
Langoa

Beychevelle
Saint-Pierre
Branaire

Fourth Growths
4 'Purs'
Daux (Talbot)
Pouget
Giscours
Pontet-Canet
Grand-Puy-Lacoste
Grand-Puy-Ducasse
4 ⅛ Dubosc, Saint-Julien (?)
Deyrem, Saint-Julien (?)
Popp (Camensac)
Coutanceau (Belgrave)
Desmirail
Marquis-de-Terme
Tronquoy, Saint-Estèphe
Morin, Saint-Estèphe
Deleveau, Saint-Estèphe
Durand (Prieuré-Lichine)
4 ½ La Lagune
Du Tertre
4 ¾ Massac, Cantenac (now part of Boyd)
Leroy, Cantenac (?)
Monbrun, Cantenac
4 ⅞ Legras (D'Angludet)

Allowing for divisions and absorptions and the general ups and downs as a result of changes of ownership, this list is not that different from the 1855 Classification except in that some of the thirds have moved up a place and the fourth division was later sub-divided. One or two notable châteaux are missing: Durfort-Vivens, several Pauillacs and what was to become Château Palmer (then no doubt in a state of abeyance prior to the General's arrival as proprietor).

What is also noteworthy is that, even before the Rothschild arrival, Lawton unequivocally puts 'Brane-Mouton' at the head of his second growths.

ANDRÉ JULLIEN

Meanwhile, there was Jullien. His first growths are the same consistent four wines which dominated Bordeaux from the start and would continue to remain unchallenged until the full emergence of Mouton soon after the arrival of the Rothschilds, and Cheval-Blanc, Ausone and Pétrus a good while later. The seconds consist of Rauzan, Durfort and Lascombes in Margaux, Gorse (Brane-Cantenac in Cantenac). Léoville and Gruaud-Larose in Saint-Julien, Brane-Mouton (Rothschild) in Pauillac and, interestingly, Pichon-Longueville. In the next category, more comprehensive than earlier tables, we find the following:

Cantenac: Kirwan, Issan, Pouget, Desmirail, De Terme.
Margaux: Malescot, D'Alesme-Becker, Dubignon-Talbot (a growth classified in 1855 which was later to disappear), Ferrière, and La Colonie and Loyac, both of which were to be absorbed into other growths before or soon after 1855.

Saint-Julien: Ducru, Lagrange, Saint-Pierre, Branaire, Dauch (sic) (Talbot), Beychevelle.

Saint-Laurent: (La Tour) Carnet, Popp (Camensac), Coutanceau (Belgrave).

Cussac: Lachenay, Delbos, Legalant (Lanessan and its neighbouring dependent Lachesnaye and Caronne-Sainte-Gemme).

Pauillac: Pontet-Canet, Grand-Puy-Ducasse, Grand-Puy-Lacoste, Lynch-Bages, Croizet-Bages.

Saint-Estèphe: Calon, Cos d'Estournel, Tronquoy, Merman (Le Crock), Meyney, Lafon-Rochet, Cos-Labory, 'Morin', 'Lebosc-Delaveau'.

Pessac: La Mission, Pape-Clément, 'Cantelaut', 'Cholet'.

Once again, there are some curious omissions: Giscours this time as well as de Gasq/Palmer, though the list is more comprehensive than most. What is interesting is the inclusion of four wines in Pessac for the first time and the large selection of Saint-Estèphes. Jullien's classification, it should be noted, was of all the red wines of Bordeaux. The Lawton list just covered the Médoc.

WILHELM FRANCK

We now come, said Wilhelm Franck in the preamble to his classification in the second (1845) edition of his book, 'to the most delicate part of our work', and he goes on to make a point which has no less relevance today. A classification is an uncertain business; one broker's opinion will differ from another's; there is no unanimity. Moreover, wines vary from vintage to vintage. One year one château, however lowly, may produce wine better than its superior classed neighbour. The next year the reverse may be the case.

The hierarchy in Franck's first edition and the number of growths listed are much the same as that of André Simon quoted above. There are only the four consistent seconds: Brane-Mouton, Rauzan, Léoville and Gruaud-Larose. Kirwan has been dropped to fourth, Cos d'Estournel appears as a third but Talbot and Beychevelle do not appear.

More interesting is a very much fuller classification in the second edition. This was the last important independent list before the 'official' assessment of 1855. Sixty-four wines are divided into five categories, with an honourable mention for a further eight *bons bourgeois*. The prices of the first growths fetched between 1,800 and 3,500 francs and, allowing for a hypothetical 2,400 francs, the seconds would obtain 2,050 to 2,100, the thirds 1,800, the fourths 1,200 to 1,500 and the fifths 1,000 to 1,200. So a lowly *cinquième* would earn 40 per cent of a Château Lafite. Today, the spread is greater. The first growths open at 220 francs. Those fifths which are not, like Lynch-Bages and Grand-Puy-Lacoste, patently above their 1855 station, fetch a mere 55 or so francs, a quarter of the price of the firsts.

For interest, I reproduce not only the entire 1845 Franck classification but quote his production figures as well. Within each category except for the first, it should be noted, the wines were listed in alphabetical order. I have given the present-day name where this has changed.

WILHELM FRANCK'S 1845 CLASSIFICATION

First Growths	*Tonneaux*	Cos d'Estournel	70–80
Margaux	100–120	Durfort-Vivens	30–35
Lafite	120–150	Gruaud-Larose	100–150
Latour	70–90	Lascombes	15–20
Haut-Brion	100–120	Léoville:	
		Las-Cases	80–100
Second Growths	*Tonneaux*	Poyferré	40–50
Brane-Cantenac	50–60	Barton	50–70

Second Growths (continued)	Tonneaux	La Lagune	40–50
Mouton (Rothschild)	120–140	Clerc-Milon	25–30
Pichon-Longueville	100–120	Marquis-de-Terme	20–30
Rauzan	50–70	Prieuré-Lichine	25–30
		Palmer	50–60
Third Growths	Tonneaux	Saint-Pierre:	
Desmirail	30–40	Bontemps	25–35
Dubignon-Talbot	15–20	Dubarry	25–35
Ducru-Beaucaillou	100–120		
D'Issan	50–70	*Fifth Growths*	Tonneaux
Brown	60–70	Batailley	60–80
(later Cantenac-Brown and		Bédout-Dubosq, Saint-Julien	50–55
Boyd-Cantenac)		(since disappeared: NB Bédout	
Ganet, Cantenac	20–25	was a former proprietor of	
(now part of Pouget)		Batailley)	
Giscours	80–100	Dauzac	40–45
Kirwan	35–40	Pontet-Canet	100–120
Lagrange	120–150	Cantemerle	120–130
Langoa	100–120	Chaillet, Pauillac	15–18
Lanoire, Margaux	35–40	(since disappeared)	
(since disappeared)		Constant, Pauillac	80–100
Montrose	100–120	(since disappeared)	
Pouget	25–30	Cos-Labory	40–50
Malescot	60–70	Belgrave	20–30
		Croizet-Bages	50–60
Fourth Growths	Tonneaux	Grand-Puy-Ducasse	80–90
Talbot	70–80	Grand-Puy-Lacoste	50–60
Marquis d'Alesme	15–20	Lynch-Bages	100–120
Beychevelle	100–120	Haut-Bages-Libéral	20–25
Calon-Ségur	120–160	Liversan	40–50
La Tour-Carnet	100–120	Lynch-Moussas	30–40
Duhart-Milon	40–50	La Mission-Haut-Brion	30–40
Dubignon, Margaux	12–15	Mouton d'Armailhacq	100–120
(since disappeared)		Haut-Bages-Monpélou	25–30
Branaire	80–90	Camensac	30–40
Ferrière	10–15	Seguineau-Deyries, Margaux	10–12
Lafon-Rochet	30–40	(since disappeared)	

The *bons bourgeois* are Marquis-d'Aligre-Bel-Air and Paveil in Soussans, Le Bosq, Morin, Le Crock and Tronquoy-Lalande in Saint-Estèphe, Lanessan in Cussac, and Pédesclaux, later to become a fifth growth, in Pauillac.

How much does the 1855 Classification differ from that of Wilhelm Franck? The 1855 Classification listed the wines in order of quality and not alphabetically within each section, so Mouton in 1855 is top of the *deuxièmes*, Kirwan top of the *troisièmes*, Saint-Pierre top of the *quatrièmes* and Pontet-Canet top of the *cinquièmes*. Montrose and Ducru-Beaucaillou rise from thirds to seconds. Palmer, Ferrière, La Lagune, Marquis d'Alesme and Calon-Ségur are elevated to third growths. Pouget is relegated to a fourth. Clerc-Milon is demoted to fifth growth. Out altogether go La Mission (a surprising omission as Chiapella, the owner, was a notable *vigneron* and became *régisseur* of a number of important Médoc growths), Liversan and Haut-Bages-Montpélou, as well as a number of estates which have since disappeared. In come Du Tertre and Pédesclaux.

BORDEAUX CLASSIFICATIONS OF THE RED WINES: 1855 AND AFTER

'Too often,' says Edmund Penning-Rowsell in his *Wines of Bordeaux* 'the 1855 Classification has, by inference, been presented either as the beginning of things – rather like the Creation – or, to use another Biblical simile, like the Tablets of the Law, handed down by the brokers of Bordeaux to Médocian proprietors . . . with Haut-Brion's owner being smuggled in on the old boys' network.'

What was so special about 1855 and why has no other 'official' classification of the top Médocs appeared since?

It is easier to answer the first part of this double-barrelled question than the second. The Victorian part of the nineteenth century was studded with grand, showy, universal exhibitions, the first of which was that held in Crystal Palace in London's Hyde Park in 1851. Not to be outdone, Napoleon III, the year after his proclamation as Emperor, set up a commission for an Exposition Universelle de Paris to take place in 1855. One of the attractions was to be a display of the best of Bordeaux wines and the commissioners invited the Bordeaux Chamber of Commerce to produce '*une représentation complète et satisfaisante des vins du Département*' – the Bordeaux region as a whole, it should be noted, not just the Médoc. The Chamber of Commerce decided that the wines of the Gironde should be represented by examples of communal wines except for those already referred to and accepted as *crus classés*. The drawing up of the list of *crus classés* they delegated to the *courtiers*, the brokers who acted as middlemen between the proprietors and the *négoce*.

On 18 April 1855, the joint Committee of the Chamber of Commerce and the Syndicate of Brokers presented their classification of the red and white wines of Bordeaux. As Cyril Ray has put it in his *Lafite*, all the wines of the Gironde were called but, with the exception of Château Haut-Brion from Pessac in the Graves, none but the red wines of the Médoc and the white wines of the Sauternes were chosen. Therefore, not only were the rest of the red wines of the Graves as well as those of Saint-Emilion and Pomerol not considered up to *cru classé* standard but neither were any dry white wines. Moreover, the classifications, it is interesting to note, were based not only on the brokers' experience of the reputation and prices, past and present, of the wines in question, but on blind tastings of recent vintages submitted by the châteaux themselves. Further, the arrangement of the wines within the various levels of growth were in order of precedence, not alphabetical.

So the 1855 Classification was, firstly, the contemporary view of the best of all Bordeaux, not just the Médoc, with Haut-Brion admitted as a sort of afterthought. Secondly, it was 'official' in that the joint considered view of the brokers had been authorized by the Bordeaux Chamber of Commerce. The hand-written list is stamped with their official seal. When the same bodies accepted the invitation to send a similar range of wines to yet another Universal Exhibition, this time in London in 1862, a duplicated list of wines was submitted with a statement that '*Les Vins désignés sous la dénomination de classes sont divisés en cinq catégories et leur rang est indiqué selon leur mérite.*' It is therefore misleading to reproduce the 1855 Classification in a different order. The late Alexis Lichine was guilty of this, promoting his beloved Prieuré to head of the fourths. It is also an error to persist with the common misconception that it was a classification of the Médoc only and to repeat the myth that Ausone, for example, was only left out because its production was too small.

However, there was certainly no intention that the 1855 Classification should be permanent. I am sure it never occurred to anybody involved in its production that it would still be cited and discussed 130 years later. How did this happen? I would suggest that the original defect was the failure of those at the time to realize what a momentous object they had created. This lack of imagination only goes to prove the point I made in the previous paragraph.

If they had had the foresight, the Joint Committee could have decreed that the classification should be reviewed every 25 years or so. They didn't; and since then nobody, official or otherwise, has had the legal or political authority – or the will – to replace the 1855 Classification with anything else. The only change has been the Presidential Decree of 1973 promoting Château Mouton-Rothschild to the ranks of the first growths.

CHANGES SINCE 1855

There have been, though, minor changes as a result of divisions and absorptions of territory by one property of another. In 1855, Léoville, like Latour and Gruaud-Larose, is listed as one growth but with three owners. Rauzan, however, is shown as divided; Pichon is still a single property.

Boyd, in Cantenac, is shown as being possessed by '*plusieurs propriétaires*'. Some 30 years later, after a legal wrangle, a new third growth, Cantenac-Brown, managed to demonstrate that it was entitled to be so classified as it origins lay in vineyards which had been Boyd in 1855. Batailley was split in the 1940s.

One château in the 1855 Classification no longer exists; another ceased to function but has since been resurrected. Dubignon, later Dubignon-Talbot, was always a tiny vineyard. It ceased production after the phylloxera epidemic but was later revived, the *courtiers* of Bordeaux admitting it to the ranks of the Bourgeois Supérieurs as '*ancien troisième cru*' in the 1949 edition of Cocks and Féret. In 1960, Cordier bought the brand name and the vineyard was divided between Ginestet of Château Margaux and Durfort-Vivens and Zuger of Château Malescot-Saint-Exupéry.

Château Desmirail also disappeared from view, though more recently. In 1938, it was absorbed into Château Palmer, though earlier other sections had been sold off. In 1981, Palmer sold the brand name to Lucien Lurton of Château Brane-Cantenac and by this time of Durfort-Vivens also, and Lurton has since re-established the cru.

OTHER CLASSIFICATIONS

With the arrival in the twentieth century of the laws of *appellation contrôlée* and a body, the Institut National des Appellations d'Origine (INAO) to administer and control them, the necessary authoritative machinery for further classification was, in theory, established. Sadly, the INAO has failed to tackle the roots of a plant which is now antiquated, if not in parts diseased, and has merely been content with tinkering at the edges. The difficulty, I suggest, is the division of responsibility, if that is the correct word, between the INAO and bodies such as the CIVB in Bordeaux. In 1932, a list of *crus bourgeois* of the Médoc was established and during the 1950s separate lists of classed growths of the Graves and Saint-Emilion were also decreed. The 1932 *cru bourgeois* list has been revised twice since – in 1969 and 1984 – and the Saint-Emilion list also, in the same years. A reclassification of the Graves is also overdue, though there was nothing in the original 'rules' which stipulated it should be. Pomerol has never had – nor as far as I know, ever wished to have – a classification. But I cannot help feeling all these separate classifications merely confuse the issue from the point of view of the consumer.

Meanwhile, there have been occasional rumours of a new classification of the Médoc. At one point in the 1950s, the classed growth owners conferred together, deciding by a majority that there should be a new classification, according to Edmund Penning-Rowsell (*The Wines of Bordeaux*), and in 1959 a committee was established to look into the matter. Their conclusions were sweeping. No fewer than nineteen growths classified in 1855 were to be demoted, including all three in Saint-Laurent – La Tour-Carnet, Belgrave and Camensac – as well as Lagrange, Dauzac and even Saint-Pierre, among others. A dozen *bourgeois* – Gloria, Lanessan, Siran, Labégorce and others – would be promoted according to the off-the-record reports. Not surprisingly, this radical readjustment caused such a furore that the proposals were dropped.

To counter these and later moves, several proprietors announced that they would boycott any attempts at a reclassification. Others, some aspirants for elevation such as Gloria, for instance, boycotted the revision of the *bourgeois* list in 1969 and so in theory are currently not classified at all.

There were further proposals in the 1970s. In 1970 itself, there was an official announcement that there would be a *concours* or competition to establish a new hierarchy, this time embracing all the top wines of Bordeaux, those of the Libournais and Graves as well as the Médoc. In 1972, another decree was signed but this time the contest was to be between the Médoc proprietors alone.

Yet nothing has happened. Inertia among those content with their 1855 position, antagonism from those threatened with de-classification, the lack of political will to establish an authority which could defend itself against the legal consequences of its actions and perhaps a feeling of doubt about how to establish an expert jury who would be seen to be 'expert' and independent enough, have all combined to preserve the old, creaky status quo.

UNOFFICIAL CLASSIFICATIONS

Yet quite clearly there should be a new classification. Any comparison between production figures in 1855 and those today, bearing in mind improvements in the husbandry of the vineyards in the interim, will show that there has been quite a change in the size of many properties. Some châteaux indeed occupy quite different land. Many produce much better wine than they did, or could have done, 130 odd years ago. Some produce wine of a quality which in no way merits the elevated position they can still quote, if they so wish. To some extent, today's prices reflect the current quality and reputation of the respective properties; but not entirely. And it is surely unfair on those who are striving to produce the best wine they can to deny them the accolade of a higher rung in the hierarchy.

In 1959, the late Alexis Lichine, then proprietor of two classed growths and a member of the original Examination Committee, produced his own classification of all the red wines of Bordeaux. The list included some 150 wines and to avoid the problems of numerical categories, he called his five ranks *Crus Hors Classe*, *Crus Exceptionnels*, *Grands Crus*, *Crus Supérieurs* and *Bons Crus*. He revised his list subsequently, lastly (as far as I know) in 1978. This list appears in the latest (1985) edition of his *Encyclopaedia of Wines and Spirits* and now includes 191 wines. In each category except the top one, certain wines are marked with an asterisk indicating that these, in his view, are considered better than their peers in their rank.

Lichine was one of the few who has dared to put his head in the noose. Given that the list is dated 1978, it is idle to criticize it for not being as up to date as it might be and for failing to take into consideration the great strides made by some properties in the last decade. I am puzzled, though, that La Lagune, Canon and Vieux-Certan are mere *Grands Crus*, the third category, and Grand-Puy-Lacoste merely a *Cru Supérieur*; also, that Léoville-Poyferré, at the time, was considered a *Cru Exceptionnel* and Cantenac-Brown was placed as high as a *Grand Cru*. It is a pity that Lichine did not find time to revise his list before his death in June 1989.

I produced a somewhat smaller list on the same lines in my *Claret* published in 1982. I confined myself to the top 60 or so wines, the same number as the brokers in 1855, and I divided them into four categories: First Growths, Outstanding Growths, Exceptional Growths and Very Fine Growths. The list was based on the performance and prices of the properties concerned during the 1960s and 1970s and allowed for their particular standing in 1982.

Since then, ten more vintages have arrived and we can see more clearly just how good the wines of the late 1970s are as they have matured in bottle. It is time I revised and extended this 1982 list. Here is this revision based on the quality, reputation and prices of the properties concerned over the last decade or so and with particular reference to the performance in the vintages since 1982. The wines are listed in alphabetical order within each category. Second wines have not been included.

First Growths
These are the undisputed top wines of Bordeaux.

Médoc
Lafite
Latour
Margaux
Mouton-Rothschild

Graves
Haut-Brion

Saint-Emilion
Ausone
Cheval-Blanc

Pomerol
Pétrus

Outstanding Growths
These are the super-seconds, wines which, more than occasionally, produce wine of first-growth quality. One could argue very forcibly that in terms of absolute quality (if there is such a thing), these should all be included in the category above. Prices, however, push the first growths into a category apart.

Médoc
Cos d'Estournel
Ducru-Beaucaillou
Léoville-Barton (from 1985)
Léoville-Las-Cases
Lynch-Bages (from 1985)
Palmer
Pichon-Longueville,
Comtesse de Lalande
Pichon-Longueville (Baron) (from 1986)
Rausan-Ségla (from 1985)

Graves
Domaine de Chevalier
La Mission-Haut-Brion
Pape-Clément

Saint-Emilion
Canon
Figeac
Magdelaine
Pavie

Pomerol
Vieux Château Certan
Certan-de-May
La Conseillante
L'Evangile
Lafleur
Trotanoy

Exceptional Growths
These wines are often as fine as those in the category above, and many are clearly of equal standing as a general rule, if not as prestigious or as expensive.

Médoc
Beychevelle
Branaire
Cantemerle
Clerc-Milon
Duhart-Milon
Gruaud-Larose
Grand-Puy-Lacoste
d'Issan
La Lagune
Langoa-Barton (from 1985)
Léoville-Poyferré
Montrose

Graves
de Fieuzal
Haut-Bailly
Malartic-Lagravière

Saint-Emilion
L'Arrosée
Belair
La Gaffelière
Le Tertre-Rôteboeuf

Pomerol
Beauregard (from 1985)
L'Eglise-Clinet
Gazin (from 1988)
Lafleur-Pétrus
Latour-à-Pomerol
Petit-Village
Le Pin

Very Fine Growths
Many of these regularly produce wine in the 'Exceptional' category and some, I am sure, will join the ranks above before too long.

Médoc
d'Angludet
Batailley
Boyd-Cantenac
Brane-Cantenac
Calon-Ségur
Chasse-Spleen
Cos-Labory
Desmirail
Durfort-Vivens
Fonbadet
Giscours
Gloria
Grand-Puy-Ducasse
Haut-Bages-Libéral
Haut-Batailley
Haut-Marbuzet
Kirwan
Labégorce-Zédé
Lafon-Rochet
Lagrange
Lalande-Borie
Lanessan
Lascombes
Malescot
Marquis-d'Alesme
Marquis-de-Terme
Meyney
Monbrison
Mouton-Baronne-Philippe
   (now d'Armailhac)
Les Ormes-de-Pez
de Pez
Phélan-Ségur
Pontet-Canet
Poujeaux
Prieuré-Lichine
Saint-Pierre
Talbot
du Tertre
La Tour-de-Mons

Graves
Bouscaut
Carbonnieux
Larrivet-Haut-Brion
La Louvière
Olivier
La Tour-Haut-Brion
La Tour-Martillac

Saint-Emilion
L'Angélus
Beau Séjour-Bécot
Beauséjour-Duffau-Lagarrosse
Cadet-Piola
Canon-La-Gaffelière
Clos-Fourtet
Dassault
La Dominique
Fonroque
Larmande
Pavie-Decesse
La Serre
Soutard
Tertre-Daugay
La Tour-Figeac
Troplong-Mondot
Trottevieille

Pomerol
Le Bon-Pasteur
Certan-Giraud
Clos-du-Clocher
Clos L'Eglise
Clos-René
L'Enclos
Le Gay
La Grave-Trigant-de-Boisset
   (now La Grave-à-Pomerol)
Lagrange
La Pointe

Fronsac
Canon (Moueix)
Canon-de-Brem
Dalem
La Rivière
Villars

PAUI

PAUILLAC IS THE MOST IMPORTANT COMMUNE OF THE MÉDOC, CONTAINING AS IT DOES THREE OF THE FOUR GROWTHS, AND NO FEWER THAN FIFTEEN OTHER CLASSIFIED CHÂTEAUX – THOUGH PERHAPS SOME OF THESE ARE IN FACT NO BETTER THAN THE BEST OF THE *BOURGEOIS* PROPERTIES.

The commune is split in two by a stream, the Pibran, which flows diagonally across the parish, in a north-easterly direction, to meet the Gironde at the northern end of the town of Pauillac itself. North and west of this stream, the land rises steeply (in Médocian terms) to some 27 metres above sea-level, and includes the vineyards of both the Rothschilds and Pontet-Canet. South and east lie the Bages and Grand-Puy-Lacoste plateaux, the Batailleys, the Pichons and Château Latour.

The Pauillac soil is heavy gravel, thicker to the north than to the south, based on a sub-soil of larger stones, and iron-based sand.

The wines of Pauillac are the archetype of Bordeaux, and the taste of the Cabernet Sauvignon, which in some cases – such as at Château Mouton-Rothschild and Château Latour – forms the vast percentage of the *encépagement*. The wines are full-bodied, dense and tannic; austere when young, rich and distinguished when mature; and the longest-lived of all Bordeaux wines. At their best they are incomparable: the fullest, most concentrated and most profound of all red wines.

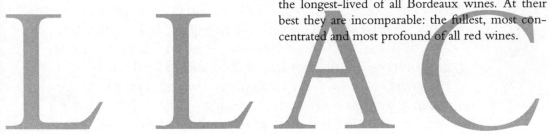

LAFITE

It would be invidious, not to say unwise, to describe any of the first growths as 'The Best'. At this level it is a matter of personal opinion, a question of preference for a particular style. To say that Lafite is better than Latour, for instance, or Mouton better than Margaux, is to attempt to discriminate in value between two things which are not alike – as if one were to try to compare Cheddar cheese with Cheshire. This is not to deny, of course, that one will not find more satisfaction in one wine or one property than in another: the wines may be from different vintages, the properties may make their wine in different ways, levels of competence and dedication may vary. Moreover, it is quite fair to point out that some estates have at times in their history produced wine which was not as good as it should be, not as fine as the price charged should deserve. Yet this is not the same as grading the five *premiers crus* – or eight, if one includes Pétrus, Cheval-Blanc and Ausone – in an order of merit. That would be a task both impossible and ridiculous.

However, one of the first growths has always had a pre-eminent place, not only in professional and wine-drinking circles, but among the public at large. If any wine can be said to be synonymous with 'The Best' it must be Lafite. Lafite, graded the top wine in the 1855 Classification (when the brokers *did* attempt to put the wines within their five categories in an order of merit), occupies a particular niche in our imagination. In a sense it has nothing any more to do with its intrinsic merit or superiority, any more than a Rolls-Royce, caviar or a diamond. In some ways it is beyond comparison. It is unique.

Lafite, though one of the oldest estates in Bordeaux, was not the first to establish its reputation. That honour falls to Haut-Brion, then known as Pontac after its owner. It was Haut-Brion which was the first single-property wine to be marketed as such, around the middle of the seventeenth century, and it is Haut-Brion which is the first single-estate wine that one finds mentioned in diaries, sales records and promotional material at this time.

Soon after, however, Haut-Brion was joined by three other estates, Margaux, Latour and Lafite. From the beginning of the eighteenth century these four were supreme – the same four wines as were recognized as first growths in 1855.

Why out of these four it should be Lafite which has the extra cachet is difficult to establish. Is it purely because it was the first wine to be mentioned in the 1855 Classification? No, the reputation predates this. Is it the price paid for the wine? Again, no, though the multiplicity of selling arrangements, long-term contracts and the different dates each wine was put on the market makes this less easy to establish. The prices the top châteaux demanded, contained in the records of the brokers Tastet and Lawton, together with figures supplied by Wilhelm Franck and other writers, tend to disprove any hypothesis that Lafite fetched more than the other first growths in the first half of the nineteenth century. Other figures culled by René Pijassou in his thesis on the Médoc from Abraham Lawton's earliest records show that in the mid-eighteenth century Haut-Brion fetched substantially more than the other three firsts, whose averages were all within a percentage point or two of each other. Has Lafite, indeed, always been first of the first growths? Again, no. Though it increasingly is at the top as one gets closer to 1855, earlier classifications, such as that of the future American President Thomas Jefferson, who paid a visit to the area in May 1787, list the four in a different order. His order was Margaux, Latour and Haut-Brion, with Lafite fourth.

One can perhaps date Lafite's pre-eminence from around the turn of the eighteenth and nineteenth centuries, perhaps reinforced by the celebrated wine it produced in 1811, the year of the comet. In 1815, Guillaume Lawton, Abraham's son, wrote, 'I regard [Lafite] as possessing the most elegance and delicacy of flavour of the three' (Médoc first growths: they did not deal in Haut-Brion). This view has been echoed, in one form or another by just about every wine writer since.

EARLY HISTORY

Just as the Eskimos have a multiplicity of words for snow, the Médoc has many words for a mound, knoll or height. *Motte*, from which comes Mouton, is one. *Tertre*, commemorated in the Arsac fifth growth, is another. *Cos* is a third; *fite* is a fourth. The origin of the name of Lafite is as simple, as mundane, as that. The word has been misspelt throughout its history, though now is standardized with, correctly, one 'f' and one 't'. There are other Lafites in various spellings in Cocks and Féret, though not as many as there are variations on La Tour.

A certain Gombaud de Lafite was abbot of the monastery of Vertheuil, a few kilometres north of Pauillac, in 1234. Whether he had any connection with the estate we do not know. According to the Abbé Baurein, a charming old gossip who wrote various essays about Bordeaux, its wines and its history in the 1780s, Lafite was an old *seigneurie*, dating from the fourteenth century, owing allegiance to the senior domaine at Lamarque, but itself having suzerainty over two or three neighbouring hamlets or parishes. Baurein alleges that there is a mention of a Jean de Lafite in documents dated 8 March 1355.

In 1558 Jacques de Bécoran, *seigneur* of Lafite, sold Simon de la Bégorce the '*agrières*' due to the *seigneurie*. *Agrières* were dues to a landlord from tenants who farmed on a share-cropping basis. According to Pijassou, it is probable that there were vines on the land at this time, though they would not have been the most important crop.

Soon after this the estate passed into the family of Sauvat or Saubat de Pommiers, Baron du Breuil, a councillor of the Bordeaux *parlement* (not so much a parliament in the British sense, more a judicial appeals court, independent of the Crown). In 1653 the *seigneur* was a Joseph Saubat de Pommiers, who died childless in 1670. His widow was one Jeanne de Gasq, daughter of Blaize de Gasq, Baron de Portets, also a councillor, and Jeanne de Monthis. On 7 October, Jeanne de Gasq married for the second time, her husband being Jacques de Ségur, owner of Calon and *seigneur* over numerous other domaines in the Gironde.

THE SÉGUR FAMILY

It is highly probable that it was the arrival of Ségur which prompted the quite rapid change from mixed farming to large-scale wine production in the Lafite estate. On the 1680 *terrier* (manifest of the estate), there are six references to vines and vineyards. Moreover, these refer to recent planting. It is likely that having seen what his friend Arnaud de Pontac was doing at Haut-Brion, and the success he was enjoying, Jacques de Ségur was determined to do likewise. His son continued the work.

Ségur died in 1691, his widow surviving him until 1704. They had seven children and it was the second, Alexandre, born in 1674, who became the heir. In 1695 Alexandre de Ségur married Marie-Thérèse de Clauzel, heiress of Château Latour. So, within a generation, the Ségur family had married into two of the greatest vineyards on earth. It is not surprising that Nicolas-Alexandre, their son who was born in 1697, was destined to become known as the Prince of Vines.

The years 1705 and 1706 saw the first appearance of Haut-Brion and Margaux in announcements of 'new French clarets' for sale in London. Lafite and Latour followed the next year. The diaries and registers of wine drinkers and merchants at the time, of John Harvey, Earl of Bristol, the Duke of Chandos, Colonel Walpole and his son Sir Robert, refer often to Lafite and the other three first growths. Fine claret was fast becoming big business.

Both Alexandre, who died in 1716, and his son Nicolas-Alexandre, who lived until 1755, must have continued to expand the vineyard area. In 1728 the Lafite *cuvier* was enlarged and rebuilt. In 1732 Nicolas-Alexandre bought the *seigneurie* of Pauillac from M. Brassier of Beychevelle, and this involved land as well as the title, on which no doubt he intended to plant more vineyards. Despite laws passed from 1725 onwards, restricting if not forbidding the planting of new vineyards (for the state was fearful that there would be not only a glut of wine but a dearth of corn and other crops), the extension of Lafite and other vineyards continued. Between 1735 and 1744 the mean yield on the estate was 108 *tonneaux*. As production averaged about 15 to 20 hectolitres per hectare at the time, the surface area of the vineyard must have exceeded 50 out of a total estate of 110 hectares. Lawton's figures from about that time indicate an average price of 1,278 *livres tournois* per *tonneau* of wine.

Nicolas-Alexandre, then, with Lafite, the slightly smaller Latour, Calon and numerous lesser estates under his belt, was a rich man, and was soon created a marquis by Louis XV. He spent most of his time in Paris, where he lived in the Place-le-Grand in the parish of Saint-Roch. When he died in 1755 he was the richest man in Bordeaux and his fortune was evaluated at 2,400,000 livres. Of this Lafite's portion was 707,000 and Latour's 522,400. Pijassou has pointed out that Latour was sold for 64,000 in 1670, so the two estates had risen in value some eight times in 85 years – as a result of producing fine wine.

On Nicolas-Alexandre de Ségur's death the domaines of Latour and Lafite were separated, though until 1785 they shared the same manager, the redoubtable Domenger. Ségur had four daughters of whom the eldest, Marie-Thérèse, married Alexandre de Ségur-Calon, prefect of Paris. Lafite passed to their son, Count Nicolas-Marie-Alexandre, in an act of settlement dated 1763. Because the boy was minor, the estate was at first administered by his father.

Nicolas-Marie was spoilt, weak and profligate. Hardly had he attained his majority that he ran rapidly through his fortune. Despite the protection he enjoyed from his uncle, the Marquis de Miromensil, who was Keeper of the Seals, one of the top government ministers, he had to flee to Holland to escape his creditors, and in 1784 was forced to put Lafite up for sale.

One of the potential purchasers was the Beaumont family, part owners of Latour, but in the end they could not raise the funds, and the property passed to the mysterious M. de Monthieu on 9 November 1784, for 1,012,000 *livres*, a considerable sum of money for the time.

However, using a rather obscure loophole in French law, still incorporated into the deed of Lafite, known as *'retrait lignager'* which gave first option to relations, President Pichard, a distant cousin, was able to acquire it two years later for the same sum.

Pichard, President of the Bordeaux *parlement*, was another man of immense fortune, and for a time was the owner of Château Coutet, as well as numerous other Bordeaux properties. Though surprisingly few members of the Bordeaux landed gentry were guillotined during the Revolution, Pichard was unfortunately one of them, for aiding the emigration of his daughter and son-in-law, the Comte and Comtesse de Puységur.

Three years later, on 12 September 1797 (or *25 Fructidor, l'An V*, according to the revolutionary calendar), Lafite was sold as a *bien national*. The price had almost doubled. Though valued at 1,286,606 francs and 25 *centimes* (such exactitude!), it fetched 2,003,000 francs and was bought by Jean de Witt, a retired minister of Betaive, one of the federal constituents of the Netherlands. In the deed proclaiming the sale, now framed at the property itself, Lafite is described, somewhat tautologically, as *'premier cru de Médoc et produisant le premier vin'*. It also says the vineyard does not suffer from frost and is well maintained throughout.

De Witt, however, could not hold on to Lafite for long. He was over-stretched financially and was unable to meet the payments he had arranged to secure the estate. So, once more, Lafite was put up for sale. This sale took place in December 1800, and the purchasers were again Dutch: three *négociants* called Vos van Steenwyck, of Zwolle, and Berg and Goll de Franckenstein, of Amsterdam.

THE NINETEENTH CENTURY

The turn of the century coincided with the arrival of one of the great *régisseur* families in the history of the Médoc. For the next three generations Lafite's affairs were managed by the Goudals, the first of whom was Joseph, who began in 1797. Coincidentally this is the earliest vintage remaining in the Lafite *vinothèque*. Joseph was a *négociant* in a small way in Bordeaux, and was paid on a commission basis for his duties at Lafite: 5 per cent on the value of the harvest. With 120 *tonneaux* of wine on average, of which three-quarters became *grand vin*, and a price of over 1,700 francs a *tonneau*, Goudal was comfortably off, to say the least.

It is from the arrival of Goudal that we have accurate records of the administration of Lafite and details of the viticulture, viniculture and marketing practices. From these we can see that Lafite in the early nineteenth century was planted with Cabernet, Malbec and 'Verdot', even Syrah, but not yet any Merlot, as well as a number of lesser varieties, some producing white grapes. Gradually over the first 30 years of the century these non-'noble' plants were replaced, though it was not until mid-century that the Merlot began to arrive.

Very little château-bottling was carried out at this time apart from a small amount of private stock for the owners and staff. Nearly all the produce left Lafite, via the port of Pauillac, in the spring following the vintage. Most of this was destined for Britain, sold via the English or Anglo-Irish section of the *'négoce'* in Bordeaux, the Johnstons, Bartons and others. As Wilhelm Franck says, Lafite *'se consomme presque tout en Angleterre'* ('the majority of Lafite is drunk in England').

The Dutch syndicate remained owners of Lafite until the Restoration. In 1816 it sold the estate to Mme Barbe-Rosalie Lemaire, estranged wife of Ignace Joseph Vanlerberghe, a wealthy businessman who had made a fortune supplying Napoleon's armies.

Soon after this purchase there followed a 'pretend' sale. For a long while it was thought that Mme Lemaire had sold Lafite in 1821 to Samuel Scott, a British Member of Parliament and senior partner in his father's banking firm: Sir Claude Scott, Bart and Co., of 1 Cavendish Square. Indeed, this was what everyone was supposed to think, and it is under Scott's name that the property is listed in guides to the wines of Bordeaux at the time, and in the 1855 Classification.

Such was the complication of the matter and the extent of the concealment, that it is only in the last twenty years that the true and, one now assumes, complete story has come to light. Original excavation was by Cyril Ray in his book *Lafite*. The full story was finally uncovered by Professor René Pijassou. The Scott sale was a complete fabrication.

The Code Napoléon had abolished primogeniture. It had decreed that the right of inheritance belonging to the first-born did not exist. Mme Lemaire and her three daughters, however, did not want the estate divided on her death; she wished Lafite to pass solely to her son Aimé. Hence the fake sale in 1821 and the fact that for the next 45 years Joseph Goudal and his son Emile, who took over in 1834, corresponded with the Scott Bank in London, who kept the accounts on the behalf of Aimé-Eugène Vanlerberghe.

In 1866, however, Aimé Vanlerberghe died, childless, and his three sisters decided to come out into the open and face the consequences. The three, all Countesses (de Villetreys, de Cornudet and Duchâtel) were fined no more than a nominal sum, but decided to put Lafite up for sale.

THE ROTHSCHILD PURCHASE

The sale took place in Paris in 1868. At this time, Lafite, now *premier* of the *premiers crus*, was an estate of 135 hectares, of which 74 were under vines. This produced 160 to 200 *tonneaux*, of which 120 to 150 were normally the *grand vin*.

The vineyard area had been enlarged by the acquisition of land on the Carruades plateau from the owner of Château Mouton-d'Armailhacq (later Mouton-Baronne-Philippe, now D'Armailhac) in 1844. This followed a protracted correspondence between Goudal and his employers during which he successfully lobbied for permission to acquire this land, and preceded an even longer, rather agitated correspondence in the early 1850s when Samuel Scott Junior (second son of the original Scott and putative owner of Lafite) was toying with the idea of selling the Carruades, by then planted with vineyards. Goudal was determined they should not go, particularly to Mouton, already a rival.

The auction was fixed for 20 June, and a reserve of 4 and a half million francs, plus a further quarter million for the Carruades, was placed on the property. It failed to reach this figure. No bidder was present. Six weeks later it was auctioned again.

Despite the efforts of a Bordeaux syndicate, led by Gernon, one of the leading *négociants*, who rightly feared the influx of powerful financiers on to the Bordeaux scene, Lafite was sold to a representative of Baron James de Rothschild. For more than 80 years, during a time of relative slump, the Bordeaux *négociants* had called the tune, much to the frequent apoplectic fury of *régisseurs* such as Goudal; now, however, with the rise in wine prices following the prosperity engendered under the Second Empire, an aggressive, moneyed proprietorship could be seen as a threat. The price was 4,140,000 francs, plus 300,000 for the Carruades, plus 400,000 for taxes, stock, etc.

Various people have suggested a number of motives for the Rothschild purchase. Baron James was ailing: he died later in the year. There is a legend that he never visited Lafite. In fact he was there in the spring prior to the sale. Correspondence between him and his sons indicates that he had a good grasp of the Bordeaux wine market. It has been suggested that his sons persuaded him to make the acquisition. A letter shown to Cyril Ray, where James tells his sons, 'We are bankers, not agriculturists', would indicate the truth of this. Others, startled by the price, four times, after all, what it had been in the false sale of 1821, have put the motive down to mere rivalry with other bankers, particularly the cousins at Mouton, or just fashion. If one were a millionaire it was the done thing to have a classed growth under one's belt, and it is mooted that the Rothschilds, who could well afford to do so, were only indulging an expensive whim.

Reality, however, indicates otherwise. No doubt romanticism came into it, but it was based on solid financial fact. Even at over 4 million francs (44 million at 1978 prices according to Pijassou, and therefore well over 100 million today) it represented no more than eight times the value of one vintage. Lafite was bought as an investment.

Since 1868 Lafite has belonged to the Rothschild family, particularly to the branch associated with the French bank. It is a neat coincidence, though it has no bearing on the purchase, that the bank is in the Rue Laffitte (two fs and two ts), in Paris.

On his death, Lafite became the property of James's sons (his daughter Charlotte had married Baron Nathaniel, owner of Mouton, but, following Rothschild tradition, could not inherit). These were Baron Alphonse, Baron Gustave and Baron Edmond. Ever since Lafite has remained in the hands of a partnership of Rothschilds normally five or six with one member taking the most active part. After the war, though the major shareholder was Baron Guy, the senior member of the family, and Alphonse's grandson, the major administrative burden was in the hands of Baron Elie, a grandson of Gustave. Since 1974 Baron Elie's duties have passed to Baron Eric, his nephew, who was born in 1940.

Successive generations of Rothschilds, then, have owned Lafite for over a century, save only for the last war, when it was sequestrated by the Vichy government in order to save the property from being confiscated by the Germans – as it would have been, the owners being Jewish, and particularly as Goering had made known his intention to acquire it personally. It was, however, temporarily taken over to billet the occupying forces, and this had at least one advantage; electricity and mains water supply were finally installed in the château.

Ownership, however, does not mean occupation; moreover ownership by a number of members of the family has tended to preclude the sort of personal commitment by a proprietor resident at the property and to its wines that one finds, for example, in their different ways at Léoville-Barton, Ducru-Beaucaillou or across the Carruades at Mouton in the days of the late Baron Philippe. The Rothschild involvement at Lafite has always seemed to have been a little more distant, more at second hand. Even the manager, the late M. Némès, who ran Lafite from 1961 onwards, was based in Paris and paid only occasional visits to Lafite, though it is fair to say that under him was a resident *régisseur*, André Portet. Baron Eric is now down there at least once a month and the man on the spot is Gilbert Rokvan.

THE VINEYARD

Lafite is the largest of the *premiers crus*, with 92 hectares under vines, a handful more than in 1868, and lies at the extreme north of the Pauillac commune. The château and its outbuildings can be seen from the main road between Pauillac and Saint-Estèphe, and stand in the top right-hand corner of the estate. Between the road and the château, gardens slope down toward a stream and duck pond, sheltered by weeping willow trees. To the north the ground descends towards the Jalle de Breuil which separates the commune of Pauillac from that of Saint-Estèphe. Behind the château lie the vineyards and here the ground rises to 27 metres, the highest point in the commune.

South-west is Château Mouton-Rothschild, whose vineyards dovetail in with those of Lafite, particularly on the plateau known as the Carruades. Further west lies the property of Duhart-Milon, bought by the Rothschilds of Lafite in 1962.

About two-thirds of the Lafite vineyards lie in a homogeneous piece immediately surrounding the château on either side of the road. Intermingled with those of Duhart-Milon lies another portion, and there is a third, a mere three hectares, across the border in Saint-Estèphe, the other side of Cos d'Estournel. Particular permission has to be sought to include this as Château Lafite, AC Pauillac.

The soil at Lafite consists essentially of a deep bed of gravel, as much as four metres thick. This lies on a bed of marl which itself lies on limestone, the so-called *calcaire* of Saint-Estèphe.

Much has been made of the *encépagement* at Lafite, in order to explain, by demonstrating a difference in the proportions of grape varieties, the difference in style between Lafite and Mouton, whose vineyards, by and large, share the same soil. It is certainly true that Lafite is planted with a great more Merlot, roughly speaking one-fifth, than its great rival, and it also has more Cabernet Franc. The figures are officially given by the château as 70 per cent Cabernet Sauvignon, 10 per cent Cabernet Franc and 20 per cent Merlot – the Merlot having been increased recently at the expense of Cabernet Franc. These proportions, though, will vary from year to year. Edmund Penning-Rowsell has shown (in an appendix to the Christie's edition of *Lafite* by Cyril Ray) that the percentage of Merlot in the grand vin has been as high as 24 per cent (1975) and as low as 10 per cent (1971) in recent years.

However, not all is *encépagement*. Some differences, if not in the general make-up or texture of the soil, must be due to micro-differences. Others to microclimatic variations. More still, perhaps, to differences in wine-making. It is worth pointing out that as early as the first decades of the nineteenth century, long before grape varieties were as clearly defined and separate from each other as they are today, and before the introduction of the Merlot to the Médoc, it was accepted that a first growth such as Latour required an extra year in cask compared to Lafite. It would seem that Lafite has always produced a softer wine than the other Pauillac first growths.

THE CHAIS

There has recently been a considerable investment in the *chais* at Lafite. You pass the entrance to the cellar as you drive up to the château and as this road is on an incline, what is ground level at the entrance is effectively underground, below the central courtyard and various outbuildings, further in.

An entirely new circular *cuverie* with twenty new stainless-steel fermentation vats with a total capacity of 4,400 hectolitres was installed and used for the first time in 1988. The old Bosnian oak *cuves* have been retained though, at least for the time being. As at Château Palmer, *égrappage à la main*, destalking manually by pressing the grapes through a slotted table, was persisted with here later than elsewhere, but an *égrappoir-fouloir* has now been in use for some years.

The long, low, dimly lit, traditional first-year cellar remains. What is new and more startling lies behind it. There is an impressive circular *chai de deuxième année*, capable of holding 2,200 barrels, and a splendid colonnaded bottling hall, one of the most up-to-date in the Médoc.

In the cellars and in the vineyard there has been more continuity. The *maître de chai*, Robert Revelle, now approaching retirement age, succeeded his father Georges many years ago. His number two is Michel Bissiriex. J. Paul Baney is the *chef de culture*.

Lafite now produces about 300 *tonneaux* of wine in total. According to the vintage, between a half and two-thirds is bottled as the *grand vin*, and the rest as Carruades or as Pauillac. Until 1967, the second label was Carruades de Château Lafite, not necessarily from the Carruades, merely the wine from the younger vines and other less successful vats, and Moulin des Carruades was an exclusivity of the firm of Nicolas. In that year, though, it was decided to abolish the Carruades label, which many restaurants and merchants had been passing off as Lafite Between 1967 and 1974 a small amount of wine was bottled with a very low-key Bordeaux Supérieur label. Subsequently, the name Moulin des Carruades was revived, starting with the 1974 vintage, and this was the sole name for the second wine. But from 1985 it was decided to rename the *deuxième vin* Carruades de Château Lafite.

THE CHÂTEAU

The small, charming château of Lafite is one of the oldest buildings in the Médoc. While most châteaux are eighteenth if not nineteenth century in construction, Lafite dates from the mid-sixteenth century. In style it is a two-storey *manoir* with a turret at one end. In atmosphere the château, its terrace and overhanging mature trees are as quietly discreet and as restrainedly distinguished as the label itself.

Inside there are no more than four major rooms downstairs, the *salon rouge*, the *salon d'été* (drawing room and morning room respectively), the library and the dining room. These are furnished in the comfortable, opulent, rather heavy Second Empire style of the time of the Rothschild purchase. Most of the furniture was imported by Baroness Betty, an English cousin who was the wife of Baron James, and who spent much of her early widowhood at Lafite, and came from the Château de Ferrières, the Rothschild home in the suburbs east of Paris.

One piece of furniture is the desk on which the schedules of the Franco-Prussian treaty were drafted in 1871. The terms of this were draconian, the French being compelled to pay an indemnity of 5 billion francs, intended to cripple their economy, as well as to cede Alsace and Lorraine. Thanks to the Rothschilds, this enormous amount was quickly paid and the table bears an ink stain said to have been caused when Bismarck smashed down his fist in anger on the table, upsetting the inkwell, on hearing the news.

In the hall stands the notice of sale in 1797, previously referred to, and down from the walls sternly stare successive generations of the family, whose emblem, five arrows representing the five original members of the family who left the ghetto in Frankfurt in Napoleonic times, serves as a weathercock on the roof.

Under the château is the celebrated private cellar, one of the great private collections of old vintages in the world. This occupies a series of deeply vaulted, long, narrow galleries and runs right the way under the house and under the courtyard.

The *vinothèque* was begun by *régisseur* Joseph Goudal in the early 1800s and holds wine going back to the 1797 vintage, including a solitary bottle of the comet year of 1811, which was served to 300 guests at the château in 1926 and described by Maurice Healy as drinking graciously without more than a suspicion of fading. He thought it must have been the greatest claret ever made.

THE WINE

How does one begin to describe a wine like Lafite? I have quoted Abraham Lawton, writing in 1815: 'The most elegant and delicate of flavour.' Cyril Ray neatly resolves the question in two words – 'perfect balance' – and between these two phrases we have most of it.

The wine is lighter than that of Latour and Mouton; the intention is style, finesse and suppleness at the expense of weight and power. This is not to say that Lafite does not possess what the French call *puissance* (not quite the same as power, certainly in the sense of muscular strength), nor that a bottle will not last. Lafite, though, will mature quicker than the other two, and perhaps only in exceptional cases will last as long. For a wine of its size it is bottled surprisingly late, rarely less than two years, at a time when most clarets, even wines as full as Léoville-Las-Cases, are bottled in the early summer some 21 months after the vintage. Some of the difference in weight, and certainly some of the disappointments in lesser vintages – though Lafite was good in the generally disappointing 1969 – may be due to this.

To drink Lafite at its mature best is indisputably one of the great taste experiences in the world: round, soft and velvety, with a complex mixture of soft fruits, delicate flowers and spices combined with a subtle touch of oak, and a depth of flavour which lingers and evolves on the palate long after one has swallowed the wine.

There was a time in the not-too-distant past when Lafite was not as consistent as it ought to have been. The vintages of the 1950s (not only the celebrated 1953) are excellent, though most now show a little age. The results from the 1960s are patchy: I have found the 1961 disappointing on more than one occasion, though I have notes of other 1961 tastings where it shone. These variations, I would imagine, resulted as much as anything from bottling having taken place over several months, and without a general prior *assemblage* to produce a uniform product. The 1962 is very fine but in 1964 the property was caught by the rain (though the wine in fact has lasted better than I expected); but so were others whose wine resulted a great deal better. The 1966 saw the commencement of a decade of substandard wines – in first growth terms. The 1966 shows some class but lacks the concentrated exquisiteness one anticipates. It now shows age. Indeed I have taken it for a 1967. The 1967 is charming, but is now on the decline. It was never as good as Latour. The 1970 is disappointing, the 1971 astringent and the 1973 well past its never very exciting best. It was in 1975 that the tide turned, and since then, especially from 1979 onwards, Lafite has been back on form, as the notes which follow will amply demonstrate. Elegance personified is just about it.

THE TASTING

Jack and Thelma Hewitt live in the middle of the most beautiful part of Vermont's lovely countryside. I first met them on a World Wine Tour to Bordeaux, several years ago, and we have been fast friends ever since.

Subsequently Thelma decided to lay on a surprise, once-in-a-lifetime tasting of Château Latour for Jack's birthday. It was such a splendid occasion we decided once-in-a-lifetime was too seldom and accordingly set about preparing another for the subsequent year. Lafite, in the fall of 1992, was the fourth such magnificent Hewitt extravaganza. Paul Provost, Bob Feinn, Carl Conaglia and Greg Cook, as well as Jack and Thelma, generously provided the wines. Most of the bottles, as you will see, were magnums. This was a deliberate attempt to get samples in as vigorous a condition as possible. It was a great weekend.

1990 2000–2025

No samples at the Hewitt tasting, but I considered this even better than the 1989: more definition, more concentration and more finesse.

1989 1988–2018

Full colour. Classy nose. Neither too hot nor too alcoholic, but rich and concentrated. Fat and oaky; round and voluptuous. Medium-full. Good tannins. Balanced, fresh, full of fruit. Intensely flavoured. But by no means a blockbuster. Long. Complex. Very fine.

1988 1998–2018

Full colour. Rich Cabernet nose, a little more austere and even earthier – in the best sense – than the 1989. Ripe and concentrated with very good grip. Blackberry flavoured. Fullish, some tannin. Good acidity. A little reserved, even a touch hard on the attack, but riper and more generous on the follow-through. Very long. If not fine, proof that at the top levels there are some exciting wines in 1988.

1987 **Drink soon**

Very good colour for the vintage. Classy nose, a little one-dimensional, quite naturally, after the 1988, but by no means weak or slight. Medium body. Fresh. Fully ready. Quite classy. Quite charming. Reasonably positive on the finish.

1986 1998–2026

Excellent colour. Much more intense than the 1988 and 1989. Splendid nose. A wine of structure, depth, harmony and intensity. This really is excellent, though it is a bit adolescent at present. Full, tannic, very rich and very concentrated. Masculine on the attack: with the breed and superb harmony and complexity of Lafite showing through on the finish. Potentially great. Second best of the decade.

1985 1996–2016

Medium-full colour. Just a hint of development. Rather more reserved than most 1985s on the nose. But one can see a wine of medium structure and potentially lush fruit underneath. Medium-full. A little adolescent still, but ripe, slightly spicy, gently oaky and quite concentrated. Doesn't exactly sing today but a lovely long complex, elegant finish shows the potential. Fine plus.

1984 **Drink up**

Surprisingly good colour and nose. Fresh, fruity. Neither sour nor herbaceous. Medium body. This is at its best but needs drinking soon. Reasonable fat and style, even length. But the grip is loosening and it is losing what finesse it ever had. Attenuated flavours of old tea and astringency lurk underneath. Good for the vintage.

1983 Now–2008

Fullish colour. Just about mature. Deeper than the 1985. Lush, accessible, blackcurrant nose. Medium-full body. Good ripe tannins if not a wine with enormous grip. Elegant, concentrated fruit. Good acidity. Long. This is a fine 1983, now approaching maturity. Best at the end. But the 1985 is better – more intense.

1982 1997–2027

Very full colour. Backward, no hint of development. This is quite brilliantly concentrated. Chocolatey, lush and intense on the nose. Full, still quite reserved and tannic, but with heaps of depth and oodles of fruit. Fat, very, very rich. Brilliant. Best of the decade.

1981 Now–2002

Very good colour for the vintage. Open, stylish nose. Ripe, cedary, almost a touch of roast chestnuts. Most attractive. Medium body. Plump, fruity, charming. Good balance. If it has no great concentration or depth it has good vigour, plenty of finesse and is long and positive on the finish. Very fine for the vintage.

1979 Now–2005

Fullish colour. Now mature, but rather deeper than the 1981. Fine, classy but slightly austere nose. Medium-full on the palate. Balanced. Very fine fruit on the follow-through, complex, a lot of depth but a bit austere. Long. Vigorous. A lot of finesse. Very fine for the vintage.

1978 Now–2010

(Magnum) Very good colour. Barely mature. Slightly leafy fruit. Fullish, intense and oaky on the nose. Still vigorous. Complex, concentrated and ripe. Shows very well. But it isn't a great wine. Underlying all there is is a slight herbaceous element. Fatter but less stylish, yet more concentration, more enjoyment than the 1979.

1976 **Drink quite soon**

Good colour. Fullish, still vigorous. Funky nose. Figs, cooked fruit, some astringency. Yet riper and more vigorous and more stylish than most. Fat, sweet, still fresh. As it evolved I got a hint of cooked apples. Medium-full. Plenty of enjoyment here. But not, of course, a classic. Some astringency. But quite fresh. Fine for the vintage. Exotic. But I have had it better than this.

1975 Now–1999

Good colour. Slightly fuller. But more mature than the 1976. Fullish nose. A little dryness. But rounder, mellower on the palate. Surprisingly rich and mellow. Soft, stylish, balanced. *A point.* Even complex. Not the real Lafite elegance but then that is the vintage. Yet long. Plenty of vigour. Fine for the vintage.

1974   **Past its best**

Mature colour but some size and not unduly aged. Smells like packet chicken-noodle soup. Rather watery. A bit astringent. Getting coarse. Over the hill. Strange sweet-sour aspects now.

1973   **Drink up**

This looks a little past it. Light. Very tawny. Old but quite elegant and even with a hint of violets amid the decay. Light but fresh. Old but not aged. Sweet, old roses. Still positive on the finish. Even elegant. Very charming. Long. Even grip. Plenty of enjoyment here despite the age.

1971   **Drink up**

Well-matured colour. Medium weight. Well-matured, old even, and just a little touch mean. The fruit is beginning to dry up and the acidity shows a bit. It was never that fat. On the palate more body than the 1973 but less charm and less elegant. Yet enjoyment to be had here. But there is a little astringency on the palate. Not as exciting as the 1973 or 1975 but there is old claret sweetness at the end, nevertheless.

1970   **Drink soon**

(Magnum) Good mature colour. Aromatic nose. Just a little barnyardy, a little unripe acidity. Well matured. Medium body. A little astringency. A little loose-knit. This has fruit and some elegance but no real concentration and zip. Reasonably sweet on the finish. Charming but not of first growth seriousness.

1967   **Drink soon**

(Magnum) Medium mature colour. No undue age. Soft, mature – but by no means aged nose. Still elegant: very subtle. I prefer this to the 1970. It has more style. Now very soft, and never very intense or concentrated. But balanced. Fresh and round and most enjoyable. Good fruit. Good complexity. Still most attractive. Full of interest.

1966   **Now–1998**

(Magnum) Very good vigorous full colour. Much more vigorous than the 1970. Much richer and more stylish too. Very elegant fruit on the nose. On the palate this also shows a little age, like the 1967 and 1970. But it is the richest, ripest and plumpest of the three. Good concentrated fruit. Fatter than the 1970. Much more elegance. Long but not that intense or concentrated. Very good indeed, but not a great 1966.

1964   **Drink soon**

(Magnum) Very surprisingly, a fuller, more vigorous colour than the 1962. The nose is soft, ripe and pleasant. The palate even better. They must have bottled the best vat in magnums! This is surprisingly good. Round, ripe. Not a bit astringent. No great concentration or dimension but very pleasant.

1963   **Drink soon**

For age and vintage the colour is really quite good. Nor is there any astringency or decay on either nose or palate. Some fruit. Reasonable acidity. No rot. Still has style and interest. A great surprise.

1962   **Now–1999**

(Magnum) Medium-full mature colour. Complex nose. Vigorous. A touch of spice. Medium-full. Very elegant. Round, vigorous without being muscular. Subtle. Long and lovely. Real Lafite. Class and harmony. This is better and more vigorous than the 1966. A fine 1962. Yet lost a bit of vigour as it developed in the glass.

1961   **Now–2000 plus**

(Magnum) Fine colour. This took time to come out of the glass. It was a bit tight at the start. Richer and richer as it developed. Splendid intense fruit. Less *rôti* than the 1959. Violets and plums. More concentrated. On the palate really intense: a *coulis* of marveleous fresh fruit. Velvety. Impeccable class and balance. Just went on and on and on to the finish and got better and better. Splendid. A great wine.

1959   **Now–2000 plus**

(Magnum) Brilliant colour. Full, intense, exciting. Rich, fat, full, concentrated nose. Marveleous mature Cabernet fruit with the extra *rôti* of 1959. Coffee and cedar, crème brûlée and roasted nuts. Not a trace of astringency. Full, very very ripe. Fat. Beautiful balance. Sweeter and more aromatic than the 1961. More muscular. A marveleous pair. No age. No toughness. No astringency. Sweet on the finish. Great wine. As you went from one to another each added an element to the previous wine, building up to a phenomenal pair, each contrasting and complementing the other. A remarkable experience.

1957   **Drink soon**

Medium to medium-full colour. No undue maturity. Slightly austere on the nose. A little lean. A little unyielding and tough. But not astringent. Fresh but a bit rigid. Leafy blackcurrant. Good but lacks charm.

1955   **Now–1997**

(Magnum) Excellent colour. Soft, round, elegant raspberry and other soft fruits on the nose. Good vigour. Great class. Medium-full. A ripe wine, mature but with no undue age. Balanced. Very graceful. Fine long sweet finish. Delicious.

1953   **Now–1998**

Fine colour. Marveleously complex nose. I get roasted almonds and all sorts of soft fruits here. This is – as, luckily, in my experience, always – simply great. Quite fabulous. Enormous depth and complexity. Sweetly ripe, round, complex.

Great length. Faultless balance and finesse. Indisputably *grand vin*. But don't push your luck for ever.

1949   Now–1996

(Magnum) Fine mature colour, no undue age. Lovely rarified elegant nose. Sumptuous, complex delicate soft fruit. Raspberries and roses. This is slightly more structured than the 1953 but in the same mode. Ethereal at the end, showing just a little sign of drying out, but by no means getting short. Supremely elegant. A great wine.

1948   Now–1997

(Magnum) Very fine colour. More than the 1949. Rich, quite substantial but not solid, let alone chunky. Much more black fruits than the 1949. Fullish, fresh, good grip. Plenty of fruit if just a little austere. But stylish, enjoyable and rich on the attack if a little less fat at the end. Yet very long. Very complex. Very classy. Fine.

1947   Drink soon

Medium colour. Lighter than both 1948 and 1949. Ample, cooked fruit. Almost jammy nose. Quite high acidity. But no undue volatile acidity. And not astringent. Sensual, gamey. A touch of caramel. A touch of the cooked fruit flavours of Madeira – though the wine is not maderized. But older than the 1948 and 1949. Beginning to thin out. I prefer the 1948, let alone the 1949. Got rather coarse in the glass.

1945   Drink quite soon

Medium to medium-full colour. Sweet nose, rich, ripe and voluptuous though perhaps it has lost a little of its grip. Medium to medium-full. Plenty of interest, sweetness, depth, style and complexity. But at first it seemed as if it was beginning to lose its vigour. Yet a splendid if residual concentration of fruit, and still long and multidimensional on the finish. The beginning of the end of a great wine, I thought at first. With the grilled veal dish which followed this was explosively vigorous and classy. And in fact it held up better than all the surrounding vintages. This is still a great wine. And seemed to be even more vigorous than it seemed at first an hour and half later.

1937   Drink soon

(Double Magnum) Ullaged to low shoulder. But despite that a good full colour and fresh and vigorous on the nose. Despite the vintage, too, this is not a hard and astringent wine. Round, ripe, raspberry flavour. The malo has obviously taken place in the bottle because there is still a slight touch of SO2. As it evolved got drier and tougher especially on the nose. Fullish. A bit mean and tight on the attack eventually but still sweet on the finish.

1934   Now–1996

(Recorked 1981) Medium to medium-full colour. Caramel and Merlot on the nose. Soft, earthy fresh, elegant. On the palate medium to medium-full. Ripe and old viney concentration. Full of interest. This is an opulent wine but with structure as well as spice. Good acidity. No undue age. Very elegant. Very long. Still plenty of life. Fine and with the usual Lafite class and complexity. A lovely example.

1928   Now–1997

(Recorked) Very good colour. Fine nose. Rich, almost porty. On the palate a little rigid, but very ripe and concentrated. Slightly tough at first but long and classy and vigorous if at the same time a touch astringent. Long. Austere. Cool. Cabernet flavoured. Much much better with food. Not quite great but very nearly there. Bigger than the 1934. Tougher. But if less supple and seductive, greater depth and class. Still plenty of life.

1926   Now–1996

Medium to medium-full colour. No undue age. Concentrated, masculine nose. Just a little tough. Softened as it evolved. Good grip. Medium body. Classy but austere. Complex. It lacks a little generosity but is still sweet. It could have been a little more supple. High acidity but not too astringent. And lots of finesse. Held up very well in the glass. Lovely.

1924   Now–1996

Medium to medium-full colour. No undue age. Sweet, caramelly nose. Great elegance. Lovely, soft, mulberry, cedary, voluptuous fruit. A very aromatic wine. And very fresh. On the palate it shows a little of the chewed lead-pencil taste of old wine. Yet long and classy and sweet on the finish. More charming than the 1926. Silky smooth. Fine. Held up well.

1918   Now–1996

Very good colour for a wine of this age. Rarified, elegant nose. Old but not faded. Cool and full of finess and complexity. Lightish now, but still dignified. Medium body. Very good fruit. Good vigour. I find the 1924 has more charm and quality and depth. But this is long and full of interest. Lovely sweet finish.

1912   Drink soon

Medium colour. Now well matured. Lovely, delicate, pure nose. It may be a little faded but it has great class. The oldest of these last flight (1926, 1924, 1918, 1912) in terms of its state of health but by no means finished. Shows a little acidity at the end. But the finesse of Lafite is still very apparent. And with food (cheese) was still sweet, still complex. And once again lovely.

LATOUR

The difficulty with writing most of these monographs is that often the history is lacking. The proprietor, together with others who have written on the subject, is largely dependent on nineteenth-century writers, who have themselves for the most part borrowed from one another. Many of the stories are largely myth; documents are missing; evidence is deficient. A lot of what one finds cannot be checked; a lot of what one guesses must remain conjecture. One does what one can, but it is not very much.

With Château Latour, on the other hand, there is almost an *embarras de richesse*. In 1963, soon after control of the estate finally passed from the de Beaumont family, owners for almost 300 years, Pierre Brugière, the 84-year-old *régisseur*, retired. This gave a dual opportunity for a general clean-up and in the process a bureau was discovered to contain an important hoard of documents. David Pollock, chairman of the new Latour board, was quick to see the significance of the find, and called in the help of the University of Bordeaux to work on them. There are a number of parchments dating from between 1359 and 1499, then a somewhat patchy selection covering the next two centuries, but, most importantly, a very detailed collection dating from 1775 onwards.

They have provided ample scope for research, and are an invaluable source of material not only for the history of this property, but also, incidentally, on others, and on how vineyards were managed and wine made, matured and marketed over the last few hundred years.

The history of Château Latour has since been published in two fascinating tomes, in French, totalling some 700 pages of text, tables and footnotes – *La Seigneurie et le Vignoble de Château Latour*, edited by Professor Charles Higounet, 1974. The following notes owe much to this work.

EARLY HISTORY

Latour, unlike many of today's châteaux, has its origins in a real castle, or at least a fortification, built as one of a chain along the Gironde to protect the Médoc from the incursions of pirates. This castle was originally square with an enclosed courtyard and a keep of two storeys, and stood roughly on the site of the present *chais*.

It is first mentioned in documents in 1378. At this time south-west France had divided loyalties. Some nobles supported the Plantagenets, represented by Jean de Neuville, King's Lieutenant at Bordeaux, others the French. On 19 September the Tor à Saint Mambert en Médoc was besieged and eventually retaken from a French nobleman who had seized it earlier. This was not the only time the Tower changed hands by force. The Hundred Years' War was a bloody time, and there were a number of skirmishes in the Médoc (hence Batailley, whose vineyards some three kilometres to the west are said to lie on a battlefield). Most of the Médoc supported the English, and when the remnants of the English Army, routed at the Battle of Castillon in 1453, left the shores of the Gironde for England, and three centuries of Plantagenet hegemony came to an end, many of the local nobles left as well. One of these was the Sieur de Larsan, Seigneur of Latour. After his departure the Tower was burnt to the ground and demolished. Nothing remains, though the present tower, built as a dovecote about 1625, and largely restored a few years ago, is said to have been constructed from the stones of the old fortress.

The domaine of Latour was one of the most important in the area. In the fifteenth and sixteenth centuries, with Guyenne and Gascony once again in French hands, there were two leading *seigneuries* in the Médoc, at Lesparre and at Blanquefort; lesser *seigneuries*, of which Latour was one, owed allegiance to these (in Latour's case to Lesparre) and in turn held sway over the smaller estates and minor families in their own immediate area.

By the end of the sixteenth century the *seigneurie* of Latour extended over several neighbouring hamlets, and as far north as Bages and Cordeillan in the parish of Pauillac – Latour being in a hamlet whose name has gradually evolved over the centuries from Saint-Maubert to Mambert, to the present-day Saint-Lambert. At this time there was a house and small park, surrounded by a moat and farm outbuildings. The estate produced mainly wheat and rye, but certainly cultivated wines as well, for in 1595 the local road was called '*Le chemin des vignes*', and in 1634 a document mentions vines on the domaine.

PHASE ONE OF THE MODERN ERA

The modern era for Latour, and probably the start of its history as a serious wine-producing estate, dates from 1670. In that year it was bought by a M. de Chavannes, a private secretary to Louis XIV, from whom it passed by marriage in 1677 to a M. de Clauzel. It must have been either Chavannes or Clauzel who saw the opportunity of fine wine production. Remarkably quickly, along with a small number of other newly planted estates, this foresight was rewarded. As early as 1707 Latour wine was offered to discerning gentlemen of society in the *London Gazette*. By 1714 it was being sold to Holland at 400 *livres* a *tonneau*. Lafite fetched 410 and the slightly longer-established Pontac (Haut-Brion), then the top wine of Bordeaux, sold for 550. Latour was already a first growth. While Prime Minister Walpole, a considerable buyer of fine Bordeaux, drank Pontac, Lafite and Margaux – but no Latour – it is possible that Latour was drunk at court. A letter dated October 1723 from a Bordeaux merchant, J. Bruneval, to Henry Powell, wine-buyer for the future George II, refers to 'four topping growths . . . La Tour, Lafite, Château Margaux and Pontac'.

By this time Latour had passed into the hands of the Ségurs, one of the grandest families of the Guyenne. Alexandre de Ségur married Marie-Thérèse de Clauzel in 1695 and as she was heiress to Latour, the estate joined the many in the Médoc that Ségur owned. He owned

Lafite, where he liked to stay on his visits to the Médoc, there being no suitable grand building at Latour, and his son Nicolas-Alexandre, a member of Louis XV's privy council and *président à mortier* of the Bordeaux *parlement*, was briefly owner of Mouton. Not for nothing were members of his family known as *'Princes des Vignes'*! For a time in mid-century the estate of Latour was run from Lafite, and later, after the death of Nicolas-Alexandre, and the division of the Ségur properties among his four daughters and their heirs, by *régisseurs* on behalf of absentee landlords. It is the preservation of the correspondence between a succession of managers and the owners which has provided the source material for the Latour history.

One aspect demonstrated by this history is how vital the British market was to the fortunes of a top-growth claret. As much as 80 per cent of the Latour crop was shipped to Britain, almost invariably, at this stage, in cask. When France was at war with Britain in the 1750s, and again in Napoleonic times, prices were very depressed.

During the eighteenth century the area under vines was gradually increased, reaching 36.7 hectares by 1790, some 70 per cent of the total domaine. The property itself was considerably smaller than the other *premier cru* estates and even now, with 60 hectares under vines, Latour produces less than the other first growths. By the end of the century production had risen to about 75 *tonneaux*.

Wine at this time was made not so much by 'old-fashioned' methods, as according to rote. There was no way of scientifically assessing the maturity and quality of the grapes, and thereby conditioning fermenting techniques to the standard of the essential basic product. All wine was fermented with the stalks, matured for a considerable length of time in new Baltic oak; in the case of Latour, from four to seven years. In this way, much as many Italian wines today, the maturity was largely achieved in wood, and the wine bottled when required for drinking. This is not to say that it would not keep thereafter, but it does not seem to have been the custom until after the Napoleonic wars to keep stocks of old wine in bottles.

Gradually, however, new methods began to be investigated. *Egrappage* was tried and adopted. The maceration was shortened to five days in 1811 to avoid making the wine too bitter. Chaptalization was first used in 1816 and found wanting, but no doubt after a while it replaced the habit of adding wines from Hermitage and elsewhere, or even of adding a large dollop of Armagnac.

It should be mentioned that at this point the responsibility of the property ceased fairly early. In the spring following the vintage, more often than not, merchants from Bordeaux would send their cellarman up to Latour to rack barrels of the new wine into fresh casks, load them up at Latour's little private quay on to shallow barges, and ship them back to Bordeaux. Very often the wine remained in casks until it reached the final (private) purchaser, where it would be carefully bottled by the cellarman of his supplier.

On the death of Nicolas-Alexandre de Ségur in 1755, the history of the property becomes somewhat complicated. He had had four daughters, and the eldest, Marie-Thérèse, married a cousin, Alexandre de Ségur-Calon, who took charge of both Lafite and Latour. In 1760, however, he passed Latour to his three sisters-in-law, thus enabling the property to pursue an existence independent of Lafite.

One of these three, Charlotte Emilie, Comtesse de Coëtlogan, had no issue; the second, Angélique-Louise, had a son, the Comte de Ségur-Cabanac. The third, Marie-Antoinette-Victoire, had two daughters, who married the Comte de la Pallu and the Marquis André de Beaumont (later to be Chamberlain to the Empress Josephine). By the time of the Revolution, the estate was in three hands, Beaumont, Pallu and Ségur-Cabanac.

The latter then fled the country, and Poitevin, the *régisseur*, advised Beaumont to buy up his share to avoid it being sequestrated by the state. For some reason Beaumont neglected to do this, and in 1794 his portion, some 20 per cent of the property, was put up for auction. It was divided and subdivided and passed through several hands before being acquired during the 1830s, partly by the Bordeaux *négociants* Barton and Guestier, and partly, somewhat later, by another local merchant, Nathaniel Johnston.

Barton and Guestier were happy to take their share of the profits in kind, while Johnston was also advancing money to cover production expenses. Letters to the owners from Lamothe, the *régisseur* from 1807 to 1835, and obviously a temperamental man, frequently denounce both the brokers (middle men between the properties and the Bordeaux trade) and the *négociants* themselves. These messages obviously took root. When, in 1840, Johnston, having only just acquired his portion of the property, announced that he was giving up his banking role, the aristocratic proprietors obviously decided they would try, at all costs, to rid themselves of this trade encumbrance. They put Latour up for auction – and bought it, but all of it, back.

So Latour once again belonged exclusively to the 'family'; the price had been 1,511,000 francs, but of this, only about 20 per cent had had to be paid out to Barton and Guestier and to Johnston. In 1842 the family formed a private company, which still exists today, in which they each took shares. And, as compensation, from 1844 to 1853 Barton and Guestier had exclusivity for the whole crop.

PHASE TWO OF THE MODERN ERA

At this point Latour enters phase two of the modern era. The owners, members of the Beaumont and Courtrivon (successors of the Comte de la Pallu) families, were still absentee landlords. The manager was a M. Roux, a notary and mayor of Pauillac (who had his own property at Bages, a short way to the north).

During the nineteenth-century, château-bottling was at first cautiously, but increasingly widely, adopted; the first growths led the way, and at Latour, this was done from 1863 onwards – the whole crop from 1925. The *encépagement* began to adopt its current proportions, with the elimination of Malbec, Syrah and lesser grapes, the adoption of a small proportion of Merlot (never found at the beginning of the century), and the concentration on Cabernet Sauvignon. The production rose to 100 *tonneaux*. Finally, a proper, if modest, château was built, a square, compact, two-storey Second Empire building with servants' bedrooms in the mansard roofs.

Official recognition as a *premier cru* came in 1855. Latour was one of four, the same four as enumerated by Bruneval 132 years earlier. And this accolade was followed by a succession of glorious vintages.

The 'golden age' of vintages of the mid-nineteenth century was rudely interrupted by the advent of the phylloxera epidemic, exacerbated by an outbreak of mildew. Latour was first hit in 1880, but not until the winter of 1901/1902 were any grafted vines planted. By the First World War about half the vineyard was under new vines. It was probably not until the late 1920s that Château Latour was made from totally grafted wines.

These setbacks, however, did not stop the property producing marvellous wine. By now 40 hectares, producing 110 *tonneaux* of *grand vin* – nearly double in prolific years like 1893 and 1900 – Latour was firmly established as the epitome of Bordeaux, the professional's claret, and had already made its reputation for producing surprisingly good wine in off vintages.

PHASE THREE OF THE MODERN ERA

The third phase of the history of Château Latour started in 1962 when the Beaumont and Courtrivon families decided to sell a majority share in the estate. Thus it was acquired by S. Pearson and Sons Limited, the family company of Lord Cowdray (53.5 per cent) with Harvey's of Bristol taking 25.2 per cent and the balance remaining in France, with the Counts Hubert and Phillip de Beaumont representing them on the board. Harry Waugh, at that time buyer for Harvey's, became another director. The price the British paid is said to have been $2.7 million – over £900,000 – for their 79 per cent share. As Alexis Lichine pointed out, it was a bargain price.

As might be expected – and as happened fifteen years later with Margaux – French chauvinism did not allow this sale to foreigners to pass without comment, but as General de Gaulle is supposed to have remarked (according to Edmund Penning-Rowsell), Pearson's could hardly remove the soil.

The new ownership produced a new regime. Firstly, two dynamic managers were appointed, Henri Martin, the owner of Château Gloria, and Jean-Paul Gardère, a noted broker. These two have now retired, and the wine-maker and technical director is Christian Le Sommer. Secondly, a thorough investigation of the property was undertaken. Old maps revealed that part of the estate, parcels totalling 12.5 hectares, and lying fallow to the west near Château Batailley, had previously been planted with vines. These were replanted in 1965. Other plots to the north-west, which had once belonged to Latour, were bought back. This part of the vineyard had been known as Les Forts de Latour. Meanwhile a vineyard known as Gradalatour in Saint Lambert to the north was also bought. From the younger vines on these new plots of land and elsewhere, a second wine has been created, Les Forts de Latour.

Further investigation of the old maps helped identify and relate a number of poor patches in the vineyard to drains sunk at the end of the nineteenth century, which had since become blocked. These, of course, were opened up again and the drainage from then on improved.

The most radical change, however, was in the vat-house. In 1964 nineteen stainless-steel vats were installed, fourteen of 200-hectolitre capacity and five of 150 hectolitres. Automatic cooling – by pouring cold water down the outside (operated by a thermostatic control from the middle) in order to prevent the fermenting temperature rising above 30°C – was also introduced. At that time *égrappage à la main* – manual removal of the grape-stalks – was also discontinued and a *fouloir-égrappoir* was put in.

Some of these changes were revolutionary – particularly the idea of stainless steel (though Latour was to follow Haut-Brion in this respect) – and particularly for a *premier cru*. Lesser properties, one could suggest, have less to lose. Yet Latour's example, if slowly at first, has now been almost universally followed, and the principle – not what material the wine ferments in, but how successfully that fermentation can be controlled – is accepted everywhere.

In March 1989, further changes in the ownership of Château Latour took place. Allied-Lyons PLC, owners of Harvey's of Bristol, bought Pearson's shareholding on terms which valued the whole property at £110 million. At the same time they bought much of the Beaumont family's equity, with the result that their holdings encompassed 144.5 of the 155 shares in Latour.

Four years later, in June 1993, after twelve months of speculation that Allied-Lyons were seeking to sell Latour, a new owner was announced. It was not AXA-Millésimes, though their interest had been widely speculated, but Artemis SA, owned by French industrialist, François Pinault. The price was £86 million.

THE VINEYARD

If I have spent a long time on the history of Château Latour it is because it is archetypal, exemplary of a leading Médoc property: medieval beginnings as a local *maison noble* or *seigneurie*; an aristocratic eighteenth century with the establishment as a *grand vin*; a prosperous nineteenth century; and finally, if belatedly, the full appreciation of modern scientific methods and the realization that the use of these need not adversely affect quality.

The vineyard has been extended considerably since 1963, and now occupies some 60 hectares in three plots. The largest surrounds the château, extending from the commune boundary, across which lies Château Léoville-Las-Cases, up to the road which runs down to

Château Haut-Bages-Libéral. The second parcel is called Comtesse de Lalande and lies midway between the main road between Saint-Julien and Pauillac and that which runs further inland between Pauillac and Saint-Laurent. The third plot is the Petit Batailley mentioned earlier. These are planted in the ratio 80 per cent Cabernet Sauvignon, 10 per cent Cabernet Franc and 10 per cent Merlot, and produce, on average, about 200 *tonneaux* of *grand vin* and Les Forts de Latour. This second wine was until recently deliberately kept back from sale until more or less mature – or at least drinkable, in France if not in England – and not sold *en primeur*. It started with the 1966 and 1967 vintages, launched in 1972.

Most of the vineyard occupies the right-hand (estuary) side of the D2 road, the road from Saint-Julien to Pauillac, and partly encircles the château of Pichon-Lalande, whose vineyards lie both farther west, and also south (some in the commune of Saint-Julien). This makes Latour the nearest great vineyard to the estuary itself; the land rising more steeply here – the château itself is about fourteen metres above sea level – with less *'palus'* or alluvial land. Possibly because of this proximity, the soil, part of a continuous strip of gravel which extends south as far as Beychevelle, yet thicker at Latour, has a quality denied elsewhere. At Latour there is a metre to a metre and a half *croupe* of this solid gravel, above a sub-soil of gravel and clay mixed with a little sand. The bed of gravel or gravel-mix is particularly deep, and so gives excellent drainage and allows the vines to penetrate deep – often four or five metres – into the soil. Finally, the gravel beds rest on clay – while at Mouton and Lafite for instance, several metres higher in altitude, further to the north and more inland, the subsoil is permeable sand, and at Margaux there is chalk.

THE WINE

What is it about Latour which makes it so fine: so distinguished in good years, so uncannily successful in bad?

In a large part, it must be the soil and its drainage, and the microclimate afforded by the proximity of the Gironde. It must also be the skill of the managers; and it must also be a selfless determination to reject anything second-rate from the final *grand vin* blend. In 1974, for instance, only 25 per cent of the crop was bottled as Latour – the remainder becoming equally Les Forts, Pauillac and *ordinaire*. On average only 60 per cent of what is produced becomes the *grand vin*.

And how does one describe the wine, a wine which is one of the greatest red wines of the world, which is my – and I imagine others' – yardstick for fine claret? Full, yet never overpowering, let alone coarse and robust; aristocratic and elegant, without being effete; deep, rich and powerfully complex in flavour; not voluptuous, like Mouton, yet nevertheless massive in its size and regal in its bearing. If its owners, once, were the *'Prince des Vignes'*, Latour, for me, is the King of Wines.

Having said that, which the tasting notes which follow will amply demonstrate, I must take a deep breath and add that in my view the vintages of the 1980s have not invariably been the yardstick by which all fine clarets should be measured. The renaissance of Châteaux Lafite and Margaux, and the return to form of Château Mouton-Rothschild after a brief hiccough at the end of the 1970s, has coincided with a period when the quality at Latour, though fine, has not been outstanding. I am sure though that this was but a temporary setback, for the 1990 is certainly the wine of the vintage; and I am ready to eat my words if the development of these wines turns out better than I expected!

THE TASTING

Over two successive days in March 1988, I was privileged to attend what I am sure all those who were present would agree was the finest vertical tasting we could ever imagine taking place. The tasting was organized by Thelma and Jack Hewitt, then of Dover, Massachusetts, now of Woodstock, Vermont, to whom my eternal heartfelt thanks. The first session consisted of a complete set of the sixteen vintages from 1985 back to 1970, and took place before lunch. In the evening that day, over a splendid dinner, we sampled another dozen vintages at leisure – 1967 back to 1948. The following evening, at the Fondulas' Hemingway's Restaurant at Killington, Vermont, near the Hewitt's holiday house in the mountains, we repeated 1982 and 1961, just to get us on our mettle, and then progressed backwards through all the best vintages from 1947 to 1920, with the 1893 – a 'pre-phylloxera' wine, in the sense that it was made from ungrafted vines – as a *bonne bouche* to finish. It was a simply magnificent occasion, not competitive, and in the company of good food and good friends. This is how fine wine should be drunk and appreciated.

We had incredible luck. *Le Bon Dieu* was smiling on the Hewitts and their friends. Not a single bottle of the older wines, though they had come from a variety of sources, was anything less than in prime, vigorous form. The notes on the more recent vintages come from a tasting I made at the château in April 1992.

1991 — Optimum Drinking 1998–2008

Very good colour. Fine nose – very fine in fact. There is nothing off-vintage about this. Full, concentrated, ripe, aristocratic. A lot of depth. Fullish, very good tannins. This is fine. Lovely fruit. Not as full or as dense as usual but subtle, complex, very long and above all balanced and classy. A great success. The wine of the vintage.

1990 — 2001–2021

Very good colour. Marvellous nose. Rich, classy, concentrated, splendid blackcurrant-blackberry fruit. Great depth here. Full body. Very good tannins. Oaky, concentrated, rich and aristocratic. Ample but not a bit too fleshy. Succulent though, plump, heaps of lovely fruit. Very harmonious. This is *grand vin*. The wine of the vintage.

1989 — 1999–2016

Good colour. Ample, rich nose, no aggressive tannins, but without the depth of the 1990. Doesn't have the same mark of the new oak, nor the grip of acidity. On the palate it is oaky and ripe, but there is insufficient backbone and complexity. It is medium-full, lush, but almost as much astringent as tannic. Round and rich and long. But not classic Latour. Very good indeed at best.

1988 — 1998–2016

Good colour. Cool, classy nose. Very good Cabernet fruit. Not too dense but very aristocratic and nicely ripe and complex. Medium-full for a Latour, but with lovely finesse, very good fruit and very good balance. It is not a blockbuster but it is harmonious and has real first growth breed. Excellent grip for the vintage. Fine plus.

1987 — 1994–1997

Medium colour. Soft, uncomplicated nose. Lacks a bit of austerity. Medium body. Reasonable fruit and grip. Reasonable finesse. Just a bit one-dimensional. Not short but a bit dilute. Will get astringent. Nearly ready. When it is, it will need drinking soon.

1986 — 1995–2005

Very good colour. Curious nose. Slightly cooked, burnt aspects, and a lack of real grip. For a Latour and for 1986 – so good elsewhere in Pauillac – this is disappointing. Ripe and fruity. Medium-full, but lacks class, grip, austerity and authority. No first growth elements here.

1985 — 1995–2012

Good colour. Ripe and ample nose. Just a suggestion of being a bit too loose-knit. Medium-full. Good grip. Just a little tannin. Most attractive (mainly red) fruit: raspberry, cherry, strawberry. Plump and seductive. Open and accessible. Yet the finish is positive. Most enjoyable. But not classic, serious Latour.

1984 — Now–2000

Not at all a bad colour. Fresh, fullish, vigorous. The nose is a bit austere and stemmy, a bit dense. Better on the palate. Medium to medium-full. Good fruit. Good grip. This a lot better than the 1987. Not a bit unripe or too austere. Very good. Surely one of the few enjoyable wines of this sad vintage! Will keep well.

1983   **Now–2000**

Medium-full, mature colour. What this nose lacks is real class. It is fruity and soft and round and *agréable*. But it is not Latour! Medium to medium-full body. Little tannin now. Balanced – well, reasonably balanced – and fruity. Even quite long and complex. But it only adds up to a nice wine, not a first growth.

1982   **1995–2025**

Full colour. Little sign of development. Smoky-rich nose. Still closed. Full, quite tannic still on the attack. Rich and concentrated. Fat and with very good grip. This is extremely good. Slightly spicy, and not as classy as the 1990, but ample, plump and exciting fruit here, especially on the follow-through. For the vintage it is fine but it does not have the sheer exhilaration to be scored higher than that. It is not quite austere, profound and aristocratic enough.

1981   **Now–2001**

Good colour. Medium to medium-full with no sign of maturity. A little bit of astringency on the nose, lacks a bit of suppleness, but good, basically Cabernet fruit as it evolved. Medium body, a little tannic. Ripe, quite good concentration. Certainly very good for the vintage but equally certainly not top class. Compared with the 1979 it lacks real power and depth by a long way.

1980   **Drink soon**

Medium colour; very good for the vintage. Not much sign of brown. Reasonable nose; there is a faint element of old tea underneath but reasonably fresh and fruity if a little one-dimensional. Good, but certainly not one of the greatest 1980s. Has ripeness and sufficient acidity to keep the wine fresh for a few more years but it may get a bit astringent in due course.

1979   **Now–2008**

Very fine colour, full and dense to the rim; no sign of maturity. Profound blackcurrant nose, with a lot of depth. Fullish, still some tannin. Still a bit of the Latour austerity. This wine has a lot of concentration, depth and size for the vintage. Complex, concentrated and extremely impressive. This is surely one of the superstars of the vintage.

1978   **Now–2010**

Similar colour; a little deeper and slightly more developed. Splendid nose. Very rich, oak and concentrated and more aromatic than the 1979. Full body, some tannin. Marvellous Cabernet Sauvignon richness and concentration but still a bit adolescent in 1988. Potentially very fine.

1977   **Drink soon**

Medium-full mature colour. Mature on the nose without undue age or elements of old tea. Slight-ly dry on the palate but a certain succulence and fat making it more interesting than the 1980. Not astringent; reasonably positive attack and finish. Not bad at all.

1976   **Now–1996**

Quite full colour; little sign of brown. Quite a blowsy nose but not dry on the palate. Full, aromatic, a little overblown. There are elements of over-ripe tomatoes and other vegetables. The wine has a reasonable acidity and therefore is fresh, but is not very elegant. Yet rich, ripe and has good length. Certainly very fine for the vintage. But by no means a really exciting wine.

1975   **Now–2013**

Full colour; a little sign of brown at the rim. Quite firm and dry on the nose but some of the dryness becoming absorbed as it evolved in the glass. Full, tannic and masculine; a little brutal as this vintage often is. But has good richness underneath and good acidity. Very fine quality.

1974   **Drink up**

Surprisingly full colour; no undue brown. Rather lean but smoky nose, some acidity and a little astringency though I understand that other bottles from the same lot have been better (and this is a wine I have not seen for a long time). I don't think this was ever very inspiring. Medium body. Rather tired finish. The 1977 was rather better and I think it always has been.

1973   **Drink soon**

Good fullish colour; now mature. More positive than 1974. Spicy, cedary nose, medium body, generous and round. Not that complex but has concentration and charm, warmth and grip. Finishes long. Shows well.

1972   **Drink up**

Medium colour; mature. Not a bad nose at all, aromatic, oaky, slightly overblown but no attenuation or fade and reasonable depth. This isn't quite as fresh and interesting as 1977 but by no means disagreeable. Getting a little pinched and bitter in the middle.

1971   **Drink soon**

Full colour; a little maturity but not unduly so. On the nose there is some maturity but the wine lacks a bit of grace and charm. There is something dry, pinched and cardboard-boxy about it. Fuller than 1973, with a certain amount of astringency, and though there is some richness and ripeness the wine lacks a certain amount of balance as well as class. I don't think this will ever get it together.

1970   **Now–2010**

Very full colour, indeed the best so far. Little maturity. Marvellous concentrated nose of real class, real depth and complexity of fruit. Full, still some tannin. Very Latour, slightly austere Cabernet. Now beginning to get fat, rich and complex. Excellent quality.

1967   **Now–1997**

Very good colour for the vintage. Still deep almost to the rim; soft, aromatic, plummy, mature nose. Ripe Cabernet, still fresh. No undue age. Fullish, still has good backbone and vigour. Ripe, concentrated and surprisingly complex. Plenty of life ahead of it. Good length with a fragrant aftertaste. Very fine indeed for the vintage.

1966   **Now–2000**

Good colour but not a blockbuster when compared with the 1967 and 1970. A profound nose; now mature with more depth, class, quality and complexity than 1970 at present. This is wine of real distinction which is now fully mature. I have seen more vigorous bottles but this has a splendid essence of blackcurrants, is fullish, has a good grip and is long and complex. Very high class.

1964   **Now–1997**

Slightly less colour; a little less dense to the rim. Solid, less complex; sturdier, not the complexity or velvetiness yet has nuances of sweetness, cigars and coffee. Fullish. While it doesn't have the suppleness and breed of 1966 there is nevertheless good fruit and reasonable length for a Médoc. This is both vigorous and classy.

1962   **Now–1997 plus**

Very fine, full colour; mature. Fat, aromatic, rich nose with a touch of toffee and butterscotch. Alive, rich and full of interest. Full, vigorous, good rich fruit kept fresh by acidity; does not have the nuance or indeed charm on the finish compared with 1966 but it is better than the 1964. Will still last.

1961   **Now–2040**

Fine, full, rich colour; barely mature. The nose is simply marvellous. Magnificent fruit, incredibly fresh; enormous depth, complexity and concentration. Really perfumed. Very full. Still has tannin and will improve. Splendid follow-through and aftertaste. The quality is almost beyond description; very complex, well-nigh perfect.

1959   **Now–2000**

Ullaged just to the top shoulder. Very fine full colour with no undue maturity. Fine mature nose showing good blackcurrants, richness and a slightly roasted quality at first. Less vigorous after a while. Quite full, ripe and complex; more depth and interest than 1966. A great element of ripe fruit and an extra aspect of spice. This is very fine and at first appeared to have bags of life but

after a while in the glass it seemed to lose a bit of its interest.

1955   **Drink soon**

Ullaged to top shoulder. Fullish, mature colour. Soft, fragrant, gently sweet nose with a lot of finesse. This is fully mature and quite full, particularly for a 1955. Ripe, slightly chunky but still fresh. Good class and still very much alive.

1953   **Drink soon**

Ullaged to top shoulder. Medium-full colour. Less than 1955. Fully mature. Slightly dry on the nose with aspects of smoke and vanilla. Medium body. A soft, round, gentle wine. Less structured than the 1955 and not as concentrated. Yet though it has less power and vigour it is no less complex. Long and ripe on the finish.

1952   **Drink soon**

Ullaged to just under the top shoulder. This is the fullest colour of all of the 1950s vintages but is also fully mature. Rich, quite full and powerful nose; still showing fine, ripe Cabernet in a slightly chunky way. Full and quite powerful on the palate. Rich and solid, even a little tannin, but good, ripe, fat, concentrated Cabernet fruit. This is the best of the last three and still finishes vigorously, but it showed a certain astringency as it developed.

1949   **Now–1998**

Fine, full, mature colour. The nose shows real finesse and fragrance; simply lovely fruit, fullish body. Very delicious, lovely, complex, rich and raspberry fruit on the palate, almost sweet in its concentration. A vigorous, quite powerful wine showing real breed. Lovely finish. Splendid balance.

1948   **Drink soon**

Ullaged to just under the top shoulder. Fuller, more vigorous colour. Firm, full, solid and tannic, almost inky. Charcoal as well as chocolate on the nose. This is a more structured, more muscular wine than the above, with plenty of fruit in a chunky sort of way, but it lacks the finesse and there is a certain astringency on the finish.

1947   **Drink soon**

Very fine colour showing not a bit of age. Very impressive nose, opulent, ripe fruit, blackberries and plums. Really sweet with something of a chocolate blend as well. Full and ripe on the palate with a touch of acidity giving it a slightly robust, astringent aspect. Very fine nevertheless. Fat and still vigorous though it did not hold up very well in the glass.

1945   **Now–2000 plus**

Even better colour. Close to being as dark as the

1961. Marvellous nose. All the depth, concentration and profundity this vintage leads one to hope for. There is a power, a concentration and a dimension here which the other wines do not have. Solid, full and tannic. Still very youthful. This is an absolutely magnificent wine with unbelievable richness, depth and complexity. Marvellous finish.

1937   Drink soon

Ullaged to the base of the neck. Extremely dense colour. Solid, structured, dense nose showing chocolate and stewed fruit. Fat and ripe but a touch rigid. A ripe, full classically Cabernet Sauvignon wine with a warm finish. No undue astringency. The wine lightened a little on aeration but held up much better than 1947. Very fine.

1934   Will still keep well

Another splendid colour. Lovely mature colour; blackcurrant, complex nose. Much more subtle than the above, showing real ripeness. Full-bodied but not dense or astringent at all. Really very, very fine. A bit like the 1949 but slightly bigger in structure. Big but round. Lovely ripe, full, complex finish. Marvellous fruit. Very special.

1929   Will still keep well

Splendid colour. Deep to the rim still but no undue brown. Magnificent nose, perfumed, complex, aristocratic but not a bit dense. The epitome of subtlety, elegance and complexity. This is a medium-full wine with a brilliant, soft, fragrant velvetiness and an essence of fruit balanced with a ripe acidity. Very, very long and fragrant and complex. Though it is less structured, I prefer it to the 1945. Will the 1961 get like this? With the 1893, this of all the old vintages lasted the best on ullage. Remarkable finesse, a privilege to drink.

1928   Will still keep well

Ullaged to the base of the neck and the cork crumbled to pieces. Fine colour. Higher-toned nose, less weight it seems. Less intensity of flavour, a bit astringent. On the attack this is a very youthful wine. Full with a very ripe chocolate, aromatic flavour and no undue astringency. It does not have the elegance of the wine above but there is still plenty of ripe, cooked, sweet fruit which continues to the finish.

1926   Will still keep well

Even better colour yet. Still black to the rim. Full on the nose, rich with burnt caramel, coffee and chocolate. Very profound and not astringent. Full-bodied. In a way this has a combination of the robustness of 1928 and the finesse of 1929. Fat, rich, chocolate cake flavour. High acidity, therefore still very fresh. Full and generous. This is like a 1962 but with extra concentration, size and dimension. Amazingly fresh and vigorous.

1924   Will still keep well

Upper shoulder. Fine, full colour. Really one of the very best of these old wines. Lovely round nose with a touch of chocolate and mint. Very rich, round and concentrated. This is firmer than 1934 and indeed has not a hint of undue age. Compared with 1934 with which it has a masculine similarity, it has less perfume of fruit but is nevertheless fine and complex with great depth and length. A classic, still vigorous wine which held up very well in the glass.

1920   Drink soon

Upper shoulder. For the first time a colour with a bit of real age. Soft, aromatic, chestnutty nose: dill, pine needles and cedar. Though the acidity is beginning to show on the palate, the wine has not begun to lighten up. Though soft, it is rich and fat underneath. There is plenty of evidence that this is a ripe year.

1893   Will still keep well

Recorked I believe as the fill was very fine and the capsule was new. A really remarkable, excellent colour. Soft nose, aromatic with a touch of brown sugar. Full body but gentle, really ripe and succulent. Feminine, complex and full of finesse. Supple and fresh, very, very ripe. On this showing it will last for years.

MOUTON-ROTHSCHILD

Baron Philippe de Rothschild was born in Paris on 13 April 1902, and died there on 20 January 1988. Following his wishes, his body was returned to Bordeaux to be buried in the family vault at Mouton a week later.

Few people would disagree with the assertion of the Mayor of Pauillac in his eulogy. This was a great man, one of the greatest men of the Médoc. With his death we had come to the end of an era. Like that other grand old man, the late Ronald Barton, his contemporary, Baron Philippe had a connection with his beloved Mouton dating back to the early 1920s, to a time when the vinification of wine was a largely unscientific affair, when the wine trade was dominated by the *négociants*, not by the proprietors, and when the ownership of a top Bordeaux estate was hardly a profitable undertaking. Baron Philippe's part in the changes which have taken place since then is larger than most.

In contrast to the restrained, typically British demeanour of Ronald Barton, Baron Philippe's approach was anything but diffident. He lived the life of an old-fashioned, almost fictional, theatrical actor-manager. Habitually dressed in a collarless silk jacket, a kimono or a flaring cloak, accompanied by a never-ending series of labradors and other gun-dogs, and radiating a supreme self-confidence in his ability to solve almost any problem, Baron Philippe dominated his surroundings, his acquaintance, his life.

Baron Philippe was a polymath, a man of prodigious energy – he swam half a mile a day until he was nearly 80 – with a multitude of interests and a relentless attention to detail. He also loved the company of women, an enthusiasm which seems to have been warmly reciprocated.

Two of Baron Philippe's chief, interconnecting passions were literature and the theatre. He published his own poetry and translated that of Donne and Marvell. For Jean-Louis Barrault he translated Christopher Fry and Christopher Marlowe. With his father he built and managed the Théâtre Pigalle in Paris in the late 1920s. He produced an early sound film, *Le Lac aux Dames,* which is still occasionally shown on French television. His only child – his daughter Philippine – inherited his love of the theatre and was herself a professional actress.

Baron Philippe was also a sportsman. In the 1920s he drove Bugattis in the 24-hour Le Mans race and the Monte Carlo Rally and came in the first three in both. He was even more successful sailing eight-metre boats, winning two *Coupes de France.*

Above all, he was a man of extraordinary flair and brilliance. Whatever he did, he did well. Everything he created or was involved in was touched with a particular flamboyant theatrical elegance: the genius of Baron Philippe.

Château Mouton-Rothschild was the Baron's lifelong labour of love. He transformed a dilapidated conglomeration of buildings in a remote backwater of the Médoc into one of the wine showpieces of the world. With his second wife Pauline he installed one of the finest small museums of art, each item an object of beauty in its own right but each with a vinous connection. He had the arrogance not only to insist on château-bottling his entire 1924 harvest at a time when this was a revolutionary idea, but then labelling this vintage with a Cubist design by the poster artist Carlu, an innovation denounced by Maurice Healy as 'Bolshevist'. From 1945 onwards, he commissioned a new label design for each vintage from artists as varied as Dali and Warhol, as internationally famous as Braque and Chagall. The payment was five cases of a drinkable vintage of Mouton followed later by another five cases of the artist's vintage itself.

With the wine of the first three years of the 1930s all successively dreary, rather than demean the reputation of Mouton-Rothschild, Baron Philippe created a second wine under the name of Mouton-Cadet, a double pun which referred not only to the secondary status of the wine but to himself, a second son. How long Mouton-Cadet remained exclusively the produce of the young vines of Mouton-Rothschild and the newly acquired Mouton d'Armailhacq is not precisely recorded. It soon ceased to be a by-product and became a brand. Today, it is the world's largest-selling Bordeaux Rouge, and the success of the company, now called Baron Philippe de Rothschild, SA, responsible for marketing Mouton-Cadet and other wines, is as remarkable as any of Baron Philippe's other achievements.

But perhaps Baron Philippe's greatest coup was his successful correction of what he always termed 'the monstrous injustice' that Mouton-Rothschild had not been deemed a first growth in the Classification drawn up by the Bordeaux brokers in 1855 and had to rest with the consolation prize of being placed top of the *deuxièmes crus.*

Why this omission should have occurred is somewhat of a mystery. Mouton had for some time fetched prices well above the rest of the second growths though it never appeared as *premier* in any of the unofficial classifications which predate that of 1855. In 1854, the year before the Classification, and again in 1858, it was sold for the same price as Lafite. Yet the property was somewhat run-down. There was no château. It had recently changed hands and, moreover, the proprietor was English; for Baron Nathaniel de Rothschild, who had bought the 37 hectares of vines of what was then Château Brane-Mouton, for 1,125,000 gold francs on 11 May 1853, was of the English branch of the famous banking family. Personally, I would suggest that it was mere inertia; a lack of courage to interfere with the 150-year-old tradition that the four original first growths – Lafite, Latour, Margaux and Haut-Brion – were in a category of their own at the head of all the other red wines of Bordeaux. Upstarts were not admitted.

Yet, almost as soon as the Classification was on paper, it was apparent that a glaring omission had occurred. By the 1880s, when the superb wines of the great pre-phylloxera vintages of the 1860s and 1870s were being drunk, it was obvious to all that Mouton's wine was of first growth quality. The injustice, however, had to be accepted. As the château's motto put it: *'Premier ne puis, second ne daigne, Mouton suis'* ('First, I cannot be, second, I do not deign to be, I am Mouton').

Unfortunately, though, the 1855 Classification originally had no pretensions to permanency, by the time the Bordeaux trade had recovered from the upheavals of phylloxera and mildew, the First World War and the economic depression of the 1920s and the 1930s, the famous sequence of names from Lafite to Cantemerle, grouped into their five categories, had become hallowed by time. Almost as soon as he arrived at Mouton, Baron Philippe was determined to correct this mistake and everything he did at Mouton was with this in view, to ensure the highest possible quality of the wine sold under the château label while boosting the image of Mouton-Rothschild. The culmination of his efforts finally came in 1973. Jacques Chirac, then Minister of Agriculture, signed a decree elevating Mouton-Rothschild to first growth status. To celebrate and, coincidentally, to commemorate the death of Picasso, Baron Philippe designed a special Mouton label using a watercolour of a Picasso *Bacchanale*, a possession of his museum. For the first and only time, the label also proudly displays the property's first growth classification and a new motto: *'Premier je suis, second je fus. Mouton ne change'* ('First I am, second I was. Mouton does not change').

HISTORY

Opinions are divided as to the derivation of 'Mouton'. The most favoured is that from *motte (de terre)*, or mound, the word was corrupted to *mothon* and then to *mouton*. Alexis Lichine states that in Pauillac they say that the plateau of Carruades behind the village of Pouyalet was where the sheep used to be grazed. I prefer the mound. Mouton, like Lafite, Cos and Du Tertre, owes its name to its most important natural asset – the ground on which it stands.

The early history of Mouton, before it became an important vineyard, is shrouded in obscurity. According to one or two nineteenth-century sources, it was a *manoir* or *maison noble* owing allegiance to the Barony of Lamarque and was confiscated from the Pons de Castillon family and given towards the end of the Hundred Years' War to Humphrey, Duke of Gloucester, youngest brother of Henry v.

Humphrey was murdered in 1447 and was so deeply embroiled in English politics that I cannot see that he could ever have been personally involved in Mouton. After the expulsion of the English from Bordeaux in 1453, the estate passed to members of the Foix family, having also belonged to Jean, Comte de Dunois, Bastard of Orléans and commander of the French army.

BRANE-MOUTON

Modern history begins with the remarkable de Brane family. It would seem that it was Joseph de Brane who developed the vineyard from 1720 onwards, having bought the seigneurial rights of the Barony of Mouton plus a small vineyard, then known as Château Pouyalet, from a man called Grammant. (He did not buy any major buildings – these were later acquired by d'Armailhacq, so giving the latter justification for adding the prefix Mouton on to what was to become a fifth growth.) Previously, Mouton had briefly been part of the magnificent de Ségur estate, which included Lafite as well as Latour.

By the second half of the eighteenth century, Mouton had firmly established itself as the leading growth in the commune, after Lafite, and was fetching prices on a par with those of Pichon in the then-neighbouring commune of Saint-Lambert: 400 to 600 *livres* a *tonneau* as opposed to 1,500 to 1,800 for Lafite and Latour (Latour being in Saint-Lambert too).

Over the next few decades, during revolutionary, Napoleonic and Restoration times, successive de Branes worked hard to improve the standing of their vineyard. The reputation of the wine grew. By the 1830s it was clearly in a class of its own – not quite up to the firsts but certainly superior to even the best of the seconds, Rauzan, Léoville and Gruaud-Larose. The vineyard, some 50 hectares, produced 120 to 140 *tonneaux*. It was Hector de Brane, grandson of Joseph, who, with his neighbour d'Armailhacq, was responsible for the promotion of the Cabernet Sauvignon as the major grape variety in the vineyards of the Médoc. De Brane's reputation was such that he was styled the 'Napoleon of the Vines'.

Then, having established one vineyard, de Brane's enthusiasm turned to another. In 1830 he sold Mouton or Brane-Mouton, as it was known, to Isaac Thuret, a Parisian banker, for the enormous sum of 1.2 million francs. Langoa, Beychevelle and Calon, all large estates which, moreover, had châteaux which could provide suitable residences for their proprietors, had all sold for no more than half this amount in 1825. De Brane concentrated his attentions on the Château de Gorse further south, renaming it Brane-Cantenac, the name it has now.

Thuret seems to have neglected the property and it is perhaps this factor, plus the mildew epidemic of the early 1850s, which sealed Mouton's fate in the 1855 Classification. In 1853 he sold it to Baron Nathaniel de Rothschild for 1.125 million francs, less than he had paid for it 23 years earlier. The vineyard was then somewhat dilapidated, as were the outbuildings. For the first few Rothschild years, there were only the farm buildings and the *chais* for the wine. There was still no place for the proprietor to live. Baron Nathaniel, who died in 1870, devoted his attention only to the *chais* and vineyard. It was left to his son, Baron James, to construct a small château, Petit Mouton, in 1880.

The Rothschilds, for the most part absentee landlords, appointed Théodore Galos as *régisseur* and he soon made good the deficiencies of the Thuret regime and continued the good work of de Brane. He also found time to manage Lagrange and Château d'Arcins. In the last half of the nineteenth century, the property encompassed some 55 hectares of vines and produced about 150 *tonneaux*, exclusively, according to Cocks and Féret, from the Cabernet Sauvignon. The price the wine fetched was high. Increasingly, the 1855 Classification was being seen as unjust.

Baron James died at the age of 37 in 1881 and his widow, Laura Thérèse, remained in charge until 1920. The property then passed to her son Henri. A doctor of medicine, a man of the arts and a pioneer racing motorist, Henri was not interested in leaving Paris. His second son Philippe, however, had been evacuated to Mouton during the war and, as Cyril Ray says, fell in love with the place.

BARON PHILIPPE DE ROTHSCHILD

So it was that on 22 October 1922, Baron Philippe, then aged 20, took over. He did not in fact acquire ownership until 1947 when, on the death of his father, he bought back his brother's and sister's shares in the property. But effectively Mouton was Baron Philippe's after 1922.

Mouton-Rothschild in 1922 was unprepossessing in appearance. Everything was still very much as it had been in the nineteenth century. The house, a small gabled villa with pointed turrets and a coloured glass veranda, extensively submerged under creeper and ivy, had been built, as I have said, in 1880. Baroness Thérèse had made regular visits to the Médoc despite the slow train journey and the long drive in a horse and cart over the 40 miles of rutted roads from the station at Bordeaux. Yet the accommodation was spartan. The estate was without running water, electricity or proper roads.

Baron Philippe set to work with his characteristic energy. With the decision to bottle the entire harvest on the estate, it soon became apparent that more space would be required as the wine would have to be kept on the spot for the two to three years it would require before being ready for bottling. The Baron commissioned the Parisian architect Charles Siclis to design a new building to his specifications. The magnificent, awe-inspiring *chai de première année*, forerunner of many imitations, was born. The design is simplicity itself, the effect emphasized by subdued, indirect lighting.

The year 1927 saw the beginnings of what would become Mouton-Cadet. The harvest was not worthy of labelling as Mouton-Rothschild. It was marketed, not entirely successfully, as Carruades de Mouton-Rothschild. In 1933, he bought the neighbouring Château Mouton d'Armailhacq from the Comte de Ferrand and the Count's rather moribund Société Vinicole de Pauillac. During the remainder of the 1930s the reconstruction continued, now at increasing speed. Electricity was installed, roads built, the telephone connected. An elegant *salle de banquet* was built alongside the *grand chai*. Revolutionary at the time, visitors were encouraged. The Baron would later add his considerable weight to the inauguration of the Commanderie de Bontemps, a promotional organization for the wines of the Médoc and the Graves, and allow the *salle* to be used for local dinners and the entertainment of distinguished visitors.

Since the shock of the Carlu design, the Mouton label had gone through several modifications. In 1929 the device of the Rams Rampant had first appeared. It is partly a pun on the word Mouton, partly an illusion to Baron Philippe's birth sign Aries, the Ram. From 1934 onwards, the annual production in numbers of bottles and the Baron's signature was added. This format was unchanged until 1945 with the exception that the labels of 1938, 1939, 1940 and 1941 remained unsigned. The Baron was not there when the wines were bottled.

During the Second World War Mouton was confiscated, the Baron's French nationality revoked, and he himself incarcerated in a Vichy prison. Between 1940 and 1944, Mouton was occupied by the Germans, who turned the house into a military headquarters and built barracks for the troops. An officer, known locally as the *Weinführer*, and personally appointed by Goering, supervised the business side and ensured the continuity of wine production. The house itself, however, suffered considerably.

While Baron Philippe escaped from Vichy and managed to make his way to London to work with the Free French, and his daughter Philippine miraculously remained safe in France, his wife, the Vicomtesse Chambure, was transported to the Nazi concentration camp at Ravensbrück and died there in 1945.

After the war, now *de jure* master of Mouton, Philippe continued to make improvements on the estate to restore the château and to expand his *négociant* business in Pauillac. The splendid 1945 vintage, with a label commemorating the *Année de la Victoire* designed by Philippe Jullian, was followed by an excellent 1947, a highly successful 1948 and a simply magnificent 1949, my favourite of all the Mouton vintages and surely one of the greatest wines ever made in Bordeaux.

In 1954, Baron Philippe married Pauline Fairfax-Potter, an American who had lived in Europe for many years and who had been his constant companion since 1951. Surrounding the original château, known as Petit-Mouton, several old haylofts and lumber rooms above garages and stables were converted into elegant modern apartments for the Rothschilds and their guests. This was christened Grand Mouton.

Together, the couple transformed Mouton-Rothschild and scoured the art galleries of the world, building up the collection which would eventually become the Museum. This was the happiest period of the Baron's life. The Baroness's taste, charm and wit were a splendid foil to Philippe's sense of style, energy and flair. We worked together as a team, he would later record. Sadly, the Baroness Pauline died in 1976. In homage, the name of Château Mouton-Baron-Philippe was changed to Baronne-Philippe – the authorities would not permit a change to Baronne-Pauline it seems (it has since been changed, yet again, to Château d'Armailhac) – and later, the *négociant* company then called La Bergerie was renamed La Baronnie. I do not think Baron Philippe ever really got over her loss.

THE VINEYARD

The Mouton vineyard stretches west from the village of Pouyalet, south of that of Lafite and on slightly less elevated land except for the Carruades plateau which the two properties share. In all, there are 75 hectares of vineyard, with perhaps 70 in production at any one time producing about 225 *tonneaux* of *grand vin*.

The soil is gravel, on a bed of larger stones, mixed with sand rich in iron. Underneath this, the subsoil consists of clay, marl and so-called *calcaire* (limestone) *de Saint-Estèphe*.

Mouton shares with Latour the highest proportion of Cabernet Sauvignon in its *encépagement* in the Médoc, as much as 85 per cent. The rest is Cabernet Franc (7 per cent) and Merlot (8 per cent).

THE *CHAIS*

Mouton is fermented traditionally, with a long *cuvaison* with the skins in 27 oak vats. The Mouton *cuverie* is on two levels as at Pontet-Canet. When the grapes arrive they are first elevated to the upper storey in order to fill the vats from above.

After the *égalisage*, the wine is transferred to the celebrated *chai de première année* through which all visitors pass on their way to the museum. This is the archetypal long, low, dimly lit cellar with the new oak casks, one deep, in serried ranks on the floor.

From here, in the second year, the wine passes to a deeper *chai*, a proper, below-ground cellar which runs underneath the central courtyard and part of the *chai de première année*. Nearby, the bottled wine is binned and behind locked doors lies the private cellar, probably one of the most extensive collections – and not only of the claret – in the world.

THE MUSEUM

Today, Mouton is one of the important places to visit in Bordeaux, indeed a must for anyone who comes for the first time. The Musée de Vin, located in a seventeenth-century cellar, one of the oldest existing buildings on the estate, was the brain-child of the Baron and particularly of his American wife, the late Baroness Pauline. It is one of the most beautiful small museums in the world. Each object, from prehistoric pottery to Picasso, from glassware to tapestry to *objet d'art*, has a vinous association, but each is of the highest quality. The museum is brilliantly lit. To anyone interested in the lore and history of wine-making and drinking, it is a fascinating place, an enviable collection, assembled with taste, care and love.

PRICES

Since the war, Mouton's assertion of its rightful status as a First Growth has been confident and unequivocal. Mouton regularly fetched opening prices *en primeur* higher than most of the other First Growths, principally Margaux and Haut-Brion, and this was confirmed by the auction levels of mature vintages. The price rivalry between its fellow Rothschild château, then owned by Baron Philippe's cousin, Baron Elie, was notorious, reaching a peak in 1971 when Lafite's price of 110,000 francs a *tonneau* was upstaged by Mouton's price of 120,000 francs, equivalent to nearly £8.00 a bottle before any other charges at the then rate of exchange of 13.25 francs to the pound. Today, all the *premiers crus* seem to go into a private huddle in order to agree the same opening price.

THE WINE

The wines, though not always recently of *premier cru* quality, are at their best. Latour and Lafite have their disciples – and, at this level, one is talking more of a preference of style rather than making a comparison of quality – and there is no doubt that Mouton cannot match Lafite's superb balance and elegance, nor Latour's uncanny knack of producing good wine in a bad vintage. Nevertheless, the concentration of flavour, the sheer opulence, the massive amount of fruit, allied with the unmistakable, seductive, cedarwoody aroma of a mature Mouton, makes truly exhilarating drinking. Bended-knees wine indeed. There is a warmth, a weight, which makes one think fleetingly of areas outside Bordeaux such as the Côte de Nuits or Hermitage, a suspicion unlikely to be evoked by a Lafite or a Latour. I recall a colleague referring to Mouton as the best Pomerol in the Bordeaux area. Although I think this is putting it a bit disparagingly, I can see what he was getting at.

The particular style of Mouton is, of course, a result of the very high proportion of Cabernet Sauvignon in the vineyard as well as longer vinification. The wine will stay in the vats with the skins for as long as a fortnight after the fermentation is over before transference to the brand-new oak casks most of the top growths use for their new wine.

I have always maintained that wine is an expression of the personality and art of the person responsible for it. Hence, if one wishes to uncover the real character of a domaine one must attempt to understand the nature of the proprietor. Nowhere is this more evident than at Mouton. Baron Philippe de Rothschild was a complex, renaissance man, of profound intelligence, great energy and a totally unselfconscious flamboyance of character. So is his creation. The result (apart from a hiatus between 1971 and 1981 when the results by *premier cru* standards were somewhat disappointing) is a wine of undoubtedly first-class magnificence.

THE TASTING

The following wines were sampled during a splendid weekend arranged by Jack and Thelma Hewitt in Vermont in October 1990. My eternal heart-felt thanks to them for such a fine opportunity.

Optimum drinking

1987   **Now–1999**

Good colour for the vintage. Attractive oaky nose. The oak does not dominate though. There is certainly fruit here as well. Gentle, already a bit cedary. While there is a slight absence of generosity at the moment, there is enough substance and grip here to suggest that this will arrive as the wine mellows. Medium body, still some tannin. A little austere but not weak or feeble. Positive finish. Very good for the vintage. Evolved well in the glass, became rounder and fruitier. Very classy.

1986   **2000–2030**

Very full immature colour. Still very young indeed. Rich, fat, concentrated, smoky and aromatic. This is quite splendid. Still very reserved. A classic wine. Very full, very concentrated, very tannic. A real baby but one of great potential. Has the right (promising) sort of bitterness of a blockbuster in its infancy. Real depth. Great character. A much more austere wine than the 1982 but with more intensity of fruit and inherently more breed. *Grand vin!*

1985   **Now–2004**

Fullish colour but a shade more development than the 1986. Even allowing for the 1986, which obviously overshadows this wine, I find the nose a bit disappointing, for there is an absence of both fat and concentration. Only medium to medium-full body. Not a great deal of tannin. An absence of real power, depth and dimension. Stylish but merely pretty, judged by *premier cru* standards. Forward.

1984   **Now–2000**

Full colour for the vintage, only a little development. Good nose. Oak and blackcurrant, the fruit almost in a Ribena sort of way. Seems more substantial than the 1987. Very promising for the vintage. No one would guess this was an off year. Though it lacks a little real richness there is substance, depth and style here. Remarkably good but the 1987 is more seductive.

1983   **Now–2005**

Just a little more colour than the 1985. A little more development. Good rich blackberry nose but just a little musty or something on the nose (this I think is this particular bottle). There is plenty of depth here. Seems better than the 1985. Medium-full body, the tannins now beginning to soften. This is an attractive, balanced wine with ripe fruit – if no real concentration – which is quite obviously the product of a plentiful vintage. Good definition. Good class. Finishes long. But ultimately lacks the dimension, power and richness of classic Mouton. Better than the 1985 though.

1982   **1997–2027**

Very full, rich colour; still immature. Excellent nose. Very rich and concentrated. Cooked and exotic. Fat and voluptuous. A lot of spice. Very full, still very tannic. Hugely rich. Opulent and oaky. This is a splendid example. Marvellous fruit and great depth. Balanced by an excellent acidity. A brilliant wine. Multidimensional. Real power and intensity of flavour here. *Grand vin* again.

1981   **Now–2002**

Very good colour for the vintage. Full, still immature. Quite developed nose. Round and plump, quite sweet fruit. This seems ready. It doesn't have a great deal of grip. Medium body. Just a little tannin but at the same time a little astringency. There is something a bit ungenerous about this. Slightly stewed and hard in the middle. Reasonable length though. Yet not very attractive.

1980   **Now–1996**

Good colour for vintage. Fullish. No undue brown. Lightish but fragrant nose. Good grip for a 1980, but quite high-toned, without much depth. On the palate this has medium body, reasonable fruit and enough grip, but not only a lack of depth – as one might expect in this vintage – but also class. Good for the vintage but not exciting.

1979   **Now–1999**

Fullish colour, still quite youthful looking. Less developed than the 1978. Fullish, blackcurranty nose. Quite austere but almost a suggestion of swimming baths, tanks. There is substance here, but a lack of opulence and dimension. A touch four-square even. Similar palate. Quite full but dull. The tannins are now resolved but there is no depth here, nor class. Disappointing.

1978   **Now–2005**

Medium-full, mature colour. This is very similar to the 1979 on the nose, but less four-square, slightly higher toned. A bit superficial. Yet this is quite the best of the last four, because it has some dimension and a lot more class. Medium-full body. Tannins now resolved. Good acidity. Quite rich fruit. Not the greatest 1978. It lacks real concentration. But has balance, length and finesse.

1976   **Drink soon**

Good full colour, just about mature, similar to the 1975. There is fruit and opulence here though in a somewhat flabby sort of way. Ripe, spicy but also some astringence on the nose. On the palate, in its burly way, this is one of the better 1976s. Good fruit, some richness, no lack of acidity. So still fresh and quite long. Medium body. As with all 1976s there is a lack of real

class. Very good for the vintage. (I have had better bottles of this wine. The latest, as I write, in November 1993, had none of the astringence, and was plump and voluptuous, with no lack of vigour. Very fine for the vintage. Now–2000.)

1975   **Drink soon**

Good full colour, just about mature, like the 1976. Tannic nose. Somewhat dry and burnt, aspects of bitter chocolate. There is a sort of arid austerity here which is a bit putting off. Quite full, as much astringent as tannic. But has a lack of fruit and also finishes a bit short. Unexciting. Won't get any better. Disappointing for the vintage.

1974   **Drink up**

Medium to medium-full, mature colour, no undue brown. Still alive but somewhat meagre and dilute, lacking class. As 1974s go this isn't at all bad. But it is now getting to the end of its useful life. Medium body. Was fresher, fruitier and classier a few years ago.

1973   **Drink soon**

Medium colour, mature, no undue age. Soft, round and pleasant on the nose. Fully evolved, of no great pretention. Fresh and fruity. Medium body. Very good for the vintage. This still has a long finish. No better than pretty but that is the 1973 vintage.

1971   **Drink soon**

Medium-full, mature colour. The nose is soft, quite classy, with good ripe Cabernet fruit. Lacks a bit of richness and depth though. On the palate this has medium body. Fully ready. No astringency. The attack is pleasant but the finish is a bit mean and insipid. The fruit is drying out. A bit astringent on the aftertaste. Disappointing after the nose deteriorated.

1970   **Now–2000**

Fullish, immature colour. Quite a powerful nose but a touch hard. It lacks a bit of flesh. Better on the palate, but I don't think this is a really great 1970. Fullish, just about ready. Good, indeed fine fruit and good grip but an absence of opulence and real concentration. I don't find this very exciting but as it developed it got less lumpy as it aerated. Fine, but the 1966 is much more powerful, much more complex, much more classy.

1967   **Drink soon**

Medium to medium-full colour. Mature but not unduly so. The nose is beginning to lighten up a little but there is good depth and class underneath nevertheless. Medium body, soft, fragrant. Attractive fruit. Good acidity. Never a wine of great concentration, and without the breed of Latour 1967, but definitely a success. Needs drinking soon though.

1966 Now–2000

Full colour; still very youthful. This took a bit of
time to evolve. A bigger wine than the 1970,
with more depth and interest. Ready. Quite
structured. Still austere on the attack, a touch of
green peppers. Plenty of concentration and fruit
and class underneath, but just a little four-square.
A wine of depth and complexity though. And
above all breed. Very fine. Much longer and
classier on the finish than the 1970.

1964 Drink up

Medium to medium-full colour. Soft, aromatic
nose. Not at all bad. There is cedarwood here.
The fruit, though, is light and high-toned and
rapidly gets thin as it aerates. For such a denigrat-
ed wine this isn't at all bad. Ripe but one-dimensional. Now shortening and losing what
class it ever had.

1962 Drink soon

Fullish colour. Still youthful. This is a bit dumb
on the nose. Very Cabernet Sauvignon. More
Latour than Mouton. Fullish on the palate. A little austere. The acidity shows and on the attack it
could be a little more generous. Quite structured. Long. But it has lost a little of its fruit and
fat. Was it always a bit too structured? Very good
class though, but I think I've had better bottles.

1961 1995–2035

Very full colour. Still youthful. Intense, powerful, concentrated nose. Closed at first but with
real depth and potential. This is indisputably
great. Powerful, intense essence of fruit. Iron in
the soul but opulence and velvet enveloping it.
This is still a baby. Quite brilliant.

1959 Now–2000 plus

Very fine colour. Splendid nose. This is open
where the 1961 is still closed. Yet real depth,
character and complexity, cedar and eucalyptus.
Breed as well, and none of the hot, alcoholic,
baked, astringent aspects of some 1959s. This is
an excellent example. The best of all 1959s perhaps. Full, ample, rich, concentrated. Splendid
balance and complexity. Real breed. Very long.
Very lovely. Still very vigorous.

1957 Drink soon

Full colour. Typical 1957 nose. Hard, unyielding, austere. Yet it put on a bit of flesh in the
glass with a touch of interesting mint. On the
palate full, a bit brutal and solid. Some tannin
and astringency. Also a bit vegetal and slightly
bitter and stalky on the finish. Better with food
but essentially lacks charm.

1955 Drink soon

Very good colour. Still vigorous; youthful even.
Lovely nose. Rich, round, supple, mellow, aromatic. Ripe and seductive. Plenty of depth.
Medium-full. Still sweet. An elegant, plump example. Perhaps showing the beginnings of beginning to loosen up and lose a bit of its class on
the finish but a lovely example. Still good length.
Very classy. Fine.

1953 Now–1997

Medium-full, mature colour. It took a bit of
time to come out of the glass. On the nose delicate, fragrant, complex and classy. Red fruit
rather than black. Yet this has a certain earthiness
to it. On the palate full and rich especially for a
1953; good acidity. Plumply fruity. But it lacks
the refinement of Lafite and Margaux. Fine but
not as great within its vintage as the 1955. Acidity shows a bit. Good vigour. Finishes well. Plenty of life still. Plenty of class. Better than the
1952.

1952 Drink fairly soon

Full, vigorous colour. Rich, mellow, open nose.
None of the toughness here which characterizes
many left-bank 1952s. Depth and cedarwoodi-
ness. Fullish, ample and aromatic. A little astringency especially on the follow-through but fine;
a touch of bitter chocolate perhaps. For food. A
bit chunky but plenty of fruit. It was rather better five or ten years ago. Yet still has a good, vigorous finish.

1950 Drink soon

Medium-full, fully mature colour. Mature, quite
fragrant, quite complex nose. Still has plenty of
vigour. This has very Cabernet fruit. Classy. But
compared with the 1953 – for example – a bit
one-dimensional; more so as it evolved in the
glass. A lightish wine, both now but also for a
1950. Has it lightened a bit? It seems to have lost
a little of its fruit. Yet there is breed and still
length here. As it evolved the acidity showed a
bit.

1949 Now–1997

Fullish colour, still vigorous. Simply exquisite
nose. Plumply fruity, quite lovely and fragrant.
Real breed and in a sumptuous, ripe, voluptuous
way concentrated. As I have always thought, this
is one of the greatest wines produced since the
war. Fullish, fragrant, balanced, complex, ethereal. Soft and perhaps not for the millennium,
but quite disarmingly lovely. Very very long and
multidimensional.

1948 Now–1997

Even fuller colour than the 1949 but quite
evolved. Very classy nose. As good as ever! Sturdier than the 1949. Fuller but cedary, opulent
and Moutonny, almost nutty. Elegant. Fullish,
rich, quite austere but classic, balanced, long and
complex. A lovely example which will still last
well.

1947   **Now–2000**

(Magnum) Full, rich, vigorous colour. Intensely
fruity in a chunky but porty way. Typically
1947. I must say I find the 1948 more elegant on
the nose. This wine is better on the palate than
on the nose though. Full, vigorous, intensely
rich. Even sweet. Heaps of concentration and
ripe fruit. A great wine. I prefer the sheer breed
of the 1949, but this is a splendid example which
has bags of life ahead of it.

1945   **Now–2000 plus**

Very fine, full colour. Still vigorous. A firm, full,
rich, concentrated blockbuster. Great power on
the nose but not burly, indeed a touch minty.
Very meaty blackberry fruit. Fine acidity. Still
very fresh and vigorous. Marvellous concentrated fruit. This is *grand vin* without a shadow of a
doubt. Smoky, gamey character and chunky. As
usual quite a toughie. Will still last for ages.

1943   **Drink up**

Medium, mature colour. High-toned nose. This
is a leanish, elegant wine. Not chunky. Not astringent. The acidity shows a little. Stylish but
lacks a little succulence. Good length. Has complexity. But was better ten years ago, I would
suggest.

1937   **Drink soon**

(Magnum) Fullish, well matured colour. This
has a touch of maderization. Stewed, tannic,
chunky, vegetal. Even compost heapy, smells of
Marmite. Reminds me of a 1957 twenty years
on. But I've had far worse 1937s. This is by no
means as tough and fruitless as some.

1934   **Now–1997**

Fullish colour, still vigorous. Rich, ample nose.
No sign of age. Full bodied, rich, meaty, tannic.
Very good grip. Quite an austere Cabernet-
flavoured wine. A little tough. But has the breed
of Mouton. Developed well in the glass. Finishes
long. Will still last well. An outstanding and vigorous 1934.

1933   **Drink up**

Surprisingly good colour. I expected much
lighter. This is medium-full. Soft nose. No
undue structure. Vegetal and, oddly, crustacea,
and something herbal on the nose. Cleared up a
bit on aeration. Medium body. Better on the
nose than on the palate. Mellow but the fruit has
disappeared a little, leaving it a bit austere and
unripe. Yet has elegance. Slightly dry and short
on the finish. I'm sure this was one of the better
1933s in its prime.

1929   **Will still keep well**

Fullish colour. Mature. Marvellous fruit on the
nose. Fragrant. Very classy. Real complexity and
very very vigorous. This is a brilliant wine. Indisputably *grand vin*. Medium-full. Lovely fruit,
real intensity and vigour and great breed. Marvellous. Still bags of life. Very, very fine finish.
Fragrantly sweet. Quite fabulous. Perhaps the
1949 is better – or better now, but this runs it
very, very close.

1928   **Now–2000**

Very fine colour. Still – if that is possible – vigorous. This is a bigger, denser wine than the 1929.
Fuller on the palate. Richer and more aromatic.
Where the 1929 is fragrant, this is fat. This will
last better. But it doesn't have the breed. Yet a
fine wine. Liquoricy, spicy and slightly four-
square but long and delicious.

1920   **Drink soon**

Medium colour. Well-matured. Soft, cedary,
lead-pencil nose. Soft, elegant, somewhat faded.
But a fine old wine nevertheless. The fruit has
disappeared to some extent. And the acidity
shows a bit. But there is fruit, charm and class.

1900   **See note**

Label shows Petit Mouton, MR in a seal; but is it
château-bottled? It doesn't say. Very full colour.
Full but maderized on the nose and palate. A
pity. Certainly a wine of substance and vigour.

PICHON-LONGUEVILLE, COMTESSE DE LALANDE

Château Pichon-Longueville, Comtesse de Lalande, to give it its correct title – it is often lazily truncated to Pichon-Lalande or Pichon-Comtesse – is the larger of the two Pichons. Suitably, it produces a more 'feminine' wine than its neighbour Baron. Always one of the top wines of Pauillac, in recent years its reputation has increased enormously. It is now recognized as producing one of the best of all the Médocs outside the first growths, often their equal if not occasionally their superior.

Strangely, the growths in Pauillac are biased at the top and at the bottom of the 1855 Classification. Since the elevation of Mouton-Rothschild in 1973, Pauillac has been able to boast three of the five first growths; at the other end, there are no fewer than twelve of the eighteen fifths. In between lies a solitary fourth, Duhart-Milon-Rothschild, no thirds, and two seconds, the Pichons – Comtesse and Baron.

The site that is now Pichon lies between the villages of Saint-Julien and Saint-Lambert and was formerly called, variously, La Batisse, La Bastide and La Baderne. The land on the right or river side of the road belonged to the *seigneurs* of Latour, that on the left was the fief of the family Montguyon who themselves were vassals of the lords of Latour, and belonged around 1500 to a family called Brun de Boysset.

Coincidentally, a few years previously, the proprietor of Latour had been a Jean de la Lande, Baron de la Brède, and on a map from a half-century later there is a vineyard a little to the north of where the Pichon-Lalande château lies now called '*Aux Vignes de Lalande*'.

HISTORY

The first Pichon to concern us is Bernard, son of François de Pichon and Catherine de Bavolier, who was born in 1602 and who on 8 September 1646 married Anne Daffis de Longueville, the only child of the Baron de Longueville. I had assumed that these Longuevilles were relations of the Duc de Longueville, Governor of Normandy and one of Condé's supporters at the time of the Fronde, the French civil wars during the minority of Louis XIV. Recent research into the château archives shows this not to be so: the Daffis de Longueville family was local Gascon nobility – Longueville is a village near Agen – and *présidents à mortier* in the Bordeaux parliament.

The Barony of Longueville appears to have passed into the Pichon family together with Anne's dowry, and their first son François acquired another, the important Barony of Parempuyre, south of Macau (his father was already owner of the Château Parempuyre), at the same time as he married Benoîte, the only daughter of Jacques d'Alesme in 1671. The Alesmes were one of the most senior families in the Médoc and held important estates just north of Bordeaux. Jacques, Bernard's second son, was styled Baron de Longueville, like his father, when he married the heiress Thérèse des Mesures de Rauzan on 9 February 1694. Thereafter, there were two Pichon branches: Pichon-Parempuyre, descendants of François, and Pichon-Longueville, descendants of Jacques.

THE SUN KING

Somewhat before this time, there is a story of Bernard de Pichon, Baron de Longueville, twice entertaining the twenty-year-old Louis XIV, once in 1659 and again the following year on his unwilling way to Saint-Jean-de-Luz to marry Maria-Theresa, Infanta of Spain. To cheer the young king up (for he was marrying Philip IV's daughter in order to comply with a treaty negotiated by Mazarin), great banquets and hunting expeditions were arranged and Louis was the guest of Longueville, then first president of the Bordeaux *parlement* at his noble residence, the Cours du Chapeau Rouge, now a bank, in Bordeaux.

JACQUES DE PICHON

Jacques de Pichon, born in 1649, married Thérèse de Rauzan in 1694 and thereby acquired estates in Saint-Lambert which Thérèse's father, Pierre, had recently begun to plant with vines. Pierre des Mesures de Rauzan, *'le Sorcier de la Vigne'* as he seems to have been known, had bought an estate called Gassies or Garsies inland from that of Château Margaux in 1661. A few years later he acquired the estate we now call Pichon. Having planted vines in Margaux and being so near the vineyard of Latour, it was logical that vines should be planted here as well. Within a few years the reputation of the wine was established. By the mid-eighteenth century the property was recognized as second only to that of Latour in the commune of Saint-Lambert – later to be absorbed into Pauillac – producing 30 *tonneaux* of *grand vin* which fetched 400 to 500 gold *livres* a *tonneau*, on a par with Brane-Mouton, Gruaud, Bergeron (now Ducru-Beaucaillou) and Brassier (now Beychevelle).

Jacques de Pichon died in 1731 and was succeeded by his son, also called Jacques. Whilst the Parempuyre branch of the Pichon family busied itself in the Bordeaux parliament, the Longueville branch occupied itself with its vineyard, enlarging the area under vines and consolidating its reputation.

After Jean-Pierre de Pichon, son of Jacques, the Longueville title had passed to Joseph, who was born in 1755 (and died, at 95 years of age, in 1850). Joseph was married in 1784 to a Mlle de Narbonne de Pelet d'Anglade and they had five children. Raoul, the sole surviving son, became the Baron of Pichon-Baron; Louis had died unmarried in 1835. Of the three daughters, one – Sophie – became a nun, the second, Marie-Laure-Virginie, married Count

Henri de Lalande in 1818, and the third, Gabrielle, married the Comte de Lavaur. What complicates the story is that their older brother Raoul also married a Lalande, Félicité, sister of Henri, in 1819.

THE DIVISION OF PICHON-LONGUEVILLE

By this time, the laws of inheritance had changed. Under Napoleonic law, inheritance was divided equally. No longer could the estate pass, as in Britain, to the heir. Indeed, the title of Baron was not exclusive to the first born either; all male heirs took the title of their father.

Thus, on the death of the old Baron in 1850, the Pichon estate was divided. Two-fifths (28 hectares) of vines – the share of the late Louis included – went to Raoul; three-fifths (42 hectares of vines) went to the three daughters. However, for the next decade, the estate continued to be run as a single entity. It was only after the death of her brother Raoul in 1860 that Marie-Laure-Virginie, Comtesse de Lalande, started to administer the 'feminine' share of Pichon separately. Sophie, *chanoinesse* of Saint Augustin, had died in 1858.

History is the death of legend. The well-known, if somewhat lascivious, story that Marie-Laure de Lalande was the mistress of the Count de Beaumont of Château Latour – and that there being at the time no château at Latour, of the Count giving some of his land to Marie-Laure on which she could construct what is now the Pichon-Lalande château – turns out, under the sober scrutiny of the archives, to be no more than a malicious myth. Marie-Laure had brought this land as her dowry and the château was constructed by the architect Duphot in 1840. Lalande was still alive in the late 1850s, by which time both he and his wife must have been well into their seventh decade.

It was only in 1851 that Raoul, then aged 64, began to construct the château we know now as Baron, modelled, it is said, on Azay-le-Rideau (if so, the architect must have had a slightly surrealistic memory). This replaced the old *maison noble*, La Baderne, which had stood, together with its ancillary buildings, on this site for over 300 years.

So it was not until Raoul's death in 1860 that the Pichon estate was finally split and the wine made separately. Curiously, none of this generation had any children. Raoul's portion went to his cousin and adopted heir, also called Raoul, a Pichon of the Parempuyre branch, who took the name of Baron Raoul de Pichon-Longueville. Marie-Laure, Comtesse de Lalande, took over her sisters' share when they died and bequeathed her larger part of Pichon to her niece, born Elizabeth de Narbonne-Pelet, who was married to another Lalande, the Comte Charles. Marie-Laure died in Bordeaux on 3 March 1882. Like her father, she must have lived to over 90 years old.

At the time of the 1855 Classification, Pichon was a large estate, some 80 hectares under vines, with a production of 100 to 120 *tonneaux*. The portion that went to the Baron was that part of the vineyard immediately to the south and west of the Château Baron and the main road, the D2. The Lalande vineyard, though it includes a few hectares on the Latour side of the road, is mainly further west still towards Batailley, and there is a substantial portion lying in Saint-Julien, interspersed with vineyards of the three Léoville estates.

Both parts of the Pichon estate remained in the family until after the First World War. The last of the Pichon-Longuevilles sold Baron to the Boutellier family in 1933 and died in 1980 – and by this time the Comtesse château had already been sold, in 1925.

The Comte and Comtesse Charles de Lalande had two children, both daughters. Henriette, the eldest, was born in 1866 and remained unmarried. Sophie married Joseph de la Croix and had five children. On her death in 1926 these children, together with their aunt Henriette, sold Pichon-Lalande to a syndicate headed by Louis and Edouard Miailhe. The price, complete with all the furniture in the château, was 700,000 francs.

THE MIAILHES

The Miailhe family have been vineyard owners, brokers and *négociants* in the Bordeaux area since the eighteenth century and came originally from Portets, 30 kilometres south of Bordeaux. Frédéric Miailhe, who was born in 1869, was a *courtier* (a broker) and had two sons, Louis and Edouard, who followed him into the business after the First World War. The brothers started to buy properties in the 1920s. Louis bought Château Coufran and Verdignan, which face each other at Saint-Seurin, at the extreme north of the Haut Médoc. These are now owned by his son Jean. Together in 1930 they bought Château Citran in Avensan, a commune inland from Margaux. This used to belong to Jean's sister, Mme Cesselin, but was sold in 1987 to the Japanese Société Touko Haus. As well as Pichon-Lalande, they became part owners of Château Palmer in the late 1930s and acquired Château Dauzac in 1966. Since 1848, through their antecedents, the Barbiers, the family have owned Château Siran.

Edouard Miailhe died in 1959, but his estates were not divided amongst his children until 1978. Château Dauzac was sold in this year to pay death duties; the share of Château Palmer went to his eldest daughter, Mme Monique Sichère, and has since been sold, and Château Siran to his son William-Alain. The Miailhe share (55 per cent) of Pichon-Longueville-Lalande went to the youngest daughter, May-Elaine, wife of the late General Hervé de Lencquesaing. The Lencquesaings immediately bought the shares of four of the associates, giving them 84 per cent, and took over the control of the estate in 1978. Today Mme de Lencquesaing and her children are the owners of Pichon in its entirety.

The transfer, however, was not as smooth as it would seem from the sequence of events broadly outlined above. May, married to a career officer in the French army, was away from Bordeaux. She originally had little thought of devoting her interest and energies to Pichon. At first – from 1960 to 1972 – Pichon was administered by William-Alain Miailhe.

Then difficulties began to arise. Some of the minor shareholders wanted to sell out. There were queries about the accounts. Eventually, a major family row broke out. In 1972, William-Alain resigned and, from 1975 to 1978, the stewardship of the estate was entrusted to Michel Delon, proprietor of the neighbouring Château Léoville-Las-Cases and old school contemporary of Mme de Lencquesaing.

THE VINEYARD

The estate of Château Pichon-Longueville, Comtesse de Lalande now comprises 86 hectares, of which 60 are under vines. In the 1960s the area under vines had only been some 40 hectares. Towards the end of the decade the vineyard was considerably increased by a parcel of almost ten hectares located between Pichon-Baron, Latour, Haut-Bages-Libéral and Batailley. This land had been so divided, hitherto, into some 70 lots, that it had been almost impossible to cultivate. A further five hectares was acquired during the management of M. Delon. All but four and a half hectares (which are between those of Latour and the road just north of the château) are situated, as I have said, on the west and south of those of Baron, on the large plateau which runs away towards Grand-Puy-Lacoste to the north, Batailley to the west and Talbot to the south.

Quite a bit of the Pichon-Longueville-Lalande vineyard is, in fact, situated not in Pauillac but across the commune boundary in Saint-Julien. Old vintages – up to 1959 – were bottled partly as AC Pauillac, partly as AC Saint-Julien. The wine, of course, was identical.

The soil here is a *graves* dating from the Gunzien period. At the top it is almost pure gravel but deeper down there is more clay. Under this is what are called *Molasses du Frondasais*, a greenish sandstone of the Miocene age and, below that, limestone and *marnes de Saint-Estèphe* (*marnes* is marl, a clay-limestone mixture).

The vineyard contains more Merlot than most in these parts. It is planted in the ratio 46 per cent Cabernet Sauvignon, 12 per cent Cabernet Franc, 34 per cent Merlot and 8 per cent Petit Verdot and produces around 200 *tonneaux*. The second wine is called Réserve-de-la-Comtesse.

THE *CHAIS*

In recent years, the *chais*, virtually a small village of outbuildings and cottages for the vineyard workers and their families, have been completely rebuilt. The *cuverie*, with its old wooden fermentation vats, was reconstructed and the wood replaced with a battery of epoxy-resin-lined cement vats in 1953, added to in 1972. In 1980, they began to install stainless steel and eight large cylindrical *cuves* were bought.

The cellars themselves have also been enlarged. A very fine *chai de première année* was constructed in 1966. This runs across the back of the garden behind the château and has been earthed over, forming a sort of roof-terrace from which one can look out over the Latour vineyard and the Gironde estuary. Another *chai*, this time facing on to the road and above ground, was built in 1980, carefully in the style of the existing buildings, and is used for bottling and the stockholding of bottled and cased wine. This replaced a further *chai* adjacent to one of Château Latour which was owned in the village of Saint-Lambert. In 1986, the underground *chai* was enlarged, to give a *chai de deuxième année*, a considerable engineering achievement. In 1988 a second *cuverie* was constructed across the courtyard behind the *régisseur's* office.

Briefly, as I had said, in the interregnum of the mid-1970s, the management of Pichon was entrusted to M. Delon of Léoville-Las-Cases, but this arrangement ceased when Mme de Lencquesaing took over as principal owner in 1978. From 1975 onwards, the *régisseur* was the able Jean-Jacques Godin, who arrived in 1970 as *chef de culture*. He was assisted by Francis Lopez, the *maître de chai*. Late in 1992, following an internal dispute, Godin was fired.

THE CHÂTEAU

The château is an elegant Restoration-style mansion built on two storeys with servant quarters above. It lies in a little park on the right-hand side of the road just over the Saint-Julien-Pauillac border, not quite facing its more fantastic neighbour, Baron. Unlike Baron, the château of Lalande has been continuously lived in since it was constructed in the early 1840s, and this has preserved its character as a home as well as a showpiece.

It is furnished almost entirely with the original, mainly mahogany, restoration and Second Empire pieces bought by the first three sisters. It appears to have been Sophie, the sister who took Holy Orders but who also studied in the *atelier* of the painter Gérard, in Paris, who had the most influence, and the rooms are decorated with a number of her paintings, both original and copies by her of old masters.

The ground floor, approached by a short flight of steps, contains five main rooms, two on each side of a wide central hall. At the back and in the corners, a circular stone stairwell leads you to the floors above and to the private cellar underneath.

THE WINE

Pichon-Longueville, Comtesse de Lalande, is today one of the superstars of Bordeaux, one of a small handful of wines now enjoying the rating of super-second, denoting a wine which, *en primeur* or later at auction, achieves a price 50 per cent or more than that of the first growths.

It is really since the arrival of, first, M. Godin, who elevated the quality of the wine from very good to even better, and, second, May de Lencquesaing, who with her boundless energy was fully prepared to get around the world and tell everyone about it, that this Pichon has produced at this level. Consistently since 1975 the quality has been excellent. Previous vintages, though very fine, only occasionally produced bottles to this very high standard. It was a fine partnership. I regret it no longer exists.

Today, Pichon-Longueville-Lalande, though never the austere, tannic blockbuster of its neighbour Latour, is a wine of immense richness and succulence of ripe fruit. The concentration and complexity, the silk and velvet, the remarkable intensity of fruit – above all the sheer breed of the wine – is of a character which is more like Lafite than Latour. It is a warm and generous wine, deceptively enjoyable, even when it is many years from maturity. It attracts high prices – equal with Palmer, Ducru-Beaucaillou and Léoville-Las-Cases – and deservedly so. It is one of the great wines of the Médoc.

THE TASTING

In July 1993 I sampled the vast majority of the following wines thanks to the generosity of Murphy L. Clark of Eagle Point, Oregon. The tasting took place at his ranch near Medford. I have added notes on the 1950, the 1947 and the 1945 from a tasting which took place at the château in March 1988.

Optimum drinking

1990   1999–2019
Medium-full colour. Rich nose, plenty of fruit, but a little raw. Not a blockbuster but certainly very ripe and succulent. Medium-full body. Ripe tannins. Very good grip. Plummy fruit, potentially opulent. On the feminine side. Very long and complex. Fine but lacks the extra flair for great.

1989   1998–2012
Medium-full colour. Lighter nose than the 1990. Less intense; lower acidity. A little drier. On the palate this is a wine of the same size as the 1990 but it is less complete. The tannins are lumpier, the wine less elegant, less balanced. It is a little bitter at the end. Very good, but the 1990 is better. Yet the wine is certainly long.

1988   1999–2019
Medium-full colour, still very youthful. Classic Pauillac. Firm, the tannins not as ripe as in 1986. Very good acidity though. This wine has class. Medium-full. Lovely Cabernet-Merlot fruit. Not a blockbuster. Excellent grip and a lot of character and complexity. Really concentrated for a 1988. Fine. Will keep well. Very long. I prefer this to the 1989. Lovely finish.

1987   Now–1998
Medium colour. No undue brown. Quite fruity, but no means light. On the nose a certain lack of generosity, obviously, but not wishy-washy or too lean. Medium body, fresh, quite ripe. Quite fat and lush, even, and with good acidity. Inevitably a bit one-dimensional compared with the neighbouring vintages, but a very good result. Will still last.

1986   2000–2025
Full, somewhat dense-looking colour. Currently adolescent, but a lot of structure here. A little dense at present on the nose. But rich underneath. Splendidly ripe tannins. This knocks the spots off the 1990 and 1989. Fullish, marvellously intense and harmonious. Really rich and concentrated. Splendid Pichon fruit and dimension. This is a great wine. Very, very long and lovely at the end. Fine.

1985   Now–2008
Medium to medium-full colour, just beginning to show some signs of maturity. Very Merlot on the nose. Some tannin evident. Ripe, with a touch of spice. A little adolescent as well. I'm sure I've had better bottles of this. It seems a little unbalanced. Smoky, the tannins a bit dry, the wine a bit hollow. Disappointing. An unlucky bottle. Not off. The finish is better especially as it evolved. Medium body. Ripe. Good acidity.

1984   Drink up
Good colour for the vintage. Now mature. Nose getting a little stringy. On the palate the wine is more generous. Medium body. The new oak is evident and gives it a little lushness. Not too lean. A very good result. But drink now.

1983   Now–2005 plus
Good fullish mature colour. Plump, accessible nose full of bramble fruit. Most attractive. Medium body. A fine result for the vintage. Good acidity. Generous and seductive. Ripe and fat. Absolutely à *point*. Very long and lovely finish.

1982   1995–2015
Full colour just about mature. Rich on the nose. Still needs time, still a bit unfocussed. Lush, fat, fullish, very rich on the palate. It doesn't have the grip and therefore poise and class of the 1986,

but it is still a lovely example. Opulent, potentially velvety. But no means lacking acidity. Long, lush. Fine. Better still in two years. Second best of the 1982–1990 flight. But not as classic as the 1986.

1981　　　　　　　　　　　Now–1999
(Imperial) Direct from the château. Vigorous colour for the vintage. Only a touch of brown. Good nose. Ripe, medium weight. Slightly more evolved and with less grip than the 1983. A *point*. Charming. Very good indeed for the vintage. But the 1979 is better.

1980　　　　　　　　　　　Drink soon
Good colour for the vintage, but quite brown at the rim. Mellow nose, but beginning to lose its fruit and elegance now. Still attractive on the palate though. Good grip. Quite plump. Reasonable structure. Shows very well for an 1980. Plenty of attraction.

1979　　　　　　　　　　　Now–1999
Full, vigorous colour. Only barely mature. Attractive nose. Firmer and fresher than the 1981: more structure, higher acidity. Good Cabernet fruit. Rich but a little hard at first. More generous on the follow-through and the finish is ample and balanced. Medium-full. Good grip. This is fine for the vintage and will last well.

1978　　　　　　　　　　　1995–2010
Good colour. More intense in the middle but more evolved at the rim than the 1979. More evolved on the nose as well, but richer and more concentrated. Good depth here. Fullish, ample ripe tannins. Very good concentration. This will still improve. Very good grip. Fine plus. Very lovely fruit. Very complex. But the 1975 is richer and more concentrated. Marvellous finish.

1977　　　　　　　　　　　Drink up
Direct from the château. Good colour. More vigorous than the 1980. A little dry and herbaceous on the nose. Certainly not unpleasant, but beginning to dry out and lose what fruit it had.

1976　　　　　　　　　　　Now–1998
Fullish, quite vigorous, mature nose. No undue brown. Sweetish on the nose. Chocolate blancmange and cooked plums. Not too dry or at all coarse. This is an attractive 1976 which is holding up well. Medium-full. Good grip. Really quite classy. Plenty of fruit. Good backbone. Finishes positively.

1975　　　　　　　　　　　Now–2005
Full colour. Vigorous, only just mature. Unexpectedly ripe – mulberry fruit – and concentrated and generous on the nose. Not a bit hard and tannic. On the palate there is a little astringency, but only on the attack, and this would not be no-

ticeable with food. Fullish, very good grip. Very good concentration too. Very well balanced. Unexpectedly harmonious. Ripe and classy. Fat. Evolved well in the glass. Even better than the 1978. Excellent.

1974　　　　　　　　　　　Past its best
Direct from the château. Reasonably full and vigorous colour. Sweetness, oakiness and mint on the nose, not dried out or coarse. Weak, old and rather dried out and vegetably on the palate.

1973　　　　　　　　　　　Past its best
Direct from the château. Medium-full colour. Mature, lightening at the rim. No undue age though. Sweet and slight warm brick Graves style on the nose. There was some plump fruit here once but it's now beginning to crack up. Finishes coarse.

1972　　　　　　　　　　　Past its best
Direct from the château. Old colour. A bit dirty on the nose. Acid, coarse and astringent.

1971　　　　　　　　　　　Drink up
Crumbling cork. Old colour. Some substance. Some sweetness on the nose. But a bit chunky and old-fashioned, especially compared with the wines made today. This has also seen better days. Has lightened, got astringent and got a bit coarse. Not much enjoyment here now. But was very good for the vintage in its time. In fact it got better in the glass. I've had better bottles of this.

1970　　　　　　　　　　　Now–1998
Fine, fullish, mature colour. More old-fashioned on the nose than the wines today. A little dense. But plenty of ripe fruit underneath. A fullish, meaty wine, quite unlike the wines today. Not nearly as stylish. Ripe but a bit solid, and the wine lacks personality. Good but not great. Lacks a bit of class.

1969　　　　　　　　　　　Drink up
Dry crumbling cork. No undue age on the colour though, less than the 1967. Sweet, roast-chestnutty nose at first. Not fruitless. Nor coarse. Getting a little astringent on the attack and just a little stringy at the end. But not at all bad. Really quite a lot of substance. Acidity shows now.

1967　　　　　　　　　　　Drink soon
Well-matured colour. Stylish nose. Mature and mellow, beginning to lose a bit of its fruit and elegance as it evolved. Medium-bodied, now more or less at the end, but a balanced charming round example. Very good for the vintage.

1966　　　　　　　　　　　Now–1999
Fullish mature colour. Very good nose. This has balance and depth and rather more style than the 1970. Fullish, complex, generous, classy. Round, fullish, harmonious and still with vigour. Very

good indeed. Lovely finish. Third best of the 1959–1970 flight, marginally after the 1959.

1964 **Drink up**

Direct from the château. Fullish mature colour. No undue age. A little four-square on the nose, the acidity showing. Fullish, reasonable fat, a little hard at the end. No astringency though. Best with food. Good but not great. No worse than the 1970 though today.

1962 **Now–1998**

Direct from the château. Fullish vigorous colour. Not as classy on the nose as the 1966, but rather more succulent than the 1964. Beginning to get a little diffuse but medium-full, balanced, ripe and quite classy. Good finish. I prefer this to the 1964 and 1970. Very harmonious. Very smooth. Very intense and stylish at the end.

1961 **Now–2000 plus**

Direct from the château. Recorked. As with all 1961s, an excellent colour. Full, mature, but vigorous. Lovely concentrated nose. No undue size. Splendid intensity of fruit. Full, quite chunky, much more old-fashioned than Lalande today. Rich and concentrated, but the structure shows a little. Much better with food. Fine, but not fine in a 1961 context.

1959 **Now–1998**

Good, fullish, mature colour. No undue brown. Lovely ripe, fat, vigorous and meaty – in the best sense – nose. Fine mature claret. Fullish, fat, generous, concentrated, rich and very ripe. Second best of 1959–1970 flight. Sweet, lingering finish. fine.

1958 **Drink up**

Direct from the château. Recorked. The colour, though well matured, shows no undue age. Ripe nose, a touch sweet, but not unstylish. Soft, lightish. No astringency. A little mean at the end now. But a surprisingly good bottle in its time. Still reasonably positive, neither astringent nor coarse on the finish.

1955 **Now–1997**

Direct from the château. Recorked 1986. Fine colour for the vintage. Full, no undue age. Lovely nose. Soft, naturally sweet. Old rose fragrance. Very stylish. This is a lovely example. Medium-full, silky, balanced. Very elegant. Lovely complex lingering finish. A fine wine. Still it seems with plenty of life.

1953 **(In bottle drink soon)**

(Magnum) Fine full vigorous colour. Marvellously ripe vigorous fat nose. This is even better than the 1949. Full, rich and concentrated. It didn't hold up as well in the glass as the 1952. But an excellent example, and no doubt as good as this because of the bottle size. Lovely fruit nevertheless. And neither short nor astringent.

1952 **(In bottle now–1997)**

(Jeroboam) Fullish mature colour. Fragrant and elegant on the nose. Slightly more diffuse than the 1953. Softer on the palate but with immaculate fruit and balance. Medium-full. Long. Quite delicious. Very, very lovely. Marvellous condition. Breed and very high quality. Beautiful. Will still keep. Great. Better than the 1949. Held up well.

1950 **Drink soon**

Medium colour, full mature. The nose is soft and there are elements of volatile acidity. Medium body. Perhaps a little past its best but there is grip, warmth and generosity. Certainly classy. Still most enjoyable.

1949 **Now–1999**

Direct from the château. Recorked 1982. Very fine full vigorous colour. Lovely nose. This has real class and even intensity. Splendid complex fruit. On the palate the wine is medium-full. It has splendid balance and concentration. And a particularly fine multidimensional finish. Much more class than the 1961. Fine plus. Best wine of the tasting. Plenty of life ahead of it.

1947 **Drink up**

Full, mature colour. This was a chunky wine which has now begun to age and show too much of a rustic element. A little oxidation. Slight burnt leather touches as well as a certain attenuation. Quite sweet. Past its best.

1945 **Now–1998**

Very full, mature colour. Full, aromatic, *crème brûlée* nose – cooked in the best sense. Structured but heaps of richness and concentration of fruit. Bags of life still. A magnificent, vigorous, complex bottle. *Grand vin!*

1940 **Drink soon**

Direct from the château. Recorked. Good colour. A little age now. Interesting nose with a hint of sweet mint. A little lean but neither mean, coarse or astringent. Vigorous for a wine of over 50 years old. Surprisingly good. Medium body. Positive finish.

1937 **Will still keep**

(Magnum) Medium full colour. Fresh, not too dense. Fresh nose. Still holding up. Not too inky. This is a really fine and enjoyable 1937. It has suppleness and fruit and no astringency or rigidity. Fresh. Round. Elegant. Ripe. Not that complex but one of the best 1937s I have ever had. Generous.

PICHON-
LONGUEVILLE-
BARON

I have reported on the early history of the Pichon-Longueville estate and followed the fortunes of the 'feminine' part, that known as Comtesse de Lalande, after the split in the middle of the nineteenth century. I now turn to the Baron.

In the Pichon-Baron brochure it states that though the two properties were officially divided in 1850, and the wines made separately from 1860, the estate was not legally split up until 1908. On the death of the second Raoul, Baron de Pichon-Longueville, a widower for nearly 30 years, the ownership of the two Pichons had reached the third generation from the Joseph who had originally decided to divide the estate, and finally the legal niceties were tidied up.

According to the Pichon-Lalande archives, however, this is a myth. The Comtesse de Lalande did not get on with the nephew Raoul, and in the 1860s all the formalities of separation were completed. Be that as it may, the Pichon-Longuevilles were to remain at the Baron until 1933, when it was acquired by the Bouteillier family.

The Bouteilliers are direct descendants of a wine-steward to Louis XIV, and have been intimately connected with a number of important Bordeaux estates. In 1907 Etienne Bouteillier married Marie-Louise Delbos, heiress to Château Lanessan in Cussac, the commune immediately to the south of Saint-Julien. Shortly afterwards the family entered into an agreement with the Deroy de Suduiraut family of Château Grand-Puy-Ducasse, taking on an *en fermage* role as well as the majority of the shares. In 1971 Ducasse was sold to a group which included the Bordeaux *négociants* Mestrezat-Preller. Through family connections with the Mahler-Besses, Bertrand Bouteillier, of the present generation, is involved in the direction of Château Palmer. The prize in the family portfolio, however, was Pichon-Baron, acquired by the Bouteilliers in 1933.

THE BOUTEILLIER FAMILY

For nearly 30 years, under the aegis of Jean Bouteillier, Pichon-Baron, placed higher than the Comtesse in the 1855 Classification, continued to produce wine which, if 'old-fashioned', i.e., long-macerated and somewhat dense in style, nevertheless enjoyed a high reputation. It was on Jean Bouteillier's death in 1961 that the troubles began.

Bouteillier *père* had produced his children late in life. Bertrand, the eldest son, was only in his early twenties when his father died; his brother Hubert, who today runs Lanessan and the adjacent Château Lachesnaye, was still at school. Bertrand was inexperienced and he was badly served by an incompetent *maître de chai* who was not as meticulous as he should have been in carrying out the orders he had been given. There was also a lack of investment. The resources were inadequate and the equipment became increasingly out of date.

The result was that Pichon-Baron in the 1960s (after a fine 1962) became rather inky and coarse. The quality was even more disappointing in the early 1970s. From 1978 onwards I detected an improvement: the wine became less 'masculine', more supple and elegant. I was told the temperature of fermentation had been reduced, as also had the length of maceration. Yet the wines of the next decade have been maddeningly inconsistent. In cask they have often showed very well indeed. In bottle they never seemed quite to live up to their earlier promise, yet hinted enough to make it beyond doubt that the estate was of super-second potential. Part of the difficulty was a rapid turnover of *maîtres de chai*; the *élevage* was not all it should have been. Another contributing factor was the lack of a bottling hall. The crop was bottled in the courtyard by a contractor, irrespective sometimes of the fact that it was 30 degrees in the shade.

AXA

Then in 1987 came the news that Pichon-Baron had been sold. The ownership of the estate, it appeared, was split up between a number of members of the Bouteillier family, and the majority of these shareholders, it was further rumoured, against the wishes of Bertrand Bouteillier himself, were attracted by the price offered by the company AXA-MIDI, the second largest insurance company in France.

Over the previous seventeen years Claude Bébear, chairman of AXA, had built up a vast enterprise, which now enjoys a turnover of 36 billion francs and employs 12,000 people. In 1974 they bought – as an experiment, so they put it – Château Franc-Mayne, one of Saint-Emilion's many *grands crus classés*. On the acquisition of Château Pichon-Baron a subsidiary company, AXA-Millésimes, was created. Jean-Michel Cazes, proprietor of Lynch-Bages and Les Ormes-de-Pez, and contemporary of Claude Bébear – they were both born in 1935, and first met at school – was brought in as administrator. Cazes, as well as running the family vineyards, is also an insurance agent. Having known Claude Bébear since he was in short trousers and having raised the quality of Lynch-Bages from its already high level to that of super-second in the last decade, Cazes was a natural choice. His appointment has ensured that the full potential of Pichon-Baron was quickly realized.

The price AXA paid, though, was startling. Pichon-Baron was then a vineyard of 33 productive hectares with an inadequate *chai* and an attractive but dilapidated château. The investment required completely to rebuild the *chai* and renovate the château was estimated at 40 million francs. This would come on top of the initial cost of 200 million for the property plus a further 80 million for stock on hand and other items. Would it be worth it? In the words of Claude Bébear, 'There is a future in top-quality wines. It's a good investment, similar to top-quality real estate, provided it is top quality, and aimed at the top end of the market.' Putting it another way, given that Pichon-Baron is potentially equal in size to Pichon-Longueville, Comtesse de Lalande, if it can sell its wine for the same price (which it does now that it makes wine of comparable quality), it will provide a suitable return on invest-ment. AXA are not the only insurance or investment group to have seen the potential in qual-ity vineyard real estate.

THE VINEYARD

At the time of the AXA acquisition Pichon-Baron had 33 hectares under vine, five of which had come into production over the last five years. On top of this there was a further large vineyard called Sainte-Anne to the west near Batailley and Larose-Trintaudon, where Pichon-Lalande also has land, which was at the time *en friche*, or scrub. When this and other plots are in full production there will be 50 to 52 hectares under vine. together with other parcels which have been recently bought, the intention is to raise the production area to 60 hectares, the same as the Comtesse. The vineyard is planted with 75 per cent Cabernet Sauvignon, 24 per cent Merlot and 1 per cent Petit Verdot and currently produces 200 *ton-neaux* of wine. Though a second wine has been made since 1983 it was discovered that the name chosen – 'Baronet' (de Pichon) – had been registered by Philippe de Rothschild's company, La Baronnie. This is now marketed under the name Les Tourelles de Longueville.

THE CHÂTEAU

The Baron château, gaunt, shuttered, romantic, is one of the most striking in the Médoc. It was constructed by Charles Burguet in 1851 and though its outside structure – particularly the imposing witche's-hat turrets – seemed still to be in good condition, the property had not been inhabited since pre-Bouteillier days. There was neither electricity nor hot water throughout. During the war it was briefly occupied by refugees from the bombing of Pauillac's oil refinery in 1944. Two rooms on the ground floor were used for twenty years by the Rotary Club of Pauillac, and the basement has always been used for the storage of wine in case or in bin. Effectively though it was a mere shell, which was a shame, because it is a splendid building. Now after more than 50 years of neglect it has been sumptuously restored.

THE *CHAIS*

Up to the 1990 vintage the wine was being vinified in fifteen cement, epoxy-resin-lined *cuves* installed in the 1960s. These were temperature controlled by means of heat exchangers. This *cuverie* connected with a single large *chai* at the end of which was a raised dais used as a tasting and reception area. All this, as I have said, was in a somewhat run-down condition, and any-way was inadequate for the yield of a prolific year even today, let alone when Sainte-Anne comes into production.

So it was decided to build entirely new *chais*, which in the modern world of public rela-tions and marketing would incorporate proper facilities for receptions and the welcome of parties of tourists. There will even be a wine museum.

With typical flair it was decided to have a competition among four carefully chosen teams of architects. The winners, announced early in September 1988, were Patrick Dillon and Jean de Gastines. The design involves a circular *cuverie* and it came into full use in the 1991 vintage.

TOWARDS A NEW LEVEL OF QUALITY

It is of course impossible to transform the quality of a wine overnight, especially without the proper equipment and resources, but a number of important changes were immediately inau-gurated by Jean-Michel Cazes, his deputy and *directeur technique* Daniel Llose, who arrived at Lynch-Bages in 1976, and *régisseur* Jean-René Matignon, who arrived at Pichon in 1985.

Firstly the harvesting machine was sold. This had been acquired in 1982, when tests were run, and employed since the 1983 vintage. Secondly the proportion of new oak was raised.

Half the 1987 vintage was matured in new wood and the proportion raised further for the more substantial vintages which followed. From now on all movement of wine, racking and so forth, will take place in anaerobic conditions, *sous azote*, a mixture of nitrogen and carbon dioxide. The old, rather brutal pumps, which tended to oxidize the wine, have been dispensed with. Finally, bottling now takes place using the property's own machinery and personnel – and not in the open air. The quality of the 1987 and the 1986 vintages showed the progress which could be made in one year. Subsequent vintages have been even better. Pichon-Longueville-Baron is now firmly in its rightful place as a super-second, a worthy rival, in its different way, to the Comtesse across the road. It is a true Pauillac: full, firm, backward, rich and concentrated – suitably masculine. A splendid wine which is going from strength to strength.

THE TASTING

I sampled the following wines at Pichon in September 1988. For notes on the later vintages see Vintage Assessments.

Optimum drinking

1987   Now–1996

Medium-full, youthful, purple colour. Young, fresh, slightly stalky aromas; some richness but not a great deal of depth. Not mean though. This is better than many 1987s. It has richness and good oak underpinning. Good acidity. No great level of tannin. A simple but attractive wine. Good result for the vintage.

1986   1996–2010

Full, youthful, purple colour. Firm, full, richly concentrated, Cabernet nose. Good, ripe blackcurrant and blackberry. This is very much better than either the 1985 or the 1983 with more power and new oak. Full, firm, rich, oaky and concentrated. Good ripe Cabernet fruit. Finishes long. Has recovered well after bottling in June. Very good.

1985   Now–2007

Fullish, quite youthful colour. Quite rich, soft and ripe on the nose. Attractive if no great weight. Medium body, a little tannin. Pleasantly fruity. Lacks a bit of concentration and will evolve quite soon. This is a forward wine lacking a bit of structure and the true Pauillac austerity. Slightly disappointing for 1985.

1984   Drink soon

Light to medium colour; some development. Lightish nose, now quite soft; reasonably fresh if a bit slight. Now drinkable. Lacks a little fruit and freshness on the palate. Indeed a bit watery. Light to medium body. Dull – indeed poor for a 1984.

1983   Now–2000

Medium-full colour; a little development. Quite some development on the nose compared with the 1982. Ripe and fruity but lacks a little concentration and weight. What puzzles me about this wine is that I get an element of old tea as well as astringency. There is a slight bitterness from too much old wood. Too loose. Bottled a bit too late. Medium body. Only 'good' for a 1983.

1982   Now–2008

Very full concentrated colour; little sign of development. Very big, rich, fat concentrated nose, now with extra elements of leather, tobacco and spice. Very ripe indeed. Big but voluptuous. A big tannic wine. More old-fashioned than the 1986 but with greater (Merlot) richness, spice and amplitude.

1981   Drink soon

Medium-full colour; a little development. Somewhat four-square and unforthcoming on the nose; a little stewed and dense even. Reasonably full and fresh. Good fruit, an absence of selection is all that is the matter with it. Less dense on the palate than on the nose. Just about ready in 1988.

1980   Drink soon

Medium colour; some development. Quite fresh but lacks a bit of real ripeness and concentration. No undue age though. Lightish. Mature. Fruit a little artificial and lacks acidity; but if slight at least reasonably attractive and finishes not too short. A good example of the vintage.

1979   Now–1998

Medium to medium-full colour, still youthful for a 1979. Medium weight, quite plump and ample, fresh and attractive, blackberry-mulberry nose. Less structure but less dense than the 1981 and a better wine. Medium to medium-full body, fresh, ripe, a little tannin. This is more supple than not only 1978 but also the 1981 and a better example within the context of its vintage than the 1983 or the 1985.

1978 Now–1998

Slightly fuller colour, still quite youthful. Richer and fuller but a bit dense and solid on the nose. Yet this has merit. Quite full, quite rich. Slight solidity. More concentration and more quality than the 1979. Also just about ready. Good but not great. Very typical Cabernet and Pauillac flavour.

1977 Drink soon

Quite a full colour; brown at the edges. Spicy and slightly blowsy, lightening up on the nose. Quite full, no undue astringency. Indeed an element of leanness to the fruit keeping it fresh. Fullish, still quite vigorous if it lacks class. Quite different on the palate than on the nose – *herbacé*, but drinkable.

1976 Drink up

Medium colour; fully mature. Rather weedy and old, lacking ripeness and freshness on the nose. This is now a little over the top but wasn't at all bad once. Now a bit astringent but underneath there is reasonable fruit. It was quite acceptable originally. Good for the vintage in its time but disappointing now.

1975 Drink up

Medium-full colour; fully mature. Old nose. Attenuated, light. Medium body. A little faded but some (if slightly old) fruit underneath. Did not hold up well in the glass. Astringent finish. Disappointing.

1974 Drink up

Medium-full colour; less brown than the 1977. Fullish nose. Slightly dry and a bit dense. Lacks richness. Some astringency. Medium body. Lacks a bit of generosity. 1971-ish. Not at all bad for a 1974. At least drinkable.

1973 Drink up

Medium-lightish colour; mature but no undue age. Quite fresh on the nose if not some meanness; no richness, slight spice and H2S. Medium body, high acidity. Reasonable effort for the vintage but never very attractive.

1972 Past its best

Lightish-mature colour; fully mature if not a bit of age. Light, weedy nose. Slightly watery, fresh because of high acidity. Spurious, slight boiled-sweet elements. Lacks fruit.

1971 Drink soon

Medium to medium-full colour; fully mature but more vigorous than the 1974. Round nose with a touch of spice, quite full and rich. Some size but quite high acidity. A curious flavour, lacking generosity.

1970 Now–1998

Deepest colour of this series (1975–1970); little sign of maturity. Fullish nose, quite solid, vigorous; still young. Ripe if a bit dense and lumpy. Fullish, slightly dense on the palate. Lacks generosity and will never round off satisfactorily. Not bad.

1969 Drink soon

Fullish, mature colour. Soft, ripe, full slightly spicy nose. Somewhat burly as usual. Quite full, getting to the end of its useful life. A certain astringency yet quite round and generous underneath. Quite flexible. Good for the vintage. Getting a bit bitter at the end but shows better than the 1967.

1967 Past its best

Medium colour; fully mature. The nose is somewhat old and faded; never anything special, with mint tea flavour. Not too astringent but fruit has dried a bit. Somewhat sour and acidic on the finish. Past its best.

1966 Drink soon

Full, mature colour. The nose shows touches of oxidation and volatile acidity. A bit inky underneath. Difficult to judge. Seems less structured than 1964. Quite warm and spicy. Round and with flexibility. Some astringency on the finish.

1964 Drink soon

Medium-full colour. More lightened than brown at the rim. Slightly forthcoming nose, a touch dry. Fullish, rich, good Cabernet. A little tough on the attack but very good for the vintage. Good concentration and richness underneath. Finishes well. Still vigorous.

1962 Drink soon

Very full, mature colour; less mature than the 1961. Very fine, full, rich nose; full, still closed it seems. This is similarly structured but has slightly more richness, ripeness and concentration. Once again a full, burly wine but has depth and generosity. I preferred it to the 1961 at first but it didn't last quite as well as the 1961 in the glass. Very good for the vintage.

1961 Now–1996

Full, mature colour. Very rich and concentrated on the nose; bitter chocolate, liquorice and cedar; somewhat tough originally as is the Pichon-Baron style but quality here as well as generosity. Full, rich, tough and solid; slight elements of astringency but not without length. The burly, roasted *sur maturité* elements detract from the quality. Only 'good' for the vintage.

1960 Drink soon

Fullish colour; not a lot of maturity. Rich, ripe, generous, mature. Still vigorous if now soft and round. Full, firm, solid and masculine but not dense. Good freshness. Fine fruit. Will keep. Fine for 1960.

1959   **Drink soon**

Full colour; not a lot of maturity. Full, quite firm nose. A bit solid. Similar on the palate. Rich but a little astringent. Good but not great. The wine is a bit inky but there is acidity and muscle here. Has depth.

1958   **Drink up**

Fullish, mature colour. The nose seems to have lightened up but not faded. Slight denseness of age. Quite full, round, rich and generous at first if a bit slight. A shade short and uncomplex on the finish as well as slightly bitter. A good result for the vintage though.

1957   **Drink soon**

Fullish, mature colour. This has some intensity, and is also slightly corked, but had quality in a slightly faded but supple way. A second bottle was fresher and much more serious: richer and solider with supple, flexible fruit if no great class.

1955   **Drink soon**

Full colour; not a lot of maturity. Quality here on the nose but a bit of age; slight sweetness and oxidation yet fullish and solid. Full, concentrated and rich but a little burly. This has more to it than the 1959: solid and old-fashioned yet richer. But I don't think this is the best bottle of this vintage. Will still keep.

1954   **Drink up**

Medium-full mature colour. A lightish, stylish, supple nose, but not that of a great vintage. Still quite fresh, supple and straightforward but fruity. Still just about alive. Quite stylish. Good for the vintage.

1953   **Drink soon**

Fine, vigorous, full colour; little evidence of age. Full, rich, very concentrated nose: high quality; lovely, rich, ripe Cabernet fruit. Classic. Full, rich and concentrated on the palate, and no astrin-

gency. Splendid vigour with flavours of cooked plums. Big for a 1953. Fine.

1952   **Drink soon**

Fullish colour. Somewhat dense on the nose but nevertheless a good concentration of fruit. Full-ish, ripe, vigorous and a little astringent. Slightly more spicy than the 1953. Very good for the vintage. No undue age.

1950   **Drink soon**

Very fine colour; somewhat muddy and inky. Full, rich, concentrated nose; not quite the nuance of some. Full, rich, solid, a little tough and astringent. Lacks a bit of flexibility but quite good.

1949   **Drink soon**

The biggest colour of all. Lovely *coulis* of fruit on the nose, less tough and solid than the 1950, a supple pureé. Yet less richness on the palate than the 1953. Fullish, getting a little astringent on the finish. Yet still much enjoyment here. Very good.

1947   **Drink soon**

Good, mature colour. Evolved, complex, leath-ery flavours, yet delicate. Lots of style here. Medium-full, balanced, long, generous, supple and lovely, *à point* now.

1945   **Drink soon**

Very fine colour. Little evidence of age. Slightly inky, acetaldehyde nose but has concentration underneath. Not as much structure or density as the 1953 or the 1949, but ripe, even sweet de-spite the off flavours. Perhaps a disappointing bottle.

1937   **Drink up**

Medium-full colour. The nose is a little coarse and the palate somewhat four-square and brutal; yet not astringent, merely inflexible. Fullish; has good ripeness. The acidity is quite evident. Good but getting a little old now. The wine has always been too tough, I would guess.

DUHART-MILON

One of the more obscure of the fourth growths, little seen until relatively recently, is Pauillac's sole example in this category, Château Duhart-Milon. The reason it was overlooked was that the vineyard evaporated in size from the 1930s onwards; the explanation for the revival of its fortunes is that it now belongs to the Rothschilds of Château Lafite. They took over the run-down vineyard in 1962. Extensive replanting was required and finally the vines are now beginning to require a respectable average age. Hitherto a somewhat four-square, even dense, wine – quite unlike the style of Lafite, though made by the same hands – it has in the later half of the 1980s begun to acquire an element of richness and concentration which should now put it on every wine-buyer's tasting list. I date the coming of age of Château Duhart-Milon from 1982. Others are more generous, suggesting 1978. Be that as it may, it is now making a wine fully worthy of recognition.

Part of the title comes from the location. Milon is a hamlet west of Château Lafite, north of the Carruades plateau up in the top left-hand corner of the Pauillac commune. This is where the bulk of the vineyard has always been situated.

Of M. Duhart, after whom the estate takes its name, we know very little. He was obviously the proprietor in pre-Revolutionary days and he must have been a man of means. When the property first appears in the unofficial classifications and brokers' notebooks in the early years of the eighteenth century, it was not only of substantial size – it produced 75 *tonneaux*, indicating a vineyard of some 50 hectares – but well regarded.

HISTORY

Abraham Lawton, writing in 1815, gives his opinion that Duhart-Milon was one of the better fourth growths. We must conjecture that the vineyard took full form later rather than sooner in the eighteenth century. The name of Duhart is absent from the archives of the Lawton ancestors from which Professor Pijassou has produced, based on price, a classification of the top wines as they stood in the 1770s.

By the time of the Restoration, the proprietor was a M. Mandavi or Mandavit (spelling was not as precise as it is today). Mandavi owned vines both at Milon and on the Carruades plateau, and seems to have produced a special *tête de cuvée* from the former. Sometime during the 1830s Mandavi passed away, and the property seems then to have been divided, for in the 1845 edition of Wilhelm Franck's *Traité sur les Vins du Médoc*, a M. Duroc is listed as owning 'Mandavy' while a Pierre Castéja appears at Milon as proprietor of what 'formerly belonged to Duhart'. Had Pierre Castéja, born in 1799 to a family of Pauillac lawyers and later to become mayor of Bordeaux, married a Mlle Mandavi? Indeed, was M. Duroc his brother-in-law?

Castéja succeeded in reuniting the estate in the 1850s, in time for it to be included in the 1855 Classification, and it remained in the hands of his successors until 1939. The size of the vineyard is confirmed in turn-of-the-century editions of Cocks and Féret as 50 *tonneaux*, at which time the yield had risen to some 150 *tonneaux*. The property was then owned by a Castéja heir – the Christian name is not given – and his sister, Mme Jules Calvé whose family owned Croizet-Bages). After the First World War, a younger brother, Jean Castéja, bought Château Lynch-Moussas and this branch of the family was to marry into neighbouring Château Batailley. The tentacles spread wide!

But back at Duhart, the economic vicissitudes of the 1930s depression and the subsequent world war were taking their toll. In the 1920s, the Castéja heirs had entrusted the administration of the estate to André Delon, grandfather of Michel who is today the owner of Léoville-Las-Cases, and he made a fine 1926 and an excellent 1929, both still vigorous today; but he was starved of capital. Fifteen hectares were ceded to the then-undivided Batailley in the 1930s. Gradually, as the old vines gave up the ghost, the acreage declined. In the immediate postwar period the property changed hands several times and the vineyard declined to seventeen hectares. Much of the land was left to the weeds and the wine seems to have all but disappeared from the market. I have no tasting notes of any vintages of the 1940s and 1950s.

THE ROTHSCHILD ACQUISITION

The Domaines Barons de Rothschild – owners of Lafite, Duhart's immediate neighbour to the east – acquired Duhart-Milon in 1962. The amount they paid is not disclosed but it cannot have been much, for a considerable long-term investment was required to put the property back into the state it deserved.

In fact they had to start from zero. The land was completely cleared of vines in order that a proper system of drainage could be installed in the vineyard, and it was replanted in the same ratio as that at Lafite: 70 per cent Cabernet Sauvignon, 10 per cent Cabernet Franc and 20 per cent Merlot. There are today 64 hectares under vine of which 54 are in full production. Stage two was the innovation of the cellar. This is located not at Milon but in a quiet little street which runs down to the quayside in the town of Pauillac. A battery of enamel-lined vats was installed, replacing the old wooden *foudres* in 1974. This *cuvier* has recently been enlarged, this time with stainless-steel *cuves*, and the adjacent barrel cellar extended. This long, low room houses both the new wine and that of the previous vintage and is 110 metres long. One-third new wood is used and a second wine, Moulin-de-Duhart, has been established since the 1986 vintage.

THE CHÂTEAU

Like the cellar, the Duhart-Milon château lies – or used to lie – not up at Milon but in Pauillac, more precisely on the waterfront a little south of the town. It is still illustrated on the label, though not belonging to Domaines Rothschild. (I trust this does not break the law.) When the Rothschilds took over in 1962, the château (dating from 1650) was sold to André Cazes, mayor of Pauillac and father of Jean-Michel who runs Château Lynch-Bages. He razed it to the ground to build a modern mansion.

THE WINE

Duhart-Milon is a true, full-blooded Pauillac. The wine is well coloured, today rich, concentrated and fleshy but reserved and tannic. It is built to last. There is an amplitude which recalls not so much Lafite as Mouton, but as well a sort of residual, earthy solidity which suggests the second or third ripple of gravel rather than the first *croupe* nearest the estuary. What has been most apparent since the vines have reached full maturity – for the average is now nearing 30 years – is the arrival of an element of what I can only describe as sex appeal. The 1970s vintages were somewhat brutal. Today Duhart-Milon has charm as well as size. It can only go on getting better and better.

THE TASTING

I sampled the following wines in Pauillac in January 1990. I have added a note on the 1926, one of a tasting of miscellaneous 1920s vintages offered by Nick Davies of Hungerford Wine Merchants in December 1988. It was the wine of the tasting.

1988 — *Optimum drinking* 1997–2012

Good colour. Ample, oaky nose. This has more charm and approachability than most, though not fined yet. Good substance underneath. Medium-full, good, ripe tannins. Attractive, plump fruit. Well balanced. A more-ish wine which is long and seductive.

1987 — Drink soon

Good colour for vintage. Fine nose for the vintage. Soft, ample soft fruits, no meanness or weakness. Has style. Light-medium body. A little lacking ripeness at present but will get rounder and more charming as it develops. Reasonable acidity. Good oak.

1986 — 1998–2016

Very good colour. There is a lot of depth here on the nose and fine, rich, concentrated fruit. Classy and backward. Fullish, quite a lot of tannin, almost too much. But good fruit and grip even if not quite as concentrated as it appeared at first. Very Cabernet. Finishes fat.

1985 — Now–2006

Medium to medium-full colour. Soft, ample nose, plump blackberry-mulberry fruit. Good grip. Medium body. A wine with a lot of charm, even elegance. A little tannin. Good grip. Quite rich. Rather more accessible and forward than the 1986. Good but lacks richness and depth.

1984 — Drink soon

Good colour for the vintage. Good nose for vintage. A bit one-dimensional but there is fruit here. Now evolved. This has more charm than the 1987 at present. Lightish but some backbone. Reasonable fruit and good grip. Still fresh. Good for the vintage. Not a bit disagreeable.

1983 — Now–2003

Good colour. Some evolution on the nose. Seems soft and not massively structured. Lacks a bit of concentration though. Medium body. Fresh and fruity. This is balanced and attractive but lacks real dimension. Certainly finishes long and stylishly. A little more forward and more supple than I expected.

1982 — Now–2010

Very good colour. Solid nose. Some tannin. Quite a bit bigger on the nose than the 1983. Full, slightly austere. Good tannin. Very good concentrated fruit, which now that the wine has softened a bit is very apparent. This is very good. Long, rich oaky and with very good acidity. Ample and stylish. Very good finish.

1981 — Drink soon

Medium colour. Mature. Quite soft and ample on the nose. Balanced, mature, fresh and attractive. Medium body. This lacks a certain dimension and richness on the palate. Somewhat slight. Yet no sign of attenuation. Just a bit dull.

1979   **Now–1997**

Medium-full colour. Just about mature. Interesting cedar-mahogany flavour, supported by good black fruit and chocolate on the nose. Medium body. Just about ready. Not exactly rich but ripe and quite stylish, with the fruit continuing long on the palate. Rather better than the 1981.

1978   **Now–2000**

Medium-full colour. Much more evolved than the 1979. Good nose. This has rather more depth and concentration than the 1979. Medium-full colour. A little sturdy but good richness and fat. This shows well, though it is a little reserved. Long, quite complex. Still youthful. Very good. Finishes well.

1976   **Drink soon**

Medium to medium-full colour. Also, like the 1978, quite brown. Fuller than the 1975. Typically 1976 on the nose but somewhat fresher than most. Medium body. Ripe, spicy. Not exactly elegant but fresher and a better grip than most. Quite good finish. Good for the vintage, certainly.

1975   **Drink soon**

Medium colour. Fully mature. Smells like a 1976. Medium body. Somewhat thin and attenuated with dry tannins, little fruit and no charm. Has begun to dry out. Unexciting.

1970   **Now–1998**

Still a very youthful colour. Fullish. A little solid on nose and palate. Fullish, good acidity but lacks a little generosity. Ripe but a little rigid. Will still improve as it softens. Good to very good.

1962   **Drink soon**

Fine colour. Still very youthful. Lovely, supple, fragrant nose. Warm, cedary, smoky. On the palate quite full but the fruit has lost its sugar and the acidity. Needs drinking soon. Not bad. Second bottle less acid, much more generous and enjoyable. Good vigour. Holding up well. Very good.

1929   **Will still last**

Very fine colour. No sign of age. Soft, ripe nose, this is very fine and not faded. Touches of chocolate and cedar. Truffles and *sous-bois*. Medium full, lovely generous fruit. Got better and better in the glass. More and more complex. Still very vigorous. Very fine.

1926   **Will still last**

Amazingly vigorous colour and nose. Could be a 1959. Ripe, oaky, concentrated. Full and rich, now soft but a big wine with good grip and plenty of fruit. Long and complex. Quite lovely. Still very vigorous. Held up very well. Very fine.

BATAILLEY

A glance at the famous 1855 Classification will show that the fifth growths are dominated by Pauillacs. Out of eighteen properties, no fewer than twelve are from this commune; and this includes all the first seven châteaux in this section. Second in the list is Batailley, followed by its neighbour Château Haut-Batailley.

Some of these fifth growths are rarely seen. Belgrave and Pédesclaux, for example, have seldom come my way. But others are well known: Lynch-Bages and Grand-Puy-Lacoste are deservedly popular. Pontet-Canet, the two Batailleys and the Rothschild châteaux, Clerc-Milon and d'Armailhac, all made good wine. In 1969 Cocks and Féret gave Batailley itself the accolade *'actuellement supérieur à son classement'*. It has a good reputation, and one for consistency too.

In the original 1855 Classification there is only one Batailley where there are now two. Like the Pichons, the Rauzans and the Léovilles, the estate has been split, but unlike them this has occurred in this century.

Batailley is a *lieu-dit* or place name, and lies about a kilometre or two as the crow flies due west of Château Latour. The name is said to originate from a pitched battle which occurred there shortly before the siege of Latour itself in the Middle Ages. It is said that this is the place where the French defeated the remnants of the fleeing English army after the rout of the Battle of Castillon in 1453. On the local maps produced by the firm of Belleyme in the late eighteenth century, the site is given as Bataille.

Malvesin and Féret's *Le Médoc et Ses Vins* (1876) states baldly that there never was such a battle, and suggests that Batailley was the name of a Bordeaux *courtier*, or wine-broker, who was the first to clear the land and plant a vineyard at the beginning of the eighteenth century. I cannot find any corroborative evidence for this.

HISTORY

The first clear records of Batailley date from 1791. At this time the owners were two spinster sisters, the Mesdemoiselles Marianne and Marthe Saint-Martin, one of whom was a nun, together with their brother, who was a priest. On 16 September 1791, the sisters sold their two-thirds of the estate to Jean Guillaume Pécholier, a Bordeaux wine merchant, for 43,000 *livres* plus an annuity of 1,096 *livres* to the sister who was a nun.

Lorbac, in his handsome *Les Riches Gastronomiques de la France*, states that one of the sisters – one assumes the one who wasn't a nun – married Pécholier, but this seems unlikely; for, if this were the case, her share would have automatically passed to her husband, and it would have been the other sister and the brother who would have to have been bought out. It is the ladies' names which appear on the document of 1791, and, moreover, when the estate was sold again some twenty years later, it was still in two parts.

From Pécholier, who died early in the new century, Batailley passed to Admiral de Bédout, his son-in-law, a French Canadian who had fought in the battle of Chesapeake Bay in 1781. Bédout died in 1816, and the entire estate was then put up for auction before the Bordeaux tribunal in order to settle the inheritance. Batailley was acquired by Daniel Guestier, partner in the Bordeaux firm of Barton and Guestier. It would appear, though, that this purchase took place in several stages. The bulk of Château Batailley passed to him in 1818 for 118,000 francs, and he bought more shares somewhat later. He also bought up a number of neighbouring parcels of land, thus enlarging the domaine from 34 to 39 hectares of vines.

By now Batailley, producing about 50 to 60 *tonneaux*, was important enough to be specifically named in contemporary books on the wines of Bordeaux, but not quite renowned enough to be placed in classifications. Mostly, these only had four categories, it was not until about twenty years later that a fifth category appears, and then Batailley is mentioned. Guestier was rich, powerful and active in local affairs, both economic and political. He was just the person to put Batailley on the map. He renovated the château, rebuilt most of the outbuildings and enlarged the vineyard by acquiring parcels adjacent to the vineyards of Grand-Puy-Lacoste and Lynch-Bages. He introduced new methods of viticulture and viniculture, and, of course, through the firm of Barton and Guestier, he could ensure a ready market for his wine. It is from this period that the wine of Batailley began to be exported, and to make a name for itself.

Guestier died in 1847, and there was another legal wrangle about the inheritance. He had three children: his son Pierre-François, by then owner of Beychevelle, and two daughters, the Mmes Phélan and Lawton, married to other leading figures in the Bordeaux wine trade. The tribunal adjudicated that half the shares should go to Pierre-François, a quarter each to the ladies. By 1866 the daughters' shares had reverted to the next generation, to Mme de Coursson, daughter of Mme Phélan, and to Mme Demarolles, daughter of Mme Daniel Lawton. On 27 March the family sold Batailley to Constant Halphen, a Parisian banker, for 500,000 francs. Halphen was one of a number of financiers, like the Perrières, Heines and, of course, the Rothschilds, who made purchases of classed growths at this time. The act of sale was drawn up by Maître Castéja, notary and Lord Mayor of Bordeaux, who was owner of Duhart-Milon, and whose successors were in 1919 to buy Lynch-Moussas.

A letter from William Guestier to the broker Tastet in 1867 states that at the time of the Halphen sale the estate comprised 55 hectares of vineyards. With the better husbandry of the vineyard the production was then 60 *tonneaux*, and was to increase to 100 by the end of the century. In 1865 the wine had sold for 1,500 francs a *tonneau*.

The Halphen dynasty lasted until 1932, when Edmond Halphen sold Batailley to Marcel and François Borie. The Bories had farmed the estate for some years during the 1920s, and also produced the wine on the neighbouring Halphen estate, Château La Tour d'Aspic (*aspic* means serpent). The price was identical to that of nearly 70 years previously, 500,000 francs. In 1934 they bought the neighbouring Château La Couronne.

The Borie brothers jointly ran Batailley until 1942. In this year François acquired Château Ducru-Beaucaillou, and it was decided to divide the Batailley estate in order to avoid further inheritance difficulties. The château and the larger portion of the vineyard went to Marcel, the smaller together with the *marques* of La Tour d'Aspic and La Couronne went to François, and was regrouped in 1951 together with fifteen hectares which had been acquired from Duhart-Milon in the 1930s under the name of Haut-Batailley.

Marcel Borie died in 1961, and Batailley passed to his daughter, Mme Denise Castéja. Mme Denise's husband is Emile Castéja, now Managing Director of Borie-Manoux, the Bordeaux *négociants*. Since 1949 Batailley has been sold exclusively through the family firm together with an impressive array of other family properties or exclusivities. From Mme Castéja's side comes Trottevielle; Emile inherited Lynch-Moussas from his father Pierre in 1969. They also have Château Beau-Site in Saint-Estèphe in their portfolio and own Domaine de L'Eglise in Pomerol. Additionally, Château Baret in the Graves and Gressier-Grand-Poujeaux in Moulis are exclusively distributed by Borie-Manoux.

THE VINEYARD

The plateau of Batailley lies inland, behind the Pichons and Latour, at the southern end of the Pauillac commune on either side of the Pauillac-Saint-Laurent road. When the vineyard was divided the larger portion of some 26 hectares of vines together with the château itself remained 'Batailley', and these are the vineyards to the north-west, opposite the château, on the left-hand side of the road stretching in the direction of Lynch-Moussas to the west and Grand-Puy-Lacoste to the north. The ground is some 25 hectares above sea level, gently undulating, comprising a deep bed of gravel on a base of clay and *alios*, a hard sandstone.

Since the division the Batailley vineyard has been extended, and now covers some 52 hectares out of a total estate of 90. I was informed a decade ago that the Merlot percentage was being increased, but at present the ratio is 74 per cent Cabernet Sauvignon, 5 per cent Cabernet Franc, 20 per cent Merlot and 1 per cent Petit Verdot. The latter variety is no favourite of Emile Castéja, and is now being replanted. The production is now some 225 *tonneaux*.

THE CHÂTEAU AND THE *CHAIS*

The château itself is one of the most attractive in the Médoc. It was rebuilt over with grey sandstone over the old structures in a Regency style in the early nineteenth century, and is a two-storey building with smaller wings on either side set in a handsome park. The park contains a large number of different trees from all over the world planted by successive owners, and a fine collection of different species of cyclamen which make a riot of pink and white colour, especially at vintage time. Batailley has the benefit of being the permanent residence of the Castéja family, so as well as being filled with fine examples of different periods of furniture, china and other *objets d'art*, it also has the atmosphere of a home rather than a museum.

Adjacent to the château are the *chais*. A new *cave de vinification* was constructed in 1980 and computer-controlled temperature regulation was installed later in the decade. The wine is fermented in a mixture of vats of oak, stainless steel and cement after which it is transferred into smaller oak in the first-year *chai* next door. Some 25 per cent of the *barriques* are annually renewed and the wine is bottled after eighteen months in wood. Since 1978 Professor Pascal Ribereau-Gayon has been consultant oenologist.

THE WINE

The atmosphere at Batailley is quietly efficient rather than showy, and the wine, it is fair to say, has the reputation of being competent rather than compelling. Perhaps as a fifth growth it would be idle to expect this. But Batailley does not possess the sort of *réclame* enjoyed by

Jean-Michel Cazes at Lynch-Bages or by the Borie cousins at Grand-Puy-Lacoste, nor does it fetch the same sort of prices at auction.

Even in vintages like 1982 Batailley is never a *vin de garde*, the sort of densely coloured and tannicly structured wine that we regard as classic Pauillac. It does not have the power of some of the properties that lie nearer the river. It is never more than medium-full-bodied, yet in the best of its recent years it has had plenty of richness and depth.

Moreover, prices are not excessive. Emile Castéja does not suffer from the sort of *folie de grandeur* of some of his neighbours. He is content to produce a highly reliable if second-division Pauillac, and one at a price everyone can afford. If not all properties can be superstars, certainly not everyone has the means to pay superstar prices. Batailley is good value for money and a fine, dependable claret. It deservedly enjoys a wide distribution and plenty of regular customers throughout the civilized world.

THE TASTING

The following wines were sampled at the château in April 1987. Of the vintages not listed below, I have found the 1979 more satisfactory in its vintage than the 1978 is in its. The 1976 is not a conspicuous success and needs drinking, but the 1973 was good, though it too is nearing the end of its useful life. The 1966 is *à point*, round and fruity, good but not great; the 1964 and 1962, the former better than most Pauillacs in this vintage, are both at least 'quite good' but now again showing a little age.

	Optimum drinking

1986   **Now–2006**
Not a blockbuster but a harmonious, rich, amply fruity wine for the medium term. Round, quite concentrated. Finishes well. Plummier and more Cabernet than the wine below.

1985   **Now–2004**
Another very attractive wine for the medium term. Round, rich, ripe, good warm grip. Shows well. A good to very good 1985.

1984   **Drink soon**
Quite oaky, straight, fresh; above all, ripe. Another 1984 which demonstrates that this vintage is not bad at all in Bordeaux, and indeed may turn out to be more satisfactory than 1980.

1983   **Now–1998**
Good colour. Not quite as fresh as I would have liked on the nose but good, plump, ripe fruit on the palate. Possibly not that stylish but good stuff. Medium-full, some tannin, but will evolve sooner than some.

1982   **Now–2002**
Good colour. Surprisingly accessible on the nose. A really plump, ripe wine. Much concentration but soft and round. Ample and velvety. I miss a little of the power of the vintage. Good though.

1981   **Now–1999**
Again a good if not very deep colour. This is a very good 1981 because it has an adequate acidity. Fuller, riper and better balanced than the 1983. Very good stuff. Will last well.

1975   **Now–2000**
Fullish colour, now with a bit of brown at the rim. Slightly dense on the nose but better on the palate. The wine lacks a little suppleness, as do many 1975s, but there is depth here and at least some concentration. Finishes well. Good.

1970   **Drink soon**
Good, full, mature colour. Quite developed on the nose. Medium-full body, complex, quite a lot of depth. If not a truly great 1970 it nevertheless shows very well.

1961   **Now–2000**
Very good colour. Vigorous, rich, complex, concentrated nose. Real depth and quality here! This would stand up to all but the really tip-top 1961 Pauillacs. A really lovely wine which will still keep very well. Indeed it will last rather better than the 1970.

1949   **Drink soon**
Fullish but well matured colour. This is an old man but an aristocrat. Ripe, very great finesse. Very Pauillac fruit. Long on the palate. Still very alive. Real breed. Lovely.

1943   **Drink up**
This has certain elements of old tea but is still pleasant to drink. Was very Cabernet-flavoured in its youth, I would have thought.

1937   **Drink soon**
The 1937 was a tough vintage. This still has a very fine colour, and is in its dense way rather more vigorous than the 1943. Has depth and fruit if it lacks, as it always did, a bit of charm.

HAUT-
BATAILLEY

Château Batailley, as I have described in the previous chapter, was divided between the Borie brothers in 1942, the last time a Médoc *cru classé* was so split. As decreed by the courts, the larger portion went to Marcel, the elder brother; the smaller part, plus the vineyards of La Couronne, a 1932 *cru exceptionel* created in 1874 by Armand Lalande, and La Tour d'Aspic went to François. Marcel's share remained 'Batailley'; François decided to call his 'Haut-Batailley'.

In the same year, 1942, François bought Ducru-Beaucaillou, and it was this which absorbed his energies at first, for there was more to be done there. He died in 1953, leaving Ducru to his son Jean-Eugène and the Pauillac vineyards to his daughter Mme Françoise de Brest-Borie. Mme Brest-Borie, married to a doctor, lives in Limoges. The estate is managed by Jean-Eugène and his son Xavier, and the rest of the Ducru-Beaucaillou team.

These three Pauillac vineyards are now run as a single entity, based on the old La Couronne *chais*, in part a curious Swiss-chalet construction, and it is fair to say that La Couronne is now a selection of the Haut-Batailley vats. It is not exactly the second wine, for that is La Tour d'Aspic, and nominally the three hectare vineyard exists in its own right and produces about 20,000 bottles a year. But it is little seen today.

THE VINEYARD

While Batailley's vineyard lies to the west of the Pauillac-Saint-Laurent road, Haut-Batailley's is situated in two parts on the eastern side. One section lies behind the *chais*, on either side of the railway, and adjacent to those Latour vineyards known as Petit-Batailley. The more substantial part, however, is on the Bages plateau a kilometre due north. The Couronne vineyard lies between the two.

Haut-Batailley now occupies 22 hectares, planted with 65 per cent Cabernet Sauvignon, 10 per cent Cabernet Franc and 25 per cent Merlot. There is land available to increase this to 35 hectares, but no intention, said Jean-Eugène Borie in 1990, to plant just yet.

THE *CHAIS*

There being no château, save a couple of apartments for one of the vineyard workers, we have merely the *chais*, a rectangular building decorated with squares of coloured brick and enlivened by an outside guttering at first-floor level. The *cuvier* was re-equipped in 1974 and consists of a double battery of fermentation vats: ten vitreous enamel-steel *cuves* over concrete vats. The wine from the higher vat can easily be run off its deposit into that underneath. In 1986, in a neighbouring building, a large *chai à barrique* was constructed. Up until the early 1970s the wines were made at Ducru-Beaucaillou.

THE WINE

I find it curious that both Michel Dovaz in his *Encyclopédie des Crus Classés du Bordelais* and Bernard Ginestet in *Pauillac* find the Haut-Batailley wine lighter than the Batailley, more of a Saint-Julien than a Pauillac. I must demur. In the past decade I have made two major vertical tastings of Haut-Batailley, on both occasions sampling back to the early 1960s (my acquaintance of the 1950s vintages is scant). I have also sampled Haut-Batailley frequently in horizontal tastings, usually alongside its neighbour.

The wine is not lighter than Batailley; and it is a true Pauillac. The style is on the austere side, with mulberry-plummy fruit and just a touch of solidity, particularly when it is young. There were a couple of disappointing results in 1978 and 1979, but by and large the quality is well superior to that of a fifth growth, though not as good as the Borie's other Pauillac, Grand-Puy-Lacoste. But, like all Pauillacs, it does need time to soften up and adopt the more mellow generosity of a mature wine.

THE TASTING

I sampled the following wines at Ducru-Beaucaillou in January 1990.

1988 *Optimum drinking* **1996–2006**

Medium-full colour. Quite a firm nose. Good oak. The tannin is a bit hard. Has just been fined. Underneath there is good weight and ripeness but the effect is still a little bitter. Medium to medium-full body. Good grip. Needs time to round off and show its charm. Better on aeration. Good.

1986 **1998–2010**

Good colour. The nose is still closed. Firm, yet rich underneath. A backward wine. This is typical Pauillac in a fine year. Rich but restrained. Firm and tannic but not hard. Best of all on the finish which shows good concentration and balance. Fullish. Good grip. Finishes well. Good to very good.

1985 **1995–2010**

Medium-full colour, still purple. Soft on the nose, after the 1986. Quite a bit more open. Mulberry fruit. Good depth underneath, though. Good substance for a 1985, and good grip. Fullish for the vintage. Ripe and balanced. Round and almost opulent. This shows well. Has a lot of charm. Lovely finish. Real personality here. Today shows better than the 1986.

1984 **Now–1996**

Good colour for the vintage. This has a good

nose for a 1984. Reasonable substance and fruit. Still has vigour. Good acidity. On the palate this has a certain tannic-bitter astringency. The follow-through is riper and more charming. One-dimensional but not short. A good result for the vintage.

1983 Now–1998

Medium-full colour. The nose is quite fruity but it seems to lack a bit of zip. Quite evolved. This is more diffuse than I expected and is not nearly as good as the 1985. Medium body. Seems to lack acidity. No freshness. Indeed there is already a certain astringency in the unresolved tannins. Disappointing.

1982 1995–2009

Fullish colour. Firm, full, rich and spicy. Quite a bit bigger on the nose than the 1983. Full, rich, smoky and firm. Quite solid for a 1982, but that is Pauillac in this vintage. Just a little four-square and lacking elegance for great. Needs time. Good.

1981 Now–1996

Medium colour, a little mature. Open, frank, stylish nose. Good fruit. Attractive. This is a nice wine: better than the 1983. Medium body. Balanced ripe fruit. Now just about ready. Mulberry flavoured. Good positive finish.

1980 Drink up

Good colour for the vintage. Now mature. A little diffuse on the nose but not too weedy. Good for a 1980. Medium body. Still reasonably fresh, fruity and positive.

1979 Drink soon

Medium to medium-full colour. Not a lot of maturity. A shade stringy on the nose. Doesn't sing. On the nose I prefer the 1981. On the palate too. This is a bit light and anonymous. Reasonably fresh and fruity but rather boring. Finishes cleanly and positively though. Not bad.

1978 Drink soon

Medium colour, mature. Both lighter and browner than the 1979. Lightish, mature nose. Seems fully developed. Doesn't have a lot of personality and depth. This, like the 1979, is also a bit light and anonymous; but has a little more substance. A little more spice. But also somewhat uninspiring.

1976 Drink soon

Fullish colour. A bit brown all the way through. Good nose. Not too dry and coarse. Still seems quite fresh and vigorous. Fullish, yes, ripe and vigorous. Rather good, fat and fruity, the fruit in a slightly cooked, spicy, voluptuous sense. But good grip keeps it all fresh and a great deal more elegant than most. Still holding up well.

1975 Now–2000

Medium-full colour. Mature. This again is a fresher, more supply-fruity nose than most in this hard, tannic vintage. Like the 1976 this is a very good result for the vintage. Firm, full, rich and concentrated. Now just about ready. Good flesh and acidity. No hardness. Finishes rich and long. Will last well. Very good.

1970 Now–2000 plus

Good colour, still youthful. Good rich, fruity nose. This has vigour and class. Very Pauillac. This will improve. Medium-full. Vigorous. Good fruit. Fine balance. Lacks a bit of concentration for great. But good to very good.

1966 Now–1996

Medium-full, mature colour. Fine mature nose. This is at its peak. Medium body, round, balanced, elegant. Softer and more succulent, and therefore more charming than the 1970. Very lovely. Very good, vigorous finish. A lot of style here. The best of the three (1970, 1966, 1962).

1962 Drink soon

Very good colour. Little sign of brown. Lovely subtle nose, generous, ample, roast chestnutty and truffles. Not a trace of age. Medium-full body. Concentrated, vigorous attack. The follow-through is a little less vigorous but nevertheless this is a lovely wine with both charm and depth, as well as ripe fruit.

1961 Now–2000 plus

Fine colour. Marvellous nose. Truffles and concentrated blackcurrant and certain leather, sandalwood spices. Has such intensity and seemingly indestructible vigour it could only be 1961. Fullish, quite full. Fresh, ripe, lovely. Harmonious and succulent. Quite delicious. Will last for ages. This is a particularly good bottle. Fine if not very fine for a 1961.

GRAND-PUY-LACOSTE

While there are, sadly, one or two 1855 second and third growths which few would hesitate to demote today, there are also, encouragingly, several fourths and fifths we would seek to elevate. Pauillac has at least two of these but, while the wine of Lynch-Bages has long been popular, it is only recently that I feel Grand-Puy-Lacoste has received its due. Since 1978, the property has been owned by Jean-Eugène Borie of Château Ducru-Beaucaillou and his son Xavier, and this has given it a higher profile. Yet it has been making excellent wines for decades, not just since this change of ownership. The fact that it has been, and still is, unfairly unappreciated is shown by the bargain prices older vintages still fetch at auction: in the spring of 1993, for instance, the 1970 was fetching £230, before buyer's premium and VAT were applicable. This is much less than Lynch-Bages, for instance. Today, the quality of Grand-Puy-Lacoste is hardly any significant margin below that of the 'super-seconds'. Yet pricing remains reasonable, for Jean-Eugène Borie preserves a healthy difference between his Ducru price and what he asks for Grand-Puy-Lacoste. Those for the 1990 vintage opened at 100 and 63 francs, respectively, ex-château.

HISTORY

On the west side of the commune of Pauillac, beyond the hamlet of Bages, is the plateau of Grand-Puy. The origin of Grand-Puy-Lacoste is the same, not surprisingly, as that of its neighbour in the 1855 Classification (if no longer on the ground), Grand-Puy-Ducasse. *Puy*, like *tertre*, *fite*, *motte* and other words now incorporated into vineyard titles, is a word for a ridge, mound or hillock. A kilometre or two behind the town of Pauillac, as the crow flies, overlooking a stream which bisects the commune in a diagonal south-west to north-east direction, is the Grand-Puy, or *Grampuing* as it is in Claude Masse's map of the Médoc in 1709, a rolling *croupe* of gravel some 20 metres above sea level. Here, in the late Middle Ages, a M. de Guiraud owned a fairly substantial estate.

De Guiraud had two daughters: one married a M. Labégorce and the other a M. Dejean or De Jehan, a councillor in the Bordeaux parliament. The Dejeans had a son called Bertrand and he had two daughters and it is at this point that the Grand-Puy domaine began to be dismembered. When exactly this took place, however, is open to dispute.

If you consult the old books, you will be told that the property was split as early as 1587. In fact it was not so much a split as a splintering off of a small parcel; and it took place in 1750. Professor Pijassou has shown that the owner in the 1720s and 1730s was the Bertrand Dejean referred to above. He was also proprietor of what is now Château Lynch-Bages, which he sold in 1728. In 1750 he disposed of part of his estate to Pierre Ducasse, one of his creditors.

Dejean seems to have been survived only by a daughter. She married a M. d'Issac, another Bordeaux parliamentarian. Their daughter married a M. de Saint-Guiron, owner before the Revolution, and from him the domaine passed to a François Lacoste.

Neither of the Grand-Puy châteaux figure prominently in eighteenth-century records, perhaps indicating that they were later than most to plant vines extensively as well as fetching lowish prices. They do not feature on the list of top wines M. Pijassou has drawn up from the records of the broking firm Tastet and Lawton between 1740 and 1770. On the other hand, in Wilhelm Franck's list of mid- to late-eighteenth-century prices in the 1845 edition of his treatise, a Lacoste is quoted as a Saint-Estèphe third growth and a Ducasse as a fourth. These must be errors. It can hardly be a coincidence.

The first real evidence of both size and value begins to appear in the first years of the nineteenth century. The classification of the broker Abraham Lawton in 1815 placed both Ducasse and Saint-Guiron, eventually to be Lacoste, among seven *quatrièmes crus purs*. Both seem to be quite large estates, Ducasse marginally the most extensive and producing 80 to 90 *tonneaux*. Wilhelm Franck agrees with this rating and gives the yield of Saint-Guiron as 70 to 80 *tonneaux* and in later editions mentions that the proprietor is François Lacoste.

François was succeeded by his son Frédéric, proprietor at the time of the 1855 Classification, and it was at about this time that the present château was constructed alongside the remains of an earlier manor, on which the date 1737 can be seen. From him it passed to his daughter Mme de Saint-Legier and from her, in the years following the First World War, to M. Hériveau and M. Neal. These two sold Grand-Puy-Lacoste to Raymond Dupin in 1932.

I met Dupin but once and briefly, only a few years before his death in July 1980. It was a bitterly cold March afternoon. His reputation, though, was already known to me. A bachelor and a *bon vivant*, he was one of the best-loved characters of the postwar Bordeaux period and never one to miss a chance of opening a few historic bottles to accompany a superb meal.

He never lived at Grand-Puy, preferring the comforts of central heating in the middle of Bordeaux to the cold draughts of the country, and consequently the château was sparsely furnished and not regularly redecorated, especially after its occupation by German soldiers during the Second World War, when a lot of the wooden panelling and wainscotting was torn out and used as firewood. What still remain, however, are four large carved cask-ends representing earth, air, fire and water. These occupy what, in Dupin's day, was the dining room. They were originally destined for Russia but the boat sank in the Bordeaux harbour and the carvings found their way into Dupin's possession.

Dupin was a rich man, with extensive woodland holdings in the Landes, but he spent little on the château and not a great deal on the property. While the quality of the wine did not suffer, the acreage under vine declined. From a peak of perhaps 55 hectares out of the 90 in total that the estate occupies, the figure declined to 25 or so by the mid-1960s, and the production, despite improvements in yield, from 140 *tonneaux* in the Saint-Legiers' time to 100. In the early 1970s, a slow process of enlargement was begun and this has been accelerated under the new regime, for in 1978 Dupin entered into an agreement with Jean-Eugène Borie. Borie immediately acquired half the shares in Grand-Puy-Lacoste and bought the rest in instalments. From this vintage, he took over responsibility for the wine.

Jean-Eugène's son Xavier is now the man in charge and on the spot, for he and his wife have converted what used to be the *tonnellerie* into a flat for themselves. They have extended the vineyard by twenty hectares or so and constructed a new fermentation cellar complete with enamelled-steel 200-hectolitre *cuves* to replace the dozen or so wooden fermentation vats which were used in the Dupin era. The barrel cellar has also been completely restored.

THE CHÂTEAU

The château is a fine building and is now being carefully restored. It is a substantial three-storey affair, having a mansard roof with a short pointed tower at one end and stands just above where the land falls away abruptly to the west. In the nineteeenth century, the stream which runs at the bottom of this hollow was dammed and extensive water gardens were laid out. These too, like the château itself, have been restored. Two swans, a gift from Peter Sichel of Château d'Angludet, now serenely disport themselves on the water.

THE VINEYARD

The vines which make up Château Grand-Puy-Lacoste lie on two separate *croupes*. The first is to the front, the west of the château, and runs up to the Pauillac-Saint-Laurent road, across which is the Bages plateau. The second *croupe* lies to the south-west, on the other side of the lower, marshy land of the stream and the railway line. Here it touches the vineyards of Batailley and Lynch-Moussas. At present, there are 60 hectares under vines producing 125 *tonneaux* of *grand vin* on a soil of the usual thick gravel bed over a limestone base. A second wine, Lacoste-Borie, is made from the younger vines. Curiously, the land is planted with only two varieties – Cabernet Sauvignon making up 75 per cent and Merlot the remainder.

THE WINE

The wine making has continued the tradition of the Dupin era and will capitalize on what is now a vineyard of mainly very old vines. The *maître de chai* is Philippe Bouze and the *chef de culture* is Marc Duvocalle. Now under the meticulous and perfectionist eyes of Jean-Eugène Borie and his son, they continue to produce the full, firm, long-lasting, ripe, almost creamy-rich Grand-Puy-Lacoste which we have become used to from Raymond Dupin. Let us be grateful, when we enjoy them, that the property will continue to be in good hands.

THE TASTING

Grand-Puy-Lacoste was featured at the New Haven wine weekend in March 1988. My thanks to Russell Norton, Bob Feinn of Mount Carmel Wines, Hamden, Connecticut, and to the remainder of the New Haven team.

1984   Now–1996

Medium colour. A little raw and green at first on the nose, lacking a bit of flesh. Some structure and tannin on the palate. This will get rounder and more generous as it evolves but lacks a bit of charm at present. Finishes better than it starts. Quite good to good for the vintage.

1983   1996–2010

Medium-full colour but not that full or dense, especially compared with the 1982. The nose is a bit adolescent at present. Elegant but a little lighter than I expected. Quite full. Some tannin. Rich and stylish but backward. Has depth and concentration. Quite firm. Very Pauillac. Good, complex, balanced finish. Long. Good but not an exceptional 1983.

1982   1998–2020

Excellent colour. Very full indeed. Impenetrable, almost black. Excellent nose. Rich, fat, concentrated, creamy old-vine character. There is a lot of depth and quality here! Clearly superior to 1983. Very full, very tannic but not a bit dense. Indeed, less adolescent than the 1983 at present. Lots of depth and concentration of fruit. This is excellent. Rich, balanced, complex. Quite a blockbuster. Very fine indeed. Even for a 1982, this is fine quality. Held up very, very well in the glass.

1981   Now–2005

(Double magnum) Fine colour. Surprisingly, marginally more depth than 1983, perhaps because it is from a double magnum. Still very youthful. Fine, ripe nose. Rich, creamy, old-vine character. Succulent and concentrated. Medium-full, some tannin. Good, ripe acidity for the very lovely elegant fruit. A seductive wine. Fine for the vintage.

1979   Now–2005

Very good colour. No maturity. Slightly high-toned nose; blackcurrant. More forward than it looks. Medium-full, plump wine, very pleasant, very stylish. By no means a blockbuster. Some tannin. Balanced. Most attractive but less depth and structure than expected. Possibly marginally disappointing in the context of 1979 compared with the 1981 in the context of 1981. Merely good plus.

1978   1995–2015

Very good colour. Full, little maturity. More than the 1979. Very fine concentrated nose. More size, more depth. Lovely complex fruit. This is excellent. Full, quite some tannin. Very Pauillac. Real depth. Masculine, very concentrated. Lovely complex, rich finish. Needs time. A very good 1978 indeed.

1977   Drink up

Extraordinarily good colour. Even a little bead, no undue brown. Slightly old tea and attenuated on the nose but not at all bad for the vintage. Ditto on the palate. This has richness and even depth in the context of the vintage. Quite ripe. Still alive. Very good indeed for the vintage. Getting vegetal as it evolved though.

1976   Drink soon

Medium colour but still quite fresh looking. Lightish nose, not very intense but not blowsy or dry. Similar on the palate. A little ineffectual, getting a bit astringent on the finish. Somewhat weak and one-dimensional but is holding up better than I expected – for I have never considered this a great success. Drink reasonably soon.

1975   Now–2000 plus

Medium-full colour; just a little sign of maturity. Quite dense, smoky nose, a little dry, a little robust. Very typically 1975 but richness underneath which came out as it evolved. Medium-full, some tannin. Good, rich wine, not too tough. Beginning to soften up. Like many 1975s, one wonders quite how fat and generous this will eventually be but it is a lot better than most. Finishes positive, fat and vigorous. Rich finish. Certainly very good for the vintage.

1970   Now–2000 plus

Fullish colour. Little evidence of maturity. This is still youthful and vigorous. Plump, plummy, seductive and classy. Quite full, ripe and rich. Still some tannin. Very Pauillac, concentrated Cabernet Sauvignon blackcurrant fruit. Still youthful. Lovely now but will still improve. High class.

1966   Now–1998

Medium-full colour, fully mature. Lovely mature nose, really classy. Discreet, balanced, ripe and complex. Medium-full, ripe, good grip. Similar flavours to the 1978. Vigorous but *à point*. Very classy, very fine. Very harmonious, understated. Less succulent and sweet than the 1970. Less charm but equally classy.

1964   Drink soon

Just a little less colour. Fully mature. A little tough and unforgiving on the nose but a lot better than most 1964s. A touch astringent but good richness, even fatness. Medium-full, more structure apparent because it is less supple compared with the 1966. Rich, even fat and good length. A very good 1964. Finishes long. Classy.

1962   Drink soon

Sample direct from the château. Excellent colour. Even more than the 1966. Aromatic nose, slight sweetness and spice – gingerbread. Soft. Fully mature, if not showing a little age and showing signs of lightening up on the finish. Quite full, ripe, plump. Just lacks a little bit of zip but a lovely, generous, charming wine. It held up very well in the glass.

1961 **Now–1996**

Fine colour but fully mature. Fullish, slightly cooked prunes nose. Not as intensely rich and ripe as I would have expected. Is this a slightly disappointing bottle? Nevertheless full, aromatic, lovely, ripe, succulent fruit. Slightly fuller and more tannic and more vigorous (in a chunky sense) than the 1959 but not as superb for the vintage. Nevertheless, even if this is not the best example, very fine and better than 1959.

1959 **Drink soon**

Excellent colour. More intense than the 1961. Marvellous nose. Really rich and multidimensional. This could be a 1961. Stupendous quality, breed, depth and complexity. Fully, fully mature, old vine flavour. More developed than the above but succulent, sweet, fat, ripe, with a touch of caramel. Lovely, complex, vigorous but ethereal flavour. Very excellent.

1952 **Drink soon**

Sample direct from the château. Fullish, very mature colour. Ripe, mature nose, no undue astringency. Fresher than it looks. Good character. Medium-full, fragrant, mellow, ripe, complex. A lot of class and elegance. Now perhaps beginning to show a little age but a lovely, mature, complex wine. Very fine, long, lingering finish.

1949 **Drink soon**

Splendid colour. Stupendous nose. This is the best of these last three vintages. Lovely, ripe, plump wine, complex, fresh, supple and generous. This is a *grand vin* without a shadow of a doubt. This really does have class and depth. Full, vigorous, long. Marvellous fruit. Excellent.

1947 **Drink soon**

Splendid colour, just marginally less than the 1949 or 1945. This is a bit more astringent than the above, showing a little age. Ripe and rich on the nose, lovely blackcurrant fruit but a bit chunky on the palate and astringent on the finish. Better with food. Has a lot of grip, richness and substance. Finishes very well. Still vigorous. Held up very well. A lovely, rich, fat wine.

1945 **Drink soon**

Splendid colour. A little maderized on the nose but rich and, though full, not too solid and astringent on the palate. Ripe with a lot of depth and concentration. Fullish. More supple than I would have expected and a little lightening up on the finish. Both the wines above are better today. Lovely nevertheless.

LYNCH-BAGES

Is it an insult or a compliment to be 'the poor man's Mouton-Rothschild'? I keep meaning to ask Jean-Michel Cazes, the man who runs Château Lynch-Bages. Lynch-Bages was classified in 1855 as a *cinquième cru*, but is now rated, judging by prices, a *deuxième*, if not a super-second.

That Lynch-Bages is justly popular today is due to three successive generations of the Cazes family and 60 years of hard work. In the 1920s, before the Cazes era, Cocks and Féret considered the wine inferior to Pontet-Canet, Batailley (then undivided) and both Grand-Puys. Today it is placed at the head of the Pauillac fifth growths, and marked '*actuellement très supérieur à son classement*' (as is also, it is fair to say, Grand-Puy-Lacoste). Both are 'currently very much better than their classification' as fifth growths.

Lynch-Bages is the dominant edifice and farm in the hamlet of Bages, a little south and inland of the town of Pauillac. I use the word farm deliberately, because while it is no more than a few hundred metres off the beaten track of the main road back to Bordeaux, the atmosphere in the Lynch-Bages courtyard is rustic and peaceful. If it were not for the curious Giacometti-grasshopper-like tractors one can see within the barn-like garages, and the gleaming new, golden sandstone facade of the château itself, recently restored, one could be back in the nineteenth century.

The hamlet of Bages surmounts a little knoll from which the southern half of the Pauillac commune spreads out before one. To the left are the yellow muddy water of the Gironde estuary, and further away, the tower and vineyard of Latour. In the foreground lie the villages of Saint-Lambert and Daubos, behind them are the Pichons. To the right, unbroken vineyards extend towards the Saint-Laurent road; more unbroken vineyard beyond it. In Bages itself the buildings huddle closely together, shuttered and anonymous, the silence broken only by the savage sudden fizz of a small motorcycle or the lumbering contortions of a large *camion* winding up a narrow path to collect from Lynch-Bages or its neighbour Croizet-Bages.

The wine of Lynch-Bages, as I have indicated above, is said to be similar to Mouton-Rothschild. In a celebrated blind tasting of the 1955 vintage, organized by the late Alexis Lichine and held two years later, everyone thought they could recognize a particular bottle of magnificent quality: it turned out not to be Mouton but Lynch-Bages. Yet the same voluptuously rich Cabernet and lead-capsule flavour had been recognized. That occasion was perhaps the kernel of the 'poor man's Mouton' reputation. Today I would suggest the wine of Lynch-Bages can stand in its own right, and needs no such back-handed compliment. At the time, however, the wine was little known, though thunderingly good, and I am sure some coat-tail hanging did not do it any harm at all.

The area was originally known as Batges, and was a fief of the Seigneurs de Lamarque. It is mentioned in the *terriers* (estate records) of Lafite in the sixteenth and seventeenth centuries; and the estate is said to have existed as a single property as far back as this, though the first official records in the archives date back only to 1728, when Pierre Drouillard, then General Treasurer of the Guyenne province, purchased the property from Bernard Dejean, a Bordeaux merchant.

Pierre died in 1749, and though he had a daughter called Marie-Anne whom he intended to make his heiress, Domaine de Batges, as it was known, passed to his younger brother Jacques Grégoire, who followed him to the grave a year later. Their sister Elizabeth then became the heir, and, as she had married Thomas Lynch in 1740, Bages passed into the Lynch family.

HISTORY

The Lynch family tree is said to date back to the Norman Conquest, and at some time an Irish branch was established in Galway, from where they spread all over Ireland. It is now a far more common name in Ireland than in England. Our branch of Lynches were Catholics, and a John Lynch (born 1669) was a soldier in James II's army, deserted by their exiled king at the Battle of the Boyne in 1690. James's force had included seven battalions of French soldiers who had come over the previous winter under the Duc de Lauzun and were later shipped home from Galway. It is possible that John Lynch travelled with them.

He settled in Bordeaux, at that time one of only three French ports – the others were Rouen and Saint-Valéry at the mouth of the Somme – through which British woollen goods were allowed to enter, and he set up as a wool and leather merchant.

John Lynch soon prospered, married a local beauty, Guillemette Constant, who bore him two sons, and became thoroughly French. The family had assumed French nationality in 1710, so Thomas was by no means a foreigner when he married Elizabeth Drouillard in 1740.

Their son Jean-Baptiste was born in 1749 and though he was nominally the proprietor of Lynch-Bages, it was in fact his younger brother Michel who cared for the family vineyard after Thomas's death around 1785, and remained in control throughout the Revolution, First Empire and Restoration.

While Michel remained in Pauillac making the wine – they also owned Lynch-Moussas and Dauzac in Labarde – Jean-Baptiste embarked upon a political career. Though he had been created a count by the King in 1775, and was a *président à mortier* in the Bordeaux *parlement* until 1790, he re-emerged as Mayor of Bordeaux in 1809, a post he still held in 1814. By this time, as can be seen from the archives, he had demoted himself from '*comte*' to '*citoyen*' and even '*viticulteur*'.

Nevertheless, with Marshall Beresford's troops breathing on the gates of the city, and the population understandably somewhat anxious for the restoration not so much of the monarchy as of their export markets, *citoyen* Lynch knew where his duty lay. Tearing off his tricolour he donned the white Bourbon sash and throwing the keys of Bordeaux at Beresford's feet he mounted the tower of Saint Michel to declaim '*Vive le roi! Vive les Bourbonnais!*' to the assembled townspeople and soldiers below. Not surprisingly, Louis XVIII promoted him to the Chambre des Députés de Paris, allowing him, following a petition from the inhabitants of Bordeaux, to remain mayor for a further term.

Jean-Baptiste died in 1835 and Michel in 1841, but Lynch-Bages had been sold in 1824 for 300,000 francs to Sebastian Jurine, a Swiss wine-merchant. At that time there were some 37 hectares under vine, producing 75 *tonneaux* of wine.

After the death of Jurine's son André-Louis in 1861, and an abortive attempt to settle the inheritance between the heirs, the property was sold to the brothers Jérôme-Maurice and Henri Cayrou for 325,000 francs in 1865. Both the Cayrous, *négociants* in Bordeaux, and their *régisseur*, M. Skawinski, enjoyed high reputations in the Gironde. Danflou describes Maurice Cayrou as a '*viticulteur très distingué*' and incidentally mentions that the wine is much appreciated in England. It passed from Maurice's daughter to General Félix de Vial, to whom it belonged until 1939, when it was purchased by Jean-Charles Cazes for 265,000 francs.

Jean-Charles Cazes, having recently bought Les Ormes de Pez in Saint Estèphe, had arrived at Lynch-Bages in 1934 as a tenant, and in fact the Cazes family have been responsible for the wine ever since; but it was not until 23 February 1939 that the transfer was made, and only from the 1937 vintage that the name Cazes appears exclusively on the label. The three previous years cite both names.

When Cazes took over, Lynch-Bages was in a sorry state. The General did not live at the château, and in the depressed economic conditions of the time, could not afford to maintain the vineyard. In some of the best sections they were even growing potatoes! Cazes was a clerk in the local bank at the time, and was able to make a better go of it because he lived locally and did not have to rely on the vine for his everyday income. When the General offered him responsibility for the property – not charging him rent but obviously hoping for a share of the dividend – Jean-Charles was pleased to take it on.

Jean-Charles, known throughout the Médoc for his skill as a wine-maker and as one of the characters of Pauillac, lived to be 95, dying in 1972. It is largely due to his skill that the property was established in the consciousness of wine-drinkers. When Cazes took over only half the present surface was under vine. He gradually increased the *vignoble* – a lot of replanting was necessary – and the wines he made in the first postwar decade were simply marvellous. His son André, born in 1913 and a charming man with a fund of amusing stories, took over in 1966 and nominally runs the estates together with his son Jean-Michel, born in 1935. In practice, as Cazes *père* has his own insurance business in Pauillac, Jean-Michel is the one in charge. André Cazes is also the local representative on the Conseil Général de la Gironde, and at the end of the 1970s celebrated his thirtieth anniversary as Mayor of Pauillac. As Mayor, he was occasionally given parcels of wine as presents by other proprietors. He claims the most extensive range of off-vintages in the Gironde!

THE PROPERTY

Lynch-Bages occupies some 80 hectares of vines, situated mainly in two large plots, one immediately adjacent to Bages between the château and the D2, the other a little further north on both sides of the road which runs from Pauillac down to Batailley and Grand-Puy-Lacoste. The vineyard produces some 300 to 350 *tonneaux* on average (though in 1977 the harvest was only 50 *tonneaux*) and this makes it one of the largest in the Médoc.

The *encépagement* is as follows: Cabernet Sauvignon 75 per cent, Cabernet Franc 10 per cent and Merlot 15 per cent plus a little residual Petit Verdot and Malbec which is not to be replaced. There is a second wine called Château Haut-Bages-Avérous.

A recent development (the first vintage was the 1990) is a white wine, Blanc de Lynch-Bages. This is made from 40 per cent each of Sauvignon and Sémillon and 20 per cent Muscadelle, vinified in barrel. This first vintage was already very approachable in April 1991.

The château itself is architecturally undistinguished, though a charming building. It is a solid, square, three-storey construction thought to have been built by Sebastian Jurine soon after he arrived in 1824 but using parts of the older buildings which existed already. The 1825 act refers to very old buildings and a '*maison de maître*'. The present château was extensively restored in the mid-1980s.

The wine is made and stored in a series of interconnecting, modernized barn-like buildings clustered nearby. On one side the wine is fermented in 30 temperature-regulated *cuves* of enamelled steel, installed in 1975. The maximum temperature is maintained at 29° to 30°C. Adjacent lie the hogsheads of maturing wine, renewed 50 per cent each year, while upstairs are the old iron rails and pulley system used in the last century before the days of pumps for transporting the arriving grapes to the wooden fermentation vats. The whole set-up before restoration in the 1980s was rather like a farm in appearance; indeed, they used horses in the fields until the end of the 1970s.

THE WINE

In such a setting it is not perhaps surprising that Lynch-Bages produces a traditional wine. It is full and sturdy in texture, warm and fruity in flavour, richly perfumed and concentrated in character. Even without cognisance of any past comparisons one can easily see that it aspires to Mouton rather than to Lafite. While it may lack the absolute distinction of either, it is distinctly superior to most other Pauillac classed growths, fully justifying the price it fetches – on a par with the better second and third growths, and the particular accolade in Cocks and Féret. Anyone who gets the opportunity to taste any of the 1945 to 1955 Lynch-Bages can be confident of an exhilarating experience (provided the bottles have been correctly stored, of course).

More recently, I felt that there was a slight falling off in quality in the 1960s and 1970s. The main reason for this was that, following the investments by Jean-Charles in the late 1930s, very little had been done. The capital necessary to bring the installations up to date had been lacking, exacerbated by problems of inheritance tax and death duties following the demise of Jean-Charles Cazes in 1972. There was a lack of space and the best equipment, and an ageing team in the cellar.

The first step was the retirement of the old cellar master, Roger Mau, in 1976 and the appointment of the 26-year-old Daniel Llose in his place. From 1979 onwards the cellars were completely transformed: the old wooden vats were systematically replaced and six metal, thermostatically controlled *cuves* were installed in this year, with a further seven added in 1980. For the first time they had sufficient space to vinify the whole crop properly. At the same time anti-rot sprays began to be generally used, not only here but throughout the Médoc. This, together with the understanding and control of the malolactic fermentation – only appreciated in Bordeaux from 1973 onwards – an increasing use of new oak and a more rigorous selection between *grand vin* and the second wine, Haut-Bages-Avérous, resulted in a return to form in the 1980s. The 1980, for its vintage, is a much, much better wine than the 1978 and 1979 for theirs. The 1981 is a splendid result, and since then Lynch-Bages has consistently been one of the stars, though I felt at the tasting I report on below the 1983 did not do itself justice. The 1985 and subsequent vintages are particularly excellent – real super-second quality. The future for Lynch-Bages looks bright.

The Lynch-Bages estate is now a model for anyone who wishes to see the best of the old preserved together with the best of the new. Surrounding an inner patch of grass the offices, *cuverie*, bottle storage cellar, barrel cellar and tasting room form a compact and efficient whole. Outside, the architecture, though largely new, is traditional in style. Inside the cellar has been transformed into one of the most up-to-date in the whole of the Médoc. It is a fitting source for one of the very best wines of the area. It is also fitting that, as the château publicity will tell you, Château Lynch-Bages was the first wine in space, having been to the moon and back on one of the Apollo missions, for Jean-Michel Cazes is one of the best-known and most respected Médoc proprietors in the USA.

THE TASTING

The following wines were sampled in Britain in October 1988, at a tasting organized by Steven Browett and Lindsay Hamilton of Farr Vintners. Jean-Michel Cazes had flown over specially for the occasion and supplied several of the more *recherché* bottles.

	Optimum drinking

1985   1996–2010

Full colour; no development. Rich, meaty and concentrated on the nose, with a certain roasted nuts element. Much bigger and more concentrated than the 1983 or 1982. A very fine wine: rich, fat, very ripe and with real depth. An excellent result for the vintage: unanimously preferred to the 1982.

1984   Now–1996

Medium-full, immature colour; good for the vintage. Fullish nose, quite plump and rich; still closed. Medium body, a little tannin and oak, but dominated by neither. There is fruit here. Ripeness indeed. Quite obviously this is not a wine of great depth and concentration but it is an attractive bottle, and it shows very well for the vintage. Another fine result.

1983   Now–2003

I felt this bottle was unrepresentative, and Jean-Michel Cazes agreed. Medium colour, a little development. On the nose it seemed a bit green and stalky, though there was more richness on the palate. Quite full but not at all together. Adolescent.

1982   Now–2008

Fullish, youthful colour. Yet quite round and
aromatic already on the nose. Medium-full
body, some tannin. Youthful but a little more
evolved than I had expected. Good richness,
warmth and grip. Ripe, even fat. Will become
voluptuous. A very good but not outstanding
example of the vintage. Finishes well.

1981   Now–2003

Fullish colour for the vintage, little development. Quite a firm, closed nose for a 1981, but
there is depth here. Fullish body, some tannin.
Good oak and concentration. Balanced fruit and
acidity. This is a fine, youthful 1981. Shows very
well indeed.

1980   **Drink soon**

Medium-full colour, some maturity but no
undue brown. Good weight and grip, even fat,
for a 1980. Fullish for the vintage, a certain leafy,
vegetal aspect from the *vin de presse*. Some tannin. This is a very good 1980 though.

1979   Now–2000

Fullish colour, not much sign of maturity. Some
weight on the nose but a little nondescript. On
the palate quite evolved. Medium body, not a lot
of grip and depth. The large vintage and the absence of real selection are evident here. Lacks
real concentration and still a shade raw. No better than 'good'.

1978   Now–2004

Similar colour. Reasonably fresh nose but an absence of concentration and generosity. Medium-
full body, a little tannin. Less lean on the palate
than the nose would indicate. Quite attractive
but lacks real depth and definition.

1977   **Drink up**

Medium colour; mature but not unduly so. By
no means a poor wine – indeed I prefer it to the
1976 – for there is freshness and fruit. Medium
weight, with a touch of astringency now.

1976   **Drink soon**

Medium colour, mature and a bit murky. This is
rather more weedy and attenuated on the nose.
It smells of old tea. Medium body; an old wine
now. Attenuated on the attack but a little richer
on the finish. Disappointing.

1975   Now–2008

This is the best Lynch-Bages of the decade, and a
fine wine in an inconsistent vintage. Fullish
colour, just about mature. Firm, rich and chocolaty on the nose, still closed. Full body, still a
touch of tannin but just about ready. Neither
burly nor aggressive. This has depth and concentration, length and quality. Very good indeed for
the vintage.

1973   **Drink up**

Medium-full, mature colour. Richness, warmth
and a certain spice on the nose, if without a great
deal of class. Medium body. An attractive wine,
and a successful 1973 with both fruit and depth,
but it is now beginning to loosen up.

1971   **Drink up**

Fully evolved colour, if not looking a bit too old.
This is definitely a bit old and faded on the nose.
This was a pleasant ripe wine but, judging by this
sample (which had come straight from the
château), it is over the hill.

1970   Now–2004

Fullish immature colour. Rather chunkier and
less evolved on the nose than the 1975. Fullish,
solid, tough and tannic on the palate. Rather
more old-fashioned. There is warmth and richness but not the charm or the class of the 1975.
Very good though.

1967   **Drink up**

Medium colour, mature. A mellow attractive
nose if with no great depth. Medium body. Similar on the palate. This was a good to very good
1967 but it now needs drinking.

1966   Now–2000

Full colour, not a lot of maturity. Like the 1970
this is a full, chunky wine which shows power at
the expense of grace on both nose and palate.
Rich, blackcurranty, old-fashioned. Still vigorous. Certainly very good for the vintage.

1964   **Drink up**

Medium colour; fully mature; now lightening
up. The nose is a bit dead. On the palate medium
body, with a touch of astringency, now beginning to lose its fruit. It never had much class.
Lynch-Bages is well-known for having been
caught by the rain in this vintage.

1962   **Drink soon**

Medium-full colour, no undue maturity. Quite
rich on the nose, blackberry fruit, a shade austere. Quite full on the palate. Certainly a wine of
quality, if never having had a great deal of class.
It is now beginning to show signs of drying up.
Very good mature claret, but drink reasonably
soon.

1961   **Drink soon**

Medium-full colour; not as full as the 1959; fully
mature. Depth, richness and class on the nose,
but on this showing not as concentrated as the
1959 – though M. Cazes said he did not think it
was a representative bottle. Medium-full body,
ripe, vigorous and distinguished, but it evolved
fast in the glass.

1960   **Drink up**

Medium-full, mature colour. Quite rich and fragrant, but at the same time quite evolved on the nose. A slightly more vigorous example of the 1958, and like it certainly a success for the vintage. This is meaty for an 'off-vintage' wine. Good fruit and finesse in a slightly earthy way.

1959   **Now–1998**

Fullish colour, just about mature. Rich, fat, concentrated, caramelly-chocolate nose. Full, rich and meaty on the palate. Quite old-fashioned. There is a little more structure than fruit. But a fine vigorous wine, still with plenty of life.

1958   **Drink up**

Quite an old colour. Fragrant but faded on the nose, still shows breed though. This is just about at the end of the road. But a good wine for a lesser vintage; the old-vine concentration is still there.

1957   **Drink soon**

Medium-full colour, still vigorous. A meaty nose with good depth. A full, solid, quite tannic wine which now shows some astringency. This again has depth and concentration, but is rather tough. Vigorous but lacks a bit of generosity and suppleness. Earthy but rich. Needs to be drunk with food. Good though.

1955   **Drink soon**

Medium to medium-full, mature colour. This is a very fine mature claret with a classic rich, concentrated, distinguished nose and flavour. Complex and full-bodied, chocolate, coffee and old-rose fragrances. Mellow and a shade spicy. Still vigorous, indeed more so than the 1953. High class.

1954   **Past its best**

(Shipped by Calvet and believed bottled in Holland) Good mature colour, but really quite old and faded on the nose. Again this was a great success for an off-vintage though. There is – or was – class and richness and no lack of fruit. Still has interest – for those who like really aged wines.

1953   **Drink soon**

(From the château) Medium-full, mature colour. Fine, rich, vigorous, slightly gamey nose and at-

tack on the palate, but it evolved fast in the glass and became somewhat astringent. Essentially the best of the early 1950s vintages but on this occasion not as vigorous as the 1955.

1952   **Drink soon**

(Belgian bottled) Medium colour, not unduly mature. Soft, mellow, fragrant nose. On the palate this is a mature wine, interesting and complex if with no great power now. Fragrant, even flowery in a red wine sense. It still has length, class and freshness, and no astringency, though it has lightened up somewhat.

1949   **Drink soon**

(Two examples; one château-bottled, the other bottled in Holland) The Dutch example was at first rich, sweet, honeyed and meaty but rapidly became coarse. The château-bottled wine was rather more solid, full and chocolatey but showed rather a lot of astringency. Yet there was good acidity and vigour underneath. Full wines, both of them, and in their time of high class.

1948   **Past its best**

(Bottled by Hankey Bannister in the UK) Full colour and a very good level but quite past it.

1947   **Drink soon**

Full vigorous colour. Quite solid on the nose, ripe and concentrated and masculine, still with plenty of life. A full, rich, meaty, quite solid wine with depth and concentration and a fine warm finish. Will still keep. Delicious. A lovely wine and the best of the tasting.

1945   **Drink soon**

(Danish bottled) Very full colour. Full, concentrated, solid and austere on the nose. Plenty of depth and quality at first. Not as chunky as the 1947. Indeed it was rather more supple and probably a richer, more sumptuous wine in its prime. But it declined quite fast in the glass.

1934   **Drink up**

Ullaged to mid-shoulder. Faded but ripe. Sweet underneath. Not so much dried out as having given up the ghost.

MOUTON-BARONNE-PHILIPPE AND CLERC-MILON

There are two quite separate Rothschild domaines in Bordeaux, both extensive. The Rothschilds of Lafite possess Château Duhart-Milon, Pauillac's sole fourth growth, and Baron Edmond personally owns Château Clarke in Listrac. They also have a majority shareholding in Château Rieussec in the Sauternes and Château L'Evangile in Pomerol. Cousin Philippine, daughter of the late Baron Philippe at Mouton, owns the best-selling brand, Mouton-Cadet, produced and marketed by her company La Baronnie, and two Pauillac fifth growths. The first, once called Château Mouton d'Armailhacq, until recently Mouton-Baronne-Philippe, has been known since April 1991 as Château d'Armailhac. The second is Château Clerc-Milon. Neither of these is particularly well known nor, until recently, very highly regarded compared with other neighbouring fifths such as Lynch-Bages and Grand-Puy-Lacoste. Though the first has been under the Rothschild aegis for 50-plus years, Clerc was only acquired in 1970. Like the former in the early 1930s, Clerc was in a pretty distressed state when Baron Philippe took it over. However, as the motto has it: '*Bon sang ne peut mentir*' (literally, 'good blood cannot lie', i.e., good breeding will out). Mouton-Baronne-Philippe (I shall refer to it in the main by this name, under which the wines I discuss have been bottled) and Clerc-Milon, now refurbished, are making increasingly good wine. Mouton-Rothschild's younger brother and sister have now come of age.

The History of Mouton d'Armailhacq

This begins with Nicolas-Alexandre, Marquis de Ségur and a *président à mortier* in the Bordeaux *parlement*. On his father's death in 1716, he had inherited not only the domaine of Latour, the dowry of his mother, but also the larger property of Lafite, acquired by Alexandre de Ségur shortly before his demise. Two years later, Nicolas further increased his holdings by the acquisition of Calon and Mouton. Not for nothing was he to be known as the 'Prince of Vines'!

While there were, indisputably, vines at Latour and Lafite in the first years of the eighteenth century, it is not certain whether there were any at Mouton and when the domaine became detached from the rest of the Ségur empire is also unclear. What seems more positive is that the territory, then known as Mouton, provided the nucleus of three classed growth properties and that some time between 1718 and 1740, in circumstances still to be unearthed, Joseph de Brane acquired the land which is now Mouton-Rothschild, Chevalier François de Pontet became owner of Pontet-Canet and Dominique d'Armailhacq took over the land sandwiched between the two. All three gentlemen were members of the *noblesse de la robe*, Bordeaux's newly rich aristocracy, a different generation as well as an emerging class in competition with the older, landed gentry.

By the early 1740s, Mouton d'Armailhacq, as it was now known, was already a vineyard. Dominique applied for tax exemption on the wines he brought to Bordeaux in 1743 and this request was granted.

He was also not slow to increase his holdings. Frequently in competition with his neighbour De Pontet, D'Armailhacq, like many of his peers, enlarged his estate by the rather unscrupulous method of lending money to the local peasantry and then foreclosing on their land when inevitably they fell behind on their repayments.

Mouton at the time was a hamlet surrounding an old ruined château. By acquiring the château, whose owner had once been a M. Romat, D'Armailhacq became entitled to use the name of Mouton. Joseph de Brane, however, bought a dwelling called the Maison du Grammant in nearby Pouyalet from a M. Saint-Duval. With this went the ancient seigneurial rights to the barony of Mouton. So he was entitled to use the name of the *lieu-dit* too.

Although the size of the estate was not inconsiderable, the wine of Mouton d'Armailhacq seems to have been somewhat eclipsed by those of its immediate neighbours throughout the rest of the eighteenth century. It appears on not one of the various unofficial classifications of the time nor does it seem to feature in the archives of the broking firm of Tastet and Lawton. Yet 'Brane-Mouton' was soon to rival Léoville, Rauzan and Gruaud-Larose at the top of the *deuxièmes* and Pontet-Canet, already, as now, prolific in production, was a regular member of the fourths or fifths.

Yet the D'Armailhacqs must have flourished, for their property, too, soon became extensive. During the Terror, the family attempted to acquire a substantial parcel of land on Pauillac's famous Carruades *croupe* which had recently become available. This purchase was contested by the town itself, no doubt considering that in these newly egalitarian times the land should go to the peasants rather than the landed gentry. In what seems, even by legal standards, unduly protracted proceedings, the case was finally settled in the D'Armailhacq favour in 1838, 40 years later.

Financial Problems

By this time, however, the family had sunk into financial difficulties. The 1830s were worrying times for the Bordeaux wine industry. The reimposition of tariff barriers, briefly lifted after the Napoleonic era but promulgated once again at the behest of northern French industrialists fearful of the cold wind of free competition, had closed down a potentially thriving export market for fine wine. The D'Armailhacq brothers, successors of Dominique, were deeply in debt. About 1840, they even attempted to solicit a loan of 400,000 francs from their neighbour Isaac Thuret, successor to the De Brane family at the other Mouton. Thuret was in no position to help. The market situation had affected him too (and, indeed, when he sold his land to Baron Nathaniel de Rothschild in 1853, he failed even to obtain as much as he paid in 1830). Finally, in November 1843, the D'Armailhacq creditors foreclosed and the property was put up for sale at the Tribunal de Première Instance at Lesparre. Was this to be the end of the D'Armailhacq era?

Curiously, the answer is no. M. Joseph Odet d'Armailhacq *ainé* and his wife were legally separated and she had her own fortune. In March 1844, Mme d'Armailhacq was awarded the property, valued at 398,000 francs, not including 'expenses'.

Not being able to raise this sum entirely from her own outside resources, Mme d'Armailhacq decided to sell the plot of land on the Carruades plateau over which there had been this long legal battle with the township of Pauillac. Comprising 32 *journaux* – there are roughly three *journaux*, the amount of land one man could work in a day, to the hectare – but at that time, naked of vines, this was a prime piece of land. Goudal, *régisseur* of Lafite, quickly wrote to his superiors advising purchase. His opposite number, Lestapis at Mouton, also asked for permission to make a bid. (The rivalry between Lafite and Mouton had already begun well before different branches of the Rothschild family had arrived!) In the end, it was Goudal who won, but only just. Half an hour after his offer of 96,000 francs was accepted, signed and sealed, Lestapis arrived ready to pay 100,000 francs. This was an enormous sum for ten hectares of unplanted vineyard, particularly by comparison with the valuation of 398,000 francs for the entire 70-plus hectare D'Armailhacq domaine!

ARMAND D'ARMAILHACQ

Mme d'Armailhacq entrusted the estate to her son Armand, born in 1798. Armand was a true example of nineteenth-century man. Scientific methods were beginning to arrive in vineyard and *chais*, and Armand, an agricultural engineer and author of *De la Culture des Vignes, de la Vinification et des Vins dans le Médoc*, was one of those in the forefront. Better husbandry in the vineyard, the use of only noble grape varieties and modern techniques of wine-making and *élevage* would not only improve standards but increase efficiency and competitiveness. The way to compete was to produce more wine at a cheaper price without lowering standards. The argument is still true today. D'Armailhacq's book ran to several editions between 1855 and his death in the 1870s.

D'Armailhacq and Hector de Brane, the last of his family at the other Mouton, are credited by many as having 'probably introduced' the Cabernet Sauvignon to the Médoc. This is an exaggeration. Actively promoted at the expense of lesser varieties – yes; introduced – no. D'Armailhacq himself writes that the Cabernet Sauvignon was 'almost exclusively' cultivated in Saint-Julien and Pauillac and, moreover, had been so for some time. This is substantiated by letters in the Latour archives. Even prior to the Revolution, the Cabernet was recognized as the quality grape variety. If D'Armailhacq introduced anything, it may have been the Merlot, which only arrived in the Médoc in the 1850s.

Meanwhile, the wine of the estate, finally appearing in the unofficial classifications just before that of 1855, was formally decreed a *cinquième* along with arch-rival Pontet-Canet and others. At 63 hectares and producing 140 *tonnieaux* (D'Armailhacq's own figures in his book), it was the third largest estate in the commune. The vineyard occupied all the slope crossed by the road from Pauillac to the little village of Hourtins plus another adjoining parcel which ran down east of Pontet-Canet towards Pibran. Despite the sale of the Carruades parcel mentioned above, there were still vineyards on the plateau and a second wine called Carruades d'Armailhacq was produced.

From Armand d'Armailhacq, the property passed into the hands of the family of the Comte de Ferrand, his sister's husband. Production increased as these successors followed D'Armailhacq's careful husbandry, reaching a peak of 250 *tonneaux* by the turn of the century. The second Comte de Ferrand, in his capacity as Vice-President of the Syndicat des Crus Classés, tried to organize a united front of owners against workers. Just as the latter won and forced their bosses to increase their wages to more reasonable levels, war broke out. It was August 1914.

Postwar France was a different country. It was another period of economic difficulty, another time of losses rather than profits as prohibition followed inflation and the economic depression worsened. The ageing Comte de Ferrand formed a *négociant*'s business in Pauillac in 1921 in 'an attempt to make good his losses', as Joan Littlewood puts it in *Mouton-Baronne-Philippe*, but could not prevent vineyard and cellars falling into a dilapidated state. It is doubtful if the Société Vinicole de Pauillac, at it was named, made money either.

BARON PHILIPPE DE ROTHSCHILD

Meanwhile, however, the other Mouton at last had a Rothschild on the spot. In October, 1922, Baron Philippe was summoned by his father. 'I've never been to Mouton,' he said, 'and I've no wish to go there.' 'But someone should be there,' Baron Philippe replied, 'the place is going to rack and ruin.' 'Do you think you could take it on?' 'Yes.' 'Well, get on with it.' 'So I did,' he told Joan Littlewood. 'I came back to Mouton.' (He had previously stayed there temporarily, when evacuated during the war.) In 1923 he arrived just in time to find the accountant burning his books in the backyard.

From the start, Mouton d'Armailhacq was a thorn in Baron Philippe's flesh. Both the vineyards and the other land surrounding the respective châteaux and their dependent buildings dovetailed. The estate of Mouton d'Armailhacq restricted the access to Mouton-Rothschild and prevented Baron Philippe laying out a suitably impressive park, part of his long-term plans for convincing the authorities that his château should be raised to *premier cru*. Simply, Mouton d'Armailhacq was in the way.

In 1933, the opportunity arose. Ferrand was persuaded to sell. The old Count and the young Baron dined to toast the deal in the faded glory of the D'Armailhacq château. Would the Count prefer to remain in residence for the rest of his days? He would. And would M. le Baron accept, in return, M. le Comte's trading company – the Société Vinicole de Pauillac? Why not? In 1954, retitled La Bergerie (later La Baronnie), this proved just the vehicle through which to sell a new brand called Mouton-Cadet made from de-classified wine of the poor 1930, 1931 and 1932 vintages.

There was much to do: the vineyard needed substantial replanting. The ivy-covered *chais* were falling apart. The *cuverie* was a mixture of old *foudres* and concrete vats, installed in 1900. There was no second-year cellar, no room to install a bottling line, and the press machine was out of date. Even Rothschilds, though, do not have unlimited money. A start was made in the vineyard, reducing it in size while the process of replanting was undertaken. But little could be done immediately in the cellars and nothing in the château itself during the final years of the old Comte de Ferrand. He died in 1938. And then came the war.

MOUTON-BARON-PHILIPPE

From a peak of 75 hectares, the vineyard had declined to 60 hectares in the 1930s and was to decrease further, reaching a level of 45 hectares under production in 1949 and descending as low as 32 hectares in 1960. This figure has now been increased to 50 hectares and production today stands at 200 *tonneaux*. The vineyard is planted in the ratio 70 per cent Cabernet Sauvignon and 30 per cent Merlot.

In 1968, the *chais* were finally gutted and rebuilt and the surrounding courtyard and its extended outbuildings now serve as the agricultural centre for the entire Rothschild empire. Mouton d'Armailhacq's *cuvier* is on two storeys, as at neighbouring Pontet-Canet, the grapes being winched up to the upper floor in order that they can be poured into the concrete fermentation vats at vintage time. Fermentation takes place at 32 degrees and the new wine is matured in wood, one-third new from 1985; the rest in old Mouton-Rothschild casks.

Baron Philippe could, quite legally, have incorporated the entire D'Armailhacq estate into Mouton-Rothschild but, in his determination to do nothing that might undermine the quality of the senior wine by one iota, the two productions are kept entirely separate, though produced by the same team. It should be stressed also that neither is Mouton-Baron-Philippe, as it was eventually renamed in 1956, in any way a second wine. Lesser *cuvées* of Mouton-Rothschild are demoted to Pauillac, as are those of Mouton-Baron-Philippe and, now, of Clerc-Milon. The team is against second wines.

With the change in name – it was felt that D'Armailhacq was difficult to pronounce and spell, as well as being historically redundant and possibly leading to confusion with Armagnac – came a change in label: Two sphinxes, couchant, garlanded with beads, facing each other under a gold canopy.

MORE CHANGES OF NAME

Baroness Pauline, beloved wife of Baron Philippe for 25 years, inspirer and creator with him of the celebrated Mouton Museum, died in 1976. In her memory, the Baron attempted to have the name of Mouton-Baron-Philippe changed to Mouton-Baronne-Pauline but this was refused; Mouton-Baronne-Philippe, however, was approved. Simpler, perhaps, but a sort of strange, halfway house.

In April 1991, following her father's death, Baronne Philippine de Rothschild decided to change the name again. She felt that there was not only a risk of Mouton-Baronne-Philippe being taken to be the second wine of Mouton-Rothschild, but also confusion with Mouton-Cadet. The new label, Château d'Armailhac, was officially unveiled at the June VINEXPO of that year.

THE CHÂTEAU

The tourist driving up to Mouton-Rothschild and its museum will miss the Mouton-Baronne-Philippe château, hidden as it is among the trees, and thereby fail to notice a real architectural curiosity. The building literally consists of half the architect's original plans. Not half horizontally but half vertically, as if it had been sliced like a loaf. Halfway along the pediment, the house just comes to a stop. It is rather surreal. It was started in the 1820s and building stopped presumably when the D'Armailhacq brothers' money began to run out. The style is classical Charles X; two-storeyed, raised above the park to permit basement kitchens and other offices. It is now being restored.

THE HISTORY OF CLERC-MILON

The background to Clerc-Milon is less dramatic and not as well documented as that of Mouton-Baronne-Philippe. Clerc was the name of the proprietor at the time of the 1855 Classification, Milon, the name of the *lieu-dit*. It used to be Clerc-Milon-Mondon, but the last name, of another proprietor, was dropped after the Rothschild purchase.

The hamlet of Milon lies in the extreme north-west of the Pauillac commune near the Jalle de Breuil which marks the commune boundary. Here, in the 1820s, under the name of Mandavit or Mandavi, was the nucleus of what was to become Duhart-Milon, at the time a fourth growth and now belonging to the Rothschilds of Lafite. Here, also, a Jean-Baptiste

Clerc, though he lived in Pouyalet, must have also owned land. As the yield quoted for Mandavit fluctuates widely at this time, I would not be surprised if M. Clerc's domaine did not originate as part of a larger, pre-Revolutionary, nucleus. But the proof of this hypothesis is not available.

The Clerc domaine, producing 40 *tonneaux* of wine, was classified towards the end of the fifth growths in 1855. Meanwhile, M. Clerc had been increasing his holding by buying up land in the hamlet of Mousset, nearer the river. After his death in 1863, the property passed to the widows Clerc and Germain, presumably his wife and sister. There was then a court case over who was entitled to the name Clerc-Milon. M. Jacques Mondon, who had bought from a M. Lamena the part originally belonging to M. Clerc, was the victor, but it would seem that it was M. Meynieu who held most of the land actually in the locality of Milon.

Be that as it may, the estate of Clerc-Milon, 'divided some years ago into *several* parcels' [my italics] as it says in Cocks and Féret in 1922 and producing some 35 *tonneaux* from its ten hectares, passed through the hands of several of Pauillac's notaries. Lamena had been succeeded by Mondon in this post and he was succeeded as the local lawyer as well as at Clerc-Milon by his son-in-law, Maître Jacques Vialard.

In 1970, after the latter's death, his sisters Mlle Marie Vialard and Mme Louis Hedon sold Clerc-Milon to Baron Philippe de Rothschild. For 23 years the wine had been the monopoly of the *négociants* Dourthe. Its reputation was not of the highest.

AFTER THE ROTHSCHILD PURCHASE

The vineyard was particularly dismembered. There was no real château as such, the small collection of cottages and *chais* being indistinguishable from the rest of the village of Mousset and the property was rundown. The price – a million francs – was derisory. At barely over 80,000 francs a hectare, Clerc-Milon was a bargain compared with Grand-Puy-Ducasse which exchanged hands in 1971 on the basis of 235,000 francs a hectare. Even in the middle of the slump four years later, the better-known Pontet-Canet sold for 480,000 francs per hectare, fetching 32 million francs. Now, even lesser châteaux sell for a million francs a hectare or more.

At the time, the area under vine was ten and a half hectares and production 50 *tonneaux*. The vineyard has since been both rationalized and extended. There are now 32 hectares, still much parcelled but most of which lie between the D2 road and the river near the Shell refinery, and which are planted in the ratio 70 per cent Cabernet Sauvignon, 10 per cent Cabernet Franc and 20 per cent Merlot. Today, 100 *tonneaux* is a normal yield, matured, like Mouton-Baronne-Philippe, in old Mouton-Rothschild casks and, since 1984, using one-third new oak.

During the 1970s, the *chais* and *cuverie* were much renovated. The old vats were dispensed with and, unique in Baron Philippe's three Pauillac domaines, eleven stainless-steel *cuves* were installed. The *cuverie* itself is tiny; Edmund Penning-Rowsell describes it as 'no bigger than a good-sized drawing-room'. Baron Philippe and his wife also redesigned the label. This is modelled on a silver wedding beaker dating from 1609 and emanating from Augsburg in Germany, now in the museum. The beaker is in the form of a lady raising a *coupe* above her head. This *coupe* forms one vessel and the skirt of the lady the second. The married couple were supposed to drink from both parts of this beaker at the same time – without spilling a drop. In 1983 the label was changed again.

THE WINES

Appropriately, Mouton-Baronne-Philippe, as much because of the situation of its vineyard as a result of having the higher proportion of Merlot, is a more 'feminine' wine than Clerc-

Milon. In the past, it seems to have been on the light side for Pauillac. It is described as 'soft' by the anonymous author of *Clarets and Sauternes*, published in the early 1920s, and as 'delicately perfumed' by Alfred Danflou in 1867. Baron Philippe was aware of the difference in its structure compared with Mouton-Rothschild itself, and thought that it might mature better contained in larger volumes than in the usual Bordeaux *barriques*.

Today, I would certainly not suggest that it is light, but it is a wine of charm rather than austerity, plumpness rather than solidity, style and balance rather than backbone and structure. It has become more elegant in recent years. Mouton-Baronne-Philippe matures in the medium-to-long term.

In contrast, Clerc-Milon is normally a little sturdier and a little more tannic. What was, in pre-Rothschild times, a burliness, even a coarseness, has been changed to a real masculine Pauillac depth, a weight and a capacity for profound concentration and longevity in the really big years like 1982 and 1986 which I find very impressive. Mouton-Baronne-Philippe is an ample wine with a really seductive appeal, good to very good but without ever perhaps the potential for 'great'. Clerc-Milon, on the other hand, is showing signs of being able to produce something really *sérieux*. I am very enthusiastic about the 1986 and later vintages. Could this be a super-second of the future?

THE TASTING

The vintages from 1987 back to 1982, of both châteaux, and the 1975 Clerc-Milon, were sampled in February 1990, at a tasting in London. The notes on earlier vintages come from a tasting at Mouton-Baronne-Philippe in the autumn of 1986.

My experience of the older vintages of Baronne-Philippe is more extensive than that of Clerc. The 1971 is beginning to loosen up now and become less generous but it still finishes well and interestingly. The 1970 is certainly a success, the wine being more Mouton-Rothschild-ish than it is today, more 'old-fashioned' in its size and weight. The 1966 is in a similar mould – full, chunky, lead-pencilly. The acidity now is beginning to show, if the last bottle I saw is any judge. Similarly, the 1961 has had elements of being a little too large for its own good, though other bottles have also shown rather more supplely and elegantly. Vintages of the 1950s, the 1955 and 1953, for instance are elegant and fragrant. But the 1945, last time out, was a little solid, now getting astringent.

Clerc-Milon, in the pre-Rothschild days, was always full and firm, occasionally a bit too solid and chunky, even rustic, but never too farmyardy, just a bit unyielding. The 1970 was not bad and the 1971 OK, if lacking charm; and the property produced a better 1973 than most. Prior to 1970, my experience has been limited almost entirely to Bordeaux or English bottlings and is not recent enough to make useful specific comments.

Optimum drinking

MOUTON-BARONNE-PHILIPPE

1987   **Drink soon**
Reasonable colour. Light nose. Light on the palate. A pleasant but rather nondescript wine for early drinking.

1986   **Now–2000**
Good colour. Good rich nose. Not a block-buster. Medium body. Good ripe tannins. Has fruit and balance. Shows well.

1985   **Now–2000**
Medium-full colour. Good rich nose, more open

than the 1986. More succulent. A most attractive wine. Medium to medium-full body. Good balance. A wine which will be ready fairly soon. Rich, quite complex. Finishes well. Very good.

1984   **Drink soon**
Reasonable colour. The nose is soft and has some charm. Lightish but not mean on the palate. A good result.

1983   **Now–2006**
Medium-full colour. The nose is succulent and rich, but still closed. Medium body, just a little tannin. A more austere wine than the 1985 but longer and denser on the finish. Complex. Very long. Again very good.

1982 1995–2015

Fullish colour. Rich, full and concentrated on the nose. A big wine which is quite a bit more tannic than the rest. Good chocolatey, roasted-nuts fruit. Fat, rich, concentrated. Very good.

1981 Now–1998

Fine colour. Good, open, ample nose. Plump fruit. Medium body, tannins now softening to show an accessible, elegant wine, with a good fresh finish. Not that powerful but has a lot of charm. Certainly good for the vintage.

1980 **Drink up**

Pleasant, straightforward, slightly one-dimensional but not unattractive wine. A bit dull in this company and only quite good to good for the vintage.

1979 **Drink soon**

Medium colour, some brown. Softer, slightly more dilute and less grip on nose and palate than I expected. Pleasant but obviously a large harvest. Soft and fruity, no great length. If anything, a bit short.

1978 Now–1999

Quite a bit more colour but also some brown. More concentrated by quite some way on nose and palate. Good, red-fruit concentration and ripeness and a very good finish. Medium body. Lovely balance. Good for the vintage.

1977 **Drink up**

Good colour for the vintage. Light, soft, pleasant – even elegant – wine. No cold-tea elements you now find in many 1977s. Still fresh in 1986. Good for the vintage.

1976 **Drink up**

Good colour for the vintage. Quite full, no undue brown. A little sign of attenuation on the nose but has at least some freshness. Medium-bodied, quite good fruit. Better structured than most, not weakening or drying up but perhaps now losing whatever elegance it once had.

CLERC-MILON

1987 **Drink soon**

Reasonable colour. Soft, plump nose. A little more to it than the Mouton-Baronne-Philippe. A little tannic in the attack. Fresher on the follow-through. Good.

1986 1996–2010

Good colour. Rich full substantial nose. Fuller and fatter than the 1985. Fullish, good concentration, rather more depth than the Mouton-Baronne-Philippe. This is very good indeed. Lovely balance and depth. Fine finish.

1985 Now–2003

Medium-full colour. Soft, aromatic nose. There is a greater difference between 1985 and 1986 Clerc as between the Mouton-Baronne-Philippe. Medium body. Doesn't have the charm of the Mouton-Baronne-Philippe. Balanced though. Finishes well. Will show more positively as it develops. Good.

1984 **Drink soon**

Reasonable colour. Good nose. Some oak, not mean. Stylish and not at all unripe on the palate. Good positive follow-through. Very good for vintage.

1983 Now–2007

Medium-full colour. Good nose, fresh and firmer than most. Medium to medium-full body. Still a little tannin. A certain dryness behind it, and not as well balanced as the Mouton-Baronne-Philippe. Yet finishes well and positively.

1982 1997–2017

Full colour. Fullish youthful nose. Rich, fat, opulent wine with fine grip. There is a lot of depth here. Better than the Mouton-Baronne-Philippe.

1981 Now–2001

Similar colour to Mouton-Baronne-Philippe but a better nose, more structured and a better acidity. Fullish, rich, plenty of depth. Less charm but this is because it is less evolved. Marginally better quality.

1980 **Drink up**

Quite good colour but now browning. Evolved, open nose. Not a lot of depth and grip but quite plump and fruity. Just a little more structure than Mouton-Baronne-Philippe and finishes well. A little more definition.

1979 **Drink soon**

As usual, slightly more colour than Mouton-Baronne-Philippe. Medium-bodied, fresher, more positive, less wishy-washy. This has good structure and fruit and will still improve. More interesting, if not a great 1979.

1978 **See note**

The only really disappointing wine of the tasting. There is an element of *sur-maturité* attenuation, a lack of grip, which reminds me more of 1976 than 1978. Fat and spicy but a touch chunky, with a bit of astringency on the finish. Lacks the grip and elegance of Mouton-Baronne-Philippe. Has shown well in the past. 'Very Pauillac' I noted at a tasting in 1984 and 'typical Pauillac' if a bit dense, the year before. Was this a rogue bottle?

1977   **Drink soon**

More evolved than Mouton-Baronne-Philippe and less interesting. Not bad, though but will get progressively more astringent as it develops.

1976   **Drink soon**

Sturdier, fresher colour than Mouton-Baronne-Philippe. More powerful nose, with hints of caramel and *crème brûlée*. This is certainly good for the vintage. Has richness and fat, plenty of grip and depth. More life if a touch tough and astringent on its own. Would be better with food.

1975   **Now–2005**

Good colour. Ripe nose. Fresh, vigorous. Not too hard. Shows well. A very good example. Fullish, even rich, good age and good grip. Very good.

SAINT-
JUL

SAINT-JULIEN LIES IMMEDIATELY TO THE SOUTH OF PAUILLAC AND IS THE SMALLEST OF THE FOUR MAIN HAUT-MÉDOC COMMUNES IN TERMS OF ITS PRODUCTION. THE COMMUNE IS COMPACT AND DOMINATED BY ITS ELEVEN CLASSED GROWTHS, ALL OF WHICH PRODUCE EXCELLENT WINE AND MANY OF WHICH PRODUCE WINE ABOVE THEIR 1855 CLASSIFICATION LEVEL. THERE ARE FIVE SECOND GROWTHS, TWO THIRDS, AND FOUR FOURTHS.

At the northern end of the commune lie the three Léovilles, at the southern end Beychevelle, Ducru-Beaucaillou and Gruaud-Larose. Langoa is in the middle, between the villages of Saint-Julien and Beychevelle; set back from the river are Talbot and Lagrange.

The Saint-Julien soil is predominantly gravel, particularly in those vineyards nearest to the Gironde, where it is based on a subsoil of the iron-based sandstone known as *alios* and clay. Further inland the soil has less gravel and more sand, and beneath this is a richer subsoil containing clay, *alios*, and occasionally marl.

Saint-Julien wines are the closest to those of Pauillac in character, and like their neighbours contain high proportions of Cabernet Sauvignon. Indeed, with the exception of growths such as Mouton-Rothschild, Latour and Lafite, there is not a great deal of difference in weight or style between the wines of the two communes. Properties such as Léoville-Las-Cases and Barton can produce wine every bit as full-bodied and slow maturing as Lynch-Bages and Grand-Puy-Lacoste.

The quintessence of a wine of Saint-Julien is its balance and its finesse. The wines are well coloured, have plenty of body, are full of fruit, rich and elegant. It is harmony rather than power which gives longevity; so a Saint-Julien, if without the firmness and reserve of a great Pauillac, nevertheless keeps exceptionally well. The top estates produce simply superb wines.

LÉOVILLE-
LAS-CASES

At the northern end of the commune of Saint-Julien, opposite the vines of Château Latour across the boundary in
Pauillac, an old stone wall encloses a 50-hectare piece of
vineyard. This is the *grand clos*, the heart and nucleus of one
of the best, and certainly one of the longest-living, of all the
Saint-Julien properties – if not of the entire Médoc. Since
the late 1950s Château Léoville-Las-Cases has consistently
produced one of the best clarets in Bordeaux – perhaps of all
wines the nearest in quality to the first growths. At a comparative blind tasting in 1988 of Château Léoville-Las-Cases
and Château Ducru-Beaucaillou (and you can't find many
super-seconds better than Ducru), I was not alone in marking the Las-Cases the higher in most of the vintages of the
last decade or so, though prior to 1975 it was the Ducru
which was generally preferred. The 1975, indeed, is probably
among the best three wines of that difficult year in the entire
Bordeaux region.

Why is it that Léoville-Las-Cases produces such good
wine? Obviously the base, the soil, must be suitable; the
blend of grapes planted in the vineyard correct; and the vinification and maturation techniques applied with understanding and dedication. Above this there must be a perfectionism, embodied in a man who not only loves his wine, but is
determined that absolutely nothing second-rate should leave
the property under the *grand vin* label, and who has the resources, in terms of manpower as well as cash, to ensure that
no corners are cut, everything done to make the wine as
perfect as possible.

To illustrate this, let us take the arrival of a lorry-load of
grapes one recent, rainy vintage. Most proprietors would
have covered the fruit with a tarpaulin on the way from the
vineyard to the press house – and, anyway, would have

avoided picking the grapes while it was actually raining if they possibly could. Would it, however, have occurred to them to tip the lorry up, without removing the tailgate, thus ensuring that as much moisture as possible drained off the fruit before it went into the fermentation vat? I was there. It was five o'clock in the afternoon. It had rained the previous night and since dawn there had been alternate spells of drizzle broken up by fitful sunshine, thankfully, with a cool wind to aid the evaporation of the rain. I was amazed by the amount of delicately pink juice which trickled through the gap under the tailgate and was sluiced away down the drains of the *chai*'s forecourt. Dozens of gallons of water were lost in this way and, as a result, the wine of Las-Cases was less thin, less anaemic than the wine of its neighbours.

The man behind Château Léoville-Las-Cases is Michel Delon, one of the few 'working proprietors' in the Médoc who combines the roles of owner and general manager. Delon is the third generation in charge of Las-Cases, and his family have gradually acquired the majority holding of the property since it was first formed as a limited company in 1900. He is a man who is steeped in wine, at the same time both a traditionalist and one who is prepared to experiment. When he says that in a lesser year, such as 1987, only one-half of the crop goes into new oak, for more than that, even with a full-bodied, muscular wine like Las-Cases, would make the wine excessively oaky, too *boisé*, you can bet this is no idle speculation: he has tested and tasted. He has proved he is right.

The Léoville estate, one of the largest as well as one of the oldest in the Médoc, was originally called Mont-Moytié. The Mont bit refers to the fact that when the domaine was created in 1638, as the surrounding land had not yet been drained – this was done by Dutch engineers later in the century – it formed a little peninsula bounded both to the north and the south by marsh, land which was flooded at high tide. The intervening mound of gravel was the Mont. Moytié was a wealthy Bordelais of Charentais extraction, though not, as far as records indicate, a *parlementaire*, and it was under his aegis or that of his son, Grand Treasurer of France, during the last few decades of the seventeenth century, that vines were first planted in a large scale on the estate.

HISTORY

In about 1740 the property passed into the hands of a M. Blaise Alexandre de Gascq, *seigneur* of Léoville in the Saintonge, and a president of the Bordeaux parliament, who had married a Moytié heiress, and it is under this ownership that the wine first became well known. Other branches of the family were, variously, owners of what is now Château Palmer and estates in Barsac. By 1750, Léoville was recognized as the senior property in the commune of Saint-Julien. It fetched higher prices than any other wines outside what were to become the four First Growths in the 1855 Classification, and in unofficial classifications ruling at the time was one of only three wines consistently rated as second growths. The others were Gruaud-Larose and Rauzan, then undivided. Mouton-Rothschild, at the time called Branne-Mouton, was not to rise until after Napoleonic times.

M. Gascq-Léoville, by this time a baron, died without issue in 1769, and at the time of the Revolution the estate belonged to four of his heirs, M. le Marquis de Las-Cases-Beauvois, his brother and two sisters, all from the family D'Abbadie, under which name the wine was also known. The Marquis himself, head of the family and fearing for his head, fled the country in 1794, and the state at first wished to sequestrate the entire property. They were persuaded that this should be divided first, and a quarter only was sold, on *3 Thermidor l'An IV*, to a consortium of two brothers called Lechevalier and a M. Monbalon. This was the origin of Léoville-Barton, and would pass to Hugh Barton in the 1820s.

Meanwhile Pierre-Jean, *Maréchal de Camps*, was now Marquis de Las-Cases, having succeeded his father in 1815. A man of different political sympathies from his father, perhaps, he had risen in the army to his exalted position of Field Marshal under Napoleon, and accompanied his hero to Elba, where he was to write his biography. His was the majority holding in the remaining three-quarters of Léoville, having no doubt been left the holding of his aunts – we don't know what happened to his uncle – and his sister Jeanne had the rest, though for the time being this part of the estate was run as one piece. It has been pointed out that the Code Napoléon had abolished primogeniture. Thence-forth all property and other inheritance had to be divided equally among all the direct heirs, male and female.

Jeanne de Las-Cases married her distant cousin, Bertrand d'Abbadie, a member of one of the oldest Gironde families. His full name was D'Abbadie de Saint-Germain, Baron de Nocarelles, and a relative was proprietor of Château Cantemerle. In 1840 the Léoville estate was further divided. Two-thirds of the remaining Las-Cases portion, that is half of the original, remained with Pierre-Jean, and is today Léoville-Las-Cases. One third passed to Jeanne. This would become Léoville-Poyferré.

So by the time of the 1855 Classification the original Léoville estate was in three parts. Las-Cases, the senior portion, produced 120 *tonneaux*, Poyferré 90 and Barton 60. All were equally distinguished, all were judged second growths, and frequently, from whatever portion, labelled merely as Léoville.

Pierre-Jean was succeeded by his son Adolphe, and Adolphe by his three children, Gaston, Gabriel and Clothilde, in 1880. Soon after, Gaston, Marquis de Las-Cases, sold his third to Gabriel.

In 1900 Gabriel wanted to sell his portion and the estate was formed into a company. Clothilde, now Mme d'Alauzier, remained the largest shareholder with eight out of twenty shares. The remainder were bought – or allocated, one each – by various members of the Bordeaux wine trade. Christophe Calvet, Hermann and Maurice Peyrelongue, and Edouard Tastet, the broker, each bought one, as did Théophile Skawinski, the general manager of the estate.

Skawinski was succeeded by his son-in-law, André Delon, and he in his turn by his son Paul. For some years now a third generation of Delons has been in charge in the person of Paul's son Michel. Over the years the Delons have acquired the majority shareholding, owning thirteen shares, the remainder being with various members of the D'Alauzier family and their descendants, all of whom can trace their ancestry back, not only to the Marquises of Las-Cases, but to Léoville, and even Moytié himself.

THE ESTATE

While the Poyferré and Barton vineyards are much intermingled, not only with each other but with those of Talbot and Pichon-Longueville-Lalande, the Las-Cases vineyards are largely separate. Most of the Las-Cases vineyard is nearer to the river than any other Saint-Julien property, for between Las-Cases and Latour at the top end of the commune the alluvial band of *palus*, used for grazing sheep and cattle, is narrower than elsewhere. The biggest part of the vineyard is enclosed within a stone wall, surmounted by the stone lion we can see on the label, and lies north of the Saint-Julien village, east of the main road, immediately to the south of the vineyard of Château Latour, and this occupies some 50 hectares. This is the *grand clos*, already mentioned. South of the village, and on the same side, is the *petit clos*, some five hectares. On the western side, among the other Léoville vineyards, is another piece of twenty hectares. Finally, Delon bought some seven hectares of land, formerly wooded, off the late Ronald Barton in the 1970s and, finding the soil excellent, cleared the ground and has planted vines. (Nineteenth-century documents show this plot to have been previously planted.)

All this, some 95 hectares of productive vines, is planted in the ratio 65 per cent Cabernet Sauvignon, 13 per cent Cabernet Franc, 3 per cent of very old Petit Verdot and 19 per cent Merlot, and produces about 250 *tonneaux* of wine a year.

Las-Cases has two second labels. Clos du Marquis was first put on the market in 1904, with the 1902 vintage. More recently, since 1977, some of this has been bottled as Château du Grand Parc, no doubt because the word *château* sounds grander than *clos*. Michel Delon prefers the original, and Grand Parc is hardly used, reserved only for two small clients. There is even a third wine, the Domaine de Bigarnon, but not necessarily in every vintage.

The château and many of the outbuildings proved less easy to divide than the vineyard. Delon has a map, dating from the 1880s, when they tried to rationalize what was in truth a hopeless mess, with adjoining rooms in different ownership, though with the same entrance. Even then they only partially solved the problem, and to this day it is a complicated matter to explain precisely where Las-Cases ends and Poyferré begins.

The bulk of the château, which lies on the river side of the road in the middle of the village of Saint-Julien, belongs to Las-Cases, chiefly most of the facade of the château itself and the north wing, where Delon has his office and where the wine is made.

Part of the *cuverie* was renovated in 1977. It contains eleven large, polished, wooden vats, a reception chamber with a modern *fouloir-égrappoir*, and stainless-steel pipes. Adjacent lies an old cellar, with fourteen smaller, unlined cement vats. More recently a third vinification centre was constructed, replacing the old *chai de première année*. This contains a dozen or so stainless-steel vats of different sizes between 80 and 200 hectolitres, to give the greatest possible flexibility; these vats being thermostatically controlled, of course. Opposite, and a little to the south, lies another large *chai*, built in four parts from 1902 onwards, the last extension being made in 1985. This is used for the maturation of wine in barrel, the bottling and the storage of wine in bottle. This is an impressive, modern construction, each section independently temperature and humidity controlled. The last extension was to the south, towards the château of Langoa, and now houses the first-year wine.

HOW THE WINE IS MADE

On arrival at the *cuverie* the grapes are completely de-stalked and then vinified at 25 to 26 degrees, raising the temperature slightly at the end of the two to two and a half week maceration, except in very hot years – which would result, in M. Delon's view, in a wine which was too robustly, even coarsely tannic – to about 28 degrees. *Remontage* (pumping over) is frequent. This produces a wine with a fine colour and concentration and a fine expression of fruit: a typically austere, slow-to-mature, claret-lovers' claret.

The amount of new oak at Las-Cases varies from year to year. In lighter years 50 per cent is considered sufficient for the *grand vin*, in bigger vintages it can be 80 per cent, even the totality. The Clos du Marquis is matured in about 25 per cent new oak. Following this the barrels go to Delon's excellent property in the Bas-Médoc, Château Potensac. Bottling usually takes place from June onwards in the second year. The Clos du Marquis is dealt with first (occasionally, in lesser years, such as 1987, at the end of April) and the Las-Cases follows a month later, except in exceptional vintages, such as 1986, when bottling was delayed until September.

THE WINE

'*Sui le lion qui ne mord point*
Sinon quand l'ennemi me poing'
('I am the lion which does not bite
Unless the enemy attacks first')
Léoville motto

Las-Cases is the senior part of the Léoville estate. Its claim to senior partner status rests not only on its size but also on its history. The Barton and Poyferré sections were divided up on separate occasions; the large Las-Cases section is what is left, and so could claim to be the original. Moreover the Las-Cases family, full owners until 1900 and still part-owners to this day, were descendants of the original Blaise-Alexandre de Gasq, Baron de Léoville, while the Bartons and the Lalandes, Lawtons and Cuveliers, variously owners of Poyferré, were not. This senior status is exemplified by the label: '*Grand Vin de Léoville*', it says, and then in much smaller letters, '*du Marquis de Las-Cases*'. The label also shows one of the many stone Léoville lions which guard the estate.

Las-Cases is a full, firm wine, the biggest of all Saint-Juliens and enjoys a fine reputation. Like all properties (or almost all, I should perhaps say), it has had its ups and downs. In the 1930s and for some years after, the property was in decline. A major scheme of replanting after the Second World War left the average age of the vines too much on the young side for '*grand vin*', and the wines of the run of good vintages between 1945 and 1955 were not as good at Barton and Poyferré. By 1959, however, the vineyard was in better shape, and since then Las-Cases has been remarkable in its consistency and exhilarating in its quality.

The wines are the most Pauillac-y of all the commune; full and firm, rich and concentrated, classic in their taste of oak and the Cabernet Sauvignon grape. In comparison with most Saint-Juliens they need a year or two more to mature. Léoville-Las-Cases is currently not only the best wine of Saint-Julien, but among the top wines of the whole Bordeaux region.

THE TASTING

The following tasting was hosted by Dr Marvin Overton – and 'moderated' by myself – in San Francisco in May 1992. I have added notes from recent vintages sampled at the château in September 1994 on the 1924 and 1918 which were sampled at the Las-Cases *versus* Ducru tasting in October 1988; and on the 1934 I sampled in May 1991.

1993

Optimum drinking
1999–2009

Very good colour. Very lovely concentrated nose. Rich and classy. Structured yet with none of the structure showing. Medium-full body. Good attack. Ample and fruity. If it doesn't have the grip and power and intensity at the end of a great vintage it is certainly a wine of great interest. Harmonious, quite complex, certainly attractive and generous and quite long on the palate. Very good.

1992   **1996–2001**

Very good colour for the vintage. This has a lot more depth and interest on the nose than most. Very good marriage between the oak and what is really quite a lot of fruit. Medium body. Fresh and quite ample and fruity. One and a half dimensions rather than three. But reasonable length and interest on the finish. Very good for the vintage.

1991   **1996–2002**

Similar colour to the 1992, a little more development though. Lovely nose. Seems older than it is. The nose is spicy and aromatic: cinnamon and nutmeg, allspice and sandalwood and cigar boxy. Really Christmas cakey. This is a lot better than the 1992. It has balance and personality and depth. Medium body. Now getting mellow. Lovely ripe complex finish. Most enjoyable. Fine for the vintage.

1990   **2000–2020**

Very good colour. The nose is a bit hidden but it is obvious that this is a wine of profound depth and aristocratic style nevertheless. Really rich and chocolaty. Full body. Immaculately ripe tannins. Excellent grip. The fruit is marvellously rich and concentrated and multidimensional. Above all there is breed. A splendid example which is very very long and fat on the palate. Everything is so ripe it gives great pleasure now. But a shame really to attack it before 2000.

1989   **1999–2015**

Very good colour. Less classic than the 1990 on the nose. Richer perhaps, slightly more evolved. Certainly more aromatic. This is fullish, but not as full as the 1990; rich but not as profoundly complex, balanced but not as harmonious or as long. Or as composed, because the tannins are drier. But it is a wine of great, almost exotic ripe fruit. Very ample and very seductive. Very lovely. But I prefer the 1990 – just.

1988   **2000–2025**

Even better colour than the 1990 and 1989. Firm, backward, classic nose that got more and more interesting as it evolved. On the palate a wine of real breed and very lovely Cabernet fruit. Medium full, splendid balance. Very very long. A very fine example with a splendid finish. Real breed here. Will keep very well indeed. All it lacks is the extra concentration and dimension the 1990 has.

1987   **Now–1997**

Very good vigorous colour for the vintage. Soft, fruity, but elegant nose nonetheless. Not a wine of great weight or dimension but one with character and sufficient ripeness and backbone to give plenty of enjoyment. Finishes positively. Drink quite soon though.

1986   **1997–2026**

Excellent colour. Still very young. Lovely ripe concentrated Cabernet nose. First growth complexity and breed here. A very fabulous wine. Classic blackcurrant. Real depth. Fullish. Some tannin but now beginning to soften. Is coming out of its adolescence. Very very lovely ripe rich follow-through and finish. Really profound. Really classy. Even better than the 1990. More depth and intensity. Brilliant. A great wine!

1985   **1995–2015**

Excellent colour. Only a hint of brown. Rich, ample, aromatic nose. Not the backbone of 1986 but fine and profound nonetheless. Medium-full, ripe, now getting mellow. Indeed just about ready. This is a generous, attractive, seductive wine, with excellent balance. Warm and approachable on the finish. Lovely. One of the best of the vintage.

1984   **Now–1997**

Surprisingly good colour. Better than 1987, fuller and more vigorous. On the palate this is mellow and at first more interesting than the 1987. Less round, but more definition and breed. The finish is also good. Certain astringent elements lurk, so drink quite soon. But a fine 1984 with plenty of dimension at the end.

1983   **Now–2013**

Splendid full vigorous colour. The nose is ripe, aromatic but just a little loose-knit in comparison with the 1985. On the palate the same reproach could be made, except that there is more Cabernet flavour here, so the follow-through is classier and the finish no shorter. Medium-full. Classy. Complex. Long. In the end I prefer this. *A point* now. A very fine example of the vintage. Up with the top Margaux and Graves.

1982   **1996–2026**

Excellent colour. Still young. Still closed on the nose. Very very rich and aromatic. Almost hot chocolate, even caramel. Full bodied, still some tannin. Splendidly rich and ample, even sweet. Very good grip. This is flamboyant like the 1989, though I think it has better acidity. A potentially hugely enjoyable combination of Pauillac/Saint-Julien 'seriousness' and the exotism of the vintage. Very long. Very lovely. *Grand vin* again. Still needs time.

1981   **Now–2003**

Medium-full colour. Good vigour, barely mature. Stylish, supple but not a bit weak on the nose. Very good, balanced fruit. Merlot shows. Medium to medium-full body. Just about ready. Subtle. Balanced. Poised. A delicious example. More elegant and more complex than most.

1979   **Now–2005**

Medium-full colour. Ripe blackberry, blackcurrant nose. More Cabernet than the 1981. This has good richness and depth. Very Cabernet in flavour on the palate. Medium-full, just about mature, balanced, elegant. Fine but it lacks just a little fat and concentration on the attack. More generous on the finish. Long. Classy.

1978   **Now–2014**

Fullish colour, just a little more brown than the 1979. Rounder, richer and fatter on the nose than the above. This has very good concentration. A highly satisfactory 1978. Medium-full, just a little tannin left. Ripe, concentrated, chocolatey. Good fat, good depth. Good dimension. Complex and full of finesse. Very fine. Lovely long finish.

1976   **Now–1997**

Good colour. Now mature. Ripe, luscious, summer fruit nose with a hint of chocolate. Not a bit dry or blowsy. Surprisingly fresh. On the palate there is a touch of the coarse and pedestrian. But it is very much better than most. Ripe and fresh on the attack. Medium to medium-full. But the aftertaste is a little astringent and a bit hard and vegetal. Very good for the vintage though.

1975   **Now–2014 plus**

Good colour. Not quite as full as the 1978. A touch of brown at the rim. Full, rich, concentrated, new oaky nose. Even more depth and harmony (and breed) than the 1976. Fullish, still tannic. Rich and very concentrated. This is the best wine of the decade. Lovely fruit. Very long. Bags of vigour. Very consistent. Very classy.

1973   **Drink up**

Medium-full, mature colour. Ripe nose with a hint of toffee and caramel, but beginning to get a little pinched. Lightening up now. Medium body. The finish is a little charmless, even attenuated. Unexciting. Uncharming.

1971   **Now–1997**

Medium-full, well-matured colour. Lacks a little generosity on the nose. On the palate the wine is better. Medium to medium-full, harmonious, subtle. Individual. Very good fruit. Not too charmless because it is very well-balanced, complex and long. Surprisingly good. Will keep.

1970   **Now–2005**

Fullish colour. Just about mature. Ripe, rich nose. But not exactly compelling. On the palate full, fleshy, generous and full of fruit. Good acidity. But not quite the definition and breed, the grip and dimension of the 1975. Very good plus. At best at the end.

1969   **Drink soon**

Good colour for the vintage. Fullish. No undue age. Pleasant, soft nose. Fresh, not pinched. A touch astringent on the attack and a little lightening-up at the end. Medium body. No decay. Fruity and attractive. A little one-dimensional, a little short, but by no means beneath contempt.

1967   **Past its best**

Good colour. No sign of age. Broad nose. A little attenuated. There is ripeness and style here but it has loosened up now. Medium body. Dry on the finish. Past its best if this bottle is any correct indication.

1966   **Now–1997**

Full mature colour. Very fine classy nose. This has excellent ripe fruit. There is even an element of the super creamy concentration you only usually find in 1961s. Full, concentrated, structured, lovely balance. Excellent fruit. *A point* now. Saint-Julien and Cabernet Sauvignon in all its glorious breed. Very complex long finish. Very fine indeed. But won't last for ever.

1964   **Now–1997**

Fullish mature colour. Firm nose. But not too hard. This is certainly a very good 1964. Medium-full, ripe, quite flexible. Lacks a little dimension and breed but not short. Not unstylish. Very Cabernet in flavour.

1962   **Drink soon**

Fullish mature colour. The nose is a little faded. But still neat and stylish. On the palate a little dry. I think this bottle is older than most. Medium-full. Ripe and fruity nevertheless, but it doesn't have the grip, vigour, generosity and complexity of some other 1962s. Finishes a bit dry. Very good but not better.

1961   **Drink soon**

Fullish mature colour. Ripe and very Cabernet on the nose but it lacks the super-abundant fruit of the 1959. There is even something a little herbaceous here. Medium-full, some astringency. Not a great wine by any means, and hardly even 'good' for a 1961. Too much age.

1959   **Now–1999**

Very full colour. Not a hint of age. Brilliant on nose and palate. Fat, concentrated, ample, luxurious and very vigorous. Puts the 1961 into the shade. Full, rich, abundant and velvety. This is very lovely. Huge amount of fruit, together with all the benefits (and none of the disadvantages) of a hot year. Long, vigorous. Very fine.

1957   **Drink soon**

(Magnum) Very good colour. Slightly vegetable soupy on the nose but not decayed and this did not evolve as the wine remained in the glass.

Fullish, a little astringent. Not exactly classy. But fruity, fleshy and still alive. A very good 1957.

1955   **Drink soon**

Good fullish colour. Just a suggestion of being mean and pinched on the nose, as if the fruit had begun to dry up. As it evolved a hint of maderization too. Fullish, generous and still vigorous on the palate with very good fruit. Long, complex. Another surprisingly good 1955. Much better on palate than nose. Not a bit astringent. Alive and fresh at the end.

1953   **Drink quite soon**

Medium-full colour. Soft, mature, complex, classy nose. Old roses, a little faded, but a little old lady with plenty of personality left. A little rounder and fleshier, but also more intense and classier than the 1955. Ripe, medium-bodied, very fine complexity, intensity and balance. Yet another lovely 1953. The best, because it is the classiest, of the decade. Though the 1959 is equally delicious.

1952   **Now–1997**

(Danish bottled by K. Dorplu-Petersens Vinhandel, Copenhagen) Fullish colour. Not quite as vigorous looking as the 1955. Just a little tough on the nose. But full and firm, not hard. On the palate the structure shows a little but there is plenty of classy Cabernet fruit here. This has breed and balance on the follow-through. No undue astringency. Vigorous. A fine 1952. Holding up better than the 1953.

1948   **Drink up**

Good colour. Firm nose, but a hint herbaceous. Good Cabernet. More generous as it evolved. A little tough. High acidity. Quite classy but a little astringent. Yet long and ripe and not too austere on the palate. This still has interest despite being a little past its best.

1947   **Past its best**

Very full colour. A bit dense. The nose is sweet but has fallen apart. Sweet, astringent and soupy on the palate. Getting coarse and vegetably very quickly.

1945   **Drink soon**

Very full colour. This is big, full, concentrated and brilliant. An austere example. Full and rich and concentrated. A bit tough – but complex and long and multidimensional. As usual with

1945s the structure threatens to overpower but the distilled intensity of the fruit wins in the end. Still has life. Splendid finish. Yet I have had even better.

1940   **Drink up**

Lightish colour. Fully evolved if not a bit aged. The fruit has lightened leaving the acidity and a finish which is a touch coarse, but the wine is quite fresh. Even if it lacks charm.

1937   **Drink soon**

(Halves) Medium colour; still fresh. Lively, ripe nose. Medium body. A little four-square, but fresh and fruity. There is a lack of generosity. Good though. A touch rigid and four-square but less so than I feared.

1934   **Drink soon**

Good colour. Quite brown at the rim but clear and vigorous in the middle. Good nose, round, aromatic, no real fade. Complex, gentle. On the palate this has lost a little of its grip but it is still sweet and fruity. A gentle wine. Still long. Plump. Lovely but not great. It finishes just a little flat.

1928   **Will still keep**

Splendid, full, vigorous colour. Lovely concentrated fruit on nose and palate. Full, vigorous, great depth, great class. A big wine. Splendidly ripe and concentrated if a little astringent. But very good acidity. Fine with food, still lots of life. Very complex. Still sweet on the finish and held up in the glass. This is the third time I have seen the wine in the last three years. On the other two occasions it was even better.

1924   **Drink soon**

Medium-full colour. Fully mature. Old but fragrant, oaky nose. Slight hint of mint as it evolved. Fullish, nice touch of spice and caramel, even butterscotch. Long, complex and fragrant. Less chunky than the 1926 Ducru sampled at the same time. More class. Better finish as very little astringency. Good grip. Holding up very well for a 1924.

1918   **Drink up**

Good colour. Full and rich and cedary and fragrant. A little fade on the palate. Has lightened but still soft and fruity and with good acidity. Ripe and rosehip fruit. Redcurrant and raspberry. Rather more than just a pleasant memory.

LÉOVILLE-POYFERRÉ

Bordeaux now has more than one Léoville super-second. With the exception of the 1988, the generality of the vintages of Château Léoville-Poyferré since 1982 is collectively as good as anything produced by the other, better-known estates in Saint-Julien and Pauillac whose wines for a decade or more have rivalled the *premiers crus*. As demand, fuelled by the world-wide recognition that Ducru-Beaucaillou, Léoville-Las-Cases, Pichon-Longueville-Lalande and the rest regularly produce wine of first growth quality, has pushed the prices of these wines to ever more ridiculous levels, it is cheering to report that these are not unique, and that a property recently in the doldrums can shake off the bad habits of yesteryear and once again produce wine of the very highest order.

For high quality is not something that has always been foreign to Léoville-Poyferré. Penning-Rowsell writes that, 'for elegance combined with fruit', the 1929 was perhaps the best of all in 'this glorious vintage' and speaks in general of superb wines in the 1920s. The 1874, says André Simon, was close on the heels of the Lafite, itself second only to the Haut-Brion, and he speaks highly of the other vintages of this period.

Yet, like many a property in Bordeaux, Léoville-Poyferré went into decline in the 1930s. Unlike others, however, there was no large-scale replanting after the war, and though not as good as its neighbour Barton, the immediate postwar wines produced many successes. As well as the 1947, 1953, 1955 and 1959, I remember a soft, elegant 1945. The 1950 and 1952 were also good, though in some cases a little astringent as they aged. In the 1960s, though, a decline set in. The wines lacked richness and concentration of fruit, they seemed a bit slight; they lacked elegance; and as the vineyards at Las-Cases and Ducru matured, for there *had* been widespread restoration in the late 1940s, Poyferré was left behind. The background to Poyferré's renaissance is given later. First, we must go back to its origins.

HISTORY

I have described the history of the Léoville estate in the previous chapter. Following the sale of what was to become Léoville-Barton during the Revolution, there was a further division in 1840. Two-thirds of what was left remained Las-Cases, the other third passed to Jeanne d'Abbadie, *née* Las-Cases, and was immediately given by Jeanne to her daughter, Mme de Bonneval. Some years later Mme de Bonneval sold this to her sister, wife of the Baron Jean-Marie de Poyferré de Céres, a member of an old Gascon family.

Despite being christened, and remaining thereafter, Léoville-Poyferré, the property was to rest only briefly in these hands. Jean-Marie's son, ill-advised by his financial consultants, invested in Russian railways, and soon lost his fortune. In 1866 he was forced to sell up, and Poyferré was acquired by the Baron d'Erlanger and Armand Lalande, the latter a respected Bordeaux *négociant*, for the price of a million francs. A Poyferré descendant, though, remains proprietor of part of the ancestral estate in the Armagnac, and produces a fine brandy under the name of Domaine de Jouanda at Arthez.

THE CUVELIER FAMILY

Poyferré was to remain in the Lalande family until after the First World War, by which time it was also connected with the Lawtons, another well-known name in the Bordeaux wine trade, for Edouard Lawton had married the daughter of Armand Lalande towards the end of the century. In 1920 the owners sold the property to the Cuvelier family for 1,300,000 francs, and it has remained in their hands ever since. Whether this figure included Château Moulin-Riche, a *cru bourgeois* in Saint-Julien, and also sold at the same time, I do not know.

The Cuveliers already had interests in the Gironde. In 1903 they had acquired Château Le Crock in the southern part of the commune of Saint-Estèphe. A year later they set up a *négociant* business back in Haubourdin, near Lille. For a time they were also proprietors of Château Camensac, until they sold that property in 1964 to a consortium of three people headed by Emile Forner of the well-known Rioja enterprise of Marques de Cacares. Eventually, in 1947, they set up as shippers in Bordeaux.

Originally, management of Léoville-Poyferré was entrusted to various generations of the Delon family, proprietors until very recently of Château Phélan-Ségur. Roger Delon, who died in the early 1980s, was the uncle of Michel Delon, proprietor today of Château Léoville-Las-Cases. Originally, as we have seen, this was a good arrangement; the wines in the 1920s were of fine quality. As time went on, however, it became patently clear, at least to outsiders, that standards were slipping. No money had been invested in Poyferré; the equipment was antiquated; there was little use of new oak; and Delon was getting old. The wine making, as Bernard Ginestet puts it, was '*un peu trop habituel*'.

Enter Didier Cuvelier in 1978 at the age of 30. Didier has not been trained as a winemaker (in fact he has a high-powered accounting qualification), but his heart and soul are in Poyferré. He was the driving force in convincing the rest of the family that a major programme of investment was required, a change of personnel was necessary, and a change in aspiration and dedication was essential. More importantly, that these changes would eventually justify themselves, not only in a higher reputation for the wine, but in increased profits.

A PROGRAMME FOR A RENAISSANCE

The first step was to ask the advice of the renowned Professor Peynaud. What was the potential of Léoville-Poyferré? What was needed to be done? How much time would be required to put the improvements into effect? How much would they cost?

We start with the soil – or perhaps I should say the *terroir*, the site of the vineyard, where it is and how it lies. I do not know Professor Peynaud's view, but I can quote Nathaniel

Johnston, well respected and much loved *négociant* and friend. Nathie has often told me that in his view the Poyferré soil – by and large on the west side of the D2 road, as is that of Barton, while Las-Cases' vineyards are on the river side – is the best of the three, perhaps second only to the first growths.

Then the *encépagement*. The vineyard was replanted to a large extent in 1962. Previously the mix had been biased towards Merlot: 50 per cent of this variety, 30 per cent Cabernet Sauvignon and 20 per cent Cabernet Franc. Now the proportions have been reversed to a more typical Médoc blend: 65 per cent Cabernet Sauvignon, 2 per cent Cabernet Franc, 8 per cent Petit Verdot, 25 per cent Merlot. Despite this replanting, however, the average age of the vines remains high – 35 years is claimed; no doubt this is the result of the incorporation of Château Moulin-Riche into the Léoville-Poyferré vineyard. Moulin-Riche, once a *Cru Exceptionnel*, is used solely as a *deuxième vin*. Today, the vineyard comprises 75 hectares and will be progressively increased to 80 over the next few years. Production is currently some 250 *tonneaux*.

The right soil was therefore there, and so were mature vines in the correct proportion. The first phase, begun in 1978, was to acquire shallow plastic trays for use in the harvest, in order to protect the fruit from being crushed before it arrived at the winery. It was also decided that priority should be given to completely rebuilding the reception area and the *cuvier* – the former was completed in time for the 1980 vintage, the latter constructed in stages between 1979 and 1984. Lastly, inevitably, the proportion of new wood was increased to between a third and a half each year. In 1984, 50 per cent new oak was used, in 1982 and 1983 it was 33 per cent.

In 1979, Roger Delon, then aged 78 years old, suffered a heart attack and gave up his position as administrator, one imagines to the relief of all, for no one had dared contradict him. Didier Cuvelier, who had been responsible for the financial side of things for some months, now took control. With part of the *cuvier* in bright, new, enamelled steel and temperature-controlled, the improvement was already noticeable – so they say. I must admit I do not find the 1979 a success.

It was the turn of the vineyard in 1980. All the individual parcels were analyzed and the soils adjusted by means of manure, fertilizer, minerals and lime. Anti-botrytis spraying commenced the next year.

Robert Lopez, the old *maître de chai*, was killed in a car accident in 1982, and was succeeded by François Dourthe, who had been in charge at Le Crock after having trained at Mouton-Rothschild. The next year, as a result of experiencing difficulties with the water pressure in the dry 1982 harvest, a large underground water storage tank was built, in order to facilitate the control of the fermentation temperature. Since then there have been: a new *cuvier*, that constructed in 1990 replacing the one installed in 1984; a brand new *chai* capable of holding 1000 barrels; the doubling of the bottle storage capacity; and a *salle de dégustation*. The renovation of the *chais* is now complete.

THE CHÂTEAU AND THE *CHAIS*

It has been explained that the dependencies of Las-Cases and Poyferré are much mixed up. The two properties share the château itself – though it is not in regular use – and both have *chais* on either side of the road. The buildings are situated at the entry to the sleepy little village of Saint-Julien. On the river side of the road, the right as you drive north, is the château. This consists of an undistinguished, single-storey *chartreuse* with two-floored early-nineteenth-century additions topped by mansard roofs. Extending from either side in a westerly direction are low, single-storey wings. That on the north is the *cuverie* of Las-Cases, as well as this property's offices. That on the south was – up to 1991 – the first-year *chai* of Poyferré.

Across the road lie the main buildings of Poyferré, described above. Separately, a few metres to the south, is the bottling hall, second-year *chai* and storage area of Las-Cases. It is all rather incestuous, and must have been even more complicated when both the properties were run by gentlemen called Delon!

THE WINE

As I have stated at the outset, the rise in quality at Léoville-Poyferré over the past ten years has been startling. The new blood – in the personality of the dynamic Didier Cuvelier – and the heavy investment have worked wonders in a very short space of time. Gone are the days when Poyferré presented a hangdog, scruffy face to the world and made wine to match. Now what Poyferré makes – and if the 1989 and 1990 are anything to go by (sadly, the 1988 is undistinguished) I would simply describe the style of wine as Mouton-ish, if Las-Cases is Latour-ish – is as good as any second growth. With a similar but less flamboyant improvement at Léoville-Barton (not that Barton was inferior before, just perhaps occasionally a little dull), the battle for who is to be the best Léoville each year is well and truly on!

THE TASTING

Marvin Overton, surgeon, wine-collector and Texan, organized a splendid series of Saint-Julien tastings in various venues in the USA in May 1992. When he invited me to moderate the Léoville-Poyferré vertical I accepted with alacrity (provided I could join him and his friends for the whole tour). It was memorable – and fun as well. Most of these bottles came from his own cellar. Stephen Kaplan, Herb Francis and Danny Oliveros generously provided other bottles.

Optimum drinking

1991 — **1995–2000**
Good colour. Fresh fruity nose. No weakness nor leanness here. Medium body. Good fruit and good acidity. This is balanced and lively. Not herbaceous. Shows well. Good elegant follow-through.

1990 — **1999–2015**
Good colour. Fuller than the 1989. Full, rich, satisfyingly oaky and concentrated nose. Very good. A very good example indeed. Fullish, lovely ripe fruit. Good structure and grip. A balanced, concentrated, subtle wine. Very harmonious. Very fine fruit. Long. Very classy. Very complex. Probably the best Léoville-Poyferré of the current generation. Very good indeed.

1989 — **1997–2009**
Medium-full colour. Ripe, mulberry-flavoured nose. But not the depth and intensity of the 1990. Medium to medium-full body. The tannins a little hard, the wine not as fat and as fruity as the 1990. Not as much dimension. Ripe and certainly good. But outclassed by the 1990. (When I tasted these two together at the château in April 1992 I preferred the 1989. Time will tell which will prove to be the better bottle.)

1988 — **Now–1998**
Medium colour. Oaky nose. Pretty, but it misses a bit of concentration and depth. Rather superficial. Medium body. Forward. Little tannin. Quite fresh, but a bit one-dimensional. Pretty but a little nondescript. Clean though. Drink quite soon.

1986 — **Now–2005**
Medium-full colour. Ripe, elegant, plummy Saint-Julien nose. Medium body. A little tannin. This is good but it lacks a bit of grip and real concentration and fat. It seems to lack thrust and real depth. But it is very adolescent at present. I marked as very good plus before it went into its shell.

1985 — **Now–2007**
Medium to medium-full colour. Not a lot of intensity on the nose but harmonious and pretty. Better than the 1986 within its context today. Lovely plump ripe fruit on the palate. Medium to medium-full body. A little tannin. Balanced, stylish, gentle, full of charm. Good positive finish. Very good.

1984 — **Now–1997**
Rather a light evolved colour. Clean, attractive nose though. This is a good effort. A lot of fruit. You can see the new oak. This has attraction and personality. Very good indeed for the vintage. Still vigorous.

1983 — **Now–2010**
Very good colour for an 1983. Very good rich, classic Saint-Julien nose. Fullish for the vintage.

Good acidity. Fresh, concentrated, plummy fruit. This has grip and dimension. This is a fine 1983. Very Saint-Julien. Will still improve.

1982   **Now–2008**

Good colour. Slightly dense and pedestrian on the nose. Medium-full. Rich and ripe, but an absence of the class noticeable in the subsequent vintages. Over-ripe fruit, slightly cooked elements. Lush, good grip. But it lacks a touch of elegance. Good but not great.

1981   **Now–1999**

Medium to medium-full colour. Mature. Open, stylish, ripe, round nose. Attractive attack. Medium body. A little more ordinary on the follow-through. It lacks a little real class, as well as concentration and depth. But fresh, balanced. Good plus for the vintage. Good fruit. *A point.*

1980   **Drink soon**

Light to medium, fully mature colour. For an 1980 (and after the disappointment of 1979) this is not at all bad. But it now loosening up. Medium body. Fruity. A bit one-dimensional.

1978   **Drink soon**

Medium to medium-full colour. Mature. Interesting nose. Black cherries, a little hard tannin. But ripe and vigorous and good dimension. On the palate medium-full. Sweet but without dimension and class. Fruit lightening up. Getting coarse at the end. Acidity shows. Unexciting. Will only get worse.

1975   **Drink soon**

Medium to medium-full colour. Mature. Slightly more evolved nose than the 1978. There is a sweetness behind the structure. Weak as it developed in the glass. A little vegetal. Astringent and sweet on the palate. Medium body. Not bad but no real class. Best of the decade though.

1973   **Drink soon**

Medium colour. Fully mature. Interesting cedary, caramelly nose. Not weak. Still plump and fat. Medium body. Pleasant but a little sweet and vegetal. Will deteriorate fast. Reasonable acidity. But no class.

1971   **Past its best**

Medium-full colour. Fully mature. Rather dried out. Astringent nose. Fruit has disappeared. Vegetal in the sense of bark. Mean now. Poor, astringent, charmless. Medium body.

1970   **Drink soon**

Good colour. No undue brown. A little bland and non-descript on the nose. Plump and fruity but no depth or class. Aspects of dank-penicillin covered cellars. Medium to medium-full body. Some acidity and fruit. Rather one-dimensional and now getting astringent. Unexciting.

1967   **Drink soon**

Medium, fully evolved colour. A little sweet on the nose. But fragrant and stylish. Medium body. Now getting towards the end, but balanced and plump and elegant. A good example. Complex.

1966   **Drink soon**

Medium to medium-full colour. Mature. Quite a vigorous nose but not exactly stylish. Medium to medium-full body. Quite classic and stylish. Cool, balanced. Lacks a bit of generosity but good acidity. Has lost a little of its fruit but a good example.

1964   **Drink soon**

Medium colour. Fully mature. Light nose. Not a lot of interest. This has ripeness and sweetness and old vine fruit. Better than the nose would indicate. Medium to medium-full. Not short. Has lost a little of its intensity. A good plus 1964. Six years.

1962   **Now–1996**

Medium-full colour. Mature. More interest than the 1964 here. Round, ripe, stylish. Fresh. Medium-full. This is mellow, rich and even fat and concentrated. Still has vigour and life. Better than 1964 and 1966. Good grip. Long. Stylish. Mellow. Very good indeed.

1961   **Now–1996**

(Magnum) Fullish colour. Mature. Rich and ripe even concentrated on the nose if not exactly classy. Fat, concentrated and rich. Fullish. There is a little age here, a little rigidity. So there is a lack of thrust at the end. Good but not great. (Herb Francis's cellar.)

1961   **Now–1998**

(Bottle) Fullish colour. Mature. Good nose. More definition and concentration than the magnum. This is better. Fullish, fat, rich, concentrated. Real intensity of fruit. Again it shows a little evolution now. But there is class and balance. Still life. Very good. (Marvin Overton's cellar.)

1959   **Now–2000**

(Magnum) Fine vigorous colour. Better than the 1961. Fine nose. Classy, fragrant. Very fine and concentrated. Very complex. Multidimensional. This is almost first growth quality. Fullish, vigorous, intense with lots of lovely ripe, mellow, voluptuous fruit. Fine. Long. Very well balanced. (Stephen Kaplan's cellar.)

1959   **Now–1996**

(Bottle) Very good mature colour. A little more evolved and less intense than the magnum. Round and ripe. Mellow and rich. A little spicy but a very classy wine. *A point.* Fullish. No undue age. (Marvin Overton's cellar.)

1957   **Now–1996**

Good mature colour. No hardness on the nose. Quite rich and classy even. A very good 1957 here. Medium-full. Quite high acidity but plenty of fruit and not a bit hard or astringent. This is surprisingly good. A success which can be ranked at the Ducru level. Long complex finish. Even charm. Long. (Herb Francis's cellar.)

1955   **Drink soon**

Good mature colour. Slightly earthy on the nose. Lacy cedary. Has lost a little of its fruit. Medium body. Mellow. Definitive. Great style and charm. Is getting to the end of its life but fragrant and lovely. Great class. Very long, complex, delicate finish.

1953   **Now–1999**

Medium-full mature colour. Very lovely on the nose. Vigorous, fragrant ripe and classy. Very very round and concentrated without being a blockbuster. Medium to medium-full. Lovely fruit. This is honeyed and rich, but delicate and distinguished. Still has life. Marvellous balance. First growth class and quality here again.

1952   **Drink up**

Not shown. Rather dried out, but residual fruit and charm.

1949   **Drink up**

Not shown. Seen only once in the last decade. Pleasant, probably originally very stylish, but now old.

1947   **Drink soon**

Splendid colour. Rich, full. Coffee and hot chocolate on the nose. Not a bit dense or volatile. Fat and clean and creamy rich on the palate. Medium-full, good grip. Just a bit of astringence on the palate. Yet fresh rather than cooked fruit. Perhaps it tails off a bit leaving a slight malic effect but fine and full of interest. A very fine 1947. Very intense fruit. (Danny Oliveros's cellar.)

1945   **Will still keep well**

Not shown. Full, muscular, but rich and profound. A wine for food. High quality.

1934   **Can still be kept**

The colour is full but a little cloudy. Full, firm, ripe nose. Classic Cabernet. Still vigorous. On the palate full, sweet, very ripe concentrated fruit. Good grip. Complex. Cool, long, classic. Fine.

1929   **Will still last**

Very good colour. Sweet, honeyed, *crème brûlée* and caramel nose. Concentration here. Ripe and voluptuous and silky. Great concentration on the palate. Fullish and very complex fruit. Multi-dimensional. This is a great wine without a doubt. Great intensity and depth yet never a blockbuster. Brilliant! It goes on and on and on on the palate. Still plenty of life. One of the really great wines of my life.

1928   **Will still last**

Not shown: structured, very concentrated, very classy. Fine.

1921   **Drink up**

Very good colour. Rich, caramelly and cedary, sweet nose. Fresh. No sign of age. Slightly lactic perhaps. Just a touch dried out (especially after the vigour of the 1929) but lots of enjoyment still. Good classy fruit.

1874   **Still plenty of life**

Good colour. Alive and fullish. Fresh if old nose. But no sign of decay. Molasses, chocolate and coffee. A lot of depth here. This is simply extraordinary! Fullish, immensely concentrated. Immaculately assembled. Brilliant concentration of fruit. So much flavour! Class, dimension, harmony. Luscious and rich. Everything is here. Great complexity, intensity and quality. One of the great wines of my life again. (Stephen Kaplan's cellar: recorked Whitwhams, 22–1–1988)

LÉOVILLE-BARTON AND LANGOA-BARTON

This story has two threads. Firstly there is the history of the vast Léoville estate, at the northern end of the Saint-Julien commune. Secondly, there is the story of the Barton family; in particular, of three people, 'French Tom', the founder of the dynasty, his grandson Hugh, who bought two famous growths in Saint-Julien, and the late Ronald Barton, who died in January 1986. It is the story of the two *crus classés* of Bordeaux which have remained longest in single family ownership.

Like the Lynches of Lynch-Bages, the Bartons came from Ireland, though unlike them, they were Protestants. Tom Barton, eldest son of a prosperous landowner, was born in Enniskillen, County Fermanagh, in what is now Northern Ireland, in 1695. He was 'bred up' (as he put it himself) as a merchant by his Uncles Dickson (there were two of them) and was sent abroad as a factor, firstly to Marseilles and Montpellier, later to Bordeaux.

THE BARTONS

Tom Barton arrived in Bordeaux, newly married (to his mother's cousin) in 1722. Why did he decide to remain there? It is impossible to be certain, though interesting to conjecture. At the time, one of Ireland's main products was wool, and moreover the wool was of very high quality. But it was discriminated against by the English Parliament, which, in various Acts to protect the home trade, forbade export of all wool and woollen goods from Ireland except to England, and that under prohibitive duties. Meanwhile, the French were prepared to pay the market price for the wool, three or four times what the English would pay, and this was naturally an open invitation to organized smuggling. Firstly the payment was in gold, but later, inevitably, as Bordeaux was one of the major entry ports, and as the amount of money dribbling out of France drew attention from the authorities, the return contraband became wine.

As Cyril Ray has suggested (*Fide et Fortudine, The Story of a Vineyard*, 1971), it is natural to assume, even if Tom Barton was not directly involved in these illegal affairs, that he should have noticed the thriving legitimate trade in wine between Bordeaux and Ireland, and perhaps compared it with the difficulties of a young merchant in Ulster, even for a Protestant.

Thomas Barton was 27 when he first went to France and 30 when he set up his own business in Bordeaux in 1725. By 1743 he had acquired a considerable fortune and had established himself as the most important buyer and shipper of fine wine in Bordeaux; he had also bought the Saint-Estèphe growth of Château Le Boscq, and had paid the enormous sum of £30,000 for an estate in County Tipperary. Tom had but one son, William, whom he had taken into partnership back in 1743, but who seems to have quarrelled with both his father and his sons, and spent his life more in Ireland than in France. William himself had six sons, one of whom became an MP, two generals, and two lived on their Irish estates; of three daughters, one married a peer and another a baronet. 'French Tom's' drive had raised the family from modestly well-off merchants to wealthy landed gentry in a couple of generations.

The next Barton in the story is Tom's grandson Hugh, born in 1766, and the fourth of William's sons. Hugh, having been taken into partnership when he was twenty, took an active interest in the Barton wine business, unlike his father. Here he was considerably helped by the *de facto* head of firm, Daniel Guestier, a French Huguenot of Breton origin, and son of the *régisseur* of the Marquis de Ségur, proprietor of Lafite and other important estates. This Guestier connection was to prove invaluable, not only in the ensuing Revolution and Napoleonic wars, but in other wars in the twentieth century.

The Barton family, let us not forget, had remained Protestant and retained their Irish citizenship. When the new Republic declared war on England in 1793, all British subjects in Bordeaux were arrested and interned, including Hugh, his baby daughter and his wife Anna (known as Nancy), herself a daughter of the Bordeaux/Irish wine family, Johnston. William Barton, 70 years old, and a dying man, was at Château Le Boscq and was not disturbed.

Internment, however, seems not to have been too much of a hardship. Hugh and his family were soon released, and, having obtained a passport, he left the business in the hands of the capable Guestier and busied himself outside France with the Irish and English end of the business.

Not even Napoleon could stop the wine business between Britain and France, and the Bartons, helped by the loyal Daniel Guestier, naturally thrived on the fact that much of it was done via Ireland and Guernsey by neutral ships. Once Napoleon had been disposed of, firstly to Elba and finally to Saint Helena, the market in claret really boomed. Between 1811 and 1820, Hugh Barton's fortune, and the firm of Barton and Guestier – as it had finally become in 1802 – doubled in value.

Naturally Hugh thought about converting some of this capital into land, into becoming a vine-grower as well as a wine-shipper, and it is said that he even had his eyes on Lafite. As early as 1810 Daniel Guestier informed Barton that he had learned that Lafite might be for sale. Guestier was on good terms with Joseph Goudal, *régisseur* on behalf of the absentee land-lords, three Dutch wine merchants. Discussions ensued, a price (1 million francs) was pro-posed and in principle accepted, but subsequently the vendors got cold feet. Yet even as late as 1821, by which time Lafite belonged to Mme Barbe-Rosalie Lemaire, Barton and Guestier were still hoping to become proprietors of Lafite. But it was not to be. The famous fake sale of Lafite to the British financier Sir Samuel Scott took place that year. What Hugh Barton did buy in December 1821, was Château Langoa, from a M. Bernard Pontet, for 550,000 francs (£22,000 at the then rate of exchange).

LANGOA

'Goa' is an early French version of *gué*, a ford, and probably here refers to a marshy brook, running from west to east, at the southern end of the property. The word 'Langoa', in vari-ous forms, exists on various documents going back to 1554. The land was bought in 1704 to 1705 by an earlier Bernard de Pontet, a local judge who was later to become private secretary to the King, and in retirement Major-General of the Médoc coastguards. De Pontet came originally from Saint-Laurent, the village behind Saint-Julien, where he also had vineyards, and it was he who had the Langoa château constructed in 1757 to 1759. Some 60 years later, his successor, Pierre Bernard, sold both house and vineyard, then producing some 80 *ton-neaux* of wine, in order to concentrate on the other family property, now known as Château Pontet-Canet, in Pauillac.

Hugh Barton made this purchase on his own account, not that of the firm, and through-out the next few years rounded off and enlarged the property by buying up small vineyards from neighbouring owners. One of these extra purchases was an amount of £620, deposit on the great Léoville estate, now about to be broken up.

LÉOVILLE

The Léoville domaine, one of the oldest as well as one of the largest in the Médoc, was origi-nally called Mont-Moytié, having been named after a Bordeaux merchant who founded the estate in 1638. It passed into the hands of Alexandre de Gasq-Léoville, President of the Bordeaux Parliament, who died in 1769 and who had married the heiress of the estate, a Mlle Moytié, in about 1720. At the north end of the Saint-Julien commune, and situated on a gravel plateau directly facing that of Latour, it shared with Gruaud-Larose at the southern end of the parish, the distinction of being one of only four second growths of the entire Médoc in the earliest, unofficial classifications of the area.

At the time of the Revolution, the estate belonged to four people: M. Le Marquis de Las-Cases-Beauvois, his brother and two sisters. The Marquis himself, head of the family, and fearing for his life, fled the country in 1794, and the state at first wished to sequestrate the en-tire property. They were successfully persuaded that it should be divided first, and so a quar-ter only was put on the market. This sale took place on *3 Thermidor l'An IV*. The purchaser was a consortium of two brothers called Lechevalier plus a M. Monbalon.

It was Monbalon's portion, effectively one-twelfth of Léoville, which Hugh Barton first bought in March, 1822. In May, 1826, he bought the Lechevalier share at auction, altogether paying 242,550 francs (£13,361) in three lots for his quarter of Léoville, some 35 hectares of vines but no château. Both Langoa and Léoville properties have remained in the Barton fam-ily ever since.

HUGH BARTON AND HIS SUCCESSORS

Hugh Barton was a considerably wealthy man, and more than just a château owner and Bordeaux wine-shipper. Back in Ireland he was the proprietor of a vast estate at Straffan,

County Kildare, which he had acquired during his 'exile' from Bordeaux. He became High Sheriff of the county, and he was also a partner in the wine-shipping firm of French and Barton in Dublin. In his 1825 accounts, Langoa is valued at £30,000 out of a total fortune of £526,000.

In 1830, at the age of 64, he retired from the Bordeaux scene, leaving the faithful Daniel Guestier (by this time a château proprietor himself, at neighbouring Beychevelle) in charge. Hugh Barton lived on until 1854, the year before the Classification which would confirm Léoville as a second growth and Langoa as a third.

During the nineteenth century, as in the eighteenth, responsibility for Langoa and the French end of the wine-shipping business was to skip a generation. After Hugh's death it was his grandson Charles Thomas Hugh, fifth son of his eldest son Nathaniel, who took charge. Charles died at the relatively young age of 37, and it was to be Bertram, son of Nathaniel's third son, also called Bertram, who bought up the Barton family shares in Bordeaux.

Bertram, however was more interested in spending money than making it. As the present proprietor Anthony Barton says, I quote from Harry Eyres's book, *Wine Dynasties of Europe*, 'Grandad did the London season . . . . [he] took a house in Half Moon Street and just quietly walked through the money. The story is that if he'd lived a few months longer the banks would have foreclosed.' Anthony's father, the eldest son, inherited the Irish property, his uncle Ronald inherited Langoa and Léoville and the partnership in Barton and Guestier.

RONALD BARTON

Ronald Barton, great-great grandson of Hugh, was born in 1902, and educated at Eton. At the age of 25, he took over from his father (killed in a hunting accident in Ireland) in 1927. In June 1940, on the fall of France, Ronald, like his forebear Hugh, was forced to become a refugee. But also, like Hugh, he had his loyal Guestier partner to whom to entrust, not only the fortunes of Barton and Guestier, but also, in as much as he could, the vineyards of Langoa and Léoville, though they did not belong to the firm. With a half-full suitcase and a few thousand francs as his sole personal possessions, Ronald landed in Falmouth a few days later. He joined the Royal Inniskilling Fusiliers, for it was from Enniskillen that 'French Tom' had set out to make his fortune nearly 250 years earlier.

While Ronald Barton was fighting his war, mainly as a liaison officer with the Free French, Daniel Guestier was persuading the German forces of occupation that Barton, as an Irishman, was neutral – in this supported by letters from Ronald's sister, herself a genuine citizen of the Republic, enquiring for details of the 'family property' – and succeeded in saving the estate, house, vineyard and contents from confiscation, though this did not stop German soldiers from being billeted in the château.

Ronald served with the battalions of the Free French in the desert, and followed soon after General Tassigny and the Americans when they landed at Cavalaire in the south of France in August 1944. On his return to Langoa he surprised an old peasant woman quietly shelling peas in the courtyard; she thought she had seen a ghost and spilt the lot.

The vineyard, of course, was in a terrible state: chemical sprays, farmyard manure, stakes and wire on which to train the vines, had all been well-nigh unobtainable. For several years the ploughing had been minimal, and perhaps a quarter of the vines were missing.

Many of Ronald's neighbours, finding themselves in the same position, did what you could say was the logical, certainly the economic, thing; they pulled up entire sections of the vineyard. But, as Ronald was to point out later, such a wholesale replanting would mean considerably reducing the average age of the vineyard, with a noticeable effect on the quality of the wine. He was, of course, too much of a gentleman to mention specifically those of his neighbours whose wines suffered in this way: but there are many whose quality suffered in the years between 1945 and even as late as 1959.

Ronald, with the help, so Cyril Ray says, of a pair of oxen and an immensely strong Basque driver, ploughed the vineyards, cleared the fields and replaced the gaps without large-scale replanting. As the tasting notes which follow will show, this ensured that both Léoville and Langoa-Barton could take full advantage of the opportunities provided by the wealth of good vintages which immediately followed.

Financially, however, it was an unhappy time. Ronald Barton can have made little profit out of his beloved Langoa and Léoville before the war, and he certainly made none in the immediate postwar years. The 1951 was a disaster, and if 1952 had been equally unsuccessful he would have sold out. Prices were static, though costs were rising inexorably. Wine revenues began to increase in value in the mid-1950s, but then the terrible frosts of February 1956 wiped out a quarter of the vineyard. It was not until 1962 that production returned to 1955 levels, and even as late as that, the price of the wines, bottled in Bordeaux by Barton and Guestier, or shipped in wood (the Barton wines were not château-bottled until 1969) barely covered their production costs.

Meanwhile Barton and Guestier had been sold. Seagrams took a 50 per cent share in 1954 and full control in the late 1960s, the last Guestier having been killed in a car crash in 1960. They also took over the exclusive contract for the marketing of Léoville and Langoa-Barton until 1976. Ronald, a confirmed bachelor, or so it seemed until he married in his seventies, retired to Langoa. His nephew Anthony, heir apparent, was waiting in the wings. Anthony, like Ronald a younger son, arrived in Bordeaux in 1950 and married his lovely Danish wife Eva a few years later. He worked as export director for Barton and Guestier before setting up his own company. But he was not allowed to take any part in the activities at Langoa.

The 1970s were a moribund time for the Barton properties. Ronald was charming and hospitable, generous with his old bottles, as committed in his quiet way to his wines as his almost exact contemporary, but total opposite in temperament, Baron Philippe de Rothschild. But he was cautious to the point of being obstinate. He did not move with the times. Nor would he delegate control and responsibility to Anthony, despite several times promising to retire. And as he grew older, the quality of his wines slipped as a consequence: not much, but enough. While neighbouring Las-Cases and Ducru were elevating themselves to super-seconds, Barton continued as merely a 'good' classed growth. There was an ageing team in the cellar, a lack of investment in new oak and the equipment necessary for the proper control of vinification, and a failure to anticipate the resources that would be required to cope adequately with the growing quantity of wine that resulted from more prolific clones and better husbandry in the vineyards. In 1979, for the first time, the combined vineyards produced over 350 *tonneaux* of wine. The cellar was simply unable to cope. The Langoa is a charming wine. The Barton, insufficiently macerated because of sheer pressure on vat space, is insignificant.

ANTHONY BARTON

Perhaps it was this, perhaps it was merely old age, but finally in the early 1980s Ronald began to concede some of the decision-making to his nephew. In 1983 he made over the properties to Anthony. When Anthony began to thank him, he replied, 'Don't thank me. Thank your ancestor Hugh. It was he who bought Langoa and Léoville. I have never felt other than merely the guardian of the estate until it was time to hand it over to my heir; which is what I am now doing.'

It was not long before super-second wines were once again being made. While the 1982 and 1983 are merely good or very good, within the context of the vintages, the 1985 and 1986 – and the wines made subsequently – are excellent. The 1986 is the best Léoville-Barton since the 1953; it has significantly more breed and concentrated excitement than the 1982.

Following Uncle Ronald's 'retirement', his health gradually diminished. It was not that he was ill; merely, like an old soldier, slowly fading away. The last time many people saw him was at the marriage of Anthony's daughter Lilian to Michel Sartouris in 1985. Early in 1986 Ronald Barton died. He was 84 years old.

Anthony Barton is a tall, elegant, handsome, youthful-looking man in his late fifties. Educated at Stowe and, briefly, at Cambridge (he was sent down for neglecting his studies), he fell into the wine trade almost by accident; a *faute de mieux*, as he will admit. Beneath the charming exterior there nevertheless beats a heart every bit as committed as that of his uncle. He replaced André Leclerc with a new *régisseur*, the bearded Michel Raoult, who came from Lagrange in 1984. The percentage of new wood has been increased to 50 (more would be an error in Anthony Barton's view), and there is greater emphasis on selection. A second wine labelled at first simply as Saint-Julien but now renamed Lady Langoa is produced from the rejected vats. One thing he has not changed is the pricing policy. Since the other super-seconds started charging super-second prices, Léoville-Barton has regularly sold for half the price of Léoville-Las-Cases: in 1985 for 62 francs ex-cellars as against 140. As, since this vintage, it has been as good, this makes the Barton absolutely splendid value. I am sure, in Britain at any rate, it sells much more than twice as fast.

THE CHÂTEAU AND VINEYARD

The Langoa château, as I have said, was built in the late 1750s (there is no Château Léoville-Barton) and has been little altered since. Indeed, much of the interior decoration and furniture, if not original with the property, dates from the period of its construction.

In essence, the building is a single-storied *chartreuse* and consists of three ground-floor rooms; an entrance hall, flanked on the one side by a drawing room and on the other side by a dining room. These rooms stretch the width of the house, and lie over extensive cellars and kitchens at ground-floor level, and are approached at front and back by large stone and wrought-iron double staircases. At each end of the building there are extra stories for bedrooms. At the back is an extensive formal garden, as at Villandry, combining flowers with produce and herbs, and a small park with mature trees, roses and box hedges. Adjacent are the *chais* and *cuvier*, said to be from a plan of a M. Gérard and constructed soon after Hugh Barton acquired the property in the 1820s. Both Langoa and Léoville wines have been made here ever since then.

On the opposite side of the main road – the side towards the estuary – the Langoa domaine has a considerable holding of pasture in alluvial land unsuitable for vineyards. This Anthony Barton lets off to local farmers who graze sheep and cattle.

The vineyards themselves consist of some 65 hectares (40 Léoville, 25 Langoa) and produce respectively about 150 and 100 *tonneaux* of wine. Each is planted in the same proportion: Cabernet Sauvignon 70 per cent, Cabernet Franc 8 per cent, Merlot 20 per cent and Petit Verdot 2 per cent. Over the last few years the Merlot has been increased from 15 to 20 per cent, and the quantity of Petit Verdot reduced.

The vineyards of Poyferré and Barton are much intermingled. While the Las-Cases portion is separate, largely behind the wall one passes on the estuary side, along which is the lion-dominated portico depicted on the label, the Barton and the Poyferré sections lie to the west, running down to Pichon-Longueville on the one side, and towards Talbot on the other. The Langoa vineyards continue southwards from here, and are as much in the hamlet of Beychevelle as in that of Saint-Julien.

THE CHAIS

The *chais* occupy a series of buildings surrounding a cobbled courtyard and adjoin the château on the southern side. They have been recently extensively modernized, more oak fermentation vats added and a new tasting room added at the end. In 1989 the roof had to be entirely renewed. It was neither fire nor dry rot, just old age and the depredations of a large beetle called a *capricorne* which had caused the damage. For months part of the cellar was exposed to the elements. Incongruously vacant like the empty eye of a statue to any who might have passed overhead in a balloon.

THE WINES

It needs to be emphasized that the produce of the Léoville and Langoa vineyards are kept entirely separate. One is not a subsidiary of the other. It is instructive to compare the two. The Léoville is invariably the more sturdy, the more backward. Langoa is more feminine, more charming in its youth, the earlier of the two to evolve. But it never has quite the depth, quite the concentration, quite the breed. If ever you wanted to demonstrate the difference that *terroir* can bring (and I use the word in its fullest sense, to include aspect, drainage and micro-climate as well as the soil and its geological and physical composition), this is it. There is no other variable.

Barton wines are rich, they are full, and they are concentrated, yet they are never tough, never too 'stewed' or robust, never inelegant. They are firm and Pauillac-y for Saint-Juliens, though there is no fundamental difference between the wines of the two communes, in my view. Some say the distinction is that Pauillacs have power, and Saint-Juliens finesse; if so, Léoville-Barton and Langoa-Barton combine both.

THE TASTING

This was another in the Overton series, May 1992.

Optimum drinking

LANGOA-BARTON

1991   **Now–1998**

Medium colour. A little herbaceous on the nose but there is soft fruit here too. Medium body. Good fresh acidity. Not much tannin but no lack of fruit. Better than the 1987. Pleasant. For early drinking.

1990   **1997–2010**

Medium-full colour. Rich, fat, plump nose. Very ripe indeed. Medium-full, abundantly fruity. Good rich tannin. Heaps of fruit. Ample. Generous. Good grip. Good plus.

1989   **1996–2006**

Medium-full colour. Lush, chocolatey nose – chocolate blancmange. No undue tannins. Medium to medium-full. A little astringent as much as tannic. Reasonable acidity. Good but not quite the flair of the 1990.

1988   **1997–2009**

Medium-full colour. Slightly austere on the nose but good style and balance underneath. Very Cabernet. Medium to medium-full. Some tannin. At present on the attack it lacks a little richness and concentration. Good acidity so will improve as it rounds off. But not *that* exciting. Good, merely, for the vintage.

1987   **Drink soon**

Light to medium-colour. Now mature. Soft, a little vegetal, a bit one-dimensional on the nose. Fully ready. A pleasant, lightish wine. Reasonably positive. Not bad.

1986   **1997–2015**

Good colour. Firm, rich, concentrated nose. Good ripe Cabernet fruit and plenty of depth. A bit adolescent on the palate but fullish, composed, concentrated wine with good intensity. Potentially the best of the decade.

1985   **Now–2009**

Good colour. Lightish, soft, fragrant nose. Without the power and intense richness of the 1986. Very pretty though. Medium body. Ripe, round. Softening now. Typically elegant, balanced, slightly feminine Langoa. Good balance, long and charming. Very good.

1983   **Now–2000**

Medium to medium-full colour. Mature. Evolved nose. A little dry, lacks a little vivacity. This seems a bit thin on the palate. Medium body. A touch astringent. Lacks grip, concentration and charm. And richness. A bit disappointing.

1982   **Now–2014**

Medium-full colour. Ample, plump, rich nose. But without the depth or class of 1986. Fullish, lush, ripe, concentrated. Good acidity. This is a typical 1982 but one with freshness as well as sex appeal. Just about ready but will still improve. Good plus.

1981   **Now–1998**
Medium colour. Mature, neat, attractive nose. Not a blockbuster but harmonious and stylish. A wine of two rather than three dimensions. Medium body. Not a lot of concentration. But fresh and balanced and charming. Good for the vintage. In its prime now.

1979   **Now–1997**
Medium-full colour. Just about mature. Open, accessible, stylish nose. Good fruit and balance if not really profound. Medium body. Fully ready. Ripe and plummy. Good acidity. Just a little austere but balanced and pleasant. The 1981 is better. Good for the vintage.

1978   **Now–2000**
Medium-full colour. Just about mature. Rather richer, fuller and meatier than the 1979 on the nose. Much more to it. On the palate it is quite substantial. And balanced and fruity as well. Perhaps not a lot of class but consistent and good for the vintage.

1975   **Now–2003**
Medium-full colour, mature. Good nose. Fresh and concentrated. No undue tannins. Not dry. More structured than the 1978. Richer as well. Fullish, stylish. Fat even. A ripe, well-made wine with depth and dimension. Cedar and plums. A very good 1975. Just about ready. Good future. The best Langoa of the decade.

1971   **Drink soon**
Medium colour. Fully mature. This has the nose of a well-matured wine. Medium body. It is beginning to lighten up and dry out on the attack. The follow-through is rounder and quite complex. But drink soon. Never had much concentration. Good for the vintage.

1970   **Now–1998**
(Half bottle) Medium-full colour. Mature. Full, rich nose. Still firm. Still very vigorous. Fullish, but a little four-square. Good rich fruit but a little austere; and the structure shows a bit. Better with food. Lacks a little smoothness, elegance and richness. A little old-fashioned. Quite good for the vintage.

1967   **Drink soon**
(Magnum) From a magnum, with a low fill. Good mature colour. Rather maderized on the nose. A little astringent on the palate. I suspect that a bottle in better condition would be still vigorous and a good 1967. But difficult to judge.

1966   **Now–1997**
Fullish mature colour. Fine nose. This is ripe and round, complex and concentrated. Very stylish. A lot of depth. Classic. Medium-full. *A point.* Rather better than the 1970. Fatter and with very good fruit and grip. Good plus but not quite the style and concentration of great. Not as good on palate as promised on the nose.

1964   **Now–1996**
Fully mature colour. Slightly earthy, charcoal nose. But neither too dense nor too astringent. Good freshness. A bit more structure than the 1966 but as good, if not as complex on the finish. Fresh. Medium-full. Not a trace of astringency. Yet lacks a little real fat. Good plus again.

1962   **Now–1997**
Fine full vigorous colour. Round and rich on the nose. Not quite as fat as the 1966. A little more acidity and a bit less ripe fruit. But lots of finesse and character. On the palate seems fatter and riper and more complex than the 1966. Indeed I prefer it. Great charm and really quite complex. Very good.

1961   **Drink soon**
(Half bottle) Good mature colour. Concentrated but slightly dense. Coffee beans aspects on the nose. Rich though. Better on the nose than on the palate. Has got a bit astringent. Has begun to loosen up. A bit disappointing. In a bottle it would obviously be much better.

1959   **Now–2000**
Good mature colour. Full, concentrated, creamy nose. This is an old wine but a profoundly good one. Full. Very fruity. Super concentrated. Aromatic. Silky smooth. An excellent wine. Old viney. Very long. Bags of life.

1955   **Drink soon**
Fine colour. Surprisingly full and vigorous. Voluptuous full nose. Aromatic. Slight touch of tobacco. Fullish on the palate. Just a hint of age. Ripe and round. Graves in flavour. Very good fruit. Good grip. Very good but not as exciting as the 1953.

1953   **Drink soon**
Very good colour. Ravishingly lovely complex nose. Caramel. Flowers, fragrances and soft fruits. Delicate and multidimensional. Soft and silky. Ethereal and harmonious. Approaching the end of its life but still complete, positive, distinctive and lovely. But the nose is better than the palate. Marvellous nevertheless.

1949   **Past its best (but see note)**
Very good colour. A little too much age on the nose sadly. It is a little dried out and lumpy. Mushroomy. Still enjoyable. You can see the

fine fruit and classic balance. But a bit too old really. An unlucky bottle.

1947   **Drink soon**
A full mature colour. Rampant, almost over-ripe cassis fruit. Honey and nuts as well. Fine nose. Fullish, fat. Very very fruity. Fresh. Exotic. Animal. A little volatile. But I find it most enjoyable.

1945   **Now–2000**
Very fine colour. Excellent nose. Classic, profound, full, rich, very vigorous. Full, marvellous concentration. Still very, very fresh. Totally complete. A big wine but not a bit dense. Lovely fat, rich fruit. Very complex. Very long. Magnificent.

1925   **Drink up**
Old light colour. Real pencil nose. Touch herbal/thyme. Still quite fresh but there was never a lot of concentration and fruit. Yet clean. No decay. Old roses. Elegant.

LÉOVILLE-BARTON

1991   **1995–2000**
Good colour. Fuller, richer and more concentrated on the nose than the Langoa. Fat and ripe. Medium body. Oaky. This has charm. Good acidity. Plenty of attraction. Very good.

1990   **1999–2015**
Fullish colour. Ripe, plummy nose. Good richness. Plenty of depth. A little austere still. It has substance, depth and grip. A little adolescent on the attack but the finish is fine. Complex, full, very good grip and dimension. Fine.

1989   **1997–2012**
Fullish colour. Much more aromatic and chocolatey than the 1990. Ripe and very seductive on the nose. Lush and sexy on the palate. Exotic and attractive. Doesn't have the depth, firmness and grip of the above. But fine for the vintage.

1988   **1998–2015**
Fullish colour. Rich, new oaky, classic. A lot of depth. Very fine fruit on the nose. Much more personality than the Langoa. This is full, rich and has lovely balance. One of the very best 1988s. Medium-full. Very good tannins. Great finesse. Very fine for the vintage.

1987   **Drink soon**
Medium colour. Now mature. A bit herbaceous but there is interest and depth on the nose. Medium body. Quite stylish. Still fresh. Has style and attraction. Very good for the vintage.

1986   **1998–2015**
Full colour. Firm, masculine, concentrated. Lots of backbone. But a little adolescent on the nose. Full, tannic. Difficult to taste. The finish is firm, rich, very, very concentrated. Very good tannins. Good oak. Fine. But needs time. Lovely finish. Very complex.

1985   **1995–2013**
Fullish colour. Ripe and accessible and full of depth and charm on the nose. Lovely soft red fruits. Redcurrant and raspberry. Medium-full. Very stylish, lovely oaky fruity wine. Delicious. This will be like the 1953. Excellent grip will keep it fresh. Fine.

1983   **Now–2000**
Medium-full colour. Mature. Like the Langoa this is a bit dry and herbaceous on the nose. Rather over-evolved and not enough freshness. Medium body. A little pinched. Lacks concentration. A touch mean. OK but no better.

1982   **Now–2009**
Medium-full colour. Just about mature. Full, fat and rich. Ample, generous and lush on the nose. Fullish, meaty. Not as stylish as the 1985 or quite as concentrated as the 1986 but the finish is positive, complex and very long. This is certainly very good.

1981   **Now–1999**
Lighter colour than 1983, mature. Light nose but balanced and classy. Good depth. I prefer this to the 1983. Medium body. Just about ready. Good grip if not that much flair. Ripe Cabernet fruit if not that concentrated. Long. Ready. Very good for the vintage.

1979   **Drink soon**
Medium colour. Still quite fresh looking. Light nose. Not too weedy, but little substance here. Light, thin, but reasonable acidity keeping it quite fresh. One-dimensional. No depth.

1978   **Now–1996**
Medium colour. Just about mature. Ripe and meaty on the nose. Good fruit and good concentration. Old viney. A touch sweet-sour. Chunky on the palate. A little ungainly. Lacks a bit of style. But good grip. Fullish. Good but not great. Will get a bit astringent.

1976   **Now–1996**
Good fresh colour for the vintage. Full too. Slightly corky but a wine of grip and depth. Slightly dense but very good for a 1976. This has spice and fat, but also acidity and voluptuous fruit. Very good for the vintage. Will still last.

1975   **Drink soon**
Medium-full mature colour. Fuller but slightly more austere on the nose than the 1978. Good depth. Not a bit dry and tannic. On the palate the attack is reasonable but it tails off. Lacks fat. Good but not better than the Langoa. Slightly austere. Lacks grip.

1971   **Drink soon**

Medium colour. Fully mature. Slightly herbaceous on the nose, but in a herbal sense. Not green. But it lacks a little generosity and richness. Verbena flavours. Medium body. Not very stylish. Some fruit.

1970   **Drink soon**

Medium-full colour. Mature. Ample, rich but this bottle quite evolved on the nose. I have had better bottles of this one the previous night in fact – see below. This is a bit dead. Lumpy. One-dimensional. Rather tired.

1970   **Now–2000**

(The bottle tasted at dinner the previous night) Good mature colour. Slightly sturdy but chocolatey nose. Rich, full, slightly old-fashioned. But ripe, old-viney, not a bit astringent. Slightly funky flavours, indeed the volatile acidity a little high. But most enjoyable.

1966   **Now–1998**

Good colour. While not being the greatest – in terms of finesse – the nose here is much better than any of the 1970s. Fullish, ripe, concentrated Cabernet. Balanced. Fresh. Complex. Not great but very good plus. Long. Plenty of life.

1964   **Now–1996**

Good colour. A bit unforthcoming on the nose but quality here. Fresh, fullish. Just a shade hard on the palate. Ripe, fresh – not a bit astringent. Neither the dimension nor the fat of the 1966 but very good for the vintage.

1962   **Past its best (but see note)**

(Magnum) Very good colour. Herbal but slightly oxidized on the nose. Leek and potato soup. Full body. Ripe, fat and complex. Potentially better than the 1964 but a bit past it. Other samples in recent years have been delicious.

1961   **Drink soon**

Good colour. Animal, gamey, spicy nose. Not the greatest of 1961s, this is a bit astringent, drying out a bit, but fresh and concentrated. Good intensity. Best on the finish. Long and quite powerful and elegant. Very good but not great.

1961   **Drink soon**

(English bottled by Justerini and Brooks) Good colour. Less gamey than the château bottling. A little less alive. A little dry on the palate. In principle better than the above. This is elegant but a little old. Yet underneath the intensity of the vintage is clear to see.

1959   **Now–2000**

Good colour. Firm nose. Closed at first. Prunes, sweetly concentrated. Bags of life. Very, very ripe. Much better than the 1961. This is glorious. Funky, individual, lush, very ripe wine. Heaps of fruit. Very fine indeed. Full and delicious.

1955   **Now–1998**

Very good colour. Still vigorous. Splendid old vine-old rose nose. Rare and delicate. Complex. Splendid on the palate. Lovely fruit. Complex and fragrant. Full and rich and old viney. Fine. Still vigorous.

1953   **Drink soon**

Good colour. A faded version of a wine with great style and intensity on the nose. Full. This is getting a little old now, sadly, but the fruit and concentration must have been remarkable a few years ago. Gentle and still lovely nevertheless.

1949   **Past its best (see note)**

Good colour. Sadly this is a little over the hill. Rather oxidized but the residue of lovely fruit. I've had them both in the last three years and they were lovely.

1947   **Now–1997**

Well-matured colour. Slightly burnt on the nose. A touch of oxidation. Concentrated and sweet and enjoyable nevertheless. Very ripe indeed. Fresh on the palate. This is ample, sweet and very seductive. Fine. Will keep well still.

1945   **Now–1997**

Excellent colour still. Ripe and fat. A smell of vanilla custard and *crème brûlée*. But on the palate a little astringent. The Langoa is better today. Yet this still has concentration and intensity and the finish is rich, fat, grand and flamboyant. Not quite as magnificent or as fresh and harmonious as the Langoa but very fine indeed nevertheless.

1943   **Past its best**

Surprisingly good colour. Lightish nose. A little astringent on the palate. Ripe but has lightened up a bit now. Elegant and fruity but a little past its best.

1937   **Past its best**

The colour has lightened a little. Collapsed in the glass. Smelled of cornflakes at first but got dirty and decayed very quickly.

1871   **Will still last**

(Recorked 1977 by Whitwhams) Light to medium colour. Still very much alive. Amazing nose. Fresh. Fruity. Caramelly. Elements of crabapple and mulberry. Full, rich, meaty, ripe. This is surprisingly vigorous and very, very youthful. Good acidity. Good structure. Still plenty of life. Fine fresh, complex finish. Real essence of fruit here. Remarkable. Held up very well indeed. Was still fresh half an hour later.

GRUAUD-
LAROSE

Château Gruaud-Larose is one of the largest and best-known classed growth properties in Bordeaux. Together with Château Meyney in Saint-Estèphe, Clos-des-Jacobins in Saint-Emilion, Château Lafaurie-Peyraguey in Sauternes, the addition in 1981 of Château Cantemerle, and a number of lesser estates it makes up the impressive portfolio of wines of the Domaines Cordier.

The Cordiers are relatively recent arrivals on the Bordeaux scene. The family comes from Taoul, near Nancy in the Lorraine, and the business was founded by Désiré Cordier in 1877. It soon prospered, concentrating on bulk wines at the lower end of the market, and this success reached its peak when Désiré Cordier landed the contract to supply the entire French army with its daily ration of *ordinaire* during World War One.

Soon after, Cordier came into contact with Fernand Ginestet, who had himself set up as a Bordeaux merchant in 1899. The two soon became fast friends. Cordier moved his business and his family to Bordeaux, away from the threat of the German invader, and like his friend Fernand was soon on the outlook for properties to buy. While Ginestet acquired Cos d'Estournel and Clos-Fourtet in 1919, and was to be part of the syndicate which bought Château Margaux in 1925, Désiré reunited Gruaud-Larose, then divided, and purchased Château Talbot for his son Georges. At the same time Meyney, Lafaurie-Peyraguey and others were obtained, and the firm of Cordier soon became one of the most powerful concerns in the area.

On 1 January 1985, the banking group Société La Henin, owners of the Domaines Viticoles des Salins du Midi (Listel) among numerous other concerns, acquired a controlling interest in Cordier the *négociant* and the above properties (though not in Château Talbot, which remains the personal property of Jean Cordier).

In the summer of 1993 the Compagnie de Suez, into which the Société La Henin had been absorbed, sold Gruaud-Larose to the French conglomerate Alcatel Alsthom for 310 million francs, itself a shareholder in the Compagnie de Suez. Alcatel are proprietors of the *cru bourgeois* Château Malescasse. Domaines Cordier, however, will continue to look after Gruaud-Larose, and Cordier the *négociants* will retain exclusivity over the distribution of this and the other domaines in the portfolio.

Château Gruaud-Larose has for long been recognized as one of the leading wines of Bordeaux. Indeed, originally it was second only to the undivided Léoville in the commune of Saint-Julien (though there are others which would dispute this title today), and one of only three consistent second growths – Rauzan in Margaux, then undivided, is the other – in classifications which pre-date that of 1855.

HISTORY

The property is traditionally said to have been formed in 1757 by the brothers Gruaud, one of whom was a priest and the other a magistrate. Records show that in fact it must have been in existence long before that, for in the early 1750s the wine was already established and sold for higher prices than all but the four first growths. The Gruaud brothers amalgamated two family vineyards they had inherited called Sartaignac and Du Derle with a third known as the Domaine de Tenac. This made an estate of 116 hectares, and it was at first known as Fond-Bedeau, taking this name from the *lieu-dit* of this part of the commune. The Chevalier de Gruaud, the one who was a magistrate, had a reputation as a disciplinarian and is said to have erected a watch-tower overlooking his vineyards to see if anyone was slacking. Two other stories indicate his eccentric character. After each vintage he would run up a flag to indicate which nationality would most appreciate the style of the wine: a German flag indicated a soft, supple wine; a British flag a firm and full-bodied wine; a Dutch flag meant something between the two.

On one occasion he drove into Bordeaux and began to auction his wine in the market-place, causing a great rumpus. When no one would offer the asking price of 200 francs a *tonneau* he insulted both their taste and judgement in the most sarcastic terms and drove off into the Médoc, only to reappear a few months later with a base price of 250 francs a *tonneau*. Such, it is said, was the reputation of the wine, and such was the *négociants'* knowledge of the rich M. Gruaud's idiosyncracies – after all in another couple of months the price might well have risen to 300 francs – the entire harvest was bought on the spot.

Le Chevalier de Gruaud died in 1778 and the property passed to Joseph-Sébastian de La Rose, who had married Gruaud's daughter. He had bought out the remaining heirs. As was the custom La Rose added his name to the title of the wine, and it has been Gruaud-Larose ever since.

Larose also owned a vineyard a few kilometres away, on the border of Pauillac and Saint-Laurent. This was known as Château-Larose-Trintaudon and had a high reputation at the time, though it later fell into disuse. He was the Lieutenant-Governor of the Province of Guyenne in the years running up to the French Revolution.

Unlike Gruaud, Larose was an absentee landlord and moved in exalted circles. The wine quickly became popular at court and among the nobility, occasioning Larose to invent the motto which still adorns the label – '*Le Roi des Vins, le Vin des Rois*'. When Larose died in 1795 the reputation was well-established outside France, and the wine was even shipped to the new United States.

Unfortunately, Larose's heirs could not settle the question of ownership of the estate and the family fight went on and on for many years. In the end the legal costs had mounted up so much that the property itself had to be auctioned to pay for them.

On 21 December 1812, while Napoleon's troops were fighting their way back through the snow from Moscow, Château Larose was bought by a consortium of three people for 291,000 francs: Pierre Balguerie, a well-known Bordeaux *négociant*, Jean Auguste (later Baron) Sarget, and David Jean Verdonnet. At that time it was making 120 to 150 *tonneaux*, fetching, according to André Simon, around £20 a hogshead, and firmly established as a leading second growth. In 1815 the broker Lawton wrote that 'Larose is the sturdiest, but at the same time rich and smooth, of all the top wines in Saint-Julien.'

Verdonnet died in 1836, and his heirs sold his share of the property back to the other two. Meanwhile Balguerie, who was also soon to die, had married Sophie Stuttenberg, daughter of a colleague (there is a Cours Balguerie-Stuttenberg in the old wine merchants' quarter of Bordeaux), and they had three daughters.

The eldest, Marie Henriette, married Isaac Charles Alexandre de Bethmann, one-time Mayor of Bordeaux, and they were also to have three children; the second, Marie Clémence married François Edouard Lemercier de Boisregard, though they were childless; the third died unmarried in 1842. By the time of the 1855 Classification the property was once again shared by three people: Baron Sarget had 50 per cent and the other half was divided between the two surviving daughters of the Balguerie-Stuttenbergs, Mme Bethmann and Mme Boisregard.

Some ten year later there were further inheritance problems. In 1865 Madame Bethmann died, and her share, which now included the portions of both her sisters, was divided among her three children, and they found it hard enough to agree among themselves, let alone with Baron Sarget who owned the other half. As a result the vineyard was split, at the insistence, it seems, of the Baron, though the wine was still made as a whole for a couple of seasons while a second *chai* was constructed for the vinification and storage of the Sarget wine.

So, from 1867 we have two separate Gruaud-Laroses. At first sight Sarget seems to have managed to get the best of the bargain, for the 1883, English edition of Cocks and Féret describes the vineyard as 'divided in quality as well as in quantity', and the Sarget wine as 'happy rivals of Châteaux Lafite and Margaux'. However, one suspects these 'puffs' in Cocks and Féret were written by the proprietors themselves. According to Bernard Ginestet contemporary opinion generally favoured the other. For quite some time, as evidenced by the two pre-phylloxera Gruaud-Laroses (1870 and 1875) that I have tasted myself – the former in October 1985, thanks to Michael Broadbent of Christie's – both wines were sold with the original, pre-partition labels.

The Bethmann half remained in the joint ownership of the three children until 1889. In that year Edouard Bethmann died and Sophie, now Mme Adrien Faure, bought out her remaining brother Charles. Gradually the name Gruaud-Larose-Bethmann became Gruaud-Larose-Faure.

In 1917 the Sarget portion was up for sale. The purchase was finalized on 2nd October, the vendor being Mme Adrienne Lavielle, Baronne Sarget de Lafontaine. It took Cordier another eighteen years to acquire the Faure portion, now a limited company owned by Madame Faure's heirs. This part of the sale was completed on 8 November 1935, at a price of 361,000 francs.

THE VINEYARD

Gruaud-Larose, even in Médoc terms, is a large property; and this is a region of large domaines. The estate covers 150 hectares, of which 82 are under vines planted in a sandy, gravelly soil on a subsoil of *alios* or *marnes calcaires*. The situation is superb. The bulk of the vineyard lies in one piece at the southern end of the commune of Saint Julien between Châteaux Branaire-Ducru and Lagrange and facing south-east on a *croupe* which runs down to the Jalle du Nord which marks the commune boundary. Opposite, in Cussac, lies Château Lanessan. There are two further parcels. The first lies to the north of the D101 which runs from the hamlet of Beychevelle to Saint Laurent and the second lies further west adjacent to Château Talbot. The vineyard is planted in the ratio 62 per cent Cabernet Sauvignon, 10 per cent Cabernet Franc, 25 per cent Merlot and 3 per cent Petit Verdot. This is marginally more Merlot and less Cabernet Sauvignon than a decade or so ago.

THE CHÂTEAU AND THE *CHAIS*

Like all the Cordier properties, everything about Gruaud and its surrounding dependencies is impeccable. The *cuvier* and *chais* are as clean as a new pin, the billiard-table lawns and formal flower beds which surround the château are immaculate, and the gravel courtyard invariably freshly raked over and free of weeds.

Yet at Gruaud, as opposed to Talbot, the atmosphere is somewhat distant, somewhat museum-like. Talbot is the home of the Cordier family. Gruaud is unoccupied, though used for receptions. The château, though in the eighteenth century *directoire* style, was constructed by Baron Sarget in 1875. It is a substantial two-storey, rectangular edifice, approached up a long drive, and lying in a small *jardin français*. Inside the *chais* everything is very modern and scrupulously clean and tidy. Glass or tile-lined metal fermentation vats hug the walls, facing huge oak vats into which the wine is racked after the fermentation.

While the wine is undergoing its malolactic fermentation, it will remain in large wooden vats, of a maximum capacity of 160 hectolitres; above this level the ratio becomes unequal between volume and surface area, and it is difficult to maintain an even temperature between the liquid and the surrounding air, necessary for a smooth maturation.

While at Talbot the wine until recently was kept in these large wooden vats for up to eight months, at Gruaud it will be racked into hogsheads, containing 300 litres, or the equivalent of 25 dozen bottles, after two months. The wine is racked off its lees every three months or so, and fined in the spring eighteen months after vintage, using five beaten egg whites and one egg yolk per cask, to settle the less solid impurities. This takes 40 to 45 days, after which racking is continued periodically until bottling two years or more after the vintage. There is no filtration.

All the Cordier estates come under the responsibility of their director of properties, the *oenologue* Georges Pauli. At Gruaud the day-to-day management is in the hands of *maître de chai* Philippe Carmagnac, assisted by *chef de culture* Henri Puzos. Production now averages some 380 *tonneaux*, distributed exclusively through Cordier and their agents abroad. The wine is not sold on the general Bordeaux market-place.

THE WINES

Inevitably, when discussing the wine of Château Gruaud-Larose, one cannot escape mentioning Talbot. Both Gruaud and Talbot are always full and sturdy wines; solid, yet soft and very fruity. Talbot is consistent; a good bottle; yet rarely, except in years like 1959 – a vintage which suited the Cordier properties – of absolute top class. It fits its *quatrième cru* classification.

Château Gruaud-Larose, on the other hand, made in the same way, is invariably better, invariably among the top of the classed growths, and, in some years, like 1961, at the very top. I have noticed that Gruaud – indeed both these two Saint-Juliens – are not wines which show a lot of charm in their adolescence. In cask they are easy to judge, but in bottle, for the first five or more years, often fail to do themselves true justice. At this stage they often seem burly, somewhat too sturdy, a bit peppery, and lacking grace. They are wines which take longer than the norm, not merely to mature, but to show their real quality. Château Gruaud-Larose is a wine which has an elegance and a breed which the other sometimes lacks, and it can be very good indeed. In the 1980s I have noticed that it has acquired an extra element of polish and finesse *vis-à-vis* its stable-companion. Though it is always in the same mould as Talbot, and for me, lacks the exquisiteness of a Ducru or a Las-Cases, the wine fully earns in second growth classification.

THE TASTING

Most of the following notes come from two sessions: the younger wines in Bordeaux in January 1990, the older vintages at a tasting organized by La Vigneronne in October 1991. I have inserted other recent notes to fill in a few gaps.

	Optimum drinking
1990	**1997–2007**

Very good colour. A little vegetal on the nose. Not as rich, classy or as concentrated as it should be. Medium body. Not a lot of tannin. Some-

what thin and mean, lacking guts. It lacks opulence and richness too. Quite forward. No better than quite good.

1989	**1997–2007**

Fullish colour. Soft and fruity on the nose and on

the palate. But rather herbaceous nevetheless. Quite ripe and sweet but lacks a bit of grip as well as class and concentration. Good but not great.

1988   1998–2013
Good colour. Better than the 1990. Fullish nose for a 1988. Good new oak. Nicely austere. Medium-full, stylish. Good blackberry fruit. The tannins nicely ripe. Well-made, well-balanced. Complex on the finish. Very good plus.

1987   Now–1998
Good colour for the vintage. Good oak. Good plump blackcurrant fruit. No lack of substance. Nothing off-vintage about this 1987! Ripe, quite fat, good balance. A little tannin. Good grip. Fresh and attractive.

1986   1998–2015
Fullish colour. Firm, full, concentrated and rich. The size of Gruaud, but not without fat, and not too closed-in. Fullish, good rich tannins. There is a fine concentration here and a lot of depth. Cabernet Sauvignon-based wine. Good grip. Very good.

1985   1995–2003
Medium-full colour. An ample wine on the nose. The higher proportion of the Merlot in this vintage is evident here. Really quite soft and supple for a 1985. Medium body. I can't really get excited though. I find an absence of complexity and breed. Merely 'good'. The 1988 is better.

1984   **Drink soon**
Good colour. Has weight and depth on the nose and seems to have quite a bit more to it than Talbot. Quite full, has a good level of flesh and ripeness as well as tannin. Good structure. Finishes long. Shows well.

1983   Now–1998
Full colour; just about mature. Soft nose with a touch of spice. Less chunky than the 1991. Medium to medium-full body. Stylish but mature – and more evolved than the 1981. A little loose-knit but adequately balanced. Good.

1982   1995–2020
Very good colour. Rich but slightly adolescent barnyard elements on the nose. Quite a lot of astringent tannins on the attack. Rich, fullish, a little muscular but the follow-through is velvety and concentrated. Good grip. Plenty of wine here. Very good.

1981   Now–2003
Good colour. Quite substantial on the nose. A rich vigorous wine with good acidity and plenty of fruit. Still some tannin, fullish, ample, concentrated, even elegant. Very good.

1979   **Now–1999**
Good colour, only just mature looking. Not as exciting as the 1981. Rather dense on the nose. Fullish, still some tannin. Ripe but lacking dimension and generosity. Good but not great.

1978   **Now–2000 plus**
Quite good colour but browner than the 1979 though more intense. The tannins are a bit dry on the nose. Good Cabernet fruit on the palate. Medium-full. A little tannin. Lacks a little generosity at first but the follow-through is more enticing. Very good. Just about ready.

1976   **Drink soon**
Quite full colour, distinctly brown at the rim. The nose is rather dry and ungenerous. Medium-full but somewhat four-square and astringent. Lacks flesh. Not exciting.

1975   **Now–1998**
Quite a full colour, like the 1976 now brown. A rather solid nose, not exactly dry or astringent, but burly and lacking richness. On the palate equally a bit unwieldy. There is fruit here, but the whole thing is rather dense and charmless. Not exciting.

1971   **Drink soon**
Fullish, fresh colour. This is rather austere, though quite substantial on the nose. Better on the palate. Quite substantial. Good acidity, and if not exactly rich, has fruit, depth and some class. Finishes well. A wine for food. Good.

1970   **Now–2000**
Good colour. No undue maturity. Slightly burly on the nose. Full but rich though. Again a touch astringent on the attack but richer on the follow-through. There is though a certain bitterness at the end. Good plus. Finishes long though.

1966   **Now–2000**
Full colour, now mature. I prefer this to the 1970. There is more generosity. Good nose, rich and aromatic. Fullish on the palate. Quite solid, but plenty of depth. This expanded and improved as it aerated in the glass. Long, meaty, satisfyingly warm finish. Very good. Will still keep well.

1964   **Now–1996**
Good fullish mature colour. Fairly substantial nose, though a bit four-square. This has substance, class and good length for a 1964. Now completely *à point* and not for keeping that much longer. Medium-full, ripe, fresh. Good length. Very good plus, especially for a Médoc.

1961   **Now–2000**
Fine mature colour. Rich, opulent nose. Now quite evolved. A fullish wine, somewhat astringent on the attack but quite concentrated and

meaty on the follow-through. Fat and rich. Long. Still vigorous. But a very good rather than a great 1961. What it lacks is a bit of intensity.

1959   **Now–1996**

(English bottled, Hedges and Butler) Fine mature colour. Sturdy, quite dense but rich nose. The tannins/astringency shows. Full, rich, and with more intensity of fruit and grip than the 1961. Sweeter. Always a burly wine. But with plenty of quality and interest. One of the best wines of the vintage. (Judging by my notes the château–bottling is not materially different).

1957   **Drink soon**

Very fine colour, mature but no age. Structured but sweet and rich on both the nose and the palate. Not hard at all. Quite full, plenty of depth. This is rich and enjoyable and fine for the vintage, but at the end it is now a little astringent.

1955   **Drink soon**

Good rich colour. A wine which still has vigour and class on the nose, if beginning to get to its end. Fullish, old-viney, concentrated, fragrant and classy. A lovely example. Beginning to lack a little grip but not astringent at the end.

1953   **Drink soon**

Very good colour. Sweet, ripe, elegant nose, no astringency. Not aggresive either. Full for a 1953: still vigorous. Lots of fruit. Complex. Balanced. Long and distinguished. Very fine.

1952   **Drink up**

Full colour; little brown. Rich full and chunky but a lot of sweetness on both the nose and the palate. Very ripe but rather old-fashioned and a certain amount of astringency. Good finish but a little too structured to be really elegant. Very good nevertheless.

1949   **Drink soon**

Good colour. This is very like the 1953. Similarly rich, elegant, concentrated, old-viney and sweet at the end. Slightly more cassis than raspberry on the nose: a bit more Cabernet in flavour. Fullish, velvety, rich and indeed opulent. Not a bit astringent. Mellow and concentrated. Fine quality.

1945   **Drink soon**

Very deep colour. Two bottles circulating. The first was rather tough and inky. The second was suppler. Sturdy nevertheless. Rich, austere, concentrated, but the structure is beginning to dominate, even in the better bottle. I prefer the 1949.

1934   **Past its best**

(Sarget) This is rather old, judging by the colour. And too old judging by the palate. Similar to a sample I saw at a Christie's pre-sale tasting in October,1987. Perhaps this is where it came from!

1929   **Drink soon**

(Sarget) Full colour. Round, rich, full, fat, robust and sweet on the nose. Remarkably full and vigorous still. Was solid for a 1929. Very ripe and blackcurrant. Perhaps it lacks a little finesse but it is certainly fine and most enjoyable.

1929   **Now–1998**

(Bethmann) Very fine colour indeed. Splendid complex nose: great depth, plenty of vigour, mellow and blackcurranty, with a touch of astringency. Full, very good grip, a surprising amount of oak too. Very fine indeed.

1928   **Drink up**

(Sarget) Fine, rich, mature colour. Rich, full and meaty on the nose. Full and tannic, fine and ample, solid but succulent. Started well, but did not last in the glass. But at first it was lovely.

1924

(Belgian bottled) Doesn't stipulate which half of the divided Gruaud-Larose. Well-matured colour. Old nose but neither too dry nor too maderized. Still sweetness here and good but not excessive acidity. No astringency. Old roses. Plump fruit. An old gentleman, but long and elegant.

DUCRU-
BEAUCAILLOU

I have a very soft spot in my heart for the wines of Ducru-Beaucaillou. It is not that I have lunched or dined at Ducru with the charming Jean-Eugène and Monique Borie more than at any other château – though that must be very nearly true. It is not that Ducru was the first Bordeaux growth about which I wrote a château profile – though that is very nearly true as well. It is not even – and this *is* true – that it was at Ducru-Beaucaillou that I sampled my first pre-phylloxera wine: the 1867, which I had a chance to sample again twenty years later on the occasion on which I report below.

No, the reason that I have a soft spot for Ducru is quite simply that during the time I cut my teeth on claret and formed my yardsticks – the collective vintages from 1953 to 1970 – it produced the best Saint-Julien and, with Palmer, the best wine outside the first growths. The 1953, though fading, is a great wine. The 1961 is my favourite Bordeaux after Latour and Mouton – but then I am a Cabernet Sauvignon man – and the 1970 is pretty damn good too. But then most of the other vintages in this period are conspicuous successes. Ducru, as I shall demonstrate, is the quintessential claret.

Ducru-Beaucaillou was originally part of the giant Beychevelle estate which extended over the whole of southern Saint-Julien and the neighbouring communes. When this was dismembered at the end of the seventeenth century, a number of domaines, including Branaire, Saint-Pierre and Beaucaillou, began a separate existence. But the details of these first few years are scanty.

HISTORY

The history of the property as we know it now begins in the latter half of the eighteenth century, the 50 or so years before the Revolution. This was the heyday of the nobles of the Bordeaux *parlement*, the '*noblesse de la robe*'. Newly endowed, rich and competitive, these lords extended their estates and bought out, by fair means or foul (usually foul), the peasant proprietors. It was at this time that most of the estates we know today were set up and many of the present châteaux constructed. Just as, a hundred years later, *nouveaux riches* bankers were to descend from Paris to do the fashionable thing by buying a vineyard, so in the 1750s, 1760s and 1770s, the newly rich lawyers from Bordeaux − especially following the terrible frosts of 1766 − extensively replanted and modernized their new estates and cellars.

Among this fraternity was a M. Bergeron at what is now Ducru. At that time, the vineyard was known as Beaucaillou, though the wine as Bergeron. Originally, in fact, the *lieu-dit* had been rendered as *Maucaillou*, the pebbles (*cailloux*) being *mauvais,* or bad, because they were hard to work and good for growing nothing but the vine. It was only later, when the wine was found to be rather good, that attitudes to the place changed; the *mau* then rapidly became *beau* (fine).

The first reference to the wine occurs in the ranking list Professor Pijassou has culled from the notebooks of the broking firm of Abraham Lawton. Between 1741 and 1774, the average *prix de vente* of Bergeron − and we think it was only sold from 1760 onwards − was 483 *livres tournois* per *tonneau*. This is more than Beychevelle itself, Branaire or 'Pontet' as Langoa was known at the time, but significantly lower than Gruaud (average 734 *livres*) or Léoville (810). The third most important Saint-Julien property at the time was Lagrange, then known as Brane-Saint-Julien, which made an average of 800 *livres*. The first growths fetched 1,200 plus.

This would place Bergeron as a fourth or third growth, a position it was to hold for 60 years or more. At the time it was producing 30 to 40 *tonneaux* a year. The vineyard was obviously not as extensive as it is today.

Little is known about this M. Bergeron. At the time of the Revolution a François de Bergeron is listed as a member of the Bordeaux parliament. One assumes this is the same gentleman. He certainly established many contacts abroad for the sale of his wines, particularly in northern Europe, in the Low Countries and Scandinavia. There is a story that in 1792 he was forced by law to surrender two expensively decorated pistols to the authorities but tried to conceal two swords which belonged to Swedish friends of his. According to Charles Lorbac, this original Bergeron had three sons. The two eldest predeceased him. The third was the *curé* of the neighbouring village of Lamarque.

In 1795 − perhaps following the death of François de Bergeron, perhaps as a consequence of the Revolution − the property was bought by a M. Bertrand Ducru, whose father-in-law, M. Dulasson, was chairman of the Bordeaux chamber of commerce. Hubrecht Duijker, in his lavishly illustrated book, *The Great Wine Châteaux of Bordeaux*, mentions that this gentleman appreciated his son-in-law's wine so much that he had it substituted for the customary water at committee meetings. We can only speculate on the outcome!

Ducru gave his name to the vineyard which he extensively renovated and extended. It was he who built, over the old cellars, the bulk of the present château. During the first half of the nineteenth century, the reputation of the wine steadily improved and production increased, reaching 140 *tonneaux* by 1850. Though regarded only as a third growth at the outset, by 1840 it was fetching prices equal to Rausan, Léoville and Larose. This improvement was confirmed in the famous 1855 Classification in which Ducru appears three from the bottom of the second growth table between the Pichons and the two Saint-Estèphes, Cos d'Estournel and Montrose.

Bertrand Ducru and his wife Marie had two children, a son and a daughter. The son Gustave was to marry the young and wealthy widow of Jean–Baptiste du Luc, whose family were connected with Issan and neighbouring Branaire. The daughter Marie-Louise espoused Antoine Ravez. Ravez *père*, Auguste, was *député* for the Gironde from 1816 to 1829 and became an Under-Secretary of State and President of the Chamber of Deputies. Bernard Ginestet in *Saint-Julien* states that this gentleman, having been a passionate defender of the freedom of the press, subsequently became its fierce adversary. Charles X ennobled him and Louis XVIII once said of him: 'Nature created him and then destroyed the mould.' A street is named after him in Bordeaux. It was he, Ginestet suggests, who played a decisive part in increasing the quality and reputation of the wine from third to second growth.

From the death of Bertrand Ducru in 1829 until May 1860 the two children owned the property in common. In 1857 or thereabouts, however, Gustave Ducru had bought Branaire from his cousin-in-law, Léo du Luc. In 1860 he ceded his share of Ducru-Beaucaillou to his sister, the transaction taking place by private auction. Six years later, Marie-Louise decided to sell Ducru-Beaucaillou and on 3 March 1866, it passed to Mme Nathaniel Johnston, *née* Dassier, for the enormous sum of 1 million francs, about £40,000 at the rate of exchange at the time. The domaine comprised 82 hectares, of which 48 were under vines, and produced about 100 *tonneaux* of wine a year.

A number of properties changed hands in this year, among them the two Rauzans, Durfort-Vivens and Batailley. Not all were bought by Parisian bankers, however. At this time, many Bordeaux *négociants* were also on the scene. Herman Cruse had paid 700,000 francs for Pontet-Canet the year before, and was to pay a million for Giscours ten years later.

One of the most enterprising young merchants was Nathaniel Johnston, whose ancestors had arrived in Bordeaux from Ireland 150 fifty years previously. Unlike his Irish compatriots, the Barton family, and others from this side of the Channel, the Johnstons became thoroughly absorbed into French culture, taking French citizenship and marrying Roman Catholics.

Johnston had bought Château Dauzac, the Labarde fifth growth, in 1863, and was already the proprietor of several lesser estates. Ducru-Beaucaillou was bought in his wife's name because the money had come from her family, the Dassiers. It became the most important feather in the Johnston cap, so much so that he used the name for a sparkling wine made and matured in cellars under the old fortress of Bourg, the citadel guarding the junction of the Dordogne and the Garonne on the opposite side of the river. When he first arrived, he had tried to change the name of the Ducru wine back to plain Beaucaillou, which was all he allowed on the letterhead. But without success. So Ducru-Beaucaillou it stayed.

The twenty years before phylloxera were a manic and expansionary period in Bordeaux, with a magnificent and plentiful series of vintages, properties changing hands at ever more inflationary prices and the rise in Britain of a prosperous wine-drinking middle class following the Gladstone and Cobden budgets of the early 1860s. It could not last and, with a mildew epidemic exaggerating the ravages of the phylloxera bug, a slump set in from which the Bordeaux châteaux only began to emerge after the Second World War.

It was at Ducru-Beaucaillou, quite by chance, that the remedy to mildew, the copper sulphate solution known as Bordeaux Mixture, was discovered. The manager at the time, Monsieur E. David, was plagued by thieves stealing grapes from his vines. To put them off, he painted those which were most vulnerable, i.e., closest to the road, with a lurid blue-green mixture he had developed. To everyone's surprise, these plants seemed to be immune from mildew attack. Two professors, Millardet and Gayon, heard of this phenomenon and got together with Skawinski, a member of a famous agronomist family which managed a number of Médoc and Graves estates (including La Mission-Haut-Brion, Léoville-Las-Cases and Pontet-Canet), and they persuaded Johnston to carry out further experiments on a larger scale. Not wishing to risk the vines at Beaucaillou, Johnston agreed to the trials being carried out at Dauzac. They proved a triumphant success and the 'Bordeaux Treatment' was born.

Cushioned as it was by the reputation and success of the Johnston business in Bordeaux,

Ducru did not suffer immediately from the bad times which were to follow and, though profitability was not easy, especially with the *beau monde* in Paris increasingly drinking nothing but Champagne, there was enough money to keep the vineyard and *chais* in good condition.

It was not until the 1920s that the Johnston business began really to suffer. They had always had very good contacts in the USA and now this market, thanks to Prohibition, was at a standstill. The Johnston fortunes were low and this was exemplified by the profitability of the wines from their most famous property. The quality, however, judging by the wines below, does not seem to have suffered. Nevertheless the reputation of Ducru, according to such critics as Penning-Rowsell and David Peppercorn began to decline.

In 1928, reluctantly, the Johnstons sold Ducru-Beaucaillou to Monsieur F. Desbarats de Burke. Desbarats was a partner in another firm of Bordeaux merchants, Gernon, Desbarats, and was the grandfather of Alain Miailhe who owns Château Siran in Margaux and of Mme de Lencquesaing of Château Pichon-Lalande. Desbarats, however, was no more able to make a profit out of Ducru than the Johnstons. The property was neglected. Finally, in the early part of the war he died; the property was up for sale again.

Late in 1941, Ducru-Beaucaillou, somewhat run down and dilapidated and regarded by many as unworthy of its second growth classification, was bought by Francis Borie and the following year a programme of reconstruction, renovation and replanting of vineyard, *cuvier* and *chais*, not to be completed until 1958, was started.

Borie died in 1953, and was succeeded by his son Jean-Eugène, but not before he had seen some return on his efforts. Already by the early 1950s the reputation had recovered and has since gone from strength to strength. It is not an exaggeration to say that since 1953 M. Borie has produced at Ducru-Beaucaillou a wine consistently in the top flight, every year among the top three or four wines outside the first growths; more than just sometimes their equal, as in 1961 and other vintages.

THE BORIE DOMAINE

The Bories had arrived in the Médoc from the Corrèze in 1890 and set up a *négociants* business. Five years later they bought Château Caronne-Sainte-Gemme in Saint-Laurent, which is now owned by a cousin, Jean Nony. In 1929 Francis and his elder brother Marcel acquired Château Batailley from Edmond Halphen. In 1942, shortly after Francis acquired Ducru-Beaucaillou, the brothers divided their Pauillac interests. The château, outbuildings and the heart of the vineyard went to Marcel; other parcels, to be named Haut-Batailley, as well as the *bourgeois exceptionnel*, Château La Couronne, and the quaintly-named La Tour d'Aspic, went to Francis. These then passed to his daughter Mme de Brest-Borie and are now run on her behalf by Jean-Eugène.

In 1970, Jean-Eugène Borie bought 32 hectares of land from Château Lagrange, the third growth Saint Julien, whose vineyards lie away from the river on the border with the commune of Saint-Laurent. He planted eighteen of them with vines. The land being AC Saint-Julien, Borie was legally entitled to absorb this parcel into Ducru-Beaucaillou as numerous other proprietors had done elsewhere. However, he decided that these vines would not produce wine of equal quality as Ducru and the wine is now sold as Château Lalande-Borie. It is not Ducru's second wine as, quite naturally, many people assume (for Château La Croix, the *real* second wine, is seldom seen), but sells for roughly the same as second wines such as Las-Cases's Clos du Marquis or Mme de Lencquesaing's Réserve-de-la Comtesse.

Raymond Dupin of Grand-Puy-Lacoste, bachelor, *bon viveur* and an old boy of great charm and personality, died in 1978. Having no heirs interested in succeeding him, he had made over his estate to his friend Jean-Eugène Borie shortly before his demise. Xavier, one of Jean-Eugène's two sons, now resides at Grand-Puy and has continued the Dupin tradition of a wine well above fifth growth levels.

Finally, on the acquisition of Saint-Pierre in 1983 by Henri Martin, the old Saint-Pierre-Sevaistre château and *chais* and five hectares of surrounding vineyard were sold by Martin to Jean-Eugène Borie. These buildings are now used for Château Lalande-Borie.

THE VINEYARD

The vineyard of the beautiful pebbles is aptly named for it is these pebbles which help to make the beautiful wine. Like most of the Médoc, the *vignoble* is situated on gravel and this is very apparent in that unbroken stretch of vines which extends, parallel to the river, from Beychevelle to Latour.

At Ducru-Beaucaillou the stones are particularly large and the thickness of the gravel particularly deep. The vines can reach down far into the subsoil for the essential but esoteric minerals and trace elements which give great wine its character and complexity. The soil, being gravel, is aerated and so drains well and, being close to the river, contains, as well as chunks of iron-bearing clay, subtle deposits of old alluvial soils washed down the Dordogne and Garonne into the estuary of the Gironde from high up in the hills many years ago. There is a lot of truth in the old Médoc saying that the best vines are those which have a sight of the river. Not all the property is under vines. Between the château itself and the river lie several acres of land, previously marshy and boggy, now drained meadows which, being alluvial *palus*, are too rich, paradoxically, to grow good wine, though sometimes this soil can be used as humus or nitrogenous fertilizer for the vineyards.

The estate itself comprises some 215 hectares, of which 49 are under vines. Of these, 26 are around the château, another 20 lie inland between Gruaud-Larose and Talbot, and three are in the commune of Cussac. The *encépagement*, or proportion of vine varieties, is typical of the Médoc: 65 per cent Cabernet Sauvignon, 25 per cent Merlot and 10 per cent Cabernet Franc and Petit Verdot. Production is some 150 *tonneaux* per year.

THE CHÂTEAU AND *CHAIS*

Set away from the main road, at the point where vine gives way to grass and on the lip of an incline overlooking the Gironde, is the château itself. This magnificent building is familiar from the label, where it is depicted in half profile, making the frontage appear less wide than it really is. The central part is a sort of *chartreuse* and was built in the Directoire style about 1820, facing the river. Later, in 1880, two square Victorian towers – 'Les Tours Johnston', as they are known in the family – were added at each end and the aspect was changed. In front of the courtyard, a park of mature trees, some reputedly 100 years old, runs down to the river's edge. Beneath the main part of the mansion is the oldest part of the building: a huge vaulted *chai*, dating to 1730, where the new wine is kept maturing gently in new oak casks (there is a second *chai* in the nearby village); connecting with this is the cuvier where the wine is made. Above, on the first floor, live Jean-Eugène Borie and his charming wife, Monique. Borie is one of the few owners in the Médoc to live literally over the shop.

THE WINE

Jean-Eugène Borie and his team at Ducru make a wine worthy of the term super-second. Indeed, the wine was of that quality before the expression was even invented. If Saint-Julien wines are the quintessence of claret, as they have been described, then perhaps Ducru is the most quintessential of them all; well-coloured, full-bodied, yet supple, elegantly fragrant in its aftertaste. A Ducru from a fine vintage is everything good claret should be.

What is it about Ducru which makes it such a good wine and so consistent? One reason is certainly the dedication and scrupulous avoidance of anything but the best which accompanies the tending of the vines and the production of the wine. Another is the scepticism with which Jean-Eugène and his team view untried but fashionable ideas and new methods which occasionally seduce other Bordeaux proprietors. A third may be the ambient temperature of the *chai* which, being within thick stone walls and underground, is noticeably colder than some others in the Médoc, allowing the wine a slower but perhaps steadier maturation during the crucial period while it is in cask.

Whatever the answer, the wine is splendid and all praise is due to the man who makes it, one of the most respected but most modest men in the Médoc – Jean-Eugène Borie.

THE TASTING

Dr Marvin Overton's Saint-Julien extravaganza of May 1992, began in New York with Jean-Eugène Borie and Ducru-Beaucaillou. Here are my notes. Others are from a Ducru *versus* Las-Cases tasting held in New Haven, Connecticut, in October 1988.

Optimum drinking

1991 **1995–1999**
Good colour. Ripe nose. Stylish. Good fruit. Not too Cabernet. Has grip and definition. Medium body. Promising quality.

1990 **2000–2020**
Good colour. Full, rich Cabernet nose. Much more classic than the 1989. Lovely ripe fruit. Fullish. Good tannins. Very voluptuous, potentially. Good grip. Giving it very good definition. Very elegant especially on the follow-through.

1989 **1998–2015**
Good colour. Ripe nose. More oaky than the 1990. Less Cabernet but more lush. Very ripe on the palate. Medium-full. The tannins show a little but this has very good acidity for the vintage. Oaky and elegant and will be voluptuous too. (NB This wine is variable. Part of the stock has a strange taint to it. See also the wine below.)

1988 **1998–2018**
Medium-full colour. Lovely nose. This has the generosity and flexibility a lot of 1988s lack. Cabernet fruit but ripe and balanced. Youthful, backward, fullish. Good tannin. Very good acidity. A little austere but fine for the vintage. (NB There are variable bottles of Ducru 1988. On at least six occasions I have found the wine to have a distinctly odd taint to it.)

1987 **Drink soon**
Medium colour. Some maturity now. A little vegetal but soft, slightly attenuated. Pleasant but some old tea aspects lurking in the background.

1986 **2000–2020**
Very good colour. Closed, backward nose. These 1986s are rather adolescent. Fullish, super-concentrated palate. Very good tannin. This has a lot of promise on the palate. Fine. Long on the finish. Lovely Cabernet fruit. Needs time.

1985 **1995–2007**
Very good colour. Still youthful. Ripe, round, stylish nose. Lovely fruit. Mulberries here. Good grip. Rather more accessible than the 1986. Medium-full, soft, ripe, oaky. Very good ripe fruit. Very sexy. Fine. Long.

1984 **Drink soon**
Medium colour. Mature. A bit hard and vegetal. A bit dry on the palate but the fruit is quite respectable. Good length. I prefer this to the 1987.

1983 **Now–2000**
Medium to medium-full colour. Just about mature. Good breed, quite accessible. Just a hint of attenuation compared with the 1985. On the palate this seems to lack a bit of grip. I prefer the 1985 today. Medium body.

1982 **Now–2010**
Medium-full colour. Raspberry-mulberry *rôti* flavour. A little cooked fruit. Fullish nose. Medium-full. Very good ripe fruit. Surprisingly classy and freshly balanced. This has a lot of style. A fine wine.

1981 **Now–2000**
Very good colour for the vintage. Still very vigorous. Soft, ripe blackberry nose. Open. Very good fruit. Medium to medium-full. Slightly earthy on the palate but fresh, ripe, positive and elegant. A fine 1981. One of the best. Plenty of vigour.

1979 **Now–2000**
Medium-full colour, now mature. Good stylish Cabernet nose but not the depth and concentration of the 1978. Medium to medium-full body. Tannins now resolved. Good grip. Stylish rather than fat and sumptuous but good depth and length. Very good.

1978 **Now–2010**
Vigorous colour. Little maturity. Fine rich nose, still a little austere, but style and depth here. Fullish. Good Cabernet fruit. Lacks a little real richness but elegant, balanced and quite concentrated. Just about ready. Will last very well. Fine.

1977   **Drink soon**

Medium colour. Mature. Soft nose. Not too weedy. A perfectly agreeable fruity bottle. Fresh. A little lean but no sign of astringency or decay. Very good for the vintage.

1976   **Now–1998**

Good colour for a 1976. Ripe and ample on the nose. Not a bit dry. Medium-full, fat, plump and enjoyable. Not the greatest of class but fleshy, fresh and quite long. Very good indeed for the vintage. Still has life.

1975   **Now–2008**

Full colour. Corky in May 1992. Yet nevertheless a wine of breed and fruit without any undue tannins. Fullish. Good grip. Long. Fine for the vintage. Will still improve.

1974   **Drink soon**

Quite a full colour. Mature. A little decayed and sweet-sour on the nose. But quite pleasant on the palate. Quite ripe. Not astringent. Positive finish.

1973   **Drink soon**

Medium mature colour. Ripe nose. Roast chestnut and butterscotch. Now loosening up a bit. Medium body. An open plump ripe wine. Good fruit. Reasonable acidity. Another very good result indeed which still has life.

1971   **Now–1996**

Good mature colour. Fine nose. Balanced, full of finesse. Plums and blackcurrant. What it lacks is a little richness. On the palate the fat is there. Medium to medium-full. Quite plump. It doesn't have the concentration and fruit of the 1970 nor quite the breed. But it is a very good result. Long finish. Fine for the vintage.

1970   **Now–2020**

Good colour, not a lot of maturity. Very lovely succulent fruit on the nose. Beautiful balance and heaps of elegance. Saint-Julien at its best. Quite clearly the best of the decade. Still young. Only just ready. Very fine fruit. Excellent grip. Balance, depth, concentration and breed here. Marvellous finish. Fine.

1969   **Drink soon**

Good colour. No undue age. Plump nose. Not a bit off-vintagey. Could have been a 1967 (did they add some surplus 1970 to it?). Medium body. Fruity. A bit one-dimensional but no undue age.

1967   **Drink up**

Not shown: Medium colour, some age now. This bottle lost vigour quickly in the glass. Originally a wine of concentration and depth but now a little old and astringent.

1966   **Now–1999**

Good fullish colour. Mature. Lovely nose. Fully ready, which the 1970 isn't. Great fruit beautifully balanced. Fullish. Harmonious. Very long. A classic.

1964   **Drink soon**

Very full colour. Full nose, ripe and vigorous but somehow a touch four-square. Full-bodied, rich and spicy, good grip. A masculine wine, has mellowness and warmth, but may possibly start to get a little astringent and loose on the finish from now on. Very good though.

1962   **Now–2000 plus**

Very good colour. Still vigorous. Fine nose. A little caramelly, but balanced and ripe. Soft red fruits. Not the classic cassis of the 1966. It has less breed but is more vigorous. Generous, balanced, full of fruit. Lovely.

1961   **Now–2000**

Good colour. But more evolved than the 1962. Lovely nose but softer than I expected. I have had better bottles. This is delicious but not as mind-blowing as it has been on other occasions. Great fruit. Very long. Subtle and full of breed. Fine but not great. Yet intensely flavoured.

1959   **Now–1998**

Fullish colour. Ripe, rich, ample, fleshy, a touch gamey. Certainly opulent. Fullish, lovely fruit. Soft but still vigorous. Harmony and breed here. Even – in a 1959 context – delicacy. Lovely. Still has plenty of life. Long and subtle on the finish.

1958   **Drink soon**

Medium-full. Lightening at edges. Soft nose but not without breed. A bit one-dimensional but stylish, fresh and balanced. Still fruity. Not bad at all. Positive finish.

1957   **Now–1996**

Fine colour. Not too hard. This has always been one of the most successful 1957s. A little astringent on the palate now. Good fruit, high acidity. Style here. Not too dense. Still vigorous at the end. Very good.

1955   **Drink soon**

Full colour. Mature. Good nose. Lovely old roses, old Bordeaux. Soft and ripe, loosening a bit but a fine Graves flavour to it. Very good. Medium-full body.

1953   **Now–1999**

Full colour. No undue maturity. Round but fat, lovely fruit. Great finesse on the nose. Medium-full body. Enormous breed and complexity. Great concentration of fruit but all in lace. Yet still very intense. A great wine. Still multidimensional. Lots of life.

1952   **Drink soon**

Very full colour. Good nose. Sturdier than the 1953 but not too four-square. Fullish, chocolatey, old vines, a little astringent at the end and getting a little dry and loose. Was better five years ago but still a lot of enjoyment. Fat and fruity still. And positive at the end. Very good.

1949   **Drink soon**

Good colour. No undue maturity. A little volatile acidity but great breed underneath. Fullish. Again just a little past its best, but really lovely structure and concentrated fruit. Great finesse. Long, complex. A great wine – almost.

1947   **Past its best**

Low shoulder. Old in appearance. Somewhat faded on the nose but neither maderized nor oxidized. Better on the palate. Somewhat past its best but was a fine wine once. A bottle with a better fill could still be very good.

1945   **Drink quite soon**

Full colour. Full, sturdy and rich on the nose. Masculine, austere and concentrated like all 1945s. Very good fruit. A little too much structure for its balance and fruit; too much backbone and not enough flesh. Generous nevertheless. Rich, classic Cabernet in flavour. Very Pauillac. Fine but I prefer the 1949 and 1953.

1934   **Drink quite soon**

Full colour. Fresh on the nose still. Lovely Cabernet. Fullish and ripe. Still vigorous and full of fruit. This is a little four-square but has more suppleness at the end. Good positive finish. Long. Complex. Fine.

1929   **Drink quite soon**

Lightish colour and a bit cloudy. A touch dry and inky on the nose. Yet sweet, soft, very ripe and lovely on the palate. Marvellous fruit. This is complex and has real breed. Long and great quality. Very positive still despite the colour and the nose.

1928   **Will still keep**

Good colour. Touch of lead pencils on the nose.

Full, rich, mocha chocolatey. This is a splendid example. Big, hot, rich, cooked fruit, chocolate fudge cake flavours. A wonderful wine. A real original. Voluptuous and almost over-ripe. Bags of life still. Very good grip.

1926   **Past its best**

Decidedly old colour. Rather maderized on the nose. A bit of volatile acidity. Past its best but was a fine wine once. You can see the breed.

1924   **Drink soon**

Vigorous colour. Slightly dumb on the nose. A touch earthy on the palate. With quite high acidity. A little lumpy now. But not, indeed never, I would suggest, either the lovely soft fruit of the 1929 or the great ripe originality of the 1928. Yet healthy, lively, improved in the glass. Lovely finish. Fine.

1916   **Drink up**

Good colour. Fragrant, round, soft and elegant on the nose. Reasonable substance and vigour. Has fruit and grip. Still plummy. Shows very well. Not past its best by any means.

1898   **Drink up**

Fine clear colour. A little age, but intriguing nose. The fruit has dried a little. On the palate the wine is ripe, complex, has a fruit salad flavour and no sign of undue age. A lot of breed here. Held up in the glass reasonably well.

1887   **Drink up**

Medium colour. No undue age. Silky and lacey. Soft, boiled-sweet nose. Turkish delight in fact. Ripe; the acidity shows a little; but fresh and soft and complex. Still alive. Fascinating. But faded quite fast.

1867   **Will still last**

Lightening colour but still alive. Complex vigorous nose. Elements of mountain herbs, angelica and coffee beans. Even cheese. Butterscotch and other things (candied peel as it evolved). Figs said someone. This is a great wine. Fullish in body. Complex and still very vigorous. No undue astringency or high acidity. Brilliant.`

LAGRANGE

For more than two generations, as Bernard Ginestet evocatively puts it, the reputation of the wine of Château Lagrange was 'in quarantine'. You could express it more cruelly: for a *troisième cru classé* the quality was a disgrace. Of all the modern vintages only the 1955, the 1959 and the 1962 have any merit. Here was a large property with an ancient and illustrious history which had fallen on hard times and was under-achieving with such a consistency that no one would even consider it. It was tragic.

That the saviour of Lagrange should have been the Japanese wine and spirits giant Suntory should not come as a total surprise. Firstly, Suntory have got the resources. A huge sum of money would obviously be required to turn things round after all the years of neglect; and Suntory are one of the world's largest wine and spirit enterprises. Secondly, they are not unfamiliar with the world of fine wine. They are the largest importers and distributors of French wine in Japan. They are also vineyard owners. At the foot of Mount Fuji, planted with a dozen of Europe's top grape varieties, lie the 160 hectares of the Yamanashi vineyard. For some inscrutable reason the produce thereof, instead of some confidently Japanese name, hides under the label of Château Lion. (I have not had occasion to sample it, but Michael Broadbent tells me it is Climens-like, and surprisingly good.) Suntory even have their own research laboratory for oenology and ampelography. They had also already made a foray, albeit unsuccessful, into the Gironde before they took over Lagrange in 1984.

The Suntory take-over and subsequent renovation of Château Lagrange has been done with tact, taste and intelligence. And the resulting transformation in the wine's quality has been swift and dramatic. For the first time in a lifetime we can begin to understand why Lagrange should have had such a high reputation in the eighteenth century, and why it should have been classed as a third growth in 1855.

HISTORY

Legend has it that the land on which the Lagrange vineyard now stands once formed part of the manor of a local order of the Knights Templars. One night in 1307 the entire French complement of the order was arrested on the instructions of Philip the Fair and five years later the order was dissolved by Pope Boniface (at which point the Grand Master of the Templars placed a curse on each of them; as his spell commanded they were both dead within the year). The land then passed to the De Cours family, *seigneurs* of Pauillac and Lagrange. Vineyard plots which are still today known as La Chapelle and L'Hôpital give some credence to this Templar story.

In the early eighteenth century Lagrange belonged to the Baron de Brane of Mouton. It is likely that it was De Brane who transformed the land into an important vineyard. By mid-century the wine makes its first appearance, as Brane-Saint-Julien, and (this was prior to the emergence of Gruaud-Larose) was firmly established as the second most important growth in the commune after Léoville, fetching 800 *livres* a *tonneau*. One of the subsequent owners was M. Arbouet de La Bernède. It may have been Arbouet who constructed the main part of the present-day château, an elegant building in the Louis XVI style. Until not so long ago there was a bell with the date 1771 (and the title *Seigneur de Pauillac et Lagrange*). Was this the date the château was completed? It was as Arbouet or Brane-Arbouet that the wine first appears as a third growth in the unofficial classifications of the period. Jefferson ranks it alongside Calon-Ségur, Mouton, 'Pontette' (Langoa), Issan and Marquis-de-Terme.

In 1796 Lagrange was purchased by Jean-Valère Cabarrus, shortly to become a Count of the First Empire and Napoleon's finance minister in Spain. Cabarrus was father of the brilliant, beautiful and promiscuous Thérèse, Mme Tallien, said to have saved many from the guillotine. (One of her lovers was the financier Jules Ouvrard, at one time owner of both Clos-Vougeot and the Domaine de la Romanée-Conti.)

Cabarrus is said to have considerably enlarged the area under vines. He also acquired a property further north in Saint-Seurin and his name is still commemorated in the title of this estate: Château Pontoise-Cabarrus. Sadly, in 1820 he constructed a large Italianate tower at one end of the classic eighteenth-century facade of the château. It makes a complete nonsense of the sober elegance of the original edifice.

The next owner was the rather mysterious John Lewis Brown: he who gave his name to Château Cantenac-Brown, another third growth. Brown was a Bordeaux merchant and was related by marriage to Jacques Boyd. The two bought and expanded a domaine in Cantenac in the early part of the nineteenth century. Brown then bought Lagrange from Cabarrus in 1832 – it cost him 650,000 francs – and continued the developments of his predecessor. From this period can be dated most of the present day *chais*, now considerably refurbished if not replaced.

But Brown obviously over-reached himself. In 1842 he sold Lagrange to Charles-Marie-Tanneguy, Comte Duchâtel, for 775,000 francs, and the following year the Cantenac domaine was split up. It would seem that his bank foreclosed on him, for it was they who were to become owners of part of the Cantenac estate.

Duchatel, like Cabarrus, was a minister of state, this time for Louis-Philippe. He entrusted the management of Château Lagrange, now one of the largest properties in the Médoc with some 120 hectares of vines in an estate totalling 300 hectares, to his bailiff, M. Galos, who was one of the first to install a proper system of drainage in a Bordeaux vineyard.

This was the zenith of the fortunes of Château Lagrange. The wine had been confirmed as a third growth in the Classification of 1855. It was large, producing 200 *tonneaux* of wine; it had one of the most up-to-date vinification installations in the area; and it was efficiently run. On his retirement Duchatel lived and entertained at the château, proudly basking in the reputation of his wine.

He was to die in the 1860s, to be succeeded first by his widow and subsequently by his son and son-in-law. This latter gentleman was the Duc de Trémouille, whose own son was eventually to succeed, through his father-in-law, to Château Margaux. Such are the almost incestuous interstices in the history of the Bordeaux estates.

Meanwhile, in 1875, Lagrange once again changed hands. The proprietors now were the Mouicy-Loucys family. Some 50 years later, having briefly belonged to the Société Immobilière des Grands Crus de France, the somewhat mysterious proprietors of Issan, Brane-Cantenac and others during the 1920s and 1930s, Lagrange passed to Manuel Cendoya, a vineyard proprietor from the Basque region of northern Spain.

Times were already hard. Lagrange had been forced to sell off a large proportion of its crop under a mass of subsidiary labels such as Château Saint-Julien, Château La Tour-du-Roi, Clos des Chartrons and others. Following the phylloxera and mildew crises and exacerbated by the First World War, the demand for fine Bordeaux had slumped. No doubt the Cendoya family had good intentions. But they were impossible to realize in the economic depression that was to follow.

Piecemeal the outlying parts of the estate were sold off, one 32-hectare parcel passing to Jean-Eugène Borie of Ducru-Beaucaillou in 1970 (Borie replanted eighteen hectares and this now produces Château Lalande-Borie), and others being acquired by Henri Martin in his creation of Château Gloria. The château was left uninhabited and was ravaged by fire in this same year.

One Cendoya succeeded another but as activity gradually ran down an aura of gloom descended on the estate. By the 1980s the property had contracted to 157 hectares, the vineyard to 50, and moreover the *encépagement* was out of proportion to be the production of fine Médoc with over 50 per cent of the vineyard planted in Merlot.

THE SUNTORY ACQUISITION

Some ten years prior to their purchase of Lagrange, Suntory made a brief and unsuccessful attempt to buy into Bordeaux. Their object then had been a modest *petit château*, Château de Caillavet. This move attracted considerable unfavourable publicity and in the end the French government decided to veto the transaction.

This time Suntory were more discreet. One of the first to be involved was Michel Delon of Château Léoville-Las-Cases. Delon was approached, in confidence, and asked for his opinion on the value and potential of the estate. He pointed out that Professor Emile Peynaud was already – I assume only marginally – involved with Lagrange, having been approached at the request of Alexis Lichine and Co. at the time when they were the property's exclusive representatives in the 1970s. I am sure Delon urged the potential new owners to make more use of the eminent *oenologue*. He also undertook to keep them appraised of any rivals who might demonstrate an emerging interest in the estate. After months of negotiation and lobbying in Paris governmental permission was approved and the contract was finally signed in November 1983. Suntory became the owner of Château Lagrange. The price paid was around 54 million francs.

Suntory's original desire was to entrust the administration of Lagrange to Michel Delon. When he refused – though he continues to take an active, paternal interest – he and Peynaud proposed the name of Marcel Ducasse.

MARCEL DUCASSE AND THE RENAISSANCE OF CHÂTEAU LAGRANGE

Marcel Ducasse was born in the Hautes-Pyrénées in 1943. He studied physics and chemistry at Bordeaux University and passed his diploma at the Institut D'Oenologie. For thirteen years he acted as technical consultant for the Institut Technique de la Vigne et du Vin before briefly working for SOPRA, a subsidiary of ICI, specializing in viticultural and agricultural products.

At Lagrange he found himself in the enviable position of having not only Delon and Peynaud (the latter retired in 1990) to call on for assistance and advice, as well as Kenji Suzuta, himself a qualified oenologist who had been working with Suntory for close on twenty years, but the availability of almost unlimited funds for the express purpose of doing everything that was necessary to produce wine of the optimum quality. The investment was immense. On top of the original purchase price some 200 million francs has been required to restore the estate and allow it to fulfil its potential.

The first priority was the vineyard. Each parcel was examined, and the soil analyzed. The land was divided into what would produce *cru classé* quality and what would not. Half the vineyard needed to be replanted. So it was immediately necessary to create a second label, Les Fiefs (pronounced 'fee-eff')-de-Lagrange. The area under vines was increased from 50 to 113 hectares, now planted in the ratio 66 per cent Cabernet Sauvignon and 27 per cent Merlot and with 8,000 vines per hectare. A further seven hectares of Petit Verdot (bringing the percentage up to 7 per cent of the surface area) were planted in 1988. Lagrange is now the largest *cru classé* in Bordeaux. Not only were vacant sectors of the estate replanted, but some 100,000 missing vines in the existing vineyard replaced. Over-vigorous rootstocks such as S04 were disdained. Only Riparia, 101/14 and 3309 have been used. There is a crop-thinning in July each year if there proves to be too many bunches of grapes on some vines. The entire crop continues to be collected manually, with a *triage* (hand-sorting of the fruit and elimination of anything sub-standard) before the grapes enter the fermentation vats.

The buildings were in ruins. Utilizing what they could of what still existed, they built from scratch a new 2,800 square metre winery complex, essentially completed in time for the 1985 harvest. There are two large *cuviers* containing a total of 56 individually thermostatically controlled stainless-steel vats of capacities from 60 to 220 hectolitres. ('This is the sort of *cuverie* I have always dreamt of,' said Peynaud.) There are larger vats for the *assemblage*, and the wine is then matured in three adjacent barrel cellars, again temperature controlled. There is, of course, a laboratory, a bottling hall, a storage warehouse and a reception centre. They can produce their own water and power. ('No-one can make great wine without being completely self-sufficient,' says Ducasse.) And there is now a growing model village of small houses laid out in groups on the edge of the vineyard for the 70-odd staff who work on the estate. While the 1983 vintage was matured entirely in new wood, because all the old barrels Ducasse inherited had to be rejected, the *grand vin* is in principle raised in 60 per cent new wood and the second wine, Les Fiefs-de-Lagrange, is given a quarter new oak. My only sadness is that the charming, somewhat Heath-Robinsony Cendoya label, with its two giant medieval conquistadors dwarfing a representation of the château, has been replaced by something rather more mundane.

THE CHÂTEAU

The Lagrange château, the personal property of Keizo Saji, Suntory's president, has been restored, redecorated and refurbished in keeping with the original classical design. The Tuscan belvedere has also been rebuilt. The only Japanese notes are in one of the rooms on the first floor and the presence of a *teppan-yaki*, a Japanese grill-room. The park, gardens and lake, too, have been rescued from their former neglect and desolation. All this was officially opened in the presence of the Japanese ambassador and other dignitaries when Lagrange played host to the Confrèrie des Bontemps de Médoc et des Graves in September, 1986.

THE WINE

Not counting 1983, which the new team did not make, though they were responsible for the *assemblage* of the *grand vin* and its *élevage*, there have now been nine vintages of Lagrange under the Suntory ownership. We are now in a position to assess the character of the wine.

Ducasse, as he puts it, doesn't like 'thick wines'. 'I like fragrant wines. So I am against very high fermentation temperatures. 28 degrees is the maximum. And I only pump over for half an hour every day.' Currently, as most of the vines are still young, only a third of the yield is bottled as Lagrange. The rest becomes Les Fiefs.

It seems clear that we have a wine of true Saint-Julien-Pauillac structure, one that is going to take a good decade in the best vintages to reach its peak. Surrounded as it is by the vineyards of Gruaud-Larose and Talbot on the north and east, and bordering the Saint-Laurent growths of Belgrave and Camensac on the west, we would expect – and indeed we find – a wine with a mixture of the classic, firm, gravelly Cabernet Sauvignon blackcurrant, exemplified, say, in Léoville-Las-Cases, and the rather more solid, earthy, spice elements – chocolate, coffee, leather – of its immediate neighbours; all this supported but not dominated by the two-year new-wood rotation. The wine is rich, ripe, balanced and meaty: certainly good. The 1986 – for a good vintage – and the 1987 – for a poor vintage – are very good, even very good indeed. The 1990 is spectacular. It was one of my stars of the vintage. (And don't tell Suntory, but prices are still cheap.) As the new vines age it can only get better. I look forward to celebrating my eightieth birthday in 2021 with a mature fifteen-year-old Lagrange of the next millennium.

THE TASTING

The following wines were sampled in New Orleans in May 1992, on the fourth leg of the Tribute to Saint-Julien extravaganza organized by Dr Marvin Overton of Fort Worth, Texas. In 1988 I made a similar comprehensive tasting at Lagrange itself. I have added brief comments on other wines sampled on that occasion.

Optimum drinking

1991　1996–2002

Not tasted in New Orleans; April, 1992, at the château. Good colour. This has a meaty, supple nose. But there is depth underneath. Fullish and succulent for a 1991. Ripe, indeed rich. Good depth. An elegance and a good oaky base, and even an intensity which is very laudable for the vintage. Very good. Four to five years.

1990　1999–2019

Not tasted. Here is a note from the tasting at Lagrange in April, 1992. Very good colour. Full, rich, concentrated Cabernet on the nose. This has plenty of depth. Full, rich and concentrated: triumphantly fine. Very good grip. Heaps of rich ripe fruit. Long, aristocratic. A splendid example. Very long and complex.

1989　1997–2012

Fullish colour. Ripe, sturdy nose. Good backbone. Good grip. A lush wine. Medium-full, cedary. Good ripe tannins. Aromatic and fleshy. Sexy and opulent. Long. Good plus.

1988　1997–2012

Fullish colour. Fine integration of oak and fruit here. Stylish if not a blockbuster. Good acidity. Reserved. Medium to medium-full. This is dis-creet and elegant and balanced. Good personality. Good plus but not great.

1987　Drink soon

Good colour for the vintage. This is a good 1987. It has fruit and charm and no weakness. Positive. Medium body. Reasonable acidity.

1986　1997–2017

Full colour. Fat, concentrated, blackberry fruit on the nose. Plenty of depth here. This has style. Fullish, meaty, lots of depth and concentration. Very good tannins. This is a wine of class, dimension and personality. Very good plus.

1985　Now–2009

Medium-full colour. A little maturity. Ripe, gently oaky, soft fruit nose. Medium-full, open, generous, complex. A little tannin. Good acidity. A round wine with good character. Long. Attractive. Very charming.

1984　Drink soon

Good colour for the vintage. Not too hard and vegetal. Some fruit here. A little lean but not at all bad for the vintage. The 1987 is rounder and more generous though.

1983　Now–1997

Medium-full colour. Some maturity. A little

earthy on the nose. Less new oak evident than the wines today. Not the class. Ripe, open and fleshy. Plump and ripe. A little lacking grip and backbone, but quite attractive if not very elegant or very long. Not bad plus.

1982   **Now–1999**
Medium-full colour. Rather nondescript nose. Ripe and concentrated on the palate. This isn't rustic. It is accessible, fat, even rich, and it has good acidity. In fact rather better than one is entitled to expect after the wines of the 1970s. Not bad plus again.

1978   **Drink soon**
Medium to medium-full colour. Earthy nose. Mellow but not very stylish. Somewhat late bottled. Medium body. Rather high acidity and not enough fruit. Not one of those properties which had the courage to wait and harvest late, evidently. Not astringent though.

1977   **Drink up**
Medium colour. Fully mature. A little dry and astringent on the nose. More so on the palate. A bit thin and mean. Not too vegetal though.

1975   **Now–1996**
Medium-full colour. *Tabac* nose. Rather dry on the palate but at least some fruit here. Medium body. As ready as it will ever be. Not too bad. But it lacks style and concentration.

1974   **Past its best**
Wasn't too bad once. Reasonably fresh but now attenuated and dried up.

1973   **Past its best**
Sweet-sour aspects. Spurious. Unstylish.

1971   **Drink up**
Medium colour. Well mature. Vegetable soup, over-evolved nose. Attenuated palate. Medium body. The balance in fact is reasonable and the wine still long. But the flavours are coarse and cheap.

1970   **Now–1996**
Medium to medium-full colour. Mature. Ripe earthy nose. A touch of volatile acidity. There is reasonable fruit here. It is a little astringent now, and the acidity is beginning to show but there is pleasure to be had. Quite good.

1967   **Past its best**
Well-coloured. Was quite full. Now excessively acid.

1966   **Drink soon**
Medium to medium-full colour. Cedary nose, quite ripe. Earthy but fuller and richer, possibly even more stylish, than the 1970. On the palate medium-full. A bit hard. Now a little astringent. Acidity showing at the end. But quite good once.

1964   **Past its best**
Big, beefy, farmyardy. But there is ripeness and richness underneath. Now astringent. Again could have rated quite good once.

1962   **Drink soon**
(Half bottle) Good colour. Fat, generous and fruity. Quite sturdy but no undue astringency. Even stylish. Good.

1961   **Drink up**
Medium-full colour. Resin, bonfires, pinetrees on the nose. Wood-sealant flavours. Medium-full, sweet-sour, astringent. Ungainly. Very odd.

1959   **Drink soon**
Fullish colour. Oxtail soup on the nose. Full but rather astringent on the palate. Yet this is not too bad. Meaty. Some fruit. Quite rich. But essentially coarse. Now drying out.

1955   **Now–1996**
Medium-full colour. No undue maturity. Some quality on the nose. Sturdy but not too coarse or dirty. Tarry aspects. Yet quite stylish fruit. Drying up a little but with food this would be by no means beneath contempt. Fullish for a 1955. Still alive. Good.

1926   **Past its best**
(Magnum) Colour indicates that it is past its best. Full though. But now totally dried out. From Daniel Oliveros's cellar.

SAINT-PIERRE AND GLORIA

This is the story not only of the fortunes of one particular property in the Médoc and the creation of another, but of one man's ambition, obsession even, to be the proprietor of a classed growth. Both parts of the story, I am glad to say, have a happy ending. After years of neglect and division Château Saint-Pierre has been reunited and is now recognized as not only making good wine today but having done so for many, many years. After a lifetime collecting together parcels of well-situated vineyards in Saint-Julien, and making a wine – Château Gloria – which is freely acknowledged to be of classed growth quality, but also waiting in vain for a new official classification, the late Henri Martin became the owner of the neighbouring Château Saint-Pierre at the age of 78. He was unsuccessful in his efforts to get Gloria its deserved recognition. But he died on 28 February 1991, owner of a classed growth.

Saint-Pierre goes back to 1693 when, according to the château archives, it was known as Serançon or Serançan and belonged to a family called De Cheverry. In 1767 it was acquired by a M. Le Baron de Saint-Pierre, and, as was customary at the time, he gave the property and its wine his name. Whether the wine that was made on the estate at this period had any reputation is uncertain. The name does not appear in the list of leading wines Professor Pijassou has culled from the records of the brokers Tastet and Lawton in the mid-eighteenth century; neither is Saint-Pierre mentioned by Jefferson.

HISTORY

In Wilhelm Franck's *Traité sur les Vins*, there is a section entitled '*Prix des Vins Rouges dans les Bonnes Années de 1745 etc*'. In Saint-Julien, Léoville, then undivided, fetched 800 to 1000 *livres*, Gruaud *Frères*, Bergeron (Ducru-Beaucaillou) and Brassier (Beychevelle) 400 to 600 *livres*. Among the 'third growths', making 300 to 400 *livres*, are Pontet (Langoa-Barton), Delage (Talbot), Duluc (Branaire-Ducru), and also 'Clauzange' and 'Tenat'. 'Tenat' is one of the present-day constituent parts of Saint-Pierre. Was this the Saint-Pierre of the day?

Proper records begin in the years after the fall of Napoleon. By this time Saint-Pierre is firmly established as a third or fourth growth. The Lawton notebooks in 1815 comment that Saint-Pierre and its neighbour Beychevelle are '*sèveux et plus légers*' (best translated as 'vigorous but lighter') than Langoa-Barton. Paguierre, another broker, singles out Saint-Pierre as having a most distinguished bouquet. The hierarchy among the properties in Saint-Julien was then precisely the same as was enshrined in the 1855 Classification a generation later. According to André Simon in his *Bottlescrew Days*, Château Saint-Pierre than made 60 *tonneaux* which sold for £12 or so a hogshead. This was about half that of the *premiers crus*. There were then some 40 hectares under vine.

Following the death in 1796 of the Baron de Saint-Pierre the estate passed to his heirs. One of these daughters had married a M. Bontemps-Dubarry, the other a M. Dubouilh. The property remained until 1832 in indivision (legally divided but run as a single entity) and the death of Mme Dubouilh. It was then split. Half, plus the château, went to Lieutenant Colonel Bontemps-Dubarry, grandson of Saint-Pierre, the remainder to the daughters of Mme Dubouilh, Mmes Galoupeau and Roullet.

Some 32 years later, subsequent to the 1855 Classification which decreed the divided Saint-Pierre as a fourth growth, there was a further sale. Mmes Galoupeau and Roullet sold the bulk of their inheritance to their cousin Bontemps-Dubarry, a part to his daughter, wife of Oscar de Luetkens, proprietor of La Tour-Carnet, and a few minor parcels to a M. Cayx, a Saint-Laurent lawyer, and to a M. Monnereau. Both these gentlemen sold their wine for a time as Saint-Pierre, *cru bourgeois*. Cayx's wine, called also Chalet Saint-Pierre, is the nucleus of what today is Château du Glana, whose rather clumsy red-brick château, constructed by M. Cayx, lies on the main road opposite the entrance to Château Ducru-Beaucaillou.

Colonel Bontemps-Dubarry had four children, a son and three daughters. One of these ladies married Georges Kappelhoff, head of the Bordeaux *négociants* Journou Frères, Kappelhoff et Cie. She and her husband bought out two of her siblings, and so conserved the vineyard of Saint-Pierre-Bontemps-Dubarry, as it became known. Meanwhile, in 1892, Mme Oscar de Leutkens sold her smaller part of Saint-Pierre to Léon Sevaistre, a parliamentary *député* for the *département* of Eure in the Ile de France and mayor of Elbeuf. As a consequence of the phylloxera epidemic, Sevaistre had to replant most of the vineyard. Nevertheless, the wine enjoyed a high reputation. According to the Tastet and Lawton records it often fetched second growth prices – though which Saint-Pierre is not often clear. At the turn of the century the Sevaistre portion represented a quarter of the original domaine; the Kappelhoffs owned the remainder.

After the First World War a firm of Antwerp *négociants* called Van den Bussche arrived on the scene. In 1922 they bought the Sevaistre section and a year later they acquired the majority of the Bontemps-Dubarry vineyard from the widow of Georges Kappelhoff. Mme Kappelhoff retained the château itself – an elegant construction built in two stages in the nineteenth century, lying in a little park at the entrance to the village of Beychevelle – and part of the vineyard, sufficient to produce twenty tonneaux of 'Château Bontemps-Dubarry'. Château Saint-Pierre was therefore reunited, though for a time the two halves were listed separately in Cocks and Féret. Eventually the name Saint-Pierre-Bontemps withered away. Château Saint-Pierre-Sevaistre was the name under which the wine was marketed.

HENRI MARTIN AND CHÂTEAU GLORIA

We now come to the late Henri Martin, who died at the grand old age of 87 in February 1991. Martin, for over 40 years Mayor of Saint-Julien, for many years Président of the Comité Interprofessionel of Bordeaux and co-founder and Grand Master of the Commanderie du Bontemps du Médoc et des Graves, the local promotional organization for the region's wines, was one of the great personalities of twentieth-century Bordeaux. Naturally, having built up practically from scratch not only the reputation but the vineyard itself of Château Gloria, he was one of those in favour of a reclassification of the wines of Bordeaux. Equally, he was an enthusiast for the application of the benefits of modern viticulture and viticultural techniques. As joint manager of Château Latour from the time of the Pearson acquisition in 1962 until his retirement, he was responsible for the introduction of stainless-steel vats into the *cuvier* – considered revolutionary at the time. Moreover, he was a fund of background information on the wines, the personalities and the politics of the area. Martin's overriding ambition, however, was to own a classed growth.

Henri Martin was born at Château Gruaud-Larose, where his grandfather was *maître de chai*, in 1903. His father Alfred set up as a cooper in 1918, but was also, from 1921 onwards, *maître de chai* and subsequently manager of Saint-Pierre-Bontemps. In return he was allowed to use one of the *chais* for storing the barrels he made. In 1923, however, Georges Kappelhoff, owner of this part of Saint-Pierre, passed away, and his widow decided to put the estate on the market. Sadly, Alfred Martin could only raise enough money to acquire the barrel cellar he was using and a few rows of vines, and the majority of the vineyard was sold to the Van den Bussches.

Martin Senior seems to have been a man of certainty of conviction and extremes of temper. He ruled with a rod of iron and his son Henri was only one of those much in awe of him. In 1936 the local workers called a general strike. Despite being paid more than their colleagues, Martin's employees joined their brothers. The furious Alfred, in retaliation at this insult, for he was, in principle at least, a radical socialist, sold off his cooperage business and the vineyard land he had acquired and he and his son took over a local food cooperative.

The story moves to 1942. Jean-Charles Cazes, grandfather of Jean-Michel, today's *chatelain* of Lynch-Bages, was, as well as proprietor of this famous Pauillac *cru classé*, an insurance broker. And he did a little financing on the side. One day he offered Henri Martin the possibility of purchasing a six-hectare parcel of vines in Saint-Julien. 'I'll have to talk to my father about it,' said Henri, at nearly 40 years of age still very much under the thumb of his parent. But it was not an opportune time. Alfred Martin was engrossed in a card game with a group of cronies and refused to be interrupted.

After an hour's hesitation Henri decided to accept the offer. At dinner in the evening, when he announced what he had done, Alfred hit the roof. 'How on earth do you think you are going to find the money to pay for these vines?' he thundered. Next morning, however, the father had cooled down somewhat; and after he had seen the terrain for himself he agreed to go into partnership with his son. Château Gloria – the name comes for a piece of land in the village of Beychevelle where the Martin family house was constructed – was born.

The first of what was to be a number of additions to the Gloria *vignoble* occurred a couple of years later. Henri Martin was driving Armand Achille-Fould, owner of Beychevelle, to Arcachon in his food-cooperative van. On the way they passed an outlying piece of the Beychevelle vineyard and Martin persuaded Achille-Fould to sell it to him.

A trend had been set. After the Second World War, Henri Martin wound up the food co-operative business and started enlarging the vineyard. From the original six hectares of vines he built up a domaine of 48 hectares, increasing production from 20 *tonneaux* to 120 or more. Often at second hand, Martin acquired a fairly sizeable chunk of Saint-Pierre-Bontemps and by purchase or exchange bits of others from Gruaud-Larose, Léoville-Poyferré, Léoville-

Barton, Lagrange, Ducru-Beaucaillou and even Duhart-Milon, who owned some land in the commune of Saint-Julien. It was a time when many proprietors were trying to rationalize their vineyard holdings and make them more of a homogeneous entity. Small parcels were often available for swapping or direct sale. Slowly but surely, based almost entirely on classed growth vineyards, the property of Château Gloria began to emerge. From the late 1950s onward, the reputation of the wine grew as well. Eventually Martin began to have a decisive effect on the Bordeaux market and the price of its wines, particularly as Château Gloria was often the first 'name' to appear as the campaign for the new vintage opened.

Château Gloria was not all Martin acquired. In addition to two second labels – that bottled as Haut-Beychevelle-Gloria, originally a monopoly of Gilbey's of Loudenne, seems in my experience to be a better wine that Château Peymartin – there is Château Bel-Air from across the commune boundary in Cussac-Fort-Médoc.

ATTEMPTS TO BECOME A CLASSIFIED GROWTH

As the reputation of Gloria grew, so, in parallel, did demands for a reclassification of the old 1855 order. As proponents such as Alexis Lichine were to point out, many properties were not only considerably different in size, but occupied land quite different from that which they had possessed in the mid-nineteenth century; more than a few produced wine inferior to their classification; more produced wine which was better; and others did not exist then and now produced wine of classed-growth quality. Like, well, like Château Gloria.

Martin was ambitious. The meek son of the 1930s had become a much-respected château proprietor and local man of influence. To prove that you made classed growth wine you had to sell it for classed growth prices. This he was able to do without difficulty. He was, not surprisingly, a firm supporter of reclassification. In 1966 Gloria had been appointed a *cru bourgeois supérieur*. This Martin considered but a stop gap. He made it plain that inclusion among the classed growths was his goal.

Sadly, all the efforts of the late 1960s and early 1970s came to nothing. The vested interests of those nervous of demotion carried the day. That the committee set up to revise 1855 got as far as producing a proposal, which included Gloria and excluded others, was an open secret. But it was not to be. Nevertheless, as late as 1978, when the *crus bourgeois* were again reclassified, Martin refused to let Château Gloria be included, lest this should preclude the wine being considered for elevation to a higher rank. Gloria at present is merely AC Saint-Julien.

But we must return to Saint-Pierre . . .

THE PURCHASE OF SAINT-PIERRE

By the end of the 1970s the situation in Saint-Julien consisted of three strands. On the one hand there was Château Saint-Pierre (Sevaistre), owned by the Van den Bussches and operated by Paul Castelein, a Belgian who had married a Mlle Van den Bussche. They operated from the old château of Saint-Louis-de-Bosq, situated west of that of Gloria, and a name used as a second wine. Opposite the large Saint-Julien bottle, a famous landmark on the bend of the road as it straightens towards the north after passing Château Beychevelle and Château Branaire-Ducru, was the original Saint-Pierre château, occupied by Mme Kappelhoff. Adjacent, across the road which leads down to Gruaud-Larose and Saint-Laurent lay Château Gloria. In 1981 Martin bought the château of Saint-Pierre and the following year he acquired the name and the vineyards from the Castelein family. He was a classed-growth proprietor at last.

RATIONALIZATION

Subsequently, in order to rationalize what were now, in effect, two separate wine-making installations, and perhaps to help finance the deal, Martin himself disposed of part of the combined *chais* and sections of the much-parcelled combined vineyard. Five hectares of vineyards and the Saint-Louis château and *chais* were sold to Jean-Eugène Borie of Château Ducru-Beaucaillou. This is now the premises where Château Lalande-Borie is made and matured. Another two hectares lying adjacent to Gruaud-Larose were bought by Jean Cordier. However, none of the old Gloria vineyards, so I have been assured, have been transferred to Saint-Pierre. They remain as they were prior to 1981. Finally, the Saint-Pierre château has been renovated and is now occupied by Martin's daughter Françoise and her husband Jean-Louis Triaud, who is in charge of making the wines.

THE VINEYARDS

Most of the Saint-Pierre vineyard lies near the old Saint-Louis château and on either side of a second, subsidiary road which runs parallel to the main D2 from the back of the village of Beychevelle towards Saint-Julien. Some seventeen hectares now produce Château Saint-Pierre. These are planted roughly in the ratio 70 per cent Cabernet Sauvignon, 20 per cent Merlot and 10 per cent Cabernet Franc, plus a few plots of Petit Verdot, and produce about 90 *tonneaux*.

The Gloria vineyard consists of three main parcels. One of these lies up near the Pauillac boundary, inland and roughly opposite the vineyards of the Batailleys and Pichon-Lalande. Another is closer to Beychevelle. A third is on the western side of the village. There are 48 hectares, planted in the ratio: 65 per cent Cabernet Sauvignon, 25 per cent Merlot and 5 each Cabernet Franc and Petit Verdot.

THE WINES

The wines are made in the recently extended Gloria *chais* which once belonged to Saint-Pierre-Bontemps. They are given a long maceration with the skins in a battery of enamelled-steel vats and then matured partly in new wood, partly in large wooden *foudres*.

Why the *foudres*? These are rare in the Bordeaux area. I posed the question to Jean-Louis Triaud. 'If you use new wood entirely you will over-oak the wine,' says Triaud. 'So what then do you do with the one third or so of your wine which you are not going to put into new oak? Some use older barrels; some keep it in stainless steel; I prefer the *foudre*. I find it combines the retention of freshness and fruit I would get from keeping the wine in stainless steel and the gentle oxidation the wine will benefit from if it stays in small wood.'

Today Saint-Pierre is aged one third in *foudre* and two thirds in new oak, in a brand-new barrel cellar; for Gloria the per centage of new oak is less, about 40 per cent.

Selection is a major concern of Jean-Louis Triaud. He could, he says, produce 90 *tonneaux* of Saint-Pierre a year. In fact he usually produces 50. The rest is declassified into one of the joint second wines.

As I have said at the outset, Saint-Pierre has produced a fine wine for a number of years, well prior to the Martin takeover. It has always puzzled me that it was not more widely bought, nor more widely recognized as a high-quality product. That it was not better known on the English market is doubly surprising. Just about every British wine merchant, I would imagine, would pay an annual visit to Peter Sichel, in order not only to buy some Angludet and stake a claim for some Palmer, but because Peter is a wizard at *petits châteaux* and a delightful and very knowledgeable man about Bordeaux and its wines. For years Peter Sichel followed Château Saint-Pierre (Sevaistre). I myself bought most vintages from 1970 onwards. The wine was excellent: full, richly old-viney, plump and succulent; good value – and consistent. I don't remember a disappointing vintage. A letter a 1987 issue of *Decanter* from a reader who had analyzed marks given by various authors of articles on claret vintages in the magazine, showed the high position of Château Saint-Pierre. Within the wines of the 1855

Classification Saint-Pierre follows the first growths, Palmer, Las-Cases, Ducru, Pichon-Lalande, Cos d'Estournel and Beychevelle, ahead of Issan, Grand-Puy-Lacoste, Gruaud-Larose, Léoville-Barton, Lynch-Bages and many other illustrious names. This, as the author of the letter freely admitted, was not exactly either comprehensive or statistically sound, as some vintages were not covered and several châteaux only appeared once or twice; but it was at least an indication.

Gloria too is – or at least was – more than just a reliable wine. Throughout the 1960s (my experience of older wines is scant) it consistently produced wine which was not merely of classed-growth quality but better than many of what should have been its peers in the commune. The wine was elegant, balanced and of medium weight, with an admirable complexity of fruit. And it also lasted well.

And yet . . . and yet I must confess to a slight element of disappointment with both of the wines that have been produced since the Martin/Triaud Saint-Pierre takeover in 1981. The price of Saint-Pierre has risen. But why indeed should Saint-Pierre not sell for the same price as Talbot and Branaire, even if it cannot command that of Beychevelle? But the creamy-old-vine element I used to admire seems no more. And Gloria seems to have lost its flair. Good the wines certainly are. But they are no longer as good as they were. Yet the 1989 and 1990 Saint-Pierres promise well. And the 1991s – when they used their new cellar extension for the first time – are by no means disasters. Emmanuel, Jean-Louis Triaud's son, is a trained *oenologue*, and joined his father at the beginning of 1993, following his military service. Let us hope that two heads will be better than one, and the disappointments of the mid-1980s are just an aberration.

THE TASTING

The following wines of Château Gloria and almost all of those of Saint-Pierre were sampled in New York in May 1992, at a tasting organized by Marvin Overton of Fort Worth and hosted by Château and Estates. The notes on the 1973 and 1966 Saint-Pierres come from a previous vertical tasting set up by Bill Baker of Reid Wines in 1986.

GLORIA

Optimum drinking

1991   1995–1999
Reasonable structure and depth, if not a great deal of richness, but the tannins seem quite ripe and the wine has length.

1990   1997–2007
Corked. Good richness, depth and vigour. Better than the 1989 in my experience.

1989   1995–2002
Reasonable colour. Soft, ripe, quite spicy nose. A little astringent on the palate. The tannins are a bit lean and herbaceous and the wine lacks freshness and zip. Medium body. Quite good.

1988   1996–2004
Medium-full colour. Fresh but a little unforthcoming on the nose. There is a hardness here and a lack of style, elegance and generosity. On the palate there is quite good Cabernet fruit but a lack of real richness and depth. A bit four-square. Quite good.

1987   **Drink up**
Reasonable colour. A bit weedy and vegetal on the nose. Quite pleasant on the palate. But a bit superficial. Hints of impending astringency now. Medium body.

1986   1996–2006
Good colour. Closed, charcoaly, plummy nose. Fullish, tannic, good grip. Quite ripe but not really as rich or as concentrated as others in the commune. What it lacks is real sweetness and personality. Quite good at best.

1985   **Now–2003**
Good colour for the vintage. Just a hint of approaching maturity. A little herbaceous on the nose. Lacks charm and finesse. On the palate this is medium to medium-full-bodied, with a little tannin and good grip. The balance is here. But the wine lacks personality.

1984   **Drink up**
Reasonable colour. Elements of mint on the nose. Also old tea underneath. Not bad for the vintage. Now getting astringent. But never too lean or austere.

1983   **Now–1997**
Medium colour. Now mature. Soft, evolved
nose. Plump and fruity but a lack of grip and
backbone. Medium body. Lacks real concentration and depth. Elements of attenuation.

1982   **1995–2002**
Medium-full colour. Just about mature. A certain
herbal element on the nose here. Can't take a
shine to this. Touch of caramel but rather lumpy.
This lacks breed and it doesn't have the concentration of this vintage. Disappointing. Dense.

1981   **Now–1998**
Medium colour. Fully mature. Light to medium,
pleasant nose. Good fruit. Not as lumpy as 1978
and 1979. Medium body. Some fruit. Ripe.
Good grip for the vintage. Better personality and
balance than the 1983.

1979   **Now–1996**
Good colour. Still vigorous. Slightly lumpy and
sweaty on the nose. A little astringency. Rather
herbaceous again. Medium body. This is unexciting. Lacks class. Lacks attraction. Quite good.
Finishes lean and hard, but better than the 1978.

1978   **Now–1996**
Less colour than the 1979. Fully mature. Can't
get a lot of style on the nose. Lacks richness too.
Pedestrian, herbaceous. Medium body. The fruit
lacks real ripeness. Slightly hard. Not bad at best.

1976   **Now–1997**
Medium-full colour. Colour a little brown.
Smoky, drying up nose. An unglamorous wine,
slightly over-ripe, yet not astringent. A little tarty
but better than the 1975. More supple. Reasonable grip. Medium body. Good.

1975   **Now–1997**
Medium-full colour. Slightly hard and unforthcoming on the nose. A touch astringent. Medium-full. Tannic. Ripe but without grace or
charm. Quite good at best. And I don't think it
will soften.

1971   **Drink soon**
Medium colour. Fully mature. Somewhat weak
on the nose but better on the palate. This has, in
a slightly lean way, good stylish Cabernet fruit.
Ripe but austere. Medium body. Good grip.
Good for the vintage.

1970   **Now–2000 plus**
Good colour. Still vigorous. Rich, chocolatey
nose. Coffee beans as well. Fullish, meaty, still
with a little tannin. Slightly over-macerated perhaps; it has got a 1964 touch to it. A touch rigid,
but good richness underneath. Good.

1967   **Now–1996**
Medium to medium-full colour. Still vigorous.

Soft, round, ripe nose. No undue age. Plump
and fruity. This has held up well. Classy Cabernet fruit. Very Saint-Julien. Good grip. No sign
of drying up. Very good.

1966   **Drink soon**
Medium to medium-full colour. No more than
1967. Nose has lightened up a bit. On the palate
it is a little attenuated. Stylish, medium-bodied
and fruity once, but now a little past its best.

1964   **Now–1997**
Good colour. Quite a four-square nose. Full and
rich on the palate. Very good old-viney fruit.
This has vigour and grip. It is not too old, and
has style and depth. Not as four-square at the end
as at the beginning. Very good.

1962   **Drink soon**
Good colour. Still vigorous. Round, slight cinnamon spice on the nose. This shows a bit more
age than the 1964, but is richer and more complex. It is slightly sweeter and certainly more
voluptuous. Fullish. Good acidity. But a touch
of astringency now. Very good.

1961   **Now–2001**
Lovely full rich colour. Splendid nose. Pauillac-y
rather than Saint-Julien. Rich, profound very
concentrated Cabernet fruit. Full body. Lively,
marvellous depth. Very lovely, very 1961. Fine.
Bags of life still.

1960   **Past its best**
Medium colour. Perhaps a little old now. The
nose is a bit faded. There is – or was – plenty of
quality here but it is now a bit old. There was
ripeness, balance, grip and interest. Certainly a
good 1960. Ample proof of the classed-growth
quality it made even at this time.

1948   **Drink soon**
Good colour. No undue maturity. Slightly dense
on the nose. Showing a little age. Fullish and tannic, a little clenched. High acidity. But not too
hard. Certainly good. But typically 1948.

SAINT-PIERRE

1991   **1995–2001**
Medium colour. Ripe, quite lush nose. Good
fruit. Good oak. This is really quite concentrated. Very good fruit and depth. A real success.

1990   **1998–2015**
Medium-full colour. Slightly unforthcoming on
the nose. But good fruit underneath. Medium-
full, very ripe fruit, old-vine concentration. Ripe
tannins. Good grip. Voluptuous and lush. Fine
finish. Very good plus.

1989   **1996–2008**
Medium-full colour. Elegant, soft, balanced and

with plenty of backbone but, it seems, not a great deal of depth. Good oak base, lush, classy almost over-ripe attack. It doesn't have the grip and therefore the class of the 1990 but it is a good 1989. Medium to medium-full.

1988   1998–2012
Medium-full colour. A little hard on the nose. But good Cabernet fruit underneath. Medium-full, slightly austere. But ripe tannins and quite concentrated fruit. Above all good acidity. Will improve as it softens. Good plus.

1987   **Drink soon**
Medium colour. Rather vegetal on the nose. But better on the palate. Some fruit. Pleasant if a little rigid.

1986   1996–2004
Medium-full colour. A little bit dense on the nose. Yet concentrated and rich as well. Medium-full. As much astringent as tannic. A bit disappointing and a little lumpy. Tannins don't seem very ripe. Quite good for the vintage. A bit dry.

1985   Now–2002
Medium-full colour. A little weedy on the nose. Like the 1986 this is a disappointment. The wine lacks real fruit. And it doesn't have breed or balance either. Lumpy. Quite good at best.

1984   **Drink soon**
Good colour. Herbaceous nose. Now getting weedy. Medium body. A little astringent but the fruit is reasonable.

1983   Now–2000
Medium to medium-full colour. No maturity. Ripe, open, evolved nose. Good fruit here. Medium body. Again a lack of real grip. Soft and fruit and accessible. Quite stylish, but a lack of real concentration and breed. Only good.

1982   Now–2009
Medium-full colour. Rich, full, fat nose. Good concentration here. An 'old-fashioned' wine. Full, concentrated, tannic. Backward. This is a very good 1982. Lots of lovely rich Cabernet fruit. Very good. Much better than the 1986.

1981   Now–2000
Medium to medium-full colour. Good vigour for the vintage. Stylish, ripe, complex nose. Now round and mature. Medium-full, very stylish. Very good grip. This is an impressive bottle. Long, complex. Lovely.

1979   Now–1997
Good colour, less evolved than the 1978. Ripe, rich nose. Straight old vine Cabernet. Medium-full. Just a little four-square, but good grip and depth. Would be better with food. Just a little over-macerated. Good plus.

1978   Now–2000
Medium-full mature colour. A little old-fashioned on the nose. Extracted, tannic, slightly lumpy, but rich and balanced. A fullish wine with a lot of fruit and depth. Almost creamy. A bit too structured perhaps but very fine concentration. Long and very good indeed. But a wine for food.

1975   Now–1999
Medium-full mature colour. Full, ripe, rich and not a bit too tannic on the nose. Good grip here. Good old vine richness. Not the concentration and grip of the 1978 – or the size – but good without a doubt.

1973   **Drink soon**
Very good colour; full, barely mature. Good for the vintage though on nose and palate now showing signs of lightening up. Full of rich Cabernet fruit, quite fat, not robust. Medium body. Drink it now while it is at its best.

1970   **Drink up (this bottle)**
Very good colour. Slightly old on the nose. The fruit having dried out just a little. I have had better bottles than this. It shows a little age. Lovely ripe fruit but it is now fading. This is a very good 1970.

1969   **Past its best**
Old brown colour. Old but not decayed nose. A bit astringent. High acidity. Past its best but not at all bad once.

1966   **Drink soon**
Medium-full colour, now mature. A fully mature wine, with a good chocolatey, leather, cigar-boxy background underneath the Cabernet fruit. Rich, mellow, a certain amount of acidity on the finish which is characteristic of this vintage. Not as exciting as the 1970 but good nevertheless.

1962   **Drink soon**
Good colour. Plenty of vigour still. A curate's egg on the nose. Very interesting fruit and balance but an element of decay as well. Now a bit old, this bottle, but there is (or was) style, complexity and fruit here. I have had better bottles. A very good 1962 in its prime.

1961   Now–1996
Fuller colour than the 1962 but less vigour. Full, ripe, rich, meaty and old-fashioned. Full, a little four-square, quite tannic. A little dense. But good.

1959   **Drink soon**
Full, vigorous colour. This, sadly, is a little old and faded on the nose. Didn't fall away in the glass, though. Rich and fat, even on the attack. A little astringent, and a little decayed at the end. But there was quality here.

TALBOT

North of Gruaud-Larose, isolated in a remote sea of vines, lies Château Talbot. With 109 hectares under vine, it is the largest of the classed growths. Only Lascombes, boasting 94 hectares, comes anywhere near it in size. Like Gruaud-Larose, Talbot is a Cordier wine. But unlike it, it still belongs to the family of Jean Cordier. Until recently it was made and marketed by Cordier the *négociants*, now part of the Compagnie de Suez group, but in late 1991 Jean Cordier decided on independence.

Talbot is said to take its name from John Talbot, Earl of Shrewsbury, Commander of the English expeditionary force defeated at the battle of Castillon in 1453.

The English had been fighting a rearguard action in south-west France against the recently revivified French army, under the personal control of Charles VII, and by 1451 had been driven out of Bordeaux and reduced to a garrison at Lesparre in the northern Médoc. Talbot, an old man already in his eighties, was despatched by Henry VI, and was welcomed by the town of Bordeaux – who knew well where their best markets lay – with open arms. After some initial success he was lured out to Castillon, the other side of Saint-Emilion, and persuaded to do battle without waiting for the arrival of his main army, with results fatal for both the English and himself. He is said to have gone into battle unarmed as a result of a pact given to the French for his release from captivity on a previous occasion (In 1449 he had been captured at Rouen by Charles de Valois.) The date of the battle of Castillon, 17 July 1453, should be engraved on the heart of every claret-lover. It represents the end of English hegemony over the greatest wine area in the world.

The routed troops held out in Bordeaux for a while, but were eventually pursued through the Médoc in the late autumn. Legend has it they sailed for England from the quay at Château d'Issan, taking a large amount of the 1453 vintage with them.

HISTORY

There is no evidence that John Talbot ever owned any property in Bordeaux, let alone in the Médoc, yet his name persists in many locations in the area, and his exploits, as the tragic saviour of the city, survive in medieval texts. In Gascon patois he is described as '*Lo noble et poyssant* (noble and powerful) *senhor mossen Johan, Comte de Cherosberi, Senhor de Talbot*'.

In the mid-eighteenth-century map produced by Belleyme, the name 'Talabot' (*sic*) can be found in Saint-Julien, and the earliest records of the property describe it as this or as Delage, from an owner at the end of the seventeenth century.

The owners in more modern times were the Marquises d'Aux de Lescout, a family originally from the Armagnac, and they occupied the property for nearly two centuries during which time it was known as Talbot d'Aux. Originally, the yield was far smaller than the current level, averaging around 100 *tonneaux* throughout the nineteenth century.

After the death of one Marquis in 1872, Talbot passed to his son Arnaud, and, when he himself died in 1884, to his three children. In 1899 it was put up for auction and bought by Monsieur A. Claverie, who was to retain it for nearly twenty years before it was bought by the Cordiers in 1918.

THE VINEYARD

The estate covers 160 hectares of which 109 are under vines. The vineyard was doubled in size in the first eight decades of this century, and has been increased by a further 25 hectares since 1981. Surprisingly, for such a large estate, the vineyard is in *un seul tenant*, in one piece inland from Langoa above the road which runs from the village of Saint-Julien inland to Saint-Laurent-et-Benon.

The geology is similar to that of Gruaud, a gravel and sand mixture, mixed with clay in parts, on a subsoil of the hard iron-rich sandstone known as *alios*, but the elevation is higher, and the vineyard is on a plateau which faces both east and west. The *encépagement* is little different: 75 per cent Cabernet Sauvignon, 5 per cent Cabernet Franc, 18 per cent Merlot and 2 per cent Petit Verdot. Untypically, a little patch (six hectares) of clay soil is planted with Sauvignon and a small quantity of white wine, Caillou Blanc, is produced. Hitherto, this has been vinified in stainless steel following a period of skin contact, and has not seen wood at any stage. The Cordier team is now experimenting with fermenting it in oak. It is a light, clean, crisp wine, intended for early drinking.

THE CHÂTEAU AND THE *CHAIS*

The Talbot château lies in the centre of its vineyard, within a little park, and surrounded by the cellars which have recently been extensively enlarged and reorganized. Unlike Gruaud-Larose, this is a home, not a rather sad anonymous shell with a few sticks of furniture. The building is in the Directoire style, dating from Napoleonic times, and is covered in creeper. It looks as if it was built in two stages. It is now the family home of Jean Cordier. A new fermentation cellar was constructed in 1987 and enlarged in 1989. Within it there are 25 172-hectolitre wooden vats, specially commissioned from the barrel-makers Seguin-Moreau. In addition, there is a battery of enamelled-steel tanks dating from 1985. In contrast to most *cru classé* practice, the wine of Talbot used to be kept in these large vats after the malolactic fermentation. Only after several months was it racked into barrel. This practice is changing now, though some of the *grand vin* and all of the second wine is still matured in *foudre*. There is a large *chai de première année* (30 per cent new wood each year) and three small cellars for the second-year wine. Like the wine of Gruaud, Talbot is not filtered.

THE WINE

Like Gruaud, Talbot has changed its style during the 1980s. It used to be somewhat solid, peppery in its youth; four-square, and what the French call *sauvage*, rather aggressive, lacking grace and charm. It took a long time to mature. It was dependable, 'quite good', but it was rarely a wine of great depth and finesse. It is now perceptibly richer, potentially more elegant. And still the reliable wine it always has been. While I have to say I am unenthusiastic about both the 1990 and the 1989 (see Vintage Assessments section), there are few, if any, other poor vintages of Talbot, and the off-vintages are often surprisingly good. The second wine is Connétable de Talbot.

THE TASTING

This is an amalgam of two tastings. The younger vintages were sampled in Bordeaux in January 1990. Most of the older wines come from a tasting in London in April 1991.

Optimum drinking

1988   **1996–2006**

Full colour. Ripe, ample, fullish but somewhat adolescent nose. This needs a racking (the vintage was in the process of being fined) and is not on form. Medium body. Somewhat raw and stalky-resiny. Lacks a bit of charm. But best to defer judgement.

1987   **Now–1997**

Medium to medium-full colour. Good for the vintage. This was still recovering from the bottling when I tasted it in January, 1990, and shows a little dry on the nose. But there is substance and fruit underneath. Light-medium body. Not a bit weedy or mean. Good oak. Reasonable fruit and grip. Good for the vintage.

1986   **1996–2012**

Fullish colour. Firm, closed, Cabernet nose. Good depth here. Medium-full body. Good ripe tannin supporting fine rich fruit and balanced with good acidity. This is a fine result. And it is both less aggressive and more elegant than most youthful Talbots. Good to very good.

1985   **Now–2006**

Fullish colour. Similar to the 1986 but a little more developed. A lighter nose than the 1986. Less tannin. More supple. The fruit is more apparent. This is softer, more accessible wine. Medium body, a little tannin. Good ripe, amicable attack, but not quite the vigour and complexity on the follow through to be rated more than 'good'. Reasonable balance though.

1984   **Now–1999**

Very good colour for the vintage. Very Cabernet on the nose and not at all without fruit. Meaty and still youthful. This is really very good for this unexciting vintage. Touch of oak. Good fruit. Even quite ample and complex. Good finish. A great success.

1983   **Now–2009**

Good fullish colour. Ripe, smoky nose. Good fruit. Not aggressive. More accessible than I had expected. Medium-full, ripe, attractive, balanced, with a gentle base of oak. This has style and more depth and complexity (as well as more body and vigour) than the 1985. Good long finish. Has charm. Good to very good.

1982   **1995–2015**

Full colour. Rich, opulent nose. Quite a lot more tannin than the 1983. More backward. Fine ripe fruit. Fullish, still some tannin. Still youthful. The finish is better than the attack, as it often is with young wines in a big vintage. Rich and concentrated on the follow through. Very Saint-Julien in flavour. Good balance. This again is a success. Long and fat and ample on the finish.

1981   **Now–1997**

Good fullish colour for the vintage. No sign of maturity. This is back to the old style of Talbot, a little solid and hard and aggressive on the nose. Medium body. A little dominated by the tannins which are a bit dry. Too stewed and vin de presse-y. Yet reasonable fruit underneath. Not bad but lacks charm.

1979   **Now–1998**

Fullish, slightly aggressive, a little herbaceous. But there is fruit here, and some fat, if not really a great deal of finesse. Good though. Will keep well.

1978   **Now–2000**

Medium-full, mature colour. Seems less alive than the 1975. The nose is at the same time solid, but rich and mature. There is depth here. This is just about ready, and it shows better than I expected. Medium-full, a little tough still on the attack but there is a fine rich Saint-Julien finish sustained by good acidity. Vigorous. Good.

1976   **Drink soon**

Quite a full colour. Brown at the rim. Rather too solid and too dry. Lacks fruit and class. Unexceptional.

1975   **Now–1998**

Medium-full, mature colour. But less brown than the 1978. This is also solid on the nose, like the 1978, but it is drier and the fruit certainly seems less rich and ample and less concentrated. Improved on aeration though. Medium-full body. Yet the fruit still didn't have the richness of the 1978. The tannins are rather drier and the net result is the usual 1975 astringency. Hard to enthuse over.

1970   **Now–1997**

Medium-full, mature colour. Once again solid on the nose. Medium-full body again. This seems rather anonymous. There is some fruit, reasonable acidity. The residue of a rather firm, tannic structure. But it doesn't sing.

1967   **Drink soon**

Good fresh colour still. This has no great finesse but is quite substantial and still holding up. Fruity, ample. Pleasant.

1966   **Now–2000 plus**

Good colour, less brown than the 1970. The nose has more style and better balance than the 1970. Rather good, in fact. A typical Cabernet-based Saint-Julien; more vigorous than some. This is a much better wine than the 1970. Medium-full, rich, ample, concentrated, vigorous and

full of character. Even improved in the glass. Very fine finish. Very Saint-Julien. Lots of future here. Very good.

1962   **Now–1998**

A good example. Quite substantial, and with plenty of vigour. An ample, fruity wine. Generous, long on the palate. Very good.

1961   **Now–2000**

Fullish colour. Fine ripe nose, as usual with a 1961 this has an intensity of fruit missing in, for instance the 1966, good as that was. Fullish, vigorous, ripe, ample. A very good 1961 which will still keep well, but has less vigour than the 1966.

1959   **Drink soon**

(English bottled by Hedges and Butler) Good colour. Fullish, vigorous. A meaty example, but a wine of richness, dimension and depth – even class. Round, fat and spicy in the best sense. Very good.

1949   **Drink soon**

Good colour. This is fragrant, round, sweet and classy. No longer obviously Cordier in style. Gentle, long, lingering finish. A wine of great charm: very Saint-Julien.

1945   **Now–1997**

Like the 1949 – and despite the solidity of the vintage – this is more Saint-Julien than Cordier. Very rich, quite concentrated, and with no undue astringency. Finishes long. Very good plus.

BEYCHEVELLE

Château Beychevelle is one of the most impressive properties in the Médoc. Its wide, single-storied, Louis xv facade, flanked by towers, and set in a magnificent park laid out in the style of Le Nôtre, is one of the grandest in the country, and one of the best known. Every *bureau de tabac* in Bordeaux will have a postcard of Beychevelle, and countless friends and relations of visitors to the area who may never have been to Bordeaux themselves, must be familiar with the view of this property, if of no other.

One of the region's most famous legends is the origin of the name Beychevelle. According to the story, this arises from the words '*bêche velle*', Gascon for '*baisse voile*', or 'lower sails'. This was done by ships passing along the Gironde estuary, supposedly as a salute to a former owner, the Duc d'Epernon, who became senior admiral of France in 1587.

Recent research has cast doubt, however, not on the lowering of the sails, but on the salute to Epernon. It seems he may never have lived at the château. It could also be that the ships had to lower their sails in order to stop and pay taxes to the Bordeaux authorities or to allow customs officials to come aboard and investigate their cargo. Moreover the name 'Bayssevelle' can be traced back to land registers dating from as early as the fourteenth century. Does the name, as Bernard Ginestet has suggested, merely mean sailing boat: from the Gascon word *beychet* (a boat) and *velo* (a sail)?

Be that as it may, Beychevelle is the name, not only of one of the most popular classed growths in Bordeaux, but of a village in the Saint-Julien commune and, sadly, a no longer active little port in the Gironde estuary. Beychevelle is an old estate, and has for a long time been the centre of activity in the area.

HISTORY

Beychevelle has its origins in the *seigneurie* of Lamarque. Some five kilometres to the south, Lamarque was one of a number of important *seigneuries* in the Médoc in the Middle Ages. Like Latour and Calon to the north, and Margaux and Issan further south, these were feudal castles, one of a number of fortified *manoirs* set up along the Gironde estuary to protect the Médoc from the incursions of pirates. One of the dependencies of the Château de Lamarque was a *maison noble* at what is now Beychevelle.

In the fourteenth century this *manoir* belonged to Archambault de Grailly, who had inherited it from his mother-in-law, Assahilde de Bordeaux. From him it passed in 1446 to their cousins the celebrated family of Foix de Candale, associated with a number of properties in the Middle Ages and, later, particularly with Issan, as well as with the *seigneurie* of Lamarque itself.

In 1587 the heiress of Beychevelle – then called the Château du Médoc – was Marguerite, only daughter of the Comte de Foix de Candale. In this year she married Jean-Louis Nogaret de la Valette, Duc d'Epernon and Grand Admiral of France. The *seigneurie* of Lamarque was sold to the Maréchal de Matignon in 1593, but on the Maréchal's death four years later, both the estate and the titles that went with it were acquired by Jean-Louis de la Valette.

Epernon, a favourite of Henri III, was soon appointed Governor of Guyenne. He was an autocratic individual, as was his son Bernard. Both were more concerned with using the position to extract as much money for themselves and the royal exchequer from the local inhabitants as they could, as with their subjects' welfare, or with representing their interests at court. Bernard, in particular, rapidly became extremely unpopular. It is perhaps from this time that the local rumours of a meadow on the Beychevelle estate known as Prat Laouret being the centre of black magic rites originates. Tales are told of midnight masses, werewolves and virginal sacrifices to the devil. Certainly, the despotic Epernons could quite easily have insisted on deference being shown to their exalted position by the boats passing up the Gironde estuary. The *baisse voile* theory may after all have a semblance of truth.

By the 1650s there was a state of open warfare between the Governor on the one hand and the city of Bordeaux on the other. The young king Louis XIV eventually sided with the city. It was the beginning of the end. Bernard was isolated and disgraced. When he died in 1661, the Beychevelle estate had to be split up and sold to pay his debts. It reverted to the crown, and a number of parcels, including what became Ducru-Beaucaillou and Branaire, were sold off.

Beychevelle was bought by the Duc de Rendan, Baron de Beychevelle, in 1674, and passed to the President (of the Bordeaux *parlement*) d'Abbadie, a member of another old Bordeaux family, in 1692. The Abbadie family were associated both with Léoville and with Cantemerle at the same time, but through collateral branches.

The Abbadie family, it is said, neglected Beychevelle, yet it must have been under their ownership during the first half of the eighteenth century that vines were first planted at Beychevelle on a large scale and wine-making began to assume the sort of importance it has today. By mid-century, shortly before the estate changed hands yet again, Beychevelle was one of the second growths of Saint-Julien together with Gruau *Frères* and Bergeron (Ducru-Beaucaillou). It fetched 400 to 600 gold *livres* a *tonneau*, second only to the Léoville wine, which could fetch 800 to 1000.

By 1757, Beychevelle was in the hands of François-Etienne, Marquis Brassier de Budot, Baron de Lamarque, another Bordeaux parliamentarian, and it was in this year that the old fortified *manoir* was pulled down, the present château constructed and the gardens and park laid out.

Brassier succeeded in uniting a number of estates which had formerly been part of the fief of the Foix-Candales: the château of Lamarque itself, and Poujeaux in Moulis, among others. In addition, he laid roads, developed the port, then the only sensible means of shipping wine down to Bordeaux, and refurbished the Beychevelle vineyard, said to have been in a poor condition. The vineyard at this time occupied some 40 hectares, about half what it does today.

Brassier *fils*, François Arnaud, continued the good work, and the property remained in the family until the time of the Revolution. Though it is said that they had secreted Lafayette at Beychevelle before he set sail for America in order to recruit support for the French cause, the Brassiers were identified with the old order, and soon ran into trouble with the local inhabitants. François Arnaud was a very rich man whose domaine extended over six parishes. At the time of the revolution his annual income was said to be no less than 400,000 *livres d'or*.

He was forced to make over a large part of the alluvial pasture to the community, but this did not stop him being first locked up in his château, and later when he tried to escape being hunted like a wild beast through the marshy land, and, as a contemporary report darkly states, 'not by strangers to the locality'.

A large part of the Lamarque domaine passed to M. Bergeron, owner of Château Ducru-Beaucaillou, whose name is to this day commemorated in the bourgeois growth Château Lamothe-Bergeron lying to the south of Beychevelle in the commune of Cussac. Another domaine which emerged as a separate vineyard was De Bédout, a fourth growth in the early years of the next century. (De Bédout was the owner of Château Batailley in Pauillac at this time.) Bédout was eventually parcelled out and lost its status. The bulk was absorbed into Saint-Pierre-Sevaistre and Bontemps.

Following a duel during which he killed his opponent, Brassier was exiled. His widowed mother remained in the château, and when she died a few years later, the son's name was added to the list of *émigrés*, and steps were taken to sequestrate Beychevelle on the part of the state.

Brassier's sister, Mme de Saint-Herem, stepped in and managed to persuade the authorities that she was the sole heir and rightful owner of the estate. No sooner had she succeeded in doing this, however, than she sold it in 1800 to a M. Jacques Conté, a Bordeaux ship owner and manufacturer (records describe him as an '*armateur de corsaires*').

At this time the reputation of the wine of Beychevelle seems to have been in decline. Reports speak of both château and vineyard being in poor condition. There are a number of unofficial classifications of this period, and if the wine, still known as Brassier, appears, it is low on the list. Production seems to have been in the region of 100 *tonneaux*.

Nevertheless, when Beychevelle once again appeared on the market, it fetched a high price. The total estate was large, some 250 hectares, and produced wheat, pine wood and cork as well as wine, and it fetched 650,000 francs when sold in 1825 by Conté to his nephew, Pierre-François Guestier, son of the faithful Daniel who had managed the Barton properties and wine business during the self-imposed exile of Hugh Barton during the Napoleonic era.

The Guestiers were firm '*Orléanistes*' or supporters of Louis-Philippe. Soon after the inauguration of the 30 July monarchy they received the royal dukes of Aumale and Nemours at a grand banquet. A toast was given to '*Le meilleur des rois*'; in response, the Dukes toasted Beychevelle, '*Le meilleur des vins*'.

Pierre-François was also a keen man of the turf. In 1821 he founded a stable at Beychevelle known as the *Ecurie* Guestier. From England he imported a thoroughbred stallion called Young Governor who soon sired a generation of champions. Guestier was accorded the great honour – for a provincial – of being elected to the exclusive Jockey Club de Paris, and started a fashion of horse-racing which persists in Bordeaux to this day.

Having been brought up in England, and seen the march of constitutional reform, culminating in the 1832 Reform Bill, he was also a man of progress, though by no means a republican. Elected to the Bordeaux Chamber of Deputies in 1834 he was the leader of a new generation of Chartronnais liberals, believers in free-trade, 'good works' and a certain amount, but not too much, of social mobility.

Guestier, unfortunately, had six daughters and only one son, François. By the 1860s, successive dowries and the effects of the mildew epidemic of the 1850s had taken their toll. In 1864 Guestier was forced to sell Batailley, which his grandfather had bought in 1819. Ten years later, the family's prized possession, Château Beychevelle, now officially confirmed as a fourth growth, and producing 150 to 180 *tonneaux* of wine from some 70 hectares of vines, also had to be sold. Beychevelle was sold to M. Armand Heine in 1874 for 1,600,000 francs. Heine was a Parisian banker, and his daughter Marie-Louise married into one of the richest and most influential banking families of France, the Foulds. The Foulds were to remain in charge of Beychevelle until 1986.

The original Achille Fould was Minister of Finance under Napoleon III, and his successors have continued the family involvement in political affairs. In the most recent generation the late Aymar Achille Fould was Secrétaire d'État of both Defence and Transport, and his father, Armand, who died in 1969, was for a time Minister of Agriculture. Aymar represented the seventh successive generation who have served in the French Chamber of Deputies. In 1983, as a result of the problems of *indivision*, Beychevelle being split between a number of members of the Achille Fould family, a minority holding in the estate was sold to an insurance company, the Garantie Mutuelle des Fonctionnaires (GMF). Following Aymar Achille Fould's death in 1986, GMF acquired total control, and three years later set up a subsidiary company, in which the Japanese firm of Suntory have a 40 per cent share, called Grands Millésimes de France. This company also owns Château Beaumont in the Haut-Médoc and the Château de Bligny in Burgundy.

The last few years have seen a number of changes at Beychevelle. The cellars and the *chais* have been modernized and enlarged. The château has been carefully modernized and kept decorated and furnished, though it is not normally occupied, and the park and gardens maintained in immaculate condition. The wine, with its distinctive label depicting an old-fashioned galleon fronted by the large head of a gryphon or some other such mythical beast, has remained one of the most popular of all the Médoc classed growths, regularly fetching a second growth price, despite its fourth growth classification.

THE VINEYARD

The size of the vineyard in 1855 was 44 hectares, and this was raised soon afterward to 73. After the Second World War it had declined to 48 hectares but has now been increased to 70. The average production is 325 *tonneaux*.

The vineyard of Beychevelle occupies much of the field which lies north and east of the main D2 road, on the right in front of Château Ducru-Beaucaillou as one drives up towards Langoa. There are other plots further north and west, and even a separate 15 hectare section to the south in Cussac, where a wine called Les Bruliers de Beychevelle is produced.

This is the heart of the Médoc. The soil is a deep bed of gravel, resting on a subsoil of larger stones, clay and *alios* (sandstone). It is fair to say that this particular unbroken bed, the stretch on the *croupe* nearest to the Gironde which begins at Beychevelle and extends north past Léoville into the vineyards of Latour, is probably the best vineyard land for the Cabernet grape in the whole world. Certainly some of the world's greatest wines are produced here.

Beychevelle is planted in the ratio 59 per cent Cabernet Sauvignon, 8 per cent Cabernet Franc, 30 per cent Merlot and 3 per cent Petit Verdot. This is a slight decrease in the amount of Merlot than which pertained in the 1960s and early 1970s. There is a second wine, appropriately called Amiral de Beychevelle.

THE CHÂTEAU AND THE *CHAIS*

The domaine in total extends over 250 hectares, and still produces a large quantity of wheat, as well as having meadows stretching down to the Gironde estuary – about one kilometre from the château itself – for the grazing of cattle and sheep. The château and its surrounding houses, barns and *chais* form a miniature township, and house much of the permanent staff, as well as the 100 or so pickers who arrive each autumn for the vintage.

One of the delights of the Médoc is the courtyard and garden in the front of the château. Beychevelle is famous for the display of its bedding plants, often picking out the name of the property itself, as well as for the magnificent venerable cedar which dominates the front courtyard, planted, it is said, in 1757, the year the château was constructed.

At the back, the grounds fall away towards the Gironde, and there is a marvellous view of the estuary over a formal garden and then over the park, meadows and vineyards towards the river. A 50-metre-wide terrace, beneath which is a splendid cellar extending under the château itself, is the best place to take in this view.

The *cuverie, chais* and other outbuildings lie on both sides as well as beneath the château. The first-year *chai* is to the left, as one faces the river. After this the wine goes into the deeper, cooler second-year cellar under the château itself, where also are stored the impressive reserves of older wine, serried ranks of binned bottles from floor to ceiling, slowly maturing under ideal conditions until released on to the market.

In the past few years a programme of extension to the cellars and investment in material has been carried out. On the south side of Beychevelle a new warehouse has been constructed – it doesn't blend in very easily with the existing buildings, I am sad to say. In here the bottled wine, in cases and on pallets, waits for despatch. Within the cellars themselves a nineteen metre extension has been excavated. A dozen or more large stainless-steel vats are available to supplement the battery of 25 smaller concrete and enamelled-steel *cuves*. With yields today regularly exceeding 350 if not 400 *tonneaux* – and 60 hectolitres per hectare, not an unusual yield these days, would make as much as 462 tonneaux before losses through evaporation and so on – one must make sure one has adequate storage capacity. In 1983, cellar-master Lucien Soussotte will admit, they could not allow the must to macerate on its skins for as long as they would have liked, as the vat space was too limited for the rapidly arriving harvest. The wine is marginally disappointing as a result.

Up to a few years ago the proportion of new wood was 25 to 30 per cent annually. Today 60 per cent of the barrels are renewed every year. The oak comes from the Allier.

THE WINE

Though there have been vintages where I have felt there has been a lack of the sort of concentration and depth one finds in, say, Ducru and Las-Cases, the quality of Beychevelle is usually, at least, good, often very good. I find the wine has a power and a meaty richness which makes one first think of a Pauillac – though I would be hard put to differentiate between Saint-Julien and Pauillac anyway, unless the wine was unmistakably Latour, Mouton or Lafite. It is full, well-coloured, ripe and elegant; dumb when young, complex and distinguished when ready for drinking. A good vintage will mean a firm, tannic wine, and, like all good claret, the usual ten years' patience after the vintage needs to be observed until the wine attains maturity.

As readers will know, Saint-Julien is a commune rich in excellently run classed growths. Indeed, today, unlike Margaux and Pauillac, there is not a single *cru classé* which produces disappointing wine. Another feature is the consistency of these domaines. Beychevelle, in my horizontal vintage tastings, regularly achieves 15 or 16 out of 20, though rarely marks in the 17s or 18s. This places the property firmly in the Exceptional Growths category, the rung immediately below the super-seconds.

THE TASTING

This was another splendid Saint-Julien vertical tastings organized by Dr Marvin Overton across the USA in May 1992. Additional bottles were provided by Stephen Kaplan, Herb Francis, Arthur Halle and myself.

Optimum drinking

1991   1995–2000
Medium colour. Ripe, round nose, good touch of new wood. There is fruit and personality and style. And good acidity. Finishes positively.

1990   1997–2005
Medium to medium-full colour. Not exactly concentrated on the nose but ripe and stylish. Good blackberry fruit. Medium body. Pretty but lacks a little backbone and concentration.

1989   1996–2004
Medium to medium-full colour. Spicy nose. Interesting; fat, balanced, new oaky. Medium body. A little richer than the 1990 it seems, but again a lack of real concentration (and grip here) on the follow-through. Quite good only.

1988   1997–2010
Medium-full colour. Good new oak on the nose. Classic Cabernet but richer than most in this vintage. I prefer this to 1990 and 1989. Medium-full. Good tannin. Concentrated and balanced. Above all consistent and stylish.

1986   1998–2018
Good colour. Firm, full, concentrated, tannic. This has a lot of potential. Full, tannic meaty palate. Rich and oaky. Plenty of depth and character. Size plus concentration. Very good.

1985   1995–2007
Medium-full colour. A little development. Medium body. Open, attractive. But perhaps not an enormous amount of fat and complexity. Good balance though.

1983   Now–2000
Good vigorous colour for a 1983. Rather evolved on the nose though. Fat but it lacks grip and style. On the palate not too bad. Medium to medium-full. Supple, balanced, but lacks real finesse. Finishes positively though.

1982   Now–2009
Good colour. Ripe, abundant nose. Not a blockbuster but plenty of high fruit here. Medium-full. The fruit could be a shade more concentrated but a good 1982 with a good acidity.

1981   Now–1999
Fresh fullish colour for an 1981. A little neutral but fresh and round and fruity on the nose. Medium body. Attractive, balanced. Not great, but a good plus example of the vintage.

1979   Now–1999
Very good colour. Still vigorous. Full, meaty, rich nose. Not a lot of finesse but plenty of fruit. Full body, ripe if not very elegant. Good grip. A bit lumpy but good for the vintage.

1978   Now–1999
Medium to medium-full mature colour. Open nose. Ripe but lacks a bit of flair and concentration. Medium body. Soft and round. Quite classy. Good blackcurrant fruit and good acidity. But lacks a little subtlety and finesse.

1976   **Drink soon**
Medium to medium-full mature colour. Gamey nose. Quite fresh, but on the surface only. Medium body. Opulent, slightly spicy cooked fruit but a little astringent as well. Quite good plus.

1975   Now–1999
Medium-full colour. Just about mature. Some structure on the nose, but fresh and fruity as well. Ample, cedary, good grip. Fullish. There is a touch of astringency but also richness and depth.

1971   **Drink up**
Medium to medium-full colour. Still vigorous for a 1971. A touch attenuated on the nose. But ripe and with interest nevertheless. *Tabac* flavours. This now needs drinking.

1970   Now–1999
Medium-full colour. Good vigour still. Meaty, fat, raspberry blackberry fruit. Cedary. Fullish, ripe and concentrated. Balanced and fat and complexity. Good extract. Very good.

1967   **Drink soon**
Light to medium colour. Fully mature. Attractive sweet, fruity nose. Medium body. Ripe, succulent, good fruit. Good balance.

1966   Now–1997
Good colour. Mature but not quite as brown as the 1964. Firm on the nose at first. A full, meaty wine on the palate. Ripe, old viney. This is concentrated and stylish. Very good fruit. Long. Positive. Very good plus. Better than the 1970.

1964   Now–1996
Good mature colour. Good flexible nose for a 1964. Fruit here. Ripe and full of fruit on the palate. A great success for a 1964. Not a bit rigid, astringent or short. Full, succulent. Long. Stylish. Will still keep well.

1961   **Drink soon**

Very good mature colour. Rich but for a 1961 not *that* concentrated. Medium-full. Has the fruit started to dry out a bit? Seems a bit dense. Ripe but not a very impressive 1961.

1959   **Drink soon**

Medium to medium-full colour. Fully mature. Ripe, very fruity nose. A fullish, opulent and balanced wine. Very good.

1958   **Drink soon**

Medium to medium-full colour. There is still fruit. Medium body. Elegant, balanced, if one-dimensional. But long. No decay. Lovely finish.

1957   **Drink soon**

Medium-full colour. Mature. Not too hard on the nose. Still plenty of fruit. On the palate a little dense and unforthcoming. It lacks suppleness. Good acidity and no lack of fruit, but I get more pleasure out of the 1958.

1955   **Drink soon**

Fullish colour. Mature but vigorous. Lovely cedary, cigar-boxey nose. Medium to medium-full. Very fine fruit. Complex, graceful. Elegant and still lovely. This has great charm and class.

1953   **Drink soon**

Medium to medium-full colour. Mature. This is very delicious. Complete, elegant, intensely fruity nose still. On the palate it is lightening up a bit but nevertheless a wine of great class.

1952   **Drink soon**

Medium-full colour. Mature. Fuller on the nose than the 1953 but not too hard or rigid. No astringency. On the palate I find it ripe, succulent, and rich, but it is a little astringent on the finish.

1948   **Past its best**

Very good colour. No real sign of age. A touch oxidized on the nose. On the palate a bit old and astringent. Acidity shows. Has lost its fruit. (Not otherwise sampled recently.)

1947   **Drink soon**

Medium to medium-full mature colour. Ripe, opulent cedary nose. Not a bit dense. Heaps of fruit. Intense. Rich, over-ripe, sweet palate. Medium-full. Very well balanced. Voluptuous.

1945   **Now–1998**

Good colour. This is brilliant on the nose. Rich, concentrated, and powerful. Austere but fine quality. Pauillac-ish. Very full, structured and concentrated. First growth quality here.

1943   **Drink soon**

Excellent colour, bigger than the 1945, if a little dense. Fine nose. Ripe, plenty of fruit. Stylish. Yet at the same time a smell of old gym-shoes.

This is fullish, ripe, elegant. Surprisingly good. Long. Classic Saint-Julien. Fine.

1937   **Drink soon**

Good fullish colour. Not a bit too dense. Good fruit. Very Cabernet. A little astringent on the palate but good fruit. Still enjoyable. A little austere. Best with food. Medium-full.

1934   **Past its best/Drink soon**

Good colour. Fully mature. A little maderized on the nose. Yet ripe, fullish, and elegant on the palate. A second bottle was ripe, gentle, supple. Medium-full, balanced and structured. Plenty of fruit. Sweet. This is fine and lovely. Very long. Lovely. Drink soon.

1929   **Will still keep**

(Magnum) Excellent colour. A little more brown than the 1928 but very full and intense. Ripe, cedary, hazelnutty, almost honeyed. Medium-full. Lovely opulent, classy ripe fruit. Lazily round and silky. Quite lovely. Great charm. A great wine. Bags of life.

1928   **Will still keep**

(Magnum) Even better colour than the 1929. Firmer nose, with a touch of old wood. Bigger, more rigid on the palate. Still tannic. More austere, but lots of lovely ripe Cabernet fruit. Less opulent, less silky but essence of Cabernet, almost in a 1961 sense. No rigidity. A great wine. Even more concentrated than the 1929.

1926   **Past its best**

Fine colour. Full and vigorous. Full, austere, a touch lactic, but interesting. Slightly rigid on the palate. A little astringent too. A fine wine. Very good concentration with lots of class but possibly a little past its best. Cedary. Better with food.

1924   **Past its best**

Light colour. Light nose. A touch of cork/bad wood – or is it decay? On the palate a little past it but ripe, sweet and classy underneath. Medium-full. Balanced. Still enjoyable.

1923   **Past its best**

(English bottling, slip-label says R.M. Jefferson, Whitehaven) Light quite evolved colour. Rather evolved and vegetal on the nose. Vegetable soup. Yet underneath ripe and rich but fatter and less classy then the 1924.

1893   **Will still last well**

(Half bottle, Barton and Guestier bottling) Brilliant colour. 99 years old – and a half bottle – and it looks like the 1978! Vigorous, fat and opulent. This is an amazing wine. Cedary, complex, has a late bottled aspect but fresh and vigorous. Complex and voluptuous. Abundantly fleshy and fruity. Brilliant.

SAINT-EST

SAINT-ESTÈPHE IS THE LARGEST AND MOST NORTHERLY OF THE GREAT MÉDOC COMMUNES, AND LIES ABOUT 50 KILOMETRES NORTH OF BORDEAUX. IT PRODUCES THE MOST WINE OF THE FOUR, PREDOMINANTLY FROM ITS CLUTCH OF HIGHLY REPUTED *BOURGEOIS SUPÉRIEURS* SUCH AS CHÂTEAUX PHÉLAN-SÉGUR, DE PEZ AND MEYNEY. THERE ARE ONLY FIVE CLASSED GROWTHS, TWO SECONDS, A THIRD, A FOURTH AND A FIFTH.

The soil is varied. In the south-east corner it is heavy gravel on an *alios* base, similar to that in Pauillac. Progressively west and north the soil contains more clay and becomes heavier and more fertile, and in parts contains limestone.

Naturally the wines vary too, particularly as some properties have quite high proportions of Merlot compared with those of Pauillac. In general the wines are tough, more aromatic and less elegant than those of the neighbouring communes. They are solid rather than austere; firm, full and tannic, but in a less distinguished way; less obviously richly blackcurranty in flavour, and more robust and spicy – even sweeter – in character. Some Saint-Estèphes do not age too gracefully, though the top growths – like Cos d'Estournel and Montrose, both from the south-eastern end of the parish – can last as well as any Haut-Médoc.

ÈPHE

Cos d'Estournel

The first thing to establish about Cos d'Estournel is its pronunciation: it is 'cosse', not 'coe' – lettuce rather than athlete. Yet the name has nothing to do with Cos, the Levantine island, nor is it, as some have suggested, a corruption of *clos*, meaning a walled enclosure with ecclesiastical connections (cloister, etc.). There is no evidence of either. The word comes from the old Gascon word *caux* which is itself a telescoping of *colline de cailloux* (slope of stones). Yet it is pronounced with the final 's': this is custom in south-west France. Any tourist who is unfortunate enough to ask for 'Coe d'Estournel' in a French restaurant is unlikely to impress the wine waiter!

Colline de Cailloux precisely describes the Cos d'Estournel vineyard. As you proceed up the road from Pauillac, with the kitchen garden and willow trees fronting Lafite on the left, crossing the Chenal de Lazarat, the ditch which is the commune boundary, the ground begins to rise steeply: there is a definite ridge up to a plateau of higher ground. On this ridge, opening out like a fan around the winery, lie the vineyards of Cos.

If you are making your first visit to Cos, however, you are in for a shock. Not here a stately eighteenth century *chartreuse*-style building as at Langoa or Malescot, let alone the nineteenth-century edifices of the Pichons or Palmer. What you see is literally fantastic; oriental arches and towers, surmounted by three Chinese-style pagoda turrets, all in soft, golden sandstone. Moreover the main door, which once formed the entrance to the harem of the Sultan of Zanzibar, is carved with vine leaves, bunches of grapes, flowers and exotic animals. This, you gasp, is not the normal sober Médoc château. No, it isn't. It's just the *chai*. There is no Cos d'Estournel château as such. This folly is where they make and keep the wine, not where the proprietors live.

HISTORY

Louis Gaspard d'Estournel was born in Bordeaux on 3 January 1762. He was a sickly baby, it seems, and his parents hastened to have him christened, just in case. In fact he was to live to the ripe old age of 91, surviving from the time of Louis XV to that of Louis Napoleon.

The origin of the D'Estournel family was the Quercy, the region in the Lot *département* whence comes the wine of Cahors. On the death of Guy d'Estournel de Maniban in 1791, the *maison noble de Pommies et de Caux* passed into the hands of Louis Gaspard. He was 29.

Land seems to have had a fascination for Louis Gaspard. He had hardly taken receipt of his inheritance when he bought the Abbaye de L'Isle at Ordonnac, declared a *bien national* by the new Revolutionary government. He was ceaselessly acquiring a parcel here, or disposing of a less well-placed piece of terrain there, the deals being by no means always to his financial advantage. It seems he was more of a romantic than businessman.

At the time there was little in this part of Saint-Estèphe in the way of vines. Unlike most of the other major properties in the Médoc, established in the early eighteenth century, if not before, Cos d'Estournel as an important vineyard is an upstart.

We can date its creation precisely. It is a summer afternoon in 1811. D'Estournel is standing in the vineyard of Lafite looking north towards his own land at Cos. He is well aware of Lafite's reputation. He compares the soils, he compares the aspects. He returns to his house at Pommies (today's Château Pomys) with his head spinning: 'I too can produce a *grand cru*.'

There were then twelve hectares of vines. A few years later the broker Abraham Lawton noted in his diary: 'I notice that M. d'Estournel wants to make a second growth out of his vines at Cos . . . . It would not be impossible.'

Yet, in the same year as Louis Gaspard made this momentous decision his creditors foreclosed on him. He was forced to sell up. The beneficiary was Jean-Louis de Lapeyrière, a Parisian tax collector; the sum derisory, 250,000 francs. But D'Estournel managed to get a strange *réméré* clause inserted into the contract, giving him the option to rebuy the estate, if of course he could raise the money, within a five-year period. More curiously, he remained in Bordeaux, nominally for all the world to see, as proprietor of Cos. More curiously still, not within the five-year deadline, but in 1821, ten years after the forced sale, he persuaded the mysterious Lapeyrière to sell him back his estates. He had found five local businessmen to finance him. It would be 30 years before they received a return on their investment.

From then on Louis Gaspard d'Estournel rapidly expanded the vineyard. Between 1821 and 1847 he bought 80 parcels of vines, increasing the size of Cos to 57 hectares. These efforts culminated in the acquisition of Cos-Labory from the Labory family, themselves heavily in debt, and the permanent transfer of the best parcel of this other Cos estate into that of Cos d'Estournel.

D'Estournel had always had connections with the Orient. He used to breed Arabian stallions, shipping them to and from India and the Far East. He then attempted to sell wine in the same way. This was a less successful venture, but on the other hand it was soon found that a voyage to India and back transformed the quality of the wine. It was judged 'very good' before it set out. 'Perfect' when it had returned. It was this that made the wine's reputation. As Abraham Lawton had foreseen, Cos rapidly rose in the ranks of the private and unofficial classifications of the time; and as we all know, it would be accepted, along with Montrose, another upstart, as a Second Growth in 1855.

From the 1830s onwards D'Estournel started to renovate his *chais* and cellars. These, inspired by his voyages east, were decorated with oriental arches and towers, and surmounted with the three sandstone Chinese-style pagodas already mentioned, now recently restored. Finally, he built a triumphal arch leading on to the main Pauillac-Saint-Estèphe road. This is inscribed with the D'Estournel coat of arms, and the motto '*Semper Fidelis*'. All this gives the place a most bizarre effect, particularly when one appreciates that the *chinoiserie* merely decorates the place in which they keep and make the wine. D'Estournel may never have built a place to live in, for he had a perfectly good home at Pommies, but he succeeded in creating a model vineyard and cellars, and to greatly increasing the reputation of his wine. Sadly this was at the expense both of his inheritance and his health. In 1852 he was forced to sell up, and in 1853 he died.

The price the estate fetched was considerable; at 1,150,000 francs, admittedly including Pomys, Cos-Labory and a few smaller properties as well, it compares favourably with the 1,125,000 francs paid for Mouton a few months later. At the time, Cos produced 140 *tonneaux*, Cos-Labory 40 and Pomys 80. The purchaser was a London businessman, Charles Cecil Martyn, who lived in Paris. Martyn was a friend of the banker Fould, soon to buy Beychevelle, and who helped him with the purchase of this property. Little else is known of Martyn; he was very much the absentee landlord, and only remained owner until 1869, when he sold Cos d'Estournel to a man called Errazu, having already disposed of Cos-Labory to M. Louis Peychaud in 1860.

What Martyn did, however, was to appoint an administrator, the vastly experienced Jérôme Chiapella, a Bordeaux *négociant* and proprietor of Château La Mission-Haut-Brion. Chiapella further improved both the wine – which by the mid-1860s was fetching prices on a par with the top second growths, Rauzan and Léoville – and the vineyard, which in 1866 won a medal for the local agricultural society for the cleanliness and concentration on modern methods, and also for the humanitarian way the management treated the workers. As today, they were given free medical treatment, and retired personnel housed free on the estate. (Perhaps this is why a contemporary writer called Aussel described Martyn as 'a perfect gentleman'.)

The Errazu ownership lasted twenty years, and was noted for the high life, expensive living and grand parties. In 1889 the property was acquired by the Hostein brothers, and in 1894 passed to Louis Charmolüe, owner of Château Montrose, who had married a Hostein daughter, heiress to Cos. In 1917 Cos was bought by Fernand Ginestet, as also was the neighbouring Château de Marbuzet. It is still in the same family. Fernand had two children, Pierre and Arlette. Arlette married into the Prats family, vermouth manufacturers in Sète, and originators of the Saint-Raphaël brand. In 1970 the family properties were divided, and Cos d'Estournel passed into the hands of Arlette's three children, Jean-Marie, Yves and Bruno. It is Bruno who takes the day-to-day responsibility for Cos, together with Jacques Pelissie, *directeur technique, maître de chai* François Carle, and with the advice of Pascal Ribereau-Gayon of the Institut d'Oenologie de Bordeaux.

Cos d'Estournel now has 70 hectares of vines. Officially these are planted in the ratio 60 per cent Cabernet Sauvignon, 2 per cent Franc and 38 per cent Merlot. In practice the Cabernet Franc has only once been used in recent years, in 1986. The mean production is 250 *tonneaux*. The amount of new oak varies from a third, in a weak year like 1987, to as much as 100 per cent, in 1985.

THE CHAIS

The wine is vinified in stainless-steel vats, quite squat, as at Haut-Brion, in a clean, modern *cuvier* installed in 1984. The fermentation temperature is of course controlled, and never rises above 32 degrees. In 1990 a further programme of extension and modernization of the *chais* was inaugurated, both inside and out. The facade has been cleaned and restored, a new reception area installed, and a roof terrace overlooking the surrounding vineyards has been constructed. Air-conditioning has been added to the barrel-ageing cellar, and an entirely new bottling cellar has been built.

THE WINE

Cos is really quite a different wine from any other Saint-Estèphe. In part this must arise from the soil, which is more gravelly and has less clay than the rest of the commune. This gives a wine which is somewhat softer and more elegant, less aggressively powerful, than other Saint-Estèphes. Most of these are full-bodied, rich and robust yet occasionally a little too tough for their own good; as a result they sometimes do not age gracefully. Cos, however, has both the power and the finesse, both the body and the delicacy, both the backbone and the fruit.

Cos d'Estournel has consistently made remarkably good wine as the following notes will show. Since the mid-1970s, following the advent of Bruno Prats, it has improved even more. There is no longer the background of vinosity and austerity which is the hallmark of other wines from the commune; instead, an ample, rich complexity, a mouth-filling fruit, and a concentration which can only come from meticulous wine-making, a rigorous selection, and a good percentage of very old vines.

THE TASTING

The following magnificent collection of vintages of Cos d'Estournel was assembled by physics professor Dr Bipin Desai, and tasted in Los Angeles in March 1990.

Optimum drinking

1989   **1996–2006**

Good colour. Succulent, rich, plump, quite Merlot-dominated nose. No new oak as yet. A soft wine, without a great deal of obvious tannin and yet what tannins there are are very ripe. Very good concentrated fruit. But not a very high level of acidity. Plump and sexy. Generous, stylish and long on the palate. When I saw the wine again at the end of April, alongside the rest of the vintage, I marked it very highly indeed.

1988   **1998–2006**

Medium full colour. This has softened up – become more accessible – in the ten months since I first saw it in cask. Ripe, new oaky, concentrated, complex nose, though without the power, concentration and interest of the 1986. Medium to medium-full body. Some tannin and the tannins ripe but not a great deal of weight and depth. Very good style though. More character than most 1988s. Very fine for the vintage.

1987)   **Drink soon**

Light to medium colour. Quite a bit less purple than the above. Light but elegant nose. Neither too weak nor too lean. Medium body. Still a little tannin but the tannins softening now. There is also an element of new oak. As 1987s go this has better structure and depth than most.

1986   **1998–2018**

Medium-full colour. Excellent nose. This has lovely concentrated fruit, a cedary sort of oak, and ripe tannins; real concentration, complexity and depth. Very promising! Full, rich and tannic on the palate. A wine whose elements are all separate, especially on the attack. On the aftertaste the depth, complexity and very finely balanced fruit coming welling up. Very fine indeed.

1985   **1995–2010**

Medium colour. The nose has now gone into its adolescent shell a little. It seems a little lumpy. It also shows its alcohol. On the palate the wine is more easy to judge. Very finely balanced ripe fruit. Full, rich and spicy. Currently a little adolescent but there is more weight, depth and eventual quality in this than in 1988, though it is outclassed by the 1986. Very good finish though.

1984   **Drink soon**

Light to medium colour. Quite fresh on the nose, and a little soft fruit, but not much charm. Yet has reasonable fruit and definition on the palate. Slight austerity and a little bitterness on the finish. As far as I am concerned it lacks a bit of generosity, but I've had worse 1984s.

1983   **Now–2005**

Medium to medium-full colour. A little sign of maturity now. Round, ripe, complex nose. Not aggressive. On the palate now getting nearly there. Medium to medium-full body. Cedary, gentle, elegant, and good plump fruit. Well balanced by acidity. Not a great wine but harmonious and stylish. Very good but not great. Softer than I had expected.

1982   **1994–2014**

Fullish colour. Rich, fat, cooked black-cherry nose. Lovely rich hot-chocolatey wine on the palate. The usual cooked fruit of the vintage. Fullish, the tannins getting soft now, but the wine still needs to knit together. Fat, plump. Very appealing. A wine of overwhelming attraction but not great elegance. Good length. Fine. Perhaps the 1986 is better still though.

1981   **Now–2002**

Very good colour for a 1981. Fine, fresh, vigorous nose. Medium-full, more like a 1983, and with less sign of maturity. This shows really well.

A lovely elegant definition of fruit. I find it almost as full and as interesting as the 1983. Good balance. Good length. An excellent success for the vintage.

1980   **Drink soon**

Medium colour. Now mature but no undue age. Light nose, with no great interest. Medium body. Quite ripe but with no real grip. A little weak and blowsy on the palate. Yet fresher and fruitier than most 1980s. Good but not great for the vintage.

1979   **Now–2000**

Very good colour. Fuller and more purple than the 1978. Ripe, plummy and cedary on the nose. Fullish, still vigorous. Just a little tannin still. It lacks a little generosity, richness and complexity but is good for 1979. Will still improve. I prefer the 1981 though.

1978   **Now–2005**

Good fullish vigorous colour. Quite ripe but not exactly generous. Medium full, softer than the 1979 but richer and more concentrated. A stylish, reserved wine with good depth and balance. Long. Very good.

1977   **Drink soon**

(Magnum) Good colour. Deeper than the 1976 but a lot browner. Soft on the nose. Not too mean. Lightish in body, but fresh and by no means fruitless. No age and no cold-tea flavours. Very good for the vintage.

1976   **Now–1998**

(Magnum) Medium colour. Fully mature. Fresh, fragrant nose, without any of the dryness of the vintage. Medium-full, ripe and cedary. Above all balanced and fresh. Long and complex. Slightly rounder and more aromatic than the 1978, and more interest today. Very fine for the vintage. Better than the 1975.

1975   **Drink soon**

Good fullish colour. Slightly vegetal on the nose. Not that full. Slightly dry and dense. Lacks both richness and zip. Similar palate. No great size and as much astringency as tannin. Medium body. This is not going to get any better. Only fair.

1973   **Drink up**

(Magnum) Medium, ageing colour. The nose has lightened now but is still reasonably fresh. Medium body. There is not a great deal here, and it is beginning to dry out now. Reasonable style and balance. Good for the vintage though.

1971   **Drink up**

(Magnum) Medium-full colour, fully mature. Fresh, stylish nose. There is complexity and depth here. On the palate the wine shows a bit of age and the fruit has begun to dry out. Yet good

fruit. Medium to medium-full body. But it lacks a bit of generosity on the finish.

1970   **Drink soon**

Fullish colour. Still vigorous. Just a little solid on the nose. Rather more Saint-Estèphe-y on the palate than the rest of the 1970s. A bit solid, with some astringency. Slightly stalky and bitter on the palate. Fullish, but lacks generosity and class. Lacks sex appeal, and I don't think it will get softer – merely dryer.

1969   **Drink up**

(Magnum) Reasonable colour but a little old at the edge now. Smells a little weak. Underneath not too faded, nor unstylish. Medium body on the palate. The fruit has begun to dry out, and the wine rapidly got short, blowsy and elegant as it developed in the glass. A reasonable effort for the vintage though.

1967   **Drink soon**

(Magnum) Medium colour. Fully mature. Soft, aromatic nose. Mellow medium body on the palate. Elegant and fruity, round and well balanced. Perhaps there is a suggestion of age at the end but a stylish 1967. Very good.

1966   **Drink soon**

(Magnum) Full, barely mature colour. Round, ripe, rich nose; rather more style of the Cos of today than the 1970. A little more rigid on the palate, especially as it developed, but rich, with leathery and liquorice, spice and sandalwood flavours. Fullish, the tannins now soft. Good but not the greatest distinction and complexity.

1964   **Drink soon**

Good full colour. Just about mature. Soft and reasonably flexible on the nose. Medium-full. Reasonable grip and acidity but a slight lack of fruit now. It is beginning to dry out a little. Good for the vintage. But drink soon.

1962   **Now–1997**

Fullish colour, fully mature. Lovely round, ripe, soft aromatic nose. Rich and succulent and gentle. Slight elements of toffee and barley sugar and Horlicks. Fullish, rich, spicy and sweet. This has more charm and sex appeal than the 1966. Rounder and better balanced. Long, harmonious and elegant. Delicious. My favourite of all the 1960s vintages.

1961   **Now–1997**

This has an older colour than the 1962. But more depth inside. Firm and rich but quite rigid on the nose. On the palate similar with a certain bitterness and earthiness. Bitter chocolate, leather. There is a lack of charm and finesse. Not the greatest 1961. The sheer essence of fruit is missing.

1960   **Drink up**

(Magnum) Rather a light colour but not too aged. Light and soft on the nose. On the palate this is now a bit past its best but the wine is not astringent; it has just lost a little of its vigour. Still sweet, still some style. But getting a bit weak.

1959   **Now–1997**

Fullish colour. Still vigorous. Round, ripe and vigorous on the nose. Good depth, good style. No undue robustness. Fullish. A little astringency/solidity. Ripe, vigorous and concentrated but not exactly stylish. A typical 1959. Very good.

1958   **Drink soon**

(Magnum) Light to medium colour. Now showing a bit of age. Fragrant nose, interesting freshness, a hint of mint, no undue age. This is a stylish wine which is still fresh. Medium body. Good fruit. Very good for a 1958.

1956   **Drink soon**

Surprisingly good colour. Much fuller than the 1958. No undue age. Fresh nose, still very much above. Ripe and cherry-flavoured. Medium body. Fuller than the 1958. But a little astringency now at the end. A very interesting, complex, individual flavour.

1955   **Drink soon**

(Magnum) Good full colour. Now mature. Shows a little age on the nose, just a little astringent and lumpy, it seems. Dried up quickly in the glass. Yet nevertheless a very complex flavour. Ultimately (or originally) a wine of greater breed than the 1959. Round, harmonious and less bulky. Still very enjoyable.

1954   **Past its best**

(Magnum) Medium colour. Fully mature. This has now dried out on the nose. Rather old. The fruit has disappeared, and there is a certain astringency. The acidity shows.

1953   **Now–1997**

Good full colour. Still vigorous. Very classy and ripe on the nose. Complex and fragrant but beginning to lighten up now. This is holding up better than the 1955. Still sweet. Equally complex, slightly fuller and more concentrated. Lovely. Will still keep. Very long.

1952   **Drink soon**

(Magnum) Full mature colour. Surprisingly good nose. No undue solidity. Still concentrated and ripe. Full, rich but chunky and astringent. Roasted, nutty and caramel flavours. The dryness is almost too much on the attack, but the finish is cleaner. Would still be fine with food. A very good 1952.

1950   **Drink soon**

(Magnum) Medium colour. Now lightening up

a bit. Would have expected a deeper colour after the Libournais I've seen. A little H2S on the nose which is a bit light, but there is some fruit here. I would have expected more muscle though. Good balance, mellow and fruity, but not astringent. Has lost a little of its sweetness but nevertheless complex and fresh. Better than nose and colour would indicate.

1949   **Can still be kept**

(Magnum) Full mature colour. Slightly four-square on the nose with a whiff of chlorine. Full and rich and ripe, but somehow a lack of generosity about it. And a certain bitterness on the finish. Yet undoubted style and dimension here. But in the end I expected and remembered better, even though I found it softer and sweeter as it developed.

1947   **Can still be kept**

(Magnum) Medium-full mature colour. Round. Soft, sweet, aromatic, roast chestnutty nose. Medium to medium-full, sweet and ripe. This is soft and silky, with, as usual, quite a high volatile element. Intriguing, an attractive and spicy wine which will still last well. Very good length. Today I prefer this to the 1949.

1945   **Can still be kept**

Medium-full colour. But quite a bit of age. Rather more so than the 1947. Rich, full, masculine, concentrated, baked nose. A bit solid perhaps but plenty of depth here. Full and rich and not too tough. But still quite rigid. Black-cherry and bitter chocolate/coffee flavours. Like the 1949 a little lack of real sweetness and succulence. But very good nevertheless. But I prefer the 1949 and the 1947. Will still last.

1943   **Drink soon**

Just a little fuller and more vigorous looking than the 1945. One bottle was ripe on the nose, but showed just a vestige of decay. Yet was stylish, fullish, concentrated and balanced. The other bottle was fresher. The first example fell away in the glass, leaving a rather cloying finish. The other bottle was fragrant and delicious. A wine of grace and elegance. Holding up well.

1942   **Drink up**

Good fullish vigorous colour. Still quite firm and fruity on the nose. Certainly fresh. Solid, tannic and a bit dried out on the palate. Fresh but too austere. A bit inflexible.

1937   **Past its best**

Full but slightly cloudy colour. Full but inky nose yet sweetness here as well. On the palate this is not too bad. It seems to have lightened up a bit. The solidity and tannin have softened. But the fruit is a bit light and one-dimensional.

1934 — Will still keep

(Magnum) Full, ripe, meaty nose with an interesting aspect of roasted nuts; still vigorous. This is fine. Ripe, sweet and full-bodied, even concentrated. A rich, stylish wine with good structure which is still holding up well.

1929 — Drink soon

Fine mature colour. Lovely nose; fragrant, complex and fresh. Great breed. On the palate it is soft and round, still reasonably alive though. But after a while in the glass I detected just a little decay. Yet delicately elegant, fragrant fruit. Long and complex. Delicious.

1928 — Drink soon

Full, very vigorous colour. A certain amount more solidity and astringency on the nose. On the palate rich, vigorous, plummy and blackcurranty, but a little overlying astringency. The second bottle was fresher, more complex and more vigorous. Rather better. Plenty of life.

1926 — Drink soon

Medium-full colour. Still fresh. A certain density, but reasonably fresh, cedary, slightly minty, fruity elements. Now a little dried out but there is real breed here. The acidity and the astringency show a little. Still has length and complexity. Finishes long and concentrated. Very fine.

1924 — Drink soon

Medium colour. Soft, slightly faded but a lovely elegant old-roses nose. I find a taste of crab-apples on the palate. Quite full, fresher, more vigorous and slightly fuller than the 1926. Interesting hazelnutty, plummy flavours. Good grip. Individual and complex. Fine.

1921 — Past its best

Very light on both colour and palate. Yet not astringent and dried out. There is a touch of strawberry jam on the nose. Plus also a sort of decayed herbal honey flavour. Yet not a bit disagreeable. But the least good of this 1920s flight.

1920 — Drink soon

(Magnum) Fullish but aged colour. Cedary nose. The fruit has disappeared a little, leaving the wood predominant. Yet on the palate there is vigour and good Cabernet fruit. Full; fuller than 1924, ripe and rich. Still vigorous. But it doesn't have the class of the 1926 or 1924, let alone the 1929. Very fine though.

1917 — Past its best

Good fullish colour. Still quite vigorous. Not a lot of nose. Some wood and though it has substance, an absence of fruit on the palate and the acidity shows. A little rigid and charmless. But softened a little in the glass. Not too bad. The first year of the Ginestet era.

1905 — Past its best

A light colour now. This really is quite light and faded and a little dry on the nose, but soft and stylish. Not too bad on the palate. Ethereal echoes of old roses and blackcurrant, but has lost its grip and the acidity begins to show a little. Elegant but a little over the hill.

1904 — Past its best

Quite a light colour now. Lightish, high-toned nose, but still fresh, with some red fruits. Spicy and just a little sweet, but not as elegant as the 1905. Earthier. On the palate this is now a bit mean and dry. More structure than the 1905 but less fruit, less attraction.

1899 — Drink up

Medium colour. A little age. Fine nose originally, reminding me of the complexity and finesse of the 1929. After a while the wood began to obtrude as the fruit died away, but yet fragrant and fruity and delicate and with plenty of dimension. Fine.

1898 — Drink soon

Medium colour. Interesting smoky nose, not too faded. A touch of mushrooms. A fullish, ripe, quite meaty wine originally, more muscular than the 1899. (A 1929/1928 pre-echo.) Still has fruit. Still has depth. Good grip. Has lost a little of its sweetness but still has length and interest. Very good.

1890 — Drink soon

Good fullish colour. No undue age. Rich, roast chestnutty and cedar nose, with a touch of roast mushrooms again. A fullish, slightly four-square wine, but with good depth and interest. Probably always a little tough and solid. Still has interest, indeed a little more fruit than the 1898, but not the depth or the finesse.

1870 — Will still keep

Amazingly full and vigorous colour for its age. Full nose; roasted, cooked plums and a little burnt. Liquorice and wood smoke here, plenty of vigour, and quite a lot of bulk and solidity. There is a touch of astringency. But rich, meaty, creamy and concentrated. Splendid quality. Still very much alive. One bottle, mine I'm pleased to say, was much better than the other. And this held up well in the glass.

1869 — Drink soon

Medium colour. Still fresh. But a little sweet and decayed. The second bottle was more delicate but fragrant and vigorous and complex on the nose. Quite lovely. Real depth. An elegantly poised wine, with flowery fruit, and aspects of plums and peaches. Very long. Lovely.

MONTROSE

Unlike many famous properties of the Médoc, the origins of Château Montrose are not lost in the mists of time. Indeed it is one of the most recent of the classed growths, having been planted only in 1815. Again, unlike some other estates, Montrose's fortunes have been smooth and successful, and its history is well documented, helped, no doubt, by a succession of dedicated, on-the-spot proprietors and by few changes of ownership. Montrose even *looks* happy, prosperous and efficient, and there are neither scruffy cellars nor a dilapidated empty château. The neat, unpretentious Montrose country house, the *chai* and the outbuildings form a little village, and the whole estate is immaculately kept.

Château Montrose lies a couple of kilometres south of the village of Saint-Estèphe, surrounded by its vineyards, on a hillock overlooking the Gironde. Most of the commune of Saint-Estèphe, including the Montrose territory, was formerly part of the giant Calon estate, one of the oldest in the Médoc.

HISTORY

At the end of the seventeenth century Calon passed as a result of a marriage settlement into the hands of the celebrated Ségur family. About a hundred years later, in 1778, the Calon estate was sold to Etienne Théodore Dumoulin.

The Revolution passed uneventfully for Calon and for Dumoulin, who died in Bordeaux in 1808, leaving two sons and a daughter. After some difficulty in buying out his siblings, the second son, also Etienne Théodore, became sole proprietor in September 1812. Dumoulin *fils* was an enterprising young man and noted that there was a parcel of land lying some distance from his Calon vineyard that seemed promising territory for the vine. This area, known as 'La Lande de l'Escargeon' was covered in heather, gorse, broom, stunted trees and brambles; but underneath this scrub was a gravel *croupe*, and excellently situated for making wine of quality. Accordingly, he cleared several plots and started planting a few vines. Pleased with the results, he began to extend his plantations, and, about 1820, built a small château and one or two buildings in which to make and store the wine.

By 1825 the *lieu-dit* had changed its name from Escargeon to Montrose, and the château and vineyard appear on local maps. Why and where the name Montrose comes from we shall never know with certainty. We do know that it was Dumoulin who performed the baptism, and that at first the vineyard and its wines were known as Montrose-Ségur. We can conjecture that the name derives from the pink flowers of the local heather. Perhaps seen from the estuary, the main thoroughfare before the days of macadamized roads, the area in midsummer was a '*mont-rose*'. Certainly 'Montrose' is more euphonious than 'Escargeon', with its connotations of snails. It is a pity the answer to the matter died with Dumoulin. Up to 1825, the vineyard and its wine must be considered as a mere appendage to Calon-Ségur, and a small one at that – for the vineyard was a mere 15 to 20 *journaux* of vines, about 5 to 6 hectares – and there is as yet no record of wine under the Montrose name.

On 6 May 1824, Dumoulin sold the bulk of his estate, including the château of Calon-Ségur and its vineyard, to Firmin de Lestapis for 600,000 francs. He retained the Montrose parcel, however, and from then, over the next few years, inaugurated a major programme of scrub clearance, vine plantation, and the construction of cellars. By 1832, only seven years later, Dumoulin had 31 hectares under vines, out of a total area for the domaine of 40. Given the absence of modern machinery this redevelopment is no mean achievement. About half the original buildings are still in use.

Dumoulin continued to increase his domaine by buying and exchanging parcels with his neighbours. By the time of the 1855 Classification, when Montrose, the upstart, and Cos d'Estournel, also a relatively new vineyard, were recognized as second growths – surpassing Calon-Ségur which was classed as a *troisième* – the estate was 96 hectares, of which 50 were under vines, and was producing 100 to 150 *tonneaux* of wine.

Dumoulin died in his Bordeaux apartment, in the Rue de Palais Galien, on 13 September 1861, and was succeeded by his two adopted children, Jean-Camille Eugène and the Baroness Travot, together with her son Jean-Baptiste Ernest. They do not seem to have been interested in Montrose. Five years later they sold the estate to Mathieu Dollfus for 1,050,000 francs.

Dollfus continued the expansion of the vineyard, put in hand some renovations and extensions to the cellars, and built residences on the estate for the workers, naming the small streets which run between the buildings, Rue d'Alsace and Avenue de Mulhouse, after that part of France where he was born. He was also a very progressive employer. The staff had 10 per cent of the profits divided among them, free medical attention and even paid maternity leave. A well was sunk and fresh water produced from it by a windmill for the benefit of the estate, which was by now a self-contained village.

When Dollfus died, childless, in 1887, his heirs sold the estate to Jean-Justin and Jean-Jules Hostein, owners of the neighbouring Cos d'Estournel and Pomys, for a million and a half francs. By this time it had reached its present size, with some 65 hectares under vines, and a production of over 200 *tonneaux*.

A few years later, on 9 December 1896, Jean-Jules Hostein, having acquired sole owner-ship of Montrose, sold it to his son-in-law, Louis Victor Charmolüe, but for only 800,000 francs. It has remained in the Charmolüe family ever since.

Louis Victor Charmolüe was born at Château Figeac in 1860. His mother was Augustine, *née* Lareine, daughter of the proprietor of Figeac at the time. His father's family came from Compiègne, in northern France, and had settled in the Libourne area at the beginning of the nineteenth century. He was owner not only of Montrose, but of Cos d'Estournel, Pomys and several lesser domaines in the Médoc, as well as the island of Fumadelle in the Gironde estu-ary. He died in 1925, having been mayor of Saint-Estèphe continuously since 1900.

The interwar years were not a happy time for the Bordeaux wine trade. Prohibition in the USA, unrest in Europe, and the slump all affected wine sales, particularly in the 1930s, and this was exacerbated by perhaps the worst decade for quality since the phylloxera outbreak. Louis Victor had sold Cos d'Estournel to Fernand Ginestet in 1919, and Pomys had also gone. Albe, Louis Victor's son, was forced to postpone some much-needed renovations to the *chais*, and to reduce the vineyard area to some 50 hectares. Moreover, in 1933 the *cuvier* burned down. This was before the days of electricity, and the cellars were illuminated by lighted candles. The fire occurred at lunchtime, when everyone was indoors, and was well-established by the time a neighbour raised the alarm. A part of the 1932 vintage was lost – perhaps it was used to put out the fire.

The Charmolüe family remained at Montrose during the whole of the Second World War, when the outbuildings were commandeered by a unit of Wehrmacht artillery, set up to guard the Shell petrol refinery at Pauillac. Part of the vineyard was used as a rifle range.

In 1942, an RAF bomber, overshooting its target by some four kilometres, loosed some bombs into the estate. Luckily, they missed the château, but the explosions produced several large craters in the vineyard.

Albe Charmolüe died in January 1944, and for a while Montrose was run by his widow, together with the help of Marcel Borie, mayor of Pauillac, and owner of Château Batailley. From 1948 Mme Charmolüe managed Montrose on her own. Her son, Jean-Louis Charmolüe, the present proprietor, took over in 1960.

THE ESTATE

The estate, now some 95 hectares, lies on the first *croupe* immediately overlooking the Gironde estuary, at this point some five kilometres wide. There are some 68 hectares of vines, planted on sandy gravel in the ratio 65 per cent Cabernet Sauvignon, 10 per cent Cabernet Franc and 25 per cent Merlot, and producing more than 300 *tonneaux*. There is a tiny bit of Petit Verdot left, but it is not being replaced; M. Charmolüe doesn't find it satis-factory from either the quality or the quantity point of view.

Partly because of the proximity of the Gironde estuary, and partly because of the excellent aspect of the vineyard, Montrose enjoys a peculiarly beneficial micro-climate. The Merlot vines suffer less *coulure* than its neighbours, and it normally harvests a few days in advance of the rest of the Médoc, or, alternatively, by waiting until they pick, can obtain grapes of a riper standard.

Comparing Montrose's harvest dates with those quoted in Edmund Penning-Rowsell's *Wines of Bordeaux*, one can see that, with one or two exceptions, they regularly commenced harvesting three or four days in advance of the rest and had normally finished by 12 October. In 1964 Montrose began picking on 18 September and had finished by 1 October, so clearly avoiding the well-known rains.

Bearing in mind how the weather tends to break up once into October, diluting the last of the grapes to be harvested and rendering them prone to rot, one can see the benefit of this precocity: riper grapes in healthier condition and thus better wine.

Charmolüe has recently installed the 33-year-old Bruno Lemoine as *oenologue* and technical director. He joins Jean-Louis Papot, the cellar master, and M. Barreille, the *chef de culture*.

There has been a considerable investment in *cuvier* and *chai* in recent years. The *cuvier* was extended in 1985, twelve extra 100-hectolitre stainless-steel tanks being added to those which exist from 1973. A new barn-like first-year *chai* was built in 1983, the same year it was decided to produce a second wine, La Dame de Montrose. This is named in honour of Mme Charmolüe, Jean-Louis' mother, who ran Montrose from 1944 to 1960.

THE CHÂTEAU

Montrose is a small, elegant family house rather than a grand château, comfortably furnished, and with a splendid collection of paintings. It lies adjacent to a little park, enclosed within a brief low wall, facing the Gironde and surrounded by vines. At the back there is a curious extension, somewhat reminding one of a Swiss chalet. There is a wooded outside gallery which leads to bedrooms on the first floor. This was originally a private chapel, built by Dumoulin in 1820s, but was converted during the Dollfus era.

THE WINE

With only one major exception, Montrose is a consistent wine, producing honest bottles even in mediocre years. One of the few 1956s I have ever drunk – the bottles came from the cellars of All Souls College, Oxford – was a Montrose, a vineyard which escaped the worst of the frost and produced 107 *tonneaux* – more than it had in 1949 or 1952; the wine, drunk towards the end of the 1960s, was light, but fruity and generous. The 1958 also had more substance and depth than most.

The style of the wine has changed in recent years. Montrose used to be, if not a robust wine, certainly a solid, austere one. Both the 1970 and the 1961 can be criticized for being too tough for their own good, having a tannic element which continues to obtrude even now that the wines are well matured. In recent years the wine has been deliberately softened up: there used to be more Cabernet Sauvignon then there is today, and there was, in the 1950s, a significant element of Petit Verdot. This resulted in the one 'failure', the 1983, admittedly a vintage which was generally unsuccessful in Saint-Estèphe. Here at Montrose they suffered badly from *ver de la grappe* (grape-worm). The 1983 is light and diffuse and the 1982 and 1985 lack a bit of richness and concentration. But this brief lapse was rectified in 1986 and since then Montrose has been back on form.

THE TASTING

The following wines were sampled at the Hotel Krone, Assmannshausen, Germany, in May 1993. The tasting was organized by Jan Paulson, with the generous help of Jean-Louis Charmolüe himself.

Optimum drinking

1991 — 1997–2004

Very good, very full, young colour. Young, rich, new oaky nose. Still unformed, but plenty of depth. For a 1991 this has good concentration. Full but not a blockbuster. Good grip too. At present it is raw, but there is fat there, complexity, and really quite a lot, potentially, of generosity. Fine for the vintage. Needs keeping.

1990 — 1998–2020

Youthful colour. Fullish. Rich, fat, rôti nose. Some tannin. Spicy on the palate. Fullish. The tannin a touch vegetal, almost stemmy; this gives a certain bitterness. There is plenty of very ripe fruit here, but a slight lack of real charm and generosity at present. Rich, fat, concentrated and impressive but it hasn't got the class of the 1986.

1989   **1998–2015**

Good full colour. Intense to the brim. Firm nose. Quite rich but a touch hard and unforthcoming. Yet there is depth here. Quite full on the palate. Good ripe tannins and very good acidity. It is a little austere at present but it finishes richer and more opulent than it starts. This is very good for the vintage. But it needs time. It doesn't have the richness and opulence of the 1990 though.

1988   **1995–2002**

Medium-full colour. Still young. Yet the nose is soft and ripe and pleasant, if a little one-dimensional. Medium body. Lacks a little flesh, but is quite ripe, certainly fresh, and there is a little tannin to give it structure. Just about ready. Quite good for the vintage. But most 1988s have more to it than this. This, for Montrose, is a little disappointing. Forward.

1987   **1995–2000**

Medium colour. Youthful. Quite a soft nose. Still a bit raw. Quite full on the palate. Good oaky base. The fruit is ripe and quite concentrated for the vintage. Only one dimension; it lacks a bit of real richness. But certainly a success for 1987. Still needs time.

1986   **1996–2016**

Full colour. Still young. The nose is beginning to develop. Good richness and depth. Fullish, rich and concentration. Now showing some advancement towards maturity. This has good depth and grip. Very good tannins. Nicely fat Cabernet fruit, and the follow-through is beginning to open out. Very good for the vintage.

1985   **1995–2003**

Quite a full colour. A little dense-looking. Quite rich and ripe on the nose. A hint of sweetness and spice. A bit four-square though. This is better than the 1982 – indeed the best of all the early 1980s. Medium-full. Still a bit of tannin. Ripe. Not a great deal of style. But reasonable grip. Good for the vintage but by no means great.

1984   **Drink up**

Medium to medium-full colour. Just about mature. More than a slight hint of the herbaceous and the minty on the nose. On the palate rather astringent. A wine which never had much generosity and is now beginning to dry out.

1983   **Drink soon**

Medium to medium-full colour for the vintage. Fully mature. The nose is lightening up a bit, but underneath there was at least some fruit. Medium body. Ripe, reasonable grip if not much dimension. This is still enjoyable. But the 1981 is more vigorous and much more interesting – as is the 1985. Rather a disappointment for a 1983.

1982   **Now–1999**

Good colour, just about mature. Some fruit on the nose but slightly diffuse. Medium to medium-full. Reasonable grip. But it doesn't have the concentration and voluptuousness of the vintage. Ready. Quite good at best.

1981   **Now–1999**

Medium-full colour. Mature. A bit unforthcoming at present, but good richness, if in a slightly earthy way. I find this fresher and more stylish than the 1982. And with more interest. It has better acidity and the most class of these early 1980s wines. Good Cabernet fruit. Will keep well.

1980   **Drink soon**

Medium colour. Mature. The nose has fruit, but it is getting a little pinched now, and was never that full or fat. For the vintage quite fat and structured. Still fresh on the palate. Even a bit of charm. Beginning to exhibit traces of astringency. But by no means a disaster.

1979   **Drink soon**

Medium to medium-full colour. Mature. This is not exactly corked, but it is certainly stewed and unclean. Dank. Underneath one can see rather a rigid wine. Medium-full. Somewhat four-square. And though there is acidity, beginning to get astringent. It lacks fat. Not exciting.

1978   **Now–1998**

Medium-full colour. Fully mature. There is good Cabernet style here, but a little dense and unforthcoming. Rather four-square. On the palate there is fruit and structure, but not much integration between them. The wine would be better with food. Will a couple more years improve it? It has reasonable grip. The finish is positive. Good, but lacks the balance, finesse and concentration for great.

1977   **Drink up**

Medium colour. Fully mature – even brown. Light on the nose. Never had a great deal of fruit. Not completely finished though. Light but not astringent. At least some fruit. A bit lean, of course, and now a little astringent on the finish. But not a bad effort for the vintage.

1976   **Now–2000**

Medium-full colour. Mature. Slightly austere on the nose, but has fat, some concentration and reasonable fruit. Now *à point*. Medium-full. Good tannins, though the tannins quite apparent. Good grip and really quite concentrated fruit. This has depth. Finishes long. This is the best of the late 1970s, and much better than the 1975 and 1978. Very good plus for the vintage. Still plenty of life.

1975 **Drink soon**

Medium-full colour. Mature. Diffuse on the nose. The fruit is beginning to collapse and the wine lacks style and grip. Medium body. A certain astringency. But the fruit on the palate isn't too bad, and not too short either. Yet a bit dry and papery, and now losing its intensity and fruit. Quite good.

1974 **Drink up**

Not a lot of brown to the colour. But somehow a bit dull and unpromising. Acidity on the nose. Not exactly lean but the fruit a bit dried out as well. There is a touch of spice here which gives it a bit more personality than 1972. Medium to medium-full. No real class, but not as bad as I feared.

1973 **Drink up**

Medium-full mature colour. Somewhat faded, though chunky, on the nose. As 1973s go this is vigorous and still interesting. Medium to medium-full. The attack has sweet fruit and some complexity, and though the follow-through lacks vigour and finesse, this is not at all bad.

1972 **Drink up**

Medium colour. Fully mature. Dilute nose. On the palate medium body. Quite high acidity. Not too much astringency or age, but a lack of charm and real interest. Finishes hard. Not as bad as I feared. Not over the hill.

1971 **Will still keep**

Full colour, mature. Tough, tannic, spicy, slightly dry, old-fashioned nose. Now showing age, even oxidation. Fullish for the vintage. Still sweet. Has, despite the oxidation, class, grip, balance and complexity. This, if in good condition, would still be very vigorous and very good.

1970 **Drink soon**

Quite a full colour. Not a lot of maturity. Not a lot of generosity on the nose. Not a lot of intensity either. On the palate really rather too astringent. Full, rich and concentrated, even fat, but the tannins have always been too obtrusive, and now they are drying out. Better with food. I have had better examples. Good but not great.

1969 **Past its best**

Medium-full colour, fully mature. A light nose, but fragrant. But getting towards the end of its useful life. Lightish on the palate. The fruit has nearly gone. And it is difficult to see what interest it ever had. Seems rather one-dimensional: rather dead.

1967 **Drink up**

Medium to medium-full mature colour. Some fruit on the nose but a little diffuse now. It is losing its class, and it never had a great deal of con-

centration. On the palate, though, a pleasant fruity wine. Not too faded. Reasonable acidity. Medium body. Good example for the vintage.

1966 **Drink up**

Medium-full mature colour. Fresh, medium-weight nose. Quite succulent. This has fruit and generosity and is not too tough. But it evolved fast in the glass. Light to medium body. Has style, but has got a bit astringency now. Yet the fruit has interest still and the finish is long. This bottle seems to lack vigour. Are other bottles better? Rather disappointing today.

1964 **Now–1998**

(Magnum) Good full colour. Still youthful. This is quite substantial, even a little tough on the nose. But there is richness here. Good essentially Cabernet fruit. On the palate perfumed, blackcurranty. Good acidity. Not short. A very good 1964 and one which still has life.

1962 **Drink soon**

Medium-full mature colour. The nose shows substance, but it is a bit four-square. It has lost much of its fruit and charm. Quite substantial on the palate. A bit chunky and solid. But good fruit – if not much fat – and good acidity. It lacks generosity. And it will dry out now. This wine has seen better days.

1961 **Now–2000 plus**

Very good colour. Still very young. A substantial, chunky, solid wine on the nose. Rich and very Cabernet, but somewhat inflexible. Took time to come out in the glass, but when it did a wine of very fine richness and blackcurrant fruit was revealed. Very good acidity. Concentrated, classy, balanced. Still young. Just a little rigid at the attack but very lovely at the end. Still lots of life. Very good indeed.

1960 **Drink soon**

Medium to medium-full colour. Fully mature. This is a bit light on the nose, and though it has lead-pencilly residual oak and some acidity and interest, it has lost a lot of its fruit. Light to medium body. Quite ripe, blackberry fruit. On the palate this still has charm, and the wine is very balanced as well. Finishes better than it starts. Good length. Surprisingly good.

1959 **Now–1998**

Even better colour than the 1961. Full and rich, but much less rigid. Much less 100 per cent Cabernet, of course, and all the better for it, on today's showing. Yet on the palate, while rounder, is a little more astringent. So this is rich and mellow, even fat, but has a bit of dryness as well. Yet the fruit is lovely: complex and mulberry-like. Drink with food. Very good indeed. Almost as good as the 1961.

1955 **Drink soon**

Very good colour. Still vigorous, mature. Just a little hard and unforthcoming on the nose. Full and rich, tannic, just a little tough. But the follow-through is sweet and complex. Very good. Long lingering finish. Classy and subtle. Very good indeed for the vintage.

1953 **Now–1997**

Medium to medium-full colour. Fully mature, a little more so than 1952. Slightly more dried out on the nose. Slightly corky unfortunately. On the palate, though a little tough, one can see more fat and suppleness than the 1952, and I think perhaps more class. This, if not corked, would be a lovely wine. Still with life.

1952 **Now–1996**

Medium colour. Fully mature. Gentle, fragrant, classy, soft. On the palate this has more substance and depth than the 1955. More vigour too. Classy. Fullish, not too solid. This has balance and concentration. And is really quite supple and alive for a 1952. Not a bit too dried out. Very good indeed. Will still keep.

1950 **Drink soon**

Full colour. No undue maturity. Rich, aromatic, sweet-fullish, spicy nose. Cream caramel aspects. Not undue structure. This is a great delight. While there is a little astringency, almost in a 1947 sense, high levels of acidity and a bit of sweetness, it is fat, full, rich and substantial. An old-fashioned wine, but surprisingly good. It doesn't have the class of the 1955 or 1952, but it has plenty of substance. On the palate, as it developed, it began to dry out.

1949 **Now–1998**

Good colour. Lovely nose. This has all the splendid ripe concentrated elegant red-and-black fruit one could wish for. Marvellously balanced. Fresh. Holding up well. On the palate this has much less of the sturdiness of Montrose of some vintages. Medium to medium-full. Round. Complex. Very elegant. Quietly successful. Fine plus. Will still keep well.

1947 **Now–1998**

Medium-full colour. This is fat, rich and succulent on the nose. Not a hint of volatility. This is one of the best 1947 Médocs I have had. Rich, ripe, complex, stuffed with fruit. Fresher than the 1949, possibly not quite as elegant, but more sumptuous and seductive, without, once again, the solidity of some Montroses. Marvellous fat, rich, opulent, *rôti* finish. Fine plus again.

1945 **Drink soon**

Good colour. Firm, impressive. Very, very concentrated nose. Substantial, but not too tough. Rich but very Cabernet, just like the 1961. On

the palate a little rigid and tannic. The fruit is there, as is the acidity, not to mention the concentration, but it is all a little severe, lacking fat. But this is quibbling – it is nevertheless a wine of great depth and quality. The fruit as it developed was very, very rich. But I prefer the 1947 and the 1949 today.

1938 **Past its best**

Quite an old colour now. Interesting nose. Smells of consommé, apples and port. It has lost most if not all of its fruit, and it was never a great vintage.

1937 **Drink soon**

Fine colour for the vintage; vigorous, fullish, mature. Good nose. A little dry and dense, though. Medium body. This is elegant, and still has fat and fruit, even suppleness on the palate. Most 1937s are solid and dried out. This isn't at all. Must be one of the very best. Very good. Not a bit dried out.

1934 **Drink soon**

Good full vigorous colour. Strange nose. Slightly 'off', maderized plus a hint of cork. On the palate rather better. Ripe but chunky. Much more solid and substantial than the 1937. Good residual fruit. Very good again. I prefer the 1937 though, it seems more elegant.

1929 **Now–1998**

Very good colour. Fully mature. Full, fat, concentrated, vigorous nose. There is a lot of depth and quality here. Mocha coffee and blackberry fruit. This is excellent. Fullish, rich, complex and multidimensional. Excellent grip. A very fine wine. Will still keep.

1928 **Drink soon**

Very good colour. Fully mature. Caramel on the nose. Some substance. Rich. *Rôti.* A suspicion of astringency. A fullish, chocolatey, slightly dry wine on the palate. It has more fat but not quite the balance and class of 1926 and 1929. Not a bit too dense. Very good though.

1926 **Drink soon**

From the château. Good colour. Fully mature. Soft, ripe fragrant nose. Getting a bit fragile. But elegant nevertheless. This is a lovely old wine. Real class. Medium to medium-full body. Balanced, gently fruity in a soft red fruit and old roses way. Long. Subtle. Lingering finish. Fine quality.

1924 **Drink up**

Medium colour. Well-matured. Soft, red fruit flavours on the nose. Not a blockbuster. Mature and complex and has good acidity though. This has the least refined tannin of the 1920s flight. And it is a little past its best. Medium-full, balanced, ripe, but has lost a little of its intensity. Yet still enjoyment to be had.

1921   Drink soon

Good colour. Well matured. A little old on the nose. Still fragrant and classy but a little dried out. A lovely wine nevertheless. Medium body. Softening and lightening, but still subtle, complex, classy and multidimensional. This is fine as well. And by no means over the hill. Splendid finish.

1920   Will still keep

From the château. Good colour. Fully mature. Subtle, laid-back, concentrated nose. This is a great wine. Complex, medium to medium-full, lovely complex ripe fruit. Velvety and subtle and very long and lovely. Fullish, ripe, aromatic. Real depth here. Very long. Very vigorous. Not a hint of astringency. *Grand vin.*

1919   Past its best

Good colour. Fully mature. Overblown, sweet, slightly sweet-sour nose. Interesting but a little vegetable soupy. This is past it. No more than a curiosity.

1918   Will still last

Sample from the château. Very good, vigorous full colour. Old-fashioned. Rich, fat, blackcurranty. But dense on the nose. But on the palate fullish, really quite vigorous, balanced and full of interest and finesse, even complex. Not a wine of enormous concentration, but certainly very classy and very good indeed. And with plenty of life. Delicious.

1896   Drink up

This has a reasonable colour, but the wine rapidly faded as it developed in the glass. Still elegant, good substance. Good fruit. Good acidity. Still sweet. There is still enjoyment to be had though. Medium body. Cherry fruit. More alive on the palate than on the nose. Very good.

1893   Drink soon

Bottle direct from the château. Surprisingly vigorous colour. Ripe, very cedary – even lead-pencilly – on the nose. On the palate not a trace of astringency. Round, rich, soft and velvety. The acidity is beginning to show at the end. But this is a lovely wine. Complex, vigorous, elegant, red-fruity. Finishing well. Lovely sweet finish. Very fine plus. Held up very well indeed. As vigorous as the 1940 vintages.

CALON-SÉGUR

Calon-Ségur is not only the most northerly *cru classé* in the Médoc but one of its oldest properties. If Château La Lagune, with one's tongue in one's cheek, can be referred to as the 'first growth' because it is the first major property one reaches from Bordeaux, so Calon could be the last. In fact, for a long time it styled itself *premier cru de Saint-Estèphe* (which indeed it was), but in recent years other proprietors have objected and the practice has been dropped. Calon is Saint-Estèphe's sole third growth. From the historical point of view, however, it is the senior estate, and, by comparison, Montrose and Cos, graded as *deuxièmes crus* in the 1855 Classification, are but interlopers.

Calon lies immediatcly to the north of the village of Saint-Estèphe and the vines run down to the back gardens of the nearest houses from which they are separated by an ancient brick wall. The estate predates the village itself and is said to have existed in Gallo-Roman times. Originally, the whole locality was known as Saint-Estèphe de Calon.

The root of the word '*calon*' is somewhat obscure. Various authorities have suggested that *calon* is an old word for wood or forest and that the boats which ferried timber across the Gironde estuary were known as '*calones*'. Research by the Médoc Archaeological and Historical Society recommends that the origin lies in the old Gallic '*onna*', meaning water, and the pre-Indo-European '*kal*' meaning stone, and has drawn parallels between Calon and Chalonnes-sur-Loire. Far be it for me to quibble with etymologists, but I would have thought that while connotations of rock − i.e., a natural shelter near running water − were appropriate in a Loire context, as they would be in the Dordogne Valley, this hardly applies on the gentle sand and gravel banks of the low-lying Médoc.

HISTORY

Calon was the principal fief of the Lords of Lesparre, one of whom was a Monseigneur de Calon, Bishop of Poitiers in 1157. There are documents in the Bordeaux University, archives dating from soon after, which relate to levies on wine. In 1331, the Seigneur at Calon was a *Mossen* (Old French for *Monsieur*) Gombard, who married Jéhanne de Peyregort, the daughter of the Baron of Lesparre. Their granddaughter Saltida, heiress to Calon, married a Mossen de Pomés in 1362. After the English had been driven out of the Bordeaux area, the estate became the property of the D'Albret family and one of them, Alain d'Albret, known as '*le grand*', gave Calon to his favourite, Jéhan de Lur, in 1481. Some 30 years later the domaine was acquired by Pierre de Marsan. His heirs sold Calon to the Vallier family and in 1581 it passed as dowry to Jean de Gasq.

In the next century, Calon again passed through the female line and this time into the hands of the celebrated Ségur family, eventual owners of Lafite and Latour and much else besides. It was Nicolas-Alexandre, Marquis de Ségur, who married a Mlle de Gasq, heiress to Calon, around 1718, and it was he, the 'Prince of Vines', who is reported to have uttered the well-remembered phrase 'I make my wine at Lafite and Latour but my heart is in Calon', since commemorated by the heart on the label. Ségur died in 1755, and in documents after his death he is styled, amongst other titles, Seigneur de Calon. The property, though, seems to have been assigned to his cousin and son-in-law, Alexandre de Ségur-Calon, Provost of Paris, some time before his decease, as it does not figure in his will. Pierre Butel, the Bordelais historian, has suggested that this gift may have been in 1742, at the same time as he disposed of his post of *président à mortier* in the Bordeaux parliament and when Ségur-Calon married his eldest daughter, Marie-Thérèse. It is probably about this time that the current château was constructed.

After the death of Ségur-Calon, the estate passed to his spendthrift son Nicholas-Marie-Alexandre, heir to Lafite, who was soon forced to sell his inheritance. Calon was bought by Etienne Théodore Dumoulin on 6 March 1778, for 300,500 francs.

Some 34 years later, as the Napoleonic armies were retreating from Moscow and being hounded out of Spain, Calon was the subject of a legal battle between Etienne Dumoulin's son, also Etienne, and his brother Charles. In the end it appears to have been the former who won some sort of Dutch auction. The estate was valued at half a million francs but Etienne junior paid another 50,000 to secure it. Dumoulin, however, soon became more interested in creating a new vineyard out of the scrubland which lay to the south of the parish of Saint-Estèphe and in 1824 he sold the bulk of the Calon estate, including the established vineyard, to Firmin de Lestapis. What he retained became Château Montrose.

Calon at this time was a substantial *vignoble*. There were 55 hectares under vines and production averaged 140 *tonneaux* according to Franck in 1824. In the classifications of this period, it is rated a third growth of the Médoc but the first growth of the commune. This is somewhat of a reduction in status from its position 50 years or more previously. At that time, no doubt helped by the Ségur name and the association with the family first growths, Calon fetched a higher price, indeed higher than all the other potential second or third growths with the exception of Léoville and 'Brane-Saint-Julien', a property which became D'Arbouet, then Cabarrus and is now Lagrange.

The Lestapis were a well-known Médoc family and had estates all over the Gironde, though no other important vineyards. They remained proprietors of Calon throughout most of the rest of the nineteenth century, during which time Calon was confirmed as a third growth and its production slowly increased, following the general trend in the Médoc, to around 225 *tonneaux*. Towards the end of the century, however, the vineyard was neglected. Subsequent generations of Lestapis had left the Gironde and the estate was allowed to run down. Finally, they decided to sell it.

Calon-Ségur was acquired by Georges Gasqueton and his uncle Charles Hanappier in 1894 for half a million francs. The Gasqueton family have been proprietors at Château Capbern in Saint-Estèphe since before the French Revolution, as they still remain, and the Hanappiers were descendants of a Léon Hanappier who had arrived in Bordeaux in 1816 from Orléans and set up as a *négociant*. Charles' daughter Henriette married Maurice Peyrelongue, and it is their grandson Bertrand who is now one of the principal proprietors together with Philippe Capbern Gasqueton, grandson of Georges.

Since the joint purchase, it has always been the Gasqueton side who have managed Calon, though normally living at neighbouring Capbern which lies adjacent to Saint-Estèphe's church, a mile or so away. At first it was Georges Gasqueton who was the administrator, but from 1931 until his death in 1962, it was the celebrated Edouard who ran the estate and he lived at Calon with his wife Elaine. It was under Edouard's aegis that Calon achieved the formidable reputation it enjoyed with its wines of the 1940s and 1950s, when there were many for whom it was not only certainly the best in the commune and the best of the third growths but one of the top wines in the Médoc outside the *premiers crus*. While Edouard Gasqueton was continuing and improving his father's work on the wine, Elaine was refurbishing the château, filling it with antiquities and tapestries, pictures and furniture.

Philippe Capbern Gasqueton is the current administrator. In 1961, the same year as he assumed responsibility for Calon, he bought Château du Tertre, at the time a derelict property in Arsac and one which, purely coincidentally, had also once belonged to the Ségurs. Du Tertre, totally replanted, is now making increasingly good wine. The family also owns Château d'Agassac, a fairy-tale-like château and a *grand bourgeois exceptionnel* in Ludon.

THE VINEYARD

The area under vines at Calon has hardly altered since the Lestapis' purchase in 1824. Then it was 55 hectares; this is approximately the area of mature vines now, though the total possible is perhaps another seven or eight hectares.

The vineyard occupies all the land immediately to the north of the village of Saint Estèphe and much of it is surrounded by a wall forming a large (by Burgundian standards) *clos*. At the northern edge stands the château itself. The vineyard falls mainly to the north and east towards the Gironde and the *palus* on either side of the Chenal de Calon, a drainage ditch excavated by Dutch engineers shortly before the time the estate first became a primarily vine-growing enterprise early in the eighteenth century. Not only is Calon the most northerly of the classed growths, it is possibly the lowest in altitude. The land does not rise above twelve metres and, at points, is barely two above sea level.

The soil is comprised of various gravels of stones of differing sizes mixed in parts with sand and in parts with limestone or clay, and the bed varies in thickness up to five metres deep. This is based on a subsoil of 'Saint-Estèphe limestone', a marly limestone rich in iron. From the sandy gravel comes the finesse, from the heavier soil comes the body.

The vineyard is made up of 60 per cent Cabernet Sauvignon, 20 per cent Cabernet Franc and 20 per cent Merlot. Production averages 240 *tonneaux*. Some years ago there was a much higher proportion of Merlot, as much as 50 per cent, but this was reduced during the 1960s to the present *encépagement*.

THE CHÂTEAU

The château of Calon-Ségur is a substantial edifice. It was constructed in the early eighteenth century and consists of two solid storeys. Unlike *chartreuse*-style buildings such as Langoa, the depth of the Calon château is more than a single room. Moreover, unlike some of the nineteenth-century constructions, the roofs of the side towers are curiously blunted. The stonework is a soft creamy limestone, and the château stands enclosed by a small garden at the bottom of the vineyard on the estuary side of the *chais*.

The interior of the château is a delight. The rooms are well-proportioned, light and airy, housing the Gasqueton family's fine collection of furniture and antiques. Particularly fine are the tapestries which adorn the walls of the main rooms. It is worth a visit.

THE *CHAIS*

Across a courtyard are the *chais*, a number of interconnecting outbuildings in which the wine is made and stored. As you enter, you will pass through an impressive *cuverie* of large wooden vats. Although carefully preserved, these have not been used since 1973. The wine has since been vinified in a battery of 24 100-hectolitre enamel-lined steel vats under the control of André Ellisade, *maître de chai* and under the supervision of Professor Pascal Ribereau-Gayon, Director of the Institut d'Oenologie of the University of Bordeaux. In 1984, a new underground L-shaped cellar was completed, 60 metres in each direction. This houses both the first- and second-year wine.

The vinification is traditional; a little chaptalization, if necessary, to raise the alcoholic degree to 12, a fermentation controlled at 28 to 30 degrees and a *cuvaison* of three weeks according to the vintage. The *vin de presse* is introduced to the blend by using it to top up the evaporation in the barrels. One departure from the norm used to be that the wine stored in a new wood (then about 25 per cent) was kept separate from that stored in old. (At most properties, the opportunity given by the periodic racking is used to move from new to old and vice versa, so, in principle, all the wine has the same amount of time in new and older wood.) This policy was changed recently and Calon now racks in the same way as most. One-third of the barrels are now renewed annually.

THE WINE

Calon-Ségur is a wine which has always shown well when one tastes it young, straight from the cask. It is full, rich, solid and fruity. Often, though, in the 30 years that I have been tasting the wine *en primeur*, it has failed to live up to its early promise and I have heard it said locally that the *élevage* was suspect. It would not be unfair to add that for some time it has not been as fashionable as it was following a run of splendidly successful vintages in the 1940s and 1950s. It is certainly now seen less on British wine lists than one would expect from the size of the vineyard and its past prestige.

One of the explanations for its relatively disappointing showing in bottle is, I believe, the property's insistence on leaving even lighter vintages such as 1984 a full two years in cask. Most top 1984s were bottled in May or June after sixteen months. I would accept that a vintage such as a 1982 could have been held until December 1984, or January 1985, before bottling. For lesser vintages, however, I consider this length of time a serious mistake.

THE TASTING

The majority of the samples below had come straight from the château and were presented by Christie's at a pre-sale tasting in June 1987. Both the 1918 and the 1928 had recently been recorked, but the 1945 still had its original cork. The older wines had been decanted. The vintages from 1989 back to 1982 were sampled at the château in April 1990.

1989 1999–2018

Good colour. Quite a powerful wine. Full, rich, concentrated, substantial. Not aggressive though. This has good grip and a lot of fruit. The nose shows depth. The palate shows quite a lot of tannin but the tannins are ripe and balanced. The finish is long and the acidity is good. Very good indeed.

1988 1998–2015

Good colour. This is *sur colle*. Closed and firm but also stylish on the nose. Difficult to taste but I get a lot of concentration and intensity of flavour on the finish. Very good, I think. Certainly long on the palate.

1987 **Drink soon**

Medium colour. Light but quite pleasant nose. This is not bad for the vintage. Some fruit but a bit rustic.

1986 1995–2008

Medium-full colour. On the nose, there is a little of the Saint Estèphe smokiness and vinosity. Richer and fatter on the palate. Medium-full. Some tannin which is quite but not totally ripe. Good but not great. In the final analysis it lacks concentration and real finesse. There is a touch of astringency. The 1989 is rather superior.

1985 Now–2003

Medium colour. Seems quite a bit more developed than the 1986. The nose has begun to evolve but doesn't show much breed. The palate is medium bodied. There is a little tannin and some quite plump fat. Quite pleasant. Good length. Rather more charm than the 1986. Good.

1984 **Drink up**

Medium colour, mature. Not much nose. A bit watery on the attack. Then a lean follow-through and an astringent finish. Uninspiring.

1983 **Drink soon**

Light to medium colour. Rather less promising than the 1985. Evolved and uninspiring nose. More like a 1973 than a 1983. Weedy, dilute and getting coarser by the finish. The fruit has dried out. Light to medium body. No tannin. Getting astringent on the palate. Lacks grip. Poor.

1982 1995–2008

Good, fullish colour. This is very good. Full, firm, rich nose. Fleshy and spicy. Plenty of fruit. This is continued through on to the palate. Youthful, vigorous, concentrated and fat. A meaty wine, but one which is not without style and dimension. Very good. Still needs time.

1981 **Drink soon**

Medium colour, a little sign of development.

The nose hints that the wine may be a little pinched. A little bland and dilute on the palate, lacking a bit of freshness and zip. As much earthiness and spice as fruit. Better on the finish though, longer and richer than the attack suggests. Quite good to good.

1980 **Drink up**

Reasonable colour for the vintage, not too brown. Fresh enough on the nose. On the palate fully developed. Rather one-dimensional, naturally, but quite pleasant. This seems better than my memories of it. Finishes reasonably fresh. Not bad.

1979 Now–1998

Medium-full colour, not a lot of development. The nose is a bit pinched and the palate a bit dry. Medium dry; as much astringency as tannin. Lacks a bit of flesh and concentration and hence generosity and style. Not too tough or coarse though, just bottled a bit late and therefore not having the intensity of fruit that it should. Quite good at best.

1978 Now–1997

Slightly lighter in colour, more brown. Looks like a fully mature wine. Broad, mature, aromatic nose, with a hint of hydrogen sulphide. Medium-full body, like the 1979 a little dry. Earthier, spicier and coarser-flavoured but it finishes quite positively. Again, only quite good. Just about ready.

1976 **Drink soon**

Good colour for the vintage. Full, vigorous, mature. Similar nose, spicy but not dried out. Fullish, cedary, good earthy fruit. This has depth and interest in a slightly earthy way. Finishes well. Good for the vintage.

1975 **Drink soon**

Medium-full mature colour. Slightly diffuse and dry nose with a touch of spice. Medium-full body. Reasonably plump, not too rustic. A little bitter, a little astringent. Good but not great.

1974 **Drink up**

Medium, mature colour. Quite well-matured and even a bit astringent but not at all without merit. Has fruit and is still reasonably fresh. Not too weak in body.

1973 **Drink up**

Similar colour, less intense, slightly older. Bland, slightly spurious boiled sweet plus attenuated on the nose. This was probably not too bad once but is now a little weedy.

1970 **Drink soon**

Good, full, mature colour. A bit dense on the nose. Similar on the palate. There seems as much astringency as tannin and the fruit behind it is beginning to dry out. I don't think this was ever that stylish and it is now getting clumsy. Too tough for its own good.

1967   **Drink up**

Medium, mature colour, still surprisingly vigorous-looking. Similar nose. The Merlot is evident; the wine is ripe and still reasonably fresh and full of interest. On the palate it is getting a bit astringent but there is depth and complexity and even style for a 1967. Was good. Now needs drinking.

1966   **Drink soon**

Good full mature colour. Soft, fragrant, classy nose. This is a surprisingly good – comparing it with the 1970 – fullish, round, fragrant wine. Good fruit. The Merlot is apparent.

1962   **Drink soon**

Good, full, mature colour. Good nose, quite vigorous. A good wine. Quite full and structured. Now more or less at the end of its useful life but ripe and fleshy and concentrated. Has the usual 1962 generosity if without the style and finesse of Cos d'Estournel for example. A little astringent at the end and beginning to dry up now.

1961   **Drink soon**

Full, mature colour. A smoky nose, with a typical Saint-Estèphe robustness, now a bit dry and tough. A chunky wine with some richness, but it is a bit four-square, and has seen better days.

1959   **Drink soon**

Rather better than the 1961. Full, mature colour. Ample, rich, *rôti*-and-spice nose. Fullish but not robust, sweet, quite complex. Now beginning to lighten up a little but there is still plenty of charm and enjoyment here.

1952   **Drink soon**

Very fine colour, could be a 1970. Lovely nose: rich, blackcurrant and black cherry fruit; complex and fragrant. There is a certain sturdiness here, but the wine is not a bit too tough. Concentrated, old viney, full of finesse. Lovely long finish. Very fine indeed.

1945   **Drink soon**

Still a very splendid colour even after all these years. Full, rich, solid but not dense. Very concentrated. Very structured but has real old-vine, reduced-harvest intensity of flavour. Very rich, not a bit astringent. A masculine, uncompromising wine but very fine.

1928   **Drink soon**

An even more amazing colour, still practically black in the middle. Hints of oxidization as it evolved. Very dense, even stewed, but rich underneath, finishing better than it starts for the attack is almost impossibly astringent. Still sweet, still bags of fruit. Finishes rich and long.

1918   **Drink up**

Excellent colour. The nose is a strange but not at all unattractive blend of consommé and vegetable soup. These flavours remain on the palate but not in such an intriguing way. Full, not as dense as the 1928 but certainly quite structured. Not astringent either.

HAUT-
MARBUZET

Henri Duboscq, fiercely proud proprietor of Château Haut-Marbuzet in Saint-Estèphe, is a man of abundant energy with a voluble and exuberant personality. If wines, like pets, resemble their owners, the proof is at Haut-Marbuzet. 'My wine is like me,' says Duboscq: virile, *caressant* (which I can only inadequately translate as tender, fond), vigorous, larger than life. Haut-Marbuzet is an excitable and exciting up-front wine – exotically perfumed, softly and voluptuously oaky when young. These are sensuous wines. You think they are a bit obvious. Somewhat, as has been said, like a young lady who doesn't need much persuasion to say 'yes'. But when you taste older mature vintages like the 1978, 1970, 1966 and 1962 you realize you were misled. There is more to them than you thought. They, like Henri Duboscq himself, are both highly individual and absolutely charming. *Qualité est ma vérité* (quality is my truth), it proclaims in the cellar, and for this sort of *qualité* and perfectionism you are going to have to pay. Duboscq demands, and has no difficulty in obtaining, the same price for Haut-Marbuzet as the market will pay for Château La Lagune. This makes Haut-Marbuzet easily the most expensive *cru bourgeois*, 20 per cent pricier than stars such as Chasse-Spleen, Angludet and Labégorce-Zédé. You may think this excessive. Yet at a tasting in the US, the 1982 was voted number one and believed by the majority to be Cheval-Blanc. High praise indeed! And, I would suggest, no great error of attribution. There is an element of the heterodox, the arbitrary, even the exotic, in both wines.

HISTORY

The hamlet of Marbuzet lies about a kilometre to the north-east of Cos and today contains a number of properties with titles which are variations of names such as Marbuzet and MacCarthy, plus Château Le Crock, owned by the Cuvelier family of Léoville-Poyferré. In the eighteenth century the *bourdieu* of Marbuzet or Marmuset was part of the estate of Alexandre de Ségur, proprietor of Calon, Lafite and Latour. On his death in 1776 it was bought by Marc-Antoine Domenger, *régisseur* of Château Latour. Perhaps it was from this time onwards that vines became the main crop of the estate.

The other main estate in the area was owned by the MacCarthy family. The origin of the MacCarthys was Ireland, from where they had emigrated at the turn of the century, perhaps as a consequence of the Battle of the Boyne. In Bordeaux their fortunes flourished. One MacCarthy set himself up as a wine merchant; another became director of the Bordeaux Chamber of Commerce; a third was a high-ranking naval officer. They were ennobled as Counts by Louis XV and given the *seigneurie* of Marlière. They too must have had vines on their lands in Saint Estèphe.

While the Domenger domaine was sold to the Merman family during the French Revolution – and from this issued Château Le Crock and Château de Marbuzet – the MacCarthy estate remained in the family until 1854. In this year there was one of those inheritance crises so directly consequential on the Code Napoleon and the 61-hectare vineyard (it produced 60 *tonneaux* in 1845) was split. It was divided into seventeen parts. The total price the domaine fetched was 144,329 francs. One part was bought by a Monsieur Poissonnier who called his seven hectares Château Haut-Marbuzet. It was more than 100 years before it would be reunited.

HERVÉ DUBOSCQ

We turn to the 1930s and to Hervé Duboscq, the sort of Gascon of whom D'Artagnan would have been proud. The Duboscq family was poor. They marginalized a living tending sheep in the uplands of the Lot-et-Garonne. They were largely illiterate. In Hervé, however, chance dealt a trump card – or was it a joker? Though unable to read or write at the age of nine, Hervé was patently a bright lad. He was apprenticed to the local railway company at fourteen, learned his letters, and shortly after returning from completing his national service was appointed the youngest inspector in France. Further promotion followed, and he found himself deputy manager of the station at Langon in 1937.

Hervé was now in his twenties. He had learned to live well. Wine, women and song (as he puts it) were his pleasures, and he soon found his income exceeding his expenditure. As a sideline, acting under the name of his wife, he became a cork salesman – the family home at Lavardac is the cork capital of France – and he soon had an extensive network of contacts in the Gironde, particularly in the Sauternais. This brought him into the *milieu* of such as Georges Bert, the not entirely scrupulous proprietor of the *négociants* Louis Bert et Fils of Barsac. (It was Bert's son, the engaging rogue Pierre, who was the central cog in the 'Winegate' scandal of 1973.) Georges Bert had a huge business, dealing mainly in *petits châteaux* and generics, and specializing in sweet wine which, whatever its origin, was inevitably bottled as Sauternes. At the end of the war Bert encouraged Duboscq to go into wine. 'You can become a *négociant en chambre*,' he urged. 'Sell my wine under your name in the north of France, send me the orders, and I will supply the wine under your label.'

This is what Hervé Duboscq set out to do. But he soon began to fear that his customers would discover the true origin of the wine they were purchasing from him and would deal direct. He decided to look to the export market. Despite speaking not a word of English he arrived in London in 1951 and went to see Bill Kopp of Bouchard Aîné. To his amazement he not only succeeded in obtaining orders but was asked by Bouchard Aîné if they could represent his firm in the United Kingdom.

But he didn't have a firm, as such! He bought a moribund company called Brusina-Brandler, rented a warehouse, and such was the success of Bouchard Aîné that by 1955 he had become the largest exporter of Bordeaux to Britain. The speciality was in *petits châteaux*, bought, blended and shipped in bulk for bottling as generic wine: Saint-Emilion, Médoc, Saint-Estèphe.

One of the wines he regularly purchased was that of Haut-Marbuzet. He liked the wine, and subsequently found out that Monsieur Lambert, son-in-law of the descendants of Monsieur Poissonnier, wanted to sell out. So in 1952 Duboscq became proprietor of Haut-Marbuzet. From then on the wine was sold under its château name. As you might expect this did not go down too well with the Ginestet family, now proprietors of Château de Marbuzet. Bernard Ginestet recalls Duboscq's arrival, describing him as looking like a half-starved wolf. When Duboscq painted the name Haut-Marbuzet in large, gleaming red letters on the side of his *chais* there was consternation. No one, it seemed, had been aware that there *was* a Château Haut-Marbuzet! This must be stopped, demanded the female members of the family. Ginestet *père*, however, was more sanguine. 'Come, come,' he said. 'We belong to the landed gentry. Everyone knows there is only one Château de Marbuzet, and it belongs to us. And, after all, everybody's got to live.'

The vineyard was practically *en friche*, devoid of vines. But Hervé Duboscq was to prove himself as much a genius as a wine-maker as a salesman. In 1953 only 44 barrels were produced. When Bouchard Aîné arrived with some customers in the spring of 1954 a blind tasting of all the top Saint-Estèphes was arranged. Everyone preferred the Haut-Marbuzet. Bouchard Aîné wanted to buy 300 casks. In the end all 44 were purchased by one of my predecessors at British Transport Hotels, the redoubtable Mr Sweeney, and George Potts of the Savoy Hotel. But, said Hervé Duboscq, as you have placed this wine higher than all the other Saint-Estèphes, you are going to have to pay me the price as Château Montrose is asking. This was agreed.

Thus began the Haut-Marbuzet empire. In 1956 Duboscq bought Château MacCarthy-Moula; in 1962, Chambert-Marbuzet; and gradually over the years the remaining parts of the original MacCarthy estate have been acquired, culminating in the purchase of Château MacCarthy itself in 1987. (These thirteen hectares cost the same – 10 million francs – as Grand-Puy-Lacoste had fetched a decade previously, points out Henri Duboscq.)

Britain has always been the chief export market, taking 2,500 cases a year. A thousand cases are reserved for the US, but no more: Henri Duboscq is somewhat wary of the hot-one-day, cool-the-next attitude of the Americans towards vintages. Most is sold to a clientele of some 25,000 private individuals in France.

HENRI DUBOSCQ

Henri Duboscq joined his father in 1962 and has been entirely responsible for the wine since 1973. It was at about this time that the wine first came into my ken, for one of the wines I found in the BTH inventory when I took over was the 1971, an excellent purchase in what was largely ultimately to prove a disappointing vintage. From 1962 onwards 50 per cent new wood was employed in the *élevage*, and from 1970, 100 per cent.

Born in 1944, Henri Duboscq is vibrant, persuasive, voluble and engaging, as passionate about wood as he is about everything else. You must choose the *provenance* of your oak according to the character of the vintage, he proclaims. Allier and Tronçais in the good years. The Allier gives aromas of coffee, chocolate, caramel and spice; the Tronçais is aristocratic, giving balsamic flavours of resin. The 1988 was matured using 60 per cent of the former and 40 per cent of the latter. Wood from the Nièvre is more exotic: honey, vanilla and cinnamon. The Jupille in the Sarthe produces more floral cadences, violets and fruit such as black-currant and raspberry. The Vosges is for lesser vintages. It gives a tannic backbone necessary in wines which lack a little structure, and in a classy sense too.

Henri Duboscq is equally discursive on the *encépagement*. In the vineyard the 45 hectares are planted with 60 per cent Merlot, 10 per cent Cabernet Franc and 30 per cent Cabernet Sauvignon. This is usually more Merlot than he needs. The composition of the 1988 was 50 per cent Merlot, 10 per cent Cabernet Franc and 40 per cent Cabernet Sauvignon. It is the Merlot which gives the richness and the fat, but it is also the variety which is most prone to rot. It is vitally important to sort through the fruit and eliminate anything substandard before the grapes are allowed to enter the fermentation vat.

Château Haut-Marbuzet is vinified in a battery of concrete tanks. To concentrate the must a *saignée* is regularly performed. Fermentation progresses at a high temperature and the maceration is prolonged as long as possible, often for as much as five weeks.

THE WINE

Duboscq produces four wines from his Saint-Estèphe domaine: Château Haut-Marbuzet and its second wine, Tour de Marbuzet; Château Chambert-Marbuzet from a separate sixteen hectare parcel and its second wine Château MacCarthy.

I have already described the wine. It is simply today the third best wine – sometimes the second best wine – in the commune. Only Château Cos d'Estournel is clearly and consistently superior. How does Henri Duboscq describe his produce? 'If Chambert-Marbuzet is a Saint-Estèphe made by Henri Duboscq,' he says, 'then Haut-Marbuzet is a wine made by Henri Duboscq which just happens to come from Saint-Estèphe; an expression of my personality.'

THE TASTING

I tasted the following wines at Château Haut-Marbuzet in April 1989.

Optimum drinking

Chambert-Marbuzet, 1988   1994–2000
One-third new oak. A less exuberant wine than its stable companion. Good colour. Solid, with good blackberry fruit. Fullish. More obviously Saint-Estèphe. Slightly four-square. Finishes well.

Haut-Marbuzet, 1988   1996–2008
Allier wood: Good colour. Not that marked by the wood on the nose. Full and rich and sumptuous. Medium body, quite sustained oak on the palate. Glossy, spicy, rich. Quite fat. Good grip. Long on the palate.

Troncais wood: Rounder, fatter, creamier but less structure.

Blend: Better than the sum of its parts. Rich. Very long and complete. High class.

1987   Now–2006
Bottled a week previously. Medium colour. Vosges wood. 60 per cent Merlot. Fat, rounded oaky nose. No weakness. Medium body. Shows well despite the recent bottling. Long on the palate. Very good for the vintage.

1986   Now–1999
Medium colour. Slightly chalky nose. 15 per cent Cabernet Franc, 50 per cent Merlot, 35 per cent Cabernet Sauvignon. One can taste the higher per centage of Cabernet Franc. Medium body only. A little tannin. Honeyed and stylish. Long but I would have expected a bit more concentration and muscle.

1985   1995–2008
Medium-full colour. Gamey nose, exotic and perfumed. Coffee and chocolate. Good ripe tannins. This is rich, concentrated and full of fruit. Rather more to it than the 1986. Very good ripeness, but also a very good grip. Well balanced. Long on the palate. Already quite complex.

1984   Drink up
Good colour for vintage. Somewhat sturdy, stalky and vegetal, dense on the nose. Rather better on the palate than the nose would indicate. The exotic violet, blackberry perfumes of Haut-Marbuzet are there and the wine is by no means either lean or short. Enjoyable if without real class.

1983   Now–2002
Good colour, not as good as the 1985 though. Smoky nose, rich and fat. Milk chocolate as it

evolved. Now beginning to show some maturity. Quite full. Some tannin but the tannins a little drier than those of 1985. Not quite as rich or as complex. Good. Finishes well.

1982 — Now–2005

Very good colour. Fat, ripe *sur maturité-fruit* element. Coffee and chocolate again but covered by this very rich, almost cooked fruit element. This is very fine indeed, certainly on the attack. Very rich and creamy and complex. Does it quite have the backbone? I ask myself. Full, still some tannin.

1981 — Now–1998

Good colour for vintage. Not a lot of maturity. Very fine stylish nose. Complex. Medium to medium-full body. A little unresolved tannin but just about ready. Good fruit in the usual perfumed, new oaky way. Not an enormous amount of depth underneath but good to very good for vintage. Not quite as long on the finish as the attack would invite us to expect.

1979 — Now–1999

Very good colour. Little sign of maturity. Quite a solid, earthy nose. A sturdy wine. Better on the palate. Full, rich, just about ready. There remains a certain four-square element but ripe and concentrated, even quite sweet at the end. Certainly good. Long.

1978 — Now–2010

Very good mature colour. Fine classy fruit on the nose. Depth, elegance and quality here! Lovely concentration. Full, rich, distinguished wine. Finely balanced. Very classy. This has excellent concentrated ripe fruit and a fine balancing acidity. An exciting wine. Real finesse.

1977 — Drink up

Good colour. No weakness. Light but not unduly faded, dirty or attenuated. This surprisingly good. A little one-dimensional but quite ripe. No weakness nor astringency.

1976 — Drink soon

Good colour. No undue brown. A plump, fat nose with a little heaviness and lack of zip behind it. As it evolved I could smell toast. Medium-full. Rich and fat. A certain astringency welling up. No great finesse or dimension but a good example of the vintage.

1975 — Now–2000

Very good colour. Good ripe nose with a certain structure underneath. Class here if not in the abundance of the 1978. A good 1975. Possibly a bit all upfront, i.e. with no reserves of subtlety to show on the follow-through, but ripe, balanced, long and satisfying. Medium body. Just about ready.

1973 — Drink up

Very good colour for vintage. Slight paper-dryness on the nose. Dead leaves. Medium body. A certain astringency and beginning to get a little coarse. Past its best.

1972 — Drink up

Good colour. Curious nose. A touch of celery and asparagus. Not at all bad. I prefer it to the 1973. Curious flavour. Some fruit. Not astringent.

1970 — Drink soon

Very good colour. Not a lot of maturity. Good mature rich wine on the nose. Not the class of the 1978 but with good depth. A little more four-square perhaps. There is a certain sturdiness and astringency on the palate now, but a good rich wine nevertheless.

1970

(Second bottle) A second bottle was rather richer and fatter. No undue astringency. Indeed with all the laid-back generosity of the vintage. A little solider than the 1966 nevertheless. Good grip. Rich finish. Very fine.

1966 — Drink soon

(Magnum) Very good colour. Not a lot of maturity. Classy nose. Fine blackberry fruit. Complex and elegant on the palate. Subtle on the follow-through. Harmonious. Lovely finish. Delicious.

1964 — Drink soon

Medium colour, now mature. Fully matured nose. Good complexity though lightening up a bit. A rich, cooked element just like a fruit cake, and certainly with candied peel. Very good but beginning to show its age and shortening up.

1962 — Drink soon

Very good colour; not a lot of maturity. Slightly dense and inky on the nose at first. Good fruit but smells older than it is. This has a real old wine smell, which is not to indicate that it is faded. Complex, slightly spicy. Certainly classy. Still very much alive. Lovely.

1957 — Drink soon

Good colour. Smells of burnt plum tart. Medium body. There is a certain amount of astringency on the palate but there is – or was – good fruit and not too much solidity. Now beginning to lighten up. Old vines I would judge. Still enjoyable.

1953 — Drink soon

Very fine colour. Little sign of age. Very lovely distinguished classy nose. Subtle, complex, creamy rich. Marvellous fruit. This is very high class indeed. Quite full. A touch of astringency. Very rich and concentrated. Exceptional old-vine concentration. Splendid. Holding up well.

MARG

WHILE THE OTHER THREE GREAT COMMUNES OF
THE MÉDOC FORM A CONTINUOUS CHAIN OF VINE-
YARDS – FROM BEYCHEVELLE TO CALON-SÉGUR –
MARGAUX LIES SEPARATELY TO THE
SOUTH. IN BETWEEN THE LAND
IS MORE MARSHY, THE GRAVEL
CROUPES LESS WELL DEFINED, AND
NO GREAT PROPERTIES ARE TO BE
FOUND.

However, Margaux is not one but five communes: Labarde, Arsac and Cantenac, the communes to the south, and Soussans, neighbour to the
north, all have the right, in whole or in part, to call
their wines Margaux.

This conglomeration of parishes boasts no fewer
than 21 classed growths: one first (Château Margaux), five seconds, no fewer than ten thirds, three
fourths and two fifths. The soil varies but is generally a sandy gravel, thinner than in Saint-Julien and
Pauillac, and lighter in colour. This lies on a base
which in Margaux itself is partly marl, partly clay.
Elsewhere the subsoil is sometimes gravel, sometimes iron-rich *alios*, and in Labarde is sand and
'*gravier*' (grit).

I find it difficult to generalise about the style of
Margaux wines, for they vary greatly. While they
are softer, have less backbone, develop sooner than
Saint-Juliens, and have less of the pronounced
Cabernet Sauvignon and oak flavour (one is supposed to find a scent of violets in a Margaux), there
are some Margaux wines – Lascombes and Marquis-de-Terme, for example – which are every bit
as 'big' as wines further north. The classic character
of the commune, however, which others have
called feminine, is that found at Château Margaux
itself, Château Palmer, and in wines like Issan and
Rausan-Ségla. These have an inherent delicacy and
elegance right from the start, which is not to say
they do not have plenty of body and potential for
ageing well.

On the whole the *encépagement* in the five
Margaux communes contains more Merlot and less
Cabernet than further north, and this gives a 'soft
fruits' flavour I also find in wines of the Graves.
Like them Margaux may be less successful than
Pauillac and Saint-Julien in lighter, poorer years.

MARGAUX

'The most delicate and the most poetic of the three greatest Médocs,' wrote Morton Shand. 'Certainly no wine can equal a fine Margaux in delicate fragrance and subtlety of taste,' according to Warner Allen. If it has, and rightly, been occasionally criticized for producing disappointing wine in poor years, few would dispute the potentiality of Château Margaux's greatness in successful vintages. Since the war the 1953 and the 1961 have found their way into wine writers' 'first eleven'. I suspect later vintages, like the 1983, will be chosen as 'desert island bottles' in the years to come.

As Nicolas Faith, to whom this profile is much indebted, has pointed out in *Château Margaux*, while all wine estates depend for their success on the interest, dedication and financial resources of their owners, Margaux, with its tendency to produce a 'fragile' wine, is more susceptible than most. Margaux, under the Ginestets, often produced wine which was not really worthy of a first growth estate, particularly in the late 1960s and early 1970s. When the Ginestet empire crashed in the Bordeaux *crise* of 1973 to 1974 both vineyard and reputation were in a sorry state. In the last two decades, however, there has been a dramatic reversal of quality. This is the Mentzelopoulos phenomenon. In 1978, in 1981, even in 1980, Château Margaux made a wine which was as good, if not better, than anything produced elsewhere in the Gironde. The 1983 is the best yet. This is a magnificent bottle, which I am sure will go down as one of the greatest both the property and Bordeaux itself have ever created. Vintages since have confirmed a triumphant return to first growth quality.

HISTORY

Château Margaux, as befits a *premier cru*, has a long and distinguished history, but it has also had a bewildering succession of owners, and as a result its fortunes, and the standard of its wines, have had their ups and downs. The manor or domaine of Margaux dates back to the early Middle Ages. According to one source, there was a fortress here in the thirteenth century, one of a number at intervals up the Gironde estuary protecting the countryside from pirates. In those days the area was called '*La Motte*' (the mound) or '*Lamothe*'. Much of the lower land would spend large parts of the year under water, and settlements tended to be concentrated on those small ridges, guaranteed dry whatever the season, and lying between the forest, which in those days occupied most of what is now the Médoc, and the river.

According to another source the domaine at one time belonged to Edward II of England, though there seems little evidence of this. There is a more dependable record of two of the *seigneurs* in the fifteenth century named Montferrand and De Durfort, a name which survives in Margaux to this day. It had certainly belonged somewhat earlier to the family D'Albret, one of France's senior families at the end of the Middle Ages, and from whom the French Henry IV, the first French Renaissance man, chose his wife.

From Durfort the estate passed in 1480 to Jean Gimel, a rich Bordeaux merchant, and then through the female line to the Lory family. A sixteenth-century deed refers to Jehan Lory, *seigneur de la noble mothe de Margaux*, and mentions lands, not only in the Margaux commune, but in Soussans and Cantenac.

Towards the end of the sixteenth century, the estate passed from a Jean de Lory to his cousin, Guy de Lestonnac. It was under successive Lestonnacs that the estate began to assume its present form; parcels were bought or exchanged with local peasants and the Margaux holding gradually changed over the years from a number of scattered plots into a compact and homogeneous estate centred on the *maison noble* and surrounding farm buildings on the first *croupe* of gravel just east of the village itself.

At the beginning of the seventeenth century Margaux passed into the D'Aulède family. Jean d'Aulède had married Françoise de Lestonnac in 1582 and in 1612 his son Pierre inherited the Margaux estate on the death of his uncle, changing his name to Pierre d'Aulède de Lestonnac. The D'Aulèdes were a distinguished family, one of the oldest in Bordeaux. Pierre's son, Jean-Denis, was to marry into an even more distinguished family, the Pontacs, when he married Marie-Thérèse de Pontac in 1654.

By this time Margaux had attained its present size. A register in 1680 states that the domaine covered about 260 hectares, of which about a third was let off to tenant farmers. Under his direct control D'Aulède had about 70 hectares of vines, much the same size as the vineyard today.

In some of the earliest references in England to specific vineyard wines, the records at the beginning of the eighteenth century of the purchases of the Earl of Bristol and Robert Walpole, the wine appears frequently and variously as Margaux, Margouze, Margooze, Margeau, Margau and even Margot.

Through Marie-Thérèse the D'Aulèdes acquired a half share in Haut-Brion, and Jean-Denis' heir, Pierre-François, who succeeded his father in 1694, and was reputed to be 91 when he died in 1755, became not only Baron of Margaux but also a Marquis. Together with the Marquis de Ségur, owner of Lafite, Mouton and Latour, he was the most powerful vineyard-owner in Bordeaux.

On François' death, his second wife, Marie-Antoinette-Charlotte de Lenoncourt, whom he had married when he was over 80, assumed control of the estate. D'Aulède was childless, and eventually, again through the female line, Margaux passed to Comte Joseph de Fumel.

Fumel had one child, his daughter Marie-Louise-Elizabeth, now heiress of both the Fumel and D'Aulède estates. Not surprisingly she was a prime target for the unscrupulous.

These were the Du Barrys, the infamous Jeanne herself, and the family she had married into. The youngest of her brothers-in-law, Elie, was perhaps the least awful of the family, and was an army officer whose career had been considerably assisted by his royal connections.

After some pressure the marriage took place. Elie du Barry's original intention was to assume his wife's name for himself, but the Fumels forbade this. Instead, he took his mother-in-law's maiden name. Margaux passed to the self-styled Comte d'Agricourt.

One of the more interesting guides to French wines during the immediate pre-revolutionary period is contained in the letters that Thomas Jefferson, then American Minister in France, but later of course to become President, sent back to the United States following a tour in 1787. Jefferson was more than just an enthusiastic wine buff, he actually planted vineyards from imported cuttings in his home state of Virginia, and he took a keen interest in both the economics of the wine trade and the latest methods of viticulture and viniculture.

Jefferson placed Margaux at the top of a list of four first growths – the same four as were classified in 1855 – and goes on to mention the owner, the Marquis d'Agicourt (*sic*); the quantity produced (150 *tonneaux* of 1,000 bottles each); and the price – the excellent 1784 was fetching 2,400 *livres* the *tonneau* and was now ready for drinking. In fact he bought some of this wine in Bordeaux. 'It cost me 3 *livres* a bottle. This is very dear.'

However, the sands of the old order were rapidly running out. D'Agricourt emigrated, and his wife and her father were both guillotined. Margaux was sequestrated by the State, leased to a man called Migeau, who milked the estate dry and allowed it to run down. After having been briefly owned by Laure Fumel, a niece of Joseph, it was bought in 1802 by another Marquis, Douat de la Colonilla, for the low price of 650,000 francs (Lafite had sold five years previously for 1,200,000). The new owner ordered the demolition of the existing building without ever having visited the estate, and commissioned the château we see today. This was completed in 1810.

In 1836 the property was acquired by a banker – the first of many to move into classed-growth ownership – Viscomte O. d'Aguado, Marquis de las Marismas, a man of Franco-Spanish origin and a patron of Rossini. His son sold to another banker, the Comte Pillet-Will, for 5 million francs in 1879.

Pillet-Will, of course, had soon to face the problem of phylloxera, and he was by no means an absentee landlord. He introduced a number of vinicultural improvements, and was quick to poach good ideas from neighbouring proprietors. After him the ownership passed to his godson and son-in-law, the Duc de la Trémoille.

It is perhaps fitting that after the 'war to end wars' this long succession of aristocracy at Margaux should die out, that the commoners should have their chance, and, moreover, that the ownership should be vested in a limited company.

A syndicate, headed by Pierre Moreau, a Bordeaux broker with Herault connections, bought out the Duc de la Trémoille in 1921. From 1935 onwards Fernand Ginestet began to buy the shares of the other members, and his son Pierre completed the purchase in 1949, having sold the family property in Saint-Emilion, Clos-Fourtet, in order to finance the deal, restore the building and furnish it inside.

Not only did they restore the château, they transformed the vineyard and the wine. Under the Moreau aegis the entire production had been sold as Château Margaux, and though mandatory château bottling was introduced, this obviously diluted the quality of the wine. Nicolas Faith mentions that when the Ginestets arrived they found that each of the eighteen fermentation vats led to a single outlet, making nonsense of the tradition of a careful assemblage of the best vats for the *grand vin*. Ginestet dismantled this, and diverted the less good wine to the firm's generic Margaux.

He reconstructed the estate, exchanging land with Rausan-Ségla, acquiring some of the holdings of Château Abel-Laurent, which lies between Margaux and Palmer, and buying

Durfort-Vivens from the Delor family, who, like many in the 1930s, were having financial problems at this time. Finally, the Ginestets were able to complete the purchase, swapping Clos-Fourtet with Lucien Lurton of Brane-Cantenac, in exchange for the 40 per cent share of Margaux the latter had inherited from his father-in-law, 'Père' Récapet.

Meanwhile, the policy of compulsory château bottling had been reversed. British Transport Hotels, as with other select importers, shipped in wood until as late as the 1949 and 1953 vintages. During the 1940s, 1950s and 1960s the wine of Durfort-Vivens was made at the château, and this name effectively became the second wine of Margaux.

The Ginestets remained proprietors until 1976. Pierre Ginestet had sold the adjoining second growth of Durfort-Vivens – the vineyard, but not the château, where his son, Bernard, currently lives – to Lucien Lurton, proprietor of Château Brane-Cantenac, in 1963; and Château Cos d'Estournel was transferred to Madame Prats, his sister, in 1971, and is now run by her son Bruno; all this to concentrate his proprietorial skills on Margaux. But then came the wine madness of 1972 and 1973 and the savage slump which succeeded it. Margaux was up for sale.

One interested purchaser was the American conglomeration National Distillers, but with Latour and Haut-Brion already foreign-owned, and a number of other classed growths in alien hands, this was too much for French pride. Some 82 million francs were offered but the sale was vetoed by the government. Finally an acceptable purchaser was found, the French supermarket group Félix Potin – whose Greek owner, the late André Mentzelopoulos, was a major shareholder in the French wine firm of Nicolas – and a price was agreed at 72 million francs, to include three vintages, the 1974, 1975 and 1976, lying in the château's cellars.

Mentzelopoulos

Mentzelopoulos was a financial wizard and a perfectionist, and just the man to rescue Margaux in its hour of need. Yet his purchase of Margaux, and the substantial investment he made in it since, was no mere act of charity. Running a first growth property is big business, and there is no reason why it should not be a profitable one. Yet it confers a responsibility: a duty to produce the best that the estate is capable of producing. This is what Mentzelopoulos set out to do.

He made one major new appointment, the introduction of Philippe Barre as *régisseur*, but otherwise the staff, headed by Jean Grangerou as *maître de chai* (who like many in the Médoc, took over from his father Pierre) and Jean-Pierre Blanchard, *chef de culture*, remains as it did at the end of the Ginestet era.

Land was drained, the stream running through the vineyard was thoroughly dredged, and nearly twelve hectares replanted. A new underground second-year *chai* was constructed. Curiously, and contrary to the advice of Alexis Lichine, a good friend of Mentzelopoulos, when the time came to renew the fermentation vats, oak was re-employed, stainless steel was not introduced. Finally, Professor Emile Peynaud, lately director of the Bordeaux Institut Oenologique, was appointed as an adviser. However, it was not only the vineyard and the *chais* which were undergoing restoration. This also applied to the château.

Firstly, the facade was cleaned. More importantly the interior has been transformed. Up to now it had always been furnished in the Second Empire style of the time of the Aguados. It has now been restored in the style of the time of Victor Combes, the architect of the château: the French Regency of the first Napoleon.

André Mentzelopoulos, sadly, was unable to see the fruit of his efforts come to full maturity; for he died suddenly in 1980 at the age of 66. Undaunted, his widow Laura and daughter Corinne decided to carry on: 'At first we continued my father's work out of pride,' Faith quotes Corinne as saying. 'We simply didn't have the right to let it fail.'

In Corinne Mentzelopoulos, attractive, determined and fiercely intelligent, André had a worthy successor, and the media an instant star. After her mother married again Corinne took over Margaux in her own right, sharing the equity with IFINT, a company belonging to the Angelli family, and one in which she herself is a significant shareholder.

THE ESTATE

The visitor approaches Château Margaux through an avenue of trees, leading down to the four Doric pillars and portico incongruously stuck on to the frontage of the mansion as if it had been temporarily borrowed from the British Museum. To the right, beyond the garden, is the main *chai*, an impressive low-ceilinged building about 100 metres long by 30 wide, and containing the first year wine maturing away in new oak casks, vividly stained crimson with spillage from the *ouillage*, or weekly topping up. The barrels here lie on the floor one deep. Adjoining this is the *cuverie* with its 26 much larger, oak fermentation vats.

Adjacent to the first-year cellar is a reception room and small museum, complete with signed photographs of the famous, menus of state and royal banquets, old vinous knick-knacks and historical maps and documents. Beneath the courtyard is the second-year cellar.

The estate occupies some 250 hectares at the north-east corner of the Margaux commune. Some 57 people work here, and live close by in a self-supporting commune with its own electricity and water supply. As well as vineyard workers and those in the cellars, these include masons, electricians, plumbers, painters and mechanics, as well as coopers, for Château Margaux has its own cooperage, producing 600 barrels a year.

Some 75 hectares are planted with vines, in the ratio 75 per cent Cabernet Sauvignon, 2–3 per cent Cabernet Franc, 20 per cent Merlot and 2–3 per cent Petit Verdot, producing about 250 *tonneaux* of wine a year. This is a higher percentage of Cabernet Sauvignon and a lower per centage of Merlot than in pre-Mentzelopoulos times. The second wine is Pavillon Rouge du Château Margaux.

Most of the Château Margaux vineyard is situated on the first *croupe*, or ridge, overlooking the fertile meadows that run gently away towards the Gironde estuary, which here divide around the Ile de Macau. The soil is thin. On the surface is a fine layer of stones or *graves* mixed with sand. Beneath this is grittier coarser gravel, known as *gravillons*, containing sand and lime, and underneath this is purer calcareous soil, combined with clay, known as the Calcaire de Plassac, and unique to this commune in the Médoc.

THE WINES

As well as the vintage red wines, Margaux has made two other blends, uncommon in the Médoc in recent years. The first of these is a white wine, now grown on a particular 12-hectare section of the property at Virefougasse, two kilometres west of the village of Margaux. There is a small plateau here of soft-water chalk, high enough not to be alluvial, but without the classic Médoc gravel. Originally another part of the vineyard was planted 50–50 with Sémillon and Sauvignon, and produced a wine labelled as Pavillon Blanc du Château Margaux. I met it both with and without a vintage, and it always struck me as stylish and attractive. These vines were then grubbed up for a time and production ceased. More recently, from the 1977 vintage, Pavillon Blanc from the Virefougasse plot has recommenced. I am glad the wine has reappeared, for we were at one time led to believe it had been permanently discontinued, and though the wine does not aspire to the heights of Laville-Haut-Brion, it is pleasant wine, and white Graves without a famous name has been until recently very hard to sell at anything much above generic price. It is now made 100 per cent from the Sauvignon grape, fermented in Allier wood, of which half is new oak, and bottled in the summer following the vintage.

The other was an experimental non-vintage, first produced as a blend of 1963 and 1964, and later presumably using some of the 1965, a vintage which never appeared under the château label. Ginestet also tried this idea at Cos d'Estournel, as did a few of his neighbours. I must confess I am not enthusiastic. Without a vintage date or a bottling date on the label, the consumer is totally in the dark about when to drink it; so it may have been my misfortune to have aged bottles. Anyway, the experiment did not last.

As at Ausone, and at the same time, the transformation from second-rate – in all its pejorative sense – to true *premier cru* was almost instantaneous. The 1975 is clumsy and uninspired, but the 1976 is certainly one of the better wines of this disappointingly evolving vintage, though this was not made – only *élevé* – under the new regime. By 1978 we are firmly back in the land of the *sérieux*, the first-rate.

A central explanation of this achievement was simply a more rigorous selection of the vats. Pavillon Rouge, the second wine, was, in fact, reborn in 1975, before the change-over, when Jean Grangerou decided that only half the enormous 1974 crop was fit to be labelled as the *grand vin*. The name had been used in the nineteenth century but then forgotten. In 1980 this 1974 Pavillon, bottled in November 1976, was launched on to the market, and Pavillon Rouge is now a permanent feature on Bordeaux wine-lists, selling, like Les Forts de Latour, for the same sort of price as a good second growth.

A second change was a policy of earlier bottling, and, importantly, bottling off at one time. A glance at the *Vintage Notes* in Nicolas Faith's book on Margaux shows that not only did the *mise* take place two and a half years and more after the vintage, even as late as 1970, and even with lesser vintages such as 1967, but the bottling often took place in two stages. The 1959 was bottled in November 1961, and May 1962. I was told at the château on one occasion that there had been three separate bottlings of the 1961. No wonder bottles of older vintages vary so much!

Today, bottling takes place either in the late summer or in the autumn about two years after the vintage. This, together with the increased proportion of Cabernet Sauvignon in the *encépagement* has increased the structure and grip which is necessary to underpin and give long life to the silky, complex delicacy which is the essence of the Margaux commune and which, now in practice as well as in theory, achieves its quintessence in the wine of Château Margaux itself. Château Margaux is now in the capable and elegant hands of Corinne Mentzelopoulos and Paul Pontallier, an able young man who has written a thesis on the ageing of wine in wood, and who was appointed in 1983 to work with and then succeed Philippe Barre on his retirement. With the wise counsel of that wizard, Emile Peynaud, it is once again in its rightful position.

It was 200 years ago that Thomas Jefferson wrote: 'I may safely assure you that . . . there cannot be a better bottle of Bordeaux produced in France.' A hundred years later Armand d'Armailhacq, proprietor of the Pauillac fifth growth, and perceptive commentator on the wines of his neighbours, wrote of Margaux: 'This famous wine is remarkable for its incomparable sweetness of perfume.' Today both these observations are as true as ever.

THE TASTING

The following splendid range of wines were tasted over a weekend at the fifth of the grand tastings organized by Jack and Thelma Hewitt of Woodstock, Vermont, in September 1993.

Optimum drinking

1991   **1995–2000**

Surprisingly good colour. There is certainly no lack of flesh and fruit on the nose. A little leanness nonetheless, but not too herbaceous. Good oak. Medium body. Good grip. Not a bit ungenerous, and with very good style. An excellent effort. Really most enjoyable.

1990   **2003–2030**

Very good colour. Full, closed-in, firm nose (quite different from a bottle sampled two days previously which was a lot more accessible). Rich, very concentrated and oaky underneath. Full, tannic, quite powerful on the attack. Splendid rich concentrated fruit on the follow-through and a complex, very classy, very ripe finish. Harmonious. Very, very long. High class. A great wine. Got better and better and better as it developed.

1989   **1999–2020**

Very good colour. Opulent nose, an exotic aspect which fleetingly suggests Mouton. Rich but without the backbone of the 1990. Not as structured as the 1990 on the palate. Medium-full. Good tannins but not quite the grip. Rich and ample and plump nevertheless, and a fine wine. Long, fragrant, ripe and classy on the finish. As it developed, and the 1990 opened up on the nose, this closed up.

1988   **2000–2035**

Very good colour. Classic nose. Very lovely, creamy blackcurrant and violets. Firm, even a bit austere. But very classy indeed. Medium-full body. Quite a lot of tannin, and these less ripe than the 1990. At present these dominate the attack. But the follow-through is elegant and very enjoyable: if a little – not exactly ungenerous – but *less* generous than the two above. Best of all at the end. Fine for the vintage. I am not at all sure this won't turn out more satisfactorily in the long term than the 1989.

1987   **Now –1996**

Good colour. Good nose. Soft, ripe, elegant and charming. With a good base of oak. Medium body. Still just a little raw, but quite drinkable now. Good quite plump attack, but the follow-through is a little one-dimensional, and the finish is a bit weak. It will get attenuated eventually. Drink quite soon. Very good for the vintage though.

1986   **1996–2004**

Very good colour. Ripe blackberry fruit on the nose, but without the fat, concentration and sheer flair of the 1985. The wine shows its tannin as it develops. Medium-full body. A little tannin. Still quite closed and a bit adolescent. Good intensity and class but not great intensity and class. Has balance though and a positive finish. But the least good of the fine vintages of the 1982–1990 period.

1985   **1996–2020**

Very good colour. Still very young. Lovely nose. Ripe, concentrated, full and very intense. Quite structured. Quite backward. Full body. Beautifully balanced and sumptuously fruity. Fullish, rich, oaky, very classy indeed. Lovely. Potentially very silky. Very fine, long, fragrant lingering finish. Very fine.

1984   **Drink soon**

Medium-full colour. No undue age. Good nose. Soft, harmonious. And there is fruit and class here. Medium body. I prefer this to the 1987. Surprisingly ripe for the vintage.

1983   **Now–2020**

Very good colour. A little more development than the 1985, but less than the 1982. The nose was a little pinched at first, and although this blew off after a bit, it was still discernible. Full on the palate. Very good tannins and structure. Particularly lovely blackcurrant, blackberry-raspberry fruit. Approaching maturity. More to it in concentration and flair as well as structure terms than the 1985. But I have had better bottles.

1983   **Now–2025**

(Second bottle) Excellent colour. Still very immature. This is quite different. Closed, but rich and very exciting nose. Heaps and heaps of very classy concentrated fruit. Fullish, very good grip. Great intensity and consistency from start to finish. Now just about ready. This is very lovely and very much better than the 1982, good as that is. Essence of fruit. Great complexity. Finely balanced. Great depth. Great class. Great wine.

1982   **1995–2020**

Very good colour. More development than the 1983. Rich, exotic, flamboyantly beautiful nose. Chocolate and mulberries. Crammed with fruit. Full, fat, concentrated, still with some unresolved tannin. Very good grip. Today superior to the first bottle of 1983 – but not to the second. A very lovely seductive wine and a very fine one. Excellent.

1981   **Now–2001**

Very good colour. Barely mature. Soft, ample but vigorous on the nose. It doesn't have the concentration or grip of the 1982 and 1983, but there is no lack of depth and freshness and even richness. Medium-full, ripe, mellow but with surprising structure and harmony for the vintage. Must be one of the very best wines of the vintage. Lovely. Plenty of life.

1980   **Drink soon**

(Double magnum) Good mature colour. Soft nose. Plump and fruity. Soft, ripe, surprisingly mellow and elegant, balanced, classy. Not too short. Very nice indeed.

1979   **Now–2001**

Medium-full colour. Not as intense as the 1978. Attractive blackcurrant nose. No great depth, but fresh and plump and elegant. But it doesn't show as much attraction as the 1981. Medium-full, a little more structure and acidity than the 1981, and a more positive finish. But the structure shows a bit more. The 1981 is better on its own and it is more classy – but the 1979 better with food. The finish is long and very impressive. Lovely fresh damson fruit.

1978   **Now–2001 plus**

Fullish colour. Richer-looking than the 1979. And more concentrated on the nose too. Fuller, fatter, more depth. This shows a lot of promise. Like the 1979, this has less finesse than the wines of the 1980s. But there is structure and depth, even concentration here. Better than the 1979. Full body. But the backbone shows a bit. Fine. Like the 1979 the tannins are less sophisticated than the wines of the 1980s. Better with food. Finishes very well.

1976   **Drink up**

Medium-full mature colour. Somewhat over-ripe. Slightly astringent nose. A lack of grip. Not very classy. Not very Bordeaux. Better on the palate. Medium body. Chocolatey. But overlaid by astringency and rather short on the palate. Not exciting at all.

1975   **Drink soon**

Fullish, mature colour. Farmyardy nose. A bit astringent. Lacks finesse. But it is better than the 1976 at the very least. Some freshness. Not too astringent on the palate. No undue tannins. The finish isn't too bad.

1974   **Past its best**

Fresh-looking colour. Medium to medium-full. Vegetal nose. Cauliflowers. Dried out. Short. A bit unclean at the end.

1973   **Past its best**

Old-looking colour, but fullish. Slight volatile

acidity on the nose. Gamey, maderized. But unsophisticated. Thin and souped-up on the palate. Suspiciously sweet/sour.

1971   **Drink soon**

Quite fresh, medium-full, mature colour. Rather dried out on the nose. But there is some class here. Medium body. Reasonable fruit and balance though a bit old now. But the finish is still positive. Good.

1970   **Drink soon**

Good mature colour. A little bit dank on the nose. Rather rigid, lacking life and generosity. Medium to medium-full body. The fruit is getting a bit dried out and the wine lacks dimension and style. The finish is dull and uninspiring. Disappointing.

1967   **Drink soon**

Good colour. Still vigorous, surprisingly enough. Soft nose, elegant and supple. This has merit and is still lovely. Medium body. I much prefer this to the 1970. Fragrant and plummy. Reasonable freshness and grip. Not great, but pleasant. Has held up well. Very good plus for the vintage. Drink soon though.

1966   **Now–1998**

Fullish colour. Still vigorous looking. Good quality on the nose. Ripe blackcurrant with good freshness. Not as concentrated or as elegant as the very best, but much better than the 1970. Developed in the glass to show a quite rich cedary and even complex character. Medium-full, good oaky background. Rather classy fruit and plenty of interest and complexity. Finishes well. Long. Unexpectedly good. Very good indeed for a 1966 but of course not up to the quality of Palmer. Will still last well.

1964   **Drink soon**

(Magnum) Lowish fill. Good colour though. Quite fragrant on the nose. Not too pinched. Not too faded. On the palate this is more alive and more enjoyable than I had expected. Medium to medium-full. Quite ripe. A little astringency though. It doesn't have the character, depth and, especially, the finesse and complexity of the 1966, but it is certainly still pleasant and still fresh. Drink soon. Didn't hold up very well in the glass.

1963   **Past its best**

Old colour. Not dried out. But lean, mean and beginning to dry out. Spurious sweetness underneath. Past any best it ever had. But I didn't expect anything better.

1962   **Drink soon**

Medium to medium-full colour. At first a little pinched on the nose. But mellowed after a quarter of an hour in the glass. Complex, but it is showing a little age now – the fill could have been higher: mid shoulder. Medium to medium-full body. A little sign of loosening up but residual class, fragrance, complexity and sweetness. More concentration than the 1964. Held up well in the glass. And went very well with food. Lovely.

1961   **Now–1997**

(Magnum) Very fine colour still. And still vigorous on the nose. Indeed the nose took a little time to come out in all its sumptuous glory. Absolutely lovely ripe fruit without a hint of over-ripeness. Rich, concentrated and intensely complex and fruity on the nose. Full, well-matured. Velvety. Rich. Very ample. Very classy indeed. This is subtle and distinguished. Lovely finish: complex; lingering; fragrant. Great wine.

1959   **Now–1996**

(Magnum) Low neck fill. Very good colour. Not quite as vigorous as the 1961. This is classic old claret on the nose. There is life here, but – perhaps because of the fill – not the vigour of the 1961. Yet there is a funky and very enjoyable complexity nonetheless. It is sweeter and spicier and more structured than the 1961. More backbone. Different fruit. Redcurrants rather than raspberries. Full. A touch of astringency. Less class than the 1961. But lovely nevertheless. Good grip. Long sweet finish. Fine.

1957   **Drink soon**

Good colour, still youthful. Not a bit too tough on the nose. High acidity. Plummy fruit. A little rigid but fresh. On the palate this is solid. But not dense or tough. There is structure here and the acidity on the finish is quite marked. But there is also fruit and sweetness. A little rigid again at the end. Good though. Not unbalanced. Enjoyment to be had.

1955   **Drink soon**

Mid-neck fill. Well-matured medium to medium-full colour. Soft, sweet, old-roses nose. This is nearly the end of its useful life but the wine is nevertheless fragrant and very elegant. Medium body. Very mellow now. Yet still sweet. Classy. Good grip. Long. Complex. Lovely lingering sweet finish. Very good indeed.

1953   **Now–1997**

(Magnum) Medium-full colour mature but no undue age. Most beautiful fragrant nose. Soft raspberry fruit of great delicacy and splendid finesse. This is a great wine. On the palate, soft and smooth, sweet and silky and complete from start to finish. Is this even better than the 1961? Medium to medium-full. Very ripe. Very fragrant, very spectacular. Absolutely lovely. *Grand vin!*

1952   **Now–1997**

Medium-shoulder fill. Medium-full colour. Mature but no undue age. On the nose ripe and sweet and spicy, but a certain structure. On the palate a little astringency, but there is ripeness and sweetness and plenty of interest and enjoyment to be had. Vigorous. Long. Will remain like this for several years still. Better with food. Classy finish. Fine.

1950   **Now–1997**

Good colour, still vigorous. Firm, spicy, slightly four-square and dense on the nose. Better on the palate. Not too astringent. Medium-full. Ripe, nicely cool, acidity elements, leaving the palate clean and classy. This is very good indeed. Complex. Full of interest. Long. Lovely, in fact. One of the most feminine examples of 1950 I have had for a long time. Will still keep well.

1949   **Drink soon**

Medium colour, well-matured. Soft, mellow, fragrant nose. This is very elegant, but has lightened up a bit. Medium body. Sweet, gently fading now, but still persistent to the end and a wine of ripeness and distinction and complexity. Very long and sweet and lingering at the end. Great breed. Very fine indeed.

1947   **Now–1998**

(Bottled Vandemeulen, Belgium) Very good colour: youthful still. Rich, fresh, higher-than-normal-volatile-acidity nose. Sweet and almost over-ripe fruit on the palate. A shadow of astringency but very good grip. Fullish, lively, fresh and long. After the mellow sweetness of the 1949 this is a little rigid and has less finesse. The château-bottled is fatter as I remember. But complex and very good indeed.

1945   **Now–2000**

Good colour. Rich, glowing, vigorous. This is a marvellous bottle. Youthful, concentrated, rich and balanced. A lot of depth here and not a bit unduly structured. On the palate this is full and very concentrated. The wood shows more than on the two wines above to give a cedary backbone. Splendid fruit. Very good grip. This has a lot of dimension and a marvellous flesh. The best of these 1940s vintages. Bags of life still. I have never had it as vigorous and as magical as this before. Great wine.

1937   **Drink up**

Medium to medium-full colour. Well matured. Quite dense, slightly burnt nose with an aspect of reduction. Ripeness and sweetness there too, though. But essentially a little rustic. It died quickly in the glass. Medium to medium-full. A little astringency. Quite ripe but getting a bit coarse and short.

1934   **Now–1997**

(Magnum) Very youthful colour. Ripe, succulent, vigorous nose. But a little reduction, not
very classy. Fullish, rich, sweet. Good vigour and
good backbone. Slight burnt sugar aspects. Quite
structured. This is enjoyable, but it is not very
soft or round and it lacks real first growth distinction. Yet sweet and vigorous on the finish. Held
up well in the glass. A wine for food. Classier as
it developed.

1929   **Drink soon**

Quite an old-looking colour. A little dry and
faded on the nose at first. Ripe but faded and
getting thin. Elegance can be discerned. Sweet,
nutty, pruney as it developed. Still enjoyable;
and not short. Even after half an hour it was still
sweet, fragrant and lovely.

1928   **Now–1998**

Very good colour. Full, vigorous. Muscular,
gamey nose. Rich and fat, not exactly distinguished at first, but alive and plumply fruity.
Fullish body. The tannins still there. It has a
chocolate and mocha flavour, but is rich and distinctive. No undue toughness. Complex. Long.
A wine for food. Splendid condition. Developed
very well in the glass and became more classy.
Very fine.

1926   **Now–2000 plus**

(Magnum) Very good colour. Full, vigorous:
like the 1928. Full, ripe, concentrated, quite
structured nose. Not dense, but one can see the
backbone and tannin. Not as chunky as the 1928
on the palate. Full but abundantly fruity. This is
exciting. Still fresh. But has the complexity of
age. Very long, classy, vigorous, youthful. Splendid fruit. Amazingly lively. This is great wine.

1924   **Now–1997**

(Magnum) Fullish mature colour. Oaky nose.
Interestingly spicy. Ripe but slightly caramelly:
burnt custard and vanilla. On the palate well-
matured but ripe and fragrant and cedary. Much
less tannic and Cabernet than the 1926. This, like
the 1929, could be taken for Burgundy. Round
mellow and complex. There *is* structure here,
but the wine is, though still fresh, quite delicate.
Fine finish. Fine quality. Still has life. Still sweet
and lovely at the end.

1921   **Drink soon**

Very good colour. Very youthful indeed.
Cedary nose. Ripe and sweet and raspberry-fra-
grant, but lead-pencilly now. Suggestions of
Rioja here. On the palate very ripe – almost
over-ripe. Medium body. A little astringent, but
juicy nevertheless and no lack of grip. This is
fresh but lacks a little fat and succulence on the
follow-through. Yet certainly classy, and still
very long and complex. Lovely finish in fact.
Very good indeed.

1918   **Past its best**

Good mature colour. No undue age. A little oxidation and maderization on the nose. Better on
the palate. But a wine which got more and more
maderized in the glass. Underneath medium
body. Ripe. Good acidity. Indeed the acidity beginning to show on the finish. Classy, nevertheless. But past its best.

1900

Recorked at the château, according to the cork,
though the bottle came from the Nicolas cellar)
Fine colour. Still very vigorous. Splendid nose.
This is great wine. Very rich concentrated fruit.
Fresh and with great finesse. Fabulous palate.
Some age. But sweetness, concentration, depth,
class, and real harmony and intensity. And has as
much vigour as the 1959. Very lovely indeed.
This is very *grand vin*.

RAUSAN-SÉGLA

At the top of the second growths in the 1855 hierarchy (as amended in 1973 when Château Mouton-Rothschild was promoted to *premier cru*) are the Rauzans. To be pedantic, according to the current spelling there is one Rauzan with a 'z' and one Rausan with an 's'. Ségla, the senior of the two in the 1855 Classification, is Rausan. Though spelt Rauzan in 1855, it is Rausan now. Going by my editions of Cocks and Féret, this idiosyncratic change of spelling took place some time between 1899 (seventh edition) and 1908 (eighth edition). Why it did so, no one seems to know. In the archives and parish records the name is spelt variously as Rosan, Rozan, Rausan and Rauzan. People were less worried about consistency in the old days!

Rausan-Ségla, like many estates, has had its ups and downs. It is fair to describe the situation and the quality of the wine in the last couple of generations as rather more down than up. Though the senior of all the second growths, there was nothing 'super' about Rausan-Ségla's wines. Today things are different. From rough-and-ready, rather dried-out wines in the 1950s, Ségla improved to elegant, if sometimes slight wines in the 1960s and the first half of the 1970s. Since 1982, however, the quality has improved dramatically. Rausan-Ségla is now not just a wine to watch but wine to buy: a major rival to Palmer for the title of 'number two in Margaux'.

HISTORY

Originally there was a single estate. Its history begins in the Middle Ages with a *maison noble* called 'Gassies', owing allegiance to the Seigneur of Margaux, and located a kilometre or two away, on higher ground and slightly to the north. A document dated 1573 relates to a sale of land near the '*Bois de Gassies*'. Variously spelt and perhaps even having the same etymological source as Gorce (now Brane-Cantenac) and the ecclesiastical Gorces to the north, Gassies, or Garcies, belonged in 1530 to Gaillard de Tardes. At the beginning of the next century it passed to Bernard de Faverolles, who married Marie de Montferant. Bernard was made '*Seigneur de la Planche et de Gassies*' in 1615.

On 7 September 1661, the estate was acquired by Pierre de Mesures de Rauzan, who co-incidentally was to create another vineyard which was later divided, that of Pichon in Pauillac. Rauzan was a *bourgeois* merchant in Bordeaux, and he had obviously seen the potential business to be had from wine, particularly the premium a really good wine could fetch on the export market. According to some of the more romantic nineteenth-century monographs on the Bordeaux châteaux, Rauzan, for a time, leased or in some way was involved in making the wine at both Margaux and Latour. This is not substantiated by later historians such as Pijassou, but it is reasonable to assume that he was involved in *selling* their wines, and having had success in so doing, to want to be a vineyard proprietor himself. What would be more natural, then, than to buy up land immediately adjacent to the great estates themselves.

In 1700, after his death, Rauzan's estate was divided. Thérèse, his only daughter, took the Pauillac vineyards, and her three brothers Simon, Jude Jean and Simon Jude (I'm sure this must have created great family confusion) shared the Margaux estate. The deed refers to the '*maison appelée de Gassies*' and to 2,042 *reges* and 234 *presses de vigne haute*, about 25 hectares. The vineyard was made up of a number of separate parcels, perhaps indicating that Rauzan had had to make a number of purchases to build up a viable estate.

The Rauzans were now aristocrats, and successive generations were councillors in the Bordeaux *parlement* during the reigns of Louis XV and XVI. It was during that period that the vineyard was first consolidated and then later divided, and it was also during the eighteenth century that the reputation of the estate improved from run-of-the-mill to top of the second growths.

Rauzan in the 1730s must have been a considerable domaine, for it contained not only what exists now as Ségla and Gassies, but also the vineyards of Desmirail and Marquis-de-Terme. Desmirail was the first to be formed as a separate estate. In about 1750, Mlle Rauzan du Ribail married Jean Desmirail, and took some fourteen hectares of vineyards with her as dowry. Similarly, in 1762, another young lady of the Rauzan family married Seigneur de Peguilhan, Marquis de Terme, and a further 30 hectares or so were lost.

Meanwhile, Jean de Rauzan, now a marquis, was adding an extra wing to the château, enlarging the vineyard, and transforming the quality of the wine. Such was the change that the local peasants thought he was in league with the devil. He explained that he had excluded all but 'noble' varieties in the vineyard, and had also been helped immensely by his good friend and neighbour, the Comte d'Agricourt. The reason his wine was so good, said Rauzan, was only that he made it like Agricourt made his at Château Margaux!

In his *Vins de Bordeaux* (*Les Richesses Gastronomiques de la France*), Charles Lorbac tells another story of Jean de Rauzan. Dissatisfied with the price he was receiving for his wine in Bordeaux, he chartered a ship, filled it with good vintages and sailed to London. Berthed in the Thames, he attempted to auction the wine, but still found the price insufficient. 'If you are not prepared to bid the price the wine deserves,' he announced, 'I will throw my wine in the river.' And so saying, one cask was launched into the Thames. After four more, the crowd could stand no more waste of wine, and Rauzan was granted the price he was seeking.

More concrete evidence of the growth of the château's reputation is found by following successive classifications of the Bordeaux wines throughout the century. Between 1741 and 1774, according to the prices culled by Pijassou from the records of Tastet and Lawton, Rauzan fetched an average of 603 *livres* a *tonneau*, less than Pouget and Malescot, let alone Gorse and Lascombes, the latter in this period the leading growth, after Margaux itself, in the commune. Indeed, the price was even substantially lower than Marquis-de-Terme!

After this period, however, there was a radical shift in the prices of certain properties. Some – Lascombes, Pouget and De-Terme – fell back, and, over a period of a generation, three properties detached themselves from the bulk of *crus* to form a distinct group of second growths, Léoville, Gruaud-Larose and Rauzan. This is borne out by Thomas Jefferson. On 6 September 1790, he ordered ten dozen bottles of Rauzan (the vintage is not indicated). Earlier, in the summer of 1787, he had made a thorough tour of the French vineyards. In his report following his Bordeaux visit, he mentions five 'red wines of second quality' (after the first growths). The first he lists is 'Rozan'.

The proprietor at this time was the formidable Mme de Rauzan, or 'Rozan', as she is spelt in contemporary documents. She was as determined as her predecessor to secure top prices for her wines. Mme 'Rozan' seems to have been the instigator of a running battle to prevent too much of a gap opening up between the prices of the first growths and those of the top seconds. A number of letters in the Latour archives and elsewhere attest to her stubbornness. The first growth price was normally around 2,000 *livres* a *tonneau*, and Poitevin (*régisseur* of Latour) as well as the Bordeaux *négociants* considered that three-quarters, i.e., 1,500 *livres*, was a just price for a good second growth. Not so Mme 'Rozan'. A discount of 350 *livres* was the most she would accept. In the end she got it.

At about this time – unfortunately the records are meagre and somewhat of a mist obscures the details – Rauzan was divided. Some records refer to a Mlle de Rauzan who married Seigneur de Gassies. What is more certain is a second Mlle de Rauzan (perhaps they were both daughters of the lady above), married the Baron de Ségla. This lady, Catherine Jacquette Clémentine de Rauzan, married Pierre Louis de Ségla, Baron de Montbardon, Seigneur de Sarcos, Monties, Aussos, Bezues, Panassac, etc., in 1780. He was inadvertently killed in 1789 by a pistol shot while standing by the window of his library in Montbardon. The Baroness lived from 1761 to 1828 and is commemorated in the garden of Château Rausan-Ségla today. A stone tablet records her delight in growing hydrangeas.

That the estate was divided in the last few years of the *ancien régime* we do know. In precisely what circumstances we do not. It would seem that originally the vineyard was divided into three, but later the Baroness de Ségla absorbed one of the sections into her third. In the earliest edition of Franck, the three sections have identical *rendement* figures (25–35 *tonneaux*) and are listed as belonging, respectively, to 'de Ségla', 'Descage', and 'Pelier'. Twenty years later, he specifies Rauzan Rauzan (*sic*) owned by De Ségla (40–50 *tonneaux*) and Rauzan-Gassies, De Puyboreau (30–40 *tonneaux*). Elsewhere, and in other accounts at this time, it is plain that the combined estate is regarded as second only to Margaux in the commune, and top of a much smaller list of second growths than was to emerge in 1855.

RAUSAN-SÉGLA AFTER PARTITION

Of the two properties since the division, it is Ségla which has had the more settled history, and, perhaps because of this, has always had the higher reputation.

The Baroness de Ségla was succeeded by her daughter, who married the Count of Castelpers, a scion one of the oldest and most noble families of the Haut-Médoc in 1803. They both seem to have died in the 1850s, for by 1860 the estate is administered by a son, the Baron d'Adeler. In 1866, the heirs sold Ségla to M. Eugène Durand-Dassier, a 'minister of the reformed church', for 730,000 francs. Under Durand-Dassier's ownership, the fortunes of Rausan-Ségla hit their highest peak. Production increased considerably, prices frequently matched those of the first growths, and the wine was widely bought and enthused over.

In 1903, Rausan-Ségla passed from Durand-Dassier to Frédéric Cruse, who had married his only daughter. Frédéric Cruse was the second son of the founder of the Cruse business, and he installed Charles Skawinski, *régisseur* of Pontet-Canet, another family property, to take charge at Rausan-Ségla. The property at this time was making some 60 *tonneaux*, and had 35 hectares under vines.

Shortly after Frédéric Cruse inherited the property from his father-in-law, the present two-storey château was erected. This replaced an earlier, modest, *chartreuse*-style building which itself had been largely constructed out of the ruins of the original *maison noble*, parts of which are still in evidence nearby.

The Cruse château is also a modest building. It has a tiled roof – red, not the usual slate – a curious round, dumpy tower, and faces south-west, away from Margaux. There are barely half a dozen rooms on each floor, and the atmosphere is elegant but informal – even cosy, if that is not too pejorative a word to use these days. During the Cruse ownership, which lasted until 1956, the rooms were furnished (from another château nearer to Bordeaux which had also been pulled down) in the style of different French periods, as in a museum. Nowadays, the decoration is more uniform, and the furniture British, of the eighteenth and nineteenth centuries. The building is not permanently occupied, but is used for entertaining and for accommodating foreign guests.

Though the wines produced in the 1920s were up to standard, the vineyard by this time was in eclipse, and production declined to twenty *tonneaux* in the 1930s. Rausan-Ségla, on the death of Frédéric Cruse, was in *indivision*, the property of all his heirs. In 1956, they sold it to a M. de Meslon. I have read elsewhere – perhaps M. de Meslon himself claimed it – that he was in some way a descendant of the old Rauzan family. This is thought by present-day historians to be improbable.

The area under vines by this time had been reduced to twenty hectares, and, moreover, consisted only of old vines. The cellar equipment was primitive – indeed, they were still treading the grapes by feet, the last major Bordeaux estate so to do. Meslon's idea was quantity rather than quality and a quick return on his capital. He instigated a rapid replanting programme, but only of the Merlot variety. Four years later he sold the estate. The price it then fetched was some three times that of the 36 million (old) francs for which he had bought it.

The purchasers were a group new to the wine business, the Liverpool firm of John Holt and Co., now part of Lonhro. A local agent, having seen this sale, then put Holt in touch with the Bordeaux *négociants*, Eschenhauer, also on the market following the death of 'Oncle Louis' in 1958 at the age of 88. Holt's bought Eschenhauer and from then onwards, until the mid 1980s, Eschenhauer was the exclusive distributor of the wine.

Towards the end of 1988, Lonhro sold its Bordeaux wine interests to Brent Walker, after which Rausan-Ségla was transferred to a family company owned by George Walker personally. Since then Château Smith-Haut-Lafitte in the Graves has been sold, Eschenhauer was the subject of a management buy-out (sadly, it went into receivership in 1994), and Rausan was acquired by the Wertheimer Group, owners of Chanel.

AN IMPROVEMENT IN WINE-MAKING

Under the Eschenhauer regime, much was achieved at the property. The programme of vineyard extension has been continued, though some of Meslon's young Merlots were grubbed up and replaced with Cabernet Sauvignon, and the old wooden fermentation vats replaced with twelve squat, round, epoxy-resin-lined steel vats in 1970.

More recently, with the increase in the size of the *rendement* as well as of the vineyard, it was found that this 1970 equipment would rapidly become inadequate. In 1983 Eschenhauer took a deep breath and decided it was time to make the investment in the right sort of personnel and equipment if they were really going to produce 'super-second' wine.

Across the garden, therefore, where the wild cyclamen used to thrive in the long grass in the late summer, a new *chai de deuxième année* and *cuverie* were built in time for the 1986 harvest. The wine is vinified in automatically temperature-controlled stainless-steel vats – eighteen of them with a capacity of 220 hectolitres plus an 800-hectolitre giant for the *assemblage*, and the old *cuvier* has been transformed into a *salle de réception*.

Once, when we were jointly making a vertical tasting of the wines, I talked to Emile Peynaud, who had been brought in as a consultant, about wine-making at Rausan. 'What was the ideal temperature of fermentation?' I asked. 'A maximum of 30 degrees,' he said, 'irrespective of the grape variety, if one seeks to make a *vin de garde*' (25 degrees was a more appropriate temperature for generics). One can seek therefore a rather longer maceration – fourteen days for the Merlot in 1985, while the Cabernet was run off after eighteen days, but above all this must be flexible; each year according to the quality, state of health and degree of ripeness and concentration of the fruit. Be gentle with the pressing, he advises, so that one can produce a *vin de presse* which can be used, not one which is exhausted. 'The *vin de presse* is a concentration of the wine – with all its faults and with all its virtues.' If one presses too hard one might find oneself with the bitter tannin of the pips. This is particularly likely if the maceration is too prolonged in a 'little' year. What about the question of the amount of new oak? 'Wood is like the spice rack in the kitchen,' Peynaud said. 'And here in Bordeaux we are not *amateurs de la cuisine indienne*,' he added with a smile. To support a lot of new wood the wine needs to be well-structured, very rich both in extract and tannin; for this reason he has decreed that the percentage at Rausan should be reduced from one-half new wood each year to one-third. It is a mistake to use too much new wood in a feeble year, he considers. Again, flexibility is the keynote.

THE VINEYARD

Since its origins, the combined Rauzan estate has been made up of numerous parcels of vineyard, scattered throughout Margaux and Cantenac. The division into Ségla and Gassies only made things more complicated. Up to 1933, there were as many as 240 separate plots of land, but in this year there was a major consolidation and a series of exchanges between the two Rauzans, as well as with other neighbours. The major part of the Ségla vineyard is now in front and to the south of the château, running down across the railway towards Cantenac-Brown. This section comprises twenty hectares. A further ten hectares lie between Château Brane-Cantenac and Château Kirwan, and there are two smaller sections on the Château Margaux *croupe*. There are 46 hectares under vine, planted in the ratio 65 per cent Cabernet Sauvignon, 5 per cent Cabernet Franc and 30 per cent Merlot, plus residual rows of Petit Verdot. Production averages 180 *tonneaux*. The potential, however, is 50 hectares, which is destined to be in the ratio 70 per cent Sauvignon and 30 per cent Merlot, with Cabernet Franc and Petit Verdot eliminated. With yields sometimes reaching 50 hectolitres per hectare, 250 *tonneaux* are possible.

THE TASTING

The older wines were sampled at the château in November 1985. I supplemented this with a further tasting in April 1992.

	Optimum drinking

1991   1995–1998

Good colour. A little thin on the nose but not too weedy. Similar on the palate. There is something good here. Quite plump at

the end, though not a lot of grip. Not bad.

1990   1998–2018

Good colour. Very good fruit on the nose. Really intense and classy violets and raspberries. Medium-full body, very good ripe tannins. This is concentrated, elegant, complex and beautifully balanced. Very good indeed. More harmony and depth than the 1989. Very lovely.

1989   **1997–2016**
Good colour. Fine oak and fine fruit on the nose. No undue tannin. Complex and fragrant. Real Margaux. On the attack there is a little dry astringency, but this is quickly swamped by the fruit. Medium to medium-full. Harmonious, well-structured, long, distinctive, and with no lack of finesse. The 1990 has more to it but this is very good plus.

1988   **1995–2015**
Good colour. Fine, rich, oaky nose. This again is a typical Margaux. Fullish but not a blockbuster. A lovely perfumed example of ripe, balanced fruit. Medium to medium-full body. Very long and complex. Much more personality than many 1988s. Fine for the vintage.

1987
Not declared.

1986   **1994–2009**
Good colour; rather better than the 1985. Still very youthful on the nose. It is a little dominated by the oak but it is stylish and well-balanced. But I think the 1988 is better still. Finishes better than it starts, though. There is plenty of richness underneath. This is the bigger wine. Good length, but not quite the harmony. Very good plus.

1985   **Now–2000**
Medium colour, a little development now. Round, ripe and spicy on the nose. The Merlot shows. Soft, round and aromatic. Much more developed than the 1986. Medium-bodied and elegant and very good. But I find the 1986 more exciting. It has more depth.

1984   **Drink up**
Good colour. Ripe, ample nose with a touch of oak. Good for the vintage because it is more generous than most. Medium body, quite complex. No weakness. There is a touch of dryness and a slight bitterness, but there is fruit underneath and the wine finishes well.

1983   **Now–2008**
Very good colour. Nose at first a little blunt but aeration improves it considerably. A rich, ripe wine, very much in the Margaux character with its soft, violet essences. Medium-full, some tannin. Balanced, ripe, harmonious fruit. A concentrated but delicate wine with a lot of depth. Lovely finish. This is really excellent.

1982   **Now–2010**
Very good colour. Rounder, more aromatic nose. Fuller and richer than the 1983. Flavours of

chocolate, mulberries and liquorice. Full, good round tannins. A very rich, fat wine with a lot of concentrated fruit, like a summer pudding. Long, ample and generous, with a good, fresh finish. Impressive quality!

1981   **Drink soon**
Medium colour, not a lot of development. Interesting high-toned nose with a touch of cigars as well as *sous-bois* and roast chestnuts. Medium body, very little tannin. Fresh, delicate and quite complex though. An attractive wine, but lacks a bit of muscle, and, like most 1981s, is not *that* long on the palate.

1979   **Drink soon**
Similar colour but more developed. Light, quite elegant nose; a mixture of oak and spice but a little hollow underneath, if not slightly watery. Medium body, slightly dilute, elegant enough but lacks power. Fully evolved, indeed some signs of impending astringency.

1978   **Now–1996**
Medium-full colour. Good concentrated fruit on nose and palate. Not a blockbuster. Now quite evolved, and with some of the spices of maturity. Medium-full body, ripe, aromatic, generous wine. Well-made, if without the depth and 'size' of some. Good if not great.

1975   **Now–1997**
Fullish colour, some brown. Slightly inky and dense on the nose, the fruit having softened but the tannin still being there. Fullish, has fruit and is more supple than most. Professor Peynaud – we were tasting together – admired it (it was the one wine we disagreed on). But in my view it has all the lumpiness of the vintage. Quite good – or perhaps I should say, 'quite good for the vintage'.

1971   **Drink soon**
Medium colour. Mature without being unduly brown. Elegant, ripe, mature nose. Quite complex. Medium body, fully ready. Surprisingly stylish wine with good, sweet, ripe fruit, a soft delicacy and good length. Most attractive.

1970   **Now–1997**
Very fine colour indeed. Full and showing very little age. Attack excellent. Rich, undeveloped but concentrated nose. Full on the palate, possibly a bit dense, some tannin. In the context of this property and this commune this is a powerful wine. Finishes well. An hour and a half later though – for this was a bottle we decanted and took to lunch – the wine was less exciting, the fruit less opulent. It was still good, but not 'very good'. 'Too much *vin de presse*,' said Peynaud.

LASCOMBES

Château Lascombes is one of the largest properties in the Haut-Médoc. Like many, it has increased both in size and in prosperity since the war as a result of a change of ownership and the injection of foreign capital. Like Loudenne and Latour, Lascombes is British owned, in this case by the brewery group Bass. Like others it has had historical connections and alliances with other classed growths.

Sometimes these alliances are as a result of common ownership, Gruaud-Larose and Talbot, for example; or because, once a single property, they have since been split up and so are closely regarded in the public imagination, like the Pichons, the Léovilles or Rausan-Ségla and Rauzan-Gassies. In Lascombes' case it is both: the estate once included both Lascombes and Durfort-Vivens. More recently Lascombes and Prieuré have been connected through the personality of the late Alexis Lichine. And more recently still, an agreement was made with the proprietors of Château Ferrière, and up until the 1991 vintage Ferrière was farmed and produced by the personnel at Lascombes.

The Lascombes estate has its origins in a *maison noble* belonging to the Durfort de Duras family. The name Lascombes first appears with a Chevalier Antoine de Lascombes who was born in 1625. Whether he gave his name to the estate and the area, or whether the name Lascombes is a corruption of *la côte* or *la coste*, meaning a small hill, is not known. Nor do we know the exact connection between the Chevalier and the successor of the Durforts de Duras who by the early eighteenth century were a family called Montalambert.

HISTORY

By 1700 the vineyard was well established. The Lascombes of the day was a councillor to Louis XIV and *procureur de l'amirauté* (naval prosecuting attorney) for the Guyenne. Berlon, *régisseur* of Château Margaux, records that this estate was paid, as feudal dues, two barrels of wine a year by Lascombes, which was welcomed for use for topping-up the home product.

By this time, we can conjecture, the estate had been long separated from that of Durfort. Both appear as second growths of Margaux in a table quoted by Wilhelm Franck, which gives the price of wines in 1745 and similar good vintages in the mid-eighteenth century.

At this time Lascombes was owned by Jean-François de Lascombes and his sister Anne. Jean-François was a councillor at the Bordeaux Parliament in 1761 and the king's prosecutor at the admiralty just like his father or grandfather (was this a hereditary position?). Mlle de Lascombes seems to have remained unmarried and also to have survived her brother. From her the estate passed briefly into the hands of Johnston, of the Bordeaux *négociants*, soon after the Revolution, then to someone called Fabre, and finally to a man called Loraigue or Loraique who was the owner by the early 1820s. At this time the property, though it had diminished from its pre-Napoleonic size – it only produced around 30 *tonneaux*, and was later to decline even further – was firmly established as a second growth.

In 1844 Loraigue's heirs sold Lascombes to a Monsieur L. A. Hüé for 90,000 francs. He spent a lot of money on the vineyard and is said to have extended it (though contemporary figures do not seem to bear this out). From him it passed to his son-in-law, M. Petit, who sold to M. Gustave Chaix-d'Est-Ange, secretary to the Gironde senate, in 1867. In the early 1870s Lascombes covered 27 hectares and produced 16 to 20 *tonneaux*. The château, such as it was, was a simple, but elegant, single-storied edifice, enclosed in a neat, tidy park, dating from around 1780. In 1887 Gustave Chaix-d'Est-Ange died, leaving the property to his two children, Jean-Jules Théophile and Jeanne-Marie. Jean-Jules was a famous man: he was president of the French Bar, and the lawyer responsible for having won the celebrated Suez Canal case for France against Egypt. In grateful thanks Louis-Napoleon gave him a Sèvres coffee service, profusely decorated with portraits of Louis XIV's mistresses!

By this time the vineyard had further decreased. Parcels had gradually been sold off, and it was down to a mere thirteen hectares, and managed, in the absence of Chaix-d'Est-Ange, who rarely visited, by a M. Valbord Hugen. One infers that Lascombes had no great reputation.

Late-nineteenth-century vintages of Lascombes are mentioned neither in Saintsbury's *Notes in a Cellar Book*, nor in André Simon's *Vintagewise*. Other contemporary writings allude more to past glories than present prominence. Nevertheless, at about the turn of the century, Chaix-d'Est-Ange felt sufficiently involved with Lascombes to construct a new château, and this is the building we see today. Essentially it is rather an ugly building, of yellow-grey sandstone, and with more than a touch of heavy Victorian Gothic about the style. The rooms, though, are large and airy, looking directly out on to the vineyards on the western side, and are both tastefully and comfortably furnished.

At the same time, Chaix-d'Est-Ange bought the neighbouring Marquis-d'Alesme-Becker, intending, it was said, to add its fourteen hectares to that of Lascombes and combine the two estates. The amalgamation plans fell through, however, and in 1923 Chaix-d'Est-Ange died, leaving the properties to his adopted son, the Comte Emmanuel du Bourg du Bazas (he was to sell Marquis-d'Alesme to UK Chaplin and Co., owners of Malescot). In 1926 Lascombes was formed into a limited company, with the firm of Ginestet as majority shareholders.

The Ginestets, in their relatively brief existence as Bordeaux wine merchants, have been involved with a surprising number of different Bordeaux estates. Besides the best known – Margaux, Clos-Fourtet in Saint-Emilion, Petit-Village in Pomerol, and Cos d'Estournel – the Ginestet family were involved with Lascombes in the 1920s. They then moved to neighbouring Durfort-Vivens, which they owned until 1963.

Despite the earlier efforts of the Ginestets, by the end of the Second World War the Lascombes vineyard was still no more than a patchwork of scattered plots, not much more than a dozen hectares under vines in total, and producing 25 to 25 *tonneaux*. During this time it was the headquarters of the Canadian General Brutinel, chief intelligence adviser to the Allied Armies for the south west of France and Spain. The majority shareholding was held by Charles Mallet.

ALEXIS LICHINE

Alexis Lichine, as he says in his *Guide to the Wines and Vineyards of France*, had always wanted to own a Bordeaux vineyard, and his preference was for one in the commune of Margaux because of the elegance and finesse of its wines. In 1951, having delivered the manuscript of his *Wines of France* to his publishers, he began to look seriously for a property of his own. At this time a number of estates were run down and sorely in need of an injection of money and enterprise. Prieuré was one, and Lichine bought it afterbriefly toying with the idea of La Lagune. A year later, Lascombes came on the market. With a syndicate of American friends Lichine, as he puts it, 'plunged for a second time'.

Not surprisingly, the arrival of Lichine at Lascombes soon saw radical changes. Lascombes was cheap – some £50,000 – but a lot of money needed to be spent. Vineyard, château and *chais* had suffered a decade or more of neglect. Previously, parts of the domaine were replanted, raising the production to 70 *tonneaux*. By patient cultivation of local smallholders other parcels were bought, bringing the area under vine to 60 hectares, and the production up to 200 *tonneaux* by the early 1970s. The château was modernized, and for eleven successive years an annual exhibition of painting and sculpture, '*La Vigne et le Vin*', was held in the ground floor receptions rooms.

Lascombes had always belonged to Lichine's American syndicate, rather than to Lichine himself or to Alexis Lichine & Co. In 1965 this latter firm was taken over by Bass Charrington Vintners/Hedges and Butler, of London. In 1990 Bass sold it and most of the rest of their wine and spirit interests, and in 1971 Bass Charrington Vintners bought Lascombes, which they still retain. The price was $1.9 million. For some years therefore, Lichine himself, though he remained at Prieuré, had nothing to do with either Alexis Lichine & Co. or with Lascombes. To his continuing chagrin, however, most people continued to assume that he was in some way associated with both.

THE VINEYARD

Between 1971 and 1980 the Lascombes vineyard was further enlarged, and it now possesses 83 hectares under vines, making it one of the largest classed growths in Bordeaux.

The vineyard of Lascombes consists of more than 100 parcels of land in little plots throughout the communes of Margaux, Soussans and Cantenac, but the nucleus, comprising 50 hectares, lies on a plateau north of the village of Margaux, about 15 to 20 metres above sea level, and perhaps a kilometre inland from the Gironde estuary. Here the soil forms a very deep bed of pebbly earth, over a subsoil of iron-rich sandstone and clay.

The vineyard is planted with 50 per cent Cabernet Sauvignon, 2 per cent Cabernet Franc, 45 per cent Merlot and 3 per cent Petit Verdot (rather more Merlot, at the expense of Cabernet Sauvignon and Franc, than a decade ago), and now produces an average of 350 *tonneaux*, though not all of this, of course, is bottled as Lascombes. There is a second label, Château Segonnes, which is used for the less good wine, and was introduced in 1982. What they also make, from a plot of flatter land lying down by the river and from a *saignée* of the younger vines, is a rosé, bottled as Chevalier de Lascombes. This is merely Bordeaux *appellation contrôlée*, not Margaux. Some 2,000 dozen bottles are made each vintage.

CHÂTEAU FERRIÈRE

In 1962, Lascombes entered into an agreement with Mme André Durand, proprietor of neighbouring Château Ferrière, and have since 'farmed' the Ferrière estate and made the wine on her behalf. Ferrière is a tiny vineyard – the smallest of the classed growths – partly enclosed within a stone wall near the village of Margaux, the rest in a plot adjacent to Lascombes itself, but in total no more than four-and-a-bit hectares under vines. Ferrière was completely replanted between 1958 and 1964, and now produces fifteen *tonneaux* of wine, sold almost entirely to a large French restaurant chain known as the Relais de Campagne.

In 1989 Ferrière was bought by the Merlaut family consortium, owners of Chasse-Spleen, Grand-Puy-Ducasse, Haut-Bages-Libéral and others. From the 1992 vintage it resumed full independence, under Jean Merlaut.

THE CHÂTEAU AND THE *CHAIS*

After Bass took over in 1971, further improvements were made at Lascombes to both the *chais* and the château. The *chais* were altered and enlarged, a modern reception chamber installed, and sixteen concrete red-tile-lined *cuves* put in a new vinification hall. A system of stainless-steel pipes was set up, somewhat similar to that at La Lagune, in order to transfer wine from *cuve* to cask by compressed air.

The château itself is now used as a sort of private hotel for visiting staff and guests as well as the administration office, and was also modernized and redecorated. A swimming pool was built in the internal courtyard-cum-garden between it and the *chais* and I can personally recommend it as a very pleasant place to relax after a typical wine-trade lunch on a hot Médoc summer afternoon. The pool doubles as a reservoir of water in case there is a fire.

LASCOMBES IN THE 1970S

The quality of the wine, though, took a turn for the worse. Up to 1966/1967 Lascombes was entirely worthy of its second growth classification: fullish, rich, mulberry fruity; more in the style of Malescot than Palmer, but this is Margaux rather than Cantenac. After that it remained quite full, but it lost its concentration and finesse.

Partly this was due to the expansion of the vineyard. The average age of the vines declined, and it is fair to say that little of the new land was capable of producing classed growth potential. You cannot produce classy wine from peripheral, *bourgeois*-quality vines, however good the wine-making is. Partly, also, the fault can be laid at the feet of the management. Lascombes gave the impression of a smoothly efficient but rather impersonal estate: and the wine had the same character. There was no one there with any flair for wine, so it was not surprising that the wine did not show any flair either. It was all rather sad, especially as at the same time more and more of what we now call the super-seconds were beginning to detach themselves from the rest of the body of classed growths. The disappointing run during the 1970s, broken only by the 1979, continued into the early 1980s. Bass then took an imaginative step. In 1985 they decided to appoint René Vannetelle.

RENÉ VANNETELLE AND THE NEW *CUVERIE*

Vannetelle, a Bordelais, had spent fifteen years as *directeur technique* at Pol Roger in Champagne. His wife's sister is married to Christian Pol Roger. But Bordeaux remained his first love, and he was quick to seize the opportunity to make Lascombes the '*premier des seconds*', as the late Alain Maurel of Alexis Lichine and Co. put it at the time. 'My personality responds to a challenge,' said Vannetelle.

He arrived during the 1985 vintage and the experience was to prove seminal. He could see what was coming in, and he could taste what the existing winery made out of it. The first thing he did was to demand a brand new *cuverie*. 'Before 1986 we did what we could, but we didn't really have the means to make good wine. We had neither the space, nor the control.' To produce wines of balance and finesse, says Vannetelle, one of the things which is crucial is the time of maceration. 'After the alcoholic fermentation is finished, it's necessary to taste every vat every day, and to decant the wine off its skins and pulp precisely when the time is right, not, as in the olden days, when the personnel could get round to it.' So the *cuverie* was designed especially so this could be done as quickly and as efficiently as possible. The fermentation vats, stainless steel and temperature controlled of course, are mounted above the storage vats, as at the new winery at La Mission-Haut-Brion. Decantation, at the press of a button, is by gravity.

But it all starts in the vineyard, says Vannetelle. From 1986 on he followed the vineyard workers round the Lascombes estate, watched the development of each parcel of vines, and, once the vintage had taken place, monitored the progress of the wine each sector produced. He became more and more convinced that in order to produce a *grand vin* worthy of the name it would be necessary to restrict its provenance to what he calls the nucleus of Lascombes; those vines immediately adjacent to the château, and on the highest *croupe* of gravel. Not surprisingly, this bears remarkable resemblance to the land which the Lichine-led consortium bought in 1951. It is this 50-hectare parcel which now produces Lascombes.

LASCOMBES TODAY

Success does not come overnight. And the weather has not been kind. Nevertheless the 1986, despite the rain which fell in Margaux before the vintage, is a distinct improvement on the 1985. The 1987 is a good result, as is the 1988, though it lacks a bit of real personality. Both 1989 and 1990 were vintages stressed by great heat and drought, and in neither vintage was the commune of Margaux particularly favoured. Vannetelle prefers the 1990. I am not sure. What is apparent, even if they have not got there yet, is a step in the direction of elegance, away from the robust; towards definition and distinction, away from the merely solid and four-square. Progress is being made at Lascombes.

THE TASTING

The majority of the following wines was sampled at Château Lascombes in October 1991. Notes on the 1971, the 1967 and the vintages from 1964 to 1955 come from a tasting at Lascombes in April 1986.

	Optimum drinking

1990   1996–2006

Racked a month ago. The colour presently is not as deep as the 1989. The nose is a little uneasy and superficial. It is better on the palate. Medium-full, quite rich if without a great deal of tannin. Lacks a bit of zip but the wine is certainly long enough on the palate. I sampled three separate elements, progressively better.

1989   1997–2010

Bottled a month ago. So the colour is not as full as the 1988. Ripe ample nose. Almost sweet. Not perhaps a great deal of strength. Inherently soft, but it is upset by the bottling. Medium-full, some tannin and oak. Plump and fleshy. Fresh and accessible. Lacks a little power and drive and depth on the follow-through but is balanced and the fruit is stylish. Good plus.

1988   1995–2005

Good colour. Quite firm, reserved nose. Fresh blackberry fruit. Medium body. A little tannin. Good balance and style if not a wine of great concentration or depth. A much more classic wine, of course. Good acidity, but the fruit merely ripe rather than super-concentrated. There is a lack of real generosity and dimension on the finish. Quite good.

1987   Drink soon

Reasonable colour. No undue age. Soft, plump accessible nose. This is ripe and by no means feeble and it is a great deal less disagreeable than the 1984. Somewhat light and inconsequential though. On the palate the wine is not too slight, but there is not much richness. Drink now while the fruit remains fresh.

1986   **1996–2010**

Good colour. Marginally less than the 1985. Plump, aromatic nose, elements of cherry as well as mulberries and the black fruits. Complex though, and with a Margaux softness. Medium-full. Good tannins. This has depth and style, and there is also complexity. Interesting fruit, well-balanced with acidity. Not as lumpy as Lascombes often is. Long. Good oak base. I like this. Very good.

1985   **1996–2006**

Good colour. Just a little more than the 1986. This has a fatter, more structured nose than the 1986, but it is not as elegant. Meatier and solider, but rather driven, over-macerated. Rustic touches. Medium-full. A bit farmyardy. It doesn't have the elegance of the 1986. Indeed I find it rather unstylish. It finishes astringently.

1984   **Drink now**

Reasonable colour. No undue age. Hard, fleshless nose, now getting coarse, dried out and unattractive. I can't see much merit here. On the palate it isn't too bad. There is some fruit but it is now drying out. A mean wine without charm.

1983   **Now–1999**

Medium-full colour. A touch of brown at the rim. Soft nose. Indeed now mature if not even loosening up. Fruity but neither very complex nor very stylish. Better than the 1985 though. Medium body. No tannins obtrusive. The attack is round, fruity and quite fresh but the follow-through tails off a bit. It lacks real grip. Yet not too short. Quite good plus. Better than the 1982 today.

1982   **1994–2004**

Fullish colour. Beginning to show signs of development. But the nose is a bit dense. It might be rich but it is certainly ungainly. There are unattractive burnt fusel oil aromas here. The palate is a little better, but the wine is as much astringent as tannic, and there seems to be a lack of fat and richness, volume even. Not showing well today. Will it ever show any better?

1981   **Drink soon**

Good fullish colour. Only barely mature. Fullish quite fresh nose. There is fruit here but also an element of the rustic. It is a bit loose and more than a bit farmyardy at first, though this disappeared after a while. An open, medium-bodied fruity wine. But it lacks grip. The attack is fresh. The follow-through less elegant and more astringent. Lacks depth, style and complexity. Drink quite soon. Not bad at best.

1979   **Now–2000**

Medium-full colour, fresher looking than the 1978. Fullish, meaty, even solid nose, with a touch of reduction. Rather more structure than the 1981. More depth too. A fullish, quite concentrated example with plenty of fruit. The grip is there too and after the reduction had disappeared one had a very pleasant example with balance, volume and vigour. Will keep well. Very good for the vintage.

1978   **Drink soon**

Marginally more colour than the 1979 but more brown at the rim. It seems more evolved too on the nose, lighter and looser, with less grip and now beginning to lose its style. Medium-full. Originally this was more elegant and complex than the 1979. Now it is beginning to get attenuated. Drink soon.

1976   **Drink soon**

Medium-full mature colour. Smoky nose, a bit dry, doesn't seem to have a lot of fruit. Better on the palate. Medium to medium-full. Reasonably fresh and fruity and not too astringent. This has neither a great deal of depth or class, nor complexity. A touch of cooked fruit about it. Yet pleasant and still quite vigorous. A pleasant wine of no great consequence. A little short and one-dimensional.

1975   **Now–1998**

Medium-full colour. No undue maturity. Good rich fat nose, no astringency. Toffee and hot chocolate, as well as quite Merlot-ish fruit. Fresh for a 1975. It doesn't have the greatest depth, class or dimension, but it is medium-full, round, quite long on the palate and mature. There is pleasure to be had here. Good. No hurry to drink it up.

1973   **Drink soon**

Well-matured colour but quite substantial for a 1973. Fragrant nose. Some age now, but this wasn't at all bad once. On the palate, though a little dried-out at the edges, it is by no means over the hill. Interesting spices. Not astringent. A good example of the vintage.

1971   **Drink soon**

Fullish colour, now lightening up. Fully mature, quite brown at the rim. Soft, slightly ethereal, wood-smoky nose. Medium-bodied. Attractive, good acidity, a complexity missing in some of the later vintages. Good length. Doesn't have enormous class but good for the vintage and will still keep well.

1970   **Now–2000**

Good fullish colour. Still plenty of vigour here. This is a typical old-style Lascombes which makes up in size and flesh for what it lacks in style and complexity. Fullish, a bit four-square. The fruit ripe but not that concentrated but with good acidity. Cabernet flavours. Still plenty of life: a good wine. But the 1966 has more finesse and subtlety. The tannins are a bit chunky and drying out.

1967   **Drink soon**

Reasonably full, mature colour. Attractive nose, blackberry and *sous-bois*, nice spicy fruit. Little sign of age. Quite a full wine, and meaty for a 1967. Has depth and no sign of astringency. Good for the vintage. No hurry to drink up, I wrote in 1986. Today I would suggest you drink it soon.

1966   **Now–1999**

Fullish colour, little sign of maturity. This is rather impressive. Ample. Quite fat, very ripe, still young. All the black fruits. Complex with the violet flavours of Margaux. Fullish, elegant, silky. Balanced and complex. This is very good. It hasn't perhaps quite the extra finesse for 'fine' but it has none of the acidity apparent at the finish of many 1966s. Plump and voluptuous and long on the palate. Plenty of life. Very good.

1964   **Drink up**

Good, fullish, mature colour. Nose has lightened up a bit. More astringent than the 1967 and less alive, less fresh. Fullish, sweet and spicy but finishes a bit dry. Lightening up. I prefer the 1967.

1962   **Drink soon**

Good, medium-full, mature colour. Aromatic nose, much fresher and more complex than the 1964. Lovely mature Cabernet and violets. Quite full, a warm, generous wine which is yet another example of how good the 1962s are, and how well they have aged. Lovely long finish. Delicious.

1961   **Drink soon**

Very good colour. Perhaps it is this particular example but the wine shows a bit of age now. Underneath the richness of fruit lurks a little astringency. Ripe, concentrated, and real quality nevertheless. Lovely.

1959   **Now–1998**

(Served at lunch from Imperials and Jeroboams) Very fine colour, like all 1959s. Fine fullish, distinguished old claret nose, not a bit dense, baked or chunky. Cedar wood and old vine creaminess. Fullish, soft, velvety, voluptuous. Essence of cassis and all the delicacy of Margaux. Very long and complex. None of the Lascombes chunkiness. Delicious. (A Belgium bottling, by H. Grafe-Lecoq, sampled around this time, was equally impressive in the bottle size in London.)

1955   **Drink up**

Old but not aged colour. Nose and palate have lightened up a bit, but generous, elegant, still has length. Very pleasant and quite concentrated. Old vines again. Very good.

D'ISSAN

Regum Mensis Arisque Deorum ('For the table of kings and the altars of the gods') is engraved in the stone above the main entrance to Château d'Issan. Issan, a third growth in the commune of Cantenac, is one of the few real castles in the Médoc. It even possesses a moat. Château d'Issan lies somewhat off the beaten track; not, like others, because it is secluded somewhere in the country away from the Gironde but because the castle lies between the first gravel bed of vineyards and the more alluvial meadows and pastures, on the river side of the main D2 road which winds north of Bordeaux into the classed-growth country. Between the château and this road, enclosed within a venerable stone wall, lies the main part of the vineyard.

Issan has a long and interesting history. Legend has it that the wine was served at the wedding breakfast of Henry II and Eleanor of Aquitaine. Further legends state that Issan was the last stand of the retreating English army after the battle of Castillon in 1453, and that from the shore nearby – the Port d'Issan – this army embarked the following spring, taking a good quantity of Issan 1453 on board with them. The Comte de Foix had been instrumental in the rout of the English and was given Issan and a Barony as a reward by Charles VII.

HISTORY

Sifting through to separate myth from reality we can isolate Issan, then called Château Théoban, as a fortified *maison noble* in the early Middle Ages. This manoir, a *seigneurie* which owed allegiance to the senior *seigneurie* of the southern Haut-Médoc at Blanquefort, was one of a number of fortifications established on high ground near the coastline to protect the Médoc inhabitants from robbery by pirates. Théoban had a near neighbour, what was then called Lamothe de Cantenac. This is now Château Margaux.

The Charles VII donation story may confuse Issan with another *seigneurie* further north, that at Lamarque, which was in the hands of the Foix de Candale family for several generations in the fifteenth and sixteenth centuries. The *seigneurs* of Théoban at this time were a family called Meyrac who had inherited it from a family called Noalhan, *seigneurs* of 'La Motte de Ludon' as well as of Cantenac itself. From Thomas de Meyrac (who died in 1464) the domaine passed to his son Jean de Meyrac and then in 1507 to Isabeau de Meyrac, 'Dame de Théoban et Cantenac', who married Giron de Ségur. Their granddaughter married Helies de Salignac in 1527 and the property passed through a number of hands before emerging as the dowry of another heiress, a Mlle la Ferrière, who married Pierre Escoders de Boysse, Captain of Ordnance to Henry IV, in 1609.

About 40 years later the heiress was Marguerite de Lalanne. She married a man called Pierre d'Issenhault, or d'Essenhault, a councillor of the Bordeaux parliament. He demolished the existing *maison noble*, constructed the present château out of the ruins and gave it his name. Issan remained in the Essenhault family until 1760 by which time it was the jurisdiction centre for Cantenac and Labarde. In that year it was acquired by M. de Castelnau, another Bordeaux councillor. In 1776 it was divided between the Castelnau family and that of the Foix de Candale. The Candales took over the castle and attempted to rename it, and it is under the name of Château de Candale that it appears in the earliest Bordeaux records.

There is one fascinating earlier English reference, however. Henry Powell looked after the cellar of the Prince of Wales, later George II, and in October 1723 received a letter from J. Bruvenal, a merchant or agent in Bordeaux. After mention of the four 'topping', that is, top wines, La Tour (*sic*), Lafite, Château Margaux and Pontac (Haut-Brion), and the market for the vintage ('indeed charming wines'), Bruvenal goes on, 'Never in my life have I tasted the Château d'Issan so good as this vintage'. This is testimony to the established status of the Issan vineyard, rather early in history of the Médoc, for it was not generally until the period between 1720 to 1740 that most of the classed growths were established.

As Château de Candale, Issan was a second growth of the communes of Margaux and Cantenac, and fetched between 1000 and 1300 *livres* a *tonneau* in the last years before the Revolution, according to Wilhelm Franck in 1845. Thomas Jefferson, later to become American president, was a keen wine-grower as well as a wine-drinker, and made a number of visits to Bordeaux. He refers to Candale as a third growth (of the whole of Bordeaux) in a letter he wrote on 24 May 1787.

By 1825 the vineyard, split between the Candales and the Castelnaus, was producing about 60 *tonneaux*. In this year Justin Duluc acquired both parts and the château for a quarter of a million francs and set about some much needed improvements to the vineyards. A M. Blancy bought the property from Duluc 25 years later for 350,000 francs, and when he died in 1859 it was valued at 470,000 francs. The heirs sold it to a M. Gustave Roy in 1866 for 790,000 francs, by which time Issan was producing 80 to 100 *tonneaux* from its 45 hectares of vines, and, now proclaimed officially as a third growth, could expect a price of between 2,500 and 3,000 francs a *tonneau*.

Gustave Roy, then also the owner of Château Brane-Cantenac, was a rich Parisian textile manufacturer, and rarely visited the estate, yet Issan enjoyed a high reputation throughout the rest of the century and spread to the Austro-Hungarian empire. It is said that Emperor Franz-Josef would drink no other claret, and particularly liked the 1899.

After the First World War, Issan was sold by the Roys to M. Grange, at that time also proprietor of Château Giscours, for 800,000 francs, but under the Grange ownership the property went into decline. The production declined to 70 *tonneaux* by 1931, and to a mere two *tonneaux* by the end of the Second World War. It was rescued from perhaps total eclipse by the arrival in April 1945 of Emmanuel Cruse.

Emmanuel Cruse, who with other members of his family was part owner at the time of Château Rausan-Ségla, was on the outlook for a *cru classé* of his own, and had toyed with the idea of Giscours, then in an equally dilapidated condition. But he decided on Issan, perhaps attracted by the romance of the castle and the moat, though it was some years before he could begin to restore the building, which had been considerably damaged by German troop occupation during the war. He died in June 1968, and Issan is now the property of his widow, Marguerite. The estate is run by his son Lionel.

Since 1945 much has been done at Issan. Firstly the vineyard was replanted, for the area under vines had declined to barely a couple of hectares. Much-needed improvements were also devoted to the *chais*, and a new first-year cellar was constructed. Once the Cruse family had sold Rausan-Ségla, in 1956, work could begin on the Issan château itself. Since then it has been carefully and lovingly restored and renovated. Not only has a great deal of money been spent on the decoration itself, but furniture, pictures and other antiques have been introduced.

THE VINEYARD

The first stage of Emmanuel Cruse's replanting was to extend the vineyard to just over fifteen hectares, in the ratio 75 per cent Cabernet Sauvignon, 5 per cent Cabernet Franc and 20 per cent Merlot. Since the mid-1960s it has been further enlarged, to 30 hectares, and the proportion of Cabernets has been increased to 85 per cent. At the beginning of the 1980s a harvesting machine was introduced. This has now been dispensed with. Picking is once again manual.

The rest of the 110-hectare estate, much of it fields full of sheep or cattle, runs down behind the château towards the estuary. Once upon a time, a wine known as Moulin d'Issan – you can still see the ruined mill – was made from vineyards in this area. It has now been revived. Château de Candale, the name which failed to take on as the proper name of the château, is now the name used for the second wine.

THE *CHAIS*

The *chais* are partly very old, but carefully renovated, partly mid-nineteenth century, and partly new. One section with a timber-beamed roof dates from the start of large-scale wine production, which we can date in the early 1700s, and is a protected building. It is now occasionally used for celebrity concerts, recitals and chamber music. The modern section of the cellars had its capacity doubled in 1988, a new *chai* having been constructed alongside the existing one. A new stainless-steel *cuverie* was installed in 1989. Until 1972, the *mise en bouteille* was carried out in the Cruse cellars in Bordeaux, where, like other château-owning *négociants*, they were better equipped to do this, and some wine sold in bulk. Since then, in common with all other classed growths, the entire crop has been château-bottled.

THE CHÂTEAU

Surrounded by its moat and by lawns, shrubs, roses and trees, Issan lies in a beautiful, peaceful setting. The building, allowed to deteriorate in the inter-war period, and subsequently further defaced by enemy occupation in World War Two, was in a sorry condition in 1945 when the Cruses took over, and it is no doubt because of this, as well as the state of the vineyard, that the price the Cruses paid – a mere 5 million (old) francs – was so low.

The structure itself, however, appears to have been sound, and now the interior has been restored, the château is also a listed building. With its treasury of beautiful things, particularly china, it is almost a museum. Indeed the two remarkable Renaissance fireplaces in the drawing room and dining room are classified as national historical monuments. Mme Emmanuel Cruse lives there in the summer.

THE WINE

The first Issan which regularly came my way was the 1961 vintage, a year when the production totalled only nineteen *tonneaux* (in 1979 it was 150). This is a most attractive wine which I have enjoyed on a number of occasions, and it has always shown well even among its peers in this memorable vintage. More recently I have seen a magnum (unfortunately decayed) of the 1929 and some oddballs such as the 1965 which was unexpectedly clear, fresh and fruity as late as 1983. But my main experience of its property lies in the good vintages of the 1960s and the wines it has produced more recently.

With a Merlot percentage as low as 15 per cent, which would be small in Pauillac, let alone Margaux, one would expect a firm, full wine. This is so, but, while it is full and rich, and less soft than some of its neighbours (Brane-Cantenac for instance), it does not have the slightly burly quality one sees in, say, Lascombes or Marquis-de-Terme. There is a refinement, similar to Palmer, which I suspect is due to the location of the vines, on the first of the gravel *croupes* which ripple away from the Gironde – further inland the soil contains more clay and sand and consequently the wines are sturdier.

Coupled with this refinement, a fine richness and concentration of fruit has become evident in recent years, as the vines have attained a ripe old age. Issan has really come into its own in the 1980s, when some splendidly ripe wines, full of depth and finesse, have been made.

If we measure a property by its quality (and long may prices remain reasonable), Issan is surely a major contender for 'super-second' status.

THE TASTING

I sampled the wines of the last decade, plus the 1975 and 1947, at the château in April 1992. The older vintages were shown at a tasting presided over by M. Lionel Cruse for Les Amis du Vin customers in June 1984.

Optimum drinking

1991   **1995–1998**

Good colour. Ripe nose but a hint of old tea disturbs me. This is soft and fruity on the palate. Medium body. A gentle wine which is not without style and length. But it lacks backbone. Not bad.

1990   **1996–2005**

Good colour. The nose is quite firm, a bit hidden. On the palate there is good raspberry fruit: very Margaux in character. Medium to medium-full body. Has balance and finesse, and dimension on the finish. What it lacks is real concentration and grip. Yet it is a subtle wine, and I prefer it to the 1989. Good plus.

1989   **1996–2004**

Good colour. Compared with the 1990 this is fuller and has a better grip. Indeed it seems much more positive on the follow-through. The nose is spicy, with a touch of sweetness. There are no obtrusive tannins. The fruit isn't as stylish but the wine has a bit more to it. But, on aeration, I find it less complex and has less finesse than the 1990. Good plus again.

1988   **1996–2007**

Good colour. The nose is not very expressive. On the palate it is also a bit closed. But there is stylish fruit here. Medium to medium-full body. A soft, understated wine. There is grip and personality but it lacks a bit of concentration. Yet the wine is long on the finish. Good plus.

1987   **Drink soon**

Medium colour. Soft, quite ripe but essentially nondescript nose. A lightish but round, elegant wine, with a cheerful if somewhat one-dimensional fruit. Yet reasonable grip. More style and length than most.

1986   **Now–2000**

Medium-full colour. Good ripe nose, but some development now. Slight aspect of washed-out tannins. A touch of slightly dry spice. On the palate this shows the same character though there is at the same time some ripe fruit. Yet the net effect lacks a bit of style and finishes a bit flat. Lacks zip and elegance and a bit of concentration. Only quite good.

1985   **1995–2008**

Medium-full colour. A little more than the above. Fuller and richer on the nose than the 1986. Quite spicy. This has an aromatic, roasted nuts element I had not remembered. A riper, more positive, more Merlot wine than the 1986. Ripe, fat, quite concentrated but in a more exotic and spicy, more Libournais way than a typical Margaux. Medium body, quite soft already. Good though, even very good. Positive finish.

1984   **Drink soon**

Good colour for the vintage. It lacks a little concentration but not a lack of ripe fruit and grip. Indeed this has a lot more to it than the 1987. Slightly austere but stylish and still has good length. Very good for the vintage.

1983   **Now–2009**

Medium-full, more evolved than the 1985. A ripe, fragrant, stylish wine which still has good grip. This has more backbone and better grip than the 1985. It is more classic and has better balance. Medium to medium-full body. Still a little tannic. Ripe, quite fat, even quite rich and long on the palate. Very good without a doubt. Better than the 1985.

1982   **1995–2010**

Fullish colour. Full, fat, backward nose. This is even better than the 1983. For a start it is fatter and more concentrated. There is more backbone and no lack of grip. Rich, aromatic, meaty and concentrated. This is firmer and fresher. Fat and satisfying. Finishes well.

1981   **Now–1999**

Fine colour. Not as fat as the 1982 or as classic as the 1983 but certainly not outclassed. Lovely ripe fruit. Cedary Margaux flavour. Concen-trated and long on the palate.

1980   **Drink up**

Lighter, weaker colour. Slightly thin and stringy on the nose. I have seen other 1980s with more grip and fruit. The wine has a slight background flavour of old tea. No better than pleasant.

1979   **Drink soon**

Medium colour, not a lot of development. Fresh, elegant, oaky nose. Soft, round, quite ripe, pleasant wine but without a great deal of depth. Stylish finish. Good but not great.

1978   **Now–2000 plus**

Full colour, some development. Quite a lot fuller, richer and more backward than the 1979. Still a bit of tannin. Good depth. Will keep well. Good.

1976   **Drink soon**

Good colour. Quite solid and rich on both nose and palate. More substantial and less developed than most. Very good for the vintage. Holding up well.

1975   **Now–2000**

Good vigorous colour. Not a bit dry on the nose. This has grip and life and good concentration. Medium-full, balanced, even rich. There is a touch of spice. But good ripe tannins and a long finish. Good plus at the very least.

1971   **Drink soon**

Good, mature colour. Elegant nose, not too developed. Medium-full body, just a little tannin. Slightly austere fruit. Clean, gravelly Cabernet flavour. This is a good 1971 which has held up well.

1970   **Now–1999**

Good colour, still youthful. Full, quite solid, good fruit and acidity. It is all here, but just lacks a little richness, roundness and concentration. Very good if not exceptional.

1962   **Now–1997**

Vigorous colour. Little sign of its age. A little pinched at first on the nose. Mellow and full of fruit after it opened up in the glass. Medium to medium-full body. Ripe, perfumed and balanced. This is an elegant, mature wine: not one with the greatest concentration and intensity but complex and without any undue astringency. Good plus.

1947   **Now–1997 plus**

Fine, full, mature colour. This is not a bit 1947-ish: indeed I thought it was a 1949. Yet it is rich and sweet, but there is neither density nor any suggestion of volatile acidity. Fullish, classy. Very good concentration, depth and dimension. Plenty of life still. Fine.

MALESCOT-
SAINT-
EXUPÉRY

I am continually surprised, when I delve into the historical background of a famous Bordeaux estate, by the unevenness of history. Even at the most exalted level, properties rise and fall, reputations improve or decline. There is decay and there is renaissance; attention and neglect. Nowhere is this more so, for some reason, than in Margaux. The first 45 years of this century saw the effects of the aftermath of phylloxera, two world wars and a continuing slump in the demand for wine. Profitability was non-existent. A large number of estates – Prieuré and La Lagune among them – almost ceased to exist. Others fared better, but only just. Throughout the southern Médoc in particular, the *vignoble* declined, as did the reputation of many of the *crus classés*.

One such was Château Malescot-Saint-Exupéry. Happily there has been stability for the last 50 years, since the current family, the Ritz-Zugers, arrived. And during this period some very fine wines have been made. The general standard of the Margaux classed growths is lower and less consistent than those communes further north. But Malescot is one of the better wines.

Malescot, as the name is now more commonly contracted, has a long and complicated history. There are not many properties which can trace their ownership back to the beginning of the seventeenth century, not long after the Dutch first drained the marshy land of the Médoc, and therefore first made it suitable for major wine production. But the Malescot estate was then already in being, belonging to the family Escousses.

HISTORY

According to tradition the Escousses, notaries to the King, arrived in Margaux in 1608, and the estate dates from 1616. On 1 August 1697, Mlle Louise Escousses sold the estate to Simon Malescot, Attorney-General to Louis XIV and a *procureur* in the Bordeaux parliament. It remained in the Malescot family until the Revolution, when it was divided between three members of the family: l'Abbé Malescot, his sister and their sister-in-law. During the eighteenth century the reputation of the wine, according to Wilhelm Franck, writing almost a century later, was that of a third growth, and this is substantiated by the first comprehensive classifications produced by the brokers Tastet and Lawton and others in the 1820s.

During Napoleonic times the property seems to have been broken up, for the next recorded proprietor, François Benoit Dunogues, later under the Restoration to be made a viscount, only bought half the estate, in 1813, and that from a consortium of three people. This was sold again in 1825 to a Louis Pierlot; when he died, shortly afterward, his heirs put it up for sale and the purchaser was then Comte Jean-Baptiste de Saint-Exupéry, who paid 90,000 francs for the buildings and estate, but without the wines of the cellar, i.e., as this was in February 1827, the 1826 crop, and any unsold wine of the 1825 vintage (a large but mediocre year). This was not a very large figure (Château Margaux itself would shortly change hands for 1.3 million) but the vineyard at the time only seems to have been about ten hectares and produced 10 to 15 *tonneaux* of wine.

Saint-Exupéry had recently married and settled in the Gironde. His wife, whose dowry provided the money for the purchase, was a Mlle Antoinette Lehoult, daughter of a *négociant* in Bordeaux. (Antoine de Saint-Exupéry, the airman and author, was their great-grandson.) Saint-Exupéry enlarged the domaine by acquiring Château La Colonie, the domaine of his wife's family, and another called Loyac. This gave him a combined holding capable of producing some 70 *tonneaux*. As is customary, Saint-Exupéry added his name to the wine, which from then on has been known as Château Malescot-Saint-Exupéry – and threw himself enthusiastically into the affairs of the Médoc, becoming Mayor of Margaux in 1830.

During the 1840s Saint-Exupéry died, leaving a widow and a son who was still a minor. The buildings consisted of a small two-storey country house within a walled courtyard, with an adjacent *chai* for the wines – not an imposing affair. Nevertheless, the expenses of maintaining the buildings were as much as that of the vineyard, and Mme de Saint-Exupéry soon began to get into debt.

Meanwhile, a M. Fourcade, a Bordeaux banker, had arrived in the commune, and was busy acquiring land. In 1853 he bought an estate known after its owner, the Prévôt de La Croix, and other parcels. He was also soon to be the new owner of Château Dubignon-Talbot, one of the classed growths which no longer exists.

Later in 1853, the creditors finally moved in on Mme Saint-Exupéry and tribunal was arranged for the disposal of the assets. But before this could take place, Fourcade had acquired Malescot for 115,000 francs, and paid off the widow's debts.

By means of further purchases and exchanges, Fourcade built up a considerable vineyard holding in Margaux, well over 100 hectares, and the best of this was reconstituted under the Malescot name. He set about rebuilding and reconstructing the cellars and outbuildings, an undertaking which was finally complete by 1871, and, now that the oidium epidemic had been controlled, replanting the vineyards. Between 1850 and 1865 some half a million new vines were planted, increasing production from 75 to 200 *tonneaux*. Fourteen oxen and six horses were stabled on the property in order to keep the vineyards tilled, and some 300 pickers were required for the harvest. Edouard Guillon, an interesting contemporary source, describes in *Les Châteaux Historiques et Vignobles de la Gironde* (1867) the combined estate of 70 hectares as being as big as Château Margaux, possessing a 'very ordinary' *bourgeois* mansion flanked by two large *cuviers* and no fewer than six *chais*, each capable of holding 500 barrels.

This collection of buildings was at the north of the village of Margaux, not where the current edifice now stands. The present château was constructed in 1885, to the plans of a Monsieur L. Garros, and from, it is said, the profits of a single year's vintage. It is an attractive three-storey mansion situated in the middle of the village of Margaux.

The energetic M. Fourcade passed away in the middle of the 1866 harvest and after some discussion his heirs decided to sell. Malescot exchanged hands in July 1869, for 1,076,000 francs. Ownership of Malescot passed to a consortium: a M. Deroulède, who had married Fourcade's daughter Adèle, M. Bernos, M. Charles Couve, and a M. de Boissac who insti-gated the building of the present château. M. Bernos soon disappears from the scene, but the remaining owners seem to have continued Fourcade's expansionist policy. During the 1880s and 1890s pastureland in Arsac was replaced by a huge 95-hectare vineyard called Arnaud Blanc. By now, we also begin to get some concrete detail about the Malescot holding. It comprised 26 'prixfait' of which twenty were in Margaux and six in Cantenac, situated on the two large croupes which ran through the communes. Cabernet Sauvignon and Cabernet Franc comprised seven-eighths of the encépagement. Despite the furious plantation, which might in-dicate the proprietors were interested in volume rather than quality, the reputation was high, but judging by its non-appearance in Professor Saintsbury's cellars, and a single mention only in André Simon's Vintagewise, probably not at the very highest level.

Then at the turn of the century, and this is where the history becomes very unclear, Malescot was put up for sale. Had the proprietors fallen out? Did one of the consortium die? We do not know. The auction took place in May 1900. The price was only 400,000 francs. A year later it was resold, fetching a mere 150,000. The new owner was German, a Herr Lerbs of Bremen.

Reading between the lines, the apparent fall in value from a million francs to 400,000 or less does not give a true picture. As far as I can make out, the domaine was split. Château Arnaud Blanc, La Colonilla (La Colonie) and Dubignon-Talbot, I suspect, were sold off sep-arately – they each appear in different hands a few years later. Lerbs soon got into financial trouble and, by way of a debt, Malescot passed to the firm of Seignitz (still a much respected source of fine wine), also in Bremen.

During the First World War, Malescot, as the property of an enemy, was confiscated. It became a convalescent home for officers. It was re-acquired for the French by a M. Fouquet in 1917, but he sold it in 1919 to the British wine firm of W. H. Chaplin and Co. Ltd. A few years later Chaplin's also bought the title and vineyards (but no château) of Marquis-d'Alesme-Becker from Lascombes.

THE ZUGER FAMILY

Shortly before the last war, in 1938, Chaplin's appointed Edmund Ritz, formerly a mining engineer, to run their two Margaux estates for them. In 1937 Ritz and his son-in-law, Paul Zuger, had bought from a M. Michel the château of Desmirail, plus four hectares of vines and a small chai in Margaux, and in Arsac, a fifteen-hectare domaine called Baudry. With these four hectares of vines Ritz and Zuger produced twenty tonneaux of wine, which they called Château Ritz-Desmirail, but sold it in bulk, there being no space to set up a bottling line, or to store the cased wine.

Edmund Ritz died in 1943, at about the same time that financial pressures forced the fami-ly to dispose of the Baudry vineyard to Château Martinens. (From Martinens it passed to Du Tertre and eventually to Lucien Lurton of Brane-Cantenac who, having acquired the name of Desmirail, has now revived this growth.) During the war the château at Malescot became first a maternity home, later the military headquarters for the area. The Malescot vineyard, deprived of materials such as fertilizer, stakes and wires on which to train the vines, as well as pesticides, was allowed to contract and decline despite the fact that the administrator during this period was a grandson of the Seignitz of the pre-First World War period. No doubt he was hoping to get it back! Even after the war, little was done. It seems as if Chaplin's had forgotten about it. There was further and further dilapidation. Less and less wine was produced, though that which did appear seems to have been satisfactory and in the case of some vintages such as the 1945 and 1947, very fine indeed. The value of the estate in the Chaplin accounts was reduced to a token £1.

In 1955, on the death of Michael Henderson, the chairman of Chaplin's, the board decided to sell its Bordeaux interest and asked Paul Zuger, now joined by his son Roger, to find a buyer. After much hesitation and at Roger Zuger's suggestion, the Zugers decided to buy it themselves. A company owned by Paul and Roger was formed to buy Malescot, and a second company, that owning the Ritz-Desmirail brand, acquired the vineyard of Marquis-d'Alesme. The combined price was 6.5 million (old) francs. In the absence of separate cellars the wine of Marquis-d'Alesme continued to be made at Malescot until, in 1972, Palmer, after much prompting, finally decided to sell the *chais* of Desmirail. Paul Zuger bought them from a doctor who had bought them from Palmer and this is now the new Marquis-d'Alesme.

Shortly before Paul Zuger's death in 1981, the combined domaine was split. Roger Zuger owns Malescot, where he lives with his wife Nicole and two children (the eldest, Jean-Luc, is now working alongside his father), and a large friendly boxer called Magnum. Jean-Claude, Roger's younger brother, has inherited Château Marquis-d'Alesme and lives about 200 metres up the road.

THE VINEYARD AND THE *CHAIS*

Malescot is now somewhat smaller than during Fourcade's heyday. There are in all about 40 hectares, of which 27 are under vines. The property has been enlarged slightly in recent years by the addition of part of the vineyard of the classed growth Château Dubignon-Talbot. In 1960 a consortium of three people – Pierre Ginestet of Château Margaux, Jean Cordier, proprietor of Château Talbot, and Paul Zuger of Malescot – combined to buy Dubignon-Talbot. Cordier wanted to buy the name, to prevent any confusion with his Saint-Julien fourth growth. Ginestet and Zuger wanted the land, which lay between their own vineyards. Château Dubignon-Talbot has now ceased to exist.

The vines are situated in four main plots on the two large Margaux *croupes* on either side of the D2, the main road and *route du vin* which passes through the village of Margaux. In places the Malescot vines are directly to the north and west of those of Château Margaux itself, occasionally intermingling with them.

The *encépagement* is 50 per cent Cabernet Sauvignon, 10 per cent Cabernet Franc, 35 per cent Merlot and 5 per cent Petit Verdot. The average production is now 170 *tonneaux*.

The *chai* is on two floors, and has undergone much reconstruction in recent years. A new reception chamber has been built, together with a number of cement, enamelled-steel and stainless-steel vats for fermentation and *égalisage*, and a large extension for bottle and storage has also been constructed. These lie to the south of the château, which is itself on the left-hand side of the main road through Margaux. The second wine is known as Château Loyac, the name of the neighbouring vineyard incorporated during the Saint-Exupéry era. A further property associated with the Zugers is the Domaine de Balardin, a vineyard in the *palus* near the new Relais de Margaux.

THE WINE

Malescot has been described as austere for a Margaux. It often undergoes a *cuvaison* of as long as three weeks and it can certainly be fairly hard at the outset – though this is no bad thing. A hardness, even a bitterness, is expected in a young Médoc of a good vintage, and is an indication of substance and depth in the mature wine to come. Oddly, Malescot (because of the extra tannin from this long *cuvaison*, maintains Zuger) puts on colour as it ages.

In the past Malescot was fuller than many in the commune. But while richly fruity and with plenty of body it did not lack style and elegance. *Au fond* it was a true Margaux. And a very good one indeed.

Then came a period of adjustment. For a decade between 1975 and 1985 there were some disappointing vintages. Quality was inconsistent. The wine seemed to have lightened up.

More recently, since Michel Rolland of Libourne has been consultant oenologist – from 1989 onwards – I feel a grip has been taken on things. The wine is more focussed now and quality is back where it should be at the very good level. We may well have another super-second on our hands.

THE TASTING

Most of the older wines come from a tasting I took part in at the château in November 1985 (I have added a note on a splendid magnum of 1947 sampled at dinner with Tom and Frances Bissell in May 1993). Most of the 1980s decade was sampled at Malescot in April 1992.

1991 *Optimum drinking* **1996–2000**

Good colour. Plenty of fruit in a slight cool way on the nose. Light-medium body. This is round and ripe and has good grip. Ample and plump. Just a little tannin. Finishes long, elegantly and positively. A good result.

1990 **1998–2016**

Good colour. Ripe, lush nose. This is stylish and fragrant, very Margaux. Good depth in quite a delicate way. On the palate no lack of intensity. This is rich and concentrated with very good acidity. Fresh and with plenty of complexity. Medium-full body. Gently oaky. Harmonious. Long. Very good plus.

1989 **1997–2012**

Medium-full colour. Rich nose, but a little more four-square than the 1990. Medium to medium-full body. The tannins show a little, and it is not as concentrated or as definitive as the 1990. Very good though. Good intensity of flavour, good depth and good length.

1988 **1997–2009**

Good colour. This has a lovely nose. Ripe, ample, fresh, blackberry and raspberry fruit. Medium body. Some tannin. Good grip. Positive finish. Good plus, but it lacks the dimension for better than that.

1987 **Drink soon**

This is a good wine for a 1987. Round and fruity. Not short. Reasonable style. There is a good oak base which does not dominate.

1986 **1995–2005**

Good colour. Somewhat unformed nose, but the elements show promise. Currently adolescent. A medium-full, ungainly wine but there is concentration and at least reasonable grip. I can't see

much style at present but the finish is positive. Good. Perhaps good plus.

1985 **1995–2005**

Medium-full colour. This is also a bit adolescent. There is good concentration of fruit though. It is ripe and balanced and has good grip. More depth than the above but it also needs time. Medium-full body. Positive finish. Good plus.

1983 **Now–1997**

Medium to medium-full colour. Fully mature. Ripe bramble fruit on the nose but not very concentrated or stylish. On the palate there is medium body but the wine lacks real grip and personality. Not a rigorous enough selection. Quite good at best.

1982 **Now–1998**

Medium-full colour. Rather blunt on the nose. A bigger wine than the 1983, with a more cooked-fruit flavour. Medium-full body, but a little lumpy. It lacks real grip and concentration. It lacks flair and zip. Quite good only in 1982 terms.

1981 **Drink up**

Medium colour, really brown at the edge. This was never a very concentrated wine, and it is now loosening up and losing what elegance it had (which wasn't much). Not one of Malescot's successes.

1979 **Now–1999**

Good colour, not that big but little development. Good fruit on the nose with a touch of spice. Medium-full, rich, quite solid, good structure and grip. Round, ripe tannins. Still youthful. Good.

1978 **Now–1995**

Marginally more colour. Spicy nose, less zip. Medium body, something a little weak and tired, as much astringent as tannic. Pleasantly fruity but lacks a bit of backbone, freshness and depth. A bit disappointing. (M. Boissenaux, until recently Malescot's *oenologue*, said that he thought too much *vin de presse* had been added.)

1976   **Drink soon**

Good colour for the vintage. Not too brown nor lightening up. Roast chestnutty nose. Soft, spicy, quite ripe. Medium body; fully developed. Fresher than most. As with most 1976s there is a slight lack of real class, but this is still fresh and has length, and it tasted well in the glass. Good for the vintage.

1975   **Now–1995**

Not an enormous colour. Soft nose, showing Merlot; a bit dense in the 1978 way, even robust. Not that exciting. Medium-full body, some tannin. Certainly there is ripeness and richness there but in addition the slight clumsiness of the vintage which gives an impression of astringency. Yet the finish is fresh, even fat. Quite good.

1971   **Drink soon**

Good, fullish, mature colour. Soft, slightly spicy, ripe nose. Medium-full body, now *à point*. Round, elegant, good fruit, still fresh. Has depth and interest, style and charm. Finishes long. Very good for the vintage.

1970   **Now–1995**

Very fine, full, dense, immature colour. Initially very rich and concentrated on the nose, became a touch inky and spicy as it developed. Full body, possibly slightly dense, still has tannin, still youthful but opened up after a while. Plenty of fruity and concentration yet a certain unsuppleness prevents it from being great. Bottles I have had *chez moi* have been more generous. Certainly good.

1966   **Drink soon**

Quite a difference in colour from the 1970. Fullish, fully mature. Mature, refined, gently fruity nose. Not a blockbuster like the 1970. Medium full, ripe, mellow wine, much lighter and less concentrated than the 1970. As it developed, the aftertaste became a little acid, a characteristic of this vintage, and the finish a shade unclean (from the old barrels?). Despite this I like this wine. Not bad for the vintage.

1962   **Now–1997**

Very fine, full colour, little brown. Much more in the style of the 1970 than the 1966. Fine nose, very ripe and fruity, even concentrated. Really quite full, still tannic, plump and meaty. Richly ripe and fruity; a classy, almost sweet wine which has a lot of depth and still bags of life ahead of it. A wine in the 'old-fashioned' style. Very fine indeed – has 1961 touches.

1961   **Now–2005**

Fantastic colour, still immensely dense. Good as the 1962 is, this knocks it into a cocked hat. Very, very ripe, rich and concentrated. All a 1961 should be. Absolutely packed with fruit. Excellent, even by 1961 standards.

1959   **Now–1997**

Very fine colour, still very full, now some brown. Fine nose, a touch chunky and *crème brûlée*/truffles but not sign of age. Solid, ripe meaty wine. A little tannic astringency now apparent yet still full of fruit. Fine combination of different fruits, spices and aromas. A bit wine in the 'old-fashioned' style again. Finishes well. Better than the 1962. Very fine.

1955   **Drink soon**

Very fine, very full colour, now mature. Fine full nose. Fullish, round, rich and mellow with plenty of depth. No sign of age at all, even after half an hour in the glass. A very fine, elegant bottle with a lovely sweet finish. Delicious.

1947   **Now–1999**

(Magnum) This is a very lovely wine. Splendid colour. Could be a 1978. Excellent fresh, ripe nose and marvellous rich complex fruit. Not a bit astringent. Not a trace of volatile acidity. Simply mellow, vigorous, concentrated and multidimensional. No sign of age. Surely one of the best Médocs of the vintage. Fine plus.

1945   **Will keep well**

Marvellous colour, still brown. Full, rich, very complex, concentrated nose. A very big wine but no hardness or astringency at all. Elegant, supple, delicious, still very fresh; one might have guessed 1961. Marvellous, even porty concentration of fruit. This really must be one of the best and most alive 1945s.

1938   **Drink now**

Surprising colour. Full, brown-rimmed but not at all old. Soft nose, a little shallow. Still fresh, mellow and fruity on the palate with only a slight sign of decay at the end. No astringency. Acidity showed on the finish as the wine developed but initially the finish was stylish and sweet.

PALMER

Long before anyone coined the phrase 'super-second', one château in Cantenac-Margaux – and a *troisième*, not even a *deuxième* – had already achieved super-second status. It did so with a single wine. The château was Palmer. The vintage was 1961.

The 1961s were scarce and very expensive. But fabulous. Almost as soon as the must had been fermented into wine it became clear that the quality of the Palmer was exceptional – indisputably first growth.

As time went on and as the reputation of the wines in bottle could be accurately measured by the prices of the then new Christie's wine auctions, Palmer 1961 repeatedly fetched record levels only matched by the *premiers crus* and their Libournais equivalents. It continues to do so to this day.

But the quality of the 1961 was no flash in the pan. The 1950s Palmer vintages were very fine and those of the 1960s would be equally good if not better. The 1966 Palmer is another wine which is clearly of first growth quality and so is the 1970. Coincidentally, this was the period when its illustrious neighbour across the vineyards was in decline. At this time, Château Palmer was producing the best wine in Margaux. Today, happily, Château Margaux is all that it should be, a wine that amply justifies its three-century-old reputation as one of the top four in Bordeaux. The quality of Palmer continues to be exceptional though; good enough to keep the wine-makers at Margaux on their mettle; and, despite enormous progress elsewhere in the *appellation*, still indisputably the number two in the area.

Although the vineyard, as Palmer, only dates from 1814 and the château from 1860, the origins lie almost a century earlier amidst the ramifications of the family De Gasq or De Gascq, a name, one assumes, deriving from Gascony.

THE DE GASCQ FAMILY

For over 200 years prior to the Revolution, the Gascqs were intimately connected with the wines and properties of the Médoc and were leading figures in the Bordeaux *parlement*. As early as 1587, a Jean de Gasq married Mme Vallier who was the heiress of Calon in Saint-Estèphe. Later, another Gasq, a M. de Gasq-Léoville, married another heiress, the daughter of the Chevalier de Moytié, who had a large estate in Saint-Julien. The domaine of Lafite was passed on by Mme Jeanne de Gasc, widow of Joseph de Pomiers, to her second husband Jacques de Ségur, a *président à mortier* (one of nine vice-presidents) in the Bordeaux *parlement*. (When she died he married Mlle Thérèse de Clauzel, who brought him the estate of Château Latour.) Later, in 1785, another Gascq, Antoine, was a sort of unofficial guardian to the young Françoise d'Yquem.

Meanwhile, in Cantenac and Margaux, the substantial Issan estate was being dismembered. First there was a division in 1729 between the Foix-Candales and the Castelnau-Essenhault family. On 17 December 1748, that part owned by the Foix-Candales was further divided. Most remained with the heir, Bernard de Foix-Candale, part went to his sisters Marguerite and Hippolyte-Euphrasie but it seems that a further section was acquired by a member of the De Gascq family. Professor Pijassou, who wrote a paper on the origins of the Palmer estate in 1964, has shown that in the 1740s only some one-seventh of the commune of Cantenac was under vine. One would assume, therefore, that it was the De Gascq purchase which provided the impetus to establish an important vineyard. Certainly by the late 1760s Château de Gasq was an established wine, fetching the same price as Issan and Giscours according to the Tastet and Lawton archives, though rather less than the somewhat older estates in the commune of Margaux itself, such as Lascombes, Malescot, De Terme and 'Gorse', later Brane-Cantenac.

Pijassou states that by Napoleonic times there were 50 hectares of vines at Château de Gasq. Yet it does not figure in the earliest classifications which emerged shortly after the turn of the century. The reputation of the property, along with a change of name, would be the creation of its next owner.

MAJOR-GENERAL CHARLES PALMER

Into the story now comes the engaging, yet ultimately tragic, figure of Charles Palmer. Much of what we know about General Palmer and his purchase of Château de Gascq comes from the *Reminiscences and Recollections* of Captain Gronow. Gronow is not always to be trusted, however. There is a large seasoning of poetic licence in his account and he has confused a number of different people called Palmer (a common enough name, after all) whose activities and interests overlapped. For straightening out my earlier version of General Palmer's life (*Claret*, 1982) I am much indebted to Sally Davis, archivist of the Bath Postal Museum.

The Palmers originated in Bath where, in the 1740s, they were a wealthy *bourgeois* family whose fortune was based on the running of a brewery and a chandlery. John Palmer, Charles' father, was perhaps part of the first generation to be brought up as a gentleman. He wanted to go into the army but parental pressure was put on him to enter the church, thought social-ly more acceptable at the time. Following a family quarrel, after which John Palmer worked for a while as a labourer in the family brewery, where he made himself ill, the matter was al-lowed to drop. But it was neither the church nor the army for him.

Instead, he planned and inaugurated the first mail-coach service from London to Bath. He took over the local theatre from his father and succeeded in obtaining a Royal Patent for it in 1768. The Bath Theatre Royal was one of only three – the others were Covent Garden and Drury Lane – to have this distinction at the time, and he became, after his resignation from the Post Office, the local MP. He was also Mayor of Bath on two occasions.

John Palmer was by now a man of substantial means. In keeping with his higher social status, the family moved to London in the 1780s, the brewing and chandlering background were quietly dropped, if not sold, and all his children were brought up as proper members of society, with the men entered for careers which would befit their true standing as gentlemen.

Charles Palmer was born in 1777. After Eton and Oriel College, Oxford, he fulfilled his father's best hopes – and thwarted ambitions – by joining the 10th Dragoons. This crack regiment was a mixture of Continental exiles and English aristocracy, including George 'Beau' Brummell, the leader of the young blades of London society. Its Colonel-in-Chief was the Prince Regent. Charles Palmer rapidly became a leading member of the Prinny set in Carlton House and the Brighton Pavilion, rose steadily in the army until he became a Colonel and was appointed Aide-de-Camp to the Prince Regent in 1814. Palmer, handsome, socially popular and accomplished, had the highest society of the country at his feet.

In 1806, John Palmer, approaching 70 years of age, decided to resign as MP for Bath. Charles was a very natural successor and there seems to have been difficulty in combining the career of a politician with that of one in the army. At the time, Bath was a pocket borough, in the hands of the Corporation, consisting of 30 apothecaries. In return, no doubt, for free access to the theatre for themselves and their families, they had elected John Palmer as their MP. They would now transfer their allegiance to his son Charles – an elegant piece of corrupt electoral practice that was perfectly in keeping with the times.

By then the State had adopted John Palmer's reform of the postal-delivery system. Yet nothing in recompense had been paid. Charles was able to sponsor two bills in Parliament which led to £50,000 being paid to his father in belated recognition of his efforts.

The Napoleonic Wars were now nearing their conclusion and General Palmer, as he now was after the Peninsular Campaign, was part of the victorious British Army under Marshal Beresford which arrived at the gates of Bordeaux on 12 March 1814, after the Battle of Toulouse – incidentally, finding the inhabitants, whose trade had been in somewhat of a turmoil for the past 25 years, only too well-disposed to accept any kind of change that was likely to restore tranquillity.

Some time later, Palmer found himself travelling in the *diligence* from Lyons to Paris – a journey then requiring three days – and met an attractive lady, Marie Brunet de Ferrière, widow of Blaise Jean Charles Alexandre de Gascq. Her husband had just died and she was on her way to Paris to sell the property – one of the finest estates in Bordeaux and second only, she said, to Château Lafite – in order that the inheritance might be divided up, according to the law of France, amongst all the family. Unfortunately, she went on, the urgent necessity of the sale would mean that she would only get a quarter of its value. By the time they had arrived at their destination, General Palmer had bought the Château de Gascq. Palmer paid 100,000 francs. The date of the purchase was 16 June 1814.

Although from then on Charles Palmer was to devote a considerable amount of energy and capital to his new Margaux estate, he first had one or two things to settle in London. The 10th Dragoons had another Colonel, a man called Quentin. A letter had been circulated accusing Quentin of cowardice and inattention to duty. Although he had not signed this letter, Palmer was appointed Chief Prosecutor when it was decided to bring Quentin before a court martial. This took place at Westminster in a blaze of publicity, filling the public galleries to the brim and the newspapers for a fortnight. In the end Colonel Quentin was acquitted on three of the four charges and given a mild punishment on the other.

The Prince Regent, however, was furious about the whole affair. As Colonel-in-Chief, his own honour had been besmirched. He ordered that the men who had complained, Palmer included, should be publicly reprimanded at the regiment's barracks in Romford and seconded to other, less prestigious regiments.

But the scandal was not over yet. Colonel Quentin went to Paris, and when Palmer arrived there in February 1815, he received a letter from Quentin demanding personal satisfaction. Charles Palmer was not one to refuse this sort of challenge. Against the advice of his friends, he met Quentin at the Barrière de l'Etoile, then just outside the city, at noon on 3 February. They used Quentin's pistols at a distance of twelve paces. Quentin fired first and missed; Palmer discharged his bullet into the air and honour was apparently satisfied.

But once again the Prince Regent was angry. This latest incident had been reported in the London papers, raking up all the old controversy over the court martial and in tones very hostile to both duellists. Palmer's army career was never the same afterwards. Perhaps more importantly, as will be seen, his relations with the Prince Regent were also never quite the same again, although he did not retire from the military until 1830.

Charles Palmer returned to Bordeaux. He installed an agent, a Mr Gray, a personable but incompetent rogue, and promptly set about enlarging the estate by buying up adjacent parcels of land. In 1814 the property had consisted of 60 hectares, about half of which were under vine. Between 1816 and 1831 he enlarged this to some 162 hectares, of which 82 were vine-yard, absorbing about a dozen other properties, many of which – in the straitened economic circumstances of the time – would have been deserted and available for sale as those who had originally taken advantage of the sequestrated land in Napoleonic times found that they could not make their holdings pay a profit. As Pijassou points out, the Palmer acquisitions had a major influence on the changing face of the surrounding area. Among his purchases were two parcels – 30 hectares in all – of woodland near the village of Virefougasse in a *lieu-dit* called Boston which he had cleared and planted with vines. Others included the Domaine de Monbrun, a property which continues today; two vineyards belonging to members of the Dubignon family, one of which went on to be the now-redundant *cru classé* Dubignon-Talbot; and parcels called Rondeau and Raze. In all, over a period of fifteen years, he spent some 370,000 francs, about 20 million in today's money. Although vineyards in the prime area of the Médoc have exchanged hands for rather more in recent hyper-inflationary years, this was a vast fortune at the time.

Meanwhile, he was energetically promoting his wine in the London clubs and in society. The soft and charming 'Château Palmer' began to become fashionable and a dinner was given by the Prince Regent at Carlton House to test it. The wine was pronounced excellent. Unfortunately, when it was compared with the Prince's own wine, a more robust claret well cut with Hermitage called Carbonel, and to the accompaniment of anchovy sandwiches (!), it appeared thin and anaemic and the banquet terminated with the old Prince urging Palmer to try some experiments on his estate to produce a better wine. No doubt if Palmer had still been in the best of odour with the Prince Regent, things would have been different.

Accordingly, Palmer, much mortified, rooted out all his old vines, planted new ones and tried all sorts of experiments at immense cost but with little or no result. Continually fleeced by the corrupt Mr Gray, he rapidly ran through his fortune. His political career was also in decline. In 1826 he lost his seat after a recount to Lord Brecknock by just three votes, but re-gained it again as a supporter of the Reform Bill in 1831. He spoke vigorously in Parliament in favour of reform. After a procession down Milsom Street in the run up to the vote he was presented with a goblet and a silver salver. A toast was proposed: the Bill, the whole Bill and nothing but the Bill. Palmer drank deeply and replied 'with all my heart'.

He had always been very popular in Bath but after losing another election in 1837 he did not stand again. The problems of his vineyard were beginning to overwhelm him. Gray had been dismissed. Palmer could hardly afford to pay his *régisseur*, Jean Lagunegrand, to whom he owed 10,000 francs. He separated from his wife Mary Elizabeth Atkins (they never had any children), and was left to cope with the mounting debts alone. He was forced to sell his house in Wilton Road in London and his mansions in Bordeaux on which now stands a block of flats called Parc Palmer. Parts of the estate were sold off to meet his more urgent debts and, finally, the remainder of the vineyard was sold to Mme Françoise-Marie Bergerac, wife of one of his creditors, for 274,000 francs in 1843. A year later it passed to the Caisse Hypothécaire in Paris, the major creditor, for 312,840 francs.

After 1843 Palmer disappears from view, dying on 17 April 1851, not exactly in penury – for he continued to live in Mayfair – but no doubt lonely and miserable, ill-tuned to the new Victorian age. The *Bath Herald*, however, published a sympathetic obituary, praising his generosity and kindness but alluding to the financial difficulties of his later years. It would appear that his theatrical investments – for he had always retained his interest in the Theatre Royal in Bath – were also a drain on his resources. Quite simply, Charles Palmer, like others, had more enthusiasm and energy than sound financial sense.

The first mention of the wine in the Palmer era is in the first edition of Franck's *Traité* in 1824. Though not judged a classed growth, the wine '*De Gasq et Dubignon Aîné*' owned by 'Palmer' is listed twelfth in the commune of Cantenac after M. Durand at Le Prieur (now Prieuré-Lichine) and Desmirail. Production is given as 50 to 60 *tonneaux*.

It appears as 'Château Palmer' in the magazine *Le Producteur* a dozen or so years later, as a third growth, and in the later editions of Franck's *Traité*, when the vineyard was the property of the Caisse Hypothécaire, is rated a fourth. In the 1855 Classification, despite the depredations of oidium – the entire vineyard except the Boston parcel had been destroyed – it made the list as a *troisième*. The 1854 vintage had, in fact, fetched a price up with the average of the seconds (3,658 francs) rather than the bulk of the thirds which made some 800 francs less.

ISAAC AND EMILE PEREIRE

The second quarter of the nineteenth century had introduced a new era of stability and with the increased industrialization, a new class of rich man had emerged: bankers, financiers, 'captains of industry' and railway barons. One of the great names was the Pereire family, of Portuguese-Jewish origin, developers of the newly fashionable watering place place of Arcachon on the Atlantic coast. In 1853 they bought the best part of the Palmer estate, now reduced to some 85 hectares but with only some 27 under mature vines, from the Caisse Hypothécaire for 410,000 francs, and shortly afterwards set about constructing an elegant château somewhat in the same style as Pichon-Baron, for on the site at the time there were only the bailiff's house and the buildings used for making and storing the wine. This is the building which still stands, though it has not been lived in since the mid-1930s.

The estate was obviously in some disarray, and the Pereires, Isaac and his son Emile, made the excellent move of installing as *régisseur* a M. Lefort, a distinguished viticulturist and *oenologue* and the proprietor of a very good property in Cussac.

The Pereires ('more than twenty times millionaires' as a contemporary reverently remarks in an aside) had both more money and more business sense than General Palmer and soon succeeded in creating a model vineyard, well administered and making excellent wine. Despite the vicissitudes of phylloxera and mildew (when the Boston segment was completely destroyed and had to be replanted), the property expanded and prospered. By 1870, according to Pijassou, the property occupied 177 hectares of which 109 were vines. This, I feel, must be a somewhat exaggerated figure unless it includes the vines in the *palus* (see below). By the latter part of the century, the production was averaging some 170 *tonneaux*.

THE CONSORTIUM

However, not even the Pereires could survive the First World War and the slump which arrived in Médoc soon afterwards. By then there were some 30 members of the Pereire family, all of whom had to be consulted before any major decision could be made. The vineyard and its wines went into decline. Moreover, for most of the vintages between the wars, especially during the poor run in the 1930s, the property was running at a loss. The family, reluctant to continue pouring money into a bad investment, started to sell off bits and pieces of the large estate. In 1929, the vineyard had occupied 65 hectares., and, in addition, there were some 50 hectares of vines in the *palus* at Port Aubin. But by 1936 the vineyard was reduced to a mere 36 hectares, only some twenty of which were productive vineyard. The vineyard at Boston, for example, had been allowed to fall into disuse.

In 1938, these remains were bought by a consortium of four famous local wine names: Sichel, Mähler-Besse, Ginestet and Miailhe, for, it is said, hardly more than the cost of a year's upkeep. When the Société Civile de Château Palmer was originally formed, it was capitalized at 25,000 francs: 10,000 provided by Fernand Ginestet and 5,000 each by Frédéric Mähler-Besse and Sichel and Co., the remainder jointly by Louis and Edouard Miailhe. Almost immediately Ginestet sold part of his holding to Mähler-Besse and Sichel and in 1950 Louis Miailhe sold his shares to the same people. In order to provide the capital to finalize his purchase of Château Margaux, Ginestet sold the remainder of his shares to Mähler-Besse early in the 1950s and, in 1982, Monique Sichère, daughter of Edouard Miailhe and sister of May de Lencquesaing of Pichon-Longueville-Lalande and William-Alain of Siran, sold her shares to Mähler-Besse and Sichel in the proportion of their existing holding. Currently, therefore, the ownership of Château Palmer is divided between the Sichel family company, Société Sichel, which possesses 34 per cent of the equity, and a number of individual members of the Mähler-Besse family. (Frédéric Mälher-Besse and his wife Marguerite have seven children and twenty grandchildren.) One of Frédéric Mähler-Besse's daughters, Olga, married Jean Bouteillier who for many years was the *gérant*, or manager, of Palmer. When he died his son Bertrand, lately of Pichon-Longueville-Baron, took over the job and he is still the manager. Three flags, English, Dutch and French, representing the countries of origin of the three proprietors, fly from the château rooftops.

The troubles were, however, not completely over. During the war, like many Médoc properties, the château was taken over by the German army. Though the cellars were out of bounds to the troops, the building itself suffered considerable damage and the lack of maintenance affected the condition of the vineyard, though not as badly as many surrounding properties. Though the end of the war coincided with the start of a run of excellent vintages and some very fine wines were made, there was a great deal to do and it was not until 1958 that the property covered its costs and 1962 that it began making a profit. In 1957, the proprietors acquired the small neighbouring vineyard of Desmirail, also a third growth but one which had hardly been in production in recent years. Part of the vineyard was incorporated into the main property, and in 1981 the name and other sections of vineyard were sold to Lucien Lurton of Brane-Cantenac.

ALLAN SICHEL

In any mention of Château Palmer it is impossible not to mention in the same breath the name of Allan Sichel. If the excellence of the wine is due to the dedication of the *régisseurs*, the late Pierre Chardon and his two sons, Claude and Yves, and to the twenty men who work under them in the *chais* and the vineyard, the popularity of the wine, especially in Britain, owes most to the energetic and enthusiastic advocacy of the late Allan Sichel, head of the English side of the Sichel family. Sichel died in 1965 and was succeeded at Palmer by his son Peter in 1961, the date he (Peter) bought the nearby Cantenac property of Château d'Angludet, where he has lived ever since.

THE VINEYARD

The main body of the vineyard is directly to the south of that of Château Margaux and on a small plateau, the first of several that ripple away from the estuary of the River Gironde.

Here the soil is at its most refined, consisting almost entirely of rough gravel with little in the way of what would serve as nourishment to other crops. The vine has to delve deep but, in doing so, picks up minute traces of minerals which combine to give the wine its complexity of flavour and nuances of character.

There are some 45 hectares of productive vineyard out of a total domaine of 52 hectares, producing about 200 *tonneaux* (150,000 bottles) in a good year – though only 30 in 1961. As with many Margaux properties, the proportion of Merlot in the *cépage* is high, though not as high as some authorities would have us believe and in any case slowly diminishing as some of both Merlot and Petit Verdot as well much of the Cabernet Franc are replaced with Cabernet Sauvignon. The mix at present is roughly 50 per cent Cabernet Sauvignon, 7 per cent Cabernet Franc, 40 per cent Merlot and 3 per cent Petit Verdot. Cabernet Franc is no longer being planted.

Opinions differ in Bordeaux on the correct proportion of Petit Verdot. While traditionalists such as the late Ronald Barton insisted on the necessity of the Petit Verdot – a small grape susceptible to disease and late to ripen – others equally dedicated, such as Robert Dousson of Château de Pez (who separately bottled a cask from each of the four varieties in the 1970 vintage), have now rejected it. Palmer used to be one of the traditionalists for there was 10 per cent Petit Verdot a dozen years ago, but more recently the Petit Verdot has not been replaced. As Peter Sichel will tell you : 'In the poor years, when you need it, it doesn't produce ripe and concentrated grapes. In the years when it does, it is superfluous.'

Equally traditional is – or was up to the 1994 vintage, for in 1995 Palmer will inaugurate a new stainless-steel *cuverie* – the way the wine is made. The fermentation vats are of oak – two new ones were recently installed – and, uniquely, as late as 1983, the *égrappage*, or de-stalking of the grape bunches, was carried out by hand by pushing the grapes through a lattice-work table like a giant sieve. Today, there is a more usual *fouloir-égrappoir*. As with all top properties, the wine is matured using a high proportion of new oak casks.

The Palmer blend is made in two stages. In January or February after the wine has settled down following the malolactic fermentation, the vats are tasted and divided into three categories, A, B and C. Category A consists of those judged indisputably worthy of being blended and later bottled as the *grand vin*. The Cs are the rejects and will find their way into the second wine – Réserve du Général, the first vintage of which was the 1983. The Bs are left for further judgement. Meanwhile, the As are racked and blended together. If appropriate, some of the B vats will be upgraded and added subsequently.

It is instructive to taste these blends at an early stage. A few years ago, as an exercise, Peter Sichel presented many of his earlier visitors with two samples asking which they preferred. One was a blend of the A vats, the eventual *grand vin*, the other was a blend of the lot. Many of the guinea-pig tasters, including a number of Masters of Wine and others who should have known better, picked the second sample as their preference. Being a little lighter and more forward, it was easier to appreciate. They were then given a sample of C which, of course, they instantly rejected, only to be confounded when they learned that their original choice was the global blend, *sans élimination*, of the worst vats.

A salutary lesson, I am sure. And in case you are wondering, I cannot boast that I picked out the *grand vin*. The opportunity was never offered to me!

THE CHÂTEAU AND THE *CHAIS*

On the right-hand of the château an alley leads down to the first of the *chais*. Beyond lies the *cuverie* and the first-year *chai*. A new, second cellar, from whose raised entrance you can look down over the series of barrels through a window at the other end directly towards Château Margaux, was recently constructed by roofing over a gap between two other *chais*. A new reception, office and tasting room were built in 1994.

The château is a typical mid-nineteenth-century family mansion, neither very grand nor very extensive. There are only two main rooms, a dining room and a salon on the ground floor. But, as I have said, the building is normally unoccupied.

THE WINE

There is nothing coarse or robust about a Palmer. Though it may lack body in poor years and, indeed, never have the power of a good Pauillac, there is a finesse, a silkiness, alloyed with a soft fruit and violets perfume of unmistakeable and unforgettable delicacy.

It is no exaggeration to state that Palmer, since the war, has consistently produced wine to rank with the very best of the Médoc. Indeed, in 1961 and again in 1966, as I said at the outset, the wine is certainly of first growth quality. How then to describe it?

As with all the best Margaux, it is never overpowering, never very full in body, yet it is perfectly balanced; aristocratic and accessible while still young, it attains in maturity, a soft, generous, almost velvety character, a bouquet of elegant, rich, complex fruit and finish of delicate distinction. Would that there more wines like it!

THE TASTING

Most of the following wines were sampled in New York in March 1993, at a tasting hosted by Amaganesett Wines of Long Island. I have added other vintages tasted in March 1990, at a Jeroboam Club tasting in Bristol.

1990   *Optimum drinking*   **1998–2018**

Good colour. Round, fresh, elegant nose. There is lovely refined fruit here. Fullish, very ripe tannins. This has breed and manners. Subtle, stylish, concentrated fruit. Very complex. Lovely harmony. Fine quality.

1989   **1997–2007**

Good colour. Fat nose, but a little dry. The tannins show rather more than in the 1990. Medium-full. The tannins are a bit obtrusive on the attack. This is not nearly as balanced as the 1990. There is richness here. But which will win, the fruit or the structure?

1988   **1998–2012**

Medium-full colour. Corked nose. Slightly herbaceous. Nevertheless one can see rather an austere wine. The tannins a little firm. The wine lacking a bit of charm. Yet the grip is here, the finish long. Medium-full body. This will improve.

1986   **1996–2006**

Good colour. Very black and red currant on the nose. Slightly lean elements though. On the palate though the wine is medium-full and the tannins are a little astringent. It lacks the harmony and richness of the 1990. Very good but lacks a little dimension and concentration.

1985   **Now–2002**

Medium-full colour. Not as full as the 1986 but still youthful. Complex, delicate fruit on the nose. This has breed and distinction, without being a blockbuster. Medium-full body. Very harmonious, very Margaux. The finish is elusively intriguing. Very good indeed.

1983   **Now–2014**

Medium-full colour. Just about mature. Lovely nose. Real distinction and class and individuality here. Violets, truffles. Quite structured. Fullish, still has a bit of tannin. Good grip. This is vigorous, alive, still not quite ready for drinking. Lovely complex fruit and really long and subtle on the finish. Very fine.

1982   **Now–2012**

Medium-full colour. Just a bit more mature than the 1983. Less distinction on the nose. Fat and opulent but not as balanced or as complex. Full but ample. Rich and brambly-fruity, with a sweetness and a good acidity. Sweeter than the 1983. Fine finish. Rather better on the palate than the nose. Shows very well. Fine.

1981   **Now–1998**

Medium colour. Fully mature. Soft, mature and elegant on the nose. Though obviously not the depth of the 1983. This has a little lack of punch and thrust. It is medium body. Round and ripe. With a gentle velvety finish. But don't hold it too long. Very good.

1979   **Now–2000 plus**

Good colour. This has much more depth and weight – and class of fruit on the nose than the 1981. A real charmer. This is one of the best 1979s I have had for a long time. It has real concentration and dimension, as well as grip and lovely elegant Margaux fruit. Plenty of life still. Fine for the vintage.

1978   Now–2000
Good colour but more mature than the 1979. Nose more closed, slightly smoky, slightly *tabac*. Took a bit of time to come out of the glass but this bottle not as good as the 1979. Fullish, slight structure showing. Ripe but lacks a bit of zip, life and complexity. Badly stored? Judgement reserved. Twenty minutes later still a bit tight but the fruit classy, the wine longer on the palate than the 1979. Firmer, richer, better. More Cabernet than in the 1979. Fine.

1976   Drink soon
Good colour for the vintage. Medium-full if not entirely brown. Fullish, firm and vigorous for a 1976. This is not too dry. It even has good fruit, though not a great deal of dimension. Quite full, quite fat. There is a little astringency but the wine has good acidity for a 1976, and is neither too blowsy nor feeble. Better with food. Very good for the vintage. Holding up well.

1975   Now–1998
Good fullish colour. No undue brown. A little hard on the nose. But the tannins don't obtrude too much. Plenty of flesh and plenty of class. On the palate the wine is fullish, has reasonable acidity, but a bit more structure than real concentration and real depth – and therefore balance and complexity. Yet quite long. Very good for the vintage.

1973   Drink up
Light to medium colour; fully matured. Evolved, somewhat dilute nose. Yet reasonably fruity, fresh and stylish. This has now lightened up but the wine is stylishly balanced and enjoyable though the acidity is beginning to stick out. Good for the vintage. Now needs drinking.

1971   Drink soon
Medium-full colour. Mature, no sign of age though. A touch lean on the nose. This is undeniably complex and elegant. Just a touch astringent on the attack but much more vigorous on the finish. Medium to medium-full. Good acidity. Cool but classy, subtle and interesting fruit – the violets are here. Will still last, but this bottle came direct from the château. Other bottles, I fear, will be less vigorous.

1970   Now–2000 plus
Full, vigorous colour. Lovely voluptuous nose. Full, fat, deliciously ample and fruity. The palate vigorous, plump, alive and joyful. Full, balanced, long, fat, very very ripe. A wine of real generosity and charm. Fine.

1967   Drink soon
From the château. Medium colour fully mature. Soft and fragrant on the nose. Still alive and charming on the palate. Round, mellow, medium body. Very charming fruit. Soft, ripe. Still long. Fine for the vintage.

1966   Now–2000 plus
Released from the château too. Full, vigorous, barely mature colour. Marvellous intensity and depth and substance on nose and palate. Indeed the nose evolved and improved in the glass. A wine of real concentration and power of flavour. The tannins even are still obtrusive. Doesn't have the fat of the 1961 though. But first growth quality without a doubt.

1964   Drink soon
Medium colour now; mature. Quite fragrant but a little four-square on the nose. Medium to medium-full body. This is a lot better than its dismissive reputation would suggest. Slightly bitter but not too rigid, and no shortage of fruit or length. Just lacks a bit of charm and class. Still fresh.

1962   Now–1999
Medium-full colour. Still looks fresh. Round, aromatic, stylish nose. Sandalwoody spices, even a touch of caramel. Still plenty of vigour. Fullish, mature, ripe and complex. Still very vigorous. This is a lovely round, stylish wine. Very complete. Excellent for the vintage.

1961   Drink soon
Full colour. Very concentrated but now showing a bit of age at the rim. Getting towards the end this might be, but this is still disarmingly lovely. Creamily rich, super concentrated. Old-viney and with amazing complexity and class of fruit. A great wine. And a lovely bottle of it.

1959   Drink soon
Fullish colour. Vigorous still – more so than the 1961. Soft nose. A touch dry. Medium full, just a hint of dryness imminent now but fragrant, classy, balanced, long and lovely on the palate. No sign of the heat of the vintage. No astringency. Real length and elegance. But the 1966 is better. Fatter and more refined.

1958   Drink soon
Very good colour for a 1958. Not much less intense, or more aged than the 1959. Has lightened up a little on the nose. More importantly there is a touch of attenuation. Amazingly good for a 1958 and a bottle of this age. Still alive. Good fruit and balance if not exactly concentrated or classy. Quite full for the vintage. Still long and reasonably fresh.

1955   **Drink soon**

Fullish mature colour. Lovely nose, ripe old vine concentration. Delicious Margaux soft fruits. Very complex. A medium-bodied, ripe, very concentrated wine (for a 1955). Generous but now slightly fading, but has real depth and finesse. Very long and subtle. Delicious.

1953   **Drink up**

Medium-full colour. Still alive. The nose has lost most of its concentration and vigour, but though past its best, has a softness and a fragrance which still shows a vestige of its inherent class. Still sweet.

1952   **Drink soon**

Full mature colour. Very fine nose. Full and vigorous but not a bit dry or muscular, or astringent. Fatter and riper than the 1959. This is rather good. Indeed even better than the 1959. The fruit is richer and more ample. Lovely old vine concentration. Still fresh. Surprisingly fine. Excellent.

1951   **Drink soon**

This is one of the rare occasions that I have had a 1951 recently. The colour is by no means light and faded. Nor is the nose, though a little light. On the palate there is fruit and complexity, and no undue signs of age. Good grip. A curious aspect of flowery honey as well. I didn't expect it to be this good.

1950   **Drink soon**

Medium-full colour. Still alive. Crisp, elegant nose. Fresh, complex, still vigorous and fruity on the palate. There is no undue age astringency here. A fine wine for the vintage. Still has life. Classy. Medium to medium-full. None of the density of a Libournais 1950.

1949   **Drink soon**

Not shown: lovely old rose and violet fruit. Very distinguished. Can still be lovely but nearing the end.

1948   **Drink soon**

Full, mature colour. Slightly dense nose. Full and dense, less fruit and richness than the 1947. Full, a little astringent. Some tannin yet ripe and even (underneath) fat. Still vigorous. No undue astringency on the finish. Very fine. I prefer the 1952 which is more supple, yet the finish is long and delicious.

1947   **Drink soon**

Recorked at the château in 1981. Good vigorous fullish mature colour. Round, velvety, ripe, fragrant perfumed nose. A lot of complexity. Heaps of concentrated fruit. No undue age. Fullish but very soft and mellow. Very ripe fruit, excellent. And the fruit still fresh. Rich, complex finish. This is long and exotic.

1945   **Drink soon**

Not château bottled. Mähler-Besse label. Good vigorous colour. Full, somewhat chunky. Got a little dry as it evolved in the glass. But a fine, concentrated, rich, full, if somewhat four-square wine. This has real depth and old vine, low *rendement* intensity.

1945   **Drink soon**

(Château bottled) Similarly full colour to the 1947 but more vigour. Rather more vigour, by some way, on the nose. Fresh, ripe, concentrated, solid, meaty and rich. Earthy and truffle. On the nose much the best of the three late 1940s vintages. Full, very concentrated, very classy, unexpectedly magnificent. Ripe, quite succulent despite being a full-bodied masculine wine. The best, by far, since the 1961, although the 1952 is not far behind it and the 1959 is also close. The further you go back, the more old-fashioned and structured and dense the wine.

1940   **Past its best**

From the château. Medium colour. Not too old, it would seem. This, though a little lean, has now undue astringency. And it is certainly elegant. The fruit has lost a little of its sweetness. But there is enough there to give plenty of enjoyment. No undue age. Medium body.

1931   **Past its best**

Perhaps the first time I have had a 1931 claret. A reasonable colour. And by no means disagreeable on the nose at first. Yet a touch of H2S. And did not hold up in the glass. Cabbagey. As it evolved it became rapidly dirty, thin and cheap on the palate. Past whatever best it ever had.

1929   **Drink soon**

Medium colour. Fragrant and classy and complex and delicious on the nose. Beginning to lighten up. But a great deal of depth and attraction here. Makes up for the disappointment of the 1928. Exquisite. Really subtle. Great class on the palate. Soft and mellow and getting light now. But has not lost its vigour or its grip. Very excellent. Quite lovely. Multidimensional.

1928   **Past its best**

Low fill. Full colour still amazingly thick looking. A little maderized on the nose. Full, sweet, tannic, dense on the palate. High acidity so finishes clean. Definitely a wine for food. Old-fashioned acidity and structure and maderization shows but the fruit is intense. I have had better.

PRIEURÉ-LICHINE

Alexis Lichine, proprietor of Château Prieuré-Lichine, author of the *Encyclopaedia of Wines and Spirits* and *Guide to the Wines and Vineyards of France*, and ambassador for fine wine throughout the world, died in Bordeaux from cancer on 1 June 1989. He was 75.

Alexis was a friend, a man of great, occasionally overwhelming, character and personality, with a fund of interesting and often libellous anecdotes about the world of wine and its personalities. He made me welcome at the Prieuré. He also gave me much encouragement and support when I started up *The Vine* in 1984. In his memory I leave this text as I wrote it in 1987. I have added a postscript to bring things up to date.

Art Buchwald, the American humorist, has written in Alexis Lichine's visitors' book at Prieuré:

> 1959 was a great year for Bordeaux. It was a great year for me because I visited Bordeaux. I'll never look at a grape again without thinking of him [Lichine] and his chicken-loving dogs. The deal is for every chicken of the priest that your dogs kill, the priest gets a bottle of wine, for every dog one of his chickens kills, you get a high Mass.
>
> Cheers
> Art Buchwald
> October 5, 1959.

It must be emphasized that Le Prieuré is Lichine's and Lichine's alone. Now that other enterprises bearing the name Lichine, such as Alexis Lichine et Cie, the Bordeaux shippers, have nothing to do with him, this needs stressing. Le Prieuré is Lichine's home in France, and he tries to spend as much time there as possible, particularly, obviously, at vintage time, or if he is writing a book. It is one of the most charming of the smaller Médoc properties, a relaxed and refreshing place to stay, and the home of one of the best wines of the commune.

HISTORY

Even before the establishment of the Benedictine Priory in Cantenac – a branch of the Abbey at Vertheuil, further north in the Médoc – there was a church in the village. The current version, directly adjacent to Château Prieuré-Lichine, was built to replace an earlier version, burnt down during the Revolution.

What is now the front courtyard and kitchen garden of the Prieuré château was once the cemetery of this church. In the late 1970s, when renovating the kitchen, stone sarcophagi, dating from the fourteenth century, were unearthed. On this site, in the late Middle Ages, the Priory was established.

The Benedictines were at one time substantial vineyard owners in this area. Both Château Boyd-Cantenac and its neighbour Pouget were also in monastic hands. Like ecclesiastical establishments elsewhere grapes were planted, firstly to provide communion wine, later as a commercial enterprise.

The *chais* at Prieuré still contain part of its original structure. This is particularly noticeable in the roof, where the original beams, often a whole oak, date from the sixteenth century. The château itself, though with an eighteenth century face-lift, and extensively modernized within, also dates from this period. The rooms have been converted out of the monks' cells.

When wine was first made on a large scale to sell to the merchants in Bordeaux is not known. It was certainly no later than the turn of the seventeenth and eighteenth centuries, for, soon after, records show what was then called 'Le Prieur (*sic*) de Cantenac' as a third growth of Margaux and Cantenac, fetching 600 to 1,000 gold *livres* a *tonneau*, on a par with Malescot, Issan and the De Gasc vineyard which later was to become that of General Palmer.

As with most if not all French monastic institutions and properties, the Revolution spelt the end of this vineyard ownership, and the ecclesiastical estates in Cantenac were split up and sold. Pouget and Boyd-Cantenac emerged as separate estates, and other parcels were bought by General Palmer, then rapidly expanding his new estate. Le Prieuré was bought by a man called Durand. Judging by the normal vineyard yield of the time the vineyard must have been about 20 hectares: the production was 25 to 30 *tonneaux*.

From M. Durand the estate passed to a M. Pagès, in the hands of whose widow it was at the time of the 1855 Classification. From her it passed to a Mme Rosset, who was probably her daughter – the property is in their joint ownership in the 1868 Cocks and Féret, then producing 30 to 35 *tonneaux* – and from Mme Rosset to MM. Rulh and Rousseau. Not a great deal is known about these proprietors, nor of their successors, a M. Victor Saint-Ubéry who 'long ago devoted considerable attention to the estate and effected improvements' as the

1920 *Clarets and Sauternes* states, and his son-in-law, Frédéric Bousset, who was owner in 1925. Under Saint-Ubéry the wine was first known simply as Château Prieuré, later as Château Le Prieuré de Cantenac.

From this time on the vineyard seems to have gone into decline, like so many during the 1930s. By the time Alexis Lichine came on the scene in 1951, it was in a sorry state. The area had declined to eleven hectares, and the production to a mere 30 *tonneaux*.

Alexis Lichine had recently finished writing his *Wines of France*, and was about to realize a long-standing ambition to become a proprietor of a classed growth. Despite the dilapidated state of both château and vineyard, and the well-intentioned advice of such friends as the Duc de Montesquiou-Fézénac, owner of Château de Marsan in Armagnac, and Georges Delmas, *régisseur* of Haut-Brion, Lichine bought Cantenac-Prieuré, as it was known then, changed its name to Château Prieuré-Lichine, and promptly began to enlarge the vineyard and renovate both château and *chais*.

It was on the second attempt, however, that the sale went through. At the first try Lichine was unsuccessful, and it was only when the new owner, an old French lady, fell ill that Lichine could step in and snap it up. The price was a mere £8,000.

The place was in a sorry state. Bats roosted in the *chais*, the château was a dilapidated shell with more holes than roof, and the vines were in sad need of proper training, vigorous pruning and nutrient in the soil.

Lichine immediately set about to extend his territory. Emmanuel Cruse was seeking to round off his vineyard and so parcels outside the Issan *clos* were absorbed into the Prieuré *vignoble*. Other land was rented on an *en fermage* basis.

By careful cultivation of neighbouring château owners and local peasants, plots of land were bought or exchanged and the vineyard grew. In all there were over 50 transactions. Lichine's sale of Château Lascombes in 1971 enabled him to increase his holdings further. The vineyard area is now 58 hectares, and included parcels which once belonged to most of his classed-growth neighbours, Durfort, Brane-Cantenac, Palmer, Ferrière, Kirwan, Giscours and Boyd-Cantenac as well as Issan.

Lichine is still attempting to extend his domaine, and I travelled with him and his son Sacha this spring to inspect a parcel north of Lascombes, on the plateau on the opposite side of the road to the various Labégorce châteaux. Land is now at such a price that these transactions have come to a standstill, however. The local peasants see properties exchanging on the basis of a million francs per hectare and fondly think they should charge the same for a couple of rows of vines.

THE VINEYARD

Though Prieuré has vineyards in all the Margaux communes from Labarde to Soussans the bulk of the vineyard lies north of the village of Cantenac on a gravel plateau on either side of the local single-track railway. On the western side the vines march with those of Kirwan and Brane-Cantenac, on the east with those of Palmer and Issan. The land is about fifteen metres above sea level, almost pure gravel, particularly as it gets higher, away from the village of Cantenac itself, and lies on a base of larger '*graves*' and *alios* (hard sandstone).

Prieuré-Lichine is made up of 58 per cent Cabernet Sauvignon, 4 per cent Cabernet Franc, 34 per cent Merlot and 4 per cent Petit Verdot. The proportion of Merlot has recently been increased at the expense of the Cabernet Franc. Average production is 220 to 250 *tonneaux*.

Some of the vines are of considerable age. They were old when Lichine bought the property, and have only been replaced very gradually, when more than half of a plot has died. These parcels can be easily noticed. The vines are trained lower than is now fashionable, and are planted closer together. While the age of the vine has its merits, producing, even in a lesser quantity, wine of greater complexity, the new method of training has its advantages. By training higher, the circulation of the air through the vineyard is increased. Spring frosts are avoided, and maturity in the autumn accelerated.

THE *CHAIS*

The Prieuré *chais* are both up-to-date and carefully preserved. The old roofbeams have been retained, and the buildings modernized and enlarged in the style of the original construction. In 1974 a new reception chamber was completed, surfaced with small red-brown coloured tiles, and the old wooden fermentation casks replaced with stainless steel, though the bulk of the wine is fermented in concrete vats.

From this one passes through a rather touristy reception area, off which lead the first- and second-year cellars, the whole *chais* forming three sides of a square round a gravel courtyard. Behind, an extension was constructed in 1980, to further increase the area of cask storage. Both Prieuré-Lichine and Château Clairefont, Lichine's second property, and second label, are matured here. The bottled and cased wines used to be kept at Clairefont but are now stored in this new extension.

The courtyard, dominated by a huge magnolia tree, and facing the creeper-clad château itself, is approached through an arch leading directly off the main Médoc vineyard road. A parking place lies directly opposite for those tourists who answer the invitation to '*vente directe*'. There are those who consider it beneath a classed growth's dignity to offer direct to the public: Lichine is not one of them. The Prieuré is open 365 days of the year including Christmas, and you can buy all Lichine's books in a number of languages, as well as wine. The 'Pope of Wine', as he has been dubbed, may offend the conservative with his attitude to marketing, but he has done much to put Bordeaux on the tourist map. Along the side of the roadside walls, the courtyard is decorated with Lichine's extensive collection of glazed cast-iron firebacks, collected from all over Europe.

THE CHÂTEAU

The château, as I have indicated, is not pretentious. Very much a home rather than a muse-um, it is comfortable and friendly, and generously strewn with modern paintings acquired by Lichine from the artists who exhibited at the annual wine exhibition he used to hold at Lascombes. One eats in the old kitchen, a dim room decorated with copper pans facing an open fire, round a table which seems to have been there for centuries.

As I have said, Prieuré is Lichine's base in France. Thanks to the laws of France and the USA being less strict than those in Britain, he can travel from continent to continent with his dogs. At one time there were two magnificent collies. Now there is a black labrador. Sadly, from time to time a dog is knocked down on the main road. The current one, having thank-fully survived such a mishap, has learned her lesson, and warily stays within the garden. I also remember his shrew of a housekeeper: she cooked superbly.

While Lichine is away, the estate is managed by the *régisseur* M. Bourgeois, a man with an uncanny resemblance to Lenin. The wine, however, is in the hands of *maître de chai* Armand Labarère, and the vineyard is the responsibility of *chef de culture* Albert Birades.

Together they produce a wine which is firm and meaty for a Margaux, a wine which is a true Cantenac rather than Margaux itself. It is full and plummy and it lasts well.

During the 1970s Prieuré was under contract to Alexis Lichine et Cie, a subsidiary of Bass Charrington Vintners/Hedges and Butler. It was not until the 1979 vintage that the wine was placed on the open Bordeaux market. Since then I feel the quality has improved out of all recognition. From being run-of-the-mill, it has become one the leading lights of the com-mune. Today, when the *assemblage* takes place, Lichine invites friends such as Jean Delmas of Haut-Brion and Emile Peynaud, and all the possible constituent parts are tasted and assessed.

It is obvious that a much more rigorous selection takes place now than hitherto. And this is as it should be. In 1986, for example, 30 per cent of the produce was eliminated, and a similarly high amount of 1985. Some 60 per cent now goes into new wood. Today the quality of Prieuré-Lichine is beyond reproach, and yet prices are not at all greedy. For *rapport-qualité-prix*, Prieuré-Lichine is one of the best classed growths on the market.

POSTSCRIPT

A major extension of the Prieuré *chais* took place in 1990, further enlarging the barrel and case storage areas, and dramatically improving the facilities for welcoming the thousands of tourists who visit the château every year (some 36,000 of them, according to Sacha Lichine).

The vineyard continues to be expanded, and now encompasses 70 hectares. At the same time the Merlot element has been upped to 44 per cent and the whole production team has changed, as the older generation has given way to the new. Michel Rolland of Libourne has taken over from Emile Peynaud as consultant oenologist.

THE TASTING

I sampled the four most recent vintages of Château Prieuré-Lichine in April 1992. The remainder were sampled in the spring of 1987.

Optimum drinking

1991   1996–2000
Reasonable colour. Plump nose. Medium body. A touch of new oak. Ripe and succulent. Good grip. This has length and dimension. A positive wine, and a good success for the vintage.

1990   1996–2009
Medium-full colour. Plummy, fruity nose. Ample and balanced if not showing that much backbone. Ripe on the palate. Medium to medium-full body. Good acidity. Not a blockbuster but an elegant, plump, fruity wine with balance and interest. Good plus.

1989   1995–2004
Just a little less colour than the 1990. Soft nose. Medium-bodied. There is just a little astringency evident here, and not quite enough grip. This deadens the fruit aspects a bit. It is not unbalanced but it is a bit dull. The 1990 is better. Quite good plus.

1988   Now–2000
Medium-full colour. Round, ripe nose. The Merlot apparent. Medium body. A cheerful accessible wine but one which is essentially just a bit superficial. There is a lack of richness and concentration on the follow-through. Not short, just a little neutral. Quite good.

1986   1995–2005
Medium-full, not a blockbuster but quite firm nevertheless. Splendid almost fat fruit and plenty of depth. Certainly very good.

1985   Now–2000
Recently racked. Shows well despite this. Soft, quite oaky. Has charm and balance. Will be bottled in early June to preserve the fruit. A wine with a lot of attraction.

1984   **Drink soon**
Good colour. Fresh, supple, attractive fruit. Medium body, a little tannin. No leanness. If all 1984s were as good as this there would be nothing to worry about! Stylish if no great dimension but very good for the vintage.

1983   Now–2005
Slightly less colour than the 1982. Full, concentrated, chocolatey nose, a lot of depth. Ripe, round, very good complex fruit. Fullish. Not a blockbuster but has good grip and great attraction. Very seductive. Very classy.

1982   1995–2009
Slightly more colour than the 1983. Rich, fat, earthy. Alcohol and tannin dominate. Fullish. Still a little adolescent. Not as seductive as the 1983 today. Bigger and richer. Meatier, less advanced. Which is going to turn out better? Certainly good.

1981   Now–1998
Medium-full colour, some development. Getting soft and cedary on the nose. Soft, not a lot of weight or grip. Is this beginning to get a bit astringent? Not quite as good as I had expected. I've had better bottles.

1979   Now–2001
Good colour. Little development. Good, fresh, slightly minty nose. Medium body. Some tannin without being very full. Still a bit unformed. Plum-damson fruit. Good acidity. Quite long but

a bit one-dimensional. Best on the finish where there is a bit of warmth. Quite good.

1978   **Now–2002**

Good colour. A little solid and unforthcoming like a 1975. Medium-full, some tannin, quite sturdy. Riper and more substantial than the 1979 but a bit four-square. Quite good.

1976   **Drink soon**

Good colour for the vintage: just about mature but not unduly brown. Broad, slightly spicy nose. Very 1976 but not too blowsy. Some fruit, freshness and length but not a lot of style. Again a bit one-dimensional compared with the wines produced today. But a good example.

1975   **Now–2000**

Fullish colour. Some brown. Very typically 1975 on nose and palate. Fullish, four-square with an element of dryness and hardness about the tannins. Yet there is at least some roundness and richness. Not bad.

1974   **Drink up**

Medium, mature colour. Slight attenuation on the nose, with a touch of H2S. Yet still quite youthful. Reasonably fruity on the palate. No astringency. Rather one-dimensional and without a great deal of class, but better than I had expected.

1973   **Drink soon**

Slightly lighter in colour. Aromatic nose, no fade. Medium-full. Soft and ripe, almost sweet. Still fresh. A lovely drinkable wine, if of no great penetration. This has always been one of the better 1973s.

1971   **Drink up**

Full colour, less brown than I had expected. Elegant nose. Soft, fully mature. Yet complex, round and classy. Better than I remembered. I would give this 15 out of 20 but it needs drinking soon.

1970   **Now–1995**

More colour, indeed still quite immature. Fullish, chunky wine, plummy but dense. Rich but a bit clumsy. The correct ingredients are here but the wine is a bit too tough for its own good. Quite good though.

1967   **Drink soon**

Very good colour for the vintage. No undue maturity. Fully mature on the nose if not showing a little bit of age. Fullish, plump, round and ripe. Quite concentrated. A very good 1967, which has held up well.

1966   **Drink soon**

Very good colour, not a lot of brown. Still full and fresh, with a bit of spice and liquorice, rather than plums or cassis. Evolved well though. Medium-full, quite classy. Good concentrated fruit. Needs drinking reasonably soon. A good, stylish 1966.

1964   **Now–1996**

Medium-full colour. Fully mature. Fragrant, stylish, vigorous nose. On the palate this is fully mature, round and fruity. A ripe wine which is not short of finesse and which finishes long. A very good bottle.

1961   **Now–1998**

Full colour. Slightly dry and dense on the nose. A solid, somewhat four-square wine but quite rich. Certainly vigorous and quite concentrated, and it doesn't lack grip. A full-bodied, meaty wine which finishes sweet. Not a great 1961, but a very good one. It still has plenty of life.

1955   **Drink soon**

Quite full, slightly fading colour. Lovely fragrant, old-vine, concentrated nose. This is gently getting to the end of its life but still has plenty of fruit. A lot of elegance. Very good indeed.

1953   **Drink soon**

Excellent colour. Full, mature, no undue age. Aromatic nose, just beginning to lose a little of its grip. Quite full for a 1953 but not astringent. Round, fragrant and honeyed. Delicate subtle and old-rose-and-raspberry flavoured. Still vigorous at the end. Very good indeed.

MARQUIS-DE-TERME

Château Marquis-de-Terme is the last Margaux *cru* (as opposed to Labarde or Arsac) you will see if you look at a list of the properties classified in 1855. It stands at the bottom of the fourth growths. Until recently it was a wine little seen on the export market. This obscurity was not, as might be the case with Ferrière or Marquis-d'Alesme-Becker, because of its tiny size, for with 30 hectares the estate is substantial enough. It was because the sales activity was almost entirely devoted to domestic customers. Additionally, it must be said, the reputation was not of the highest. Doubts were cast about the high *rendement* – 150 *tonneaux* is the figure given in the 1969 edition of Cocks and Féret – and the character of the wine, hard, beefy and tannic, neither concentrated enough when young nor rich enough when mature, did not attract many friends.

Recently, as with so many properties in the Bordeaux area, improvements have been made. The *encépagement* and the *élevage* have been changed, a new *chai* has been constructed, and a higher proportion of new wood has been introduced. The net result is yet another estate which, if not a super-second, is certainly producing quality wine. Marquis-de-Terme is a property to watch.

The origins of Château Marquis-de-Terme begin with Pierre des Mesures de Rauzan who, as I have already described, created an estate alongside that of Château Margaux in the latter part of the seventeenth century.

History

On 16 December 1762, a Mlle Elizabeth de Ledoulx d'Emplet (described as a niece of Pierre Rauzan, but I feel sure more of a grand-niece) married a Gascon nobleman, the Seigneur François de Peguilhan de Larboust. This gentleman, through his mother's family, had inherited the title of Marquis de Thermes (*sic*). Part of the vast Rauzan estate was transferred to the Marquis as his wife's dowry. Other sources suggest that the domaine was the union of several smaller properties – Léoville-Cantenac, Cordet and Phénix. Perhaps these were the names of the particular parcels which changed hands.

Originally the reputation of the wine was high. In the third quarter of the eighteenth century it fetched prices not far short of 800 *livres* a *tonneau*, higher than that of Rauzan and more or less the same as the wine of Lascombes, then the second wine of the commune after Château Margaux itself. Thomas Jefferson, on his famous visit to the Bordeaux vineyards in 1787, describes Marquis-de-Terme as a third growth, but thereafter, on the death of the original Marquis, and with the difficulties which followed, imperceptibly, in successive unofficial classifications, Marquis-de-Terme slides from a good third growth, even at times a second growth, to bottom of the fourths.

The history of Marquis-de-Terme then becomes somewhat complicated, if not self-contradictory. In the original, 1824 edition of Franck's *Traité sur les Vins du Médoc, etc.*, the estate seems to be divided: Mme 'Determe' produces 18 to 20 *tonneaux*, and a M. Solberg at 'Marquis de Terme' produces 20 to 24 *tonneaux*. Sometime later both halves seem to be owned by a man called Mac-Daniel. Yet, later still, in the early 1840s, Sollberg (spellings vary between one and two 'l's) and this time with the Christian name Oscar, reappears as the proud possessor of a united Marquis-de-Terme, now producing 50 *tonneaux* – more as the century progresses – and confirmed officially in 1855 as a fourth growth. What is the explanation for all this ducking and weaving? Who is the mysterious Mac-Daniel?

The answer – and for this I am much indebted to Bill Blatch of Vintex SA, through whom Château Marquis-de-Terme is marketed, and who dug up a detailed and fascinating history of the estate written by Armand Feuillerat, a later proprietor – is as follows.

After passing through the hands of two intermediaries after the Marquis himself, the property was acquired by a Halvorous Sollberg, a Bordeaux *négociant*, for 32,000 francs in January, 1809. Sollberg was of Swedish origin, a Protestant recently arrived on the Chartronnais, but one who had quickly made a success of his wine business, not to mention having married a rich heiress from Calais. As well as Marquis-de-Terme he also bought a domaine called De L'Isle or Delille and one called Sibille, as well as several other small plots in the neighbourhood. This made a total of some 120,000 vines producing 35 *tonneaux* of wine. One of the new recruits to this now impressive estate was a young lad of eleven years from the Ariège, Thomas Feuillerat.

Fairly soon, however, Sollberg found himself with financial difficulties. Rather than face the debtor's tribunal he disappeared, probably to Argentina. The estate was liquidated and split up, and, in 1834, on discharging a sum of 72,700 francs owed to the courts, a M. Mac-Daniel became proprietor of Marquis-de-Terme. Mac-Daniel was another Bordeaux *négociant*, this time of Scottish or Irish descent, one assumes. He was also the lover of the abandoned Mme Sollberg, and there is more than a suggestion that his ownership was a sort of blind, keeping the property warm, so to speak, while the wife and son, Halvor Oscar Sollberg, worked to discharge the rest of Sollberg senior's debts. By 1845 this was complete, and the Sollbergs could return to Marquis-de-Terme, now a domaine of some 45 hectares.

Meanwhile Thomas Feuillerat, shortly to be married, had prospered. Now *régisseur*, he was building up a vineyard of his own. Over the next 35 years, as well as running Marquis de Terme, Feuillerat was creating Domaine de Gondats.

Oscar Sollberg – the family was soon to acquire Château Siran, still owned by their descendants, the Miailhes – was also a *négociant*, and under his ownership much was done in the vineyard and to the outbuildings in an attempt to re-establish the wine's former glory. This was only partly successful. The wine is mentioned neither in André Simon's *Vintagewise*, nor was it cellared by Professor Saintsbury. Admittedly Warner Allen states that the Marquis-de-Terme is 'justly famed for its fine quality' (*Wines of France*, 1924, repeated in *Natural Red Wines*, 1951), but he gives no concrete evidence for ever having met this fine quality himself. Neither does Maurice Healy (*Claret*, 1934), who rather curiously states that 'The modern Marquis-de-Termes [*sic*] is palpably a cockney'. Does this mean that the name reminds him of some East-End pub?

In 1886, the Sollbergs found themselves in financial difficulties for the second time, and Marquis-de-Terme once again was put up for sale. Jean Feuillerat, son of Thomas, *régisseur* in his place, and a man of some substance, would have loved to buy it, but he could not raise the capital. Instead, Marquis-de-Terme was acquired by Frédéric Eschenhauer, son of Louis, the original founder of the *négociant* business. Frédéric was a great friend and long-time admirer of Jean Feuillerat. In effect, he undertook to hold title to Marquis-de-Terme until such time as Feuillerat could build up the finances to acquire it in his own right. By 1898 Jean Feuillerat had achieved this and more besides – a *cru* called Marian, and another called Pontac-Lynch. In addition Armand Feuillerat, his son, was later to acquire Château Ferrière in 1913. This is still owned by his descendants, the Durand family.

In 1935, however, on Armand Feuillerat's death, and in difficult economic times, Marquis-de-Terme and other parts of the family holdings had to be sold. In this year the father of the current proprietors Pierre Sénéclauze, a wine-merchant from Marseilles, bought Marquis-de-Terme at auction. It is now jointly owned by Pierre's sons, Pierre-Louis, Philippe and Jean.

THE VINEYARD

Château Marquis-de-Terme occupies 35 hectares, a little more than the reunited vineyard of Oscar Sollberg's day, and the parcels lie mainly in Margaux and Cantenac. The biggest segment is on the Labégorce plateau hard by the château of Lascombes, another piece surrounds the château itself, and there are two further parcels between Prieuré and Issan. Formerly the vineyard was high in Cabernet Sauvignon and particularly high in its percentage of Petit Verdot. Both of these have recently been reduced somewhat in favour of the softer Merlot, and the *encépagement* stands at roughly 60 per cent Cabernet Sauvignon, 3 per cent Cabernet Franc, 30 per cent Merlot and 7 per cent Petit Verdot. Despite these changes, the average age of the vines remains high, with some parcels which are 70 years old and an overall age of 30.

THE CHÂTEAU AND THE *CHAIS*

Château Marquis-de-Terme and its dependencies lie on the southern outskirts of the village of Margaux, behind Durfort-Vivens and the Rauzans, and most of the buildings appear to date from the Sollberg area. The château itself is a modest two-storey house with a gabled roof in the normal Médoc gunmetal-coloured slate. This building has been recently restored, and the rooms on the ground floor are used as offices. It adjoins the *cuvier* and faces on to a small gravel courtyard opposite, while a series of low, rectangular, white-painted outbuildings continue towards the south-west. At first sight these would seem to be more than enough to store a couple of vintages worth of wine and more besides, but until recently the wine spent its first year in the *chai* at the other end of Margaux. In 1981, however, a new *chai de première année*, complete with a bottling and storage cellar – the whole thing insulated and thermostatically controlled to maintain an even temperature – was constructed in the château gardens. This spotless new *chai* is symptomatic of the new approach at Marquis-de-Terme.

THE WINE

The wine is vinified in a battery of concrete vats, white-tiled on the outside, and somewhat aseptic-looking. Formerly it was invariably given a long (20 to 30 day) maceration, after which it spent a year in these vats and then a further two years in cask before being bottled. The result, as much because of the soil, according to Alain Gouinaud, *maître de chai*, as because of the *encépagement* or the vinification methods, was something very tannic and burly, sometimes a little robust, and was usually hopelessly purple and inky until the wine was far too old and had begun to dry out.

Today the approach is more imaginative and more flexible. The grapes are harvested later and riper, and this, together with the reduction in the amount of the late-developing Petit Verdot means that the wine is less 'green', more plump and fruity. The maceration time has been reduced, and varies with the vintage, and the wine is transferred into wood, one-third to one-half of which is new, immediately after the *égalisage* and the creation of the château blend. Vats not used for the *grand vin* are set aside for blending with the produce of the vineyard called Gondats, a Bordeaux Supérieur plot of land on lower ground south east of the village near the *palus*.

Since 1978 the improvement in the quality of Château Marquis-de-Terme has been significant, and it is still progressing as the team on the spot, led by *régisseur* Jean-Pierre Hugon, develop their techniques and bring new investments into play. Interestingly, the average yield is now given as 110 *tonneaux*, two-thirds that of the quantity in the late 1960s.

With this rise in quality has come a more export-oriented approach to sales. The objective is now to sell 50 per cent of the crop abroad, and to sell more *en primeur*. This is being done by the appointment of exclusive agents in all the important export markets.

My acquaintance of Château Marquis-de-Terme's older vintages is not exactly extensive. My comments on vintages in the 1950s and 1960s frequently describe the wine as solid and four-square. One-dimensional at best; dense, inky and astringent at worst. Since 1978, and particularly since 1983, things have got better. Marquis-de-Terme is still, in Margaux terms, a full-bodied wine, but this is now the structure of depth, concentration and quality, not just the size of a wine too tough for its own good.

THE TASTING

The notes on the older wines come from an amalgamation of two comprehensive tastings I attended in 1986; the more recent vintages were sampled at the château in April 1992.

1991 — Optimum drinking **1995–1999**

Good colour. A little closed on the nose, and there doesn't seem to be very much fruit. But it is better on the palate. A bit astringent, and not much style, but some succulence and length. Not bad.

1990 — **1998–2012**

Medium-full colour. This is rich and blackcurranty on the nose. More backward than the 1989. Good depth and grip. Medium-full body. Meaty. Concentrated. Ripe and quite rich. Good balance and plenty of depth. An ample, long, satisfying wine. Very good plus.

1989 — **1997–2010**

Medium-full colour. Good nose. Soft and with quite pronounced oak, but ample and rich at the

same time. Lighter than the 1990 though, and less fat, yet ripe and very enjoyable. Balanced. Long. Good plus.

1988 — **1995–2003**

Good colour. The nose is restrained and more classic. Fruity and gently oaky and ample on the attack. It doesn't have a great deal of nuance or depth on the follow-through but is competently made and quite long. Quite fat and quite stylish. Quite good plus.

1986 — **1995–2005**

Fullish colour. A little denser and less focussed than the 1985 on the nose. Medium-full, quite good grip. Ample and plummy with a touch of new oak. Finishes well. Good.

1985 — **1995–2010**

Ripe, rich, meaty, solid. Good new oak background. On the firm side for the commune. Shows well. A good 1985.

1984   **Drink soon**
Good colour. Good new oaky nose, quite plump for a 1984. Slightly lean and a little short but has some fruit and enough structure. Certainly not weak. Finishes well. Good for the vintage.

1983   **1996–2010**
Very good colour. Firm, concentrated, earthy, liquorice, new oaky nose. Good fruit. Full, some tannin; a rich, solid, meaty with plenty of depth.

1982   **1996–2010**
Another very fine colour. Dense, unforthcoming nose, even possibly a bit hard. Big, full-bodied tannic wine. At first seems possibly a bit too dense and solid, but there is richness and concentration underneath. Lacks a bit of charm at present but finishes better than it starts, and should prove another good bottle from the mid-1990s onwards. The 1983 seems more stylish though, as is the case with many wines in the commune.

1981   **Now–2000**
Quite good colour, just a hint of development. Not much nose, closed but not dense. Medium body, a little tannin. Straightforwardly fresh and fruity. Again it finishes better than it starts. At present it seems to lack a bit of personality but it may acquire more character and charm as it softens. Not bad.

1980   **Drink up**
Light-medium colour but no undue brown. Soft nose, quite mellow in a Merlot sort of way. Ready for drinking. Quite fresh and fruity, if a bit one-dimensional, but finishes well with a bit of warmth. Not bad at all for the vintage.

1979   **Drink soon**
Medium colour, some maturity. Soft, round nose if a little dull. Medium body, a little tannin. Quite advanced for a 1979. Not a lot of structure. Soft, plump. Quite pretty and quite elegant. Like the 1981 it finishes better than it starts but essentially both a bit short.

1978   **Now–1997**
Fuller colour. Still immature. Chunky nose but quite rich in a blackberry-cassis way. Medium-full body. Solid, tannic. Rather more old-fashioned wine-making, making the character similar to that of a 1975. On the one hand the wine is ripe but on the other there is not enough freshness and zip, though there is something a little raw and inky about it. Yet again it finished better than it started. Not bad.

1976   **Drink soon**
Quite good colour for the vintage – medium-full, no undue brown. Pleasant nose, round,

mellow, ripe, quite rich. Neither too blowsy nor too spicy. Medium body, ready for drinking. Good fruit and reasonable length. Pleasant if no great elegance. Good for the vintage.

1975   **Now–1997**
Fullish, some development. Quite dense on the nose. Some of the toughness of the vintage but not as much as one might expect with this château. Has fruit, medium-full, some tannin but supple and ripe at the end. Good.

1973   **Drink up**
Good colour for the vintage and not too brown. Not a lot of elegance but reasonable substance, fruit and acidity. Still has life. Not bad at all.

1971   **Drink soon**
Good colour for the vintage. Quite full, just about mature. High-toned nose, no oak, has fruit if no great richness, and is still fresh. Quite full, firm for a 1971. Solid, four-square wine. A bit dense but more agreeable, and less evolved than expected. Not bad.

1970   **Drink soon**
Fullish colour. Ripe, full, a bit solid but it has enough fruit underneath. A bit dense. Needs two to three years. Fullish, some tannins, becoming astringent. Not bad.

1966   **Drink soon**
Full, mature colour. Solid, tannic, earthy wine. Now full mature but not yet soft. Rather dense and four-square.

1962   **Now–1994**
Well matured colour. Similar on the palate, at the end of its active life but not dense or solid like the above. The warmth of the vintage if without much elegance. Quite pleasant. I prefer it to the 1966.

1961   **Drink soon**
Medium-full body, mature. Mellow nose, quite some age, rather more than I would have expected for this property and in this vintage. Medium body, as with all 1961s there is a richness and a complexity, an almost porty sort of fruit. In 1961 terms not special, and needs drinking soon, but has depth if not a great deal of class.

1959   **Drink up**
Full, solid but not too tough. Generous and ripe. Now a little old and therefore slightly astringent.

1955   **Past its best**
Medium weight, was a generous fruit wine once but now a little over the hill.

1937   **Past its best**
Reasonable colour. Very tough. Still has fruit but very astringent on the finish.

D'ANGLUDET

In the bottom south-western corner of Margaux, at a point where the communes of Cantenac, Arsac and Labarde inter-connect, there is a large gravel plateau called Le Grand Poujeau. The vines thereon are shared by three important domaines. One is Giscours; the second is Du Tertre. The third belongs to Peter Sichel, Bordeaux merchant, co-owner of Château Palmer, and wise and warm friend to many an Englishman who has travelled to Bordeaux to learn a little about its wines. Peter has owned Château d'Angludet since 1961, and he has lived there with his wife Diana and six children since 1962. Angludet is not a pretentious place. Indeed it is a farmhouse, though an attractive one, rather than a château in the normal Bordeaux sense of the word. On the one side are fields and pasture, and a duck pond – I suppose, given that they now have swans, I ought to dignify this and call it an 'ornamental piece of water' – fringed by trees. Behind the house and the buildings where the wine is made, the land inclines and the *croupe* begins. Here are the vines which make one of the most popular of Margaux's non-classified growths. Angludet, though regarded in the eighteenth century as a fourth growth, never made it into the official 1855 list and had to be content with a consolation prize as one of six *crus bourgeois exceptionnels* when the lesser properties were first classified in 1932. Today it would be a *troisième*, at the very least. But 30 years ago it was derelict.

The property is ancient. There was a *maison noble*, a manor house, on the site in the thirteenth century, and the *seigneur* in 1319 was the Chevalier Bernard d'Angludet. Later it belonged to the family Donisan, who sold it in 1350 to a man called Rampnol de Corn. A century later the proprietor was Jehan de Treulon, through whose daughter it passed as dowry to a Pierre de Makanan, described as an 'English gentleman' but possibly, if you anglicize the name to Macannan, Scottish rather than English. Raymond de Makanan was the *seigneur* in 1509 and his son Geoffrey in 1560.

HISTORY

According to James Seely in *Great Bordeaux Wines*, the property was confiscated from the Makanans in 1631 during the fierce religious wars of the period and bought by a M. Pommiers. Edouard Guillon, a nineteenth-century historian, gives the new owner as Marc de Jousset, described as an *écuyer* (an *écuyer* was a trainee *chevalier*, so to speak). Be that as it may, Angludet soon passed into the hands of Pierre du Mons, a man of Flanders as his name might suggest. Mons was a rich man. He was to buy his way into the Bordeaux parliament, and it is he who gave his name to La Tour-de-Mons in Soussans, the commune which adjoins Margaux to the north. Coincidentally, the proprietor of what was then known as La Tour Noble de Soussans in 1563 was a Louis de Makanan, surely a kinsman of those at Angludet, though in the intervening period La Tour had passed into the hands of a third and separate family, that of Thomas de Lannefronque.

Detailed evidence to support the family history during the next 100 years is sketchy. La Tour-de-Mons passed as part of a marriage settlement to Jean-Baptiste de Secondat, son of Montesquieu, in 1740, but he does not appear to have been *seigneur* of Angludet as well. William Franck mentions some Demoiselles Dengludet (*sic*) as proprietors of a fourth growth in the area when he offers a list of the senior properties and their prices in the middle of the eighteenth century. But the wine does not appear on the list Professor Pijassou has culled from the archives of Tastet and Lawton which covers the prices they paid at this period. On the Belleyme map (1785) one can discern both 'Angludet' and a site called 'Mlle d'Angludet'. As one can see from the map there were certainly vines on the estate by this time as there must have been 30 years previously. Margaux and its surrounding communes were the first areas to be extensively planted in the Médoc.

The next documented fact is the purchase of the domaine by one Pierre Legras in 1776. Legras certainly developed the existing vineyard, creating an extensive property which produced 100 *tonneaux* of wine, a considerable figure for the period. He had four sons, and on his death in 1791 the property was divided between them. It was further divided in the next generation, but not all the heirs were interested in wine. Nevertheless, they all continued to live on the estate, forming a sort of commune – and here I use the word in its unparochial sense – known locally as La République. Production dwindled, declining to 35 *tonneaux*, and the twin effects of neglect and oidium, which hit the Médoc in 1852, resulted in the wine missing out in the 1855 Classification, despite being included in an unofficial list by Abraham Lawton – admittedly right at the very end, as his single 4 7/8 *cru* – in 1815.

Anarchy prevailed at Angludet. In 1867 the resident proprietors included Henri Legras, M. Danglade, M. Bignon, and Mmes Mouchon and Lalanne, both widows. Shortly afterwards it was formally split. Two-fifths, including eleven hectares of vines, seem to have been acquired by Paul Promis, grandson of an erstwhile proprietor of Château Giscours, who sold his wine as Domaine d'Angludet; three-fifths passed into the hands of Jules Jadouin, owner of Château Monbrun and heir to Château Vincent, both originally part of the Palmer domaine. Promis doubled the area under vines in his part and made numerous improvements to his property, only to be seduced into passing over his share to Jadouin in 1891, perhaps as consequence of the phylloxera epidemic. Some 100 years after the death of Legras, Angludet was again in single hands. By the end of the century, despite phylloxera, there were 55 hectares of vines in a domaine which totalled 130 hectares, planted with Cabernet Sauvignon, Cabernet Franc 'and especially Carmenère' (a variety which has since disappeared in Bordeaux, though still officially recommended by the authorities). Some of these Carmenère vines were 100 years old. The property made 150 *tonneaux*. Jadouin was now additionally the owner of Château Martinens. One curious fact is that the château depicted in the Cocks and Féret of this period corresponds neither with that in the 1883 edition nor with the photo in the edition of 1922. No doubt there were a number of dwellings on the site, all dating from the time of La République.

Jadouin's daughter married the merchant Jules Lebègue, and in the next generation Angludet passed to Maurice Addé, Lebègue's son-in-law. Shortly before the Second World War Addé sold Angludet to Paul Six, a Biarritz industrialist. Six was more interested in the dairy produce of the estate than its wine. The old vines were not replaced and the vineyard declined. When Six's widow sold the property in 1953 to Mme Rolland of Château Coutet – the latter bought it for her son by her first marriage, M. Thomas – Angludet had virtually ceased to exist as a wine-producing domaine. Thomas replanted a few hectares but the majority of these young vines were wiped out by the terrible frost of February, 1956. It was the nadir of the fortunes of Château d'Angludet.

PETER SICHEL

Enter the saviour. It was 1961. Peter Sichel had just become engaged to Diana, and they had decided that they wanted to live in Bordeaux (Peter's father Allan had always lived in England). So he was looking for a house. He heard that Angludet was for sale, though he was not sure exactly where it was, and after lunch at Château Palmer one rainy day he and Diana walked across the vineyards to inspect. What they saw was dereliction: a rather dilapidated though habitable farmhouse, but an abandoned vineyard; yet a potentially attractive site, well away from any main road, silent and peaceful. A good place to rear a family.

The formalities were soon arranged, and within the year they had moved in. At the same time M. Thomas has sold off part of the estate separately to Lucien Lurton of Château Brane-Cantenac. This was a piece of a vineyard called Notton, now used by Lurton as one of the names for the second wine of Brane-Cantenac. So what Peter Sichel acquired was an estate of a total size of 80 hectares.

The vineyard Peter inherited stretched to barely seven hectares of vines. Most of this was the rather badly planted residue of the vines Thomas had installed in 1954/1955. A couple of hectares were of really old vines, dating from the end of the nineteenth century. Peter's first harvest, the short but glorious 1961 vintage, amounted to eleven barrels – 275 cases.

Slowly but surely the vineyard has been extended to its present 34 hectares, planted in the ratio 60 per cent Cabernet Sauvignon, 30 per cent Merlot, 3 per cent Cabernet Franc and 7 per cent Petit Verdot. The Cabernet Franc is gradually being replaced with Cabernet Sauvignon. About 130 *tonneaux* (13,000 cases) is the average harvest. A second wine is bottled as Le Ferme d'Angludet. The wine is vinified in plastic-lined concrete vats, installed progressively as the quantity of the harvest has increased, and matured using one-third new oak.

THE CHÂTEAU

As I have said, Angludet is a comfortable home, not a pretentious Victorian edifice. Above the entrance used to be, until recently removed, the words '*Ancien 4e Grand Cru*', although there is no indication of the date this memorial was carved. The château dates from 1767. In the drawing room, copied from an original by the Austrian painter Reidinger, are wall-canvases depicting the Spanish Riding School in Vienna in the eighteenth century. Elsewhere there are dogs, tennis rackets, gumboots, books and the generally friendly untidiness that you would expect in a house with six children and, so far, six grandchildren.

THE WINE

Compared with the majority of the wines of Margaux and its surrounding communes, Angludet is normally one of the fuller wines. There is an aspect of *arrières côtes* which I also find in the wines of Du Tertre and Chasse-Spleen. Partly this is due to its position, on the second *croupe* of gravel away from the estuary of the river Gironde; partly it is a result of a highish percentage of Cabernet and Petit Verdot in the *encépagement*. By this *arrières côtes* as pect I mean a certain sturdiness, an earthy solidity, which, while it gives the wine weight and backbone, also means that it needs a good decade to mature. Yet underneath there is depth, balance and richness. A wine like the 1983 is fine by any standards. It will still be drinking well twenty or more years after the grapes were first harvested. Since 1976 (1975 is a bit of a puzzle) the property has not put a foot wrong, and the style has become more and more refined. It is one of the most reliable of all the Margaux wines and usually excellent value for money. It is not only because they want to get their hands on some of Peter Sichel's Palmer that merchants flock like flies to Angludet every season!

THE TASTING

In 1989 I was delighted to receive an invitation to taste just about every wine Peter Sichel has produced since his arrival at Angludet. Bookseller Clive Sharples of Coningsby, Lincolnshire, had amassed a remarkable collection of eighteen vintages. It gave us all a splendid opportunity to put Angludet in context and to watch the evolution of its wines over the last 25 years. Here are my notes. The four most recent vintages were sampled in 1992.

Optimum drinking

1991   1996–2000
Good colour. A little tough on the nose, as Angludet often is in its youth. On the palate light to medium body; not a lot of tannin but ripe and with good acidity and definition, even style. Well made.

1990   1995–2002
Medium-full colour. Rich and ample on the nose, but perhaps not quite fresh and austere enough. This is on the light side for Angludet. It has elegant fruit and reasonable balance and complexity. There is plenty of charm here, but not quite enough structure and concentration. Quite good.

1989   1996–2006
Medium-full colour. A more masculine nose than the 1990. More tannin, more structure. But with a better grip as well. Medium-full, rich, good oaky base. Good fruit and acidity as well. Long, positive. Good plus.

1988   1995–2002
Good colour. This seems to show more new oak than the 1989. Stylish, good blackcurrant fruit. Medium body, ripe, not a great deal of tannin. But positive and charming with a good fresh finish. Not a great deal of power and complexity though. Quite good plus.

1986   1995–2005
Medium-full colour with rather more to it than the 1985. Good structure on the nose, ripe tannins and some new oak. Quite full, rich, meaty and fat. Good ripe fruit. Some tannin. Finishes well. Good.

1985   **Now–1999**
Medium colour. A lovely complex aromatic nose, but a feminine wine, quite soft. It lacks the usual density of Angludet. Medium body. Not a lot of tannin. A ripe, raspberry-flavoured, quite soft wine. A balanced wine but one which has come forward. Subtle finish.

1984   **Drink soon**
Good colour for the vintage. Now just about mature. Good nose too. Lacks a little fat and warmth but certainly has fruit. Medium body. A little one-dimensional. But neither mean nor too lean.

1983   **Now–2005**
Fine colour. Clearly richer and deeper – and less advanced – than the 1982. Still youthful and tannic, but plenty of depth on the nose. Fullish, tannic, concentrated wine. Still a bit raw and adolescent. Good depth and fine balance underneath. Very good indeed.

1982   **Now–2001**
Good colour, now showing some development. Soft and aromatic on the nose. Cigar-boxy. Quite developed compared with the 1983. Medium body. Some tannin. Spicy and slightly roasted. Aromatic. Good finish. But the 1983 has more depth and quality and rather more of a classic flavour. Good.

1981   **Now–1999**
Medium colour. Now just about mature. Good mature Margaux-flavoured claret. New oak evident on the nose. Quite structured for a 1981. Very stylish. Just about ready and with the slight earthiness and *arrières côtes* element of Angludet. Good fruit. Good balance. Very good for the vintage. Good future.

1980   **Drink soon**
Medium colour; mature but not unduly aged. Slight spice on the nose but a lack of definition as one might expect in this vintage. Yet better than

this would suggest on the palate. Good acidity keeping it fresh and preserving the fruit. Medium body. Very good for the vintage.

1979   Now–1995

Medium-full colour; just about mature. Less finesse than the 1981 on the nose. A rather dumb, sturdy wine which has now softened but doesn't have the fragrance of the 1981. Medium to medium-full body. A little lack of character but not bad. Quite fresh. A bit dull. Perhaps this was a badly stored bottle. My memory of it is of something better.

1978   Now–1998

A little more colour. Richer and more glowing. Just about mature. Similarly solid but more richness and more structure. There is depth here. Quite full. A rich sturdy wine with good depth and a fatness to the fruit. Quite elegant. Good finish. Good future.

1977   Drink up

Fresh colour for the age. Rather less brown than the 1976. Light nose. Some fruit. A bit dilute but without the old tea element in some 1977s. This began to develop after a while in the glass. A certain leanness and astringency. A good effort for the vintage but essentially rather uninspiring.

1976   Drink soon

Decidedly brown at the edge. Fat, caramelly, spicy and aromatic. Not dry. This is a lot better than most 1976s. Elements of chocolate blancmange. Fresh with a touch of spice. Medium body but short, but it will still keep. Lacks class as always with this vintage.

1975   Drink up

My notes suggest there is something faulty about the 1975: excessive volatile acidity in some of the samples. Not tasted.

1974   Drink up

Lightish colour, but not too brown. Soft nose, a bit dilute but neither mean nor unduly old. Medium body, a touch of astringency and a certain suspicious sweetness. Rather better and fresher than I had expected. Good effort.

1971   Drink up

Mature colour. Getting a little cool and lean on the nose but not drying up. Medium body. An elegant but rather austere and ungenerous wine. Lacks a bit of flesh. Acidity shows on the finish. Quite good.

1970   Now–1996

Medium-full mature colour. Fat, ripe, succulent nose. Fruity and meaty. Roast chestnutty. Depth here. Quite full, quite sturdy. Good richness and concentration but definitely a *bourgeois* wine. Lacks a little class. Good though. Will still last.

1969   Drink up

Medium colour, mature, beginning to lighten up on the rim. Similar on the nose. Light, faded, lacks zip and definition as well as class. Similar on the palate. Weak and unstylish. Now beginning to dry out and lighten up. Undistinguished.

1968

No Angludet produced.

1967   Drink soon

Good mature colour. More vigour than the 1971 for instance. Fragrant and fruity on the nose but some age now, it seems. This was stylish and not at all bad once. Fruity and balanced. Now shows a bit of age.

1966   Now–1996

Fine colour, barely mature, still vigorous. Lovely nose – concentrated old-vine flavour, almost with a lactic element. This is still very fresh. Fullish, very ample, rich fruit. Complex. Essentially sturdy and I would have said if I had seen this wine blind, a good vigorous example of the 1950s rather the 1960s. Fine. Will still last well.

1965

No Angludet produced.

1964   Drink soon

Good colour. Less glowing than the 1966 though. Rather sturdier than the 1966 on the nose but good old-vine fruit again. Ripe, even sweet. Quite full but not too four-square. Shows well. Good rich fruit here and no lack of class.

LABÉGORCE-
ZÉDÉ

If one were to compose a list of candidates for promotion into a revised classification of the top red wines of Bordeaux – whether this would be a separate Médoc hierarchy based on that of 1855 or a more comprehensive survey of all the wines of the Gironde – several of the best *crus bourgeois* of the Haut-Médoc would immediately spring to mind. Chasse-Spleen, Haut-Marbuzet, Angludet, Poujeaux, Monbrison, Gloria and Sociando-Mallet would all be sure-fire candidates. So too would Château Labégorce-Zédé in Soussans. Since 1979 the property has been owned by the Belgian Thienpont family, elsewhere involved in Vieux Château Certan and Le Pin in Pomerol and Château Puygueraud in the up-and-coming area of the Côtes des Francs.

Labégorce-Zédé is one of three properties – the others are Château Labégorce and the currently defunct Château L'Abbé-Gorsse-de-Gorsse – which have their origins in a single estate which once straddled the border between the communes of Margaux and Soussans, or so we have been led to assume. According to early editions of Cocks and Féret, there are documents dating from 1332 which attest to a *maison noble de La Bégorce*. In 1611 the *seigneur* was Louis Gordon de Genouillac, Baron de Bessan; in 1641 Gaillard Millon; in 1683 de Beaucorps and in 1728 the Chevalier de Mons, additionally involved variously with Angludet and, of course, Château La Tour-de-Mons. Cocks and Féret also mention an owner in 1793 called Weltener. Now it should be remembered that though the order in which the wines appear is determined by the editors, the little blurbs in Cocks and Féret are in fact written by the owners, and many, I have noticed, have in the past not been above 'inventing' a little history, or just simply misremembering details and dates. What the above account fails to acknowledge is the Gorsse, or Gorce, family itself.

HISTORY

The origins of the Gorsse family were *bourgeois*. They were merchants in Bordeaux. An antecedent, Pierre, became a court prosecutor in the seventeenth century, and this seems to have been the start of a rise in the Gorsses' social standing. They bought themselves into the Bordeaux Parliament, adopted the aristocratic prefix '*de*' and, like their peers, set about purchasing a country estate in the Médoc. It seems a curious coincidence that what they found in Soussans should have so conveniently already been called La Bégorce. I would like to see this fourteenth-century deed! Was the domaine named after them? It is improbable that they should take their name from a *lieu-dit* of what was only a minor part of their landholdings. Their major property was in Cantenac.

The Cantenac property was that of Guilhem Hosten. It later passed into the hands of Baron Hector de Brane. It is now Brane-Cantenac. In 1735 or thereabouts the Cantenac domaine was acquired. It must have been later that the Gorsses bought land in Soussans. And it is probable that the land they acquired belonged to the neighbouring estate of La Tour-de-Mons. The De Mons family had arrived in Bordeaux from Belgium and bought what was originally called La Tour-de-Marsac in 1623. Like the Gorsses they bought their way into the *noblesse de la robe*, the parliamentary aristocracy, and they soon established a considerable estate in Soussans. In 1740 the heiress to the domaine, Marie-Catherine de Mons, married Jean-Baptiste de Secondat, son of Montesquieu. As a result he became the *seigneur* not only of De Mons but of Bessan, Marsac and Labégorce. We do not, however, have any details of any sale of land to the Gorsse family.

Francis de Gorsse died in 1766, and it is from letters written to the trustees of the estate by a *Sieur* Estèbe, grandfather and tutor to the infant heiress Marie-France de Gorsse, that the first documentary evidence of wine on the Soussans estate exists. At Soussans the family kept a herd of cattle and owned a granary where they stored wheat. They also had a vineyard of some eleven or twelve hectares but the wine did not achieve the same high prices as that at Cantenac. What was to become Brane was already a second growth.

The next thing we know about the Labégorce which was to become Zédé is that it was sequestrated by the State at the time of the Revolution and sold as a *bien national*. Had it passed back into the hands of Secondat? Or had this parcel never been part of the land owned by the Gorsse family? There is no record of the Gorsses at Cantenac falling foul of the new authorities. But at La Tour-de-Mons, Secondat's son Charles having emigrated, we do know that part of the estate was seized.

On *25 Thermidor l'An III* (12 August 1795, in the non-revolutionary calendar) Barthélémy Benoist acquired the 'Domaine de La Bégorce', otherwise known as Petit Barbot, for 425,000 *livres*, to be paid for in instalments. Benoist had two daughters. The first married Jean-Emile Zédé, a merchant from Paris; the second Michel Boué, a local broker. In 1840, at a time of economic crisis in the Gironde and on the death of Mme Benoist, the property was valued by the tribunal and awarded to Pierre Zédé, son of Jean-Emile. Of a total of 28 hectares some fifteen were under vines.

Meanwhile the two other Labégorce estates had emerged, and these certainly seem to have had their origins with the Gorsse family. A man named Capelle owned a property called Marcadie in 1824 and he seems to have acquired part of the Gorsse land in subsequent years. This is what is now called simply Château Labégorce. What became Château L'Abbé-Gorsse-de-Gorsse was a rump of twenty hectares which remained in the family until the 1890s when it was acquired by a Monsieur Pérès. Back at what was now Château Labégorce-Zédé we come to the children of Pierre Amédée Zédé and his wife, Esther Henriette Chevassus, in particular to the three sons. They must have been a remarkable trio. The eldest, Emile Hippolyte, became an admiral and a Grand Officier of the Légion d'Honneur. Charles Jules went into the army and rose to the rank of General. He was a Commander of the Légion d'Honneur.

Gustave Alexandre, the youngest, was a brilliant engineer. He was born in 1825 in Paris and at the age of 48 was appointed Director of Naval Construction. Eleven years later, less than 40 years after the first propeller-driven naval vessel was launched, Zédé presented the world with a new method of submarine propulsion, the greatest revolution in marine circles since the invention of the internal combustion engine. Sadly, in 1891 he fell victim of his researches into torpedoes when a experiment went disastrously wrong in his laboratory. But his name lived on. The first non-experimental naval submarine, a vessel of 266 tons, was launched in 1893, armed with a torpedo. It bore his name.

Following Gustave's death, Admiral Emile bought out the rest of the family interest in Labégorce-Zédé. His children remained owners of the property until 1931, when they sold the estate to Pierre Hubert Eyrin, the *régisseur*. The deed of sale notes that the size of the vineyard was 28 hectares. The price was 212,000 francs.

During the next 30 years Labégorce-Zédé changed hands no fewer than five times. The vineyard contracted and the reputation of the wine declined. It was a difficult time. Salvation came with the arrival in 1961 of Jean Battesti. Battesti, a builders' merchant in Constantine, Algeria, decided not only to move to France when colonial rule came to an end but to embark on a new career. From his arrival the fortunes of Labégorce improved. He doubled the size of the vineyard and renovated the cellar. For the first time for over a 100 years the property had a resident proprietor.

LUC THIENPONT

In 1979 Battesti decided to retire. He was 85. As neither his children nor his grandchildren were interested in carrying on, Labégorce-Zédé was again put up for sale. The new proprietors were a branch of the Belgian Thienpont wine-merchant family: Luc Thienpont and his four brothers and sisters. The price was 6 million francs. Newly married, Luc and his wife Annick, herself also the daughter of a *négociant*, moved in in June 1979.

THE VINEYARD

Since his arrival Luc Thienpont has planted a further nine hectares to supplement those added by Battesti. Out of a total estate of 42 hectares, 27 are therefore now under vines. And these lie both in Soussans and in Margaux. A third of these date from the 1950s and earlier, a third from the early 1960s and a third are still young vines. Fifty per cent of the vineyard is Cabernet Sauvignon, 35 per cent Merlot, 10 per cent Cabernet Franc and 5 per cent Petit Verdot.

THE CHÂTEAU AND THE *CHAIS*

Labégorce-Zédé is the nearest to the Gironde estuary of the three Labégorce châteaux. In contrast to the sober elegance of Château Labégorce, constructed in the 1830s in the Directoire style, Zédé has the appearance of a Swiss or Bavarian chalet. There are two storeys and an overhanging roof. In front is a little garden. Behind are the *chais*. The wine is made in a battery of 23 unlined cement *cuves* and ages in barrels of which 35 to 40 per cent are new.

THE WINE

In the last decade, carefully nurtured by Luc Thienpont, the quality and reputation of Château Labégorce-Zédé have risen enormously This improvement has been the result of a multitude of little adjustments which add up to something of significance. One interesting feature is that all the collected fruit is picked over by a team of cellar workers as it travels up to the *fouloir-égrappoir*. Another is that it is not filtered. A third detail is that the *rendement* is regularly substantially inferior to that of its neighbours as a result of crop-thinning in July. This is a rising estate which has kept its prices reasonable. Labégorce-Zédé is a wine to buy.

THE TASTING

Thienpont sent a decade of his wines to *Decanter*, who passed them on to me, and I sampled them in September 1989. The four most recent vintages were tasted in Bordeaux in April 1992.

Optimum drinking

1991   1996–2000

Good colour. Ripe nose. Soft, supple and stylish. Good substance. On the palate this is gently oaky, and has balance and depth. A wine with a positive follow-through and finish. Good plus.

1990   1998–2010

Medium to medium-full colour. This is a little closed, but it's balanced and the fruit is ripe and stylish: violets and cherries and raspberries. This is very concentrated and stylish, without being a blockbuster. Gently oaky, ample, succulent, richly ripe. Long. Very seductive. Very good.

1989   1997–2007

Medium to medium-full colour. Ripe nose, slightly *rôti*, ample, not unduly tannic. On the palate medium body. A little bit of astringency, not as long or as fresh as the 1990. Yet good nevertheless. There is a good warm, plump follow-through. But the 1990 has more elegance and definition. Good.

1988   1995–2005

Good colour. A wine of medium weight but with real grace and elegance. Supple fruit. Ripe and balanced. Not a blockbuster but good intensity on the follow-through. Good to good plus.

1987   **Drink soon**

Medium colour. Reasonable substance on the nose for the vintage. Evidence of selection here. A lightish but not feeble wine. Little tannin. Has both fruit and personality. Good for the vintage.

1986   Now–2005

Good colour. This is a rather more substantial wine than the 1988 – though it is not as rich as the 1985. Plummy nose. The tannins obtrude more than they do in the wine below, and they are not as covered or as ripe. Medium-full body. At present it lacks the fat and flesh of the 1985 but has balance, depth and interest. Better than the 1988. Good positive finish.

1985   Now–2008

Good colour, just a little development compared with the above. Richer, more concentrated, and with more depth than the 1988. This is a fine bottle. Lovely ripe, subtle fruit on the nose. There are elements of cedar and sandalwood as well as blackcurrant and plum. Medium-full. Good ripe tannins. Balanced. Long. Charming and classy. A lovely example.

1984   **Drink up**

Good colour for the vintage. No undue sign of age. Good positive nose. Neither austere nor weedy. Inevitably somewhat one-dimensional after the 1985, but no mean achievement. Medium body. As round and ripe as it ever will be, and may begin to dry out. Lacks a little charm but a good effort for the vintage.

1983   Now–2013

Very good colour. Little development compared with the 1982. The most substantial wine of the early 1980s. Firm, fullish, backward, classic nose: a fine wine still in its infancy. Lush, meaty, rich and concentrated. This has very fine fruit. Still quite a lot of unresolved tannin. Good grip. Plenty of depth. Fine finish. Potentially the best of the early 1980s by a significant margin. Still needs time.

1982   Now–2008

Medium to full colour. Now a little development. Softer and more aromatic on the nose than the 1983. Medium-full. Ripe, cedary and succulent. A more exotic example of the 1985 perhaps. And it is a bigger wine with more fat and sweetness. Engaging, even and will give much pleasure. Not as good as the 1983 though.

1981   Now–2001

Very good colour for the vintage. Almost as deep as the 1982. Approaching maturity now. I have long regarded this as a very successful vintage for Labégorce-Zédé. Still backward on the nose but more approachable on the palate. Medium to medium-full body. Stylish fruit. Good length. Beginning to round off. A most attractive example. Just about ready.

1980   **Drink up**

Medium mature colour. Somewhat neutral on the nose, and beginning to get a little astringent. Quite attractive – certainly not weak. But getting towards the end of its useful life.

1979   **Drink soon**

Medium to medium full colour. Not as deep as the 1981. Approaching maturity. Slightly weak on the nose. Medium body. The tannins now soft. This seems a little neutral, even a shade dilute. It lacks the fat and flesh it would have had if the rejection of lesser *cuvées* to make a second wine had been in operation at the time. Not bad but not exciting.

MONBRISON

'Across the gravelly hillside five yolks of yellow oxen drag five chains.
I sent them forth at daylight to pull up the deep-rooted vineyard.
Today and tomorrow and every day throughout the winter they will
pace up and down the ordered channels,
With heavy breath and gritting iron, hauling out the damp tap roots.'

So wrote Robert Meacham Davis at Château Dauzac in
1921. Robert Davis was an American protestant minister,
poet, artist and journalist, and was Commissioner for the
Red Cross in the Balkans during the First World War. Why
was he at Dauzac? He had fallen in love – it was a *coup de
foudre* – with Kathleen Johnston, daughter of the famous *négociant* family, at the time proprietors of this Margaux fifth
growth. Seeking somewhere to live after their marriage, the
couple decided on Monbrison, a kilometre or so inland in
the commune of Arsac. There have been some ups and
downs since, not least because the vineyard was uprooted in
1939 and not replanted until 1963. But now the vines are 30
years old, and for at least a decade Monbrison has been as
high a flier as neighbouring Angludet and not-so-far-away
Labégorce-Zédé: one of the *super-bourgeois* of the Médoc.

It is tempting to try and connect the history of Monbrison with the Marquis de Montalambert, owner of the combined Durfort-Lascombes estate in the mid-eighteenth century. In 1768 the widow of the Marquis de Montalambert
divided this estate between her nephews, the Viscomte de
Vivens and a M. Montbrizon (a 'T' and a 'Z'). In fact, what
is now Château Monbrison was a *métairie* of the neighbouring Château d'Arsac, which belonged to the powerful Ségur
family. In 1749, it was ceded as an independent estate to a
M. de Copmartin, a *conseiller du roi* in Bordeaux, and it remained in the hands of the Copmartin family until 1818.

HISTORY

On the 26 February 1818, Mme François-Pierre Copmartin, *née* Anne Faure, sold her Arsac domaine, at this time relatively small as regards vineyard, to Paul George Conquère de Monbrison for 75,000 francs. Was he a descendant of Montalambert's nephew? We do not know. Monbrison enlarged the vineyard, adding land in Margaux itself from a M. Teychonneau in 1836, and assembling more parcels locally to form a coherent whole, but in 1848 his sons Jacques Edouard and Jean-Henri Dominique sold the estate to Isidore Feuillebois, a lawyer resident in Margaux. It produced about 25 *tonneaux* of wine at the time.

Eighteen years later, in 1866, Monbrison changed hands once again. This time the purchaser was Gustave Chaix-d'Est-Ange, another lawyer, and also to become proprietor of Lascombes a year later. According to Guillon in *Les Chateaux Historiques et Vignobles de la Gironde*, the vineyard was extended. Perhaps it was merely replanted. Production figures seem to remain stable.

Gustave Chaix-d'Est-Ange died in 1887, and, though his heirs remained at Lascombes, they decided to dispose of Monbrison. It was acquired by Jean Clanis, a *négociant*. Early in the new century the domaine passed to Jean Lavendier, who had married Clanis's daughter Jeanne-Marie. The Lavendiers do not seem to have resided at Monbrison. He was Mayor of Margaux, and they lived at Château La Gurgue. But for a time the two properties were combined, and production increased to 60 *tonneaux*. It was Lavendier who sold Monbrison, but not La Gurgue, which he retained, to Robert Davis after the First World War.

THE DAVIS AND VONDERHEYDEN FAMILIES

Though he did not acquire La Gurgue, Robert Davis was able to tack on to his estate a parcel of vines which lay on the Giscours side of his vineyard called Cordet, Kathleen Johnston's dowry. At some stage, according to Cocks and Féret, this produced a white wine. Today it produces red wine again. This, though, is not the second wine of Monbrison. That is known as Bouquet de Monbrison.

The Davises resided at Monbrison, encircled by a gently peaceful, isolated patch of vines, surrounded in the far distance by forest, until the outbreak of hostilities in 1939. Being of alien nationality Robert Davis decided to take the advantage of cash incentives offered by the government to rip up his vineyard – wine-making was barely profitable at the time – and use this money to flee the country. The land was made over to his eldest daughters, and he and Kathleen spent the war in Morocco. He died in 1949.

It was his youngest daughter Elizabeth who decided to take up the reins of Monbrison. Married (until she divorced in 1972) to Christian Vonderheyden, originally of German origin, it was she who bought out her sisters, rented back some of the land her mother had sold off after the war, and supervised the replanting of the derelict vineyard. Once, causing much aeronautical confusion, she released an anti-hail rocket into a threatening cloud. It hit an aircraft which had just taken off from Bordeaux's Merignac airport!

Elizabeth Davis, bright, white-haired, the spitting image of Mrs Bun the baker's wife, is still the dominant figure at Monbrison. Her second son, Jean-Luc, was responsible for the wine from 1976 until his tragic early death from leukaemia in 1992. Today it is the third son, Laurent, who had lived and operated his own wine business in the US for a dozen years or so, who has returned with his wife Cécile to take over.

THE VINEYARD

From 1974 to 1983 six of the ten hectares of Monbrison were leased to Alexis Lichine of the Prieuré, and went into Prieuré-Lichine. Now reinstated, the domaine has been further increased by Elizabeth Davis' own farming arrangements nearby to a total of 13.2 hectares, plus a further 7.4 hectares at Cordet. The vines are planted in a ratio of 50 per cent Cabernet

Sauvignon, 15 per cent Cabernet Franc, 30 per cent Merlot and 5 per cent Petit Verdot, and lie more or less in one piece, on the edge of the plateau known as the Poujeaux, adjoining Du Tertre and Angludet on one side, and Giscours on another, alongside the road which runs from Arsac to Macau.

THE CHÂTEAU

It is an attractive farmhouse, Château Monbrison, a hotch-potch of architectural periods and styles, partly originating in the seventeenth century. Bits seem to have been added on to the sides at intervals, so that you are continually travelling up and down corridors from one side of the building, to the other in order to gain access to the adjacent rooms. There is a small tower in the middle, a porch covered in wisteria, and a swimming pool under the pine trees at the back. And there are at least three friendly dogs. Legend has it that there is a secret passage from the Château d'Arsac to Monbrison, and from Monbrison onwards to the river. I have not travelled it.

THE WINE

The wine is vinified in enamelled-steel vats at a maximum temperature of 32 to 33 degrees, given a long *cuvaison* and aged, in the best years, in as much as 50 per cent new wood. There is, of course, a *vendange verte* – Jean-Luc Vonderheyden was one of the first to adopt this crop-thinning technique – though not in 1988 or again in 1992 when hail reduced the harvest naturally. A new barrel cellar was constructed in 1978, and a new storage cellar and reception area in 1987.

The wine of Monbrison has, since 1982 at least, not put a foot wrong. Partly this is as a result of what is now a respectable age of the vineyard. Principally though, it was the application of the considerable talents of Jean-Luc, now continued by the equally able Laurent Vonderheyden. The wine, not surprisingly, is similar to Angludet and, the vineyards being replanted at the same time, has undergone a parallel process of refinement, becoming richer and more concentrated over the years, remaining sturdy for a Margaux, yet nevertheless showing an inherent plummy velvetiness, or at least promising it for maturity, which is characteristic of the Margaux commune. '*Actuellement parmi les plus réputés*,' says Cocks and Féret: today, among the most esteemed (of the non-classified growths). Shed a tear in fond memory of the late Jean-Luc. But his legacy lives on.

THE TASTING

I sampled the following vintages at Monbrison in September 1993.

	Optimum drinking
1992	**1996–2000**

Good colour. Good oaky nose. Plump and ripe. Almost sweet fruit. No lack of substance and depth. On the palate a little raw, and not a lot of tannin and grip. But better than most, plump and ripe.

1991	**1996–2001**

Good colour. This again has fruit and charm. No lack of warmth. Medium body. Some grip. Fresh, persistent. Even classy. Shows well.

1990	**1999–2014**

Good colour. Rather closed at present on the nose. A little hard on the nose, but rich, full and concentrated on the palate. Good new oak. Good grip. Plump, ripe, classy and harmonious. Plenty of dimension. Very good finish. Good plus to very good.

1989	**1998–2010**

Very good colour. Like the 1990 this has gone into its shell. The tannins are more evident than in the above. The wine is more adolescent. Yet it has good grip and fruit. Slight spice. At present not only less potentially velvety but less charming and with less class. Good though.

1988	**1999–2014**

Very good colour. Lovely nose. Perfumed, plummy, oaky, intense. Quite firm on the palate. Good fullish body. The tannins not too austere. Very good grip. This finishes long and persistent and classy. Very good.

1987   **Now–2000**

Good colour. Attractive, plump nose and palate. Good grip. Medium body. Charming, even seductive. Long, positive. This is an excellent 1987. Just about ready. But will keep well.

1986   **1995–2003**

Good colour. A little hard on the nose. The tannins a bit rough at first. But ripe and new oaky after a bit of aeration. Medium-full body. Good plump fruity attack, but it tails off just a bit. It is stylish though. Quite good plus.

1985   **1996–2006**

Very good colour. This is full and concentrated, but slightly more rustic on both nose and palate. Still youthful. Good acidity, plump and even rich, but the tannins less refined than the wines today, a slight bitterness somewhere, and less new oak. Got more stylish and a bit more obviously new oaky as it evolved. Long complex finish. Good plus.

1984   **Drink soon**

Good colour for the vintage. This is a good 1984, but it is not a patch on the 1985. Good substance. Not too lean. Now a slight astringency. And it is much less classy.

1983   **1995–2008**

Very good colour for the vintage. Still very youthful. Typically *arrières côtes*, just like Angludet. Full, rich, quite tannic and structured. Backward. Slightly brutal. But the finish is ample and ripe. Good plus. Still needs time.

1982   **Now–2005**

Fullish colour, now suggestions of maturity. Less solid than the 1983. Ripe, velvety and concentrated nose. On the palate medium-full. Good grip. More evolved than the 1983. Lovely fruit. Good plus. This has less vigour, perhaps a little less depth, but is currently more stylish.

1981   **Now–1997**

Medium-full colour, just about mature. Interesting aspects of coffee and chocolate on the nose. Medium body. Similar palate but there is a little astringency. It is a little lumpy, but it is also rich, curate's eggy. A touch short. But quite good.

THE REST OF MÉ

Outside the four great communes of Margaux, Saint-Julien, Pauillac and Saint-Estèphe, the best wines of the Médoc peninsula are found on a ridge which begins at Saint-Seurin-de-Cadourne, north of Saint-Estèphe, and then curves round behind Pauillac and Saint-Julien – through Saint-Laurent, Listrac and Moulis – to stop at Avensan. Below le conglomerate communes of Margaux further leading estates are found in Macau and Ludon.

THE

DOC

LA LAGUNE

La Lagune, sometimes jokingly referred to as the *premier grand cru du Médoc* because it is the first that one reaches on the wine road, is a *troisième* cru, and one of only five properties in the 1855 Classification, apart from Haut-Brion, which do not lie in the classic communes of Saint-Estèphe, Pauillac, Saint-Julien and Margaux. Of these, three are in Saint-Laurent, which is situated west of Saint-Julien and Pauillac: La Tour-Carnet, Belgrave and Camensac. The remaining two are Cantemerle in Macau, just north of Château La Lagune, and La Lagune in the commune of Ludon.

Some 40 years ago La Lagune was a ruin. The vicissitudes of world war, slump and yet again world war had left it neglected if not abandoned. It was allowed to fall into disrepair and it hardly produced a dozen barrels of wine a year. Today it makes as much as 1,000 hogsheads, and the wine is very good indeed; consistently one of the top wines of the region. The marketing policy is to make it and sell it, to leave others to sit on the stock until it is ready for drinking. No reserves are held. Perhaps because of this the administrators are never greedy about the price they ask, so this makes Château La Lagune splendid value for money. It has won many friends in the past 30 years and well deserves its current high profile and great popularity. Here is another super-second!

HISTORY

The estate is established on Ludon's highest land and dates from at least the seventeenth century. It was probably first planted with vines at the end of this era, in common with much of the Médoc. The first mention of wine appears in documents dating from 1724 when it belonged to the family Seguineau de Lognac. It passed, by dowry given to two sisters, to MM. Parrouty and Dumas de La Roque, and, again through the female line, to a man called Buret.

By Napoleonic times La Lagune was shared between at least a dozen members of the Seguineau family and their descendants; and perhaps this plethora of owners, none of whom seem to have been prominent in local politics, helped to prevent punitive action, as elsewhere in the Médoc, by the new revolutionary state.

In 1819, a wealthy Périgord landowner named Jouffrey Piston became the owner and it seems to have been under his ownership that the quality of the wine first achieved renown. Yet some early-nineteenth-century classifications, while consistently recognizing the wine as the top growth of the commune, do not include it in their lists of the top wines of Bordeaux.

It does not appear in the classification in Wilhelm Franck's first edition of his *Traité* in 1824, for instance. However, Abraham Lawton, writing in 1815, after admitting that he found La Lagune's reputation somewhat exaggerated (it was very popular in Holland and that meant that it sold for 1100 francs a *tonneau*), has to acknowledge that it must be considered a fourth growth. Franck's second edition (1845) rates it as a fourth *cru* too, and records it as producing 45 to 50 *tonneaux*. In the 1855 Classification La Lagune is rated a *troisième*.

Meanwhile Jouffrey Piston had died, eventually to be succeeded by his son, who added the name Eaubonne to his name, whether as a compliment to the mythical lagoon, after which the property is said to be named, I do not know. By the end of the century the property consisted of some 50 hectares, producing 80 *tonneaux*, and in 1898 it was sold to M. Louis Sèze for 340,000 francs. La Lagune passed to M. A. Galy, Sèze's son-in-law, in 1911, and when Galy died, Lagune fell on hard times. There were 40 hectares under plantation in 1923, 35 but containing 40 per cent less vines in 1935, 9.5 hectares in 1949 and only four in 1954. The property was shared between a number of successors of M. Galy, all financially constrained. Production dwindled, the vineyards and *chais* were left uncared for, and the whole estate allowed to run down.

RENAISSANCE

In the mid-1950s La Lagune was acquired by Georges Brunet. Brunet was an agricultural engineer who had made a fortune in real estate, but had always had an ambition to make wine. From 1958 onwards he set about an ambitious scheme of replanting, restoring and renovation. The scale of this project may be indicated by the fact that the late Alexis Lichine, ever the go-ahead entrepreneur, on the look out for properties to buy in the early 1950s, had also inspected but rejected La Lagune, so dilapidated was the estate. The success of Brunet's achievement was such that by 1962, at least, the property was once again producing classed growth wine.

By 1962, though, as a result of a rather messy divorce, Brunet had moved on. La Lagune was bought by M. René Chayoux, of the Champagne house of Ayala (the price valued the vineyard at 83,330 francs per hectare; Latour sold in the same year for 300,000 francs per hectare), and he and M. Boirie, the *régisseur* he had inherited, continued Brunet's good work. Parcels of land, originally part of the estate, were bought back and replanted. The elegant château was restored, and the cellars completely modernized. Some 26 metal fermentation vats (they have since added six more), epoxy resin lined, were installed, and an automatic piping system to take the wine from the vats to the waiting barrels in the various *chais*, was introduced. All the new wine now normally goes into new oak casks, and all is château-bottled.

THE VINEYARD

The name of the property, as I have mentioned, is said to come from the word 'lagoon', which in French is spelt exactly as the wine. Frankly I find this hard to believe; Lagune is on Ludon's highest *croupe*, a full fifteen metres above sea level. This may not sound much, but is mountainous by Médoc standards. Also, I cannot see where the lagoon could have been. There is marshy land to the east, running down to the estuary the other side of the village of Ludon, and also to the south, past the imposing Château Agassac, and even far to the north between Labarde and Cantenac, north of Château Giscours; but nothing near to La Lagune. On the other hand, I have no alternative to offer.

The plateau, a little to the north of the château and *chai*, falls away in all directions and is entirely planted with vines. In all, the estate consists of some 152 hectares, of which 73 are under vines, 57 in a single parcel of land – this, itself, is uncommon in the Médoc – now producing 200 to 250 tonneaux of wine. The second wine is called Moulin de Ludon.

The soil is grey in colour, very light, and is essentially a sandy gravel on a basis of *alios*. This sort of subsoil is said not to be as good as the basic *graves* encountered elsewhere, as it tends to be more solid and therefore humid, but fortunately at La Lagune, at the top of its little plateau, the vineyards drain well. They are planted in the ratio 55 per cent Cabernet Sauvignon, 20 per cent Cabernet Franc, 20 per cent Merlot and 5 per cent Petit Verdot.

THE CHÂTEAU AND THE *CHAIS*

The château itself dates from the early eighteenth century. It was built to replace a more ancient edifice in 1715, just about the time when Bordeaux began to be transformed from a medieval town into the city of the *grands boulevards* we know today. It consists of a *chartreuse*-style, raised, single-storey building overlooking one courtyard, while next door the *chais* (recently doubled in capacity) open on to another. All this is bounded on three sides by vines, reaching almost to the walls, and fronted by a small park on the other. Elegant wrought-iron gates encircle the whole complex. The château itself is now rarely occupied. The property is administered from Champagne by Chayoux's successor, Jean-Michel Ducellier.

In 1964 the *régisseur*, M. Boirie, died, and the estate was managed until 1986 by his widow Jeanne, a fairly formidable, late-middle-aged lady, exuding competence. On her death in November of that year she was succeeded by her daughter Caroline Desvergnes, who had worked alongside her mother since 1972, and Patrick Moulin, the *maître de chai*.

THE WINE

La Lagune used to be known as Grand La Lagune, but in 1958 they bought up a neighbouring piece of land known as Petit La Lagune which had belonged to the domaine in ancient times, and have since dropped the 'Grand'. It is a wine quite different from its neighbour Cantemerle, whose vineyards it touches, and different too from neighbouring Margaux wines.

While Cantemerle is soft and elegant, fruity and refined – and has more Merlot – La Lagune is sturdier, more fleshy, fuller in colour and body, and richer. Alexis Lichine describes it in his revised *Wines and Vineyards of France* as combining Médoc elegance with Graves' earthy richness, and I would not quarrel with this neat juxtaposition. It has shown a remarkable renaissance since the early 1960s and now can rank amongst the top growths of the Médoc.

THE TASTING

Most of the following notes are based on a combination of two tastings. The first was organized by the London-based Wine and Dine Society in December 1988. The second took place at La Lagune in April 1989. I have added notes on the four most recent vintages, sampled at the château in April 1992.

1991   **1996–2000**

Good colour. The nose is ripe. The wine is reasonably classy, has concentration and even depth. Finishes well. Very good.

1990   **1997–2009**

Good colour. Rich, ripe, soft, oaky nose. A gentle ample wine for La Lagune. Not a blockbuster but round and stylish. Medium body. Oaky on the palate but with no hard tannins. Good ripe, succulent fruit. Long, rich finish. Good plus.

1989   **1996–2006**

Good colour. Soft, round nose; oaky and plump but not very intense. Medium body. Plummy. Reasonable tannins. Gently oaky on the palate. The 1990 is marginally better.

1988   **1995–2009**

Very good colour. Quite new oaky on the nose. Rich, full and satisfying. Very good fruit: blackberry and blackcurrant flavoured. Medium-full body. Good grip. This is more classic than the 1989 and 1990, and I prefer it.

1987   **Now–1997**

Round, cedary nose with good fruit behind it. Medium body. Ripe, even fat. A very good 1987. Good length and depth for the vintage.

1986   **Now–2004**

Very good colour. Firm, quite closed, oaky nose. Medium-full body. Fat, old viney. Long and rich and blackcurranty on the finish. Fine. This is better than the 1985.

1985   **Now–2001**

Good colour. Rather more open nose than the 1986. Soft, more red fruit flavours plus oak. Not the weight of the 1986. Medium to medium-full body. Ripe and generous. Good grip.

1983   **Now–2008**

Good colour. Just a little development. Fine, fresh, elegant nose. Good Cabernet-based fruit with a fragrant Margaux softness. Medium-full, still some tannin. A very classy wine with a lot of depth and lovely complex fruit.

1982   **Now–2014**

Fine full colour. Big, fat, with hints of chocolate and liquorice. Very ripe tannins. Quite substantial. A full-bodied tannic wine with a lot of concentration. 1983 may be more classic but this has the power, the depth and the intensity.

1981   **Now–2004**

Excellent colour for the vintage. No sign of maturity. Fine ripe nose. Good concentration. No lack of grip. Blackcurrants and blackberries. Medium-full body. Another success. More sub-stantial within the vintage than the 1983. Very good length.

1979   **Now–2000**

Very good colour. Good ripe fruit on the nose. An element of coffee and roast chestnut, even praline, as well as blackcurrant. Medium body. Beginning to get there. Not as ample as the 1981, which I prefer, but certainly very good.

1978   **Now–2004**

Excellent colour. Quite a cool, unevolved nose. This is more austere, because of being less advanced, than the 1979. Good blackcurrant. Quite full, still some tannin. Ripe and rich and concentrated. Good length. Very stylish. Fine.

1976   **Drink soon**

Medium-full, mature colour. Aromatic overblown nose, slightly dry but not uncomfortably so. A certain astringency on the attack but this is soon replaced by a spicy, rich, mellow quality. No drying off on the finish. Good length for a 1976. Once again very good indeed.

1975   **Now–1999**

Fullish, mature colour. Still vigorous looking. Firm elements to the nose but not hard, underneath now getting soft. Fullish, a little tannin. This is rounder and more generous than most 1975s and has more concentration. Not the style of the 1978 though, nor the complexity or freshness. Good length though. Again very good.

1971   **Now–1997**

Very good mature colour. Fresh, aromatic cedary nose. Very stylish. Fullish, vigorous, cedary-oaky background, attractive fruit. Very good grip. Mellow. *A point*. Vigorous, complex. Lovely.

1970   **Now–2000**

Fine full colour, just about mature. Complex nose, quite sturdy. Fullish, ripe, good tannins. Ripe and concentrated. Very good.

1966   **Now–1996**

Fullish, mature colour. Fullish, mellow nose, touch of spice, hint of bonfires, good grip, toasted oak now mellowed into cedar. Fullish, ripe, mellow, mulberry fruity, plump and soft. Good grip. Fine balance. Complex and long on the palate. Very good indeed again. No sign of age.

1964   **Drink soon**

Full mature colour. Sturdier, more burnt nose. Quite full, a little astringency but basically another mellow, ripe, cedary, balanced wine. More rigid structure than the above. Not quite the finesse or the complexity. Good grip though. Long on the palate, especially for a 1964. Very good again.

CANTEMERLE

A few 100 metres north of the Lagune plateau, the D2 Médoc road enters a small wood. After another 100 metres or so, a white gate indicates a drive to the left. At the end of this long drive, past rhododendrons, oak, beech and fir, you will emerge once again into the open. Opposite stands the château of Cantemerle, shaded by plane trees. Cantemerle is the last of the classified growths of 1855, but is by no means the least important of the 60-odd properties listed.

There are at least two stories attempting to explain the origin of the château's name, which literally means 'blackbird song'. In the first story a dragon came to live in the wood and frightened all the birds away. A bold and handsome (of course!) knight slew the dragon, and all the blackbirds gathered in the wood to sing and celebrate his victory. The second story is on the face of it equally fanciful, but may in fact contain a grain of truth. A large black cannon, nicknamed the '*merle*' or blackbird, successfully disrupted bands of looting English soldiers, fleeing up the Médoc after the battle of Castillon in 1453. In Old French '*merlon*' meant battlement and we know that Cantemerle in the Middle Ages was a fortified *manoir*: it would seem quite natural to take advantage of the double meaning and name one's trusty old cannon the '*merle*'.

The domaine of Cantemerle, like other Médoc properties I have already described, begins with one of a number of feudal castles built as part of the defensive system of the Gironde. According to some authorities, it possibly dates back in its original form to the ninth century.

HISTORY

In the early Middle Ages Cantemerle was a *seigneurie* in its own right, with its lords direct vassals of the king – unlike most of the southern part of the Haut-Médoc, which was dependent on the *seigneurie* of Blanquefort. Charles Lorbac mentions a document dated 1270 which attests to this. A Pons de Cantemerle is recorded in 1242, and was succeeded by his son Gaillard, who had a son called Raymond. Presumably Raymond died without an heir, for the estate then reverted to the king (Edward I). His grandson Edward III gave it to Louis Chabot in 1369, and for a couple of centuries the *seigneur* of Cantemerle owed allegiance and paid tithes and taxes to the Lord of Blanquefort.

From the Chabots the estate passed through a family called Cauperie (a *procès verbal de convocation* of the local nobles in 1491 mentions a Medard de Laupenne or Cauperie – it depends on how you read the handwriting – '*Sieur de Cantemerle*'), and then in 1510 to the Larroques. From them it passed to François de Geoffre, and the document of his sale, on 20 August 1579, to Jehan de Villeneuve, is still extant. This parchment, some four and a half metres long, is in the château archives. What François de Geoffre sold were his *maisons nobles* at Cantemerle, La Raze and Mesterieu, with their *dépendances*, for 12,500 *livres*. Interestingly, the document refers to the produce of wine of the estate – a mere 3 *tonneaux* in the year 1575, which had been affected by frost.

Jehan de Villeneuve was *seigneur* of several estates near Toulouse, privy councillor to the King and a deputy president of the Bordeaux *parlement*. Moreover, he was a descendant of earlier *seigneurs* of Cantemerle – perhaps of the Ponses, Gaillard and Raymond. Because of this, Cantemerle re-assumed its independence of Blanquefort, though not, intermittently, without a few arguments between them.

Jehan de Villeneuve's heir was his youngest son, also called Jehan, who married Antoinette de Durfort of the house of Duras de Blanquefort, another of the great Bordelais dynasties. From then on the family was known as Villeneuve de Durfort. All this time, however, the main seat of the domaine was not where the current Château Cantemerle stands, but a kilometre and a half to the east, nearer to the village of Macau, on the boundary of the parishes of Ludon and Macau. Included in the Cantemerle dependencies was a *maison noble* called 'Sauvges'. This was where the wine was made. When the castle itself became so dilapidated that it had to be demolished, the whole family moved inland to Sauvges, and the house there was modernized, enlarged and renamed Cantemerle.

A few years later, in December 1683, Marie de Caseau, widow of Baron Louis de Villeneuve de Durfort, re-asserted her 1270 rights by refusing to pay dues on trees she had cut down and sold. The tax was claimed by a bureaucrat with the magnificent title *Fermier Général des Domaines de Guyenne*. Records do not state who won the action. What intrigues me, however, is why the trees were being cut down. Were the Villeneuves enlarging the vineyard?

Cantemerle remained in the Villeneuve family throughout the next two centuries, despite the fact that the head of the family emigrated during the Revolution. Details of the period are scant, but it was about this time that the seventeenth-century *manoir* was demolished and the first parts of the present château constructed. Originally, this was a simple two-storey edifice with another at right angles to it, forming an L shape. Where these two join there is a rounded turreted staircase, said to date from the original building.

Subsequently, two further towers have been built at each end; one round, one square, with long thin roofs like witches hats, in the Médoc nineteenth-century fashion. Last of all, late in the century, the central portion, a three-storied structure, again with a steep roof, was added, and stuck on to the front of the original, eastern L. All this sounds like – and is – an architectural hotch-potch; but it is not without charm.

The first records of Cantemerle as a wine occur in Wilhelm Franck's account of the prices wines fetched in 'the good years from 1745 onwards'. This was published 100 years later, and in some cases needs to be taken with a pinch of salt. Villeneuve is a *premier cru* of Macau, and made 300 *livres* a *tonneau*. This is less than wines such as Angludet, then a fourth growth of Margaux and Cantenac, at the time the leading Médoc commune, and hardly half of its nearest important neighbour, Giscours. According to Franck, the wine had been sold in its entirety to Holland for decades, the first purchases having been made in the first half of the eighteenth century by the Maison Couderc of Amsterdam. This Dutch connection persisted.

Variously classified in the early nineteenth century as a fourth or fifth growth, Cantemerle only squeezed into the 1855 Classification as an afterthought. Not only is it the last of the names, but it has been entered in an alien hand, close and precise, rather than the flowery script of the rest of the document. Others have already argued that its original omission was probably because the wine was not normally brokered on the Bordeaux market. I see no reason to disagree with this reasoning.

The proprietor at the time was the Baroness d'Abbadie de Villeneuve de Durfort; a grand title, and, from all accounts, a *grande dame*. The property, an estate in total of some 340 hectares, contained 110 hectares of vines, and produced 150 to 170 *tonneaux*. Running the estate for the Baroness was the Comte de la Vergne, a distinguished agricultural engineer, and the man who in 1852 discovered that dusting the leaves of the vine with sulphur powder was an antidote to oidium (powdery mildew), an epidemic of which threatened to ravage the vineyards of France. To this day, this treatment, successfully pioneered at Cantemerle so long ago, is still used.

The Villeneuve association with Cantemerle, said to have spanned seven centuries, finally came to its end in 1892. Some doubt surrounds the reasons for the break, but one suspects that once again it was problems of '*indivision*' following the death of the old Baroness. Cantemerle probably now belonged to several descendants, none of whom could agree how financially to manage the estate, and none of whom could afford to buy the others out.

In one of those deals one would love to know more about, the *négociants* Calvet bought Cantemerle on 29 June 1892, for 600,000 francs, and sold it a fortnight later for 770,000. The buyers were Théophile Dubos of the firm Dubos Frères and his associate Maurice Thomas.

Philippe Dubos, son of Théophile, was owner of both châteaux for over 60 years, and kept a detailed, daily record of the local climatic conditions. Each morning, afternoon and evening, without fail, Dubos would record the temperature, atmospheric pressure, wind velocity and direction, amount of cloud, and so forth, together with a note of the development of the vine and its fruit. When he died, in 1962, the property passed to his two daughters. The elder, Pia, was married to Henri Binaud, head of the *négociants* Beyermann, a firm of Dutch origin, and for the next fifteen years, until his retirement, Binaud was effectively proprietor of Cantemerle together with his nephew, Bertrand Clauzel.

THE VINEYARD

In the first 80 years of the twentieth century the vineyard of Cantemerle contracted considerably. In 1868 it was 110 hectares, and produced 170 *tonneaux*; 50 years later production was 250 *tonneaux*, including the second wine, created by Dubos, called Château Royal-Médoc. Since the 1920s the crop evaporated to 100 *tonneaux* in 1949, 75 in 1969, and an average of 57 *tonneaux* during the 1970s. The vineyard area declined to a mere 22 hectares.

It has been suggested that this failure to replant was due to a reluctance on the part of Beyermann, the exclusive agents for Cantemerle, to raise production to more than they themselves could market. Another reason, no doubt, following the economic difficulties of the 1930s and the immediate postwar years, was just a simple lack of cash.

Not surprisingly, then, with the Cantemerle estate run-down and ripe for development, rumours began to circulate in the late 1970s that it was up for sale. Nathaniel Johnston was one of those interested in buying but at the time Henri Binaud was reluctant to sell. A few months later, in December 1980, Johnston was astounded to hear that a deal had gone through, moreover, for 16 million francs, 2 million less than he had been prepared to pay.

The purchasers were a consortium of which the majority share was held by the French group Goulet-Turpin. The Bordeaux house of Cordier were one of the minority owners. Jean Cordier and Goulet-Turpin were old friends and the *raison d'être* of the partnership was that the Cordiers would farm the estate and make and market the wine. At the beginning of 1985 both parties were absorbed into Société La Henin.

Since this time Cantemerle has been transformed. A major expansion of the vineyard has taken place. The cellar has been completely reconstructed, and the château has been renovated. Most importantly, after a decade and a half of rather dull wine, Cantemerle is back to what one remembers from the Dubos days, a wine of remarkable elegance, of a quality which belied its position at the very end of the 60-odd classed growths.

In December 1980, there were 33 hectares under vine. Fifteen hectares were immediately planted the following year. By 1991 the surface area had risen to 60 hectares; eventually there will be 64. This was what was originally under vine, so no planting permission was required. The total estate comprises 325 hectares or so, and it is not hard to envisage that there is further land which is suitable. I am sure we will see a further expansion of the vineyard, subject to the usual bureaucracy, over the next decade. The land is planted in the ratio 45 per cent Cabernet Sauvignon, 10 per cent Cabernet Franc, 45 per cent Merlot.

THE CHÂTEAU

I remember Cantemerle in the 1960s. It still rattled with the ghost of Philippe Dubos. Edwardian in furnishings, somewhat gloomy in atmosphere, it seemed to be a rambling building with every possible surface covered with photos, prints, knick-knacks and memorabilia. It was not without its attraction. For many years it lay empty, part being used as an office, another room converted into a vineyard kitchen. It has now been restored. The ground floor has been completed in the somewhat anonymous style of a luxury hotel. There is a dining room for groups and for those employed at vintage time. Upstairs there are four opulent suites. No expense has been spared.

Across an expanse of noisy, crunchy gravel are the *chais*, and to the west, a number of dependant buildings, once stables, now house the tractors and other agricultural implements, or have been transformed into dwellings for the vineyard workers. There is also an impressive *salle de réception* and tasting room. Much has been changed in *cuverie* and *chais* in the last decade. Fermentation still mainly takes place in wood, though there are a number of stainless-steel vats. Within the original shell the entire cellar from reception of the fruit to the quantity of new oak employed (meagre in the latter days of the old regime) has been transformed. Even the floor has been retiled. The last extension was in 1990.

THE WINE

Cantemerle makes a wine which is in complete contrast to its neighbour, La Lagune. Where the latter is firm, full and rich, Cantemerle is soft and elegant. The Merlot shows. La Lagune uses 100 per cent new oak. At Cantemerle the new-wood percentage is not so exaggerated.

I had expected more of a change in style, in character and personality, as a result of the arrival of the Cordiers in 1980. There is, it is obvious, a Cordier style: full, meaty, round and plump; a wine which may be a bit rude in its infancy but which has fruit and structure (possibly at the expense of breed) and which is always reliable; never weedy in the poor vintages.

The change at Cantemerle has been more one of quality – a return to the finesse of the 1950s – than of style. There is more new oak, giving a cedary flavour. There is more concentration of fruit. There is more sex appeal. This is a renaissance which I can wholeheartedly welcome.

The Tasting

The more recent wines were sampled at Château Cantemerle in April 1992, and January 1990; those from the 1983 backwards at a tasting I presented to customers of La Vigneronne in November 1988.

Optimum drinking

1991   1995–1998

Good colour. Soft nose, quite fragrant; quite elegant. But a bit slight on the palate. Quite pleasant but lacks backbone. Forward.

1990   1996–2003

Good colour. Elegant and fruity, but a little superficial. What it lacks is real depth and concentration. Yet the fruit is ripe and charming. The 1989 is better though. Quite good.

1989   1997–2009

Medium-full colour. Smoky nose. Ripe and lush on the palate. This has good grip and more dimension than the 1990. Medium body. Ripe. Quite intense; with good tannins, and good length. Good plus.

1988   Now–2003

Good colour. This is gently oaky, restrained and refined on the nose. Soft and complex fruit. Medium body. Essentially it lacks a bit of concentration, but it is balanced and elegant. Will come forward quite soon. Quite good plus.

1987   Now–1996

Medium colour. Light nose but there is some fruit and grip here. Neither weak nor mean. Light, little tannin. This is a good, if forward, result for the vintage. Good grip. Attractive fruit. Positive finish.

1986   1993–2003

Medium to medium-full colour. Medium weight nose. Quite ripe and ample. Good mulberry-type fruit but not a great deal of concentration or depth. Medium body; soft charming. But essentially a bit weedy.

1985   Now–2005

Medium to medium-full colour. Just a little more evolved than the 1986. Rather fatter and richer on the nose. Medium to medium-full body. Ripe, balanced. Quite rich. Good depth and the habitual Cantemerle elegance. Again charm but this is a more serious result than the 1986. Quite good.

1983   Now–2008

Good colour. Full, rich, meaty, plummy. Good acidity – more than the 1985 – more concentration, more depth. Fullish, some tannin. Plenty of depth here, chocolate and cooked plums. Good grip. This is a serious wine. Very good.

1982   Now–2005

Good colour. Fat, spicy, cigar-box and liquorice, touch of coffee. Full, rather more closed and adolescent than the 1983, but essentially not as stylish. Some tannin but a bit chunky. Plenty of wine but lacks a little finesse.

1981   Drink up

Medium colour, still youthful. Fresh nose, reasonable fruit. A medium-weight wine which lacks a bit of substance and interest. A bit dull. One-dimensional finish.

1978   Drink soon

Good colour, still immature. Nose now getting soft but seems a little insignificant. Medium body. Not a lot of tannin. Fully ready. Round and pleasant and with good acidity. But not a great deal of interest or depth. Not bad though.

1975   Now–1996

Fullish colour, little sign of maturity. Slightly more substance than 1978 but not a lot of depth. Medium-full, as much astringency as tannin, and I don't think these are ever going to go, as the wine inside is already soft. A little more concentrated than the 1978, and more interest. But the dryness invades. Better with food.

1966   Drink soon

Medium-full colour. Just about mature. Fragrant, mature, complex nose. There is a lot of depth here. This is well-matured, almost nearly the end of the road in fact, but a very stylish mellow fruit wine with length and complexity. Fine. Fresh on the finish.

1961   Drink soon

(Halves) Medium colour only for a 1961. Mature. Ripe, very slightly caramelly nose, but soft and on the light side. A delicate 1961. Fragrant and with more ripeness and concentration than the 1966 – as well as more class – but really quite evolved. I remember it better in bottle a few years back.

1959   Drink soon.

(Bottled by Liggins, Birmingham) Medium-full colour. Fully mature. Old claret nose. Sweet on the palate. Quite full but now very soft and mellow. No astringency though. The château-bottling has more grip and more class but this is a most enjoyable old bottle.

CHASSE-SPLEEN

Bernadette Villars and her husband died in a mountaineering accident near their holiday home in Barèges in the Hautes-Pyrénées in November 1992. In their memory I leave this chapter, apart from amendments to the tasting notes, as I originally wrote it for *The Vine* in July 1989.

Currently the Villars estates are being run by Jean Merlaut, Bernadette's brother, and Alain Sutre, property manager of the estates of the Groupe Taillan. Eventually Mme Villars' elder daughter, Claire, will take her mother's place.

Château Chasse-Spleen has been the senior growth in Moulis for over 100 years. Though none of the wines of Moulis and neighbouring Listrac were considered worthy of classification in 1855, Chasse-Spleen was one of six properties decreed a *Cru Bourgeois Supérieur Exceptionnel* in 1932. Since 1976, in the able hands of Mme Bernadette Villars, the quality of the wine has reached even greater heights. If it would be exaggerating to class it a super-second, it would certainly be a *troisième cru* in any re-classification of the red wines of Bordeaux. Château Chasse-Spleen is a *super-bourgeois*.

Though the property's brochure claims that part of the estate was under vines as early as the twelfth century, the first documentary records date from 1560. These show certain parcels of vineyard east of the village of Moulis belonging to a local *seigneur* named Grenier, plus others which he rented, on both a cask and a share-cropping basis, from other landlords. One of these landlords was also the owner of the domaine of La Tour de Saint-Mambert, as it was then known, what is now Latour in what is now Pauillac; another was a *chevalier* of the Knights of Malta, who had a base in the nearby village of Arcins. These documents are supported by further evidence dating from 1630 which shows that in the interim M. Grenier had enlarged his vineyard.

HISTORY

The property lies on the hamlet Grand-Poujeaux, and it is as Château Grand-Poujeaux that the wine was first known. As a result of inheritance difficulties, the estate was divided in 1822. Not only did they divided the land, but they also divided the château and its surrounding garden. This division was carried through with such meticulousness that they even attempted to divide the well. You can still see this today. The sturdy iron railing which separates the two gardens continues across the face of the well, thus rendering it impossible for either of the part-owners to lower a bucket to collect any water! This seems a little excessive and dog-in-the-mangerish; but perhaps the well was not functioning anyway.

The Grenier family name had in the meanwhile evolved to Gressier, and it is as Château Gressier-Grand-Poujeaux that the non-Chasse-Spleen half continued its existence. The other part passed to a Grenier or Gressier daughter, Mme Castaing.

The Castaing family had made their fortune in the West Indies and had recently arrived in the commune of Moulis. They already owned another large estate immediately to the west – what is now Maucaillou and Poujeaux-Theil – which had formerly belonged to the owners of Beychevelle and was called Brassier after the previous proprietors. A subsidiary vineyard was known as Gastebois or Cattebois. Altogether they had a considerable holding. The combined vineyard produced 150 *tonneaux* in the 1830s. For a while it would seem that Madame Castaing's estate was incorporated into that of her in-laws. It is not until later that it gained its independence. It is in the 1860s that the new name, Chasse-Spleen, begins to emerge, and by this time we are on to the next generation: Jean-Jacques Castaing.

There are two explanations of the origin of the name Chasse-Spleen, which can be roughly translated as 'dispels melancholy'. The first is that Lord Byron, when visiting the property in 1821, fell in love with the wines and exclaimed: '*Quel remède pour chasser le spleen*'. The alternative suggestion is that the château took its name from Baudelaire's poem 'Spleen', which begins, '*J'ai plus de souvenirs que si j'avais mille ans*' ('I have more memories than if I were a 1000 years old').

Jean-Jacques Castaing died in the 1880s, and on his widow's death in 1909 the property was acquired by the Bremen shippers, Seignitz. They were also owners of Château Malescot, and their local estate manager was the well-known Théophile Skawinski, administrator of Château Léoville-Las-Cases and a highly regarded wine-maker throughout the Médoc.

Confiscated in 1914 as a *bien appartenant à l'ennemi* (those who picked the 1914 harvest were regarded with hostility because they were 'working for the enemy'; later the cellar was broken into one night and cleared out of wine), Chasse-Spleen was put up for auction in 1922. It was acquired by a M. Lahary who had made his fortune in the forests of the Landes and administered from the late 1930s onwards by his son Frank.

Frank Lahary's daughter married Michel Bezian, a nephew of M. Dupin of Grand-Puy-Lacoste, but Bezian was no businessman. The crisis of 1973 to 1975 was too much for him. In 1976, he decided to put Chasse-Spleen up for sale. The purchasers were the Merlaut family: the price 10.25 million francs, valuing Chasse-Spleen at just over 200,00 francs a hectare (40 per cent that of Pontet-Canet which had sold the year before). In addition there was the stock in the cellar, the entirety of the 1973, 1974 and 1975 vintages, at ten francs a bottle.

BERNADETTE VILLARS

Bernadette Villars, a daughter of Jacques Merlaut, was born in Bordeaux in 1945, but though her father's family were deeply involved in the wine business she was brought up in Paris and she did not set foot in a vineyard until she was eighteen years old. She returned to Bordeaux at the age of eighteen to study geology at the university, married Philippe Villars in 1966, had two daughters, Claire and Céline, in rapid succession, and taught history and geography.

Her husband's family were also in the wine trade, and the exposure to fine claret in the early years of her marriage was a revelation. Rather than being a teacher for the rest of her life she decided to enrol for a course in oenology. She studied, of course, with Professor Emile Peynaud, then in his last year of full-time teaching, and having graduated, started on the accounts and sales side of the family business. Her opportunity arrived in 1976 when her father asked her to take over responsibility for Chasse-Spleen.

Was it difficult? At the start there was a certain amount of suspicion, if not derision, at the idea of a woman in charge of the administration of an important Bordeaux château. But this was soon dispelled. The veteran cellar-master, André Raspaud, was quick to compliment her: 'If the previous owner had had a daughter like you he wouldn't have sold up.'

At the beginning she adopted a cautious approach. 'From 1976 to 1980 I listened a lot, but changed little.' With Professor Peynaud installed as consultant, she adapted rather than innovated. It was not until later, in the 1980s, that a series of major improvements was set in train.

The first of these was an extension of the semi-underground barrel-ageing cellar which had been constructed in 1956. The second was the introduction of machine harvesting for part of the crop. Six large stainless-steel fermentation vats were installed in 1982, and more have been added since. A new reception centre, on top of which is a large salon where parties can be held, was built in 1986. A system of modern, efficient drainage is gradually being extended throughout the vineyard. In 1985 she added a modern laboratory and more recently a computer to help determine the ideal picking pattern. Each morning during the harvest a technician tests the sugar level of fruit from all over the domaine. This is fed into the machine, and it will quickly report exactly in which order the different parcels should be collected.

But the innovation of which Bernadette Villars is proudest is the installation in 1984 of a steam-cleaning machine for cleaning the casks. This allows her not just to diminish the sulphur level in the wines but also, because the steam drains off some of the most aggressive tannins in the new wood, to employ more new oak for the *grand vin*, especially in the lesser vintages, so the wine can have more structure. 'As I know my cellars are clean, I can afford to use less sulphur,' she is quoted as saying. 'I follow the process from the grape to the bottle, ensuring that no detail has been missed. It's like a woman with her children.'

THE VINEYARD

The vineyard of Chasse-Spleen is much divided. There are parcels all over the *appellation*, and even a small parcel of old Petit Verdot (which they very nearly made the mistake of uprooting in the early days) over the border in Listrac. Some 82 hectares are under production, planted in the ratio 55 per cent Cabernet Sauvignon, 4 per cent Cabernet Franc, 35 per cent Merlot and 6 per cent Petit Verdot. The average production is 250 *tonneaux*. The second wine, inaugurated in 1982, is L'Ermitage de Chasse-Spleen, named after a little chapel in the vineyard.

Machine-harvesting started with trials in 1983, and by 1986 about two-thirds of the Cabernet was harvested in this way. This will be the limit; not just because the vineyard is divided in such a way as to make certain sections impractical for anything but manual harvesting, and not only because there are considerable parcels of old, low-trained vines to which the machine cannot be adapted. The main reason is that the Merlot is not suited to automatic picking. The Cabernet skins are tougher but the Merlot with its softer, larger grapes easily get crushed. The makers of the machines suggest you can harvest four hectares per day, but at Chasse-Spleen the maximum is two.

THE WINE-MAKING

On arrival at the reception centre the grapes are completely de-stalked, fermented at 28 to 30 degrees and macerated for up to three weeks, depending on the vintage. Today this takes place almost entirely in stainless steel, the latest of which have the external jacket, cummerbund approach to temperature control. There is now, even in the weakest vintages, 50 per cent new oak. In 1985 it was 65 per cent. The bottling normally takes place in June, though the 1983 and 1986 were bottled in September. An outside contractor arrives, sets up shop in the courtyard, and completes the job in two weeks.

THE CHÂTEAU

The château of Chasse-Spleen is a curious construction. It is, firstly, half of the original property, with additions, and, secondly, one of two distinct and architecturally uncomplementary styles. And yet it has a certain charm. Beauty is in the eye of the beholder, not just in the opinion of the art expert.

The oldest section of the building dates from the end of the eighteenth century, and on to this extensions at either end which were added at the end of the 1860s, at the same time as part of the more formal gardens were turned into a wilder, English-style park. The château has a tower at one end, recently turned into an acoustically insulated hi-fi room by Philippe Villars. The middle has two stories; the right-hand side one. As I have said, a bit of a hotchpotch. The Villars family live mainly in Bordeaux, but the château is fully furnished and equipped. Indeed I have spent a night or two there myself.

FURTHER VILLARS DEVELOPMENTS

Not content with merely running Chasse-Spleen, Bernadette Villars persuaded her family to acquire the run-down Château La Gurgue in Margaux in 1978. With vineyards which adjoin those of Château Margaux and some very old vines, Mme Villars considers La Gurgue potentially better than Chasse-Spleen. In 1983, just before the arrival of large insurance groups in Médoc real estate, Château Haut-Bages-Libéral, the fifth growth neighbour of Château Latour in Pauillac, was added to the portfolio. As you might expect the improvements at both have been impressive.

THE WINE

The wine of Chasse-Spleen has traditionally been full, firm and long-lasting, with the customary hardness, even robustness of a wine from the *arrières côtes*, away from the estuary. The Villars' input has not so much softened it up as given it an extra element of cleanliness, richness, concentration and maturity of tannin, so that it appears less aggressive. Yet it will still last just as long. The quality is certainly exceptional today. And yet the price remains ungreedy. Château Chasse-Spleen is certainly one of the best values-for-money in the Bordeaux region. The danger is that it has now become a 'name' itself. But a stable long-term pricing policy is close to Mme Villars' heart. It is much easier to sell the best *bourgeois* growth than a minor classified growth at a more pretentious price, she says. And will she buy any more estates? 'No,' she laughs in reply to my question, 'I think I have enough on my plate for the time being.'

THE TASTING

I have made a number of visits to, and made a number of tastings of, Chasse-Spleen in recent years, in particular two major verticals, one at the château in January 1988, and another in London later in the year. Here are my notes. I have added notes on the more recent vintages, sampled at the château in April 1992.

1991   1996–2000

Medium-full colour. Quite rich on the nose. Fat and earthy. At present it is a little slight on the palate, but the addition of more *vin de presse* will give it a bit more substance. Certainly a competent result.

1990   1997–2007

Good colour. Good rich, oaky, chocolatey nose. Medium body. A little tannin. Ripe complex fruit. Long, quite profound. Certainly stylish. A typically well-made wine. Good plus to very good.

1989   1996–2005

Medium colour; that of the 1990 is more intense. The nose is ripe, if a little four-square, and the palate, though quite rich, rather dominated by hard, dry tannins. There is grip though, and the wine is long on the palate. It will need time to soften. But I much prefer the 1990. Quite good plus.

1988   **Now–2005**

Good colour. This has good depth and concentration for a 1988. It really has complexity and depth on the follow-through. Medium to medium-full. Ripe, balanced, classic. Good plus.

1987   **Now–1997**

Good colour. Has more structure and definition than most in this vintage. Good.

1986   1998–2018

Very good colour. Rich, oaky nose, concentrated, plenty of depth, not a bit tough. Full; quite tannic, lovely fruit. Excellent balance, classic, quasi-Saint-Julien sort of flavours. Ripe and rich. Long on palate. Very fine. The best Chasse-Spleen ever?

1985   **now–2010**

Good colour. Fine, elegant, fragrant nose. Lovely soft red fruit element and also oak which has a touch of cedar and sandalwood. Medium-full, some tannin. Ripe and quite rich. Rather more feminine. Not quite the power or concentration but elegant and well balanced. Fine finish. Very good and again a lot of charm.

1984   **Drink up**

Rather a light colour. Light, a little weedy on the nose. Quite pretty, quite stylish. Good oak and fruit but essentially a little slight. Drink early.

1983   **Now–2013**

Good colour. This nose has a lot of quality. A bit in between the character of 1986 and 1985 but real depth and finesse. A little closed in, in an interim, if not adolescent stage. Fullish, some tan-

nin. Good acidity and freshness of fruit. Concentrated, positive. Long on the palate. Very fine. Third best to 1986 after 1978. Better than 1982.

1982   **Now–2005**

Similar colour to the 1983. Fat, rich, ripe, aromatic nose but just a faint element of coarseness compared with the above. Elements of chocolate mousse. Quite full but by no means the biggest, most tannic, most concentrated of 1982s. Lacks the power of some. Good but not great. Does it really have the acidity?

1981   **Now–1999**

Good colour. Plump but firm nose. Slight bitterness of young wine (in January 1988) but no undue hardness or tannin. Ditto on the palate. Was drunk at lunch and was quite drinkable. Ripe, well-made. Good length. Good quality.

1980   **Drink up**

Better colour than most and nice fresh, quite plump nose. A shade dilute and one-dimensional but no spice, blowsiness or old-tea flavours. Medium body. Ripe, fresh, straightforward. Fully ready. Good for the vintage. Reasonable length.

1979   **Now–1997**

Very fine colour. Purple almost to the rim. No development. Open, ripe, damson and mulberry, almost raspberry nose. Not the backbone and youthfulness of 1978 though. Medium body. Just a little tannin. Velvety, quite cassis. Just about ready. Plump and ripe. Shows well but nowhere near the concentration and depth of 1978. Good but not great.

1978   **Now–2000**

Medium-full colour. No real signs of maturity. This is really very good indeed! Fine, classic, Cabernet nose; ripe, a little reserved like all good claret should be; plenty of depth and dimension. Fullish, a little tannic still. Concentrated blackberry flavour. Complex, classic. A lot of character and finesse. Lovely Cabernet finish.

1977   **Drink up**

(Half bottle) Very good colour for the vintage. Still fresh. Fresh nose, has fruit. This shows very well. Quite ripe, no astringency. No weakness. Positive finish. Not a lot of dimension, of course, but not bad at all.

1976   **Drink soon**

Fullish colour for the vintage. No undue maturity. Fullish, ripe, rich nose, warm and aromatic. Not a bit too spicy or blowsy. This is another very good wine for the vintage. Medium-full, ready, good acidity for the vintage keeping it fresh and vigorous. More style and better (blacker) fruit than most.

1975   **Now–1997**

Medium-full, mature colour. Quite full, ripe nose. Not too dense though there is a certain solidity, as much the old-fashioned Mou-lis/Listrac flavour as the vintage. Not quite the elegance of the later vintages but still very good, has a *puissance*. A full, fully mature wine with some of the spices of maturity. Ripe, rich, plenty of flavour. Vigorous. Has balance. Better than most, indeed not at all without merit. Long, warm finish.

1970   **Now–1997**

Good colour. Less brown than the above. Good nose, rather fine, ripe fruit – mulberries. Complex, mature but no real age, still fresh. Mellow. Fullish, ripe, rich, plenty of depth. No rustic or robustness. Yet another fine example of this vintage. Very elegant.

1967   **Drink soon**

(English bottled by Justerini and Brooks) Good colour, not a lot of brown. Soft yet still quite full, clean, not-too-spicy or weak fruit. Soft, plump, mellow. Medium body, no undue age. Ripe, no obvious chaptalization, in fact really very good. Most charming and attractive. Very nice, clean fruit. Long, quite complex. Surprisingly good!

1966   **Drink soon**

Medium-full, mature colour. Interesting nose. Touch of honey and cedar, spice in the roast chestnut sense. No fade. Medium-full, less concentrated and less vigorous than the 1970, less dimension. Finishes well but a certain element of astringency on the finish. A nice wine.

1964   **Drink soon**

(From a half bottle) Good, full, mature colour. Vigorous nose; not tough. Full body. Good blackcurranty fruit. Still fresh. This is a nice wine with plenty of depth and a mellow and charming finish. Unexpectedly good.

1961   **Now–1999**

(English bottled) Very fine colour indeed, little brown; concentrated but a slightly high-toned colour. A touch of volatile acidity. Not sweet but very ripe, blackcurrants and cream. Very concentrated fruit, delicious. Earthy, more 'old style'. Some tannin, rich but solid, concentrated fruit, ripe finish. Still will develop and improve.

1958   **Drink soon**

(English bottled) Surprisingly good colour. Dense, solid, little brown. Old wine on the nose but has substance. No age. Elegant fruit, loose knit, slightly astringent but fresh, alive, and with a good finish. No fade, no chaptalization.

POUJEAUX

To my great regret I have never sampled Château Poujeaux
1953. It is, it seems, a legendary wine. Two of these legends
will suffice. At a blind tasting of Poujeaux and the Médoc
first growths, attended by a number of luminaries in the late
1970s, Lafite and Poujeaux were unhesitatingly placed first
and second by every taster. On another occasion President
Pompidou gave a dinner at the Elysée Palace. Among the
guests was Baron Elie de Rothschild of Lafite. 'Thank you
for doing me the honour of serving my 1953,' said the
Baron. 'But it is Poujeaux,' replied the President. Only when
the bottles were brought in from the still-room, for the wine
had been served from a decanter, was Baron Elie persuaded
that he was not drinking Lafite!

I have, however, sampled the 1961, I am happy to say, and
on a number of occasions. It is surprisingly fine, and still
holding up well. More relevantly, perhaps, for speaking of
old, rare bottles without being able to share the glass with
one's audience can be a tedious pastime for both sides, I can
pronounce with confidence on vintages such as 1982, 1985,
1986 and 1988. Château Poujeaux can be ranked alongside
its neighbour Chasse-Spleen as one of the top half-dozen
crus bourgeois which would unreservedly take their place
among the classed growths if ever the 1855 Classification
were to be revised.

Gaston de L'Isle, Baron de la Brède et Beautiran, *seigneur*
of considerable lands in the Gironde, is the first recorded
proprietor of what was then known as La Salle de Poujeaux.
There is a title deed referring to this '*noble et puissant*' gentleman dated 18 January 1544. De L'Isle was also proprietor of
what is now Château Latour, and Poujeaux was still associated with this property some 60 years later, in the time of
Denis de Mullet. In the seventeenth century it seems to have
been detached, and the next recorded squire was the
Marquis de Brassier, proprietor of Beychevelle in the time of
Louis xv.

HISTORY

One can conjecture that it must have been about the time of Louis xv that vines were first planted on the gentle, gravelly slopes of eastern Moulis on a commercial scale, and a reputation began to be established for the wine. This is confirmed by the records historians have unearthed in the account books of brokers such as Tastet and Lawton from about 1750 onwards. Brassier passed Poujeaux to one of his sisters, Mme de Montmontin Saint-Herem, and it was subsequently sold to André Castaing on 18 July 1806. In the first edition of Franck's *Traité* the wine is listed second in the commune, but still under the name of Brassier. It produced 75 to 90 *tonneaux*, indicating a vineyard of a considerable size for the time.

The Castaings rechristened the wine Poujeaux, and it was passed down through successive generations of the family until 1880. A younger son, Jean-Jacques Castaing, had taken over at what is now Chasse-Spleen in the 1850s, and was also proprietor of a domaine called Gastebois. Between them the Castaings produced as much as a quarter of the commune of Moulis. In 1880, as part of an inheritance settlement, Poujeaux was divided into three parts. The new owners were Philippe Castaing, Elizabeth Clauzel, *née* Castaing, and their sister Jeanne Claverie. Eugène Clauzel, husband of Elizabeth, was co-proprietor of nearby Château Citran. The two sisters' portions subsequently passed through the female line to Pierre Marly and Louis Jacmart, but both of these estates seem to have suffered as a result of the vicissitudes which were to exact such a terrible toll in the Bordeaux vineyard between the wars. It was left to the Theil family to reunite the estate and bring it back to its former glory.

THE THEIL FAMILY

Like a great many of today's Bordelais – the Bories, the Manoux and the Moueix – the Theils hail from the Corrèze. The Corrèze is an isolated, impoverished *département* in the Massif Central, and it was from here that François Theil, from a family of local wine-wholesalers, arrived in the Gironde in the early years of this century. Theil set up on his own as a wine-merchant, and in 1903 acquired Château Le Pape in Léognan. Late in 1920 he disposed of this estate in order to purchase one-third of Poujeaux from the heirs of Philippe Castaing who had died on the 24 November. His son Jean later managed to acquire the other two segments, but it was not until 1957 that the final portion, Poujeaux-Thibaut, previously Poujeaux-Marly, was brought in and the domaine was reunified into its pre-1880 proportions. Jean Theil died in March 1981, leaving seven children. Three of them, Philippe, Jean-Pierre and François, run the domaine today.

THE VINEYARD

Château Poujeaux occupies 50 hectares which are situated in one piece at the eastern end of the commune of Moulis. Moulis lies between Margaux and Saint-Julien, but rather more inland. Much of the coastal land hereabouts, in the communes of Arcins and Lamarque, is low-lying and marshy, unsuitable for the vine. It is not until you get a couple of kilometres away from the river that the terrain rises sufficiently for the gravel *croupes* which characterize the whole of the Haut-Médoc to be fully exposed. Here, 25 metres above sea level, just about where the little local railway cuts through the vineyards, is the best part of Moulis. Here are the vines of Château Poujeaux. 'Poujeaux' is Old French for 'the high place'.

The vines are today planted in the ratio of 50 per cent Cabernet Sauvignon, 40 per cent Merlot, 5 per cent Cabernet Franc and 5 per cent Petit Verdot, both the last two varieties having been reduced in the last decade in favour of the first two. As at Chasse-Spleen, the Cabernets are today harvested by machine.

THE CHÂTEAUX AND THE *CHAIS*

There are two buildings which could be called Château Poujeaux, neither imposing, both comfortable *maisons bourgeoises*. The first is occupied by the widow of Jean Theil; the second divided between François, who is responsible for vinification and marketing, and Philippe, who looks after the vineyards and the general financial management of the domaine.

A couple of hundred metres away lies the *chai*, constructed in the early 1970s. The wine is vinified in epoxy-resin-lined cement *cuves* and stainless steel, given a prolonged *cuvaison* of as long as six weeks with frequent *remontages* (pumping over). It is not filtered. Since 1980 there has been not only an increase in the proportion of new wood employed – now 30 to 40 per cent, even 50 per cent in the most structured vintages – but also an increasingly severe selection, the rejected *cuvées* being bottled as La Salle de Poujeaux. The wine spends a year in cask before being returned to vat for fining and eventual bottling in June of the second year.

THE WINE

Poujeaux is dominant in the *vente directe* market with a mailing list of 12,000 customers, and indeed most of the second wine is disposed of in this way. The property is open every weekday afternoon and all Saturday for the travelling tourist to stop by and fill up his or her boot with a few cases of wine. The Theils also take an active interest in all aspects of the wholesale commercialization of the wine, preferring to control both domestic and export sales via a number of selected agents rather than to sell the wine on the open Bordeaux market.

All this indicates a rather higher degree of personal involvement, indeed passion, in what is in the bottle, what is eventually going to be enjoyed by the private consumer. The Theils mail a little brochure, '*secrets du château*', to their customers twice a year and this may give, *inter alia*, a tasting note on a vintage as old as 1959 or 1961. You can still buy these, at a price, if you call. I applaud this attitude. Too often, the château approach seems to imply that the wine estate's sole duty is to make the wine; beyond that their responsibility ceases. It is particularly encouraging in the case of Château Poujeaux, for the wine is built to last.

Poujeaux is a wine of deep colour and a determined structure. In most vintages it is a bigger, more meaty wine than most. Today the size is balanced by ripe tannins and concentrated fruit, and, with the introduction of a severer selection and more new oak in the early 1980s, a depth and style it did not always possess in the earlier years. The 1983 I found a little disappointing, and the 1975 suffered from a hail attack on the first day of the harvest, as well as the more usual difficulties of this vintage. The 1979 is better than the 1978 and I currently find the 1985 more engaging than the 1986. But it is a consistent property, even in the disappointing 1977 – and 1987 – making a surprisingly good wine. My friend Giles de Maré speaks highly of the 1928. Perhaps one day I shall sample this as well as the 1953. . .

THE TASTING

The following wines were in the main sampled at Château Poujeaux in January 1990. I have filled in a couple of gaps from an equally comprehensive tasting presented in London by La Vigneronne in 1987, and added notes on recent vintages sampled in Bordeaux in April 1992.

	Optimum drinking

1990 1997–2012

Fine colour. This is lovely and rich on the nose. Real depth and concentration. Very good new oak base. On the palate a wine of elegance and quality. Medium-full-bodied. Very well balanced. Very good.

1989 1997–2010

Fine colour. Good nose. Not as opulent as the 1990, but balanced, rich, positive and ripe. Medi-

um-full; good tannins; good grip and finesse. Not as fine as the 1990 but certainly good.

1988 1997–2012

Medium-full colour. Fine oaky nose. This has good concentrated ripe fruit. A reduced harvest as a result of spring hail, and it shows in the depth in this wine. This is a very good 1988. Fullish, good ripe tannins, plenty of fruit. A bigger, more meaty, more concentrated wine than many. Finely balanced. Finishing rich and ample.

1987   **Drink soon**

Medium colour. Lightish, a bit one-dimensional, but not too weedy on the nose. This is rounder and more fruity than most. Slight touch of oak. Good fruit and grip for a 1987. Fresh. Reasonable finish. Not bad.

1986   **1995–2008**

Medium-full colour. Good nose, ripe, plump and rich and quite concentrated. Good tannins underneath. A little adolescent. Medium to medium-full body. Good oak. An attractive ripe wine. It lacks a little richness at present, but will become more generous as it rounds off. Well balanced. But not a wine of great power. Finishes well. Good.

1985   **Now–2002**

Medium-full colour. Softer nose than the 1986. Plump mulberry fruit. Medium body. A little tannin. Good grip if not a great deal of concentration or power. Good oaky base. Attractive, plump fruit. Easy to enjoy. Will come forward soon. Good finish. Good complexity.

1983   **Drink soon**

Medium-full colour. Little development. I find the nose both a bit more evolved than I had expected, and less intensely flavoured. The 1982 seems a lot more promising. Slight touch of coffee on the nose. Medium body, not a lot more than the 1985. Little tannin. Pleasant fruit. But lacks a little depth and grip. No better than pleasant. Slightly disappointing. The 1985 is better.

1982   **Now–2008**

Fullish colour, a little more brown than the 1983. Full, rich, oaky on the nose, beginning to be cedary. A lot of attraction. Fullish, some tannin. Quite sturdy. Rich, spicy and concentrated, well balanced with good acidity. This shows very well. Finishes long and vigorously.

1981   **Drink soon**

Good colour for the vintage, only just about mature. Quite a fleshy nose for an 1981. Good substance. Still fresh. A very good 1981. Rich and ripe. Medium-full body. Reasonable grip. Ample, plump and even fat. But drink quite soon because it ultimately lacks a bit of zip. Very good though.

1979   **Now–1998**

Like the 1981, a good colour for the vintage. Only just about mature. This shows well on the nose. Ample, rich, good richness and depth. No lack of class. Medium-full body. A little more backbone, better acidity. On the attack slightly less charm but a fresher, more vigorous follow-through. This has plenty of depth and personality. Very good.

1978   **Now–1998**

Even better colour. No sign of age. Closed nose but in no way burly or inelegant. Full, rich, concentrated, youthful. Bigger, more masculine. Slightly hard tannins and possibly a little too solid. This is a firm wine which currently lacks a bit of generosity. Will it get astringent? A bit solid and four square. Not the style of the later vintages.

1976   **Drink soon**

Good colour for the vintage. Only a little brown and quite full. Voluptuous, ripe, aromatic nose. Slight cherry and strawberry boiled-sweet fruit plus spice. Fullish, quite fat, a little astringent on the attack but not at all without grip. In fact very fine on the finish. Long, warm and aromatic. Very good.

1975   **Drink soon**

On the first day of the harvest half the harvest was lost through a hail-storm. Full colour, a little mature. One can smell the dry tannins and slight. Lack of grip on the nose. This has not got much style or attraction. Better on the palate though. Medium-full body. Quite soft. A little astringency but enough acidity to keep the fruit reasonably fresh. Has a finish. Quite good.

1973   **Drink up**

Good colour again for the vintage. No undue age. Slight element of vegetable (braised celery?) on the nose but fruit as well. Medium body; soft mature wine, now beginning to lighten up and dry out. Good wine for the vintage. Stylish fruit, good acidity. Ripe and in 1973 terms concentrated – as well as elegant. Still has a good finish.

1970   **Now–1996**

Full colour, barely mature. Full, rich, chocolatey nose. A meaty wine, typically Moulis. A rather more old-fashioned wine. Blackcurrant fruit, quite austere. A little rigid. Quite full. Some acidity. A wine for food. Lacks a bit of class and generosity but not bad at all.

1966   **Drink soon**

Very good glowing full colour. If anything a little fuller than the 1970. Lighter – or less meaty – nose. Good refined, mature Cabernet, classy nose. More elegantly made. Better balanced than the 1970 but beginning to show a bit of age. Classy fruit. Medium-full. Still very good on the finish, even complex. Good length benefitting from the extra acidity of the 1966 vintage. The fruit is beginning to dry a little now. Was very good.

SOCIANDO-MALLET

Sociando-Mallet has been recognized for at least a decade as a wine of classed-growth quality. Yet as recently as 1969 it was almost derelict. This is the story of a single-minded passion. It is also, if proof were further sought, an example of the perfect marriage that can be achieved between a gravel soil and the Bordelais grapes.

The history of Château Sociando-Mallet is sparse in detail but intricate in complexity. A document dating from March 1633, refers to the '*terres nobles*' in Saint-Seurin-de-Cadourne which belonged to an aristocrat of Basque origin called Sociando. This family, one assumes, also owned land on the opposite bank of the Gironde estuary, at Cars near Blaye, where there is today a château called Haut Sociondo (note the difference in spelling).

In the archives there is a notice of the arrest in 1793 of a prominent royalist lawyer called Guillaume de Brochon. Brochon owned substantial property in Saint-Seurin and lived at Sociando. He fell foul of the new revolutionary regime and his estates were sequestrated and broken up for sale. A man called Lamothe bought Sociando. Neighbouring Pontoise (and Coufran further north) passed to the Cabarrus family, owners of Château Lagrange in Saint-Julien. A few residual hectares were acquired by or remained in the hands of Cadet branches of the Brochon family.

Some 40 years on we find Sociando, or Lamothe, as it is referred to in early editions of Franck, in the hands of a naval captain called Mallet. It produced 35 *tonneaux* and was rated among the top handful of properties in the village. Mallet dropped 'Lamothe' in favour of Sociando, and, as was customary, added his own name. Sociando-Mallet it has been ever since.

HISTORY

Mallet's widow sold the estate in the early 1870s to a M. Alaret – when the *encépagement* was five-sixths Cabernet Sauvignon and 'Cabernet Gris' and one-sixth Malbec – who retained it only until 1878, when ownership passed to Léon Simon. During the next 90 years successive owners included Delor the *négociants*, Louis Roullet, one-time mayor of Saint-Seurin, and François Téreygéol, deputy director of technical affairs for the INAO in the Médoc. Together with a partner, this latter gentleman bought both Sociando-Mallet and Pontoise-Cabarrus in 1959. He was responsible for an excellent Sociando-Mallet in 1961. Subsequently, he bought out his colleague, and in order to concentrate on Pontoise, sold Sociando to Jean Gautreau in 1969.

JEAN GAUTREAU

Gautreau was a wine man, but a salesman, not a wine-maker. He had worked for the Miailhe family in their *négociant* business, and based on his own account was later in Lesparre, at one time additionally working as a broker in the upper Médoc. What attracted him to Sociando? After all, he knew nothing of viticulture and vinification. It was, he will tell you, quite simply, the view. The situation of the Sociando-Mallet vineyard is superb. If you stand outside the *chai* and look east you can see for miles. The estuary unfolds beneath you about 800 metres away and stretches on either side from the fortifications of Blaye to the Point de Grave. On the opposite bank the vines of the Bordeaux area give way to those which will produce Cognac. As light, as open and as dominated by sky as a Dutch painting, the landscape is serene and magnificent. It is a place to collect one's thoughts and gird one's determination.

A sense of purpose Gautreau certainly required. The vineyard was down to five hectares of productive vines, the outbuildings were dilapidated, and the château uninhabitable. It would take him fifteen years of patient application to get everything straight. But Jean Gautreau is nothing if not painstaking. Like the wine he makes, he has a notion of the long term. From the outset his objective was to make quality, and from the start there were to be no compromises in the pursuit of the sort of oaky *vin de garde* we know today.

The first target was the vineyard. The fallow areas were tilled and drained, exposing the excellent gravel *croupe* which lies at the base of the wine. Despite a setback in 1975 when hail destroyed a large part of the potential harvest and wiped out some young vines, the area was expanded to 30 hectares by 1982 and has gradually been further increased since. With eight hectares Gautreau acquired in 1990 Sociando-Mallet can now boast 50. These are planted in the ratio 60 per cent Cabernet Sauvignon, 10 per cent Cabernet Franc, 25 per cent Merlot and 5 per cent Petit Verdot.

The next step was the *cuvier*: concrete and stainless-steel vats, plus four modern wooden *foudres* he only uses for the second wine (the name Château Lartigue-de-Brochon has now been superseded by La Demoiselle de Sociando-Mallet). The *chai* was restored, an office transformed out of a stable on the other side of the courtyard, and finally the château itself, a modest, architecturally unpretentious *maison bourgeoise*, was modernized.

THE WINE

By this time the wine's reputation was well established. Mounting production enabled greater circulation. Flattering publicity ('*pourrait figurer dans un nouveau classement*', said Cocks and Féret in their 1982 edition) helped to stoke the fires, and soon Jean Gautreau was being besieged on all sides.

Originally Gautreau had sold Sociando himself through his own small firm. He concentrated on the domestic market, allocating exclusivities to one or two clients abroad. But it then became time to expand and offer the wine to the Bordeaux *négoce*. Most is now sold through Bill Blatch of Vintex. At first his pricing policy was cautious. As a merchant himself,

Gautreau knew about *en primeur* pricing and the danger of getting so greedy that there was nothing left for those who were holding on to stock in the pipeline. The 1982, in retrospect, was cheap. It was not until 1988 and 1989, when in two successive years the price of Sociando jumped from 35 to 55 francs for its first *tranche*, that prices began to climb.

Sociando-Mallet now sells for the same price as Haut-Marbuzet and Chasse-Spleen, and that means at the same price as La Lagune and De Fieuzal: 75 francs ex Bordeaux *négociant* for the second *tranche* of 1989. This is no longer cheap.

The wine, however, is consistently good. My first experience of it was the 1970 vintage, firm but succulent, sampled some five years later. Then my notes move on to the 1975, which I saw in its infancy and have continually rated one of the successes of this uneven vintage: this is a tannic wine, but the tannins are ripe and fat. It is only now coming into its own. The 1978 and 1979, neither of which have I seen for some time, were also promising. Finally, some twenty years on, I had occasion to enjoy the 1961 twice in rapid succession: excellent!

But it is with the 1980s vintages, matured in an increasing amount of new oak – now normally entirely new for the *grand vin* – that Sociando reached its present apogee: a triumphant 1982, a lush and succulent 1985, an impressive but currently somewhat surly 1986, and a discreetly classic 1988. Sociando is a less exuberant, more austere wine than Haut-Marbuzet, another overachiever (Gautreau and Duboscq are good friends), but is similarly out of the ordinary. Neither project hints at the earthy, somewhat rustic aspects one sees in their neighbours' wines. Both are full-bodied, tannic, oaky and assertive. Both are examples of what *can* be done. The only puzzle is why it is not repeated more often elsewhere.

THE TASTING

The following wines were sampled at the château in April 1990 and April 1992.

1991 *Optimum drinking* **1997–2002**
Good colour. Oaky, rich and substantial on the nose. Quite full for a 1991. Good rich tannins. Ripe and lush. The finish is rich, even quite powerful and certainly long. Very good.

1990 **1999–2019**
Very good colour. Rich, oaky and structured on the nose. Firm, with a lot of depth and personality. Quite a lot of tannin, but these are very ripe. Fullish, concentrated, intense and with very good grip. Very good plus.

1989 **1997–2012**
Good colour. This is softer and spicier. But round and rich on the nose. Medium-full body. Good tannins. Ripe and sweet with very good acidity. But not the depth or sheer excitement of the 1990. Very good though.

1988 **1997–2012**
Good colour. Rich and oaky. More classic than 1989. Quite austere tannins but rich and ripe underneath. This has a good future. Fullish, structured, balanced and classy. Very good.

1987 **Drink soon**
Reasonable colour. Quite fat on the nose for a 1987. A little lean on the fruit side but has substance. Not bad at all. Reasonable grip.

1986 **1996–2015**
Very good colour. On the nose and the attack this has gone into its shell. Fine oak base. Very good concentration. Very good acidity. A fullish wine with quite a lot of tannin. On the follow-through the fruit comes out. Better than both 1988 and 1989.

1985 **1995–2010**
Medium full colour. Aromatic nose – more so than the 1986 – slightly higher toned. Has also closed up somewhat. A touch of balsamic spice. Fullish, rich, good grip. Plenty of depth. This has good structure and balance and plenty of personality. Good to very good. Good length.

1983 **Drink soon**
Medium colour. Rather more evolved on the nose than the above. Less grip and less freshness, and less elegance and complexity. Medium to medium-full. A little tannin still. Round and quite fat but not as good or as much future as the above. A shade diffuse. Quite good at best.

1982 **1995–2015**
Fine colour. Lovely, succulent, concentrated, ripe nose. Oaky, of course, but with real depth and fruit. Very fine. Full, rich, tannic, balanced and complete. I rate this really very highly indeed. Still has some tannin.

GRA

THE GRAVES COMMENCES A FEW KILOMETRES NORTH OF BORDEAUX (THOUGH THESE DAYS FEW VINEYARDS HAVE SURVIVED THE INCREASING SPRAWL OF SUBURBS, INDUSTRIAL ESTATES AND SHOPPING PRECINCTS), AND CONTINUES SOUTH, ROUND THE BACK OF SAUTERNES, BARSAC AND CÉRONS, AS FAR AS THE COMMUNE OF LANGON. THOUGH THE GRAVES IS LARGER IN AREA THAN THE HAUT-MÉDOC, ITS PRODUCTION IS LESS THAN HALF, AND OF THIS QUANTITY, ONLY A PORTION — THOUGH A LARGER PROPORTION THAN MOST PEOPLE REALIZE — IS RED WINE.

The best red wines are found in seven communes at the north of the region: in Pessac and Talence, in the suburbs of the city of Bordeaux, and in Gradignan, Léognan, Villenave d'Ornon, Cadaujac and Martillac, where the best vineyards form a sort of horseshoe or inverted V along the banks of the river Rau l'Eau Blanche and alongside the *route nationale* which connects Bordeaux with the south-east. In 1987 this northern part of the Graves — these seven communes above plus three others — was designated with a superior *appellation*: Pessac-Léognan.

The name Graves derives from 'gravel'. Not unnaturally, this is the base of the soil. In general, except at Pessac and Talence, the gravel is finer and thinner than at Pauillac and Saint-Julien, more like that at Cantenac. This is mixed with sand and occasionally clay, and lies at Pessac and Talence on an *alios* or iron-rich sandstone base. Further south, at Léognan — the most important of the other communes — the soil is more varied, and there is clayey limestone and clayey marl, as well as gravel and sandy gravel, and the subsoil is equally varied: large gravel boulders, *alios*, and other agglomerations.

Graves wines are generally not as full as the sturdiest Médocs, though made with more or less the same *encépagement*. They are similar in weight to those of Margaux and the rest of the southern Médoc. The wines, however, are more aromatic — a sort of roast chestnut, soft-fruits flavour — rounder and looser-knit. When mature, a fine Graves is among the most elegant wines to be found in Bordeaux, and a characteristic flavour redolent of a warm, south-facing brick wall, the so-called earthiness or '*goût de terroir*', becomes apparent.

The top wines of the Graves were classified in 1953, and this classification was confirmed in 1959.

HAUT-BRION

It is commonly but erroneously supposed that the famous 1855 Classification of the wines of Bordeaux was a classification of the Médoc only, with Château Haut-Brion from the commune of Pessac in the Graves somehow muscling in because it was too prestigious to be left out. This is untrue. It was a list of the best wines of the entire Bordeaux area, and if no Saint-Emilions or Pomerols appear, and indeed no other Graves, it was because they were not considered good enough, nor fetched high enough prices.

Haut-Brion, however, is on the list, as one of four *premiers crus*, and it can claim to be the most senior of them all – the oldest wine-producing estate in the Bordeaux area. Not only was it the first to establish itself, and not only did it fetch a much higher price than the other first growths for nearly a century after, but it is the first single-property Bordeaux wine to be mentioned in English literature.

This is Samuel Pepys's diary, on 10 April 1663: 'to the Royal Oake Taverne. . . . And here drank a sort of French wine called Ho Bryan, tha hath a good and most perticular taste that I never met with.' Pepys several times refers to claret in his diary, at least once to clarets in the plural, denoting that several alternatives were on offer, but nowhere to any other Bordeaux wine by name.

The wine at the time was more commonly known as Pontac after the name of the owner: though, as the Pontac family were extensive vineyard owners, owning Château de Pez in Saint-Estèphe among other domaines, not all the wine sold as Pontac was in fact Haut-Brion. Pontac, at the end of the seventeenth century, was almost a generic word for claret in England. Richard Ames, in a rather affected poem called 'The Search after Claret' (1691), refers to: 'sprightly Pontac . . .

the best of the sort', which no doubt refers to the specific wine, but Joseph Addison in *The Tatler* in 1708, in a piece about wine fakers, used the word as a synonym for good Bordeaux, and incidentally refers to the very deep colour, darker than Hermitage and Burgundy. (The resultant home-made brew was tasted by Addison's cat which was 'flung into freakish tricks, quite contrary to her usual gravity'.)

Haut-Brion, or Pontac, is mentioned by Dryden, Defoe, Swift and John Evelyn who, in July 1683, mentions having 'much discourse with M. Pontaq . . . owner of that excellent *vignoble* of Pontaq and O'Brien, from whence came the choicest of our Bordeaux wines'. This was in London. More interestingly, the property was actually visited by John Locke on 14 May 1677. He wrote: 'It is a little rise of ground open to the west, in a white sand mixed with gravel; scarce fitting to bear anything. The vines are trained, some to stakes, some to lathes. . . . The yield [is] 50 tuns which sells for 105 *écus* a tun. . . . Some years since [it used to be] 50 or 60 *écus*, but the fashionable, sending over orders to have the best wine sent them at any rate, have by striving who should get it, brought it up to that price.' Locke goes on to mention that the best quality 'at Bordeaux' is 'Médoc or Pontac' but very good wines can be had for 35, 40 or 50 *écus* a tun.

There are records of Haut-Brion as a place-name dating back to the fourteenth century, though at that time it is more commonly rendered D'Aubrion. Aubrion was a *maison noble* and passed through a number of hands until it was acquired in 1509 by a Jean de Ségur, an early member of the family later to be intimately connected with Lafite and Latour.

In the early 1520s it passed, according to one account, to Philippe de Chabot, one-time Mayor of Bordeaux, and a companion of King François 1 when they were taken pris-oner after the disastrous battle of Pavia. Chabot was known as the Admiral de Brion. Soon after, the property passed into the possession of the Mayor of Libourne, Pierre de Bellon. He bought land at Haut-Brion as a dowry for his daughter Jeanne, and on 23 April 1525, she married Jean de Pontac, born in 1488. According to another history, Jean de Pontac bought the *maison noble* at Haut-Brion in 1533 from a Bordeaux merchant of Basque origin, Jean Duhalde, for 2,650 francs. With this combination of land and buildings a *grand cru* was born.

HISTORY

The founder of the Pontac dynasty, a family which was to be connected with Haut-Brion until Napoleonic times, was Arnaud de Pontac, who died some time after 1518. He was a successful merchant and ship owner, and the first of his line to be mayor of Bordeaux, in 1505. His son Jean expanded the business and rapidly became one of the richest and most powerful men in the province as well as one of its largest landowners. It is Jean de Pontac who is credited with creating the Haut-Brion vineyard. Certainly for the next twenty years after his marriage he bought up neighbouring parcels of land, so consolidating the estate, and from 1549 onwards had a château constructed, parts of which (the north-eastern section of the present edifice) are still extant. He died, aged 101, on 14 April 1589, having served as notary and secretary of the province under six kings.

Jean was succeeded by his son Guillaume, and he in his turn by his son Louis, who was succeeded by another Arnaud. Each became in due course a *premier président* of the Bordeaux *parlement*, a hereditary honour in those days. Arnaud's son was François-Auguste, a man who, according to Alexis Lichine, had 'neither the temperament nor the aptitude for the legislative life'. He was more interested in wines and the money he could make out of them.

London after the Restoration was a cosmopolitan place. The king had returned from exile in France where he had acquired a taste for many things French, including wine. Britain was a potentially lucrative export market for Pontac and his Bordeaux wines. In 1666, shortly after the Great Fire, Arnaud de Pontac sent François-Auguste to London to promote his wines, where he opened up a tavern called The Pontac's Head. According to André Simon, it soon became the most important and fashionable eating house in the city. One could dine in great style for one or two guineas a head, including seven shillings for a bottle of Haut-Brion. Spanish or Portuguese wine, meanwhile, was a mere two shillings. Moreover, it is suggested that Pontac may have had an interest in the Royal Oak in Lombard Street, scene of Pepys' encounter with the wine.

The Pontac's Head, though fashionable, was not a nine days' wonder. It remained open until 1780, when it was demolished to make way for redevelopment. Its opening was an astute move; it consolidated the reputation of the property and gave London society a chance to sample fine Bordeaux in what one must assume to be the best and most honest condition. The future of Britain as Bordeaux's best customer for its best wines owes a lot to M. de Pontac.

It would seem that François-Auguste spent some time in London (Lichine says he sold his presidency), but he was back in Bordeaux in 1689. The Grand Alliance, created that year, had decreed an economic blockade of French goods. Exports of Bordeaux to England were officially outlawed. By this time his father, Arnaud, was dead, and the Pontac domaines were now shared by François-Auguste and his two sisters, Thérèse and Marie-Anne. François is said to have got into debt, and, either because of this or because he had no heirs, it is through the female line that the succession of Haut-Brion passed.

Both the daughters, impressive heiresses in their own right, married well. Marie-Anne married Jean-Baptiste de la Tresne, also a President of the Bordeaux *parlement* and later to be made a marquis, and Thérèse married Jean-Denis d'Aulède, owner of Château Margaux. At the turn of the eighteenth century, Haut-Brion had 42.5 hectares (133 *journaux*) under vines, and was producing upwards of 100 *tonneaux* of wine. In June 1705, the *London Gazette* offered '230 hogsheads of new Pontac and Margoose' (*sic*) for sale, and in 1707 'new French Obrion claret'. The wine went for £60 a tun, while ordinary Bordeaux fetched £18.

The D'Aulèdes had a son, Pierre, and a daughter named Catherine, who married Comte Louis Fumel. This side of the family seem to have acquired the share of François-Auguste, for, when in 1749 the vineyard was divided, it was in the ratio of two to one. The larger went to Fumel; the smaller section, owned by the Marquis de la Tresne, remained detached from the main body of the estate until 1840.

The Fumels remained owners of the major portion until the revolution. Louis's son, Joseph, was born in 1720, had an illustrious career in the army of the *ancien régime*, and finished up as a Field Marshal and Governor of the Guyenne, the province of Bordeaux.

He was passionate about Haut-Brion. Irked by the presence of the Tresnes, he decided to simplify things by dividing the vineyard, and in about 1780 a small portion known as the *chai neuf* became detached. Now the sole owner of what was left, he embarked on an ambitious programme of renovation to the château and the estate. The buildings were enlarged, taking on their present form, and lavishly decorated. Parks, both large and formal and small and intimate, were laid out. An orangery was constructed.

One of his visitors was Thomas Jefferson, who noted on 25 May 1787, 'The soil of Haut-Brion particularly, which I examined, is a sand in which is near as much round gravel or small stone, and very little loam'. The third of his 'four vineyards of first quality' was 'Hautbrion; belong two-thirds to M. le Comte de Femelle . . . the other third to the Comte de Toulouse, the whole is 75 *tonneaux*'.

In July 1789, after the storming of the Bastille, Joseph Fumel relinquished the Château Trompette, the Governor's fortified castle in Bordeaux, and gave away a lot of his fortune to the poor. In March 1790, he was acclaimed mayor of Bordeaux. Nevertheless, when the Terror came he was betrayed by his own butler and guillotined on 27 July 1794. His part of the property was sequestrated by the state but later reacquired by his nephew Jacques Poris, who also bought up the share owned by Joseph's sister, Mme Branne. On *9 Ventose l'An IX* (28 February 1801), Fumel sold Haut-Brion to Charles-Maurice de Talleyrand-Périgord, Prince de Bénévent, better known simply as Talleyrand, Foreign Minister of France, for 255,000 francs.

The Talleyrand ownership did not last long. It may even be that he never visited the estate, for the château had lain abandoned since Joseph Fumel's execution, and Talleyrand was busy elsewhere negotiating the Peace of Amiens and Napoleon's coronation as Emperor. In July 1804 he sold the estate to M. Michel Aîné, a banker, for 300,000 francs, and Michel in his turn sold it to M. Beyerman, a *négociant*, and Louis Comynes, a Parisian stockbroker, in 1825 for 525,000 francs. This joint arrangement was for Beyerman to 'farm' the estate and market the wine, for which he paid Comynes a rent of 25,000 francs a year, a rather curious arrangement. One might have thought a partnership, dividing the dividend according to the share of the equity, after the expenses had been met, would have been more appropriate. Anyway, it did not last, and in 1836 Château Haut-Brion was put up for auction.

At this time, Château Haut-Brion's reputation, so fine in the eighteenth century, had declined. A number of contemporary writers bear witness to this. The broker Lawton wrote in 1815: 'In Pessac in the Graves we have a growth, Château Haut-Brion, which for a long time has been classed with the three *premiers crus* of the Médoc. But for a number of years we have found it no longer up to this level. It is difficult to know what to attribute this change to. Perhaps the reputation has always been higher than it deserved. Or perhaps it is due to the poor state of the vineyard.' Others, such as Franck in 1824, stated that the vineyard was over-manured. He also asserted that the wine needed six or seven years before bottling, while other first growths were 'drinkable' after five years.

The estate, valued at a quarter of a million francs, fetched 296,000 and was bought by a Parisian banker, Joseph-Eugène Larrieu. At this time there were 91 hectares, about 35 to 40 of which was vineyard. The Larrieu family were also owners of Château Bastor-Lamontagne in the Sauternes.

Meanwhile the De La Tresne portion had also changed hands. In 1802, Tresne's heirs, the Count of Toulouse's family, had sold it to the Marquis de Catellan for a price of 70,000 francs' worth of *assignats* (paper promissory notes). Catellan died in 1838, and Larrieu was able to acquire his section from the successor Mme de Gramont, Comtesse de Vergennes, for 60,000 francs.

The combined production during the 1840s was a little over 100 *tonneaux* on average, but no sooner had the vineyard been just put into good order when the first of the three great Bordeaux disasters, oidium, took its toll. Oidium seems to have hit Haut-Brion worse than others, for Cocks and Féret, in 1868, speaks of replanting, and the wines then being trained on wires. The estate now comprised 165 hectares, of which 50 were under vines.

Joseph-Eugène was succeeded by his son Amédée in 1856, and Amédée by his son Eugène. By the turn of the century there were 56 hectares under vines, and the production was given as 100 *tonneaux* of *grand vin* and 20 *tonneaux* of second wine, sold as Bahans Haut-Brion.

The Larrieu dynasty lasted until the First World War, at which time Haut-Brion passed to Eugène's nephew, M. Milleret, and his niece, now Mme Taconet. The former bought out the latter but during the 1920s he was foreclosed by his bank, the Companie Algérienne. This firm sold the estate to the Société des Glacières de Paris. In 1924, one of their directors, André Gilbert (who according to Edmund Penning-Rowsell had made a fortune in Algeria as well as in France), decided to retire, and as his share of the company took over Haut-Brion. Shortly afterwards part of the estate's 30-hectare park and other land was sold off as building plots.

Almost immediately Gilbert initiated court proceedings between Haut-Brion and a number of properties which were incorporating Haut-Brion into their names. Most of these were successful, though the law suits were prolonged and expensive. There were, however, no proceedings against La Mission and Larrivet-Haut-Brion. The former quite obviously was situated in and originated from the same *lieu dit*, and there had previously been an unsuccessful case in the 1890s involving the latter.

It is alleged by some that the inter-war period was an unhappy time for the wine of Haut-Brion, as well as for the property as a whole. I beg to differ. I sampled the 1919 and the 1933, on either side of the Gilbert ownership, neither of them 'great' vintages, at a Wine and Food Society tasting in February 1981, and both were remarkably good for age and vintage. The others I have seen, such as those reported on later, seem eminently respectable. Some, indeed, are great. I find no lack of first growth quality at this time.

Unhappy for the wine or no, it was not a happy time for the trade. The Haut-Brion vineyard had been allowed to contract, it was now a mere 31 hectares of vines out of an estate which had been reduced to 50 hectares. By the mid-1930s, following three abysmal years, the property was again put up for sale.

The purchaser was Clarence Dillon, an American financier, and he paid 2,350,000 francs, a little over £100,000 at the rate of exchange ruling at the time. Cheval-Blanc, it is said, was also on the market, for the same very reasonable price, and so was Ausone, but Dillon and his party got lost in the fog and never reached either of these properties. He settled for Haut-Brion, comfortably accessible, now encircled by the expanding suburbs of Bordeaux.

In 1962, the company 'Domaine Clarence Dillon SA' was transferred to Douglas Dillon, former United States Ambassador and Finance Minister under Kennedy, and the president is now his daughter Joan, Duchesse de Mouchy. Dillon senior died in 1979 at the age of 96, almost as old as his predecessor, the founder of Haut-Brion.

The last 25 years have seen an extensive programme of modernization of Haut-Brion under the direction of the resident administrators Georges Delmas, who arrived at Haut-Brion in 1921, and his son Jean-Bernard, the current director of affairs, who took over in 1960.

In 1959 the *chai de première année* was considerably enlarged, and two years later the wooden fermentation vats were replaced by stainless steel, Haut-Brion being the pioneer in this respect among the top estates in the Bordeaux region. There are twelve vats, especially designed by Jean-Bernard Delmas. Unlike Latour, for example, whose vats are tall and cylindrical, Haut-Brion's are squat and measure roughly three cubic metres. Delmas's belief is that it is important for the macerating must to have as much contact with the *marc* as possible, but that one should avoid moving the *marc* around too much, as it gives the wine a herby taste. In his view the smaller, squatter vat gives a better result.

The new *cuverie* was followed by a new reception bay and *fouloir-égrappoir* in 1970, and this, four years later, by the construction of a large underground *chai de deuxième année* under the central courtyard. Meanwhile, the château itself underwent modernization and redecoration as well as cleaning of the outside stonework. Haut-Brion is now much less sombre than hitherto. Finally at the end of 1983, the Dillon empire acquired neighbouring La Mission.

THE CHÂTEAU

The château itself was built in 1550 and enlarged in the 1740s and is familiar to anyone who has seen the label on a bottle of Haut-Brion. In the courtyard outside, a male and female stone lion crouch on guard, and inside the first thing one notices is a large portrait of Eugène Larrieu in the hall, and the fine dining-room table. Also in the hall is a plaque commemorating the fact that Clarence and Anne Dillon equipped the château as a hospital and gave it to the French for use during the Second World War.

The building faces west, away from the vineyard, and lies in a small *parc anglais*. Deeper in this garden are tennis courts and a swimming pool, and further on is the back entrance to the house of Jean-Bernard Delmas and his wife Annie, a modern building with a Roman-style atrium and a fine collection of modern paintings.

THE VINEYARD

Haut-Brion is in Pessac, some five kilometres from the centre of Bordeaux, and lies adjacent to the Bordeaux-Arcachon road. Across the road, technically in the commune of Talence, though both vineyards dovetail in with one another, is La Mission-Haut-Brion, once perhaps part of Haut-Brion, certainly a dependency in the Middle Ages. These are the nearest major vineyards to the heart of the city, and it is not for nothing that it should be these two, virtually alone, which have been able to withstand the march of concrete from the city outwards.

This is the northern end of the Graves area, and the part which was once the most prosperous vineyard in the Gironde. Now Mérignac is the airport, Pessac and Talence are suburbs, and most of the important properties lie in Léognan, twenty kilometres to the south, on the edge of pine forests of the Landes.

The vineyards are on a small mound, some 27 metres above sea level. The gravel is particularly deep here, as much as eighteen metres in places, though there are parts of the vineyard where clay is also predominant. The vineyard straddles both sides of the main Bordeaux-Arcachon road and railway, overlooked by a larger water tower. Some 70 per cent, however, lies in one piece surrounding the château and the *chais*. There are now 42.5 hectares of vines, planted in the ratio of 55 per cent Cabernet Sauvignon, 20 per cent Cabernet Franc and 25 per cent Merlot, a higher Cabernet and lower Merlot percentage than a few years ago. The mean production is now 130 to 150 *tonneaux*.

Delmas, one of the most able and respected wine-makers in Bordeaux, was one of the first to see the implications of the right root-stock as well as of clonal selection of the vines. For the last fifteen years, and more particularly since 1977, he has been conducting experiments to produce the best clone for each of the three grape varieties, the one most suitable to the soil of Haut-Brion. To this end, in collaboration with the INRA (National Agricultural Research Institute), he has planted a collection of specially selected strains, some originating from old Haut-Brion stock, others developed by the INRA. In total there are some 550 individual clones, planted in 1977, now coming into fruition. These researches will enable poor-quality clones and sterile plants to be progressively eliminated, and these will be replaced by those proven to be best adapted to the Haut-Brion soil.

Similar research into rootstocks have discovered that the best for Haut-Brion is Riparia Gloire de Montpellier, followed by rootstocks numbered 420-A and 3309, though the latter is never used for Merlot as it produces a lot of *coulure*. Number 101–14, widely used in Pomerol for gravelly-clay soil, does not work at Haut-Brion because the soil is too well drained. This rootstock does not produce well in a dry soil.

THE *CHAIS*

At Haut-Brion the first task after the grapes have been picked is to work over every berry on every bunch and to eliminate not only any leaves which might have fallen into the harvesters' shallow wooden trays but also every green, rotten or split grape. This *triage*, as it is called, is done on a series of large stainless-steel shallow trays, mounted on tables.

Thereafter there is a complete elimination of the stalks by means of the *égrappoir*, the berries are pumped into the stainless-steel vats, and the must is allowed to begin its fermentation. At Haut-Brion this is done at a relatively high temperature, between 30° and 33°C, and the must allowed to macerate with the skins for about a fortnight. A high temperature, in Delmas's view, aids extraction of colour and flavour from the skins of the grape, without obtaining too much tannin. All Haut-Brion is matured in new oak.

HAUT-BRION BLANC

The reason Haut-Brion's white wine did not appear on the original Graves classification is that the production was so small that Dillon expressly requested that it be left off. Some three hectares are normally under vine, half Sauvignon and half Sémillon, and the wine is fermented and aged in new wood and bottled fourteen to sixteen months after the harvest.

It is a wine which is rarely offered on the Bordeaux market, and not often seen on wine lists except in the top local restaurants. My experience is almost entirely confined to bottles I have enjoyed in private houses and châteaux in Bordeaux, for I have only recently owned any myself (the 1983, I am happy to say). In 1977, two-thirds of the vines were uprooted for replanting, and thus the average age is currently low. The quality of the wine, however, is very high indeed. Until recently, the old 'serious', i.e., vinified-in-oak, white Graves were the triumvirate of Chevalier, Laville and Haut-Brion itself. Haut-Brion Blanc was usually the best of the three, a wine of a quality equivalent to the best of *grand cru* Burgundy.

BAHANS-HAUT-BRION

Haut-Brion used to be unique among the top Bordeaux properties in producing a non-vintage wine, sold exclusively on the Bordeaux market by the firm of Nathaniel Johnston. This was marketed when ready for drinking, and was a relatively soft, round, fragrant wine, typically Graves, typically elegant but possibly lacking a little power and depth. It sold for the equivalent of a classed growth in a medium-to-good vintage (such as a 1979), and it was certainly not over-priced. In 1976 a vintage Bahans was launched as well. I said at the time that I felt that to have both a vintage and a non-vintage Bahans would lead to confusion, and I urged Haut-Brion to find an alternative name for one of them. What they did, as from the 1982 vintage, was to cease production of the non-vintage wine. Bahans, therefore, is now just like Les Forts de Latour and the rest, a proper second wine.

THE VINTAGE RED WINE

The word to sum up the wine of Château Haut-Brion is elegant. One could also add charming and consistent. If Haut-Brion does not have the *réclame* of Lafite or Pétrus, or fetch the same sort of astronomical prices at auction, that is the fault of the consumer. This ignorance is our good luck. On several occasions in recent vintage tastings, Haut-Brion has come out top. Moreover it is normally ready for drinking somewhat sooner than the bigger wines of Pauillac and Saint-Julien. It is a wine I myself have regularly bought, and I confess it to be one of my favourites.

Haut-Brion is always a balanced, distinguished wine, perhaps more typically 'Haut-Brion' than typical of the vintage, and one which is accessible at an early age. When young it has a rich, elusive, soft-fruits, violets and truffle flavour. When mature this is underwritten by the typical 'warm-brick' earthy spiciness which is characteristic of Graves. Haut-Brion is a wine which is quite unlike its neighbour, La Mission. Of all the other top Graves, I find it is Domaine de Chevalier with which it has most in common.

THE TASTING

In 1989 I was delighted – privileged, indeed – to be invited to a splendidly comprehensive vertical tasting of not only the red Haut-Brion but the rare Haut-Brion Blanc. This was organized by my friends Jack and Thelma Hewitt in Vermont, at the height of the fall colours. My everlasting thanks to them for a marvellous opportunity to taste such splendid wines. The younger vintages were sampled in 1992.

HAUT-BRION BLANC

Optimum drinking

1990   1999–2020
Lovely fruit on the nose. A wine of real breed and complexity. But it appears to be a little more delicate than the 1989. Very subtle, very clean, very concentrated. Long and ripe, but perhaps for perfection it could have had just a bit more acidity. Fat and very good indeed.

1989   1998–2020
Unlike the Laville I find this better than the 1990, though it is early days. Honeyed, oaky, very rich and opulent. But at the same time very well balanced. A wine of real depth and complexity. Fine.

1988   1997–2010
This is ripe and plump and fullish. There is a certain adolescent hard edge about it at present. It doesn't have the succulence of the two more recent wines. Yet there is plenty of depth and grip here. I am easily prepared to give it the benefit of the doubt. Very good at the very least.

1987   Now–2000
Straw-gold colour. Delicate nose. No sulphur. A mixture of slightly herbal Sauvignon (but not grassy) and a gentle Sémillon fatness. Developed in the glass. By no means unripe. Medium body. Good oak. Though the attack is a bit neutral the follow-through is better. This has more to it than I expected. Will still develop. Round and gently fruity. Intriguing; elegant. Good but lacks a bit of real richness. Best on the finish.

1986
Not declared. Though the wine seemed to me to be delicious in cask, it did not evolve as well as was hoped. In retrospect they feel they did not

vintage early enough. There will not be any Laville either.

1985   Now–2008
Crisp, youthful colour. A certain amount of built-in sulphur on the nose. Fuller, more vigorous, more concentrated and more depth than the 1987. But rather more adolescent. Good oak base. This has a restrained aloof elegance I really like. Long and complex on the finish. Getting more honeyed and ripe as it developed. Excellent.

1984   Drink soon
Slightly more colour than the 1985. Lightish nose, somewhat four-square. On the palate there is quite an ample, gently oaky attack, but then a lack of dimension on the follow-through. Yet gentle and charming on the finish. Reasonably ripe. Light/medium body. Certainly enjoyable. Good but not great.

1983   1995–2015
Slightly less colour than the 1984. Like all these the nose is still hidden: aspects of plasticine. This is quite a big wine but very adolescent. I can't see a lot of richness and concentration at first. The follow-through is rather better. There is depth here; the wine is still very fresh and youthful. On the finish the wine is gently oaky, flowery and – finally – rich. A lot of potential here but it is difficult to see really how much. Got better and better in the glass. Inherently a more austere, masculine wine than the 1985. At present it is less seductive. As it evolved became very subtle and elegant. Lovely. Indeed, I suspect, better still.

1982   Now–2005
Still a youthful green-gold colour. Round and nutty on the nose. Beginning to open out. Less sulphur than the younger vintages. Fresh appley-

peachy fruit. Good concentration and grip. Good oak base, honeyed. This is a ripe, fullish, promising wine which will still develop. Very good indeed but not great.

1981   **Now–2001**

More colour than the 1982 – mid gold. Leaner nose, more vegetal. Some nutty oaky aspects underneath – but kernels of fresh nuts not roasted. This is beginning to evolve. Once again best on the finish. Quite full, quite rich. Stylish, still youthful. Not as potentially rich or ample as the 1982 but good.

1980   **Drink soon**

Quite a deep golden colour. An evolved nose, without a great deal of depth, lacking fruit and concentration. Similar palate. A bit of built-in sulphur – which makes the wine and its finish a bit coarse – not a lot of dimension. Ready soon and should be drunk. Only quite good.

1979   **Drink soon**

Quite a deep golden colour. If anything, this is less opulent even than the 1980; similarly lacking fruit and concentration. This I find rather thin and disagreeable. Less grip than the 1980. Less body. Rather tired vegetal flavour. Collapsed in the glass. Disappointing.

1978   **Now–1997**

Deep golden colour. Rich, opulent, new oaky nose, plus an aspect of dry Sauternes. Very ripe. Quite different to the 1981–1979 trio. An intriguing flavour. Both developed and fresh with quite high acidity. Ripe on the palate but not as opulent as the nose. A bit disjointed. It doesn't quite come off. Yet round, fresh, fat, and ripe. Good but not great.

1977   **Drink soon**

Light golden colour. Interesting nose. Fruity and nutty. No fade. Still fresh. Medium body. A little built-in sulphur on the attack, but this is not evident on the finish. Good richness and fruit – a surprising amount for an off-vintage. Much more enjoyable today than the 1980 and 1981, and always better than 1979.

1975   **Now–2012**

Quite a deep golden colour – more than 1971 and 1970. Very concentrated nose. Still closed at first. High quality. Ripe and sumptuous. This is still in its infancy. Fat, rich, concentrated, still powerful. A lot of wine here. High class but the 1971 is even superior.

1974   **Drink soon**

(Bottled as Les Plantiers de Haut-Brion) No Haut-Brion Blanc was declared this year: this is it. It was only released recently. Light golden colour. Fresh herbal nose. Higher toned. No

built-in sulphur. Youthful. Elegant. This is quite a different style: supple, touch of sweetness, aspects of Condrieu. Intriguing. Still fresh. Rather good.

1971   **Now–2020**

Medium golden colour. Excellent nose. Very concentrated. Lovely rich opulent fruit. Still youthful. This is a great wine. Very rich and concentrated. Real depth and class. Lovely firm Sémillon. Voluptuously ripe, yet masculine and austere. Very exciting.

1970   **Drink soon**

Medium golden colour. A more evolved nose than the 1971. Neither as concentrated nor as ripe. Nor as vigorous. Medium body. Seems to be loosening up and drying out. Basically an elegant ripe wine but it was always lighter and less concentrated than the 1971. The acidity now shows on the finish.

1969   **Drink soon**

Quite a deep golden colour. Good clean, ripe, reasonably fresh, dry Sauternes-style nose. Touch of honey. This has maturity and depth. Seems firmer and fresher than the 1970. Beginning to dry out a little but still finishing positively. Good. Most enjoyable. In its prime the 1970 was a wine of much more depth and concentration though.

1967   **Drink up**

Lightish colour, still fresh. A little built-in sulphur on the nose. The wine seems to be lightening up. Not as exciting, it seems, as the 1969. Some depth but the fruit has lightened up and there are now rather lean, even metallic, vegetal aspects.

1966   **Drink soon**

Deep golden colour. Very curious nose. Solid, clumsy, oily and volatile. Not mushroomy or maderized but certainly off in some way. A full coarse wine, with some built-in sulphur. Try again.

1962   **Drink soon**

Good colour, still youthful mid-gold colour. Lovely nose, seems sweet. Good fruit, velvety, long, complex. Dry Sauternes again. A medium-full, round, fragrant wine with a little sweetness on the attack. Showing a little age and built-in sulphur. Good fruit, good class; a gentle, feminine wine which now needs drinking reasonably soon. Yet a long positive finish. More delicate than most of these wines. Fine.

HAUT-BRION

1991   **1996–2004**

Good colour. Very good nose. This has richness and ripeness and above all generosity. Medium body. Good tannins. Has dimension and complexity, and good fruit and length. There is real first growth class here. Very good indeed.

1990   1998–2020
Good colour. Fine nose. A little closed, but ripe, rich, complex, classy. This is excellent. Fullish; very good tannins; very good oak. Lovely fruit. Very intense and concentrated without being a blockbuster. Classy, persistent finish. Very fine indeed.

1989   2000–2030
Medium-full colour. Lovely nose. This is ravishing and complex and has very lovely ripe, lush, fragrant fruit. Real class, depth and intensity. Fullish, opulent, very mature tannins. Excellent harmony. Very fine grip. *Grand vin!*

1988   1998–2018
Good colour. The nose has gone into its shell a little. Yet, coaxing it out, one can see, if muted, the breed of Haut-Brion quite clearly. Medium-full body. Lovely fruit. Very well balanced. The follow-through is rich and complex and ample, and the wine finishes very long and subtle. Very fine mulberry fruit. More classic than the 1989 and 1990. Fine quality.

1986   1996–2015
Good colour. The tannins are somewhat aggressive but there is richness underneath if a lack of real concentration and charm at present. Not, in essence, a very big wine, though it is somewhat raw at present. Similar on the palate. Quite full, some tannin. Good breed, length and balance on the finish. A fine well-made 1986. Good cedary follow-through. For a Graves a triumph. Got better and better in the glass. More substantial than the 1985 and preferred by many to it.

1985   1995–2015
Good colour. Very fine concentrated nose. A lot of depth and breed here. Medium-full, even soft – certainly gentle – but a very complete wine. Lovely succulent ripe fruit, with the Merlot showing. Long and complex. Heaps of class and subtlety. High quality. Fine character. Not as big as the 1986 but I find it more interesting.

1984   Now–1997
Surprisingly good colour. Stylish nose, good new oak; surprisingly supple, fruity and charming. Medium body. The tannins are rapidly getting less green and unripe as it softens up. The acidity is keeping it fresh. A little lean, inevitably, but shows real first growth class. Ready soon.

1983   Now–2015
Fine colour. Full, rich, very complex nose. Better on nose than palate. Cedary and almost chocolatey. Fine ripe red and black fruit mixture. There is concentration and succulence here. High class.

Quite full, concentrated, very good tannins. There is an intensity of flavour on the attack and a vigour which at first shows a size and character greater than the sum of both 1985 and 1986. Yet it seems to tail off in the glass. I have seen better bottles, and on occasion preferred it to the 1982. It will evolve sooner than I expected if this bottle is any indication.

Bahans 1982   Now–2000
Medium-full colour. Lightish, essentially loose-knit nose bolstered up by *vin de presse*. Some new oak underneath. Medium body, not much tannin but rather herbal and grassy on the attack. I prefer the 1984 Haut-Brion: it has much more breed. An astringent touch. Somewhat disappointing.

1982   1997–2020
Very full colour. Full, rich nose, but rather closed, dense, and adolescent compared with the 1983. Yet on the palate, on this occasion, more exciting. And this has the extra substance and power. Rich, fat concentrated fruit. Balanced by good fresh acidity. Long on the palate. A really fine complexity and freshness on the finish. Excellent.

1981   Now–1997
Surprisingly deep full colour – looks like Pétrus! – some development on the rim. Soft, but intense, mature, complex nose, very smoky and autumnal and as it evolved showing ripe Cabernet more than Merlot. Most attractive. Medium body. Now mature. Not a great deal of grip but round, soft, complex and full of charm. A wine of breed, and one of the best examples of the vintage.

1980   Drink soon
Good colour for a 1980, now mature. Good nose for the vintage, lighter but a little similar to the above. Not as ripe or as intense, and now drying somewhat: getting a little pinched. This is now showing signs of getting to the end of its useful life. Medium body. Cheerful uncomplicated character. Soft and still fresh.

1979   Now–2000
Very fine colour, still seems to be a long way from maturity. At first a little closed, rigid and four-square, but has plenty of fruit and character within. A fullish wine, which while remaining a little inflexible on the attack, is now evolved on the finish. Somehow a bit disjointed, while the follow-through is round, ripe, complex and balanced, perhaps it essentially lacks a little real breed for great wine, though certainly fine.

1978   Now–2000 plus
Fullish colour, but more forward (less vigour) than the 1979. Good class and fruit on the nose.

A mature wine now. Somehow on the follow-through and finish it doesn't quite sing really aristocratically. Just a little less full than the 1979. Very fine and elegant. Long and complex with a fine finish but lacks just a little complexity on the follow-through for great.

1976   **Drink soon**

(Magnum) Good, very full mature colour. Aromatic nose, not typically either Haut-Brion or Graves. As much Merlot as Cabernet. Ripe and fresh and smoky at first but less impressive after a short while in the glass. Fullish for a 1976, like most a little short, showing a bit of astringency. Evolved in a downward direction in the glass. Drink while it retains its vigour. Reasonable finish.

1975   **Drink soon**

Almost identical colour to the 1976 (but then that was from a magnum). Good slightly burnt and roasted nose. Smoky. No aggressive tannins. These are a bit more obvious on the palate. There is fruit underneath, even concentration on the follow-through, but like so many 1975s the fruit is lightening before the tannins are softening, and I now get an element of uncleanliness in these tannins. Yet still has length. I would drink this now. Good but not great.

1974   **Drink soon**

Good colour for the vintage, better than the 1973. Not a bad nose at all for a fifteen-year-old wine of an off-vintage. No age, no attenuation. Fresh, good oak elements; has fruit. On the palate the wine is quite full, certainly still vigorous, and there is a ripe cedary attack. The finish is less exciting, getting a bit mean and insipid. But a fine effort for the vintage. Surprisingly good.

1973   **Drink soon**

Medium-full, mature colour; no undue age. Evolved nose; round, the fruit has dried up a little. Medium body. Soft and pleasant, quite ripe attack but thinner, less vigorous and more astringent on the finish. Yet no undue age. Still has class – and charm.

1971   **Drink reasonably soon**

Good full mature colour. Interesting nose when first poured but light and a little dull as it evolved. There is a lack of intensity here. Medium-full, a mature, soft wine, which shows good class and balance. Yet there is something lacking: real vigour and concentration – compared with the La Mission for instance.

1970   **Now–2000 plus**

Similar colour, surprisingly, yet this has more vigour. Much more vigorous on the nose. Elements of chocolate mousse, blackberry, red fruits

and cedar. Rich and complex. This is a very fine mature claret. Full and vigorous. Rich, even meaty, rather more structured than later vintages would suggest. Lots of fine ripe fruit, well balanced with acidity on the palate. Long, complex, concentrated: quite powerful and aristocratic on the attack. Very fine – but not ethereal enough on the finish for great.

1967   **Drink soon**

Medium-full colour. No undue age. Attractive, plump, fruity nose, though without great complexity or richness. Fullish for a 1967. Good fruit if no great depth. Has style and no sign of decay. Shows well. Still sweet.

1966   **Drink soon**

Good colour. Interesting smoky nose, quite high-toned. Well matured. More so by comparison with the 1967 than I would have expected. Slight roast-chestnut touch. Medium to medium-full body. More vigorous and intensely flavoured than the nose would suggest but a fully matured wine. Not exactly rich but quite refined. The level of acidity shows. Getting a little herbaceous on the finish.

1964   **Drink soon**

Medium-full colour; browner than the 1966 on the palate. Complex nose, nutty, slight touch of caramel. More vigour than the 1966. More richness and sweetness. Fuller than the 1966. Richer too. A more solid wine but neither four-square nor short-and-finishing-astringent as is the case with some 1964s. Quite concentrated. Good fruit. Good richness and vigour on the finish. A very fine 1964 for the Médoc and Graves. More class than the Latour (which would make it the best in the region).

1962   **Drink soon**

Very good colour, remarkably purple for the year. Round, ripe nose but softening now. Fuller and chunkier on the palate than the nose would indicate. Some tannin. Quite a powerful wine. A little dense perhaps, and so lacking breed. But long and vigorous. Perhaps it lacks a little class; perhaps it was a bit stewed. I have seen better. Improved in the glass.

1961   **Now–2010**

Fine full mature colour. Full, rich, very concentrated on the nose. Similar palate. A vigorous powerful wine, which evolved considerably in the glass. Roasted. Still very youthful. A lot of concentration and depth here. Will go on getting better and better. Excellent.

1960   **Drink soon**

Lightish colour, well matured. Soft, attractive aromatic, cedary-*marron glacé* nose, still sweet. Not attenuated. Medium body. This still has vigour, and it certainly has plenty of class. Good fresh fruit. Acidity showing on the finish but not lean. Long. Fine for the vintage. No decay. Yet went downhill quite fast in the glass.

1959 See note
Fine vigorous full colour. Some maderization on the nose. Not undrinkable on the palate. Full and vigorous. Ripe, concentrated and sweet. Will still last well. Quite a powerful wine compared with later vintages. Other tasting notes suggest one of the best wines of the vintage – and a wine which will still last well.

1957 Drink soon
Another very fine colour. Slightly pepperminty on the nose. Big and dense. Lacks grace but clean. Yet on the palate this is not lacking merit. Powerful, solid, full, rich. Still youthful. Still sweet. May still round off to its advantage. A very good 1957. Will it get astringent soon? Holds up well in the glass. Lost density and acquiring roundness.

1955 Drink soon
Medium-full, mature colour. No undue age. Lovely nose. Complex, fragrant, fresh, subtle and full of breed. Very high class. Medium to medium-full body. Getting towards the end of its useful life but lovely complex fruit. Real character. Still very long and subtle on the finish. But did not last too well in the glass.

1953 Drink soon
Good fullish colour. Quite an evolved nose but a lot of class here. Much less vigorous and on this occasion less exciting than the 1952. Yet the breed is evident. Round, sweet, complex and delicate. Still with life on the finish. Lovely fruit. Not as ethereal as it was six months ago at a 1952/1953 comparative tasting but a great bottle.

1952 Still plenty of life
Full, vigorous colour. This is a fine, vigorous 1952. There is a fresh slightly herbaceous, high-toned aspect to the nose. Yet a lot of depth and quality. Quite full. Cool Cabernet fruit, still very blackcurranty. Good grip. Very good vigour. In contrast to the 1953 this is a better bottle than six months ago, very fine indeed. Indeed excellent. Ripe and succulent. The best bottle of Haut-Brion 1952 I have seen. Very fine indeed.

1949 Will still last well
Very full colour, still intense. Quite an old nose. Maderized and a little porty. Getting rather astringent. Some volatile acidity. Another bottle six months ago was also past its best but still enjoyable. I would like to see a bottle in its prime.

1948 Will still last well
Full colour, fine, classy, vigorous nose, a slightly chunkier, drier, less succulent wine than the 1952. Quite powerful. Good grip. More austere. Good Cabernet fruit. Long on the palate. Opened out somewhat as it developed, softened, got rather more classy. Fresh, long. Very fine indeed in its slightly solid way.

1947 Will still last well
Very fine colour. There was just a faint touch of maderization on the nose as it developed but essentially very ripe, rich and vigorous. No astringency. High-toned of course. Fullish, the usual fresh but cooked fruit with high acidity aspect of many 1947s. Slightly inflexible. A little hard even. But despite this rigidity, vigorous and fine. Will still last well (was still very fine an hour later).

1945 Will still last well
Full colour. Very classic, rich concentrated nose. Vigorous and powerful. Essence of Cabernet. Aristocratic. Very fresh and delicious. The best Haut-Brion 1945 I have seen. Full on the palate. Absolutely crammed with fruit. A masculine wine but triumphant class. No undue muscle. Almost sweet. Very, very concentrated. Lovely. Still youthful. Perfect condition. *Grand vin*.

1943 Will still last well
Very good colour. A slight earthy, astringent touch to the nose. But there is nevertheless high quality underneath. This shows very well. There is, inevitably, less concentration than the 1945 but good depth nevertheless. Old vine fruit. No undue age. Rich, classy still long and fragrant. Very fine indeed. Will still last. Gentle and aristocratic. Quite lovely. Held up very well in the glass. Not at all overshadowed by the 1945.

1934 Will still last well
Very fine full colour. Still barely mature. Smells of hot chocolate. Elements of burnt toffee and spice. Full, quite dense and solid. This was always, I think, quite a tough, tannic wine. Yet rich and concentrated and vigorous. If it lacks a bit of sheer class for great, there is a lot of vigour and rich fruit still here. Still plenty of life. Very fine.

1929 Will still keep well
Very fine full colour. Amazing nose. Great concentration of fruit but in a more supple, flexible sense than the 1945. Complex, concentrated. Great finesse. Fabulous! Still very vigorous. Medium-full body, smooth and velvety. Quite high acidity so still very fresh. Lovely plummy fruit. Very long on the palate. The palate not quite as magnificent as the nose though, but a great finesse and quality of fruit. *Grand vin* without doubt. Will still keep very well.

1928   **Drink soon**

Very fine full colour. Still barely mature. Liquorice, leather nose, almost a touch of Syrah. Firm dense and masculine. Yet high quality. Still vigorous. A very full, tannic (still), masculine wine. Sweet, spicy, exotic, complex: a gypsy of a wine. The most vigorous yet the most evolved, in the gamey sense on the palate; and the most interesting on the finish, compared with the 1929 and 1934. Excellent. Almost *grand vin*. The 1929 has more finesse though. And this did not hold up so well in the glass.

1926   **Will still keep**

Excellent colour. Full but round, concentrated and somewhat spicy – cinnamon, allspice – and red fruit. Very Graves. Still gently vigorous. Firmer, more bitter chocolate-coffee as it evolved. A chunky slightly cooked wine on the palate. The fruit seemed to have dried up to a certain extent. But this seemed less apparent as it evolved. Good concentration. Rich, meaty. Masculine (without being dense – perhaps I really mean austere) and classy. Vigorous finish. Held up well in the glass. Good with food.

1924   **Drink soon**

Very fine full colour, barely mature. Quite a big, full, solid chunky nose, somewhat aggressive. A certain astringency. Sweet and porty. Quite full. Good attack but lacks a bit of concentration on the finish, and a bit of power to carry it through.

Not exactly short, just tailing off a little. Dried up somewhat as it evolved. Probably always, like some 1952s, a little tough for its own good.

1921   **Will keep**

(Recorked at the château, 1987) Medium-full colour; no undue age. On the nose there is a touch of filter-papery dryness, hiding the fruit. Opulent and perhaps slightly overblown underneath. On the palate medium-full, velvety, very harmonious. Lovely succulent fruit. A wine of class, seductive charm and great luscious attraction. A cornucopia of fruit. Very, very long. Excellent. Still real vigour. *Grand vin*. Very strange that it is so unpromising on the nose and so fabulous on the palate.

1920   **Drink soon**

(Magnum) Full colour. Roast chestnut aspects to the nose but a certain astringency, and as it evolved a certain maderization and oxidation. A full, old, quite tough wine. A bit inky now. Yet good elderberry, leathery fruit underneath. Shows a bit of age but still enjoyable.

1918   **Drink soon**

The cork fell into the bottle. Medium colour. Still vigorous. Fresh nose though. No oxidation. Soft, elegant, fragrant wine. Medium body. Still very classy. Some age, naturally, but still fresh and no astringency. Very fine. Still sweet. A lovely wine. Held up well in the glass.

LA MISSION-HAUT-BRION, LA TOUR-HAUT-BRION AND LAVILLE-HAUT-BRION

The 1855 Classification and its rather less official predecessors were based on firmly practical criteria: the price a wine could command. Less tangible or verifiable data such as the reputation of the property or the opinions of experts – though these did have a bearing – were not what mattered most. What really counted was money.

No doubt, as in 1855, the brokers in the 1960s looked at the opening prices of all the relevant châteaux year by year. Today, they would also, one assumes, take the auction price of mature wine into account as well. If they were to do so, they would find one property in a sort of limbo somewhere in the gap between the eight first growths (the current five plus Pétrus, Cheval Blanc and Ausone) and the next category: Château La Mission-Haut-Brion. La Mission's opening price is always half as much again as the better second growths and about three-quarters that of the firsts. If ever there is a reclassification, the judges will be in somewhat of a quandary. In which category will they put it? To put La Mission with the seconds would be demeaning the château but to include it among the firsts would seem to diminish them. There are more problems to reclassification than coping with irate proprietors whose wine has been downgraded!

It is assumed that the vineyard of La Mission originally formed part of Château Haut-Brion itself. This is hard to establish for there is no deed of separation of the former from the latter. As I have written, Haut-Brion as a place name dates back to the fourteenth century.

HISTORY

The original Pontac, Jean, bought land from 1533 onwards to consolidate his estate and lived until 1589. It seems, on the face of it, unlikely that he would be selling off on the one hand whilst he was acquiring with the other. Nevertheless, what is now La Mission-Haut-Brion already had a separate existence early in the seventeenth century. I would suggest this always was independent of its illustrious neighbour.

The first records show ownership in 1650 in the hands of Dame Olive de Lestonnac, widow of Antoine de Gourges, a president of the Bordeaux Parliament. She bequeathed to Jean de Fonteneil, directeur général of the clergy of Bordeaux, '*icelle maiterie d'Aubrion, située en la paroisse de Talence, dépendant de l'hérédité de la dite Olive de Lestonnac et une chambre basse a loger les valets et ensuite un grand chay cuvier garni d'un fouloire en pierre de taille, une cuve assez grande and une autre moyenne et deux autres petites cuves et 22 journaux de vignes . . . et cinq autres ou environ de bois taihis . . . plus six journaux de vigne ou environ.*' ('This farmhouse . . . situated in the Parish of Talence . . . together with a lodging house for the farmhands and also a large wine shed containing a tiled crushing vat and a large storage vat (and various others), in all 22 plus 6 *journaux* [approx. 10 hectares] of land under vines.') It goes on to note that it adjoins the property of M. de Pontac on the west.

It was not until 1664 that her heirs finally handed over the property. In 1682, one of the Fonteneil's successors, Monsignor Louis de Bourlemont, transferred the property to R.P. Simon, Superior of the Congregation of the Priests of the Mission.

The *Prêcheurs de La Mission*, a missionary order, were commonly known as the Lazarites, having been formed in 1634 by St Vincent de Paul and established in the College of St Lazare in Paris. The Bordeaux branch enlarged the vineyard by clearing a small wood and built a small chapel, Notre Dame de La Mission, which was consecrated on 26 August 1698. From then on, the vineyard and its wine were known as La Mission-Haut-Brion. The château itself was constructed in 1713.

In the eighteenth century, the wine was well established as a second *cru* of the parish. Unlike Pape-Clément, whose wine seems to have been reserved for ecclesiastical throats, La Mission must have been traded on the Bordeaux market, for Wilhelm Franck quotes prices of 1200 to 1300 *livres* per *tonneau* (higher than anything from the Médoc apart from the first growths) for La Mission in mid-century.

The Lazarite era lasted until the Revolution. La Mission was confiscated by the State and judged a *bien national*. On 14 November 1792, it was acquired by Martial Victor Vaillant for 302,000 *livres* in paper money (about a third that in actual silver). This was a high price and exemplifies the standing of the estate. At the time there were some fifteen hectares of vines and the production was in the region of 25 *tonneaux*.

Vaillant was succeeded by a M. Ledoux and a man called De Catalan, whose name appears in the Tastet and Lawton archives in 1815. He was followed by Celestin Coudrin-Chiapella in 1821. Coudrin was the adopted son of a rich Genoese, whose name he also took over. He is described as a '*colon*', a repatriated colonial – he was born in Louisiana in 1774 – and was also a *négociant* in Bordeaux. He and his son Jérôme managed other properties, particularly Cos d'Estournel, on behalf of absentee owners and seemed to have had a considerable reputation as progressive viticulturists and wine-makers.

Franck, in 1845, lists La Mission as a fifth growth, producing 30 to 40 *tonneaux*. In the text, somewhat more up to date in terms of the production figures than the classification, Chapella (*sic*) is listed as producing 10 to 12 *tonneaux* in Pessac and 45 to 50 *tonneaux* in Talence. The vineyard, divided by the Bordeaux-Arcachon railway, straddles both communes. These production figures seem a little excessive. By 1868, having failed to make the 1855 Classification, La Mission is down to 30 to 40 *tonneaux* in total and is surpassed in that year's Cocks and Féret by Pape-Clément.

Around 1880, La Mission passed to the Société Anonyme des Etablissements Duval of Paris and in 1895 was bought by Monsieur F. de Constans of the Bordeaux firm of Schröder and de Constans, later bought by Cruse. Eight years later, de Constans sold to a M. Victor Cousteau. The property was still fifteen hectares, producing 30 *tonneaux*, but since the late 1860s had been selling for the same price as the Médoc second growths.

THE WOLTNERS

The modern era for Château La Mission-Haut-Brion begins with the Woltner family and, in particular, with Henri Woltner, son of Frédéric, who bought the property in 1919. Henri Woltner was one of the most dedicated and engaging working château proprietors in a part of the world not short of 'committed' owners.

Henri's father, Frédéric, was born in Riga in 1865 and was originally a partner in the firm of Schröder and de Constans. As such, he was a friend of both de Constans himself and of Victor Cousteau and is said to have agreed with the latter that if he ever contemplated selling La Mission to give him (Woltner) first refusal. In 1916, Cousteau decided to retire and duly did as they had arranged. The deal was completed three years later.

La Mission, after the war and in the hands of its new owners, was in a parlous state according to Harry Waugh, a good friend of the late Henri Woltner. There were no old vines and the whole property had been neglected for some years.

Frédéric Woltner soon set matters to rights. One of the things he did, revolutionary in its time, was to install vitrified-steel fermentation vats, the first two of which were set in place in 1926, followed by ten others acquired from a brewery in 1950. The idea behind these, as with the later stainless-steel vats now commonplace even in the top growths of the Médoc, was to control the temperature of the fermentation. In the old days, this could only be done by suspending sacks of ice in the must, a cumbersome and expensive exercise as well as having the inbuilt disadvantage of diluting the wine. With a metal vat, a simple cooling system involving running cold water down the outside can be easily applied. Moreover, being metal, the heat of the fermentation is more quickly dissipated in the first place.

Frédéric Woltner had two sons, Fernand, who was born in 1899, and Henri, born in 1902. There was also a daughter who became Mme Le Gac. It was Henri, a graduate of Bordeaux University where he studied oenology, who was the active partner, first working alongside his father, then taking over on Frédéric Woltner's death in 1933. He was a passionate believer in '*fermentation froide*'. *Froide*, of course, is a relative term in this context, denoting a control at 26° to 28°C rather than a free reign above 30 degrees. Too high, say up to 35°C, and there is a major danger of volatile acidity as the fermentation yeasts get killed and vinegar bacteria are free to feed on the unfermented sugar. No wine-maker would ever allow a temperature as high as this.

Research has substantiated, however, what the Woltners pioneered. By lowering the temperature marginally, a reduction in the loss of volatile, flavour-producing trace compounds is maintained. These remain in the wine, increasing its complexity. Moreover, by its very nature, a metal vat is easier to keep spotlessly clean. It is inert and, unlike wood, does not get eaten away by the acid in the wine, so creating little crevices where dirt and bacteria can thrive.

CHÂTEAU LA TOUR-HAUT-BRION

Meanwhile, adjacent and exclusively in the commune of Talence, lay the small property of La Tour-Haut-Brion. The first records show that at the time of the Revolution it belonged to a Mme de Saige. It is first mentioned in Cocks and Féret in 1868 when it is listed third in order of preference in this commune and produced 7 to 8 *tonneaux*. The owner then was a Louis Uzac. Uzac sold to a M. Parent who, in his turn, sold it to Victor Cousteau, the transaction having taken place between 1886 and 1893. In this edition of Cocks and Féret, La Tour is listed first in the parish and the production (exaggerated in my view) is given as 30 *tonneaux*.

When Cousteau bought La Mission ten years later, he decided to abandon the cellars at La Tour and make all the wine at La Mission, though he continued to live, no doubt more peacefully, in the château of La Tour. From this time, La Tour has, to a greater or lesser extent, been the second wine of La Mission as M. René Rondeau, who is engaged in a history of these two properties and to whom I am much indebted for this and other information, has shown. A contract, dated 1917, with the firm of L. Rosenheim et Fils, who had undertaken to sell the wines of both properties for a five-year period, states, *inter alia*, 'the seller has complete liberty to make the wine of the two châteaux at his convenience: he will select, at his choice, the product of the two châteaux, it being understood simply that one quarter of the total will be labelled Château La Tour-Haut-Brion . . .'

When Cousteau, on his retirement, sold La Mission to Woltner, he retained La Tour as his home but, no longer having the facilities to make wine, he entered into an '*en fermage*' agreement with Woltner. In exchange for running the vineyard and making the wine, Woltner would take a third of the production. This was marketed through the family firm of F. Woltner et Cie, later to be called Woltner Frères and now Société Woltner, for a long time domestic agents for Pol Roger Champagne in France. (On the death of Fernand Woltner, the Paris office was closed but the firm still maintains its activity in Bordeaux.)

Cousteau died in 1923 and his widow, Marie, found herself with few friends among the rather stuffy society that existed at the time. One of these was her neighbour Mme Woltner, herself not a Bordelaise and, more in contact with the outside world, unconcerned to keep in step with restrictive Bordeaux opinion. This friendship blossomed to such an extent that in 1933, on Marie Cousteau's death, Mme Woltner found herself the owner of La Tour-Haut-Brion.

Henri Woltner died in October 1974, on the eve of his fiftieth vintage at La Mission, and overall direction than passed to Francis and Françoise Dewavrin, Mme Dewavrin being the late Fernand Woltner's daughter. The two Woltner brothers had had a son and two daughters between them but the son, a distinguished civil servant, did not wish to be actively involved and Henri's daughter lived with her husband in Switzerland. The two widows, Hélène and Yvonne Woltner, resident in Paris, continued to take a keen interest in the estate.

Francis Dewavrin comes from a very ancient northern family, the Dewavrins having been *sénéchals* of Flanders in the Middle Ages. He was originally trained as a chemist. Dewavrin divided his time between his retail wine business in Brussels and Paris, Bordeaux and California, where he and his wife established a vineyard at St Helena in the Napa Valley. The day-to-day affairs were entrusted to the *régisseur* Henri Lagardère who joined Henri Woltner in 1954, and his son Michel, a trained oenologist.

Dewavrin continued the good work of Henri Woltner and, in an era where proprietors began to climb into aeroplanes to conduct tastings of their wines in San Francisco, Tokyo and Buenos Aires, was not shy in making sure that La Mission was esteemed the world over. He established that the red wine should sell for 75 per cent of the price of the first growths and gradually raised the price of the white until, in 1982, it was selling for 170 francs, comparable with a *premier cru rouge* or the best of white Burgundy, and equivalent, in real terms, to more than three times that of the 1975.

Sadly, the difficulties of getting family agreement in the way the domaine was to be run and the profits distributed led to the Dewavrin-Woltners deciding to liquidate their interests. La Mission and La Tour were put up for sale. At the end of 1983 they passed, so to speak, across the road. The purchaser was Château Haut-Brion; the price 75 million francs plus over 20 million for the revenue from the 1982 and 1983 vintages. Lagardère took his *retraite* and responsibility for the wine passed to Jean-Bernard Delmas.

However, it should not be suspected that La Mission is, or is now intended to be, in any way amalgamated into Haut-Brion. The two estates and the five wines they make between them will be kept entirely separate. La Mission continues to retain its old character, big and powerful, as distinct from its neighbour's softer elegance. The new owners intend to keep it this way. Delmas is a very astute wine-maker and I have no doubt that changes and improvements have been made (some of which are outlined below) but the inherent personality of La Mission, that which comes from the soil and its particular microclimate, will be preserved.

THE VINEYARD

The vineyard of La Mission straddles both sides of the Bordeaux-Arcachon railway and is therefore in both the Talence and Pessac communes, though most is in the former. In part, it is contiguous with that of Haut-Brion. There are some eighteen and a half hectares planted in the ratio 60 per cent Cabernet Sauvignon, 5 per cent Cabernet Franc and 35 per cent Merlot. The La Tour vineyard comprises four hectares. It is planted in more or less the same proportion but does not contain any Cabernet Franc. Total production of red wine over the past twenty years has averaged about 65 *tonneaux*. Of this, between 50 per cent and 70 per cent was bottled as La Mission. The rest became La Tour, itself also a *cru classé* of the Graves. Under the new regime, this second wine aspect has been dropped. La Tour is now a wine in its own right from the original pre-Cousteau-amalgamation section of the vineyard surrounding the La Tour château.

Both these vineyards, as well as that of Haut-Brion itself, lie on a mound of gravel 25 metres above sea level, overlooking the surrounding terrain. Though, as this is increasingly built on with high-rise offices and flats, one should perhaps say that these overlook the vineyards. The bed of gravel here is particularly thick and rests on a subsoil of coarser gravel and *alios*.

CHÂTEAU LAVILLE-HAUT-BRION

The estate produces a third wine, a really top-quality white Graves, a wine which, at its best, can be ranked with top *grand cru* white Burgundy. Part of the original La Tour vineyard was found in the early 1920s to be unsuitable for the production of quality red wine as it had less gravel and more clay in the soil. This was planted with white grapes in 1923. The first vintage was produced in 1928 – incidentally, with a La Mission label. In 1931, this was changed to 'Château Laville, Terroir du Haut-Brion, Premier Cru de Graves'. Later this was reconciled to Château Laville-Haut-Brion. Today, some seventeen *tonneaux* per annum is made from 60 per cent Sémillon and 40 per cent Sauvignon.

THE CHÂTEAUX AND THE *CHAIS*

While there is no Château Laville there is, of course, both a Château La Tour and a Château La Mission. The former is the more elegant building being a smallish, square, two-storey mid-nineteenth century construction with a mansard roof. It is now an hospice. The La Mission building is less attractive but more individual. At one end is the tiny chapel of La Mission, no longer used as a church and now a museum. Rather incongruously stuck to this is the château itself, the other end of which connects with part of the *chais* which bend back to form a U. Surrounding the château is a small, neat garden and the whole is enclosed by a wrought-iron fence. A large new *chai* was constructed in 1987, and all cellar operations were transferred there just before the vintage.

Frédéric Woltner was a great collector. Prompted by Notre Dame de La Mission, he built up a collection of holy-water stoups which decorated the hall and staircase of La Mission. He also acquired a number of Bacchus figurines and a superb assembly of Delft dishes. These were sold at Christie's after the Haut-Brion purchase.

THE WINE

La Mission is a distinctive wine. It is totally different from its neighbour Haut-Brion, and it is the fullest and sturdiest of all the Graves *crus classés*. During the Woltner-Dewavrin period, the harvest took place noticeably later than at Haut-Brion. The wine at La Mission was given a particularly long maceration with the skins and because of the temperature control, the fermentation itself was drawn out over a number of weeks, coinciding, when things went well, with the malolactic fermentation.

All this produced a wine of exceptional depth of colour and one of great tannic austerity when young, in its way similar to Latour. For years young La Mission was habitually unyielding, hard, tough and seemingly too dense for comfort. One occasionally began to wonder if there was not too much maceration in the first place, whether the wine was not, in fact, too 'stewed', whether it had enough long-tasting fruit within it to last until the hard edges had softened and the tannin broken down.

Eventually, patience was rewarded and a wine of considerable depth, character and complexity began to emerge as if from a chrysalis. I have heard many opine that La Mission is every bit as good as Haut-Brion and, further, that they even prefer its style. One can see similarities between these pairs. I, too, have found vintages when La Mission is superior but there are others where the verdict goes the other way.

RECENT QUALITY

Was there a small trough in the quality of La Mission at the end of the Dewavrin era, a descent from the very high standards we have come to accept? Not in the 1982 and the 1983 vintages but in the 1976, 1978 and 1981, and in the white wine as well as the red. Over the past decade I have made several comprehensive tastings of La Mission-Haut-Brion. On each occasion, the feeling of those present was that the 1960s vintages were in general superior to the late 1970s. The 1960s had real concentration and richness. The late 1970s, seemingly, were just solid, a little unyielding and four-square. Was it just the age of the wines – the later wines still being in their adolescence? Was it too much *vin de presse*, a criticism I have heard levelled at La Tour-Haut-Brion? Interestingly, this period was precisely when the services of Professor Emile Peynaud were used as consultant. The new owners will suggest that the slump occurred during the last few years of the Woltner era, in particular between 1967 and 1974. The Woltner brothers were old and unwell. There was a lack of supervision, and the wines suffered from an excess of volatile acidity. This I accept. But I add that high volatile acidity has been noticed in stocks of both the 1961 and 1962. From the arrival of Emile Peynaud in 1974 these volatile acidity problems were eliminated, but, with the exception of the 1975, I continue to maintain that there was a lack of severe enough selection.

The white wine, too, as the price mounted, declined in quality. The 1975 and 1971 are magnificent and the 1970 and 1976 also extremely good as was the 1978; but the 1979, 1980 and subsequent vintages, though some seemed fine in cask as far as one could judge, suffered from that old white Bordeaux failing – over-sulphuring. They also seemed to have been deprived of new oak. When Jean-Bernard Delmas took charge of the new Laville 1983, he was appalled to find that it had so much sulphur in it he did not have to add any more until it was bottled eighteen months later – and there was hardly a new oak barrel in the entire *chai*.

Thankfully, the new regime put a stop to all this. The white wine is once again splendidly concentrated, full and rich, with a firm but subtle oaky background from the – now new or newish – barrels in which it is not only matured but fermented. Normally, the new oak percentage is now roughly 75 per cent; the 1987 has been given 50 per cent. It is a wine of delicate structure and Delmas does not want to risk over-oaking it. Recently, for the first time, skin contact techniques have been applied.

The new *cuverie*, completed in time for the 1988 harvest, have also allowed Jean-Bernard Delmas to bring the red wine-making up to date. A battery of twelve double '*auto-vidante*' stainless-steel *cuves* have been installed, six on each side. The upper vat in which the alcoholic fermentation takes place, now, for the most part, at 30° to 33°C, is 180 hectolitres in capacity. The lower, into which the new wine is decanted afterwards, contains 125 hectolitres. Here, the malolactic fermentation will ensue. *Remontage* is controlled to take effect with the minimum amount of oxygenation to the wine and occurs several times per day, unlike at Haut-Brion where this takes place once every twelve hours.

Will all this change the character of La Mission? Precisely what aspects come from the soil and what from the wine-making? This is an argument which has occupied the correspondence columns of wine magazines for years. My guess, drawing a parallel with Cos d'Estournel before and after the arrival of Bruno Prats, and with the wines Delmas had made at La Mission over the last few years, is that the essential La Mission will not change but the elements will become less brutal and better defined. Moreover, there will continue to be the same sort of difference between La Mission and Haut-Brion itself as there is, say, between Latour and Pichon-Lalande.

THE TASTING

Laville-Haut-Brion

The following notes are an amalgam of two tastings, one at the château in April 1992, and another which took place in 1987 and was organized by Liz and Mike Berry of La Vigneronne, plus a couple of other recent notes.

Optimum drinking

1990   1999–2020

Fatter, richer and a little more oaky on the nose than Haut-Brion Blanc. Ripe, seductive and honeyed. Closed on the palate. Very good grip. A lot of depth. Fine.

1989   1995–2005

Soft and rich but a little awkward at present. Lush and spicy, but without the grip of the 1990. This will evolve soon. Very good, but not great.

1988   1995–2003

Rich, gently oaky, fragrant, elegant nose. Medium body. Ripe, honeyed, good fruit. A feminine wine more on the lines of 1986 (elsewhere – they didn't make a 1976) than 1985. Complex but very good rather than great.

1987   Now–1998

Soft, round and gentle; an elegant wine though at present a little overwhelmed by its sulphur. A little slight, but not inconsequential. More depth than I expected.

1986

Not declared.

1985   1995–2015

This is full, rich and concentrated. Gently oaky; ripe, honeyed, concentrated and subtle. Lovely fruit. Medium-full body. Still in its infancy, but has a depth and concentration which promises very well indeed.

1983   Now–2000

Rather lumpy and ungainly on the nose: toffee, petrol and sulphur. A little more stylish on the palate. Rich and fat, full-bodied but somewhat coarse. Doesn't sing. And I don't think it ever will. Haut-Brion Blanc is much, much better.

1982   Now–1996

Quite full if not a bit heavy on the nose. Sulphur evident but quite plump and fruity underneath. Fullish, firm, possibly a little hard. Sulphur masks the fruit. Does it lack a bit of zip? Indeed, a bit of fruit? Not much evidence of new oak.

1981   Drink soon

Quite a lot of sulphur on the nose. Medium · body. Essentially dull. An absence of fruit on the attack though better on the finish. Again, not much new wood.

1980   Drink soon

Softer nose, more fruity but perhaps a little one-dimensional. A little oak. The fruit seems to be drying up on the palate though. Not bad but not exciting.

1979   Drink soon

A lot of built-in sulphur on the nose, rather more than the above. Again seems to lack fruit and depth. Medium-full, not a lot of oak. Again dull.

1976 Now–2000

Quite a deep golden colour. Big, full, fat nose, even an illusion of noble rot. A bit, rich wine, somewhat like a dry Sauternes. Fat, honeyed, slightly oaky. Voluptuous but balanced with acidity. Plenty of character. Ready but will keep well. Lovely.

1975 Now–2000 plus

Crisp, full colour. Classic, full, ripe, nutty, concentrated nose. A wine of really fine profundity. Rather more oaky than the above. Only just ready. This is a brilliant wine. Real depth and enormously long on the palate. Quite marvellous. Here the 1975 is better than the 1976. The opposite is the case at Chevalier.

1973 Drink soon

This wine followed the 1979 at the La Vigneronne tasting and was a great relief. Deeper colour, very fine, ripe, honeyed nose. All you would expect. Very Sémillon, even an element of botrytis. Fully mature, if not a bit of age. Ripe, elegant, balanced, medium-full-bodied. Very good.

1971 Now–1998

Very golden colour indeed. Lovely rich Sauternes-type nose, quite high in alcohol, but rich, vigorous and delicious. Full. Individual, very ripe, very good grip. Luscious but dry. Very fine. Will still keep well.

1970 Drink soon

Less colour. On the nose this is ripe but not that positive, especially after the 1971. Medium body, stylish and balanced, but not *that* rich or concentrated. Good but not great.

1968 Drink soon

Mature but not aged colour. Delicate flowery nose, venerable but still fresh and with plenty of interest. A little lean but not without fruit. Quite high acidity. Elegant.

1967 Drink soon

Ripe nose, broad and quite full. Some age, a little drying up on the palate. Less obviously elegant than the 1968 but riper and fuller. A bit dull and four-square perhaps but still has a positive finish.

1966 Drink soon

Fine colour, full but not aged. This has more personality than the 1970. Complex on the nose, mellow and fragrant. On the palate the wine is fullish, still vigorous, rich and spicy. Very good indeed.

1965 Drink up

Light but elegant nose. Still quite fresh and complex. Showing a little age, not unexpectedly but, like the 1968, not at all without interest. Indeed, this is fuller and fatter and finishes better. Surprisingly good.

1964, Crème de Tête Drink soon

Really quite deep colour. Firm nose with elements of petrol like an old Moselle. Fat and full, not quite as complex as I had hoped. Ripe and honeyed though but lacks a bit of zip. Yet reasonable length. Four years ago I had a chance to compare the 1964 *crème de tête*, a selection produced occasionally prior to 1964 (but not since) with the 'ordinary'. It was fatter, richer and more vigorous.

1962 Now–1996

Quite a deep colour. More botrytis on the nose. Less firm, more ample. A soft, plump, rich, fat, honeyed wine which is now beginning to show a little age. Yet there is plenty of fruit and a better finish than in the above. This is the superior vintage.

1947 Drink soon

Deep golden colour. Like the 1971 this smells like a Sauternes: rich, full, concentrated and honeyed. Quite full, still reasonably fresh. A fat wine, aromatic and slightly exotic in flavour. Voluptuous yet finely balanced. Delicious.

1945 Drink soon

Old golden colour. The nose has more of an old Sauternes than an old Graves, as so often. Elements of toffee and grilled nuts; drying out slightly as it developed. Medium-full body, quite dry. Complex fruit well balanced by acidity which is now tending to dominate. Fresh, appley aspect. Long on the palate. Certainly fine quality.

1945, Crème de Tête Drink soon

Similar colour, slightly lighter. Much drier nose, no old Sauternes, even an element of petrol like an old raspberry, plus a herbal element, ivy, camomile. Nevertheless, full, rich and indeed sweet on the palate. Deceptive. An old wine, complex, interesting. Quite high acidity. But more alcohol and less finesse than the above, but richer. Held up better in the glass though.

La Mission-Haut-Brion

In January 1989, I sampled the following splendid range of the wines of Château La Mission-Haut-Brion in New York at a tasting set up by Daniel Oliveros. *Merci, mon ami*! The more recent vintages were sampled in Bordeaux in April 1992.

1991 1997–2001

Medium-full colour. Ripe, complex and structured on the nose. A soft, unaggressive wine but one which is balanced and stylish and has depth and grip. Shows well.

1990 1997–2019

Medium-full colour. Good ripe Cabernet fruit on the nose. Not a blockbuster but plenty of depth. This is certainly fine: fullish, very ripe, very good grip and intensity. Lovely opulent Fruit.

1989 2000–2025

Better colour than the 1990. Full nose, rich, intensely concentrated. Not a trace of excess tannin. Full and rich on the palate. Oaky. Fine concentrated fruit. Very good grip. Ripe, rich, harmonious. Not far short, in its different way, from the Haut-Brion.

1988 1998–2018

This is excellent. I am not sure I don't prefer it to both the above. Full colour. Lovely, concentrated, classic, blackcurrant fruit. Full body. Good ripe tannins. Real breed. Very well balanced. Splendid. A lot better than 1985 and 1986.

1986 1995–2007

Fresh, youthful colour. Quite full. A little tannin on the nose. Attractive fruit. Quite lush and elegant, with a bit more backbone than the 1985, but lacks real concentration and power.

1985 Now–2005

Medium colour. Youthful, plump, ripe, oaky wine without a great deal of depth. Seems more insignificant than I found it at a 1985 tasting the previous week. This has the attraction of youth. New oak. Good appealing fruit but not the depth and backbone nor the grip. Forward and pleasant but not as good as the 1986.

1984 Now–2000

Medium to medium-full colour, still immature. Nose will evolve. More to it than the 1980. This is a better wine. Ripe, good oak. Good acidity. Quite rich for a 1984. Not too obvious acidity. Finishes well. Will still improve. Cool, but certainly a success for the vintage.

1983 Now–2006

Medium-full, youthful colour. Closed, fat, rich, chocolatey nose. Fat, rich, ripe, caramel, liquorice, bitter chocolate and coffee. Medium-full body. Fat and almost roasted. Tannin and chocolate mousse. Long. Fine but not really great.

1982 1997–2017

Full, rich, immature colour. Dumb, tannic, young wine. Rich though. A bit adolescent. Fullish, tannic. A big, fat, rich, chocolatey wine. Good grip. Not too solid or dense. Long. Dumb. Has adolescent, rubbery elements and finishes in the glass with a flavour of prunes. Very fine but not great.

1981 Now–1999

Medium-full, youthful colour. Not a great deal of nose. Medium-full body, ripe, not too tannic and tough. This is not too ungainly. Blackcurranty, reasonably balanced. Has charm. A good wine without being great. Inherently soft.

1980 Drink soon

Medium colour. Slightly hard nose, lacks fruit and richness. A little rigid. Medium body, reasonable ripeness but not a great deal of charm. One-dimensional. A little hard and ungenerous but a good effort for the vintage. Cabernet leafiness. Tougher but coarser than the 1984.

1979 Now–1997

Medium to medium-full colour. Just a little maturity. Again a fundamental lack of richness on the nose. This has got some merit, there is an element of new oak. Some fruit but not a great deal of depth or dimension.

1978 Now–2007

Another fine, full colour, barely mature. Chunky, chocolatey, tough but rich and toffee-caramelly flavours. A powerful, muscular, tough wine, with a certain evidence of *vin de presse*. A certain hardness but not too tough. Needs time but rich and concentrated and good quality. A very good 1978.

1977 Drink up

Medium colour, quite brown. Vegetal, dilute, old. Weedy and herbaceous. Now lightening up. Light, thin and one-dimensional. Artificially sweet. Acidity shows. On the way down.

1976 Drink soon

Medium-full, mature colour. Somewhat sweet and bland, attenuated nose. Medium-full, somewhat bitter and astringent. This lacks charm and grace. Not special.

1975 Now–2014

Fine, full colour, tannic mature. Lovely nose. This is really *grand vin*. Ripe, concentrated, distinguished. Not a bit of solidity. Real depth though. Fullish, complex, long, delicious. Great character. Lovely. Cool and classy. This is totally un-1975 because it lacks the chunkiness. Unexpected breed and balance for the vintage.

1974 Drink up

Medium-full colour, not a great deal of maturity. Plummy, slightly earthy nose. A certain lack of real richness. A bit hard and ungenerous. A little stewed and tough. Fuller and firmer than the 1973. Not undrinkable though.

1973   **Drink up**

Medium, mature colour. Herbal, vegetal nose. Touch of celery. Medium body. This lacks class and character. Something a little spurious and sweet/sour and coarse about it. Like a cheap Chinese meal. Pretty dreadful.

1972   **Drink up**

Medium-full, mature colour. Fat, minty nose, leafy. Ripe, quite solid. Rich but somehow a bit heavy and four-square. Lacks concentration and zip. Good but not great. Will still improve? Medium-full, a little tannin. Better than the 1973 and 1974 but not really that good. Very good for the vintage is the best I can say for it.

1971   **Drink soon**

Medium to medium-full colour, some maturity at the rim. Quite a lot of breed. Slightly hard and certainly unforthcoming on the nose. Green and ungenerous. Sugar lurks underneath. Medium to medium-full body. A little rigid. A bit sweet, with a leafiness. Lacks charm. Disappointing for the vintage. Is this typical?

1970   **Now–2005**

Fullish colour, little maturity. Fat, rich, nutty nose. Ample, some age – more than the colour would indicate. Soft, voluptuous, very ripe tannins. Aromatic. Sweet. Lovely. Long and classy. Fatter, riper, sweeter and richer than the 1975 but not as fine. Very good length. Like a 1947 but younger. A touch of excess volatile acidity?

1969   **Past its best**

Medium colour. Open, dilute, somewhat blowsy and faded nose. A light wine. But again not too bad. Getting a little astringent. Better than 1963 but older.

1968   **Drink up**

Medium, mature colour. Nose is a bit dried, and was never *that* exciting, but there is at least some merit (or was). Riper and richer than the above. More structure. This was a success for the vintage. Reasonable vigour if a little sweet. Excellent effort. Better than the 1969.

1967   **Drink soon**

Medium to medium-full colour; light at the rim but not unduly brown. Interesting nose. Not a blockbuster, but smoky. The fruit is not super ripe but there is enough of it and it is balanced by acidity. More structure than the 1960. Medium body, a little astringency. This is a pleasant wine but lacks real concentration and depth. A bit one-dimensional but straight and fresh and reasonably balanced. Not bad. A pleasant wine without being in any way really good.

1966   **Now–1999**

Fullish mature colour. Ripe and rich, elements of volatile acidity – or suggestions of it. Aromatic. Rich and spicy and very, very ripe. Fullish, good grip. No astringency. Long, fat. Fully mature. Fuller and more tannic than the 1964. Slightly riper but to me less class and attraction. Long, complex and classy. Better than the 1970.

1964   **Now–1997**

Full, barely mature colour. Full, fat, concentrated but masculine nose. This has a lot of depth but has an austere quality. Tough, firm, full and masculine, some tannin. Will still develop. Concentrated. Fine grip. Long. A claret-drinker's wine. A certain astringency on the finish. Very ripe. But long and complex and very classy. I prefer the 1966 though.

1963   **Drink up**

Medium-full, mature colour; a little vegetal and weedy on the nose but a great deal fresher than the 1977 for instance. A little sweet on the palate. No great distinction, but better than the 1969. A very good wine for the vintage.

1962   **Drink soon**

Medium-full colour; not a great deal of maturity. A bit dumb on the nose at first. Typical La Mission solidity, even density. Good but not great. Medium-full, some tannin. Not too solid, though there is a little tannin. Riper than the nose suggests. Well balanced. Good class. Good length.

1961   **Now–2000**

Fullish colour, just about mature. Fine, classic, really aristocratic, cassis nose. Great breed, really classy. Rich, fresh, full, still tannic. Still youthful. Ripe and seductive. Enormous depth and concentration and complexity. A wine of structure but not *too* much density. Earthy on the finish. Very good indeed but not a great 1961.

1960   **Past its best**

Medium-full, mature colour. Soft, aromatic nose. Something just a little fading and inelegant about it. Medium body. Slightly spurious sweetness. Short on the palate and one-dimensional. Reasonably fresh but coarsening up. Some decay as it developed. Past its best.

1959   **Drink soon**

Full colour just a little sign of maturity. Rich, voluptuous nose. More evolved than the 1961. Lovely fruit. A certain threatening incipient acidity. Ripe and succulent. Roasted and fat. Not the class or concentration of the 1961 but a very fine wine nevertheless.

1958   **Drink soon**

Fullish colour, a little sign of maturity. Ripe,

soft, mellow nose. This is another surprisingly good off-vintage. Lightened in the glass but plump and fresh. Much much better than the 1960 and still vigorous.

1957   **Drink soon**

Full, mature colour. Full, masculine, even solid, even austere nose. But has depth underneath. Full, concentrated, certainly has a family resemblance with 1950; rich and complex, very good grip. Solid. Rather too monolithic. Too muscular. Too much press wine? A fine 1957 though.

1955   **Drink up (see note)**

Fullish colour but no great maturity. Still barely mature, concentrated nose. Ripe and leafy, no great dimension but good class. Now beginning to show a bit of age on the palate. Slightly dirty elements on the finish. This is a bit astringent. Fullish. A bit chunky. Was better ten years ago. Yet still rich and concentrated. Coarsening rather than drying out. I've had better – and more vigorous – bottles. This has always been one of the best 1955s.

1953   **Drink soon**

Medium-full, mature colour. Fat nose, ripe, with a tendency to H2S. Round. Good grip, seductive and warm. A vigorous wine still. Very fine but not really with great class. Will still keep. Still sweet. Has more charm than the 1952.

1952   **Drink soon**

Medium-full colour, now a bit mature. A little rigid on the nose. But ripe and rich. Full, a bit of tannin but ripe and sweet and succulent, if not really complex and concentrated. Yet a great deal less tough and both fleshier and fresher than most 1952s.

1951   **Drink up**

(Recorked 1979) Fullish, mature colour. Open, aged, dilute nose. Not as aged on the palate. A certain hardness or greenness in the background. Fresh, pleasant but lacks real concentration. Quite good. Will still keep. Not a great wine but a good effort, particularly for a really off year.

1950   **Drink soon**

(Recorked 1979) Very good, mature colour: full, rich and glowing. Rich, concentrated, berry-like nose, a little dry and clenched. A full, solid, tannic wine, both sweet and somewhat astringent. Ripe but slightly earthy. Good but not great. Still vigorous though.

1949   **Will still keep well**

Very fine, full, barely mature colour. Almost black still in the middle. Fine nose. Aristocratic. This is in a class of its own. Ripe and concentrated but really so. Full, tannic, porty sweet. Structured and brilliant. Long. Aristocratic, lovely. Marvellous

blackcurrant extract. Great wine. Superb. Complete. The best of the tasting.

1948   **Will still keep well**

Fullish colour. Fine, aromatic, cedar and roast chestnut nose. This has not only ripeness and depth but breed. Fullish, mature, classy. Not a bit too solid. This has finesse and concentration and personality. Delicate for La Mission. Intensely flavoured. Generous and plump. Very high class.

1947   **Drink soon**

Medium-full, mature colour. Ripe and sweet and voluptuous and rich. Velvety. Soft and plump and smoky and sweet. Good concentration but has neither the breed of the 1949 or the backbone of the 1945.

1946   **Drink soon**

(Recorked 1979) Medium-full, mature colour. Firm but a touch dry and pinched on the nose; yet good quality underneath. Just perhaps a bit solid. Still seems quite youthful. This is surprisingly classy and clean. Medium-full, rich and complex. Amazing for a rarely-encountered off-vintage which I expected to be totally past it.

1945   **Now–1998 plus**

Fullish, mature colour. This is perhaps the oldest on the nose of the 1949, 1947, 1945 trio. Yet also very classy. Fuller, more aristocratic and more structured than the 1947. Indeed the firmest of the three on the palate. Long, very fine grip. Great class. A certain coolness and austerity about it. More subtle. Quietly confident. Lovely subtle finish. Great wine again.

1943   **Drink soon**

Fullish, still barely mature colour. Ripe, mulberry bouquet; good acidity, not too tough, but there is something a little four-square about it? Again some hardness evident on the nose as it evolved. Yet fullish, quite vigorous and ripe. A good but not fine vintage, yet a success for La Mission. Ripe and balanced. Good grip and depth. Very good but not great. Lacks a bit of personality but no undue density.

1940   **Drink soon**

Lightish, mature nose. Fragrant but old nose, light but at least not too brutal. Yet an element of vegetal hardness. This is not a vintage to be reckoned with. Better than the 1951 though. Medium body, quite sweet. Reasonable vigour if a bit one-dimensional. A touch of astringency surging up. Average quality.

1937   **Drink soon**

(Recorked 1979) Another fullish, mature colour. Again a bit tough on the nose, there is a hardness within. A brutal, tannic, solid wine. Quite good concentration though. Mouth-filling astringency on the attack but richer on the follow-through. An austere wine. Also beginning to dry out.

1936   Drink soon
(Recorked 1979) Medium-full, mature colour. The nose has a touch of attenuation in its favour. Has acidity, it seems but not concentration. Good but not great. Will not improve. Better on the palate than the nose though. Amazing vigour for a 50-odd-year old-off-vintage.

1935   Drink soon
(Recorked 1979) Good, fullish, mature colour. Firm, aromatic, spicy nose. Fullish, still some tannin but also an aspect of astringency. Ripe and fat and sweet. Very Cabernet; even Franc and leafy. Solid, rich and fat but lacks real class. Extraordinary vigour for its age and the pretention of the vintage.

1934   Drink soon
(Recorked 1979) Full, vigorous colour. Another solid, tannic wine: somewhat unforthcoming. Some astringency on the palate. Seems older than the 1933. Again quite high acidity. Riper and sweeter. More attractive. This is beginning to dry out though. Yet still finishes rich. Best of the 1930s flight, as you might expect.

1933   Drink soon
(Recorked 1979) Full, mature colour. Powerful, quite rich and concentrated nose, once again dense and masculine, a little bit too much so for its own good. Elements of burnt caramel and bonfires as it evolved. Full, earthy, quite high in acidity. Has both tannin and astringency. Has good grip and balance but a lack of real richness and concentration to the fruit. Now beginning to lighten up. Finishes a bit bitter.

1929   Will still keep
(Recorked 1979) Full, rich colour, not much sign of maturity. Serious stuff here. Rich, concentrated and fat; older that it looks but plenty of depth and character. Fully mature again. Rich and velvety. Concentrated and sweet. A certain over-voluptuous richness but greatly seductive. Long and complex. Very classy. The best of the three later 1920s vintages. Or is the 1928 superior? It's a question of taste. Crammed with ripe fruit. Still vigorous. Super-duper.

1928   Will still keep well
(Recorked 1979) Medium-full, mature colour. Fragrant nose, supple, aromatic. Has depth and subtlety, even class. Medium body. Round, rich; a little age – certainly fully mature. Complex, less structured than the 1926 but subtle and fragrant. Long on the palate. Very fine indeed. Very complex. Held up very well in the glass. Splendid.

1926   Drink quite soon
(Recorked 1979) Medium-full, mature colour. Fullish nose, the usual La Mission solidity. Somewhat four-square but there is good wine here. Medium-full. Ripe and balanced. Lacks a certain concentration and nuance and is a little rigid but is good, if not great. Acidity beginning to get obtrusive. Not as good as the 1928 or 1929.

1924   This bottle is past its best
Medium, mature colour. Smells of vegetable soup. Old, astringent and totally over the hill and decayed. Maderized. Earlier notes indicate a fine wine.

1921   Drink up
(Recorked 1979) Medium-mature colour. A little dry but no real fade on the nose. Some class at least. Medium body. Fresh and balanced. No great depth but a pleasant fruity bottle. Still agreeable and sweet. Soft and no undue age but no depth. Though after a while it got a little dry. Fresh for the age.

1920   Past its best
Lightish, slightly brown and faded colour. Sweet, watery, faded lead pencils on the nose. Not unattractive. No decay. Acidity shows. Lightish. Drying up and getting astringent. Too dry on the finish.

1919   Drink up
(Recorked 1979) Medium-full, mature colour. The nose seems a bit old and pinched. Doesn't have quality or charm. A lighter wine than either of those below and the oldest of the three on the palate. Yet good acidity and fruit. On the feminine side. Flowery and plump. Acidity begins to get obtrusive. Still sweet on the finish. Still very enjoyable.

1918   Drink soon
(Recorked 1979) Medium-mature colour. Mellow, soft, evolved nose. More new oak than the 1916. Ripe and complex. This is the most vigorous of the three. Fullish, concentrated fruit, good grip. Quite powerful. Certainly a wine of depth and breed with a good oaky background. Long, vigorous, complex wine. Very fine indeed.

1916   Drink up
(Recorked 1979) Medium-full, mature colour. Quite a full, firm, solid nose. Touch of liquorice and a shade burnt. Is it a bit dry as it develops? Fullish, certainly quite a bit of age. Mellow with a shade of astringency on the attack. Ripe, almost sweet-sour follow-through. High acidity but beginning to show a bit of age now. Gently sweet as it evolved.

DOMAINE DE CHEVALIER

As the late Nancy Mitford points out in *The Sun King*, the word *château* in French means a gentleman's country seat; not a castle, '*château fort*', nor something grandiose, which would be a '*palais*'. Versailles is a palace; Azay-le-Rideau a *château*; so are Beychevelle, Palmer, Haut-Brion and many others. However, while many of the famous properties of Bordeaux fully merit their title of château there are many more mere farmhouses, whose use of the word I find a little pretentious, for neither the buildings, the estates, or even the wines are of any great distinction.

In the Graves, however, out in the wilds of the country at the end of the commune of Léognan, is a property whose buildings may be modest, but whose wines are consistently of top quality, and which is content to exist under the honorific of *domaine* – Domaine de Chevalier.

The top Graves properties were classified in 1953 and codified in 1959, and Chevalier is included as one of thirteen reds: it also makes a little white wine, and is one of nine white Graves *crus classés*. I would put Chevalier even higher than this, as one of the three top reds with Haut-Brion and La Mission; and also as one of the top dry white wines of Bordeaux: Laville from La Mission and Haut-Brion Blanc again being the only rivals.

Some of the Graves properties, particularly those in the suburbs of Bordeaux, surrounded but not yet swallowed by municipal housing and shopping centres, are among the oldest in the area. While the Médoc was still marsh, and Saint-Emilion an undiscovered region of rustic vines and rude peasants, the landowners of Bordeaux had vineyards outside the city in what are now the suburbs of Pessac, Talence and Mérignac. Most of these have now disappeared.

HISTORY

In the seventeeth and eighteenth centuries, as the city grew and communications improved, and as the Dutch dug ditches and drained the land, the Médoc was developed and the Graves declined in importance. Some landowners, however, looked to the south, and discovered that underneath the pine trees of the nearby Landes, on certain plots of higher ground where the sand had eroded away, gravel beds lay exposed; substantially the same sort of soil then being successfully exploited in Margaux and the communes further north. One such entrepreneurial spirit, we can conjecture, was a man called Cibaley, who planted a few acres of vines amid the trees of Léognan in about 1770. This is the name under which the domaine appears in the map drawn up by the French geographical engineer, Pierre de Belleyme, a few years later.

By 1824 the name of the property and its wine had become corrupted to the more obviously French word 'Chevalier', and the vineyard, then producing 12 to 15 *tonneaux*, was ranked one of the five top wines of Léognan. Franck, in one of the first books which gives a detailed account of the wines of Bordeaux, described Léognan wines as firmer and with more body and colour, but less easy to drink than those of the commune of Mérignac, also in the Graves. Chevalier, however, then suffered an eclipse, the vines were uprooted, and the land given back to the pines; for almost 30 years it disappeared.

What happened to the Cibaley or Chevalier family we do not know. In the 1868 edition of Cocks and Féret, a Chevalier is listed as proprietor of a property called Bacalan in Pessac, a growth which no longer exists; and this may be the same family. But 'Chevalier', like the English surname 'Squire', has its origins in minor gentry titles, given or assumed, and is common enough in France.

THE RICARD FAMILY

Meanwhile, also in Léognan, there was a family called Ricard, whose main activity was barrel-making. This affair seems to have prospered, and they decided to diversify into wine-trading and vineyard ownership. In 1850 *Veuve* Arnaud Ricard bought Malartic-Lagravière. Ten years later, together with her son Jean, the Chevalier land was acquired, the pines were ripped up, and the land planted with vines.

From Jean Ricard it passed to his son-in-law, Gabriel Beaumartin, at the turn of the century. Beaumartin was a timber merchant in Bordeaux, which gave him the advantage of a plentiful supply of inexpensive wood at a time when wine-makers were beginning to realize the advantage of new oak for new wine, and also a ready supply of extra labour at vintage time. It is said that because he was able to import temporary hands for the harvest, he was able to pick in two or three days, at the optimum time, instead of over ten days or a fortnight.

Most of the day-to-day administration, however, was left in the hands of Marcel Doutreloux, particularly towards the end of Beaumartin's life and after. Between them, they brought the reputation up the very high present-day level.

In 1942 Beaumartin died, and the domaine passed to his son-in-law, coincidentally called Jean Ricard, and a direct grandson of the original Jean. Jean's son, Claude, took over in 1948, and one of the first things he had to do was to supervise the replanting of sections of the vineyard ravaged by frost in 1945. Claude, once a professional pianist, continued the perfectionism of his predecessors. Both he and his manager, Louis Grassin, went to study oenology under Professor Peynaud at Bordeaux University, and they looked after the wine with the same care as Beaumartin and the Ricards before them, with Peynaud as an expert advisor.

Claude Ricard was not only one of the most charming hosts in Bordeaux – I have been lucky enough to enjoy many memorable meals and fine bottles at his table – but one of the most perfectionist. At vintage time he would follow his small troop of *vendangeurs* round the vineyard like a bloodhound, telling them to reject this, trim that bunch of green or rotten berries, all to ensure that what arrived at the *cuverie* was as healthy and as ripe as possible.

In 1983 I was dismayed to hear that Ricard had sold Domaine de Chevalier to the distilling firm of Lucien Bernard et Cie, at a price, it was said, of 20 million francs. The reason was the perennial problem which has beset France since the Code Napoléon was established in the 1790s: the problems of inheritance. In 1983 Chevalier was divided between three Ricard brothers and two sisters, and producing a return after tax which was barely non-existent. The relations wanted Claude to buy them out, but he was unable to do so. In the next generation there would be even more shareholders (Claude and his wife Monik themselves have six children) and the family squabbles could only get worse. The only solution was to sell.

The terms of the contract, however, were eminently sensible. Claude and Monik were to remain at the château for the time being, and he was to continue to manage the estate. Olivier Bernard and his wife Anne moved in next door and it soon became apparent that the relationship between Claude and Olivier was one more of father and son than that of vendor and buyer. Olivier began to learn his craft from a willing mentor and when Claude finally began to take a back seat in 1988 had become as much of a perfectionist as his predecessor. Continuity has been maintained. The Ricards have only moved a kilometre or so away, and remain frequent guests. Though none of the Ricard boys are involved in the wine business, the three girls all are. Nathalie, the eldest daughter, serves as secretary to Olivier Bernard, Virginie is married to Lionel Bord who has a vineyard in Loupiac, and the youngest, Eve, is now married to Rémi Edange, Olivier Bernard's partner.

THE VINEYARD AND THE WINE

At the end of the Ricard era the active Chevalier vineyard was not large, a mere fifteen hectares of black grapes and three of white planted on a gravel bed with a clay-iron subsoil. The *vignoble* was roughly rectangular and almost entirely surrounded by forest. This was further reduced in 1985 when as a result of winter frost five hectares had to be ripped up: one of Sauvignon Blanc, two of Merlot and two of Cabernet Sauvignon.

All this is now in the process of being considerably enlarged. Land has been cleared. Other plots, hitherto fallow, have also been planted. The white wine vineyard has been increased to four hectares, this being the maximum that Bernard believes can be operated in a manner as meticulous as the Chevalier vineyard always has been. The red wine vineyard will eventually total 32.5 hectares. From the young vines and rejected vats a second wine, originally cunningly named Bâtard-Chevalier, but now called L'Esprit de Chevalier, is made. Moreover, in September 1993, Bernard and Edange took over the 25-hectare (twenty red, five white) Domaine de la Solitude in Martillac on a *fermage* basis.

Currently, as a residue of 1985, the red wine *encépagement* is 80 per cent Cabernet Sauvignon and 20 per cent Merlot. Eventually a more habitual 70-30 ratio will be achieved. The white wine is made from 70 per cent Sauvignon and 30 per cent Sémillon.

The domaine's principal problems are frost and hail. Year after year, if other parts of Bordeaux, even of Léognan, are spared, Chevalier is hit. In 1982, for instance, as a result of hail, Ricard only produced nine hectolitres per hectare, i.e., ten barrels of white wine, and only 27 hectolitres per hectare of red. In 1981, as a result of frost, there were only fourteen hogsheads of white wine. In 1978 there were eighteen barrels but in 1977 only six. One of the few recent vintages when the vineyard was not affected was in 1983.

The production of white wine is the most difficult. The actual optimum date of picking is more difficult to define, and needs to be more accurately adhered to. The grapes must not be too ripe or the wine lacks acidity, nor too unripe, or the wine lacks fruit. The white grapes are vintaged eight days in advance of the reds, usually by means of several '*passages*' through the vineyard to pick each bunch in prime condition. The fermentation needs to be controlled most carefully. It takes place in individual oak barrels (but never in new oak which would give too much of an oaky taste to the wine), at a temperature of between 15° and 20°C. After the alcoholic fermentation the wine falls bright of its own accord (it is never fined), and it is racked and its sulphur content raised to prevent a malolactic fermentation. The malolactic fermentation, so necessary in Sancerre, Chablis and Germany, where the wines would be hard, raw and tart without it, is resisted firmly where the weather is better further south, for the wine would lose acidity and firmness, become too soft and too flabby. Maturation is in oak barrels from the Allier, of which there used to be a maximum of 30 per cent new wood – six out of 30 in 1979, six out of 20 in 1980 – more would leave the wine too oaky, Ricard used to consider. Subsequently he and Olivier Bernard changed their minds and 50 per cent is now the new wood percentage.

The white wine is left in barrels for about a year and a half before bottling and at its best this is one of the most splendid wines to come out of Bordeaux. It is full, honeyed and rich, without being sweet, with a hint of the oak barrels, so far very Burgundian; but has a distinctive fruitiness which, just in time, prevents one from declaring it a fine Corton Charlemagne. It is one of the few dry white wines which ages well in a bottle.

But, as is often the call in Bordeaux, the wine often seems over-sulphured – delicious in cask, but rather dead when you see it in bottle a couple of years later. Even Chevalier can sometimes be criticized for producing, in a minor vintage, a wine which when mature exhibits more sulphur than fruit.

The vinification of the red wine is fairly classic. Nine specially constructed 104 hectolitre-capacity cubic steel vats are used enabling a frequent immersion of the *chapeau*. The *chai* can be warmed so that fermentation takes place at 32 degrees, and the *cuvaison* is long, lasting for about three weeks. The first *vin de presse* – sometimes the second – is added to the free-run juice. Until recently, the fermentation temperature was lower, but in 1974, as a result of an accident, one vat fermented for a time at 34 degrees, and this was found subsequently to be better than the rest. There is one vinification detail at Chevalier which is uncommon elsewhere in the region. The *chapeau* is regularly broken up and mixed with the fermenting juice by the means of long poles. This Burgundian practice is known as *bombage* or *pigeage*.

To accommodate the larger harvest coming from the new vines, Olivier Bernard enlarged his cellar in 1991. The old *chai* now forms one element of an H-shaped winery, a dozen squat, cylindrical, stainless-steel fermenting vats, wider than they are high, forming a circular vinification centre in the middle of the axis. The enamelled-steel vats, however, have been retained. In most years, at least half of the wine goes into new oak. Owing to a very severe pruning and to the ravages of frost or hail, the *rendement* is rarely more than 30 hectolitres to the hectare. The permitted maximum is 40, and in 1970 Chevalier was the only property in the Gironde not to exceed that figure.

The red wine is one of the most elegant of all Bordeaux. Never aggressively hard and solid, yet never without plenty of body, depth of character, and length on the palate. A mature Chevalier has a subtle yet rich, soft fruit flavour, and is delicately but very well balanced, able to mature with finesse and last better than some of its originally tougher and heavier brethren from further north or across the water.

THE TASTING

The following notes have been taken from a number of tasting opportunities. The younger whites were sampled at Chevalier in April 1992; the older wines at a special blind tasting held at the château in March 1988. The four younger reds were also sampled at Chevalier in April 1992. Most of the remainder of the reds were tasted in New Haven, Connecticut, in March 1992.

WHITE WINES

1991   **1996–2003**

Lovely nose. Very classy, very good oak base. Deliciously honeyed and flowery. On the palate it is more hidden, more austere. Less rich than the nose would suggest. Not that structured but balanced and elegant. Very good indeed.

1990   **1997–2012**

Ripe, complex, clean, balanced. Full of flavour. The oak has given it a slightly marked, rigid touch, but the wine is fat and rich on the follow-through, so I am sure the rigidity is temporary. Classy, harmonious, complex. Needs time. Very good indeed.

1989   **1995–2005**

Opulent, rich and very ripe indeed. The 1990 has better grip and finishes more positively and elegantly, but this is very good. Potentially exotic. Certainly long enough. Shows well, but I prefer the 1990.

1988   **1995–2008**

Good depth here on the nose, though a bit of SO2. There is fat and concentration underneath. Fullish. Currently somewhat adolescent. Rich though. Good grip. Quite a masculine sort of wine. This has a fine future.

1987   **1993–1999**

Charming nose. Not unripe. A little more flowery and herbal than the fatter and richer vintages. Soft, Sauvignonny, subtle and reasonably supple. Yet it still has the size and grip to improve. Some honey. Does not lack depth. Very good for the vintage.

1986   **1993–2003**

This is the vintage which currently seems to be the most deadened by the SO2 on the nose. Less body and less depth than the 1985. The sulphur makes it taste a bit insipid at present. There is fruit here, and this fruit is ripe and subtle if a bit delicate. Reasonable acidity.

1985   **1995–2010**

Rich, full nose. Still firm. Fullish body. Honeyed, concentrated. A bit adolescent at present but there is grip and depth here. This is the best wine between the 1983 and 1990 vintages. Still needs time. Good fruit. Good grip. Still a bit of residual SO2.

1983   **Now–2000 plus**

Excellent quality. Good oaky backbone. Great depth and concentration of honeyed fruit. A very long and complex wine. Still youthful, but very, very intense and multidimensional. Marvellous!

1982   **Now–1998**

Sulphur dominates the nose. Underneath rich and honeyed, with flavours of vanilla and apricots. Not the structure and length of the 1983 but very good.

1981   **Now–1994**

Light-green gold colour. Youthful nose, no SO2, some oak, Sauvignon rather than Sémillon. Depth here, and fat, still a bit closed. There is a bit of age here and some wet wool on the nose and palate as it evolved. It has less fruit and richness than appeared on the nose. A bit like the 1979. Some astringency. Better as it developed.

1980   **Drink up**

Light, green-gold colour. A little mean on the nose. Lacks richness and ripeness. A bit neutral. Clean though. Like the 1978, a bit vegetal though not as marked. A *petit millésime* now drying up.

1979   **Drink soon**

Fresh, mid-lemon-gold colour. Some complexity if not great richness or fat. No SO2, less honeyed than the 1981. Discreet. Quite full, quite fat, has depth but not the breed and balance of the 1983. Not bad. Is the fruit beginning to dry a little? As it developed became somewhat one-dimensional.

1978   **Drink soon**

Light, green-gold colour. Smells of fresh cobnuts. Less SO2 than some but a slight vegetal element. Higher acidity. Also youthful. There is something a bit unripe and ungenerous about this. Medium body. Lacks depth and concentration. Lean. Now beginning to age. Average.

1976   **Now–2000**

Fresh, mid lemon-gold colour. Fresh nose, some oak, a touch of sulphur, still quite youthful. Not a great deal of depth (or concentration of fruit at first) but not bad. On the palate there is slightly more depth. Round, medium-full, honeyed, discreet, classy. Fine. Elegantly long. Stylish. Very good indeed. Will keep well.

1975   **Drink soon**

Light, medium colour. No undue sulphur though a little fade, slightly green-leafy, perhaps a touch of sulphur. Lacks a little fruit but there is, or was something here. More SO2 on the nose as it evolved. Got coarse, showed age. Similar palate. Still reasonable fruit and acidity. A pleasant, ripe, fruity wine, now a little faded but still finishes vigorously. Good. But curiously at Chevalier 1976 is better than 1975. It is the reverse at Laville-Haut-Brion.

1973   **Drink up**

Slightly lighter, greener colour. Neutral, slightly

flat nose. A bit of SO2, some fade, not very intense. Seems to have at least some depth and fruit underneath but not a lot of dimension. Similar palate. Reasonably fresh. Medium weight. Not too much SO2 but one-dimensional. Quite good.

1972   **Drink up**

Just a touch cloudy in colour, but this seemed to settle after a while. Quite a different nose. This is old and slightly unripe. Somewhere between old Alsace and old Loire. Highish malic acidity. Still quite alive and no undue SO2, fat and buttery in a vegetal way. Lacks style. Quite full. Average.

1971   **Now–1995**

Medium-full, golden colour. Some weight, complexity and some richness on the nose. No SO2. Depth here. Honeyed with a slightly green-spice (green peppercorns?), slight bitter aspect, very faint touch of resin. A little age? Discreet attack. Better finish. Quite full, complex and balanced. Shows a little age. Interesting. Very good but not great. Finishes well and long. While at Laville-Haut-Brion the 1971 is better than the 1970, here the reverse is the case.

1970   **Now–1995**

Slight weight of colour. This has more richness, without being too Sémillonny and heavy, though there is certainly some Sémillon evident. Full, rich, ripe and fat on the nose. Still youthful and vigorous. Class here. Peachy. Possibly a slight touch of botrytis. Full, with a definite aspect of dry Sauternes. Rich and fat, buttery in the best sense. Plenty of life. A big wine, quite powerful.

1969   **Drink up**

Medium colour. Again no SO2 on the nose and not very intense; now fading a bit? On the palate the fruit has dried up a bit, but reasonable freshness brought by high acidity. Clean, no SO2, not much richness but was stylish. Some fruit. Reasonable length still but needs drinking.

1968   **Drink up**

Medium colour, a little like the 1962. Nose is not very intense but seems stylish; no SO2. Similar palate. Mature, quite full, delicate, even subtle. Playing hard to get. Attack subdued but fragrant, finish rich, with complex fruit and long. Good acidity. This is what I wrote at first. When I went back to it I found it had faded fast and the fruit and richness had gone. Better than the 1969 though.

1967   **Drink soon**

Fresh colour. Still a hint of green/lemon. This has a typical old Graves – slight element of sulphur nose. On the palate the wine is ripe and stylish, gently oaky, quite complex but slightly

austere. Quite a high level of acidity keeping it fresh. Good fruit. Interesting rather than really appealing. Very good. Will still last.

1963   **Drink up**

Similar colour, a little lighter. Light nose, soft, quite aged, even less to it than the 1962. Now showing age. A lot of SO2 as it evolved but also botrytis. Less SO2 on the palate but quite a lot of acidity. Fresh but lean and a certain astringency on the finish. Austere. Lacks fruit and ripeness.

1962   **Drink up**

Slightly fresher colour, mature, less age. Medium-light nose, a little innocuous, as it evolved became heavy and coarse, touch of old SO2. Was once quite a delicate and gentle wine perhaps. Now a little faded. Light, leaves the palate as a bit mean. Now drying up. Was quite good at least once upon a time. More and more SO2 as it evolved.

1961   **Drink up**

Full, golden colour, mature but not aged. Oldish nose seems to have a bit of built-in sulphur. Round and spicy but lacks a bit of class and zip on the palate: fullish, quite rich, Sémillon shows, rather better than the nose would indicate. Some freshness. Some weight and depth, a bit like a dry Sauternes, but showing age on the finish.

1959   **Now–1997**

Medium colour. Light golden; very youthful for the age. Fat, rich, ample nose. This is round and almost honeyed, in a flowery, rich, dry way. Ripe and oaky, long and lovely. Still vigorous. Very complex and rich and fat on the finish. Super.

1942   **Drink soon**

(Tasted at the domaine, March 1988) Deep golden colour. The nose is aged but by no means finished. Slightly botrytis. Fullish, fat. Drying out a little but it has held up well. Rich and nutty. Clean finish. Surprisingly good.

RED WINES

1991   **1996–2000**

Reasonable colour. Clean, upright nose, not without elegance. Indeed it is balanced, fruity and fragrant. Light to medium body but has reasonable acidity and fruit on the palate. Quite long. Certainly very stylish. This has charm. Positive. Good plus.

1990   **1997–2007**

Medium to medium-full colour. Delicate on the nose but elegant and harmonious, with a gentle touch of new oak. It doesn't have enormous weight and intensity but it is stylish and balanced. And very long and lovely. Yet I prefer the 1988.

1989   **1997–2008**

Medium-full colour. An exotic wine with a
more pronounced oaky flavour than the 1990.
Seems fuller and richer and more substantial.
Ripe, balanced, no obtrusive tannins. Charming,
complex and very good indeed. Better than the
1990, but the 1988 is better than either.

1988   **1995–2007**

Good colour. Good oak. Quite firm on the
nose. Even a shade austere. But closed. Medium
body. Not an enormous amount of tannin. More
accessible quite quickly as it evolved in the glass.
Stylish, oaky base. Reasonably fruity: certainly
ripe but an absence of real concentration. Good
grip. A pretty wine. Good length though.

1986   **1996–2006**

Medium-full colour, less advanced than the
1985. The nose is a bit neutral at first. A little
four-square compared with the 1985. Better on
the palate. Slightly dry on the finish. Good fruit
and good acidity. Medium body. No washed-
out tannins. This lacks a little richness and concentration, and especially fat. But is a good result
for the vintage.

1985   **1995–2010**

Medium-full colour. Some signs of development.
Fragrant nose. Quite delicate, but very complex,
very lovely. There is an element of plums and
vanilla but it has still got plenty of reserves. It is a
more backward wine on the palate than it seems
on the nose. A bit hard on the attack. Better on
the finish. Good concentration. Not great. Merely very good. It doesn't quite have the depth and
complexity. Classy though.

1984   **Drink soon**

Surprisingly good colour. More intense than the
1985 or 1983. I have for a long time reckoned
Chevalier as one of the very best 1984s. Not austere. Good oak. Even chocolatey. Medium
body. Some length. At its best now.

1983   **1995–2015**

Fullish colour. Now some signs of maturity. Altogether fatter and more ample than the 1985. A
fuller wine with more depth. Medium-full body.
Rich, fat, concentrated, classy. A lot of depth.
This is better than everything they have produced since, and better than the wine below.
Very long. Still a bit of tannin. Very good fruit
and real dimension on the finish. Fine. Still needs
a year or two.

1982   **1996–2016**

Fine full colour. Just a hint of maturity. Still a little closed on the nose. A little herbaceous and
dense, even, and dry, compared with the 1983.
Still youthful on the palate, but concentrated,
full, and with plenty of depth. Very good grip.

Quite structured. The elements are here but not
together yet. Very good fruit on the finish.
Long, quite complex. Very good but not fine.

1981   **Now–2002 plus**

Very good colour for the vintage. Now just
about mature. Ample, plump, very classy cedary
nose. Round and mature. Good concentration
and grip. Medium to medium-full, ripe, seductive, complex, balanced. This is a delicious example for the vintage. Very good acidity, especially
for a 1981. Very long. Lovely. Almost ready.

1980   **Drink up**

Good colour for the vintage, fully mature. Obviously by comparison with the above this is a
small wine. Medium body, a touch of tannin
still. Good structure, enough fruit. Plenty of
charm. Good for the vintage but outclassed by
these other immediate vintages.

1979   **Now–2002 plus**

Fullish colour. Less mature than the 1978. Some
development on the nose. Just a touch of the
mulberry plumpness and the warm brick of the
Graves, but more of the class and gently integrated oak of Chevalier together with a slightly
herbaceous element. Almost ready, but it doesn't
have the fat and the seductive appeal of the 1981.
Medium-full, good grip, but a shade of astringency lurking in the background. It doesn't
quite have the fruit. Very good though.

1978   **Now–2005 plus**

Fully mature colour. There is a slightly dry element, even slightly vegetal, from the tannins on
the nose at first. As it developed, quite firm on
the palate, concentrated and classy. Long and
subtle. Fullish, complex, really elegant. Multidimensional and very, very long. Just about
ready. Soft and sweet and lovely on the finish.

1976   **Drink soon**

Fullish, fully mature colour. Soft, ripe, fleshy and
fresh nose – for a 1976 – not a bit too astringent.
On the palate it is a bit dry. The fruit has began
to dry out. Spicy, but lacks generosity. Not too
bad. Still some fruit and charm. Drink up soon.

1975   **Drink soon**

Good colour. Now mature. Not a great deal of
nose. On the palate, like the 1976, there is some
astringency; the wine lacks real charm and fat.
Medium body. A bit one-dimensional. Nothing
special. Will dry out as it evolves further. Has already lost a bit of its flesh.

1973   **Drink up**

Quite a big colour for a 1973, now mature.
Broad nose, fullish, slightly spicy. Much more
developed than the 1976 and with less class.
Signs of both astringency and attenuation.

1971   **Drink soon**

Medium colour. Fully mature. Quite evolved, if not slightly aged, on the nose. A touch fruitless and stemmy/herbaceous. Elements of old tea as it evolved. On the palate a little more generous, but it lacks roundness and fruit and fat again. This is an uninspiring trio. Again drink soon. But this did at least have some quality five or ten years ago.

1970   **Now–1997**

Fullish mature colour. Lovely nose. Ripe, round, complex. Very stylish fruit. Beautifully *à point*. Very subtle and soft. This is fullish and fat, long and ripe. Finely balanced. A round wine but one which still has plenty of intensity. Very attractive. Very fragrant. Very long and lovely.

1967   **Drink soon**

Medium to medium-full colour. No undue maturity. Soft, fragrant, delicate but not a bit too old or too astringent. The fruit is still here. The wine is still sweet and elegant. Delicious for a 1967. Old roses and *pot pourri*. Medium body. Good acidity. Still has very good fruit. This is a lovely example. Very subtle and fresh still. Very positive on the finish.

1966   **Now–2000 plus**

Full colour. Mature. Richer, more vigorous, more concentrated than the 1970. This is excellent. Marvellous fruit. Even better than the 1970. The fruit is very ample and concentrated. It has more structure and depth. Summer pudding fruit. Vigorous. Fat. Very very long on the palate. Fullish. Very fine. Plenty of life still. A great 1966.

1964   **Now–1997**

Full colour. A little more brown than the 1966. A little drier on the nose. But plenty of depth and fruit still. No lack of fat. This is a fine example of the vintage. Fullish on the palate. Ripe and ample – indeed really quite fat. Doesn't have the complexity or poise of the 1966 but this is certainly a very attractive wine. Above all, it has balance and freshness. Not a bit astringent.

1962   **Drink up**

Good, mature colour. Round, fullish nose. Shows a little age and didn't last as well in the glass as the 1964. Fullish, good fruit. Very good nevertheless, but now needs drinking.

1961   **Drink soon**

Very good colour. Marvellous nose. Super concentrated fruit. Classically proportioned. Enormous intensity and sweetness. Not a hint of age. Old vine. Creamy. Medium-full body. On the palate the wine does have a hint of astringency, but at the same time it is rich and ample, subtle and understated, balanced and long and very very classy. But the end result is a little dry. Didn't hold up too well in the glass.

1955   **Drink soon**

(Magnum) Medium-full colour, mature but youthful or its age. Soft, fragrant nose. Now a touch of lightening up to leave the warm-brick, faded-roses smell of an old Graves. Medium body. Getting a little tired but sweet and ripe, not short of length. Classy. Still vigorous. Proof again of what a very good vintage 1955 was. Long. Fragrant, ripe, even complex. Elegant.

1953   **Now–1996**

Splendid colour. Close in intensity and vigour to the 1961. Splendid nose. Marvellous soft, elegant fruit, with an aromatic, spicy hint – sandalwood, cinnamon. Exotic and complex. This is medium bodied. Soft, round, sweet and complex. Without a touch of astringency. It is absolutely *à point* and is really very lovely. I wouldn't keep it too long. Marvellous class. Very lovely, very fresh, very complex fruit. Very, very lovely lingering finish. A great wine.

1948   **Drink soon**

Big colour. Solid, chunky, tannic, but very rich and complex underneath in a firm, slightly austere sort of way. Has a lot of depth. Very fine quality; very long finish.

1947   **Drink soon**

Splendid colour. Rich, round, mature nose. Heaps of fruit and concentrated ripeness. Full, complex, very rich and ripe. Has the concentration and even the essence of fruit which resembles the 1961 vintage, but in a more mature way. Very long indeed. *Grand vin!*

1929   **Now–1998**

Full colour. Old, a little cloudy. Smoky nose. Aromatic. Sweet but powerful. Like a 1947. This is remarkable. Old but really intense fruit, really quite sweet. Alive and concentrated and fragrant, soft but still quite full and vigorous. Another great wine (after the 1953). Very lovely concentrated fruit. Still surprisingly fresh. And very intense in flavour. Very long indeed. Plenty of life still. *Grand vin!*

1928   **Drink up**

Fine mature colour, tawny obviously but not over-old. Lovely, refined nose; still sweet, vigorous and full of finesse. Delicate old-rose and violet aromas with a touch of nuts. Became progressively more mushroomy as it developed in the glass.

1921   **Drink up**

Less colour. More age on the nose. Bigger, chunkier, still sweet. Was rich but now has a very slight touch of astringency. Complex, spicy, very fine but not the elegance of the 1928.

DE FIEUZAL

South of Léognan, just before the winding road disappears into the forests of the Landes, lies Château de Fieuzal, one of the Graves's most important classed growths. This is an up-to-date, dynamic establishment, the quality of whose red wine has been high for a generation or more, yet has languished unsung until the last decade or so. The white wine is very fine too, though this is a newer development. To describe De Fieuzal as a rising star is therefore only partly the truth: it is really only the reputation which has belatedly risen. There is still, though, in recent books on Bordeaux, an element of damning De Fieuzal with faint praise, a not-bad-considering patronizing attitude. This is unjust, as the tasting notes which follow will demonstrate.

Why was it that De Fieuzal did not hitherto receive the recognition that it deserved? Is it because it has only relatively recently been available on the ordinary Bordeaux market-place? Prior to 1973 it was sold directly to agents abroad. The price was depressed below its real level, and the wine was not sampled by the commercial buyers on their annual visits to the area.

De Fieuzal is an old estate, though relatively new as a vineyard as far as I have been able to establish. Its creation as a serious wine-producing domaine dates only from the first half of the nineteenth century.

HISTORY

Before the Revolution the land belonged to the La Rochefoucaulds. One of the maxims of the writer of the family was 'Sobriety is a sort of impotence', highly apposite in the present circumstances (not of course that one wants to encourage inebriation, just a happy medium!). No doubt there were some vines on the estate then; after all, prior to the Revolution there were some 35 per cent more vines planted in the whole of the Gironde than there are now. But Léognan was not the centre of Graves wine-growing it is today: the important vineyards were closer to the city walls of Bordeaux. The Rochefoucauld family would have derived their local income primarily from the pine rather than from the vine. Such vines as there were at Léognan would probably have mainly provided *vins blancs secs*.

The vineyard of Château de Fieuzal seems to have been created in Napoleonic times at the same time as the locality was turning from white wine to red. There is no doubt that the owner was a follower of the Emperor, for Napoleon's emblem, the bee, has for long been commemorated on the capsule, but who this owner was we cannot be sure. The first clear indication of the estate appears in Franck's 1860 edition, in which 'De Fieuzal', owned by 'Griffon', is listed 13th in the commune, producing 20-25 tonneaux of wine.

Alfred de Griffon, a brother or cousin of whom owned neighbouring Château Gardère (now Haut-Gardère), a *vignoble* newly created in the 1850s, sold Château de Fieuzal in 1893 to Abel Ricard. This was the branch of the Ricard family which was already involved with Domaine de Chevalier and Malartic-Lagravière.

In the same year − or was it bottles of this early, exceptional and abundant vintage? − the wine was sold to the Vatican cellars and was enjoyed by Pope Leo XIII. De Fieuzal was said to have enjoyed a high reputation at the time, and to have sold for higher prices than the other Ricard estates, though it is listed below them in the Cocks and Férets of the period. Like many Bordeaux estates, its fortunes suffered in the 1930s slump, and the vineyard was allowed to run down. it was rescued, after Abel Ricard's death during the Second World War, by his daughter Odette and her husband Eric Bocké. Bocké, a 'tall, lean man with a laugh I shall never forget', to quote Hubrecht Duijker in *The Good Wines of Bordeaux*, was born in Sweden. He left for America in 1918 but returned to Europe to marry Mlle Ricard in 1920. He then settled in Bordeaux and was owner and manager of the Alhambra theatre until 1970.

On their return from Morocco, where they had spent the war, the Bockés set about the resurrection of the dilapidated De Fieuzal. Fifteen hectares of vines were planted, including, for the first time in the modern era, a few rows of white grapes. Their efforts were rewarded by the inclusion of De Fieuzal in the Graves classification of the 1950s, though as the white wine production was only sufficient for private consumption, this was for the red wine only. In December 1973, after Odette Bocké's death (Eric Bocké died in 1976), the property was sold to Georges Négrevergne. It changed hands again in 1994, when Négrevergne's heirs sold De Fieuzal to the Banques Populaires for 130 million French francs.

GÉRARD GRIBELIN

Gérard Gribelin, son-in-law of Georges Négrevergne, has been running De Fieuzal since the end of the Bocké era − he continues under the new regime − and it is his energy and perfectionism, capitalizing on the good grounding of the Bockés, which has been largely responsible for the high quality at De Fieuzal today. The vineyard has been extended to 40 hectares, 32 of which are currently in production. The red wine part of the vineyard is planted in the ratio 60 per cent Cabernet Sauvignon, 5 per cent Cabernet Franc, 30 per cent Merlot and 5 per cent Petit Verdot. The white wine section contains 50 per cent Sauvignon and 50 per cent Sémillon. Production averages about 12,000 cases of red wine and 1,500 of white. The white wine vineyard is being increased.

Gribelin has transformed the cellar. A battery of eleven fermentation enamelled-steel vats (plus two larger ones for the *assemblage*) replaced old wooden *foudres* in 1977, though two concrete *cuves* have been retained. The vinification hall connects via a section currently used for some of the cased storage and the bottling with a traditional long, low *chai*, used for the retention of the wine in barrel. These two form two sides of a hollow square in the form of an L. A third side has now been constructed, which means that Gribelin has been able to move the De Fieuzal element out of his warehouse in the centre of Léognan which he currently shares with Château Malartic-Lagravière. This has given him more room for storage there of wines for his *négociant* and retail business.

THE CHÂTEAU AND CHÂTEAU DE FERBOS

There has never been much of a 'château' at De Fieuzal. Old photographs show a simple farmhouse, but this, like the vineyard, was neglected in the 1930s and early 1940s, was never restored, and was finally demolished at the end of the 1970s to make way for more vines. Paradoxically, the extension of the *chais* has necessitated the uprooting of these plants.

Instead, Gribelin and his wife and children live at Château de Ferbos, an attractively restored, early-nineteenth-century construction which lies about a kilometre due west, on the road down to Domaine de Chevalier. Ferbos also has a small vineyard, the wine of which goes into L'Abeille de Fieuzal, De Fieuzal's second wine.

THE WINE

De Fieuzal *rouge* is fermented in the coated-steel vats, temperature-controlled by means of water aspersion down the sides, macerated at a high temperature for a long time – as much as 21 days, according to the vintage – and matured in an increasing amount of new oak. There was 70 per cent new oak for the 1986 vintage, though only 40 per cent in the weaker 1987, when 40 per cent of the wine was eliminated from the *grand vin*. The result is a wine which has a fine colour, is high in tannin and extract, is fat and substantial, but which retains an inherent Graves softness, though this latter aspect can be masked when the wine is young.

As elsewhere in the Graves, but blazing a trail ahead of the majority, the white wine vinification and resultant quality has been revolutionized. Up to 1983 the wine was vinified in tank and never saw any new oak (a pity, this particular vintage would have been a splendid wine if it had been made in the modern way). Following trials in 1984 the wine is now, after *débourbage* (being allowed to settle its gross lees after pressing), fermented in new oak. It is left on its fine lees for six months, with the occasional *bâtonnage* (stirring up of these lees), and bottled after sixteen months. The results are startling. We now have a white wine with an explosion of flavour, an almost exotic fruit element, good but not excessive new oak underpinning, and a character, depth and complexity which can rank it among the very best in the region. Like the great estates such as Domaine de Chevalier, the white grapes are collected by *passage*. The rows are picked over three times to ensure each bunch is in optimum condition. Prices of De Fieuzal *blanc* are high, indeed higher than for the red wine, but it is worth it. It is indisputably of *cru classé* quality.

THE TASTING

I sampled most of the following wines at Château de Fieuzal in September 1988. The younger vintages were retasted in 1992.

WHITE WINES

1990   **1997–2009**

Rich, fat and oaky on the nose. Full and opulent and exotic on the palate. A firm wine, with plenty of depth, and very good balance. I marginally prefer this to the 1989. Very good. But needs time.

1989   **1996–2006**

This is similar to the 1990, but softer, riper – sweeter, even – more luscious and exotic, but slightly less grip. Very seductive. Very good.

1988   **Now–2000**

Not as marked by the oak as the 1990 or the 1986. Ripe, balanced, medium-bodied wine with plenty of depth, but not the power and the weight of the two younger vintages. Most attractive though, but more forward. Good plus.

1987   **Now–1996**

Lightish, green-gold colour. Stylish, delicate, oaky nose, but the oak does not dominate. Medium body. Fresh and elegant, quite oaky, good fruit. This does not have the depth and sheer flair of the 1985 or 1986 but is balanced, complex and finishes well. Very good.

1986   **Now–2003**

Similar colour. Rich, concentrated, oaky nose. There is a lot of depth here, very fine balance and lovely, fresh, complex fruit. This is really very good. Fuller than the above. Good grip. A fine result for 1986.

1985   **Now–2003**

Slightly deeper colour. Fatter, plumper, nuttier, more oaky nose. I had had fears originally that this wine was over-oaked but I no longer think so. Rich and ripe, more substantial than the above. This is even better. Very fine indeed.

1984   **Drink up**

Similar colour. Half vinified and matured in oak; half in tank. A little oak but also a bit of the dead hand of SO2. Better on the palate. Medium body, the sulphur less apparent after a while in the glass. Reasonable fruit. A good effort for the vintage. Drink it while it is still fresh.

1983   **Now–1999**

Rather more colour. Ripe nose, no oak, a touch of SO2 which soon disappeared. Old Graves flavour. A broad, ripe, balanced, substantial, meaty wine with plenty of depth. Finishing long and rich. This will last well. Essentially this was the best of the early 1980 vintages. All it needed was the oak.

1980   **Drink soon**

Mid yellow-gold colour. This has a bit of built-in sulphur. Medium body; crisp, quite elegant fruit, better on aeration. Not at all bad if a bit one-dimensional. Fresh.

1979   **Drink up**

Similar colour. Rather more sulphur: a classic example of how not to do it. This shows more age. The fruit has begun to dry out and the wine finishes rather bitter.

1974   **Drink soon**

Quite a deep colour. No undue sulphur and not faded. Indeed there are interesting camomile elements on the nose. Round, quite ripe, medium bodied; slight bitterness on the finish but not past it. A fine example of this vintage.

1966   **Drink soon**

Old green-gold colour. No fade here either. Rich, fat and plump, with plenty of interest. Fullish, nutty, interesting. Good acidity keeps it fresh but there is no lack of fruit and no undue sulphur either. Finishes long.

RED WINES

1990   **1997–2006**

Good colour. This is rather more substantial, as well as very much more successful, than the 1989. Rich, fat, firm nose. Plenty of fruit, though not a great deal of backbone on the palate. But balanced and attractive. Good plus.

1989   **1995–2001**

Medium-full colour. Somewhat diffuse on the nose. The wine is less rich and has less grip. Earthy and a bit stalky. Medium to medium-full body. A bit of a disappointment.

1988   **1996–2006**

Good colour. Fullish, firm nose. A little four-square. There is plenty of substance here, and good acidity, but it lacks a little richness. Medium-full body. More positive at the end. Slightly hard, but there is fruit here, and the finish is long. Good to good plus.

1987   **Drink soon**

Good colour. Merlot shows on the nose. Neither unripe nor watery by any means. Medium body, a little tannin. A very good effort.

1986   **Now–2002**

Very good colour. A rich plump nose with a hint of chocolate, essentially soft-centred. Medium body, some tannin. A much more complete wine than most Graves 1986s. Good plummy fruit, good grip and quite complex finish.

1985   **1995–2010**

Very good colour. Better nose. More accessible and riper and richer, complex black fruits with a touch of liquorice; lots of interest. Medium-full body, some tannin. A ripe, balanced, complex, positive wine with fine fruit and plenty of depth. More substantial than a lot of 1985s. Very good.

1984   **Drink soon**

Excellent colour for the vintage; little development. Good Cabernet nose, not a bit unripe. Medium body; positive, oaky, no unripe tannins, good fruit, even rich. This will fool many. A splendid effort for the vintage.

1983   **1995–2015**

Medium-full colour, a little development. A good substantial wine with plenty of depth which has now gone into its shell. Better on aeration. Medium-full, some tannin; very good fruit, lovely concentration. Long, harmonious finish. Very fine. Perhaps the best of all the 1980s vintages.

1982   **1995–2010**

Quite full colour, a little development. Ample, fat, rich nose with a touch of spice: hot chocolate and raspberries and an element of burnt toast. Quite powerful and tannic if no more real size than the above. Slightly hotter and more alcoholic though. A good, rich, concentrated finish after a slightly aggressive start. Long, fat and ample. Very good for the vintage.

1981   **Now–1997**

Good colour for the vintage: pretty well similar to the 1982. Fresh, still a bit closed on the nose. On the palate the tannin is still there. Quite full. Underneath there is good fruit and the wine is soft, but the effect of the tannin – or was it an excess of *vin de presse*? – is to make it a little foursquare. It may round up in a year or two.

1980   **Drink soon**

Good colour for the vintage: fullish, mature. No undue age: round, fruity and quite stylish on the nose. Good substance, fruit and freshness on the palate for a 1980.

1979   **Now–2004**

Good colour for the vintage: very full, still youthful. Good fresh blackberry flavour. A substantial, backward 1979. Full, still tannic. Somewhat tough on the attack but with good richness and concentration underneath. Still needs time. Very good for the vintage.

1978   **Now–2008**

Fullish colour – a little development. Good fresh, plump fruit, slightly fatter than the above. A similar wine, substantial and concentrated, only more so, with an extra element of spice. Shows very well. Still youthful.

1976   **Now–1996**

Quite full colour, now mature. Interesting,

slightly cooked, summer pudding fruit. No dryness. Still very fresh. Once again a wine with no lack of grip or life and therefore with more style than most. Ripe and fresh. Good length. Will keep well. Very good for the vintage.

1975   **Now–1996**

Full but quite mature colour. Quite fat if a touch chunky, with slight bitter elements as well, yet some complexity of maturity to go with it. This is a rather austere wine, though not too tough, but it lacks charm and suppleness though there is reasonable fruit. A typical 1975. I can't get enthused.

1973   **Drink soon**

Good colour for the vintage; fully mature but no undue age. Pleasant fruit on the nose. This is fresher than most but now beginning to loosen up. Good for the vintage though with no real finesse.

1971   **Drink soon**

Very fine, full mature colour; better than the 1970 indeed. Fresh nose, slightly austere; for the wood element is quite fierce (I am told Bocké bought a lot of new wood for this wine but the wood was not of very high quality). This gives the wine a certain bitterness, but there is very good fruit as well. Vigorous but somewhat unbalanced. 'Good' at best.

1970   **Now–2000**

Good full, mature colour. Lovely complex nose. Full, rich, very Graves, less chunky than some of the wines here and all the more elegant as a result. This is lovely, exciting, balanced, concentrated wine. Ripe all the way through. Complex, harmonious and with plenty of vigour. Delicious.

1967   **Drink up**

Very good colour for the vintage. A touch of spice on the nose but no fade. This is a very good 1967. It is in the same style as the 1970 but has less concentration and finesse. It is now getting towards its end but still finishes fresh, stylish and vigorous.

1966   **Drink soon**

Fine mature colour. Fine nose with complex leather, liquorice and almost burnt black fruit. A more austere, less mellow wine than the 1970, with a touch of astringency. The finish is much better than the attack though. This is complex, concentrated and very stylish, will still keep well. Very good.

1964   **Drink soon**

Good mature colour. Good nose: somewhat four-square but not undue chunkiness nor astringency. Also vigorous and stylish. Good length. Ripe, fullish, blackcurranty. Yet another example of how good the Graves is in this vintage.

1962   Drink soon

This was from a magnum. Good colour. Much more evolved on the nose. Slightly tough and dense, losing a bit of grip and suppleness. Better on the palate though. Fresher than the nose would indicate. Fullish, generous and fragrant. A typical 1962, in fact. Very attractive. Still vigorous.

1961   Drink soon

No more colour than the 1962. Full but slightly burly on the nose, though rich underneath. A bigger, richer wine but slightly tough at the edges. Would be better with food. This is a rather more old-fashioned style of wine. Good but not great in 1961 terms.

1959   Drink up

Very full colour. Slightly chunky on the nose with a touch of maderization. The wine shows a bit of age and astringency but there is fine, ripe fruit underneath. Was certainly good.

1950   Drink soon

Very full colour, as is usual in this vintage. Also a little aged on the nose but less dense. Smoky, complex character. Good grip. Surprising concentration and breed. Could have been a 1949.

HAUT-
BAILLY

While Pessac is the best-known commune in the Graves – for it houses Château Haut-Brion, Château Pape-Clément and some of Château La Mission-Haut-Brion – the commune of Léognan, some ten kilometres to the south, is the most prolific in classed growths. Six of Graves's thirteen *crus classés en rouge* lie here. Four of these are also classed for white wines. A fifth property, Château de Fieuzal, also, in fact, produces some white wine and very good white, too, but is not a *cru classé en blanc*. It is the remaining château, however, Haut-Bailly, one of the few Graves properties which produces only red, which is the subject of this chapter.

In standing, Château Haut-Bailly can rank at the top of the commune. Like many properties, it has had its ups and downs. In particular, it suffered between the wars. But, in the last 35 years, in the hands of new proprietors, it has had a renaissance, and it now produces wine which can rank among the top six or so in the Graves.

Léognan lies south of Bordeaux, several kilometres inland from the Garonne, and the vineyards are hidden among pines, heathland and the occasional field of other crops. Unlike the main communes of the Médoc or further south in the Sauternes, there is no unbroken sequence of vines. North-east of the village of Léognan itself, however, the area comes nearest to being monocultural. Along a small, winding road leading from Léognan to Cadaujac, on a ridge some 40 to 45 metres above sea-level, lie the vineyards of Larrivet-Haut-Brion, Haut-Bailly, Louvière (a property very highly regarded a century and a half ago and today meriting classification) and Château Carbonnieux.

HISTORY

In the 1820s, Château Haut-Bailly, as such, appears not to have existed. Franck (1924) and Paguierre (1829) seem to agree, more or less, on the top few estates, all fairly large, for their combined production was over 300 *tonneaux*, a very considerable quantity in those days. One of these was Carbonnieux, much of whose vines lie in the neighbouring communes of Villenave d'Ornon and Cadaujac; another was the afore-mentioned, neighbouring Château La Louvière, owned by a long-established noble family named Mareilhac. A third called 'Bustat' was owned by the Marquis de Canolle. This became Larrivet-Haut-Brion. The fourth mentioned property was called Branon, and owned by De Literie. This does not appear to have survived to the present day, though it still existed at the end of the century.

It is possible that Haut-Bailly has its origins in this property, if only in part. What is perhaps an equally likely possibility is that some enterprising people, noticing the success of Carbonnieux and Louvière, bought up land further along the ridge, cleared the trees and scrub and planted vines. Certainly by 1845 (the second edition of Franck), Haut-Bailly was an established vineyard, producing fifteen to twenty *tonneaux* and is listed ninth in the commune.

The owner then was a M. Ricard. Coincidentally, the name Ricard crops up several times in the history of the top Léognan estates. But Haut-Bailly's proprietor was not a member of the family connected with Malartic-Lagravière, Domaine de Chevalier and De Fieuzal. Nevertheless, as we shall see, there is a family connection with one of these properties later in Haut-Bailly's history. Originally, the property was called Bailly. It steadily expanded its production and consolidated its reputation over the next 30-odd years when, on the death of M. Ricard, his son Pierre sold the estate to a M. Bellot de Minières.

THE 'KING OF WINES'

Alcide Henri Bellot de Minières, even by confident, flamboyant nineteenth-century entrepreneurial standards, was a remarkable man. He was born on 30 September 1828, at La Réole in the Gironde, the son of a local magistrate. For the first half of his life he was an engineer and economist. In 1859, he married Fanny Olivari, the widow of a M. Heirweg. His brother was a priest and private secretary to Monsignor Bonnet, Cardinal Archbishop of Bordeaux; and it appears to have been the ecclesiastical brother who brought the availability of Haut-Bailly to Bellot de Minières's notice. He seems to have been a man of great energy and enthusiasm, coupled with a rigorous attention to scientific detail and method. All of this he threw into Haut-Bailly once he had completed the purchase, on 20 April 1872, for what was described as a high price, although 115,000 francs does not seem excessive – a M. Labar was to buy Château Carbonnieux for 400,000 francs in 1878. Admittedly, there was, as yet, no château at Haut-Bailly and the Carbonnieux vineyard was considerably larger.

Before long, having completely reorganized and enlarged the property and constructed the château – which still stands today (though now unoccupied) – Bellot de Minières had elevated Haut-Bailly to number one among the Léognan estates, producing 30 *tonneaux* and fetching between 3,000 and 4,000 francs a *tonneau*, as much as a good Médoc second growth. In addition, he had acquired for himself the title '*Roi des Vignerons*', the Gironde's accolade for a man whose scientific knowledge and courageous approach produced some major and widely-copied viticultural and vinicultural improvements.

One of his innovations – but one he kept to himself – is mentioned by Penning-Rowsell in *The Wines of Bordeaux*. 'According to the firm of Mestrezat which used to buy the whole crop around the turn of the last century, one at least of the "secrets" of Haut-Bailly's success was that he "cleaned" out his *cuves* before the vintage with a few litres apiece of Grande Fine Champagne cognac. This drop of spirit at the bottom of each vat was conveniently "forgotten" when the grapes were shovelled in.'

Where perhaps he also got his reputation from was in his reaction to grafted vines. The solution eventually found as the answer to phylloxera was to graft the European grape variety – Cabernet, Merlot, and so forth – on to a phylloxera-resistant American rootstock. Bellot de Minières found this a foul abomination. '*Tout vin issu de vignes gréffées est un vin incomplet, un vin issu de race bâtarde, issu d'un métis et frappé de dégénérescence, ne se bonifiant pas en bouteille.*' ('Any wine produced from grafted vines is not a complete wine; such a wine coming from mixed origin and threatened with degeneration will never improve in the bottle.')

Firm words from a strong man, who was adamant to retain his '*vignes françaises*' and who invented a special copper-ammonia solution to treat his vines with. From records kept at the time, we have the *encépagement* in the 1890s: one-twelfth each Syrah, Merlot, Malbec, Petit Verdot, Carmenère and Cabernet Franc; the remainder Cabernet Sauvignon.

Bellot de Minières died at Haut-Bailly in November 1906, aged 78, and the property passed to his daughter Valentine Heirweg and her cousins named Tétard. Immediately after the First World War, they sold the estate to M. Franz Malvesin, author of the important *Histoire de la Vigne et du Vin en Aquitaine* for 350,000 francs.

Malvesin, who also had a reputation as a 'wine expert', continued the adherence to un-grafted vines and introduced further innovations. In order to prevent the wines degenerating in any way, he started to pasteurize them. Having done this, he was able to demonstrate that the wines could be bottled much earlier. The 1918 was bottled eight months after the vin-tage. At first, these techniques were approved and admired but after a while it could be seen that these 'improvements' had gone too far. It would also appear that they were discontinued soon after Malvesin's death in May, 1923, for certainly by the 1928 vintage the property had reverted to producing wine of traditional style.

Via Malvesin's two children, both born illegitimately but later 'officially' recognized, Haut-Bailly passed to a man called Paul Beaumartin, a relation of Gabriel Beaumartin who was then the owner of Domaine de Chevalier and, like him, involved in the family timber-merchant and railway-track construction business. The price Beaumartin paid, however, was only 200,000 francs. Today, the Beaumartin 'clan', if this word does not demean them, is widely spread in the world of Bordeaux wine. One grandchild of Paul Beaumartin is Mme Jean Tari of Château Giscours, another is the charming wife of Christian Moueix. Both these ladies are cousins, if removed at several paces, of Claude Ricard, erstwhile proprietor of Domaine de Chevalier.

At first Beaumartin shared Haut-Bailly with Comte J. Lahens, a Parisian banker whose daughter married a member of the Lur-Saluces family. Their son, the late Comte Pierre de Bournazel, was owner of Château de Malle in Preignac. In 1937, though, after a dismal peri-od for Haut-Bailly, during which part of the vineyard was grubbed up (the Government gave compensation to do this), Beaumartin bought the Lahens share, paying 100,000 francs, the cost of it in 1923, such were the economic conditions of the time. There was no return on the Count's investment.

Rather than neglect, it was probably as much the run of poor vintages and the general world recession which led to Haut-Bailly's deterioration in the 1930s. The reputation certainly suffered and the production waned. But it was the war which almost finished the estate. Early in the war, Beaumartin, now an old man, sold the property. After one or two more deals, a M. Boutémy, a textile manufacturer from Lys-Lannoy in the department of Nord, emerged as majority shareholder together with a M. Louis Tyberghien, an industrialist from neighbouring Roubaix. Under this ownership the wine of Château Haut-Bailly almost disappeared.

DANIEL SANDERS

Meanwhile in Bordeaux there was a wine-merchant called Daniel Sanders. The Sanders fam-ily were linen manufacturers in Belgium. Daniel, wounded in the First World War, convalesced first in England and later in Bordeaux. In 1919, he married the daughter of a Bordeaux wine-merchant and eventually inherited the business. Subsequently he acquired Château du Mayne in Barsac and, through his wife, the similarly named Cru Mayne-Pompon, a little estate situated next to Château Coutet. Sanders bought heavily in the 1945 vintage, including Haut-Bailly. Having seen the wine develop, he began to make enquiries about the estate.

By this time Château Haut-Bailly was extremely run-down. Many of the vines had died and had not been replaced, leaving the vineyard in a very deteriorated state. Only some nine or ten hectares out of the 35 in the property were still planted and the château and chais were much in need of renovation. As Sanders said, anyone could have bought Haut-Bailly. He did; and although the legal technicalities were not completed until December 1955, Sanders took over in midsummer and this was the first vintage he made. He died in May 1980, and the property is now run by his son Jean.

THE VINEYARD

Since 1955, the vineyard has been carefully and gradually brought nearer to its full potential. There are still only 28 hectares under vines, some of which are still young and not used in the *grand vin*. One of the reasons for this cautious approach is what attracted Sanders to Haut-Bailly in the first place – the average age of the vines. Some 25 per cent or so still remain from Bellot de Minières's ungrafted vines, giving an impressive average age of 40 years to the vineyard. Too hasty an approach to extending the area under plantation would destroy it.

As far as one can tell, the '*vignes françaises*' are Cabernet. The remainder are 60 per cent Cabernet Sauvignon, 10 per cent Cabernet Franc and 30 per cent Merlot and now produce an average of 120 *tonneaux* of wine a year. As is usual in the Graves, the pruning is by single *guyot*.

The vineyard of Haut-Bailly is all in one piece and is situated on one of the highest *croupes* of the left bank of the River Garonne, some ten kilometres inland from the river bank. The croupe is rich in the so-called '*feluns de Léognan*'. *Feluns* is a petrified sandstone containing a great deal of fossilized shellfish and is peculiar to this part of the Graves in the Bordeaux region, although it can be found widely in the Anjou. Underneath this gravel-*feluns* mixture, the subsoil, about two point five metres down, is *alios*. The *alios* here is not very permeable which means that the soil can suffer when the weather is excessively dry or wet. It is also not very acid. Neither is the wine, which makes it ample and supple.

THE CHÂTEAU AND THE CHAIS

The property, though it contains one or two bits of furniture, has not been inhabited since 1955, the end of the Boutémy era. In recent years, some of the ravages of time have been repaired and one room is now in use as an office. Others such as the dining room can be used during the vintage time by the harvesters. It is a solid, simple, two-storey building, with a red-tiled roof, much as a child would construct with Lego, fronted by a courtyard and backed by a small flower garden leading directly into the vineyard.

To the side are the *chais* managed by Serge Charitte, the *régisseur*, who, like so many in Bordeaux, has inherited the job from his father. The entrance to the *cuverie* has the appearance of a grotto, the walls at the front being constructed of rough rocks of *feluns* showing the fossils. Inside is no Mouton showpiece, merely a battery of fourteen small cement *cuves*. Across the yard, a large, new aircraft-hangar of a *chai* was constructed in 1982.

Today, in the good years, the wine is matured using 50 per cent new wood. In lesser years such as 1984 – a wine which is surprisingly successful, as well as charming, for the vintage – less new wood is employed and the wine is bottled earlier.

A recent development, in line with most other estates, is a second wine, La Parde de Haut-Bailly. This absorbs the produce of the young vines as well as any other vats not deemed by Jean Sanders, Serge Charitte and Emile Peynaud, here as elsewhere consultant, to be worthy of the *grand vin*.

THE WINE

As I have said, Haut-Bailly is an ample, supple wine. Well coloured, elegant, plummy and generous, it is concentrated and has a richness which sometimes makes me think of a Pomerol, especially one of those with quite a lot of Cabernet in it such as Vieux Château Certan. It is made with considerable dedication to quality, as is evidenced by the fact that even in these, at last, profitable days for well-known Bordeaux growths, they have not rushed to fill every part of their 35 hectares with vines. In 1979, they declassified between 30 per cent and 40 per cent of the crop: some of the wine in this prolific harvest was simply not up to standard and again in 1985 and 1986.

I first encountered Château Haut-Bailly in the 1960s and with the vintages of this decade. At that time, production was much smaller than it is today, particularly as the vineyard had been severely damaged by frost, not only in 1956 but in 1959, 1960 and again 1961. The wine was somewhat fuller and denser, more old-fashioned in those days than it is today.

Château Haut-Bailly, now, is one of the wines which is regularly on my shopping list. Some years ago, a previous proprietor – perhaps Bellot de Minières – decided to designate the wine and the property '*Premier Grand Cru Exceptionnel*' and, such was the reputation, this was soon how it was described by all. The label still says '*Cru Exceptionnel*'. So is the wine, thanks to the patience and attention to detail of the Sanders family.

THE TASTING

Most of the following wines were sampled at Haut-Bailly in June 1987. I have added notes of younger vintages sampled in 1992, and an assessment of the 1953 tasted in January 1991.

Optimum drinking

1990   **1997–2009**
Good colour. Rich, mulberry nose, round and accessible. This is by no means a blockbuster, but balanced, subtle and has a lovely soft-fruit flavour. A feminine wine. Long on the palate. Good plus.

1989   **1995–2003**
Medium-full colour. Stylish, oaky nose, with more of a Graves *goût de terroir* than the above. On the palate the wine has medium body, and like a lot of Graves in this vintage is just a little deficient in acidity. Quite good plus. Will come forward soon.

1988   **1997–2012**
I prefer this to both the above. Good colour. Plummy nose with good grip and complexity. On the palate fullish, rich and harmonious. This has plenty of depth and a more black-fruit flavour than the 1989 and 1990. Long and complex at the end. Very good.

1986   **Now–2004**
One-third eliminated, the *grand vin* being 95 per cent Cabernet. Good colour. Plump Cabernet, no stark tannins and no weakness on the nose. Medium-full body. A slightly austere Cabernet flavour but plump and ripe underneath and a

good acidity. Elegant. Very good indeed for a Graves of this vintage.

1985   **Now–2006**
43 per cent eliminated. Good colour. While not showing quite as well as it had done five weeks previously, the wine has lovely ripe Merlot fruit, now melting in with the oak to produce a mulberry-cedary flavour. Full, rich and plump. An ample wine with plenty of character and a rich, abundant finish. Very good.

1984   **Drink soon**
Good colour for the vintage. An attractive, even fat, nose showing plenty of fruit. This is rather good for 1984! Quite fat, ripe and plump. No weakness, no hard, uncovered edges. Quite long on the palate. Surprisingly full of charm.

1983   **Now–2008**
Very good colour. Full, rich nose. More structured, more depth than the 1985. Very good concentrated fruit. A full, rich wine, still with some tannin. Very elegant, velvety, plummy character and excellent balance. Better than the 1985, good as that is. A demonstration of how good the Graves are in this vintage. High class.

1982   **Now–2002**
Less colour than the 1983 and browner too. This

does not have the weight or quite the concentration of the above. Higher tone, more spicy nose, redolent of bonfires. Very fat and rich though. Plump, almost summer-pudding flavours and good length. Rather less tannic and more forward than most. Good plus.

1981   Now–1999

Surprisingly good colour. Soft, round, plump, blackberry and spice nose. Medium to medium-full body, now evolved to give an ample, fleshy wine with a touch of chocolate. Good grip. A wine with a lot of charm. Good to very good for the vintage.

1980   Drink up

Medium colour, now some brown. Lightish nose with a faint whiff of attenuation. The attack is plump enough with a touch of coffee, caramel and vanilla but it tails off and loses elegance on the finish. Quite good for the vintage but *à point* now and should be drunk.

1979   Now–1999

Very good colour indeed for the vintage. I remember this wine as being better than it shows today. This bottle was medium-bodied, fully evolved but lacked a little freshness and acidity. Quite Merlot in flavour. Other bottles have had more depth as well as length.

1978   Now–1998

Medium-full colour, browner and less intense than the 1979. Fullish, slightly clumsy nose but with good fruit and freshness. A more old-fashioned wine, the product of a longer maceration. A meaty, spicy wine, slightly earthy, tasting older than one would expect. In contrast to previous tastings more alive and more attractive than the above – if not exactly elegant.

1977   Drink up

A better colour than the 1980, though more brown. Slightly burnt, spicy nose, not dried out though. Brisker than most 1977s, a little bitter and austere but there is fruit. Not on its last leg by any means. Good for the vintage but, nevertheless, uninspiring.

1976   Drink up

Fullish nose, decidedly brown. Typical, slightly blowsy 1976 nose, lacking a bit of bite and acidity. Ripe but aspects of old tea lurk underneath and it is getting a little bitter on the finish. Quite full and still plump. Reasonable quality for the vintage.

1975   Now–1999

Full, mature colour. Good, plump nose, not too dense. Fullish, has the density of more traditional wine-making rather than the vintage. Rich and ripe, good fruit, finishes well. Good.

1970   Drink soon

Full colour, mature but less so than the 1975. Full, rich, sumptuous nose. Ready but showing no signs of age. Lovely, ample, blackberry flavours. Fullish, fat, still fresh. Quite structured compared with the younger wines. Meaty but classy. Finishes long.

1966   Drink soon

Slightly less colour than the 1970. Quite brown at the rim. Very elegant, blackcurrant fruit. Less powerful, more evolved. Medium-full body, complex, full of breed. This is not as vigorous as the 1970 but is rather more stylish. A really lovely bottle – all in finesse.

1964   Drink soon

More colour than either of the above. Solid nose, drier, more structured, denser. An example of how good this vintage was in the Graves, though this is a solid wine. Long, concentrated, ripe. Good quality.

1962   Drink soon

Another excellent colour. Lovely, full mature, classy, complex nose. Has neither the power of the 1970 nor the sheer finesse of the 1966 but a ripe, sweet, lovely bottle.

1961   Drink soon

Marvellous colour. Full, still vigorous. Very full and intensely rich in a slightly solid way. Opened up considerably in the glass. Even by 1961 standards, this is a very fine wine. Heaps of fruit. Very long, concentrated finish.

1959   Drink soon

This resembles a 1947. Very rich fruit on the nose but roasted, unlike the above. Quite high acidity, even, like the 1947s, an element on the volatile side. But not the heaviness or robustness of some 1959s and no sign of astringency. Full, very rich indeed. A fine bottle, if not a typical 1959.

1953   Drink soon

Good colour. Still vigorous. Two bottles: one of the bottles was a bit more rigid than the other. The better bottle was ripe, vigorous and delicious, with breed and complexity and no sign of age. Fine quality.

OLIVIER

Château Olivier, one of the last of the Graves *crus classés* to undergo the renaissance from the *bourgeois* humdrum to true classed-growth quality, has perhaps the best *terroir* of all the top growths in the Léognan commune. It also has, for its white wine, the correct *encépagement* for a wine of longevity, a full 65 per cent Sémillon. The château is grand, moated and medieval, the vineyard extensive, enclosed in an even larger forest on a patch of complex but essentially gravelly soil; remote, isolated but hardly a handful of kilometres from Bordeaux's encircling *rocade* (bypass). This property is going places. Current indications promise a superstar of the future. Watch this space!

Olivier dates back over more than eight centuries, and is well documented, despite an act of archival sabotage by an owner in the last century. As a *seigneurie* it is rivalled in the Graves only by La Brède to the south, with whom it has had more than one family connection over the years. The first of these was the marriage of Rostang d'Olivey (*sic*) in 1350 to Elizabeth, daughter of Guittard de la Lande, and heiress of Arnaud de la Lande, proprietor and *seigneur* of Château de la Brède. But well before this there are documents relating to other Olivey or Olivier transactions on the estate: homages to royalty, payments of feudal dues, and the like.

This Rostang was obviously one of the leading nobles of Aquitaine. He often played host to that romantic brigand, the Black Prince, who resided in Bordeaux between 1362 and 1373. The royal entourage would go hunting in the forests of Talence and Gradignan and Léognan, seeking deer and wild boar, even wolves, which were common at the time. Hence names such as La Louvière . . . Duguesclin was another guest, in 1374.

HISTORY

In 1409 the town council of Bordeaux took over a neighbouring *seigneurie*, the Comté of Ornon. They then laid claim to jurisdiction over and dues from, the parish of Léognan and the *seigneurie* of Olivier. For over two and a half centuries, despite the French King Henri II siding with an Olivier in 1552, a legal battle wrangled on. It was not until 1680 that the matter was finally resolved.

Meanwhile, during the sixteenth century, the last of the Oliviers having taken holy orders, the *seigneurie* passed through the female line to the Lasserre family. A century later, in 1663, Marie, only daughter of Jacques de Lasserre, *seigneur* of Olivier, married Pierre Penel, Baron de la Brède. Their daughter, another Marie, married Jacques de Secondat, Baron de Montesquieu. These were the parents of the celebrated man of letters.

Penel-Secondats sold Olivier – perhaps with La Brède they felt it superfluous to their requirements – to Bernard Joseph de Malet, a councillor of the Bordeaux parliament, in 1687. His widow in her turn sold Olivier to M. Fossier de Lestard in 1715, and Lestard disposed of the estate in favour of Jacques Legris, *Président Trésorier de France*, in 1747. In 1784 it passed to the Souberrie-Dugarry family; in 1827 it was sold to M. Sergent-Bardwich; nine years later it was acquired by a M. W. Fousset; and in 1846 Olivier changed hands once again. The new owners were the Count and Countess Charles-Joseph Maurice d'Etchegoyen.

It is at this juncture that the vinous possibilities of the Olivier estate begin to surface. Up to this period Léognan was not regarded as a place to produce serious wine. Prices were low by Médoc standards, and the huge Olivier estate, then as now, gained most of its income from forestry, cereals and the rearing of cattle. The vineyard was modest. It produced 30 *tonneaux* of red wine, ten of white.

The château, however, was in need of renovation. A century earlier, during the time of Fossier de Lestard, much of the old medieval fortified manoir had been rendered more elegant, in keeping with the times. Two of the three remaining turreted towers in the corners of the château had been pulled down, the windows had been enlarged, the interior courtyard covered over and a south door, communicating over the moat by a drawbridge to allow access into newly constructed gardens, had been opened up.

The Etchegoyen 'improvements' were less successful. Mid-nineteenth-century taste was less stylish. The north facade has never been the same since. On 7 December 1886, following an auction, Olivier was allocated to M. and Mme Alexandre Watcher, to whom the estate had been mortgaged since 1879, but not before the Bousset-Salvat family, briefly the successors of the D'Etchegoyens, had burned a considerable chest of archives and other historical documents. Luckily the library of La Brède possessed a similar collection.

Today Olivier belongs to the De Bethmann family – the family is of German banking origin – whose antecedents once owned part of Gruaud-Larose; Jacques de Bethmann having married Agathe Watcher earlier this century. Jean-Jacques de Bethmann, who lived for a decade in the USA, and who is an American citizen, bought out his brother and sister in 1984, and is today the man in charge.

THE VINEYARD

For much of the century, until Jean-Jacques de Bethmann took over, the vineyard of Olivier was leased to the firm of Eschenhauer, as at Smith-Haut-Lafitte. This arrangement ceased after the 1981 vintage, but the Bordeaux *négociants* retained the exclusivity for the wine until 1987.

Eschenhauer were more interested in the white wine than the red, and as a result the red vines – there are now 27 hectares, planted in the ratio 60 per cent Cabernet Sauvignon, 10 per cent Cabernet Franc and 30 per cent Merlot – are still young, the vineyard having been largely reconstituted in the 1970s. The seventeen hectares of white wine grapes – 30 per cent Sauvignon, 65 per cent Semillon and 5 per cent Muscadelle – are somewhat older.

These 44 hectares lie in one piece to the north of the château, isolated within an extensive estate of ancient woodland, newer pine trees and fields of pasture and cereals. The soil, however, is what excites the *oenologues* and land engineers. There is a diversity of gravels of different origins, depths and sizes, resting on a subsoil which contains *alios*, a hard sandstone rock, clay and various types of limestone, in different proportions in different parts of the vineyard. The potential to produce great wine is there because of this complexity. All De Bethmann has to do is to realize it.

THE WINE-MAKING

There is now the equipment to do this. On the east side of a wide grassed-over courtyard is a large *cuverie* of enamelled-steel vats. Temperature control is by means of mobile coiled heat exchangers, of which M. de Bethmann is very proud, for they can extend or collapse according to the volume of the must in each vat, and, if required, more than one can be inserted into a tank at the same time. Prior to 1985 the red wine was fermented at too low a temperature, and the tannins are hard as a result. Now maceration temperatures can be raised to 32 degrees. In the Eschenhauer days there was no wood employed at all in the production of Olivier. Now there is 25 to 40 per cent new wood – the rest being one or two years old – for the red wine, and the white wine, since 1990, has had its vinification started in tank, but as soon as fermentation is under way the must is transferred into barrels, one-third of which are new, two-thirds of which are of the previous year. Up to now the white wine bottling has taken place after nine months. Henceforth this wine will be given eighteen months in cask, just as at Haut-Brion, Laville and at Chevalier. De Bethmann has tried skin contact. He has tried *bâtonnage*. But he has rejected these procedures. He wants to make a *vin de garde*. He has also reduced yields from 70 hectolitres per hectare to 40; and there is a severe *triage* in the vineyard. The second wines are labelled Réserve de J.J. de Bethmann.

THE CHÂTEAU

The château is one of the glories of Bordeaux, and a national monument, though not open to the public. Partly feudal bastion, partly Renaissance, somewhat, I would imagine, damp, cold and austere in the winter (how *do* you keep a place like that warm and dry?), the castle – and it is a proper castle – stands imposing and four-square encircled by its moat. A lake to the west feeds the moat, and the water then runs under the courtyard in front of the *chais*, which helps keep them cool and humid, before emerging into a fishpond on the other side.

From each side of the château you are presented with a different view. The front, the north face, has a square tower on the one side. There is a raised double staircase to the main door. The east face is massive, dominating, relieved only by the Renaissance-style windows. From the south you have the sole remaining round medieval tower to your left, another square tower to the right; and this feudal reminder softens and romanticizes the west facade.

Inside, the walls are thick – in part excavated to provide bathrooms and lavatories – and the first-floor living space is not as large as you might imagine. There is no vast hall, merely a sizeable *salon* with a typically beamed Renaissance ceiling, a morning room and a dining room. Where is the kitchen? Hidden away, and connected to the dining room by a concealed entrance. Look again and it has merged into the wallpaper. On the ground floor there is a small chapel, originally consecrated in 1500, redecorated in the Viollet le Duc style in the middle of the last century.

THE WINE

Olivier is a wine which needs time, both in red and in white. There is depth here, but its expression can be a little ungainly at first. The red wines have progressively become more serious, more elegant, since 1985, and if the 1989 and 1990 are anything to go by, have a size and a substance which recalls more the wines of Pessac and Talence rather than those of the rest of Léognan. The white wines did not really come of age until the 1992 vintage, and even this was bottled after nine months rather than eighteen as it shall be henceforth. 1992 is a good year for white wine – rather better than for the reds – but not a great one. But if one extrapolates the depth of the 1990 and the finesse of the 1992, anticipates a better vintage in the years to come and adds the concentration and complexity which a more prolonged maturation in cask will give it, one can but shudder with excitement. I am convinced this is going to be one of the great Bordeaux whites. I look forward to it!

THE TASTING

I sampled the following wines at Olivier in September 1993.

WHITE WINES

Optimum drinking

1992   1997–2007

Delicate, elegant, gently oaky nose. This has got depth and grip and plenty of potential for development. It's clear that the large per centage of Sémillon gives extra fat, and an aromatic weight which bodes well for long-term keeping. This is the year when Bethmann got it all right. Not as much depth as the 1990 but more finesse. Very good.

1991   1995–2000

This has got into its shell a bit after bottling. A touch of SO2 is evident. After fifteen minutes in the glass it opened out. Ripe, slightly exotic fruit. Not the weight of the 1992 but has depth and charm. Good.

1990   1996–2010

Not as complete as the 1992. The attack is a little rigid. The aftertaste full and ripe, again with an exotic touch from the Sémillon. Good grip. A shade adolescent. Very good plus though. Needs time.

1989   Now–2002

Softer, more forward, more floral. Matured in wood but vinified in tank. A lighter wine with good acidity. There is an intriguing mixture of grape, fruit and flowers on the follow-through. This is also good. But it will be ready sooner. And it has less depth and less complexity.

1988   **Drink soon**

More SO2 on the nose. I find this a little dead on the palate. There is much less sign of oak here. Ripe and balanced underneath the SO2. Medium body. But a bit one-dimensional and anonymous.

1987   **Drink soon**

Much cleaner. A neat little wine. Still quite fresh. Not without interest. No undue sulphur. Positive at the end. Good.

1986   **Now–1999**

Clean nose. A little rigid. But good acidity, and complex peachy fruit. The *matière première* was rather fine here. This is still youthful. Quite rich. Needs food. All it lacks is the flair that vinifying in wood would have given it.

1985   **Now–1998**

Ripe but a little heavy. A bit of sulphur deadening it. Fullish. Good concentration. The finish is complex and positive. Like the above it shows the possibilities.

1984   **Drink soon**

No undue sulphur. More vegetal than fruity. But not too lean. Indeed there is fat here. But it is beginning to lose its style. Not at all bad, but drink soon.

1983   **Now–1998**

Despite no wood this has complexity. The flavours are gently floral. Not too rigid, as in the 1985 and 1986, any longer. There is good depth and acidity. It shows the quality of the *terroir*. Will still keep well. Enjoyable.

1982   **Drink soon**

This is beginning to show its age. There is less grip here, and less concentration. And it is now getting a bit diffuse. No undue sulphur.

1981   **Now–1996**

This again has interest. It is better than the 1982. Ripe, with an interesting nutty hint. Medium body. Good grip. Clean. Finishes well. Will still hold up a bit.

1978   **Drink soon**

This is a little rigid and anonymous, and has a little built-in sulphur. Ripe and fruity and quite fresh. But a little neutral. Not bad.

RED WINES

1992   1997–2001

Good colour. The nose is fruity but raw. On the palate this is gentle but charming. Some oak. Quite fruity. It lacks a bit of depth, structure and grip. But it is positive at the end. Quite good.

1991   1996–2001

Light to medium colour. Lightish nose, but positive and oaky, not a bit mean. Ripe and fruity. A good 1991. Well made, balanced and charming. Finishes well.

1990   1999–2015

Medium-full colour. Firm nose. Good depth here. Closed-in though. Fullish, ripe and spicy, with a good oak base. The finish is rich, even opulent. It is currently a bit adolescent but there is both elegance and complexity here. Very good on the finish. Very good indeed.

1989   1997–2012

Fullish colour. Slightly more expansive. The tannins are more in evidence. But there seems to be more size and substance as well. Fullish also, richer and more opulent, ripe and spicy too. The new oak is more evident. A flamboyant wine. And very good indeed again.

1988   1998–2015

Full colour. Still very youthful. Backward, stylish nose. This is balanced and has plenty of depth. The tannins are tougher – in the sense of less rich – than in the 1989, and this makes the attack a bit aggressive. The follow-through is much finer. Good blackberry damson fruit. Medium-full. Good plus.

1987   **Drink soon**

Good colour for the vintage. No undue maturity. Gently ripe and stylish on the nose. Fresh, *à point*, medium-bodied. A touch anonymous and not that long on the palate. But a well-made wine.

1986   **Now–1997**

Medium-full colour. Little development. A bit burnt and burly on the nose. But better mannered on the palate. For a Graves this is ripe, even quite concentrated and has good grip. Ripe fruit. Really quite good. Just a bit of astringency at the end.

1985   1995–2008

Very good colour. Still very youthful. The nose is closed still. A fullish, quite tannic wine for the vintage. Ripe fruit, but slightly burly. This is good but the wines today have more elegance. Still needs a few years.

1984   **Drink up**

Medium colour. No undue brown. This is a little weedy and astringent now. But there is some ripeness.

1983   **Now–1999**

Good mature colour. The nose smells of the stalks of flowers like iris and peony, and with some of the flower as well. On the palate medium full, there is good fruit, even depth and finesse. But it is a bit rigid. It would be better with food. Good *matière première*. Plenty of grip and life.

1982   **Drink soon**

Good colour. Still youthful. Quite rich and burly, but a little unforthcoming on the nose. This has much less grip than the 1983. And as a result, though less rigid, and more velvety-fruity, has less interest. It tails off a bit at the end. And it lacks a bit of finesse. Pleasant but lacks depth. Quite good.

1970   **Drink up**

Medium colour. Mature. This is almost ruined by volatile acidity. Has got a bit thin. Underneath there is a suspicion of classy fruit, and the wine is not astringent. But it is not very good.

PAPE-CLÉMENT

Château Pape-Clément can fairly claim to be the oldest wine-producing property in Bordeaux. It can trace its history back to the year 1300, since when the vineyard has been in continuous production; firstly as the main source of supply for successive Archbishops of Bordeaux; latterly, since the French Revolution, as a commercial enterprise.

Pape-Clément is situated in Pessac, a suburb of Bordeaux, and lies near the encircling motorway known as the Rocade and the main road to Arcachon, some six or seven kilometres from the centre of the city. While it is not quite so hemmed in by housing estates and office blocks as its neighbours Haut-Brion and La Mission-Haut-Brion, it still nevertheless gives the impression, as do the others, of a last bastion against the relentless march of concrete out of the city. There are now few wine-producing estates this close to the centre. Only those with a reputation and prices to match can withstand the pressures of the property speculator.

The Pope in question is Clement V, elected to the Papacy in 1306; and it was he who, fearful of the strained relations between the Vatican and the King of France, and mindful of the continual internecine warfare between the Italian city states, chose to remain in his native France and remove the papal seat to Avignon. This is near where, incidentally, his successor built a summer palace and established a vineyard — an area now known as Châteauneuf-du-Pape.

HISTORY

Clement V was born Bertrand de Goth at Villandraut – a castle south of Sauternes. He was a younger son of a noble family, and like many such, chose to make a career in the church. His rise was rapid. From Bishop of Comminges he was elevated in 1299 to the Archbishopric of Bordeaux by Pope Boniface VIII. His elder brother Béraud decided the new spiritual lord should hold lands commensurate with this high position and made over a property a short distance from the city between an estate called Magonty and the road to Merignac. Were there vines there at the time? It is natural to assume so. What is more clear is that De Goth extended the vineyard. On his translation six years later, he left the estate to Cardinal Arnaud de Canteloup, his successor as Archbishop of Bordeaux, and to the Cardinal's episcopal descendants.

The estate remained in ecclesiastical hands until 1789, its produce being known as '*Vigne du Pape-Clément*'. It does not appear to have been commercially marketed, for, despite its high reputation, attested as early as 1619 in the *Chronique Bordelaise*, the wine does not appear in a list of the prices of red Graves properties around 1745 quoted by Franck a century later, nor in the Lawton archives. One can assume it was reserved for entertaining guests at the Archbishop's court. There is, however, a fascinating reference in Rabelais – a *bon viveur* if ever there was one – to '*vin clémentin*'. Was this the wine of Pape-Clément? If so it predates by almost a century and a half Samuel Pepys's mention of '*Ho Bryan*'.

During the revolutionary years, Pape-Clément, along with other ecclesiastical estates such as La Mission-Haut-Brion and Carbonnieux, was confiscated and sold. In 1824 it was owned by a man called Jarrige; from him it passed to De Fortmanoir in the 1840s and then to a M. Clouzel a few years later. At this time it was producing between 30 and 40 *tonneaux* and was considered the second most important château in Pessac after Château Haut-Brion.

In 1858 M. Clouzel sold the major portion of the estate, retaining an adjacent part called Château Sainte-Marie, which he renamed Château Cazalet. The purchaser was a Monsieur J.B. Clerc, and it seems to be Clerc who established the present-day reputation for the wine. He greatly improved the vineyard, ensured that it was entirely planted with noble vines, and generally renovated the property to such an extent that he was awarded the Gironde Agricultural Societies' gold medal in 1861, with a national medal to follow in 1864. The vineyard was enlarged to 37 hectares, and was producing 75 *tonneaux* by Clerc's death in the late 1870s, selling for some 3,000 francs a *tonneau*, on a par with a Médoc second growth.

From Clerc, Pape-Clément passed to a M.J. Cinto, a stockbroker. He restored and enlarged the château from a small, elegant, essentially single-storey country house into a rather ugly, grey sandstone three-storied pile, with a pseudo-Gothic tower and crenellated battlements.

Cinto's heirs sold the property sometime after the First World War to an Englishman called Maxwell and from then it went into decline. During the 1930s it was neglected completely and wine production almost disappeared. The final straw was an unusually heavy hailstorm which severely damaged the dilapidated vineyard on 8 June 1937. Pape-Clément was on the verge of being wound up, and the land, now in Bordeaux's ever increasing suburbs, sold for redevelopment – indeed, there were rumours that this had happened. Instead Château Pape-Clément was bought in 1939 by Paul Montagne, wine-grower and poet, author under his *nom de plume*, Pol des Causses, of *Les Chants du Cygne* and *Chants d'Exil*. Montagne set about replanting the entire vineyard and restoring the château, but owing to the war it was not until 1950 that the programme of renovation was completed, and not until 1953 that the property produced a wine which could be set against the standard of the wines it had produced up until the 1920s.

Paul died at the age of 94 almost twenty years ago, having been blind for the last fifteen years of his life. His son Léo is now co-proprietor along with other members of the family and shareholders in Montagne et Cie; although the running of the property is left to M. Bernard Pujols, the director of the estate.

THE VINEYARD AND THE WINE

There are now some 29 hectares under vines, and these occupy two plots. One of these is immediately in front of the château and comprises 20 hectares; on the other side of the road are several smaller sections. These are planted almost exclusively with Cabernet Sauvignon (60 per cent) and Merlot (40 per cent), with one or two rows of Petit Verdot and Cabernet Franc.

The soil here is less gravelly than at Château Haut-Brion. There is more sand and clay, and the subsoil is a mixture of clay and *feluns*, a mixture of compacted sandstone and fossilized shells. Further down lies limestone.

Château Pape-Clément is one of the few Graves properties – Château Haut-Bailly is another – producing only red wine: on average about 120 to 130 *tonneaux* a year. A few casks of white wine are also made, but only for private consumption and local restaurant sale, from 33 per cent Sémillon, 33 per cent Sauvignon and 33 per cent Muscadelle; a curious, almost Sauternes *encépagement*, yet the wine is dry. It is a very elegant, stylish wine, bottled at present after six to nine months in oak. They are now experimenting to see if delaying the bottling will improve it. In 1989 it was decided to enlarge the white wine vineyard to two and a half hectares, and to adjust the *encépagement* to something more traditional for the Graves.

In recent years there has been considerable renovation to the *chais* and *cuverie*. The first improvement was in 1974, when a long, low *chai de première année* was constructed. Mouton-like, this vast room contains 1,000 *barriques*, one deep, stretching away in the gloom of the subdued lighting towards the far well where the papal arms and cross keys are emblazoned. At the entrance end is a raised reception area, decorated with orange and lemon trees in shrubs, which is occasionally hired out for receptions and parties.

Next to this is the *chai de deuxième année*, but between the two, recently added, is a spanking new *cuverie*. Fermentation now takes place in twenty stainless-steel, 145-hectolitre vats, temperature controlled from a console more appropriate, you would have thought, for launching a space ship.

Up to the installation of this new vinification centre the wine was made in concrete vats, and given one-third new oak. Today, under the supervision of Professor Pascal Ribereau-Gayon, the proportion of new oak has been increased. It was 50 per cent in 1985 and 70 per cent in 1986; the remaining wine is kept *en cuve*. Since 1986, as well, there has been a second wine, Le Clémentin.

Château Pape-Clément is the most Médocain in taste of all top Graves properties. While Château Haut-Brion and Domaine de Chevalier are characterized by their elegance, La Mission by its firm masculinity, and Haut-Bailly by its rich plumminess, Pape-Clément has a certain reserve one does not often find in Graves. This is allied with a more obvious Cabernet ripe fruitiness, a decisive cut from the new oak, and when young, quite a lot of tannin for a Graves. This combination will mellow into a wine of great complexity. But only after ten years or so, in a good vintage, will it show at its best.

As I have already said, the renaissance of Château Pape-Clément really begins with the 1953, and my experience of older bottles has been scanty. A magnum of 1924 – alas, past its best in July 1978 – has been one of the few older bottles of Pape-Clément which has come my way. The vintages of the 1950s I used to know well, having bought both the 1953 and the 1955 myself, the latter a very fine bottle in what was an often disappointing vintage. I would now hazard that it will be showing age.

The 1957 was not at all bad either, and the 1959 has given much pleasure. This run continued in the 1960s with a string of noticeable successes.

In the 1970s, sadly, the quality of Pape-Clément went into decline. Both the 1970 and the 1975 have had their uninspiring moments, though the 1975 now seems to be softening up better than most, and I have found myself getting more enthusiastic about it in the last two or three years. The Graves suffered more than most of Bordeaux in 1973 and 1974, and these wines are best left as unexciting memories. The 1978 is 'good but not great', but after that one has to wait until 1984 for top class quality again. The wines from 1979 to 1983 are disappointing.

Since 1984, however, it would appear that a stricter selection is being made, the influence obviously of Ribereau-Gayon. This vintage is a wine with not only the tannic structure of the year, but a surprising amount of flesh. The 1985 and 1986 are both certainly successes and have shown well in subsequent blind tastings in bottle. The earlier year is fragrant and complex; the latter vintage is good and sturdy, especially considering the downpour. The vintages since then have shown that Pape-Clément is now right up with the very best in the Graves. Indeed today it is no less than a super-second, especially when you rate its performance in 1989 and 1990 against most of the rest of the Graves *crus classés*.

THE TASTING

The older wines which follow were sampled at a tasting organized by Russell Norton, photographic antiquarian *extraordinaire*, and hosted by Bob Feinn of Mount Carmel Wines in New Haven, Connecticut, in May 1986. I have added some notes from tastings held in London in April 1990 and in Bordeaux in 1992.

Optimum drinking

1990   **1998–2014**
Good colour. This is stylish, quite rich, certainly ripe. But not a blockbuster. Good balance though. Medium-full body. Good tannins. This has classy blackberry-blackcurrant fruit. Good grip. Elegant and stylish and not without depth. Shows very well. Very good indeed.

1989   **1997–2009**
Medium-full colour. Not as intense as the 1990. The nose is quite fat, rich and ample, but doesn't have quite as much grip and elegance. On the palate medium to medium-full body. A little dry on the attack, but the follow-through is better. Ample, ripe and quite intense. A bit more substance but the 1990 is better balanced and more stylish. And more concentrated. Very good plus though.

1988   **1995–2009**
Fullish colour. Better than the 1989. Stylish nose: good fruit and very good balance and depth. A gentle wine, harmonious, complex and understated. Medium to medium-full body, very elegant fruit, very good grip. Less intense and less concentrated than the 1990 but long and subtle. Very good plus.

1987   **Drink soon**
Reasonable colour for the vintage. Reasonable structure on the nose but the tannins are a little dry and lean. Some concentration and fruit though. A good effort.

1986   **Now–1999**
Good colour. Good richness, fat and new wood on the nose, slightly grilled toast. No lack of fruit. Medium to medium-full. A little tannin but essentially quite a soft, forward wine. Pleasant. Not dilute, nor weedy. A good effort.

1985   **Now–2002**
Good colour. Ripe, quite substantial, but a little four-square on the nose at present. On the nose this has more personality but nevertheless not a great deal of character or depth. Balanced but not very complex or much *puissance*. Very good at best.

1983   **1995–2005**
Good colour. The nose is rather more dense and artisanal than the 1985. Medium-full. There is substance here, even richness and depth, and the wine has good acidity and reserves. I prefer it to the 1982. But it lacks a little flair. Good plus.

1982   **Now–2008**
Fine full purple colour. Full nose, there is plenty of fruit, but there is something a bit clumsy about it. Quite full; rich, tannic, a little burly. Good better as it developed but this is nevertheless not a really exciting example of this vintage.

1981   **Drink soon**
Medium-full colour. High-toned nose, a little vegetably. Medium body, not a lot of tannin. Soft, supple, pleasantly cedary and fruity but the acidity is on the low side. Charming initially but didn't hold up very well in the glass.

1980   **Drink up**
Medium colour; some brown. The nose is a bit dry and uninspiring, and the palate more so. Dull; even for the vintage.

1979   **Drink soon**
Medium-full colour; a little development. Open nose, plummy; quite attractive if without a great

deal of depth and concentration. Reasonable finish, quite fresh and fruity but a bit loose and lacking personality. Quite good.

1978   **Now–1999**

Medium-full colour; less developed than the 1979. Denser nose, more closed, with a touch of cloves. Medium full body, some tannin. This has depth but seems to lack a bit of richness. Has grip but not quite enough warmth and charm. Finishes better than it starts though, so may improve as it ages further. Yet after aeration didn't seem to get any better.

1976   **Drink soon**

Good colour for the vintage; mature. The nose has more weight than most of the 1976s, as well as less development. Fullish, not a lot of finesse – there is even something a little earthy and farmyard about it – yet no fade, and not coarse or rustic. Fat. Quite good.

1975   **Now–2000**

Fullish colour; no development. Closed nose, but seems to have less density and more flexibility and fruit than most. Fullish, some tannin, plump and ample for a 1975. Not too tough and has fruit and grip. Finishes well. Very good.

1971   **Drink soon**

Quite full, mature colour. Good, reasonably mature, elegant nose; has depth and fragrance. Medium body, fully mature Has finesse if no great weight or depth. Soft, round, quite generous. Good but not great, yet certainly better than most 1971s. Holding up well.

1970   **Now–1999**

Fullish, mature colour. Not much nose. Fullish on the palate, with a little bitterness, as well as tannin. A chunky, four-square wine which lacks charm. Has fruit, but it is the solidity which dominates. Will still develop, but will it develop more generosity?

1967   **Drink soon**

Very good colour for the vintage. Good, quite full and concentrated nose, with no undue age. Rich, plummy, ripe and fruity. More structure than most of this vintage. Mature but not aged. Good finish, even complexity. Very fine for the vintage.

1966   **Drink soon**

Good full, mature colour. Fragrant, complex nose, delicate, blackcurranty. Soft, round, quite

developed, even a little past its best (or is this just a more advanced bottle than some?). Lacks a bit of zip but finishes well. A very elegant wine.

1964   **Drink soon**

(Tasted April 1990) Good colour, still vigorous. Mature but not a bit faded. Good Cabernet fruit. Medium-full, ripe, generous and stylish. Still very fresh. Now mature, complex, long and attractive. Still very much alive. Very good.

1964   **See note**

(Château bottled, low level) Even better, full, mature colour. The nose is a little pinched compared with the other bottle. Medium body. Some signs of dryness but still a good wine.

1964   **Drink soon**

(Bordeaux bottled? Barrière label) Similar colour. Fine, complex, fragrant nose. This has a lot of elegance. A fine, medium-full bodied wine; ripe, balanced, classy. This is fresher and better than the above. Very good.

1962   **Drink soon**

Very fine colour, only just mature; no sign of age. Delicious, plump, generous, plummy nose. Fullish, ripe, fragrant, complex wine. Quite lovely and still plenty of life. At first even better than the 1964, but as it developed in the glass the wine above caught up and overtook the 1962. Very fine indeed nevertheless.

1961   **Drink soon**

Very fine full colour. Little brown. Rich, firm, meaty nose. A wine of structure, full and sturdier than most Graves. Very fine perfumed concentrated fruit though. Not perhaps the greatest of 1961s, but good.

1959   **Drink soon**

Fullish, well-matured colour. Quite an old nose. This bottle has seen better days and is outclassed by both the 1961 and the wine below. Nevertheless an elegant gentleman, still showing his class. Medium body; not the toughness and roasted quality of many 1959s. Smells a little of figs.

1953   **Holding up well**

(Magnum) Full colour, mature. Lovely nose, a real concentration of fruit. Rich, very complex, still amazingly fresh for a wine of over 30 years' age. Fullish, sweet and fragrant. A very lovely bottle indeed. The best of the entire tasting without a doubt.

LA TOUR-MARTILLAC

On two separate occasions, in two different vintages, I have recently marked the white wines of La Tour-Martillac ahead of all its peers in a blind tasting (it is fair to say that the ranges did not include Haut-Brion, La Mission and Domaine de Chevalier). The vintages were 1988 and 1989. As a result I went straight out and bought a case of each. I have also noticed a distinct improvement in the quality of the red wine. Things are obviously happening down there, I said to myself, and the next time I was in the area I decided to pay a visit to my old friend Jean Kressmann to ask if I could make a vertical tasting of his wines and find out more about what has been going on recently. The Kressmanns are merchants as well as château proprietors, and I have known them for ages. But I had never before found much to admire at their Martillac domaine. As elsewhere, this château in the Graves has undergone a renaissance.

The property takes its name from a small, thin, isolated tower which stands in the central courtyard in front of the château. The tower was in fact once a staircase of a small twelfth-century fort – a *castagne*, as it is described in old plans. The rest of the fort, or the ruins thereof, was used to build the present château towards the end of the eighteenth century. The domaine was once part of the vast estates of Château La Brède, which lies four kilometres to the south, and the fort was probably one of its outer defences.

HISTORY

The château of La Brède is inseparable from the name of Montesquieu, who was brought up at the neighbouring domaine of Rochemorin. Part of the La Tour-Martillac vineyard, it is said, belonged to his wife, Jeanne de Lartigue. Though Montesquieu exported considerable quantities of wine to England, the reputation of the wines of Martillac was slow to evolve. No specific estates are mentioned in the early editions of writers such as Wilhelm Franck and Charles Cocks. It is not until Franck's fourth edition in 1860 that 'La Tour' – or indeed any others – get a specific mention. M. Charropin, an important Bordelais jurist, acquired the property in 1853 from a 'marchand de Brienne'. He is listed last out of eleven proprietors in 1860, producing 10 to 12 tonneaux of wine.

The Kressmanns arrived on the scene in 1871, soon after Edward Kressmann, of German extraction, had founded his firm in Bordeaux. Firstly, they were merely distributors of wine. Subsequently they farmed the estate. In 1929 they purchased it from Pierre Langlois, successor to the Charropins.

ADELINA PATTI

One of the Kressmanns' most successful wines was the Graves Monopole Dry. The base of the wine came from La Tour-Martillac and the brand was launched in London in 1892. Its great sponsor was the soprano Adelina Patti (1843–1919). Patti was the most celebrated vocalist of her time, and insisted that she would only tour the United States provided that 'the dry white Graves wine Kressmann had the monopoly of' was available at every stopover.

THE KRESSMANNS

White wine was the mainstay of the domaine at the time. Red grapes do not appear to have been planted on a large scale until after the Second World War, though the 1929 was served at the coronation of King George VI in 1937. In 1929 there were twelve hectares under vines, of which eight were white grapes.

In 1940 the vineyard was enlarged, a section between the château and the village being acquired, and since then the area under vines has been extended to 30 hectares, of which 24 are under red grapes. A further extension occurred when the neighbouring Château La Garde was sold to the négociant CVBG in 1990. Some of the Merlot vineyard opposite the château was acquired by the Kressmanns. They would have liked to have bought more.

The red-wine vineyard is planted in the ratio 64 per cent Cabernet Sauvignon, 25 per cent Merlot (an increase since the 1970s), 6 per cent Cabernet Franc and 5 per cent Malbec. The six hectares of white wine vineyard contain 55 per cent Semillon, 35 per cent Sauvignon, 3 per cent Muscadelle and 7 per cent of 100 year old vines of diverse origins from a vineyard called Grattecap.

Jean Kressmann took over responsibility of La Tour-Martillac in 1940, and inherited the property when his father Alfred died in 1955. He has now been succeeded by two of his six children: Tristram on the business side, Loic in the winery.

It is since the arrival of these two, and the appointment as consultant oenologists of Denis Dubourdieu in 1986 and subsequently Michel Rolland for the red wines in 1989, that the quality of the La Tour-Martillac wines has been transformed. What was first of all necessary was a renovation and extension of the cuvier and chais. This is now a thoroughly modern, temperature-controlled establishment with a tasting room and reception centre at the upper level, overlooking the vineyards.

Below, on one side, are twelve large vats for the vinification of the red wine, four of wood (for the produce of the older vines) and eight in stainless steel. Round the corner are nine smaller cuves which used to be used for the white wine. Beyond is the chai for the vinification of the white wine. This now takes place in Allier oak, half of which is renewed each year. Until 1990 the wine is kept *sur lie* for seven to eight months before bottling. It is now bottled after fifteen months. In 1986 half the crop was vinified and matured in wood, the rest in tank. Since then all has been fermented in oak.

On the other side of the reception centre is the red wine cellar. One-third to 45 per cent new oak is employed and there is now a second label: La Grave-Martillac Rouge. The red is bottled 20 to 22 months after the vintage and in recent years I have seen it expand from something medium bodied but diffuse in character – merely *bourgeois* in quality, despite its classification in 1953 – to something altogether richer and more exciting. I am sure the introduction of the second wine has played an important part. Judging by the recent vintages of both colours, this is a property to watch.

THE TASTING

Most of the following wines were sampled at La Tour-Martillac in April 1990. I have added further notes from 1992.

WHITE WINES

Optimum drinking

1991   **Drink soon**
Youthful, fresh, new-wave nose. Ripe and gentle. Good style, good fruit. Quite high acidity but not unripe. Elegant. For early drinking.

1990   **1997–2008**
Kept fifteen months on the lees. Good depth here, richer and fatter than the 1989. Youthful. Serious. Lovely fruit and great harmony. Very good plus.

1989   **1995–2005**
Fragrant and peachy. Rather more accessible and forward. Also rather more elegant and high-toned than the 1988. The Sauvignon comes out a bit more. Balanced, crisp, medium-bodied, supple and stylish. Very good.

1988   **1995–2007**
On the nose this is a touch hard and adolescent. There is a bit more built-in sulphur. In principle this is a better wine than the 1989. It is fuller and better balanced. But at present the 1989 is cleaner and more elegant. On the finish though this is very good. Long. Plenty of depth. Will last well.

1987   **Drink soon**
Slightly rigid on the nose. A little built-in SO2. Better as it evolved. It has neither the depth nor the fruit of the 1988. And there is a little SO2 on the palate. Stylish but one-dimensional. Wait until the SO2 disappears and then drink soon.

1986   **Drink soon**
This was the year Dubourdieu was called in to advise, but they didn't get their act together immediately. There doesn't seem to be a lot of fruit (nor oak for that matter) on the nose and there is a bit of built-in SO2. Wet wool on the palate hiding the fruit.

1986   **Not commercially available**
Held another six months in wood. This has got less SO2, seems richer, but it is also more rigid. Interesting oak/apricot flavours. Good acidity, good ripeness. This is more like it. Good.

1985   **Drink soon**
Old-style Graves on the nose. No oak, a bit of SO2, but a ripe fullish wine underneath nevertheless. As a result of frost, their old vines did not produce a drop of wine this year. Plump, ripe, even honeyed on the palate. Not bad. Has the depth to endure until the SO2 diminishes.

1984   **Drink up**
This has less SO2 but less fruit as well. On the palate it is not too bad at all for a 1984. There is fruit if not a great deal of concentration of depth.

1983   **Drink soon**
Fuller and richer and more concentrated than the 1985, but nevertheless the built-in SO2. A full, rich, aromatic wine. Plenty of concentration. A bit ungainly as are all these tank-fermented and bulk-aged wines but there is depth here. Finishes long and complex.

1982   **Drink soon**
A ripe aromatic wine, the SO2 is disappearing. On the palate it is ripe and supple and really quite attractive. Good style. Good length, none of the heaviness I associate with the vintage. Will still keep.

1981   **Past its best**
This has begun to lose its fruit. The SO2 still remains. A dead wet dog. The fruit is beginning to dry out. The SO2 dominates. I find this barely drinkable.

1975   **Drink soon**
Good colour. There is a little pinched and bitter-

ness of slight fading fruit on the nose. But on the palate no lack of freshness, nor fruit. Ripe, fruit salady. Fragrant, stylish. Almost a suspicion of honey. Good.

1964   **Drink soon**

Fresh colour. Complex, fresh, fragrant nose. Fat, rich, slight suggestion of oak. This has given it structure and depth. Lovely, rich complex finish. Long and warm and satisfying. Very fine. Yet the attack is a little blunt. Curious.

1962   **Past its best**

This is richer but rather more evolved on the nose. On the palate the wine is very soft but there is a suggestion of sweetness. Yet not really like a Sauternes (or even a dry Sauternes). Individual. If anything it has a touch of Frascati. Basically this is a bit too old. But it is not without interest.

RED WINES

1991   **1995–2000**

Medium colour. Positive nose. This is not too weedy. There is fruit here and no lack of grip. Not bad at all. There is no real depth or concentration, but it is attractively balanced and has a reasonable finish.

1990   **1996–2006**

Medium-full colour. Rich, positive, gently oaky nose. Medium to medium-full body. Ripe and balanced; has fat as well as fruit. Good tannins, good finesse. Good grip. This is one of the few 1990 Graves with real interest and merit. Long. Complex. Good plus to very good.

1989   **1995–2002**

Medium to medium-full colour. Not as interesting on the nose as the 1990. Less weight. A little dry from the tannins. Less fat, less power, less interest. It is balanced but it lacks a bit of richness and concentration. Quite good at best.

1988   **1995–2004**

Medium colour. Cool, balanced, discreet, stylish nose. Not a blockbuster but a harmonious wine with good gentle fruit. I prefer this to the 1989, but it is not as promising as the 1990. Medium body. Good tannins. Lively, stylish, subtle and balanced. Finishes positively. Good.

1987   **Drink up**

Good nose for the vintage. Fresh and ripe. Not feeble. Medium body. Not much tannin but reasonable fruit and grip. Positive finish. Good for the vintage.

1986   **Now–2001**

Good colour. Reasonable nose for the vintage though the tannins lack a little flesh. Medium body. There is good concentrated Cabernet fruit

here and not a bad grip at all. Some tannin. Also a little astringent on the attack but the finish is more succulent. A very good Graves.

1985   **Now–2001**

Very good colour. An ample, round, spicy nose though it lacks a little class and zip. There is something a little rustic here. On aeration not so much rustic as earthy. It seemed to improve. A meaty wine. Quite full. Ripe, rather more Merlot-ish. Just a little four-square. The structure obtrudes. Good balance but lacks a little elegance. Quite good.

1984   **Drink up**

Reasonable colour for vintage. Now some development. The unripe, slightly vegetal tannins have now softened, but the wine lacks charm as well as depth. On the palate it lacks a little fruit and the finish is astringent but I suppose it's not bad for a 1984.

1983   **Now–2000**

Medium-full colour. Now a little development. A pleasant, soft, round nose. More class than the 1985 perhaps, but less grip. A little one-dimensional. This is medium to medium-full, the tannins now all but absorbed, and is ripe and succulent, with better length than apparent on the nose. Has charm if no great class. Reasonable length. Quite good.

1982   **Now–1997**

Fullish colour. Not much sign of development. On the nose the tannins are a little dry but the wine is quite full and meaty. Yet it lacks the real 1982 richness. Not that much bigger than the above. It seems a little diffuse and there isn't a great deal of finesse. Lacks a bit of grip. Not exciting.

1981   **Drink soon**

Medium colour. Mature. Lightish nose. Fully evolved. Not a great deal of excitement to offer. A medium-bodied wine which is now ready. Reasonable fruit if no great style or concentration. Not bad at best.

1980   **Drink soon**

Lightish colour; fully mature. Soft, diffuse nose. Not much style here. This isn't too bad at all on the palate. Reasonable fruit. Good grip for a 1980. Still quite fresh. Not yet at the end of its life. Not bad.

1979   **Drink soon**

Light to medium colour, mature. Nose is a little light and herbal. On the palate the large vintage is all too apparent. Some fruit. Even some style and indeed not that short. But essentially dilute.

1978   **Drink up**

Lighter colour than the 1979, more evolved in

colour too. Quite plump on the nose but lacks style and grip. A bit over-evolved. There is a certain astringency and a certain attenuation. Light. Feeble really. Unexciting.

1977   Drink up

Lightish colour, less brown than the 1976. Light nose. Not too weedy but nothing much here. Not bad for a 1977. Not too evolved. Some fruit. Not too lean. Rather a better effort for the vintage than 1978 and 1979.

1976   Drink up

Medium colour, mature. The usual, rather coarse, dry, diffuse 1976 nose. This is a bit short, the fruit is drying up and the whole thing is rather astringent. Another uninspiring 1976.

1975   Drink soon

Medium to medium-full colour. Still reasonably vigorous. Some fruit on the nose and no undue hardness. This is not bad at all. There is an element of tough (now slightly astringent) tannins but there is fruit and even depth as well. Not bad. Still has a positive finish.

1974   Drink up

Good colour. Still vigorous. A reasonable nose. A little lean but not to aged. This is in fact surprisingly stylish. Lacks richness but neither dilute nor astringent, nor too lean. Still quite fresh and enjoyable.

1973   Past its best

Light to medium colour, fully mature. Light, rather slight and weedy nose. This is light and now past its best. There is a little residual fruit but it is now overwhelmed by the astringency.

1970   Drink soon

Good colour. Quite full and no undue maturity. On the nose full and meaty if not a great deal of style. The wine has reasonable substance but was never excitingly ripe. Did the malo take place? I think there was always a little toughness and four-squareness about it. Lacks style.

1967   Drink up

Good colour for the vintage. A lot more vigorous than most of the 1970s examples. Soft, spicy nose. Reasonable body and depth. Ripe. Now a bit diffuse but I suspect might have had a bit of elegance once.

1966   Drink soon

Good colour. Fullish, no undue maturity. This is rather better than the 1970. Ripe nose not without style or balance. Reasonable substance and depth. Even still length on the palate. Good.

LARRIVET-
HAUT-BRION

Prior to the French Revolution the most important estate in
Léognan was that of the Marquis de Canolle, a member of a
family which had once been English, under the name of
Knollys, but had stayed in the Bordeaux era after the end of
the Hundred Years War. The Canolle family, also associated
with Château Belair in Saint Emilion, managed to survive
the Revolution, but ran out of male heirs in the middle of
the nineteenth century. Part of their Graves estate was absorbed into Château Haut-Bailly; the remainder is what we
today call Larrivet-Haut-Brion. This latter property almost
disappeared between the wars, and was a small young vineyard when the Graves Classification was first drawn up in
1953. The vines are now mature, and the property has recently been given a new lease of life and has been expanded.
I am sure that if there were a reclassification of the Graves
today Larrivet would be elevated into the ranks of *cru classé*
for both its white and its red wine.

The first mention of the wines of Léognan, historically
rather later to be exploited as a vineyard area than Pessac and
Talence, nearer to the city of Bordeaux, is in André Jullien's
Topographie de Tous les Vignobles Connus in 1816. The best
wines of the commune, he says are comparable in quality
with fourth and fifth growth Médocs, and these are the estates of the Canolles, the Literics and the Mareilhacs.

It is hardly a coincidence that these three lay in a line on
the same ridge of gravel between the eastern end of the village and Château Carbonnieux: Literic first, then the
Canolle estate, then the domaine of the Mareilhacs.
Mareilhac became Château La Louvière. Literic evolved into
Branon-Literie (*sic*), and was owned towards the end of the
nineteenth century by the Clavé family. The aftermath of
phylloxera and the expansion of the village of Léognan in
the early years of this century saw the demise of this growth;
part of it too had been absorbed into Haut-Bailly. Which
leaves us with the Canolles.

HISTORY

It must have been a large estate. In 1824, according to Franck, production averaged 70 to 100 *tonneaux*, indicating 65 or more hectares under vine. Franck's 1824 edition lists the wines in alphabetical order. In 1845 he has more courage. The wine of the Marquis de Canolle is rated in second place. With Charles Cocks, writing in 1850, we come to the first allusion to the current title of the estate: La Rivette. As this suggests, there is a small stream which runs across the land, helping to drain the vineyard. '*Brion*', so some writers have claimed, is a local word for gravel.

The Canolle era was drawing to a close. Successive accounts show production evaporating as parts of the estate were sold off – including a parcel which went to Haut-Bailly – and by 1860 what was now Brion-Larrivet belonged to Mmes de Tafford and de Sulzer, daughters of the Marquis de Canolle-Lescours.

A decade later the property was bought by Ernest Laurent; he was a Bordeaux *négociant*. At this time, out of a total landholding of 125 hectares, still sizeable, there were 40 hectares of vineyard. Twenty years further on, now Haut-Brion-Larrivet, the estate had changed hands yet again. It was owned by Thomas Conseil, a Bordelais ship-fitter. The vineyard was to remain in the Conseil family, slowly falling into desuetude, until 1935.

In the meanwhile, the name had been drawn to the notice of a rather important property in Pessac. Legal proceedings ensued. It was one of two (Les Carmes is the other) which the first growth failed to win. An appeal in 1929 upset a judgement of 1926. Larrivet could retain its Haut-Brion, but to avoid confusion it was suggested that the order of the words should be reversed; so as Larrivet-Haut-Brion it has continued.

In 1935 the estate was broken up. Encouraged by the government offer of *primes d'arrachage* (a bounty for uprooting vines), most of the vineyard was destroyed. The three-hectare rump that remained was acquired in 1940 by Jacques Guillemaud. Slowly but surely after the war, Guillemaud replanted the twelve hectares of land he had acquired, and in 1973 bought a further four hectares. At an equal pace, the reputation of Larrivet-Haut-Brion, so high in the past – for throughout the nineteenth century it had been rated either first or second in the commune – began to revive.

Jacques Guillemaud died in 1973, and responsibility for the wine passed to his grandson, François Boutémy. Boutémy is still in charge, though in 1987 his grandmother decided to sell out to the Société Andros, better known as jam manufacturers.

THE VINEYARD

Since the Andros arrival there has been an expansion of the vineyard. Currently there are 14.8 hectares in production under black grapes (55 per cent Cabernet Sauvignon and 45 per cent Merlot) and 1.2 hectares under white (50 per cent Sémillon, 50 per cent Sauvignon), making 625 cases. A further 25 hectares have been planted, in two separate plots; one lies immediately south of the existing vineyard and was formerly part of the domaine; the other is further away, near Smith-Haut-Lafitte; and there is a possibility of a further fifteen. This will increase the presently tiny white wine exploitation to ten hectares.

THE *CHAIS* AND THE WINE-MAKING

The wine-making and the place where it takes place are also changing. At present there is rather a cramped *chai* which houses three stainless-steel vats and a battery of nine epoxy-resin-lined concrete *cuves* next to a tiny barrel cellar. This is already barely adequate. A new *chai* is being constructed a short distance away. An underground cellar will connect the two.

What has changed in the red wine production is the amount of new wood. Formerly this was changed on a four-year rotation basis, that is, 25 per cent new each year. Today there is

70 per cent new wood, and Boutémy might even go to 100 per cent new oak, but rotate between rackings so that some of the wine was kept in tank.

Like many, Larrivet-Haut-Brion began using wood for the white wines in 1985. At first it was only *élevé* (matured) in wood. From the 1987 vintage the wine was fermented in wood. And 70 per cent of this is now new. Originally the wine was bottled after six months. Today the wine is kept a year before bottling.

THE CHÂTEAUX

There are two châteaux at Larrivet-Haut-Brion. The 'proper' château is a modest single-storey *chartreuse* with a tiled two-storey tower at one end, not dissimilar to Vieux Château Certan. The designs in old editions of Cocks and Féret show that there were originally two towers, one at each end. This château lies in a little park on the same side of the road, that is the south side, as the existing *chai*. François Boutémy lives here.

This building, though the original château of the estate, was never part of the Guillemaud acquisition. It had been previously sold off separately and it was just fortuitous that it happened to be on the market at the time of the Andros purchase. Where the Guillemauds lived, and where Philippe Gervoson, director of the property on behalf of his father, boss of Andros, lives today, was on the other side of the road, in what was once a series of farm-workers's cottages. As a result of the acquisition of the original château, the label of the wine has recently been changed – or should I say perhaps changed back: I have never seen an old bottle of Larrivet-Haut-Brion.

THE WINE

The Larrivet-Haut-Brion white's sole defect, currently, is that there should be so little of it: something we white Graves lovers are going to have to endure for the time being, until the new vineyard is mature. At least we will not have to wait quite as long as if it were red grapes, for a white wine vineyard seems to give of its best earlier.

The red wines, as the notes will show, are elegant and subtle, rich in the best years such as 1985, and evolve in the medium term. They are certainly of *cru classé* standard. Indeed they have more interest and depth than some of the current classed growths. Boutémy is an exigent wine-maker (he has done wonders at Clos-Saint-Martin and elsewhere in Saint-Emilion where he is also in charge) and he has not finished yet at Larrivet-Haut-Brion. With a second label, Domaine de Larrivet, to absorb the produce of the young vines, Larrivet-Haut-Brion can only go from strength to strength. This is a property to watch.

THE TASTING

The following wines were sampled in January 1990. I have added a note on the 1989s and 1990s which I sampled in April 1992.

WHITE WINES

1990 *Optimum drinking* **1996–2012**
This seems less rigid than the 1989. Fatter and plumper, better balanced, more concentrated. Firm, but there is good richness and grip underneath. Fine finish. Very good plus.

1989 **1995–2008**
Clean, fresh, oaky, slightly rigid nose. The structure and the oak are quite apparent. Underneath the wine is ripe and succulent, with good depth

and balance. Currently a little four-square, but it will round off. Very good.

1988 **1995–2010**
A deep colour for a wine this young. Fat, rich, full, ample nose. Depth and concentration here. Quite delicious. Very fine oak. Firm but quite evolved and exotic in flavour already. Reminds me of De Fieuzal. Good grip. Still raw. Lots of potential, and the size to last for a long time.

1987 **Now–1998**
Good nose. Not the dimension of the 1988 but

clean, gently oaky and stylish. Good palate. Balanced, fruity and charming. Medium body. Will evolve soon. Finishes ample and plump.

1986   **Now–1997**

This has the lightest colour of the three. This shows SO2 on the nose. Difficult to see what is underneath. Medium full, ripe but a bit raw and a little rigid. Good grip but not the depth of the 1988. Underneath quite stylish, especially on the finish.

RED WINES

1990   **1996–2003**

Good colour. Quite ample on the nose. Pronounced new oak. Underneath though the wine is plump, there is not a lot of substance. Quite good only.

1989   **1997–2007**

Good colour. Quite pronounced toasty new oak on the nose. Here I find the 1989 better than the 1990. It is ample, rich and long. And it seems better balanced. Good.

1988   **Now–2000**

Good colour. Stylish nose. Gently oaky. Not too hard. Not a blockbuster; a medium-weight, fruity, elegant wine with good balance and a subtle oaky base. Has charm. Shows well.

1987   **Drink soon**

Very good colour for the vintage. More substance than most though a touch of *vin de presse* is evident. A lot better than most on the palate. Mainly Merlot in flavour. Has fruit. Reasonable grip and a positive finish. A very good result.

1986   **Now–1999**

Medium colour. Not a blockbuster on the nose but there is balance and style here. Good fruit. A soft Cabernet-ish wine. Medium body. Not too

obtrusive tannins. Pleasant fruit. Plump. Positive finish. Lacks a bit of depth but has balance and charm.

1985   **Now–2004**

Medium-full colour. Rich nose, fuller than the 1986. Some spice. Opulent. There is depth here. A little fuller than the 1986 on the palate. More complex fruit. A little more tannin. This has good grip and plenty of style. Positive finish. Good.

1984   **Drink up**

Medium colour. Mature. Getting a bit attenuated on the nose. Some sweetness on the attack but a bit coarse and dry on the finish.

1983   **Now–2000**

Medium colour, a surprising amount of brown. More so than the 1984. This is rather more evolved on the nose than I had expected. Soft and spicy but less rich than the 1985, it seems. Medium colour. Quite mature. Pleasant but lacks a bit of depth and excitement. A slight disappointment after the 1985. Yet is soft, has good grip and finishes better than it starts.

1982   **Now–2002**

Medium-full colour. Just beginning to show signs of brown. Full and rich on the nose but a little adolescent. Good ample attack. Opulent fruit, rich and spicy. Medium to medium-full body, the tannins now quite round. Reasonable grip. An attractive plump wine.

1981   **Drink soon**

Good colour for the vintage. Just about the same as the 1982. Now mature. Medium weight on the nose. Interesting complexity. Good freshness. Full ready. Round and fruity; fresh but not that long. *A point* now and not a keeper. Lacks a little dimension on the follow-through. Pretty.

SAINT-EMIL

THE COMMUNE OF SAINT-EMILION IS LARGER THAN MOST OF THE IMPORTANT MÉDOC PARISHES, AND LIES NORTH OF THE RIVER DORDOGNE, SOME 50 KILOMETRES EAST OF BORDEAUX. IT CAN BE DIVIDED INTO THREE SECTIONS. SOUTH OF THE TOWN OF SAINT-EMILION ITSELF, THE LAND FALLS AWAY STEEPLY TOWARDS THE RIVER, AND THE BEST VINEYARDS LIE ON THESE SLOPES OR OCCUPY THE PLATEAU ON THE OTHER THREE SIDES OF THE TOWN. THIS IS THE AREA KNOWN AS THE *CÔTES-SAINT-EMILION*. THE SOIL CONSISTS OF A THIN LAYER OF LIMESTONE DEBRIS AND CLAY OVER A SOLID LIMESTONE BASE, WITH SAND AS ONE DESCENDS INTO THE VALLEY. TO THE NORTH THE LIMESTONE IS MIXED WITH OLD WEATHERED SAND, AS WELL AS CLAY. TO THE WEST, ACROSS A LESSER AREA WHERE THE SOIL IS TOO SANDY FOR TOP-CLASS WINE, IS THE SMALLER *GRAVES-SAINT-EMILION*. AS THE NAME WOULD SUGGEST, HERE THERE IS MORE GRAVEL IN THE SOIL. THERE IS LESS LIMESTONE AND CLAY THAN IN THE BEST SITES OF THE *CÔTES*, BUT MORE SAND. THE SUBSOIL IS OF THE SAME COMPOSITION.

The different areas produce quite different wines, although (with the exception of Château Cheval-Blanc, which is made from two-thirds Cabernet Franc, and Château Figeac, which has a substantial portion of Cabernet Sauvignon), the top growths have similar *encépagements*: roughly one-half to two-thirds Merlot and one-third Cabernet Franc. The *Côtes* and northern wines start off well coloured, quite full, without being particularly dense, and develop quickly, being ready for drinking a few years before Médocs and Graves of similar standing. In character they are loose-knit, somewhat warmer and sweeter than in the Médoc, and with a spicy, fruit-cakey flavour which derives from the predominant Merlot grape.

The *Graves*-Saint-Emilions have more power. They are fuller and more concentrated, rich and firmer than those of the *Côtes*, though still in the main with the predominant flavour of the Merlot grape. They tend to require longer to mature, and last better.

Saint-Emilion was first officially classified in 1954, and this was brought up to date in 1969 and again in 1984. The eleven *premiers crus* are divided into two sections: A (Châteaux Ausone and Cheval Blanc) and B, and these are followed by 63 *grands crus classés*.

AUSONE

That wine was made in the Bordeaux area in Gallo-Roman times is well established; there is ample evidence, both documentary and archaeological. Whether, however, it was the Romans who first brought vines to the Gironde, and when these were first planted, is less certain.

It would appear that the city of Bordeaux, or 'Burdigala' as the Romans called it, was a centre for wine-trading and shipment – no doubt of the wines made further up the Garonne and Dordogne valleys in Gaillac, Cahors and elsewhere – before it became a wine-growing region in its own right.

The late William Younger, in his *Gods, Men and Wine*, thought it was 'probable' that vines were grown in the area in the first century AD but he pointed out that the progress of the vine through Gaul, northwards and westwards from the Mediterranean, was slow. Further expansion would have been discouraged by the edict of the Emperor Domitian who in AD 92 gave instructions that all vineyards outside Italy were to be pulled up because there was a dearth of grain in the Empire.

While it is unlikely that a great deal of notice was taken of Domitian's edict, such vineyards as there were in Bordeaux would have produced poorly by comparison with these vineyards further inland where the weather was kinder. It does not seem to have been until the fourth century AD, perhaps encouraged by the revocation of the Domitian edict by the Emperor Probus in AD 280, that the Gironde became a widespread vine-growing area. Although some vines may have been grown on the land around the town of Burdigala itself, evidence suggests that cultivation was more common on the higher ground of the Entre-Deux-Mers and above the Dordogne valley around the town of Saint-Emilion.

Most appropriately, one of the first chroniclers of Bordeaux wines and vineyards has a property named after him – Ausonius.

AUSONIUS

Ausonius was born in Bordeaux about AD 310, the son of a doctor, and spent the first half of his life as an academic, being appointed Professor of Rhetoric at Bordeaux University, a post he was to hold for 30 years. During this time he was appointed tutor to Gratian and when Gratian became Emperor of Rome he was appointed Governor of Gaul and, later, Consul. He died in AD 394 or 395.

Ausonius was also a poet and a vineyard owner. In his retirement, he lived on his 'little inheritance', a piece of land of 1,000 acres, of which 100 were vineyard. He speaks of the famous wines of the Gironde and describes his own vines as 'casting their reflections on the yellowing Garonne'. From this last statement, we might conclude, sadly, that the connection between Ausonius and Château Ausone is tenuous at best. Nevertheless, there is no doubt that the Saint-Emilion vineyard is of considerable antiquity and there is other evidence to associate Ausone with Lucianacum, as Saint-Emilion was known at the time. The vineyard overlooking the Garonne had belonged to Ausonius' father. Subsequently, Ausonius acquired other land, on the outskirts of Bordeaux, in the region of Saint-Emilion, and in the Saintonge.

Evidence for the local tradition that Ausonius lived at Lucianacum has been the recent uncovering of the remains of an important Gallo-Roman villa called the Moulin du Palat at the foot of the Ausone vineyard in the grounds of Château La Gaffelière. Was this the villa to which Theon was so enthusiastically invited?

If one approaches Saint-Emilion from the south by the long straight road on the north bank of the Dordogne, one will drive between Château La Gaffelière – the *chais* on the left, the château on the right – and then up a narrow valley towards the narrow cobbled streets of the town itself. On the steep slopes up on the left is a small vineyard whose aspect is south and east. There are the seven hectares of Château Ausone. Behind the château of Ausone are further vineyards on the plateau itself which belong to neighbouring Belair. In one of these, now hidden behind clumps of bramble and broom, are some ruins. These show clearly how the vine was cultivated from the time of Ausonius until the early eighteenth century.

This ancient method was to plant the vines in a straight line trench cut out of the local rock, here only a few centimetres below the surface. The sides of the trench were protected by stones, these being excavated from the local limestone caves, thus enlarging them into useful caverns within which the wine could be stored. The Romans had a number of techniques and these were exported and adapted throughout the Empire and over the centuries.

HISTORY

The modern history of Château Ausone begins in the early nineteenth century. The property was given by a local gentleman, Jean Cantenat, to his son Pierre in 1808, and appears to have been in the hands of the Cantenat family since 1718. In the 1868 Cocks and Féret, Ausone is listed fourth in the commune after neighbouring Belair, Troplong-Mondot and Canon. It produced 10 to 12 *tonneaux*. Soon after this it passed to a nephew of the Cantenats, a M. Lafargue, and it was during the ownership of Lafargue, and later, his widow, that the property really seems to have established itself.

The three superior *crus* were all at the time in more aristocratic hands but their fortunes were in decline. Canon was sold, Belair was in '*indivision*', split up between a large number of heirs, and ably directed by M. Lafargue, Ausone was perhaps better able to withstand the triple effects of the great nineteenth-century scourges: oidium, phylloxera and mildew. By 1874, Cocks and Féret list it second; in 1898 it is first, and by the 1920s it 'heads the list of the *premiers crus* and is the finest growth in all Saint-Emilion', as *Clarets and Sauternes* somewhat tautologically puts it.

By this time Ausone had changed hands again. For the second time it went to a collateral branch, to Edouard Dubois who had married a Mlle Challon, niece and heir of Mme Lafargue in 1891. For some years before the death of his aunt by marriage in 1892, Dubois had managed the vineyard, and it is he who is accorded the credit for the reputation of Ausone in the twentieth century.

Edouard Dubois-Challon bought neighbouring Château Belair in 1916, and the two properties have been worked together ever since, although the wines are of course kept entirely separate. After his premature death in 1921, the property was managed by his widow and their children: Jean, who was born in 1896 – a leading figure in the Saint-Emilion *Jurade* and who died in 1974 – and Cécile who married a M. Vauthier.

The property now has several owners. Mme Dubois-Challon, the widow of Jean, owns half, and the other half is divided between Marcel Vauthier, son of Cécile, and his four children. This side is represented by his son Alain who was born in 1950. Belair, however, belongs solely to Mme Dubois-Challon.

THE VINEYARD

Practically all the Ausone vineyard is on the slope running down towards the valley from the terrace in front of the château. The soil, a mixture of limestone and clay, is the most valuable of the *Côtes*-Saint-Emilion, giving a wine with richness and concentration. Lower down, the soil has more sand in it and the wine is thinner. On the plateau, above the château, it is almost pure limestone. The subsoil, not that far down, is limestone.

The vineyard comprises just over seven hectares making it the smallest of all the topmost Bordeaux estates (it is also the only one on limestone soil and the only one on a slope – triply unique) and is planted with 50 per cent Merlot and 50 per cent Cabernet Franc. There is a vestige of Cabernet Sauvignon. The slope faces south-east and is protected from the cold north wind and westerly rain. Because it is raised above the valley and sheltered, Ausone escaped most of the worst damage of the dreadful February 1956 frosts which devastated Pomerol and many of the *Graves*-Saint-Emilion vineyards.

The production, even with the application of modern methods, is hardly generous. A century ago it was no more than 10 tonneaux. By the 1970s, this had been enlarged to 20 *tonneaux* (2,000 cases). Even in 1982, Ausone only produced about 28 *tonneaux*. The age of the vines is venerable, the soil exhausted after two centuries of mono-culture.

THE CHAIS

Ausone has one of the most impressive 'natural' cellars in Bordeaux, enlarged over the centuries by stonemasons excavating the stone from which the houses of Saint Emilion were to be built. The cave is extensive – much more than enough for the needs of such a tiny vineyard whose production, in a poor year, is made to look even more pathetic – in 1984 there were a mere twenty barrels – and is said to have existed in its present form from the sixteenth century. At one point one can look up a chimney through several metres of rock and at other points one can see the roots of vines protruding through the ceiling. Above are vineyards and a tiny ruined thirteenth-century chapel, the Chapelle Madelaine after which a number of neighbouring vineyards are named.

The wine is made in another cellar, half inside the rock, half under the château, and fermented in oak vats, four of which were renewed in 1979. Ausone is now fermented at 28 to 30°C together with between 10 to 40 per cent of the stalks, depending on the vintage. The *cuvaison* lasts between three and four weeks after which, following the *écoulage*, it is removed back into a corner of the barrel cellar where a battery of small stainless-steel *cuves* was installed in 1980. Here, the malolactic fermentation and the *assemblage* of the *grand vin* will take place. The wine is then matured in new oak for sixteen months or so before bottling. It is never filtered. There is no second wine, what is rejected from the *grand vin* – all in the case of vintages such as 1991 – is sold off in bulk.

THE CHÂTEAU

The buildings at Ausone have an incongruous appearance, being the result of several nineteenth-century reconstructions of and additions to a sixteenth-century château and its adjuncts. Architecturally it is a dog's dinner, yet, largely hidden by the chestnut trees in the courtyard, it has its charm. The atmosphere is peaceful and sedate, and from the terrace there is a splendid view down the valley. One of the two main buildings is used as an office. The other has been divided and is occupied by Alain Vauthier and Mme Dubois-Challon.

THE WINE IN ECLIPSE

The wine of Ausone lay under a cloud for a long time – far too long. Why this happened has been the subject of much discussion. Alexis Lichine says it was a lack of sufficient new oak. Others have suggested that the *élevage* was suspect; for instance, that the casks were not topped up assiduously or racked frequently enough. Others still have suggested that too much of the crop went into the *grand vin*, that no selection of only the very best casks or vats was made. The fact that no 1963, 1965 or 1968 was bottled under the Ausone label (nor under Belair for that matter) would tend to contradict this assumption.

At the property, they will admit that the *cuvaison* during the couple of decades prior to 1975 only lasted for 10 to 15 days and that the wine was kept too long in barrel. The sanitary conditions, moreover, were not all that they might have been, necessitating an immoderate use of sulphur and too frequent rackings. Alain Vauthier will also suggest that, perhaps as a result of over-manuring, the yield in the vineyard during the 1960s and early 1970s was excessive, all of which resulted in wine which, though elegant, lacked body and soon began to lose its fruit. Whatever the reason or combined reasons, this is now history, for in the past fifteen years Ausone has undergone a renaissance.

RENAISSANCE

In the early 1970s Ausone was in a sorry state despite having been classified together with Château Cheval-Blanc as a *premier grand cru classé* 'A' in the 1950s. Jean Dubois-Challon was a sick man, the *régisseur* M. Chaudet, who had come from Château Carbonnieux in the 1950s, was now in his eighties and the *maître de chai*, M. Villalba, was about 65. Mme Dubois-Challon, a lady of considerable energy and determination, was occupied with caring for her husband and, on the Vauthier side, it would seem that it was not until Alain Vauthier came of age that anyone took an interest in the affairs of the estate.

The first step was an important investigation which was carried out by Mlle Cazenove-Malu and M. Chaine, local *oenologues*. This isolated the problems and suggested the remedies. The next was to find the person to carry them out. After her husband's death in 1974, Mme Dubois-Challon took matters in hand. She asked M. Palatin, an old friend of hers who was *régisseur* of Château Ferrand and owner of Domaine de La Vieille Eglise in Sainte Hippolyte, if he knew someone suitable. He suggested Pascal Delbeck, a young man who was a distant relation and who had just finished his viticultural studies. In 1975, Delbeck, aged twenty, arrived on a three-month trial. Eighteen months later Chaudet retired; Delbeck was in complete control. In 1978, a new, young *maître de chai*, M. Lanau, was appointed.

THE WINE NOW

Up to 1975, Ausone had been rather light – a pretty and elegant wine, but essentially lacking in what the French call *puissance* and tending to show age rather sooner than befits a *premier cru*. I have, however, had good old Ausones. During the 1920s and 1930s it was a marvellous wine, as many of those who have been privileged enough to enjoy more bottles than I have attested to. Up to 1953 this standard was maintained. The 1947 does not have the power of Cheval-Blanc or Pétrus but is nevertheless excellent. The 1952, in its prime, was better than the 1953, and on the single occasions that I have seen the 1950 and the 1954 – despite the latter not being a conspicuous success as a vintage – the wines were worthy of Ausone's position at the head of the *Côtes*-Saint-Emilions.

Subsequently, the punch and concentration seemed to have been lost, leaving an empty if stylish shell. From 1955 until 1975, Ausone was no more than adequate in the great vintages and too watery in the others, ageing fast; although as will be seen the wines of the best years in *grands formats* still have life. By and large, however, I would be wary of risking money on any of these older wines.

Since 1975, though the change has been radical, and particularly since 1978 the quality has been fine, though it has yet to consistently achieve the flair and excellence of Cheval-Blanc. Nevertheless, there is concentration, richness, meatiness, flesh and power, but on top of this a particular distinction and elegance that is found only in the very finest wines, together with a character which, dare one say it, is unique; for only Ausone, among the first growths, comes from a limestone soil and from a sheltered vineyard which is situated on a slope.

'What does it take to make great wine?' you ask Pascal Delbeck, a modest man with a quiet determination and a delicate sense of humour hidden behind a thicket of dense, black beard. 'Simply, great grapes;' is the reply. 'Which is the best wine you have made?' you press him. 'My greatest vintage? Perhaps it will be the 1988,' he says with a smile. (This was in April of that year.) In view of its tiny size, I dare say it will not be long before Ausone fetches the same prices as Pétrus.

THE TASTING

The majority of the following notes come from a triple vertical of Cheval-Blanc, Ausone and Figeac which took place at a wine weekend in New Haven in October 1990, and was organized by Bob Feinn of Mount Carmel Wines and his friends. I have filled in one or two gaps with other notes taken in recent years.

1986   *Optimum drinking*   **1996–2010**
Medium-full colour. Somewhat adolescent nose. Full and rich though. Full, ample, rich and spicy on the palate. Ripely tannic. Good underlying flesh and grip. A satisfying wine. Less elegant at present but a little fuller than Cheval Blanc. Very good but not as much personality or richness.

1985   **1995–2014**
Fine colour. Distinguished, classy, subtle nose. Medium-full body, warm and spicy, rich and succulent. Good base of oak. Neither as full, nor as concentrated, as Cheval-Blanc but certainly fine.

1983   **Now–2008**
Good colour. Ripe, almost over-ripe nose, with hints of cloves and spice and burnt wood. Medium-full, accessible, still some tannin. Plummy fruit but compared with the top Médocs lacks a bit of depth and concentration. Fine for a Saint Emilion though.

1982   **1997–2020**
Very, very full colour. Still immature. A wine of alcohol and burliness compared with Cheval Blanc. More adolescent. Less sumptuous, less breed. Slight liquorice. Slight tar aspects. Rich, fat and tannic. Doesn't have the distinction of Cheval-Blanc but plenty of *matière* and depth. The class will come as it develops. Better than Figeac. Fine.

1981   **Now–2000**
Good colour. Cardboardy nose. Lumpy. A suggestion of herbaceousness. Medium-full. Slightly rigid tannins, with a suspicion of astringency. Good acidity. Ripe and rather more stylish on the finish. Needs to throw off this somewhat rustic nose though. A bit dry at the end. Elements of bitterness. The 1979 and 1978 are much better today, though I have good notes of other bottles of this 1981. Good, merely.

1980   **Drink soon**
Medium colour, now with some maturity. Sur-

prisingly ripe and substantial with good, positive acidity. Medium body. Good fruit. An excellent Libournais 1980 which has held up well.

1979   **Now–2000**

Full colour, little sign of maturity. Strange nose. Rich but very dark and inky at the same time. There seems to be a lot of *vin de presse* here. A second bottle also had a certain *vin de presse* solidity/inflexibility on the nose but was very much better. Ripe, fullish, quite stylish. Finishes a little bitter.Good to very good. But it got better in the glass. As good as Cheval-Blanc perhaps.

1978   **Now–2008**

Full colour. Quite a reserved nose, some structure. Good grip, quite rich. On the palate quite a lot of tannin, but the rigid tannins of new oak. Ripe, good acidity. Essentially classier than the above but a bit solid. This has length. Will improve. Finishes well. Improved in the glass. More depth and class than Cheval-Blanc. Very good indeed. Will last well.

1976   **Drink soon**

Very good colour for the vintage. Rich, fat, aromatic, spicy, summer-pudding nose. Full and ripe though there is a touch of astringency on the palate. Not as long or as rich on the finish as on the attack but a good, gamey wine which has held up well. Fresher and better than most.

1975   **Now–2000**

Full colour, still not much sign of brown. Tough, slightly dense nose. An element of tar and tobacco box; hard, slightly bitter tannins. Full, a bit solid and stewed, yet has rich, concentrated fruit underneath. Just about ready.

1971   **Drink up**

Medium-full colour, mature. Mellow nose. Attractive. Mature but vigorous. On the palate medium-full, a little astringent. The fruit lacks the class and definition of Cheval-Blanc but good length. Less complex though. Getting a bit astringent at the end as it developed. Lost fruit fast.

1970   **Drink up**

Fullish colour, mature. Soft nose, a little attenuated. Slightly *tabac*/lean as it evolved. Medium body. Has lost quite a lot of its fruit. The elegance has also disappeared a bit. Reasonable acidity though. Not too bad.

1967   **Past its best**

Medium-full colour. Mellow but thinning nose with a curious sweet/sour element. This has dried out a lot on the palate. Elegant once though. Medium body. Getting bitter at the end.

1966   **Drink up**

Fullish colour. Slightly maderized on the nose. This is not a good bottle, but I think there is/was

size and fat here. Bigger than expected. Last time out I noted: stylish but austere, but now beginning to lose its fruit and show its acidity.

1964   **Drink soon**

Medium-full colour, fully mature. Seems a little dried out on the nose. Yet on the palate, if fading, shows elegance and balance. At the end of its life yet still long on the palate. Delicately refined. Finishes better than it starts.

1962   **Drink up**

Medium to medium-full colour. Rather a tough nose, a bit cardboardy at first, but got richer and richer as it developed. A fullish, burly quite solid wine. Sweetly fruity on the attack but a bit empty on the follow-through. A bit short and watery on the finish.

1961   **Drink up**

Medium-full colour. Class here on the nose, but delicate. Complexity rather than size. Showing a little age. On the palate there is some astringency and the wine has become a bit short. But quality here. Lacks intensity now.

1955   **Drink soon**

Fullish, mature colour. Classy nose. Soft. Lots of depth. Rich and quite structured. Good acidity. Fat. Ripe. Will still keep well. Classier and more complex on the finish than the Cheval-Blanc. Food for 1955 and holding up surprisingly well.

1953   **Drink soon**

Medium-full colour. Well matured. Classy nose but quite evolved. Quite full, a bit more astringency than the above. Good grip and plenty of finesse. Still is long, but not as mellow as Cheval. Not as luscious. But undeniable class and discretion. Pleasureable, but today the 1955 is fresher.

1952   **Drink soon**

This must originally have had more depth and richness than the above, but now shows a little more age and astringency. Medium-full colour, quite some brown. Classy and complex but now lightening up, especially on the nose and finish.

1947   **Can still be good**

Two bottles, one full, very ripe and concentrated, with a splendid complex richness and great depth, without ever having been the sort of real blockbuster some other Libournais wines were (and indeed still are). This first bottle was marvellous. The second was rather faded.

1945   **Drink soon**

Fine full colour. Spicy nose. Exotic, liquorice, bay leaves, toffee. On the palate a little astringent but essentially a full, vigorous wine, quite tannic – the tannins perhaps always a little hard like the 1975s – yet classy and rich. This is surprisingly good and fresh. Has held up well.

CHEVAL-BLANC

Château Cheval-Blanc makes one of the most glorious wines of the Bordeaux area. While the great growths of the Médocs are firm and austere and can lack an element of charm until the tannin begins to round off, Cheval-Blanc, like other top Saint-Emilions – and Pomerols too – has a richness and voluptuousness and an illusion of sweetness which makes it even in its infancy an immediately appealing wine. Indeed it used to be said that the wines of Saint-Emilion were half-way between those of the Médoc and those of Burgundy, as if a blend of Chambertin and Château Latour would produce Cheval-Blanc. I fear this is muddying the waters somewhat, and it indicates a rather odd idea of what top Burgundy tastes like. I would prefer not to draw parallels from other areas, particularly those growing a quite separate grape variety, and to stick with words like plump and ample to describe the texture of a top Saint-Emilion and to rely on the differentiation between the fruit-cakey, allspice flavour, deriving from the Merlot grape, of the Libournais wines, and the drier, blackcurranty character and inherently denser structure of a Médoc.

Cheval-Blanc lies in the smaller, more westerly and more open terrain of the two parts of the Saint-Emilion *vignoble*. Almost on the border with Pomerol, and in more gently undulating country than round the village itself, is the *Graves-Saint-Emilion*. The soil here, as the name would suggest, contains gravel. Indeed it is a complex mixture of gravel, clay and sand, with pockets of limestone over a bed of hard iron rock, known as *crasse de fer*.

Cheval-Blanc itself is right on the Pomerol border. Part of the vineyard lies opposite that of Château L'Evangile, part marches with La Conseillante. This is home to one of the greatest wines not only of Saint-Emilion, but of the whole of Bordeaux; a wine which is full, generous and fruity, accessible when young, warm-hearted, rich and silky when mature.

HISTORY

The earliest records show two 'maisons nobles' in what is now the Graves-Saint-Emilion; one at Figeac, whose lands extended over Cheval-Blanc, and the other at Corbin, to the north. In two stages, in 1832 and 1838, the Cheval-Blanc section was detached and was acquired by a family called Ducasse, owners then and now of Château L'Evangile, Cheval-Blanc's immediate neighbour across the Pomerol border. Ducasse also owned land in the Côtes, commemorated to this day in the name of Château Larcis-Ducasse, neighbour to Château Pavie.

Meanwhile the Fourcaud family, originally from Lugon in the Dordogne, were also vineyard owners in the area. Franck lists a Fourcaud-Duplessis at Trois-Moulins, and an Edouard Fourcaud at Château Franc-Mayne, both Côtes first growths at this time.

In 1852, Jean Laussac Fourcaud married Mlle Henriette Ducasse. She brought as her dowry a property known as Cheval-Blanc, at that time slightly more than 31 hectares and producing 25 to 30 tonneaux of wine.

Where the name Cheval-Blanc comes from is uncertain. Hubrecht Duijker, in his The Great Wine Châteaux of Bordeaux, quotes an old family story that the vines lie on the site of an old post house. The ubiquitous Henri IV was said to have changed horses here on the road to Pau. As his horses were always white, the inn was named Cheval-Blanc. As Duijker says, local historians dismiss all this as pure fancy. But it's a nice story.

At the time of the Fourcaud-Ducasse marriage the wines of the Graves-Saint-Emilion (and, similarly, those of Pomerol) were reckoned second class. All the premiers crus of Saint-Emilion were on the Côtes, headed by Belair. The senior Graves property was Figeac.

Jean Laussac Fourcaud set about buying up adjoining parcels of land and converting suitable sections of it to vineyard. He was the first agriculturalist in Saint-Emilion to install a proper system of drainage in his land. By 1868 Cheval-Blanc was producing 50 to 70 tonneaux and its 40 hectares, according to Cocks and Féret, would be yielding 80 to 100 tonneaux when all the newly planted areas were in full production. This is the size of the vineyard today. The illustration in Cocks and Feret shows an elegant, small two-storied country house with a curious steep tower peeping out from behind it.

By the 1886 edition of Cocks and Féret, though the production is still quoted as 60 tonneaux, Cheval-Blanc is ranked first of the Graves châteaux, and, though still a second growth, is said to sell for the price of the firsts.

In 1893, Jean Laussac Fourcaud died, and was succeeded by Albert, one of his eight children. He bought out the rest of the family and changed his name to Fourcaud-Laussac. Albert himself had five children, and, before he died in 1927, made over Cheval-Blanc to a Société Civile, a limited company owned by his children.

Meanwhile the reputation of Cheval-Blanc was being established. It started, no doubt, with the great prewar vintages, the remarkable 1893, the earliest harvest on record, and that magnificent pair, 1899 and 1900; but it was considerably consolidated by the 1921, a vintage where Cheval-Blanc produced, as it did in 1947, an incredibly rich, sweet, almost porty wine. This was the wine which really made Cheval-Blanc, and with it took Saint-Emilion into the consciousness of claret drinkers as wine to rank with the best of the Médoc first and second growths. After the war it gradually made its way higher and higher. Nowadays all the first growths, in which I include Cheval-Blanc as well as Pétrus and Ausone, sell for about the same price.

Cheval-Blanc's Société Civile is now owned by ten members of the Fourcaud-Laussac family. Up to 1989 it was managed by the genial, somewhat Fernandel-like Jacques Hebrard, husband of a granddaughter of Albert. The direction is now in the hands of three ladies. Brigitte Hamelle and Martine D'Arfeuille are granddaughters of Fourcaud-Laussacs. Claude de La Barre was née Fourcaud-Laussac. Pierre Lurton, formerly of Clos-Fourtet, is the régisseur.

THE VINEYARD

The Cheval-Blanc estate now occupies some 41 hectares, of which 36.8 are under vines. These are planted in the ratio two-thirds Cabernet Franc (known as Bouchet in Saint-Emilion) and one-third Merlot, and produce about 120 *tonneaux* (188 in the record year of 1982). There is a little Cabernet Sauvignon, planted at the insistence of the INAO in 1964, and even less Malbec, but these are never used in the *grand vin*.

THE CHÂTEAU AND *CHAIS*

The château itself is a modest but elegant building; a white painted, two-storey country house set in a little park facing the vineyards of Pomerol. It was built around 1860. Adjacent on the one side is an orangery and a small chapel; on the other lies Château Cheval-Blanc's gleaming new *chai*.

Up to 1974 the *chai* was not large enough to store two vintages' worth of wine. The second-year wine had to be moved to cellars in Libourne where it was eventually bottled and from where it was subsequently dispatched. In order for them to be able to say legally '*mise en bouteille au château*', these Libourne cellars were officially licensed as part of the property, a neat piece of French having-your-cake-and-eating-it. The only other property to have had a similar arrangement with an annexe, to my knowledge, was Château La Mission-Haut-Brion in the time of the Woltners.

The wine is now made in concrete vats, dating from 1964, and housed in a clean new cellar above which is a terrace from which one can view the vineyard, and behind which is a reception area. The whole effect is cool and refined, a discreet atmosphere of quality.

Up to 1969, some of the wine was shipped in wood – the last wine of *premier cru* level to allow this – but since then all has been 'château bottled', and since 1974, actually *in situ*.

THE WINE

Cheval-Blanc is always a wine of great appeal. Its lack of Pauillac backbone and tannin makes it a wine easy to appreciate when young. Yet the richness and abundance of fruit is balanced with plenty of body, and the regular use of new oak adds to the substance and mixes with the spicy, fruit-oaky taste of the Merlot grape to create cigar-box and other complex but elusive flavours. Cheval-Blanc is a first-class, and very consistent wine. It has hardly ever not produced *grand cru* quality. And it keeps remarkably well. From the 1988 vintage a second wine, Le Petit Cheval, has been introduced. Previously what was rejected from the *grand vin* was labelled merely as Saint-Emilion.

THE TASTING

Most of the following range of Cheval-Blanc was assembled by John McNulty of Philadelphia for the June 1990, meeting of the Society of Bacchus America, and tasted blind in flights of decades. He was kind enough to invite me along too. Many thanks, John! I have added notes from recent vintages sampled at the Atlanta Wine Festival in 1993.

Optimum drinking

1990   2000–2025

Very good colour. Marvellous nose, at present much more opulent and rich than the 1989. Rich, cedary, ripe, concentrated and full-bodied, with excellent tannins and grip. This seems even better than the 1989 at present. Very high class indeed. Marvellous long, complex, aristocratic finish. Needs time.

1989   2000–2025

Very good colour. Much less expressive on both nose and palate. Full-bodied, spicier, more adolescent. Underneath, though, there is great depth, backbone and dimension. I am sure this is also a wine of really great quality. But whether the 1990 is yet better only time will tell.

1988   2000–2025

Very good colour. Firmer tannins than the 1990;

slightly drier; not quite as ripe. Very classy on the palate though. Fullish. Splendid grip and concentration. Rich plum and damson flavours. Lovely long finish. A wine of real finesse. Very fine.

1987   **Drink soon**
Light to medium colour; still youthful. A lack of real succulence and richness on the nose. Somewhat leafy. But a discernible new oaky base. Not bad for the vintage. Medium body. Quite ample on the attack. Reasonable fruit, but a little lean on the finish. A good result for the vintage though.

1986   **1995–2005**
Fullish colour; still youthful. Youthful, new oaky nose. Inherently quite soft; good fresh charming fruit, but not a great deal of depth and concentration. Medium-full, new-oaky; still with the primary fruit flavour of fresh plums and blackberries. Good acidity and plenty of style, though not enormous concentration. Yet this has depth. A very fine result for the vintage in this part of Bordeaux.

1985   **1998–2020**
Fullish colour; little sign of maturity. Rich, fat and spicy on the nose. A lot of depth and quality here. Good new oak base. Very concentrated fruit. Chocolatey. Still a little unresolved tannin. Good concentration. Full and succulent. Rich, ample and voluptuous. Still youthful. Great depth. Fine quality.

1983   **Now–2005**
Fullish colour. A little development. Somewhat closed on the nose. There is something a little lumpy and adolescent about this. Fullish on the palate. Still a little unresolved tannin. Rich and concentrated. Still closed. Good grip. Plenty of depth. Rich mulberry fruit, well supported by acidity. This is a fine wine, but a bit of an ugly duckling at present. This is a bigger wine than the 1981, and rather more backward.

1982   **1995–2020**
Medium-full colour; now some maturity. Ripe, stylish nose. Very rich and chocolatey with a hint of ginger biscuits. On the palate full, concentrated and voluptuous with very good ripe tannins and very good grip. The follow-through is very intense and vigorous. Classy. Multidimensional. A splendid wine with a very lovely finish. Perhaps the best wine – certainly the best Libournais wine – of the vintage. *Grand vin*!

1981   **Now–2001**
(Magnum) Medium colour; now some maturity. More than the 1982. Soft nose. A little spice, lovely ripe damson-blackberry fruit. On the palate this seems more alive than it does on the

nose. Medium body. The tannins now just about absorbed. Not as full as the 1983 but seems to have more class and better balance. Good depth for the vintage. A fine result which has good length. Just about ready.

1979   **Now–2007**
Medium-full, mature colour. Fragrant nose. Refined, stylish. Fully mature. Balanced. A little tannic still. Good depth and complexity but not a blockbuster. A fresh, medium-bodied, mature wine. Elegant fruit. Long on the palate. Not the greatest concentration but a fine stylish, complex effort. I prefer this of all the 1970s. Needs two years.

1978   **Now–2000**
Full, mature colour. Quite an opulent but open, spicy nose. Not quite the class of the 1979. Fuller than the 1976. More tannin. There is complexity, concentration and vigour here. Very good but not great. A little herbaceous.

1976   **Drink soon**
Fullish mature colour. Ripe, plummy-mulberry-toffee nose. Ample and rich and attractive, but perhaps not *that* concentrated. This is a bit overblown, lacking real grip, and the fruit is beginning to dry out. Good but nothing special.

1975   **Now–2000**
Full mature colour. An ample, meaty nose: sweet, fresh and spicy. Doesn't have the depth and concentration of the 1982, but fat, rich and chocolatey. Some oak. On the palate this is quite full, it has good depth and class, no austerity or astringency and plenty of charm. The tannins are not as sophisticated as in the 1989 but the wine has very good grip. Finishes well. A fine 1975 but not a great wine.

1974   **Drink up**
Medium-full, just about mature colour. Quite firm nose. Cedary, chocolatey. Good grip. Surprisingly attractive. Fullish, still has youth and tannin. Not very full though. Good acidity. Long. Does it lack a bit of ripeness? Medium-full colour, not a lot of maturity. Cool, herbaceous nose. Fullish, fresh, high acidity. An austere wine. Good residual oak. Lacks fruit but no fade or astringency. Very good for vintage.

1973   **Drink up**
Medium-full mature colour. Ripe, aromatic but somewhat lumpy and tough nose. Slight element of volatile acidity. Quite evolved. Perhaps just a little thin. Somewhat old and drying out on the palate. Not the greatest of vintages and bottles. Uninspiring. The least good of the 1970s flight.

1971   **Drink soon**
Quite a dark colour but seems a bit tired. Some-

what old and dried out, yet quite substantial on the nose. Some fruit underneath, and certainly some elegance. Medium body. The usual Cheval chocolatey flavour. Not as thin on the palate as it seemed to be on the nose. Finishes better than it starts. Fresher and sweeter as it developed. Held up well in the glass.

1970   **Now–2000**

Fullish, mature colour. Fat, ripe, vigorous mature colour. Rich and earthy, elegant, balanced and vigorous. Good quality. Plenty of depth. Rich, ripe. Quite full. Not exactly a blockbuster; but has style. It is more classy than the 1975. Round and spicy but not with a great deal of acidity. Yet good grip. Long. My second favourite of the 1970s. A fine example.

1969   **Drink soon**

Medium-full, mature colour. Fullish, but somewhat four-square on the nose. A meaty wine, but seems a little inflexible. Quite full. Chocolatey and fruity but there is a little astringency. Yet rich. This is a bit like a fresher version of 1967 but the 1967s were variable. Will still keep. Quite high acidity. I would have liked a bit more richness of fruit.

1968   **Drink up**

Quite full but an old colour. Aromatic nose but a certain attenuation. Somewhat high-toned. A light wine which is now getting towards its end. The acidity is beginning to show. Unexciting.

1967   **Drink soon**

Good, full colour; no undue maturity. Bottle variation here, my bottle is less fresh than the other. Tasting note on the better bottle: rich, spicy nose. Quality and succulence here. On the palate less exciting. This has begun to dry out a bit, though there is a residual richness on the palate.

1966   **Over the top**

Fullish but old. Old and attenuated on the nose. My bottle is better than my neighbours but rather past it nevertheless. Was reasonably vigorous wine once but not very pleasant now.

1966   **Now–2000 plus**

(From a La Vigneronne tasting in December 1992) Excellent colour. Fuller and more vigorous than the 1970. A bigger, more tannic wine than the 1970. The structure shows a bit. Very fine grip, depth and distinction though. Just a touch of astringency at the end, but this would not be apparent with food. I think this is classier, if less seductive than the 1970. Marvellous complex finish. Fine plus.

1964   **Now–2000 plus**

Medium-full colour, no undue maturity. Good

nose. Fat but slightly austere, compared with the 1961. Firmer. Less rich and voluptuous but with good depth. This is very fine as well. Full, beautifully balanced. Very long and complex. Breed and multidimension here. The best of the 1960s. Not as voluptuous as 1961 but with more class.

1962   **Now–1996**

Fullish colour, relatively youthful for this 1960s flight. This has a good nose: ripe and vigorous. Elegant and fragrant. Not as firm as 1964 or as voluptuous as 1961. Less dimension but good stuff. Medium body. Elegant, balanced, plump, charming. Long and stylish. Good complexity. Shows well.

1961   **Now–2000 plus**

Good, full colour, intense to the rim. This is high quality: rich, concentrated, youthful, cedary and chocolaty. Full and fat. A big wine. Rich, concentrated, tannic. Aromatic, perfumed, voluptuous. Very concentrated. Almost porty. Black cherries, figs and caramel.

1960   **Drink soon**

Medium colour, no undue maturity. Soft nose, slightly overblown but plump, fruity and stylish. Medium body. There is a good fresh acidity here and quite ample fruit, and this is keeping the wine alive and stylish.

1959   **Past its best**

Medium colour, fully mature. A little thin and pinched on the nose. Yet there is/was quality here. Slightly leafy, I get a touch of lime jelly. Medium body, a little pinched and astringent. A little sweet. Now getting a little coarse. A little past its best.

1959   **Now–1999**

(From the New Haven Ausone/Cheval-Blanc/ Figeac tasting, October 1990) Medium-full colour. Slightly dense on the nose. Full and rich and meaty. Lacks a bit of class though. More spice than elegance. Still has vigour, and intensity on the finish. Better with food. Very good rather than great. Yet sweet and most attractive. Long on the palate. In the end more elegant than the 1961.

1958   **Drink soon**

Medium to medium-full colour, no undue maturity. Broad, quite fat, slightly farmyardy nose. Medium body. Quite evolved but not flabby. Never a wine of great concentration. Has good fruit supported by good acidity. Fragrant and stylish but now approaching the end of its useful life.

1955   **Now–2000**

Medium-full colour. Quite full and meaty on the nose. Rich but doesn't quite sing. Yet my bottle is just a bit better than that of my neighbour. Developed in the glass. Quite ripe and aromatic. Supple. Much better in fact than it seemed at first. Full, youthful, cedary, vigorous. Fine and ripe and complex. Really lovely fruit. Very elegant and long on the palate. I prefer this to the 1953. Caramel and coffee tones. A great bottle.

1953 **Now–1995**

Full colour. Rich, aromatic, quite high-toned nose, at first, yet subtle. Similarly soft like the above. This is a bit more evolved than the 1955 and 1952. Not quite as intensely flavoured but ripe and succulent, rich and aromatic. Good depth. Long. Fine but not great. Evolved quite quickly in the glass.

1952 **Now–1998 plus**

Full colour. Bottle variation here. Mine not nearly as good as my neighbours'. Note on the better bottle; splendid nose. Rich, fat, concentrated. Meaty high quality. A lot of depth. Full and rich, just a touch of astringency. A big, concentrated wine. Rich and chocolatey. Long. Very fine.

1950 **Drink soon**

Very full colour. Full nose, slightly firm, if not a bit hard. Somewhat burnt and dense. Full, tannic, tough and a bit astringent. A roasted and slightly burnt-toast aspect. Yet at the same time concentrated and rich. Not the greatest class. Good but a wine for food.

1949 **Now–1997**

Fine, full colour. Lovely rich, plump, blackberry nose. Soft, succulent, full of fruit. Still fresh but gentle not aggressive. Medium-full. Rich and plump. Round and ripe. A delightful, elegant bottle. Lovely ripe acidity. Long. Subtle, delicious. Still bags of life. Excellent.

1948 **Now–1997**

Very fine colour; still youthful. The nose too is still very vigorous as well as concentrated and opulent. This is very nearly as brilliant as the 1949 and 1947. Full, voluptuous, sweet and excellent: a more structured wine than the 1949; less porty and essence-of-fruit than the 1947. Splendid quality.

1947

(Bottled by Destree et Fils, Belgium) Very full colour. Extraordinary nose. Rich and porty but sweet and herbal and a hinge of pine trees. As always a very individual wine; rich and sweet and alcoholic and concentrated. Yet good acidity, if quite a high element of the volatile. I've had finer bottles though. Today I prefer the 1945.

This has too much of the scented pine bath-essence aspect.

1947 **Now–2000 plus**

(Château bottled, from a La Vigneronne tasting in December 1992) Brilliant colour. The usual almost porty richness. On splendid form if slightly softer – if my memory is correct – than at the Paulson tasting. Marvellous intense fruit. Super-concentrated. Magnificent.

1945 **Now–2000**

Fine full colour. Firm, full, rich nose. A little tough on the nose. Masculine. Full and tannic but rich and meaty and concentrated. Yet after a bit of aeration seemed to loosen up a bit and throw off its hardness. Very rich and powerful. A lot of concentration. Slightly austere, blackberry fruit. Very long. Very full, very fine. Still very vigorous.

1943 **Drink soon**

Medium colour. Well matured but not too old. Gentle on the nose. Not too past it. Elegant, soft, flowery. A little faded though. Gentle, sound, stylish on the palate. Not bad at all. Still most enjoyable.

1942 **Past its best**

Medium colour, rather a little too old it would seem. On the nose a little faded and oxidized. Rather past it on the palate.

1937 **Drink soon**

(Half bottle) Fullish colour. Good nose. Does not have the inkiness of most 1937s (or of the 1950). A bit dense. Sweet. Some astringency on the palate. Not a great deal of class. Second half bottle a bit thinner but less chunky. Possibly slightly classier. Good length. This is fine.

1934 **Drink soon**

(Château bottled, from a La Vigneronne tasting) Excellent colour for age. No undue maturity. Full. Distinguished nose. No undue age. Refined, classy, complex. Declined quite fast in the glass, in the sense of lightening up, but no astringency. It just leaves a classy cedary sweet aftertaste. A lovely example.

1929 **Now–1998**

(From the New Haven Ausone/Cheval-Blanc/Figeac tasting) Medium colour. Soft, sweet, almost Burgundian. Very fragrant and rich, but delicate. This is very lovely but I would never have placed it in Bordeaux. Quite highish volatile acidity. Little backbone, but ripe and raspberry flavoured. Long and complex.

BEAUSÉJOUR-
DUFFAU-
LAGARROSSE

At the extreme western edge of the *plateau calcaire* of Saint-Emilion, one above each other like the prows of two ships overlooking vineyards which fall away down to flatter, more ordinary land, are the Beauséjours. Once this was a single estate. Once they were both *premiers grands crus classés*. Beauséjour was divided in 1869. Half became Beauséjour-Duffau-Lagarrosse, and continues to be owned by this family. The other has changed hands more than once, most recently in 1969, exactly a century after the original division. The Bécot family, the new owners, were already proprietors in the area, and ten years later they acquired a third neighbouring vineyard. It was because the produce of these three vineyards was then combined under the single Beau-Séjour-Bécot name, not because of the geology, or because of the quality, that this Beauséjour was relieved of its status as a first growth. Such are the apparent illogicalities of the Institut National des Appellation d'Origine. Ironically, while you could have argued a good case a decade ago for demoting both the Beauséjours on the grounds of inferior quality, the 1980s have seen a revival at both estates. Neither is great but both are good. But one is today merely a *grand cru classé* and must continue as such until the classification is once more the subject of scrutiny.

In the Middle Ages the land both here and at neighbouring Château Canon was cultivated by the monks of the Abbey of Saint-Martin. The *lieu-dit* was known by the intriguing name of Peycoucou or Puycoucou. There is an interesting play on words here. Both 'Puy' and 'Pic' denote a mountain, or promontory. '*Pic*' is also a name for a woodpecker and '*pie*' a magpie. So we have both the headland where the birds announced their presence and a choice of either bird being impersonated by a cuckoo.

HISTORY

In the seventeenth century, as the power and vigour of the monastic order declined, the land here, as elsewhere, was taken over by the laity: in this case the Gerès family, *seigneurs* of Camarsac in the Entre-Deux-Mers on the other side of the Dordogne. In 1722 Jeanne de Gerès married François de Carle de Figeac, the younger son of a family which had ruled on the other side of the Saint-Emilion vineyard for many a century. It was their son Jacques, a general in the Bourbon army, who rechristened the domaine with the apt but unimaginative name of Beauséjour in 1787.

Jacques de Carle bequeathed the estate to his cousin André de Carle-Trajet in 1803, and twenty years later it was sold to M. Toussant Troquart, a local pharmacist and surgeon, for 32,000 francs. By this time the fourteen-hectare vineyard was well established, and when the first reliable indications of the relative status of the Saint-Emilion estates began to emerge in mid-century, Beauséjour was graded fifth in the entire region after Belair, Troplong-Mondot, Canon and Ausone. It produced 30 *tonneaux*.

By this time the property had been passed to a cousin, a lawyer named Pierre-Paulin Ducarpe. This poor man is invariably referred to in the records as Ducarpe Junior, implying some sort of inferior status. I trust it did not give him an inferiority complex.

It was during Ducarpe's lifetime that Beauséjour was divided. In 1869 his son Léopold took half the vineyard. The remainder, plus the château and its dependent buildings went to the daughter, now Mme Duffau-Lagarrosse.

The southern half of Beauséjour is currently a limited company owned by some 30 descendants of Dr Calixte and Mme Duffau-Lagarrosse, and is currently administered by a triumvirate of Dr Jean Duffau-Lagarrosse, his wife (who is also a cousin), and his brother-in-law, Jacques Redaud. This is a large extended family, most of whom rarely visit – the château is not permanently occupied – and one can criticize it for a lack of involvement and investment until recent years. I first visited the property in the early 1970s, when the *régisseur* was Jean-Michel Ferrandez, now at Château Citran. I remember sensing his frustration. The average age of the vines was high. The potential was there. The current *régisseur* is Jean-Michel Dubos. Since his arrival in 1983 the modernization instigated by Ferrandez has been continued and accelerated. At last Beauséjour-Duffau-Lagarrosse is beginning to show what it is capable of producing.

THE VINEYARD

The vineyard occupies 6.8 hectares and is today planted in the ratio 60 per cent Merlot, 30 per cent Cabernet Franc and 10 per cent Cabernet Sauvignon, the Merlot having been increased at the expense of the Cabernet Sauvignon over the past five years. The vineyard was largely replanted after the 1956 frosts, so can now boast an average age of a third of a century. They pick later but faster than they used to do, allowing the Cabernet grapes to ripen to the maximum of maturity. As they pick, the fruit is sorted through and anything substandard is rejected.

Since Dubos has been in charge, and with the prolific vintages the 1980s decade has threatened, not only an *éclaircissage* (removal of excess bunches of grapes in July) has been practised, but also a *débourgeonage* (removal of excess buds in March or April, after they have swelled). As a result, Dubos made less wine in 1986 than in 1985. The wine is all the better for it.

THE CHÂTEAU AND THE *CHAIS*

The Duffau-Lagarrosse château is the original, having been constructed early in the nineteenth century during the time of André de Carle-Trajet. Facing south, almost overhanging a parapet below which is a small garden, it is a simple but elegant Directoire-style mansion of fifteen rooms, with single-storey additions, today functioning as part of the *chais*, on either side.

The *cuverie* is attached to the north, and consists of a battery of concrete vats together with three larger stainless-steel tanks for the *assemblage*. Adjacent is a small *chai à barriques*. Across the courtyard are offices. Tucked into the hillside, hewn out of the limestone rock, are a number of caves, one an impressive bottle-storage cellar.

THE WINE

The most traditional, the most artisanal, the most 'ancestral' of Saint-Emilion, says Bernard Ginestet about the wine. He was writing before the mid-1980s renaissance, and one can see what he means. The Beauséjour of his day was solid, four-square, somewhat inky and dominated by a hard lean flavour of unripe Cabernet Sauvignon. The 1960s vintages were good; the 1970s meagre. What the wine lacked, as well as breed, was generosity and richness.

This has been changed by the decision to harvest later, by the introduction of a second wine, La Croix de Mazerat (no *grand vin* was declared in 1984), by an increase in new oak to at least one-third (45 per cent in some very structured vintages), and by the increasingly venerable average age of the vines.

The wine continues to be matured at 30 to 32 degrees, rather than at a lower temperature; and is given a long *cuvaison* of 21 to 30 days. But it now appears to have a certain richness as well as its habitual structure. It is early days, but I feel this property is on the right track.

THE TASTING

The following wines were sampled at the château in January 1990. In April 1990, and again in April 1991, I had a chance to review the 1988 and taste the 1989 alongside its *premier grand cru* peers: good to very good was verdict on both. These and the 1990 vintage show real promise.

Optimum drinking

1988   1996–2006

Fine colour. Quite rich and concentrated on the nose, though the tannins seem a little unyielding. Medium to medium-full body. The attack is a bit dumb, lacking zip and concentration, but the follow-through shows more interest. Still adolescent. Just a little solid. Needs time to come together. Certainly good.

1987   **Drink soon**

Reasonable colour, still fresh. The nose is soft but is not too hollow and has some personality and charm. Fresh attack, reasonable fruit and balance. A touch of new oak. A bit one-dimensional but rather more positive on the follow-through, as well as more attractive than most. A very good result.

1986   **Now–1999**

Medium colour. Little on the nose. This is a lighter, more open, more forward wine than the 1985. Like many Libournais 1986s there is a lack of concentration and grip. Medium body, a little tannin. This has cheerful plump fruit and good balance. But not real depth and concentration. Good to very good for a Libournais. Finishes well.

1985   1995–2003

Medium-full colour. The nose is more substantial but more closed than the 1986. Not just a fuller wine, but rather tougher. Medium-full, some tannin. Firm attack, the Cabernet showing. A little unyielding perhaps. Better follow-through but a bit adolescent at present. This is going to need time. At present it lacks a bit of charm. And the finish lacks grip and concentration.

1983   **Now–2002**

Good colour. Little sign of maturity. The nose is currently a little hidden. On the palate we have quite a full wine, with more substance, fatter fruit, and better acidity than most. Just a little tannin. Just a little hard. But positive finish, showing richness and grip. Better than I expected and remembered, particularly for a Saint-Emilion.

1982   **Now–2005**

Full colour. Little sign of maturity. Rich, fat, meaty nose. This is a fullish wine, with the richness, opulence and spice of the vintage, but also with a certain firmness brought by the Cabernet Sauvignon. Good grip. Still some tannin. Again a shade hard. The 1983, for 1983, is a better result.

1981   **Drink soon**

Medium colour. Just about mature. Medium body. The attack is fresh and fruity though the follow-through is somewhat one-dimensional.

Yet there is reasonable length here, if no real depth and richness. Pleasant but a little dull. Competent but the 1983 is rather better.

1980   **Drink soon**

Good colour for the vintage. No undue age; indeed still quite purple. Reasonably positive nose, though I wouldn't exactly call it elegant. On the palate there is substance and fruit. The finish is beginning to get a bit attenuated but this was a very good result for a 1980 Saint-Emilion.

1979   **Drink soon**

Medium to medium-full colour. Just about mature. Much fuller and more vigorous than the 1978. The nose seems a bit pinched and ungrateful. On the palate medium-full body; a little ungainly. There is some richness, good acidity, but a certain solidity, and these elements are not exactly in harmony. The finish is a bit rigid and astringent. Not bad.

1978   **Drink soon**

Disappointing colour. Somewhat light and weedy. The 1979 colour is much better. Somewhat anonymous on the nose. Fully mature, slight spice. A bit weak. Medium body. While there is little or no elegance here you can see the potential, for the wine has concentration and balance even if it is a bit light and rustic. Not bad.

1976   **Drink up**

Like the 1978, the colour is a bit thin and feeble. Now quite brown at the rim. Somewhat watery on the nose. Fully mature and with a dilute version of the usual 1976 lumpy, dry, spiciness.

Weak, curiously sweet. Old, tired, inelegant. This is poor.

1971   **Drink up**

Medium-full colour. No undue age. Very 1971-y on the nose, a sort of mean attenuation. A little more agreeable on the palate. Reasonable fruit, richness and grip; but this is overlaid by a certain astringency, and the end is bitter. Wasn't too bad once but now needs drinking.

1966   **Drink soon**

Medium-full, mature colour. Good, full, rich nose. This is a very attractive medium-full bodied wine. It may not have the greatest elegance or concentration but there is plenty of fruit, well balanced with acidity, and the wine is round, plump and complex and finishes long. Most enjoyable. A point now.

1964   **Drink soon**

Medium-full, mature colour. Fatter, spicier, more flesh and more opulence on the nose than the 1966. Sturdier on the palate with just a touch of astringency. This is a more masculine wine with rather more depth. Perhaps better with food, and certainly longer and more vigorous than the 1966. But not a great Libournais 1964.

1961   **Drink soon**

Medium-full colour, no more than the 1964, but fully mature. The nose, while rich, shows a certain attenuation. And I find this on the palate too. Medium full, ripe but a little blowsy, and it seems to be getting a bit short and astringent. Once there was plenty of fruit but this seems a little past its best.

BELAIR

Belair, not Cheval Blanc or Ausone, is the senior estate in Saint-Emilion. Indeed, with a documented history which goes back to the Middle Ages, long before the Médoc ceased to be a marshy swamp, it can well claim to be the oldest vine-growing domaine in the whole of the Gironde with the possible exception of Pape-Clément. If, in the last 100 years, its reputation has been somewhat overshadowed by the rise of Château Ausone, its immediate neighbour, Belair nevertheless continues fully to deserve its position as one of Saint-Emilion's leading growths. Its origins as a wine-making domaine provide a fascinating illustration of the emergence of Saint-Emilion *vignoble*.

Leaving aside the Roman poet and statesman Ausonius, whose connection with Saint-Emilion and in particular with this section of the Côte I have discussed in the chapter on Château Ausone, Belair's history begins with Robert de Knollys or Knollis, *Grand Sénéchal* and governor of the province of Guyenne during what the French continue to term the English 'occupation' in the Middle Ages.

It might have been expected that this alien, English presence on French soil would be a source of continual trouble and, from the start, there was intermittent warfare against the 'foreign' possessions. The English soon lost most of their northern territory and by the accession of Edward III in 1327, its overseas provinces had been reduced to a rump in Guyenne and part of Gascony, roughly from Saintes in Cognac to Bayonne but only extending as far east as Castillon just beyond Saint-Emilion.

ROBERT DE KNOLLYS

The English kings had acknowledged, at least in principle, that they held their territories in France as vassals of the French crown. They accepted their position as subordinate to the kings of France and did not lay claim to the French throne. Edward III changed all this. The succession of Philip de Valois in 1328, a cousin of the previous three French kings – Louis X, Philip V and Charles IV – all of whom had expired without issue in rapid succession, left Edward, so he argued, with a prior claim. His mother had been Isabella, the sister of the three deceased monarchs. The Hundred Years War was unleashed.

Most of the fighting, naturally, took place in the south-west. Saint-Emilion and Libourne, named after an earlier *sénéchal*, Roger de Leyburn, were on the battlefront. Facing each other across the vineyards were Robert de Knollys and the French commander Bertrand Du Guesclin. Although the war was eventually to go Du Guesclin's way, honours at first favoured the English. The French King John was captured after the Battle of Poitiers and held in exile in Bordeaux and London until ransomed in 1360. Subsequently, Du Guesclin was also taken prisoner after the battles of Auray and Navarette in 1364. It was Knollys who accepted the symbolic offer of Du Guesclin's sword in surrender. It was, so legend also has it, at Belair that Du Guesclin was housed, as Knollys's guest, until paroled.

A century later the English were finally expunged from south-west France after the Battle of Castillon. Not all decided to depart. Some families had obviously been settled in the Gironde for many years. These remained, acknowledging the new French rule, keeping their heads down for the time being, marrying into other local families and gradually becoming thoroughly French.

Amongst these, evidently, were the descendants of Robert Knollys. Words like 'knife', 'knave' and 'knot', up to Shakespearean times, were pronounced with an active 'k'. Knollys therefore became Canolle. The name reappears as such in the ranks of the Bordeaux nobles at the time of Fronde uprising during the infancy of Louis XIV and, at the same time, the family was raised to the marquisate. They remained in the possession of Belair until 1916.

MODERN HISTORY

The establishment of an important viticultural enterprise at Belair must have been one of the first in the region. By 1752, according to the late Henri Enjalbert, author of *Les Grands Vins de Saint-Emilion, Pomerol et Fronsac*, it was already an old vineyard since there were, even then, 42 *journaux* of vines, some eleven hectares. The Canolles had a house in Libourne, *manoirs* elsewhere and a château at Saint Sulpice-de-Faleyrens to the south-west of Saint-Emilion. This last estate included what are now Châteaux Lescours and Monbousquet. Through their noble contacts they were able to develop a clientele for their production throughout France. Belair was the leading *cru* of the region, a *lieu-dit* which can be discerned above Gaffelière and Fonplégade on the Belleyme map of the 1770s. The Canolles, the De Sèzes at Berliquet and the Fontémoing family at what is now Château Canon were the leading innovators in the decades prior to the Revolution. In 1786, the Canolle wine sold for 450 *livres* a *tonneau*, three times the price of most of the rest of Saint-Emilion. Unlike common practice elsewhere but like the grand Médoc estates, Belair did not produce any white wine. The red wine was often aged in cask in its own cellars and there is evidence of 'château-bottling' as early as 1802.

The local *curé*, a M. Vidal, describes the surrounding area at the time and his description still holds good today. 'On the plateau [outside the town of Saint-Emilion] huge vineyards are suspended in the air since vast quarries have been dug beneath them, with supporting columns of stone left at intervals.' Indeed, at one point in the Belair vineyard, there is, today, an enormous hole in the ground. A thin strip of turf and earth exposes a metre or so of solid limestone rock.

Underneath is a stygian darkness with cavernous passages running away in all directions.

There are a number of contradictory stories relating to what exactly happened at Belair during the Revolution. All are agreed that the Canolles emigrated to avoid the Terror. In one version, the property, sequestrated by the State to be sold as a *bien national*, was bought by its *régisseur*, a M. Goudicheau, whose family had worked there, father and son, for several generations. This faithful family retainer held the property intact until the Canolles returned in 1802. Where, you may wonder, did he get the money from? The value, we can establish, was in excess of 60,000 *livres*. Perhaps from Auguste Chaperon, a Libourne *négociant* and neighbouring landowner. The name Chaperon is later associated with Tertre-Daugay, Balestard, Couspaude, Dominique and Grand-Corbin as well as with L'Evangile, but which of these were already in the family in 1795 I have been unable to establish. Enjalbert, sweeping aside all romantic notions of devoted servants, states that Belair was seized and sold in seven lots on *24 Prairal l'An II* for a total of 60,450 francs. Chaperon bought six of them (why not all seven of them?), including the main house. He made numerous purchases of *bien nationaux* and most probably acted as an intermediary for the Canolle family. Meanwhile, the main Canolle residence, Château Lescours, had been sold to a 'rich American' – a Frenchman who had made a fortune in the West Indies – so it escaped seizure.

Whoever was the intermediary, the family was back at Belair after their years of exile early after the turn of the century and Goudicheau was, once more, installed as its manager. The family was to remain until 1897. Times were hard, though; the market for the wine in northern France had evaporated and the entire 1802 harvest, all fourteen and a half *tonneaux*, had to be sold *en primeur* to the Bordeaux *négociant* Balguerie at the knock-down price of 398 francs a *tonneau* (twelve years on, things were rather better – the 1815 fetched 588 francs).

Wherever else they may disagree, all the earliest classifications of Saint-Emilion put Belair firmly at the head of the list. Lawton wrote in 1815: 'Saint-Emilion wines are nicely coloured, very lively and very pleasant; the *premiers crus* have an incomparable bouquet. The top wine is Bel-Air belonging to the Canolles; others are Cambret [Soutard] and Dordon [?].' Jullien wrote: 'The Saint-Emilion *Côte* wines have a pleasant aromatic savour. This is particularly the case of the leading wine Château du Bel-Air.' Lecoutre de Beauvais recorded in 1841: 'First and foremost, the Chevalier de Canolle at Belair, who produces 20 to 25 *tonneaux*'. From a later Lawton account we learn that in 1831 it fetched 750 francs a *tonneau* while the other Saint-Emilions only fetched 250 to 400 francs. Cocks and Féret in 1868 say the Belair 'has always' been placed at the head of the *premier crus*.

By this time, ownership had passed through the female line to the Baron de Marignan who had married Léontine, daughter of Victor de Canolle, himself son of François-Antoine-Joseph, Marquis de Canolle de Lescours, proprietor at the time of the Revolution. This marriage was to produce three daughters, Mme de Gueringard, the Marquise de Galard-Terraube and the Countess Paul de Montbel. It would appear that the Baron died in the early 1870s and his widow some twenty years later. These were the crisis years of phylloxera and mildew. As I have stated in the Ausone chapter, as this property rose, so Belair was eclipsed. Cocks and Féret, as Belair is finally displaced as top dog in Saint-Emilion in 1899, are at pains to reassure their readers that they do not consider that its quality has declined, merely that Ausone's has improved. What they also state, though, is that the property was 'much ravaged by phylloxera'. Part has been replanted with *vignes françaises* (ungrafted vines), maintained by carbon disulphide whilst continuing to reconstitute the rest by grafting on to American rootstocks. At the time the yield had decreased to eighteen *tonneaux*.

The Canolle era finally came to an end in 1916, the year in which Edouard Dubois-Challon of neighbouring Château Ausone bought both Belair and the tiny vineyard of Chapelle-Madelaine. Since then, the estates have been run jointly though the wines are, of course, kept quite separate. The name Chapelle-Madelaine was retained as a subsidiary name, a sort of Ausone *sous marque* according to Pascal Delbeck, until 1970. It is the same Delbeck who has been manager of both properties since 1978. Ownership, however, lies solely in the hands of Mme Dubois-Challon, widow of Jean, son of Edouard.

THE VINEYARD

The Belair vineyard is enclosed by the town walls of Saint-Emilion and the vineyards of Châteaux Ausone, Gaffelière, Magdelaine and Canon. Drive out of the town from the *place* by the Hôtel Plaisance, keep turning left and you will eventually arrive at a collection of buildings, some of them troglodyte. This is Belair. (Delbeck lives in the château.) Beyond lies Ausone. On the plateau above you lie two-thirds of Belair's thirteen hectares; below on your right, reaching down towards Gaffelière, lies the remainder on the slope. The *encépagement* is 60 per cent Merlot, 40 per cent Cabernet Franc. Beneath the vines, as is evident when you go into the vast galleried cellars of both Belair and Ausone, is limestone rock. Production is about 60 *tonneaux*.

THE WINE

Up to the 1980 vintage the wine of Belair was vinified in old wooden and concrete vats, and earlier still it was stored in the Ausone part of the *cave*. The wooden vats have since been replaced by stainless steel and the whole production is now separate. The wine is vinified at 28 to 30 degrees and macerated for fifteen to 21 days, after which it is stored in oak, one-third of which is new, the remainder those of the previous year's Ausone. It is bottled after fifteen to twenty months in wood.

'Belair is the Lafite of the *Côtes*-Saint-Emilion,' said Alfred Danflou in 1867. Contrary to what you might expect from a vineyard which lies largely on the plateau, Belair is a delicate wine, and at times has indeed been a little *too* delicate. I am almost tempted to use the word 'feeble'. Like its neighbour, quality was not all it should have been in the decade or so prior to the arrival of Pascal Delbeck; and the wine of Belair, in my view, has been slower to catch up since. Very good indeed in 1979 and in 1982 but only good in 1980 and 1981 and sometimes subsequently. There is certainly more potential to be realized. As it currently stands, I would place it lower than Canon and Magdelaine, other Saint-Emilion vineyards largely subsisting on the plateau, though I would not go as far as the 1982 Cocks and Féret which places it behind Trottevieille. The wines of the last five years have been ripe and fragrant and have had depth, concentration and elegance without in any way intimating anything of a blockbuster character or real super-dimensionality. This is the style of the wine – soft-textured and harmonious, with an intensity of fruit rather than substance. My experience of 1940s and 1950s vintages of Château Belair is not extensive and as the wine is differently made today it is difficult to suggest quite in which direction its full potential lies. That it will get better still, though, I am in no doubt.

THE TASTING

The following is an amalgam of two sessions. The first was a Sotheby's wine evening I presented in December 1987. I updated my notes on the more recent vintages early in 1991 and have added one or two other notes to fill in some gaps.

	Optimum Drinking

1989   **1996–2012**

Good colour. Lovely fragrant, gently oaky nose. This is distinctly superior to the 1988. Medium-full body, delicate but intensely flavoured, very subtle and complex, with a slightly roasted and cooked flavour which reminds me of 1982. Very good.

1988   **Now–2001**

Medium to medium-full colour. After the opulence of the 1989 the nose, though balanced and elegant, is no more than pretty; it lacks a bit of intensity and richness. Medium body. Not a great deal of tannin. This is good but not great though certainly stylish. It will evolve soon.

1986   Now–1998
Medium to medium-full colour. This is similar to the 1988, though more evolved: a soft, gently oaky wine on the nose and palate which has elegance but a lack of real concentration. Medium body. Only a little tannin. Approaching maturity. Good but not great.

1985   Now–2005
The best Belair between the 1982 and 1989. Good colour. Discreet, attractively plummy nose with a touch of violets. Medium-full body. Round, balanced, fresh and elegant. By no means a blockbuster, but ripe, oaky and with plenty of character. Very good.

1983   Now–1998
Medium to medium-full colour. Now mature. Ripe, stylish nose. Medium body, the tannins now round and soft. This has attractive fruit and balance and a cedarwoody Merlot flavour. An elegant forward wine but without great concentration or depth. Good but not great.

1982   Now–2008
Good colour. On the nose this appears to have gone into its shell. There is a lot of richness here but the wine is somewhat adolescent. Better as it developed. As the constituent parts fell into place one could see the concentration and cooked fruit power of the vintage in the typically subtle and elegant Belair manner. This is lovely wine, if not great in 1982 terms.

1981   Drink soon
Good colour. Even seems to have more density than the 1983. The nose lacks a bit of intensity though. Medium body, not a lot of tannin. Unlike at Ausone, the 1983 in this case is better than the 1981. This is elegant and has good fruit but doesn't have the depth. Pleasant but tails off a bit.

1979   Now–2005
Medium-full colour. Some signs of maturity. Good nose. Straight, ripe fruit. Good acidity and depth. Not that evolved. Medium-full body, some tannin. Rich and meaty. This has depth and quality and is quite a bit more powerful than the above. Finishes well. Very good indeed.

1978   Now–2002
Full colour. Some signs of maturity. Good, ripe, plummy, blackcurrant fruit on the nose. Fullish, some tannin but a little clumsy, giving an element of astringency. Not as fragrant nor as elegant as the 1979. More substantial but a bit foursquare. I find the 1979 more classy.

1976   Drink soon
Fullish colour. Quite a lot of brown at the rim. Interesting nose, slightly caramel and roast-chestnut elements as well as blackberry. Medium body. Round, aromatic and spicy but good acidity and no blowsiness. A very good 1976. Quite rich and opulent. A second bottle was less good – more evolved, slightly attenuated.

1970   Drink soon
Very full, mature colour. Good fresh, ripe nose, classy, quite substantial – more than I had expected. Fullish, mature, rich and fat. A ripe wine, of some depth and class, with supple, attractive fruit. Certainly good but not up to the standard of 1982 and 1989, even the 1979.

1967   Drink soon
Medium-full colour, well-matured if not a trifle aged. Broad, elegant nose. This was quite full for the vintage and certainly a success though it is now beginning to lighten up and lose its fruit. Quite elegant, though acidity shows on the finish.

1964   Drink soon
(Magnum)Very fine colour. Rich and concentrated, fatter and more ample than Ausone 1966. More aromatic – violets and jasmine. Round, ripe tannins, more concentrated than the Ausone. Long and with bags of life though in the bottle size I advise to drink soon. Very fine.

1962   Drink soon
Good colour. No sign of age. Fresh, plump, fragrant nose. Light but fruity on the palate. This is really a little faded, yet ripe almost to the point of over-ripeness. Lacks a little grip. But elegant and pretty and not completely past its best. Soft and gentle, as always. Getting a bit short yet a lot of style.

1955   Drink soon
Fullish, mature colour. Elegant, fully mature nose; soft and mellow if not a touch aged. Delicate, classy and sweet. Medium body; in its discreet way a lovely wine. No astringency, but not a great deal of concentration. Getting towards the end of its useful life. Lacks a little power but by no means short or faded.

1953   Drink soon
Reasonable but quite old colour. Quite substantial fruit nose. Lovely elegant fruit with a certain plummy, blackcurranty, bramble flavour. Fullish, meaty palate. Showing a little age but a wine of subtlety and breed. But getting a bit astringent on the finish. In its prime. Very good if not even better than the 1955.

CANON

About a quarter of a mile west of Saint-Emilion, beyond the vineyard of Clos-Fourtet, lies the small Romanesque church of Saint-Martin. Next to this church, encircled by a stone wall, lies the vineyard of Château Canon. Vines were first planted on land surrounding the church in the first half of the eighteenth century. Most of this, a holding of twelve to fifteen hectares, belonged to the local *seigneur*, Jean Biès, a member of an established family of Libournais gentry. It was at this time that the vineyard was enclosed.

The Biès family was in the vanguard of vineyard exploitation in the area and it is well possible that the Domaine de Saint-Martin is the oldest monocultural property in Saint-Emilion. However, only the vineyard was planted. Before the Biès were able to consolidate their investment and modernize the *chais*, they ran into debt and were forced to let it go.

In 1760, Biès sold the domaine to Jacques Kanon for 40,000 gold *livres*. Kanon is described as a *corsaire* (a privateer) from Dunkirk, and a lieutenant in the Royal Marines. During the Seven Years' War (1756–63) he had commanded a number of ships, and the inference is that he had made a considerable fortune out of piracy and looting as was customary at the time. To the existing vineyard Kanon added seven small pieces of land outside the wall of the estate and, in place of the old farm buildings, he constructed a fine *maison de maître* (manor house), which still exists. On one of the porticos at the entrance to the estate, the figure 1767 shows the date of completion.

Kanon was certainly not short of money. In all, it is estimated he spent over 20,000 *livres* on the property in the space of ten years. Yet his ownership was not to last for long. Tempted back to the life of seafaring gentleman adventurer, he sold the Domaine de Saint-Martin to Raymond Fontémoing in 1770 for 80,000 *livres*. That the vineyard was fully mature and that the wine had already created a reputation for itself is attested in contemporary references and the substantial increase in price in the space of a decade.

HISTORY

The Fontémoing family figures widely in the early vinous history of Saint-Emilion and Pomerol. They were the leading wine-merchants of Libourne at the time and their names are associated with many properties. They intermarried with other landowners and, throughout the eighteenth century, were the dominant and most interesting personalities in Libourne and the surrounding area. Coincidentally, their original wine estates and the foundation of their wealth lay in the Frondasais, in particular with that part of Fronsac known as Canon-Fronsac after the most important property, Château Canon. The Fontémoings, of course, owned this Château Canon, as they did a number of other leading domaines. At this time, Fronsac wines, particularly Château Canon, fetched the highest prices of all the Libournais wines. The first reference in a Christie's catalogue to a named Bordeaux is to 'a hogshead of Canon Claret' which can only have been the Fronsac wine. To avoid complication, the wine of the Domaine de Saint-Martin, despite Jacques Kanon, remained Saint-Martin. The name of the estate and the wine was not changed until 1853.

Raymond Fontémoing passed Saint-Martin to his eldest son, Jean-Raymond, when he retired in 1800. From Jean, it went to his daughter Jeanne, the *Veuve* de Tranchère (her husband had been guillotined as a Girondin in 1794), in 1808. The Domaine de Saint-Martin remained in the family until 1857. Jeanne's daughter Virginie had married Jules Howyne (or Hovyne) and it was she who took the step, not without protest from the proprietors in Fronsac, to change the name of the estate to Château Canon, justifying her rather opportunistic decision on the basis of the name of the previous owner, he who had had the château constructed.

Following the sale in 1857 to the Comte de Bonneval, there were a number of rapid changes of ownership. Bonneval sold the property to M. Domecq-Cazaux in 1883. Félix Guignard acquired it in 1891 and it was then bought by Gabriel Supau for his daughter Henriette and her husband, André Fournier, in 1919.

All the way through the nineteenth century, the wine of Château Canon had increased in value and reputation. Back in 1783, there are records of the Fontémoing family having exported Canon to Brittany and Dunkirk at a price of 350 *livres* a *tonneau*, and in 1807 it fetched 450 francs but, on the other hand, the other Fronsac wines sold for 500 francs. By the mid-1850s, the wines of Saint-Emilion were beginning to establish themselves. The top four wines – Canon, Magdelaine, Belair and Ausone - would fetch 1,000 francs per *tonneau* and in 1861 made 1,500 francs with the top Pomerols at 1,200 to 1,400 and the other top Saint-Emilions at 1,100 to 1,300. In the wine journal of Lecoutre de Beauvais, *Le Producteur* (1838–41), we find the first specific mention of the property in a guide to the wines of the region. By the first edition of Cocks and Féret (1850), production had risen to twenty *tonneaux* and in the second edition (1868) it is given as 25 to 30 *tonneaux*. By the turn of the next century it was 35 *tonneaux*, and this has gradually risen to the present level of 75 to 100 *tonneaux*.

THE SUPAU AND FOURNIER FAMILIES

Gabriel Supau first arrived in the Bordeaux area in 1885 when he rented (and later bought) Château Broustet, the *deuxième cru classé* in Barsac. After the First World War he gave Broustet to his son André and bought Château Canon for his other child, Henriette and her husband, another André, confusingly enough. André Fournier was a lawyer but was also a *courtier* (wine-broker) until the difficult years of the mid-1930s, and he kept careful records, still preserved by the Fournier family. In the 1920s, such was the reputation of Sauternes that Broustet fetched more than Canon, and sometimes as much as a first growth claret. In 1922, for instance, Latour sold for 4,000 francs per *tonneau*, Léoville-Poyferré for 2,700, Broustet for 3,400 and Canon 1,500.

The Fourniers had one son, Pierre, who lived to a goodly age. André died in 1955 and his widow, one of Bordeaux's real characters, survived until May 1984. She is well remembered as one of a small number of formidably energetic lady proprietors, totally undaunted in the promotion of the quality of their wines. Since 1972, Canon has been managed by one of Pierre's three sons, the quietly determined Eric Fournier, who was born in 1948. He also directs Château Broustet which the Fourniers acquired from their cousins in the 1930s.

THE VINEYARD AND THE WINE

The vineyard, unchanged since the Kanon era and enclosed, occupies eighteen and a half hectares. It is bounded on the north by Clos-Fourtet, on the west by the Beauséjours, on the south by Magdelaine and on the east by Belair. This is the nucleus of the plateau of Saint-Emilion. The limestone base, into which extensive galleries of underground cellars have been quarried – neighbouring Fourtet has a very impressive example – is covered by a thin layer of clay soil mixed with decomposed limestone, barely 60 centimetres thick. The vineyard inclines to the west at between 50 and 85 metres above sea level and is planted in the ratio of 55 per cent Merlot and 40 per cent Cabernet Franc. The vines have an average age of well over 30 years, with the oldest dating from the 1920s. Until 1979, horses were still used to pull the ploughs.

THE CHATEAU AND THE *CHAIS*

The *maison de maître* constructed by Jacques Kanon was extensively renovated during the course of 1987. Effectively, the original structure, today flanked by the orangery – now a reception room – and the *chais* and offices, has been gutted and rebuilt. Eric Fournier lives in Bordeaux, but Canon is still used at holiday time and during the vintage.

The *chais* have recently been modernized as well. Prior to 1980, Canon was vinified in unusually small, wooden fermentation vats. The size was deliberate; the Fourniers considered that this led to a more regular vinification. The *cuverie* has been rebuilt and these have been replaced by wooden vats of a more normal size. The vinification is now entirely temperature controlled – indeed the whole cellar is *climatisé*. A new bottling room has also been installed.

Vinification is traditional: a long *cuvaison*, 15-20 days at 25° to 27°, the addition of a proportion of the *vin de presse* to give added structure, plenty of new oak, no filtration. Fournier, like others, adopts the view that it is better to have a high proportion of new oak (currently about 60 to 70 per cent) and mature for slightly fewer months in cask than the reverse. Today, Canon is bottled earlier than it was twenty years ago.

THE WINE

The wine, you would have said twenty years ago, is traditional – solid, sturdy, deep-coloured, warm-hearted. Eric Fournier and I prefer the 1962 and 1964 within the context of their respective vintages. Since Fournier has taken over, however, there has been a perceptible change in the style. The full body remains – and Canon is one of the fullest Saint-Emilions – but the muscle has been, to some extent, relaxed, allowing a concentrated richness to come through. The flavour I associate with Canon today is an almost creamy taste within this very rich base of fruit. Canon is a consistent wine. I continue to purchase it. This is a Saint-Emilion star.

THE TASTING

The following wines were sampled at a tasting organized by Jan Paulson of Paulson Weinraritäten in Assmannshausen, Germany, in March 1994. My thanks to him and to Hans-Burkhart Ullrich, proprietor of the Krone, for his hospitality.

1993 *Optimum drinking* **1998–2004**
Good purple colour. Raw, oaky nose. Very promising. Ripe and seductive. Medium body.

Round ripe tannin if not a great deal of structure. Balanced and elegant. Attractive fruit. Better than the 1992.

1992   **1997–2003**

Good colour. A little hard on the nose. Slightly herbaceous. There is an absence of real flesh. This has just been racked from its finings so it is not at its best. Better on the palate. Reasonable structure and grip if not a great deal of dimension. But this finishes well. Very good.

1990   **2000 2030**

Full colour. Quite firm, full, very concentrated nose. This has a lot of depth and dimension. Potentially fine. Full, oaky, very very concentrated marvellous fruit. This is very fine indeed. Marvellous balance. Very very long and complex.

1989   **2000–2020**

Good full colour. Just a touch of development. Good slightly austere rich nose. A little closed at present. Medium-full. The tannings are quite evident and a little dominant at present. But the wine is cool and classic and rich underneath, with very good acidity. Long. Needs time. Fine.

1988   **1999–2015**

Full, rich colour. Opulent nose. Lots of succulence and depth here. Potentially a gamey, animal wine. Medium-full. Rich. Plump. Some tannin on the attack. Good acidity. But it doesn't add up at present. There is a suspicion of astringency here. Yet very fat rich and plump. Very good indeed but not great.

1987   **1995–2001**

Medium colour. Lightish nose. Quite soft but not too evolved. Good fruit. This is a very good example. Medium body, quite persistent. Good extract and very good grip. Fruit and personality here. And a very good long finish. Even better on the palate than on the nose. Bravo!

1986   **Now–2000 plus**

Fullish, rich mature colour. Full, rich and firm on the nose. A lot of concentration here. Medium-full body. Good grip. Succulent, spicy, balanced and elegant. Surprisingly good acidity. Doesn't have dimension of 1985 but is a little more structured. Very good. Better than the 1983 now.

1985   **1995–2010**

Fullish colour. Just a touch of maturity. Just a little lumpy on the nose at first yet developed to become fullish, intense and ripe. Lots of succulent fruit here. Medium full, ripe, oaky, cedary, a touch of spice and butterscotch. Very good grip. Getting soft. Long and classy at the end. Fine.

1983   **Now–1997**

Medium to medium-full mature colour. Evolved nose. Mainly Merlot. Round, yet good grip. Medium to medium-full body. Fattish, quite rich, but a slight lack of acidity. End is getting a little attenuated now. Yet still positive.

1982   **1995–2010**

Medium full colour, just about mature. Ripe nose. Good flesh and fruit. Open and accessible and fresh. Full, rich and concentrated. Very good grip. Lovely. A meaty wine. Slightly cooked fruit elements. Fine. Will still improve.

1981   **Now–2000**

Medium, mature colour. Good concentration, in a soft medium-weight way, on the nose. Good fruit and balance too. Medium body. A little loose at the end. And beginning to get a touch astringent on the attack. Reasonable acidity but it lacks real fat and concentration. Good but not great. Better than the 1983.

1980   **Drink soon**

Light to medium mature colour. This is quite evolved now, yet has fruit and is still enjoyable. Medium body. Ripe. Getting just a little astringent and diffuse at the end. But a good example for the vintage. Still fruity and positive.

1979   **1995–2010**

Surprisingly small crop owing to a very small sortie. And it shows. Full. Very youthful colour. Firm nose. Slightly chunky. Slightly austere. This is full, tannic and structured. A wine of concentration. Best with food. Very good slightly austere acidity. Needs time still. Much better than the 1978. Fine for the vintage. Bags of life.

1978   **Now–2000**

Full vigorous colour. Soft mature nose. Not a lot of depth and concentration but elegant and well-balanced. Ripe and still vigorous. Medium full. Elegant fruit. Some acidity apparent. Lacks a little real concentration and succulence. Very good.

1977   **Now–1998**

Medium-full colour. Mature. Fresh and richer than most on the nose. But a little lumpy and diffuse and dry, like many 1977s. On the palate quite rich and ripe. Reasonable acidity and length. This is fat even elegant. Finishes well. Medium to medium-full. Very good.

1976   **Drink soon**

Quite a lot of colour. But rather old now. Somewhat dilute, but reasonably fresh; even a little elegance here. Medium body. Quite pleasant and fruity. Quite high acidity. But disappointing, loose and evolved. The 1977 is better. Getting a bit attenuated on the finish.

1975   **Now–2005**

Medium-full colour. Still quite fresh looking. Full, fat and concentrated. Rich and quite structured, but opulent. This is the best of this late 70s flight. Full, very rich and concentrated. Good structure and tannins. Very good acidity. Lovely long finish. Lots of vigour. Will last well.

1974   **Drink up**

Oldish colour. Rather old, pinched and herbaceous on the nose. Not a lot of pleasure here. Some fruit on the palate. But a little astringent. Getting coarse at the end. Yet better than most.

1973   **Drink up**

Medium colour. Fully mature. Evolved. Not a disaster. But never much here, now rather old. Thin. A bit acidic. Not very elegant any more. Slightly sour at the end. But good for what it is.

1972   **Past its best**

Medium colour. Not too evolved. Soft and very pepperminty on the nose. Getting a little dry. Medium body. A bit thin, even more astringent.

1971   **Drink soon**

Medium-full colour. Mature. Lightish, evolved nose. Reasonably plump and attractive. Medium to medium-full body. Soft, even sweet. And still positive at the end. A very good example.

1970   **Now–2000 plus**

Good concentration. Still vigorous. Full, rich and firm on the nose. A little solidity but very concentrated. Full, rich, tannic, quite solid. Good acidity. Slightly old-fashioned. Better with food. Meaty, slightly four-square. But very good quality.

1969   **Drink up**

Medium to medium-full colour. Fully mature. Fresh nose. Elegant. Medium weight only but good complexity. On the palate a little astringent. Well put together but only medium bodied, and has now begun to dry up. Not at all bad.

1967   **Drink soon**

Medium to medium-full colour. Soft, elegant, fruity nose. Plump and attractive. Medium body. Good concentration. Attractive plump old viney fruit. Very good, and very vigorous. Still has life. Complex. Almost as good as the 1971

1966   **Now–1999**

Medium to medium-full colour; fully mature. Rich, fat, soft and round on the nose. Plenty of ample fruit, but now fully evolved. Medium-full, ripe, intense, complex. Long and elegant. Good acidity. Indeed more vigourous on the palate than the nose would indicate. Long.

1964   **Now–2005 plus**

Good full mature colour. Fine rich nose. Fat and concentrated. Lots of character and breed. Medium-full to full but really very very intense. Essence of fruit. Great class. Perfectly harmonious. Marvellous complexity. Brilliant. Seemingly everlasting. Very very long and complex.

1962   **Now–1999**

Full colour; the least mature of this 1959-1966 flight. Cool nose. Good grip. Indeed the acidity quite evident on the nose. Very plummy fruit. Medium-full. Good tannins. Fresh and classy but not a blockbuster. Good acidity. Stylish. Nicely fresh. Long. Subtle. Very good. Lovely finish.

1961   **Now–2000 plus**

Very full colour. Yet the nose, though rich, is not as fat and as concentrated as 1959. It's more brutal. The acidity is quite evident. Medium to medium-full body. A touch of astringency. But a powerful, old fashioned wine. Very good. Certainly classy. But not as exciting as 1964 or 1959.

1960   **Drink soon**

Medium-full mature colour. Light, biscuitty nose. But the fruit has lightened up and the wine is getting attenuated. Medium to medium-full body. Holding up very well. Stylish, with good grip and substance. Still most enjoyable. A great success.

1959   **Now–2000 plus**

Very good mature colour. Rich, vigorous and concentrated on the nose. Nicely intense and fatter. Good element of cooked fruit. Full, good tannins. Even spicy. A fat, opulent, voluptuous wine. Very fine. Very lovely. Lots of vigour.

1958   **Now–1997**

Good vigorous colour. Open, fresh, round and fruity on the nose. But not a lot of real concentration. Alive, attractive and elegant. Medium-full, rich and mellow. Good acidity. Complex. Much better than the 1957 or 1960.

1957   **Now–1998**

Fullish mature colour. Soft, quite evolved, but certainly pleasant. Medium body. Some oak. Soft and mellow, but good acidity and vigour. Ripe, very attractive. Better than the 1960. Still positive at the end. Very good for the vintage.

1955   **Now–1998**

Fullish vigorous colour. A little solid on the nose. Good ripeness but a little rigid. A full, concentrated and very rich wine with a surprising amount of depth for the vintage. Better than the 1952. Vigorous, intense. Very long. Very complex. Very lovely. Almost as good as the 1953.

1953   **Now–2000 plus**

Fullish mature colour. Soft, evolved, complex nose. A lot of depth and interest. Full, concentrated and vigorous. A bigger wine than the 1952, which surprises me. More intensity. More depth. Really very fine indeed. Splendid finish.

1952   **Now–2000**

Very full colour. Still vigorous. Open, evolved ample nose. Elegant but not as much dimension as 1953. This is medium-full, without the grip and complexity of the 1953 but most enjoyable. And with plenty of old vine depth and intensity. Fine.

1950   **Drink soon**
Very full. Slightly dense colour. Slightly dense on the nose as well. Full and tannic. Rather brutal and rigid. Yet good acidity and no lack of class. The acidity shows at the end. A touch too lumpy and four-squre. Good but not great.

1949   **Drink soon**
Very full colour. Still youthful. Very sweet and concentrated on the nose. Full, ample, sweet and blackberry ripe. Very lovely, with plenty of vigour. A touch of astringency but there is fruit at the end. But it is not as good as either of the 1947s.

1948   **Drink soon**
Very full colour. Still youthful. Soft, plump nose. A touch of volatile acidity. Medium full. A touch of astringency. Ripe, opulent, but not quite the depth of the two 1947s. A little lumpy. Very good indeed. Very good fruit. The least good of these late 1940s examples. Yet in magnum, at dinner: vigorous, full, really very good indeed.

1947   **Now–2000**
Very full mature colour. Sweet, voluptuous, cedary, very seductive nose. This is lovely. A spicier, more cedary example than the rest of this flight. Round, seductive, warm, rich. Quietly composed. Very long. Very well balanced. Most attractive and very fine quality. But not great.

1947   **Now–1999**
(B.B. Lestapis) Fullish colour. Mature. Rich, fat, slightly cooked, slightly tarry. Slight element of volatile acidity. Full, some tannin, some astringency. A firm, slightly dense wine. Yet very very rich underneath. A wine for food. But the concentration and the follow-through are sweet and very lovely. Fine. This is really subtle and very long. But not a bit like the château bottling.

1945   **Now–2000 plus**
Full colour. Mature. Firm, rich, very very concentrated masculine and full on the nose. Marvellous depth. This is excellent. Full body. Very very concentrated indeed. Marvellous grip. A very intense, very vigorous bottle. Real depth and complexity at the end. Brilliant. *Grand vin!*

1943   **Now–2000 plus**
Good colour. Still full and vigorous. Rich and fat, ample and vigorous on the nose, if without the intensity and concentration of the best of the late 1940s. Still alive, but a touch four-square. Clearly the best of the 1933–1943 flight: rich, slightly spicy, fat, vigorous, no trace of astringency, long and satisfying at the end. Lovely. Fine.

1942   **Now–1999**
Medium to medium-full colour. No sign of age. There is a bit of fruit and fat here. But also a bit of astringency. On the palate better. Richer.

More vigorous. Better grip and more personality. This is long. Very good plus.

1937   **Drink soon**
Medium-full colour. Still vigorous. Fat, rich and really quite opulent on the nose. On the nose this is the best of the 1933–1943 flight. Because the fruit is really properly ripe. On the palate a bit astrigent and dense. Getting dry at the end.

1934   **Past its best**
Full, dense colour, brown at the rim. Rather too dense and stemmy for enjoyment. Also a bit oxidized. Still a little enjoyment on the palate. Medium full, slighly rigid. But the fruit is sweet.

1933   **Now–1997**
Medium colour. No real sigh of age. On the nose the acidity shows. Has lost most of its fruit and lacks charm. On the palate better; medium body. Cedary, rip, elegant. Yet still lots of enjoyment.

1929   **Now–1998**
Medium to medium-full colour. Fully mature. Interesting nose. Old. Some cedar. A bit of mint. A touch sweet/sour as it evolved. Dryish, but also a curious touch of peaches. Medium-full, ripe, sweet, mellow. Good vigour. Very soft and plump. Still life. Fine, yet not a classic.

1928   **Now–2000 plus**
Fullish, vigorous colour. Ample, aromatic nose. No astringency here. Slightly lactic and mushroomy. Fullish, meaty, good vigour. Nice touch of oak. Has grip and structure but no density. Long, classic, concentrated. Vigorous and subtle at the end. Very fine indeed.

1926   **Drink soon**
Medium-full colour. Now fully mature. Curious nose. An element of boiled milk. Light and fruity and attractive, soft but not astringent. Just lacks a little intensity. But still fresh and pleasant.

1923   **Drink up**
Fullish colour. Fully mature. A little old and dry and herbaceous on the nose. Has lost intensity on the palate. Yet there is evidence of a lot of style and complexity here. Still positive on the finish. But getting a bit loose.

1920   **Drink up**
Good full vigorous colour. Dense. Four-square nose. A lack flexibility here. Yet on the palace round, spicy, intense and complex. This is a round wine. A little past its best but certainly lovely.

1916   **Past its best**
Medium-full colour. Mature. Somewhat disagreeable nose. A bit of attenuation, a bit of built-in sulphur. The fruit has dried out. Very astringent. Only the acidity is left. This has seen better days. Seems to have some substance.

FIGEAC

Within the 5,000 hectares of vineyards entitled to the *appellation* Saint-Emilion, there lies, at the extreme western edge, some 60 hectares of gravel. This is the nucleus of the *Graves-Saint-Emilion*, and the reason for its separation from the rest of the commune, from the *Côtes*-Saint-Emilion and the other, lesser areas. The origin of all the properties in the neighbourhood is the ancient domaine of Figeac. What is now Château Figeac is a large estate – some 40 hectares of vines – but 200 years ago it was even larger. Originally the domaine extended from the borders of the town of Saint-Emilion itself some four kilometres to the east to what are now the outskirts of Libourne to the west. It comprised not only all the land on which there are now vineyards – there are thirteen in all – which today incorporate the name of Figeac in their title, but also the land which is now Cheval-Blanc. It is ironic that Figeac, having suffered numerous changes of ownership in the last half of the nineteenth century, and absentee landlords in the first half of this, should not have been classed with its neighbour as a *premier grand cru classé* (A) when the Saint-Emilion Classification was drawn up in 1953. Historically it was the predominant wine of the area, and even after Cheval-Blanc was separated the proprietor for several years used to sell his wine as *vin de Figeac*.

As befits its status as the senior estate in the area, the château of Figeac is a large, imposing, solid, three-storey construction, complete with a wing on either side, enclosing a gravel courtyard, and situated in a park, approached through an avenue of tall, mature trees. While many of the Saint-Emilion properties are fairly small, their buildings modest, and lie, particularly in the *Côtes* sector, cheek-by-jowl with each other, Figeac gives the impression of space, money and established aristocracy. There is nothing rustic or *arriviste* about *Figeac*.

HISTORY

The domaine was a *maison noble* at least as early as the fourteenth century, occupying at that time some 500 hectares, according to Professor Henri Enjalbert, and known by the Gallo-Roman name of Figeacus. Whether there ever was someone of this name, or where otherwise the name Figeacus comes from is not known. It could be perhaps a corruption of '*ficus*', the Latin for fig-tree, the French word being '*figue*'. On this site there was a medieval château which was razed in 1590 by Henri de Navarre. From the ruins a Renaissance-style building, parts of which still remain, was constructed in 1595 by the Cazes family, which had been proprietors of the estate for over 200 years.

In 1654 Marie de Cazes married François de Carle and the de Carle family, known later as Carle-Figeac, and eventually Carle-Trajet, remained owners of Figeac until 1838, when Félicité de Gères sold the estate to a M. Lebel, a Parisian, for 155,000 francs. By this time there was already an established vineyard producing 80 *tonneaux*, though the Cheval-Blanc vineyard had been detached in 1832, and other parts had been sold off over the previous 30 years. Meanwhile the Renaissance château had been destroyed and the present building constructed. This dates from the 1780s, though parts, a turret, a couple of columns and a wall on the right of the main entrance, remain from the original.

At first, the *Graves*-Saint-Emilion wines were considered inferior to those of the *Côtes*. In the 1853 edition of Franck's *Traité*, 42 first growths are listed, all in the *Côtes*, and Figeac is placed top of the seconds, marked '*très bon cru*'. The wine would have fetched around 500 francs a *tonneau*, only half the price of a lowly fifth growth Médoc. Figeac was producing around 40 to 45 *tonneaux*.

During the next decades, Figeac changed ownership seven times, and periodically additional lesser parcels of land were sold off, many of which were later planted with vines.

In 1868 the second edition of Cocks and Féret still places Château Figeac in front of Cheval-Blanc, but now says that these two sell for the same price as the *Côtes premiers crus*. Figeac, producing 50 to 70 *tonneaux*, is owned by a *Veuve* Laveine, whose husband, Gabriel, had acquired the estate in 1842. There are also three other Figeac vineyards owned by a M. Longa, a M. Chauvin and a M. Loyer, each producing around twenty *tonneaux*.

A few years later an heir of the widow Laveine, presumably her son, re-acquired the part of Figeac estate owned by M. Loyer. He was succeeded by a M. Fournier – there are Fourniers still in Saint-Emilion, notably at Château Canon (though this is not the same family, I am told) – and Fournier in 1892 by Henri de Chevremont, who was married to an English lady named Elizabeth Drake.

In 1875, a parcel of land – some 37 hectares, of which 32 were under vines – was split off and sold to a M. Corbière, and he immediately sold about half to a M. Marais. The former property became known as La Tour-Figeac; the latter, which has since been further subdivided, is La Tour-du-Pin-Figeac. The main Figeac vineyard was now down to 30 hectares, but in the next few years a certain amount of replanting was undertaken, and by 1893, according to *Saint-Emilion et ses Vins*, an extract from Cocks and Féret, the vineyard was up to 42 hectares of vines, and producing 60 *tonneaux*.

The De Chevremont heir to Figeac was the eldest daughter, Henriette, who married a *préfet* from Paris named André Villepigue, the man who inaugurated the *métro* before the First World War. From then on the property was run from Paris. For some 50 years the château was left empty except for occasional landlord visits.

The first *régisseur* was Alfred Maquin, proprietor of Château La Serre, responsible to André Villepigue from 1892 to 1905. He seems to have hoped that eventually he would be able to acquire Figeac for himself. When he realized that this would not be possible he decided to quit and concentrate on his own properties, and André's son Robert took over. It was Robert Villepigue who designed the present label.

The production of the estate continued to expand, reaching its current level of 150 *ton-neaux* in the 1920s, by which time Villepigue's daughter Ada Elizabeth, the heiress to Figeac, had married Antoine Manoncourt. Villepigue also had two sons: René was killed during the First World War and Robert, already mentioned, became owner of Cadet-Piola. It is Antoine's son, Thierry, who is the present proprietor. Though his father and grandfather only used Figeac as a holiday home, Thierry Manoncourt, who took over from him in 1947, has lived 'on site' since 1952. He married in 1956 and he and his wife, Marie-France, have four daughters.

Thierry Manoncourt is by training an agricultural engineer. Hardly had he finished the first part of his studies when the war broke out. It was 1939. He spent part of the next few years in a German prisoner-of-war camp, but was given an early release as a result of his professional qualifications. He finished his studies when the hostilities were over.

Manoncourt will persuasively attempt to prove to anyone who will listen – often, I must confess, at some length – that his wine is as good as Cheval-Blanc, deserving to be both a *premier cru* and to sell for as high a price; he will demonstrate that as late as the first two decades of this century the prices were comparable, this year the one achieving the better price, the next the other. Yet in 1945 he was told by his father that 'It was a disaster your mother inherited Figeac. We shall only lose money.' When the original Saint-Emilion Classification was being drawn up in the early 1950s, one member of the commission was reported as declaring 'Figeac, never a *premier cru*!' The wine hardly sold – it took Manoncourt five years to dispose of his 1947 – and had rarely been tasted by this particular individual.

Yet within five years of Manoncourt's arrival Figeac was selling for a higher price than all its peers among the *premiers grands crus classés* (B), up with what were then the super-seconds of the Médoc. And today it takes about two days to sell a year's vintage.

THE VINEYARD

The *Graves*-Saint-Emilion is characterized by five gravel *croupes* on a siliceous plateau over a flinty, iron-rich subsoil. Three of these lie in the Figeac domaine, two in neighbouring Cheval-Blanc, and it is this gravel (it continues across the border to the vineyards surrounding Pétrus in Pomerol) which gives these two estates their particular quality, distinctly superior to their neighbours. It is said that the soil is volcanic in origin, and was washed down from the Massif Central along the valleys of the Dronne and Isle rivers by the ice-age glaciers many years ago. Two-thirds of the Figeac vineyard is planted on this gravel soil, and unusually for Saint-Emilion, but specifically because of the gravel, there is a large proportion of Cabernet Sauvignon in the blend: 35 per cent of both Cabernet Sauvignon and Cabernet Franc (or Bouchet as it is known locally), and 30 per cent Merlot. There used to be a little Malbec, but this has not been replaced in recent years. There are about 40 hectares under vines, producing about 150 *tonneaux*.

THE CHÂTEAU AND THE *CHAIS*

The château, as I have said, is a large three-storey building, somewhat Georgian in appearance, and dates from 1780. Thierry Manoncourt and Marie-France live in what might be termed the 'east-wing'. On the western slide lie the *cuvier* and *chais*. Formerly the vinification took place in wood, but in 1972 a programme of modernization was inaugurated, and these were complemented by a battery of ten stainless-steel vats – the third in Bordeaux after Haut-Brion and Latour – though the ten oak *foudres* are retained for use during the first fermentation. The stainless-steel vats are for the malolactic fermentation, the *égalisage*, or when the crop is particularly large. The *chais* were also extended, and there are now not only a first- and second year *chai*, but an impressive underground cellar. Until recently Figeac was one of the few properties outside the first growths normally to mature its wines using 100 per cent new oak.

Manoncourt, elegant, hospitable, charming, in his mid-seventies, is committed to producing the best possible wine he can. For many years, beginning in 1953 he has kept back a hogshead of each grape variety in certain vintages, in order to pursue the evolution of the constituent parts, as well as of the blend. It was by following this that he decided later in the 1950s to increase the proportion of Cabernet Sauvignon and to dispense with the Malbec. When he arrived, though there was no more Merlot in the vineyard than today, there was 15 per cent Malbec, and most of the rest was Cabernet Franc.

THE WINE

Since 1947, Figeac has gone from strength to strength. It certainly has become a worthy rival to its illustrious neighbour, and is frequently as good, if not occasionally superior. The wines are somewhat akin in style, despite the difference in *encépagement* (for Cheval-Blanc has no Cabernet Sauvignon, though an equally small, un-Libournais quantity of Merlot), being equally solid, structured and tannic when young, as even the best wines of the Côtes – Ausone, Magdelaine, Canon – cannot be. The high incidence of both Cabernet grapes gives a welcome acidity in very hot years, such as 1982, and weight in weaker vintages such as 1984. It also gives Figeac staying power. Figeac lasts better than most Saint-Emilions, as the notes in the accompanying tasting will show, and it also makes good wine in poor years: Figeac was the only Saint-Emilion to obtain the right to the *premier grand cru classé appellation* for its 1968. There is a second wine, which I have rarely seen outside the château itself, called Château Grangeneuve.

THE TASTING

Thierry Manoncourt is an inexhaustible ambassador for his wine and generous with his precious bottles, and as a fortunate result I have attended a number of comprehensive tastings of Château Figeac in recent years. Perhaps the most comprehensive of all was that organized by Bipin Desai, the Los Angeles physics professor and oenophile, at the Restaurant Taillevent in Paris in December 1989. The only major absentee was the 1959, a splendid wine, better than the 1961 and almost as good as the 1964 in my view. As you will read, the vintages between 1966 and 1979 were somewhat disappointing compared with what followed and preceded this period. About half of the vines were lost in the 1956 frost and the average age of the vines as a result was severely reduced. The stars of the tasting were the 1964, 1955, 1953, the glorious 1949, 1947, 1937 and 1929.

Optimum drinking

1988 **1997–2015**

Medium to medium-full colour for vintage. The 1985 is better. Fullish, open, opulent, oaky nose. Rather more depth than the 1986. This is a fullish wine with good, ripe, stylish tannins. It shows well. Good grip. Lovely fruit. Rather good!

1986 **1995–2008**

Medium colour. Not as full as the 1986. Not a lot of concentration or weight or richness on the nose. On the palate medium-bodied, ripe, even quite sweet. But somewhat one-dimensional. No great weight or tannin. And no great complexity. But quite pretty and certainly balanced. Will evolve quite soon.

1985 **1996–2020**

Medium-full, immature colour. Fullish nose. This is a bit adolescent. Some oak. Seems fuller than the 1988. A bit stalky at present. Fine full palate. Good oak, ripe and succulent; good tannins. As it developed, round, spicy, aromatic and complex. This has style and depth. Bigger than most Libournais 1985s. The best of these first three wines. Fine.

1983 **Now–2005**

Medium-full colour. Little sign of development. I get an aspect of 1971 on the nose. This has a sort of lean attenuated touch I can't get enthused by. Riper on the palate but I still find a lean, slightly metallicy-acid wine. Not the size, nor, potentially, the succulence, nor the fat I am looking for. Medium to medium-full. Still just a little unresolved tannin but nearly ready.

1982   **1996–2020**
Good full, immature colour. Full, rich and concentrated. A chocolate, leather and liquorice nose. Fullish, very ripe tannins. Lush, aromatic, ripe. Very fine but not the greatest.

1981   **Now–2001**
First bottle corked. Medium-full colour, just a little developed. Good fruit and structure – in a medium bodied way – and balance underneath.

1979   **Now–2003**
Full colour. Bigger and more vigorous than the 1978. Good fullish fruit on the nose. At first slightly hard and with a lack of generosity. Shades of green and a lack of richness. It became better as it evolved. Quite full. Still young. The Cabernet shows. Some tannin. Good rich fruit, quite concentrated. Good grip. Good for the vintage but has ultimately rather too much of a vegetal flavour. So no better than good.

1978   **Now–2003**
Fullish colour. Little sign of maturity. I don't get a lot on the nose. A lack of concentration, personality. Better as it evolved. Has some richness. Medium-full. This has structure but no charm, nor succulence of fruit, nor real richness. Doesn't sing. And the acidity shows on the finish.

1976   **Drink soon**
Good full vigorous colour for the vintage. Fat but somewhat dry and blowsy, yet quite structured on the nose. Quite full on the palate, rather dry, and a lack of fruit and acidity. Unexciting.

1975   Drink soon for the better bottling
Fullish vigorous colour. Not a lot of maturity. Very curious 'off' mushroomy nose. Another bottle had less colour. Apparently there were two bottlings. What was obviously the later bottling (it only represented 5 per cent of the crop) was soft and pleasant, with good length; but the earlier bottling is a disaster, it seems.

1971   **Drink soon**
Medium-full colour. Fully matured. This has the characteristic lean-acid-plus-attenuated 1971 nose. Getting dry as well. This is disappointing for a 1971. Soft, weak and feeble. The fruit lacks richness and the acidity shows. At least fresh but not really inspiring. And at least not astringent.

1970   **Drink soon**
Medium-full colour. Still vigorous. Some H2S on the nose. A bit lumpy as well. Lacks real class and succulence of fruit. Quite full. Has balance but it lacks style. Four-square. Quite concentrated. But where is the finesse, the fruit and the distinction? Quite good at best.

1966   **Drink soon**
Good mature medium-full colour. Fresher than 1962. Fine, fully mature nose. This is classy but it lacks the weight, concentration and complexity. Medium body. A good wine but lacks real vigour and fat, as well as concentration. Fully ready. Yet the fruit is stylish and the wine is balanced. Certainly a success.

1964   **Now–2000 plus**
(Magnum) Fine vigorous colour. Closed nose at first. Full, rich, fat and concentrated. Very classic, very fresh. This is still very vigorous. An intensity of fruit at a really very fine level, with a slight cooked element. Well structured. Real depth. Marvellous texture and balance. A great wine!

1962   **Drink soon**
Medium-full, fully mature colour. The nose shows just a touch of fruit but a lack of concentration and vigour. The least good of these 1960s vintages. It was better last time I saw it.

1961   **Now–2000**
Fullish vigorous colour. Mature. Very fine, plump concentrated nose. Fresh expression of blackcurrant fruit. It got a bit burnt and malty as it evolved. A very concentrated slightly baked wine. A little more four-square than the 1964 yet rich, full and balanced. Fine. Still bags of life.

1959   **Drink soon**
(Sampled October 1989) The colour shows a little age: full but distinctly brown. Yet the nose is rich and fragrant. Full but ripe, sweet, concentrated and fragrant, with vigour, plenty of grip and a great deal of quality. High class. Holding up well. Splendid finish.

1955   **Drink soon**
(Magnum) Fine colour; as full as the 1952 and more alive. Fine rich chocolatey nose. Ample, vigorous and with lovely concentrated fruit. Quite full on the palate. A touch of mint and liquorice. Fresh, good grip. A fat wine, fuller and more vigorous than 1953, but not as complex.

1953   **Drink soon**
Fuller, more vigorous colour than the 1952. Lovely ripe fragrant nose. Very complex. A very classy, fully mature wine. A little less structured than the 1955 but more subtle, and with greater length. This has a lot of breed, and a lovely, long, complex lingering finish. Delicious. Manoncourt has always preferred his 1953 to his 1952.

1952   **Drink soon**
Fully mature colour. Fuller but more evolved than the 1953. More evolved on the nose too. The least vigorous of these four 1950s wines. Classy nevertheless. Medium body. This seems to be lightening and drying a little, and the

slightly burnt fruit leaves a little bitterness at the end. The least good of these 1950s vintages.

1950   Drink soon
Fine, full, mature, vigorous colour. Rich but dense on the nose. Blackcurranty in flavour. Structured, but has obviously been hard in its youth and taken a long time to mature. Big, raw, tannic and alcoholic. Lacks finesse. Will still last.

1949   Now–1998 plus
Brilliant colour. Looks like a 1978! This is a remarkable wine. Still very closed on the nose. Youthful. Very, very rich and concentrated. Amazing depth. Full body, rich, very concentrated. Lovely fruit but above all real breed. Ample, complex. Really long and multidimensional. Better than 1947. *Grand vin*!

1947   Now–1997
Full colour but more brown than the 1945 and not quite as full. Lovely soft, almost porty-rich, vanillary voluptuous nose. Creamy. Fine quality. Exotic, opulent and very, very, rich. Still some tannin. Good acidity. A big wine. Solider than the 1949 but not as classy or as subtle, yet quite delicious. Still plenty of life but at its peak now.

1945   Drink soon
Fine, fullish, vigorous colour. Fine and rich and violetty at first on the nose but got a bit hard and animal with leather touches as it evolved. Firm, solid but has lost a little fruit. A full wine, but it still has unresolved tannins. A bigger wine than 1943 but not as good. A little disappointing.

1943   Drink soon
Green glass so a later bottling (i.e., late 1945 or early 1946 rather than earlier). Medium colour. Still reasonably fresh. Good nose. Raspberry flavoured, a little boiled-sweet element but creamy, like a sorbet. Full, rich and concentrated. Similar on the palate. Old viney, rich, structured. Fine fruit, the Cabernet showing. Long. Fine. Still vigorous.

1942   Drink up
White glass. Good medium but fresh colour for this age. Denser nose than the 1943, less fruit, less sweetness. Somewhat herbal. Medium-full body and medium interest and concentration. Good acidity has kept it fresh. A bit one-dimensional.

1939   Drink up
Medium colour. A little age. Interesting fragrant nose at first though there is also a bit of dryness. Some fruit but no real concentration. Now fading. Medium body. Some fruit in a somewhat lack-lustre way but also rather astringent.

1937   Drink soon
Medium colour, no undue age. An austere nose. Good acidity and richness but a slight element of

H2S. Full but not too hard. A little tannic astringency but has good fruit, at least a little suppleness and certainly has richness. Tough but not too tough. Didn't dry out too much. Very good for the vintage. Held up very well.

1934   Drink soon
Fine colour, still vigorous. This has a full nose. Still shows a lot of structure. A big, rich, full, tannic, masculine wine. Still vigorous. A full, tannic wine. Rich underneath. Meaty. Long macerated. Good acidity. Tough but good.

1929   Will still keep
Amazing colour. Full, rich, deep and barely mature. Fine, full, ripe nose. Slightly caramelly and certainly concentrated. Quite full on the palate, rich and vigorous. A ripe, very concentrated wine which is still amazingly vigorous. Fat, plump, ample and voluptuous. A *crème brûlée* flavour. Multidimensional. Beautiful. Held up very well. A gamey wine which has the structure of a 1928. Lovely. Will still keep.

1926   Drink up
Medium colour. Still has vigour, it would appear. Held up well. A little dry on the nose, but sweet on the palate even after half an hour. Good concentration. A more classically austere flavour, less spice. Good acidity. Still fine.

1924   Drink soon
(Magnum) Medium colour. Now quite old. Quite high volatile acidity. Well matured but still round, succulent, fat and meaty. A touch of chocolate and blackberry. A lot of class and depth here. Quite full. Rich and concentrated. Again chocolatey on the palate. Still has vigour on the finish. Long. Classy. Very fine.

1911   Past its best
Lightish colour now. Well matured. Fresh mountain flowery nose, but a little dried-out now. A light wine which has now lost its fruit and become a bit dry. Past its best.

1906   Drink up
(Magnum) Lightish colour now. Well matured. A little dried-out on the nose. Better than the 1911. More genuine than the 1905. An old wine now. Yet fragrant and elegant with the old-rose flavour of a classy old wine. Faded quickly but no astringency. Was a fine wine once. Very fine.

1905   Drink soon
(Magnum) Amazingly good colour. Strange slightly cooked nose, a little papery-dry but also a touch sweet-maderized element. On the palate fullish, fresh – much fresher than the nose – blackcurrant and vigorous. Good grip. Suspiciously boiled-sweety. Very curious. Indeed possibly spurious.

LA GAFFELIÈRE

Château La Gaffelière is one of several Saint-Emilion *premiers crus* whose quality has gone through a disappointing patch in recent years. Vintages from the late 1940s right up to 1976 were very good, though there were one or two inconsistencies: I have had volatile bottles of the 1961, and as many disappointing bottles as exciting bottles of the 1966. There was a slight trough in 1978 and 1979. Since then the quality has picked up again. After Château Pavie, Gaffelière is the largest of the Côtes *premiers crus* and the vineyard contains a high proportion of old vines. That the estate can produce magnificent wine is shown by the quality of its 1945, one of the finest Saint-Emilions I have ever drunk.

Now, after this brief period of disappointment, the management reins have been tightened again. La Gaffelière was rated second only to Ausone among all the *Côtes*-Saint-Emilions in the 1969 edition of Cocks and Féret. Then in 1982 and 1991, among the *Côtes et Pieds de Côtes*, listed separately from the wines of the *plateau calcaire*, the judgement places Gaffelière in the top half of the list of first growths rather than among those fighting relegation at the bottom. Though I would not rate it a super-second, i.e, as good as Canon or Pavie, I consider that if there were ever to be a serious reclassification of the wines of Saint-Emilion, La Gaffelière would have nothing to fear.

Château La Gaffelière has belonged to the family of the Counts of Malet-Roquefort for over three centuries, a record unrivalled in Saint-Emilion and probably elsewhere among the top estates of the Bordeaux area. The De Malets can trace their history back to the times of William the Conqueror. As Normans, their origins were Viking, and the ennoblement of Roland de Malet in 1066 was as a direct result of valour on the field of the Battle of Hastings. One of Roland de Malet's three sons remained in England – there is still a British branch of the family – another branch, the Malet-Roqueforts, eventually arrived in Saint-Emilion. An ancestor, Louis de Malet, was Admiral of France in 1486.

HISTORY

The land De Malets-Roqueforts took over in Saint-Emilion in the seventeenth century included a *manoir* which had once been a hospital for lepers. Hence the name '*La Gaffelière*', from the medieval word for leper. The current château, though whether this was the original leprosarium I would beg to doubt, dates in part from the thirteenth century or even earlier. There is a stone-floored, medieval vaulted kitchen and the wings are in the Renaissance style of the seventeenth and eighteenth centuries. The whole building was extensively reconstructed in the nineteenth century, giving in parts an atmosphere which is palpably Victorian Gothic, and from the back, the main part of the house has something of the character of a converted church. Parts of the château, it is said, were modelled on the medieval '*logis de Malet-Roquefort*', still to be seen in the walls of the town of Saint-Emilion itself. The building lies on the right-hand side of the road at the foot of the town in an extensive park containing a venerable old cedar tree eight metres in circumference, said to have been planted by the first De Malet to live here 300 years ago.

The De Malet holdings were extensive, and much, one can conjecture, was originally farmed on a share-cropping basis by tenants. Vineyards, no doubt, occurred here and there, increasingly as the eighteenth century progressed. Enjalbert, in his *Les Grands Vins de Saint-Emilion, Pomerol et Fronsac*, records that there was a *bourdieux* of 25 *journaux* of vines at La Gaffelière in the mid-eighteenth century (a *journal*, the amount of land one man could work in a day, measured roughly as a third of a hectare). In the records of Beylot, a *négociant* who developed his affairs from 1770 on, there is a note of purchase of wine from a M. Trianson of La Gaffelière for 400 *livres* the *tonneau* in 1777.

By the 1840s the name of the De Malets themselves appear in lists of properties and the wines they produced. They made fourteen *tonneaux* of wine at 'Peygenoustous et Saint Georges', eight of first growth wine and 40 of second at Fondroque (*sic*), but nothing yet at Gaffelière. Down among the bottom of the second growths a M. Boitard made 40 *tonneaux* and M. Modet ten at La Gaffelière. By following the trail through successive editions of Cocks and Féret it becomes apparent that M. Boitard's *cru* became what is now called Château Canon-La-Gaffelière. The De Malet family acquired M. Modet's *vignoble* in the 1860s; Peygenestous became Puygenestous-Naudes, and the two were combined as Château La Gaffelière-Naudes in the 1890s. Meanwhile by 1886 the Fonroque vineyard had passed to J. Chatonnet, owner of Château Magdelaine. It was eventually to come into the hands of the family of Jean-Pierre Moueix who coincidentally today also own Magdelaine. The Comtes de Malet also owned Château Puy-Blanquet, a very large property in Saint Etienne-de-Lisse, one of the Saint-Emilion satellites, for some 70 years between 1880 and 1950.

Until the Second World War La Gaffelière (the Naudes was dropped after the 1964 vintage) does not appear to have enjoyed a very high reputation. Until the 1949 edition of Cocks and Féret the wine is listed towards the end of the 40 to 50 Saint-Emilion 'first growths'. Not until 1949 did the De Malets request an illustration of the property to appear, or a brief puff of the wine it made. In 1949, though, La Gaffelière-Naudes is listed eighth among the *Côtes*-Saint-Emilion *crus*, and, as I have said, in 1969 it appears in second place.

THE VINEYARD

The Gaffelière vineyard lies on both sides of the D122 road which connects Saint-Emilion with the main Libourne-Bergerac highway. This road, incidentally, was originally private but was given to the town by the present Count's grandfather when the railway was constructed and the Saint-Emilion station built in 1853. Divided by the road, the vineyard is nevertheless in one piece, running down to the railway on the east side where it marches with Pavie, and adjoining Belair and Magdelaine on the western side. The geology is complex, consisting of three of the six main soil types to be found in the area. Part of the vineyard lies on the *Côtes*, part on the *Pieds de Côtes*, both predominantly sandy-limestone or clay-limestone soils on a limestone base, while some of the lower-lying vineyard has sandy-gravelly terrain with little limestone content, if any. There are 25 hectares of vines, not all necessarily in production at one time, planted in the ratio 65 per cent Merlot, 25 per cent Cabernet Franc (Bouchet) and 10 per cent Cabernet Sauvignon. The oldest of the vines boast 70 years of age: the average is 35 or more. Château La Gaffelière had been experimenting with a harvesting machine since 1981 but this has now ceased. Production, in these prolific days, averages 100 *tonneaux*.

THE GALLO-ROMAN VILLA

In 1969 evidence of a Gallo-Roman villa was found on the estate under part of the vineyard known as *Le Palat*. This has carefully been excavated by a team of local archaeologists and they have slowly revealed the remains of a building of substantial proportions. The mosaic floor of what was certainly the main room shows a fruiting vine. Elsewhere elaborate hunting scenes with exotic animals – lions, tigers and mythical beasts – are depicted. Was it here, Léo de Malet-Roquefort will try to persuade you, that Ausonius had his villa?

THE *CHAIS* AND THE WINE-MAKING

Like the vineyard, the different buildings where the wine is made and stored straddle the road. On the château side, the wine is bottled and stored, and there are several garages for tractors and other agricultural machinery. Opposite, there is a new, square subterranean barrel cellar and *cuvier*, all rather stylish, and a small building used mainly for *vente directe*.

The wine is fermented in stainless steel, at a temperature held to a maximum of 30 degrees, and aged using about one-third to one-half new wood, depending on the vintage. It is not filtered before bottling.

CHÂTEAU TERTRE-DAUGAY AND CHÂTEAU DE ROQUEFORT

Standing on a magnificent promontory to the west, commanding an awe-inspiring view of the Dordogne valley – all the way from Castillon downstream to the hill of Fronsac and beyond – lies Château Tertre-Daugay, a property the current Count, Léo de Malet-Roquefort, bought in 1978. Until its own *chais* were reconstructed, Tertre-Daugay was made at Gaffelière; since 1984 *in situ*. The wine is a *grand cru classé*, and has been performing exceptionally well in recent years.

Château de Roquefort, a small *grand cru* lying between Pavie and La Clotte on the eastern-facing slopes opposite Château Ausone, was acquired in 1965. This label is used for the second wine of La Gaffelière.

THE WINE

There has been quite a bit of change in the personnel running La Gaffelière under Léo de Malet-Roquefort in recent years. From 1944 to 1980 the *régisseur* had been Lucien Julien. It was towards the end of his career, a sick man, that he let the quality decline a little. Briefly Jean-Marie Galari combined the roles of *maître de chai* and manager. Then, for a couple of seasons, Alexandre Thienpont, son of the late Lucien of Vieux Château Certan, was the man in charge. On his father's death in 1985 Alexandre departed to run the family property, and Edouard Belin is now installed.

Compared with some *Côtes*-Saint-Emilions, Gaffelière is a full, plump, structured wine. Normally those vineyards on the slope produce a wine which is less sturdy than those of the plateau. Pavie is less solid than Canon, for example. Belair, whose vineyard lies largely on the plateau is an exception on the one side; La Gaffelière on the other. As a result of this, a good Gaffelière from a full vintage – 1982 or 1970, for example – will need a good dozen years to evolve to full maturity. Other bottles, as the notes will show, are still vigorous after fifteen years or more, even when they emanated from less firm vintages. So the wine has power. It also has richness, and the concentration which comes from the old vines is certainly evident. It does not quite have the breed of Ausone or Magdelaine, but it is nevertheless, normally – let us forget the hiatus of 1978-79 – a very good wine, one of the best of the *Côtes*-Saint-Emilions.

THE TASTING

The following wines were sampled at La Gaffelière in April 1986. I have added a note on a 1959 and an English bottling of the 1966 which, quite coincidentally, I had a chance to taste immediately on my return, and some other notes on 1950s vintages tasted more recently.

Optimum drinking

1985   1995–2010

This wine had only been in oak for a month. Alongside the other *premiers crus*, at a tasting at Cheval-Blanc, I noted a great subtlety, finesse and concentration but without the power of, say, Ausone or Magdelaine. The next day, straight from cask, it seemed to have more *puissance*. Lovely fruit. Long on the palate. Very fine.

1983   **Now–2008**

Good colour. Lovely harmonious nose; rich, ripe and complete. Quite full, some tannin. Absolutely none of the dilution sometimes found on this side of the Bordeaux area in this vintage. Round, ripe, balanced. Long on the palate. Plenty of class. Very fine finish.

1982   1996–2018

Good colour. Full, rich, slightly earthy nose. Full and concentrated. A big, rich, meaty wine with plenty of power. More structure than the 1983, and currently, because it has retired into its shell somewhat, not the charm. But this is very fine indeed. Very long.

1981   **Now–2005**

Medium-full colour, no development. Soft, round, ripe nose. Plump and plummy if without much oomph behind it. Medium-full body. A little tannin. Good acidity and very good length. Very attractive fruit. Better than it was the previous occasion I saw it.

1979   **Drink soon**

Medium-full colour, some development, indeed more than I had expected. Quite developed on the nose, almost a touch of 1976, and less structured than I would have anticipated. Fully ready. Open, high-toned, not that much grip and a little one-dimensional. A touch hollow in the middle and astringent at the finish. Quite good but not exciting.

1978   **Drink soon**

A little more colour but also fully mature. Evolved nose; fully ready if not surprisingly so for a wine of only seven years age in 1986. Quite attractive fruit, but not a wine of long life. Lacks a bit of structure. Again quite good, but a little disappointing in this context.

1976   **Drink soon**

Better colour than expected after the two wines above; some brown but no undue age. Fullish nose, spicy but no fade. Round, still sweet but one-dimensional and lightening up now. Good for the vintage nevertheless. A 1976 with more to it than most.

1975   **Now–1997**

Good full mature colour. Not a lot of the nose at first; rich, fat and meaty as it evolved. Full, a little tannin. Good round rich fruit. A bit hard at the outset but has evolved into one of the better and more accessible 1975s. Long. Quite concentrated and complex. Shows well.

1971   **Drink soon**

Good colour for the vintage, now fully mature. Fine, fragrant, ripe, fresh, elegant nose. Good depth on the palate. A complex mature wine with plenty of fruit and which still has plenty of life. Very good for the vintage.

1970   **Drink soon**

Medium-full colour, fully mature. The nose is ripe and very attractive but softer and more gentle than one might expect. Indeed the wine is quite a lot more developed than one might anticipate after the 1971. Fuller and richer on the palate than the nose might indicate. Very ripe. Rich; good style. Good but not great.

1967   **Drink soon**

Very good full colour for the vintage. Full, vigorous nose, a lot of depth for a 1967. Quite full, meaty, old-vine concentration. A serious wine for the vintage which still has plenty of life. Excellent for a 1967.

1966   **See comments**

This bottle, surprisingly, was more evolved than the 1967. The wine had lightened and shortened, showing the faded Merlot touches – all attenuated all spice and *crème caramel* and no fresh, vigorous plummy fruit – of a poorly made Saint-Emilion. Astringency on the finish. I have had better bottles. But also other bottles similar to this.

1966   **Drink soon**

(Hedges and Butler bottling, sampled May 1986) The label said 1964 but the cork 1966. Big, full purple colour (a lot of *vin de presse*?). Still a bit tough and burly but fresh, plenty of fruit if a little lack of elegance. Vigorous though and good length. Good.

1964   **Now–1996**

Excellent colour; full, alive, vigorous. This is a lovely wine! Rich, meaty, concentrated, old-vine flavours. A lot of depth on both nose and palate. Full, vigorous, very complex, very long. Still bags of life. Excellent.

1961   **Now–1998**

Good colour. Fully mature nose. Rich and concentrated and with all the flavours and complexity of a mature wine of this superb vintage. Now mellow and velvety and wonderfully ripe and fragrant. For now rather than the year 2000.

1959   **Drink soon**

Fully developed, meaty, earthy aromatic wine now beginning to lighten up a little. Fat, sweet, caramelly finish. A wine of fine quality which now needs drinking.

1955   **Drink soon**

(Belgian bottled) Good mature colour. Still vigorous. Rich but earthy on the nose. Plenty of fruit and depth if not a lot of class. A full, originally quite tannic, wine. Good old-vine concentration to support it. A bit old-fashioned. Meaty. Still has life. Very good. Good finish.

1955   **Drink soon**

(Avery's bottling) Good colour. Plump, fresh, slightly chunky, four-square nose. Fullish, rich, old-viney. This has class, concentration and depth. This has plenty of life still. Better on the nose. An ample, full, fruity wine. Very good for the vintage and still vigorous.

1953   **Drink soon**

Full colour, mature but still vigorous. Ripe nose, quite substantial for a 1953 – no undue age. Old vines. Fine, old, meaty claret. Fat, rich. Still quite vigorous. Fuller and meatier than I would have expected. Rich, long, fat finish. Good acidity. Very good indeed.

1952   **Now–1997**

Excellent colour. Lovely, smoky, rich nose. Concentrated, old-vine creaminess. Mature but no fade or astringency. Full, still even a little tannin. Ripe, very concentrated. This is excellent. Real depth. Bags of life. Almost porty sweet. I might have said it was a 1947.

1949   **Drink soon**

Full colour; mature but no sign of age. Smoky-spicy nose with a touch of caramel and cooked fruit. Fullish, fat, rich and classy on the palate. Good fruit. Freshly balanced. Long and complex. Initially very fine, though a certain amount of underlying decay began to appear as the wine developed in the glass.

MAGDELAINE

For over 200 years Magdelaine, or Madelaine as it is alternatively spelt in the earliest records, belonged to the Chatonnet family. In the 1868 Cocks and Féret, one of the earliest books to list a wide range of Saint-Emilion and Pomerol wines, the property is listed tenth among the *grands crus* of the *Côtes*-Saint-Emilion. Four proprietors are listed: Chatonnet (producing ten *tonneaux*), Chatonnet Crepin (three to four), Bon Barat (three to four) and Domecq Cazeaux (three to four), and it is spelt Madelaine.

One presumes that the third of these smaller sections finally split off entirely and became Curé-Bon-la-Madelaine, now a four-hectare vineyard lying between Magdelaine and the town of Saint-Emilion, and, coincidentally, another property in which the Moueix company used to have an interest, though this time as distributor for M. Landé, the proprietor, rather than as owners themselves. (It used to make very good wine too; the 1978 is delicious.) Another of these subsidiaries became Chapelle-Madelaine, acquired by the proprietor of Château Belair in 1916. Yet another became Cap-de-Mourlin-Magdelaine, owned in the 1930s by the proprietors of Curé-Bon. And there is also a Clos la Madelaine.

According to Cocks and Féret, the vineyard is one of the oldest in the area, wines having been made there on a commercial scale prior to the Revolution, and bottles from the famous Comet year of 1811 still being in existence over a century later. Under part of the vineyards stretching back from the *cave* entrance behind the château, are magnificent galleries, over 100 metres long, ending in a large cavern once known as the *Grotte de la Fausse Monnaie*, a room where money forgers had once worked.

HISTORY

The earliest reference in which I have been able to trace 'La Magdelaine' is in Lecoutre de Beauvais' *Le Producteur*, published between 1838 and 1841. 'First and foremost' is Le Chevalier de Canolle at Belair; properties which are now Fonplégade, Canon, Pavie and Troplong-Mondot are next, as well as various domaines owned by the Chaperon family: 'Gouspaude', Balestard and Tertre-Daugay. Following these comes a list which included Ausone, then considered inferior to Belair, Beauséjour, Berliquet, Clos Fourtet, Trottevieille and Soutard – and 'La Magdelaine'. Prices descended from 750 francs the *tonneau* for Belair down to 300 to 400 for most of the rest. Jean Chatonnet, the last of his line, died about the time of the First World War, and the estate passed to his son-in-law M. G. Jullien, notary of Saint-Emilion, and proprietor of what was then called Château du Jardin Villemaurine, now Château Cardinal-Villemaurine. Jullien was succeeded by his son Jean in the 1930s, at which time Cardinal-Villemaurine was sold to the Carrille family.

Already Magdelaine was regarded as one of the top properties in the area. Cocks and Féret, who always list properties in what they consider to be a true order of merit, put Magdelaine third after Ausone and Belair in their 1929 edition (Cheval-Blanc and the other Graves properties are listed separately). In 1949 the order is the same despite the fact that by that time the state of the vineyard had deteriorated somewhat; the wines though, judging by their appearance in 1980, were still fine.

In 1952 Magdelaine was acquired by Etablissements Jean-Pierre Moueix. This was the second property Jean-Pierre bought. Lafleur-Pétrus had come on the market in 1950, and Trotanoy and Lagrange were to follow in 1953 and 1954. The vineyard, as I have said, was in a sorry state, and in 1954 a large section of it, including a new two hectare section cleared from scrub, was replanted. I cannot speak from any great experience of the wines of Magdelaine in the 1950s, but certainly from 1961 onwards it has been consistently one of the very best of the *premiers grands crus*.

THE VINEYARD

Magdelaine is bounded by Belair on the east, Curé-Bon and Canon to the north, and by Tertre-Daugay, Berliquet, Fonplégade and La Gaffelière to the west and south. The vineyard lies on the lip of the Saint-Emilion limestone ridge and its eleven hectares are divided between six hectares on the plateau and five on the slope into two sections which adjoin, like an inverted V. The soil of the plateau is limestone debris mixed with clay, about 20 centimetres of it resting on a bed of limestone rock. On the slope there is more clay in the top soil, the thickness of which varies, and this adds to the depth and concentration of the wine, whereas that from the flat land above tends to have more finesse.

Magdelaine is planted with 85 per cent Merlot (the proportion having been increased in the last 30 years) and 7 per cent Cabernet Franc, with the remainder being very old vines of a mixture of varieties, dating from prior to the First World War. The average age is now over 30 years old. One can easily tell a really old vineyard by the narrow space between the rows of vines. The modern habit is to plant further apart in order to facilitate the use of special tractors. At Magdelaine horses must still be used.

Since the replanted section has been included in the *grand vin*, the average production has risen. In the Cocks and Féret of 1969 it was given as 20 *tonneaux*. It is now 45.

Because the vineyard is not large the harvest can take place in one go, as at Pétrus, taking two or three days rather than being staggered over two or three weeks, and I am sure that this makes a major contribution to the quality. By waiting until the moment is optimum, and then drafting in a large team, Christian Moueix, together with Jean-Claude Berrouet, the oenologist, can ensure that the fruit is as ripe as possible, but also that there will be no chance that it will linger on and rot on the vine if the weather deteriorates. Magdelaine, hence, is often one of the latest properties to commence picking; but, again, one of the first to finish.

THE CHÂTEAU AND THE *CHAIS*

Magdelaine is no showpiece. To reach it you take the road which leads away from the *place* by the Hôtel Plaisance, and drive a few hundred metres south, taking the left-hand fork in the direction of Ausone. When you come to a T-junction, opposite you over the dry stone wall, is the vineyard of Magdelaine.

The château is no longer inhabited, sadly, and is the small, elegant two-storey edifice hidden behind a cedar tree that is depicted on the label. Behind, half in the rock under the road, are the *chais*, enlarged, as elsewhere, from natural limestone caves. The whole place used to have a rather dilapidated air, but in 1989 some renovations were put in train and the atmosphere is now a little less forlorn.

The wine is vinified in small cement *cuves*, with some of the grapes (about 20 per cent, depending on the vintage) left unstalked. The *cuvaison* with the skins is long, averaging three weeks, and the wine matured using 50 per cent new oak for eighteen months or so before bottling. It is not filtered.

THE WINE

Magdelaine is the Saint-Emilion *premier cru* with the highest percentage of Merlot in its *encépagement*. This gives a wine with abundant ripe fruit, and, as a result of the short, concentrated harvest at the optimum time, a fruit that is concentrated to the optimum. The new oak gives backbone and structure, fullness and longevity. Not here do you get a wine which, opulent and generous when young, degenerates after half a dozen years into something weak and attenuated. Magdelaine retains both fruit and structure. Above all there is class; a clean, vigorous finesse typical of what one might call the Moueix style of wine-making. In the latest Cocks and Féret – well, it's Féret solely now, officially, but I always think of it as Cocks and Féret – Magdelaine is rated the top wine in the sub-section entitled '*plateau calcaire*' (Ausone is '*Côtes and Pieds de Côtes*'). I could not agree more.

THE TASTING

In July 1986, I was asked to preside over a range of Magdelaines at a tasting organized by Sotheby's. This was followed four years later by a tasting in London I organized with a group of friends. To complete the range I have added notes on other bottles which have come my way in the last couple of years.

1989   *Optimum drinking* **1997–2012**
Good colour. Rich, fat, substantial nose: there is a lot of *matière* here. Fullish, ripe and voluptuous on the palate with good tannins and good grip. Yet at present a touch ungainly. Very good, even very good indeed. (Having since tasted the 1990 against the 1989 in April 1991, and again twelve months later, my first impression is that the 1990 is even better.)

1988   **1995–2005**
Good colour. This is also a bit adolescent though it has now (tasted twice in January 1991) had time to recover from its bottling. The finish is the best part. Medium-full body, ripe, ample and rich.

There is a good constitution here but lacks drive and freshness on the finish. Good to very good.

1986   **Now–1997**
Medium colour. Very Merlot on the nose, and a shade diffuse. This is the least exciting of these recent vintages. Medium to medium-full body. Ripe and round but with a lack of real concentration and zip. Quite good to good.

1985   **1995–2012**
A lovely example. Good colour. Concentrated, ripe, voluptuous nose with a lot of depth an intensity of flavour: an example of how good the top Libournais examples are in this vintage. Fullish on the palate. Lovely ripe fruit. Very good balance. This is fine, indeed very fine.

1983   **Now–2005**

This is better than the 1981. Good colour; no
undue signs of age. Good fruit on the nose, and,
most importantly, no sign of the dilution in other
Libournais wines of this vintage. Fresh, vigorous
palate. Fullish. Ripe Merlot fruit with no lack of
concentration. Rich, structured. Excellent result.

1982   **1995–2015**

Good youthful colour. Fine ripe, concentrated
nose. Good oak base. Very good fruit. Medium-
full. Good ripe tannins. Succulent, full of fruit.
Long and balanced. Not adolescent. Fine.

1981   **Now–1997**

Good colour, a little development. Soft nose,
quite ripe but without a lot of weight or grip behind it. Medium body, not much tannin. Lacks
concentration and depth. Reasonably fresh but a
little one-dimensional. Good though.

1979   **Now–2000**

This is better. Slightly more colour. Rounder,
ripe and richer on the nose. Attractive oak, roast
chestnut and mulberry flavours. Fuller, more
depth. Good fresh fruit. Well-balanced, long finish. Altogether more positive. Very good.

1978   **See note**

When I vertically tasted Chateau Magdelaine at
the Studley Priory Wine Weekend in December
1983, I noted 'quite lovely'. At the Sotheby 1978
vintage tasting in 1985, I marked Magdelaine as
'outstanding'. Others, I heard later, tasted from a
less satisfactory bottle, and did not find it so exciting. At a 1978 tasting in September 1990 we
had a disappointing bottle. Here in 1990 we had
two unsatisfactory bottles. Well-coloured, fullish, still tannic but somehow both a bit raw and
pinched and somewhat rubbery and peppery.

1976   **Drink soon**

Good colour for the vintage but definitely a fully
mature wine. Fullish nose, but old-tea flavours
lurk underneath. Fuller than most on the palate.
Spicy, some sweetness and fruit but also a touch
of astringency. Quite good if not very elegant.

1975   **Now–2000**

Good colour, just a little maturity. Rich and
plummy, with a creamy old-vine flavour on
both nose and palate. Fresh, full, still has a bit of
tannin. Very good quality.

1971   **Drink soon**

Rather better colour than the 1976. Very lovely,
elegant, mature, complex nose. A fragrant, re
fined, medium-full-bodied wine. Fine, balanced
fruit. Very good.

1970   **Now–2005**

Very good colour, little brown. Very fine, rich,

fruity, oaky nose. Still reserved. Big, full, complex. A fat wine. Rich and concentrated. Excellent. Now in its prime.

1967   **Drink soon**

Excellent colour for the vintage, mature but no
age. Full, slightly high-toned but elegant, fruity
nose with a touch of hazelnut. A refined, soft,
mature wine, still fresh, and moving towards the
end of its days. Very classy for the vintage.

1966   **Drink soon**

Splendid colour. An individual cooked plums
and liquorice nose. Rich, full, ripe wine which
improved considerably in the glass. Fat and aromatic. Curious but good.

1964   **Drink soon**

Very full colour, still dense, just about mature.
Full, rich but very aromatic, wood-smokey nose.
Tannic, earthy wine. Sweetly blackcurrant but
muscular and with a touch of farmyard. Finishes
long though. A good wine in its curious way.

1962   **Drink soon**

Good colour. Round, generous, warmly fruity,
richly aromatic. Roast chestnuts, Christmas cake
flavour. Long on the palate. Most attractive.

1961   **Now–1996**

(Half bottle) Very good but not great. Good
colour. Rich, ripe nose. Very concentrated. Instantly the dimension of a very fine vintage. Yet
somehow the complexity and intensity is missing, as is the breed. Very good only. Simply lacks
the concentration and richness on the finish.

1959   **Drink up**

(Belgian bottled, Graf Lecocq) Good colour but
now shows a bit of age. Stylish nose. Soft and
fading but plump and fragrant. Shows a little age.
Medium body. This is an attractive, ripe wine
but it is not as vigorous as the other 1950s Belgian bottlings today.

1957   **Drink soon**

(Belgian bottled, Graf Lecocq) Good colour, a
little more age than the 1955. Quite a firm nose.
Even a little hard. Not too hard at all on the
palate. Quite full, ripe, good acidity keeping it
fresh. This does not lack charm. It doesn't have a
great deal of dimension but it doesn't lack character or interest. Holding up well.

1955   **Drink soon**

(Belgian bottled, Graf Lecocq) Good vigorous
colour. Rich, plump, elegant nose. Still vigorous
though it has perhaps lost a little of its fruit. A softer, fruitier wine than the 1957. Looser knit but
more finesse. A pleasant wine which is beginning
to show signs of shortening and losing elegance on
the finish. Getting a bit diffuse at the end. Very
good though, especially on the nose.

PAVIE

Pavie is by far the largest of the *Côtes*-Saint-Emilion *premiers grands crus classés*. There are 40 hectares, and the average production is 150 *tonneaux*. Because of this, and because of its consistently high quality, Pavie is one of the best-known and easiest encountered of the top Saint-Emilion wines.

Few of the early works on the wines of Bordeaux note the names of any leading growths in Saint-Emilion. Paguierre (1828) lists Canolle (now Belair), Pères at Berliquet (a neighbour of Canon and Magdelaine), l'Abbé de Sèze (now Troplong-Mondot), Laborie – which even the redoubtable Professor Enjalbert has been unable positively to identify; he hazards that it might have been meant to be Laveau, variously involved with Trottevieille, Soutard and Franc-Mayne – and Fontémoing (Canon).

In the 1824 and 1845 editions of his *Traité* Franck lists no single properties, but by the first edition of Cocks and Féret (1850) there are a large number of '*cru de premier classe*', as well as even more seconds, not only in Saint-Emilion itself, but in neighbouring communes such as Saint-Christophe. The list is headed by Châteaux Belair, Troplong-Mondot, Franc-Mayne, Beauséjour and Canon (then called Saint-Martin). About two-thirds down the list of first growths is Pavie, listed four times. The first owner is Talleman (twenty *tonneaux*); Pigasse also owns Larcis and produces fifteen *tonneaux*. This is followed by Lafleur, ten *tonneaux*; and Chapuis, also ten *tonneaux*. Eighteen years later, in 1868, the second edition of Cocks and Féret gives a new picture. The Pigasse holding now produced 25 to 30 *tonneaux*; a new entry, Croisit et Dussaut, produce four to five; but 'Talleman' has disappeared. This, as we shall see, must be a mistake.

HISTORY

Adolphe Pigasse seems to have died soon after 1868, and during the next twenty years his widow gradually sold off parcels of her land to neighbours. By 1885, her domaine was down to a rump producing a mere fifteen *tonneaux* and the bulk of Pavie was owned by a family called Fayard-Talleman who must surely have a connection with the 'Tallemans' of 1850. It had, however, already established a reputation. Together with many other Saint-Emilion properties, Pavie exhibited at the Paris Exhibition of 1867 and won a gold medal. Other awards were gained elsewhere.

In 1885 M. Ferdinand Bouffard arrived on the scene. Bouffard was a Bordeaux *négociant*, and no doubt, like many of his contemporaries, had ambitions to be a vineyard proprietor as well. He had inherited from his father the curiously named Domaine de la Sable (by no means on sandy, alluvial land, but immediately below what was then Pavie, between it and the little railway line). In 1885 he bought the Fayard-Talleman vineyards. He then bought an adjacent section called Château Pimpinelle, and over the next six years added the Dussaut parcel, the Pigasse rump, and a further extension of the slope to the east known as Larcis-Bergey. All this gave him a substantial holding of well over 50 hectares of vines, capable of producing 125 to 150 *tonneaux*.

This was not the limit of the Bouffard viticultural empire. Below the railway line, where Saint-Emilion's station used to be, the Bouffards had Clos Simard, and in the Graves, adjacent to Haut-Brion, Ferdinand Bouffard was co-proprietor of Château Héritage-Haut-Brion.

For some reason, while the bulk of this holding was consolidated under the Pavie name, the Pigasse section was run as a separate vineyard. It is now called Pavie-Decesse. Meanwhile, Alfred Maquin, owner then of neighbouring La Serre, had bought the Chapus-Pavie vineyard, which together with a number of other parcels gave a sizeable property which has continued its separate existence as Château Pavie-Maquin to this day. Both Decesse and Maquin lie on the top of the slope, rather than on the slope itself.

Bouffard not only consolidated the property, he modernized the *chais*, eliminating all but noble vines, and vigorously defended his domaine against the ravages of phylloxera. According to a contemporary source, his solution was sulphur-carbonate of potassium and, for this and other efforts, the local agricultural society awarded him a gold medal in 1896.

Pavie increased in reputation during Bouffard's reign, fetching 2,800 francs a *tonneau* for the 1890 vintage – admittedly an expensive vintage, for it was one of the first moderately successful vintages after the dismal phylloxera-mildew years of the 1880s. In this year the *premiers crus* of the Médoc made around 4,000, and the Pavie price is superior to all but one or two *deuxièmes*.

Shortly after the First World War, the domaine passed into the hands of Albert Porte and some twenty years later, in 1943, the ownership changed again. The buyer was Alexandre Valette. Meanwhile, Château Pavie-Decesse had been sold to an Monsieur R. Marzelle. In 1970 it too was to be acquired by the Valettes.

Alexandre Valette, like Bouffard, was a *négociant*, though not from Bordeaux but from Saint-Oeun-Sur-Seine, near Paris, and he was also the owner of Château Troplong-Mondot. He ran his domaines from Paris, and rarely visited Saint-Emilion except at vintage-time. Normally the château at Pavie was unoccupied.

On Alexandre Valette's death in 1957, Troplong-Mondot was passed to one branch of the family, and is now run by Christine Valette, and Pavie passed to the other. Alexandre's grandson Jean-Paul is the *Directeur d'Exploitation*, though the owners are a limited company known as the Consorts Valette, owners also of Château La Clusière and Château Pavie-Decesse.

Jean-Paul, having spent his earlier years as a rancher in Chile, has lived at Pavie since 1967 with his wife, a Chilean of French extraction, and five children. The eldest, Patrick, has studied oenology and viticulture in Bordeaux and California. As well as his responsibilities alongside his father at Pavie, Patrick has a property of very old Merlot vines called Château La Prade in the up-and-coming Côtes de Francs.

THE VINEYARD AND THE WINE

The Pavie domaine now occupies some 40 hectares, of which 37 are under vines. This lies all in one piece on the slope of the hill south-east of the town of Saint-Emilion, bordered by the vineyard of Château La Gaffelière on the west and Larcis-Ducasse on the east. Part of the vineyard is on the plateau at the top, a predominantly clayey soil; the bulk is on the 'Côte' – a thin layer of earth covering friable limestone rock; and part is at the bottom of the slope, where the soil is more sandy. This vineyard is planted in the ratio of 55 per cent Merlot, 25 per cent Cabernet Franc (Bouchet) and 20 per cent Cabernet Sauvignon, and produces an average of 150 *tonneaux* a year. As usual in Saint-Emilion the vines are pruned to a single fruit-bearing cane, not to two canes, as in the Médoc, and at Pavie they prune to six buds, not eight as the law allows. The average age of the vines is a venerable 45 years, and there are even a few which were planted in the last decade of the nineteenth century.

The buildings at Pavie are at three levels on the side of the slope. Nearest to the entrance to the domaine, at the lowest level, is the vat house, where the wine is made, and, later, bottled and stored. Half-way up is the château itself, a simple two-storied construction, no more than a large, if comfortable and elegantly furnished farmhouse. At the top is the *chais*.

Like many Saint-Emilion *chais*, the Pavie cellar is a real cave, a natural hole in the limestone hillside quarried out in medieval times to secure building material for the expanding town of Saint-Emilion. The Pavie cave is one of the largest in the area, leading Valette to hazard that it could have been a commercial quarry, and that perhaps the name Pavie derives from *pavé*, a paving stone, and *pavière*, the place where the stones were quarried.

The Pavie *chai* wherein the wine is stored until ready for bottling is said to date from the eleventh century. It is deep and wet, and has on a number of occasions partially collapsed, the last time being in 1974, when 53 hogsheads of wine were lost. At the deepest point one is eight metres under the vineyard of Pavie-Decesse, the roots of whose vines can be seen penetrating through the roof.

In the last few years, in common with many in the Bordeaux area, Jean-Paul Valette and his team have used the services of Professor Emile Peynaud as oenologist and consultant. When the grapes arrive they are sorted through on a *table de triage* (one of the first to be installed in the area). Vinification is in cement *cuves* dating from 1927, the *cuvaison* is long (usually three weeks), and the temperature of fermentation controlled below 30°C. The *vin de presse* is not blended in right at the beginning, as is common elsewhere, but introduced gradually over the eighteen or twenty months the wine is kept in cask, as the barrels are topped up, and when racking takes place.

When I first wrote a profile on Pavie – some fifteen years ago – I described it as light in comparison with some of its neighbours: Canon, for example. Soft, ripe and cedary, was how I described it; ready for drinking five to eight years after the vintage.

This was the sort of wine Pavie produced during the 1960s and 1970s. Since 1981 or so the style has changed. With a severer selection and a deliberately reduced harvest the wine has become not only fuller but richer and more concentrated, more intense in flavour. There has been a considerable improvement. Most of my notes from the 1960s say 'good but not great'; those of the later 1970s are less complimentary. Since 1982 we are indisputably at the very good (or even better) level. The 1982 itself is excellent, even for this very successful vintage in the Libournais. Perhaps more importantly, both 1983 and 1986, where the Libournais was least favoured by the weather, are also fine.

What happens to the wine that is rejected from the *grand vin*? There used to be a second wine, Château Larcis-Bergey, but this has now been discontinued. Valette sells off in bulk the produce of the young vines, plus the rest which has been eliminated. Taking into consideration the extra expenses, personnel, bottling cost, reduced cash-flow, and so on, which a second wine would involve, he does not think he loses much money.

THE TASTING

The following wines were sampled at Château Pavie in April 1990.

Optimum drinking

1989 1997–2015

Good colour, good structure, good oak, plenty of depth and concentration here. This confirms the continuing high level of Pavie. Quite full. Very well balanced, giving the wine lovely ripe fruit, definition and class. Rich, complex and long. Fine. Indeed lovely. Above all a splendid concentrated acidity.

1988 1998–2015

Medium-full colour. As I thought last year this is one of the best of the *premiers crus*. Quite concentrated, plenty of character; balanced and ripe. Fullish, good tannins, oaky and balanced. Fine ripe fruit. A good long, complex finish. Plenty of concentration here. Very good to fine.

1987 **Drink soon**

Light to medium colour but no undue sign of development. Soft, ripe nose. Quite fleshy. No signs of old tea. This is supple and balanced. Very good for a 1987. Good fruit. Reasonable balance and vigour. A touch of bitterness at the end but shows very well.

1986 **Now–2003**

Medium to medium-full colour. Good vigorous nose. A touch of roasted oak. Roast chestnuts perhaps. Good freshness and concentration. This is one of the very best Libournais 1986s because it has a good cedary concentration, and no weakness. Ripe, fullish, good grip. Complex and long on the palate.

1985 **Now–2003**

Fullish, vigorous colour. Ripe, fat, concentrated nose but perhaps not as good in its context as the 1986 is in its. Medium body. Ripe but as well as a certain residual tannin there is a certain astringency. Good fruit but not quite the intensity to carry it through. Definitely not as good as the 1986 promised. Only a quite good finish.

1984 **Drink soon**

Good colour for the vintage. No undue maturity. Light nose but there is fruit here and no undue age. The fruit is a little one-dimensional but at least there *is* fruit. Good for the vintage. Because the acidity is higher this will keep better than the 1987.

1983 **Now–2003**

This has a good, vigorous colour for a 1983 Saint-Emilion. Fullish, not much sign of age. This has good cedary fruit on the nose. No weakness. Plump, mulberry fruit. Like the 1986 this shows very well for a Saint-Emilion. Round but has good grip and ripe tannins. Medium to medium-full. Only just about ready. Good vigour and good length.

1982 **Now–2012**

Full, rich colour. Still youthful. Rich, fat, concentrated meaty nose. Essence of fruit and plenty of style and balance. Fine. Fullish, still some unresolved tannin. Very ripe and concentrated but very good grip as well. Fresh, complex, voluptuous and vigorous. This is not only the best of the 1980s but very fine in its own right as a 1982.

1981 **Now–1995**

Again a good colour for the vintage. Fullish, now mature but no undue age. Round nose, a little more evolved, less grip than the colour might indicate. On this occasion (many Saint-Emilions are the reverse) not as good as 1983. A pleasant, open, not very fresh wine – the grip isn't there but good for drinking now. There is a certain amount of unresolved tannin on the palate. Fullish for a 1981. Good – indeed very good – but not great. Stylish, indeed concentrated, but lacks just that extra bit of grip. Yet by no means short.

1980 **Drink up**

Medium colour. No undue age. Soft and ripe and a little sweet and attenuated on the nose. Not bad for a 1980. Reasonable fruit and grip still. Medium body. But I'd drink it soon.

1979 **Now–1996**

Medium to medium-full colour. Still vigorous. On the nose a little four-square and rigid. Yet fresh. Medium body. There is tannin here but the tannins are a little solid and unripe. Yet quite concentrated fruit and good acidity. Quite good but doesn't really sing, and I don't think it will now really soften up properly.

1978 **Drink soon**

Just a bit more concentrated but now shows a bit of maturity. This is more aromatic, even a trace earthy and H2S-y. Ripe but a little rustic. Medium body. Tastes older than it is, and lacks a bit of real class. Has fruit, has balance, but does not have breed, complexity and concentration. Dull.

1977 **Drink up**

Good colour for the vintage. Still reasonably vigorous, indeed better than the 1976. Smells a bit of old tea but not totally finished. Yes, this was a very good effort. Fresh, fruity and balanced. Not, indeed, without class.

1976 **Now–1996 plus**

Medium-full colour. Fully mature. Very 1976. Open, ripe, smoky nose but essentially a little dilute. As 1976s go this goes far. Round, aromatic, good grip. A fat, voluptuous wine with no undue astringency. Indeed even quite a vigorous, warm, fresh finish. Very good for the vintage.

1975 **Drink soon**

Fullish colour just about mature. Fat, aromatic, meaty, soft but a little of the dry tannins of the vintage. Not exactly vigorous or complex but more flexible and more enjoyable than most. This is balanced but seems to be getting a little tired. It's more astringent than the 1976. Soft but lacks real grip and concentration. No selection.

1973 **Drink up**

Medium-full colour, fully mature. This is approaching the end of its useful life and is lightening up. But there is ripe fruit still. This was a good ripe cedary 1973. It's now beginning to dry out a bit, but it was a good result for the vintage.

1971 **Drink soon**

Medium to medium-full,mature colour. A fragrant if not very fat and generous nose. More generous on the palate. Medium-full, ripe. Quite fit. Good grip. Not exactly a very seductive wine but has depth and interest. Good length. Good but not great.

1970 **Drink soon**

Fullish colour. Still vigorous. Ripe, generous and cedary on the nose. An open, attractive, mature wine. Medium body. Good tannins. Perhaps it is beginning to loosen up a little at the end, but the attack is supple, soft and charming. Good but not great.

1967 **Drink soon**

This has got a very good colour. Even fuller – and less brown at the rim than the 1966. Good vigorous, ripe nose. This has depth. A vigorous wine for a 1967. It lacks a little grip at the end but this is ripe and has surprisingly good concentration and freshness for the vintage. Very good for a 1967. Holding up well.

1966 **Drink soon**

Good fullish, mature colour. A touch vegetal on the nose but has a certain complexity, if without the vigour and ripe fruit of the 1967. Pleasant but lightening up now. Medium body. Lacks real depth, vigour and complexity. No selection.

1964 **Drink soon**

Good, fullish, mature colour, just a little more evolved than the 1966. Fat and rich, ripe and concentrated, but quite evolved now. An earthier, meatier, more tannic wine than the 1966 and with rather more vigour. Like most Libournais, a fine example, especially as this has elegance as well as grip. Very good. Will keep well.

1962 **Drink up**

Medium-full, fully mature colour. Slightly fluid on the nose. A ripe, amicable wine with a smile on its face, but lacks concentration. Did it ever have it? This is lightening up now. A little astringent. Pleasant but lacks grip. Not bad.

1961 **Drink soon**

Good, full, mature colour. Rich and nutty on the nose. An element of cooked almond pastry but not exactly the concentration of most 1961s. Good nevertheless. A meaty, medium-bodied wine but lacks zip. The 1964 is much more interesting. This lacks a bit of concentration and oomph.

1961 **Now–1996**

(Magnum, sampled later over dinner) This is a fresher example than the wine we sampled in bottle earlier today, but all the same a wine without the concentration and sumptuous fruit of a really fine 1961. Good, fat and stylish. But by no means great.

L'ANGÉLUS

Top, at least alphabetically, of the long list of Saint-Emilion's *grands crus classés* is Château L'Angélus. While the property is old, the name is young, having being dreamed up in the early 1920s because apparently this vineyard was the only place in the area where one could hear the angélus – rung early in the morning, at noon and at sunset – from all three of Saint-Emilion's churches: the chapel at Mazerat, the old church of Saint Martin, further up the slope near Château Canon, and the Collegiate church in Saint-Emilion itself.

Being top of the alphabet in any list is a bonus. This is what strikes the eye first. Despite the wine never having been matured in wood it always found a ready market. Following various trials, instigated at the suggestion of Pascal Ribereau-Gayon, one of Bordeaux's most celebrated oenological consultants, the wine was finally given some barrel-ageing in 1981. Since then there has been a major investment in the *chais* and an increasing element of selection in the creation of the *grand vin*.

Angélus lies in the hamlet of Mazerat, west of Saint-Emilion, at the foot of the slope below Château Beauséjour-Duffau-Lagarrosse. Some 150 years ago most of the vineyards in this area were owned by two families: the Gurchys, who had been there since 1610, and were also *négociants*, and the Souffrains, who had originated in Limoges. According to one of the later editions of Franck's *Traité*, one of the Souffrains wrote an '*Essai sur Libourne*'. In it he recounts the story of a visit to the region by Louis XVI. The king, 'who was not a flatterer', pronounced the wine of Saint-Emilion 'nectar'. Meanwhile, elsewhere in Saint-Emilion, and with ancestors there even earlier than the Gurchys, was the Bouard de Laforest family.

HISTORY

The Bouards, originally from the Berry, had arrived in the Périgord during the Hundred Years War and later moved down to Bordeaux. Some time later, as a result of plague in Bordeaux itself, the regional parliament moved temporarily to Saint-Emilion. The Bouards were among this number, bought land in the area, and decided to stay. In 1564 a Georges de Bouard was a member of the Jurat of Saint-Emilion.

The modern era begins with Comte Maurice de Bouard de Laforest. Maurice was born in 1870. He is said to have been a man of a restless, fiery temperament and seems to have been something of a merchant adventurer. At the age of sixteen he emigrated to America. He later worked in Argentina and Africa, and at one time he served in the dragoons. When he was in his sixties he attempted to stop a bolting horse and had his right hand crushed by a wheel of a cart. Undaunted, he taught himself to write with his left hand. He died in 1959 at the age of 89.

Some 50 years earlier he had inherited thirteen hectares of the Domaine de Mazerat from his aunt, the widow of the Chevalier Charles Souffrain de Lavergne. In 1924 he acquired three adjoining hectares, known at the time as Clos de L'Angélus, from the Gurchy family. After the Second World War his three sons, Alain, Jacques and Christian, decided to amalgamate the two vineyards under the name Château L'Angélus. With the addition of three hectares acquired from Beau-Séjour-Bécot when it changed hands in 1969 and other local acquisitions, the area under vines now totals 25 hectares in a single parcel. The Angélus vineyard lies mainly on the *pied de côte*. The soil is a limestone-clay mixture at the top of the slope, with more sand as one descends. It is planted in the ratio 50 per cent Merlot, 45 per cent Cabernet Franc and 5 per cent Cabernet Sauvignon.

PROGRESS IN WINE-MAKING

Up to 1979, as I have already described, the wine was matured in concrete vats. The results, in the main, were rustic and four-square, but underneath one could discern a richness in the fruit. It was this which led Ribereau-Gayon to propose experimenting with maturing the wine in new wood.

This was the first step. The next was a reconstruction of the cellar to accommodate the barrels. In 1983 the wine was matured half in tank and half in wood, and 50 per cent of the wood used was new. From 1985 it was all matured in wood, and today the percentage of new oak can be as high as 80 per cent. It depends on the vintage.

The first batch of eight 125-hectolitre stainless-steel vats was installed in 1982. A further eight were added in 1989, at which time a temperature-controlled barrel cellar was constructed, doubling the storage capacity. Work is still going on. In 1991, at the time of my last visit, a new reception area and tasting room was being added. After almost a decade L'Angélus has been transformed. I am sure they will be glad to see the last of the builders.

But new equipment and new wood do not of themselves improve the wine. As important have been developments in the vineyard and in the attitude to the wine-making. Since 1985 L'Angélus has practised a green harvest, eliminating some of the fruit in July in order to concentrate on the rest. In 1987 a second wine, Carillon de L'Angélus, was introduced. The following year a *tapis de triage*, a conveyor belt on to which the incoming harvest is emptied to be picked over, was installed. Under consulting oenologist, Michel Rolland, the vinification is now controlled at 30 to 33 degrees, and the *cuvaison* has been extended to as much as 21 days.

THE CHÂTEAU

Arrive at Angélus and you will see the name Château Mazerat still prominently displayed. There is no Château L'Angélus as such. Adjoining the new winery complex is a nineteenth-century *maison bourgeoise* with extensions. Hubert de Bouard de Laforest moved in following his grandmother's death in 1987. Nearby, in a house which was acquired in 1969 with the land from Beau-Séjour, lives his cousin, Jean-Bernard Grenie. The two run L'Angélus in common. Hubert began to take over responsibility in 1979 after he had finished his oenological studies. His stockier, older cousin joined him some years later. It is since their arrival that L'Angélus has begun to climb up the ladder of quality. The most recent wines have shown the potential of the vineyard and quality is continuing to rise. L'Angelus is not yet at the Larmande or Troplong-Mondot level. But one can see that it soon might be. The future looks bright.

THE TASTING

The following wines were sampled at the château in 1991.

	Optimum drinking
1989	**1995–2009**

Medium-full colour. Fat, rich, ripe nose. Very blackberry-ish. Quite alcoholic. Fullish, tannic, quite meaty. Oaky, quite powerful. Rich, good grip. It is difficult to see the style but there is good intensity. Finishes well and improved in the glass.

1988   **Now–2002**

Medium-full colour. Neat, gently oaky, stylish nose. Good fruit. Medium body. Fresh, ripe and balanced, with a good base of oak and good grip. Not that greatest of style but an attractive bottle which finishes well. Quite good.

1987   **Drink soon**

Not a bad colour for a 1987. This is a little thin and one-dimensional on the nose, but is not too weedy. Light to medium body. This has good fruit, reasonable balance and is stylish and with a positive finish for the vintage. A good effort.

1986   **Now–1996**

Medium to medium-full colour. Not a great deal of intensity on the nose. Quite forward. Not much depth. Slightly farmyardy. Medium body. As much astringent as tannic. But a stylish wine with reasonable freshness and fruit. Not bad.

1985   **Now–2004**

Medium to medium-full colour. Good nose. There is depth and concentration here. Not as much oak as the 1988 but more to it. Quite stylish. This is a good example, better than the 1988. Medium-full. Good integrated tannins. Fat and ripe. Finishes well. Good grip.

1984   **Drink up**

Reasonable colour for the vintage. Not unduly brown. The nose is now fully evolved and getting blowsy rapidly. This needs drinking now. Quite fruity but now elements of old tea beginning to show. Slightly suave: the wine shows evidence of chaptalization.

1983   **Drink soon**

Medium colour. The 1985 is much more vigorous. Evolved, slightly spicy-Merlot nose, similar to the 1986. A pleasant medium-bodied wine without great dimension or class, but not an unattractive bottle. Medium body. Ready now.

1982   **Now–1997**

Not an enormous colour for a 1982. A rich but blowsy nose, a little rustic. Fat, ripe and spicy. Medium to medium-full body. Good acidity. But lacks concentration, grip and class. There are many better Libournais 1982s than this. Yet it finishes reasonably well. Ready. Won't make old bones.

1981   **Drink soon**

Medium colour but still fresh. Indeed it has less brown than the 1982. It's beginning to lose its fruit and its elegance, but this was originally a fat wine with reasonable depth. Good matière here, even concentration. And good grip for a 1981. But a bit artisanal. Shows the potential of the property though.

1978   **Drink soon**

Medium colour. Still quite fresh. There is a lack of style here but reasonable structure and balance. Not as good as the 1981. Blowsy, quite attenuated. Medium body. Finishes astringent. Unexciting. Needs drinking.

1970   **Drink soon**

Medium-full colour. Again quite a structured, rich wine. No great elegance, but has some depth. A richer, better balanced wine than the 1978, but it lacks style. Again, underneath, one can see good fruit. A bit astringent on the finish.

1967   **Drink soon**

Medium colour, fully mature. A little overblown but not too much on the nose. There is structure, fat and concentration on the palate. Vigorous, even muscular for a 1967. Rather too spicy and unstylish on the follow-through but a good example for the vintage.

1966 **Drink soon**

Good colour. Rich nose but a little rustic. A more elegant wine than either the 1967 or the 1970. Medium to medium-full body. This is still reasonably vigorous, and is not too spicy. Good grip. Shows well.

1964 **Drink soon**

Good colour. Full, fat and rich, but an element of reduction on the nose. Quite concentrated, almost to the point of being inky. Full, rich and concentrated, very ripe indeed. A meaty example. Rather inelegant but not bad at all. Spicy finish. Will still keep for a couple years.

1962 **Drink up**

Good colour but on the nose seems to be losing its grip. Medium body. There is a little astringency on the palate. Still sweet, still reasonable acidity, but at the end of its useful life. Wasn't bad at all once.

1961 **Now–1996**

Good colour. This is still rich on the nose, even concentrated, though not with a great deal of style. Good acidity though. Once again the enormous concentration and richness of 1961 comes singing through, even in a wine which is quite rustic, basically. This gives it interest. Medium-full. Good. Still has life.

1959 **Drink up**

Good colour. Fat, rich and spicy on the nose. Rather more blowsy than the 1961. Not bad though. Getting rather astringent on the palate. Sweet. Medium-full. Getting to the end, if not over the top.

1958 **Past its best**

Surprisingly good colour. And on the nose still fresh, if a touch dense and inky. Past its best but not at all a bad wine originally. Rustic, of course, but not without richness of fruit.

1955 **Drink soon**

Good colour. Spice and sandalwood on the nose. A little old but not without charm. Fading gently. This is really still very attractive on the palate. Fuller than I had expected. Sweet and concentrated. Ripe and balanced. Even vigorous. Artisanal but good. Better than the 1959.

1953 **Drink soon**

Very good colour. Rich, fat and concentrated on the nose, if showing a little age now. This is even better than the above because it is less artisanal. Ripe, sweet, rich and was quite a concentrated wine once. Muscular but not too rustic. Still quite vigorous. Fat and with good grip.

L'ARROSÉE

One of the most sought-after – and consequently expensive – properties in Saint-Emilion is Château L'Arrosée. It is an ample, plump, richly concentrated, new-oaky wine, and it is this latter factor, the new oak, which has caught the interest and produced the accolades of many a wine pundit. L'Arrosée is deservedly today one of the most popular of the *crus classés* and an eager contender for elevation to *premier grand cru*.

Perhaps you might be misled into imagining that the quality of L'Arrosée is a recent phenomenon; that it is only since it has been widely extolled in the press that it has made such good wine. The property, however, enjoyed considerable fame at least a century ago. Why is it not a first-classed growth? The answer lies in the fact that for 30 years earlier this century the wine was made by the local cooperative, like its near neighbour Château Berliquet; and that the co-operative was then – how can I politely put it? – more interested in the mechanics of making wine of commercial acceptability than in the art of creating top-notch quality. The irony is that it was an earlier proprietor of L'Arrosée who helped establish the cooperative in the first place; indeed donated some of his land – then vineyards – on which the cooperative could establish its winery. In 1956, though, the present proprietor, François Rodhain, wrested control away. He has since made the wine we know today. And it has been excellent since at least 1961, the earliest vintage I have sampled.

LOCALITY

The origin of the name L'Arrosée, as you might expect, lies in water, in three underground springs in the locality which flow through the limestone rock under the vineyard. Apparently these never dry up even in the most arid and torrid of summers. The vineyard lies below Magdelaine and adjacent to Fonplégade and La Gaffelière on the Saint-Emilion *Côtes*, and its ten hectares cover a variety of soils on the slope, whose nature, incline, drainage and precise geological composition can differ widely within the space of a couple of rows of vines. These vines enjoy an advantageous exposure to the south, protected from north and west, and so the fruit can soak up the calories of the sun from morning until late evening. This is particularly necessary in case of L'Arrosée *encépagement* which, contrary to the norm in the cooler limestone soils of Saint-Emilion, includes 35 per cent Cabernet Sauvignon as well as 45 per cent Merlot and 20 per cent Cabernet Franc. Nevertheless, Rodhain has to pick late in order to ensure that his slow-to-evolve Cabernet Sauvignon is fully mature. In 1980 he was still collecting on Halloween.

HISTORY

L'Arrosée was one of a number of properties belonging to the family of Pierre Magne, three times Napoleon III's Finance Minister. Magne was born in Périgueux but was senator for the Dordogne, where he lived in the château that had once belonged to Montaigne. The emperor is supposed to have stayed there during the winter of 1867/1868. One of his estates, Franc-Magne (now Franc-Mayne), was listed third in the area after Belair and what is now Troplong-Mondot in the Cocks and Féret in 1850. Château L'Arrosée first appears in the second (1868) edition. It made 8 to 10 *tonneaux* and is listed in twentieth position.

After Pierre Magne's death in 1879 the property passed to his daughter the Marquise de Reverseaux de Rouvray. Her husband Jacques-Marie was a diplomat, successively ambassador in Sofia, Cairo, Madrid and Vienna. During this period, for obviously the Reverseaux were very much absentee landlords, the vines were tended by the Dupuch family, proprietors next door and elsewhere in the area. A few years after the Marquis's death in 1907, his widow sold the vineyard to Mme Dupuch.

It was Mme Dupuch's son, Georges, who helped set up the local cooperative in the inter-war years. He donated some of his land in the flatter, more sandy soil at the bottom of the slope and entrusted the vinification of Château L'Arrosée to the co-op management. It was from this period that the reputation of the wine declined. When he died in 1938 the property passed to his son-in-law, Pierre Rodhain. Rodhain was then employed by the French inspectorate of mines and lived in Versailles. It was not until 1956, four years after Pierre Rodhain had been succeeded by his son François, that the contract with the co-op was terminated and the quality of L'Arrosée began to improve.

THE WINE

The *chais* of Château L'Arrosée lie underneath the steeply inclining vineyard – horses were the only means of dragging a plough through the vineyard until a few years ago – and are attached to a simple farmhouse which I suppose is technically the château. In fact this is the original Dupuch *maison bourgeoise*. Farmworkers live there. Rodhain has a more substantial and elegant home a few hundred metres away near the main Bergerac road.

The cellar is small; the atmosphere artisanal. The wine is fermented in concrete vats of various sizes, matured in 100 per cent new oak, and bottled after 18 to 24 months. There is not normally a second wine. In 1987 part of the crop was bottled as Coteaux de L'Arrosée.

The clue to L'Arrosée's success lies not just in the new oak but in the combination between this facet and the voluptuous, concentrated, nutty, almost exotic, richness which

Rodhain manages to achieve. He only gently crushes the grapes, hardly doing more than break the skins, so they enter the fermentation vat whole. This avoids a too-compact *chapeau*, says Rodhain, and results in a better extraction. Surprisingly, the average age of the vines is not high. But the *rendement* is low. And Rodhain's determination to harvest late, achieving the maximum amount of concentration from his fruit, has happily paid off a great deal more times than not.

THE TASTING

I sampled the following wines at L'Arrosée in January 1991.

1989 — *Optimum drinking* **1996–2006**

Medium colour. Ripe, stylish and gently oaky on the nose but perhaps not quite as concentrated or as powerful as I expected – especially when M. Rodhain told me he thought this was even better than 1982. Medium body. Ripe and ample. Good tannins. Quite oaky. Plenty of depth. Finely balanced and very stylish. Fine but not great.

1988 **1995–2005**

Medium colour. This shows extremely well. Good ripe, oaky nose. Medium body. Good structure. Ripe, stylish, balanced fruit. I like this because it has harmony, charm and balance. Very good.

1987 **Drink soon**

Light to medium colour. A soft but inherently – eventually – weedy nose. Yet on the palate not too bad. Ripe. Medium body. Now fully ready. Pleasantly fruity and not too short. But a bit one-dimensional and needs drinking soon.

1986 **Now–2000**

Medium colour. Pleasant nose but shows a little of the dilution of the vintage. The attack is also a bit dilute but the follow-through is better. Medium body, a little tannin but it seems a touch astringent as well. Ripe but no better than good to very good.

1985 **1995–2005**

Medium-full colour. Excellent concentrated, new oaky nose. Nutty and roasted. This is very fine and has a great deal of depth. Fullish, ripe, oaky, rich and complex. Finely balanced. This is very classy and has a lot of dimension. Very long. Lovely.

1984 **Drink up**

Reasonable colour. But a little bit of old tea on the nose. This is a good effort for the vintage. Ripe and fruity but is now beginning to get a bit attenuated. Reasonable freshness of acidity still.

1983 **Now–1996**

Medium colour. The nose of this wine shows a little evolution now. Medium body. The attack is ripe and oaky but I find a lack of grip and concentration on the finish. Good fruit and balance but neither very complex nor giving one much confidence in a long future. Good but not great.

1982 **Now–2005**

Good colour. Full, rich, sturdy on the nose – even a touch earthy. Full, concentrated, almost over-ripe fruit. Fat, some tannic still. Blackberries and black cherries. Good, almost exotic, voluptuous touches. Fine but quite how much finesse has it got? Good length.

1981 **Now–1996**

Good colour, vigorous for its age. This is good but not as good as the 1983. Fully evolved but leaving a little astringency on the palate. Ripe, reasonable balance but lacks a little class. Good but not great again. But finishes well.

1980 **Drink soon**

Good colour for the vintage and shows good fresh fruit and personality on the nose. This is a lot better than both 1984 and 1987 put together. Ripe. Medium body. Fresh. No undue sign of age. Shows well.

1961

(Tasted October 1990) Excellent colour. Full, rich, no sign of age. Rich, full but not dense: a touch porty. Very ample and concentrated on the nose. A structured wine on the palate. Very rich. Very concentrated. Very fat. A touch, but just a touch, dense; but fine, balanced, youthful and vigorous. Long and meaty. Fine, even by the standards of the vintage.

LARMANDE

Château Larmande is freely acknowledged, even by most of its rivals in the Saint-Emilion area, to be the best of the *grands crus classés*, and, moreover, to have been producing excellent wine for a generation or more. Until recently the property belonged to the Meneret-Capdemourlin family, many branches of which are wine growers in the commune.

Wine has been made at Larmande since 1640, as a date on the door of the *chai* will maintain. A 100 years ago the property, rather smaller than it is today, belonged to the Saint-Denis family. At the turn of the century the grandfather of M. Jean-Fernand Meneret, proprietor until December 1990, was *régisseur* here, and, together with his brother-in-law, a Capdemourlin, acquired the estate. At the time it was producing twelve *tonneaux*, while nearby, the Despagnes produced fifteen under the same name. The Saint-Denis section contained seven hectares of vines.

THE HISTORY

Since the turn of the century the Menerets have enlarged the property so that it now consists of some nineteen hectares of vineyard. They bought out their cousins the Capdemourlins and devoted everything to improving the wine. In 1955 Emile Peynaud was made consultant to Larmande, and his advice is supplemented by that of M. Guimberteau, a director of the Oenological Research Institute of the University of Bordeaux.

Jean Meneret took over personally in 1977. He is a cheerful, engaging tubby man in his late fifties, and was subsequently assisted by one of his sons Philippe (the other son, Dominique, is a partner in the *négociant* firm of Bernard et Meneret, lately Sobivi). In 1974 nine stainless-steel fermentation vats were installed. Since 1980 the proportion of new wood has been increased. Today, as a result of trials with the 1978 vintage, the percentage is normally a third, though the 1985 was matured in 50 per cent new oak.

Late in 1990, Jean Meneret sold Larmande to the insurance company La Mondiale, which has appointed M. Durup, formerly with Calvet, to look after their viticultural interests, but Philippe Meneret remains at Larmande as wine-maker.

THE VINEYARD AND THE WINE

The vineyard lies above the town of Saint-Emilion near those of Capdemourlin and Soutard, on an incline which slopes gently down to the north. The soil descends from clay-limestone, through a sand-limestone mixture to *sables anciens* over *alios* on the lowest parts. The average age of the vines is high – over 35 years – and the Menerets will proudly point out to you some Bouchets (Cabernet Franc) which are over 100 years old. The *encépagement* is 65 per cent Merlot, 30 per cent Bouchet and 5 per cent Cabernet Sauvignon, and average production runs at some 70 *tonneaux*.

The château, sadly, is unspectacular, merely an adjunct to the *chais*. Part has been converted into an office; the rest is inhabited by one of the vineyard workers. The Menerets live in Saint-Emilion, Jean with his wife Françoise in a house on one of the main, steeply inclined cobbled streets in a house with extensive cellars dating from the thirteenth century. Here until the recent sale, those bottles of Château Larmande not sold *en primeur* were stored in ideal conditions.

Recent vintages of Château Larmande are excellent, as the following notes will demonstrate. But the property has been producing fine wine for many years. Larmande is one of my premier candidates for elevation to *premier cru*.

THE TASTING

The vintages from 1989 back to 1981 were sampled at Larmande in April 1991. The notes on the older vintages date from a previous vertical tasting I made in September 1986.

1989 — *Optimum drinking* **1995–2005**

Medium-full colour. Good fat, ripe, succulent, gently oaky nose. Full, rich, lush. Good touch of oak. Good grip. There is plenty of depth here. Medium-full body. Good tannins. Long and meaty on the finish. A well-made, classy wine. Very good.

1988 **1995–2005**

Medium-full colour. Quite a firm nose, a touch austere. Quite full but seems to lack a little richness. The tannins are less ripe, but the balance is good and there is no lack of fruit. Medium-full. It will never be as lush or as seductive as the 1989, but this is a very good example which will keep well.

1987 **Drink soon**

Medium colour. Soft nose. A little rustic, lacks zip. A shade dry and astringent. Quite pleasant and fruity, if, inevitably, a little short. Lightish. Drink soon before it gets astringent. Not bad.

1986 **Now–1996**

Medium colour. Smoky, aromatic nose, but lacks a bit of class and definition. Soft now. On the palate I get a bit of astringency. Medium body. The follow-through is richer and more satisfying but there is a lack of concentration and richness. I prefer the 1983.

1985   **Now–2003**

Medium-full colour. Plump, raspberry, mulberry nose. Soft and round. Medium-full body. Still a bit of tannin. Ripe, spicy. Quite rich and concentrated. Good balance. This is long and ample. Very good.

1984   **Drink up**

Light colour. This is beginning to get a bit attenuated on the nose. Light in body, weedy. The fruit has lightened up and the wine is astringent.

1983   **Now–1998**

Medium to medium-full colour. Slightly earthy on the nose. But good freshness and fruit for the vintage. Medium to medium-full body. Good fruit. Above all, fresh and vigorous. This has kept the wine more positive than the 1986, for instance. Ripe, aromatic. A good example.

1982   **Now–2005**

Medium-full colour. Classic nose. Full, fleshy, rich, abundant. Satisfying. A typically ample, second-rank 1982 Libournais. Fullish, still a bit of tannin. Still vigorous. Very good, ample concentrated fruit. Rich and spicy and long on the palate. Very good, even in 1982 terms.

1981   **Now–1996**

Medium colour. Less colour than the 1983 and less vigour and richness on the nose. This is a neat, quite fresh example on the palate but it has less structure and depth than the 1983, and it is neither as rich nor as vigorous. Good though.

1980   **Drink soon**

Good colour. Quite substantial – quite rich and complex, ripe and oaky – especially for the vintage. Very good. Not at all without depth and character. An excellent result.

1979   **Now–1998**

This was not matured using new oak, but one-year-old barrels from Château Cheval-Blanc. Very good colour; little sign of brown in 1986. Good elegant nose of prunes and blackberries. Quite fat, not noticeably less oak than the 1978. A good wine, marginally better than the 1981. Good fruit, medium body, still a bit of tannin. Quite concentrated. Long finish. Very good for the vintage.

1978   **Now–2000**

This was a sample from an experiment with 50 per cent new wood. I can see why they decided that a third was optimum in most vintages. Very good colour. A bit, fat, ripe wine, certainly markedly oaky on the surface but a little dominating on the finish. Still needs time. One third new oak would have been splendid. NB: This sample would not be representative of 1978 Château Larmande on the market. Those, I assume would be bigger, denser versions of the 1979, perhaps not quite so elegant.

1977   **Drink up**

Reasonable good colour but a bit attenuated on the nose compared with the 1980, lacking the structure the new oak would have given. Not lean though, just a bit empty. Reasonably fresh and fruity but the suggestion of old tea on the finish will increasingly take over.

1976   **Drink soon**

Very good colour, only just about mature in 1986. Good nose, still ripe and powerful. Fullish, good grip. Fruit flavours slightly cooked, and certainly some oak in evidence. Finishes long. No hurry to drink. Good for the vintage.

1975   **Now–1997**

Similar colour, a little less brown. Nose took some time to evolve. Full, still slightly tannic. Concentrated, ripe, chewy but rich. Good caramelly, prune finish. Another example of how much more satisfactory the 1975s are here compared with the Médoc.

1971   **Drink soon**

Very fine, full colour, more than the 1975. Mature. This is a really splendid wine! A lot of concentration and a really creamy, old-vine flavour. Fresher than the 1975 if less chunky. Full, vigorous, mature, a great deal of depth. Very good.

1970   **Drink soon**

An abundant vintage – 82 hectolitres per hectare Very fine colour, little brown. Fullish nose, no oak. Fat, fresh mulberry-plummy fruit. Plenty of depth. Not as complex as the 1971 or as great as the recent vintages. If only it had had new oak! Good nevertheless.

1966   **Drink soon**

Good colour, fully mature. Less powerful on the nose but complex and elegant. An evolved, strawberry-flavoured wine, now beginning to show a little age. Fine wine nevertheless.

1955   **Drink soon**

Splendid colour. This was made by 'old-fashioned' methods. Full, dense, meaty, rich, earthy – leather, liquorice and *sous-bois* – much more vigorous than the 1966. Not the slightest bit of age in September, 1986. Excellent. Jean Meneret thinks that this is better than his 1959.

SOUTARD

Soutard is one of the largest and most individual of the Saint-Emilion *grands crus classés*, and is located north of the town at the point where the *plateau calcaire* begins to descend and the geology changes to incorporate elements of clay and weathered sand. Despite its size it is perhaps not as well-known as its quality deserves. A couple of decades ago it was marketed through a contract with Gilbeys of Loudenne and British consumers could find the wine easily enough on the shelves of Peter Dominic. Today it is sold direct, not through the Bordeaux *négoce*, and is rarely seen on the export market. It is a structured wine, vigorous and long-lasting; rich, ample and satisfying when mature but somewhat sturdy in its youth. Alongside its peers this is very definitely a *vin de garde*. It is certainly a contender for elevation to *premier grand cru* status.

The title, it is said, is a corruption of the English 'Southard', coincidentally a name long associated with wine in London. There was an important port shipping firm called Southards in the London Bridge area at the end of the nineteenth century which was managed by the Andrew James Symington who was later to acquire Silva and Cozens, proprietors of Dow and Warre. In Saint-Emilion one can postulate a medieval *seigneur* who decided to remain after the collapse of English authority over the Gironde in 1453.

HISTORY

The history of present-day Soutard is a somewhat complicated matter of dowries, adoptions and marriages between cousins, but essentially concerns two families; the first of whom, the Combrets, selling to the second, the Laveaus, in July 1811. This has been the only major change of ownership in the past 250 years.

The vineyard was created by Jean Combret de Faurie in about 1762. Faced with land too meagre for the successful production of any other crops, Combert dug trenches in the limestone rock, a practice which had been pursued in the area since Gallo-Roman times, filled them with earth, and planted some vines. This soon raised the value of the land, and with the proceeds he constructed the central portion of the present day château in the mid-1770s. Combret de Faurie died without issue in 1804, leaving his estate to a nephew, Jacques Combret de Milon. This gentleman sold the estate to Jean Laveau seven years later. The price was 65,000 francs, a very low price. One can speculate that Combret had fallen into financial difficulties owing to the blockade that followed the collapse of the Peace of Amiens in 1806.

Jean Laveau came from a family of local jurists and prominent landowners which had been established in the Libourne are since the fifteenth century. He owned an estate in Pomerol, had land at what is now Trottevieille and Villemaurine, and also was proprietor of Château Franc-Mayne, a neighbour of Beauséjour, and at the time one of Saint-Emilion's leading domaines. Both this and Soutard were properties of considerable size, much larger than they are today. Judging by contemporary records, his Saint-Emilion estates must have commanded a good 100 hectares between them.

Laveau died without direct male heirs in 1836 – he must have been almost 100 years old – and his fortune was then split up. Soutard passed to a great-granddaughter, the widow of M. Barry-Berthomieux d'Allard, owner at the time of Beauregard in Pomerol and Gazin at Saint-Michel-de-Fronsac, and from Mme Barry to her adopted nephew Adolphe. Fifteen years later the Soutard estate was divided, giving birth to what is now Château Faurie-de-Souchard (*sic*). The first owner of this domaine is given as Lavau (*sic*). This can hardly be a coincidence.

Soutard was now a property of 22 hectares of vines, the size it remains today, and producing, in these pre-phylloxera years, about 35 *tonneaux* a year. The *encépagement* was Bouchet (Cabernet Franc), Merlot, Cabernet Sauvignon and Malbec in roughly equal proportion. It remained in the hands of Adolphe d'Allard, mayor of Saint-Emilion under Napoleon III, until the turn of the century. During this time the château was enlarged – or despoiled; it depends on your point of view – by the addition of two towers with mansard roofs, and the courtyard in front enclosed by new *chais* and stables and an imposing wrought-iron gateway. By 1914 production had risen to 60 *tonneaux*.

On Adolphe d'Allard's death in the early years of this century the property passed to Henri du Foussat de Bogeron, husband of Allard's youngest daughter Marie, and it was later to pass once more through the female line to Michel de Ligneris, who had married his distant cousin Jeanne du Foussat. Comte Jacques de Ligneris, their son, today in his early seventies, is the current proprietor. The wine is made by his son François.

THE VINEYARD

One of the largest of the *grands crus classés*, Château Soutard comprises a total of 27 hectares, the 22 hectares under vine now being planted with 60 per cent Merlot and 40 per cent Cabernet Franc. Most of the vineyard lies on the limestone plateau which surrounds the town of Saint-Emilion, and here there is barely 40 centimetres of soil before you reach the rock base. Further north, as the plateau descends the land contains more clay, even, at the foot of the slope, some loam.

Château Soutard is firmly ecological. No pesticides, no chemical fertilizers, no use of anti-rot treatments. It is also traditional. It is one of the latest to commence picking: not until 3 October 1988, for instance, and while others increasingly resort to machines, harvesting is undertaken manually, with the same team year after year.

WINE-MAKING

François de Ligneris is a serious young man and dedicated wine-maker. His first ambition was to study architecture, and he completed part of his studies before transferring to wine. He travelled a lot, working with the Hill-Smith family in Australia in 1981, and it was on his return from there that he began to take over from his father. Since then, everything has been carefully documented: what he did; when he did it; what his conclusions were.

From his records we can see, for instance, that in 1982 he vinified with 47 per cent of the stalks – itself unusual for Bordeaux – and the *cuvaison* lasted 23 days. The 1988, on the other hand, was entirely de-stemmed, but macerated for 32 days. The fruit is isolated into lots of different age, origin and grape varieties, and fermented separately in vats of cement and stainless steel of different sizes. The temperature is allowed to rise to a maximum of 33 degrees.

Ligneris is against excessive use of new oak; the percentage is usually a fifth or a quarter, but zero in lesser vintages such as 1984 (when there was no *grand vin*, merely the second wine of Clos de La Tonnelle) and 1987. Equally, he is against filtration and any other unnecessary manipulation of the wine. Bottling is by gravity.

Where Château Soutard differs most from other Bordeaux properties is in its refusal to assemble the different lots into the *grand vin* until some eighteen months after the vintage, just prior to the *mise en bouteille*. This makes a firm early judgement on the wine in cask somewhat difficult! But it enables Ligneris to make a more accurate assessment of the quality of his different *cuvées*.

There is something refreshingly artisanal and engagingly idealistic about the atmosphere at Soutard. The large kitchen garden and free-range Bresse and Leghorn chickens are not unique. Nor is the somewhat rambling and decayed nature of the château and its decoration. But you are somewhat surprised when you are informed that Soutard produces its own specific tools for all the vineyard and cellar tasks, in a little workshop across the courtyard. You half expect them to be still using horses rather than tractors.

THE WINE

The wine is solid, dense and uncompromising. It is full, firm and austere in its youth, much more so than the vast majority of its neighbours, and ungenerous, adolescent and somewhat deceptively unstylish for several years thereafter. But it is undeniably rich and concentrated when mature. It just needs time. But it does keep well. The 1970 is still surprisingly youthful, the 1966 shows no undue age, and the 1964, though a touch old-fashioned, is also still vigorous. Soutard needs patience but it is usually worth waiting for.

THE TASTING

I sampled the following wines with François de Ligneris and several of his friends in January 1990. The notes on the 1989 and 1988 come from my subsequent April visit.

1989   *Optimum drinking* **1997–2012**

Not yet assembled. The Cabernet Franc I liked very much: quite structured with ripe tannins, ripe, concentrated fruit and a good acidity. The Merlot was softer but very rich and succulent. Again good grip. I sampled several other cuvées, some less good which will probably not go into the grand vin. But I think what will go into Soutard will be rather good this year. The vintage will suit this style of wine.

1988   **1997–2010**

Good colour. Full, rich and oaky, this is still a little tough and inflexible, has developed less in the last twelve months than most. A certain, almost bitter austerity. But has a good future. Plenty of ripeness and concentration and good balance.

1987   **Drink soon**

Not at all a disappointing colour. Fullish, still youthful. A little green on the nose but not weak. Medium body. Still a little raw. Lacks not so much substance as a bit of charm. This may come as it evolves. More acidity than most 1987s so should keep fresh. Not bad for the vintage.

1986   **Now–1999**

Medium to medium-full colour. Just a little hard on the nose. Lacks a bit of generosity. Better on the palate than on the nose. Medium to medium-full. A little tannin. Good fruit and quite ripe and plummy on the finish. Good grip. Will warm up as it rounds off. Good for a Saint-Emilion.

1985   **Now–2004**

Fullish colour. Full, rich nose, with a roasted nut, toasted oak character. Fatter, fleshier and more generous than the 1986. Medium-full body. Good, ripe, spicy tannins. This is currently more adolescent than the 1986 but has more depth, more richness and more complexity. A more exciting vintage. Again good, but at present lacks a bit of style.

1984

Did not declare.

1983   **Now–1997**

Medium to medium-full colour. Just a little development. The 1981 seems rather fuller. Some maturity now on the nose, but does not seem to have a great deal of substance and depth. Medium body. No tannin. A soft, fresh, balanced wine with a lot of charm. Not a blockbuster but elegant, gentle and harmonious with good plummy fruit and a long finish. Good.

1982   **Now–2002**

Medium-full colour. Rich and full bit somewhat closed and backward on the nose. This by contrast is a bit adolescent and lumpy. Fuller and richer but a touch solid and the elements are not yet in harmony. Fat and ample on the finish. Will be good.

1981   **Now–1998**

Full colour for the vintage. Now mature. Quite a backward, vigorous nose for a 1981. Quite full on the palate. Good, rich, chocolatey/spicy wine. Just about ready. This has plenty of personality and more depth than the 1983. Very good. Will keep well.

1980   **Drink up**

Lightish, mature colour. The nose is a bit attenuated now and the palate a bit weak. Getting weedy on the finish.

1979   **Now–1996**

Medium to medium-full colour. Just about mature. There isn't a great deal here, either on the nose or the palate. A medium bodied, mature wine with reasonable balance but a lack of depth and personality. Yet the finish is positive. Not bad, but I much prefer the 1981.

1978   **Now–2000**

Medium-full colour. Mature: rather more so than the 1979. Interesting, mature nose, this is now beginning to get complex and aromatic. Medium-full. Good grip. Tannins now absorbed. Yet it will still improve, getting more complex, gaining more dimension as it ages and softens. Good to very good.

1977   **Drink up**

Not at all a bad colour: medium, mature, but no undue age. Light nose. Not at all a bad effort. I prefer this to the 1980 because it is less blowsy. Yet essentially light, one-dimensional and a little spuriously sweet. Good effort for the vintage though.

1976   **Drink soon**

No more colour than the 1977, brown at the rim. Somewhat dry and spicy on the nose. Less astringent than most 1976s. Medium body. Some fruit. A bit broad and blowsy on the follow-through but has better grip than most. Not bad.

1975   **Drink soon**

Fullish colour, just about mature. Firm, slightly spicy nose. A little closed. A little clumsy. On the palate this is softer and lighter than I expected, and the follow-through is rather astringent. A lack of grip and concentration. Not special.

1973   **Past its best**

Medium colour. Now beginning to show real age. Was soft and pleasant but is now fading fast. Medium bodied. Wasn't bad once.

1971   **Now–1997**

Full colour, but decidedly brown in colour (indeed even green at the rim). Not maderized on the nose and palate however. This is a full, rich wine with real concentration and plenty of depth. It has the usual somewhat sturdy Soutard character but there is quality here. Fine and complex on the finish. Long and vigorous. Very good indeed.

1970   **Now–2000**

Good, full, mature colour. This again is very good indeed. Rich, vigorous, fresh fruit on the nose. Full, surprisingly youthful, but fat, round and concentrated so not sturdy at all. Just ample, plump and with lovely fresh, complex, vigorous, old-vine fruit. High class.

1967   **Drink soon**

Good colour. Quite full, still looks vigorous. Round, soft, gently aromatic nose. Quality here, as well as a surprisingly amount of vigour for a Saint-Emilion 1967. Medium body, soft, ample and complex. Fresh and balanced still. A lot of charm. Lovely fruit. Very good. Holding up well.

1966   **Now–1998**

Medium-full colour. No undue age. Fresh, quite complex, fruity nose. A little fuller, a little more obvious structure. This again is an ample, complex, well-balanced wine. Has more depth and concentration than the 1967, as one might expect. And also has breed. Again fine.

1964   **Now–1998**

Full colour, even dense. The best of the lot. This has more solidity, more concentration, but doesn't have the finesse of the 1966. Fullish, good grip and richness, but somewhat four-square. Yet undeniably a lot of depth. Almost 1961-ish in its essence of fruit aspect. Long. Still vigorous. Very good again.

1962   **Drink up**

Medium colour. Fully mature. This was another good wine but it now shows a little age. Still quite fresh but has lightened up and the fruit has dried out. Certainly has elegance but a little past its best.

1961   **Drink up**

Just a little more colour but looks rather older than the 1962. Again shows a little too much age. Rather more rustic than the 1966 to 1971 vintages. Less rich and full than the 1964. Now getting a bit coarse.

1945   **Will still keep**

Fine, full colour, no undue maturity. There is a certain dryness. Rusticity and late bottling. Yet essentially a wine of richness and concentration. Certainly rich and concentrated on the palate. Big, structured, beefy and solid, with a certain astringency. Good but a little artisanal. Will still keep – indeed I think it has not budged for several years and will continue to be like this for some time to come.

1924   **Drink up**

Good colour still but well matured. This is really a bit past it. A structured, somewhat artisanal wine. Rich and concentrated though. A very good vintage, quite obviously. But fading fast, a bit astringent. Dried up in the glass.

LE TERTRE-
RÔTEBOEUF

Le Tertre-Rôteboeuf. Who'd heard of it ten years ago? Who *hasn't* heard of it today? In little more than a decade, 45-year-old François Mitjavile has turned this obscure five-hectare Saint-Emilion *grand cru*, not even a *grand cru classé*, into one of the *appellation's* most sought-after superstars. And he is not even a Bordelais. Nor was his upbringing in wine.

Spend any time in France and you will hardly fail to notice the name Mitjavile. It is one of the country's leading haulage contractors. Their 40-footers thunder up and down the motorways bringing melons and aubergines from Cavaillon to the Paris markets, taking T-shirts and swimwear in the opposite direction; and, yes, moving plenty of wine too, for the Mitjaviles hail from the Roussillon, and cousins produce Banyuls.

The Mitjaviles, François and Miloute, were married in 1971. They lived in Paris. He worked for the family firm; she in a press agency. Occasionally they would come down to Saint-Emilion to visit her Faure cousins at Château Bellefond-Belcier. Nearby, Miloute's father, Emile Gilard, had a small vineyard, Le Tertre, but after his death in 1961 it was rented out to the cousins and the wine vinified with theirs: a perfectly respectable, but by no means startling, Saint-Emilion *grand cru*.

François began to get itchy. A man of great enthusiasm and intelligence, but a loner and an individualist, one can see why Mitjavile was unsuited to the corporate life. He didn't get on with his boss. They are best off working for themselves. He and Miloute decided to take back the family inheritance. But first he had to learn something about viticulture and viniculture. In April 1975 he began a two-year *stage* at Château Figeac, and after the 1977 vintage he took over at Le Tertre. As there were a number of châteaux called Tertre in the Bordeaux area, they decided to add on the suffix Rôteboeuf. This is named after a nearby slope on which oxen used to graze.

The house – an attractive farmhouse dating from the 1730s with good-sized rooms and a commanding view down to the silvery Dordogne and across into the Entre-Deux-Mers – was at least habitable. Miloute's father, a naval officer, had lived there for 40 years, though more recently it had merely been used as a holiday home. But money was nevertheless scarce. There was nothing in the cellar: no wine-making equipment, no barrels, no agricultural machines. François sensibly concentrated at first on the vineyard. 'This didn't cost much. Only the effort.' And he borrowed and begged for the rest. From the start he was determined to make his wine as good as was humanly possible. Yields were kept to a minimum; he harvested as late as he dared in order to get maximum ripeness and concentration; and he prolonged the maceration in order to obtain a *vin de garde*.

But it was tough. For eight years it was an uphill struggle. How many minor châteaux are there in the Saint-Emilionais? One thousand? Two? Who wants another one? How do you persuade people that your wine is better than your neighbours? The bank began to make grumbling noises. Was it time to call it a day?

In the nick of time, just like the last reel of a cowboy film when the relief column finally roars into view, salvation arrived. In a blind tasting of 1982s, early in 1985, conducted by the French magazine *Que Choisir?*, Le Tertre-Rôteboeuf came first. Finally the orders began to come in; the price could be put up; new oak could be afforded. You can see the immediate difference in the wines. Pre-1985 the wines are undeniably rich and concentrated but a little bit clenched and structured, one feels they have not been allowed to breathe in the open air, like a city dweller brought up entirely in artificial light. Post-1985, Le Tertre-Rôteboeuf takes on an entirely new dimension.

In fact there are four phases, so far, in the development of the wine: 1978–1981, a learning curve; 1982–1984, Mitjavile begins to get it right; 1985–1988, new oak and profitability. And then from 1989 onwards, everything is in place, and there is an increased element of elegance.

THE VINEYARD

The 5.6 hectares of Le Tertre-Rôteboeuf lie south-east of the town of Saint-Emilion, on an extension of the same slope as Pavie and Larcis-Ducasse. Planted 80 per cent Merlot and 20 per cent Cabernet Franc, this land produces about 2,000 cases a year; though less than half this quantity in 1991, when the yield was a mere seventeen hectolitres per hectare.

ROC DE CAMBES

Once he had put Le Tertre-Rôteboeuf firmly on the map, Mitjavile sought to expand, in order to spread the cost of his agricultural machinery and vinification equipment. But this he found hard to do. Suitable land in Saint-Emilion rarely comes on to the market, and then only at extortionate prices. If you cannot expand, then diversify, he said to himself, remembering the crisis of 1973 to 1975. Best not to have all one's eggs in one basket.

Early in 1988 a friend put him in touch with an expatriate, resident in Singapore, who had a vineyard in Lalande-de-Pomerol and another in the Côtes de Bourg, and wanted to sell the latter. Along went Mitjavile, and he promptly fell in love with the site and its potential. The

fourteen hectares (four of which are merely AC Bordeaux rouge) lie in two natural amphithe-
atres overlooking the Gironde estuary. The vines were old. There was a resident vineyard
worker, an Arab with the name of Tayat Abderrahmane; a neat little farmhouse-style
château; and a rather special microclimate – even in 1991 untouched by the frost. The possibilities were enormous.

Mitjavile explained his intentions to his principal clients. Would you be prepared to pay
three times the going rate for a Côte de Bourg if the wine was good enough? All of them
said yes. They were already paying distinctly over the odds for Le Tertre-Rôteboeuf, but it
was worth it, and selling the wine was no problem.

The initial sales of this wine, which he called Roc de Cambes, were no problem either,
somewhat to Mitjavile's surprise. It all sold *en primeur*, and the wine has continued to improve ever since. One reason why most Bordeaux *petits châteaux* are so dull, according to
Mitjavile, is that they are simply harvested too early. The cold clay-limestone soils of the
Bourg and Blaye, for instance, take a long time to heat up. The fruit takes a long time to
fully mature. Mitjavile sometimes finds himself harvesting a full month after his neighbours, a
cause of some embarrassment in the village to his resident vineyard worker.

Roc de Cambes is planted with 55 per cent Merlot, 10 per cent Malbec, 20 per cent
Cabernet Sauvignon and 15 per cent Cabernet Franc. He does not de-herb the vineyard,
which adds to the rustic aspect. The wine is fermented in cement *cuves* and 50 per cent new
wood is employed in the troglodyte cellar. The results are startling.

THE TASTING

Roc de Cambes

The following wines were sampled in Saint-Emilion in April 1992.

	Optimum Drinking

1991   1995–2001
Normal harvest: not frosted. Very good colour.
Ripe and exotic on the nose. Fullish, fat, sumptuous palate. Very well-covered tannins. Quite
good grip. A round opulent wine. Finishing
long. Surprisingly good.

1990   1997–2009
Fine colour. Still quite dense on the nose. The
oak is quite apparent. On the palate no dominance by the oak. This is fullish. The tannins very
ripe. The fruit cool and classy and rich and ripe.
Very complex. Needs time. Lovely fruit. Fine
finish. Refined compared with the 1989.

1989   1997–2002
Fine colour. Splendidly aromatic, spicy, gently
oaky, exotically ripe nose. There is an aspect of
Scheherezade here. Fat and opulent. Very, very
rich. This is generous and complex and long on
the palate. A wine of great expansiveness and
larger-than-life personality. Good. Excellent for
a Bourg. Fine finish.

1988   1995–2005
Fine colour. Ripe nose. An attractive gamey element on the palate. Perhaps a little more rigid
than the other two. Certainly a bit more austere.
Quite solid tannins, but it has the fruit and grip
to last while it softens up. Good. A little rude,
but not rustic. A bit four-square.

Le Tertre-Rôteboeuf

Unusually, I sampled these from old to young, rather than in reverse chronological order.

1978   Now–1998
The first vintage. Good colour. No undue
brown. A little bit rigid and rustic on the nose.
Not attenuated, but solid and a bit lumpy. Medium-full. Under-exposed to the benefit of air in
its first months. Ripe, though. Good basic fruit.
Balanced. Still alive. Best on the finish. Not bad.

1979   Now–1997
Good colour. Less rigid, but also a bit chunky
and four-square. On the palate a little less full but

more civilized. Quite rich on the follow-
through. Good positive finish. Quite good. Still
plenty of life.

1980   **Drink soon**
Surprisingly full and vigorous colour. Here there
is evidence of a development towards something
a bit more refined. It is more supple. Not weak.
Surprisingly good. Ripe and fruity. Quite full.
Good grip and vigour. This has style and quality.
Drink soon but no hurry.

1981   **Now–1997**

Very good colour for the vintage. No undue
maturity. There is now a bit of richness coming
out. Good grip. Vigorous. This is definitely
'good', in anybody's interpretation. Good structure. Medium body. Rich and even concentrated. Dimension here. And depth. Long. Good
plus.

1982   **Now–2000**

Full colour. Still very youthful. This is the first
time he got it right, and the quality of the vintage
helped. Full, quite tannic. The tannins a little
untamed and evident, but very rich and concentrated. Fat, masculine, black fruit. Long and succulent if with a slight austere aspect.

1983   **Now–1996**

Medium-full colour. No undue brown. Good
fruit. Not weak. Well, it wasn't as good a vintage
as the 1982, but the wine is quite rich. It is reasonably balanced. The tannins more elegant. But
it is very stylish. This is long and satisfying, and
would put a great many of its peers to shame
(and still no new wood).

1984   **Drink soon**

Surprisingly good colour. Good nose. There is
fruit here and no sign of old tea. Really remarkably good. Plump raspberry fruit. Good grip.
Vigour here, and style, and attraction, and balance. OK, no great dimension, but it is 1984,
after all. A great success. No hurry to drink.

1985   **Now–2003**

Very good colour. Still very vigorous. Here we
have the imposition of new wood. Instantly we
have additional flavours: vanilla, caramel, coffee
and indeed a wild herbs, south-of-France element. It is un-Bordeaux like. Medium-full.
Tannins now soft. High-toned. A very individual wine. Flowery, soft and long on the finish.
Very good.

1986   **Now–1999**

Medium colour. Very complex nose. Indeed for
its vintage this is perhaps even better. Chocolate
now as well as coffee and caramel and a touch of
mint (in the best sense). On the palate it misses
just a little fat on the attack but very concentrated
and generous on the follow-through. Intense.
Stylish. Long. Very good plus.

1987   **Now–1996**

Medium colour. Who else made a 1987 as good
as this? There is nothing off-vintage here. Fat,
rich even. Medium body. Complex, ripe and
depth and complexity. Surprisingly fine for the
vintage. Long. Only just about ready.

1988   **1995–2009**

Fine colour. Cool, very stylish, complex nose.
This is quietly successful. The end of the third
phase – or the beginning of the fourth. Everything in place now. Excellent concentration of
old vines. Very good grip. An intensity of
flavour and a length on the palate to which one
can only say 'hats off'. Fine. Long.

1989   **1997–2015**

Very fine colour. Lovely nose. Heaps and heaps
of fruit. Deliciously ripe and rich. The opulence
and richness of the vintage is very apparent. Firm
but lush. Intense and exotic. Yet classy, fresh,
balanced, vigorous and fully fleshed out. A full
wine but an open-hearted, very generous one.
Fine.

1990   **1996–2009**

Fine colour. Fat and rich and oaky on the nose.
Just a touch four-square and closed, but it had
been pumped from barrel into tank in preparation for the *collage* the previous week. Full, rich,
very good tannins; quite a lot of oak, but not too
much. Not as fat or as intense as the 1989 but
very good nevertheless.

1991   **1996–2001**

Surprisingly good colour and very good nose for
a 1991. This has richness, even depth. On the
palate the wine is fullish, rich, intense and oaky.
There is nothing off-vintage about this.

TROPLONG-MONDOT

North-east of the village of Saint-Emilion, itself high above the surrounding countryside, the land rises still further. This is the bluff of Mondot, 100 metres above sea level. Astride the hill, graceless but utilitarian, is a large water tower. No one hates this eyesore more than Christine Valette, *châtelaine* and wine-maker of Château Troplong-Mondot, on whose land the water tower lies. Convinced by the quality of old bottles of Troplong-Mondot that improvements could be made, Christine suggested to her father, Claude Valette, that she take over responsibility for the wine when the old *régisseur* retired in 1980. Since then progress has been significant. Troplong-Mondot is now one of Saint-Emilion's rising stars; perhaps the best of the *grands crus classés*; another contender for elevation in the hierarchy.

HISTORY

Troplong-Mondot is one of the oldest and noblest properties in the Libournais. Back in the early eighteenth century the owners were the influential and aristocratic De Sèze family, also masters of Berliquet, and the estate extended south, down towards the Dordogne river over what is now Pavie. It is neat, but merely a coincidence, that Pavie is today held by another branch of the Valette family, cousins of Claude and Christine.

In 1745, when the château was constructed, the owner was the Abbé de Sèze. Succession then passed to the children of his brother Raymond, one of the defenders of Louis XVI at the time of the Revolution, but some time in the 1830s the De Seze domaines were split up and sold. Paguierre in 1828 states that the first growths of Saint-Emilion are Canolle (Belair), Berliquet, L'Abbé de Sèze (Troplong-Mondot), Laborie (?Soutard) and Fontémoing (Canon). This is the last we hear of the De Sèze dynasty at Mondot, though they seem to have hung on to part of Pavie until the mid-1840s according to the Tastet and Lawton records.

The next recorded proprietor is Raymond Troplong. Troplong was both a jurist and an intellectual, both a man of letters and a politician. Friend of Théophile Gautier, he was a member of the Académie des Sciences Morales et Politiques, the author of a number of legal text-books, president of one of the Courts of Appeal and leader of the Senate. He arrived at Mondot shortly before 1850 and appears to have taken over from his father Gerus Troplong, proprietor in 1841 according to the journal, *Le Producteur*. He regrouped several parcels of land at the top of the hill to make a coherent domaine of 30 hectares (it has not changed since) and, as it is the custom, appended his name to the title of the estate. It is at this time that the wine first appears in Cocks and Féret: number two in the commune after Belair. The 20 hectares of vines produced 25 to 35 *tonneaux* of wine.

Raymond Troplong died in 1869 and was succeeded by his widow. Subsequently ownership passed to his nephew Edouard, also a lawyer, and at one time mayor of neighbouring Saint-Laurent-des-Combes. By the end of the century the vineyard had been extended to 30 hectares, production had increased to as much as 120 *tonneaux* in a plentiful vintage such as 1893, and vast new *chais* had been constructed, a few 100 metres outside the little park which surrounds the château.

Edouard Troplong was now an old man. Like his uncle he had no children; unlike him he had never married. He lived alone in the decaying splendour of the château, somewhat of a recluse. His tranquillity was rudely interrupted one evening during the vintage. A group of harvesters burst in and emptied their bowls of inedible lentils all over Troplong's Aubusson carpet. You eat this muck, was the message. We can't. It was the time of riots in Champagne. Jean Jaurès, socialist leader and founder of the newspaper *L'Humanité*, was in his prime. Unrest was in the air. Troplong decided to sell up.

This is the story. But it does not quite fit with the facts. As far I can make out, Troplong did not dispose of the property until after the First World War, when he must have been very old indeed. Into the picture now comes the mysterious *Veuve* Lasseverie. Within the space of 24 months between mid-1918 and mid-1920, and often in conjunction with her sons-in-law, Henri Gasqueton and René Dupeyron, Mme Lasseverie acquired at least half a dozen major estates in the Gironde. Equally as abruptly, she disposed of them. By 1925 the Lasseverie empire is no more. By 1921 she had already sold Troplong-Mondot to Georges Thienpont, a wine-merchant from Etikhove in Belgium. Thienpont was to acquire Vieux Château Certan in Pomerol three years later.

'I bought Troplong-Mondot for pleasure. Vieux Château Certan is for business,' Georges Thienpont is quoted as saying. He spent most of his time running his business in Belgium, but it was at Troplong-Mondot that he stayed when he visited the Libournais. In 1936, as a result of the slump, one of them had to go. Troplong was larger, and the better known; the wine fetched higher prices than its Pomerol stable-mate. Troplong was put up for sale.

It was acquired by another outsider, another merchant. Alexander Valette was a *négociant* at Saint Ouen near Paris. Troplong-Mondot was not his first venture into vineyard ownership. He had property in Fronsac and at Quinsac in the *premières côtes*. Château Pavie, back in the eighteenth-century part of the same property, was to follow in 1943. Château Troplong-Mondot is now owned by Alexander Valette's grandson, Claude. Since 1981 it has been run by his daughter, Christine.

THE VINEYARD

In a region where few vineyards exceed ten hectares, the domaine of Château Troplong-Mondot is large. The 30 hectares under vine lie in one piece on one of the commanding heights of the region on a marly soil broken up with flints and fragments of pure limestone. Streams in the rock underneath ensure that though the exposition and drainage are excellent, the roots of the vines are kept supplied with water even in the most arid of summers. The *encépagement* is now 70 per cent Merlot, 15 per cent Cabernet Franc and 15 per cent Cabernet Sauvignon. Over the past decade a few residual rows of old Malbec have been replaced. Not having replaced any other vines since 1981 the average age is now a venerable 45 years, with some which are as old as the century.

CHANGES AND IMPROVEMENTS

Much has been fine-tuned since Christine Valette took over the direction of the estate. The 1978 and 1979, she will accept, lack concentration. She engaged Michel Rolland as consultant oenologist. Together they came to the decision that one of the failings had been picking too early. In 1981 they decided to wait. Today, because of microclimatic reasons, they harvest a whole week later than the cousins at Pavie.

Another change has been the abandonment of the harvesting machine. Half of the 1982 crop was picked by machine. The result is a lumpy wine, disappointing by 1982 standards. A third has been a reduction in yield. If you're going to do an *éclaircissage*, those in the know will advise you, knocking out one bunch in four is a complete waste of time. You have got to grit your teeth and eliminate every other bunch. Like others in the region, the vineyard is gradually being changed from single- to double-cane (Guyot) pruning. The result was a gross yield, before selection, of 45 hectolitres per hectare in 1988 and no more than 48 in 1989. The extra concentration achieved thereby is manifest in the wine.

With the 1985 vintage, Troplong-Mondot 'came of age', as Michel Rolland puts it. More accurately it began to show why it had been so highly regarded a century and a half previously. The introduction of a second wine, simply called Mondot, thermo-regulated vinification, a *triage* in the vineyard for the first time, and an increase in the per centage of new oak in the cellar to one half – all this began in 1985. From 1989 a *tapis de triage*, for sorting through the fruit when it arrives at the winery, was installed. In 1990 eight new smaller stainless-steel vats were added to the battery already in place. Now the fruit from all the different parcels in the vineyard can be vinified separately.

THE WINE

This is classy wine-making, and the result is a complex, concentrated, elegant wine. Château Troplong-Mondot is very well situated. The average age of the vines is old. The yields are limited. The result, as can be seen from the wines since 1985, is something full and masculine, though not too sturdy, rich and long-tasting. Today there is no doubt that Troplong-Mondot is a very strong contender for elevation to *premier cru*.

THE TASTING

The following wines were sampled at the château in April 1990.

Optimum drinking

1989 — 1996–2016
Good colour. Good fat, ripe, meaty nose. There is concentration here. Fine old-viney fruit. Medium-full, good ripe tannins. A vigorous, stylish example. Very good.

1988 — 1996–2016
Good colour. Fine nose. Good new oak support. Ripe and stylish. Good depth. A quietly confident wine. This is fine and very elegant. Medium-full. Rich and oaky. Ripe and balanced. Must be one of the very best of the *grands crus classés*. A fine result. Long and complex.

1987 — Drink soon
Surprisingly good colour for the vintage. Quite full, still vigorous. This has a fine nose for the vintage. There is substance and ripeness, plus an element of new oak. Nothing weak and feeble about this! Medium body. Still has a little tannin. There is a lot of fruit here. Ripe, stylish. A surprisingly good result.

1986 — Now–1997
Medium colour. Less new oak evident. There is some, and the wine has better substance than most of its Libournais peers, though not exactly rich. Medium body. A little stringy. The substance is not in balance with the structure, but a good result. Ripe, damson and blackberry fruit and good acidity. Lacks a little concentration.

1985 — Now–2003
Medium-full colour. Quite full and substantial, a little reserved. Plummy fruit. Quite full. Good depth. Ripe and fat with good grip. This is a concentrated wine which has finesse. Very good indeed. Long and complex.

1984 — Drink up
Medium colour, good vigour. Lacks a little concentration but a good effort for the vintage. Not weedy, nor is there any fade. A very good 1984. Good fruit supported by good acidity. Lacks a little charm and depth but a good result.

1983 — Now–1998
Medium to medium-full colour. Round, ample and mature on the nose. Lacks real concentration and grip but ripe and pleasant. Medium bodied. Round, slightly spicy. Good substance. Has charm if not that much breed. Good grip for a Saint-Emilion. Finishes positively. Good.

1982 — Now–2001
Medium-full colour. Big, fat, rich and concentrated. Plummy fruit. A good example but one which is clearly of *bourgeois* quality rather than *premier cru* aspiration. Fullish on the palate but rather more artisanal than the vintages of the later 1980s. Ripe and balanced but lacks a bit of real richness and concentration. A bit lumpy. Quite good at best.

1981 — Now–1997
Medium colour, just about mature. This is good for the vintage. Medium weight, stylish and mature but has good grip so it is still fresh. Indeed I find it more elegant though less fat than the 1983. It is more positive. A good 1981. More elegance than the 1982 and a better result for the vintage. Medium body. Balanced. Good fruit. Finishes well. Still vigorous. Plenty of life.

1980 — Drink soon
Medium colour. No undue age. A little diffuse on the nose but not too bad. A pleasant, fruity wine which is more than respectable. Getting a little coarse now but not feeble, nor short.

1970 — Now–1996
Good colour. Mature but no undue age. Round, spicy, ample, reasonably full. Not too rustic. Medium-full, ripe and even rich. It is a little artisanal. It lacks the supple, harmonious, velvet and cedar of a more classy example. Not without depth or interest.

1961 — Drink soon
(Double magnum) Fine colour, fullish and still very vigorous. This is the proof that even with the artisanal methods of the time, in a great year like 1961 it was almost impossible not to make very good wine. Good fresh, concentrated fruit on the nose. No undue solidity. Still fresh blackcurrany fruit on the palate. But getting a little rigid on the palate as it evolved. Good though.

1929 — Will still keep well
Very fine colour. Quite a lovely nose. Three times as succulent as the 1961. Really lovely concentration. Marvellous intensity of fruit. As it evolved an aspect of exotic fruit emerged. Marshmallow. Beautifully poised. Very long – lovely. This has a fat and a freshness which reminds me of a 1947.

POM

POMEROL LIES IMMEDIATELY TO THE WEST OF THE *GRAVES*-SAINT-EMILION, NORTH OF THE TOWN OF LIBOURNE. IT IS A SMALL, COMPACT AREA OF RELA-TIVELY SMALL ESTATES, MANY OF WHICH ARE OWNED, MANAGED OR MARKETED BY THE EXCELLENT FIRM OF JEAN-PIERRE MOUEIX IN LIBOURNE. THERE HAS NEVER BEEN AN OFFICIAL CLASSIFICATION OF POMEROL WINES.

The best section in Pomerol lies between the Saint-Emilion boundary and the *route nationale* to Périgueux. Here the soil is predominantly clay and gravel, with some sand, on a hard, iron-rich base known as '*crasse de fer*', or '*machefer*'. Further to the west the soil is flatter and contains more sand, and the wines are consequently looser-knit, lighter and quick-maturing.

The best wines of Pomerol are firm and full, have a great concentration of ripe fruit coupled with a Merlot richness which matures into a velvety wine of great depth of flavour, full of distinction. Being based on the Merlot grape, they are always somewhat sweeter, less austere than the wines of the Médoc. Yet this is not to say they are not slow developing and long lasting. The top Pomerols are the rivals of the best in Pauillac and Saint-Julien, and hence for me have immense attraction. One only wishes the estates were larger and produced more wine.

PÉTRUS

Without doubt the most *recherché* claret in the world is Château Pétrus. Its production is limited – less than 40 *tonneaux* (4,000 cases) – so sales are by allocation, almost irrespective of the asking price. Pétrus is almost impossible to acquire later, when mature, except by the odd dozen or two at auction or through the brokerage network, at which time it will command a price two or three times in excess of the prices asked for Lafite and other 1855 first growths. Pétrus is probably the most valuable red wine now made.

Yet it was not always like this. The Pétrus phenomenon is recent. Some 50 years ago hardly anyone had heard of Pétrus, and fewer still were interested in buying the wine. Avery's of Bristol, then headed by the late Ronald Avery, who did so much to put Pomerols on the map (perhaps the Mayor of Libourne should commission a statue?) bought all the fine postwar vintages up to 1955, some in bottle, some in cask. But they could not sell it. It was not until the early 1960s that fame finally arrived.

Pomerol itself is recent. Up until 1900 when the Syndicat of Pomerol was founded, the commune was considered a lesser sub-area of Saint-Emilion, much in the same way that the wines of Montagne, Lussac, Puisseguin and Saint-Georges are today. Saint-Emilion itself, until well into the last quarter of the nineteenth century, was regarded as greatly inferior to the Médoc and the Graves. It is for this reason, and not because of any self-imposed restriction, that the 1855 Classification consists (with the exception of Château Haut-Brion) only of Médocs. Unlike other areas in Bordeaux, Pomerol has never had a classification of its own.

The land close to the vineyard of Pétrus was formerly a hamlet known as La Fleur. This disappeared in the expansion of the heartland of Pomerol into a monocultural, wine-producing area in the late 1700s but explains the presence of so many vineyards whose name, wholly or partly, incorporates the words La Fleur.

HISTORY

According to the late Professor Henri Enjalbert, in his *Les Grands Vins de Saint-Emilion, Pomerol et Fronsac*, the pioneer in Pomerol, an area of mixed tenant farming until the 1740s, was Louis Fontémoing at Trochau, a growth since parcellated and no longer in the front line of the top estates. He was closely followed by M. Giraud at Trotanoy and Mme Conseillan at La Conseillante and later by the Demays at Certan and the Arnaud family at Pétrus.

The first mention of Pétrus in the notebooks of the Bordeaux firm of Tastet and Lawton was in 1837. Up to 1830, the sole *grand vin* of Pomerol had been Vieux Certan. Then, in 1831, Petit-Village makes an appearance and in 1836 Trop-Ennuie (Trotanoy). M. Arnaud's wine joined these ranks a year later. The price of all these three was between 300 and 350 francs a *tonneau*. (Vieux Certan fetched 400 to 450 francs). This was a third that of a top Saint-Emilion such as Belair, but was roughly equivalent to second-rank wines such as Berliquet and Troplong-Mondot.

It was probably not until the mid-nineteenth century that wine-growing became the staple crop on the Pétrus domaine. Lecoutre de Beauvais in *Le Producteur* (1841) writes of a total production in Pomerol of 600 to 700 *tonneaux* and other statistics at this time give 261 hectares of land completely given over to vines, roughly half what it is today. The second edition of Franck (1845) states that the whole of Saint-Emilion (i.e., including Pomerol and the outlying districts) produces only 2,500 tonneaux and mentions no individual growths on this side of the river at all.

Franck's *Traité*, however, is essentially on the Médoc and perhaps he rarely visited Libourne. Certainly Charles Cocks, the English schoolmaster, and his French collaborator and successor, Edouard Féret, were more painstaking in their researches and exacting in their comments. In their 1868 second edition, a separate section is given over to Pomerol. The principal properties are described as *cru bourgeois* and Pétrus is listed third after Vieux Château Certan and Château Trotanoy, producing twelve to fifteen *tonneaux*. By this time Pomerol's reputation had risen and the top wines now fetched 1200 to 1400 francs a *tonneau*, according to the Lawton archives. This was roughly equivalent to a fifth growth Médoc.

Pétrus remained in the Arnaud family until after the First World War. By this time it was producing about 25 *tonneaux* and had fully consolidated its reputation as the top property in the area, in good years fetching prices on a par with second growth Médocs. Now a limited company, it was gradually acquired from 1925 onwards by Mme Edmond Loubat who became sole owner by about 1945.

The Loubat family was well established in the area. They owned two minor Pomerol properties at the end of the nineteenth century: one called Jeanlande, the other called Chante-Caille; and Edmond's brother was Mayor of Libourne. Edmond also founded the Restaurant Loubat in Libourne.

It was Mme Edmond Loubat who really achieved top-growth status for her beloved Pétrus. Penning-Rowsell describes her as 'a woman of great personality, who never made the mistake of underestimating the value of her product'. She was convinced that her wine was second to none in Bordeaux and was determined that everyone else should recognize it. She asked very high prices for her wine and eventually the clients collected – even if, like Ronald Avery, they had some difficulty in selling on to *their* customers. In this, she had a good ally in the redoubtable Jean-Pierre Moueix.

MOUEIX

Moueix is the second and complementary part of the Pétrus phenomenon. He started as merely the proprietor of Château Fonroque in Saint-Emilion but finding no *négociant* interested in his wine during the depressing 1930s, he set up as a *négociant* himself. Now retired, but ably succeeded by his nephew Jean-Jacques and his son Christian, the family business owns, farms for an absentee landlord or has the marketing rights, in part or in exclusivity, for the majority of the top properties in the area. The properties they own include Lafleur-Pétrus, Trotanoy, Lagrange and La Grave in Pomerol as well as Magdelaine in Saint-Emilion. In addition, Moueix sells a third of Cheval-Blanc and half of Ausone. He has been the sole agent for Pétrus since 1947.

Mme Loubat had no children and two heirs, the only children of each of her two sisters, a Mme Lily Lacoste and a M. Lignac. These two did not get on and before Mme Loubat died in 1961, she gave one share in Pétrus to Jean-Pierre Moueix in order both to enable him to have a say in the management of the property and to make an exact division of the remainder between the heirs. Moueix bought Lignac's shares in 1964 and has since, effectively, been the man in charge. Jean-Pierre's son Christian is personally responsible for managing the château, the viticulture is delegated to Michel Gillet and the wine-making to *oenologue* Jean-Claude Berrouet. Château Latour-à-Pomerol, the other property inherited by Mme Lacoste from her aunt, is similarly managed by the Moueix family and the wine marketed by them.

THE VINEYARD

The Pétrus secret begins with soil. While across the road at Lafleur-Pétrus the soil is partly gravel, as it is in part of the vineyards of Cheval-Blanc and Figeac, and elsewhere in Pomerol there are patches of sand, at Pétrus the soil is clay with a curious blue tinge to it. Underneath this clay is a subsoil of gravel and underneath this is an impermeable layer of hard iron soil known as *crasse de fer*, or *machefer*.

Planted in the soil are the vines. At Pétrus, the *encépagement* is particular to the property and almost unique in Bordeaux – practically 100 per cent Merlot. While there is 5 per cent Bouchet (Cabernet Franc) in the vineyard, the wine from these vines is not always used in the *grand vin* blend, for it is only in exceptional years that the Bouchet gets really ripe. Pétrus, then, is a 100 per cent Merlot wine.

The proportion, however, has only in recent years been weighted as heavily as this. Up to the mid-1960s, it was more like 80 per cent Merlot and 20 per cent Cabernet Franc. The vineyard is not large. Bounded by the other top growths of Pomerol, La Conseillante and L'Evangile to the Saint-Emilion side, Vieux Château Certan to the south-west and Lafleur-Pétrus to the west, it measures a mere 11.5 hectares. Until 1969 it was yet smaller but in that year five hectares were acquired from the best soils of its northern neighbour Château Gazin and the wine from this section has, partly, been incorporated in the *grand vin*.

The vines are very old, an average of 40 to 45 years, some as much as 80 if not more. Mme Loubat refused to replant after the 1956 winter frosts which killed two-thirds of the vineyard. Instead, they re-grafted on to the existing established root – a process known as *re-cépage*, and untried before in the region. It was said that these new branches would only produce for fifteen years yet they are still functioning. But it took thevineyard ten years to regain full production. In 1985 and again in 1987, the frosts hit once more. Luckily, this does not appear to have inflicted permanent damage.

The vineyard looks different from those in the Médoc. Here they will plough or weed twice a year; in Pomerol, three or four times. In addition, at Pétrus they deliberately plant a weed which helps to dry out the soil in winter. It is later ploughed in. This takes the place of chemical fertilizer and helps increase the mineral content.

Perfectionism begins with the vines themselves. Not only are they very old, but when a single old vine gives up it is not immediately replaced. This way Christian Moueix can maintain the venerability of not only individual vines but of sections of this vineyards and can thus tell you as well from which part of Château Pétrus each vat of new wine comes and almost how old each constituent drop of the final blend is.

Perfectionism is carried almost to the verge of eccentricity in the way Pétrus is harvested. In years where there has been rain at the time of the harvest, helicopters have been used to generate a down wind to dry out the grapes. In 1992 the ground was lined with plastic sheets so that no moisture should penetrate the earth. The total Moueix team, some 180 people, are detailed to pick at Pétrus on the exact day when experience, helped by present-day scientific methods, tells the family the grapes are at optimum. Pétrus is so small that they can clear it in two or three visits. But, not only is the entire squad poured in on the best day, it is not sent in until after lunch. By the afternoon the dew has evaporated, the berries are dry and warm and the grapes are thereby a half degree of potential alcohol riper.

Château Pétrus is fermented traditionally in concrete vats and with a maceration on skins for 18 to 25 days, with between 20 and 30 per cent of the stems. This produces a big, sturdy, very rich wine which, despite the amount of Merlot, will not only last but does not take one immediately to the Saint-Emilion/Pomerol side of Bordeaux. This comes later, when one realizes that the wine, though incredibly, almost overpoweringly, powerful and full in body yet does not have the austere backbone of the Médoc and does taste distinctively of very concentrated Merlot, not Cabernet. Naturally, it is matured exclusively in new oak and lodged there for two years or more before bottling.

THE CHÂTEAU

Few châteaux in Pomerol are grand buildings and in this respect Pétrus is no exception. The building is painted light turquoise blue and is a small and uninhabited nondescript country house of two storeys, hardly more than a reception hall with a couple of bedrooms on top. In the hall is a portrait of La Grande Dame, Mme Loubat, and this leads directly through to the *chais*. This was formerly in two adjacent sections, but in the early 1980s it was extensively enlarged to give more storage space, a bottling hall — heretofore the wine has been bottled by hand, cask by cask — and a larger reception area.

THE WINE

The first thing that strikes one about Pétrus is its incredible concentration. This is due, in part, to the very old vines and long maceration; in part, also, it is a direct result of deliberate attempts to keep the harvest as low as possible, to a maximum of 45 hectolitres per hectare, even in these prolific days. This was precisely the 1986 figure before selection of the *cuvées* for the *grand vin*. From other figures which Christian Moueix has been kind enough to furnish me, I can see that the equivalent figure (that is, before elimination of the lesser vats) was 42 hectolitres per hectare in 1979, a prolific year, 32 in 1975, and as low as 17.5 in 1961.

Today, yields elsewhere of 55 to 60 hectolitres per hectare are not uncommon, even in the top estates. How do they manage to keep it so low at Pétrus? The answer is by means of an *éclaircissage*, or crop-thinning. Christian Moueix was one of the first to practice this in the Gironde as far back as the early 1980s. Originally, wary that the usual vineyard workers would be naturally reluctant to chop off bunches of grapes on vines as valuable as those at Pétrus, he entrusted the task to a bunch of students — *stagiaires* — working for the Moueix establishment during their summer vacation. Today, crop-thinning is a more accepted occurrence, even tolerated by the older generation.

With concentration comes power. Pétrus is a big wine yet without being massively, austerely tannic in the same way as a young Latour or Mouton-Rothschild: rich and full and sturdy and, as I have said, not immediately redolent of the Libournais despite the quantity of Merlot in the *encépagement*. Pétrus, above all, is a wine of enormous fruit. The fruit dominates the oak, it dominates the tannin. This is as it should be. It can also overpower the taster.

It is perhaps academic to attempt to answer the question of which château produces the greatest Bordeaux of them all. Do you measure 'the greatest' in terms of prices fetched at auction? If so, what would be the effect if Pétrus was deprived of its rarity value and produced as much as Château Lafite? Even if you were to tot up the marks given for the top Bordeaux in horizontal tastings and found that Pétrus was marginally higher, on average, than the other first growths, would this really matter? Is it not, perhaps, at this level, a question of personal taste? Speaking for myself, there are moments when I consider Pétrus the greatest red wine produced in Bordeaux and others when I do not. It is an unanswerable question.

THE TASTING

Most of the following tasting notes come from the most recent comprehensive tasting of Château Pétrus that I have attended. In October 1993, George Sape offered a tasting of the vintages between 1982 and 1952 at a splendid dinner at the Montrachet restaurant in New York. Other notes come from an amalgam of a Pétrus versus the Rest session organized by Daniel Oliveros, also in New York in October 1989 (37 different pairs of wines, served blind), a La Vigneronne tasting in March 1991, and a range of Pétrus vintages from 1986 to 1926 sponsored by the Club Vinophile du Conseil de France, and organized by the late Jacques Luxey in Paris in May 1987.

Optimum drinking

1986 1997–2010
Youthful purple colour. Rich, concentrated, new oaky nose. Very plummy and seductive. Almost too much so. Medium-full, fresh, youthful and tannic. Opulent fruit and a lot of new wood on the palate. Very good, but at the Oliveros tasting I preferred the Vieux Certan.

1985 1997–2015
Fullish colour. Still youthful. Nose still a bit closed. Good acidity. This is presently a bit adolescent. Full, tannic, masculine, firm, youthful. Very good grip. This has lovely concentrated fruit and real potential. Excellent.

1984 Now–2000
Medium-full colour, not much sign of maturity. Good fruit initially on the nose but a slight herbaceous element as it evolved. This is nevertheless an unexpectedly succulent wine for the vintage. Fullish, still youthful.

1983 Now–2003
Quite full colour. Attractive, fresh, fruity nose. Fullish palate, ripe tannins. Good acidity. This has stylish fruit but not a great deal of concentration. Approaching maturity. Fresh and positive. Very good but not great.

1982 1995–2025
Full colour. Rich, fat and concentrated nose. Not too dense. Now approaching maturity, but still not quite open enough. Fullish, meaty and rich. Still some tannin. Rather less advanced than last time out. Good grip. Slightly earthy. Lots of concentration. Backward. Very fine indeed but lacks the sparkle of great. Doesn't sing.

1981 Now–1998
(Magnum) Medium to medium-full colour. No undue maturity. Attractive ripe nose. A touch of attenuation. High toned. Cedary. But lacks a little zip and depth. Medium body. Fully ready and not for the long term. A juicy sandalwoody wine with good ripe fruit and touch of spice. Very good indeed, but not the depth, vigour and concentration for better.

1980 Now–1997
Very good colour for the vintage. A substantial oaky nose, though it became a little astringent as it evolved. Very full for the vintage. There is richness but also a little rigidity, but underneath an unexpected amount of fruit. Very good.

1979 Now–2010
(Magnum) Medium-full colour. Lovely ripe blackberry plummy nose. This is a lot more interesting and much more vigorous than the 1981. Lots of concentration here. Fullish, slightly austere, still a touch of tannin. This has lovely black fruit and a lot of dimension. Slightly firm still – perhaps always. Bags of life. Lacks a little flesh and generosity. But very fine.

1978 Now–2015 plus
(Magnum) Medium-full colour but slightly less intense than the 1979. More reserved than the 1979, a little dense and unforthcoming. Fullish. More evolved than the 1979. Richer and fatter. Mellower. This is very fine indeed. Complex, very long on the palate. Shows better than the 1982 today. Lovely finish.

1977 Now–1996
Good colour, just about mature. Somewhat green and stalky on the nose, but rather more richness on the palate. Quite full. A little raw

though, and it lacks real concentration. A good effort for the vintage though.

1976   **Now–1997**

Medium to medium-full colour. Rich, sweet, pruny, evolved nose. Medium body. No astringency. Ripe, quite attractive and quite fresh. But lacks a little elegance. Certainly very good. But not great. A little lumpy.

1975   **Now–2000 plus**

(Magnum) Fullish colour. Good rich ripe nose. Just a little dense. Medium body. Quite fat and spicy, quite sweet. Good grip. But a little too structured to be great. Certainly very good. And with plenty of vigour and spice. The acidity shows a little on the finish.

1974   **Drink up**

Medium-full colour. Still youthful. Firm on the nose, a little herbaceous. Lacks charm. Quite full but an element of astringency. Undistinguished.

1973   **Now–1998**

(Magnum) Good colour for the vintage. Soft, ripe, open, accessible fruity nose. No weakness or attenuation. Medium body. Fresh. Quite oaky. A touch of spice. A very excellent 1973. Surprisingly elegant, balanced and vigorous. Still has plenty of life.

1971   **Now–2000**

Medium-full colour. Two bottles circulating at the Sape tasting. One better than the other. The best was refined and distinguishedly fruity on the nose. Full on the palate. Still with a little unresolved tannin. A touch medicinal. But as well a lot of class, concentration, complexity and depth. This is fine. It would have been even better if made today. Fresh long finish, but the tannin shows a little.

1970   **Now–2010 plus**

(Magnum) Full colour. Firm, rich, profound nose. This is quite structured and only just ready. A full, rich, spicy wine – chocolatey and mocha. Almost a little too dense. The structure shows on the palate. It is a potent wine. Very concentrated, even a touch inky. Yet it is very very rich and lovely. Very fine indeed.

1969   **Drink up**

Medium colour, mature. A cedary, sandalwoody nose: round and smooth. Spicy and rich on the palate. Yet a little astringency as well. Yet unexpectedly good. By no means past it.

1967   **See note**

A well-matured wine which now shows a touch of spurious sweetness and hints of attenuation. Very Merlot. Soft and ripe and pleasant but lacks a bit of grip and dimension. This must have ben a bad bottle because the example at the Oliveros

tasting was really excellent. A lush, ripe, concentrated example with plenty of vigour still.

1966   **Now–2000 plus**

(Magnum) Good colour. Firm nose. A touch herbaceous. Doesn't sing. Lacks generosity. Slightly hard. On the palate this is rich and concentrated though. Not too tough, slightly austere but in a true Bordeaux lover's way. Firm but very very ripe and long and complex. Very fine indeed. Really lovely.

1964   **Now–2010 plus (in this size)**

(Double magnum) Very good colour. Ripe, very elegant, very concentrated and multidimension fruit on the nose. This is brilliant. Very classy. Fullish, quite structured. Smooth and velvety. Rich and plump and generous. A touch of spice. Concentrated Merlot at its best. This is very fine indeed. Very good vigour still. Marvellous finish. Bags of life.

1962   **Now–1997**

Good colour, fully mature. Very good nose. A little chunky and 'old-fashioned' in character but of high quality. Solid, tannic, full-bodied, a lot of depth. Ripe, slightly spicy, rich. A splendid vigorous wine which will still keep well.

1961   **Now–2000**

(Magnum) Very good colour. Enormous concentration on the nose. This is splendid. Really very lovely fruit. But more evolved than the 1964. Fullish. Very mellow and velvety and silky. Marvellous intensity of fruit. Brilliant. Great wine again, and even better than the 1964.

1960   **Past its best**

Medium-full colour. At first round, attractive and cedary if without great depth or dimension. A little sweet and vegetal at the end. It died in the glass. But it was a success at the time.

1959   **Now–2000**

Very good colour. Very fine lusciously creamy nose. Full, very ripe and sweet. A little more spice and a little more age than the 1961. The second bottle at the Sape tasting a touch more vigorous, positive and rich. The finish is creamy-velvety, high class and very, very long and lovely. In fact it is even better than the 1961 – the second bottle. Great wine again though quite high in alcohol. The other bottle less sweet on the finish.

1958

Medium colour. Fully mature. This is corked but is soft and fragrant, like the 1973. Still fresh.

Note from the Oliveros tasting: Mature but fullish nose. Slightly high-toned nose with an element of H2S. Supple though. Medium-full, not that amount of class but round and ripe, slightly sweet. An element of bonfire – or is it baked potatoes? An attractive bottle – a wine with a smile. Drink soon.

1955   Drink up
(Belgian bottled by Vandemeulen) Good full mature colour. There is just a touch of maderization on the nose and it appears to be thinning out a little. But there is still plenty of enjoyment to be had. Medium body. Ripe and stylish, but getting a little better and astringent. Balanced and plump but a little past its best. Not short though, nor too dry on the finish.

1955   Drink soon
Good colour. One bottle a little drier on the nose than the other. Ripe, fragrant. Old roses-y. Raspberry flavoured. Intense and yet delicate. Old viney. Medium to medium-full. Delicious. Lovely finish.

1954   Drink up
Lightish colour, now showing quite a bit of age. Nose is attenuated and rather blandly sweet. Soft, round, ripe and boiled-sweet-flavoured. At least not astringent but in this series a distinct lack of class.

1953   Drink soon
(Belgian bottled by Vyncke-Daels) Very good full mature colour. Bigger and more vigorous than the 1955 (Belgian bottle). Full, fat, slightly burnt/roasted nose. This has plenty of interest and richness. A full, toasted, earthy wine. There is good acidity and plenty of fruit. Plump but quite muscular. Yet no lack of finesse. Very good – but not great. Will still keep.

1953   See note
Good colour. Started off quite vigorous, as well as classy. Quite full, certainly good quality, has size and depth, I noted at first. Then the wine became a little four-square and finally it lightened up and lost interest, revealing a slightly bitter element on the finish. Essentially a wine of greater breed than the 1952 though. The Oliveros example was from a magnum: fragrant and classy. Still alive.

1952   Drink soon
(Belgian bottled by Lambrecht) Medium full, quite well-matured colour. Not as full or as vigorous as either the 1955 or the 1953 (the Belgian bottlings). A very stylish, complex nose. But a little more aged. Medium body now. A touch of astringency. Yet this has the most breed and depth of the three. Much more dimension. Lovely fruit and a long, balanced, quietly fading but elegant finish.

1952   Now–1998
(Magnum) Very good colour. Lovely nose. An element of roast chestnut and sweet nutty squash. Medium to medium-full body now. Perhaps it has lightened up a bit. But rich, complex and multidimensional, with plenty of vigour and above all marvellous balance and subtlety of fruit. Great wine again. Very, very elegant.

1950   Drink soon
Very good, full, mature colour. This really does have a great, almost porty richness on the nose. Velvet as well as power. Youthful, full, tannic, very, very rich. Very ripe, with a marvellous concentration of fruit and still with bags of life. Fat and plump and beautifully balanced. Also excellent at the Oliveros tasting.

1949   Drink soon
Good full colour. No undue age. This is a wine of considerable quality, if not the size of some, which remained vigorous even after an hour or two in the glass. Medium-full, really ripe fruit: very complex. Very lovely indeed. A certain hint of astringency at the back of the palate doesn't hide a lovely, long, lingering finish. Aristocratic. Also very lovely at the Oliveros tasting.

1948   Drink soon
Very fine colour. Showing little age. This is a wine of considerable size and richness. Quite solid though. Tannic, a bit unyielding, yet plenty of depth. Rich on the finish if a little dense on the attack. Very good. In the mould of what turned out to be the 1945 but not quite as much finesse. I marked the Oliveros bottle very highly. It had a breed and a power which compensated for the density.

1947   Drink soon
(Belgian bottled by Vandemeulen) Full, dense but well-matured colour. Definitely a very old wine on the nose. Could be pre-war. The aldehydes are dominant, and there is a slight maderized, vegetal black treacle aspect. On the palate the wine is dense and rich, though there is a certain astringency. But it is more vigorous than the nose. Cooked fruit, especially plums and damsons. Full and tannic. Good acidity. Still sweet and pruny. But a shade lumpy. Not as lush as I had hoped for but plenty of interest. The 1952 is more classy. What was it like ten years ago?

1947   Drink soon
This was the very first wine of the 1987 Paris tasting and I found it excellent. I might even have given it higher marks still had it cometowards the end of the session when I had sampled all the remainder. Fine, full, mature colour. Ripe, concentrated nose. No undue age. There is a lot of rich fruit and complexity here. This is a big wine with a great deal of old-vine concentration and power. Fat, slight burnt toffee aspects.

Still vigorous. Excellent. *Grand vin*, I wrote, at the Oliveros tasting.

1945   **Drink soon**

Amazing colour. Could have been a wine of the 1960s. Chunky, solid and a little astringent on the nose. A structured wine but not unduly stewed. Full and tannic but rich and plump. Good acidity. Still vigorous again. Very fine but not great. It doesn't have the fat and richness of the 1947 or the breed of the 1949.

1934   **Drink soon**

Medium-full colour. Good, rich, velvety – silky even – nose. Rather an earthy wine but with good richness and intensity. Quite a solid example originally I would guess. But a little astringency now. Yet good fruit and plenty of enjoyment still to be had.

1929   **Over the hill**

The colour is lightening up but is still limpid. While not dry the fruit has disappeared rather, leaving a certain leanness and a dominant acidity. On the palate it is slightly more attractive. Medium bodied. A little vegetal though. Over the hill.

1928   **Can be still enjoyed**

Another light colour. Riper and gentler on the nose. Soft, a little faded but still has charm and class. An old wine but a real aristocrat. Medium body. If not exactly vigorous still very much alive. Rich, complex, real finesse. *Grand vin*, if a little past its best.

1926   **Over the hill**

Similar colour. Slightly lactic, *crème caramel* nose. This is a wine which is over the hill. Fruit is now drying up and the wine is no longer mellow but astringent, though has some sweetness still.

BEAUREGARD

Unlike most of the Pomerol châteaux, Château Beauregard is a proper gentleman's residence. Constructed in 1795 to designs by a pupil of Victor Louis, it is an elegant two-storey *chartreuse* which gives on to a wide stone balustraded terrace. This terrace is flanked by a *pavillon* (a small one-room rain-shelter surmounted by a tower) at either end, and overlooks a moat. The whole is set in a substantial park of mature trees with a view across vineyards and meadows in the direction of Figeac.

All this, however, is not the view you get from the main road. From that side, flanked by the *chais* on one side and of-fices and other dependencies on the other, the château gives a more businesslike, functional optic on life. But the private facade is rather fine.

So fine in fact that it enthused an American architect, one Mr Coffin, who had been commissioned by Mrs Daniel Guggenheim to design her country retreat at Port Washington on Long Island, to reproduce it in its entirety in 1932. In the USA the building is called Mille-Fleurs. In Pomerol, where gardeners are no doubt more scarce, the property is the residence of the Clauzel family, the erstwhile owners, though the vineyard and the wine are now the re-sponsibility of the Crédit Foncier de France.

The history of Château Beauregard can be traced back to the twelfth century and the Knights Hospitallers of St John of Jerusalem. They were active in the Pomerol area and owned a small *manoir* on the very site. On these ruins the De Beauregard family constructed a rather grander edifice five centuries later. It was this building, eventually rather dilapi-dated, which was replaced by the present-day château.

HISTORY

In the middle of the eighteenth century the property was inherited by Jérome de Chaussade de Chandos. Beauregard was not the main residence of this gentleman, who had a larger estate at Rauzan in the Entre-Deux-Mers, but his son Luc-Jermé did live there from 1755 to 1769, and it is at this period that the land was transformed from polyculture to viticulture. In 1741, according to Enjalbert, there were two *journaux* of vines at Beauregard; by the Revolution there were eighteen (6.3 hectares). Luc-Jermé Chaussade was a friend of Jacques Kanon (of what was to become Canon in Saint-Emilion), and shared his enthusiasm for the new fashion of serious vineyard husbandry. In his hands Beauregard became one of the first of the Pomerol estates to be vinously expanded.

By the time the Revolutionary Convention abolished primogeniture in 1793, Luc-Jermé had been succeeded by his son Jermé, a young man who had three sisters. Seeing his inheritance about to be quartered he put his share of Beauregard up for sale and persuaded his sisters to do likewise. It fetched 110,000 *livres* (a high price, justified only on the grounds of the reputation of the wine) on 3 July 1793, and passed into the hands of Bonaventure Berthomieux.

Despite his somewhat Italian Christian name Berthomieux was a prominent and wealthy citizen of a well-established Saint-Emilion family. He was a merchant who dealt in grain as well as wine, and he looked after his brother's estate in Fronsac as well as his own.

Prior to the Revolution he had been a member of the local appeal court and was *Trésorier de France*, a position which 'conferred nobility but for which the authorities required the security of a considerable fortune'. Yet he was a liberal. Up to the end of the Girondin phase (2 June 1793) he was a supporter of the Revolution, indeed administrator of the local Libourne district. At the time he bought Beauregard a month later he was still safe, but he subsequently fell out with Tallien, and was only saved from the guillotine by locals who were prepared to testify that in the food shortages of 1791 and 1792 he had sold his reserves of grain for two-thirds of their real value.

The end of the Terror and the fall of Robespierre in July 1794, relieved the threat to Berthomieux's life, and, with his wealth intact, he was able to set about the construction of his new château and the development of his vineyard.

If Beauregard was so obviously in respectable hands, how was it that it failed to be a serious contender to Certan and others by the time the first pecking orders of quality were being put forward some 50 years later? The answer lies in the wild schemes of Bonaventure's son or grandson, Barry-Berthomieux. This gentleman was persuaded that a fortune was to be made out of madder, which could be planted on alluvial land unsuitable for the vine. Wine prices were low in the 1820s and 1830s, and Barry-Berthomieux concentrated his energies in this direction, at the same time neglecting his vineyard.

It was a grave mistake. Following the Restoration and the end of the blockade, cochineal, imported from Mexico, dealt a mortal blow to the madder market. André de Carles-Trajet at nearby Figeac was *abandoning* madder just at the same time as Barry-Berthomieux was extending his plantations. Not only, naturally, was this a financial disaster, but, as important, the reputation of the wine fell. The journal *Le Producteur* rated Beauregard in its third class in 1841.

In 1854 Beauregard was sold to M. Durand-Desgranges. Restoration was swift. Durand-Desgranges, a local *courtier* (broker), replanted the vineyard, extended it to fourteen hectares, and by the second edition of Cocks and Féret in 1868 had raised its eminence to thirteenth place in the Pomerol hierarchy, a position, by and large, which it has enjoyed ever since.

The Durand-Desgranges family remained at Beauregard until 1920. After a brief interregnum in the hands of the brothers Chavaroche the estate was acquired by a local lawyer, M. Brulé, on behalf of his god-daughter Henriette Giraud in 1922. Henriette's father was Savinien Giraud, owner of Trotanoy, and she was wedded to Raymond Clauzel of the family which then and now owned Château La Tour-de-Mons in Soussans. Their four children remained owners of Beauregard until March 1991 when they sold the estate to the Crédit Foncier de France for 100 million francs.

The Crédit Foncier de France have long been vineyard owners in the Gironde, having been proprietors of Château Bastor-Lamontagne in the Sauternes since 1936 and Château Saint-Robert in the Graves since 1879. They also own the Château de Puligny-Montrachet. Though they own a minor estate, Château Barbe-Blanche, in Lussac Saint-Emilion, they had been on the outlook for a major Libournais domaine, one of 'classed growth' pretention.

M. and Mme Paul Clauzel, now in their sixties, have the right to remain at Château Beauregard for the rest of their lives.

THE VINEYARD AND THE WINE

The twelve productive hectares – there is the possibility of eking out one more – lie on a mixture of gravel, sand and clay soils on the south side of the Libourne to Montagne-Saint-Emilion road opposite the vineyards of Petit-Village. They are planted in the ratio 48 per cent Merlot, 44 per cent Cabernet Franc, 6 per cent Cabernet Sauvignon and 2 per cent Malbec.

Vinification takes place in stainless-steel tanks, with the concrete vats which were formally used for fermentation now solely employed for *assemblage* and *stockage*. In order to preserve the architectural harmony, the barrel cellar, unusually, was excavated below ground, underneath the *cuverie*. Today there is a second wine, Le Benjamin de Beauregard, and the wine is matured using 60 per cent new oak.

My experience of old Beauregards is not extensive, going back only as far as 1964. I have had most of the main vintages since then on several occasions. It used to be a good middle-of-the-road Pomerol; quite sturdy as a result of the high proportion of Cabernet in the blend. Sometimes a little austere, in a marginally unripe sense, as Clinet and Clos-René used to be, for the same reason. It might have lacked grace and complexity but it was a good wine. The 1964, 1966, 1970 and 1975 can be recommended, as good-but-not-great.

Things have changed since the end of the 1970s. As elsewhere, there were three major developments at this time. The first was a decision to pick the Cabernet grapes later and therefore riper; the second was an increase in the percentage of new oak; and the third was a greater emphasis on selection. This last improvement was particularly important at Beauregard. The vines, though in one piece, lie on three separate terraces. To the north, mainly planted with Merlot, the bulk of the estate lies on the clay-gravel high plateau of Pomerol, as the land declines to the south the clay diminishes, the percentage of sand increases, as does the proportion of Cabernet. It is arguable how fine any wine produced on the lower land can potentially be. Demotion to the second wine is the obvious solution.

I remember visiting Beauregard with newly appointed consultant *oenologue* Michel Rolland in 1987. We sampled the 1985 (which he had not been responsible for). It was a knock-out. Subsequent tastings of this wine have not let me to believe I overreacted. Things had obviously changed here.

At the time the property shared the same *maître de chai*, the venerable M. Zucchi, as did Vieux Château Certan, La Conseillante, and other neighbouring estates. His retirement coincided with the Crédit Foncier de France's takeover and the appointment of Vincent Priou, a qualified *oenologue*, as full-time *régisseur*, and I get the impression that from now on Michel Rolland's role will be less 'hands on' than hitherto. But I see no reason why the quality of the 1985, repeated in 1989 and 1990, should not now be the norm. The quality of Beauregard has climbed a full couple of points, from good to very good indeed as a result of following Rolland's advice. It is both more concentrated and more elegant than it used to be. The increase in the percentage of new oak – it used to be one-third – is a positive improvement. And the wine is more complex as a result of the greater selection. In style, not surprisingly as a result of the *encépagement*, it leans more towards the Certans than the more feminine Trotanoy or Lafleur-Pétrus: rich and plummy, firm and long-lasting, but with the ripe succulence of fruit underneath which is so unmistakably Pomerol.

The wine deserves greater recognition. Château Beauregard is now without hesitation one of Pomerol's (unofficial) first growths.

THE TASTING

I sampled the following wines in January 1992.

Optimum drinking

1991   **1995–1999**
Medium colour. It is early days to be evaluating this, and it has only recently been racked into wood and the *assemblage* is not really married yet. Light but with reasonable balance. They produced eight hectolitres to the hectare.

1990   **1998–2015**
Good colour. Quite firm on the nose. Good new oak. Good richness. On the palate this has concentration, style and balance. Medium-full body. Very good oaky base. Good grip. I find this very stylish and certainly a great success for a 1990. Very good.

1989   **1999–2019**
Medium-full colour. The nose is a bit hidden at present but there is plenty of depth here. This is a bigger, richer, more tannic wine compared with the 1990, but it has now gone into its shell a bit. Only on the finish do you get the great intensity properly expressed. Shows very well. Very long and complex.

1988   **1997–2010**
Medium-full colour. Fine nose. Subtle, classic. Good acidity. Elegant cassis-blackberry fruit. Medium to medium-full. The tannin is evident but ample enough on the follow-through. Balanced, stylish, fresh.

1987   **Drink soon**
Medium colour but alive. Smells a little of old tea on the nose. On the palate this is still reasonably fresh, if a bit light and one-dimensional. At its apogee. Not too short. A good result for the vintage.

1986   **Drink soon**
Not as good a colour as the 1987. This seems a little insubstantial. Not a very exciting nose. A bit loose-knit. This is rather a disappointment. It is not *that* much better than the 1987. A lack of selection. As much astringent as tannic. Lightish. Will dry out.

1985   **1995–2015**
Good fullish colour. Full, firm, rich nose. There is plenty of depth. This makes up for the failure of the 1986. Fullish, lovely, ample, rich old, viney fruit. There is a volume and an intensity here. The wine is very well balanced and very ample and rich and classy. A fine result.

1984   **Drink soon**
Reasonable colour for the vintage. No undue age. I prefer the nose of this to the 1987. Quite full, quite fresh. This isn't at all bad. There is a certain rigidity caused by somewhat inflexible tannins but no lack of fruit or grip. I find it fresher than the 1987.

1983   **Now–1999**
Good colour for the vintage. Still vigorous looking. Round attractive nose. No dilution. Good vigour and positive fruit. This is now just about ready. A medium to medium-full ripe wine with good freshness and even concentration for a 1983. Positive. Very good. Attractive. Will last well.

1982   **Now–2002**
Not an enormous colour. No richer looking than the 1983. Rich and fat on the nose but not an enormous intensity. Medium to medium-full. Round, soft, plump and ample. Velvety fruit. Good freshness. More class than the 1981 and 1983. Seductive. Ready. I prefer the 1985 though. Good.

1981   **Now–1996**
Medium to medium-full colour. Mature. This is quite evolved, especially compared with the 1983, contrary to most of the Libournais. Medium body. Fully ready. Compared with the 1983 it doesn't quite have the grip andfat, but it is a pleasant wine. It lacks a bit of class and real depth. Good though.

1980   **Drink soon**
Good colour for a 1980. Vigorous-looking too. Good fresh nose. Surprisingly so. Fresh for an 1980 of this age. Light to medium body. By no means over the hill. A fine result. It has got fruit and even complexity, and certainly breed.

VIEUX CHÂTEAU CERTAN

Vieux Château Certan, it is said, dates back to the early sixteenth century, when it was a manor house and the centre of quite a large estate dominating a little plateau, about 35 metres above sea level, two or three kilometres north-east of the old port of Libourne. If this is so, it is probably the oldest property in the area. It is certainly one of the largest in a commune where few properties produce more than a few dozen *tonneaux*. And it is also one of the best. After Pétrus itself, Vieux Château Certan can compete, if it so wishes, with L'Evangile, La Conseillante, Lafleur and Trotanoy for the title of number two in the commune of Pomerol.

It is said that the name Certan, originally spelled with an 'S', comes from the Portuguese for 'desert'. The Portuguese were in the locality in the twelfth century, looking for areas to settle, but rejected this particular site as it was too arid and dry. The soil was so poor – for anything else but vines – that its peasants were exempted from paying local taxes. Vines were certainly planted here early, and the estate was principally wine-producing – as distinct from most of its neighbours which were still multicultural – well before the French Revolution.

HISTORY

According to Enjalbert in his *Les Grands Vins de Saint-Emilion, Pomerol et Fronsac*, Vieux Château Certan was not the first of the estates to become entirely viticultural. Louis Fontémoing at Trochau was perhaps the pioneer, followed by the Girauds at Trotanoy and Catherine Conseillan at La Conseillante. In rolls dated from 1741 and 1754 the proprietors at Sertan were still at the stage of *métairies* and *bourdieux* (different forms of leasing and share-cropping) and involved in other produce as well as wine. Monoculture, under the direct control of the proprietors followed soon after, however, and Sertan rapidly established itself, becoming the leading growth in Pomerol by the end of the century.

The owners at the time were a family called Demay (or De May), a dynasty of Scottish origin, who had been landowners in the region since about 1500 and who had arrived in Pomerol at the end of the sixteenth century, the land having been granted to them by royal decree. In the late-eighteen-century maps produced by the firm of Belleyme the property is marked as Sertan and a number of neighbouring estates – Lafleur, Gaxin, Conseillante – are also recorded. The Demays were also proprietors, until 1782, of Château Nénin. This too was an active vineyard.

In 1793 Vieux Château Certan appears in the inventories of the *biens nationaux*. The *Veuve* Demay, with five children , one of whom, Pierre Demay, had emigrated, was obliged to sell part – or even all – of the domaine in order to refund the *émigré's* proportion of the estate. The property, with 16.2 hectares of vines, was valued at a very high price compared with other plots in Pomerol – 54,130 *livres*, 22 times its yearly income. It sold for double. Enjalbert is somewhat imprecise at this point. On the one hand he quotes the estimated value and the realized price of the whole estate – saying that the former for confiscated *émigré* property in general are more meaningful than the latter, owing to the inflation of government-issued *assignats*. But then he goes on to state later that only one-fifth was put up for sale and that this was bought by one of the remaining brothers and two of the sisters – and at an artificially low price; the sale being engineered to take place when only members of the family were present.

Be that as it may, the Demays were people of substance. As well as their Pomerol vineyard they had a mansion in Libourne, a farm at Tessier in the plain of Saint-Suplice and the commune of Vignonet, plus a house and another estate at Macau in the Médoc. They not only sold their own wine, but that of others, being *négociants*, in a small way, before the Revolution. It was not then, therefore, but sometime later that parts of the estate were sold off – one of them, coincidentally belonging later to a family called Giraud – and that the other two neighbouring estates with the name Certan in its title became independent estates. The area of Vieux Château Certan today is somewhat less than the figure given above.

Pomerol at this time, despite the reputation of Certan, was hardly considered an important wine-producing area. It was ignored by most of the early books on the Bordeaux region. Not until his third (1853) edition does Wilhelm Franck mention Pomerol except in passing – though he does say in a footnote in his 1845 edition that the Pomerol wines are noted for their delicacy and finesse. At the time, very few Pomerols fetched prices equal to top Saint-Emilions, and this was less even than the Médoc *bourgeois* growths, let alone the *crus*.

Nevertheless, until the time of phylloxera, Vieux Château Certan reigned supreme. The wine had been the first Pomerol to appear in the notebooks of the brothers Tastet and Lawton, earlier in the century. In the 1840s the journal *Le Producteur* placed it at the top of a list of *grands crus*. Demay protested and had his *cru* classed as a *catégorie unique*. The price it fetched was 400 to 500 francs.

In the 1853 edition of Franck, only one Pomerol estate, Château de 'Curtan', is mentioned by name. In the introduction to the 1868 edition of Cocks and Féret, mention is made of Pomerol's '*vins très renommés depuis quelques années*', indicating that it was only recently that the area as a whole began to concentrate on wine. This edition lists seventeen

Pomerol first growths: Vieux Château Certan – correctly spelt – heads the ranking, followed by Trotanoy and Pétrus, and the production is given as 20 to 30 *tonneaux*.

Meanwhile, the property had changed hands. In 1858 the Demays sold Certan to Charles de Bousquet, a Parisian, though they held on to part of the estate. One of the first growths among those mentioned above is Petit-Certan, later to be known as Certan-de-May, owned by the 'Demoiselles de May de Certan' and producing 6 to 8 *tonneaux*.

De Bousquet appears never to have lived at Certan, though he did attempt to reconstruct the château. The château, essentially a small, single-storey *chartreuse*, with a tower at each end, dates from the eighteenth century. It is an unpretentious building of great elegance, one of the few of any note in this commune. Most of the Pomerol 'châteaux' are merely farmhouses.

De Bousquet certainly had plans to enlarge or dignify Certan. He got as far as replacing one of the towers with a slightly taller example, but then apparently – perhaps because of the phylloxera outbreak – his money ran out. This gives Certan a very curious, lopsided appearance: at one end a grey slate tower two storeys high, at the other a red-tiled tower only one storey above ground level.

In 1924 Certan was sold to a Belgian, Georges Thienpont. Thienpont was a wine-merchant, and came from Etikhove, a small village near Oudenarde, halfway between Brussels and Lille. Thienpont had bought Château Troplong-Mondot in Saint-Emilion in 1921, and he continued to run his wine business from Belgium, rarely visiting Bordeaux, and staying at Troplong-Mondot when he did.

With business deteriorating in the 1930s, Thienpont found himself forced to sell one of the Bordeaux properties. It is said that he chose to sell Troplong-Mondot because he saw greater potential in Certan. I would suggest, more prosaically, that he sold Troplong-Mondot because it was larger, better-known and easier to sell, as well as fetching more money.

Georges Thienpont, who died in 1962, had six children. The eldest, Gérard, lives in Belgium and runs the family firm. The youngest, Léon, lived at Vieux Château Certan until his sad death in the summer of 1985. Léon came to manage the property in 1947, staying at first with another brother, Georges, who is a cattle farmer at Castillon, and moved into Certan, becoming the first person to live there permanently, in 1966. From the time of his arrival Léon Thienpont was responsible for the wine, and it is largely due to him that Vieux Château Certan today enjoys such a high reputation.

Léon Thienpont was a man of deceptive appearance. To be frank, he looked like a rude peasant; you would have taken him for one of the lesser estate employees rather than what he effectively was – the proprietor himself. Yet the mien was misleading. He was a man of warmth, culture and discrimination as well as having a proud and passionate conviction for his wine – and those of his neighbours: no chauvinist he.

Since his death the property has been jointly managed by his son Alexandre and his nephew Nicolas. It is Alexandre, a tall lean man in his thirties, shy but fervently determined, who lives in the château with his family and is responsible for the wine.

THE VINEYARD AND THE WINE

Vieux Château Certan lies in the heart of Pomerol, surrounded by other great names: Certan-de-May, Petit-Village, La Conseillante, L'Evangile, Pétrus. The soil is gravel, about 30 centimetres deep, and below this there is a subsoil of clay, rich in iron. There is some sand in the northern corner of the vineyard. According to Léon Thienpont, this 'plateau of Certan' enjoys a peculiar microclimate. It is, of course, prone to spring frosts – most particularly in 1956 when the whole of Pomerol as well as the Graves-Saint-Emilion was devastated (though Certan was less badly hit in 1977 than its neighbours); but on the other hand the area never gets any hail.

Vieux Château Certan has 13.6 hectares under vines, planted in the ratio of 50 per cent

Merlot, 25 per cent Cabernet Franc, 20 per cent Cabernet Sauvignon and 5 per cent Malbec, and produces about 60 *tonneaux* of wine. This *encépagement* – Cabernet Sauvignon is unusual in Pomerol – pre-dates the arrival of Georges Thienpont. The family see no reason to change it.

Alexandre Thienpont is a passionate exponent of *éclaircissage* or crop-thinning. This takes place in July, just before the *veraison*, and must be carried out with some severity – eliminating one bunch in three, even one in two to have the desired effect of concentrating the remainder.

Although a new *cuvier* and first-year *chai* were constructed in 1972, the appearance of the cellars is traditional, with terracotta floor tiles and a vaulted wooden ceiling. The fermentation takes place in eight large wooden vats, bought from the *tonnellerie* of Rémy-Martin, with two stainless-steel tanks in reserve and for use during the *égalisage*. The normal percentage of new oak has been increased by Alexandre to two-thirds, even 100 per cent in a lesser vintage like 1987. But should this threaten to over-oak the wine, Thienpont is quite prepared to decant it back into vat to await the bottling.

One curious detail is the capsule, which, unlike most clarets is not wine red or black, but shocking pink, with a gold band. This was Georges Thienpont's idea, in order to make the wine easy to pick out. The wine is matured for between 20 and 22 months and not filtered before bottling. The second wine is called La Gravette de Certan.

Because of the close Belgian connections, Vieux Château Certan's chief market is in that country, the Belgians being particular amateurs of all Pomerols. But for some time the wine could only be obtained elsewhere through Gilbey SA at Château Loudenne. Gilbeys had started buying in a small way in 1962, and were regular and increasing purchasers throughout the next few years. In 1971, Thienpont raised his price from 18,000 francs a *tonneau* to 48,000, and his Belgian brother refused to pay this price. Gilbeys bought the entire crop, and followed this up by buying all the 1972. Then came the slump, and they were unable to buy the 1973 – of which Thienpont had 100 *tonneaux*, substantially more than usual, at 18,000 francs. All this vintage was sold to Belgium, and Gilbeys later sold off their 1971 at twenty francs a bottle, and the 1972 at twelve francs. Since then the wine has been generally available again on the Bordeaux market.

Vieux Château Certan has been producing excellent wines for decades. There were splendid bottles in the 1920s, a superlative 1947, a fine 1952 and 1959, and a notable 1964. Since Alexandre Thienpont has been in charge the intensity of the wine has, if anything, increased even more. Its character, to those who know their Pomerols well, particularly Pétrus and the other properties in which the firm of J.P. Moueix is involved, is quite individual, arising, no doubt from the low proportion of Merlot and the addition of Cabernet Sauvignon into the *encépagement*. Most Pomerols have no Cabernet Sauvignon at all, and a Merlot per centage of 70 or higher practically 100 in the case of Pétrus.

This gives Vieux Château Certan a less voluptuous, more Médocian flavour; there is certainly more backbone; the wine takes longer to come round and the fruit is more blackcurrant/blackberry than plummy in flavour. Cocks and Féret speak of the '*goût de truffe si charactéristique du plateau de Certan*'. I am not too sure about the truffles, but Vieux Château Certan, the oldest estate in Pomerol, and with one of the most elegant of châteaux, produces a full, rich wine of great distinction and complexity.

THE TASTING

The majority of these wines were sampled in New Haven, Connecticut, at a tasting organized by Bob Feinn of Mount Carmel Wines and his friends in March 1993. The notes on the three pre-war wines date from 1986/87.

Optimum drinking

1990　　　　　　　　　　**2000–2020**

Fine colour. Intense to the rim. Rich, round, fat concentrated nose. Still not completely recovered from transport and bottling. Full body. Still very young and awkward, the elements not integrated. Very good ripe tannins. Good grip. Lovely fruit. Finishing slightly austerely – a cross between 1988 and 1989 – but very well. Adolescent. Improved immensely as it settled down in the glass. The fruit gained definition. The oaky underpinning settled out. Marvellous potential. Surely as good as the 1989?

1989　　　　　　　　　　**1999–2019**

Fine colour. Splendid nose. The oak more evident than in the 1990 and the whole thing much more composed and harmonious. Delicious complex, opulent, marvellously ripe, rich fruit. Fullish, marvellously velvety and harmonious. Splendid acidity. This has benefitted by the high proportion of Cabernet. Really long and multidimensional. Very fine.

1988　　　　　　　　　　**1999–2018**

Excellent colour. Deeper, firmer and more backward than the 1989. Full but austere on the nose. Doesn't have the ripeness and generosity of the 1989, but there is plenty of concentrated fruit here. It just needs time. Medium-full. Some tannin. Not as obviously oaky as the 1989. Less concentration, less warmth, more Médoc-y. But very long and classy at the end. A fine result with more personality than most in this vintage.

1987　　　　　　　　　　**Now–1997**

Surprisingly good colour. No sign of age. Fullish. Good nose. Fresh, has personality. Obviously a bit one-dimensional compared with the rest of this flight, but a good result. Medium body. Surprisingly fruity and generous, with a touch of oak. Positive finish. Excellent for the vintage. Just about ready.

1986　　　　　　　　　　**1995–2009**

Excellent colour for the vintage. Still very full and deeply purple. This is a little tough and tannic on the nose at first. Later still a bit dense but not too astringent. Medium-full. The tannins show a bit. There is just a little too much structure and not enough fruit on the attack. More fruit on the follow-through but a slight lack of fat. Yet a very good result for an 1986 Libournais though because it has balance and definition.

1985　　　　　　　　　　**1995–2012**

Fine colour for the vintage but just a little less intense than the 1986. Ripe, generous, amply plummy fruity nose. But it doesn't have the power and intensity of the 1988 to 1990 trio. Engaging, stylish. Medium to medium-full body. Ripe, perfumed fruit. Easy to drink. A very seductive wine, but two dimensions and amount of concentration rather than three. Not asserious as 1989, even 1988. The Merlot to the fore; no lack of grip but a slight lack of backbone and thrust. Very good rather than fine.

1983　　　　　　　　　　**Now–1997**

Good fullish mature colour. Ample nose. Plump and fruity. Seems fatter and more intense than the 1985. Good acidity. No weakness at all. Evolved quite fast in the glass though. Lost fat and dimension. Medium to medium-full. Still elegant and harmonious. Fruity but losing a little bit of its generosity now. Still very good but drink quite soon. 1981 and 1979 are better.

1982　　　　　　　　　　**Now–2020**

Very full colour. Just beginning to show signs of maturity. Full nose. Very rich, round, concentrated and intensely flavoured. Crammed with fruit. Full-bodied, velvety, round and smooth. Very good acidity. Very, very ripe tannins. And long and intense at the end. Very lovely. Just about ready but better still in a couple of years.

1981　　　　　　　　　　**Now–1999**

Fine colour. Fuller and more vigorous than the 1983. Mature nose, just a little less fat and a little more rustic than the 1983. Were the tannins as ripe? Good grip though. On the palate the wine is fuller, fresher, more vigorous and more exciting than the 1983. But there is a touch of the artisanal compared with the wines of today. Finishes long, sweet, attractively and vigorously. Will last well. Very good indeed – even fine.

1979　　　　　　　　　　**Now–1999**

Full, vigorous colour. Ripe nose, but without a lot of thrust or intensity or grip. Medium-full, somehow more elegant tannins than the 1981. A littleless of them. Elegant, quite rich. A little less intense. But attractive fruit. Finishing positively. Very good plus. Not as good as the 1981 but better than the 1983.

1978　　　　　　　　　　**Now–2010**

Full, vigorous colour. Good concentration on the nose here. Quite a full and originally slightly austere, even dense, wine, now soft and mellow.

Good plummy fruit. Fresh acidity. Fullish, with fine tannins and very fine fruit. Good grip. This is a most attractive wine which has much, much more to it than the 1983, 1981, 1979 trio. Very long; very good concentration. Very stylish. A super, complex, attractive 1978.

1976   Drink soon

Medium, mature colour. Spice, liquorice and leather on the nose but more life than most. An attractive 1976. Still vigorous if not exactly elegant. Fullish, aromatic, reasonable acidity. A good wine for the vintage which still has reasonable vigour.

1975   Drink soon

Good colour, now mature-looking. Good ripe, fruity nose but without any great density or concentration. Medium-full body, still a touch of tannin. Now an evolved wine, sweeter, less austere, less complex than the 1978. As it develops in the glass do I get a touch of attenuation? Good but not great.

1971   Now–1996

Fullish colour. No undue age. This is one of the best and most vigorous 1971s I've seen for ages. Lovely nose. Soft, succulent, sweet and elegant. On the palate fullish, showing just a hint of age at the end. This is a great success for a 1971. Good fruit. Quite prominent acidity keeping the wine fresh if not exactly fat or succulent. Cool, damson fruit. Still long and positive at the end. Very good plus. Drink quite soon.

1970   Now–2000 plus

Fine full colour. Very little brown. Ample, fat, succulently ripe nose. Full, expansive, seductive. Fullish on the palate. Sweet and generous. Long and lovely. Balanced, harmonious, classy and rich. This is a most attractive 1970 which still has bags of life. Very good indeed – even fine for the vintage.

1967   Drink up

Amazingly vigorous colour. Only a little brown. And still very full. A little dense and astringent perhaps on the nose. On the palate there is still a lot of enjoyment here. Fullish for the vintage. Quality and elegance. The fruit still has life. But it's just a little past its best. Eventually, inevitably, it will get astringent. But plenty of fat, structure and vigour for a Libournais of this age and vintage.

1966   Now–1999

Full, mature colour. Good nose. Old viney, quite succulent fruit. Very stylish but less voluptuous than the 1970. This is a fine example of a mature wine. A little less vigorous than the 1970 but soft, sweet, long, complex and elegant. Very good indeed, even fine for the vintage again.

1964   Now–2000 plus

Fine full colour. Still very vigorous looking. Splendid nose. Very fresh and concentrated fruit. Plummy, mulberry, but classy too. Not a bit dense or any trace of astringency. Full, very rich. Very vigorous. Great class. Excellent fruit. Beautifully balanced. Plummy-ripe lingering sweet finish. This is very fine, even for a 1964 Libournais. Bags of life.

1962   Now–1996

Excellent full colour. A more evolved nose than the 1964 and with more rustic tannins but full and ripe. Coffee grounds, a little leather, a little dryness perhaps. Smoky as it evolved. Threw off this astringency on aeration in the glass. Yet a fully mature wine which may begin to dry out quite soon. Fullish, slightly spicy. Fat, sweet. But a little denser than the 1964, not as well balanced or as complex.

1961   Now–2000 plus

Intensely dark colour but not as much so as the 1959. Browner than the 1964. Very concentrated on the nose if less rich and voluptuous than the 1959. Slightly denser perhaps. On the palate sumptuous and sweet. Fullish, quite structured but very concentrated and so not too dense on the palate. Very, very rich. Silky. Very lovely. Still bags of life.

1959   Now–2000

Marvellous colour. Very full indeed. Almost black still. Marvellous nose. Better even than the 1964, let alone the 1961. Creamy rich and old-vine concentration. Not a hard edge in view. Voluptuous and ripe and beautiful. Complex and classy too. Slightly less dense but equally concentrated as the 1961. Full, rich, ripe and tannic. A little less sweet. But perhaps even more depth of fruit and intensity here. More structure. Perhaps it will begin to dry out sooner? But in the end I prefer this to the 1961. Excellent.

1957   Drink soon

Fine colour. Very full. No sign of age. Really surprisingly mellow on the nose. No hard edges here! Fullish. On the palate a little lean, a little firm, but not ungenerous. Not astringent. The acidity shows a little, and the wine is a little inflexible and one-dimensional. But by no means a write-off. Would really be very good with food.

1955   Drink soon

Enormous colour. Now a little vegetal decay. But a voluptuous ripe wine underneath nevertheless. Fullish, round, aromatic. Sweet and classy. This bottle a touch maderized. But not a bit astringent. Generous, fat, very seductive.

1953   Now–1998

Very good, fullish mature colour. Deliciously intriguing, spicy, smoky, grilled hazelnuts and honeyed custard nose at first. Lost a little intensity after a while. Medium-full body, very classy fruit. Poised, fresh and complex. A delicious old wine. Real length and class. More sex appeal than the 1952 but less length, less depth. Fine quality. Will still keep.

1952   **Now–2000**

Fine colour. Firm, aristocratic – surprisingly elegant – refined and balanced nose. Lovely ripe fruit. Real depth and harmony. Fuller, firmer, more tannic than the 1953. Less silky, perhaps more grip and more positive on the finish. Less immediately appealing. But more class and depth. A little more structure evident. More vigour. Very fine indeed. I prefer this to the 1953.

1950   **Drink soon**

Dense black colour. Dense solid nose as so often with Libournais 1950s. Tarry. Full, sweet, very typically 1950. A little astringent. Quite a lot of unresolved tannin. Yet because there is so much fat sweet fruit – if not integrated – still enjoyable.

1949   **Drink soon**

Very good colour. No undue maturity. This is a really lovely fragrant wine on the nose. But less intense than either the 1948 or the 1947. On the palate there is a little astringency now. Medium-full. Very beautiful poise and elegance and complexity here. But, as happens to every wine eventually, now on the descent. Was brilliant. Still very long. Very enjoyable.

1948   **Now–1998**

Amazingly deep, purple, vigorous colour. Somewhat dense but very voluptuous nose. Structured but very sweet. Like a well-mannered version of the 1950. Much more harmonious and elegant of course. Fullish, a little tannin showing. But ripe and succulent nevertheless. Long and luscious. Fine quality. Still has plenty of life. But a wine for food.

1947   **Now–2000 plus**

Very good colour. Slightly less intense than the 1949. Marvellous nose. Splendidly complex. This has totally sumptuous, luscious, ripe fruit. Even in Libournais terms, this is a great 1947.

Very full, incredibly concentrated. Incredibly fresh and sweet. Absolutely fabulous! Marvellous condition! *Grand vin*!

1945   **Now–1999**

Fine colour. No undue brown. Firm, almost porty. Structured but not a bit dense. This has real, real depth concentration. Nutty, a bit leathery, grilled almonds. Slight hints of bitter chocolate and burnt toast, even truffle. On the palate a little tannic, even slightly inky, but soft, not astringent. Fullish on the follow-through, quite clean, not a bit dry. Classy, long, very elegant complex fruit. Very fine finish. Very fine quality. Will still keep.

1943   **Drink quite soon**

Very full colour. Fully mature but not undue age. Slightly dense on the nose but there is still fruit here. On the palate though, surprisingly fat and ripe. A little rustic. But the fruit is fine even if the tannins are a bit dense. This is very good and still has vigour. Would be better with food. Very good quality. Amazingly vigorous for a 1943.

1934   **Drink soon**

Fine colour, still vigorous. One bottle a bit sweeter and more vigorous on the nose than the other. Full, rich, must have been a massive wine once. Very concentrated, complex, warmly-fruity. A marvellous wine. Still very long. Still very alive.

1929   **Drink soon**

(Magnum) Enormous colour: could be a 1970, very little brown. Slightly earthy, very truffley: leather, bitter chocolate, mushrooms, liquorice, strong honey. Remarkably fresh. Real, concentrated, almost sweet fruit. Full, even a little tannin still. This is really magnificent. Held up marvellously in the glass with no hint of fade. *Grand vin*.

1926   **Drink soon**

(Magnum: recorked 1986) Medium, mature colour. No undue age. Delicate, ripe, flowery nose. Still plenty of fruit. Ethereal, fragrant, soft, sweet flavours; old roses. Good acidity, no sign of dryness. A lovely long finish still. Remarkable for a wine of this age. A real delight to drink.

CERTAN-DE-MAY

When I wrote an article on the classification of the wines of the Libournais in *The Vine* in November 1986, I placed Château Certan-de-May in the exceptional growths category, equivalent to an average mark of 16 to 17.5 out of 20. When I came to draw up this list, Certan-de-May was one of the wines which caused me much thought. Some vintages I knew well, like the 1982, were obviously superb and would indubitably place Certan-de-May in the Outstanding, that is, super-second, category. Yet other vintages had come my way so rarely that it was hard to be positive about the wine in general. This is the difficulty about many of the smaller Pomerol properties. They are simply less accessible, lower-profile than the large estates in the Médoc. The solution was to err in the classification on the side of caution; the remedy – to seek further opportunities of tasting the wine.

The occasion duly appeared. A few months later, I was asked to present a vertical tasting of Château Certan-de-May in one of Sotheby's regular series of tastings.

As described in the previous chapter, despite difficulties with the authorities at the time of the Terror, Château Certan remained in the possession of the Demay family until 1848. In this year there were further revolutions, not only in France, and once again the owner of the property decided to flee the country. Ten years later the bulk of Château Certan, which thenceforth was to be known as Vieux Château Certan, was sold to the De Bousquet family. On his return to France a few years later, Demay found himself in possession of a five-hectare rump and no château as such. He decided to stay on, however, and buildings opposite the old Certan château were converted into living and wine-making premises. He died soon after, and in 1868 we find the estate listed as 'Petit Certan', owned by the Demoiselles de May de Certan, as they styled themselves, listed tenth in the second edition of Cocks and Féret and producing 6 to 8 *tonneaux* of wine.

HISTORY

I have often wondered how the property known today as Certan-Giraud came into being and had assumed that either it had started its separate existence at the time of the first Revolution or, if not, after that of 1848. Further enquiry into the records available to me shows this not to be the case. There is no mention of this particular Certan before the 1890s.

In the 1893 Cocks and Féret, this property finally makes its first appearance, owned by one Talazac Jeune (a Talazat [sic] had owned vineyards elsewhere in Pomerol in previous editions). At the same time, the *rendement* at Vieux Château Certan, as declared in Cocks and Féret, declined from 25 *tonneaux* to fifteen. Are we to assume that, perhaps as a result of financial pressures following inheritance problems, it was decided to break off a portion of the larger estate? It is a pity that the Demay ladies were not able to take advantage of this opportunity to enlarge their own estate.

Certan-de-May remained the property of the Demay sisters until the 1920s when, following the death of the last of the line, the domaine was acquired by a M. André Badar. He was to be responsible for the wine until 1953. His daughter Odette married Jean-Pierre Barreau. Barreau died after a long illness in 1971 and the property is now owned by his widow and run by their son Jean-Luc, a graduate of the Viticultural School at Château La Tour-Blanche in the Sauternes.

RENAISSANCE

Château Certan-de-May, despite its size, has always been one of the top growths of Pomerol, listed consistently in about sixth place by Cocks and Féret in consecutive editions between the First World War and 1949. My first experience of the wine was a superb 1947, drunk in the mid-1960s, and other authorities such as Edmund Penning-Rowsell, who has longer experience of fine Bordeaux than most of us, attest to splendid wines in the postwar decade. Then, as he says, the property seemed to enter a period of obscurity. The reason was the poor health of Jean-Pierre Barreau and the fact that between 1967 and 1974 the estate was farmed by Ginestet, owners of neighbouring Château Petit-Village. Like this property since Bruno Prats took up the reins, Certan-de-May has come into its own in the last twenty years.

Jean-Luc Barreau-Badar took charge of Certan-de-May in 1975 and from this date the progress has been astonishing. The cellars were renovated in 1976, stainless-steel fermentation vats being installed, and since then the proportion of new oak has been gradually increased from a quarter to 50 per cent. The château itself was redecorated inside and out in 1979.

THE VINEYARD AND THE WINE

Certan-de-May occupies five hectares of prime land entirely situated on the south-eastern part of the gravel and clay plateau of Pomerol where the best growths are found. The vineyard lies partly behind the château that is, on the west side of the road which leads up towards Pétrus – and partly on the opposite side next to that of Vieux Château Certan. It is planted in the ratio 65 per cent Merlot, 25 per cent Cabernet Franc and 10 per cent Cabernet Sauvignon and Malbec. Production averages twenty *tonneaux* (2,000 cases).

Certan-de-May itself is given a very long maceration – as much as a month in some vintages – and is kept about two years in cask before bottling. The wine is not filtered. The result is a wine of quite substantial size and power; rich, solid and opulent. Compared with its neighbour Vieux Château Certan, it is less Médocian, with less of a Cabernet Sauvignon austerity in its youth. Yet it is a bigger wine than both La Conseillante and L'Evangile, even than Trotanoy, though Trotanoy is perhaps more silky. Of all its neighbours, it reminds me most of Château Lafleur or even of Pétrus itself.

As the Sotheby tasting amply demonstrated, Certan-de-May today produces excellent wine, the equal of every one of the best properties in the commune. If I were to revise my Libournais classification today on the basis of the wines produced by Jean-Luc, I would unhesitatingly place Certan-de-May in the outstanding category.

THE TASTING

The following wines were sampled at a Sotheby's wine evening (the two older wines later over dinner) in December 1986. The wines had been provided by Farr Vintners, who are one of Certan-de-May's major customers (as indeed they are of many Pomerols) in the UK.

Optimum drinking

1985   **1996–2010**

Production: 190 hectolitres. This wine had been brought over on the day by Jean-Luc Barreau-Badar. Good colour. Firm, rich, concentrated new oak nose. A full, fat, very ripe tannic wine. On the attack, probably because of its recent journey, the wine seemed to lack a bit of zip but there was plenty of grip on the follow-through and the finish. Very fine. Lovely concentrated fruit. Full, solid but not sturdy. Certainly one of the stars of the vintage.

1983   **Now–2005**

Production: 160 hectolitres. Medium-full colour. Very fine blackberry-blackcurrant nose. Full, rich and stylish. Full-bodied, quite a lot of tannin; very good fruit. Fine but lacks just a little concentration and zip for greatness. Very elegant though and with a good long finish.

1982   **1997–2027**

Production: 240 hectolitres. Very fine immature colour, almost black. A very powerful, backward, concentrated wine; big and tannic. Fat, rich, firm and solid; real depth. A wine of massive, stupendous quality, very much in its infancy. Quite splendid!

1981   **Now–1997**

Production: 175 hectolitres. Good, full, immature colour. Soft, stylish nose; blackberry, a touch of spice, leather, liquorice and cooked plums. On the palate, there is a slight lack of acidity so it gets a bit dry on the finish. Fullish. Good fruit but lacks a bit of grip and warmth on the aftertaste. Good to very good. But will it get astringent?

1980   **Now–2002**

Production: 90 hectolitres. Very fine colour for a 1980. Indeed bigger and less developed than the above. Full, fresh nose, accessible but no age. Very good fruit. Very full and tannic for the vintage: a Pauillac among Pomerols. Rich, oaky and concentrated. Startlingly good for the vintage. Real quality, even better than the 1981.

1979   **Now–2005**

Production: 160 hectolitres. Very good colour, little sign of maturity. A good, very slightly minty nose, fresh and quite high-toned. Quite full, still tannic; rich blackcurrant and blackberry flavour. Balanced, warm, long, stylish. Quite concentrated. Very good indeed.

1978   **Now–2005**

Production: 210 hectolitres. Two different bottles: essentially the same wine but though from the same case, one was a lot more evolved than the other in appearance and on the nose, though not on the palate. Big colour, in the case of the first bottle rather browner than the 1979. Full, fat, concentrated and rich. Meaty and voluptuous. A very stylish wine with a lot of charm. More grip on the palate than the nose of the more evolved bottle had suggested. Again, very good indeed.

1977   **Drink soon**

Production: 70 hectolitres. Very good colour. Very full for the vintage, mature but no age. Fine, elegant nose. A slight coolness but no austerity. Fresh, fruity, still vigorous, plenty of substance. Surprisingly ripe and elegant. Excellent result for the vintage. Holding up well.

1976   **Drink soon**

Production: 185 hectolitres. Good mature colour. Slightly overblown 1976 nose but good fruit and freshness if not much complexity. Ripe, medium-full. Good for the vintage, especially for a Libournais, if without a great deal of style.

1975   **Now–1997**

Production: 115 hectolitres. Fullish colour, some maturity. The nose is now beginning to evolve but the wine, nevertheless, is still a bit dumb and dense, lacking a bit of flexibility. Fullish, some tannin. Good fat fruit but lacks a bit of dimension. Finishes better than it starts – really quite warm and rich. Good but not great.

1966   **Drink soon**

Good colour. Fresh nose, rich, elegant and with the very typical noticeable acidity many 1966s now present. Quite a big, meaty wine, obviously also the product of a long *avaison*. Good fruit and high class despite a certain rustic element you don't find in the vintages today. Very good.

1953   **Drink up**

Good colour. The instant the wine was poured out it was delicious. Complex, sweet, fragrant, very classy; but it fell apart very rapidly.

CLINET

Of all the Pomerol domaines the one which has shown the greatest improvement in recent years has been Château Clinet. For many years this was just another run-of-the-mill estate, producing rather hard, charmless, fruitless wine. Only occasionally, back in vintages such as 1947, 1950, 1955, 1959 and 1964 – and one felt more by luck than judgement – did it manage to make anything better than dull and ordinary: 'quite good plus' at best. And in the 1970s it even seemed to be declining further.

But then there was a change of generation. Jean-Michel Arcaute, proprietor of Château Jonqueyres in the Entre-Deux-Mers, married Georges Audy's daughter in 1979 (Audy, himself a *négociant*, had inherited Clinet from his mother in the 1950s), and Arcaute gradually began to make his influence felt. In 1985, helped by his good friend, oenologist Michel Rolland, a number of important changes were made, both in the vineyard and in the cellar. Since then, triumphantly in 1989 and 1990, the quality has been transformed. The wine can now be described as 'very good indeed': rich, concentrated, opulent and full of finesse. In July 1991 the bulk of the equity of Château Clinet was transferred to the GAN Assurance group, but Arcaute continues as administrator and wine-maker, the public face of the revived Château Clinet. It just shows what you can do when you try.

HISTORY

The Clinet vineyards lie in the main central plateau of Pomerol, that part which surrounds the church and reaches up to Gazin and Pétrus on one side and down towards Trotanoy on the other. In the 1830s, according to *Le Producteur*, Clinet belonged to the Arnauds of Pétrus, and sold for the same price: 300 francs a *tonneau*. This placed the wine among the top half-dozen in the commune, in the next tier below Certan, which fetched 400 to 500 francs. Château Belair, the top wine of Saint-Emilion, could command 750 francs. But this was barely half of a lowly fifth growth Médoc. The Libournais wines were sadly unfashionable in those days.

In the 1860s Clinet passed into the hands of the Constant family. There was an A. Constant, later succeeded by his son Ernest, at Lafleur-Pétrus. Hyppolyte Constant owned a further three hectares in the vicinity, while at Clinet the proprietor is given as Constant Père and produced ten *tonneaux*. After briefly passing through the hands of a man called Barrat, a local lawyer called Guibert bought the estate in 1879 when it produced 25 *tonneaux* from ten hectares planted half with Cabernet Sauvignon, plus Cabernet Franc, Merlot and Malbec. The implication is that this purchase included the Hyppolyte Constant morsel or that it was absorbed into Lafleur-Pétrus itself. Guibert was soon replaced by a Monsieur P. Rideaux, and Rideaux, in the first decade of this century, by Monsieur J.P. Lugnot. It was Lugnot's daughter who married the father of Georges Audy.

THE CHÂTEAU AND THE ESTATE

The château of Clinet, a two-storey *maison bourgeoise* dating from the last half of the 1800s — and without the two incongruous towers at the end which you will see on the label of the wine (this was the artist's *jeu d'esprit*) — lies next to the church on the northern side, adjacent to Château L'Eglise-Clinet. Behind it is the *chai*.

The vineyard — there are seven productive hectares, planted in the ratio 75 per cent Merlot, 15 per cent Cabernet Sauvignon and 10 per cent Cabernet Franc — consists of three parcels. Les Grandes Vignes is on very gravelly soil and lies next to the church. Les Argilles, as the name implies, contains more clay, and runs down behind the outbuildings where the wine is made. Next to L'Eglise-Clinet you will find Le Plateau. The gravel here is finer than at Les Grandes Vignes.

CHANGES IN WINE-MAKING

Neglected in the 1960s and 1970s because Georges Audy was concentrating on his *négociant* business, and largely consisting of young vines, planted following the 1956 frost, Clinet probably reached its nadir in 1979. The estate manager was ill, the harvesters were not recruited in time, and the vines were picked far too late.

Nevertheless, one of the main explanations for the solidity and lack of rich concentration of Clinet was the influence of unripe Cabernet Sauvignon in the blend. There was rather more then — 25 per cent — than there is now, and the tendency once the harvest had begun was to get it over with and avoid the risk of rain. Cabernet Sauvignon can work in Pomerol — you only have to cite Vieux Château Certan — but patience is needed because it arrives at full maturity a good ten days after the rest of the fruit. Arcaute, the new boy (and he was only 32 at the time), had to move tactfully to impose the correct picking schedule on his father-in-law's team. He was allowed a freer hand at La Croix de Casse, another Audy Pomerol property lying on more sandy soil between Libourne and Figeac, but it took time for him to establish himself at Clinet.

Progressively from 1985 onwards the new Arcaute/Rolland regime was implemented. The picking machine which had been in operation since 1982 was abandoned, and the grapes were now harvested by hand, later than hitherto, and into shallow plastic trays rather than larger wicker boxes wherein the fruit at the bottom would be crushed before arrival at the winery. A *table de triage* to sort through the fruit was installed. A second wine, firstly Domaine du Casse, later called Fleur du Clinet, was introduced. The vatting time was extended, up to six weeks where appropriate, and the amount of new wood increased. Today the *grand vin* is matured entirely in new wood.

In the 1970s Clinet was transfered back into the fermentation tanks, epoxy-resin-lined concrete, after only a few months in oak and bottled after thirteen months. Georges Audy believed that otherwise the wine would dry out. Today the bottling does not take place until 24 months after the vintage. One Audy process, though, has been retained: the wine is neither fined nor filtered.

But it all begins in the vineyard. Like so many, Arcaute believes that the quality of the original fruit is paramount. As well as ensuring maximum concentration by severe pruning and green-harvesting in July, he is a firm believer in *effeuillage* (leaf stripping). Train the vines quite high to produce plenty of foliage, and hence nourishment for the vines, but expose the fruit to the full glare of the sun by eliminating all the sheltering leaves four to six weeks before the harvest. It also helps to reduce the possibility of rot by aiding the flow of air through the vineyard.

THE WINE

The change in the quality of Clinet has been remarkable. The first five vintages of the 1980s (there is no 1984) are one-dimensional, herbaceous and decidedly uninspiring. The 1986 shows a distinct improvement – and this was overall only an average vintage in the Libournais, though rather better in Pomerol than in Saint-Emilion. The 1987 is positive and stylish, more so than most. And the 1988, though a little firm at present, has good fruit and definition.

But it is when we come to the 1989 and the 1990 that we see the potential of Château Clinet fully and excitingly realized. My notes are below. They speak for themselves. In the current (1991) edition of Cocks and Féret, Clinet is listed seventeenth in the commune. Today it would certainly place itself among the first dozen.

THE TASTING

Jean-Michel Arcaute and I co-presented a tasting of his wines to the customers of Nickolls and Perks and the Stourbridge Wine Society, West Midlands, in March 1992.

Optimum Drinking

1991   Now–1998
Good colour. Fresh nose. Ripe, soft, not a great deal of structure but reasonable style and length. Forward but pleasant.

1990   1997–2010
Very good colour. Full, rich, meaty nose. Good new oak. (100 per cent new here). This is substantial, ripe, fleshy and balanced. Very good fruit and fine ripe tannins. Not too rigid. Potentially lush. Very good indeed.

1989   1997–2015
Very good colour. Ripe, new oaky nose with just a hint of mint. Seems more firm and closed than 1990. More concentrated and has better definition and grip. Very good indeed. Very elegant. Finishes long and complex and persistent.

1988   1997–2010
Good colour. Ripe, stylish, fresh raspberry-plummy nose. Good definition. Medium body. A little tough and hard in the middle. The tannins just a little bony. But the finish is fatter and riper. Lacks a little elegance and complexity after the 1989 but good plus for the vintage.

1987   **Drink soon**
Reasonable colour. Fresh nose. Quite fruity and positive. A little one-dimensional and a touch astringent. But reasonable fruit and balance. Nice for drinking now. Finishes well.

1986   1995–2003
Good colour. Fresher and as full as the 1985. Good nose. Not too rigid. A little more so on the palate. The tannins show, but there is concentration and grip here, style and depth. The

finish is riper and longer and more positive. Very good for a Libournais of this vintage.

1985   **1995–2003**
Good colour. Just a slight hint of brown. A rather sturdier, more herbaceous, old-fashioned nose. Better on the palate, but there is a slight inkiness nevertheless. Medium to medium-full. Ripe but it lacks a little style and charm. Not bad to quite good.

1984   **Drink up**
(Bottled as Domaine du Casse) Medium colour. No undue brown. Quite fresh nose. Essentially Cabernet. Just a little astringent and attenuated. More so on the palate.

1983   **Now–1996**
Medium colour. Mature. A little charmless on the nose. Uninspiring and coarse and hints of old tea developing as it evolved. Medium body. Ripe and quite fresh at the end but essentially one-dimensional. Not bad at best.

1982   **Drink soon**
Medium colour. Just about mature. The nose is a bit weak, and for a 1982 this is not at all exciting. It lacks acidity and finesse. And it even tastes as if it has seen better days. Short. Weak. Lacks class.

1981   **Drink soon**
Medium colour. Rather a weak, attenuated nose. Disappointing. Yet this is better for the vintage than the 1982. Medium body. Chocolate drops. Reasonable grip. A bit one-dimensional but not bad.

1980   **Drink soon**
Lightish mature colour. This isn't too bad. Fresh and quite positive. Well, at least more so than I would have expected after the 1982. Ripe, not too short. Some elegance even.

1979   **Drink soon**
Medium colour. Mature. This is rather attenuated on the nose and now a bit weak and astringent on the palate. Medium body. Simple fruit but hollow in the middle. Unexciting.

1978   **Now–1996**
Good colour. Much better nose than the 1979. A little of the usual evidence of not-absolutely-ripe Cabernet. Medium to medium-full. No enormous elegance but has substance and grip. Now soft and with pleasant slightly elderberry-flavoured fruit. Reasonable finish. Quite good.

1976   **Now–1996**
Reasonable colour. No undue age. Intriguing nose. A little sweaty/aromatic, but in quite a pleasant sense. Like the body odour of someone you love. Medium body. Reasonable grip and finish. Has interest and complexity even. Quite good plus for the vintage.

1975   **Now–1997**
Good mature colour. Slightly hard on the nose, but not too astringent, and it certainly has some concentration. Medium to medium-full. Fresh; quite lush and stylish. Lacks a bit of real class but has reasonable length. Quite good plus again.

1970   **Now–1999**
Good colour. Mature. Full nose. Slightly rigid and sweaty on the palate, though the fruit is fresh, ripe, even sweet, and quite complex. This now goes down very silkily. It is not exactly very elegantly put together but it is long and has a lot of charm. Will still keep well. Good plus to very good.

1964   **Now–1997**
Very good colour. Still vigorous-looking. As with all these older Clinets, more rigid on the nose than on the palate. A little lean now, but many Libournais are now lightening up. Still stylish and soft. Long, ripe, concentrated and elegant. Very good for the vintage.

1947   **Now–1997**
Very fine colour. The nose once again is a little ungenerous, but on the palate the wine is very impressive. Youthful, concentrated, fat, chocolatey. This is in very good condition. Not as lush or as sweet-sour as some 1947s. Still bags of life.

La
Conseillante

One of the most elegant labels among all the top growths in the Gironde area is that produced by Château La Conseillante in Pomerol. The label is white with a fancy silver shield and a broad silver border. The capsule is a rich blue-purple which will stand out in every bin. Moreover, what is in the bottle is, after Pétrus, one of the best wines in the commune.

The female councillor in the title, La Conseillante, was Catherine Conseillan, a *dame de fer*, a lady who had a business dealing in metals in Libourne in the middle third of the eighteenth century. By this I assume that the firm was neither involved in smelting the ore, which would have been unlikely in Libourne at the time, nor was she exactly a blacksmith, but that Mme Conseillan's business was somewhere between the two. Perhaps it was because she wholesaled ploughshares and wire on which vines could be trained that this lady had the idea of developing a section of land on the Pomerol-Saint-Emilion border between 1735 and 1776. She was certainly one of the pioneers of vineyard exploitation in the area. In 1756 a wine called La Conseillante was baptised. It has been one of the leading Pomerol *crus* ever since.

Originally, the vineyard was farmed on a *métayage* basis, a form of share-cropping, but after 1756 Mme Conseillan took personal charge and the vineyard was then further expanded along with those of several neighbours. On the map of the engineer and geographer de Belleyme, drafted between 1763 and 1770, the heartland of the Pomerol *vignoble*, that which runs from Gazin to Petit-Village in one direction and from the Saint-Emilion border to Trotanoy in another, can clearly be seen.

HISTORY

Madame Conseillan and her successors, if any (there is no record of either husband or children), disappear from view in the late eighteenth century, and the next records relate to a family called Leperche-Princeteau, proprietors in the 1840s. One of these was a painter and teacher in Libourne and the family was related to the Toulouse-Lautrecs in Albi.In the first edition of Charles Cocks's *Bordeaux et Ses Vins* in 1850, there is no specific mention of the top Pomerol wines though Saint-Emilions and Fronsacs are listed in some detail. The Princeteaus owned a number of top Fronsacs including de Revers and part of Château Canon itself, as well as Châteaux Gaby, Pey-Labrie and Lavalade. A solitary Conseillan (*sic*) is listed *à Lacoste* in the Côtes de Fronsac, producing 25 *tonneaux*. By the next edition this survivor, if that was what he was, is no more.

Pomerols make their first detailed appearance in the 1868 edition of Cocks, now by Edouard Féret. Château La Conseillante is listed seventh, producing 15 to 20 *tonneaux*. Shortly afterwards, in 1871, the property was purchased by Louis Nicolas. The estate has been passed down successive generations of the Nicolas family ever since. The constitution of the vineyard, then as now twelve to thirteen hectares, was one-third Merlot, one-third Malbec and one-third Cabernet (half Sauvignon, half Franc).

The wine soon became established as one of Pomerol's top châteaux. According to Féret's *Saint-Emilion et Ses Vins* (1893), it fetched 2,400 to 2,500 francs per *tonneau en primeur*. If this is indeed true, it is certainly a high price. In most of the good vintages of the 1870s and 1880s (not that there were many in the latter decade), the Médoc *premiers crus* sold for 4,000 francs a *tonneau* and the better seconds and thirds made between 2,000 and 2,500 francs, often a great deal less. As Pomerols were hardly fashionable at the time, I would regard this inflated La Conseillante figure as a bit of a hyperbole.

Louis Nicolas senior died in 1880 and there were then three further generations, all also called Louis, the first of whom was to be the founder and first President of the Syndicat Viticole de Pomerol in 1900. There is an interesting account of the measures taken against the phylloxera devastation on the Conseillante vineyard in the 1898 English edition of Cocks and Féret: 'The vineyard . . . is particularly remarkable for the age of its vines. It was first invaded by the phylloxera in 1875, since which time the proprietor has devoted himself to the preservation of the old vine plants which alone are capable of imparting to the wine that high quality which has made its reputation. Careful applications of carbonic sulphur, continually effected since 1878, combined with a triennial system of manuring, have completely attained this object. The vines are . . . healthy and vigorous.' Obviously, there was no thought of planting grafted vines at this stage and this paragraph is repeated in all editions up to and including that of 1922. Do we assume that American rootstocks did not arrive at Conseillante until after the First World War?

Currently, the property is jointly managed by Bernard Nicolas, an insurance agent and formerly deputy mayor of Libourne, and his brother Francis, a retired doctor of medicine. Neither live at Conseillante except during the vintage time.

THE VINEYARD

Conseillante lies at the extreme eastern end of Pomerol just by the crossroads where one turns off the D21 to go down to Cheval-Blanc, and is bounded by Petit-Village, Vieux Château Certan, Pétrus and L'Evangile on the Pomerol side and by Cheval-Blanc itself across the road and the commune boundary. Part of the vineyard, indeed, is in Saint-Emilion. The vineyard is in one piece and has remained the same size, roughly twelve hectares, since the Nicolas purchase. It now produces 40 to 45 *tonneaux* from equal proportions of Merlot and Cabernet Franc and 10 per cent Malbec.

The land here is some 35 metres above sea level, a plateau of gravel, clay and sand, which rises marginally to the north towards Pétrus and descends in the opposite direction towards the Dordogne and the outskirts of Libourne.

THE CHÂTEAU AND THE *CHAIS*

The château itself is a simple two-storey *maison girondine* with a tiled roof, and dates from the 1750s. One assumes it was constructed when Catherine Conseillan decided to take over the property herself. It lies just off the main road, sheltered by a number of trees. Some 100 metres or so into the vineyard are the *chais*, extensively renovated during the 1970s.

When Bernard Nicolas took charge of the property in 1971, he was quick to engage the services of Professor Emile Peynaud as consultant. Peynaud suggested that the old wooden fermentation vats should be replaced and recommended the installation of stainless steel. La Conseillante was the first in this field in Pomerol and at the time the *cuvier* was entirely re-built. Subsequently the *chai* was reconstructed and a *salle de reception* added on.

The wine-making, however, has remained traditional. The wine undergoes a long maceration with the skins, is matured in oak barrels, half of which are renewed each year, and kept 20 to 24 months before bottling. It is neither filtered nor, even when it undergoes periodic racking, ever pumped. Movement from one receptacle to another is by gravity.

THE WINE

The current edition of Cocks and Féret places the wine of La Conseillante in fifth position in Pomerol after Pétrus, L'Evangile, Trotanoy and Vieux Certan and therefore rates it superior to Lafleur, L'Eglise-Clinet, Petit-Village and Certan-de-May. In the 1969 edition, Cocks and Féret rated it third. Whether this is a reflection of the rise of these other estates Trotanoy and Vieux Certan are those which have overtaken it − or a fall in the quality of La Conseillante, I do not know. Though Edmund Penning-Rowsell 'has not found it outstanding in recent years', I have always found it up to par and would certainly include it among Pomerol's many super-seconds. The wine resembles Lafleur-Pétrus rather than Lafleur or Pétrus itself in that it is elegant rather than densely structured, perfumed and accessible rather than firm and unforthcoming, delicately rich and refined rather than voluptuously solid. This, I would suggest, is a result of the gravel and sand elements in the soil. What I find exciting about a good Conseillante is its complexity, the depth and concentration of its fruit; above all, its breed. Though it seems to mature faster than some of its more muscular neighbours, the wine is normally impeccably balanced and therefore will certainly keep. As the Conseillante motto has it: '*Faire peu mais faire bon*' ('Make little, but make it good'). It deserves its high reputation.

THE TASTING

The following is an amalgam of two main tastings: one at the Studley Priory Wine Weekend in December 1986, the other in London in 1990. I have added a couple of other notes to complete the range. Dr Nicolas says that both he and his wine consultant, the celebrated Pascal Ribereau-Gayon, consider 1989 better than 1985 and the 1985 better than the 1982: the best since 1947.

	Optimum drinking
1987	**Drink soon**

This has a lot of merit. Round, ripe, chocolatey flavour. Not weak. More velvety than most. Even has concentration. Fine within the context of 1987.

1986   **Now–2003**

Medium to medium-full colour. Good nose, elegant, blackcurrant. No lack of depth. This is ripe, gently oaky, concentrated and stylish. A wine with a smile on its face. Medium body. A little tannin. A good success for Pomerol.

1985   **1995–2020**

Fullish colour. Full and concentrated and ripe on the nose but a little more spicy and certainly more adolescent, than the 1986. Full and rich on the palate, a lot of depth here, and, above all, style. This is very fine indeed. A real volume of flavour yet without being a blockbuster. Very ample and plump.

1984   **Drink soon**

Good colour. A success for this vintage. Has fruit and balance, charm and even complexity. Rich for a 1984, and not short.

1983   **Now–1998**

Good colour. New oak, complex, sandalwoody nose. An elegant, ripe, almost opulent wine which is now beginning to open up. Medium to medium-full body. Mulberry flavours. Finishes well. Very good.

1982   **Now–2008**

Fine colour. Good fat, quite spicy nose. Rich, ample and concentrated but not as fine or as concentrated as the 1985. The acidity level is a little lower. Fullish. This is approaching its apogée. Rich, fat and voluptuous. Very good but the 1985 is finer. It has more elegance. This is long. But the 1985 is longer.

1981   **Now–2000**

Good colour. Soft but rich, quite concentrated. Very stylish nose. Medium body, a little tannin. Positive, accessible, balanced, fresh and ripe. Lovely finish. Very good indeed for the vintage.

1979   **Now–1996**

Good colour. Not a wine of great richness or concentration on the nose, but there is elegance. Medium body. Good fresh acidity if an absence of real intensity. Quite long. Good to very good.

1978   **Now–2005**

Very good colour, no sign of development. Fatter, richer, more concentrated nose. Plenty of depth and complexity. Medium-full, some tannin. Still a shade on the austere side, needing to 'warm up' as well as round off. Very fine certainly but not, as yet, very seductive.

1975   **Now–2008**

I have always considered this one of the best Libournais wines of this vintage. Good colour. Rich, full, plump nose. Complex and concentrated on the palate without the hardness or astringency of the vintage. Fullish and vigorous. Very classy indeed.

1971   **Drink soon**

Good colour, mature, no undue age. Broad, ripe, very stylish and complex nose. Good fruit, good balance, soft and full of nuance. This is a high-class wine! Rich, ripe, quite full, still vigorous. Must be one of the best of the vintage. Now this *is* seductive – in a cerebral way.

1970   **Now–1998 (see note)**

Very good colour. Having always considered La Conseillante 1970 one of the great stars of the vintage, I was disappointed to find this particular bottle a little stewed. Rather dense and chunky and with an element of H2S on the nose. Full and rich nevertheless. Last time I drank this it was magnificent.

1967   **Drink soon**

Good mature colour, no undue age. Merlot nose and flavour, now beginning to lighten up a little. Round, soft and plump. Charming and fruity. Still reasonably fresh and vigorous. Very elegant. Very good for the vintage.

1966   **Now–1996**

Good, full, mature colour. Plummy, rich and vigorous on both nose and palate. A full, fat, concentrated wine, still youthful. Just what I expected the 1970 to be. Real complexity and depth. Excellent. Evolved quite fast in the glass.

1964   **Drink soon**

This bottle, in fact, was served up at a separate occasion alongside a 1964 Evangile – and was distinctly superior to it. Ample, elegant, complex. Absolutely no sign of undue age. Got better and better in the glass. A really lovely wine. Since then, at a 1964 Pomerol and Saint-Emilion comparison, another bottle was less vigorous, less exciting.

1962   **Drink up**

This is getting towards the end of its useful life. The nose is soft but lightening up, and the elegance is beginning to disappear. Yet still fragrant. I don't think it was ever a really exciting wine, but it was certainly competent.

1961   **Drink soon**

Very fine, mature colour. Really rich and fat on the nose; the typical, almost porty, fruit you get in many 1961s. One bottle had a bit more grip than the other. Full, rich and complex on the palate. But even the most vigorous developed quickly in the glass. Very fine but in 1961 terms not quite in the top flight.

1959   **Drink soon**

(Belgian bottled by Van den Howe) Fine colour. Very full, mature. Fine, elegant nose. Fragrant and rich. On the palate it is full, slightly astringent and solid. Bottled a bit late? The nose is the best part. But still a nice, ripe, complex wine if a bit older than it should be.

1955   **Drink soon**

Very good colour. A good, blackcurranty, almost summer pudding nose. Fully mature but no undue age. Rich, round, very full and fat for a 1955. Fine, complex fruit, very well balanced. Good long finish. Excellent for the vintage. Still vigorous.

1953   Drink soon

Good fullish colour. Not a lot of maturity. Tar, liquorice, leather nose. Firm and full. Strong and vigorous. Hot and roasted. Some alcohol. Full, rich, some tannin, even slightly dense. Sweet, even slightly spicy. Ripe prunes. Long, rich finish. Quite a big wine for the vintage and for La Conseillante. Still vigorous. Very good if without great finesse.

1947   Drink soon

(Belgian bottled by Vandemeulen) Fine, full colour. Fat, solid, really creamy fruit on the nose. Full, solid, old-fashioned wine-making. An element of roasted caramelized spice. A touch of astringency on the finish. Overwhelming fruit. Very fine if a touch chunky, even robust.

1945   Drink up

(English bottled by Harvey's of Bristol) Good colour, not a lot of brown. The nose shows some age, and has dried out, but underneath it is fine, complex and very classy. Fat and rich, though it does now show a bit of age on the palate. Plenty of plummy class and depth. Sweetly round and ripe. Good finish, no astringency. Creamy old-vine taste. Very fine indeed. Lovely, but now a bit past it.

L'EGLISE-CLINET

For a number of years now, a quiet revolution has been taking place in Pomerol. That the standard of quality has improved in the 1980s is not just due to a succession of very good vintages; nor is it merely that the vines, largely replaced after the 1956 frosts, are now of a respectable age. It is because there is a new generation of working proprietors, a breed who combine expertise and dedication, who are prepared to make noble and unselfish sacrifices in order to maximise the standard of their wines. In previous chapters I have written about the effect Alexandre Thienpont has had at Vieux Château Certan, and the improvements Jean-Luc Barreau-Badar has brought to Certan-de-May's impressively high performance, to cite but two. I now turn to Château L'Eglise-Clinet, rated already as high as seventh in the commune in the 1982 edition of Cocks and Féret, and performing better than ever. The impetus behind this rising star is the 37-year-old Denis Durantou.

A few hundred metres to the north of the present-day church of Saint-Jean, in what passes for the village of Pomerol, there used to be another church, built by the Knights Templars in the twelfth century. This Romanesque edifice has long since fallen into ruins, and was finally demolished at the end of the nineteenth century and its stone pillaged to assist in the construction of more recent buildings. There is nothing left but the odd ivy-covered hump, or the brief unnaturally thick divisional wall between one vineyard and another.

It was this church, not Saint-Jean, which gave rise to various ecclesiastical-sounding Pomerol domaines: Clos L'Eglise, Domaine de L'Eglise, and L'Eglise-Clinet. The word Clinet may have its origin in the old French verb *cliner* (to incline), or indeed may be eponymous. It was certainly a *lieu-dit* for this particular part of the Pomerol *vignoble*, and remains in the title of a number of estates.

HISTORY

Delving back into the earliest editions of Cocks and Féret, we find a property called Clinet, owned by a M. Constant, and a neighbouring domaine called Clos L'Eglise owned by M. Rouchut-Frérot. Both families were well established. The Constants were also connected with Lafleur-Pétrus. The Rouchut family owned a number of estates in the area including what is now Château Plince and were in other ways influential members of the local community. One was a lawyer, another a surveyor, a third an *'agent d'affaires'*, a wonderfully vague French term meaning simply a man of business.

It seems likely that a son of M. Rouchut-Frérot, Mauleon Rouchut, married a Mlle Constant. In 1882 both domaines were divided, and an eight hectare property known as Clos L'Eglise-Clinet came into existence. It is only since the 1950s that it has been titled Château L'Eglise-Clinet. While Château Clinet has changed hands several times in the last 100 years, and is now owned by Georges Audy, Plince, Clos L'Eglise and L'Eglise-Clinet have remained in the hands of descendants of the original Rouchuts. Plince and Clos L'Eglise's owners are the Moreau family, L'Eglise-Clinet the Durantou family. Denis Durantou's grandmother was *née* René Rabier. Her father, Paul, had married the daughter of Mauleon Rouchut.

Yet for 40 vintages, up to and including 1982, the wine of L'Eglise-Clinet was made, not by the Durantous, but by an outsider. If you look at the label of an old bottle you will see the name 'Pierre Lasserre, Administrateur'. Lasserre was, and remains, proprietor of Clos-René, which he now runs with the help of his grandson, Jean-Marie Garde. Widowed early, Mme Rabier entered into a *fermage* arrangement with Pierre Lasserre in 1942. Lasserre tended the vineyard and made the wine in exchange for the proceeds of half the crop. Jacques Durantou, Denis' father, the local *préfet*, has never taken an active role in the running of the property, and it was only when Lasserre decided he was getting a bit too old to continue to operate both vineyards that Denis Durantou, who had followed an oenological course at Bordeaux University, suggested to his family that he take over.

THE VINEYARD

The total surface area under vines consists of five and a half hectares. Of this four lie on the main Pomerol plateau near the church on a gravel soil underneath which is clay, and a further one and a half are situated on more sandy soil towards the main road between Libourne and Périgueux. Since the 1986 vintage the produce from this vineyard has been bottled separately under the name of La Petite Eglise. The property is fortunate to possess a significant proportion of very old vines which escaped the ravages of the 1956 frost. The estate is now planted in the ratio 70 per cent Merlot, 15 per cent Cabernet Franc and 10 per cent Malbec, with the final 5 per cent made up of old vines whose exact botanical origin is uncertain. Production averages 25 *tonneaux*.

THE CHÂTEAU

The château is a simple two-storey farmhouse. It adjoins the *chais* and was constructed in about 1850. For most of this century it was rarely inhabited except during the holidays and at vintage time. Denis Durantou and his wife, Marie Reilhac, a painter, have lived there permanently since 1981.

CHANGES SINCE 1983

Since the arrival of Denis Durantou in 1983, several major improvements have been inaugurated. Lasserre had always worked with old barrels – not necessarily a bad thing; so did the Mlles Robin at Château Lafleur – but when Durantou arrived he found that three-quarters were over fifteen years old. Lasserre also vinified in a somewhat artisanal way, not being greatly concerned with temperature control. The wine was vinified with some of the stalks, matured in this old wood and bottled after two years.

Thankfully, the vines were old and the yield low. The result was an old-fashioned wine, dense and muscular rather than plump and elegant but with an underlying concentration and richness. It certainly deserved not only the 25 per cent premium over his own Clos-René that Lasserre was able to extract from the *négoce* but its high rating (twentieth in the 1969 Cocks and Féret but seventh in the 1982 edition) in the Bordeaux Bible.

Durantou has installed a new *fouloir-égrappoir* (crusher and destemmer), introduced a three-year turn-round of new barrels, and is now controlling the temperature of fermentation at a maximum of 31 degrees. He has renovated the old concrete vats by adding a lining of epoxy resin and added a stainless-steel tank. He completely destalks and has reduced the length of time in cask to sixteen months. Most importantly perhaps, following the lead of his friend Alexandre Thienpont, he is particularly assiduous about keeping the yield as low as feasible, pruning vigorously and reducing the harvest by eliminating excessive bunches just before the *veraison*. Since the 1986 vintage, as I have indicated, there is a *deuxième vin*.

The results are impressive, though there have been one or two inconsistencies, such as the 1985, which is only fair for the vintage. L'Eglise-Clinet is not quite in the super-second class, but it is certainly a property to watch.

THE TASTING

I tasted the following wines in Bordeaux in April 1989.

1988   *Optimum drinking*   **1996–2006**

Good colour. Fragrant ripe nose. Medium-full. Quite fat and rich. A harmonious wine, fragrant and subtle but it lacks a bit of power compared with the best. Long but delicate. This is more like a 1985. Good or even very good but not great.

1987   **Now–1997**

Good colour. Stylish fruity nose, round and attractive blackberry fragrance. Medium body. A little tannin. Good grip for the vintage. Quite rich and fat and with a good finish. This is one of the better wines of the vintage.

1986   **1995–2004**

Fine colour. An intriguing nose of chocolate and roast chestnuts and oak. There is good fat here. Good depth. This shows very well. A Libournais 1986 of substance, ripeness and concentration. Very good. Long on the palate.

1985   **1995–2004**

Good colour. The nose is higher toned than I had expected. This is not showing well. Got better as it evolved in the glass but there is a certain dilution here which is not evident in the above. Stylish wine, good fruit. Good grip. But only good, if that. Long on the palate, though. Improved in the glass.

1984   **Drink soon**

Good colour for the vintage. Good richness and fat for the vintage on the nose. Quite round, no weakness. Medium body. Inevitably a certain lack of dimension but neither dilution nor feebleness. Pleasant. *A point*. Not short. Very good for vintage.

1983   **Now–2001**

Good colour. Full, little development. There is depth here on the nose and little of the dilution of the vintage. Good. Ripe and round and with grip. Medium to medium-full body, some tannin. Good fresh blackcurranty and plummy fruit. Good length. An attractive wine. Very good especially for a Libournais 1983.

1982   **Now–2013**

Good colour. Rich cooked plum nose. Fat, rich, tough even and tannic. But with both concentration and grip. This is really very fine. Streets ahead of all the vintages from 1983 onwards. Creamy ripe. *Sur-maturité* and old vines. Lovely.

1978   **Now–1997**

Medium to medium-full colour. Just about mature. Quite ripe and fat on the nose. With a certain attenuation of the Merlot. Quite full, fruity and slightly spicy. Good grip. An attractive wine. Now *à point*. Finishes long. Perhaps lacks a little finesse but it is concentrated and fruity. Also a touch vegetal. Good though but not special.

1975   **Now–1998**

Good medium-full mature colour. Quite dumb still on the nose, but not hard. There is depth and richness here. This is a bigger, richer wine with more tannin. A certain density but has fatness and spice and a riper fatter acidity than the above. Will still improve. Good for the vintage in a slightly solid way. Rich on the finish.

1971   Now–1996
From a magnum. Surprisingly good colour for the vintage. Fullish, mature but not excessively so. Good fruit on the nose; fresh and full of interest. Lovely attack. Rich, old viney, very fine grip. Fine attack. Very long on the palate. Old-fashioned in character but no density. Very concentrated. Fresh and ripe. A long life ahead. Very fine especially for the vintage.

1964   Drink soon
(Bottled in Bordeaux by Barrière) Good colour. Mature but no age. Fat, ripe and concentrated but a certain amount of age, it seems. Fullish, fat and ripe but I think this bottle has lost a little of its vigour. It is good but it doesn't sing. Essentially a more elegant wine, with better fruit and more complexity than the wine below.

1962   Drink soon
Good colour. Vigorous, charming meaty nose with an added spice aspect. Caramel and cinnamon. This is much more vigorous. Rich, fat, ripe and concentrated. Old vines here. Has the *puissance* the 1964 lacks. Very good, if not the greatest nuance.

1961   Now–1996
Very good colour. Still very youthful. Very big and rich. Concentrated; even dense. More to it

than the 1964. Fullish, somewhat old-fashioned if not rustic. Rich, fat and meaty. Concentrated if not with any great finesse. A big wine. Even sweet.

1959   Drink soon
(Bottled in Bordeaux by Barrière) Very good colour. Little sign of age. A certain amount of volatile acidity on the nose. Fat and rich nevertheless. Fat, spicy, toffee-like. This is less rustic, more vigorous and cleaner than the 1961. Sweet, a certain astringency. Less finesse but more concentration. Still vigorous. Very good.

1955   Drink soon
(Bottled in Bordeaux by Barrière) Excellent colour. A big dense wine. Still fresh and vigorous. Solid and meaty. Old vines. A big, fullish, old-fashioned wine. Fine fruit. An essence of fruit even. Concentrated. Ripe. Lovely fruit. Very fine for vintage. Still plenty of life. Better than the 1959? It didn't hold up quite so well in the glass.

1952   Drink soon
(Labelled Clos L'Eglise–Clinet) Even better colour. Deep to the rim. Very youthful. Not quite as fat as the above. Bigger and cleaner on the nose. There is a certain astringency now about this but basically a splendid wine. Very, very concentrated. Larger than life. I would have said a 1945. Immensely rich damson fruit. Tough though, and small harvest evident. The best of all?

L'ENCLOS

The best sector of Pomerol is agreed to be that part which is enclosed by the road from Libourne to Montagne-Saint-Emilion on one side, the R98 to Périgueux on the other, the village of Catusseau to the south and the river Barbanne to the north, particularly those vines which lie on what is known as the high plateau surrounding Château Pétrus in the centre of this rectangle. One of Château L'Enclos's nine and a half hectares can be found on the high plateau. The rest are scattered all over the place. There are as many as 38 parcels. But the nucleus lies west of the R98 in the hamlet of Moulinet. A neighbour is Clos-René; another is the extensive Château de Sales. The soil is sandier here than in the heart of Pomerol, thus less propitious, yet the wine of Château L'Enclos is extremely good, and has been so for years. A new generation of the family which have owned it for a century and a half has recently taken over, and further modernization of the cellars and sophistication of the wine-making equipment have been put in train. Château L'Enclos remains priced among the lesser Pomerols. However, it *is* a bit of a bargain!

The only mention of L'Enclos in the earliest editions of Cocks and Féret refers to a *bourdieu*, or vineyard, allocated to the local priest in order for him to supplement his income. During the Revolution the little village was deprived of its man of God, the parish was annexed to neighbouring Néac, and the old church, which had existed since the time of the Templars, was allowed to fall into ruins. It was not until 1846 that the village regained its ecclesiastical independence. A rather dull new church then replaced the old one, next to which a small patch of vines, capable of producing two or three *tonneaux* came into existence under the name of L'Enclos du Presbytère. It belonged to successive, but anonymous *curés* of Pomerol. But it has nothing to do with today's Château L'Enclos.

HISTORY

Elsewhere in the area, associated at various times with a number of small estates, was a family called Larroucaud. Towards the end of the century a Pierre Larroucaud regrouped some of the family land, built himself a new château, rather Swiss-chalet in appearance, in the hamlet of Moulinet, and called it L'Enclos-Pomerol.

Why the name? His successors suggest it came from the name of the immediate locality. This part of Pomerol was a centre for hemp manufacture. The hemp was spun into yarn, dyed with madder, which was also produced in the commune, and made into trousers for the French army. While the hemp was grown extensively, within the fields nearby were one or two walled enclosures where the locals planted vines. L'Enclos, it says on the *cadastre*, or local register. L'Enclos became the name of Pierre Larroucaud's wine.

Through the female line L'Enclos passed from Larroucaud's son to a Monsieur J.F. Carteau, and from the Carteaus to their daughter Mme Xavier Marc, whose husband's family once owned Château La Grave-à-Pomerol, formerly Trigant-de-Boisset. The attractive, blonde Catherine, a teacher of Spanish, and the daughter of Mme Marc, and her husband Hughes Weydert – his family is of Luxembourg origin – have recently moved into Château L'Enclos with their two children to be with Mme Marc. He has been responsible for the wine since 1989.

THE VINEYARD

There are, as I have said, nine and a half hectares, divided among a number of parcels throughout the commune, plus an extra hectare in Lalande-de-Pomerol. One of these lies near Château Pétrus. Pierre Larroucaud originally owned a different plot, but when he ceded this to the community in order to provide a site for the local school, he was given an even better sited vineyard in exchange.

The vines are old, and are grafted on to low-yielding rootstocks. Even without green-harvesting, only necessary on the young vines, the harvest usually averages a mere 40 hectolitres per hectare. Only in 1986 and 1992 has the domaine had to ask for the PLC (*plafond limité de classement*). The domaine is planted in the ratio 80 per cent Merlot, 19 per cent Cabernet Franc and 1 per cent Malbec, and from 1984 to 1988 was in part picked by machine, but this no longer takes place.

WINE-MAKING

Since 1989 there has been much change in the cellars of L'Enclos. There are nine new 120-hectolitre, enamel-lined, steel fermentation vats and a new pneumatic Boucher press in the *cuverie*, and behind this is a small *chai à barriques*. Automatic temperature control is being installed, as will a new reception centre for the fruit. The maceration takes place at a maximum temperature of 32 degrees, and Weydert proposes to add a few stems to the must the next time the climatic conditions make this appropriate. It will give the wine a little extra strength. Future plans include transforming the old *cuverie* into a bottle-storage cellar and tasting room. The short crop of 1991, though, has temporarily halted this new investment.

L'Enclos is matured one-third in new oak, one-third in casks of the previous vintage and one-third in tank, and bottled after about eighteen months in wood. Bottling is handled by one of the better mobile bottling teams in the area.

THE WINE

L'Enclos is a very typical example of the best of second-division Pomerol: medium in weight, plump in fruit but with a style, a concentration and a harmony that sets it above most of its neighbours. The old vintages are good – I remember an excellent 1947 and a very good

1966 as well as the wines below – but the latest vintages are even better. The 1989 and 1990 have shone out since they were first in cask. And the 1991 is an unexpected success.

After the death of Xavier Marc in 1971, Gaston Vessière, *maître de chai* of Cheval-Blanc, would pop by from time to time to cast an avuncular eye over proceedings, though the official cellar-master was the ubiquitous M. Zucchi, who also looked after Vieux Château Certan, La Conseillante, L'Evangile and other properties. Vessière made his last vintage at Cheval-Blanc in 1986, and Zucchi is now retired too. But L'Enclos, with Hughes Weydert at the helm, is in extremely good hands.

THE TASTING

I sampled the following vintages at Château L'Enclos in September 1993.

	Optimum drinking

1992 1996–2001

Medium colour. Fresh fruity nose. This is 1987-ish in character. No great depth or strength, little tannin. Will be bottled early. Fresh, good acidity. No lack of fruit. This has a subtle touch of oak, and is well-made and attractive. Good.

1991 1997–2004

One-quarter of the usual harvest. This has a much better colour than the 1992. Surprising richness, with a touch of new oak on the nose. Medium to medium-full. Ample and blackcurranty. This is really most attractive. No hard tannins. Quite fat. Long and complex. Fine for the vintage.

1990 1997–2007

Medium-full colour. Just a little less than the 1989. Good firm plummy nose with a touch of spice. Plenty of ripeness and fat. Medium-full body. Ripe opulent fruit. Good mature tannins. It lacks a little bite for perfection but it is very seductive. Finishes quite long. Very ample. Good plus.

1989 1998–2012

Medium-full colour. A little more intense than the 1990, but a little more evolved as well. This has a more vibrant nose. Slightly higher volatile acidity. But this gives the fruit flesh and life. More damsony than blackberry. Medium-full body. The tannins less soft than the 1990. More depth and better grip. Long and more complex and a bit more elegant. Very good.

1988 1998–2012

Good colour. Fresh and blackcurranty, with a slightly herbaceous austerity on the nose. Medium to medium-full body. This has a good backbone and plenty of grip. But it lacks a little generosity at present. There is a certain hardness on the finish which reminds me of some 1978s. It will round off as it matures and become more generous. This finish is long and even complex with some class. Good but not exciting.

1986 Now–1998

Medium colour. Some evolution. Fat and ripe on the nose. No dilution or attenuation. Medium body. Good freshness. Round and gentle. Even has class. It lacks a bit of concentration but it is a good, even very good, 1986 for a Pomerol. Positive at the end. Just about ready.

1985 Now–1999

Medium colour. Also some evolution. If anything slightly less intense than the 1986. Ample Merlot nose. A touch spicy-sweet. A touch more rustic, nevertheless, than the wines above. Medium body, a little more depth than the 1986, more grip and vigour too. But it lacks a little finesse. Quite good.

1983 Now–2001

Good colour. Plump, vigorous, amply generous nose. This has good fat and concentration for a Libournais 1983. No dilution here. Better than the 1985 and 1986 by quite a way. Medium-full. Good vigour. Good concentration. The tannins are a touch dry at the end but the wine is ripe and satisfying nonetheless. Very good.

1982 Now–2008

Fine colour. Lovely concentrated nose. This is really exciting. Rich and intense and classy. Fullish, still very vigorous. Indeed I would still give it a year or two. Has twice as much concentration and depth as the wines above – even the 1989 perhaps. Very good grip. Very persistent. A really very good example indeed. Lovely. Very long. Bags of life.

1978 Now–1997

Good colour. Nicely cool. Good blackcurrant and bramble fruit. Slight touch of hardness. But no rusticity. Medium-full. Round, silky, elegant, *à point*. This is subtle and ripe and style with a good complex finish. Not a blockbuster but good plus.

1975 Now–1998

Very good colour. This is quite a lot more substantial than the 1978. On the nose there is an element of spice and fat, on the palate bitter chocolate and damsons. Fullish, rich, meaty but with good grip and concentration and though the tannins are noticeable they do not obtrude too much, though it is just a little dry on the finish. Good vigour. Not quite as elegant as the 1978 but good stuff. A wine for food.

1970   Drink soon

Medium to medium-full colour. Fully mature. Old viney nose, lovely if quite rarified and delicate fruit. A wine like the 1978 of subtlety rather than muscle. Good intensity. Ripe and complex. Even sweet at the end. Lots of finesse but it is showing signs of nearing its end. If this is the vigour of château-stocked wine I'd be wary of bottles which have often changed provenance. Yet developed in the glass. Seemed to gain vigour. Very good indeed.

1959   Now–1999 plus

Excellent colour. Full and vigorous. Slightly old-fashioned in its thickness. Very rich and old-viney on the nose. A sort of rugged velvetiness: the best of the old way of making wine. Full, meaty, sweet, powerful and intense. The wine could be any age from 1945 onwards: seemingly motionless in its development. Splendid fruit. Delicious. Plenty of vigour.

1948   Now–1998

Fullish mature colour. Still very young. Vigorous nose. Quite firm, even a touch of hardness. Yet ripe and concentrated and lovely. Fullish on the palate, classy, old-viney, complex; velvety-smooth all the way from start to finish. Long. Lovely. Bags of life.

1929   Drink soon

The colour is fullish but now well-matured. And on the nose and on the palate this has the personality of an old wine. Sweet, with even a touch of the sweet-sour about it. Medium body. This is silky and ripe and intense. Complex and subtle. It has lost a little of its vigour, but is still most enjoyable. A real treat.

L'EVANGILE

Turn to page 1413 of the most recent edition of the 'Bible of Bordeaux', Cocks and Féret, and you will find, listed immediately after Château Pétrus, the name of Château L'Evangile. Cocks and Féret list wines in their own considered order of merit. So in Cocks and Féret's view, L'Evangile is second in the Pomerol hierarchy, and superior to Trotanoy, Vieux Château Certan, La Conseillante and Château Lafleur, respectively the properties which follow on the succeeding pages. This edition of Cocks and Féret appeared in 1991, but even two decades ago, in the edition of 1969, L'Evangile is in the number two spot. Indeed the first six châteaux are the same properties as today, the only difference being that La Conseillante and Trotanoy have since changed places.

Without wishing to prejudge the issue, I suggested in a profile on Château Trotanoy published in February 1985, that this particular order might cause a few raised eyebrows among Pomerol lovers, and, my knowledge of the wines of Château L'Evangile being somewhat scanty, said I would go and investigate. I duly wrote to Mme Ducasse, the owner, did a bit of research on L'Evangile's history, and dusted off my rather meagre collection of tasting notes of its wines. I found that I had only tasted the wine on some four dozen occasions in the last fifteen years, not the basis to form a really convincing estimate of a property's consistency and quality. The only L'Evangile I knew well in maturity was the 1970 bought at the time Alexis Lichine et Cie had a major share in the marketing of the property in the carefree days before the slump of 1973/1974.

Sadly, I had to report that progress at the Bordeaux end was negligible. Mme Ducasse was unable to put up a long series of wines for me to taste, though she did open bottles back to 1979. Equally, back in England, when I tried to supplement a range of vintages which the enterprising Jeremy Parke had organized for a Studley Priory Wine Weekend in December 1985, I drew a blank. It was not until May 1991 that I was able to make a really comprehensive vertical tasting of Château L'Evangile.

HISTORY

The origins of Château L'Evangile lie in a Libournais family called Leglise who were active in the mid-eighteenth century in the establishment of what is now the Pomerol *vignoble*. Among this fraternity was M. Giraud at Trotanoy, Catherine Conseillan at the estate next door and the Arnaud family at Pétrus. It was originally called Fazilleau.

Briefly in the 1770s L'Evangile/Fazilleau passed into the hands of the Feuilhade family, for Jeanne Leglise, heiress to the estate, married a Jean Feuilhade. However when Feuilhade died in 1778 the domaine reverted back to the Leglises, and it was they who continued to develop the property into the early years of the Napoleonic era. It was already more or less its present size, some thirteen hectares, and it appears on the Belleyme map of the late 1780s as Fazilleau.

Soon after, the estate passed to a lawyer named Isambert or Izambert, and it was he who changed the name and gave it its present ecclesiastical connotation (L'Evangile means 'gospel'). Why, we do not know. In 1862 it changed hands yet again, but for the last time. The purchaser was Paul Chaperon, and L'Evangile has belonged to Chaperon's heirs, the Ducasse family, ever since.

Paul Chaperon seems to have been an active and competent vineyard proprietor. He owned Château Grand-Corbin and Tertre-Daugay in Saint-Emilion as well as L'Evangile. He had the present château constructed, a fairly substantial (for Pomerol) two-storey edifice in the Second Empire style, within a little park, and he soon raised the reputation of Château L'Evangile to the heights it enjoys today.

In the 1868, second edition of Cocks and Féret L'Evangile is rated eighth in the commune and is recorded as producing ten to fifteen *tonneaux*. By 1874 it has climbed to fifth and by 1898 it is third, now making 25 *tonneaux*. Soon after this date Paul Chaperon died, to be succeeded first by his widow and then by his daughter, Mme Paul Ducasse.

The Ducasses are a well-established wine family in the Gironde. One branch of the family – though the connection is extremely tenuous – gave his name to a Pauillac estate some 200 years ago. A more immediate relation was a Mlle Henriette Ducasse, heiress of Cheval-Blanc who married a Jean Laussac-Fourcaud in 1852. It was a nephew of hers who married Paul Chaperon's daughter, and it was her father, President Ducasse, who bought such an important parcel of land from Félicité de Geres of Figeac in 1832 and first established Cheval-Blanc in its own right. The family name is still commemorated in Château Larcis-Ducasse, neighbour of Château Pavie.

Madame Paul Ducasse's son, Louis, officially took over on his mother's death in 1954, though in practice he had been responsible for the wine since before the war. For 28 years L'Evangile was his pride and joy. Sadly, he died in 1982 and his widow, Louise, a somewhat formidable lady with thick pebble glasses and the air of a rather severe school-mistress, who took over, dividing her time between Libourne in the winter and L'Evangile in the summer. In 1990 the Domaines Barons de Rothschild (Lafite) bought 70 per cent of the equity in L'Evangile from the Ducasse family. As yet no major changes have been made.

THE PROPERTY

Take a straight line between Cheval-Blanc and Pétrus, a distance of some 1,200 metres, bisect it, and you will find Château L'Evangile neighbouring Château La Conseillante on the road which runs from Libourne to Montagne and Lussac-Saint-Emilion. The estate consists of fourteen hectares, planted two-thirds with Merlot and one-third with Cabernet Franc, and produces 40 *tonneaux* of wine per annum.

The soil at Château L'Evangile consists partly of gravel and sand but predominantly of clay based on an iron-rich subsoil known as *crasse de fer*. The clay soil gives wines of firmness and vigour, richness and power, but sometimes solidity. The soil and gravel balance that with suppleness and delicacy. The wine is vinified in small epoxy-resin-lined cement vats with a *cuvaison* of two or three weeks, and from grapes which are completely de-stalked. A metal grill immersed a few centimetres below the surface of the must keeps the *chapeau* submerged. The wine is then matured for 18 to 24 months in oak barrels, one-third of which are new.

THE WINE

Château L'Evangile resembles Château La Conseillante and Vieux Château Certan in style, being more structured than the former and less predominantly Cabernet Sauvignon in flavour than the latter. Despite having less Cabernet in its *encépagement* than either, the Cabernet background is nevertheless manifest, and its expression shows the minty, leafy flavour of Cabernet Franc, giving L'Evangile a weight and backbone which the softer, more Merlot-flavoured Pomerols, particularly those from more sandy soils, do not possess. It also means that L'Evangile is a wine which takes longer than most to come round and it can be a bit burly and even tarry in its youth. Quality, judging by the wines of the last half-dozen vintages, all of which I have seen reasonably regularly, and which seem to have been matured using a higher proportion of new oak than was employed up to 1983, is certainly very high, well into second growth standard. The wine is priced as a super-second, and normally deserves to be. However, whether it is currently quite as good as Trotanoy is a different matter. Perhaps not. Whether it will be in the future now that it is part of the Lafite-Rothschild stable is yet another question. I see no reason not to expect that it will be in its own way at least as good.

THE TASTING

Some of the older vintages of the following wines were sampled at the Studley Priory Hotel Wine Weekend held in December 1985. I tasted a range of the 1980s vintages in London in December 1990, and have added two or three notes of bottles which I tasted at the Oliveros Pétrus Versus the Rest event in New York in October 1989. Finally, the Domaines Barons de Rothschild (of Lafite) held a comprehensive tasting in London in May 1991.

1990   *Optimum drinking*   **1996–2008**
Fullish colour. Ripe, new oaky nose. Lush, ripe, black-cherry and hot plum tart on the nose. Medium-full. Good tannins. Quite alcoholic. Rich and fat. Not as good as the 1989 though. Not as concentrated. But potentially classy, seductive and voluptuous. Very good indeed.

1989   **1996–2012**
Good, full colour. Not too marked by the oak. More classic, richer and more concentrated than the 1989. Full, excellent quality. Good oaky background and very good acidity. This is very fine. Real breed, real complexity. The best wine of the decade and better than the 1990.

1988   **1996–2008**
Medium-full colour. A ripe, concentrated but somewhat hidden nose. I don't get a great deal of new oak. A bit more to it than the 1986. Medium-full. Good grip. A little austere at present. The elements are good but not brilliant – but this is the vintage. Good length. Very good.

1987   **Drink soon**
Good colour for the vintage. A bit dry on the nose. It lacks both fruit and zip. Potentially a tendency to attenuate quickly. This has reasonable class but is now as good as it is ever going to be. It lacks depth, dimension, richness and grip. Not bad for the vintage.

1986   **Now–2002**
Medium-full colour. Ripe and plump on the nose, but a slightly four-square aspect and a lack of concentration and richness. Currently it misses a bit of sex-appeal. Medium body. Not a lot of tannin. Ripe but just a touch bitter and herbaceous. I prefer the 1988. Good.

1985   **1995–2015**
Fullish colour. Full, rich, concentrated; quite dense and tannic. Fullish, much riper and lusher tannins. Firm backbone. Good acidity. Rich and concentrated. Bitter chocolate and black cherries. Fine. More class than the rest of the 1981 to 1988 series.

1984   **Drink up**
Reasonable intensity and vigour on the colour for the vintage. Nothing really very much except

a rather feeble old-tea aspect on the nose. Better on the palate. Reasonably fresh. Medium body. Still clean. Not bad.

1983   Now–2003
Good colour, just a little development. Good, full, lush nose; not the greatest of class but good grip. Slight aspects of gingerbread. Fullish, more dense than concentrated. But good acidity. Lacks a bit of richness and breed but a very good example of a Libournais 1983.

1982   Now–2003
Full, rich colour. Not a bit dense and ungainly. Still a bit of tannin. This has somewhat less charm than the 1983 at present. Full body. I don't get much class though. Will it ever round off satisfactorily? A bit of a disappointment.

1981   Now–1998
Medium colour. Fully mature. Fully developed nose. Not a wine of great class, but it has reasonable vigour and grip. Soft and plump and slightly spicy. Very good for the vintage.

1979   Now–2003
Very good colour. Rich, ripe nose with clean fruit and good acidity. Fullish, some tannin, backward. Ripe, concentrated, very fine fruit. Lovely, long, velvety finish. This is better than the 1978.

1978   Now–1998
Medium-full colour, just a little maturity. More Cabernet Franc than Merlot on the nose. Medium to medium-full body. *A point.* Attractive fruit. What it lacks is a bit of velvet. It is a bit too high-toned and herbaceous. Good for the vintage, but by no means great.

1976   Drink soon
Medium, mature colour. Broad, open, spicy Merlot nose with a hint of cedar underneath, not too weak. Medium body, quite fresh, ripe and fruit. Better acidity than most. Soft and mellow; no great depth or elegance but no weakness and will last better than most.

1975   Now–2000 plus
Full colour. Ripe, distinguished, classy nose. This is of high quality and has none of the dry density of the vintage. Fuller than the 1970. Richer and more concentrated. But less lush. Yet a lovely long, rich, fat finish. Bags of life.

1970   Now–2000
Good colour. No undue sign of maturity. Lush, fat, round, ample nose. Medium-full, vigorous, stylish. Raspberry and chocolate. Good grip. Long. Very good indeed, but seemed to fall away in the glass. Less good after half an hour.

1966   Drink soon
Full colour. This smells as if it was reared entirely in tank. There is an old swimming-bath aroma about it. Medium to medium-full. Quite high acidity. Rather four-square. Once again the Cabernet Franc comes out. A bit astringent as it evolved. Lacks elegance.

1964   Now–1998
Very good colour. Mature but no lightening up. Rich, ripe, complex, mature nose. Fat and concentrated, very lovely. Full body and a wine of high class. Ripe, fat, warm, just the sort of seductive voluptuousness missing in the above. Very long indeed on the finish. Delicious.

1961   Drink soon
Very full colour. Dense, tough, inky, old-fashioned wine-making. There is volatile acidity and a bit of maderization. Full and rich but more the characteristics (and the state of maturity) of a 1950 than a 1961. Lumpy. Lacks breed.

1959   See note
From a jeroboam: in bottle, probably should be drunk soon. Very fine colour, still black. Smells of leather, yew and cedar. High in alcohol. Tough, liquorice-flavoured; slightly baked, burnt aspect. Full, firm, spicy, not very Pomerol at all, but no undue hardness or astringency. Old-fashioned wine-making yet rich, earthy, concentrated and warm on the finish. Quite a blockbuster. Very fine, at least at first, but became a little inky as it developed in the glass.

1955   Drink soon
Fine colour: full, rich and dense. Splendid nose, rich, with some very faint traces of volatile acidity. Almost porty. Full, youthful, very concentrated and rich with a flavour of blackberries and chocolate. This is an old-fashioned wine in the best sense of this phrase, with a slightly earthy flavour. Still has power. Long, ripe, warm, sweet finish. High quality. Holding up well.

1949   Drink soon
Fullish colour, still vigorous. Fine classy nose, very good fruit. On the palate has body and concentration but is beginning to show a little age, and as it evolved a gamey-vegetal aspect began to show as well as a little astringency. Undeniably very good. Was very fine in its prime, I would suggest.

1928   Drink soon
Lightish, well-matured colour. Very elegant, old-roses fragrance on the nose, but a touch of astringency now. Soft, silky palate at first. Complex, classy, ethereal flavours. A wine of real breed. Now a distinguished old lady. Began to get a bit coarse in the glass after five minutes.

LA FLEUR-PÉTRUS

A number of properties to the east of the village of Pomerol incorporate the word '*fleur*' into their title. There is Château Lafleur itself, probably the most prestigious, if not as a result of its tiny four-hectare size widely known from personal experience. Adjacent to Gazin is Lafleur-Gazin. I remember a fine 1961, bottled by The Wine Society. This domaine produces a good *bourgeois* standard Pomerol and has a larger percentage of Cabernet Franc than most in its *encépagement*. Like many neighbouring estates, it is *en fermage* to Etablissements Jean-Pierre Moueix.

Between Lafleur and Pétrus, logically enough combining the two names, is where you will find another flower. It has rather a curious label showing a flag which resembles that of a shipping line. Again it is a Moueix wine. Whilst the style is quite different from either of its famous neighbours, in quality, as you would expect from these illustrious names in the vicinity, it is one of the best wines in the area.

The history of La Fleur-Pétrus begins with a family called Constant, proprietors of Château Clinet in the middle of the nineteenth century, and it makes its first appearance in Cocks and Féret in the edition of 1874 as Pétrus-Lafleur. Constant *père* makes ten *tonneaux* at Clinet; an A. Constant makes four at Pétrus-Lafleur and Hyppolyte Constant makes a further three in the area. The name Pétrus, like Lafleur, was obviously then a *lieu-dit*.

Ten years on, Château Clinet is owned by a man called Barrat, and Ernest Constant and a M. Pinau (*sic*) (was Pinau his son-in-law?) are established at Lafleur-Pétrus, and production has climbed to eight *tonneaux*. By 1893 'Pinau', on his own, has an initial 'O' and his name is spelt Pineau, more suitable for a *vigneron*. The standing of the wine is in nineteenth place in the Pomerol list. The production is given as eight *tonneaux*.

HISTORY

The property was passed down successive generations of Pineaus – from O. to A. to F., but no Christian names given except for the last, Fabien – until the 1930s. The wine, during the 1920s a *monopole* of the Belgian firm of Eugène Delgouffre, enjoyed a solid but not superstar reputation and the yield slowly increased to some twenty *tonneaux*. It then seems to have passed rather quickly through the hands of an old French family called Montouroy before being acquired by a M. Garet.

Though I have been told the vineyard was neglected at the time, the wines of the Garet period that I have had occasion to sample – and these include the 1940 as well as those below – have always shown exceptionally well. Yet it was not until after the estate was acquired by Jean-Pierre Moueix in 1953 that the reputation of the property began to rise. It finally made the top ten in Pomerol in 1969 though in the 1982 (and the 1991) edition it is listed in twelfth place.

The reason for this apparent decline was the appalling frost in February 1956. Assuming the 1969 Cocks and Féret verdict was based on wines produced from old vines in the 1950s and early 1960s, the 1982 placement results from the quality of the vintages in the 1970s. Inevitably, as the vineyard had almost entirely to be replanted after the 1956 disaster, these 1970 vintages were the result of young vines. Nevertheless, I have fond memories of both the 1971 and the 1970, vintages I bought myself, so I do not want to suggest this interim period – the 1982 would have come from 25-year-old, fully mature plants – was in any way beneath contempt. Nevertheless, a temporary weakening of both the wine's concentration and its reputation was inevitable. Happily, things are back to normal now. I would certainly not agree that Château La Violette and Nénin, tenth and eleventh in the 1982 and 1991 Cocks and Féret, are inferior to La Fleur-Pétrus.

THE VINEYARD AND THE WINE

The vineyard of Château La Fleur-Pétrus occupies 9.1 hectares and is planted in a fairly common ratio for a Moueix Pomerol: 80 per cent Merlot, 20 per cent Cabernet Franc. Production now averages 3,500 cases. The soil, unlike the clay of Pétrus across the road, is entirely a marly gravel. This would suggest a wine whose characteristic is elegance rather than power and so it is. I find the wine has much more in common with Conseillante than with either of its immediate neighbours, Pétrus itself or Lafleur.

The wine is vinified in five unlined cement vats in a small outhouse of the château; this latter being nothing more, really, than a modest two-storey farmhouse constructed in about 1850. In contrast to the blue shutters of Pétrus 100 metres away, those of La Fleur-Pétrus used to be painted a vivid, indeed hideous, yellow (repainted red in 1988). Only the first-year wine is kept at the property, the *chai* being too small. At the end of the summer, it is transferred to the Moueix cellars for the rest of its sojourn in cask, an increasing number of which, these days, are of new oak.

Various authorities – Hubrecht Duijker and Bernard Ginestet among them – consider Lafleur-Pétrus third only in quality – after Pétrus and Trotanoy – among the Pomerol wines of the Moueix stable. If this stable is to include all those the Moueix team are in charge of, not just those they own, I am not sure I would agree. Lafleur is certainly superior and so, in my view, is Latour-à-Pomerol, if by a smaller margin.

The wines, anyway, are entirely different. Lafleur-Pétrus may be less concentrated but it is a very elegant, extremely harmonious wine, with a lot of charm. In recent years it has been producing very fine wine indeed.

THE TASTING

The following tasting took place at the New Haven wine weekend in September 1987. A number of the bottles had been generously donated by Christian Moueix. This is my chance to thank him publicly for his generosity.

Not sampled on this occasion were the 1971 and the 1961. The former I know well, having cellared some myself: a complex stylish example which was still holding up well last time out in May 1993. I rated the 1961 'very good', but old-fashioned in style alongside other 1961s six months before the New Haven, Connecticut, tasting.

Optimum drinking

1983   **Now–2003**

Medium full-colour. No sign of development. Quite an open nose. Not that intense or concentrated but ripe, fruity and elegant. Medium weight. A slight absence of grip and power and it lacks real richness and concentration. Good but not exceptional.

1982   **1995–2015**

Much fuller colour. Full, fat, aromatic nose. This has much more weight, depth and power. Full, rich, spicy and concentrated, with the chocolate, liquorice, coffee and leather flavours of the 1982 vintage. Quite tannic, very classy. Does not have the density of the Latour-à-Pomerol or other Pomerol 1982s but is very finely balanced and long on the palate. Very good indeed.

1979   **Now–2002**

Medium to medium-full colour, some maturity. Ripe, seductive, plummy, flowery nose, quite developed. On the palate medium to medium-full body, just about ready. A ripe, most attractive wine but, again, a little absence of intensity and concentration. Very good fruit, fresh, stylish, good length. Good to very good for the vintage.

1978   **Now–2005**

Medium-full colour. Aspects of maturity, browner than the 1979. Bonfires and blackberry jam on the nose. Good depth and richness of fruit. This is a fuller wine with rather more to it. Quite fat and spicy. Still some tannin. Good concentration. Quite powerful. Fine quality.

1975   **Now–2007**

Fine colour, fullish, and not as developed as the 1978. Excellent nose, a lot of class and lovely harmonious fruit. Full, still some tannin – a substantial wine in both senses, size and quality. Rich, generous, plenty of depth. An example of how much more satisfactory, in general, the Libournais are than the Médocs in this vintage. High class. Rather better, in absolute terms, than either of the two above.

1970   **Now–2005**

(Magnum) Full colour again. Quite developed. Reserved, blackcurrant nose, less sweet than the above. Full, meaty, rich and powerful. Still some unresolved tannins. Good acidity. The fruit is perhaps not so ample and old-vine-concentrated as it might be but this is still very good. Rather more hard and solid than I remember the bottle size from my own cellar. The 1975 is better.

1969   **Drink up**

Medium colour. Fully mature. Both the nose and the palate are still fresh and quite fruity and attractive. Light but not too light. A little one-dimensional and signs of attenuation on the finish. Rather better than I expected, though. No undue age.

1967   **Drink soon**

Excellent colour for the vintage. Mellow, ripe, generous nose. No undue age. This is a very fine 1967. Medium body. Complex and fragrant. Lovely soft fruit flavours, still vigorous. Surprisingly good. Obviously very well stored – one of the tasters had had a much less good bottle recently – and very well balanced within its context.

1966   **Drink soon**

Full, mature colour. Lightish, fresh, elegant but 'cool' nose. Cedary, slightly herbal, lacking a bit of richness and concentration. This has lightened up a bit and doesn't show as well (for its vintage) as the 1967. Medium body. Good attack but finishes a bit mean, even a little bitter. Slightly disappointing. Only 'quite good'. At a tasting held a few months previously, the example was rather more concentrated and vigorous.

1964   **Drink soon**

Very fine colour. Full, rich, vigorous, glowing. Rich, aromatic, smoky, cedary nose, with plenty of depth. Doesn't quite live up to this promise on the palate. There is a good grip of acidity and a fine concentrated old-vine flavour but the finish is less rich and ample and shows a little astringency. This was a fine bottle a few years ago. It is still, just, 'very good'.

1962   **Drink soon**

(NB: Though château-bottled, this had a different label to the usual.) Medium-full, mature colour. Fullish, round, soft, aromatic – cedar and roast-chestnut – nose. Plumper than the 1964, not quite as full but less aged, less astringency. This is a generous wine, harmonious and seductive, if quite chunky, like lots of 1962s. Will still keep.

1959   **Drink soon**
An anonymous (non-château-bottled) bottle was sampled separately with Liz and Mike Berry of La Vigneronne a month or so later. Sadly, it was somewhat volatile and faded. I have only seen this wine in Belgian bottlings. Elsewhere, it has been full, rich, ripe and well-balanced. An ample wine, not too muscular.

1955   **Drink soon**
Good, mature colour. Gentle, fragrant, classy nose. With a faint hint of maderization as it developed. Medium body. Now beginning to show a bit of age and dryness but this was full and rich for a 1955. Still elegant and stylish. Ripe and sweet with a touch of rose-hips. Very good. Very lovely.

1953   **Drink soon**
Rather special! Fine, full colour. Lovely nose. Multidimensional, ripe, fragrant, subtle and complex. Marvellous soft fruit. Full for a 1953, must have been quite powerful. A beautifully balanced wine with real depth and class. Very long on the palate. Delicious.

1950   **Drink soon**
The usual very big 1950 colour, somewhat dense in appearance. Full, chunky nose. Tannin and astringency noticeable. Full and solid with aspects of burnt toast and spice. Always was and always will be a bit too tough for its own good.

1949   **Now–1997**
Magnificent colour. Splendid nose. Marvellous rich, mature, multidimensional fruit. Not a sign of age. This is a great wine with real old-vine, small-harvest concentration. Full-bodied, vigorous, rich, mouth-filling wine. Velvety, fat and ample. Great breed. Wonderful complex finish. Seems as if it is only just ready. Magnificent!

1948   **Drink soon**
An even more magnificent colour; almost black. The deepest yet. A brute! Tarry, liquorice nose, solid and dense, in a similar vein to the 1950 but with more fruit and less toughness, therefore more elegance. Full, solid, and less toughness, therefore more elegance. Full, solid, rich and powerful, with a bit of astringency on the finish.

1947   **Drink soon**
(Magnum) Another magnificent colour. Immense, typically porty, intensely concentrated 1947 fruit. Roasted, hot-vintage aspects. Full, quite solid, certainly meaty and tannic. Bigger and chunkier than the 1949 and drier on the finish. I prefer the 1949 because it is so supple and silky. This may be less elegant but there is still an immensely powerful concentration of fruit. So nevertheless a splendid wine.

1942   **Drink soon**
(Magnum) Quite full but definitely well-matured colour. Pleasant, soft, fragrant nose. No fade. Similar on the palate. Medium-full, elegant, quite sweet still. No undue astringency. Surprisingly good.

1937   **Drink soon**
(Magnum) Full, mature colour. A very slight element of maderization on the nose which, underneath, is quite chunky. As 1937s go, very good fruit and not at all too solid and four-square. Still sweet, still vigorous, though a little dry on the finish.

GAZIN

A number of Pomerol estates claim historical connections
with one or other of the two great military-religious orders
of the early Middle Ages: the Knights Hospitaller of St John
of Jerusalem (otherwise known as the Knights of Malta)
or the Knights Templars. Many, indeed, confuse the two.
One of these estates is Château Gazin. '*Ancien domaine des
Templiers*' it says on the château label and literature. '*Ancien
Domaine des Hospitaliers de Malte*' would be a little more accurate, for it is known that the Pomerol area was a resting
place for pilgrims on their way to Santiago de Compostella
and legend has it that the Knights of St John built a manor
house and a Romanesque church, since destroyed, in the locality, as well as a hospital on the site of Château Gazin.
Sadly there is hardly any archaeological evidence to support
this romance. There *is* a Maltese cross on a stone in the
Gazin courtyard, but it dates from the nineteenth century.
On the other hand, the cross on the lintel over the fireplace
in the château itself is considerably older.

The modern and documented history of Château Gazin –
does the word derive from *casa*, house, or *gazaille*, a place
where farmers bring their cattle to graze? – begins with
Antoine Feuilhade (1699–1776). Feuilhade, like his antecedents, was a lawyer, a politician and a wealthy local
landowner. Mayor of Libourne in 1735 and subsequently
Admiralty Commissioner for the area, a post he held until his
death, he was one of the pioneers of the gradual transformation of Pomerol from mixed farming and what wine there was
at the time was mainly white – to serious red wine viticulture.
Feuilhade chose to manage and modernize his vineyards himself rather than lease his land to sharecroppers, and he kept a
diary of his vinous activities from September 1763 to May
1773, an important source work. He owned a number of estates in the area, including one called Roussillon (now
Château Moncets) in nearby Néac, but it was only towards the
end of his life, in 1772, that he acquired Château Gazin.

HISTORY

From the Belleyme map produced around this period, we can see that there was already a substantial vineyard *in situ*. Feuilhade's son Jean, married to Jeanne Leglise of adjoining Château L'Evangile, survived his father by a mere two years, and the inheritance of Gazin subsequently passed to the children of Antoine's brother, Arnaud. Resident in Bordeaux and uninterested in viticulture, they put the estate up for sale, and Gazin was acquired by a M. Capitan-Bayonne, a Bordelais ship-fitter. This gentleman seems to have profited considerably during the Napoleonic period. He extended his viticultural activities by buying Château Rouget, also in Pomerol, and it was probably he who constructed the nucleus of the present-day château.

The next 80 years were to be a golden period for the Gazin-Rouget estate. Consistently classed among the top four properties in the commune, the combined vineyards were further developed and enlarged during the period of the Fabre family – the original Fabre was a nephew of Capitan-Bayonne – and produced between 50 and 60 *tonneaux*, a large amount for the time. After briefly passing through the hands of a J.J. Cabanes in the late 1870s the property was divided and the larger Gazin section acquired by a *négociant* called Léon Quenedey in 1885. It was to remain with M. Quenedey until 1917, in which year it was sold to Louis Soualle, another wine merchant from the north of France. At the same time Soualle bought La Dominique in Saint-Emilion. He is said to have additionally contemplated purchasing Trotanoy, Plince and Troplong-Mondot, all three of which were also on the market.

DE BAILLIENCOURT *DIT* COURCOL

Louis Soualle's daughter married Edouard de Bailliencourt, a wine merchant from the Artois. Descendants of the high Lords of Landas, the nickname *Courcol* (short neck) was given to one of them by Philippe Auguste, King of France, in 1214, for a feat of arms in the battle of Bouvines in Flanders, and subsequently adopted by all the members of the family. It has since become the family motto: 'By courage a Courcol'.

The venture into château ownership proved to be less successful than Soualle and his successors had hoped. After the Second World War, starved of profit, the Bailliencourts were forced to neglect La Dominique. It was sold, almost derelict, in 1969. They continued at Gazin, for the most part reluctantly, until the death of Edouard de Bailliencourt ten years later. Three of his four children then decided to sell out. Only Etienne de Bailliencourt wished to continue. In order to buy up his brother's shares and pay the death duties on the estate he was compelled to sell off part of the vineyard. Five hectares were transferred to Château Pétrus for a consideration of 24 million francs.

This was the nadir of the fortunes of Gazin. Profitable it might not have been, but at least the wines made in the 1940s and 1950s were very good (and earlier too if my experience of a Belgian bottled 1937 is anything to go by). The estate was sizeable and the wine popular and widely distributed. But following the February 1956 frosts, when the vineyard was particularly badly hit, necessitating a considerable replanting programme, the quality of the wines declined. The decision to pick by machine, taken in 1979, represented rock bottom.

THE VINEYARD

The vineyard of Château Gazin lies in the north-east corner of the Pomerol commune and marches with those of Pétrus and L'Evangile to the west and south. Now comprising 23 hectares, still large for the area, in a single piece, the vineyard is planted with 80 per cent Merlot, 15 per cent Cabernet Franc and 5 per cent Cabernet Sauvignon, the first planted on the clayey soil on the plateau on the western side, the two others on the more gravelly and sandy soil on the lower slopes to the north and east. You will notice, because of the decision to adopt mechanical harvesting, that the vines are wider-spaced than elsewhere.

THE CHÂTEAU AND THE *CHAIS*

The château lies in the middle of the vineyard surrounded by its dependent buildings, the whole resembling a small village. It is an attractive two-storey *maison bourgeoise*, built, so it is said, on the foundations of an earlier *manoir* and dating from the end of the eighteenth century, with later additions. One of these additions is the *cuvier*, attached to the right-hand side. Within, you will see an impressive battery of wooden vats. You have been misled. Behind the wooden facade the wine is in fact fermented in concrete.

Behind the château – you pass first through a new reception area, a large *salon* for parties and dinners, rather elegantly done – is the *chai à barriques*. This gives the usual monastic impression, a feeling accentuated by the Maltese cross echoes of the Knights Hospitaller.

A CHANGE FOR THE BETTER

Since 1987 there has been a transformation at Gazin. The arrival of Nicolas de Bailliencourt, who is now increasingly taking over from his father Etienne, produced a number of changes. The harvesting machine was abandoned. A second wine, Hospitalet de Gazin, was introduced. The vat time has been extended and the amount of *vin de presse* added to the *vin de goutte* reduced. The new oak element has been increased and the filtration, if employed, will be not as severe.

Moreover a new *cuvier* has been built across the courtyard. The fermenting vats in use up to now have really been far too large. Some 100 hectolitre *cuves*, with all the latest thermostatic controls, have replaced the old 175-hectolitre concrete vats. This size is more compatible with the quantities of fruit from the different sectors of the vineyard.

THE WINE

Prior to the February 1956 frost, and in principle, allowing for the age of the vines, prior to the transfer of the five hectares of plateau vineyard to Pétrus, Gazin was a bigger wine than it has been in recent years. It might have been a little sturdy at times, but there was an underlying richness and concentration in the best years: 1947, 1955 and 1964. It then seemed to lose not only depth but refinement, not only structure but fruit. The wines were not too bad, but they had lost their flair.

Since 1988, the same year as Etablissements J.P. Moueix took over the exclusivity for the sales of Château Gazin, this flair has begun to return. The rusticity has disappeared, and the wines are now beginning to show not only power but finesse. For the first time for a generation one can see the same sort of quality that is echoed elsewhere on the high plateau of Pomerol. Seventeen of the 23 productive Gazin hectares are on this plateau, and while it is debatable whether the remainder is capable of producing *grand vin*, the Hospitalet de Gazin will take care of this. Gazin looks as if it is on the verge of a renaissance.

THE TASTING

I sampled the majority of these wines at Château Gazin in January 1992. I have filled in one or two gaps with other recent notes.

1990   *Optimum drinking*   **1997–2009**

Good colour. Rich, fat, gently oaky. Real style and depth. Lovely fruit. Medium-full. Very good grip. Quite evidently largely Merlot. Rich, fat and ample. A succulent wine but one with good backbone. More class than the 1989. Long, very promising. Very good indeed for a 1990.

1989   **1997–2009**

Good colour. Sturdier nose. Richer, meatier. More closed. Full. Very good tannins. Has concentration and weight. Ripe and potentially very lush. Good grip. Very good for the vintage. What it lacks is the finesse of the above.

1988   **1995–2003**

Good colour. Attractive oaky nose with good

plump fruit behind it. Medium to medium-full. The attack is ample, the follow-through not as stylish or as attractive. It is balanced but it lacks a little finesse and flair at the end. Good for the vintage though.

1987   Drink soon
Good fresh colour. Quite fresh and fruity on the nose. Medium body. Surprisingly ample and engaging. No great depth or style. And the finish indicates it might get a bit astringent.

1986   Now–2000
Medium colour. No sign of maturity. Broad, somewhat unsophisticated nose. Fresh and fruity and really quite pleasant (not too rustic) on the palate, if with dry undertones. This finishes better than the nose would indicate (and better than I had expected). Good.

1985   1995–2002
Medium-full colour. Only a little sign of development. Quite full, rich and ample on the nose, if without any real class. Quite full, a bit ungainly on the palate. Meaty. Reasonable balance but it lacks depth and class. Only average. This is more rustic than the 1986. Will get skinny.

1984   Drink soon
The colour is quite vigorous for an 1984. And the nose smells more of chocolate and plums than old tea. On the palate a certain astringency lurks in the background but I've had a lot worse. Reasonable fat for an 1984. Good acidity (of course) keeps it fresh. Not a bad effort at all.

1983   Now–1998
Quite a full colour. Now showing signs of maturity at the rim. Quite fresh on the nose. Quite stylish fruit. Chocolate and plums again. Medium to medium-full. Good grip. A little touch which I could almost describe as metallic, giving an edginess. But the wine is reasonably ample and fresh. Good substance if no real class. Yet plump. Better within the context of the vintage than the 1985 perhaps.

1982   Now–2008
Fullish colour. Barely mature. Quite a rich substantial nose. Not without depth. This has the abundant fruit of the 1982 vintage. What it lacks is a touch of class and a bit of grip, but ample, lush and very ripe. Most enjoyable. Good for the vintage. Will still improve.

1981   Drink soon
Good colour. Barely mature. Very spicy and fruit cakey on the nose but also with an off flavour: slightly metallic which got worse as it developed in the glass. There is a touch of oxidation here. I think something went wrong in the *élevage*. Yet underneath there is good fruit. Fell apart quickly.

1979   Now–1997
Good colour. Not a lot of brown. Ripe nose. Quite elegant. Good freshness. Quite stylish. Medium-full. Ripe and elegant. No great weight or richness but this has life and even a certain complexity. Good plus for the vintage.

1961   Drink soon
Good rich colour. Little sign of age. Rich nose, quite high acidity. Plenty of depth and substance. Yet despite this a certain rusticity. Fullish, some tannin. Animal. Exotic. Not exactly very stylish. But rich and intense. Quite good at best for the vintage.

1955   Drink soon
Good colour. Mature. Fat Merlot nose, quite fresh. Fully mature. Slight touch of age, pinched as it developed in the glass. Full. Rich. Round. Slightly sweet spicy taste. Holding up well. Finishes long and interestingly.

1947   Now–1997
Full mature colour. Quite lovely nose. Real first growth quality. Really lovely concentrated fruit without any element of gameyness about it. Very concentrated and fat. Very fresh. Voluptuous fruit from start to finish. Very lovely. *Grand vin!* This bottle was from a perfect cellar. Stacks of life ahead of it.

1937   Past its best
(Belgian bottled by B. Destree et Fils) Good colour. Still vigorous. Pronounced sweet mint, acetone and some volatile acidity on the nose as it evolved, very mocha-chocolate in flavour. On the palate the fruit has dried up a bit. Acidity dominant. Some fruit but now essentially a bit sour. Past its best. But was good in its prime.

Other Vintages
The **1962** is round and succulent: still alive. The **1966** lacks a little finesse, but is ripe and structured. I prefer it to the **1970**, though that has merit too. The **1971** and **1975** are uninspiring but the **1978**, though a little dense, can also be recommended.

LAFLEUR

If you were to ask Jean-Pierre Moueix or his son Christian –
and you could hardly find two greater authorities on the
wines of Pomerol than these two excellent gentlemen –
whether there was any property in the area which could rival
Pétrus, you would immediately be offered the name of
Château Lafleur. In their opinion the tiny 4.5-hectare vineyard of Lafleur, potentially at least, can make wine equal
with Pomerol's *hors concours* growth.

Since the mid-1980s the wine of Lafleur has been at a
premium, and the few dozen cases released every season in
Great Britain exchange hands at high prices. I sold the 1982
for £102.50 a case ex-cellars in 1983. The value has multi-
plied ten times since.

For a wine of such high renown, the history of Lafleur is
neither very grand nor complicated, nor does it stretch very
far back. But then, by and large, this is true for most of the
neighbouring estates. On the Belleyme maps – drawn up in
1764, revised in 1774 and published in 1785 – one can see
that most of the great plateau of Pomerol was already planted
in vines, including what is now the Lafleur vineyard, and
from this and other records we know that certain estates were
already prominent in the area. As I have indicated in other
château profiles, the first to emerge included the Demays at
Certan, the Girauds at Trop Ennuie (Trotanoy), Catherine
Conseillan at La Conseillante and the Fontémoings at
Trochau. They were followed, in the years before the revolution, by the Arnauds at Pétrus, Jean Dalbet at Nénin and the
Feuilhades at Gazin.

HISTORY

Throughout the eighteenth century the Fontémoing family were the leading *négociants* and powerful landowners in the area. As well as Trochau they held land at a *lieu-dit* called Le Gay, on the north side of the Pomerol plateau. When Louis-Léonard Fontémoing's father died in 1750 this land was farmed on a share-cropping basis by a man called Jean Pignon (coincidentally 'Pignon' is today the same of a nearby hamlet). The actual ownership at the time, however, is somewhat in dispute. In the deeds of transfer from father to son, the local notary called Isambert, whose descendants were to own L'Evangile in the next century, marks the document '*Pour servir et valoir ce que de raison*' (for whatever useful purpose it might serve), and in 1782 Elie de Carle, owner of Figeac, made a curious donation to Fontémoing, ceding his rights to Le Gay, to a value of 22,000 *livres*. Was there a disputed inheritance? Had there been a lawsuit between Fontémoing senior and Vital de Carle, father of Elie?

Whether the vines farmed at Le Gay by Pignon included what is now Lafleur, and what happened to this particular parcel when the fortunes of Fontémoings began to decline after the Restoration, we do not know. The next mention of Le Gay that I have been able to unearth is in the second edition of Cocks and Féret, published in 1868. Here, under the title '*Au Gay*', a *Veuve* Greloud makes 35 *tonneaux* and the wine is rated ninth in the commune. The Gre[l]ouds are said to have purchased Le Gay from the De Béchade family, when it was called Le Manoir de Gay. Soon after, the estate was split between her sons. Henri took what was at first termed the Domaine de Lafleur; his brother Emile '*Au Gay*'. Today these are the Château Lafleur and Le Gay, though there are other neighbouring properties with both Fleur and Gay in their titles. Lafleur and Le Gay today occupy precisely the same terrain they did then, and they are still owned by the same family.

The reputation of Lafleur grew rapidly once the division had been made. By 1893 the wine was rated third in the commune after Pétrus and Vieux Château Certan. It fetched 1,700 to 2,000 francs a *tonneau* while Pétrus would sometimes fetch 3,000 francs, but nevertheless this lower price was on a par with the third growths of the Médoc. From the Grelouds Lafleur passed to a son-in-law André Robin, shortly after the First World War Robin won a gold medal for the state of his vineyard in 1925 – and, presumably because Robin was the sole survivor in his generation, Le Gay passed to him too. Since 1946 the owners of both properties have been his daughters.

Marie Robin – her elder sister Thérèse died in 1984 – is the last of the line. Neither lady ever married, and as the years went on, they lived an increasingly retiring life, the winters in Libourne, the summers at Le Gay – the château at Lafleur, such as it is, is not habitable – rarely venturing further afield, and seldom receiving visitors, especially foreign customers. Since 1985 the property has been farmed by Jacques Guinaudeau, a young cousin of Marie Robin, and his wife Sylvie. Since their arrival, a second wine, Pensées de Lafleur, has been created. All the 1987 was declassified into second wine.

LAFLEUR

The vineyard of Lafleur is in one piece, *un seul tenant* as the French say, though it is divided on the cross by two roads. It lies barely 200 metres north of Pétrus itself, the vines marching on one side with those of Lafleur-Pétrus, in another direction with those of La Fleur-Gazin. To the north and west lie the Le Gay vineyards, Le Gay itself, La Croix-de-Gay and Vray-Croix-de-Gay. The soils of both the Robin vineyards are gravelly, but Lafleur has more clay. It is this clay which gives the wine its extra power. The four hectares are planted with equal portions of Merlot and Bouchet, as the Cabernet Franc is known locally. Back in the 1920s there was Noir de Pressac (Malbec) in the vineyard, but this, in common with the other top properties in the Libournais, has been progressively phased out. As the property escaped much of the damage of the 1956 frost the majority of the vines are now of considerable age, as an average yield of only 26 hectolitres per hectare in the late 1980s would indicate. Production now averages 1,250 cases per annum.

André Robin's motto was '*Qualité passe quantité*' ('Quality before quantity'), and the vinification of the wine, continued after his death, was very much by old-fashioned methods: fermentation with the stalks in concrete vats at quite high temperatures, a long maceration and little if any use of new oak. This *vinification à l'ancienne* can pose problems, particularly where, as is the case at Lafleur, the state of cleanliness in the cellar was not such as to inspire confidence. Since Jacques Guinaudeau has been in charge things have been somewhat refined. The grapes are now de-stemmed and from one- to two-thirds new oak is employed.

THE WINE

Nevertheless, even under the old regime, the wine was of a very high standard. The pecking order in Pomerol since the war, according to successive editions of Cocks and Féret, has gone: Pétrus, then, switching places from time to time, L'Evangile, Trotanoy, Vieux Château Certan and La Conseillante, and then Lafleur, L'Eglise-Clinet, Petit-Village and Certan-de-May, followed by La Violette and Nénin before we come to Lafleur-Pétrus and Latour-à-Pomerol – succession I have disputed elsewhere.

There has been some criticism of older vintages of Lafleur. I have not myself encountered any really dirty bottles, but I have occasionally found the wine at first a little bit too much on the robust and chunky side, even a bit stewed. I have noticed however that if you let the wine breathe properly this disappears. The wine has much more in character with Latour-à-Pomerol or with Pétrus itself than with its neighbour Lafleur-Pétrus. I feel that the Lafleur vineyard must more resemble Pétrus in its geological make-up than the more purely gravel soil of Lafleur-Pétrus, despite the latter being its neighbour, and it is this which gives this extra solidity and power to the wine.

My experience of the wine of Lafleur was slight until May 1986. In that month I attended one of the most spectacular vertical tastings it has ever been my privilege to experience. Russel Norton of New Haven, Connecticut, ably assisted on this side of the Atlantic by Steven Browett of Farr Vintners and with additional bottles generously provided by Christian Moueix, Donald Kurtz of New York and others, assembled a truly comprehensive range of vintages of Lafleur. The tasting was admirably hosted by Bob Feinn of Mount Carmel Wines.

It was a remarkable tasting. I do not think there was any disagreement among the assembled company of a dozen experienced tasters that it was one of the best – if not *the* best – vertical tasting we had ever enjoyed. I think we had all expected the recent vintages such as the 1982 to show well, indeed perhaps rather to overshadow the older wines. Yet this was not the case. For me the highspots, of which there were many, included a magnificent 1979, a sumptuous 1966, an impressive 1964, one of the best 1962s I have ever drunk, a 1961 of truly first growth quality, a voluptuous 1959 and deliciously elegant and remarkably vigorous 1943. Lafleur is indeed a wine of great power as well as size, but this power is not overwhelming, the wine though dense and alcoholic is not too much of a blockbuster. It is balanced with not only a creamy old-vine concentration but with great elegance, producing an intensity of flavour rarely encountered outside the first growths and their equivalents. I emerged from a breathtaking day with the feeling that if the more direct Moueix influence could improve on that – and, yes, the 1982 is indeed stupendous – Pétrus really *will* have to look to its laurels.

THE TASTING

At the end of February 1992, I presented a 'once-in-a-lifetime' tasting of Château Lafleur at the Hollywood Wine Society's annual celebration, ably organized by Bob Maliner of Miami. The notes on the recent vintages come from that occasion, most of the rest from the New Haven, Connecticut, tasting in 1986.

Optimum drinking

1990   2000–2025

Excellent colour. Powerful and concentrated on the nose; dense and tannic, but an underlying sumptuous richness and breed – almost, indeed, over-ripe. This is very splendid, but at present rather closed. But on the finish the wine give every indication of seriously high quality, very much at 1989 levels. Excellent.

1989   2000–2025

Marvellous colour. Similarly massive in appearance and attack. But a little more accessible. Profoundly rich, old-vine, low-*rendement* concentration. Even better than the 1990, I would judge today. Fat, opulent, aromatic and very impressive. Very long and complex. *Grand vin!*

1988   1999–2009

Good colour. Fine nose. Dense, but ripe and fleshy. Firm, still closed. Fullish, tannic, very good acidity. Touch of oak. Masculine. Plenty of style and depth. Excellent for the vintage. Fine.

1986   1998–2012

Very good colour. A little more marked by new oak than the other recent vintages. Not as sumptuous as the 1985, but a splendid effort for the vintage nonetheless. Full, the tannins showing a little. But there is very good fruit and good acidity. It is the most ungainly of the younger wines and it will need a little time yet before it is ready. Fine but not great.

1985   1998–2018

Very good colour. Lush, rich, concentrated, mainly Merlot, voluptuous. This is full and rich, fat and voluptuous. This is full and rich, fat and voluptuous. Good grip. A harmonious, plummy, concentrated wine. More dimension than the 1988. Fine also.

1983   Now–1999

Medium to medium-full colour. A touch attenuated on the nose. But plenty of fruit nevertheless. What it lacks is a bit of grip. A little bit of old tea and astringency on the attack. A little weak at the knees. Now ready. Reasonable acidity but lacks a bit of style. Good at best. Won't make old bones. Just about ready.

1982   1995–2025

Fine colour, barely mature. Brilliant nose. Very, very rich and concentrated. Hugely fruity. Full,

very, very concentrated and chocolatey. Real old-vine flavour. A brilliant example. Very good grip. Massive concentration and fruit. Very fine indeed, even for a 1982.

1981   Now–2001

Medium-full colour, a little development. Good, ripe blackberry and cedarwood nose. Medium-full, some tannin but quite accessible already. Good, fresh creamy fruit – plum and mulberries as well as blackberries. Good length. Very fine indeed for the vintage.

1980   **Drink up**

Medium colour, some maturity. Broad, evolved nose, quite attractive without much fruit or grip. Medium body, a little fresher than the nose would indicate but the fruit is rapidly getting stringy and some astringency lurks underneath. A little better than I remember but no great shakes nevertheless.

1979   **Now–2010**

Very big colour indeed, no development. Noticeably a rather different style of wine-making than the 1981; firm, backward, at first rather dense on the nose. Tough, even earthy; very full and tannic. Yet as it evolved in the glass got better and better and better. Lovely bitter-chocolate and black-cherry flavours. Rich, concentrated, finishing very well. Surely as good as Pétrus.

1978   **Now–2005**

Full colour, little development. Bit, rich, almost tarry nose. Reminds me of Northern Rhône. Full, but less dense and tannic than the 1979. Rich but lacking an element of real charm because there is something slightly bitter in the make-up. Certainly good; if it can pick up a bit of generosity as its oftens will be even better. Subsequent bottles have maintained this solidity. The wine is still youthful though.

1977   **Drink up**

Medium colour, just about mature. This bottle a bit corky but the wine (discounting this) has a reasonable amount of fruit and substance and must rate as good for the vintage at the very least. Fresh if, naturally, one-dimensional.

1976   **Drink soon**

Medium colour, quite mature. Dense and chunky and aromatic on the nose, the fruit has already dried up a bit and the acidity is low. Some complexity in a spicy sort of way. Initially quite fresh and not too short but did not hold up well in the glass. Typical of the vintage.

1975   **Now–2008**

Very big colour, some maturity now. Initially very big, dense, earthy, even farmyardy on the nose, masking the richness and concentration of the wine and reminding me, in a way, of some of the Libournais 1950s. As it developed this rustic aspect disappeared, the ripeness of the fruit became apparent, and despite the size and structure – from both the vintage and the old-fashioned wine-making – one could see high quality and an excellent plummy, blackcurrant, bitter chocolate concentration underneath. This is very good indeed – the exception to many, many 1975s.

1974   **Drink up**

Fullish colour for the vintage, just about mature. A little austere and skeletal on the nose; acidity shows, but the wine is not too ungenerous. Quite full, lacks a bit of charm but by no means disagreeable, astringent or unduly aged. Has fruit. Lacks the elegance of the 1972 and the flesh of the 1973 but (though one sees few 1974s these days) must rate as good for the vintage.

1973   **Drink soon**

Fullish colour, mature. Mellow, milk-chocolate and cedarwood nose, slightly spurious. Fullish for the vintage, still a lot of life. Warm, slightly sweet if rather one-dimensional fruit; but there is structure here and the wine is very pleasant. Very good for the vintage.

1972   **Drink soon**

Very good full colour. Bigger and more alive than the 1973. fine nose, lighter and more ethereal than the 1973 but more elegant. Similar on the palate, though finishes a little astringent and hard. Remarkable for such an off-vintage.

1971   **Drink soon**

Good full colour, barely mature. Fine nose, still youthful, has depth as well as density. Fullish on the palate, slightly spicy and a touch bitter but has fruit and grip. Lacks a bit of class, generosity and richness compared with the best Libournais 1971s. Just a touch too inky, lacking suppleness. Good but not great.

1970   **Now–2005**

Full, dense colour, very little maturity if any. Volatile acidity evident on the nose but this is in no way excessive. This is clearly the *ancienne méthode* of wine-making. Full, earthy, tannic, dense wine but with heaps of concentrated, meaty, plummy fruit. This is very fine indeed.

1966   **Now–2000 plus**

Marvellous full colour and an equally marvellous

rich nose with a real 1961 concentration. Quite splendid, and with none of the toughness and density of the 1970 at all. A full wine, still with some tannin, absolutely crammed with fruit and laid out with an impressive amount of class and complexity. A complete wine. Good as the 1970 is, it will never match this. Well-nigh perfect.

1964   **Drink soon**

Similar colour. Another splendid nose, less blackcurrant and bitter chocolate, fatter, more *crème brûlée*, sweeter, slightly porty. Full-bodied, mature, yet there is a solidity of tannin still apparent. This is not overshadowed by the above. Rather more burly, less silky-smooth perhaps but with an equal amount of richness and concentration. Marginally less elegant but still of very high quality indeed.

1962   **Drink soon**

Very fine colour, mature. More mellow on the nose but again a wine of stupendous quality. This again is 1961-ish: aromatic, rich, enormous depth and class. Full-bodied and fully mature; slightly less size and solidity than the 1964. Lovely blackcurrant fruit, marvellous balance, marvellous complexity. Subtly different from the 1966 but of equal stunning quality. The best 1962 I have ever tasted? Still fresh as a daisy, and perfect for drinking now.

1961   **Now–2001**

Incredible colour, practically black. The three previous wines were so good, even magnificent; how do you describe this which is yet better! On the two most recent occasions I saw this wine I remarked on its initial solidity, leading one to suspect it was a bit too dense for its own good, and noticed that this disappeared and the wine just went on and on getting better and better. This 1961, like all the bottles, had been carefully decanted prior to the session and by the time it was poured out any undue toughness had completely disappeared. Incredible concentration of old-vine fruit on the nose and depth and complexity of flavour on the palate; real nectar. Hugh but not dense; not so much silky or velvety as engulfing you in ermine. This is *grand vin* even by the most exacting of top-class 1961 standards. Seems as it will last for ever. Magnificent.

1959   **Drink soon**

Another incredible colour. Another splendidly concentrated nose with no undue toughness. Ripe but not baked, classic Pomerol blackcurrants, warm and inviting. Medium-full body, less intensely fruity and concentrated than the 1961, slightly more roasted – a touch of coffee beans and hazelnut very nearly as multidimensional but not quite. This again is quite splendid. A powerful voluptuous wine of enormous appeal and seductiveness and no sign of age at all. The second best wine of the New Haven tasting.

1955   **Drink soon**
(Tasted in 1986) Fullish colour, mature. Nose quite developed. Perhaps this wine would have been better poured direct from the bottle because classy as it is there is a faint hint of fade. Fine, old, mellow, cedary, fullish, rich, sweetish wine. Gentle. Old roses and chocolate. Great charm.

1955   **Drink soon**
(Tasted in 1992) Fine colour. Vigorous, old-viney, plump and lovely nose. Very complex, still sweet and generous. Not a bit old. Fullish, round, sweet, soft and lovely. A great 1955. Very complex and fragrant. Could be a 1953.

1952   **Drink soon**
(Not château bottled. Bottled in Holland?) Good full, mature colour. Fine, firm, richly fruity, fragrant, classy nose. Not dense. Lovely old mature wine. Still reasonably fresh, though developing a slightly burnt finish as it oxidized in the glass. Rather better than the 1955 in 1986. Has a lot of depth and complexity. Very fine wine.

1950   **Drink soon**
Splendid dense full colour, some brown. A little oxidization, even maderization on the nose. Better on the palate. Big, dense and tannic, but at the same time fat, meaty and rich. A bit on the clumsy side compared with most but good nevertheless.

1947   **Drink soon**
(Belgian bottled by Vandermeulen, tasted in 1986) Amazing colour. Now showing a bit of age but in its prime but must have been a wine of 1961 quality. Still very rich and porty indeed on the nose, and this is the best part about it. Full-bodied but a little astringent on the palate. Voluptuous and creamy nevertheless.

1947   **Drink soon**
(English bottled by John Harvey, tasted in 1992) Medium-full but slightly cloudy colour. Very rich, damson acidity but also porty nose. Sweet and fullish, quite lush volatile acidity. Jammy and raspberry-blackberry flavoured. Still a lot of enjoyment. A very typical 1947. Over-ripe and voluptuous and almost sweet. Yet very good grip and class. Fine.

1945   **Drink soon**
(Bottled in Bordeaux ? Cruse label.) Another very full colour indeed, some brown. Fine nose, no harshness or density. On the palate full, chunky, some astringency as well as tannin. This was perhaps a bit too solid for its own good.

1943   **Drink soon**
Fine, full, old colour. Lovely old fragrant nose, rather more class as well as life compared with the 1945. A fullish, mellow, gentle wine, which still has plenty of delicious complex fruit. A lovely old wine which is still holding up well.

LATOUR-À-POMEROL

According to my 1969 edition of Cocks and Féret, there are seven properties in the Bordeaux area with Latour, as one word, in their name. In addition, there are no fewer than 75 more which incorporate the two words La Tour. Among all these estates, that which has pride of place after the Pauillac Latour itself is the Pomerol Latour – Château Latour-à Pomerol.

Unlike most of its peers in the commune, Latour-à-Pomerol is not a single vineyard. There are as many as 25 different parcels despite the fact that the vineyard, in two main sections, occupies only eight hectares, and they lie in the heart of the commune. The property and its history is the union of these towards the end of the last century and the first twenty years of this.

Château Latour-à-Pomerol has belonged to the family of the present owner, Mme Lili-Paul Lacoste, for as far back as records exist to the first half of the nineteenth century. The name of the proprietors then was Chambaud. The earliest detailed listing of the principal Pomerol properties, as I have pointed out elsewhere, does not appear until the second edition of Cocks and Féret (1868); neither Latour-à-Pomerol nor the name Chambaud is found in this book.

HISTORY

In 1875, the only daughter of the Chambauds married a M. Louis Garitey and it is under his name that the property is first mentioned at the end of Pomerol's second growths in the Cocks and Férets of the 1890s. The production was around nine *tonneaux*. Garitey died on 23 July 1914, and his estate was divided up among his three daughters – Mme Edmond Loubat inherited part of Latour and was later to buy, progressively, Château Pétrus. Firstly, however, in 1917, she acquired a vineyard known as Clos des Grandes-Vignes next to the church. This is the nucleus of today's Latour-à-Pomerol. She also added Haut-Canton-Guillot, a *cru* situated next to Château Trotanoy. By 1929, production had risen to 40 *tonneaux*.

What precisely were the respective histories of Grandes-Vignes and Haut-Canton-Guillot is unclear. In the 1899 Cocks and Féret, English edition, the 'growth of Grandes-Vignes' is listed eight amongst the first growths, owned by M. Hermel and producing eight *tonneaux*. Yet it doesn't appear at all in the 1893 (French edition). There is a 'Guillot', firstly owned by someone called Gros, then by M. Larquey and later by André Bermond, and this, with a 25-*tonneaux* production, must have been a substantial estate. However, a 'Gombaud-Guillot' is also listed and this, too, increased quite significantly in production between the turn of the century and 1929.

On the death of Mme Loubat on 5 November 1961, Latour passed to her niece, Mme Paul Lacoste. In the succeeding year the firm of Jean-Pierre Moueix was appointed *fermier* for the estate. The vineyard is now run and the wine made, reared and sold by the same team responsible for all the Moueix properties.

THE VINEYARD

The main part of the vineyard, a parcel of five hectares, surrounds the Pomerol church. Most of the rest is situated further west and to the north near the N89 Libourne-Périgueux road. Here the land is lower, flatter and more sandy, and the resulting wine is lighter. As one travels east towards Pétrus and Saint-Emilion, the terrain rises and there is more gravel in the soil. Most of the Latour-à-Pomerol soil consists of sandy clay and gravel (*limoneux-graveleux*, as the French geologists put it). The vineyard has a considerable portion of old vines, averaging over 30 years old. It is planted in the ratio 85 per cent Merlot and 15 per cent Cabernet Franc and now produces 35 *tonneaux* (3,500 cases).

THE CHÂTEAU

The château of Latour-à-Pomerol, with its *chais* behind, lies next to the subsidiary part of the vineyard between the church and the Périgueux road adjacent to La Grave-à-Pomerol (another Moueix property). It is a small, grey, elegant two-storey, building, with a little pointed tower at one end from which the property takes its name. It is uninhabited.

THE WINE

Latour-à-Pomerol is a full wine with a concentration which comes from the dominance of old vines in the *encépagement*. I find the power of the wine has more in common with Lafleur and indeed with Pétrus itself than it has with, say Lafleur-Pétrus or Trotanoy. Recent vintages, as a result of the vineyard not having had to be almost completely replanted like Lafleur-Pétrus, have been very consistent. Those like 1970 are real blockbusters. I would certainly class Latour-à-Pomerol with the very best Pomerols if not *quite* at the top of the tree.

THE TASTING

The more recent vintages which follow were re-tasted in London in 1993. The older wines come from a session at the New Haven, Connecticut, wine weekend in September 1987, the day after those of Lafleur-Pétrus. My thanks to Bob Feinn of Mount Carmel Wines for his hospitality and to Russel Norton for his organization and to both for their invitation to attend. By and large, we preferred the Latours to the Lafleur-Pétruses.

1990 — Optimum drinking **2000–2020**

Very good colour. Concentrated and old-viney, almost creamy cassis and blackberry on the nose. Fullish, rich, concentrated, quite substantial as well as ample, with a fat, opulent succulence underneath and very good acidity. Long. Fine.

1989 **2000–2025**

Very good colour. Spicier and lusher, but very much in the same old-viney mode. I think this is even more concentrated. Full, meaty, very rich. Lovely ripe tannins. Very intensely flavoured, plenty of grip. This is a lovely example. Fine plus.

1988 **1997–2013**

Good colour. Firmer than the two above on the nose, more austere too. But it isn't as exciting. Good damson and Merlot fruit on the nose. Certainly has good grip. Fullish. The tannins are ripe and the wine has length. But while certainly very appealing, it has not the concentration or depth for more than very good plus.

1986 **Now–1997**

Good colour. Compared with the 1988 this is a little diffuse. The fruit is ripe, but the wine lacks grip and definition. Medium body. Attractive but not serious. Merely good. Will come forward soon.

1985 **Now–2002**

Like the 1986, though with less excuse, this is not up to the very best in the vintage. Medium-full colour. Quite fleshy Merlot fruit on the nose. Medium-full body, ripe, round and ample, but it lacks a bit of excitement, and the finish is not as long and intense as it might be. Good plus.

1983 **Now–2008**

Good colour. Ripe and meaty on both nose and palate. This is considerably more substantial than Lafleur-Pétrus. Medium-full, still some tannin. Good grip. Ripe and rich and concentrated. A very good 1983 Libournais. Finishes long.

1982 **1995–2015**

Full colour. Fat, rich, concentrated, old-viney nose, smoky (bonfires) as it developed. Powerful and closed up but of excellent potential. Full, spicy in extract, tannic. Rich in a very fine earthy sort of way, very concentrated and with a fine residual flavour. Long, rich, ripe acidity. Fine.

1981 **Now–2003**

Medium colour, just a little maturity. Soft, plump, gentle, fruity nose, perhaps a little bland because it lacks a little grip. Medium body, just a little tannin. Good rich fruit and a little more acidity on the palate than the nose would indicate. Good finish and an attractive wine. Very good for the vintage at the very least.

1979 **Now–2008**

Medium-full colour, just a little maturity. Medium nose, attractively fruity – blackberry jam – fresher and more interesting than the 1981 because of its higher acidity. Medium-full body, still some tannin. Ripe, rich, stylish and even quite concentrated. This is quite a structured wine for a 1979. Has good depth, good length and will keep well. Again, very good, at the very least, for the vintage. Better than the 1981.

1978 **Now–2008**

Medium to medium-full colour. Less than the 1979 and more maturity. Rich, cedary, old-vine concentration. Riper, more substantial and less developed than the 1979. Yet less structured and less high a quality in terms of its vintage. Rich, quite a lot of depth. Good but not great for a 1978.

1976 **Drink soon**

Good colour for the vintage. Medium to medium-full, no undue maturity. Similar, indeed, to the 1978. Surprisingly fresh on the nose for a 1976. Cooked fruit but not too dry or blowsy. This is a very good 1976. Good grip, quite full, cedary, roast-chestnut spice. Neither that long nor that elegant but quite fat. Shows well. Holding up well.

1975 **Now–2007**

Medium-full colour, some maturity. Closed on the nose, even a bit ungenerous at first. Fullish, some tannin. Started off a bit burly and ungainly but one could see an underlying richness, if a slight absence, of style or charm. Developed in the glass acquiring an almost chocolatey fruit. Rich. Plenty of depth. Very good – almost very good indeed – for a 1975.

1974 **Drink up**

Medium colour, mature but not unduly so. Elegant, surprisingly good, fruity nose, continuing into the palate. Lightish in body but has good fruit and no sign of age. Really not bad at all. Even stylish.

1971 **Now–1998**

Good, mature colour. This has an elegant, stylish nose, with very lovely fruit. Ripe if a little austere, like so many of the best Libournais 1971s. A lovely, balanced, medium-full wine. Subtle and therefore even more seductive. High class. Delicious now.

1970 Now–2010

Stunning quality! Reminds me of a 1961 in its almost super-abundance of fruit. Full, barely mature colour. Rich, concentrated, fat nose. A huge, tannic, powerful, almost porty wine, with marvellous fruit. Meaty, old-viney. Got better and better in the glass. Really excellent.

1967 **Drink up**

Very good colour, especially for the vintage. No undue age. Fine nose, ample and plump, slightly aromatic, elegant fruit. Medium body, lightening up a little but ripe and supple with no astringency. Good stuff.

1966 **Drink soon**

This is another, almost text-book example of the disappointment of some 1966s. Good mature colour. A little pinched, a little light on the nose. Only medium body on the palate, has lightened up and the fruit has faded to leave a somewhat astringent finish and a bitter aftertaste. The acidity obtrudes. At a previous vertical tasting kindly set up for me by Christian Moueix in 1981, I remarked on the denseness of the wine. It did not sing like the 1971 and the 1970. Yet, at a 1966 tasting in 1986, though solid, it was rich and concentrated. I gave it 16/20. As I have always insisted, bottles of older wine do vary and it is dangerous to be too dogmatic.

1962 **Drink soon**

Good colour. Fine, fat, plump, smoky, aromatic nose. Medium body, round and generous, with both charm and elegance. Still very vigorous. A most attractive example of the most enjoyable 1962 vintage. Medium-full body, plenty of depth and complexity. Fine, long, ripe finish.

1961 Now–2001 plus

Very fine, full colour. Marvellous nose, an immense concentration of sweet fruit. This is a very full, porty wine of great depth and complexity. Powerful, velvety, as superb as the very best 1961s. A real *coulis* of rich fruit. Marvellous!

1959 Now–1997

Another amazing colour and another very powerful, sweet nose. The 1961 is more concentrated and porty. This is more roasted. More tannic, denser, spicier, more muscular. A swashbuckling wine, possibly a bit top-heavy, but I love it.

1952 **Drink soon**

Similar colour but older. Sweet and mellow on the nose, was never too tough but the power is now declining. Full of old-vine ripe fruit. Still most enjoyable but a wine now nearing the end of its active life.

1947 **Drink soon**

Fine, full colour. Splendid sweet, porty nose. Velvety, concentrated, plump and fruity. This has a lot of depth and extract. Still very fresh. Fullish, no undue solidity. Rather more stylish – indeed, unexpectedly refined than some 1947s. Lovely, ripe, sweet finish. Delicious.

1945 **Drink soon**

Very fine, big, dense-seeming colour, more than the above. The nose shows power, structure and tannin. Very fine, full, rich fruit, so not too solid or over powering on the palate. Yet doesn't quite have the follow-through. Very fine but the 1947 is better.

PETIT-VILLAGE

Many of the top wines of Pomerol, I suspect, are known more by their reputation than by actual tasting experience. As Lafite produces eight or nine times more wine than Pétrus, it is naturally easier to get hold of and there is no scarcity premium either! Similarly with the super-seconds: Ducru-Beaucaillou, Léoville-Las-Cases, Pichon-Longueville-Lalande and Palmer appear more frequently than Trotanoy, Lafleur, Vieux Château Certan and La Conseillante. Among these Pomerol *crus* must now be included Château Petit-Village. Petit-Village is different from its neighbours, though, because for many years it has been owned by outsiders. After the First World War it was acquired by the *négociants* Ginestet. From the Ginestets, it passed to the Prats family of Château Cos d'Estournel. In July 1989, in order to safeguard Cos from the effects of inheritance taxation, the property was sold to AXA Millésimes, who among other things own Pichon-Baron.

The origin of the rather curious name of Petit-Village arises, it is said, from the fact that, seen from afar, the small, farmhouse-style château and its dependent buildings resemble a hamlet. Another version suggests that here was the original heart of the village of Pomerol itself.

If you approach the nucleus of the Pomerol *vignoble*, the plateau of Pétrus and its surrounding neighbours, from the direction of Libourne, you will first drive through the little village of Catusseau. There is then a fork in the road. Left for Vieux Château Certan, Certan-de-May, and Pétrus itself; right for the road towards Montagne-Saint-Emilion, along which lies La Conseillante and L'Evangile, and, opposite, Château Cheval-Blanc. Directly in front of you, as the road divides, the triangle of vineyard is that of Château Petit-Village. In the middle of these vines lies the château itself.

HISTORY

The area was already under vines by the time Belleyme drew up his maps of the area in the second half of the eighteenth century. It was owned after the Revolution, if not then, by a family called Dufresnes, from whom it passed to a family called De Seguin, who were for a time also involved with Clos-Fourtet. By 1868, the first year for which we have specific records, the Seguin estate was rated fifth in the commune and produced 20 to 25 *tonneaux*.

The early history of Petit-Village is sparse. The De Seguins were followed by the Buidin-Buffins in about 1870, and they by a Monsieur J.P. Héron in the early 1890s. Details of the background to these exchanges are missing. The present-day era begins in 1919 when Petit-Village was purchased by Fernand Ginestet of the Bordeaux *négociant* house of Ginestet and Latrille.

GINESTET

Fernand Ginestet had set up at 132 Quai des Chartrons in 1899. This was an auspicious year, one of a pair of high-quality, prolific vintages – a parallel is 1989 or 1990 perhaps – and proof that despite phylloxera (though most of the great wines must have been produced at least primarily by engrafted, aged vines which had escaped the scourge), Bordeaux could still produce vintages which combined quantity with high quality.

The Ginestet business soon prospered. Their first successes were in northern France and the Low Countries, and exports soon expanded to Britain, Germany and Scandinavia. Despite the First World War, increasing sales and profitability do not seem to have been affected, and, like the Cordiers at the same time, and other, older-established *négociants* some 50 years earlier, Ginestet began to buy into the properties themselves.

Fernand Ginestet's first foray was into Saint-Estèphe. He bought Château Cos d'Estournel in 1917. Two years later he bought Château Petit-Village and Clos-Fourtet in Saint-Emilion, and in 1925 was to become a member of the syndicate which bought Château Margaux. This Pomerol purchase must have caused a bit of a stir. Hitherto the wines of the Libournais had been rather ignored by the Chartronnais. For a member to actually involve himself to the extent of becoming the proprietor himself must have been rather alarming.

Moreover, it was not as if Petit-Village was at one time one of the high-fliers of the commune. Pomerols were then unfashionable, and under the Buidin-Buffin and Héron regimes the reputation of Petit-Village itself had declined somewhat. In 1922 Cocks and Féret rate it tenth in the commune, between Gazin and La Grave-Trigant-de-Boisset. It produced 45 *tonneaux*, more or less the amount it makes today. But the buildings were modest, not exactly a country estate; there was no park, no grand mansion for putting up friends over the weekend. It was purely a functional wine farm.

No doubt the reasons for the purchase were simply commercial. Petit-Village, Clos-Fourtet and other less distinguished Libournais estates were bought in order to eliminate the middlemen and to provide continuity of name and supply for the Ginestet clientele.

In 1971 the Ginestet domaines were divided among the family: Pierre, Fernand's son, took Margaux; his sister Madame Jean Prats the remainder (Clos-Fourtet had already been sold). Groupement Foncier des Domaines Prats is the owner of Château Cos d'Estournel and Château Marbuzet in Saint-Estèphe. Bruno, youngest of Mme Prats's three sons, remained in charge until the estate and a couple of lesser Prats domaines in the Libournais were sold to AXA in July 1989. It is now administered by Jean-Michel Cazes and Daniel Llhose of Lynch-Bages.

THE VINEYARD

Bounded by Vieux Château Certan and Certan-de-May to the north, La Conseillante to the east and Beauregard to the south, the eleven-hectare vineyard of Château Petit-Village lies more or less in one piece in the form of a triangle. The land declines slightly on three sides, this being the western tongue of the Pomerol plateau, and the soil is made up of clay with some gravel on a solid, iron-rich base. The vineyard is planted in the ratio 80 per cent Merlot, 10 per cent Cabernet Franc and 10 per cent Cabernet Sauvignon and produces about 40 to 50 *tonneaux*.

THE CHÂTEAU

As I have said, Château Petit-Village and its dependent buildings are not the most architecturally impressive. A simple rectangular, two-storey farmhouse forms the 'château'. From this, enclosing a small courtyard, extend two wings wherein the wine is made and stored. The bunches are completely de-stalked, vinified in steel vats, and then transferred to concrete *cuves* for the malolactic fermentation, before being moved across the courtyard into the *chais*. Bottling takes place after eighteen months or so in wood.

BRUNO PRATS

As at Château Cos d'Estournel, the arrival of Bruno Prats in the early 1970s was to engender the decisive extra which marks the difference between merely 'good' and 'very good indeed'; bridging the gap between classed-growth quality and a wine which could be a contender for a super-second. Naturally this was not achieved overnight. For a start the vineyard had been almost completely wiped out as a result of the February 1956 frost; so in the early 1970s the average age of the vines was barely twenty years old. Additionally, at the time the bulk of the terrain was replanted, it was decided to follow the lead of neighbour Vieux Château Certan and introduce a substantial proportion of Cabernet Sauvignon. This was eventually found to be unsuitable and the percentage has since been reduced to 10 per cent.

The *cuvier* was renovated in 1976 and a battery of epoxy-lined steel *cuves* introduced. The proportion of new oak was gradually increased. It is now normally at least 50 per cent per annum. The 1985 was matured entirely in new wood. Bruno Prats also experimented with different types of oak. What succeeds in the Médoc does not necessarily work in Pomerol – and vice versa, he will tell you. The difference are slight, but crucial.

By means of all this, and simply a greater attention to the details of careful wine-making and selection, the quality of Petit-Village has shown an exciting improvement. This has been particularly evident since 1980. The 1977 was also excellent for the vintage, but neither 1978 nor 1979 are more than 'good'. Both 1975 and 1976 though, in their different ways, are very fine. However I do not wish to denigrate the wine produced before Bruno Prats took over. As you will see in the notes which follow, the 1971 is fragrant, elegant and still vigorous. The 1970 is stylish and full of fruit, if not as powerful as some of its neighbours, and the 1967 and 1966 are both very good wines in their respective vintages. In the earlier vintages the 1964 is also a success, if not quite in the top flight for what was an exceptional year for the Libournais, the 1962 is rich and still vigorous, and the 1961, on the single occasion I have seen it recently, was round, rich, sweet and still vigorous.

THE WINE

The style of the wine at Petit-Village has discreetly changed in recent years, as it has at Cos d'Estournel. In part this is due to the maturing vineyard, in part to the reduction in Cabernet Sauvignon. Mostly, I suspect, the change reflects the personality and perfectionism of Bruno Prats (we have yet to see what effect the recent change of ownership will have). There is now a warmth and a richness, a suppleness which does not deny vigour and backbone, above all concentration and complexity of fruit. Petit-Village has always been a well-structured wine. Now there is an element of flesh and fat covering the skeleton, and with this has come finesse as well as charm. Leopold, King of the Belgians, on tasting the wine, said, 'Strike out the word '*Petit*' in the title'. I would put it a different way: AXA have a right-bank wine to compete with their Pichon-Baron on the left-bank.

THE TASTING

The majority of the following wines were tasted at Cos d'Estournel in April 1986. I have added notes on more recent vintages sampled in October 1992, and on a trio of older wines sampled in 1993.

Optimum drinking

1990   **1999–2019**

This is better than the 1989. Fine colour. Full, rich and concentrated on the nose, with a lovely mulberry-blackberry fruit I find most attractive. Full, plenty of new oak. Opulent, lush and profound. Distinctive. Fine.

1989   **1998–2014**

Very good colour. Again it is rather more new oaky than earlier vintages, but it doesn't sing as much as the 1990. Good rich nose, with a hint of spice. Fullish, ripe and well-balanced, but not quite as intense or as persistent as the above. Very good indeed nevertheless.

1988   **1997–2010**

Good colour. Some new oak on the nose. Blackberry and cassis rather than mulberry is the fruit here, and the acidity is rather more obvious. But the wine is full and ample – succulent even – and the finish is long and classy. Very good plus.

1986   **1995–2007**

This has always been one of the best of the 1986 Pomerols, without the slightly austere tannins of some. Good colour. Plenty of fruit, with a touch now of spice and coffee-chocolate. Medium-full body. Good grip. Very positive and harmonious on the follow-through. A lush wine for a 1986 Libournais. Very good.

1985   **Now–2008**

Slightly more evolved colour. Sumptuous nose. Opulent and rich. On the palate it is medium-full-bodied, and is quite evolved. Aromatic and cedary, getting round and subtle. Very much *petits fruits rouges* in flavour: the Merlot dominating. Engaging. Perhaps not really profound, but most enjoyable. Very good indeed. Just about ready.

1984   **Now–1996**

This shows well, particularly so by the standards of the rest of the Libournais. Fullish, ample, even fat. Has depth and ripeness.

1983   **Now–2002**

Many 1983s, I remarked in April, 1986, are taking their time to come round after their bottling, as

did the 1982s. This was one of them. It showed a lot better after 20 minutes or so in the glass than it did initially. Medium-full. Quite rich. Certainly good but at present out-shone by 1985 as well as 1982. Judgement deferred. Subsequent tastings have shown this to be good (just) but by no means great. The 1981 is better.

1982   **1996–2020**

Splendid full, solid, rich colour. Marvellous nose, cigar boxes, cedarwood, concentrated and aromatic. This is a splendid wine. Rich, full, fat and profound. Goes on and on. Very complex. Very high class.

1981   **Now–2008**

Fine full colour, little development. Good ripe, slightly wood-smoky nose. Quite full, rich, aromatic, almost like a less intense 1982. The tannins are more apparent but the wine is still fat as well as concentrated. Full, well-structured and vigorous for a 1981. Shows very well. A wine with a lot of charm.

1980   **Drink soon**

Very good colour for the vintage. Round, mellow nose. Lacks a little zip, but has fruit and even complexity. Medium body. Fully ready. An attractive wine with more fruit and substance than most. Still vigorous. Shows very well for a Libournais 1980.

1979   **Now–2003**

Good colour, little development. Smells of summer pudding. A good meaty sort of wine on the attack. Fresh, straightforward creamy fruit. Good grip. Medium-full-bodied. In the middle it seems to miss the concentration of the 1981 but it finishes well. Ripe; charming. Good.

1978   **Now–2003**

Slightly lighter, slightly browner colour. More developed on the nose. Fresh, fruity, not *that* concentrated. A little bit more structured and a little more depth than the 1979 but not as much as one might expect for the vintage. Also good but not exceptional.

1977   **Drink up**

Good colour; quite full, no undue brown. Good

nose, a bit lean and one-dimensional but not lacking flesh. Fully developed and now some traces of attenuation and spice but very good indeed for the vintage – even plump.

1976   **Drink soon**

Very fine colour: better than the 1978. Full nose, meaty, aromatic, with both depth and concentration and still a good degree of freshness. Full body, fat, ripe, slightly spicy. Long on the palate. A most attractive wine. Very fine for the vintage.

1975   **Now–2005**

Very fine colour indeed, still youthful. The nose is still dense and undeveloped but the wine on the palate does not have the burliness and undue muscle of some of the vintage. Full, fat, rich and concentrated. A lot of depth and complexity. Quite some tannin still. Excellent for the vintage.

1971   **Drink soon**

Good colour. Lovely, elegant, ripe, fragrant, complex nose. All the style of this vintage and none of its faults. Soft, mellow, medium-bodied wine, full of fruit, very elegant and delicately balanced. Shows very well.

1970   **Now–1996**

Medium to medium-full colour. Plump, fruity, gently aromatic. Not a wine with a great deal of power but a most attractive, elegant, balanced bottle. Has charm and length. Very good.

1967   **Drink soon**

Medium body. Now perhaps approaching the end of its life. No astringency though but a little loosening and coarsening of the structure and flavours. Ripe, soft, elegant. Obviously a success if not with the sheer quality and concentration of the later vintages.

1966   **Drink soon**

Full colour, fully mature. A more structured, more masculine wine than the 1970. Rich, meaty, plenty of depth. Fat, ripe, blackcurranty. Very good.

1964   **Drink soon**

This is not one of the great Libournais 1964s, and, in my experience, not as fine as the 1966, though I have never tasted them against each other. The best part is the colour. The nose is a little four-square, but the palate is round and mellow, soft and fruity. What it lacks is a little excitement, and a little class. Good, merely.

1962   **Now–1997**

This is better. Very good colour. Full, vigorous nose: slightly robust but rich and old-viney. Cabernet influenced. Fullish, ripe, smooth, still sweet. Slightly spicy. But no astringency. Very good. Will still keep well.

1961   **Drink soon**

Fullish colour. Well matured, indeed not as vigorous as the 1962 – though I have only seen this once in the 1990s. Yet it is sweet and opulent, even silky, and it has plenty of class. Medium-full. Rich. Still very positive at the end. Even by 1961s standards this is very good.

1953   **Drink up**

(An anonymous Belgian bottling) Good colour. Fully mature. Quite an ample nose, gently fading fruit. Medium bodied. Balanced and quite classy, but it is beginning to lose its concentration and the acidity shows a little on the finish. A mellow attractive wine nevertheless.

LE PIN

The emergence of a new, high-quality wine is always the cause of much interest and celebration, but it is an infrequent occurrence. What normally happens is that when a parcel of suitable vineyard exchanges hands, normally as a result of the death of the previous owner, it is absorbed by the purchaser into his own domaine. The result is that he has more wine to sell, not that a new name appears on the scene.

It was therefore with a certain amount of surprise that I began to hear of a new name in Pomerol a decade ago, particularly when it transpired that the owners in question were the Thienpont family, proprietors of Vieux Château Certan. The Thienpont family is very extensive, however, and though Alexandre, now the genius behind Certan itself, is involved in this new enterprise, it is another branch of the family who are the proprietors of the new estate. So far, it has not been dignified with the name of a château, merely Le Pin.

The Thienponts are a Belgian family originating from Etikhove – where they remain important wine-merchants – in the person of Georges who bought Vieux Château Certan (and Troplong-Mondot in Saint-Emilion which was later sold) in the 1920s. This Georges had seven children among whom were another Georges, Gérard, Marcel and Léon. The family of this second Georges now operates Château Puyguereaud in the Côtes de Francs while Gérard runs the family business in Belgium. The late Léon, who died in 1985, ran Vieux Certan and has now been succeeded there by his son Alexandre and nephew (son of Georges), Nicolas. Marcel was chairman of the Flemish Credit Bank and, like most of his generation, also had numerous children. One of them, Luc, now runs Château Labégorce-Zédé in Margaux. It is another, Jacques, who is responsible for Le Pin.

HISTORY

A Mme Loubie acquired the small vineyard which is the nucleus of Le Pin in 1924. She sold the wines as generic Pomerol up until her death in March 1979, when the property was bought by Marcel and Gérard Thienpont for a million francs. At the date of the purchase, the vineyard amounted to no more than one hectare and six *ares* – about 2.6 acres – but in 1985 the Thienponts were able to acquire another precious hectare from the local blacksmith. This parcel had to have half of its surface replanted. The remainder of the territory, though it contains some old Cabernet Franc, is almost entirely Merlot averaging 30 years of age. It is therefore accurate to describe Le Pin as essentially 100 per cent Merlot, just like Château Pétrus.

The land lies in the heart of the plateau of Pomerol, surrounded by Petit-Village, La Violette, Trotanoy and Vieux Château Certan itself. The soil is therefore gravel and clay with a little sand on *crasse de fer*. The clay here is more extensive than that under most of Vieux Certan, as much as 2.5 metres deep, and the soil is poor, particularly as the vineyard remained unfertilized in the years prior to the Thienpont era as Mme Loubie could not afford to treat it. This results in a very low yield, usually no more than 30 hectolitres a hectare. All the better for making good wine.

The wine is vinified in stainless-steel vats for one or two weeks, depending on the state of the grapes and the ambient temperature. As soon as this initial period of fermentation and maceration has ceased, the wine is drawn off and transferred to new oak casks where it will undergo its malolactic and remain for 18 to 24 months before bottling. It is not filtered.

Though there was a little Le Pin in 1979 and 1980, this new wine really dates from the 1981 vintage. It took a bit of time to get the vineyard and *chai* into sufficient order for fine wine to be produced. Since then Le Pin has rapidly achieved a fine reputation for the quality of its wine, many already proclaiming it a 'super-second'. One of the reasons has been the high prices. Another is no doubt the scarcity. Only some 1,500 bottles per annum are currently produced, of which three-quarters are marketed in Britain.

So how good is it: and how does it compare with Vieux Château Certan? In 1987 I had a chance to compare the 1981 to 1985 vintages alongside each other. In three out of five I clearly preferred Vieux Certan. The Pins were attractive and voluptuous, very oaky, almost excessively so, and so most appealing in an upfront sort of way. But they lacked the depth and profundity of the Vieux Certans.

It must be understood, though, that one is not exactly comparing like with like. Le Pin is a 100 per cent Merlot wine, matured in 100 per cent new oak. Vieux Certan is only 50 per cent Merlot and the blend also contains a high proportion of Cabernet Sauvignon. Moreover, the wine is less obviously oaky. Personal preference obviously has a large part to play. The French, I understand from similar tastings, prefer Le Pin.

Le Pin certainly has style, balance and attraction. It is a wine which in its youth is very immediate – *flatteur*, as the French say. Equally, it is certainly one of the top wines of the area. It is clearly made with a great deal of care and attention to detail. It is certainly a star, but as yet I would not rate it a superstar.

THE TASTING

In May 1991, I had a chance to re-taste the first ten vintages of Le Pin. The occasion was set up by the wine-merchants, Bibendum, in London with the help of Mark Walford and Roy Richards, leading importers of the wines of the Thienpont family.

1990   **1996–2006**

Full colour. This is rich and meaty on the nose. Good concentration, and not a bit outclassed by the 1989, though it is not as fat or as rich. Medium-full, soft, round tannins. A wine with a lot of appeal and good length.

1989   **1997–2012**

Fine colour. Round, voluptuous oaky nose. Rich and aromatic. Full, concentrated and finely balanced. This has heaps of very lush fruit. Good long finish. Fine quality.

1988   **1995–2005**

Good colour. Ripe, raspberry-flavoured, oaky nose. Fresh, clean, straightforward. Has plenty of personality. Medium body. A little tannin. Still a touch firm and bitter, but this is no bad thing. Stylish.

1987   **Drink soon**

Surprisingly good colour and attractive nose. There is nothing off-vintage about this. Round, gently oaky. Good fruit. Not fluid. Medium body. Just about ready. This has a lot of appeal. Not a bit short. Very positive. A very good 1987.

1986   **Now–2003**

Good colour, if anything a bit more intense than the 85. Rich, oaky nose. Now cedary. Good acidity. This has a lot of concentration for an 1986 Libournais (just like Vieux Certan). Medium body. Ripe and fleshy, evolving quickly. Very good but lacks a bit of real intensity.

1985   **1995–2010**

(Magnum) Good colour. A curious nose (and flavour on the palate) – mint, resin (almost men-

thol), plus well-hung pheasant. Rich and concentrated but odd, even slightly metallic. I don't think this a good bottle. A second bottle was firm and rich, even quite austere. Much more backward than the 1986. And a great deal better. Very good indeed.

1984   **Drink soon**

Lightish, browny colour. In its context not nearly as good as the 1987, though better on the palate, which has reasonable vigour and fruit, than on the nose, which is rather weedy. Reasonable quality though. Drink soon.

1983   **Now–1997**

Good nose. Now just about mature. Like the 1985, this has a slight mintiness on the nose. Perhaps it lacks a bit of richness underneath. On the palate a medium-full, round wine which is now ready. It is ripe and quite fleshy. But it lacks just a little grip and dimension on the finish. It will not make old bones. Good but not great.

1982   **Now–2013**

Full colour. Little sign of maturity. Fat, spicy, quite powerful, still youthful, indeed even a bit adolescent on the nose. Full, still tannic. Still quite oaky. This has power and intensity. Lovely ripe, not too cooked fruit. Excellent quality. The best of the decade, quite clearly.

1981   **Now–2000**

(Magnum) Medium to medium-full colour. Fully mature. More intense than the 1983. Rich nose. More vigour than the 1983, more oak apparent and more grip. Altogether a better wine. Medium-full body, rich and fat and meaty for an 1981. *A point* now, but plenty of life ahead of it. Ripe, vigorous, good length. Very good.

TROTANOY

After Château Pétrus, which property produces the best wine in Pomerol? Historically, number two was Vieux Château Certan, and indeed for most of the nineteenth century Certan was considered the best of all in the district. In the opinion of many professionals in the area, not least Christian Moueix, Château Lafleur, potentially at least, is number two. Others, though, would cite Château Trotanoy.

The dissenter is Cocks and Féret, the 'Bible of Bordeaux', which has always, in its discreet way, listed wines within their own *appellations* and classifications in its own order of preference. In its 1991 edition, Cocks and Féret places Trotanoy third in Pomerol, after Pétrus and L'Evangile. I'm not sure that I would agree with the placement of L'Evangile this high. I have frequently taken part in tastings of recent vintages of Trotanoy. In the spring of 1988, thanks to the efforts of Stephen Browett and Lindsay Hamilton of Farr Vintners, I had the opportunity to sample a range of Trotanoys which descended as far back as the 1924. I have also tasted L'Evangile and Lafleur in depth, as well as most of the other top-flight wines of commune. It would be difficult to separate Trotanoy and Lafleur, but for me these two are a notch above the rest. If I were to revise Cocks and Féret I'd place them second equal, very closely followed by Vieux Château Certan. Yet are these strict pecking orders of any real value or meaning? They all produce excellent wines.

Trotanoy lies on the western edge of the central and highest slope of Pomerol. In the middle of this plateau lies Château Pétrus, ringed by most of the rest of the leading properties of the commune – Lafleur, Lafleur-Pétrus, Gazin, L'Evangile, La Conseillante, Petit-Village and Vieux Château Certan. Continue west for a few 100 metres and you will come across the simple two-storey farmhouse flanked by its *chais* at the centre of a small, nine-hectare vineyard of impressively old vines. This is Trotanoy, owned since 1953 by the family of Jean-Pierre Moueix, and producer of one of the most impressive, deeply concentrated and profound wines of the entire Bordeaux area.

HISTORY

The derivation of the name 'Trotanoy' comes from the medieval French *trop anoi* or *trop ennuie*: literally, too much bother, too wearisome. The soil is a very dense mixture of clay and gravel, which tends to solidify as it dries out after rain to an almost concrete-like hardness; not an easy task to plough, particularly in the pre-tractor days of a single ploughshare pulled by a horse or an ox. '*Trop Ennuie*' first appears as a wine-producing estate in the middle of the eighteenth century when it belonged to the Giraud family, minor aristocrats who lived in Libourne and worked in the service of the king. At that time the main focus for vine-growing was the more alluvial soil lying along the banks of the river Dordogne upstream of Libourne. The land was richer, easier to cultivate, and the vines produced prolifically, albeit making wine of little finesse.

Vineyards were not established in a serious, commercial way in what is now the Pomerol heartland until the 1740s. According to Enjalbert, the pioneer was one Léonard Fontémoing at Château Trochau, closely followed by the Giraud family at Trotanoy and Catherine Conseillan at La Conseillante. Enjalbert has dug up a '*procès verbal*' dated May 1761, produced for Fontémoing, which refers to '*les vignes de Savinien Giraud à Trop-Ennuie*'. The Fontémoing family were the most powerful *négociants* in Libourne at the time and owned a number of important properties, including Château Canon in Saint-Emilion. The Trochau property, which lay between Trotanoy and Pétrus, unfortunately, no longer exists. These vineyards now belong to a number of small properties which cluster round the Pomerol church. By the end of the eighteenth century, 'Pomerol-Giraud Cru de Trotanoy' as it was called at the time, was among a number of estates which had established themselves as the *premiers crus* of the area.

Yet though they styled themselves *premiers crus*, the reputation of these wines was small. At the turn of the century the leading wines of the Libournais came from Fronsac, a much larger and older-established *vignoble*. Even as late as the 1840s, prices for the first quality '*Vin Rouge de Graves de Pomerol*' and '*Haut-Saint-Emilion*' fetched barely half that of Médoc fifth growth.

The first detailed classification of the wines of Pomerol is found in the second edition of Cocks and Féret, which appeared in 1868. It is fascinating to recognize what are still today the leading wines of the area. The first nine are Vieux Château Certan, Trotanoy, Pétrus, Rouget-et-Gazin (run as one property by the Fabre family), Petit-Village, Guillot, Conseillante and L'Evangile. Guillot, now Château Gombaud-Guillot and Trotanoy's western neighbour, is the only one of these nine which could be said to have fallen from grace. Another nine properties follow, listed as '*crus bourgeois et premiers artisans*', including Le Gay, Certande-May, L'Enclos, Clinet – there are now a number of properties with variations on the name Clinet – Beauregard, La Grave (Trigant-de-Boisset), Nénin and La Pointe. Lafleur, not listed in 1868, rapidly moves up the hierarchy in subsequent editions.

Trotanoy at the time was the largest of the leading estates. It comprised 25 hectares in several separate plots, and made 40 to 60 *tonneaux* of wine. In 1898 there was a division of the property in order to settle an inheritance problem, and during the 1920s further parcels were sold off. By 1929 only eleven hectares were under vine, producing 25 *tonneaux*. During this period Trotanoy's neighbour, Gombaud-Guillot, increased in size quite substantially. Is this where some of the vineyards went? The reputation of Trotanoy had also, if marginally, declined. No longer second in the commune, in the tenth edition of Cocks and Féret (1929), Trotanoy is listed eighth, after Pétrus, Vieux Château Certan, L'Evangile, La Conseillante, Lafleur, Certan-de-May and Petit-Village.

The Giraud era, which had lasted for over two centuries, came to an end after the war. Trotanoy, now a *société civile*, was bought by a M. Pecresse. The Pecresse family owned a number of vineyards, including Vieux Château Perruchot in Pomerol and Château Bellevue-Saint-Lambert, a *bourgeois supérieur* in Pauillac. Neither of these properties exists today. Pecresse sold Trotanoy to Jean-Pierre Moueix in 1953.

THE VINEYARD

The Trotanoy vineyard slopes gently to the west. The soil at the highest point of exposure contains a good proportion of gravel, becoming progressively more clayey as the elevation declines. Under this clay is a subsoil of sandy gravel, and this lies on an impermeable layer of hard, iron-rich soil known as *crasse de fer* or *machefer*.

Even by 'classed-growth' standards – there has never been an official classification of Pomerol – the average age of the vines at Trotanoy is impressively old. When Jean-Pierre Moueix bought Trotanoy in 1953, the vineyard consisted entirely of vines which were 25 years old; since then only two hectares have been replanted.

There are now nine productive hectares in total. Some 85 per cent of these are Merlot, 15 per cent Bouchet (as Cabernet Franc is known to the Libournais) together with a few rows of Pressac (Malbec).

THE CHÂTEAU

Trotanoy is not architecturally impressive though it is an attractively decorated home; like many in the region, it is essentially a simple, two-storey *maison bourgeoise*, dating from 1890, in white brick with white shutters and a terracotta-tiled roof. It is flanked, forming three sides of a square, by the *chais*; the whole protected by several mature trees in a little park, approached by an avenue of cypress tree. Jean-Jacques Moueix, Christian's cousin, lives here.

THE WINE

Trotanoy is made in much the same way as at Pétrus. It is vinified in small concrete vats, with the fermentation taking about a week or ten days, followed by a further week's maceration with the skins. According to the vintage, between 10 and 30 per cent of the stalks are added to give the wine more muscle and tannin. Maturation is in oak, these days largely new, and the wine, contrary to the modern trend, held for over two years before bottling. The cellars are also used for the manufacture and maturing of Château Lagrange, another Moueix wine.

Old vines produce little, but produce well. Production is rarely more than two *tonneaux* per hectare, rather than as much as four or five in some prolific properties. In the short year of 1977, the total was a low as ten *tonneaux*; in the abundant vintage of 1982 only 27.

Trotanoy is a profound and richly concentrated wine with plenty of depth and very classy, almost creamy, fruit. Though it has power and weight, and will certainly last, it is never as dense as Pétrus itself, or Lafleur. Nor does it have the Cabernet Sauvignon–inspired backbone of Vieux Château Certan. In some vintages – 1975, for instance; even 1982 – it comes forward to make very agreeable drinking rather quicker than many of its peers. But so does Magdelaine. This is the result of the high proportion of Merlot. But it keeps very well, as the following notes will show. It is a lovely wine; second equal in the commune.

THE TASTING

The younger wines were sampled in London in April 1993. The notes on the older wines come from the Farr Vintners tasting held on Leap Year's Day 1988.

1990   *Optimum drinking*   **2000–2020**

Fine colour. Very splendid nose. This has sumptuously concentrated fruit, and real flair and originality. Fullish, excellent ripe tannins, very good acidity. The fruit fills the cornucopia from blackcurrant to wild strawberries. Very long. Very fine.

1989   **2000–2020**

Very good colour. The nose is more closed, less opulent. The wine needs more work as it has gone into its shell a little. It seems fatter and more spicy, rich but more tannic. Fullish again. It is on the finish one can see the quality. Even more concentrated. Perhaps even more classy and complex. Excellent.

1988   **1997–2015**

Fullish colour. Rich, ample, plummy nose. Plenty of depth here. This is harder and more obviously tannic than the two wines above and at present is a little austere. But the wine has real finesse and excellent fruit. Fullish, concentrated and profound. Lovely long finish. Fine.

1986   **Now–2001**

Medium-full colour. Closed on the nose but quite rich on the palate. Yet there is a certain astringency about the tannins. Medium-full body. Ripe but lacks a little generosity and flair. Good plus.

1985   **Now–2008**

Medium-full colour. Ripe, stylish, generously ample nose. But very Merlot. Does it lack a little grip? Medium-full. Quite rich, certainly opulent and fleshy, even concentrated. By no means a blockbuster. Positive finish, but very good rather than great. It doesn't seem to have lived up to its early promise.

1983   **Now–2000**

Medium-full colour, no undue maturity. Ripe on the nose, if without a great deal of grip or dimension. On the palate this comes across as rather a bland wine. Medium-full-bodied. Quite fruity. But it seems a little hollow in the middle. It is fully ready, and it lacks bite and flair. Many Saint-Emilions in this vintage are like this, but I would have expected better from Trotanoy. This is a bit of a disappointment. Good at best.

1982   **1995–2015**

Good full colour. Now just a little development. Fat, rich, meaty and concentrated on the nose. This has plenty of vigour. Fullish, substantial, approaching maturity. Very rich and ripe, with the fat, opulent, concentrated, cooked-fruit character of the vintage. Lovely.

1981   **Now–2000**

Good fullish, fresh colour. Fresh, stylish, plump, even quite concentrated nose. Good acidity. Medium-full. Gently oaky. This is classy and delicious now. Long and satisfying. Very good indeed. Must be one of the best 1981s. Will hold up well.

1979   **Now–1999**

Medium-full colour. Quite a different fruit on the nose, compared with the 1981 – damsons rather than mulberries. Fresh, high-toned. Elegant. Medium-full-bodied. This is vigorous and attractive, though not that concentrated. Positive, long, even complex on the finish. Very good plus.

1978   **Now–1998**

Fullish colour, just about mature. Elegant nose, not weighty and quite high-toned. Fully mature but with a touch of austerity. Quite full on the palate. Fresh; indeed the acidity shows a little. Mellow but lacks a little richness and charm. Will last well. A very good but not great example of the vintage.

1976   **Now–1997**

Medium-full colour, just about mature. A shade dry but quite firm and tannic on the nose, especially for a 1976. Full, ripe, rich and ample. Attractive but a bit dense and with some slightly burnt elements on the flavour. A fine 1976 though which will last well.

1975   **Now–1997**

Medium-full colour, just about mature: no more than the above. Quite fat and developed on the nose; mature ripe Merlot. Quite full on the palate, ripe and rich and slightly spicy. Somewhat four-square and lacking zip. Lost fruit as it developed in the glass. This is quite developed for a 1975. Very good but not great.

1971   **Now–2008**

Fullish colour, only a little maturity. Fresh, ripe, fullish, youthful Merlot, with good concentration on the nose. Just about ready. Quite full; this has a lot of depth, excellent balance and real complexity. Significantly superior to the three wines above. Very high class indeed. Probably the wine of the vintage.

1970   **Now–2010**

Very full colour; barely mature. This is a more old-fashioned sort of wine-making: big, full, firm, meaty, somewhat dense. Yet real depth and concentration to go with the size. Another wine of very high quality indeed which will still improve.

1967   **Drink soon**

This is one of the best 1967s I have seen for some time. Good full mature colour. Rich, classy, mature nose; plenty of dimension and still vigorous. Refined, slightly leafy, violets and blackcurrant flavour. Fullish, balanced. Very complex for a 1967.

1966   **Drink soon**

Full mature colour. Fine, round, mellow nose. Richly aromatic with aspects of toffee and caramel. Full, plump, ripe and concentrated. Opulent, even voluptuous. Still vigorous. Very good indeed for the vintage.

1964   **Drink soon**

From a magnum, and sampled separately at a dinner preceding the tasting alongside a magnum of La Mission 1964 and other goodies. Good colour. Ample, round and rich on nose and palate. Quite full and meaty but lacks a certain element of real class. Good but not great.

1962   **Drink soon**

Quite full mature colour. Mellow nose, hinting at a little age but still fine and stylish. A medium-full, ripe, elegant wine, classy and charming but has now lost a bit of its concentration and depth. Very good for the vintage but now needs drinking.

1961   **Now–2000**

Very full colour, not a lot of maturity. Big, meaty, rich and tannic. Old-fashioned size and muscle. Underneath this structure there is a great deal of concentration and elements of chocolate, liquorice and leather. Real depth. Very fine fruit, but slightly larger than life. In its own way like a 1948 or 1950.

1959   **Drink soon**

Full, mature colour. The nose is a touch hot and cooked; elements of *tabac*. Full structured, rich and chocolatey but essentially a certain four-square astringency, lacking a bit of nuance. It is fair to say that I liked it less than my companions. Overall, this was preferred to the 1961 and voted second equal in the entire tasting (see below).

1955   **Drink soon**

Full, mature colour. Full, vigorous, ripe and chocolatey on the nose; mellow, mature, Merlot fruit. Quite full, a ripe, even sweet wine with no sign of astringency. Very elegant and refined. Loosened up in the glass but a lovely example.

1953   **Drink soon**

Medium-full mature colour. Soft and fragrant, old tea roses on the nose. An elegant, supple, ripe, feminine wine. More age than the 1955 on this showing but more complex. Lovely.

1952   **Drink soon**

Full, rich colour, showing a little age. This is definitely an old wine, showing some oxidation. Still enjoyable though. Medium-full body. Ripe and full of fruit. Complex and classy. A better

bottle would be wonderful, I wrote. And I had one in fresher condition a year later. It was. But it still needed drinking soon.

1949   **Drink up**

Full mature colour. Very fine aristocratic nose but didn't hold up too well in the glass. Rapidly became astringent, but classy, discreet and ripe.

1945   **Now–1998**

Level to upper shoulder. Unanimously voted the wine of the tasting. Very fine, full colour. Marvellous nose: rich, voluptuous, powerful and seductive; no undue size like the 1961. An opulent, fat, full, supple, creamy, plummy wine. Powerful and multidimensional. Very excellent. Bags of life.

1943   **Past its best**

1947 on the label, not specifying château bottled. Branded cork with the name of Savinien Giraud, and the date 1943. Rather old, faded colour. Medium body. Has lightened up without drying out. Acidity shows. Certainly not at all too bad once, but today it is past its best.

1934   **Past its best**

(Recorked by Etablissements J.P. Moueix two years previously) No ullage. Slightly faded in colour and on the palate. A little oxidized on the nose. Sweet and fragrant but lacks vigour.

1928   **Drink soon**

Good, vigorous colour, still fullish. Chunky nose, chocolatey, solid and rich. Still very much alive. Ripe and full with no undue astringency. A wine of backbone with a rich complex finish. Very fine indeed.

1924   **Drink up**

Reasonably vigorous colour. Faded roses, white chocolate and vanilla creams on the nose. Was quite full. Still ripe and not too faded. Fine fruit. Good acidity has kept it fresh. Very good.

At the Farr Vintners tasting, which did not include any wines of the 1980s decade, the overall vote was for the 1945 in top place, followed jointly by the 1959 and 1928, with the 1971 fourth. I would not quarrel with three of these (see my comment on the 1959). I feel a better bottle of the 1952 would compete with the above. And for power if not breed I would place the 1970 and 1961 in fifth and sixth positions.

SAUT

THE SAUTERNES REGION LIES SOUTH OF BORDEAUX AND CONSISTS OF THE COMMUNES OF BARSAC, PREIGNAC, BOMMES, FARGUES AND SAUTERNES ITSELF. BARSAC IS ALSO AN *APPELLATION* IN ITS OWN RIGHT.

While in the Médoc and the other red wine areas of Bordeaux, as in the dry white wine areas, a yield of roughly one bottle of wine per vine is the norm in the top properties, in Sauternes the yield may be as low as one-sixth of that – a glass of wine per vine, as they will tell you at Château d'Yquem. Equally, by prolonging the harvest beyond the date of ripeness and waiting for the fruit to be attacked by the fungus, *botrytis cinerea*, in order to produce *pourriture noble*, the noble rot, the grower is at the mercy of the elements as the weather changes from summer to winter. He may wait and have his patience rewarded, he may pick early and avoid the terrible consequences of a change in the climate, or the reverse may occur. This makes Sauternes much less consistent from one vintage to the next and between one château and its neighbour.

D'YQUEM

Château d'Yquem. The very name is synonymous with sweet wine perfection, with tradition, with all that is superlative in Sauternes; with the greatest sweet wine in the world. Yquem is one of those few wine names which is known the world over, even among people who know nothing about wine, and would not know whether the wine was red or white, sweet or dry, still less where and how it was made.

The great sweet wines are quirks of nature; originally, perhaps, discovered by accident; expensive and time-consuming to produce; rare in frequency for they require precisely the right conjunction of particular climatic conditions. Luck plays a major part. Wealth, tradition and painstaking perfectionism are also vital. Perhaps it is only at Yquem that all these, together with the particular contribution brought by an ideal combination of soil, site and microclimate, can come into play and be evolved to the summit of capability. Certainly, at Yquem, the price the wine can command confers both a duty and a means to realize the absolute very best that a naturally sweet wine can produce.

Château d'Yquem lies at the top of a hill in the commune of Sauternes commanding a view over the surrounding four communes that comprise the Sauternes district. Geographically, as well as psychologically, it is the focal point of the *vignoble*. East is Fargues, with its major property, Château Rieussec, as Yquem's immediate neighbour; south is the rest of the commune of Sauternes; west is Bommes; north is Château Suduiraut, situated in Preignac, then the motorway, and across the little river Ciron, the parish of Barsac. In the distance, beyond the Garonne, is the hill of Sainte-Croix-du-Mont. From a *salle de dégustation*, hacked out of the fossilized oysters which make up the bed-rock of Sainte-Croix-du-Mont, one gets perhaps the best panoramic view of the Sauternes vineyard. Just as you can see the hill from the château, so, from the wine-tasting terrace, the most recognisable sight, away across an undulating countryside made up of vines, pastures, spinneys and silent hamlets, are the slate turrets of Château d'Yquem.

HISTORY

Château d'Yquem is an ancient, fortified *manoir* which has belonged to the same family, only changing hands by marriage, and as generation succeeded generation, since records began. It was originally owned by the De Sauvage family. In the reign of Edward III (1327–77) a Roger de Sauvage was mayor of Bordeaux and during the next 100 years, prior to the expulsion of the English from Aquitaine, the name of Sauvage can be found frequently in the archives and city records. The oldest parts of the château itself date from this time. It was originally conceived as a fortress; basically a rectangle, containing a courtyard, surrounded by a moat, and with four massive, round towers, one at each corner. At the east and west side are entrances surmounted by a machicolation, a space between the corbels supporting a parapet, from which burning oil or whatever could have been poured on to an attacking enemy.

In the more peaceful times of the early Renaissance the château was largely rebuilt, particularly the main residential part which faces north and east. Here there is a chimney piece bearing the date 1545. There were further alterations in the seventeenth century.

Towards the end of this century the *seigneur* was Léon de Sauvage d'Yquem who married Cécile de Marbotin. Their son Laurent was also *Seigneur* of Podensac, and was in the service of the King. He was a colonel in the Infantry and was decorated as a Chevalier de l'Ordre de Saint-Louis. Laurent, however, had no sons. The heiress to Yquem was his daughter Joséphine, styled *Dame d'Yquem de Podensac et de Saint-Crie*.

Meanwhile, at the Château de Fargues, and equally long-established in the Sauternes district, were the Lur-Saluces family. The family name originated when a Jean de Lur married Charlotte de Saluces, whose ancestors had originally come from Saluggia, north-west of Turin in northern Italy, and the Lur-Saluces had been at De Fargues since 1472, when one of the family married Isabeau de Montferrand, heiress to that important estate.

One 6 June 1785, a magnificent wedding, celebrating the union of two of the greatest families in the area, took place at Yquem. Joséphine de Sauvage d'Yquem married Louis-Amédée de Lur-Saluces, Comte de Lur, and colonel of the regiment known as the Dragons-Penthièvre. Louis-Amédée may have been already quite old, for he was only to live for another three years, but not before the succession had been assured. In 1786, Joséphine gave birth to a son, Antoine-Marie. She was to live to a very advanced age, surviving both her son and his wife, and not dying until 1851. For many years she would be a lady-in-waiting to the Comtesse de Provence.

In 1807, another grand wedding, again uniting two old Sauternes families, took place. Antoine-Marie de Lur-Saluces married Françoise-Eugénie de Filhot. Yet another prominent wine estate was brought into the Lur-Saluces ambit. Since then the Lur-Saluces family has always been dominant in the Sauternes district. As well as Yquem, Filhot and De Fargues, they have also been associated with Coutet, Piada and De Malle.

Antoine-Marie became chamberlain to Napoleon, and was a cavalry officer in Russia, where he was wounded and taken prisoner, not returning to France until 1814. Thereafter he became *aide-de-camp* to the Duc d'Angoulême, following him to Spain in exile, and dying at Madrid in 1823. During the Napoleonic era he was ennobled to marquis. After his death the Countess Eugénie became canoness at a nunnery at Poussey in the Lorraine before coming back to end a long illness and die at Yquem.

MODERN SAUTERNES EVOLVES

We now come to the Marquis Bertrand de Lur-Saluces (1810–67), the eldest son of this issue, and to the period where the wine made in Sauternes evolved from being a wine which was merely sweet to the luscious, rich, *pourriture noble* delicacy we know today. How, and exactly when this transition took place is difficult to pinpoint. That Yquem and Sauternes in general were sweet wines at least as early as the mid-eighteenth century we can prove from wine lists at the time, as well as from contemporary references to the wine, analogizing it with the sweet fortified wines of the Mediterranean and the Iberian peninsula.

We know also that at Château La Tour Blanche, the first of the *premiers crus* in the 1855 Classification (Yquem is in a class of its own as a *premier grand cru*), the owner in the mid third of the nineteenth century was a M. Focke, who had come from the Rhineland, and no doubt brought techniques of German sweet white wine-making with him.

However, tradition has it that the first botrytis-affected crop was made at Yquem in 1847. The Marquis Bertrand was delayed in his return from a visit to Russia, then the major customers for Yquem, and as a result the harvest, waiting his command, was delayed. When he arrived, the grapes were seen to be rotten, but nevertheless, the order was given that they should be picked. To everyone's amazement, the result was so delicious that the search for *pourriture noble*–affected grapes was undertaken every year.

Eventually, when Lur-Saluces made a return visit in 1859, the 1847 crop was sold to the Grand Duke Constantine, brother of the Czar, for the unbelievable sum of 20,000 gold francs a *tonneau*. Even today's exaggerated price levels can hardly match that!

THOMAS JEFFERSON

The Grand Duke Constantine was not the only person of renown to buy Château d'Yquem. Though he did not visit the estate itself, Thomas Jefferson had arrived in Bordeaux in May, 1787, at the end of a three-month trip round French and Italian vineyards. He reported, of Sauternes, 'the best crop belongs to M. Diquem or to M. de Salus his son-in-law. . . . They make 150 *tonneaux* at 300 *livres d'or* now and 600 old.'

On his return to Paris he wrote to M. Diquem in French with the politeness characteristic of the period. Although we have not been introduced, ran the gist of the letter, I am taking the liberty of writing to you and I hope you will forgive my effrontery in approaching you direct, in order to order some of your excellent wine (250 bottles of the 1784). Jefferson was ordering it direct, and requesting it to be bottled at the château in order to ensure that what he received was genuine. The American Consul in Bordeaux, John Bondfield, would organize delivery and payment.

Later he wrote to Bondfield, with whom he was in constant touch, buying other wines, to say that, 'The Sauternes sent to me by the Marquis de Saluces turns out very fine'. Later still, on his return to the United States, he wrote to order a further 40 dozen, 10 for himself and 30 for the President, George Washington.

THE MODERN ERA

Bertrand de Lur-Saluces was the first of the family, it would seem, to take a close personal interest in the estate and its wine. He lived and died at Yquem, made major improvements to the vineyard, beginning the installation of what is now a network of some 100 kilometres of drains within the domaine, and instigated a major reconstruction of the *chais*. During his generalship, Yquem reached markets and fetched prices hitherto and henceforth unrivalled. The 1861 and 1864 brought more than Lafite. The demand for Yquem, led by the Imperial Russian Court, was substantial. The reputation was confirmed by the 1855 Classification.

Since then, though the fashion for Sauternes as such was to diminish, Yquem has always remained protected. Lur-Saluces has succeeded Lur-Saluces; Alexandre, the present proprietor, took over at the death of his uncle, the old Marquis, another Bertrand, whose very long reign came to an end in December 1968. And *maître de chai* has succeeded *maître de chai*. The legendary Roger Bureau, whose typically French-peasant, mustachioed photo has been much reproduced, and who started work at Yquem in 1909, retired in 1970, and his place was taken by Guy Latrille, who with *chef de culture* Yves Laporte, production director Francis Mayeur, and Lur Saluces's assistant Antoine Laporte, are the present-day team at Château d'Yquem. Since the abrupt departure of Pierre Mestier in January 1990, there has been no *régisseur* as such.

THE VINEYARD

Yquem has always been one of the largest, if not *the* largest Sauternes estate, in production if not in area. A century ago it was producing 110 *tonneaux*, when only Suduiraut and Filhot among the other *crus classés* produced over 50. Today, it produces a little less, and apart from the above two, only Guiraud, Rieussec, Rayne-Vigneau and La Tour-Blanche are close rivals in surface area.

The domaine totals nearly 150 hectares. Two-thirds of this are nominally under vines, but at any one time only 80 hectares are in full production. Each year about three hectares are pulled up, when the vines reach 40 to 45 years of age, and these parcels are then allowed to lie fallow for three years before replanting. These new vines are then not fully mature until at least fifteen years after that.

From these 80 hectares of severely pruned vines, planted in the ratio four-fifths semillon, one-fifth Sauvignon, an average of only seven hectolitres per hectare is produced. This is equivalent to one glass of Yquem per vine per year.

The soil is a complex mixture: gravel mixed with sand, silt and clay, reddish-brown in colour, and subsisting on a base of *alios* and water-retaining clay, depending on position. The vineyards more or less exactly occupy the rectangle delimited by the roads which surround Yquem, but there are additional parcels to the east, towards Rieussec, and to the north-west, beyond Raymond-Lafon.

HOW THE WINE IS MADE

Everything about Yquem is traditional. It is firstly the estate with the greatest determination to pick each grape at the peak of perfection. While other, lesser properties collect bunch by bunch, with only three or four visits (*passages*) to each row of vines, the 150 Yquem harvesters will make as many as thirteen *passages*, over as much as two months, frequently only collecting enough to make a half a dozen barrels of wine a day. In a red wine vineyard one harvester can collect the equivalent of two hogsheads of wine a day. At Yquem it takes fifteen to produce one.

The harvesters are old hands, drawn from the four dozen or so permanent workers on the estate and their families, and pick two to each row of vines, one on each side, so that the most experienced can guide those less accustomed and collect each grape at its optimum.

Yquem is frequently the last property to start harvesting, and, not surprisingly, nearly always the last to finish. In 1978 the last grapes were picked on 8 December, and, as a result, the Yquem 1978 is one of the few wines in this vintage to show an unmistakable flavour of *pourriture noble*.

The grapes are crushed in three small, wooden, upright presses. There are three pressings. The first, carefully controlled at twenty kilos per square centimetre, yields 80 per cent of the juice. The next yields 15 per cent and the last 5 per cent. Each pressing produces juice which is progressively more botrytis affected.

After resting in glass-lined tanks for an hour or two, the must is moved into new oak barrels, each bearing the date of the harvest, so it can be identified later, for the fermentation to take place. Both because the must is heavy in sugar, and because by this time the ambient temperature is cool, the fermentation takes a long time. No effort is made to speed it up, and, again because the wine is so sweet, no malolactic fermentation takes place.

The team at Yquem look to produce a must with an average degree of potential alcohol of 20 degrees. Obviously some batches or barrels will be higher (as much as 26 degrees), others lower. An average of 20 degrees will produce a wine with an alcohol level of 14 degrees, and a residual sugar level of 6 degrees. At 14 degrees or so, the fermentation naturally stops. The yeasts which could work at a higher level are killed by an enzyme called botrycine manufactured by the *pourriture noble* itself.

The wine has a long infancy. Not until three to three and a half years later is it bottled (since 1922 entirely at the château), and normally not until a decade after that will it finally be mature. Only after the bottling is it put on the market. No one, literally no one, outside the 'home team' is allowed to taste Yquem before it is bottled.

THE RISKS OF PRODUCING YQUEM

Yquem is a vineyard which is prone to risk; as Sauternes by its very nature is a chancy business. In 1950 the crop was reduced by half as a result of frost, as it was in 1977 also. In 1951 and again in 1952 there was no Yquem at all as a result of hail. In 1964, as a result of a month of rain which set in at the beginning of October, and despite thirteen *passages* in the vineyard, no wine was declared at Yquem. Neither was any Yquem produced in 1972 and 1974. Nor will any be in 1992.

They did, however, perhaps unwisely, declare 1963 and 1965. 1968, on the other hand, despite being a disaster in the red wine vineyards, was a success at Yquem, as the autumn was fine. 1969, too, is a good Sauternes vintage. In 1976, the harvest was completed in three weeks, on either side of two rainy spells, as the onset of both ripeness and botrytis was very fast. The wine, however, is not as successful as the 1975, and was bottled after only two and a half years. 1982 was another year which was rain affected, much as in 1964, but, unlike that year, a few passages had been made before the rains commenced, and about 25 to 30 per cent of a potential crop has been declared at Yquem.

YGREC

In 1959 Yquem 'startled the world' to use Penning-Rowsell's expression, by introducing Ygrec, a dry white wine. This is a wine which is full, viscous, and looks and smells very much like a Sauternes. The taste though is fundamentally dry (there is a third of a degree of potential alcohol not fully fermented out) but rich.

Unlike other dry wines produced on the Sauternes estates, the idea is not to produce a *primeur*, Sauvignon-style wine, though they do recommend that it should be drunk young. I find that, in its infancy, it is rather heavy, and that it does improve, quite considerably, with age. A ten-year-old Ygrec is a much better glass of wine than one at five years. Altogether it is a curious, untypical but interesting wine.

The wine is made with equal proportions of Sauvignon and Sémillon, using up the spare Sauvignon (for in fact 30 per cent of the estate, not 20 per cent, is planted with this grape, in order to ensure that 20 per cent is always available for the *grand vin*). Additionally the *cuvées* which fail to reach 14 degrees potential alcohol are used.

In the 1970s Ygrec was produced in 1971, 1972, 1973, 1977, 1978 and 1979. It has been produced in most vintages since then.

THE WINE

How do you describe Château d'Yquem? Liquid gold? A ray of sunshine caught in a glass? Perhaps just simply the best sweet wine in the world?

For it *is* the best, quite clearly, and by quite a long way. No other Sauternes possesses quite the power, the concentration, the sheer depth of character. The others cannot or do not achieve the weight, the richness or the lusciousness of Yquem, the combination of ripe fruit and delicious fresh tartaric acidity which gives Yquem the balance to match its breed.

What is remarkable about Sauternes is its longevity, and Yquem is the longest living of them all. In the tasting whose notes I give below the colours were, for the most part, old gold, if not decidedly brown, but the wines were crisp and lively, even if some of them were 50 years old, and even after two or three hours in the glass showed not a sign of deterioration.

A Tasting of Sixty Years of Château d'Yquem

I was fortunate to be invited to a remarkable blind tasting of a large range of vintages of Château d'Yquem which was held at the property in April 1985. Here are my notes which I have supplemented with others sampled in the last year or so.

Optimum drinking

1988
2003–2028

Light, mid-gold colour. The nose is still closed. Cool, oaky, not – at this stage – *that* sweet and luscious. Fullish, but not a blockbuster. Quite oaky. Certainly concentrated. Very youthful. Lovely elegant peachy fruit. Reminds me of the 1962 at the same stage. Harmonious but not *rôti*. Very, very long and complex. Lovely.

1986
2005–2035

Slightly fuller, richer colour than the 1985. Closed, fat and concentrated. Good *pourriture noble*. Ripe and solid. A bit adolescent and foursquare at present. A lot of depth and intensity, but just a shade rigid on the attack. The finish is very fine but doesn't blow my mind. But it is still very young. Very long and concentrated.

1985
1999–2016

Just a touch of sulphur on the nose. Not too rigid. Fresh and fullish but a bit adolescent. This is very good on the palate, because it has zip and flexibility. Fullish, fine fruit. Long and complex. No lack of *pourriture noble*.

1984
Now–2004

Sweet nose, but, inevitably, a shade simple. A bit of built-in sulphur. Medium-full, vanilla, fondant flavours but no real nuance. Certainly surprisingly good for the vintage, but finishes a bit flat, a bit cloying.

1983
2005–2035

Medium-gold but still fresh colour. Still very young on the nose. Very rich and honeyed, even caramelly. Very concentrated. This seems a wine of twice the power of the 1986 and a great deal more size. I am sure this is streets ahead of not just the 1986 Yquem, but any other 1983. It has really marvellous, concentrated, multidimensional fruit. Splendidly balanced with the acidity. Size, breed, harmony, depth, lusciousness: it is all here. Real dimension. Infanticide to drink it now. But brilliant.

1982
Now–2005

Lightish colour for Yquem. Very strongly oaky on the nose, more so than Yquem usually is. Underneath the wine is soft, lemony, plump and attractive but there is not much *pourriture noble* and the wine lacks the strength and intensity Yquem usually has. Forward. Normally Yquem is streets ahead of the rest. In 1982 there is not much extra concentration and richness over the best of the rest such as Lafaurie-Peyraguey. Dull for Yquem.

1981
1995–2015

Fullish colour. Full, oaky nose, very silky and balanced but quite accessible already. Similar on the palate. Rich, voluptuous and perfumed; peaches and apricots together with cinnamon and butterscotch on the aftertaste. Very fine balance of acidity. Very fine, much fatter and more concentrated than the rest of the wines in this vintage. A lot of class. Ready soon.

1980
Now–2000

Lightish colour; fresh nose, still very young, with a little built-in sulphur (this will soon pass). Medium-full, sweet, rich. A good deal more *pourriture noble* than most in this vintage. Soft, plump, long on the palate. Just about ready. Few 1980s are really serious wines, but this is one.

1979
Now–2013

Green-gold colour. Fresh nose. Not as luscious as expected. Still very fresh, even Sauvignonny. Not as rich, fat or full as expected but lovely fruit and acidity. Quite sweet, long. Only a medium amount of *pourriture noble*. Still very young. Fine finish. Very racy. Very, very long. The best Yquem between 1976 and 1983.

1976
Now–2018

Slightly deeper colour than 1975; fat and rich on the nose but a shade heavy and clumsy. Quite full, some maturity, sweet and honeyed but lacks a little depth. Certainly not as complex as the 1975, not as long.

1975   **1995–2025**

Youthful yellow-gold colour; fresh, youthful, oaky nose, showing more Sauvignon than the above. Quite powerful, young, full wine. Not as much botrytis perhaps but sweet, peachy, Victoria-plum flavour. Very fine balance. Rich. Has a lot of depth.

1974 and 1972

No Yquem declared.

1973   **Now–2000**

Quite a lot more full and concentrated than any other 1973. Lots of depth on the nose. Good fruit and acidity. Just about ready. A good wine but not a great one.

1971   **Now–2023**

Medium colour. Powerful, youthful nose. Not yet luscious; very concentrated but youthful. Full, more luscious on the palate than the nose would indicate. Very concentrated. Still amazingly young. An exceptional wine, even better than the 1975. The best Yquem of the 1970s.

1970   **Now–2008**

Rich golden colour. Full, fat, very concentrated powerful nose. Sweet in a fondant rather than barley-sugar way. Full and still very young, quite a lot of botrytis. As yet still a bit adolescent. Very good but 1975 and 1971 are *plus fin*.

1967   **Now–2005**

Colour now shows a bit of age. Grapey, barley-sugar nose, quite developed. Full, broad palate. Older than I expected, and less good. I am sure other bottles are firmer and more complex. Quite full, and there is a slight lack of grip. Has plenty of charm and sweetness. On this showing ready for drinking, but I have had other, greater bottles.

1964

No Yquem declared.

1962   **Now–2012**

Fresh, green-gold colour; weighty, powerful, honeyed, botrytis nose. Fresh, full, very rich and concentrated. Fat, caramelly. A big, attractive wine with plenty of finesse and a feminine touch compared with the 1959. Ready and will last very well. The best Yquem of the 1960s.

1961   **Now–2005**

This has quite a deep colour compared with the 1962. Good nose but neither as fresh nor as rich as the 1962, and doesn't quite have the finesse. Fullish, some sweetness and *pourriture noble* but not that luscious. Nice but not a great wine.

1959   **Now–2009**

Slightly more colour than the 1962; fullish, round, sweet, barley-sugar nose. Very ripe, quite

a lot of *pourriture noble*, good acidity. Still remarkably young. Fullish, honeyed, slightly spicy, luscious wine. Big, fat, even slightly *brûlé* in character. Good length. Will keep well. Shows very well indeed. Splendid quality.

1953   **Drink soon**

Slightly darker, golden colour; quite a powerful, intense nose, concentrated, plenty of botrytis. Full, vigorous, rich and complex. Spicy. Showing fully mature, if not with a slight touch of age.

1952 and 1951

No Yquem produced as a result of hail damage.

1950   **Drink soon**

Lighter, greener gold colour than the 1953; the nose is a little faded though there is some sweetness underneath. Sweet, slightly *brûlé*, but not as full or as intense as most. Finishes well because the acidity level is good. Do not keep for too long.

1949   **Now–2000 plus**

This is one of the greatest Yquems of all; in my view a wine of stupendous class and magnificent balance. Not as powerful as the 1947 or 1945 but a wine of tremendous fruit, great harmony and multidimensional complexity. Sheer nectar! *Grand vin*! Will keep for ages.

1948   **Now–2000**

Full, dark golden colour, with some age. High-quality nose, full, a lot of depth and finesse. Big, full, rich, complex, honey and toffee-flavoured wine, with mint touches as it developed in the glass. Fully in its prime but will keep well. A delicious, very elegant wine.

1947   **Now–2000 plus**

Glowing, deep golden colour. Even brown. Concentrated, powerful, great depth on the nose. Very good acidity and freshness but at the same time rich, complex, fragrant. Full yet delicate, heaps of finesse. Fullish, simply heavenly fruity; lovely and delicate, yet concentrated. Complex balance. Great depth. Quite splendid. Not too rôti or barley sugar. Lovely peachy, honeyed, flowery style. What keeps this wine so alive (and will keep it for ages) is the marvellous ripe acidity. Incredible length.

1946   **Drink up**

Medium, gold-tawny colour, some lightening-up at the rim. Loosish, melony flavour, quite stylish and shows some age. Never great and now a little old.

1945   **Now–2000 plus**

Light amontillado colour. Green rim. Walnut veneer colour. Marvellous intensity of fruit but no longer full and clenched, yet an explosion of flavour. Multidimensional, fantastic cornucopia of fruit, mouth-filling. Spice, honey, peach, nuts, elements of butterscotch. Marvellously fresh, complex, subtle, mind-blowingly good. Great complexity and real class. Very well preserved despite the colour. Indisputably *grand vin*. Bags of life.

1944   **Drink soon**

Really quite a brown colour, green at the edge. The nose has both lightened up and dried out a little. Quite sweet, quite full, remarkably fresh on the palate for a wine of this age and vintage. Good grip. Interesting, slightly spicy flavour. Good length.

1943   **Now–2000**

Golden-brown colour, less green. Quite full, powerful nose, good level of botrytis, rich, ripe, sweet and with plenty of depth. Big, rich, complex, excellent fruit. Very fine indeed. Still remarkably youthful. One could almost say that it will still improve.

1942   **Now–1997**

Old-gold colour; nose shows some age but is fresh, quite powerful and concentrated. Medium weight, round, very stylish, honeyed and barley-sugar, still very sweet. A very elegant wine which will still last very well.

1937   **Now–2000 plus**

Full, golden-brown colour; full, fine, very stylish nose, a wine with a lot of depth and character. Subtle, complex, beautifully balanced wine, a lot of *pourriture noble*. Marvellously long, lingering finish. Splendid.

1934   **Drink soon**

Lighter, greener colour; quite earthy and minty on the nose. Fullish, sturdy, some of the fruit has now disappeared, and the wine has lost a dimension or two. Less honeyed, less botrytis. If this bottle is typical it is now a little past its best.

1929   **Now–2000**

Of this great pair of vintages at the end of the 1920s, 1928 is the classic Sauternes vintage. The 1929 has a deep, tawny colour and is full almost to the point of syrupiness. Very sweet with an aromatic raisiny flavour. Quite high in alcohol. Not as elegant or as balanced as the 1928 but a fine wine nonetheless.

1928   **Now–2000 plus**

Oldish colour; but still a very fine, complex, delicate, aromatic nose. Medium weight, not as vigorous as the 1937, but fragrant, very elegant, with a lot of character and a lovely, fresh finish. Excellent.

1921   **Now–2000 plus**

A legendary wine which I have sampled on three occasions and only on the third did it live up to its reputation. Then – and even though it was some time ago I can still taste it now – it was so magnificent I was rendered speechless. Utter perfection; incredible concentration and complexity of fruit; perfect balance; still incredibly fresh. Sheer heaven!

The Best Yquem

The greatest years of Château d'Yquem include, in reverse chronological order, 1988, 1986, 1983, 1976, 1975, 1971, 1967, 1962, 1959, 1955, 1953, 1949, 1947, 1945, 1943, 1937, 1929, 1928 and 1921, and will almost certainly include 1989 and 1990 though these last two vintages are not yet available for sampling. Of these the greatest mature vintages in my experience are the 1921 and the 1945, closely followed by the 1949 and the 1947, the 1943, the 1937 and the 1928. I have a particular fondness, among more recent years, for the 1962 and the 1971, while the potential of the 1983 is awe-inspiring.

The Jefferson Yquem

Though tradition has it that the first fully botrytis-affected Yquem was the 1847, in 1985 a bottle of the 1787 vintage surfaced, bearing the initials of Thomas Jefferson. Despite still having the original cork the wine was fresh and drinkable. It was opened at the château in May of that year, and, as Alexandre de Lur-Saluces reported to me, showed without any doubt that wines made before the French Revolution were made with *pourriture noble*-affected grapes.

LA TOUR-
BLANCHE

Second only after Château d'Yquem in the 1855 Sauternes
Classification is Château La Tour-Blanche in the commune
of Bommes. Since 1907 it has belonged to the French na-
tion, and since 1911, at the behest of the previous proprietor,
the Ministry of Agriculture has run a viticultural and oenological school on the property, though the students are not
involved in the making of the Sauternes.

As elsewhere in the *appellation*, La Tour-Blanche has experienced a renaissance in the last half a dozen years. Prior to
this, good Sauternes arrived more by chance than by design,
but since the 1986 vintage the improvement has been dramatic. The grapes are now harvested riper, at a higher degree of potential alcohol. The wine is now matured with a
large proportion of new wood (50 per cent in 1988, 90 per
cent in 1989), and the quality is now up with the very best
in the region. Both the 1988 and the 1989 are excellent:
Sauternes as it should be. One now can see why this domaine was placed higher than all the other first growths (bar
Yquem) in the Classification 135 years ago.

The origins of La Tour-Blanche are obscure. There is an
isolated tower on the estate, though not that depicted on the
label. There used to be, judging by the illustrations in early
editions of Cocks and Féret, a modest two-storey château, a
maison bourgeoise of no particular architectural merit, surrounded on two sides by the necessary viticultural and vinicultural dependencies. But when this was constructed and
who built it, we do not know. It still exists, now somewhat
transformed and submerged by the modern college buildings.

HISTORY

The name comes, not from any white tower, but from Jean Saint-Marc du Latourblanche, treasurer-general to Louis xiv. Latourblanche died at Bommes on 20 October 1784. Did he produce Sauternes? How highly was it rated? There is no documentary evidence.

Then there is an historical hiatus. The first accounts of named châteaux in Bommes producing Sauternes are by André Jullien in 1816 and Paguierre in 1828. Jullien refers to 'Deyne' (Rabaud), Lafaurie and Dert (?); Paguierre to En Casaux (Rabaud again) which he rates a *premier cru*, and Dufourg, Lafaurie again and Lalande. These three are his second growths.

By the time we got to Wilhelm Franck in 1845 (his first edition in 1824 does not cover the Sauternes area), the picture is clearer. Franck's first growths are headed by Lafaurie at Peyraguey, Deyme at En Rabaut (*sic*), Baronne de Reyne at the Cru de Vigneau, Focke at La Tour-Blanche and André Lacoste (Lacoste was proprietor at Château Pexiotto, a *deuxième* in the 1855 Classification which no longer exists. I can find no evidence to link Derte, Dufourg or Lalande with La Tour-Blanche. Nevertheless the supposition must be that one of them was predecessor to M. Focke.

M. Focke, legend used to have us believe, was the man who introduced the idea of waiting for the noble rot to Sauternes. He had arrived in the area from the Rhineland in the 1830s. We now know (Richard Olney has this established beyond doubt in his monograph on Yquem) that luscious wines from botrytis-affected grapes were being made at least as early at the 1750s. But all the old books credit the phenomenon to M. Focke. No doubt he played his part. Perhaps it was he who created La Tour-Blanche as a major Sauternes estate. According to Jullien, Focke was a proprietor in Barsac prior to moving to Bommes (or is this an error?).

Focke died soon after the 1855 Classification, and in 1860 his widow sold the property to Paul Maître, Georges Merman and M. Capdeville (the latter was soon bought out of this consortium). The Merman family had been proprietors in Saint-Estèphe (Château le Crock and later Château de Marbuzet) since before the Revolution. At the time there were some 35 hectares of vines at La Tour-Blanche, producing 40 to 50 *tonneaux* of wine.

Early in the 1880s Maître and Merman sold the property to Daniel Osiris. Osiris was a financier and umbrella manufacturer. He was a good friend of both Pasteur and Ulysse Gayon, the latter the first of Bordeaux's famous oenologists, and he carried out numerous experiments on the problems of micro-organisms in the cellars and the effects of yeasts in the fermentation of wine. After he died in 1907 his will revealed that he had bequeathed La Tour-Blanche to the state, on condition that it should be used as a base for an agricultural school which should be 'practical, open to all, and free'.

At first, having inaugurated the Osiris bequest, the French government were more interested in the school than in the Sauternes. From 1924 to 1955 the vines were leased out to Cordier, who owned neighbouring Lafaurie-Peyraguey, on a *métayage* basis. Under this agreement Cordier would have kept half the grapes or wine they produced at La Tour-Blanche, though whether this was later sold and blended together with the state's share is unclear. If not it would mean that we would have had two distinct La Tour-Blanche wines during this period.

The new era starts, not so much with the rescinding of the *métayage* agreement in 1955 as with the arrival as director of Jean-Pierre Jausserrand in 1983. Since then, as I have said, the wine has regained the high position it was allocated in 1855.

THE VINEYARD

The whole estate covers 65 hectares and occupies a hill overlooking the River Ciron in the north-west corner of the commune. At the summit we are 67 metres above sea level, almost as high as at Yquem, and the view is impressive, though the feeling is naturally more of a university campus rather than an agricultural estate. Behind the college the vines descend sharply. The soil is gravel over clay at the top, sand and loess over limestone below.

There are 27.5 hectares of AC Sauternes vines planted in the ratio 78 per cent Sémillon, 19 per cent Sauvignon and 3 per cent Muscadelle. The Semillon and some of the rest are pruned short, the remainder by the classical single Guyot method. There are also a few black grape varieties on the estate, but I must confess I have never sampled the wine.

THE WINES

As well as producing the *premier cru*, La Tour-Blanche, a number of other wines are made: Mlle de Saint Marc is the second wine. Osiris, exclusive to the Belgian market, is a semi-sweet wine; and there is a Sec de La Tour-Blanche.

Since 1988 La Tour-Blanche has been vinified in wood – before that it was in stainless steel – and in this same year a modern cooling/freezing system was employed to avoid the overuse of sulphur dioxide. There is equipment for cryo-extraction, utilized in 1987; but in Jausserand's view the end product is one-dimensional, 'like a German *eiswein*'. There is a limit – say 30 per cent maximum – of cryo wine you can add to ordinary wine, he says. As I have said the proportion of new wood has risen to 90 per cent for the last vintage, and the grapes are now picked at a higher degree of ripeness. In the last couple of vintages, both plentiful, the yield was seventeen hectolitres per hectare. Jausserand intends eventually to re-duce this to an average of eleven hectolitres per hectare. The wine will further improve in power and concentration as a result.

Judging by the last couple of vintages – and it would be inappropriate to use any other as a criterion – La Tour-Blanche is one of the fullest and richest of the Bommes châteaux, in style a cross between Sauternes, the most luscious of all the five communes, and that of Bommes – plump wines really of medium-full rather than full weight. Certainly both the 1988 and the 1989 seem to be among the most backward of all the top growths. Great strides have been made in a short period of time. Let us hope that the 1990s favour the Sauternes climatically as much as the last seven years have done.

THE TASTING

Of the following wines, 1987 back to 1961 were sampled at La Tour-Blanche in January 1990. The two most recent vintages were tasted in April. Of the vintages not offered I can only speak with recent experience of the 1976. Better than the 1975 but only marginally so; not a wine to get excited about.

Optimum drinking

1989   **2000–2020 plus**
Ripe, oaky, complex and honeyed. Well sup-ported by new oak. This is a closed youthful wine. Potentially brilliant. Real depth. Real breed. Very, very concentrated. Excellent quali-ty.

1988   **2000–2020 plus**
Good nose. Ripe, ample, elegant. Very good, complex fruit. There is depth here. Full, lus-cious, ample, concentrated and backward. This has a lot of class. It is still very young. Really powerful. Excellent.

1987   **Now–1999**
Greeny-gold colour. Light nose; gently hon-eyed, gently sweet, gently oaky. Stylish but

ephemeral. Sauvignon shows still. It was bottled in January 1989. This is a flowery and elegant wine with good grip. Lightish and forward but has intensity, and no vestige of SO2. Shows well for the vintage. Good positive finish.

1986   **1998–2018**
Light golden colour. Light nose, a little more concentrated but, it seems, an unduly delicate wine for this vintage. A little more weight be-came apparent as it evolved. Clean again. Subtle. Fresh, medium bodied, barley sugar and peachy wine. Good *pourriture noble*. Good grip and in-tensity. Long. Shows well. Subtle. Needs time. Very good indeed.

1985   **Now–2008**
Lightish colour, greeny gold. A somewhat fuller wine, but with a touch of SO2. This is rather

more four-square and less interesting. Medium bodied, sweet, a good residual oaky flavour. Has balance but not much dimension. Cleaner on palate than on nose. Some *pourriture noble* but not much depth. This will improve as it evolves. Only quite good to good for the vintage though.

1984   **Now–1996**

Lightish, greeny gold-colour. Sweet but a little four-square on the nose, not much depth, a little SO2. Sweet but a bit coarse on the palate, with rather too much built-in SO2. Somewhat cloying. Lacks class.

1983   **1996–2016**

Light golden colour. Medium-full, some richness, certainly not *that* intense or powerful. Sweet though, some SO2. Medium-full, rich, honeyed, fat and concentrated. Good *pourriture noble*. Good grip. This is certainly one of the best 1983s but there is nevertheless a little coarseness and four-squareness about it. Good intensity. Will improve in style as it rounds off and the SO2 disappears. A bigger, fatter, more concentrated wine than the 1986 but without as much class or subtlety.

1982   **Now–1997**

Light golden colour. Somewhat blowsy on the nose. A little SO2. Lacks intensity and breed. Not enough grip either. Sweet but sulphury. Lacks breed. More to it than the 1984, of course, but not special.

1979   **Now–2004**

Lightish colour. This was entirely *élevé* in new wood (though vinified in tank). One of the better 1979s. Clean, stylish, oaky, good grip (much better than most) on the nose though a bit of SO2 as it evolved. Some *pourriture noble*. Fullish, peachy, balanced. Very good grip. Very vigorous. Fine for the vintage, though not a wine of the greatest depth and complexity.

1975   **Drink soon**

Lightish colour. The nose seems a bit diffuse; lacking elegance. Neither selection nor patience

for the *pourriture noble* here. A little built-in SO2. Seems a bit aged. The 1979 is both more vigorous and much better. Medium bodied, soft, pleasantly fruity. *A point*. Pretty, but not real depth. Better on the palate than on the nose, though a bit coarse in the finish.

1971   **Now–1997**

Medium gold colour; a little more than the 1970. Fat, honeyed, oak and beeswax nose. A little bland and broad with SO2 dominating but a good wine struggling to emerge underneath. This has more to it than the 1975. *Pourriture noble*. Better balance. More fruit and complexity. On the palate really not bad at all. Now *à point* but a reasonable future. Yet lacks a bit of concentration really, as well as elegance on the finish. Not bad.

1970   **Drink soon**

Light mid-gold colour. A little less than the 1971. This is fresher, cleaner and fuller but more four-square on the nose. Sweet and honeyed. Less *pourriture noble* than the 1971. A fuller, more one-dimensional wine. A little lumpy, some SO2 on the palate. Ripe and sweet but without *pourriture noble* or style. Slightly cloying on the finish. Petrol on the nose as it evolved.

1962   **Now–2000**

Bright, full, golden colour. This is very fine. Classic Sauternes. Rich, mature, plenty of *pourriture noble*. Lots of complexity and class. Delicious. Fullish, mellow, mature and complex. Balanced and multidimensional. A round wine. Very Bommes/Preignac. Lovely freshness and fragrance thanks to very good acidity. Very long and complex on the finish. Very fine.

1961   **Drink up**

Slightly old-looking golden colour without the freshness and sparkle of the 1962. This is lighter, much, much drier and much more faded than the 1962. Honeyed, beeswaxy. Medium body. Shows a lot of age. Pleasant but lacks grip and never had that much depth or class.

LAFAURIE-PEYRAGUEY

North of Château d'Yquem and south of the river Ciron lies the commune of Bommes, one of the five which makes up the *appellation* Sauternes. In the 1855 Classification Bommes could boast five classed growths; four firsts and a second. The second growth, Château Pexiotto, no longer exists, the vines having been absorbed into the neighbouring first growth, Château Rayne-Vigneau. Another first growth, Château La Tour-Blanche, is now owned by the State and is run as a school for young local *vignerons*. The other two growths have both been split since 1855; Rabaud has become Sigalas-Peyraguey and Rabaud-Promis; Lafaurie-Peyraguey has spawned Clos-Haut-Peyraguey.

Lafaurie-Peyraguey, owned since 1913 by the Cordier family, is today arguably the best of all these Bommes *crus*. Less controversially, it is the largest and best of the two Peyragueys, and, possessing the original château and *chais*, can also claim to be the 'original' Peyraguey. If so, it is probably the oldest estate in the area after Yquem, and of all of them is the most castle-like in appearance.

Sauternes must have been a place of some military significance in the thirteenth century for not only the fortress of Yquem but a baronial keep a kilometre or less distant was constructed at about the same time. This latter edifice is the foundation of Château Peyraguey. Who or what Peyraguey was or refers to, is not known. *Pey*, in old French, means a hill or mound; and *raguer* is an obscure verb meaning to break up as a result of friction or wear and tear. But then *gué* is an old word for a ditch or stream – or ford. The site is certainly at the top of a little slope, and no doubt if you look closely down through the rows of vines in almost every direction you will find water running towards the river Ciron.

HISTORY

In the seventeenth century the main part of the château was reconstructed, and a century later the domaine came into the hands of Nicolas-Pierre de Pichard, owner of Château Lafite, holder of various baronies in the Gironde, a member of Louis xvi's council and a *président à mortier* of the provincial Bordeaux *parlement*. At the time it was known as Château Pichard and perhaps as a result of this purchase Pichard acquired another title, that of *Seigneur de Bommes*. Pichard fled the country at the time of the Revolution – he went to Coblenz according to Guillon – and his estates were sequestered by the State. In Year 3 (1794) Château Pichard was sold as a *bien national* for 79,496 francs to two gentlemen, M. Lafaurie and M. Mauros. Not much is known about M. Mauros, and he was bought out soon after by Lafaurie, but the latter is described as a *viticulteur très distingué* and it is as a result of his efforts in the vineyard that the wine of – first Pichard-Lafaurie and eventually Lafaurie-Peyraguey – began to achieve a reputation. At the start of the nineteenth century, Peyraguey was only deemed to be a *deuxième cru* in the commune. By 1855 it is rated third in the entire Sauternes region. Early records show a domaine of some 45 hectares, of which 30 are under vine. Production was around 40 to 50 *tonneaux* and the wine sold for 500 to 1,500 francs according to the success of the vintage. (Red wine prices were more regular, a third growth could command perhaps 1,000 to 1,200 francs.)

Sometimes prices might be a great deal higher. There is a story of a grand banquet, laid on by the French at San Sebastian, in order to woo his Imperial Catholic Spanish Majesty with the delights of the wines of France. The Spanish King – he must have been a bit of a kill-joy – rarely drank except for a little port, and proceeded to turn up his nose at all the great wines of France: Lafite, Chambertin, Champagne and the rest. It was only when a flagon of Pichard-Lafaurie 1858 arrived that a spark of enthusiasm was engendered. The King was delighted with the wine and demanded whether any was available for sale. One hogshead turned out to be left, and this was snapped up by the Spanish Court for the unbelievably high price of 6,000 francs, 24,000 the *tonneau* – more even than the legendary Yquem 1847 had been sold for to Grand Duke Constantine of Russia.

Shortly after the 1855 Classification, Lafaurie died and the property passed into the hands of Monsieur J. Saint-Rieul-Dupouy, a well-known Bordeaux man of letters who had married Lafaurie's widow. In 1865 it changed hands again, the purchaser being Count Duchâtel, owner also of Château Lagrange in Saint-Julien, and a former Minister of the Interior under Louis-Philippe. Within a couple of years Duchâtel was dead, for in 1868 the Countess Duchâtel is listed as the proprietor. Cocks and Féret also mention that the estate is managed by a M. Lassauvaju-Magey, proprietor of the neighbouring Château Barrail-Peyraguey and 'one of the most intelligent and experimental *viticulteurs* of the region'.

A decade later, in the aftermath of the death of the widow Duchâtel, there was an inheritance squabble among her children. For some reason which I have not been able to unearth, it was decided, not only to sell the estate – which would seem reasonable – but to sell it in two halves. Perhaps an attempt was made to sell it as a whole but this proved unsuccessful. Be that as it may, on 26 June 1879, part of the estate, that including the Peyraguey château and *chais*, passed to a M. Farinel and a M. Grédy. A slightly smaller part, in vineyard terms, was bought by a M. Grillon, a Parisian pharmacist, who was already proprietor of Château de Veyres in Preignac. Because Grillon's portion was on the highest *croupe* of the estate, he christened his new vineyard Clos-Haut-Peyraguey.

From Farinel and Grédy, Lafaurie-Peyraguey passed to Frédéric Grédy, presumably the son of the latter, if not the man himself, and for a time the fortunes of the wine were somewhat eclipsed by its new rival, the neighbouring growth of M. Grillon. At the time Rayne-Vigneau, La Tour-Blanche, even Rabaud, are preferred to either by succeeding editions of Cocks and Féret. In 1913, however, M. Lassauvaju-Magey's Château Barrail-Peyraguey was absorbed into the estate, this bringing it back to pre-partition size, and in 1917 Lafaurie-Peyraguey was acquired by Désiré Cordier.

CORDIER

Under the Cordier regime the reputation of Lafaurie-Peyraguey was soon restored. The 1929 edition of Cocks and Féret lists the wine second after La Tour-Blanche, a property by which time Cordier was administrating on behalf of the French government. The local *régisseur* was a M. Descamps, whose family had worked at Lafaurie for several generations, and it is at this time that someone dreams up the following elegant phrase to describe this Sauternes: '*Sous sa prison de verre, c'est un rayon de soleil de France, un chant plein de lumière*' (Imprisoned in its glass is a ray of French sunshine, a song full of light).

VIMENEY

At about the same time as Lafaurie bought Peyraguey, in the aftermath of the Revolution, he acquired an interest in Château d'Arche. D'Arche, a sizeable domaine lying to the west in the commune of Sauternes, was divided after the Revolution, though still run as a single entity for a time, and it was Lafaurie who ran it on behalf of himself and his co-proprietors throughout the first half of the nineteenth century. His efforts, therefore, did not merely result in a first growth accolade in the 1855 Classification, but that of a second as well.

Coincidentally, part of the D'Arche vineyard today belongs to Cordier and has been incorporated into that of Lafaurie-Peyraguey. Sadly it is not the original Lafaurie portion, which would be satisfactorily neat, but another quarter, that known as Vimeney, and for a time owned by a relation of Raymond Lafon. In 1960, M. Bastit Saint-Martin, who had married into part of the D'Arche estate, acquired the portion originally owned by M. Lafaurie, and at the same time he rented the Vimeney section. Twenty years later the life of his son and heir came to an abrupt end. Subsequently, the owners of Vimeney, Mme Macé and her family, decided to sell their vineyard to Cordier.

THE CHÂTEAU

Peyraguey is one of the few real castles, in the sense of a toy or medieval fort, in the Gironde. Partly dating from the thirteenth century – the entrance hall and tower date from this period – and substantially reconstructed in the seventeenth, the château, heavily covered in creeper, stands in a little courtyard shaded by trees beside and in front of the main part of the *chais*. Surrounding this courtyard in a neat rectangle is a substantial and crenellated wall giving the appearance of a fortification Beau Geste and the Foreign Legion would have been proud of. In the bucolic countryside of the Sauternais it seems unnecessarily warlike, too aggressive. Apart from an apartment for the *régisseur* and his family, the château is only used for receptions and lunches.

THE VINEYARD

Now incorporating the four and a half hectares of Vimeney, the domaine of Lafaurie-Peyraguey possesses 25 hectares of vines. These are in three parcels: running behind the château and marching with the vines of Sigalas-Rabaud; on the Yquem side of the road opposite the *chais* of Clos-Haut-Peyraguey; and between Château Guiraud and the rest of Château d'Arche. The soil is a mixture of *graves moyennes* originally washed down from the Pyrenees, and lighter, more alluvial limestones and gravels resting on *terres fortes*, or *alios*. The vineyard is today planted almost exclusively with Sémillon – there is 2 per cent of Sauvignon – a change on the *encépagement* of some years ago where the Sauvignon percentage was 30. With an average production of twelve to fourteen hectolitres per hectare, again less than what it used to be, the yield is some 140 barriques of wine. According to the Cordier literature there is a second wine, 'L.P. du Château Lafaurie-Peyraguey', but I have never tasted the wine, nor seen it on any price list.

WINE-MAKING

There has been a considerable change in the manner of making Lafaurie-Peyraguey – and indeed an improvement in its resultant quality – in recent years. Under the regime of *régisseur* Patachon, who worked at Peyraguey for 42 years until his retirement in 1983, and who from all accounts was a moody individual, difficult to deal with, it would seem that there was an emphasis more on quantity than quality. Between 1967 and 1975, the wine was largely matured in glass-lined vats, covered in nitrogen, only returning to wood for four months before the *mise en bouteille*. It was fresh, but often rather light and short-lived, lacking lusciousness and richness, without the intensity of *pourriture noble* we associate with high-class Sauternes.

Since 1977 the wine has been fermented in wood, and this is now renewed every two years. The oak gives tannin and therefore backbone and longevity to the wine. In 1978 the entire cellars were air-conditioned, a system of thermostatic control now governing not only the temperature of the fermenting wine but that of the barrels subsequently storing the wine until it is ready for bottling.

Since the arrival in 1983 of M. Laporte as successor to Pierre Patachon, the cellars have been reorganized and renovated. The wine is now passed through a cold-treatment process, thus enabling the cellar staff to be less heavy-handed with the sulphur, and the wine is bottled after eighteen to twenty months in wood. This is somewhat earlier than hitherto.

THE WINE

Lafaurie-Peyraguey is a Sauternes marked more by elegance rather than power. It is now markedly oaky, which is no bad thing, and this gives some fatness and a vanilla flavour; but crisp, flowery and honeyed rather than luscious and heavy. The colour is lighter than most, leading one to expect a Barsac, and it is certainly less sulphur-dominated, even in its youth, than many of its peers. Some of the earlier vintages, as I have indicated, can be criticized for being too light and forward, with an insufficient flavour of botrytis. But the wines have always had finesse. Recent vintages have demonstrated a more serious approach, however. Since 1983 the standard has been consistently high. Even as far back as the 1975, Lafaurie produced a major success, so things were not all bad under the previous *régisseur*. But today there is no doubt the property produces one of the best wines of the *appellation*.

THE TASTING

The following wines were sampled at the château in April 1986.

1985 *Optimum drinking* **Now–2002**

A little sulphur on the nose but vanilla and honey, pronounced oak and at least some noble rot. Quite firm, rich, ripe, sweet and quite concentrated. Reminds me of a good 1970. Finishes long. Promising.

1984 **Drink soon**

Not much nose. Some body. Quite sweet but a little one-dimensional. Better than I expected but a *petit vin* which will be best for drinking soon.

1983 **1995–2015 plus**

Medium colour. Very fine, elegant, closed-nose, classic *pourriture noble*. No undue SO2. Medium-bodied, round, fat, vanillary, new-wood flavour with a lovely apricot and marmalade fruit. This has concentration. Good depth and length if not a blockbuster. Very good, even for the vintage.

1982 **Now–1997**

Light golden colour. Fresh, sweet, good fruit. Not an enormous amount of depth or dimension but well-made and elegant. Good for the vintage. Could be drunk now.

1981   **Now–1998**

Nose a little unformed and awkward. Medium
body. At first lacked a bit of charm and class but
improved in the glass. Fruit underneath, at least
some *pourriture noble* and has grip. Difficult to decide but seems good if rather adolescent at the
moment.

1980   **Drink soon**

Didn't show quite as well as at a comparative
1980 Sauternes tasting which had taken place
some months previously. Then I marked the
wine as a bit lumpy and unstylish on the finish.
Here there seems something a little soapy about
it, and it seemed less elegant all the way through.
The nose is the best part, and there is quite good
fruit.

1979   **Now–1997**

Evolved nose with some sign of maturity. Medium sweet, a little *pourriture noble*. Medium body,
fresh, round gentle wine without enormous
depth. Quite good.

1978   **Now if at all**

The only Lafaurie-Peyraguey spoiled by too
much sulphur. Sweet and a reasonable acidity
but overloaded by an unpleasant taste of wet
wool. Not for me.

1977   **Drink now**

Better than expected. A pleasant, clean, if one-
dimensional, sweet wine. Still fresh.

1976   **Now–1999**

Golden colour, quite evolved. Nose shows maturity as well as botrytis. Full, rich, good acidity.
Fully mature. Ripe, honeyed, flowery wine: soft
but balanced by good acidity. Not a bit heavy.
This has depth.

1975   **Now–2015**

Slightly less colour. Real quality here! A quite

different wine. Full, fat, rather more oaky than
the 1976. Very concentrated and complex. Firm
and powerful and will still develop. Plenty of
noble rot. Very long finish. Excellent.

1971   **Drink soon**

Golden colour. The nose is elegant but is now
losing a little fruit. A good round, quite powerful
and quite concentrated wine; clean and classy if
without a great deal of *pourriture noble*. Still fresh
and flowery and finishing well, but getting on
the dry side and will begin to show a little age
soon.

1970   **Drink soon**

Deep golden colour. Quite a lot of age on the
nose. Sweeter, fatter and more *pourriture noble*,
seemingly, than the 1971. Plump, butterscotch,
nutty flavours. Now showing a bit of age and beginning to lose its class.

1967   **Drink up**

Even deeper colour. The nose shows some age
and not much class. The wine was sweet and
quite concentrated but has now coarsened up
and even finishes a bit dirty.

1966   **Drink soon**

Deep golden colour. Soft, fresh, ripe, sweet
nose. Lots of fruit. Much more alive and much
more concentration and depth than the 1967.
No undue age. Vigorous, honeyed, round and
rich; slight saffron flavour on the finish. Rather
good, especially for the vintage. Reminds me of
a 1962.

1959   **Drink soon**

Less brown than the 1966. Gentle, fresher than
the 1966 if less fat and concentrated. Fruity and
elegant. Was always a bit on the light side I suspect and is now lightening up further and there is
a little bitterness and dryness apparent. A wine
with elegance though.

RAYNE-VIGNEAU

This is the story of a fine Sauternes estate which, like many, fell on hard times and would not have been deemed worthy of classification had the 1855 Classification been re-examined not so long ago. Yet, in recent years, after a change of ownership and the arrival of a young team determined to succeed, its fortunes have been restored. Rayne-Vigneau is now back among the stars and a revolutionary new technique of Sauternes production, pioneered on the domaine, looks like ensuring its place in history as the source of a major innovation as well as in the local hierarchy as one of the leading *premiers crus*.

The earliest records of the estate date back to 1692 and a M. Etienne du Vigneau. Details during the eighteenth century are scanty and the next specific reference is in André Jullien's *Topographie de Tous les Vignobles Connus*, first published in 1816. In my reproduction copy of the second edition (1824), mention is made of a M. Deyne (*sic*) as the owner of the leading *cru* in the commune of Bommes which produced 20 to 25 *tonneaux*.

Now 'Deyne' could refer to Rabaud, a single estate at the time, whose owner was, in fact, a M. Deyme. Or it could be a misprint for Reyne. A Baron de Reyne, described as a high-ranking military gentleman, was certainly the owner at Vigneau at this time. He had espoused a Mlle de Pontac from a famous and established family with large property holdings in the area. It would appear that his wife brought the estate with her as a dowry. Perhaps he was getting on in years. The Baron died soon after and the union was without issue.

HISTORY

Paguerre, in 1829, lists various proprietors in the commune: Lafaurie and others, but fails to mention anything which is indisputably Rayne-Vigneau; but then, as he places Mareilhac (Rieussec) in Barsac, he cannot be wholly relied upon. In Franck in 1845 we have more concrete evidence. Third in the commune after Lafaurie and Deyme at Cru Rabaut but before Focke at La Tour-Blanche, we have the Baronne de Reyne at 'Cru de Vigneau'. Production is given as 35 to 40 *tonneaux*.

Château Vigneau was listed third in the 1855 Classification in the list of first growths which followed Château d'Yquem, separately noted as a *premier cru supérieur*. The Baroness's name is now spelt with an 'a'. In 1867, there was a memorable competition among the great sweet wines of the world. Rayne-Vigneau 1861 was declared the winner ahead of anything even Château d'Yquem could produce. The Rhineland sweet wines, even to the German members of the jury, were, it seems, classed only as also-rans.

By this time the Baroness Rayne had been succeeded by her brother Viscount Gabriel de Pontac. It was Gabriel's son Albert who rechristened the vineyard Rayne-Vigneau in honour of his aunt in 1892. Gabriel, like his late brother-in-law, was a military man, a colonel, and it seems to have been in this period, during the 1870s and 1880s, that the existing château was constructed. The domaine comprised 100 hectares, 66 of which were under vine. Production averaged 50 *tonneaux*.

From records preserved at the property, André Simon published a paper on its production and the alcoholic content of the wines from the vintages of the 1840s onwards. In 1875, the strength of the wine was 17 degrees. The lowest was in 1910 – a mere 12.

Following the Viscount Albert's death in the 1920s, Rayne-Vigneau was administered on behalf of the family by a son-in-law, the Vicomte de Roton. Roton took an active interest in the affairs of Sauternes, being mayor of Bommes and vice-president of the local *syndicat vinicole*. He was also a geologist.

He soon discovered that the hillock on which the Rayne-Vigneau château was situated was a veritable mine of precious and semi-precious stones. He unearthed onyx, sapphire, cornelian, amethyst, opal, agate, jasper, chalcedony and others brought down from the Pyrenees by glacial action in the ice ages of the Pliocene period 5 million years ago. He published a paper on them under the pen name Notor and amassed a fine collection. This has now been dispersed to local museums but some can still be examined at the property today.

Roton lived to be 98 – his mother had died aged 101, so obviously it is a long-lived family – and his son, Vicomte François, now also of some considerable years, continues to live in the château. In 1961, however, the estate was put up for sale. The new owner was a M. Georges Raoux. I never met M. Raoux and my experience of wines of this period is scanty. It would seem that the vineyard was allowed to run down but the wines, what little I know of them, were not too bad. Most of the vintages of the late 1940s and 1950s which I have tasted I have noted as full and rich if lacking a bit of elegance. The 1959 was certainly very good and I have a single, quite enthusiastic note on the 1962. The 1964 was one of the few successes of the vintage. The next entry in my files is the 1970, rated as quite good.

In 1971, the year of many changes in Sauternes, Raoux sold up. Climens, Rieussec and Nairac also changed hands at this time. The purchasers were the *négociant* company Mestrezat-Preller; the price, 3 million francs.

MESTREZAT-PRELLER AND THE MERLAUT FAMILY

The original Mestrezat came from Switzerland and set up a company in Bordeaux in 1814, later becoming the Swiss Consul in the city. The Mestrezats ran out during the First World War and control of the company passed through the female line to the De la Beaumelle family, shortly after which it joined forces with the concern of M. Preller. In 1970, a substantial share in Mestrezat-Preller was bought by Jacques Merlaut and it was soon after that the firm embarked on an ambitious programme of châteaux purchases.

The Merlaut empire is one of France's postwar success stories. Its various ramifications are extensive and their connections between one another bewildering. Jacques Merlaut was born in 1911 and trained as a lawyer. During the Second World War he worked briefly as a *courtier* in Bordeaux before moving to Paris in 1946 where he founded the firm of Bernard Taillan. This was named after his brother-in-law and first partner who died in 1961. Originally, Bernard Taillan imported North African wines, creating Chantovent in 1956, today the third largest wine company in France. In 1965, Merlaut joined forces with Enrique Forner to buy Château Camensac. Another branch of the Forner family owns Marques de Cacares in Rioja and the Forners also used to own Château Larose-Trintaudon, Bordeaux's largest vineyard.

The year after Merlaut bought into Mestrezat, the company acquired Château Grand-Puy-Ducasse and Château Rayne-Vigneau, following this with a string of five *crus bourgeois* in 1973 and 1974. In 1976, the Merlaut family bought a majority holding in Château Chasse-Spleen. Château Le Gurge in Margaux and Haut-Bages-Libéral in Pauillac followed in 1978 and 1983, with Château Ferrière in 1990. The group also owns the Bordeaux *négociants* Ginestet and Descas, Ropiteau Frères in Meursault, the Compagnie de la Vallée de la Loire in Montreuil-Bellay and the Compagnie de la Vallée du Rhône at Castillon-du-Gard.

New Wine-Making

When Mestrezat took over Rayne-Vigneau in 1971 the vineyard was in a sorry state. The vines were old but large sections of the domaine had been allowed to decay leaving gaps between the vines and patches which were not productive at all. During the first decade, the only thing that was done was to replant, and as the INAO for some inexplicable reason – for a Sauternes vineyard – would only authorize Sauvignon, Sauvignon it had to be. During this period, quantity rather than quality was the prime objective. The harvest was picked without undue patience and the wines usually lacked lusciousness, *pourriture noble* and any background of new oak. They were also frequently over-sulphured. The result, frankly, was uninspiring.

All this was to change in the 1980s. Rayne-Vigneau occupies most of the mound which lies between Château d'Yquem and the River Ciron and is bounded on the north by the two Rabaud properties – Sigalas and Promis – and on the south by La Tour-Blanche. There are 65 hectares in production, now in the ratio 80 per cent Sémillon and 20 per cent Sauvignon although some of the former are still young vines. Recently, the Sauvignon content has been reduced and the Muscadelle eliminated.

Some 100 or so metres from the handsome turreted château, a substantial three-storey edifice which possesses more than a passing resemblance to Pichon-Baron, are the *chais*.

In the last decade, a lot of money has been pumped into Rayne-Vigneau. The cellars have been extended, providing a battery of double-lined stainless-steel fermenting vats of various sizes. New wood has been bought, the harvest maturing in 30 per cent new wood in 1982, 50 per cent in 1985 and 60 per cent today. Patrick Eymery joined from Château Guiraud as *régisseur* in 1982 and the team then embarked on trials for a completely new process for the manufacture of Sauternes, a technique called cryo-extraction.

Cryo-extraction

Producing fine Sauternes requires grapes which have been attacked by *botrytis cinerea*. If the weather is suitable – a combination of humidity and warmth – the botrytis will produce rot which is noble. If it rains, though, the danger is that the rot will turn into the ignoble *pourriture grise*. Moreover, the fruit will be diluted.

Jean Merlaut, Jacques' son, started thinking about this problem in 1982. In 1982, the Sauternes harvest began early, but hardly had the properties embarked on their first couple of tris or *passages* through the vineyard to pick those grapes in suitable condition when it began to rain. It did not stop for three weeks. The remaining fruit soon became worthless.

Meanwhile, Professors Chauvet and Sudraud of the Station Oenologique at the University of Bordeaux – the latter is a consultant to many Sauternes properties – had had an idea.

Could one not pick wet botrytized grapes and then freeze them? If one pressed them whilst frozen, the excess moisture would remain in the fruit as ice, only the *pourriture noble* juice would flow. A sort of artificial ice-wine, in essence. It would not matter if the fruit was harvested in the rain for any excess water in the inflated berries would remain as ice crystals and would not dilute the wine. Chauvet and Sudraud approached Merlaut and Merlaut agreed to experiment. From small beginnings – two twenty-litre *cuves*, micro-vinification originally – Merlaut is now able to vinify, if climatic conditions should deteriorate, much more of his harvest by this method.

The major investment that is required is twofold. The first is a cold room. The grapes are collected in the usual way, in shallow plastic panniers, and stacked in an enormous walk-in refrigerator like a hotel meat store. This is maintained at about minus 5°C and the fruit remains inside from some 24 hours. It is vital that the grapes are at a uniform temperature at the time they are pressed.

A pneumatic press is essential and Merlaut imported a specially designed Buscher direct from Switzerland. Crushing must be gentle but swift before the fruit warms up. Botrytized grapes are denser than non-botrytized fruit but the *pourriture noble* juice has a lower freezing point that water. Only this juice will flow away. The non-botrytized grapes will not be crushed at all. Surplus water is not released into the must and the result will be a wine with as much concentration as if the harvest had taken place in the sun.

It should be stressed that this technique is not a substitute for traditional Sauternes harvesting and vinification in clement weather. If the days are dry and sunny, the wine will continue to be made in the usual way. Merlaut has performed tests with nobly rotten grapes collected at three in the afternoon. There is no advantage. What the extraction process does enable him to do is to start picking earlier in the morning when the fruit is covered in dew and to continue if it rains. In a vintage such as 1987, it must have been a godsend!

One can see cryo-extraction catching on fast in the Sauternes. In a region where the harvest does not begin until it has been completed everywhere else and which often continues well until November, the chances are that it will rain at some stage. The investment is large but, offset over many vintages, more and more of them now potentially successful, the effect on the price of the single bottle is negligible. Will the other châteaux join him? You ask Merlaut. They have installed the facilities at Rabaud-Promis, he will point out. Also at Doisy-Vedrines, La Tour-Blanche and Rieussec; even at Yquem. Cryo-extraction works and, meanwhile, the quality at Rayne-Vigneau has improved enormously.

THE TASTING

The following wines were sampled at Château Rayne-Vigneau in June 1987.

Optimum drinking

1986 1996–2016

Medium colour. Good oaky nose. Delicate but ripe and plump. Some *pourriture noble*. Full and honeyed on the palate. Very good fruit. Rich and stylish. Plenty of botrytis and concentration. Fine balance. Surely the best Rayne-Vigneau for years!

1985 Now–2005

Similar colour. Less intense on the nose but oaky and stylish nevertheless. Good plump fruit again. Peachy, flowery and honeyed. Elegant. Not without noble rot. Good acidity. Long on the palate. Shows very well.

1984 Now–1997

Again, a stylish nose, some oak. Obviously less

pourriture noble and less dimension but not without balance or elegance. Reasonable body, good freshness. Finishes well.

1983   Now–2000 plus
Medium colour. Rather a lot of sulphur on the nose, especially in contrast with those above. Medium body. Basically, quite sweet and reasonably balanced, but does not really have the depth and intensity it should have. Unexciting.

1982   Drink soon
Similar colour. Also, quite a bit of SO2. Similar weight and intensity. Rather less style. In fact, rather coarse.

1981   Drink soon
This is rather better. Interesting fruit and some depth, if little botrytis. Again, the wine is dominated by built-in sulphur. Quite fat and honeyed and reasonable acidity. Finishes quite well. If the sulphur taint disappears, this will make a reasonably attractive bottle.

1979   Drink up
This has so much built-in sulphur it is hardly drinkable at all let alone enjoyable. No *pourriture noble*. Now getting old. Coarse.

1977   Drink now
Surprisingly, this wine is much cleaner. No obvious SO2. Clean, fresh, ripe and sweet. No undue age. Much more enjoyable. Not bad at all.

I also have several recent notes on the **1975** and one on the **1976**. both have reasonable amounts of botrytis. The **1976** is rich and succulent with the plumpness one associates with Bommes: quite a fat wine, now ready. The **1975** is firmer, a little harder and coarser. Neither could really be described as elegant nor as stars of the vintage.

SUDUIRAUT

Immediately to the north of Yquem, some three kilometres away from the Garonne and straddling the Sauternes-Preignac commune boundary, lies Château Suduiraut.

Suduiraut is one of the oldest estates in Sauternes, probably second only in seniority to Château d'Yquem itself. In the time of the *ancien régime*, it belonged to the Suduiraut family, an early member of whom must have quarrelled with the Duc d'Epernon, Governer of the Bordeaux area under Louis XIV. At Epernon's order, the ancient mansion was razed to the ground. The Suduirauts soon recovered from this setback, however, and were sufficiently in favour at court, as well as rich enough, to have an imposing two-storey *chartreuse* constructed in its place and to lay out front and back courtyards, complete with ponds and fountains, and have the extensive park landscaped, it is said, by Le Nôtre, the designer of Versailles. Today, Suduiraut, approached through a grand avenue of plane trees, is one of the loveliest as well as largest examples of the Bordelais country manors and estates.

Suduiraut describes itself on its label as '*Ancien Cru du Roy*'. There is no regal connection, however. At the beginning of the nineteenth century, a daughter of the family married a M. du Roy. At about the same time, a neighbouring property, Castelnau, originally belonging to a M. Pugneau, was incorporated into the estate and it attained its current size, in total some 200 hectares. Meanwhile, a collateral (*sic*) Duroy branch were proprietors at Château Grand-Puy-Ducasse in Pauillac.

Suduiraut passed into the Guilhot, or Guillot, family, owners at the time of the 1855 Classification. Subsequently it came into the hands of Emile Petit de Forest, owner in 1893, an engineer. He made a splendid 1899, and I also had a fine, if marginally maderized 1904 in London in 1991. When he died, the property was neglected and, as in so many cases, failed to exploit the good vintages of the 1920s, although a 1934 (proprietor, A. de Girodon Fralong) was a lovely old fragrant wine. Nevertheless, a number of authorities attest to disappointing wines, small *rendements* and a declining reputation.

HISTORY

In 1940, Château Suduiraut was acquired by Léopold Fonquernie, a rich industrialist from the north of France. As soon as he was able, he put into effect an ambitious and costly programme of improvements to both vineyards and *chai* and it was not long before Suduiraut was once again producing *premier cru* wine. In June 1981, I was lucky enough to be asked to preside over a selection of 1949 Sauternes for the London tasting group, Tastevin. The Suduiraut, still remarkably fresh and concentrated, was the star of the show.

After Léopold Fonquernie's death in the mid-1970s the property was managed by his daughters, the most active being Mme Madelaine Frouin. Rumours repeatedly circulated that it was for sale. Eventually, in 1992, a deal was reached with AXA Millésimes, giving them, like the Domaines Rothschild at Rieussec, a sweet wine property to add to their portfolio.

Under the control of Pierre Pascaud, who followed M. Bayéjo as *maître de chai* in 1978, the vineyard and cellars are a model of tidiness and cleanliness. Between the casks, the gravel is so neatly raked, one hardly dares disrupt the precision by walking up and down!

Yet, not only wine inhabits the *chai*. In July 1979, on a visit to the property, I was quietly digesting my impressions of the 1978 when, out of the corner of my eye, I noticed a large brown toad hop across the path between one row of hogsheads and the next. '*Tiens, un crapaud*,' said I, trusting I had chosen the correct word, for toad is not normally part of one's wine vocabulary. 'Oh yes,' said Pascaud, 'he's a great friend and helps keep the cellars free of vinegar flies and suchlike. We give it the occasional dish of Suduiraut, but only the second wine of course!' So drive carefully in the leafy lanes of Sauternes, dear readers, you never know when you might encounter an inebriated toad!

THE CHÂTEAU

The château of Suduiraut is a real castle. Not in the sense of a fort but in the same sense as the grand palaces of the English landed gentry or the châteaux of the Loire. It is a really fine example of French eighteenth-century architecture. Viewed from the front, there is a courtyard surrounded by two wings behind which is an elegant, long, harmonious, two-storied facade. From the garden, in the centre of the facade, a pediment bears the coat of arms of the owners of Suduiraut: heads of wild boar for the Suduiraut family themselves, spots of ermine for the Du Roys. The garden is overshadowed by huge mature trees – beech, planes, cedars. It is a splendid setting.

THE VINEYARD

Suduiraut occupies 200 hectares, of which 75 are under vines, roughly the same as a century ago. A small parcel is given over to the production of a red wine called Château Castelnau and the rest is planted in the ratio 80 per cent Sémillon and 20 per cent Sauvignon. Sauternes is a wine which, by its very nature, necessitates a low yield. At a nominal fifteen hectolitres per hectare – a third of what the more prolific red wine vineyards are allowed to produce – this would mean a theoretical maximum of around 14,000 cases of wine per annum. In fact, after evaporation, wastage and the normal rejection of that part of the harvest which does not come up to the *grand vin* levels, the quantity bottled under the château name is hardly half this amount: 50,000 bottles in 1975, 35,000 in 1976. The 1983 harvest, though, was much larger and 180,000 bottles of *grand vin* were made.

HOW THE WINE IS MADE

Suduiraut is said to have a microclimate marginally warmer than its neighbours and normally begins harvesting a day or two earlier, certainly several days before Yquem commences. The grapes are picked in bunches, not de-stemmed and the juice extracted by means of small, cylindrical, upright manual presses. The free-run juice is decanted into 5,000-litre stainless-steel vats and allowed to ferment at 18 to 22 degrees for 15 to 21 days. The fermentation is arrested at around fourteen degrees, using SO_2, leaving 4 to 6 degrees of liqueur. In great years such as 1967 and 1976, 15 degrees plus 7 was obtained. Up to 1978, the wine spent three years in (old) oak. Now it spends part of the time in vat and part in wood, some of which is new, and is bottled rather earlier.

CUVÉE MADAME

Suduiraut, like Coutet and Caillou, produces a *crème de tête*, a special *cuvée* of superlative wine in the best vintages. This is a fairly recent phenomenon, the first vintages of *Cuvée Madame*, as it is called, being the 1982 and 1985. The 1982, the produce of a single day, 15 September, with a must weight with a potential of 22 degrees, was matured and bottled separately. Some 4,000 bottles were produced of a wine which had a residual sugar of 130 grams per litre. The wine is magnificent.

THE WINE

I find Suduiraut less fat and luscious than some Sauternes, more akin to a Barsac in fact, although there is a plumpness which is reminiscent of Bommes. It is not a full-bodied, intense wine but there is normally an elegance of fruit and a character which is not the least bit blowsy or unstylish. In the twenty years since 1949, at least, it rarely failed to produce top-class wine. The 1955 is still excellent, the 1959 superb and the 1962 honeyed and delicious. Moreover, in lesser years such as 1958 – and even 1965 – it succeeded in making surprisingly good wine. Only in 1971, when too greedy a selection for bottling under the *grand vin* label was made, did Suduiraut produce disappointing wines in this period.

In the last twenty years, however, Suduiraut has been less consistent. It began with the 1971 which I have referred to above. The 1975 is variable, sometimes very good, sometimes less than compelling although not less than competent. The 1979 and 1982 are better than most. But the 1976 is poor, the 1983 disappointing, and the 1986 is unexciting. Suduiraut has never been one of the fuller, richer Sauternes but in recent years it seems to have become lighter still and there is often an absence of real concentration and the taste of noble rot.

Suduiraut, as I have pointed out, is an early picker. Is it picking too early? Stephen Brook, in his *Liquid Gold*, states that, as a consequence, the must sometimes needs to be chaptalized by the largest amount, the equivalent of two alcoholic degrees. As he says, this is hardly desirable. Moreover, if the figure given earlier for the quantity declared as 1983 Suduiraut is correct, it hardly indicates any severe degree of selection.

Sauternes vintages are notoriously variable. Sometimes, as in 1982, the noble rot arrives early. This obviously suits the Suduiraut *modus operandi* – their 1982 is a good result. In vintages such as 1983 and 1986, the reverse is the case and Suduiraut fails to produce wines of the standard of its more patient neighbours.

If the *matière première* is not always there, the wine is nevertheless made with sensitivity and care. Suduiraut normally has finesse as well as balance. It is not dominated by sulphur as some of its peers are in their youth. It is fresh and lemony in both colour and flavour and, when it is good, as in 1988, it fully justifies its reputation (and consequent high price) as one of Sauternes's better-known *premiers crus*. I just feel they could do even better if they really tried.

THE TASTING

The following wines were sampled in London in June 1988.

1986   Now–2001

Soft, flowery nose. Rich, quite full, good *pourriture noble* and reasonable depth. Typical medium weight. Preignac/Bommes style but more honeyed than usual. Not as concentrated as most in this vintage. Lacks grip and concentration. Forward.

1985   Drink soon

Lighter nose, even a suspicion of lacking a bit of weight. Medium body. Sweet but not much *pourriture noble*. Rather one-dimensional. Rea-sonable grip but not much elegance. Not bad.

1984   Drink up

Fresh, youthfully crisp and flowery on the nose. A bit lighter and a bit leaner than above. Shorter but a good 1984. A pleasant sweet wine.

1983   Drink soon

Light nose for a 1983; not a lot of depth or *pourriture noble*. Quite full but lacks class and zip. Finishes a bit heavy. Disappointing.

1982   Now–2002

Quite a full nose with depth, indeed as much weight as the above. Flowery, camomile touches. Ripe, honeyed, positive. Will still develop. Good *pourriture noble*. More style than the above and better acidity. Very good for the vintage.

1981   Now–2005

Medium colour. This nose is a little blunt and awkward at present like many 1981s. Better on the palate. Fullish, honeyed, some botrytis. Still youthful. Finishes well. Good to very good.

1980   Now–1997

Lightish colour. Plump, flowery, high-toned nose. Medium body. A gentle, elegant, ripe wine, with a touch of oak and a little *pourriture noble* but no great depth. Better acidity than most in this vintage.

1979   Now–2005

A fully mature, medium-weight, elegant wine. Without enormous *pourriture noble* but enough. Good fruit and balance. *A point* now. Good style and plenty of interest. Good for the vintage.

1978   Drink soon

Fullish, slightly four-square. Lacks suppleness and zip. No *pourriture noble*. On the palate more generosity. Ripe, quite fat and ample. Some zip. Really quite attractive. Very good for vintage if without enormous nuance. Seems fuller and less developed than the above, but essentially no more than a pleasant sweet wine.

1976   Now–1997

Full colour. Slightly overblown, blowsy nose. Slightly oxidized. The second bottle is better but not much. Fat, ripe, honeyed nose but the nose of an old vine. Similar palate. Fullish, rich and quite concentrated, certainly has *pourriture noble* and is honeyed but it lacks a bit of zip and class. Not a keeper.

1975   Now–2000

Mid-gold colour. Certainly quite a lot fresher and more youthful than the above. Some *pourriture noble*. Good grip. Medium-full. Alive and fresh. A good to very good 1975. Rich and honeyed. Finishes well.

1972   Drink up

Lean and a bit old on the nose. Getting coarse. By no means a disaster but now a bit long in the tooth. Yet there was ripeness, certainly, as well as grip. Even some *pourriture noble*. By no means thin or lean.

1970   Now–2000

Fat and plump, full and quite fresh. Though not a lot of *pourriture noble*. Full body, indeed firm. Rich and fat. Honeyed and some *pourriture noble* on the palate. Still youthful. This lacks just a bit of elegance but plenty of concentration and attraction. Will last well.

1969   Past its best

A bit old on the nose and faded but not as lean as the 1972. Light, flowery, quite sweet. Was really quite elegant. Now a little old but not bad.

1967   Now–1997

Golden colour. Ripe, plump and luscious on the nose. Good concentration and Pinot. Good grip – which not many have. Slightly caramelly, vanillary. Rich and full but soft. Very round, fleshy wine. Very good. Will still keep well.

1962

Not offered. Not seen for some years. Delicious – and vigorous – last time out.

1959   Now–2000 plus

Very lovely, fullish colour. Very concentrated nose, a lot more finesse and breed than the above. Abundant fruit, *pourriture noble* complexity. Still quite powerful on the palate. Indeed fresher than on the nose. Will keep for ages. This is really luscious. Very lovely. Much better acidity and grip and class than the above.

1928   Drink soon

Deep golden colour. Mature, complex, slightly burnt-toffee nose. A little fade and attenuation but interesting and complex. On the palate it is fresher. Full, honeyed, velvety and luscious. Still alive. The graceful decline of a wine of breed and concentration. Lovely finish still. By no means over.

COUTET

Château Coutet is one of the best-known and best-loved of all the great Sauternes properties and one of only two estates in Barsac to have been classified as a *premier cru* in 1855. Together with its great rival, Château Climens, the domaine dominates that part of the commune once called Haut-Barsac, that section of *vignoble* that lies to the west of the town, on higher land away from the River Garonne, between the railway and the *autoroute*.

The property is one of the oldest, if not *the* oldest in the area. The ancient manor house retains, in the form of a square crenellated tower surmounted by a corbel, some vestiges of the fortified, military architecture of the early Middle Ages. This part dates back to the thirteenth century. There is a small chapel which was constructed a century later, also during the period when the English held sway in Bordeaux. The main part of the house, tagged on to the tower, and with two pointed towers on the garden side, was built over the remains of the old *maison noble* in the fifteenth and sixteenth centuries. The whole is a building of elegance and charm, not at all without architectural merit, and further evidence, together with other châteaux in the area such as Yquem and Suduiraut, that the Sauternes was a thriving region long before anyone considered developing the land in the Médoc.

While the derivation of the word Coutet is obscure – it perhaps takes its name from one of its owners in the Middle Ages or later – it was certainly an important wine-growing estate early in Bordeaux's viticultural history. In the eighteenth century it formed part of the vast agricultural holdings of the President Pichard, one of the senior figures in the Bordeaux parliament, a man of immense wealth and influence, and owner, among other estates, of Château Lafite.

HISTORY

Thomas Jefferson, in his survey of the wines of Bordeaux following a visit in 1787, mentions the property as the *premier* domaine in Barsac. It made 150 *tonneaux* of wine – indicating a vineyard area of 100 hectares or so – which sold for 280 *livres* when new and 600 when 'old', i.e., when ready for drinking four or five years later (in those days wines were matured largely in cask). This was the same price as that obtained by Yquem itself and the other top wines of the region at the time such as Filhot and Suduiraut.

In 1788 Pichard sold Coutet to his neighbour Gabriel Barthélémy Romain de Filhot, another member of the *noblesse de la robe* and proprietor of the château which bears his name. Filhot fell foul of the new revolutionary order a few years later and was guillotined in 1793 (*22 Messidor, l'An II*). His wife, Mme Thérèse Filhot Chimbaud, was also condemned to death, at the age of 60, for passing money to her children who had emigrated.

Following this one assumes that both Coutet and Filhot were sold off as *biens nationaux*, but we do not have exact details of the transaction. Fourteen years later the orphaned Marie-Geneviève de Filhot married Antoine-Marie de Lur-Saluces of Château d'Yquem. He was well in with the new regime, being Napoleon's chamberlain, and by 1810 Marie-Geneviève had been able to reacquire her patrimony. With Yquem and Fargues, Coutet and Filhot, as well as De Malle and Château Piada, Lur-Saluces was king of Sauternes indeed!

Château Coutet was to remain in the hands of the Lur-Saluces family for 115 years. Up until the 1850s it continued to produce large quantities of wine, around 110 *tonneaux* according to most sources, but then the annual production dramatically halved. For the next century it remained at about 50 *tonneaux*. What was the reason for the decrease? This was prior to the outbreak of phylloxera, but the early 1850s saw the arrival of oidium, a form of mildew. While estates such as Yquem and Suduiraut suffered a temporary reduction in harvest until a remedy against oidium was discovered, the Coutet fall was permanent. Were some sections of vineyard never replanted, and later, indeed, sold off?

In 1922 the Lur-Saluces decided to sell Château Coutet (in 1935 Filhot was also sold). The new owners were the imposing-sounding but anonymous Société Immobilière des Grands Crus de France, owners also at the time of Château d'Issan, Brane-Cantenac, Lagrange, Branaire-Ducru, and La Tour-Rauzan in Saint-Laurent. Three years later, however, Coutet was resold to a Lyonnais industrialist, M. Henri-Louis Guy. Guy was a manufacturer of hydraulic presses, and these were soon installed at Coutet. Regrettably, he did not live long enough to see the fruits of these and other investments, for he died soon after.

Henri-Louis Guy had two daughters. One of these, Mme Thomas, was widowed early. For a number of years she entrusted her children's education to an old family friend, the Abbé Rolland. Eventually the two fell in love, Edmond Rolland renounced the priesthood and married his beloved. The Rolland-Guys remained at Coutet until the death of Mme Rolland in 1977.

It was during this period that the wine for which Coutet is most renowned, the *Cuvée Madame*, was devised. In honour of his wife, Edmond Rolland decided that in the best of vintages, a few barrels of a *crème de tête* originating from carefully selected grapes, hand-picked at the optimum of fruition and *pourriture noble* and with a potential alcohol of 22 degrees, would be produced. These are not normally sold on the commercial market, but reserved for presents, grand banquets and other special occasions. In most years only 100 or so cases are made. In 1971 the quantity was six casks, from fruit selected on the 15th and 16th October, and the amount bottled was 1,408 bottles and 177 magnums. It is a superlative wine, despite the fact that after the disastrous frosts of 1956, 70 per cent of the vineyard had to be replanted. To date, *Cuvée Madame* has been produced in 1943, 1949, 1959, 1971, 1975, 1981, 1986, 1988 and 1989.

The new proprietor in 1977 was Marcel Baly, a rotund gentleman from Strasbourg, and proprietor of the Société Alsacienne, whose interests include a road-haulage business and hotels. He paid a price of 4.3 million francs for Château Coutet. Bertrand Baly, Marcel's son, now takes an increasing interest. Alexis Lichine et Cie of Bordeaux are Coutet's exclusive world-wide agents.

THE VINEYARD

Château Coutet has always been the largest vineyard in Barsac. Even now, despite the reductions of a century ago, there are 37 hectares under vine, planted in the ratio of 75 per cent Sémillon, 23 per cent Sauvignon and 2 per cent Muscadelle – the Sauvignon content having been increased slightly in recent years – and producing about 80 *tonneaux*, 8,000 cases, of wine a year.

The vineyard lies in one piece, adjoining Doisy-Daëne and near Château Climens, surrounding the château and its outbuildings and the park which lies outside the domaine's walls. The soil is a complex, heterogenous mixture: in part *limons calcaires*, a form of limestone-based loess or silt; in part there is alluvial soil; elsewhere fine gravel or clay and also old weathered sand of the Mindel glacial era. The subsoil is a hard limestone rock plateau of the earlier Stampien glaciation.

HOW THE WINE IS MADE

Coutet, like all Sauternes, is collected in a number of *passages*, often over a month or more, in order to select each berry, half-cluster or bunch at its optimum. First there is a preliminary vineyard visit to cut out anything poor, unripe or affected by insects. The first *tri*, a form of insurance, may go towards a lesser wine or even be sold off as a generic wine, and not wind up in the *grand vin*. Thereafter, the game of poker with the elements continues. Will there be, as in 1988, 1989 and 1990, a plentiful arrival of noble rot, thanks to humid morning mists and warm, dry, sunny afternoons? Or will the winter arrive, the weather break, and the rot become *grise* rather than *noble*? Sometimes the harvest will continue over several weeks – the 1985 did not finish until 28 November. Sometimes it will be over in a month. There may be four pickings, there may be ten. Neither, *per se*, will indicate a successful vintage. It all depends on the weather.

The grapes at Coutet are pressed in M. Guy's small, horizontal hydraulic presses, and the various juices derived therefrom allowed to settle for 24 hours, lightly sulphured to inhibit fermentation, in order to eliminate the *grosses lies*. This is called *débourbage*. The fermentation takes place in cask, one-third of which are new, but the rest of no great age, at a temperature of 15 degrees. Thereafter there is a cold treatment, cooling the wine to less than 0°C to precipitate out further impurities, thus reducing the necessity for loads of sulphur to preserve the wine from bacterial contamination. Bottling takes places after eighteen months. A contract bottler arrives in the spring with his machine and stations himself in the courtyard. Amongst a great clatter and noise, and much hurly-burly in the cellar, the entire crop is confined to glass within a week or so, capturing the youthful fruit and fragrance and ensuring a wine which will safely acquire depth, honey and concentration in bottle, while retaining freshness and acidity. In a very rich year, high in pectins and other elements which do not settle out in cask, a very light fining, one-sixth as strong as that required for a red wine, may be undertaken.

VIN SEC DE CHÂTEAU COUTET

Château Coutet also produces a dry wine, like many Sauternes properties. However, unlike most, the label boasts a Graves *appellation*. In part the wine comes from a Graves property under the same ownership in nearby Pujols-sur-Ciron which used to be known as Château Reverdon until it was rechristened as Château Coutet also. A dry white wine from the

Barsac estate would merely be AC Bordeaux. As from 1989 this is partly fermented in barrel. Coutet *sec* is a better wine – crisper and more fruity, less heavy – than many of the dry white wines of its neighbours.

THE WINE

In the 1855 Classification Coutet headed Climens, as it did prior to this classification in the opinions of Jullien and Paguierre, as well as Jefferson. Since then some have averred that Climens is superior. And with this view I would agree.

Climens is certainly richer, fuller, more luscious, but it is also heavier, in the past retaining an element of bound-in sulphur which is sometimes obtrusive, even when the wine is eight or ten years old. Coutet is lighter, the peachy fruit and acidity more evident. If Climens is powerful, Coutet is delicate.

Curiously, the great years for each do not always coincide. 1976 and 1975 is an example: Climens 1976 is better than its 1975. Coutet is the opposite. Equally, Climens seems generally more successful in the lesser vintages. There have been years when Coutet is a bit too light and insubstantial, not sufficiently concentrated and luscious. It can be criticized for being too variable. Yet at best, as the *Cuvées Mesdames* amply demonstrate, Coutet can be spectacular.

It can be argued that the existence of the *Cuvée Madame*, by creaming off the very best, dilutes the quality of what remains. Do you judge Coutet by the commercial wine or the *Cuvée Madame*? I must confess I regret this policy of a *tête de cuvée*. I approve of second wines, a device which manifestly produces a better *grand vin*. But I think Coutet do themselves a disservice by producing the *Cuvée Madame*. If this cream was not taken off the top the reputation of the property might be higher. As it is one admires the property for its professionalism and its seriousness, but one occasionally looks for more depth and concentration in the wine it produces in bottle. At its best though, as in 1988, 1981 and 1971 (all of which were years when a *Cuvée Madame* was produced, incidentally – so perhaps my fears are unwarranted) the wine can be outstanding.

THE TASTING

The following vintages back to the 1971 were sampled at Château Coutet in April 1986. I have added a note on a 1970 which came my way in the following July, and on other vintages which have come my way in recent years.

Optimum drinking

1985   1995–2005

Various *cuvées* before assembling. In general fairly dry on the nose but more luscious than this would indicate on the palate. Rich, firm, concentrated and oak. Good crisp, flowery fruit with the Sauvignon evident, as it always in very young Sauternes. Seems good.

1983   1995–2010

Lightish colour. The nose has a bit of built-in sulphur and is again quite dry. Fat and full and still a little unformed on the palate. Rich and sweet, oak and vanilla but though concentrated and powerful there doesn't seem to be a great deal of *pourriture noble*. A good wine but not a great 1983.

1982   **Drink soon**

Deeper colour. Quite sweet but a little one-dimensional on nose and palate. Quite full and

buttery. Doesn't have the concentration or elegance of, say, Suduiraut. Finishes a little coarse.

1981   1996–2020

Lightish colour again. Fine nose, plenty of depth and a lot of finesse. A good vintage here! This is really very fine. Concentrated, rich, plenty of *pourriture noble*; fat, flowery, vanillary-oaky. Very long on the palate. Delicious. (Despite the elimination of the following!) Must be one of the very best of the vintage.

Cuvée Madame, 1981   2006–2056

Much more colour. Even more finesse, depth, concentration and quality. This is an Yquem of Barsac! Enormous power. Essence of wine. Quite marvellous. *Grand vin!*

1979   **Drink up**

Lightish colour. Some built-in sulphur on the nose giving it a diesel-oil aspect. Medium body, no noble rot. Quite sweet but rather four-square and lacks nuance. Dull; lacks acidity and will become astringent.

1978　　　　　　　　　　**Drink soon**

Lightish colour. Quite a lot of built-in sulphur. Wet-wool smell. Fat, plump and fruity despite this. Reasonably fresh. Not bad for the vintage once the sulphur goes.

1976　　　　　　　　　　**Now–2000**

Some development of colour. Honeyed, ripe, has grip. Touch of barley-sugar. Fullish, round, quite fat. Not enormous *pourriture noble* but has good grip for the vintage. Good wine.

1975　　　　　　　　　　**Now–2005**

Similar colour. Fresher on the nose, more elegant and more depth as a result. Similar weight of wine but a better grip, more power and more concentration. Lovely stylish wine in the Barsac character. Very fine.

1973　　　　　　　　　　**Drink soon**

Quite a developed nose. Fresher on the palate. Has fruit and zip and elegance. Medium sweet. Now needs drinking but not bad at all for the vintage.

1971　　　　　　　　　　**Now–1997**

Rich and honeyed, with very attractive fruit on the nose. Now fully mature. Peachy, stylish, quite concentrated delicious wine – really elegant. Classic Barsac. A very fine Coutet.

1970　　　　　　　　　　**Drink soon**

Straightforward, full sweet wine. Some *pourriture noble* at least. Not that much style, grip or length but not bad. A little dull.

1967　　　　　　　　　　**Drink up**

Quite a full colour. On the nose the wine is rather coarse, showing its alcohol in what is now rather a diesel-oil sort of way. Some sweetness on the palate but the wine lacks balance and finesse. Not one of the best 1967s.

1966　　　　　　　　　　**Drink up**

Less colour. Sweet on the nose but without much evidence of noble rot. Has lightened up on the palate. Lacks grave and dimension. Unexciting.

1964　　　　　　　　　　**Drink soon**

Lightish colour. Round, sweet, a little *pourriture noble*. Still reasonably fresh and elegant. As 1964s go not bad at all. Not a lot of structure but sweet and fruity.

1962　　　　　　　　　　**Drink soon**

Golden colour, oldish but light. On the nose not exactly luscious but fresh, sweet and full of fruit. But it is beginning to lose its intensity. Clean and

elegant on the palate. It lacks the fat and real Sauternes structure. And there is not the amount of noble rot character that there is in the best 1962s – in the Climens for example. But it has style. Good but not great. A second bottle circulating was less vigorous than the first.

1961　　　　　　　　　　**Drink up**

Medium colour. Typically Coutet: soft, balanced, still elegant, some – but not a lot – of noble rot. Not a great deal of concentration or grip now, and never had a lot in the first place. On the way down but enjoyment to be had still.

1959　　　　　　　　　　**Now–1998**

(Bordeaux bottled by Schroeder and Schyler) Rich gold colour. Concentrated nose. There is depth and intensity here. Fullish; very good grip; finely balanced. Complex, rich, peachy fruit, but no longer *that* luscious or sweet. But plenty of life still. Very good indeed.

1955　　　　　　　　　　**Drink soon**

(English bottled by Avery's of Bristol) Light golden colour. Mature, honeyed but a little anonymous on the nose and on the palate. Fresh but not much concentration, fat or grip. Has lightened up. Balanced, fresh, attractive, but good, merely, by no means great.

1953　　　　　　　　　　**Drink up**

Light golden colour. Delicate nose, without a great deal of *pourriture noble*. Soft and gentle, ripe and fruity on the palate. This is balanced, elegant and now gently fading, but still long, still enjoyable. Fragrant and honeyed at the end. Good plus.

1950　　　　　　　　　　**Now–1999**

Tasted alongside Rieussec and Climens: and the best of the three by some way. Marvellous healthy, complex, botrytis nose. Honeyed, balanced, very vigorous fruit on the palate. Very good grip. This is concentrated and multidimensional. Very classy. Very long. Will last well still.

1948　　　　　　　　　　**Drink up**

Sercial nose. Interesting nose. Has lightened up and there is a touch of maderization. Only a little sweet now and it is difficult to see how much noble rot there was here. The fat has disappeared. Yet complex, long on the palate and interesting nevertheless.

1937　　　　　　　　　　**Drink up**

Amontillado colour. This shows quite a bit of age. The wine is fresh, with good grip, but there is a certain astringency on the palate. But as it developed in the glass it improved. Clean, sweet, elegant and with evidence of plenty of noble rot. Inevitably the concentration has loosened a little now but a fine wine nevertheless.

CLIMENS

The largest of the five communes of Sauternes, Barsac, is somewhat detached from the remainder of the area, divided from the other four by the motorway and the river Ciron. Though officially part of Sauternes, Barsac likes to keep its independence. When the *appellation* laws were laid down in 1936 the local growers managed to persuade the authorities to retain the name of Barsac as an independent AC. A wine of Barsac, therefore, can call itself Sauternes or Barsac, or even, as in the case of Château Climens, its leading growth, 'Sauternes-Barsac', thus getting the best of both worlds.

The name Climens first appears in a document dating from 1462, when one Jean Climens is reported as owning the privilege of levying customs duties at Royan, at the mouth of the Gironde estuary. No direct connection with the Barsac domaine has yet been established, but nevertheless almost a century later a deed of sale in favour of Guirault Roborel, King's Prosecutor at Barsac, refers to the estate as Climens, so one can but conjecture.

Over the next 40 years Roborel and his son enlarged the property and it was to continue in the hands of their successors until the Revolution. The last Roborel, Jean-Baptiste, like his forbears a lawyer, declared to the revolutionary tribunal that his domaine at Barsac had been almost entirely ruined. He had not been able to harvest a single barrel of wine and had had to uproot two-thirds of his vines. The reason for this misfortune, however, is not clear.

After Jean-Baptiste Roberel's death in 1800, the estate was sold to Jean Binaud. The deed of sale refers to three parcels of vines totalling 27 hectares. It is under the name of Bineau (*sic*) or Roborel that the estate appears in the pages of Paguierre (1828) and others, Jullien having declared in his *Topographie de Tous les Vignobles Connus* (1816) that, 'the wines of Haut-Barsac [that is the better, higher land, away from the river Garonne] stand out by virtue of their full body, finesse, flavour and bouquet. The First Growths of this commune are Climens, Coutet, Doisy and Caillou.'

HISTORY

In 1850 the vineyard produced 60 *tonneaux*, still occupied 27 hectares and was owned by Eloi Lacoste. He also owned Château Pexiotto in Bommes. Coutet was almost twice the size, and though it has been much reduced since this time, Climens remains precisely the same domaine it was then. Five years later they were both classed as *premiers crus* of the region, and various Doisys, Myrat, Caillou, Suau, and Broustet-et-Nairac, at the time one estate, were all classed as *deuxièmes*.

In 1871 Climens and Pexiotto were bought by Alfred Ribet. Production at Climens was now 30 *tonneaux*, reduced from the 1850 figure because not all the vineyard was in full production, and also because the yield was lower as a result of the concentration on true *pourriture noble*-type Sauternes, rather than a wine which was merely very sweet. At the time the vineyard was planted with 80 per cent Sémillon, with the remainder Sauvignon and 'Muscade' (Muscadelle).

In 1885, with the Climens vineyard three-quarters ravaged by phylloxera, Ribet decided to sell up. Nearby, at Château Doisy-Dubroca, the heiress, a Mlle Faux, had recently wed Henri Gounouilhou. Gounouilhou, a publisher, decided to buy Climens, and it was at this time that Pexiotto was absorbed into Château Rabaud, its neighbour. Climens and Doisy-Dubroca remained in the same family until 1971, when both were bought by Lucien Lurton, proprietor of numerous estates, including Brane-Cantenac, Durfort-Vivens and Desmirail in Margaux and Cantenac, and Château Bouscaut, the *cru classé* Graves.

Gounouilhou was obviously a man of energy as well as expertise. His predecessor had done much to bring the vineyard into full production, only to see his vines wasting away as a result of the phylloxera bug. On top of this, in the late 1880s, there was an outbreak of mildew. Nevertheless, by the turn of the century, the production of Climens was up to 80 to 90 *tonneaux*, and Gounouilhou had been awarded a medal for 'the rapid execution of a well-prepared programme of reconstruction of an important estate and its dependent buildings' by the Concours Régional de Bordeaux.

Under the Gounouilhou regime – Henri died about 1920 – the reputation of Château Climens reached great heights. It was considered throughout the region as the only real rival to Château d'Yquem, and in several vintages – 1929, 1937, 1947, possibly 1949 – excelled Yquem in quality. In 1926 Climens fetched 32,000 francs per *tonneau*, a record for the region, and probably unrivalled, in real terms, until the 1960s or even 1970s.

THE VINEYARD

The present vineyard occupies about 30 hectares, almost entirely planted in Sémillon with the rest Sauvignon – there is no longer any Muscadelle – and lies principally between the château and its outbuildings and the A61 *autoroute*, north of the *départementale* road which runs from Barsac to Pujols-sur-Ciron. Two further *clos* lie east of the château and on the other side of the road facing the various Doisy vineyards.

This is the highest point of Barsac. At the summit of the *croupe*, consisting of gravel and *sables rouges* on a limestone base, mixed with clay, the ground rises to twenty metres above sea level. The vines, like elsewhere in the area, are very severely pruned; the Sémillon being trained by the Cot method, a sort of very restricted Gobelet or spur type, the Sauvignon by the traditional single Guyot. They are grafted on to the Riparia-Gloire 101–14 root stock. Their average age is well over 30 years.

WINE-MAKING

Harvesting and vinification are traditional. The vineyard is picked over a period of several weeks, each bunch selected when it is at its optimum. Four to six *passages* are made over each row of vines. After pressing, Climens is vinified in oak barrels, of which about one-third are new each vintage, and matured for two years before bottling. There is a second wine, Les Cypres de Climens, which I first saw in the 1984 vintage, when no *grand vin* was declared. All the 1987 was sold as generic Sauternes. Currently, the production is 60 *tonneaux*, an average yield of eighteen hectolitres per hectare.

THE CHÂTEAU

Climens's château is a simple affair of no particular architectural merit, dating from the early decades of the nineteenth century. It consists of a single-storey, un-ornate, *chartreuse*-style building complete with an additional floor surmounted by slate-roofed, pointed towers at either end. It is presently uninhabited.

The château gives on to a courtyard, facing west, surrounding which are the rather larger *chais*, other outbuildings, and the residence of the *régisseur*. André Janin took over from his mother when she retired in the mid-1980s after over 30 years' service. The Janins have been at Climens for over a century.

A feature of Climens is its collection of old wine presses, one of a number amassed by Lucien Lurton over the years. The largest can be seen near the entrance to the *chai*. But this is a merely incidental. The atmosphere at Climens is one of a quiet farmyard, neither an aristocratic country residence, nor an attraction for the tourist.

THE WINE

Inevitably Climens must be discussed, compared and contrasted alongside the other Barsac *premier cru*, Château Coutet. The vineyards are close, at one point barely 250 metres from each other, but the wines are quite different.

Climens is fuller and richer, more of a Sauternes than a Barsac. Barsacs in general are less luscious, more racy than Sauternes, full of fruit and with a good acidity, but not as weighty – or, one might add, as heavy, an attribute which a poorly-made Sauternes can sometimes have to excess. Climens combines these Barsac characteristics with an extra fatness, and this gives it a depth and a longevity rarely found elsewhere in the commune.

While Climens has for long been considered the best wine in the district, it is only since 1969 that Cocks and Féret has given it precedence over Coutet. I think it is generally accepted that it has been consistently producing the better wine since the 1920s.

Though I have been fortunate enough to taste the 1929s of both properties – and indeed can go back to 1899 with Château Coutet – most of my experiences of the two properties are with their post-1959 vintages. Climens takes more time to come round, and in its youth the sulphur is more evident, but its extra weight makes it last better. Personally I have no hesitation in rating Climens the better estate. There have been few disappointments. Regularly, when I assess a Sauternes vintage horizontally I find I have placed Climens in the top three of the entire region after Yquem when the results are revealed.

And I do not think I shall ever forget the Climens 1929, sampled in Villeneuve-de-Marsan in February 1978. The wine looked like an amontillado sherry, but it showed not the slightest sign of age. The combination of honey and spices, barley sugar and fruit, balanced with acidity, was exquisite. It was nectar!

THE TASTING

The younger wines were tasted in London in May 1994. I have added a few notes on older vintages which have come my way in the last couple of years.

1991   **1997–2007**

Slightly lighter colour than the next two: sweet, flowery nose. Some botrytis, surprisingly; reasonable substance – again surprisingly. Rich, clean and elegant. Good lemony zip to it. No undue SO2. A splendid effort. Lighter obviously than the next three but not slight. Good length. Still youthful.

1990   **2001–2040**

Good colour. Closed, rich, concentrated nose. A lot of depth and power here. Full bodied. A lot of botrytis. Very good grip. This is still extremely young, but potentially superb. Marvellous fruit. Lots of dimension and complexity. Very, very long. Brilliant. But an infant.

1989   **1999–2040**

Good colour. Fat and honeyed and exotically nobly rotten on the nose. Good balance but less power and density than the 1990, and more evolved. On the nose it seems a little blander but there is plenty of grip on the palate. Real harmony and great class. Rich and concentrated but also flowery. Very very lovely. Not the size of the 1990 but perhaps it is more elegant.

1988   **1998–2020**

Good colour. A little bit more SO2 on the nose here, slightly deadening it. On the palate medium-full. Round, a little adolescent. No lack of either botrytis or acidity but it has a slightly hard, even petrolly edge to it at present. Currently the least good of the 1986-1990 quartet.

1986   **1996–2016**

Good colour. Just a touch of built-in sulphur on the nose here, but cleaner and crisper than the 1988. It is a slightly lighter wine, but one of immense charm and clarity of expression. Fruit salady and flowery. Medium body. Fresh, gentle, elegant. Very long and complex at the end. Fine.

1985   **Now–2005**

Good colour. Fondant nose. Less intense than the 1986. Much less noble rot. No SO2 though. Medium to medium-full. Caramelly, slightly four-square. A slight burn of alcohol. Some length but no real depth or dimension. Good for the vintage. But it is all a bit flat.

1983   **Now–2015**

Deep colour. Much less evidence of built-in sulphur than there was a few years ago, but still a touch. Underneath, though, a wine of real dimension and size – even power. Very rich, a lot of botrytis. Meaty. Honeyed, caramelly. This is now ready, and it shows the improvement of Sauternes in the last decade: rich and full and concentrated and opulent as it is, it doesn't have the class and sheer sophistication of 1989 and 1990, even 1986.

1982   **Drink soon**

Medium colour. Not a lot on the nose. Light, soft, sweet. With a touch of built-in sulphur. This is a gentle, unassuming wine, pretty but not serious. On the palate medium body. A bit slight and short. One dimensional. I remember it as having more interest than this. Today it is dull.

1981   **Now–2000**

Medium colour. Slightly heavier and more lumpy on the nose than the 1982, but more depth and interest perhaps. Much better on the palate than the 1982 but it lacks a bit of class. This is all over the place – acidity here, alcohol there and coarse over all. But quite good.

1980   **Now–2000 plus**

Medium colour. Light gentle nose. Quite elegant. A little botrytis. This is like the 1982 but with a lot more personality. Medium weight. Gentle. Harmonious. Indeed elegant. I prefer this to the 1981 as well. It is longer and it is more complex. Good. Surprisingly so.

1979   **Now–2005**

Quite evolved on the nose. Ample, sweet and plump. But no richer than the 1980, it would seem. But this is deceptive, the wine is more hidden. Similar weight on the palate. Good crisp fruit. Good grip. A little more complexity. This will still improve.

1976   **Now–2013**

Golden colour. Fresh, ripe, no sulphur on the nose. Very Barsac in the Climens way. Still undeveloped. Full but still youthful and closed in. Plump, ripe, very concentrated. Very good acidity. A lot of *pourriture noble*. A lot of elegance and quality. Very fine quality.

1975   **Now–2005**

Good fresh colour. Fine, stylish, crisp, nose. Very Barsac again. Rich but racy. Similar palate. Good acidity. Quite sweet, peachy fruit. Some noble rot if not a great deal. Very elegant. Still vigorous.

1971   **Now–2005**

Golden colour. Ripe, vigorous, barley-sugar flavour. Balanced, *pourriture noble* fruit. This has great style and complexity. Rich and complex. Fine quality.

1970   **Now–2000**

Ripe, sweet, but not much *pourriture noble*. A bit four-square. Best as it developed, as the SO2 went. Full, honeyed. Good but not great. Will still keep well.

1967   **Now-1998**

Ripe colour but still youthful and fresh. A lot of concentration. Still young and vigorous. Fat, caramelly, honeyed and very stylish. Vanillary and oaky. This is a bit more rigid and one-dimensional and less ample than the 1962. Stylish nonetheless. Not great. Merely very good.

1962   **Now-2000**

Golden colour. This is rich and concentrated and stylish. Fat and honeyed and with good *pourriture noble*. Now a fully mature wine. Succulent and vigorous.

1959   **Now-2005**

Deep golden colour. Fullish, plump and ample. Good acidity. This is very fine. Vigorous. Lovely. Bags of life left.

1955   **Now-1988**

Mid-gold colour. Fresh, ripe, Pinot nose. Good richness and fat. Full, concentrated. Similar palate. This has depth, with good spicy *pourriture noble* character and elegance. Fine quality. Still very vigorous.

1953   **Now-1998**

Barley-sugar colour. Sweet, fragrant nose. Has lost a little of its concentration. But good botrytis and class. A delicate, mellifluous, balanced wine.

Not quite as fat as it once was but fresh, Barsacy and lovely nevertheless. Fine quality.

1950   **Drink soon**

Vigorous, orange colour. Fatter and with more *pourriture noble* than Rieussec but less classy. Full and plump though, less age. Rich, honey and barley-sugar. High class. Long. Plenty of life left. Fine, fat. Good finish. Not as good as Rieussec or Coutet but very good. Not as complex.

1949   **Drink up**

This was from a fairly ullaged bottle and had a really deep tawny colour. Sweet and spicy but a little maderised on the nose. On the palate fresh and fragrant but a little sign of shortening up. Ripe and fragrant. Certainly stylish. But has lost its concentration and intensity. Still very enjoyable and not too short. I have had better examples.

1942   **Drink up**

Light-golden colour. A quite rigid wine. A little tough and even tannic. Fresh but chunky. Sweet but slightly drying out and not a lot of *pourriture noble*. Yet this has style. Light on the nose. Not that sweet and certainly not luscious on the palate. Good but not great. A little past its best.

GUIRAUD

When the five communes of the Sauternes region were first classified in 1855, there were 21 top growths. Now, as a result of some subdivision, there are twelve first growths including one *grand premier cru* (Yquem) and fourteen second growths, a total of 26 properties. Six actually lie in the commune of Sauternes itself, the most southerly and the furthest away from the River Garonne. The only *premier cru* of the village, however, apart from Yquem, is Guiraud.

Guiraud, like most Bordeaux wine estates, has had its ups and downs; it has also been associated with '*enfants terribles*'. In 1981 a new and, moreover, foreign '*enfant terrible*' arrived on the Sauternes scene, the Canadian Hamilton Narby. Narby was determined to seize the sleepy Sauternais by the scruff of their collective neck, restore some of the old glory to the reputation of this superlative sweet wine, and reintroduce a fashion for drinking it regularly. The world, we felt when we first met him, would hear of Sauternes whether it liked it or not, and if, in the process of shaking up the apathy for promoting Sauternes, a few local toes get trodden on, well, perhaps, '*tant pis*'. Sadly, Hamilton is no longer resident at Guiraud, though his family still own the estate. But nevertheless he has left his mark. Two years later the provident arrival of a superb 1983 vintage enabled prices to rise to more realistical economic levels. Nineteen eighty-five was not bad at all, and this was followed by excellent vintages in 1986, 1988 and 1990. All of which were rapidly taken up. Sauternes has become news.

In the 1855 Classification, Guiraud was known as Bayle, the name under which it also appears on the map of Belleyme (1790) which decorates the endpapers of Benson and Mackenzie's book on *Sauternes* (1979). Who or what was Bayle has not yet been unearthed. It has been suggested to Narby that Bayle might be a *lieu-dit*, offered as part of a seigniorial grant from the Crown back in the fifteenth or sixteenth centuries. It might also be the name of an early proprietor. Local myth has it that the Bayle family originated in the Pyrenees, where their immense pasture holdings at one point provided oxen to work the Bordeaux vineyards.

HISTORY

The earliest proprietors so far recorded are the Essenhault family, councillors of the Bordeaux parliament in the seventeenth century, and owners also of a large estate in Cantenac, part of which is now Château d'Issan. In 1729 the baronial domaine was split up, and in September, 1730, Marie Catherine d'Essenhault, wife of Joseph-Guillaume de Mons (a name which will also be familiar to claret lovers) bequeathed her 'estate in the parish of Sauternes, known as Bayle' to her daughter, Marie Angélique. From Marie, who, we presume, did not marry, Bayle passed to Joseph, Chevalier de Mons, her brother, and from him, 30 years later, to his nephew Léonard-Joseph, his 'héritier général et universel'.

On the 22 February, the first Guiraud, or, as it was then spelled, Guiraut, comes on the scene. Pierre Guiraut was the eldest son of a Bordeaux *négociant*. He bought Bayle for 53,000 *livres* tournois and, as is the custom, bequeathed his own name to the estate and its wine.

The first mention I have been able to trace of Guiraud the wine, is under the name Guireau as one of six *premiers crus* of the commune (not the region) of Sauternes by Paguierre in 1828 – the other are Yquem, 'Saluces', Filhot, 'Ligous' and 'Picherie' (curiously, the second growth, Château d'Arche, which was certainly known as Arche at the time, is not mentioned, but one of the other names may hide Lamothe, another *deuxième cru*).

In July 1846, Pierre Aman Guiraud, grandson of the original Pierre, sold the domaine of Guiraud or Bayle to a consortium of six gentlemen for 140,000 francs. Monsieur J.B. Depons de Grignols took half the equity, MM Coutereau and Coubet of Langon a quarter, and MM Ardusset, Auguste Depons and Roman of Paris the final quarter. It is under the ownership of Depons and Co. that Guiraud is recorded in the official documents of the 1855 Classification. Guiraud is listed ninth in the region.

Three years later, in November 1858, and for reasons not yet established, Depons and Co. put Guiraud on the market again. This time the purchaser was a Parisian, Félix (or Euryale-Aaron) Solar, who bought the estate with money left to him by a M. Mires. According to Bertall, Solar was a man who lived the life of a gourmet, surrounded himself with fine *objets d'art*, a magnificent library and entertained on a lavish scale. So liberal was he with his new inheritance, and so unfortunate in his choice of friends, who sponged off him remorselessly, that he swiftly ran through his fortune. Solar was forced to sell up in 1861, and Guiraud was transferred to Pierre Schroeder, of the Bordeaux *négociants* Schroeder and Schyler. The price was 300,000 francs. The estate at the time measured 122 hectares in total, and made about 35 to 40 *tonneaux* of wine.

It is possible that the sale to Schroeder may have been forced, i.e., in lieu of a repayment of debts, or, alternatively, that Scroeder and Schyler had, at the time, an exclusive contract to market the wine, and wished to protect their investment in the stock of vintages already purchased in view of Solar's imminent insolvency; in any case, within the year, Guiraud changed hands again. It was under this new ownership, that of the Bernard family, that Guiraud reached its greatest heights.

THE BERNARD FAMILY

The Bernard family had generated a colossal fortune, predominantly in the realms of engineering and construction. The original Bernard is said to have built many of the railway lines linking Bordeaux with the deeper south-west; but his most ambitious achievement was the creation of the dockyards of Bordeaux as they exist today.

So the Bernards were rich: like Solar and the Pereires of Palmer, they were of Jewish origin, and for the first time since the departure of the Guirauds there were the means to be able to give the estate a bit of continuity and stability, and to make some much-needed improvements to vineyard and cellars. The vineyard was enlarged to its present 70 hectares (though it diminished a little after the First World War), and the production gradually climbed from 35 to 80 *tonneaux*. The *chais* were reconstructed, and the present château, an elegant, square, two-storey building, without turrets, in golden sandstone and with a mansard roof, resurrected out of the old *maison noble* in the mid-1860s. The previous Château Bayle had been a rather modest eighteenth-century *chartreuse*, a one-storey structure with two outlying dependencies: a chapel to the east and the original *chai* to the west. These two buildings still exist and are of particular architectural interest, owing to their Frontignan-style facades and obvious Basque influence, which perhaps gives some credence to the Basque theory of the original Bayles.

A hunting-lodge was also built elsewhere on the estate, for the family kept a herd of wild boar. Stables for horses and kennels for a pack of hounds still exist today. By 1869, according to Armailhacq, Guiraud was ranked fourth in the Sauternes region (as against ninth in 1855) and fetched 3,000 to 5,000 francs a *tonneau* (Yquem made 4,500 to 6,000 francs).

The Bernard era saw some of the greatest wines Guiraud has ever made, including the 1900, which even stole the limelight from Yquem at the Grand Prix Universel at Paris. The 1904 and 1907 have an equally high reputation. By this time another generation of Bernards had passed on and the two Bernard heiresses had married into the Maxwell family, originally from Ireland. James Maxwell assumed responsibility for the property in 1910. He became Président d'Honneur du Syndicat Vinicole de la Région de Sauternes et Barsac. When the Guiraud 1907 was voted *hors concours* at the Bordeaux exhibition in 1911, Maxwell was a member of the jury!

PAUL CÉSAR RIVAL

The Bernard/Maxwell era came to an end in 1932. Following a string of disappointing vintages – those in Sauternes in the first three years of the 1930s were even more disastrous than for the red wines of Bordeaux – the Maxwell family decided to put Guiraud up for auction. It fetched a million (old) francs, and the purchaser was Paul César Rival, a young man from the Vidauban region of the Var. Rival was truly an *enfant terrible*: cantankerous, arrogant and eccentric to a fault. His great passion was flying. He built an airstrip in the middle of the vineyard in front of the château so that he could flit back and forth between Guiraud and the family estate in Provence. Once he built an airplane out of a kit, but this was not a success. It only flew on a couple of occasions, and on the second it crash-landed in the middle of the Yquem vineyard, an occurrence which, understandably, was not very well received by the Marquis de Lur-Saluces!

At the start at least, Rival did not neglect Guiraud. He trained himself as an oenologist, and is said to have introduced tractors to the oxen-worked vineyards of the Sauternes. Older vintages, the 1942 and the 1935, are excellent wines, and still fresh and alive today. Rival and Guiraud suffered during the Second World War. The château was occupied and subsequently wrecked by the German soldiers. Some of the evidence, swastikas crudely carved into the stonework and suchlike, was still visible when I visited Guiraud for the first time in 1976.

After the war Rival quarrelled with the liberation government, and as a result was refused any reconstruction grants. Rival aged with the château, divorced his wife and disinherited his son, apparently even refusing to acknowledge his paternity. He gradually became a recluse; he rarely washed or changed his clothes, never received any guests or went out to dinner, and slept on a camp bed in his kitchen. The château was allowed to sink into a lamentable state of disrepair. The roof leaked, the upper floors had fallen in, broken windows were not replaced, pigeons roosted in the rafters and rats nested in the cellar. Bottles of wine were stored all over the place, in what had formerly been bedrooms, reception rooms and pantries.

Inevitably, the wine eventually suffered. Though the vintages of the 1950s and that of 1962 are very good, the other vintages of the 1960s and those of the early 1970s are disappointing and certainly variable. Penning-Rowsell writes that he was surprised, on a visit in

1968, to find the 1961 and 1962 still in cement tanks. I remember noting, in 1976, that the whole place had a listless, depressing air and was indescribably scruffy; and I found the 1975 very heavy and clumsy. I also feel that in this era wine was bottled to order; there was no uniformity of *assemblage*, and the vintage was not bottled all at the same time.

Eventually, however, Rival decided to sell in order to return once again to Vidauban. With the house a ruin, the *chais* badly in need of renovation and not a stick of new oak or modern machinery in place, the only value was the vineyard. In order to make this as productive as possible he installed a crash programme of replanting. Sauvignon yields more than Sémillon, so Sauvignon it was; all twelve hectares of it; a decision which was to play havoc with the traditional Sauternes *encépagement*. Rival also raised his prices. Whether anyone bought the 1975 Guiraud at a price half as much again as most of the rest of the *premiers crus* I do not know (the wine is not very good), but it was calculated to look impressive on the prospectus of sale.

Yet in his heart of hearts Rival did not really want to leave Guiraud. Perhaps, an old man, he feared a change of environment: perhaps also, having quarrelled with the rest of his family, he was reluctant to return to the bosom of it in Provence. Negotiations with prospective buyers dragged on and on. One was the Champagne house, Louis Roederer, who asked the broker Daniel Lawton to act for them in the area (and who were also, or alternatively, said to be interested in buying Château Suduiraut). But in the end, they and the others (and there were many of them) lost patience. Rival was obstinate, difficult to pin down, and would often change his mind. But finally, five years later, a deal was struck. Rival had come up with a team with plenty of patience, an opponent as adept and determined as he: the Narby family.

THE NARBYS

Frank Narby, born in Egypt of an Egyptian father and Irish mother, educated and married in England, had immigrated to Canada in the mid-1950s where he was one of the first to realize the implications of the transatlantic container-shipping revolution. Having made a considerable fortune, he offered to back either of his two sons in any worthwhile new project that they might be interested in. His eldest son, Hamilton, having worked his way up through the ranks of the Narby shipping empire (no nepotism here), decided that he wanted to do something which was connected with his great passion, that of wine.

For a time the family considered buying Cantemerle, then on the market for a considerably higher sum (and eventually sold to a group which includes Cordier), but Hamilton was more attracted to Guiraud. Here was a dilapidated estate, a waning reputation and a wine which was difficult and expensive to produce. Moreover, it sold at a market price which was clearly barely economic. Guiraud, in short, represented the greater challenge, one which caught the entrepreneurial Narby imagination. Guiraud they would buy by hook or by crook.

The first hurdle was to gain an agreement with Rival himself. As outlined above, this was no easy matter. Secondly, being foreigners, the sale had to be approved by both the French Ministry of Finance and the Ministry of Agriculture. This took months, in the middle of which the government changed.

Providentially, perhaps, the price – 1,650,000 French francs, was fixed in dollars. The dollar was rising and the new Mitterand government was disposed to welcome an inflow of foreign currency. Finally, on 2 July 1981, the deal was complete. Rival departed for Provence, the Narby family was the new proprietor, and Hamilton, at the age of 28, was free to move into Château Guiraud.

THE CHÂTEAU AND THE *CHAIS*

What Hamilton found was a scene of utter desolation, but under that a certain, if decayed, majestic beauty, which was what had attracted him to Guiraud in the first place. You approach the chateau through a long avenue of mature plane trees, and the building, though then a ruin, is a fine construction. He spared no expense in setting it to rights. It was restored to its original splendour and Hamilton settled there with his wife and two sons.

The outlying buildings, too, needed much renovation and expansion if not rebuilding. New stainless-steel vinification tanks were installed, and the old cement cuves were dispensed with, or are only now used for *débourbage* and *assemblage*. Today some 100 new barrels are purchased each year, enabling about 25 per cent of the crop to be vinified in wood while the remainder undergoes its fermentation in vat. There is about one-third new wood for the maturation. More would perhaps be excessive, for the vineyard, as we shall see, contains a higher proportion of Sauvignon than most, and Sauvignon is quite tannic already. A laboratory was installed and everything began to be done with the most up-to-date techniques modern oenology could provide. The total investment was a further 4 million francs.

One innovation, not unique, but certainly one which I saw for the first time at Guiraud, was the purchase of a small stainless-steel jacketed refrigeration vat. Progressively, in the winter and spring after the vintage, all the separate pressings of the Sauternes go through a cold treatment. The wine is cooled to less than zero – Sauternes freezes at about minus 5 degrees – and this stabilizes and clarifies the wine, thus enabling the team to have to have less recourse to sulphur dioxide. The result is not only a cleaner Sauternes but one which has much more finesse.

The personnel was also changed. M. Fuegas, the old *régisseur*, and Jean Capbern, the old *maître de chai* took their *retraite*, and the young, capable Xavier Planty, ex-manager of Château La Gaffelière in Saint-Emilion, was installed as Hamilton's right-hand man. Several of the other older members of the *équipe* also departed, and the team now presents a new, confident air. Guiraud bustles with enthusiasm, as it never did in the old days.

Hamilton Narby, however, is no longer responsible for Guiraud. At the beginning of 1988 his father assumed total control, and Guiraud is now administered on his behalf by Xavier Planty. Hamilton has now bought a small estate in the *premières côtes*, but has also set up as a *négociant* in Switzerland. What I shall miss was another Hamilton innovation, a balloon which he hired for several days at vintage time, from which one could sail over the Sauternes taking a bird's eye view of the harvest.

THE VINEYARD

The *encépagement* at Guiraud has changed even more than most over recent times. During the course of the last century, as elsewhere in Sauternes, Muscadelle was gradually supplanted by Sémillon, with Sauvignon as the junior partner, but a host of other varieties, including Riesling, known in the area as Metternich, were also listed. Cocks and Féret specifically mentions Metternich at Guiraud in its 1922 edition. Riesling was prohibited as part of the Sauternes *encépagement* when the AC laws came into force in the 1930s, but can still be found elsewhere in Bordeaux, though not officially allowed, even for dry white wines.

In 1970, the *encépagement* at Guiraud was 50 per cent Sémillon, 35 per cent Sauvignon and 15 per cent Muscadelle. After Rival's crash replanting programme, the proportions in the vineyard rose to almost 70 per cent Sauvignon, by far the highest Sauvignon percentage in Sauternes, but this has now decreased to 55 per cent Sémillon and 45 per cent Sauvignon as the vineyards planted by Narby have come into fruition, and eventually will return to normal.

Traditionally Sauternes is produced from a blend of seven or eight-tenths Sémillon and two- or three-tenths Sauvignon, and this presented Narby with a bit of a problem. What to do with his excess Sauvignon? The answer was a dry white wine, known as G, matured for six months in oak, and from 1988 onwards, after trials in 1986 and 1987, fermented in new oak as well. This is a wine with more depth and personality than many a mid-priced tank-aged Graves, though it was occasionally a bit heavy-footed in the past, and complements 'Le Dauphin', a lightish Merlot-based red wine also produced on the estate. Both these wines are, paradoxically, simply AC Bordeaux. A short distance away, outside the delimited Sauternes area, they would be Graves.

The Guiraud estate now measures 116 hectares, of which 75 are under vines, 68 with white varieties and seven with red. Much of the land under red varieties, however, would produce excellent Sauternes. A total of six and a half hectares, under red vines in 1981, has now been replanted with Sémillon. Production of Sauternes is now some 11,000 cases a year. The label, though, still its traditional gold lettering printed on a black background, has been modified to incorporate the dolphin crest of the Narby family.

THE WINE

It is perhaps a dangerous generalization but I find that there are essentially three styles of Sauternes. Barsacs are more racy and have a certain steely austerity, firm in the case of Nairac, luscious in the case of Climens, soft and elegant at Doisy-Daëne. The wines of Preignac and Bommes, such as Suduiraut, Lafaurie-Peyraguey and Sigalas-Rabaud I find plumper, more like a peach to bite into than an apple. But in Fargues (Rieussec) and Sauternes itself, as at Yquem, you find the fullest, most powerful and most luscious wines. Guiraud is no exception.

Guiraud is certainly a big, sweet, honeyed wine, and while it tended to be rather blowsy in the last years of the Rival regime, Narby's investment in plant, equipment and new oak, and his determination to cut no corners and make the best wine he could, have given it an extra dimension of depth, character and grip. The new *enfant terrible* was *in situ* in time to make the *assemblage* of the 1979, declassifying a quarter of the crop, and slowly but surely the 1980s have seen an improvement in the standard of the wine (given the basic climatic conditions of course). While the 1983 did not quite live up to its potential in cask – some of the old wood was a little too old and this gave a rather coarse taint to the wine – vintages since show a lot of promise.

THE TASTING

The majority of the following wines were tasted at a La Vigneronne wine evening in December 1988. I have supplemented this with notes on other mature vintages sampled in recent years.

1983   Optimum drinking   **Now–2002**

Fullish, classic golden Sauternes colour. High-toned nose – or higher-toned than I had expected. Good vanilla. Full, still closed. Good new oak touches, fresh but without real grip or power. Still youthful though. Ripe, quite concentrated and some *pourriture noble* nevertheless. A good to very good 1983 but not a great one.

1980   **Drink soon**

Light green-gold colour. Sweet nose, quite full, a little SO$_2$ damping down the elegance. Sweetish on the attack but a bit mean on the finish. Medium-full. Reasonable grip but a little coarse.

1979   **Now–1996**

Quite a full colour. Good honey and toffee on the nose. Quite vigorous – more so than I expected. Mature, medium-full, some *pourriture*

noble. Mellow and ripe. Good fruit if without a great deal of elegance.

1976   **Drink up**

Light tawny colour. Ripe, marmaladey, caramelly nose, touch of burnt toffee. Quite a lot of *pourriture noble* but no real power or grip. This is now beginning to dry out. A fat blowsy wine once barley-sugar flavoured. Now coarsening. Falls away.

1975   **Drink soon**

Medium-full green-gold colour. Dried-up, sweet nose, lacks elegance. No concentration. Not entirely clean. Sweet and plump, more vigorous than the above. A dirty wine. Yet has a good grip. Pity.

1971   **Drink up**

Fullish green-gold colour. Fuller nose but again not entirely clean. Some sweetness and slightly loose *pourriture noble* perhaps. Loose-knit, sweet, getting dilute. Quite sweet. Like the 1975 but more evolved. Was cleaner but now getting a bit coarse.

1970   Drink soon

Medium-full, green-gold colour. Fullish, rich, fat *pourriture noble* nose. Cleaner and more vigorous than the 1971. Quite full, plump, sweet and a touch of vanilla. Some *pourriture noble* but rather more plain four-square sweetness. Still fresh and vigorous and clean than the two above. The best of these early 1970 vintages. Finishes long. Good grip.

1967   Now–1997

Deep, rich, golden colour. Rich, fat, vigorous, slightly blowsy, mature Sauternes. Full, plenty of *pourriture noble*. Clean and classic. Fullish, luscious, ripe, a touch of liquorice, said someone. Honeyed, long, classy. Very good. Plenty of life still.

1962   Drink soon

Not too deep a colour. Fat nose, honey and acacia flowers, plenty of botrytis. Youthful, caramelly, balanced, long and complex on the palate. This shows very well indeed. But a second bottle circulating had more built-in sulphur and was less exciting.

1942   Will still keep

Old gold colour. Still fresh-looking. Full of lovely fruit on the nose. Ripe, round, full and fat. Not a trace of age. Rich and surprisingly youthful. Could be a 1962. Plenty of depth. Fine.

1935   Drink soon

Deep tawny-gold colour. Soft, sweet nose, now gently fading. Caramel, butterscotch and barley-sugar on the palate. But only a medium amount of *pourriture noble*. Good though. Still fresh.

1922   Will still keep

Old, light amontillado colour with a green edge. Old but ripe, with just a shade of maderization. Still sweet and luscious. Complex and full of interest. Fragrant and not faded. This still has a lot of interest. Definitely oaky. Full and concentrated. Ripe and full of fruit. Very long. Still plenty of life. Intriguing and delicious. I sampled this again in July, 1992: still good.

RIEUSSEC

Rieussec, immediately to the south of Château D'Yquem, though in the neighbouring commune of Fargue, is the closest to it in character: the fullest, the most luscious, the richest of all the other first growths. Sadly, it has not had as settled a history. For too long Sauternes wine-making was uneconomic. Proprietors came and went with alarming rapidity. It was only occasionally that the wine of Rieussec was quite as good as it should have been.

Fortunately, at a time when Sauternes fortunes were at their lowest, a saviour arrived at Rieussec. In 1971 Albert Vuillier bought the estate. Vuillier was one of the few in this decade – Climens was another notable exception – who really seemed to be trying to produce fine wine. Thirteen years later he sold out to the Rothschilds of Lafite. But the ground work had been done. Rieussec is Sauternes 'super-second'.

Before the French Revolution the land which is now Rieussec belonged to the Carmes, a male religious order based in Langon, who also owned the property known as Les Carmes-Haut-Brion in Pessac. Where the name Rieussec comes from is uncertain. There is a small stream, separating the domaine from that of Yquem and which dries up in summer (*ruisseau* + *sec* = Rieussec?) or was there an owner called M. Rieu – the man who smiled? Sequestrated and sold as a *bien national*, the property came into the hands of a Monsieur J.B. Mareilhac who was also major of Bordeaux and the owner of a prestigious vineyard in Blanquefort, on the northern border of the Graves, and of Château La Louvière in Léognan. Rieussec was already a fairly substantial estate with a high reputation. It was mentioned by Jullien, Paguierre and Franck in the 1820s as a second growth, though erroneously placed in the commune of Sauternes or Preignac rather than in Fargues.

HISTORY

In 1846 Rieussec was sold to a M. Maille (or Maye as he is designated in the 1855 Classification) and at the same time four hectares were acquired by Château Pexiotto in Bommes. For a time this wine was sold as Pexiotto-Rieussec. When Pexiotto was absorbed into Château Rabaud at the time of the phylloxera epidemic, this portion was brought back and reunited with the rest of the vineyard. From Maye, Rieussec passed to Charles Crépin, and from him to his son-in-law, Paul Defolie, in 1892. Defolie bought the neighbouring estate of Louison three years later and did much to improve the *chais* and the vineyards after the ravages of the phylloxera epidemic. He sold Rieussec in 1907 to Edgar and Marc Bannel of Langon, owners of a number of minor properties in the Entre-Deux-Mers.

In 1920 the estate passed to the *Veuve* Lasseverie and her son-in-law, Henri Gasqueton, a member of the family which owns Château Calon-Ségur, but this association lasted no longer than most of its predecessors – or indeed most of the other purchases this lady made at the time. The next owner was the Vicomte du Bouzet, followed by his half-brother, Monsieur P.F. Berry, an American, and then by Gérard Balaresque. Balaresque, a broker, was owner from 1957 to 1971 when he sold the domaine to Albert Vuillier.

The Vuillier family came originally from the Ariège in the Pyrenees, where they still have a large estate on which they used to fatten cattle but where cereals and rape seed are now grown. They own the Aquitaine multiple grocery stores group and were at one time shareholders in Lanson Champagne. When in 1970 the *pastis* giant Ricard acquired a substantial holding in Lanson, one of the 'casualties' was the Vuillier interest, and, wishing to continue in the fine wine, Albert and his wife, Chantal, came to Bordeaux to see what was on the market.

Vuillier was attracted by the idea of making Sauternes and found that Climens, Rayne-Vigneau, Nairac and Rieussec were all for sale. Rieussec was the most prestigious, and, moreover, a 'proper' Sauternes rather than a Barsac. It also had buildings which, though modest, were habitable, though no previous owner had lived there permanently. The price was 1.1 million francs.

Vuillier always intended to be the working proprietor on the spot, but at first he left the team he had inherited in charge, and established an exclusivity arrangement with the *négociants* Mestrezat-Preller (part of the group which owns Rayne-Vigneau) for the marketing of the wine. When this was annulled during the *crise* of 1973 to 1974, Albert and Chantal moved in permanently and he took personal charge of the property.

It is fair to say, and I am sure Albert would have been the first to admit, that the first years of the Vuillier ownership had their downs as well as their ups. The run of vintages in the 1970s was depressingly poor apart from 1975 and 1976. The Rieussec harvest was completely destroyed by hail in 1977 and for the same reason there was only a tiny amount in 1973 and 1974. And when the harvest was plentiful and the climate auspicious, he was not able to realize this bounty to its fullest advantage. By the end of the decade Vuillier began to look for a source of additional finance. He was not making enough profit out of Rieussec to make all the improvements he would wish.

In 1984 the Rothschilds of Lafite came on the scene. They had acquired Château Duhart-Milon, the Pauillac fifth growth, in 1962, and were looking to diversify further. They had, as yet, no interests in Sauternes, but could well appreciate the problems and long-term nature of Sauternes ownership and investment. It seemed a natural liaison. Domaines Rothschild are now the majority shareholders in the restructured Société Anonyme de Château Rieussec, the others being the Banque Paris-Pays-Bas and Albert Frères, a Belgian finance house. For a short while Vuillier remained at Rieussec, but in 1985 Charles Chevalier, an agricultural engineer who had worked in the Anjou for a number of years before arriving as deputy at Lafite, was installed as manager. Vuillier remains as a minority shareholder and director and is especially involved in the selection of the *grand vin*.

The domaine of Rieussec has remained much as it was in the 1820s. The estate lies in one piece at the highest point of the Fargues commune and marches with Yquem at its western end. There are some 75 hectares in total of which 50 are under vines, planted in the ratio 75 per cent Semillon, 22 per cent Sauvignon and 3 per cent Muscadelle. Some 140 ago the production was 60 *tonneaux*; today it ranges between 80 and 100, an average of fifteen hectolitres per hectare.

Rieussec is effectively a little hamlet consisting of a modest single-storey farmhouse together with its dependent outbuildings on top of a little hill or *croupe*, a gravel and clay-limestone mound on a hard sandstone base 76 metres above sea level. The house itself, built in the years after the Revolution, is comfortably and elegantly furnished but of little architectural merit. More noteworthy perhaps is the three-storey tower built some 50 years ago over one of the ends of the *chais* and recently renovated. This is the office and the hub of the Rieussec domaine. The top floor commands a magnificent view over the surrounding vineyards. Elsewhere, part of the cellar is underground, a rare thing in this part of the world.

It is partly fate, partly a change in fashion but perhaps largely the arrival of a succession of fine vintages in the 1980s, but Sauternes is once again in demand and commands high prices. The production of fine sweet wine is once again an economic proposition. The 1983 vintage gave us both quality and abundance and sold for high prices. Even if not all the wines are quite as good as they might have been, at least all the estates made a profit; a profit which has been reinvested in the wine. This meant that when the equally successful (though *plus tendre*) 1986 vintage came along, all were in a position to capitalize on its delights. This has been followed by potentially magnificent vintages in 1988, 1989 and 1990. The wines are very exciting indeed.

The mood has changed dramatically. Today the growers have a confidence in their product where a decade or more ago they could only communicate a feeling of futility. Today the atmosphere is one of optimism and perfectionism, and there is an abundance of new oak. There is a rigorous elimination of lesser *cuvées* in the creation of the *grand vin*. Cooling equipment has been installed for the precipitation of yeasts, tartrates and the rest, thus producing a cleaner wine which does not have to be so highly sulphured to keep it stable. Even the lesser vintages have improved significantly in quality. There is a consistent level of high quality across the board.

At Rieussec one of the first changes was a massive augmentation of the amount of new wood. Vuillier had been gradually increasing the percentage since the 1976 vintage. But a new barrel these days is an expensive item. One will cost £300. If, like Rieussec, you produce 300 to 350 barrels-worth a vintage, and you wish to maintain a new-old ratio of 50:50, probably the ideal for this wine, the aggregate annual investment is an important addition to the overheads. Since the 1983 vintage half the wine has been matured in new oak.

The selection of the *grand vin* is now made as late as possible. I was invited to take part in the process – for the 1983 vintage – in April 1984. (I'm happy to report that we were all in agreement.) A larger percentage than hitherto is today bottled as Clos Labère, the second wine. Today none of the Sauvignon is used in the Sauternes. This goes into R, the dry wine.

Improvements have also been made in the cellar. Up to now it has been traditional in the area to persist with small mechanical presses. At Rieussec a pneumatic press – in principle more flexible – has been introduced. It came into service for part of the 1989 vintage. The results were considered favourable, and all the old presses have been replaced. Needless to say, there is also a cryo-extraction chamber at Rieussec. It was installed in 1987, a vintage where, as it happened, the investment (650,000 francs) was necessary, for it was a rainy autumn. The wine is all the better for it.

Since 1984, the date of the Rothschild purchase, land prices in the top Bordeaux estates have risen to astronomical levels. On the one hand there are high inheritance taxes and heavy death duties; on the other the arrival of insurance companies and other large groups seeking a safe investment haven in a wine-producing estate. One begins to wonder if the era of the individual owner-proprietor is doomed. One can only congratulate the Rothschilds on their foresight in investing in Rieussec before price-levels were ignited to their present excessive heights. But one cannot help feeling rather sad for Albert Vuillier. He is a hospitable, charming and dedicated man. He did all the spade-work at Rieussec. But he was unable to remain to reap all the profit and excellence from the present-day renaissance of Sauternes.

THE TASTING

The following wines were tasted at Rieussec in 1985 and supplemented by a further opportunity in September 1988. I have added some notes on older wines sampled in recent years.

Optimum drinking

1987   **Now–1998**

They sold 'a good third off' in bulk. Very rigorous selection of *grand vin*. Surprisingly rich and sweet, as well as full. There is a certain hard bitterness at the back. They had started before 10th October which was when the rain started, and had already made a *passage* in which there was quite a good amount of botrytis. This is by no means a failure.

1986   **1997–2017**

Mid-gold colour. Closed, concentrated, oaky nose. Youthful if not slightly awkward but fine quality here. Real Sauternes size. Very slight touch of SO2 which is also apparent on the palate. Firm, full, backward, rich and concentrated. There is real honey and a lot of depth. Very fine indeed. Needs time. Potentially high class.

1985   **Now–2004**

Lightish colour (compared with the 1984 and 1983). Light green-gold. There is a little bit of SO2 on the nose and not a lot of *pourriture noble*. Some, indeed quite a lot, at present, of built-in SO2 on the palate deadens the wine a bit. Fullish, honeyed rather than botrytized and slightly hard on the finish. Very young still. This is a conspicuous success for the vintage.

1984   **Drink up**

Much more evolved colour. Mid-gold. This already smells like a mature wine. This is *à point*. Medium body, no tannin. Supple, fresh, flowery, medium sweet. No hardness or bitterness. Not a great wine but attractive and well made.

1983   **2000–2020**

Mid gold, also quite evolved. Nose quite developed. No undue SO2. Rich, ripe *pourriture noble* but closed and powerful on both nose and palate. Full, a lot of wine here. Firm, vigorous, a decade from maturity. A bit in an adolescent phase but a wine of very fine potential.

1982   **Drink soon**

Lightish colour for Rieussec. Pretty, sweetish, loose-knit nose Sauvignon showing, but no *pourriture noble*. Quite an elegant wine. With a flavour of honeyed fudge. Clean and fruity. Forward.

1981   **Now–2001**

Medium colour. Some noble rot on the nose but the wine is also a little four-square, though not as clumsy as some. Quite full, a little awkward. Good spicy-sweet flavour and enough acidity, though currently it does not show much style or zip. 1981 in general is a vintage which is being curiously slow to show its paces.

1980   **Drink soon**

Slightly more golden colour. Open, fullish, plump, quite sweet, honeyed nose. Less *pourriture* than the 1981 but more than the 1982. Medium-full, fruity, quite elegant. A pleasant wine.

1979   **Now–1999**

Similar colour. Firm, oaky nose, has noble rot, good fruit and a good acidity. Not as full as it appears at first but still backward and a bit austere. The 1981 seems fatter and plumper but this has more finesse, certainly at present, and is more oaky.

1978   **Drink soon**

Full, golden colour. Developed but one-dimensional nose. Sweet but no noble rot, nor a zip of acidity. Has fruit but lacks depth and complexity. May dry out soon.

1976   **Drink soon or Keep**

A dark colour – even copper. Rather *crème brûlée*, toffee nose. Last time I tasted this wine I thought it was completely overblown. Today, while it obviously lacks the acidity and zip that it should possess, it is not at all bad: full, solid, sweet, concentrated and full of noble rot. Bottles obviously vary.

1975   **Now–2000 plus**

Mid-gold colour. A surprising amount of *pourriture noble* on the nose. Fresh, lovely fruit. Medium-full body. Sweet, balanced, rich and luscious. Very elegant and long on the palate. Delicious.

1974   **Drink up**

Golden colour, no undue age. Good, fresh, sweet nose and flavour. No great complexity but some fruit and charm.

1972   **Drink up**

Light colour. The nose is sulphury as is the attack – the wet-wool flavour of some wines of the Loire. On the finish there is more character, indeed more interest and richness than the 1974. Not at all bad.

1971   **Now–1999**

Good rich, golden colour. Full, complex nose, mature, a wine with a lot of depth. Full, rich, excellent fruit, a lot of noble rot, plenty of style and elegance. Fine, concentrated wine, long on the finish.

1970   **Drink soon**

Not quite as full a colour. Rich, plump, fruit nose. Full, fat wine but less style, *pourriture noble* and zip, making the palate a bit four-square and flat. Good though, but now needs finishing up before it gets too coarse.

1967   **Now–1997**

Golden colour. Ample, plump, fresh nose. No great finesse but ripe, fullish, sweet and honeyed. Very good.

1962   **Now–1997**

Mid-gold colour; no undue brown. Rich, barley-sugar nose. Brown sugar but with just a faint tanky aspect. A mature, gentle, sweet, spicy wine. Very good but it lacks just a little vigour, grip and finesse. Will keep though.

1959   **Now–1997**

Golden colour. This is very good. Rich, sweet nose with the slightly burnt aspect you get from a hot vintage with plenty of *pourriture noble* when the wine is fully mature. This still has vigour. Very good indeed.

1950   **Drink soon**

Orange colour, shows a little age. Fresher on the nose and palate. This has good plump fruit and is long and honeyed. No lack of botrytis. A fat wine, quite full, with a marmaladey *crème brûlée* flavour. Very good.

1945   **Now–1999**

Tawny colour: like Sercial Madeira. Honeyed, caramelly nose. Sweet, citrussy. This is a really splendid wine. Full, still vigorous. Powerful and fresh. Toffee and peaches on the palate. Very long. Very complex. Very lovely.

RABAUD-PROMIS AND SIGALAS-RABAUD

Four growths from the commune of Bommes were listed in the first division of the 1855 Sauternes Classification and one in the second. Today the commune can boast six *premiers crus*, but no *deuxièmes*. This change has come about not through promotion but through division and absorption. The Lafaurie-Peyraguey estate spawned Clos-Haut-Peyraguey; Château Rabaud is now divided into Sigalas-Rabaud and Rabaud-Promis. It is the latter into which Château Pexiotto, second growth in 1855, has been integrated.

Château Rabaud has its origins in an ancient noble family of the same name. In 1660 Marie Peyronne de Rabaud married Arnaud de Cazeau and the estate remained in the hands of the Cazeaus until 1819 when Pierre-Hubert de Cazeau, mayor of Bommes, sold it to Gabriel Deyme. It is under the names of either Cazeau or Deyme that the wine first appears in the accounts of contemporary writers, classed superior to its larger neighbours Rayne-Vigneau and Lafaurie-Peyraguey. At this time it produced 20 to 25 *tonneaux*.

HISTORY

In 1864, perhaps following the death of Gabriel Deyme, the property was sold to Henri Drouillet de Sigalas, who set about enlarging the area under vines. By the turn of the twentieth century the estate comprised 92 hectares, of which 42 were under vines, and produced 50 *tonneaux* of Sauternes. Château Pexiotto (ten hectares and eighteen *tonneaux*) was absorbed in the 1880s. The proprietor, Alfred Ribet, had acquired Climens in 1871, and afterwards seems to have lost interest in his *deuxième cru*. Perhaps Pexiotto changed hands when Climens passed to Henri Gounouilhou in 1885.

December 1903 saw the first division of Château Rabaud. For reasons which are obscure – perhaps he just simply needed the money – Gaston Drouillet de Sigalas, son of Henri, sold part of the estate to Adrien Promis. Promis came from a family which had been making sweet wine in Loupiac for a number of generations and seems to have been taken into partnership at Rabaud during the 1890s, a few years prior to the split.

This initial division was to last for 27 years. In 1930 the two Rabaud vineyards were reunited by Fernand Ginestet who formed a company whose shareholders included the heirs of Gaston Drouillet de Sigalas – one of his daughters married the Marquis Lambert de Granges – and the daughters of Adrien Promis, Mmes Montrelay and de la Motte-Rouge. Ginestet was to farm the estate and market the wine.

The amalgamation was to be short-lived, however. In 1949 René Lambert de Granges decided to re-buy his family inheritance, and when Raymond-Louis Lanneluc bought Rabaud-Promis the following year the domaine was split once again. The 1950 was the last vintage of the combined Château Rabaud. It is very good indeed; as is the 1949.

CHÂTEAU SIGALAS-RABAUD

Sigalas-Rabaud is run today by Comte Emmanuel Lambert de Granges, who took over on his father's retirement in 1983. The *maître de chai* is Jean-Louis Vimeney. The vineyard is much the smaller of the two Rabauds. There are fifteen hectares, lying on a gravelly–clay soil, planted in the ratio 90 per cent Sémillon, 10 per cent Sauvignon, and these lie immediately to the north of Lafaurie-Peyraguey.

The Sigalas château is the original of the estate, an elegant, single-storey, seventeenth-century *chartreuse*, joined at its sides by the two wings of the *chais*, the combined buildings forming three sides of a square.

After being crushed in a small vertical press the wine is fermented in stainless-steel or concrete vats. Thereafter it is stored partly in wood, partly in tank. The new oak percentage is deliberately kept as low as a quarter, Comte Emmanuel considering that more would impart too much of an oak flavour into the wine. 'I want my wine to taste of fruit,' says he. The objective is elegance and balance rather than lusciousness. The result is a wine which is 14 degrees plus 4 of sugar rather than 15 or 15.5 plus 5, 6 or even 7 elsewhere; a wine of subtlety and harmonious fruit rather than power. The 1986 is an exception, however. This, contrary to the norm, is *plus liquoreux* than the 1988.

In contrast to its neighbour, Sigalas-Rabaud produced better wine than most during the region's doldrums in the 1960s and 1970s. The 1962, 1967 and 1971 are among the successes of the vintage, and so is the 1973, albeit at a lower level. The 1975 is excellent, though the 1976 a bit of a disappointment. I have a number of notes on the 1983, not tasted below. A summary would be good-but-not-great. The wine is a little four-square. There is no second wine at Sigalas. In recent years what is not included in the *grand vin* has been sold off in bulk.

CHÂTEAU RABAUD-PROMIS

A dozen or more years ago Château Rabaud-Promis was in a very sorry state. The château was crumbling away into ruin; the outbuildings at the back were dilapidated; the *chais* were indescribably scruffy. There was not a single oak cask in the place. To describe the wine as undistinguished would have been to flatter it. Thankfully, all that has changed.

The improvement has been due to the arrival of Philippe Dejean, who married the granddaughter of Raymond-Louis Lanneluc in 1972. He had originally decided to study medicine. But the Dejean family have a small estate called Domaine du Noble in Loupiac (a fine 1988, incidentally), which his elder brother runs, and he found himself becoming more and more interested in wine and less and less in his studies. After completing his military service he became *régisseur* at Rabaud-Promis in 1974, and in 1981 he and his wife Michelle bought out the shares of her elder sister in order to command the majority of the equity.

As you drive up to the château from the main road – approaching from the opposite direction to that of Sigalas-Rabaud – you will climb up a definite hill. You will see the main frontage of the château, now being restored. This was built to an early nineteenth-century design by Adrien Promis. Looking out behind there is a curious concrete tower, totally out of place, added by Philippe Dejean's father-in-law.

In a wing on the south side live the Dejean family, Philippe, Michelle and their three children, as well as Michelle's mother. Opposite are the *chais*, offices and tasting room. All this has been transformed since 1981. There is now a battery of 50-hectolitre stainless-steel *cuves*. There is a new horizontal pneumatic press. There is a cold room for cryo-extraction. Below ground there is a series of interconnecting cellars for the storage of wine in cask.

This is a much larger estate than Sigalas-Rabaud. There are 33 hectares under vines, situated to the east and to the north of Sigalas, planted in the ratio 80 per cent Sémillon, 18 per cent Sauvignon and 2 per cent Muscadelle. The soil is particularly gravelly, on a base of clay and limestone.

For fifteen years there was not a barrel at Rabaud-Promis. The wine was fermented in concrete vats and stored in vast underground cement reservoirs.

All this began to change after 1983. This vintage is by no means a disaster. Nor is the 1982. But it was in 1986 that Rabaud-Promis showed for the first time for a generation why it had been classed *premier cru* back in 1855. The reason was a much less greedy harvest, a greater diligence with botrytized fruit and the reintroduction of wood. In 1986, Dejean began to ferment Rabaud-Promis in oak. In 1988, 50 per cent was vinified in wood, and the intention is that eventually all the *grand vin* will start life in cask. Moreover, not only is the proportion of new oak being increased – 30 per cent in 1988 – but the length of time the wine is matured in oak is also rising. The 1988 spent fourteen months in wood before being transferred to stainless steel to await bottling after a further year or so.

We can see now that Rabaud-Promis is a lusher, richer wine than Sigalas-Rabaud. It is more honeyed, the vanilla flavours of the oak are more pronounced. Yet it nevertheless has the plump amplitude of a Bommes rather than the power of Sauternes.

As you will see below, I was lucky enough to sample most of the best vintages of the last 30 years on a recent visit. Of those not listed I regret I cannot enthuse about the 1976, but the 1962 was stylish on the one and only occasion I have seen it. There is a second wine, called either Château Bequet or Domaine de L'Estremade, and Dejean also produces a soft, plump, *primeur*-style Graves from land he has recently bought at Illats.

THE TASTINGS

I sampled the wines of Sigalas-Rabaud in Sauternes in January 1990, and those of Rabaud-Promis in April.

SIGALAS-RABAUD

1988   **2000–2020 plus**

This will be bottled in two months' time (March 1990). A fine expression of fruit. Subtle, delicate, complex. This seems much more Bommes than some of the wines which follow. But it is just that it has not yet acquired the lusciousness of the 1986, for instance. Long. Very fine.

1986   **1998–2018 plus**

Medium gold colour. There is good *pourriture noble* on the nose. Ripe and honeyed but it doesn't have the raciness of Rabaud-Promis. It is rather more closed. Became complex as it evolved. On the palate good concentration, really quite a powerful wine. Sweet, luscious, balanced, youthful. Ripe and luscious. Needs time. A lot of depth. Very good indeed.

1985   **1995–2008**

Light colour. Somewhat dry and filter-papery on the nose. After a bit of aeration this disappeared but the nose is a bit dry for a Sauternes. A touch of marmalade. Opened up as it aerated. There is a little SO2 here but it is rather better than it seemed at first. Quite sweet and luscious. A little *pourriture noble* at least. Ripe and meaty. Does it lack just a little zip? Certainly less four-square than some. Very good for the vintage.

1982   **Now–2000**

Medium gold colour. Quite full and candied-peel in character on the nose. Not without *pourriture noble*. Again a little dry. Medium-full. Quite sweet on the palate though. On the attack a little straightforward. More complex and better grip on the finish. Again quite a luscious wine for a Bommes. Will still improve. Good, even very good for the vintage.

1981   **1995–2015**

Medium colour. Good depth and style here on the nose. Quite complex. Has fat, fruit and *pourriture noble*. Still youthful. Shows well. Elegant, full, rich and complex. Again fat and luscious. This has good grip and plenty of concentration. Needs time. Very good indeed.

1980   **Now–1998**

Medium colour. This is lighter and more evolved on the nose than the 1981, but there is good fruit here as well, especially for the vintage. Quite full, again sweet and concentrated and balanced, though without the depth of the above or the 1979. Quite powerful for a 1980. Still young. Finishes long. Not without *pourriture noble* even.

1979   **Now–2006**

Medium colour. Round, soft, supple, evolved nose. But good style and fruit. Some *pourriture noble*. This was a vintage without great power, but here it at least has elegance. The 1981 is fresher and firmer. Yet this is a fine bottle of mature Sauternes. *A point*, succulent, balanced. Good fruit. Still vigorous. Very good for vintage.

1978   **Now–1998**

Medium colour. An evolved fruit-salady nose. Clean but quite evolved now. No *pourriture noble* or indeed very much depth. But not without style. Medium body, medium sweet. Quite a bit more complex than Rabaud-Promis. Good for the vintage.

1969   **Drink soon**

Medium gold colour. Not exactly elegant but some fruit and interest, if a touch of petrol on the nose. Not faded. Not without *pourriture noble*. Clean on the palate. Good fruit, fresh, clean. Just a little dry and short on the palate but what do you expect after all this time? Good.

RABAUD-PROMIS

1988   **2000–2020 plus**

Light golden colour. Soft, discreet, marmaladey nose. Good *pourriture noble*. Not exactly fat and luscious but that is the character of Bommes as opposed to Sauternes. This is fine. Lots of depth. Above all a fine acidity. Reserved. Apricot and peach jam flavours. Lots of potential. High class. Very elegant.

1987   **Now–1999**

Slightly fuller golden colour than the 1988. Straightforward sweet nose. No *pourriture noble*. Lacks a little zip and finesse but not too bad. This is surprisingly good – better than the 1982 – and, dare I say it, more elegant than the 1983. Some *pourriture noble* on the palate. Good fresh, sweet fruit. Quite full. Quite concentrated. Quite complex. A fine effort for the vintage.

1986   **1997–2015 plus**

Very light colour – more like a Barsac. This has a lovely nose. Gentle, harmonious, peachy fruit. Complex and elegant. Again not a blockbuster. Round, ripe, gently oaky. Most attractive and seductive. Long, balanced, medium-bodied wine. Good *pourriture noble*. Feminine in style. A lot of depth. Very long. Very fine.

1985   **Now–2003**

Also quite a light colour. Interesting nose. Ripe, quite sweet. Good grip. Some *pourriture noble*, caramel, vanilla, touch of new wood. Has class. But a little bit four-square. Less complex than the above. Much less *pourriture noble*, fat and power. But fresh. Well made. Good for the vintage. But after the above a bit one-dimensional.

1983   **1996–2016**

Medium gold colour. A fat, rich nose. There is a

little SO2, which is not evident in the younger wines, and it doesn't have the class of them either. But there is weight and lusciousness here. Full, fat, rich and quite powerful. The SO2 is less evident on the palate and will get absorbed with time. A meaty wine. Still very young. Got better and better in the glass. Needs time. A lot of depth and concentration. Very good plus.

1982   **Drink soon**

Medium colour. This is a good 1982 because it has zip and elegance. Gentle and fruity. Ripe and quite sweet. Still fresh. Not much *pourriture noble* though. A straightforward sweet wine but has good fresh fruit and so is stylish. *A point* now. A good, indeed very good, example of the vintage.

1981   **Drink up**

Quite a light colour. Not as much fruit or freshness on the nose as the 1982. Less elegant, less vigorous. No more *pourriture noble* than the above. This is a bit one-dimensional and as it was always a bit loose-knit and the acidity not very high, it is loosing the grip of its fruit. Tails off in the mouth. I prefer the 1982.

1978   **Drink soon**

Light golden colour. The nose is a bit slight and blunt. A touch of SO2. No *pourriture noble*. On the palate the effect is more interesting. Quite sweet. Reasonable grip. Toffee-caramel elements, and at least a little *pourriture noble*. Quite fresh, and reasonably stylish on the finish. Good for the vintage. Holding up well.

1975   **Now–1998**

Quite a brownish-gold colour. The nose shows, obviously, more to it than the 1978, but nevertheless has become a little spirity, the fruit has become a little mean. In fact it shows age. No fat, no richness, a lack of class. Again this is better on the palate. It seems riper and more stylish. Caramelized orange flavour. Good grip. Finishes well. Not bad.

1970   **Drink quite soon**

Colour just a little lighter than the 1975. The nose is not too bad, there is a toffee-vanilla-fondant element which is quite attractive, though again the fruit has thinned out somewhat. On the attack this at first appears to be a rather dilute wine. The built in SO2 certainly shows. Quite sweet. A shade cloying. Medium body. Lacks a bit of class. Not bad.

1967   **Now–2000**

Similar colour, perhaps a little less alive-looking. Rich, luscious and fat, but now in a gentle way, on the nose. This seems much more alive than the 1975 and the 1970. This is really quite good. Round, ripe, plump and stylish. Good fruit. Good balance. Plenty of *pourriture noble*. Very good and still has plenty of life.

1964   **Drink soon**

Deepish colour. This also has merit. Fuller and not as complex or elegant as the 1967 but has fruit; some lusciousness, still vigorous. Fell away in the glass, though I don't think it was at all bad, or inelegant, once. Medium body. Quite sweet. Good suppleness and reasonable acidity. At least some *pourriture noble*.

1961   **Drink soon**

Similar colour. A slightly burnt element on the nose. Has lost its fat. Lightening up now. A reasonably stylish burnt caramelly wine. Sweet but never that fat and luscious I would have though. Still enjoyable.

1959   **Drink soon**

This has a proper deep gold old Sauternes colour. Rich, fullish, nutty and caramelly, if perhaps not exactly elegant. But lightened up fast. This was a fuller, more ample wine but it now shows a little age, and was not originally as classy as the 1961. Now it doesn't have the concentration of even the 1961, let alone the 1967.

1957   **Drink soon**

Similar colour to the 1959. Older, less concentrated nose than the 1959 but it seems richer and fatter than the 1961. This seems to be holding up better. Fuller and more vigorous than the 1959 as it developed. Not a lot of concentration or complexity but still a bit of plumpness and fat.

1955   **Drink soon**

The deepest colour of the lot, really quite tawny. This is the best of the older vintages. Ripe, stylish, complex; an ample, gently coffee-flavoured wine. Again this is beginning to show a bit of age, but it is the most elegant, by some way, of the older wines. Round, ample, fragrant and still complex. A gentle – almost feminine – Sauternes. Typically Bommes.

DOISY-VÉDRINES

Wine-maker or *terroir*: which is of greater importance? The debate continues. In a sense it is pointless, for the influence of both is crucial. You cannot gainsay the superiority of one piece of land over another; but neither can you deny that the expertise, philosophy and personality of the proprietor and vinifier do not play a part which can be decisive. No one can make *great* wine (as opposed to merely *good* wine) if his vines are not planted in a great soil and situation. But great wine does not manufacture itself. The difference in character between one great wine and another is the expression of the personality of the person who makes it, as much as of the *terroir* from which it originates.

An illustration of this latter point is the difference in style between the neighbouring Doisys in Barsac. The wine of Daëne, made by Pierre Dubourdieu, is peaches and cream, citronelle and acacia-honey, roses and Turkish delight; never luscious, always elegant. Doisy-Védrines, on the other hand, is richer and more traditional. It combines the raciness of Barsac with the power and *liquoreux* of Sauternes. It is more viscous, more golden-coloured. The flavour is more exotic: cinnamon and roasted nuts, marmalade and candied peel. It is a more concentrated wine; less accessible in its youth; more opulent in its maturity.

A kilometre to the south of Château Coutet lies a little group of houses: the hamlet of La Pinesse. In the eighteenth century, this land was owned by a wealthy *bourgeois* jurist family of Gaston origin, the Védrines. Thanks to the research of Jacqueline Olivier Vidrine of Louisiana, who has delved into the history of her ancestors, we have a reasonably full picture of this family.

HISTORY

On 29 May 1704, a marriage took place in Barsac between Jean Védrines and Marie Raymond. The Raymonds were Bordeaux lawyers, the Védrines came from Agen. What was formerly a mill at La Pinesse was transformed into a summer residence for the couple. This estate came from the Raymond side of the family, and vines must have followed soon after, if they were not there already. An oath of fealty made by Jean Védrines to the new king, Louis XV, in December 1716, refers to 'the noble house and fief, named de Doisic . . . in Barsac'. On the map executed by Belleyme in the 1770s, the *lieu-dit* is spelt Doysy. The building represented is the château of Doisy-Védrines today.

Jacqueline Olivier's branch of the family descends from Jean-Baptiste Lapaise Védrines, son of the above pair, a midshipman who emigrated to America at the age of 27 in 1739. It is said that he fled the country because he killed a rival (over a lady's hand) in a duel. But the rest of the family remained in the Gironde, the estate at La Pinesse being passed down the generations until 1846. One young Mlle Védrines scratched her initials within a heart with her diamond ring on a pane of glass which still exists in the château today.

Meanwhile, immediately adjacent to the north, was a piece of land under vines which was part of the estate of Château Coutet. When the owner of Coutet, Barthélémy Romain de Filhot, went to the guillotine in 1793, the estate was sequestrated by the state. This corner of the vineyard seems to have been detached, and absorbed into the Doisy-Védrines vineyard.

The first detailed account of the top wines of Barsac is given by André Jullien in his *Topographie de Tous les Vignobles Connus*, first published in 1816: 'The four *premiers crus* [of the commune] are Coutet, Clément (a misprint for Climens), Doisy and Caillou.' According to Paguierre in 1828 the leading estate is Coutet, after which come Bineau or Roborel, Perrot, Dumirail, Veuve Dubos, Dubos Mercier and Saluces de Laborde. Roborel was an alternative name for Climens; Perrot was the proprietor of Château de Myrat; the Saluces reference is to Châteaux Pernaud and Piada, then one estate; while the Dubos or Dubosq family farmed much of what was then and now Védrines.

What certainly did happen is that in the 1830s or 1840s the Doisy vineyard was split into three. One part was bought by an Englishman with the name of Daëne, another by a Mlle Faux (this is what is now Doisy-Dubroca). The biggest part remained – there is talk of a marriage settlement according to Cocks and Féret – but whether in the hands of the Védrines or with the Dubosqs is not clear. It may even have passed to the Boireau family of which more in a paragraph or so. At the time M. Daëne and Mlle Faux produced 10 to 15 *tonneaux* each and the *Veuve* Dubosq 50 to 60 *tonneaux*.

1855 ONWARDS

The subsequent history of Védrines is simpler than that of the other two. There was also, prior to 1855, a family called Boireau in the La Pinesse area who produced wine and were also *tonnelliers* (barrel-makers). The Boireaus bought out the Védrines in 1851, and at the same time seem to have taken over the Dubosq vines. The wine has since been passed down the female side of the family – from J. Boireau Fils Frères (one of whom was mayor of Barsac for a while) to Mme J. Teysonneau, proprietor also of Château Menota in the first half of this century, and from her to her daughter, the mother of Pierre Castéja, the proprietor today.

THE WINE

Védrines is the largest of the three Doisy estates, with 30 hectares under vines (rather less than a century ago), as against fifteen for Daëne (rather more) and three and a half for Dubroca (rather less again). It has recently been enlarged by the acquisition of the neighbouring Château Massereau.

The proprietor at Doisy-Védrines is the gentle, genial and hospitable Pierre Castéja. Since his retirement from the family firm of Roger Joanne and Co. a few years ago (like his brother Emile of Borie-Manoux, he took over the firm of his father-in-law shortly after the war), Castéja has lived permanently at Védrines. It is a charming two-storey family farmhouse, a hotch-potch of architectural styles, the oldest part, a round tower, dating back to 1500 or so. All this lies in a little park, the shaded parts of which are covered in wild cyclamen in the autumn and violets in the spring.

Doisy-Védrines' ingredients comprise 85 per cent Sémillon and 15 per cent Sauvignon, the Muscadelle having been ripped out in 1957. Vinification starts in stainless steel and is finished in barrel, half of which is now new, and bottling takes place two years or so after the vintage. This is an up-to-date cellar, all the thirteen vats being equipped with temperature control, so that the wine can have a *passage à froid* to precipitate impurities. There is also a cryo-extraction facility.

But the wine is traditional. It is one of the fullest and richest of the Barsacs: Climens rather than Coutet. Doisy-Védrines has been producing first-growth quality since (at least) Pierre Castéja took over in 1947. As well as the wines below I can thoroughly recommend the 1952. And the 1971 is balanced and elegant.

THE TASTING

I sampled the wines of Doisy-Védrines in January 1990.

1988 — *Optimum drinking* 1998–2118

Light colour. Rich, concentrated, honeyed nose; gently oaky. Slightly adolescent. Plenty of hidden power here. On the palate this has really lovely peachy fruit, a lot of depth and concentration; beautifully balanced. A typical, elegant racy Barsac. Very complex. Very fine.

1986 — 1995–2010

Light colour. Not quite as concentrated on the nose as the 1988 but elegant and flowery and with no absence of *pourriture noble* on the palate. Ripe and stylish but without the power and the depth of the 1988. Good but not great. Some *pourriture noble* but less than the above. Finishes well though. Will come forward soon.

1985 — Now–2003

Light colour. An elegant wine with good fruit and balance. Perhaps the Barsacs are better than the Sauternes in this vintage because they are more racy. Medium bodied. Sweet rather than luscious. Good fruit. Good grip. Shows well. Good.

1983 — Now–2008

Light colour. Fat and rich and honeyed on the nose. Fragrant and flowery at the same time. The nose is a little more open and a little more deadened by SO2 than I would like. On the palate the wine is better. Medium to medium-full. Very obviously Barsac rather than Sauternes. Some *pourriture noble*. Good racy fruit. Stylish finish. Quite forward. Very good. Very subtle.

1982 — Now–2005

Light colour. Charming nose. Fondants with a very slight touch of mint. Fresh, supple, fragrant. Like the 1985 this is sweet rather than luscious, but there is more *pourriture noble* here and very good grip. Youthful, quite concentrated. Not quite as clean and elegant as the 1985, but this may be as much due to the youth of the wine as anything inherent. A very good 1982.

1975 — Drink soon

Quite an orange colour. Quite an evolved nose. No longer exactly sweet. Complex, nutty and spicy. Medium sweet on the palate. Medium body. A fresh, mature, balanced wine, without a great deal of concentration or *pourriture noble* but with style and character. Flowery, soft and discreet.

1970 — Now–2000

Quite an orange colour. Seems fuller, richer and fatter, as well as a bit more vigorous on the nose. Sweeter and richer and more honeyed than the 1975. Medium-full. Quite voluptuous. Very good, peachy fruit and very good acidity. A lovely mature wine. Very good for vintage.

1969 — Drink soon

A little dry on the nose. I wonder if this is showing too much age. Quite a surprise on the palate. Fresh and sweet (slightly sweeter than the 1970 because the acidity is not as fresh) and plump with a good spicy-toffee finish. No lack of vigour. A little more *pourriture noble* than the 1970 perhaps, but not as fresh or as stylish.

1967   **Drink soon**

Quite concentrated and spicy on the nose, yet on the dry side, with a suspicion of old Riesling-petrol. Has also lost a bit of its vigour. This is a mellow, quite sweet wine. A bit broad and diffuse on the finish and even a shade coarse. It was richer than the 1969 but now, though it finishes reasonably vigorously, I think it is beginning to lose a bit of grip. A good 1967 though.

1966   **Drink up**

Broader nose. Toffee flavours, still sweet. Still vigorous. Medium body. A relatively simple wine, never *that* concentrated. Has now lost a little of its sweetness. The least interesting of the 1970–1966 series.

1962   **Now–2000 plus**

Full old-gold colour. Lovely nose. Rich, complex, subtle. Musk and nectar, exotic and opulent. Full, rich and concentrated. Only the vigorous grip puts it in Barsac rather than Sauternes. This is a luscious, vigorous, mature wine. Both mellow and alive. Lovely fruit. Really multidimensional. Delicious. Plenty of life ahead of it.

1961   **Drink up**

The nose is drier and more spirity than the 1962. On the palate it is better than on the nose. The attack is quite sweet, complex and mellow, and it seems balanced. The aftertaste is more coarse, even a bit cloying. And the finish lacks class, vigour and depth.

1949   **Now–2000**

Quite a deep old-gold colour. Yet still fresh and clear. Lovely nose. Very rich, very concentrated, still fresh, has harmony and great finesse. Mellow and complex, the complete, mature Sauternes. Lovely. This is richer and more concentrated than the 1962. But the 1962 is fresher.

DOISY-DAËNE

The succession of Doisy-Daëne is more complicated than that of Doisy-Védrines and the changes less accurately dated. M. Daëne remained until the 1870s, when the estate briefly passed to a Juhel Bilot. He was the proprietor in 1879. Ten years later it was Jules Debans, member of a family which was also involved with the Dubroca portion in the 1860s – before the Dubrocas arrived. Ownership then passed to M. Dejean of the *négociants* Cazelet et Fils. He was proprietor in 1922. Two years later Doisy-Daëne was acquired by Georges Dubourdieu, grandfather of the present proprietor, Pierre.

A *bourdieu* was a piece of land which lay near the church and town (*bourg* + *dieu* = *bourdieu*), and the produce therefrom was a source of income for the local priest. The people who worked it were *les dubourdieux*.

Georges Dubourdieu, before he purchased Doisy, was a proprietor in Cérons. Pierre's grandfather on his mother's side was owner of Château Roumieu-Lacoste. His wife's family own Château Cantegril, detached from Château de Myrat the year after the Classification (if it had been in 1856 and not 1854, Pierre would have two classed growths under his belt). There are other Dubourdieus at Illats (Château Archambeau), while Pierre jointly owns a property in Pujols (Château Montalivet) together with his son. Moreover this son, Denis, is the influential oenology professor and consultant who has done so much to transform dry white Bordeaux from the dead sulphury rubbish or thin green paintstripper of the 1960s and 1970s to the wine we know today. This is a family steeped in wine.

Whether steeped in Sauternes or not is a moot point. One very forcibly gets the impression that Pierre Dubourdieu – if it would be exaggerating to say actively *dislikes* Sauternes – is at least indifferent to it. Dry wines are what interest him most. Dry wines form 70 per cent of his production, and they are brilliant. There is the standard Doisy-Daëne *Sec*: 50 to 70 per cent Sauvignon, the rest Sémillon, picked at the usual time, fermented in wood, left on its fine lees and bottled in April or May following the vintage. It is classic and stylish, subtle and balanced; in my view by far and away the most successful of the 'dry Sauternes', the reason being that it doesn't taste like one. It doesn't have a sweet nose and a hard, fruitless, sulphury palate.

Doisy-Daëne, *Cuvée* Saint-Martin, is, as far as I know, unique. It is disarmingly definitive; totally individual. It was created for the delicious Hélène Coste, and is exclusive to her father's firm. The wine is made completely from Sémillon, from the same patch of old vines every year. These are picked late, in November (the festival of Saint Martin, patron saint of *vignerons*, is celebrated on 11 November). The grapes are prevented from being attacked by botrytis by the application of Bouille Bordelaise (a copper sulphate mixture) or by anti-rot treatment, but have nevertheless dried up and concentrated on the vine. The must is fermented in new wood and the wine kept on its lees for a year before bottling. This is a rich, complex, positive, quite un-Graves wine, which needs to be kept back a couple of years after going into glass. It certainly keeps well.

Pierre Dubourdieu's Sauternes, as I have indicated in the previous chapter, is a less luscious, more fragrant wine than most; more feminine if you like. Balance and elegance rather than sheer power are the objectives. The wine is made from 100 per cent Sémillon.

The grapes are picked at 18 to 19 degrees of potential alcohol, rather than the 20 to 22 degrees which other proprietors strive for, rarely chaptalized, and vinified in stainless steel. Up to 1986, rather than stopping the fermentation by the use of sulphur, or by reducing the temperature to 4°C and then filtering out the yeasts, which is what the rest do, Dubourdieu used to *raise* the temperature, up to 42, for a month. It does not seem to have done the wines any harm. Now he ferments right out.

After fermentation the wine goes into new oak for a few months. It is then blended together, returned to stainless steel and bottled during the succeeding winter, 15 to 18 months after the harvest. Throughout the entire process of *élevage*, the addition of sulphur is kept to a minimum. This results in a light, fresh, clean wine, not without *pourriture noble* in the best years, but certainly not that honeyed and luscious. It evolves early, but because of its inherent breed and balance keeps exceptionally well. The 1975, for instance, is still crisp and fragrant, a lovely prima ballerina of a wine, one of great poise and surprising finesse.

Dubourdieu does not stop there. There are always experiments going on. I remember in 1984 sampling a 1945 he had refreshed, revinified and rebottled. The result was a curious mixture of the old and the new; neither the one thing nor the other; but certainly of interest. In 1978, a fine dry autumn, too dry, paradoxically, for the development of noble rot, he covered part of the vineyard with a transparent plastic sheet in October and harvested the fruit at Christmas. This *vin de Noël* was made from grapes which were not only shrivelled up, but slightly oxidized, and the nearest thing in Bordeaux I have tasted to a *vin de paille*. The Doisy-Daëne, *vin de Noël*, 1978 has naturally high alcohol, very little botrytis flavour, is fat, oily and slightly oxidized on the nose, even a little burnt and spirity, but on the palate it is fresh, supple, complex and intriguing. Dubourdieu made four casks' worth, which were vinified in wood.

Pierre Dubourdieu is also notorious for having, unofficially, some plants of both Riesling and Chardonnay in his vineyard. The resulting grapes probably find their way into the Doisy-Daëne *Sec*. Oh, if only I were permitted to have Chardonnay, Pierre will say. He is convinced that the southern Graves could make an excellent wine with it if the local growers were so allowed. He has vinified his separately and it is brilliant.

THE TASTING

I sampled the following wines in Barsac in April 1990.

Optimum drinking

1989   1997–2012

Not a lot of *pourriture noble* on the nose but honeyed, gently oaky, fragrant and graceful. An attractive example. Ripe, quite a lot of *pourriture noble*. Concentrated, intensely flavoured. This is rich and even powerful yet has a lot of finesse. Lovely flowery complexity. Very good indeed.

1988   1996–2012

This is a little adolescent. It seems fuller and fatter but perhaps (and perhaps only temporarily) not to have as much finesse. But it had recently been fined, etc, in preparation for bottling. On the palate it shows rather better. Ripe and ample if a little disturbed. At least very good but not *en forme*.

1986   1995–2008

Fine, delicate, honeyed nose. This is very elegant and very lovely, like a very sexy mannequin from the pages of the French *Vogue*. Medium body. Ample and fruity on the palate with a good vanilla and oak background but not quite as seductive or as complex as the nose. Yet a fine example. Honeyed. Plenty of *pourriture noble*.

1985   Now–2001

The nose doesn't show *pourriture noble* and neither does it have much sweetness. Sweet and vanillary but not a great deal of *pourriture noble* on the palate. Medium body. Stylish but essentially a bit one-dimensional and four-square. Yet balanced. Good for vintage.

1984   Drink soon

Light, somewhat one-dimensional, fruity nose with a touch of SO2. This is, as you might expect, a lesser wine. Slightly coarse. Sweet but without great elegance.

1983   1995–2015

Full, fat, vigorous, rich nose. Plenty of depth here but currently a shade adolescent. A wine of really quite a lot more power and concentration than, for example, the 1986 or 1988. Rich, fat, complex, a lot of *pourriture noble* intensity. Still needs time. Very fine.

1982   Now–1997

Ripe, stylish, fruity nose but without much power or depth behind it. Elegant, balanced, ripe and plump. One of the more stylish examples of this vintage. Lovely fruit. A little *pourriture noble*. Very good indeed for the vintage.

1981   Drink soon

This is not too bad. Some *pourriture noble*. A lightish gentle wine which is now fully ready. No great depth or complexity but fresh, fruity and pretty. Attractive. Very good for vintage.

1980   Drink soon

A little one-dimensional on the nose but not without elegance. The nose is a little faded but the palate better. Yet this is merely a sweet, fruity wine without a great deal of grip. Pleasant but one-dimensional.

1948   Now–2000

The oldest thing about this wine is the colour, which is quite a deep tawny now. Lovely plump, fresh nose. Splendid vigour especially on the palate. Soft and ample on the palate. Rich and stylish. Supple and round. A feminine, delicate wine. Complex fruit. Ripe and long on the palate. Surprisingly good. Delicious. Clean and vigorous not a trace of fade. Very well balanced. Will still keep for ages.

NAIRAC

The first château that one encounters in the Sauternais as one rolls gently down the tree-lined N113 below Cérons is one of the most elegant. It also makes one of the best wines, one of the most oaky and distinctive in the area. This is Château Nairac in Barsac. Like many, it suffered from the depression in the fortunes of Sauternes in the 1950s and 1960s, but it was resurrected somewhat earlier than most. Early in 1972, sans reputation, the château a shell, and the vineyard neglected, it was acquired by the American Tom Heeter and his French wife Nicole, daughter of Nicolas Tari of Château Giscours. For fifteen years Heeter and Tari poured their heart and soul into the estate, painstakingly re-building the renown of the wine – it is now a major contender for elevation from second to first growth – renovating the beautiful château and restoring the vineyard. In 1986 the Heeters divorced, and Tom Heeter ceded his interest in Nairac to Nicole and their children. Since then she has continued the good work alone, and progress continues.

Château Nairac has its origins in one André Duranceau, a Bordeaux citizen who was responsible for the accounts of the local parliamentary court in the middle of the seventeenth century. He owned a manor house in Barsac and a number of parcels of land in the neighbourhood, most of them vineyards which he leased out to local tenant farmers. From him the estate passed to Jérome Mercade at the beginning of the eighteenth century. Mercade, a recently ennobled member of a long-standing *bourgeois* family and a parliamentary advocate, was related by marriage to two aristocratic families in the area, the Roborels of Climens and the Montalliers of Romer-du-Hayot, and it was this which perhaps prompted him, one can conjecture, also to settle in the area. He extended and dignified the existing *manoir*, though it was left to his daughter-in-law, *née* Elizabeth Prost, daughter of a wealthy Creole plantation owner from Port-au-Prince in Haiti, to enlarge the vineyard. It was Elizabeth and her son who sold Duranceau to Elysée Nairac in 1777.

HISTORY

The Nairacs were a wealthy Protestant family from the noble house of Luzies. They were merchants, ship-owners and politicians in eighteenth-century Bordeaux. Paul Nairac, Elysée's elder brother, was *député* for the Guyenne in the later part of the century and lived in the Cours de Verdun in the heart of the city, in a house built by Victor Louis.

It was one of Victor Louis' pupils, the architect Jean Mollié, who was responsible for the design of today's Château Nairac. Classical in concept, elegantly proportioned, this beautiful building, one of the best examples of the late eighteenth century in the Gironde, was constructed between 1777 and 1780 in a little park just off the main Bordeaux-Langon highway at the north of the village of Barsac itself.

Elysée Nairac only remained in possession of the property which was henceforth to bear his name for fourteen years. In 1791, just before the Revolution, he died, leaving five daughters. Two of these, Henriette and Julie-Emilie, inherited the *vignoble*. Neither was to marry but both were to live to a healthy old age. They remained at Nairac until the death of the former in 1837.

Other members of the Nairac family, however, were forced to flee the country during the Terror. They went first to Holland where, Hubrect Duijker reports, a Charles Auguste Nairac was to become burgomaster in the town of Barneveld from 1841 to 1883. Later they emigrated to Mauritius, where the family continue to play an active role in public life to this day. The Heeters have had members of the present-day Nairac family to stay at the château.

After Henriette Nairac's death the property was put up for sale. The purchaser, one Bernard Capdeville, was already the owner of a number of vineyards in the area, including both Broustet and an enclave in the western part of the Nairac estate, once owned by the Ségur family, which had been sold off as a *bien national* during the French Revolution. This he had bought in 1816, and one can speculate that he might well have farmed the surrounding Nairac vineyards on behalf of the increasingly elderly spinster sisters from that time onwards. While André Jullien, in his *Topographie de Tous les Vignobles Connus*, first published in 1816, refers to a Mlle Neirac (*sic*) as a proprietor among his *vins blancs de deuxième classe*, M. Philippe Maffre, who has researched the Nairac history, and on whose efforts this account is largely indebted, has found no reference to the name of Nairac in any of the financial transactions of the post-revolutionary period.

The vineyard, however, was small. Together with the Ségur parcel, according to Charles Cocks in 1850, it consisted of hardly eight hectares and produced fifteen *tonneaux* of wine. Joined to Broustet, under which joint name it was classified as a *deuxième* in 1855, it produced 40 to 50 *tonneaux*.

On the death of Bernard Capdeville in 1861 the Barsac estate was divided. Broustet went to one daughter, Madame Moller, wife of the owner of Château Myrat, Nairac to the other, Georgina, wife of Pierre Gustave Brunet, owner of another well-known growth, Château Piada. Brunet was an academic and a prolific writer, as well as a director of the Bordeaux Chamber of Commerce.

The Brunets were childless, and after Georgina's death in 1906 Nairac passed to a distant cousin, Madame Armichard. This latter lady, retired and living in Royat in the Auvergne, had to put up with legal proceedings, instigated by other members of the Capdeville family. Having succeeded in successfully contesting the action she promptly sold Nairac to a Lorraine *négociant*, Jean-Charles Perpezat. The deed of sale at the time refers to a vineyard of just over ten hectares in one piece. It produced eight *tonneaux* of Sauternes and fifteen of red wine.

In 1913 Perpezat won a gold medal for his work in restoring the vineyard, and by the mid-1920s production had risen to 30 *tonneaux*, as he gradually replaced the red wine plants with Sémillon, Sauvignon and Muscadelle, and enlarged the vineyard slightly to twelve hectares. Perpezat was a partner in the *négociant* firm of Mas et Mostermans (his daughter married a M. Mas), and his family were to remain proprietors until 1966, entirely replanting the Nairac vineyard after the terrible February frosts in 1956, but leaving the lovely château itself empty and forlorn.

In 1966 the Perpezats sold Nairac to Dr Jean Gabriolle Seynat, a municipal councillor from Bordeaux. Though they had maintained the vineyard in good order, the wine had no great reputation at this time. It is listed last of all in the Barsac section of the 1969 Cocks and Féret, and was to suffer further. Seynat allowed the estate to run down and sold off the wine in bulk. Why he bought the property I cannot make out. He never made any attempt to restore the château.

TOM HEETER AND NICOLE TARI

Tom Heeter is a tall, powerful man with the large feet and hands of a lumberjack. He comes from a family of industrialists from Dayton, Ohio. While at college he caught the wine bug, and after working for a firm of retailers in New York he arrived in Bordeaux in the late 1960s to work as a trainee at Château Giscours. Before too long he had captured the heart of Nicole Tari, daughter of the house, and soon after they were married they happened to hear that Château Nairac was up for sale. In August 1971, a purchase was agreed, at the attractively low price of around 800,000 francs, and, despite Seynat later trying to renege on this agreement because he had subsequently received a better offer, the Heeters became proprietors a year later.

There was much to be done. The vineyard, subsequently enlarged by the acquisition of three hectares from Château Climens, was in poor condition. The outbuildings and *chais* needed renovation, the installation of modern wine-making equipment and the acquisition of new oak; and the château had to be extensively modernized and redecorated as it had stood empty for 60 years. The Heeter family moved in the spring of 1974.

Despite the unexciting vintages of 1972 to 1974, the improvement in the wine was dramatic. In each of these three vintages, by means of very severe pruning, painstaking harvesting – eleven *passages* in 1974 – and by rigorous selection of the finished wine – only 619 cases bottled as Nairac in 1972 and 1,200 in 1974 – the wines are remarkably good for their years. Indeed I would go as far as to say that the 1973 Nairac is the best wine of the commune, superior even to Coutet and Climens. The standard of quality has continued to improve.

THE VINEYARD

The nucleus of the Nairac vineyard lies immediately behind the château and its various outbuildings – there are several small *chais*, recently restored and temperature controlled, rather than one large above-ground cellar. Here we are a mere seven metres above sea-level, and less than that above the mean level of the nearby Garonne. In December 1981, the château basement and other buildings were flooded when the river overflowed its banks. Further parcels of land lie near the motorway, beyond Château Climens. This land is the classic Barsac stoney limestone, less clayey than further inland in Sauternes itself, on a limestone base. In the main section of the Nairac vineyard this calcareous base has been covered with a fine layer of alluvial gravel.

The vineyard is currently planted with 90 per cent Sémillon, 6 per cent Sauvignon and 4 per cent Muscadelle, and produces about 2,000 cases of wine a year. Because the Sauvignon is pruned differently (single Guyot as against the *cot à deux yeux*) and, moreover, vintaged earlier, before over-ripening, in order to preserve all its fresh aromatic properties, the eventual final wine, when blended, may contain 15 to 18 per cent Sauvignon by volume. Heeter used to tell me that though the Sauvignon rots as easily as the Sémillon, it quickly loses its character. He preferred to harvest with little or no noble rot.

A team of some two dozen pickers is employed. On arrival at Nairac the first task is to pick over the fruit. This second *tri*, to add to the one already in the vineyard, is vital. Only absolutely 'clean' fruit is allowed to be pressed into juice.

THE WINE-MAKING AT NAIRAC

When they first started to make wine at Nairac the Heeters invited the renowned Professor Peynaud to act as a consultant. His recipe for making quality Sauternes recommended the use of new oak casks every year, and, moreover, fermentation in wood. Just like at Yquem.

Unlike at many less perfectionistic properties, therefore, after the grapes have been pressed and the juice allowed to settle, this juice is transferred into oak casks for the fermentation. This takes place slowly at a natural 16 to 18 degrees. Cooling is unnecessary as the ambient late October-November climate in Bordeaux is normally cold enough. Moreover the oak casks enable the heat created by the fermentation process easily to disperse. The wine ferments at a slow pace until the fermentation falls away of its own accord, at 14 degrees of alcohol or just above, without the need for heavy sulphuring.

Bottling takes place after considerable maturation in cask, the wine acquiring tannin from the oak, which will give it longevity, and being allowed to clear by natural means. The length of time the wine remains in cask, however, is flexible; sometimes 24 months or less, sometimes as long as three years. In all years a rigorous selection is made: 60 per cent was rejected in 1979, and in 1977, 1978 and 1984 no wine was bottled as Château Nairac.

THE WINE

Château Nairac is a carefully, lovingly made wine of high quality, and the style and quality do not appear to have changed since Tom Heeter's departure. As a Barsac it is a more *nerveux*, more racy, less fleshy, less *liquoreux* wine than a Sauternes. Yet it is as luscious, has as high a sugar content, even if the wine appears to have a greater austerity and will have a lighter colour. Nairac is a full, rich wine in Barsac terms, considerably more powerful, oaky and potentially longer-lasting than most. When young this element of oak is aggressive and may appear to over-dominate. When the 1981 was young I felt that the wine might have been kept too long in new wood. But it seems all right now. In most years the result is splendid, considerably superior to most of the other second growths not only in the commune but elsewhere in what one might term 'greater' Sauternes: a tribute to the efforts of Tom Heeter and Nicole Tari. It is curious that at Nairac, as elsewhere, it took a 'foreigner', albeit married to a local, to show how the locals how wine should be correctly made.

THE TASTING

The following wines were sampled at Château Nairac in April 1992.

1991   *Optimum Drinking* **1995–2003**

Firm, quite structured. Sweet, and certainly with some botrytis. Honeyed and rich. Still very youthful. This is by no means a 'lesser' vintage. It is just a pity that there is so little of it – a mere fifteen casks.

1990   **1999–2020 plus**

Medium colour. The nose is still closed, but there is quite a lot of depth and power here. Fat, rich and vanillary/oaky. Sweeter and more botrytized on the palate than the nose. Good acidity. Flowery and caramelly, with other elements such as angelica and ginger. But very youthful as yet. Very good.

1989   **1996–2020 plus**

Lightish colour. Gently flowery nose. Stylish, complex. But not a blockbuster. On the palate medium body but very intense and persistent. Lovely vanilla custard and all sorts of fruits on the palate. Very good grip. This is elegant, balanced, positive and long. Fine.

1988   **Now–2004**

Light gold colour. Fat, rich and ample on the

nose. Plenty of concentration. Medium body. The wood shows a little. A more open wine than the 1989. A little less grip. Rich, good acidity, fat, lush and oaky, but not quite the concentration for great. Good plus.

1987 — Now–1998

Some colour. A little lumpy and four-square on the nose. There is a bit of residual SO2 here. On the palate a wine which has not much botrytis, and is only a little sweet. Medium body. It is also a bit rigid. Not a wine to write home about, but as it softens will be sweet and quite pleasant. Not bad.

1986 — Now–2004

Light gold colour. Closed nose. Quite powerful. Oaky. Full but not a lot of botrytis. A little built-in sulphur. A bit four-square. A ripe wine but without a lot of noble rot. And because it is a bit top-heavy, without the real grip and nuance of a really nobly rotten wine, it lacks a bit of grace and charm and elegance. Adolescent at present. Not as exciting as the 1988. Good though.

1985 — Now–1998

Lightish colour. Full, but somewhat unforthcoming on the nose. A little SO2 on the palate. Rather a simple wine. Not that sweet. But quite positive and elegant. A little four-square at the end, a bit rigid. Pleasant but one-dimensional.

1983 — Now–2004 plus

Medium colour. The nose is not the best part, but there is some richness here. On the palate there is a bit of sulphur but in essence the wine is quite rich and powerful. Fullish. A little ungainly still. Ripe and flowery on the finish. But there is a woody element here which detracts from the velvet. Long, though, powerful and intense still. Very good.

1982 — Now–2000

Medium gold colour. A fresh, flowery example with good grip and a fruit-salady flavour. This has good grip and intensity. There is caramel on the finish. Medium body. A bit more *pourriture noble* than 1981, and a wine with more dimension as a result. Very good for the vintage.

1981 — Now–2000 plus

Medium gold colour. Slightly caramelly nose. Medium body. Not a lot of intensity, but an attracting fresh sweet wine which has at least some *pourriture noble* and good complexity and depth. Stylish. Still vigorous. Will keep, even improve. Good for the vintage.

1980 — Now–2000

Medium colour. Spicy herbal nose. Showing some maturity. Medium-full, ripe, flowery, stylish. This has depth and complexity and style. Very good for the vintage. Will still keep well. Finishes long.

1979 — Drink up

Medium gold colour. Round, honeyed nose. Sweet without being botrytized very much. Open-knit. Medium body. Now *à point*, and I don't see much life ahead of it. Caramelly. But a bit rigid and getting a bit astringent. Loosening up. This is not as good as the 1980.

1976 — Now–2000

(Magnum) Mid-gold colour. This shows honey and nuts and *pourriture noble* on the nose. Gently sweet. Medium body. Still round and fresh and elegant (a lot better than the 1979) if without ever a great deal of depth or balance. Yet good *pourriture noble*. Still most enjoyable. A little ungainly but very good.

1975 — Now–2005

Light colour. Light, pleasantly sweet and fruity nose. Still very fresh. Rich and sweet. Stylish and even complex. Medium to medium-full. Good grip. This shows well. It is not that far short in *pourriture noble* than the 1976, and it has better grip and life. It is more elegant, more complex, and will keep better.

1974 — Drink up

Mid-gold colour but showing a little age. Getting a little loose now, but sweetness, even *pourriture noble* on the nose. But losing its elegance. On the palate medium to medium-full, there is good intensity here, surprisingly good. Rich, fat and lush, even quite powerful still on the finish. But the wine is beginning to lose its elegance.

1973 — Now–2000 plus

Lightish colour. Good rich firm nose. Still vigorous. Plenty of *pourriture noble* for a 1973 and good grip. A lush fat wine, barley-sugar flavoured. Like one or two other 1973s there is good botrytis and honey here. No dilution, and plenty of life left. Very good. Fatter than 1975. Will still keep well.

1972 — Past its best

Golden colour. Vegetal, maderized nose. It is sweet on the palate but old now. But one can see ample signs that this was really not bad at all in its prime.

DE FARGUES

The southern part of the Bordeaux area is rich in medieval fortifications. Some have ecclesiastical connections, as at Villandraut. Others are proper castles, what the French would call a *donjon*. The heyday of their construction – or adaption from older buildings – was the latter half of the thirteenth century and the beginning of the fourteenth. It is no coincidence that the period overlaps the date of the election of the local Bertrand de Goth to the papacy as Clement v in 1305.

Most of the castles – at Budos, Castets, La Brède, Landiras and Roquetaillade – date from immediately after Clement's enthronement, as he flexed the muscles of his patronage by liberally bestowing the red hat of cardinalship among his friends and relations. One such was Raymond Guilhem, a nephew. In 1306, on the site of an even older fortress, he built the Chateau de Fargues. Today the property is owned by the Lur-Saluces of Yquem and the name is known for fine Sauternes. This, however, is a new development, dating only from 1942. For most of its history the Fargues estate has not been vineyard but pasture and pine trees.

After Cardinal Raymond Guilhem de Fargues the estate passed into the hands of Gaston de Foix; subsequently to the Monferrand family. The Foix and the Monferrands were two of the most powerful forces in medieval Bordeaux, liege lords of the English kings and possessors of vast *seigneuries* in the Gironde. Foix, for example, can be connected with both Margaux and Latour; Monferrand with the *seigneuries* of Lesparre and Blanquefort.

FROM GUILHEM TO LUR-SALUCES

It was the time of the Hundred Years War (1337–1453). Gascony and Guyenne were all that were left of the vast lands that Eleanor of Aquitaine brought with her when she had married the English Henry II in 1152. With the collapse of English hegemony after the Battle of Castillon in 1453 all was to change. Most of the more active combatants were forced into exile. Others decided to retire peacefully to what they could salvage of their lands, accept the status quo, and forswear politics. Pierre de Monferrand seems to have done neither. He was eventually captured at Poitiers and summarily executed.

Some of his kin, at least, continued at Fargues, but he was effectively the last of his line. In 1472 Isabeau (or Izabelle) de Monferrand, heiress of Château de Fargues, married Pierre de Lur. Some 114 years later their descendant Jean changed his name to Lur-Saluces when he married Catherine-Charlotte, only child of the Marquis de Saluces. The property has remained in the hands of the same family ever since.

THE CHÂTEAU AND THE CASTLE

Unlike Roquetaillade, for example, Fargues is today a ruin. But it is a ruin as a result of neglect rather than deliberate dismemberment. It has suffered neither at the hands of enemy cannons nor because the stone was dislodged to build other local dwellings. It was repaired at the end of the sixteenth century during the reign of Henri IV, and twice served as refuge for the locals during periods of local insurrection. Perhaps it was simply allowed to fall into decay when the Lur-Saluces moved to Yquem in 1785, following the marriage of Louis-Amédée de Lur-Saluces to Françoise-Joséphine de Sauvage d'Yquem. It must, though, have been an impressive sight in its heyday. The castle forms a large square with octagonal towers at each corner. Most of the walls still stand. Ghostly, it looms over the neighbouring village. Unconcerned the locals play soccer on a nearby football pitch.

In front of the old castle, a converted farmhouse serves as the present-day château, a couple of elegantly furnished reception rooms being separated from the offices by a covered gateway into the inner courtyard.

Adjacent is another courtyard giving access to the *chais*. Here the atmosphere is rather more artisanal. It is a little scruffy. A fine old barn has been carefully restored and converted into a temperature-controlled storage cellar, and here you will find the 100 or so casks of the new vintage of Château de Fargues.

THE VINEYARD

It is only recently that wine has been produced at Château de Fargues. Not until 1893 is there any mention at all of De Fargues in the pages of Cocks and Féret. In this year 65 *tonneaux* of red wine is declared as an average yield.

The size of the vineyard declined in the first few decades of the twentieth century, and in the last twenty years the production of red wine has evaporated into a mere couple of *tonneaux* for private consumption. But in 1935 or so, the late Bertrand de Lur-Saluces, uncle of Alexandre, the present proprietor, started to plant white grapes, and the first vintage of a Sauternes was produced in 1942. There are now twelve hectares under vine, in the ratio 80 per cent Sémillon, 20 per cent Sauvignon, producing about 25 *tonneaux* a year.

THE WINE

The wine is made by the same team as at Yquem, and with the same attention to detail, but is in no way a *deuxième marque* of its magisterial cousin. The press is pneumatic rather than hydraulic. The wine is fermented and matured in newish casks passed down from Yquem but not in new wood. But it is held almost as long in wood before bottling. The style is very similar, with the intensity of honeyed fruit and the rich mellow oakiness which is the hallmark of the greatest sweet wine in the world.

Where it differs is in the matter of power and richness on the one hand, and sheer breed and complexity on the other. The main reason, all other things being equal, is the difference in soil and microclimate. The elevation is not as high, the conditions marginally cooler and more humid, the soil predominantly a sandy loam. (At Yquem the geology is more complex: as well as sand and loam there are patches of gravel, a point at which the underlying belt of clay comes to the surface, and elsewhere a soil which is purer in limestone.) The result is at Fargues a later harvest and a less multidimensional wine; one which is less rich and intensely flavoured. Drink a Chateau de Fargues on its own, and such is the Lur-Saluces hallmark one would be forgiven for thinking it was Yquem. Drink them side by side, and the difference is palpable.

THE TASTING

I sampled most of the following wines in Sauternes in January 1990. I have added notes on two older vintages also tasted at around this period.

Optimum drinking

1986   2000–2025

This is a structured wine, and it hasn't quite recovered from the bottling. Concentrated, introspective nose. On the palate there is power and fat, richness and depth. Honeyed lusciousness. A wine of intensity, even muscle which is a little four-square at present. Will need a further ten years at least.

1985   1997–2017

Concentrated but light gold colour. Nose still closed. Full, rich, ripe and oaky. Quite firm. Ripe and concentrated rather than decidedly botrytized. More *pourriture noble* on the palate. Full, quite powerful. Splendid fruit. Good grip. Quite an opulent, almost exotic wine. Fresh. A long life ahead of it. Very good.

1984   Now–2003

Light gold colour. Not a lot of nose. A touch of SO2. Sweet and flowery-fragrant underneath, if not very rich. No *pourriture noble* of course. Medium bodied. Sweet, pretty, straightforward. No great depth or concentration but certainly fresh, balanced, flowery and pleasant. Will come forward soon.

1983   1999–2029

Deeper colour, mid-gold. Fat, rich, spicy, adolescent nose. Certainly plenty of power, but overloaded by a little SO2. Real *pourriture noble* here. Very fine acidity. Complex, concentrated fruit. A full wine but the elements not yet together. And on the attack not nearly as classy as on the finish. Rich and peachy, opulent, but in a softer, more fragrant style than Yquem. Needs time.

1982   Now–2009

Light gold colour. Soft and honeyed with a touch of beeswax. Not a greatdeal of grip. Gentle, sweet, quite forward. It lacks a bit of power but is certainly elegant and graceful. Very good for a 1982. Few have this finesse. Soft, fragrant, sweet, balanced. Some *pourriture noble*. Very stylish. Forward. Lovely.

1981   1996–2016

Mid-gold colour. Good *pourriture noble* on the nose here. More power than the 1982 but not as rich or as concentrated as the 1983. Finely balanced. Very good fruit. Once again the accent is on peaches and other fruit, and flowers like mock-orange, rather than on nuts and spice. Fullish. Very well balanced. Very good grip. Very youthful still.

1980   Now–2002

Light gold colour. Sweet but somewhat broad on the nose. Not nearly as classic or as elegant as the 1981. Similar nose. Lacks grip and *pourriture noble* and therefore real elegance. There is a slight cloying aspect. Medium bodied. Sweet. Not as fine as the 1982.

1971   Now–2010

Deepest colour so far. Full golden colour. Fine mature, honeyed and (now, finally) spicy nose. Good grip. Complex. This is delicious. Medium-full, mature but vigorous, lovely peachy fruit. Very well balanced. Very fresh and lovely. Lovely clean finish. High class.

1967   Now–2010 plus

Golden colour. Amazingly fresh. Lovely *pourriture noble*. Real concentration. Great balance. A full, honeyed, oaky, peachy and botrytized wine. Real elegance. Lovely. Quite super. Fresher and more elegant than Yquem (the bottles of Yquem 1967, in my experience, vary greatly). Will live for ages. Still powerful. Great wine.

VINT
ASSES

ONE OF THE FASCINATIONS OF BORDEAUX IS THE VA-
RIETY AND INDIVIDUALITY OF EACH VINTAGE. EACH
VINTAGE IS DIFFERENT. GIVEN THAT THE SURFACE
AREA, PROPORTIONS OF VINES PLANT-
ED, AGE OF VINES, AND WINE-MAKING
PERSONNEL AND EQUIPMENT DO NOT,
BY AND LARGE, CHANGE, IT IS THE
WEATHER PATTERN WHICH IMPOSES
THE DIFFERENCES IN STYLE BETWEEN
ONE PROPERTY'S WINE IN ONE YEAR
AND THE NEXT.

Vintages obviously vary in quality and in potential for long-term developments. Nor are they
necessarily uniform across the Bordeaux region.

Rather than mark on an absolute scale, which
would introduce the absurdity of, for example,
marking a poor vintage such as 1984 a maximum
of 10 out of 20, while 1961 was marked out of a
maximum of 20, I have decided to mark each vintage *within its context*. Thus a mark of 20 for a poor
vintage indicates an excellent result for *that vintage*,
a mark of 15 indicates a good result, and so on. I
trust the words will speak for themselves.

AGE

SMENTS

1993, 1992 AND 1991

After the years of plenty, came the years of famine. As in the 1930s, after a decade of above-average quality vintages, Mother Nature or the law of averages – or just plain chance – is seeking to regularize itself. As a result of modern techniques of viticulture, viniculture and *él-evage*, no vintage is the disaster today it would have been 60 or even 30 years ago. There is plenty that is worthwhile in 1993, 1992 and 1991. But these are vintages to set alongside 1980, 1984 and 1987, not alongside even 1981, let alone 1982, 1989 and 1990.

Unluckily for the Bordelais, these three latest vintages have arrived at the same time as a worldwide economic recession. Even if the quality had been very good they would have met with little demand. As it is, the response has been negligible. Despite lower prices, there has been no *en primeur* campaign for the 1991 and 1992 vintages (this book goes to press before the 1993s have been priced and offered). When they are in bottle the wines will no doubt find their market, probably mainly domestically in the supermarket sector where price and name seem to be more important criteria than quality. Thankfully they are evolving quickly, and will be more or less drinkable by 1995/1996.

THE WEATHER: 1993

After a dry and sunny winter, prompting fears of drought by the end of March, April was wet and generally grey, though not particularly cool. This was followed by a May which was a little warmer than usual, with average rainfall. The vegetative cycle, having begun early, was not interrupted by frost, and the vines flowered rapidly in good conditions a few days in advance of the 30-year average (*mi-floraison* 8 to 10 June). Thereafter June was more than twice as wet as usual, but also warmer than the average, which encouraged the development of mildew. A hailstorm hit the Bas-Médoc on 22 June.

July, however, was a little drier than normal and August particularly hot and sunny. Both Merlots and Cabernets underwent their *veraison* at the same time (*mi-veraison* 8 to 10 August). By the end of September, thanks to extensive green-harvesting in the better properties, the crop looked to be of reasonable size, was uniform and healthy, and its state of maturity was not far short of that of 1982 and 1989 at the same date. All looked very promising indeed. The Merlot grapes at Haut-Brion were already reading 11 degrees on 27th August.

I was in Bordeaux for a fortnight from 30 August. The first week was splendid, but then the weather broke. On Monday, 6 September, it started raining on and off, particularly heavily after the 16th and again after the 25th, for the rest of the month. Overall the precipitation was three times that of the average, and at 250 millimetres beat all previous records: 1965, with 213, and 1969, with 207 being the previous two wettest Septembers in the last 30 years.

This does not augur well. But all is by no means disaster. Firstly, the state of the fruit was excellent before the rains began. In contrast to 1992, when August was miserable, the grapes had been able to stoke up calories and thicken their skins before the weather deteriorated. The colours, the must-weights, the tannins and the overall structures of the 1993 red wines are superior to those of 1982. Oenologues were even going round warning wine-makers not to over-macerate! Obviously concentration has been diluted, but reports indicate that the aromas and flavours are nevertheless satisfactorily intense and elegant. And there was no rot.

Once again it will be a vintage where, proportionately, the top estates will do better than the *petits châteaux*. But yet again modern wine-making techniques and equipment have saved the day. It will not be an *année de garde* – or a vintage where there will be much incentive to buy *en primeur* – but the whites will be elegant and aromatic, the reds will be round and fruity, and there may be some respectable Sauternes. Overall, 1993 is definitely better than 1992 and 1991. Once again it was a very large harvest.

THE WEATHER: 1992

Bordeaux experienced an erratic and very wet year. It was alternatively wet and cold, or dry and very warm. But even when it was hot it was humid, and the vintage was interrupted by rain. It was a difficult, frustrating season from start to finish. The reward, sadly, is wine of only average-to-good quality. That there is plenty of it is, in these economically straitened times, perhaps a two-edged sword.

After a cold but dry winter, and a certain amount of difficulty with the pruning following the frost damage in April 1991, April 1992 was wet, but still cold, and the vines made a sluggish start to the growth cycle. May, however, was very warm; indeed, the vines rapidly caught up, and the flowering began eight days ahead of the 30-years' norm. June was stormy and changeable; very wet indeed. The flowering was drawn out over as much as a month. The resultant irregular maturity remained a problem for the rest of the year, but fortunately there was little *coulure* and *millérandage*. Unfortunately, though, there was an ever-present threat of rot which continued throughout the summer, even when temperatures were high. Many châteaux sprayed twice as many times as they normally do. Those that did not paid the price.

The weather continued cold and wet until 13 July, but it was thereafter warm, frequently very hot, though always rather humid, until 20 September, broken by the usual occasional thunderstorm – and one violent hailstorm on 8 August, which damaged parts of Arsac and Cantenac, and Bégadan in the Bas-Médoc.

The potential crop, however, was huge. Never before has so much *éclaircissage* (green harvesting) been practised in the top properties. Christian Moueix employed 62 people for 25 days to strip off half the bunches of grapes in his vineyards. Hubert de Bouard at L'Angélus did the same. The latter produced 42 hectolitres per hectare, while elsewhere, where there was no grape-thinning, the yield was 80. The official, authorized volume was decreed at 63 hectolitres per hectare for Bordeaux Rouge and 60 for the better *appellations*, including PLC. (In 1990 it was 66.) The harvest eventually totalled 6.26 million hectolitres of *appellation contrôlée* wine – and this, I suspect, after quite a sizeable quantity was sent for distillation.

The vintage began in good weather on 8 September for the whites, a week or more in advance of the norm, and was fully under way by the 14th. Sauvignons are crisp and delicious, certainly good, even very good. Sémillon quality is less regular. There was more rot, maturity was more uneven, and the fruit was less ripe. In general the white wines are pleasant, but are maturing quickly.

The red wine harvest was due to begin on the equinox, 21 September. Would the good weather hold up? The answer was no. The rain front which was later to cause extensive damage and even death in the southern Côtes du Rhône hit Bordeaux on the 20th. It was cloudy with only occasional drizzle until Monday, the 28th, and thenceforth there were only four days without rain until Saturday, 10 October. It was also quite cold. God did not smile on the Bordelais in 1992.

However, all was not lost. The saving grace of the 1992 harvest was, paradoxically, its size. Despite the crop-thinning, volumes were high. The encouragement to make a very severe selection was there. Moreover, many properties performed a *saignée* to balance up the ratio of liquid to solid. The result is a vintage which is softer than 1984, and fuller, but with less charm than 1987. Quite how much better than these two vintages remains to be seen after the wines are in bottle. There does not at this stage appear to be a material difference in quality between the left bank and the right, though there was more satisfaction with the Merlots than with the Cabernets, which may indicate otherwise. The dry whites are better, particularly those which are Sauvignon based. The Sauternes vintage is much like 1982 in its weather pattern. Good conditions at first, but worse after 28 September. Only those with cryo-extraction facilities have been able to salvage much.

To sum up: a very irregular vintage. Those who were in the first place able and willing to spray and spray again, and to green-harvest, and in the second place fortunate with their picking dates, have made much better wine than others. It will inevitably be proportionately at its best at the top of the hierarchy. (Not many can afford 800 pickers, as at Mouton-Rothschild.) But there is plenty of wine. Expect some agreeable bottles for drinking in 1996. You won't have to buy them until then.

THE WEATHER: 1991

Nineteen ninety-one was a very small harvest. At 2.58 million hectolitres of *appellation contrôlée* wine, it is the smallest red wine crop since 1977 and the tiniest vintage of white wine ever, and this by a very long way.

Frost towards the end of April, followed by cold weather in May, decimated the first generation of grapes. Fine weather in July and August and the first half of September encouraged hopes of a small-but-beautiful vintage like 1961. But there was rain just before the picking commenced, and further rain thereafter. The first-generation fruit, what there was of it, was ripe, even concentrated, and, if picked before it became too sodden, able to produce balanced, even praiseworthy wine. But the second generation of fruit barely reached physiological maturity, and the polyphenols therein, which produce the tannin essential for the wine's backbone, were unripe.

Paradoxically, 1991 is a vintage where those who produced the most have produced the best wine. The reason is simple: it is a question of the amount of first-generation fruit the wine-maker had at his disposal. Saint-Emilion, Pomerol and their satellites suffered most from damage. Overall the crop was 29 per cent of that of 1990. And sadly there are few wines of great interest.

Many famous châteaux have decided not to produce a *grand vin*. In the Médoc and the Graves the red wine harvest was 40 per cent of the previous vintage. And those domaines nearest to the estuary – Montrose, Cos d'Estournel, Latour, Léoville-Las-Cases, Margaux, Issan and Palmer spring to mind – have produced in many cases double that of the estates further inland. Their proximity to the Gironde alleviated the worst effects of the frost. Moreover, most of these estates were able to green-harvest the second generation of fruit in July, so not only enabling what remained to concentrate fully, but making the life of the picking team and the wine-makers behind them a lot easier when the time came to vinify the fruit.

The result therefore is a vintage of serious irregularity. It is a total contrast to 1987, the previous 'bad' vintage. In 1987 few wines – perhaps none whatsoever – are any better than quite good, but nearly all the top wines are respectable. In 1991, there are some wines which have a surprising amount of merit, but most are dilute, empty, insubstantial and forward. It is not a vintage for second wines, or for *petits châteaux*. And only at the very top levels is there anything to enthuse about.

THE BEST WINES

Saint-Estèphe: Cos d'Estournel; Montrose; Meyney.
Pauillac: Latour; Mouton-Rothschild; Pichon-Longueville, Comtesse de Lalande; Clerc-Milon; Pichon-Longueville-Baron.
Saint-Julien: Léoville-Las-Cases; Léoville-Barton; Ducru-Beaucaillou; Lagrange; Léoville-Poyferré; Saint-Pierre.
Margaux: Margaux; Palmer; Rausan-Ségla; Malescot; Du Tertre; Prieuré-Lichine; Angludet.
Graves: Haut-Brion.

1990 CLARET

Nineteen ninety ended a most remarkable Bordeaux decade. Never before had there been such a regular succession of fine vintages – only two out of ten less than very good; never before had the quantities of these fine vintages been so plentiful. In 1970 Bordeaux produced over 2 million hectolitres of *appellation contrôlée* rouge for the first time. It was considered rather excessive. In only one year in the 1980s decade was 2 million hectolitres *not* produced; and this failure, in 1984, was only by a whisker. In eight years out of ten the figure was over 3.5 million hectolitres: in three of the vintages over 4.5 million. Quantity, it would seem, is no longer inversely proportional to quality.

Following the hype which had surrounded the 1989s it was a surprise to find that when one compared the 1990s alongside the 1989s in cask that the later vintage was better. Three years on, this is still the case. The vintages are superficially similar, in that they were both early, plentiful and the products of hot and dry summers. But the 1990s are both better across the board – with certain exceptions – and more consistent at the lower levels. The tannins are riper, acidities are higher, and harmony, fruit and elegance all superior. And the vintage was cheaper. It was the cheapest in real terms since 1982, and a vintage to purchase *en primeur*.

THE WEATHER

Climatically, 1990 proved to be quite as extraordinary as 1989. It was a very mild winter, with only three light frosts between 1 November and 28 February. A heatwave in February, the thermometer on one afternoon reaching 26 degrees, produced a very early start to the vegetative cycle, the first shoots being visible by 12 March, and a prolific sortie of embryonic bunches of grapes. If it continues like this, growers were heard to say, we'll be starting the harvest on 20 August, ten days earlier even than 1989, which itself was the earliest since 1893.

The temperatures then cooled, and over the next ten days there was a little frost damage – but light, isolated and in no way on the scale which was to follow a year later. The rest of April was mild and wet, and with the benefit of all this rain the vegetation galloped ahead during a mini heatwave in the first fortnight of May, starting to flower by the week of 14 May, a full ten days ahead of 1989, and still on schedule for a 20 August harvest.

Then, right in the middle of the flowering, the weather changed. Unsettled conditions prolonged the fruit-setting. The weather was not bad enough to cause *coulure*, but sufficient to create, especially in the Cabernet grapes, an enormous variation from château to château, parcel to parcel, vine to vine, and even grape to grape. These irregular Cabernet bunches were to prove a worry right to the very end of the harvest.

The weather continued to alternate between warm and cool and wet and dry until 10th July, by which time it was clear that the harvest was going to be abundant. But if the humid weather were to continue there would be a major danger of rot. At the same time the authorities announced that the maximum harvest level for 1990, including the PLC, would be 60 hectolitres per hectare, reduced by 5 from the 1989 figure. All this encouraged many growers to perform a crop-thinning, or *éclaircissage*. Almost every property of note seems to have made a *vendange verte* in 1991. Yet even with severe crop-thinning, a conscientious cutting out of poorer-quality fruit at the time of the harvest, and, in some cases, a *saignée*, or bleeding of the vats before the fermentation commenced, yields were nudging the 60-hectolitres-per-hectare maximum. And I am talking about at perfectionist properties like Pichon-Lalande and Malescot. It seems crazy that in a temperate part of the world like Bordeaux, it should be necessary to worry about (and indeed have to absorb the expense of) restraining Nature's bounty rather than eking out her frugality, as Peter Sichel put it in his annual *Vintage Report*.

From 11 July the weather was exceptionally hot and dry. The two months of July and

August were the driest since 1961. July was the sunniest ever, and August, with an average temperature of 23.1 degrees, the hottest in Peter Sichel's records, which go back to 1928. Even though September was cool and June had been unremarkable, the 1990 summer was overall slightly hotter, slightly sunnier and slightly drier than 1989, and that vintage had been the warmest since 1949.

The extreme heat, however, occurred towards the latter half of July, reaching 40 degrees on the weekend of the 21st/22nd. The effect was to block the vegetative cycle – without water the vine simply turns itself off – delaying the onset of the *veraison*. Exposed leaves got scorched; exposed berries, where the vegetation had been thinned out to assist air circulation as a preventive anti-rot measure earlier in the month, were also scorched. If you vinify scorched berries you impart a metallic flavour to the wine, so it would become vitally necessary to cut these out at the time of the harvest.

While there were the usual odd thunderstorms in August, rainfall was barely a third of the norm and the vines continued to suffer. The more uniform Merlot grapes were looking good, especially where the soils were more water-retentive, but the Cabernets were still looking patchy. Then, thankfully, there was rain. To quote from the detailed vintage report by Bill Blatch of Vintex, to whom this account is much indebted: 'On the night of August 29th/30th, it rained hard: 10 millimetres in most places, up to 20 in the Graves, and 35 in the Entre-Deux-Mers. The whole Bordeaux vineyard, red as well as white, suddenly woke up from its lethargy and a proper ripening cycle started again.'

The white wine harvest, which had already begun, was completed during the week of 9 September, Haut-Brion collecting its Sauvignons and Sémillons on 3 September, and towards the end of this week one or two Libournais growers began to fill up a few vats of Merlot. By the following week the red wine harvest was fully under way, most Merlots being collected before a weekend of rain on 22/23 September, and most of the more competent growers then waiting until the Cabernets were fully ripe a week or so later. The harvest was prolonged, it being necessary to move the picking teams around from parcel to parcel, even to working over the same rows of vines more than once, in order to ensure that each plot was collected at an optimum state of ripeness.

Happily, not only were the grapes high in sugar, but the fruit was also physiologically ripe. This had been a problem in 1989. Moreover, apart from the 22/23 September intermission there was little interruption as a result of rain. The growers could take their time. It was not until 20 October that the weather broke. By then, even the most recalcitrant Cabernets had fully ripened and the must was happily fermenting away in the proprietor's cellars.

THE SIZE OF THE CROP

The 1990 vintage produced 4.95 million hectolitres of *appellation contrôlée* rouge, a record in modern times and higher still than 1989's 4.87 million. In 1992 this record would be once again broken, and the 5-million barrier breeched for the first time. Overall, before the elimination of surplus wine destined to be removed for distillation, the average yield in 1990 was 65 hectolitres per hectare. A table in the next chapter compares yields for 1986, 1989 and 1990. From this we can see that because the area under vine has increased, despite the overall volume, the yield per hectare is in fact less in 1990 than in 1989, and 1989 itself lower than 1986. Moreover, in the top estates, increasing emphasis is being put on green-harvesting. Top proprietors take great pains to persuade you that whatever the figures might suggest, on their own estate at least the production is kept under control.

THE WINES

One thing is sure. In 1990 the wines are a great deal more consistent then there are in 1989.

In the Libournais they are in general better in 1989 than in 1990, but there are nevertheless plenty of fine bottles to be found in the later vintage and at the lower levels less which is nondescript. In both there is a greater richness and a concentration than in any other vintage since 1982.

Moreover, some estates are making much better wine than a decade ago. Whole *appellations*, such as the Côtes de Francs, Castillon, Fronsac and Canon-Fronsac, have made a great leap forward. Properties such as Le Tertre-Rôteboeuf have appeared seemingly from nowhere. At Angélus, Pavie-Decesse, La Serre, Troplong-Mondot and Clos-Saint-Martin, among the Saint-Emilion *grands crus classés*, at the *premiers crus* of Beauséjour-Duffau-Lagarrosse, Clos-Fourtet and Trottevieille, and at Beauregard, Clinet, L'Eglise-Clinet, Gazin and La Pointe in Pomerol, to cite the major examples, the wines have more finesse, more definition and a better balance today than they did in 1982 and are infinitely to be preferred. Great progress has been made. And the vines, largely planted following the February 1956 frost, are now at their optimum age. These are exciting times.

The explanation for this greater regularity in 1990 can be found in the weather pattern; less stress on the vines, greater balance and riper tannins in the must, if nevertheless acidities which are not in general any higher; and overall, higher amounts of harmony and finesse and therefore length on the palate, interest and depth of character.

For the best wines, of course, you have to select carefully between those who reduced their total harvest – forget the protestations of how severe the selection was in the creation of the *grand vin*, though this too obviously plays an important role – and those who produced up to the limit. As always, at the top there are some very exciting wines. But the humdrum estates have produced wine which is, well, humdrum.

Fronsac and Canon-Fronsac
As in 1989 the Fronsacs are good and consistent. Canon-Moueix and Canon itself are very good indeed. Dalem, corked below, is also praiseworthy. By and large these wines are rather better value than the lower echelons in Saint-Emilion and Pomerol.

Saint-Emilion
Among the *grands crus classés* there is a lot of dross, but some gems stand out: Dassault, Canon-La-Gaffelière, Fonroque, Grand-Mayne, Larmande, Troplong-Mondot and the not-yet-classed Le Tertre-Rôteboeuf. L'Angélus is markedly oaky at present but is certainly very good. L'Arrosée and La Dominique, though not beneath contempt, are disappointing, given their reputation. The plums among the *premiers crus* are Pavie and Canon and of course Cheval-Blanc. Beauséjour-Duffau-Lagarrosse and Trottevieille are better than their recent performances would suggest. Belair seems weak; Ausone not up to first growth standard. Overall more consistent and almost as good as 1989.

Pomerol
Again, at the lower end of the scale there are rather too many wines which are somewhat dilute but at the top of the hierarchy much to admire. Among the second division La Grave-à-Pomerol and Plince stand out, as do Bon-Pasteur and L'Enclos. All the first division wines are very good, some very exciting indeed: Pétrus, obviously, but also Vieux Château Certan and Trotanoy. Many wines are as good as they were in 1989.

Graves
While only Haut-Brion can really be termed outstanding, the top Graves are commendable, and rather better than they are in 1989, though La Mission lacks real concentration. Nevertheless both here and in Margaux it is arguable that 1988 is better than both 1990 and 1989 overall.

Margaux

As always, the majority of the *crus classés* of Margaux are disappointing. Indeed after Palmer (much better than in 1989) and Margaux itself the consumer is better off with Monbrison, Angludet and Labégorce-Zédé. Why should there be this continual inconsistency in Margaux?

Saint-Julien

Very fine at Las-Cases (though the 1989 is better still) and at Barton; almost as good at Poyferré; inconsistent bottles at Ducru-Beaucaillou; disappointment at Gruaud-Larose and Talbot, Saint-Pierre and Gloria. The 1990 pattern follows that of 1989 but is overall rather more successful. Lagrange is very good, though a bit adolescent at present. Clos du Marquis is remarkably good for a second wine.

Pauillac

Latour is the wine of the vintage: a 1990 which is indisputably great. Pichon-Baron is as good as Lafite, and very exciting. Mouton and its stable companions D'Armailhac and Clerc-Milon are a little disappointing. Haut-Bages-Libéral, Batailley and, surprise, surprise, Lynch-Moussas, are good and not expensive. With the exception of Mouton and its cousins, once again these 1990s are better than the 1989s.

Saint-Estèphe

The 1990 Saint-Estèphes are rather better than the 1989s: the wines have much better balance and a lot more class. Cos d'Estournel and Montrose are the best: Haut-Marbuzet rich and luscious; Cos-Labory harmonious and pretty; only Calon-Ségur, though rich and concentrated, is a little rustic.

THE MARKET

Despite the third good vintage in a row, despite a good *en primeur* campaign for the 1988s and a record one for the 1989s, and despite the vintage not having originally been trumpeted as loudly as its predecessor, the 1990s sold well. One of the factors was a decrease in prices.

The 1989s had opened at the highest prices yet, though less in real terms than those of the 1985s. A year later the first Growths had declined from 225 to 230 francs to 205. Cos d'Estournel was at 100 as opposed to 115; Pape-Clément at 80 rather than 93; La Lagune down from 55 to 52; Chasse-Spleen 50 from 55; the up-and-coming *bourgeois* Sénéjac 23.50 from 26. All these made fine 1990s. Similar reductions were applied in the Libournais, with the *négociant* J.P. Moueix reducing the prices of the splendid clutch of wines in its portfolio by an average of 13 per cent.

The effect was a reduction of anything up to 20 per cent in the ex-cellars price asked by British *en primeur* wine-merchants. Jasper Morris MW of Morris and Verdin published the following interesting table in his opening offer, comparing and indexing his firm's ex-cellar price of Château La Lagune over the years.

	1983	1984	1985	1986	1988	1989	1990
Ex-cellar Price (£)	59	85	100	92	80	110	89
Indexed Price	59	80	91	81	62	85	63

Here is another fascinating table illustrating the price movements of four fashionable wines. These were the opening prices offered by a leading Bordeaux *négociant* to his customers in Britain (prices in French francs).

	Labégorce	La Lagune	Cos d'Estournel	Pichon-Lalande
1982	24.55	39.75	68.50	82.00
1983	28.40	50.85	70.00	102.00

1984	33.35	66.70	102.00	120.00
1985	42.35	70.60	102.00	132.00
1986	40.50	60.50	97.50	113.00
1987	n/a	n/a	n/a	n/a
1988	44.00	59.00	103.00	120.00
1989	55.00	74.00	140.00	155.00
1990	52.50	*64.00	115.00	115.00

* 100 case orders FF 61.00

I have in the past accused certain château proprietors of excessive greed and the trade who kowtowed to them of pusillanimity. I have argued that there was no economic sense in investing in stock at prices which showed no possibility of gain in the short to medium term. Certainly not with the high interest rates which persist.

In the summer of 1991 the position was different. Overall, the 1990 vintage was the cheapest in real terms for a quality year since 1982. I advised my readers to invest in it, and with the relative disappointments of the next three vintages anyone who took my advice made a sensible move. The best of the 1990s will become the gems of anyone's cellar.

THE TASTING

In January 1994, as is our custom, a group of British wine professionals met over three days at The Crown, Southwold, headquarters of Adnams Wine Merchants, to cast a comprehensive look at the 1990s, now safely in bottle. Here are my notes. I have filled in one or two gaps from notes taken during tastings in the USA in the fall of 1993.

	Optimum Drinking	Mark out of 20

CÔTES DE BOURG

Roc-de-Cambes 1997–2007 14.0
Good colour. Full, plump nose. Medium to medium-full body. Good ripe tannins. Balanced and stylish, with nicely ripe fruit and a touch of oak. Finishes well. Even has class. Very good for this *appellation*.

FRONSAC AND CÔTES-CANON-FRONSAC

Barrabaque 1995–1999 12.0
Medium-full colour. Lightish nose, not a lot of depth. Medium body. Not much structure. Nor very long. A little dull. Only quite good.

Canon-de-Brem 1995–2004 14.0
Good colour. Ripe nose. Very mulberry-raspberry. Good freshness. Good style. Medium body. Just a little tannin. Balanced and well-made. Good fruit. Good stuff and good value.

Canon-Moueix 1996–2006 16.0
Good colour. Firm, rich, concentrated, classy nose. This is very good. Medium-full, old-viney creaminess. Lovely fruit. More Merlot and a lot more character than Canon-de-Brem. Better grip. More depth. Classy. Very good.

de Carles 1996–2005 14.0
Very good colour. Plump nose, but not as much dimension as many of these other Fronsacs. Better

on the palate though. Medium to medium-full. Some oak. Good acidity. Ripe, long, harmonious and attractive. Good.

Dalem — —
Very good colour. Both bottles corked.

Fontenil 1996–2005 13.5
Good colour. Ripe, plump, round nose. Lots of soft fruit here. Gently oaky, obviously Merlot-based. Medium body. Opulent and fruity. Generous and easy to drink. Good for a Fronsac.

Mazeris-Bellevue 1995–2000 12.5
Good colour. Soft nose, a little loose-knit perhaps. Medium body. A little flat. Quite fruity, but lacks a little zip and class.

Moulin-Haut-Laroque 1996–2004 13.5
Good colour. Plump, ripe nose. Medium to medium-full, ripe and balanced, both blackberry and fruit-cake here. Not much class but well made.

Moulin-Pey-Labrie 1996–2002 13.5
Good colour. Rich nose, quite closed. But good depth. Medium to medium-full. Touch of new oak. Not much structure, but attractively fruity.

La Rousselle 1995–1999 12.0
Good colour. Plump, round nose but not a lot of depth. Medium body. Ripe and fruit-cakey on the attack but not a lot underneath. Unexciting.

Vieille-Curé 1995–2000 13.0
Medium-full colour. Just a touch forced on the

nose. A little rustic. Medium body. A touch stringy. Reasonable fruit but lacks a little finesse. Not bad.

Villars 1996–2004 13.0

Good colour. Slightly backward, slightly austere nose, but good ripe fruit nevertheless. Medium to medium-full. Some tannin. A little adolescent at present. Balanced but lacks a little excitement.

SAINT-EMILION GRANDS CRUS CLASSÉS

L'Arrosée 1996–2003 14.0

Good colour. Soft, plump nose. Not the amount of new oak there usually is in L'Arrosée. Medium to medium-full. Good acidity and attractive fruit. But rather forward. More oaky as it developed. .

Beau-Séjour-Bécot 1996–2005 14.5

Good colour. Ripe, attractive nose if without a lot of backbone and depth. Medium to medium-full. Some oak. A pleasant aspect of digestive biscuits. Good acidity but a lack of real concentration. Yet good quality and a positive finish.

Canon-La-Gaffelière 1998–2012 15.5

Good colour. Elegant poised fruit, not as substantial as Troplong, but really quite new oaky. On the palate medium-full, balanced, stylish and composed. A very well made example.

Chauvin 1996–2000 13.0

Medium-full colour. A little over-ripe, perhaps alcoholic on the nose. Raisinny and lacking grip. Lighter than most. Rather thin. Not yet too dry but it will get astringent. Already a bit attenuated.

Clos-des-Jacobins 1996–2002 12.5

Medium-full colour. Slightly vegetal on the nose. Medium to medium-full. A touch of oak. But a lack of style and generosity. Good acidity though.

Clos de L'Oratoire 1995–1999 12.0

Good colour. Quite developed nose, with some SO2 and H2S. Open and unstylish. No backbone, no grip. The fruit is ripe but it is already a bit astringent. No future.

Clos-Saint-Martin 1996–2008 15.5

Good colour. Good new oak on the nose here. Medium to medium-full. Generous, oaky, quite concentrated. Balanced. This has depth and potential and a very good finish. Good plus.

La Clotte 1996–2002 13.5

Good colour. The nose lacks class. Weedy and rustic. On the palate a curate's egg mixture of good ripe *matière première*, some new oak, but unclassy elements as well. Yet there is grip.

Dassault 1996–2007 15.0

Good colour. Balanced but a bit closed on the nose. Medium to medium-full. Good oak. Good grip. This is well made, fresh, ripe and fruity. Best

of all on the finish, which is long and complex, even quite classy. Good.

La Dominique 1996–2003 14.0

Good colour. Ample, oaky nose. But how much concentration underneath? Pleasant attack. Quite a high toast. Medium to medium-full. Reasonable balance. But lacks real depth and dimension. Quite good.

Faurie-de-Souchard 1995–1999 11.5

Medium-full colour. Somewhat weedy on the nose. This will soon get rustic. Medium body. Not much tannin and not much style. Tails off at the end. Won't make old bones.

Fonplégade 1995–2001 13.0

Good colour. Fruity nose, but a lack of backbone and style. As it developed a smell of sultanas. Medium body. Reasonable acidity but not a lot of tannin. And the wine lacks class and dimension. Not bad at best.

Fonroque 1997–2007 15,0

Good colour. Ample ripe Merlot nose. Very Moueix. On the palate certainly rich, almost over-ripe, but not too raisinny and by no means lacking grip. Medium-full. Very plump. Good length. Good.

Grand-Mayne 1998–2012 15.5

Medium-full colour. Ripe essentially Merlot fruit, plump and attractive. Medium-full body. Positive, fresh, well made. This is a good example. Very well balanced. A generous wine.

Grand-Pontet 1995–1999 11.0

Good colour. A bit weedy and unstylish on the nose. But rather astringent on the palate. Medium body. This is poor.

Guardet-Saint-Julien 1995–1998 11.5

Good colour. Lacks class and lacks structure on the nose. Slightly weedy Merlot, as usual. Very watery at the end. Medium body. No future.

Haut-Sarpe 1996–2001 13.0

Good colour. Rather rustic and reductive on the nose. Medium-full body. Some grip and some tannin. A bit lumpy. Finish is positive. Not bad.

Larcis-Ducasse 1995–2000 13.0

Very good colour. Fat and quite structured on the nose. But rather rustic. On the palate medium body. A touch of oak. Somewhat coarse and a suspicion of astringency at the end. Not bad at best.

Larmande 1998–2015 17.0

Medium-full colour. Good rich nose. Old-viney, low *rendement* concentration here. Medium-full. Classy, balanced, composed. This is a lovely example. It has real generosity and class. Very good indeed. Very complex. Very long.

Laroze 1996–2003 13.5

Good colour. A little forced and vegetal on the

nose. Better on the palate. Some substance. Some grip. Some oak. It lacks a bit of style. But it is not bad and the finish is positive.

Moulin-du-Cadet 1996–2004 14.5
Medium-full colour. Closed nose. A touch of reduction at first. Good substance here. Rich, some tannin. Good grip. This has depth. At present it is a little dumb. And perhaps not that exciting. But at least quite good plus.

Pavie-Decesse 1998–2010 15.0
Good colour. Ample Merlot nose. Ripe but lacks a little personality. Medium-full. A little oaky. Good plump ripe fruit, even rich. Balanced. But a little zip and character are missing.

Pavie-Macquin 1996–2008 15.0
Medium to medium-full colour. Good ripe nose. Concentrated, old-viney even. A little tight. Not obviously 80 per cent Merlot. Medium to medium-full. Ripe, individual. Balanced. Rather better than it showed in cask. Good thrust on the follow-through. Good concentration. Very good.

Ripeau 1995–1999 12.5
Medium-full colour. Lightish nose. Not much depth or backbone. Medium body. No structure. Watery at the end. Some pleasant fruit but this has no future. Will get coarse and astringent.

La Serre 1997–2009 14.0
Good colour. Smooth, round, ripe and oaky. Attractive. Good start, but a little one-dimensional on the follow-through. Medium body. Fruity. Gentle. Quite good, but it lacks a little drive. Yet elegant.

Soutard 1996–2001 13.0
Medium-full colour. Not as solid as usual. But not as concentrated as usual either. Very ripe. But a little sweet and superficial. Lacks zip and class. This is a bit of a disappointment. Forward too.

Le Tertre-Rôteboeuf 1999–2019 17.0
Good colour. Fine, very rich and intense nose. Lovely fruit here and plenty of depth. New oaky. Fullish. Good ripe tannins but quite a lot of power here. On the finish rich, complete and very old-viney in its concentration. Lovely finish. Very good indeed.

La Tour-du-Pin-Figeac (Moueix)
1995–2000 13.0
Medium-full colour. Lacks a bit of structure – as well as class – on the nose. Medium body. Some oak. But a lack of zip. And the wine is a bit short. Even a bit dilute at the end.

La Tour-Figeac 1995–1999 11.5
Good colour. Smells of raisins. Medium body. Over-ripe. Lacks grip. Already a bit astringent. No future here.

Troplong-Mondot 1998–2015 17.0
Good colour. Rich, concentrated and very new oaky on the nose. If it is not over-oaked this is very good indeed. Full, very good grip. Lovely concentrated, old-viney fruit. The finish is intense and classy and very promising. Backward though.

SAINT-EMILION *PREMIERS GRANDS CRUS CLASSÉS*

Ausone 1997–2009 16.5
Good colour. This is a lot better than Belair (thank God!). Rich and concentrated and intense, and quite oaky, on the nose. But compared with, say, Pavie, let alone Cheval-Blanc, this lacks real intensity and power of flavour.

Beauséjour-Duffau-Lagarrosse
1999–2015 16.5
Good colour. Firm, full, slightly austere but very good on the nose. Backward though. Fullish. Quite tannic. But very ripe and rich. A bit tough at present on the attack but the finish is long and promising. Very good plus.

Belair 1997–2005 14.0
Good colour. Pretty nose but lacks a little intensity. Only medium to medium-full body. Has fruit and balance but no concentration, no real grip. Tails off a bit on the palate. A disappointment.

Canon 2000–2017 18.0
Fullish colour. Firm nose. Closed but concentrated. Plenty of depth here. Fullish, very lovely concentrated fruit. More structure and less accessible than Pavie. But very well-balanced again. Very lovely, plummy fruit. Very long. Very fine.

Cheval-Blanc 1999–2020 plus 19.5
Good colour. Splendid nose. Very, very rich. Very, very composed and harmonious. Classy. Oaky. Intense. Full, beautifully composed. Very good oak integration. Very complex. A luscious wine. Marvellous balance. Very, very long and classy. Better than Pétrus.

Clos-Fourtet 1997–2006 14.5
Good colour. Quite oaky on the nose but not a lot of concentration or substance underneath. Good attack, plump and oaky. But lacks real grip and intensity. A bit superficial. Yet good.

Figeac 1997–2014 16.0
Good colour. Ample and ripe on the nose but a slight metallic/herbal streak. On the palate medium-full. Ripe, rich and stylish. Also quite concentrated. Yet not intense as Pavie. Lacks just that extra dimension and intensity. Very good at best. Should have been more concentrated.

La Gaffelière 1998–2012 15.0
Medium-full colour. Ripe Merlot fruit. Balanced but lacks a little depth and excitement. Medium-full, balanced, ripe, competent. But one and a half dimensions only. Finishes long.

Magdelaine   1998–2015   17.5

Good colour. Very ample and plump on the nose. Very Merlot. Fullish. Intense. Concentrated. Good acidity. This is opulent and potentially velvety. Very long. Fine.

Pavie   1998–2018   18.0

Good colour. Quite oaky on the nose, but very full and rich, fat, concentrated and intense. Lovely. Fullish on the palate. Very concentrated and intense. Lovely rich elegant fruit. This has a lot of depth and a very fine voluptuous finish.

Trottevieille   1997–2009   16.0

Medium-full colour. Not a blockbuster but fresh, stylish, ripe and complex on the nose. Medium-full body. It lacks a bit of strength and intensity on the palate. But there is balance and elegance here. Very good. But tails off just a bit at the end compared with Pavie.

POMEROL

Beauregard   1998–2016   16.0

Medium-full colour. Fullish, rich, ample nose. Nice firm understructure and grip here. Good tannins. Masculine. Fullish. Good acidity. Long. Needs time. But very good. A nice austerity.

Bonalgue   1996–2000   13.0

Good colour. Slightly closed nose. A bit tanky. Not a lot of substance here or much class and character. Yet reasonable balance. Not bad.

Le Bon-Pasteur   1998–2012   15.0

Good colour. Plump nose. A little 'hot'. Fullish, ample, ripe and rich. Good grip and freshness. Ripe tannins. Shows well. Very Merlot.

Bourgneuf-Vayron   1996–2000   13.0

Good colour. Lacks class on the nose. Some *vin de presse* or over-maceration. Rustic and coarse on the palate. Medium to medium-full body. Slightly chocolatey. Slightly astringent at the end. Not much enjoyment here.

La Cabanne   1996–2003   14.0

Good colour. Fresh and reasonably structured, but not a lot of real personality. Medium to medium-full. Good fruity attack, but tails off a bit thereafter. A pity! Because it is not over-ripe as many of these are. Quite good.

Certan-de-May   1999–2018   17.5

Good colour. The nose has gone into its shell a little. But concentrated, fat and complete. Full and rich and oaky on the palate. Very good grip. This is a fine example. Classy and complex. Very lovely long finish.

Certan-Giraud   1996–2004   14.0

Medium-full colour. Over-ripe, loose-knit nose. Not too unbalanced or weedy. Indeed the fruit is pleasant. But one-dimensional. Medium body. Only quite good.

Clinet   1999–2017   16.5

Good colour. Firm, rich, masculine nose. Good new oak. Full, ripe, meaty and concentrated on the palate. Nicely austere. Very good grip. This is a wine of real flair and depth. Marvellous fruit. Very long. Very good plus.

Clos-du-Clocher   1995–1998   11.0

Medium-full colour. Resinny nose. Thin. Astringent. Quite ripe, even a bit sweet. But no class and no future.

Clos du Vieux-Plateau-Certan

Medium-full colour. One bottle only. And it was corked.

Clos L'Eglise   1998–2008   14.5

Good colour. Ample nose. But a little alcoholic. Fullish, a touch stewed. A little astringent. And a touch inelegant. Quite good but it doesn't sing. Yet the finish is positive.

L'Enclos   1997–2009   15.5

Good colour. Composed, balanced fruity nose without being a wine of great substance and depth. Medium and medium-full. Ripe, balanced and stylish. The fruit has a lot of charm. Finishes well.

La Conseillante   1997–2004   16.5

Good colour. Elegant, quite rich, balanced nose. Class here. Medium to medium-full. Not a blockbuster but very good intensity and length. Lovely fruit. Not great but very good plus.

La Croix   1995–1998   11.5

Good colour. Plump, reasonable acidity. But not much style. Medium body. Increasingly rustic and astringent as it developed.

La Croix-de-Gay   1996–2004   14.5

Medium-full colour. Quite oaky on the nose. Reasonably fresh. Medium body. Good freshness. This is a nice plump, fruity, medium-range Pomerol with a positive finish. Quite good plus.

Domaine de l'Eglise   1995–2000   13.0

Medium-full colour. Slightly over-ripe on the nose, but some depth. Medium body. Slightly sweet. Slightly raisinny, but something here. Reasonably positive.

L'Evangile   1999–2018   18.0

Good colour. Full but not dense on the nose. Oaky. Fullish on the palate. Very ripe tannins. Very good grip. This has a lot more depth and concentration than La Conseillante. Long. Plenty of dimension. Very fine.

Feytit-Clinet   1995–1999   12.5

Medium-full colour. A little closed and unforthcoming on the nose. Slightly hard. On the palate rather short and watery. Disappointing for a J.P Moueix wine.

La Fleur-de-Gay   1996–2008   15.5

Good colour. Oaky nose. Reasonable substance

on the palate here. Medium to medium-full. Good grip. Quite rich and even quite concentrated at the end. Long. Good plus.

La Fleur-Gazin   1995–1999   12.5

Good colour. Soft, pleasant Merlot nose. On the palate a little loose-knit. Slightly astringent at the end. Disappointing for a J.P Moueix wine.

Le Gay   1996–2002   13.5

Good colour. Smells a bit of the stems. A little lumpy. On the palate it really doesn't have the depth and substance it normally has. And there is a lack of class. Reasonable grip though.

Gazin   1998–2012   16.0

Good colour. Lovely stylish balanced fruit here on the nose. Medium-full, ripe, straightforwardly fruity but charming and elegant. Fresh. Balanced. Long. Very good.

La Grave-à-Pomerol   1996–2004   15.0

Good colour. Plump, ripe, ample nose. Good Merlot fruit. If not a lot of dimension. Medium to medium-full. Rich, balanced and spicy. Good tannin. Good finish. A little too aromatic to have real class but better than most. Good.

Haut-Maillet   1996–2003   14.5

Good colour. Round, plump. ripe nose. This is a good example of a lesser Pomerol. Balanced, generous. Medium body. Long finish. Well-made.

Lafleur   1999–2015   17.0

Good colour. Quite a lot of alcohol on the nose. More than Pétrus. Big and full and tannic. But the alcohol gives the impression of a bit of oxidization, and it seems a little stewed and astringent. Yet on the finish the wine opens out. Adolescent at present. Very good but today it doesn't sing.

Lafleur-Pétrus   1998–2017   17.5

Good colour. This seems riper and more stylish and concentrated than Latour-à-Pomerol. More substance. Very ripe and rich. Fullish. Intense and long and lovely.

Lagrange   1996–2004   14.0

Good colour. Ripe, even a touch over-ripe on the nose. Some substance, indeed a little four-square perhaps. Medium to medium-full. Good ripe tannins. Chocolatey in flavour, plus fruit cake. This lacks a little zip and class. But quite good.

Latour-à-Pomerol   1997–2014   17.0

Good colour. Good fruit but not exceptional depth on the nose. Better on the palate. Ripe and concentrated and oaky. Medium-full. Very good grip. This has style and depth. Very good fruit. Lots of charm.

Mazeyres   1996–2001   13.0

Medium-full colour. Yet another wine that smells a bit raisinny. On the palate medium to medium-

full. Quite a good attack but a bit astringent at the end. Lacks zip. Not bad though.

Montviel   1995–1998   11.0

Medium-full colour. Smells of sultanas, as do many of these lesser Libournais. Astringent on the palate. Slightly chocolatey. But very short.

Moulinet   1995–2001   13.5

Good colour. Ripe nose. Quite fresh. But not a lot of depth or dimension. This is a bit watery on the palate. Yet, as yet, has charm. Not bad plus.

Pensées de Lafleur   1995–1998   11.0

Medium-full colour. Smells of raisins. A bit weedy, really. Astringent. Short. Disappointing – even for a second wine.

Pétrus   2000–2020 plus   19.0

Good colour. Very, very concentrated nose. A lot of structure but a lot of depth. Has closed in since I saw it last six months previously. Full. Very new oaky – more so than usual – backward, rich, full, powerful and intense. Very fine finish.

Le Pin   1998–2012   17.0

Medium-full colour. Concentrated Merlot fruit, without the structure of Pétrus, for instance. Medium-full, very mellow, ripe, oaky and attractive. But, compared with Vieux Château Certan or L'Evangile a little obvious. Yet undeniably well-made and seductive.

Plince   1996–2006   15.0

Good colour. Good richness and substance here on the nose. Medium to medium-full. Some tannin. Plump ripe Merlot fruit. Good grip. This has a positive finish. Well-made. Good but not enough personality for better than that.

Prieurs-de-la-Commanderie

1996–2003   14.0

Medium-full colour. Toasted oak on the nose. Ripe. But it lacks a little zip. Medium body. Quite pretty. Reasonably balanced. But it lacks real excitement.

Rouget   1995–1998   11.0

Medium-full colour. Slightly over-ripe and sweaty on the nose. Medium body. Already astringent. No future here.

de Sales   1995–2002   14.0

Medium to medium-full colour. Soft nose. Slightly attenuated Merlot. Medium body. As much astringent as tannic. Ripe and sweet. Quite developed. Reasonable grip. Pretty but lacks a little harmony and class.

Taillefer   1995–1998   11.0

Good colour. Slightly raisinny on the nose. On the palate rather watery and short, and became more so as it developed. Nothing here.

Trotanoy   1998–2017   18.5

Good colour. Very ample and rich on the nose.

Lovely fruit on both nose and palate. Full, intense, classy and very concentrated, especially at the end. Very fine quality.

Vieux Château Certan
1999–2000 plus   18.5
Good colour. A wine of real concentration and depth here, and lovely harmonious fruit. Full, very, very concentrated and intense. Huge concentration of fruit. This is most impressive. Very, very long and lovely. Splendid finish. Excellent.

Vray-Croix-de-Gay   1997–2002   12.5
Good colour. Ample nose. Very ripe. Chocolatey aspects. This is a little unbalanced. More astringency than tannin. Medium-full. Slightly spicy. I don't think this will age well. Some reduction.

GRAVES

Bouscaut   1999–2008   14.0
Good colour. Quite ripe and balanced on the nose but a slight absence of real personality and class. On the palate medium to medium-full. A little astringent. But reasonable grip and ripe fruit. Quite good.

Domaine de Chevalier   1997–2015   17.0
Good colour. Gentle and stylish as always. But a lack of real depth and complexity on the nose. On the palate not too light weight. There is intensity here. And as usual, very good fruit and subtlety and breed. Round, ripe. Long. Fine.

de Fieuzal   1998–2013   15.5
Good colour. The nose has a whiff of burnt charcoal. Quite sturdy in the tannic sense on the palate. Medium-full. Ripe. Good grip. A little burly as Fieuzal always is when it's young, but good depth and concentration, and a ripe, plump, positive finish.

Haut-Bailly   1998–2014   15.5
Good colour. Plump, ripe, balanced nose. But seems to lack a little flair and breed. On the palate fullish. Good grip, gently oaky. Very attractive. Long, indeed complex at the end. Good plus.

Haut-Brion   1999–2020 plus   19.0
Good colour. Subtle, lovely nose. Not nearly as oaky as the Margaux for instance. More laid-back. Very complex and harmonious. Clearly head and shoulders above the rest of the Graves. This is really classy and complex. Intense. Very lovely.

La Mission-Haut-Brion   1997–2012   16.0
Good colour. As often, a slightly vegetal/grassy touch on the nose, as if it was Cabernet Franc rather than Cabernet Sauvignon. On the palate only medium-full. Some oak. Ripe, but it lacks real concentration and real grip. Yet it is balanced enough. But a lack of excitement for La Mission.

Pape-Clément   1998–2014   16.0
Good colour. A little closed on the nose. Plump, some oak but a little adolescent. Better on the palate. Fullish, a little robust, but rich and meaty. And with good grip too. The finish is opulent, ripe and long. But no better than very good.

La Tour-Martillac   1996–2006   15.0
Good colour. Soft nose. Clean and plump. Not herbaceous. Medium body. This is ripe and elegant, but will come forward reasonably soon.

HAUT-MÉDOC

Cantemerle   1996–2002   13.0
Good colour. Soft nose. A little lean and vegetal. Medium body. Slightly astringent on the palate. Pleasantly fruity but lacks grip and depth. Will get attenuated. Only fair.

Chasse-Spleen   1998–2014   15.0
Good colour. More adolescent on the nose than Poujeaux. Opulent and fat, a touch spicy. But not as classy. Full, slightly lumpy, slightly untogether. Rich though, and balanced. But it hasn't the class and harmony of Poujeaux. Good to good plus.

La Lagune   1999–2016   16.5
Very good colour. Rich, full, fat, oaky nose. Plenty of depth. Fullish, very good grip. Ripe tannins. Well-made, multidimensional and very good.

Poujeaux   1997–2014   15.5
Good colour. Ripe, good oak underpinning. Stylish. Good concentration here without being a blockbuster. Fullish, composed, lovely balanced fruit. Rich. Long. Very good. Better than Chasse-Spleen this year.

Sociando-Mallet   1998–2016   16.0
Very good colour. Flamboyant oaky nose, but not an excessive toast. And plenty of wine here as well. Fullish, good tannins, good grip. This has depth and balance. Much fresher and more stylish than most. Very good.

MARGAUX

d'Angludet   1998–2014   15.0
Good colour. Lighter on the nose than Monbrison. Ripe, plump, very good fruit. On the palate medium to medium-full. A little tannin. This has more character than Monbrison but a little less substance and fat. Finishes long though. Good.

Boyd-Cantenac   1998–2012   12.0
Good colour. Good rich nose. Firm but no undue density. Like its stable-mate Pouget this is very ripe, but underneath a certain amount of the usual solidity, and very astringent at the end.

Giscours   1995–1998   11.0
Good colour. Soft, indeed a little weak on the nose. Forward. On the palate light, thin, weak and attenuated. No future. Poor.

d'Issan   1996–2001   13.0
Good colour. Soft nose. Ripe but lacks a little

freshness and zip. Reasonable attack. Medium to medium-full body. But it is a bit superficial. There is not enough grip or backbone.

Kirwan   1997–2006   13.0
Very good colour. Not much on the nose. Slightly vegetal, even a little hint of manure. Medium body. A little astringent at the end. Lacks grip and concentration. Ripe but no zip. Unexciting.

Labégorce-Zédé   1998–2014   15.5
Good colour. Balanced, stylish, complex nose. Not a blockbuster though. Medium bodied. Ripe and balanced. Lovely supple fruit and good fruit and good grip. Long, stylish, subtle. Good plus.

Lascombes   1998–2015   15.0
Good colour. Plump nose. A little sweaty. Some H2S. Fullish, good grip. Ripe tannins. But lack of sophistication to the fruit. Yet the finish is positive. Good but not great.

Malescot-Saint-Exupéry 1998–2018   15.5
Very good colour. The nose a bit closed at present. Ripe and oaky; rich and concentrated. Full, concentrated, rich and with plenty of depth. A touch adolescent. But the finish is long and promising. This is a complex wine. Good plus.

Margaux   1999–2020   18.5
Very good colour. Quite full nose, distinctly oaky in comparison with the rest of these Margaux. Only this and the Palmer, in this section, have real breed. This is the bigger wine. Oaky and rich. Flamboyant rather than subtle. But *plus fin*. The finish is very lovely.

Marquis-de-Terme   1997–2007   13.5
Good colour. Solid nose. A little over-macerated perhaps. On the palate only medium body. A touch vegetal. Lacks concentration. Not short. Just a bit one-dimensional. Dull.

Monbrison   1998–2012   14.5
Very good colour. Full, meaty nose. Firm but not dense. Medium-full. Good oaky base. Plump, fruity and balanced. Well-made. A slight absence of personality, so no better than quite good plus.

Palmer   1997–2017   17.5
Very good colour. Very good nose. Fragrant and classy. Gently oaky. Subtle and complex. This is fine. Clearly the second best Margaux – as usual. Balanced. Fullish, very harmonious. Lovely multi-dimensional fruit. Very long.

Pavillon Rouge du Margaux
                          1997–2012   16.0
Good colour. Good, firm, ripe, oaky nose. Medium-full, poised, stylish, very good plump fruit, beautifully balanced. Very good.

Pouget   1998–2012   12.0
Good colour. Rather dense and solid on the nose. Not much grace and refinement here. A little

tough but certainly ripe. Unbalanced and unstylish. Rather astringent at the end.

Prieuré-Lichine   1997–2007   14.0
Good colour. Competent fruit. Well-made. But it lacks a little class on the nose. Medium to medium-full. Just a little astringent. Plump and reasonably balanced but a little unexciting.

Rausan-Ségla   1997–2012   15.0
Very good colour. Plenty of class and concentration here on the nose. A little closed, but composed and gently oaky. Medium-full. Ripe. Good tannins. Just a little over-ripe and sweet for really exciting. Lacks, ultimately, a little freshness as well. Not as good as it seemed to be in cask.

Ségla   1996–2000   12.5
Good colour. The second wine of Château Rausan-Ségla. Soft fruit nose. Lightish, a little over-ripe and not very stylish. Not bad for a second wine but nowhere near Clos du Marquis standards. Will get attenuated.

du Tertre   1997–2007   13.5
Medium-full colour. Just a little loose and vegetal on the nose. Medium body. Lacks a little zip so a bit astringent at the end. Lacks concentration too.

SAINT-JULIEN

Beychevelle   1998–2015   15.5
Good colour. Good nose. But an absence of real concentration and style. Slightly lumpy. Fullish, nicely ripe and basically well-balanced and quite intense. Good long finish. Just lacks a little real flair. Good plus, though.

Branaire   1997–2008   14.0
Good colour. Firm nose. Quite substantial. Lacks a little grace perhaps. Fullish. Ripe but slightly four-square. Some tannin but also a little astringent. Adolescent but a lack of real excitement.

Clos du Marquis   1997–2009   15.5
Good colour. Good nose. Ripe and blackcurranty. Not a blockbuster but a lovely harmony and very fine fruit. Medium to medium-full. Breed here. Very good indeed for a second wine.

Ducru-Beaucaillou   1998–2015   17.5/0
Good colour. Slightly musty and tainted on the nose. Fullish, rich, backward and very concentrated underneath. Good intensity and fine quality. I have had a number of tainted bottles of this.

Gloria   1997–2007   13.0
Good colour. Good Cabernet but a little dry and inflexible on the nose. Lacks flesh and generosity. Medium to medium-full body. Ripe and stylish on the one hand but a little dry and slightly stewed on the other. Quite good at best. Lacks style.

Gruaud-Larose   1997–2007   13.5
Good colour. Sweet nose, like the Talbot. A little more backbone. But again a lack of style. On the

palate a dog's dinner of the vegetal, the lean and the rustic. Marginally better than Talbot but very unexciting.

Lagrange   1998–2015   16.0

Good colour. Rich, backward, very Cabernet. Lots of depth here. Fullish, good oak, very good grip. This is ripe and concentrated and fat and ample. Lovely fruit. Very good plus. Slightly adolescent at present.

Lalande-Borie   1996–2000   12.5

Good colour. A little weak-kneed and loose-knit on the nose. Quite evidently a large vintage. Lacks backbone. A bit dilute. Even attenuated. The fruit is reasonably stylish and fresh at present. But not for long. Lightish. Little tannin.

Langoa-Barton   1997–2013   16.0

Good colour. Charming, elegant, balanced Cabernet. Very typical Saint-Julien. Not a blockbuster. Medium-full. Ripe, oaky, rich and harmonious. A lovely example. Very elegant.

Léoville-Barton   1999–2020 plus   18.5

Good colour. Full, rich, intense, nicely backward. Very good fruit. Full, tannic, very rich. Good new oak. This is concentrated and intense and very classy. A lovely example. Really ripe and complex and very long on the finish. Very fine.

Léoville-Las-Cases   1999–2020 plus   18.5

Good colour. Really profound on the nose. Marvellous intense fruit. Very good oak integration. Very lovely. Full, very, very rich and concentrated. Real breed. Marvellous balance. Exceptionally complex and long on the palate. Very fine.

Léoville-Poyferré   1998–2018   17.5

Good colour. Slightly oaky, slightly fatter, slightly more opulent than Las-Cases. Mouton as opposed to Latour. Fine quality though. Fullish, oaky, ripe and rich. Very good grip. Lovely Saint-Julien style. Long on the palate again. Fine.

Saint-Pierre   1997–2010   14.0

Good colour. Just a little element of the rustic on the nose here. Medium-full, slight astringency here as well as tannic. Lacks fruit and grace and real style. Pedestrian.

Talbot   1997–2007   13.0

Good colour. Sweet nose. But no support or style behind it. Medium body. Not much tannin or structure. Not as bad as the 1989 but nothing special at all. Lacks fat and concentration and style.

PAUILLAC

D'Armailhac   1998–2012   15.0

Medium-full colour. Medium weight. Something Mouton-ish but without the flair. Lacks a little style. On the palate medium-full. Ripe and balanced. Fragrant and with good fruit. Finishes better than it starts. But no better than good.

Batailley   1997–2011   15.5

Good colour. Medium-weight, ripe nose. Open and charming. Medium-full, good rich fruit. Balanced and well-made if without the depth, concentration and flair of a super-second. Finishes long. Good plus.

Carruades de Château Lafite
                    1997–2007   14.0

Medium-full colour. Reasonable nose. But just a little *vin de presse*-stewed and a bit sweaty. Not a patch on Les Forts. On the palate just a little loose-knit. Ripe but a touch astringent. Though a reasonable finish. Quite good.

Clerc-Milon   1998–2012   15.0

Good colour. Nicely firm but concentrated and rich. Much better than D'Armailhac on the nose. On the palate a little more to it but the balance is a little out of kilter. Suggestions of astringency as well as the tannic. Like D'Armailhac good but not great. Slightly disappointing.

Duhart-Milon   2000–2015   16.0

Good colour. Firm, structured, masculine, backward nose. A little inflexible? Fullish, good tannin. A little dense. Lacks a little flair, I thought, on the attack. But the finish is longer and more complex. This just needs time. Very good.

Les Forts de Latour   1998–2013   16.0

Good colour. A lot of breed here on the nose. Composed and balanced. Ripe with just a little austerity. Fullish. Good oak. Very good tannins and very good grip. Plenty of flair and depth here. Very good. Long.

Grand-Puy-Lacoste   1998–2012   16.0

Full colour. Not a blockbuster by any means, but ripe and quite round and rich and sweet on the nose. Medium body. Surprisingly accessible. Ripe, reasonable grip. Not a lot of tannin. Round. Harmonious. Very good but lacks real depth, concentration, backbone and class.

Haut-Bages-Libéral   1998–2012   15.5

Good colour. Fat, ripe, slightly flamboyant and spicy on the nose. Plenty of *matière* here. But just a little solid and four-square. Fullish, good grip. Plenty of depth and vigour. Lacks a little grace but good plus.

Haut-Batailley   1997–2008   14.0

Good colour. A little closed on the nose. Plenty of ripeness. Fullish, but a touch pedestrian. Lacks a bit of grip and flair and dimension. Not as good as Batailley this year.

Lafite   2000–2020 plus   18.5

Good colour. This is very lovely, but tasted after Latour it did not have the same flair. Yet a lot better than Mouton. Fullish, rich, oaky, harmonious. Very long. Very fine certainly. But is it any better than Las-Cases or Pichon-Baron?

Latour 2000–2020 plus 20.0

Good colour. Brilliant nose. This is Bordeaux at its most quintessential. Understated. Very refined. Exquisitely harmonious. Quietly aristocratic. Splendid fruit expression. Full, but not a backward blockbuster. Hugely concentrated and intense. Very, very long and with real complexity and marvellous balance. Very exciting.

Lynch-Bages 1999–2015 16.5

Good colour. Fat, rich and ripe on the nose. But not the flair and class of the Pichons or Latour. Fullish, slightly spicy. Lacks a little dimension after the Pichons as well as sheer breed. But fat, quite concentrated, good grip. Very good plus.

Lynch-Moussas 1997–2007 14.0

Good colour. Round and ripe and sweet on the nose. But not nearly as weedy as usual, it seems. Medium to medium-full. Round and ripe again. Good grip. No blockbuster. Not the greatest of style and dimension, but a good wine.

Mouton-Rothschild 1998–2012 16.5

Good colour. Quite dominated by the new oak here. But there doesn't seem to be that much concentration underneath. Sadly one-dimensional for a first growth. A lack of intensity and real grip. Medium-full, balanced and ripe but a little anonymous. Very good at best.

Pichon-Longueville-Baron

2000–2020 plus 18.5

Good colour. Very lovely nose. This is slightly fuller and more obviously tannic than the Latour but has marvellous depth and complexity and class nonetheless. A true Pauillac. Full, structured, very rich and concentrated. Oaky. Very good intensity and grip on the follow-through. But more closed in than Latour.

Pichon-Longueville, Comtesse de Lalande

1997–2015 17.5

Good colour. Very lovely, ripe, intense fruit here. Complex, gently oaky. Fine. Medium-full. Balanced. Sweet but fresh. Good intensity and subtlety. Very Pichon-Lalande. Fragrant, feminine. Long. Very seductive.

Pontet-Canet 1997–2007 14.0

Good colour. Good nose. More depth and strength than I remembered. On the palate less exciting. Medium body. Some tannin. Lacks a bit of concentration but at least quite good.

SAINT-ESTÈPHE

Calon-Ségur 1998–2013 15.5

Good colour. Ripe nose. Good meaty stuff here. Fullish, quite concentrated. Good grip. Plenty of fruit and nice ripe tannins. This is well made. But the fruit lacks real breed. There is a Sainte-Estèphey slight farmyardiness to it.

Cos d'Estournel 1999–2018 17.5

Good colour. Velvety, gently oaky, very elegant and fragrant on the nose. Lovely rich fruit. Fullish, firm, concentrated. Really quite structured and intense. Splendid follow-through. Very good grip. Subtle, oaky and very long. Fine.

Cos-Labory 1997–2008 14.5

Good colour. Ripe, stylish nose. Harmonious and quite round. Not a blockbuster. Medium to medium-full body. Some tannin. Good acidity. This has very charming fruit, but it lacks a little real personality and intensity. Balanced though.

Haut-Marbuzet 1998–2015 16.0

Good colour. Rich, plump ample nose. No excessive new oak. Fullish, ripe, very good grip. Just the right sort of oak underpinning. Almost sweet in its richness. But not a bit over-ripe. This has depth. Very good.

Lafon-Rochet 1998–2009 14.0

Good colour. Slightly hard on the nose. Austere. Black fruits. Medium-full. Good acidity. There *is* richness underneath but will the wine soften up? Quite good.

Lillian-Ladouys 1997–2010 14.5

Good colour. Good balance here on the nose. And elegance too. Medium-full. The tannins just a little tough. Ripe fruit though. Reasonable grip. Doesn't have the usual rustic, slightly hard Saint-Estèphe character. Quite good plus.

Meyney 1997–2010 14.0

Good colour. Fat, rich and opulent on the nose. Very ripe, almost over-ripe. On the palate medium-full, ripe tannins. A little bitter though, as well. An opulent wine. Good grip but not classic style. (I have other notes where it showed better than this; 15.0 to 15.5 or so.)

Montrose 1999–2018 17.0

Good colour. Firm. Very blackcurrany nose. A lot of depth here. Full, structured, tannic, backward. But with very good concentrated fruit. This is the best Montrose for a long time. Lovely rich finish. Very good indeed.

Les Ormes-de-Pez 1996–2006 13.5

Good colour. Balance and elegance here on the nose. Medium-full. The tannins still stick out a bit and the wine lacks a bit of real style. But balanced and fragrant at the end.

de Pez 1997–2010 14.0

Good colour. A little tough and four-square on the nose. Not too tough on the palate though. Medium-full, good grip. Ripe. Good tannins. Lacks just a little definition and concentration on the follow-through. But quite good.

1989 CLARET

When the 1989 red Bordeaux vintage first appeared on the market in the spring of 1990 it was promoted with the sort of hype not seen since the 1982s were first offered seven years previously. 'Truly great,' seemed to be the consensus, both in Bordeaux itself and further along the chain. It had been a very early harvest, after a hot and very dry summer. The colour of the wines was very promising, and levels of alcohol and tannin were high. Things did indeed look good. On the other hand, the vintage followed the 1988, one which had sold well *en primeur*, and behind that lurked the 1986s and 1985s, the 1983s and the 1982s themselves, all still widely available. Nineteen eighty-nine was a very large crop, and the wines were expensive. Was there an element of special pleading in the enthusiasm with which it was being written up? Was it really as fabulous as it was being made out to be? Did it need to be snapped up straightaway?

In the light of events since then – an equally good and plentiful 1990 vintage and the current economic recession – it is easy to answer the last question. You can buy most of the 1989s today at prices equivalent to those at the outset. You will probably not have to pay any more in real terms if you wait a few years.

Is it the great vintage the growers and merchants promised at the outset? The answer is no. Certainly very good, even fine, particularly in Saint-Emilion and Pomerol. But it is irregular elsewhere. At the top levels most of the Graves and Haut-Médocs are commendable. But there are some shockers. It is not a vintage you can purchase with a blindfold and a pin.

THE WEATHER

Climatically, it was certainly an extraordinary year. For a start, it was not just an early but an unprecedentedly early harvest. Not since 1893 has the collection of the red wine grapes commenced in August.

A mild and largely dry winter, followed by torrential rain at the end of February, and only partly influenced by a cooler March, produced a bud-break before the end of the month. This is three weeks earlier than the average. April was miserable: very wet indeed and decidedly chilly, though thankfully not so inclement as to produce frost damage. It can be said that this was exactly what was needed, that the vines' development was retarded, except that there is always the danger that this sort of climatic see-sawing renders the poor old vines susceptible to *coulure*. This did not happen in 1989, largely because May, in total contrast to April, was gloriously sunny and warm. No less than 316 hours of sunshine were recorded – an average of ten hours a day – fully 50 per cent above normal. It was also, naturally, more than 4 degrees warmer than the average. This produced an early flowering. It began before the end of the month – and despite a cold snap between 30 May and 4 June (which caused much crossing of fingers and biting of fingernails, especially over the Cabernets), this flowering was over by 12 June, the date it usually begins. All the red varieties flowered successfully; the whites less so. The weather continued excessively warm – it was decidedly uncomfortable in the non-air-conditioned tents of the biennial Vinexpo – and the stage was set for a large harvest, and an early one.

It was to end up the second hottest summer since the war. The average temperature from June to September was 20.9 degrees, the same as 1947, and only surpassed by 1949 (21.3). It was also very dry. The yearly rainfall was again the lowest since 1949. The May-to-September rainfall measured 195 millimetres against an average of 332 but the crucial month of August – and it was August which was the prologue to the harvest rather than September – was by no means a record-breaking drought. In August, the rain fell mainly in short, sharp, violent storms, on the 7th, the 16th, and particularly on the 19th and 20th. Moreover, there had been a savage hailstorm on 7 July which ran from the north of the village of Sauternes across the vineyards of Bommes before petering out by the motorway, so avoiding damaging the vineyards of Barsac, but severely reducing the crop at Rayne-Vigneau, Clos-Haut-Peyraguey and neighbouring estates.

As August entered its final week, the grapes were approaching ripeness. Or were they? How do you measure ripeness? The normal, time-honoured procedure is to determine the sugar (and therefore the potential alcohol) content of the fruit, and to measure the acidity. At some moment, at about 12 to 13 degrees of potential alcohol, depending on the variety, the balance between the sugar and acidity will be correct. For a period just after this stage of maturity, the grape will concentrate both in sugar *and* alcohol if the weather is fine. This is the time to pick.

But this is only the opportune time if the grape is additionally phenolically ripe; if the tannins are mature. What happened in 1989 was that the grapes were analytically ripe, indeed even threatening to produce acidities which were too low for comfort, but that the tannins were unripe. This is a problem unprecedented in Bordeaux, but more common in the torrider climates of the New World. It was illustrated by a charming anecdote related by Peter Sichel, who writes of a grower who complained that he usually knew when to start picking his grapes. He would kick the vines. If the grapes fell off, it was time to start. 'This year I don't understand. The sugar is high, the acidity is low, but my toes are black and blue from kicking the vines and nothing happens!'

This factor left the grower with a perplexing problem, and gave rise to an argument about picking dates which continues today. The problem was further exacerbated by the sheer size of the crop; some 20 per cent up in red wine on the previous record, that of 1986.

With the white grapes, the problem was one of speed rather than of the ripeness of the tannins. Most white-wine producers, fearing a repetition of 1982 – high alcohol, low acidity and hence rather heavy, inelegant wines – started on Monday, 29 August, and had finished by the following weekend. Some lingered into the first full week of September, and were helped by temperatures which were in the upper 20s by day but were cool at night.

Some red-wine growers, and not just in the Libournais, normally the first to crop, also started picking before the end of the month. Alexandre Thienpont at Vieux Château Certan began collecting his Merlot on 31 August, but so did Jean Delmas at Haut-Brion. Latour also started on this date. Elsewhere, in the Médoc as well as in Saint-Emilion and Pomerol, the harvest commenced on 4 September – at Palmer and Rausan-Ségla – on the 5th at Las-Cases and Calon-Ségur, on the 6th at Cheval-Blanc, or on the 7th at Cos d'Estournel. Pétrus was collected on the 6th and 7th. Some started later, and will confess they should have begun sooner. Others claim they hit it just right. Some were forced to wait because their last vineyard treatments had been too recently in mid-August, and to pick any earlier would leave a taint in the wine. Many will accuse their neighbours of leaving the Merlots too late, with the result that the acidity was too low. Others, who picked later, will maintain their tannins were ripe and those of the early pickers were not. The debate continues.

With the Merlots, the main problems were the size of the crop, the superabundance of alcohol (nearly everybody had a *cuve* of over 14 degrees), and the low level of acidity. A tendency to big, hot, flabby wines with a 'hole in the middle', in short. Levels of tannin were also higher, much higher, than in most vintages. But if you have merely tannin and alcohol, and no acidity and concentration, you will hardly have wines of character, let alone elegance.

Picking then turned to the Cabernets. And what followed was one of the longest drawn-out harvests of recent times. With the difficulties over the ripeness of the tannins, all vineyards *should* have waited perhaps as much as a week between collecting the last of the Merlots and the first of the Cabernets. Not all could afford to leave their pickers lying around idle. Some, indeed, collected some of their youngest Cabernets and vinified them together with the last (potentially 15 degrees, but with consequent low acidity) of their Merlots. At Lascombes, one of these properties, I was told that this mixture produced the best *cuvée*.

The harvest was only occasionally interrupted by rain. There was quite a bit in the southern Médoc, the Graves, the Entre-Deux-Mers and the Libournais on Sunday, 10 September. It was then virtually dry until Friday, the 22nd, when there were storms. But fine weather returned after the 25th. Most had completed their harvest by then. Others lingered on. At Haut-Bailly the last grapes were not cleared until 6 October.

THE WINE-MAKING AND ITS PROBLEMS

If the problem with the Merlots was the acidity – or lack of it – that of the Cabernet was the tannin: the amount of it and the state of ripeness of it. As Pierre Coste has written in 'On Immaturity and Truth': One can sadly find too many wines these days which are analytically faultless, have a good colour and alcohol/acidity balance, but are disappointing on the palate. Their total polyphenol count may be the usual 50 or 60, as it is in Bordeaux in a good year, but because the vines were overloaded and the grapes harvested five or six days prior to optimum (tannic) maturity, the wines are hard on the palate, the nose is unsophisticated and ageing in bottle will always lead to disappointment. Coste was referring in particular to the 1988s, but what he says about the quality of the tannin applies equally to the 1989s.

One point in the 1989s' favour: the grapes arrived in the winery at 26 to 27 degrees, so there was good extraction from the beginning. It was less necessary to prolong the maceration. However, the tannins were high, and the question mark over their ripeness remained. With high sugar readings and low acidity levels, it was vitally important to be precise about the *remontage* (pumping over) and to do this in the absence of oxygen in order to preserve the fruit, to retain the aroma and delicacy, to ensure elegance. After all, red Bordeaux is, or should be, a wine of breed and distinction. This is what renders it supreme among all Cabernet/Merlot wines. Sadly this is what many 1989s, well-made in other respects or not, seem to lack.

THE SIZE OF THE CROP

When they finally added everything up, the amount of *appellation contrôlée rouge* produced in Bordeaux in 1989 totalled 4.87 million hectolitres. This was larger than the previous monster vintage of 1986 (4.51) but would be eclipsed a year later by the 1990 vintage (4.95).

Comparing the yields, however, gives us a different picture. The area under vine has grown, and in most cases the *rendements* in the quality villages and subregions was smaller in 1989 than in 1986, and would be smaller again in 1990.

	1986		1989		1990	
	Production (000 he)	Yield (per he he/ha)	Production (000 he)	Yield (per he he/ha)	Production (000 he)	Yield (per he he/ha)
Pauillac	59	58.1	65	59.8	65	58.6
Saint-Julien	42	56.3	50	58.6	50	56.9
Margaux	63	52.4	69	55.5	71	55.4
Saint-Estèphe	71	60.7	71	59.6	66	53.8
Pessac-Léognan	41	65.7	45	60.4	57	60.0
Saint-Emilion	305	60.5	298	58.2	289	53.6
Pomerol	43	59.0	40	53.7	37	48.3
Total Médoc/Graves	829	60.5	924	60.1	957	59.1
Saint-Emilion/ Pomerol/Fronsac	674	61.6	678	59.5	648	54.9
Total AOC Bordeaux rouge	4,514	65.6	4,870	61.1	4,950	59.5

STYLE, QUALITY, IRREGULARITY

As I normally do, three and a bit years after the vintage, I arranged a comprehensive tasting in England with a group of professional friends over three days at the end of January 1993. I had seen most of the wines in bottle in Bordeaux in January and April 1992, and more in a series of tasting seminars I conducted in the USA in September. So it was by no means the first time I had sampled these in bottle. But this was an opportunity to see all the top wines more or less in one go, to taste the top Médocs and Graves while one's memory was still fresh with the top Saint-Emilions and Pomerols of the day before.

Overall the colours are still very impressive indeed. Alcohol levels are high, and not often obtrusive. The wines are tannic, but sometimes the tannins are somewhat astringent. The explanation is not just the level of ripeness of those tannins but that acidity levels are generally low. All this adds up to wines which are big and fleshy, rich and full. But some are earthy and clumsy, some are herbaceous, and many lack freshness. Few wines have the breed, the harmony and the length on the palate of really great claret.

In Saint-Emilion and Pomerol this does not matter so much. Here, because of the preponderance of Merlot, the tannins are riper and more integrated, and the sheer exuberance of the fruit in the top wines is exciting. The stars are Le Têrtre-Roteboeuf, Troplong-Mondot, Canon, Pavie and Cheval-Blanc in Saint-Emilion; Beauregard, Clinet, La Tour-à-Pomerol, Trotanoy, Certan-de-May, Vieux Château Certan, Lafleur and, not surprisingly, Pétrus. Comparing these with the equivalent 1982s, sampled a few months previously, we decided on balance that we found the 1989s more exciting.

Lower down the scale on this side of Bordeaux, despite the success of the top wines, there is more to criticize than applaud. Few of the *grands crus classés* Saint-Emilions and their Pomerol equivalents are better than competent. Some are decidedly incompetent. The best of the Fronsacs are just as good and significantly cheaper. Overall, however, the 1989 Libournais are better than the 1990s.

Generally speaking, the reverse is the case in the Médoc and the Graves. Talk to the wine-makers, or sample the wines side by side, as I have done on several occasions, and you will note a preference for the 1990s. There are some exceptions, notably at Haut-Brion, Léoville-Las-Cases, Mouton-Rothschild and the Cazes stable (Pichon-Longueville-Baron, Lynch-Bages, etc.), but in most cellars the 1990s are better. They seem to have more balance and greater elegance.

Despite the brilliance of Haut-Brion, the Graves is a disappointment in 1989. And it is also disappointing in 1990. Château Margaux is fine but most of the rest of the southern Médocs do not inspire – and Giscours is a disaster. Cos d'Estournel is as usual delicious, but the 1990 is better still, and most 1989 Saint-Estèphes lack flair and personality.

For Bordeaux with the greatest finesse and complexity we instinctively turn to Saint-Julien and Pauillac. How do these 1989s show? Lafite is supreme among the first growths: a lovely example. Las-Cases and Pichon-Baron are the best of the super-seconds. Langoa and Léoville-Barton, Grand-Puy-Lacoste and Clerc-Milon are more than very good. But Pichon-Longueville-Lalande, while pretty, lacks intensity, Beychevelle, while very good, lacks breed, Gruaud-Larose is boring and Talbot thin and vegetal. And we had curiously tainted bottles of Ducru-Beaucaillou and Haut-Batailley (I have also had similar 1988 Ducrus). Overall there are good wines, but there are no great ones.

Nineteen eighty-nine was a difficult vintage to vinify because of the disparity between the sugar-acidity ripening optimum and the date the tannins were mature. The stress on the vines as a result of the drought added to these problems. The weather conditions, despite a lack of diluting rain or rot-inducing humidity, were not as ideal as seemed at first. The fruit was ripe, it was concentrated and it was healthy. But it was not balanced. 1989 is a very good vintage, but it is not the vintage of the century . . . or of the decade.

THE TASTING

The following wines were sampled in Southwold, Suffolk, over three days in January 1993.

	Optimum drinking	Mark out of 20

COTES DE BOURG

Roc-de-Cambes   1997–2005   13.0
Good colour. Good full earthy nose. Fullish, chunky. Good austerity. This is well-made if a little muscular. Needs time.

FRONSAC AND CANON FRONSAC

Canon-de-Brem   1996–2008   14.5
Medium colour. Good nose with a hint of caramel and chocolate blancmange. Ripe and meaty. Quite rich. Good grip and length. Good.

Canon-Moueix   1997–2010   15.5
Good colour. Rich, full and intense on the nose. This has depth and concentration. A serious wine. Good structure. Old-vine intensity. Lovely damson fruit. Fine for a Fronsac.

Cardeneau   1996–2002   13.0
Good. Slightly tanky on the nose. Lacks a little style. A bit hard on the attack but good concentrated fruit underneath. Medium-full. Finishes better than it starts.

De Carles   1996–2001   12.5
Medium colour. Good fruit but a little one-dimensional on the nose. Medium body. Quite austere. Slightly hard. Lacks a little character.

Dalem   1997–2007   15.0
Good colour. Ripe, rich and oaky on the nose. Good intensity here. Ripe tannins. Fullish. This has style and depth. Very good for a Fronsac. Lovely fruit on the finish. Complex.

La Fleur-Caillau   1995–1999   12.5
Good colour. Rich and chocolatey on the nose. But the tannins show a little. Medium-full. Tannins are a little obvious. Some fruit but not enough fat. Finishes a bit bitter and astringent. Lacks charm.

Fontenil
Good colour. A little pinched and sickly at first. Fruity. But corked.

La Grave   1995–2000   12.5
Good colour. Soft and fruity but a little thin on the nose. Medium body. A little astringent. Fruity but a little unbalanced.

Mazeris-Bellevue   1995–1999   11.0
Good colour. More evolved than most on the nose. Less structured. Merlot evident. A bit one-dimensional. Medium body. A little suggestion of attenuation. Acidities are a bit low. Fades away.

Moulin-Haut-Laroque   1997–2004   13.0
Good colour. Slightly higher volatile acidity than the rest on the nose. A bit marked by the *vin de presse* but good richness here. Good acidity. Slightly hard again. Fullish.

Moulin-Pey-Labrie   1995–2000   12.0
Good colour. This is a bit more developed than most, even to the extent of being slightly oxidized on the nose. Fruity and a little chocolatey but a bit short. Medium-body.

La Rousselle   1995–1999   12.5
Good colour. Slightly astringent tannins. But not a lot of structure on the nose. Medium body. A hint of oak. A pleasant fruity wine but a bit dull. Quite forward. Reasonable length.

Vieille-Curé   1995–2001   13.5
Good colour. Soft and gently oaky on the nose. Medium-full. Well-made. Clean and fruity without being a blockbuster. But one and a half dimensions only. Quite good plus.

Villars   1997–2005   14.0
Good colour. Rich, full and oaky on the nose. Good. Fullish. Good tannins. Ripe, good depth. Fat here, and concentration. Good. Finishes long and stylishly.

SAINT-EMILION GRANDS CRUS CLASSÉS

L'Angélus   1997–2007   15.5
Very good colour. Ample nose. Quite markedly oaky. But lacks a little real breed. Chocolatey. Medium-full. The tannins show a little. But the acidity is at least reasonable. Plump. Good plus.

L'Arrosée   1996–2001   14.5
Good colour. Soft and oaky on the nose, but lacks depth. Ripe, stylish, medium body. More elegant than most. But just a touch one-dimensional.

Balestard-La-Tonnelle   1996–2000   12.0
Good colour. A little sweaty on the nose. Medium body. Not a lot of acidity. Lacks concentration. Unexciting.

Beau-Séjour-Bécot   1995–2000   13.0
Good colour. Quite oaky on the nose. But no depth underneath. Pleasant but light and forward. No concentration. Not much excitement here.

Cadet-Piola   1997–2002   12.5
Good colour. Slightly dry and chunky on the nose. Solid but inflexible. On the palate some richness but as much astringent as tannic. Yet reasonable grip. Medium-full. Lacks style.

Canon-La-Gaffelière   1997–2009   15.0
Good colour. Ample and sexy and fruity on the

nose if without a great deal of complexity underneath. But a very attractive wine. Gently oaky. Medium to medium-full. Could do with just a little more grip. But soft and seductive. Reasonable length. Shows well.

Cap-de-Mourlin 1997–2003 13.5

Good colour. Good grip on the nose. Some fruit, but a little four-square and not exactly stylish. Slightly hard on the palate. Medium-full. Reasonable grip.

Chauvin 1997–2006 14.0

Good colour. Slightly lumpy nose. A bit adolescent. Slightly stewed and not enough grip and concentration. Medium-full. Quite good only.

Clos-des-Jacobins 1996–2000 12.0

Good colour. Chunky and stalky on the nose. Medium to medium-full. Vegetal and ungainly. Reasonable acidity but little enjoyment.

Clos de L'Oratoire 1995–1999 12.5

Good colour. Soft and pretty on the nose but a bit bland. Medium body. Fruity attack but nothing behind it. Dull but acceptable.

Clos-Saint-Martin 1996–2003 14.0

Good colour. Good oak, and substantial on the nose. This is better than most. Quite oaky. Rich and fat, but a little forced. Quite good at best.

La Clotte 1997–2006 14.5

Good colour. Dense nose. Some fruit underneath, but rather unforthcoming. Fullish, rich, structured. This has style and depth. Best of all on the finish. Needs time.

La Clusière 1995–2008 11.0

Good colour. Vegetal and high-toned on the nose. Medium body. As much astringent as tannic. Thin and young viney. Unexciting.

Dassault 1995–2001 11.5

Good colour. Quite high volatile acidity but some fruit, and good grip. On the palate rather vegetal. There is a certain edgy acidity. Badly made.

La Dominique 1996–2002 13.5

Good colour. A bit anonymous on the nose. Gentle, oaky, fruity and quite stylish but it doesn't have the depth and concentration it should have.

Faurie-de-Souchard 1996–2001 13.0

Medium-full colour. Pleasant fruit on the nose but lacks a bit of character. Medium body. Some fruit, reasonable acidity. But dull.

Fonplégade 1995–1999 12.0

Good colour. A little thin on the nose, fruity but no depth or real class. On the palate it is a bit astringent. Ripe, in a slight artificial way. But short.

Fonroque 1997–2002 12.0

Good colour. Lacks freshness on the nose. Rather astringent on the palate. Medium body. Lacks richness.

Grand-Mayne 1998–2012 16.0

Good colour. Round, ripe, ample fruity nose. An attractive wine. Fullish, ripe tannins. Fresh, positive, with a gentle oaky background. Finishes well. This is one of the best *grands crus classés*.

Grand-Pontet 1995–1998 12.0

Good colour. This is thin and undistinguished on the nose. Young viney. Medium body. Rather astringent already. Short and dull.

Guardet-Saint-Julien 1997–2003 12.5

Medium-full colour. Some oak but a bit bland on the nose. Medium to medium-full. Good acidity but the wine lacks concentration and fat.

Haut-Corbin 1996–2003 13.0

Good colour. Solid and oaky-chunky on the nose. Fullish and quite ripe on the palate. A meaty wine. But it lacks style. Not bad.

Haut-Sarpe 1996–2000 11.5

Good colour. Somewhat rustic, slightly high acidity. A bit vegetal. Rather stewed. Chunky. Ungainly. Medium-full. Not special.

Larcis-Ducasse 1996–1999 10.0

Good colour. This is rustic and slightly shitty on the nose. A badly made wine.

Larmande 1997–2010 15.5

Good colour. Ample, rich, plump, structured nose. Medium-full. This has spice and depth. Good grip. Not a blockbuster but long, gently oaky, persistent finish. Good plus.

Laroze 1995–1998 10.0

Good colour. A little thin on the nose. Young vines again? Thin, rather short. Poor.

Moulin-du-Cadet 1997–2007 15.0

Good colour. Quite closed on the nose but there is good depth. Fullish. Rich and fat. A bit tough and closed but there is *matière* here. Good grip.

Pavie-Decesse

(Corked) Other tastings indicate a better wine than most of this series (±15.0/1997–2007).

Pavie-Macquin 1995–1998 10.0

Good colour. This seems a bit rustic and edgy on the nose. And on the palate it is mean and astringent. Stewed. Poor. Not even very ripe.

Petit-Faurie-de-Soutard 1996–2000 12.0

Good colour. Slightly strained on the nose. There is an astringency and a pinched quality about this wine. The wine is rather vegetal and a bit thin.

La Serre 1997–2010 15.0

Good colour. Good fruit on the nose but not the greatest of depth or concentration. Medium-full. Stylish, round, soft, gently oaky. Good acidity. Plenty of fruit and of flair. Good. Finishes well.

Soutard 1999–2009 14.0

Good colour. A bit raw and hard. The tannins less

ample, the fruit less generous than most. A little herbaceous. This is rather an austere wine at present. Full, backward. Raw. But the acidity is there. Quite tannic. Quite good but needs time.

Le Tertre-Rôteboeuf   1997–2017   16.5
Good colour. This is very good. Excellent old-viney blackberry nose. Very rich. Plenty of depth. Good oak. Excellent grip. This is a lovely definitive wine which is not a bit outclassed by even the best of the *premiers crus*. Not a blockbuster. Long. Fullish. Accessible. Very good.

La Tour-du-Pin-Figeac 1995–1999   12.0
Good colour. Slight herbal touch. Cherry flavours but artificially so on the nose. A bit herbaceous on the palate. Medium body. Lacks flesh and style and charm.

La Tour-Figeac   1997–2006   14.5
Good colour. A bit dense and unstylish on the nose. Some substance and perhaps even depth on the palate. This has possibilities. The fruit has richness and the wine has good grip.

Troplong-Mondot   1998–2015   16.5
Good colour. Round, generous, gently oaky. Lovely ripe fruit. Real flair here. Medium-full. Concentrated and old-viney. Very harmonious. Fine fruit. Elegant. Very good indeed.

SAINT-EMILION *PREMIERS GRANDS CRUS CLASSÉS*

Ausone   1997–2017   18.0
Good colour. Not a blockbuster but very stylish. Finely oaky. Lovely, elegantly balanced fruit. This has a lot more flair than the Belair. A complex, subtle wine with a lot of dimension. Medium-full. Very long. Very fine.

Beauséjour-Duffau-Lagarrosse
                 1998–2015   16.5
Good colour. This is very good. Lovely concentrated fruit on the nose. Classy as well. Rather better than Gaffelière. Fullish, fine fruit. Very good grip. This is long and classy. The best Beauséjour-Duffau-Lagarrosse in years!

Belair   1997–2012   16.0
Good colour. Good structure on the nose. Still young. Less developed than some. But plenty of depth though. Fullish. Good substance. On the palate the fruit is old-viney, the tannins ripe, but it lacks just a bit of grip for great. Very good.

Canon   1999–2017   17.5
Good colour. This is very fine. Marvellously concentrated old-viney fruit. Good oak. Full, backward. Fine. Full, very concentrated. Intensely flavoured. Very good tannins. A lot of depth here. This is lovely. Needs time though.

Cheval-Blanc   2000–2025   19.5
Good colour. Brilliant nose. Very, very rich.

Multidimensional, ample fruit and spice. Full, backward. A blockbuster. Undeveloped. Very, very ripe, almost over-ripe. The attack is massive, the follow-through very, very rich. A tannic wine with very good grip. Excellent.

Figeac   1997–2012   16.5
Good colour. As usual, more austere than most, but good oak and plenty of quality and flair. Medium-full. Not a blockbuster. Balanced. Good oak base and plenty of stylish fruit. Long.

Clos-Fourtet   1997–2002   12.0
Good colour. Shitty nose. Rustic on the palate. Not enough body and grip. No concentration. Thin, unripe and vegetal. Disappointing.

La Gaffelière   1998–2008   15.0
Good colour. Firm but rich nose. Not the greatest of class but plenty of substance. Fullish. Good acidity. This is youthful, indeed a bit raw. Good fruit. But not the class or concentration for great.

Magdelaine   1998–2006   14.0
Good colour. This seems a bit over-evolved, indeed oxidized on the nose. A bit disappointing. It lacks acidity. There is some astringency as much as tannin. Medium-full. Is this a bad bottle?

Pavie   1998–2018   18.0
Good colour. Splendid nose. Lovely ripe, plump, old-viney fruit. Real class. Plenty of depth. Fullish, good ripe tannins. Very concentrated, splendid fat fruit. Very good grip. This is fine. Even better than Canon and Figeac.

Trottevieille   1997–2002   13.0
Good colour. Bad *élevage*. It wasn't as bad as this in cask. Seems a bit thin and weak and over-evolved. Medium body. Attenuated. Lacking acidity. Astringent and artificially sweet. Not special.

POMEROL

Beauregard   1998–2015   16.5
Good colour. Firm, full. Quite backward and masculine. Good grip. Very good fruit. Some new oak. Full, positive, very good grip and tannin. This is very good. Spicy complexity in the fruit. Long. Intense. Good personality and style.

Le Bon-Pasteur   1997–2009   15.5
Good colour. Very ripe, almost over-ripe nose. There is a spice here which reminds me of an Accad Burgundy. Medium to medium-full. Some tannin. Lots of chocolatey extract. A little ungainly and four-square at present but good stuff. Finishes long and ample and rich.

Bonalgue   1995–1997   11.0
Good colour. Plump and ripe but not a lot of character here. Little tannin. Light. Young viney. Watery even. Very short.

La Cabanne   1996–2002   15.0

Good colour. Ripe, plump, gently oaky nose. Attractive. Medium to medium-full. A touch of oak. A stylish, balanced, fruity example for reasonably early drinking. Good.

Certan-Giraud   1996–2003   14.0

Good colour. Clean and fresh. Good fruit and elegance if not a great deal behind it on the nose. Medium body. A little tannin. Not quite enough grip, though the fruit is ripe and attractive and quite stylish. Finishes a bit short and one-dimensional. Quite good.

Certan-de-May

Good colour. I have seen this better. It is almost as if it is bottle sick on the nose. I don't think this is a good bottle. Judgement deferred.

This is a wine I tasted several times in the US in September/October 1992. Here is a typical note: Rich, full and concentrated on the nose. Quite toasted oak. At first a bit closed but a big wine with a follow-through which is very intense and classy. Needs time (1999–2012, ±17.5).

Clinet   1999–2015   17.0

Good colour. A lot of new oak here. Is there too much? But ample blackberry fruit as well. A full tannic wine but one with plenty of extract and grip, enough to balance the amount of oak. This has a lot of depth. Fine. Needs time.

Clos-du-Clocher   1996–2004   15.5

Good colour. Attractive blackberry-fruity nose. Open and accessible. Medium-full. Round. A well-made wine. Good fruit and good balance.

Clos-René   1996–2001   13.0

Good colour. Fullish and solid on the nose. A little dense and vegetal. A bit of unripeness. Medium-full. Not a lot of acidity. OK at best.

La Conseillante   1997–2012   17.0

Good colour. Not a blockbuster. A feminine wine. Complex, gently oaky nose. Medium-full. Very well balanced. Lovely stylish fruit. This is round, velvety, long and very elegant. Fine.

La Croix   1996–2000   12.0

Good colour. Chunky, astringent. Stewed nose. Quite high volatile acidity. Medium body. Unripe tannins. Dry at the end. Hard.

La Croix-de-Casse   1995–1999   12.0

Good colour. Light nose. A little thin and non-descript. Pretty fruit but as much astringent as tannic. Weedy. Boring. Forward.

La Croix-de-Gay   1996–2001   13.0

Good colour. Round, fat, quite spicy nose. But a little dry. Medium body. A bit astringent on the palate. Some fruit but ungainly. Not bad at best.

La Croix-Toulifaut   1996–1999   12.5

Good colour. Soft and oaky on the nose but not much underneath. Medium body. Oaky, but a bit thin and short. Young vines. Pretty but no depth. No dimension.

Domaine de L'Eglise   1995–1998   12.5

Good colour. Somewhat weak and insubstantial. Fruity but lacks real depth. Lacks grip too. This is thin. Lightish. No tannin. Pretty but no grip or weight. As disappointing as always.

L'Eglise-Clinet   1998–2008   15.5

Good colour. A little lumpy on the nose. It lacks a bit of grace. Plenty of substance though. Some oak. Medium-full. Good tannins. Good grip. This has fat and concentration. But it lacks just a little elegance for great. Good plus.

L'Enclos   1996–2003   14.0

Good colour. Ample, fruity and oaky. This is quite full and has a lot of seductive charm. Medium body. Lots of Merlot it seems. Plump fruit but not quite the acidity. It has fat but it lacks just a little freshness. Tails off.

L'Evangile   1999–2013   17.5

Good colour. Unforthcoming on the nose. Totally different from its neighbour Conseillante. Full, tannic, oaky, but with a splendid concentration of fruit and very good grip. Needs time. Rather more youthful than most.

Feytit-Clinet   1996–2000   13.5

Medium-full colour. A little weak on the nose. Reasonable fruit though. Quite pretty. But a bit one-dimensional. Medium body. Not a lot of tannin. A touch short.

La Fleur-de-Gay   1997–2004   14.5

Tête de cuvée of La Croix-de-Gay. Good colour. Very marked by the new oak on the nose. Can't see much concentration underneath. Medium body. This seems more stylish than the Croix-de-Gay, with more richness and better balance. Oaky but not too much so on the finish.

La Fleur-Gazin   1996–2002   14.0

Good colour. Soft fruity nose. Quite stylish and balanced but not *that* much weight. Medium body. A pleasant example. The fruit is correct and attractive but it is only one and half dimensions. Not short though.

Le Gay   1997–2006   14.5

Good colour. Full and rich. A little chunky but there is depth here. Some oak. Full. Quite concentrated. Good grip. A bit ungainly but this has possibilities. But it could do with more elegance.

Gazin   1996–2002   14.0

Good colour. Slightly mixed-up on the nose. Good bits: the fruit. But not so good bits: a certain lack of style. On the palate this is medium-full but the tannins stick out a bit. It lacks zip as well as flair. Quite good only.

La Grave-à-Pomerol   1997–2003   15.0

Good colour. Plump, ripe, elegant on the nose. Less structured than Lagrange but more stylish and concentrated. Medium-full. Elegant, fat and complex. This is a neatly made wine with very good ripe fruit. Good balance. Good length. One of the best of the lesser Pomerols.

Lafleur   1999–2019   19.0

Good colour. This is very fine because it has the grip as well as the concentration. Rather more accessible than Pétrus. Very ripe and very well balanced. A big full, intense wine. Very fine indeed. Big, tannic, masculine. Very long indeed.

Lafleur-Pétrus   1996–2006   16.0

Good colour. Coming after the Latour it seemed as ripe, but a little spicier and with less acidity. Medium-full. Very Merlot. Ripe and rich, but a little bland. Very good at best. Lacks a bit of zip.

Lagrange   1997–2004   13.5

Good colour. Ripe, plump, quite substantial on the nose, but not *that* exciting. What it lacks is a bit of style. Good Merlot fruit and good grip. Medium-full.

Latour-à-Pomerol   1997–2012   17.0

Good colour. This is fine. Ripe – over-ripe – fruit. Medium-full. Good grip. An ample, exciting, generous wine. Very lovely finish. Fine.

Mazeyres   1996–2000   12.0

Medium-full colour. Sweaty and vegetal on the nose. Astringent on the palate. Medium body. One-dimensional. Unexciting.

Montviel   1996–2000   12.0

Medium-full colour. Nondescript nose. Slightly hard. Lacks generosity and depth. Medium body. A bit astringent because the acidities are low. One-dimensional.

Moulinet   1996–2001   13.5

Good colour. Fruity nose but lacks style and grip and concentration. Medium body. Decent grip and fruit. A good example of a lesser Pomerol.

Petit-Village   1997–2009   15.5

Good colour. Ample, oaky, a little ungainly but plenty of richness. Fullish, ripe, plenty of fruit. A generous wine. But ultimately it lacks a bit of zip.

Pétrus   2000–2025   20.0

Very good colour. Closed, backward, tannic. Huge fruit. Rather more oak and more tannic than the others. But not a blockbuster. This is excellent. Even better than the Cheval-Blanc today. Enormous concentration, intensity and persistence. And an immense amount of fruit. Brilliant.

Le Pin   1998–2020   18.5

Good colour. Lovely ripe fruit. Red fruit and quite oaky. Inherently very soft and silky. Excellent balance. Very good acidity. Medium-full.

This is high class. Lovely ripe fruit. Oaky. Very fine indeed. Very, very long.

Plince   1996–2004   15.5

Good colour. Reasonable substance and fruit on the nose and good grip. Less evolved than most of these lesser Pomerols. Medium-full, fat and ripe and with good grip. This has depth and balance and style. Good plus.

La Pointe   1996–2008   15.0

Medium-full colour. Soft and gently fruity and oaky on the nose. Medium body. Reasonable grip. A fresh, well-made wine without the depth of the best. Balanced though. Good style. Will come forward soon.

Prieurs-de-La-Commanderie
     1996–2002   13.0

Good colour. Neat oaky nose. Pretty and with at least some depth. Medium-full. The tannins could be a bit riper. Reasonable acidity. Some fruit. A bit rustic at the end.

De Sales   1996–2001   13.5

Good colour. Open fruity nose. Lacks a bit of grip. It is a bit bland and dilute. Medium body. Pleasant fruity attack but not much behind it. Just a little short.

Taillefer   1996–2000   12.5

Good colour. Fruity nose but little depth or richness, a bit of H2S. Medium body. Not a lot of tannin. Less style. Finishes short. Undistinguished.

Trotanoy   1997–2015   18.5

Good colour. Very harmonious on the nose. Lovely fruit. Good oak. Very classy. This is a step up from Lafleur-Pétrus and Latour-à-Pomerol. A wine of real flair and elegance. Medium-full. Round. Silky. Very fine old-viney fruit. Long. Lovely. The finish is most impressive.

Vieux Château Certan   1999–2020   19.0

Good colour. Brilliant nose. Good oak. A cornucopia of lovely concentrated fruit. Disarmingly super. This is very serious. Marvellous balance. Very good acidity. This is long, oaky, concentrated and very, very complex. Brilliant.

PESSAC-LÉOGNAN

Bahans-Haut-Brion   1997–2007   14.5

Good colour. Slightly herbaceous on the nose. Quite chunky. A little raw. Medium-full. Good fruit, though there is something a little bitter and hard in the middle. Reasonable acidity. Lacks a bit of charm and finishes a little astringently. But good for a second wine. .

Bouscaut   1995–2002   13.0

Medium colour. Slightly earthy ungenerous nose. Medium body, a little astringent. But reasonable acidity. Lacks real class and depth but not bad.

Domaine De Chevalier   1996–2008   17.0
Good colour. Soft, elegant, oaky nose. Balanced, very stylish, lovely fruit. But medium to medium-full only. Quite forward. No obtrusive tannins. Not a blockbuster but a lovely example.

Haut-Bailly   1996–2004   14.0
Good colour. Plump, ripe nose. Plummy fruit but the tannins obtrude a little. Medium body. Some new oak. A curate's egg of a wine. Doesn't quite fit together.

Haut-Brion   1998–2020   20.0
Good colour. Lovely nose. Really elegant fruit. This has real finesse and complexity. First-class breed. Fullish, harmonious. Intensely flavoured. Clearly a cut above the rest of the Graves. Real quality. Impeccable balance. Lovely fruit.

La Mission-Haut-Brion   1999–2015   18.0
Very good colour. Closed nose. Much less developed than La Tour-Haut-Brion. Still rather hard. Much better on the palate. Full, ripely tannic. Integrated, rich and concentrated. This is fine. Long.

Olivier   1997–2007   14.0
Good colour. Earthy but rich on the nose. But lacks a little generosity. Fullish, tannic. There is reasonable acidity here but a lack of richness. A little austere. Quite good.

Pape-Clément   1996–2004   15.5
Good colour. Firm, rich and plump on the nose. Not a lot of body. Not a lot of grip. The astringency pokes out a bit. Medium-full. Good fruit and style but a little unbalanced. It finishes just a little short.

La Tour-Haut-Brion   1997–2005   13.5
Good colour. Firm, rich, not as 'green' as it is sometimes. A little more structure than body on grip it seems. And a lack of real concentration and richness. Tannins stick out. Will it dry out?

La Tour-Martillac   1995–2002   14.0
Medium to medium-full colour. Slightly dry tannins on the nose at first. Medium weight, ripe, quite classy, balanced fruit. Ripe, medium body. Quite soft, a little lacking concentration and depth. Not too short, though. Quite good.

Médoc and Haut-Médoc

Cantemerle   1997–2005   14.0
Good colour. Soft fruity nose. But a little weak I fear. Medium to medium-full. Reasonable grip. Good blackberry fresh fruit. Fresh. But lacks a bit of concentration and fat. Finishes well though.

La Cardonne   1994–1999   13.0
Good colour. Ample on the nose. Well-made. Not too dense. Quite ripe and correctly balanced. Light to medium body. Not a lot of tannin. Good oak. Lacks dimension but quite neat. Quite good.

Chasse-Spleen   1997–2007   14.5
Good. Some tannin shows on the nose. But there is richness and grip enough to balance it. Medium-full. Tannins show a bit on the palate as well. But there is more acidity here and riper tannins in the first place, compared with Poujeaux. Quite good plus. Lacks a bit of generosity.

Citran   1996–2002   13.0
Good colour. Chunky nose. Something a little sweaty as well. On the palate the tannins and their astringency dominate, with no balancing grip. This will always be rather dry.

La Lagune   1997–2009   14.5
Good colour. Soft plump, oaky nose, but not a lot of weight or grip behind it. Medium-full, balanced, ripe, attractively fruity. Good but lacks depth. A bit short.

Plagnac   1995–2002   13.5
Quite good colour. Good grip on the nose. Ripe Cabernet without being too tough and too austere. A little more to it than the Cardonne. Medium body. Quite good plus. Reasonable finish.

Poujeaux   1996–2001   13.0
Good colour. Just a little cool and vegetal on the nose. Good fruit though. And good balance. Medium body. This lacks grip. And it isn't very ripe either. The effect is a little thin and ungenerous. Disappointing.

Sociando-Mallet   1998–2012   14.5
Good colour. Full and chunky on the nose. But not too dense. Good fruit. Fullish, rich and oaky. Quite tannic but the tannins are ripe and there is plenty of grip. This has an encouraging freshness. Needs time though. A bit tough.

Margaux

D'Angludet   1997–2007   14.5
Good colour. Fullish nose, a bit solid. Lacks a touch of freshness. Fullish. Good fruit. Reasonable acidity. Here the balance and length are reasonable. Positive finish.

Boyd-Cantenac   1999–2009   14.5
Good colour. This is a lot more generous on the nose than the Pouget. But it is still a bit tough. Yet the acidity is there and the fruit ripe. This is a lot better than most – and the Pouget.

Cantenac-Brown   1996–2002   12.5
Good colour. Fat and fruity but unbalanced and though oaky, not very stylish on the nose. Medium body. Fruity but rather weak in acidity. Astringent and lacks finesse on the follow-through.

D'Issan   1996–2000   13.5
Good colour. High-toned nose. Lacks a bit of generosity and fat, though it seems reasonably fresh. Medium body. Rather lightweight. Not much tannin or structure. Pretty but no depth.

Kirwan   1996–2004   13.5

Good colour. Nondescript nose. Seems fruity but hollow. Medium body. Reasonable fruit. A little fresher than Cantenac-Brown and with a better, more stylish finish. Not bad plus.

Labégorce-Zédé   1996–2004   14.0

Good colour. Rather dull on the nose. Lumpy like most of these Margaux. Medium to medium-full. This is balanced and ripe. But lacks real length and grip. Quite stylish.

Lascombes   1998–2005   13.5

Medium-full colour. Four-square nose but a bit hollow in the middle. Not very stylish either. Medium-full. Some tannin. Not too astringent. But lacks real intensity and direction.

Malescot-Saint-Exupéry   1998–2015   16.5

Good colour. Ripe, plump balanced nose. This is much better than most of the Margaux. Fullish, fresh, good grip. Good plump fruit. Harmony and depth here. A refreshing change from most of this flight. This has a future.

Margaux   1999–2014   18.0

Good colour. Not as oaky as I expected, or as the Pavillon Rouge. This is integrated, concentrated, classy and ripe. Lovely subtle nose. But it doesn't have the depth of the top Pauillacs.

Marquis-de-Terme   1998–2010   14.5

Good colour. Fresh damson nose. No obtrusive tannin. Not very classy, but at least balanced. Fullish. Good structure. Chocolatey flavour. Quite fresh. Quite long. Better than most Margaux.

Monbrison   1997–2007   14.0

Good colour. A little dense on the nose. Somewhat clumsy. On the palate it shows better. Medium-full, rich. The tannins not too obtrusive. Not a great deal of length or grip though.

Palmer   1998–2008   15.0

Good colour. Curiously clumsy for a Palmer on the nose. Where is the stylish fruit? On the palate a little astringent. But the wine is fresh and the fruit stylish. But it lacks the usual Palmer flair. Medium to medium-full.

Pavillon Rouge du Château Margaux   1998–2012   15.5

Very good colour. Rich, plump oaky nose. Very much better than most. Quite substantial. Lots of oak. Good tannins. Good acidity. Fresh. Very good fruit. Long. Surprisingly good.

Pouget   1997–2007   12.5

Good colour. Solid, well macerated, very hard and tannic on the nose. Green and stalky. Very tannic and the tannins rather vegetal. Fullish. Good acidity but hard and ungenerous.

Prieuré-Lichine   1997–2007   14.0

Good colour. Reasonably well-made, as usual. Not much real breed, as usual. Medium to medium-full. Some tannin. The balance isn't bad but there isn't much to excite. But the finish is positive.

Rausan-Ségla   1998–2012   16.0

Good colour. Plump nose. Fresh. Good oaky base. Medium-full. Some tannin but good fresh plump raspberry fruit. It is not as fat or as harmonious as Malescot but it has length and style and complexity. Very good.

Du Tertre   1996–1999   12.0

Good colour. Oaky make-up over a hollow astringent wine. This is medium body. Pretty attack. But nothing on the follow-through. Weak.

La Tour-de-Mons   1996–2002   13.5

Good colour. Quite fresh on the nose. Not too solid, reasonable fruit. But not much depth or style. On the palate a little weak and short. Medium body. Will get astringent. Doesn't have much class I'm afraid.

SAINT-JULIEN

Beychevelle   1998–2013   16.0

Good colour. Plump nose. Ample fruit if a slight lack of real class. A touch of *tabac*. Rich, fullish, plump, oaky. Good grip. This has good intensity. Finishes well. A generous wine.

Branaire   1998–2008   14.5

Good colour. A little dry and hidden on the nose. Quite good on the palate. A little lumpy at first but the follow-through is positive and long. There is good rich fruit here.

Clos du Marquis   1997–2007   15.0

Good colour. Not a blockbuster but good oak and fresh stylish fruit on the nose. Medium body. Well-made. Balanced. Fresh. Long. A lot of charm here.

Ducru-Beaucaillou   1996–2005   15.0

Good colour. Laid-back nose. There is breed here, but it is not as big or as powerful as Léoville-Barton or Léoville-Las-Cases. Medium-full, curiously understated. Pleasant fruit, balanced, but it is a bit too delicate and the finish lacks intensity. And it is a touch astringent at the end. And is it still (the first bottle was) slightly tainted?

Here is a note from a clean bottle sampled September, 1992: Good colour. Ripe, very elegant nose. Less cooked fruit aspects than most. Medium-full. Rich, balanced, concentrated. Good tannins. This has very good grip. Fine. Long, complex, full of interest. (1998–2018, 17.0)

Gloria   1996–2003   13.0

Good colour. Rather hard and ungenerous on the nose. Medium body. A bit astringent, as much as tannic. A bit driven. Lacks charm and flexibility.

Gruaud-Larose 1997–2002 13.5

Good colour. A little lumpy on the nose. Muscular and a touch coarse. A bit astringent. Fullish. Unbalanced. No breed. Unexciting.

Lagrange 1998–2012 15.5

Good colour. Stylish fruit here on the nose. Fresh, plump, plummy. This has good depth. Medium-full. Balanced. Quite rich. Finishes well. Well-made.

Langoa-Barton 1998–2013 16.0

Good colour. Good nose. Classy individual fruit. Not a blockbuster but old viney, even chocolatey. Medium to medium-full. Good grip. Well-covered tannins. Good fat and plump character. Very good.

Léoville-Barton 1999–2015 17.5

Good colour. Good oak. Fine, concentrated, stylish, balanced old-vine fruit on the nose. A bigger wine than Langoa, as always, with a bit more depth and concentration. This is fine plus.

Léoville-Las-Cases 1999–2019 18.0

Good colour. Closed but very concentrated. Excellent integration of fruit and oak. Full, backward, concentrated, splendid fruit. Real breed. Very long and complex. Excellent. Needs time. The best of the Saint-Juliens.

Léoville-Poyferré 1998–2012 15.5

Good colour. Rich nose. Ample, fat, succulent. This is promising. Good oak too. Medium-full. Good ripe mulberry fruit. This is balanced and stylish. Long and with good depth. But not as long or as fresh as Langoa.

Saint-Pierre 1997–2002 13.5

Good colour. Just a little stringy on the nose. Seems a bit hollow behind it. There is ripeness here. But it is as much astringent as tannic. Unbalanced. Medium-full. No charm.

Talbot 10.0

Good colour. This is not very inspiring. Weedy and metallic on the nose. This ends unpleasant. I've seen this wine on many occasions now and I know this is not a bad bottle. Talbot 1989 is a disaster.

PAUILLAC

d'Armailhac 1997–2007 14.5

Good colour. Fragrant and fruity on the nose. But lacks a bit of grip. Medium-full. A little tannin shows. Pleasant fruit. Reasonable balance. But a little dull. Lacks personality.

Batailley 1997–2005 14.0

Good colour. Open, plump fruity nose. A little boiled sweet and caramel like a burnt jelly. Medium body. Pleasant fruit. Not unbalanced, but a little short and without the grip and breed of a top classed growth. Will come forward soon.

Carruades de Château Lafite

1997–2012 16.0

Good colour. Good oak, good balance, good breed here on the nose. This is promising. Medium-full. Lacks a little bit of concentration and intensity on the attack but the finish is long, classy and rich. This is very good. Very fresh.

Clerc-Milon 1999–2015 16.0

Good colour. This is much better than the D'Armailhac. Fuller, more concentrated, more grip on the nose. Fullish. Good grip. Good positive attack and a long intense finish. Stylish too. There is depth here. Needs time.

Cordeillan-Bages 1999–2014 15.5

Good colour. Firm, concentrated, this has style and depth. Unexpectedly good. Backward. Spicy. Fullish, balanced, concentrated, plenty of grip. This is very good indeed. Integrated and with plenty of character. Not the class for great though.

Duhart-Milon 1998–2010 14.5

Good colour. Quite marked by the new oak on the nose. A little rigid too on the palate. The tannins obtrude just a little. But the follow-through is better. More ample. Yet in the end it lacks the grip and flair and freshness for better than quite good plus.

Grand-Puy-Lacoste 1998–2018 16.5

Good colour. Ripe and plump and quite concentrated. Doesn't have the taint I noticed in the Haut-Batailley and the Ducru – also in the Borie stable. Fullish. Good old viney fruit. Ripe tannins. This has grip and depth and style. Long and subtle and classy. Very good.

Haut-Bages-Libéral 1997–2007 13.0

Good colour. Clean stylish nose. Not a blockbuster but flesh plump and balanced. On the palate the tannins are a little brutal. Ripe and spicy and fullish but a bit lumpy. Will it always be a little astringent?

Haut-Batailley 1998–2008 14.0

Good colour. Just something a little tainted on the nose. Plump but flat and dull. A bit cleaner on the palate. Medium-full. Lacks a bit of personality.

Here is a note from a clean bottle sampled September 1992: Good colour. A little austere on the nose. A lack of generosity but no undue tannic astringency. Better on the palate. Seems much riper. Fuller, more backward than Léoville-Barton. Firm, rich, very well-balanced. Good depth. Classy. Very good. (1998–2016, 15.5)

Lafite 2000–2020 19.5

Good colour. Less flamboyant than Mouton, more depth and class perhaps. Medium-full. On the palate full, concentrated. Very good oak and breeding of fruit. This is very classy and beautifully balanced. Long and subtle at the end. Much better than Latour. Less flamboyant than the Mouton but more to it.

Latour   1998–2014   17.0

Good colour. A cool nose. More Latour than 1989. But it lacks the intensity of Lafite and Mouton underneath. Oaky, of course. Not a blockbuster. An aloof wine. It doesn't have the power and intensity of a first growth. Stylish and oaky though.

Lynch-Bages   1999–2019   17.5

Good colour. Lush, spicy nose. Ample and ripe, but without the interest and class of Pichon-Baron. Rich fat, full and chocolatey on the palate. Very good grip. This is fine. Long and lush and complex and voluptuous.

Lynch-Moussas   1995–2002   13.0

Good colour. Ripe and damson-fruity on the nose but hollow underneath. Inherently weak. Medium body. Fruity and forward. Not a lot of tannin. But reasonably fresh. Not bad.

Mouton-Rothschild   1999–2015   18.5

Very fine colour. Very cedary, lead-pencils on the nose. Very Mouton. But lush and concentrated underneath. Full, lush, flamboyant. Sexy. Oaky. Fine but I prefer the breed and class of Lafite.

Pichon-Longueville, Comtesse de Lalande
                          1997–2011   16.5

Good colour. Lovely soft mulberry-raspberry fruit on the nose. Inherently plump. Medium-full body only. Lacks a little grip, and intensity. Lynch-Bages, let alone Pichon-Baron, is better. The fruit is very pretty but it lacks a bit of depth.

Pichon-Longueville-Baron
                          1999–2020   18.5

Fine colour. Excellent nose. This is very concentrated and very ripe. A lot of power of flavour here. Fullish, rich and concentrated. Very good oak integration. Very good grip and intensity. First growth quality.

Pontet-Canet   1998–2010   14.0

Good colour. A bit sweaty on the nose, like someone else's feet. Cleaner on the palate after aeration. Good ripe fruit. Fullish. Quite a lot of obtrusive tannin but seems balanced. Has grip. Lacks just a little style and personality.

Réserve-de-la-Comtesse 1996–2005   15.0

Good colour. A gentle, very ripe, fruity wine on the nose. Medium body, balanced, amply fruity. Quite forward. Soft but charming. Good.

SAINT-ESTÈPHE

Calon-Ségur   1997–2003   13.5

Good colour. Barnyardy nose. Weak and hollow in the middle. No grip. No fat. Medium-full.

Ripe but as much astringent as tannic. An inherently unbalanced wine. Yet not too short.

Cos d'Estournel   1998–2015   17.0

Good colour. Quite easily the best of the Saint-Estèphes. The only one with real class on the nose. Lovely fruit here. Great harmony. Fullish, rich, balanced. Real finesse here. Lovely. Very long. Very well-balanced.

Haut-Marbuzet   1998–2008   15.0

Good colour. Ample, voluptuous, oaky nose. Medium-full, flamboyantly lush and oaky on the palate. Ripe and fleshy. This is good. Long on the palate. Seductive.

Lafon-Rochet

(Corked) Note from September 1992: Medium colour. Reasonable fruit on the nose. Not too hard. Quite cool in flavour. Medium-full. Not too aggressively dry tannin but it lacks a bit of flexibility and charm. Slightly dry on the finish. Not bad to quite good. (1997–2007, 13.5)

Lillian-Ladouys   1998–2008   14.5

Good colour. Good ripe fruit on the nose. A little Saint-Estèphe hardness too. Medium-full on the palate. Good oak. More style than most. This is plump, ample and generous. Shows well.

Meyney   1997–2004   13.5

Good colour. Plump nose. Inherently soft for a Saint-Estèphe. Medium-full. On the palate balanced and ripe. Quite succulent. But it lacks a bit of charm and real interest and style.

Montrose   1997–2004   14.5

Good colour. Soft nose. There is fruit here but it lacks a bit of depth and concentration. Medium to medium-full. Quite round already. Some fruit and reasonable acidity but it lacks a bit of flair and personality.

Les Ormes-de-Pez

(Corked) Note from September 1992: Good colour. Smoky nose. A little dry and papery, even. Cooked fruit and spice on the palate. Yet reasonable acidity and fat. Yet slightly hard in the flavour. Lacks a bit of charm. Quite good. (1997–2007, 14.0)

de Pez   1998–2006   14.0

Good colour. This is a bit *sauvage* on the nose. On the palate the wine has structure and depth. This has good length and harmony. It is not *that* stylish, but it never is. But a well-made fullish example.

Phélan-Ségur   1997–2003   13.0

Good colour. The tannins obtrude a bit. There is a dryness and an emptiness in the middle here. Not too bad on the palate though. Some fruit. Medium to medium-full. Ripe, reasonable balance. Lacks a bit of harmony though.

1988 CLARET

The 1980s ended with three vintages of quality, but three vintages of striking contrast one with another. The first was consistent, but somewhat cool and distant in its youth. On paper a vintage of structure and balance, but in the mouth a year of wines which lacked the ineffable character and personality of a great vintage. This was followed by a pair of prolific but early vintages ripened by great heat but retarded by drought, resulting in wines of richness but irregularity. Prices rose, only to fall again when the worldwide economic depression began to bite. Stocks of all three vintages, at the châteaux, in the Bordelais *chais* and down the pipeline to the wholesalers in Europe and America are currently high. Demand has evaporated.

Logically, 1988 being less good than the best of 1989 and 1990, this is the vintage which may turn out to be the poor relation. It is good but not exceptional. But it has improved as it has aged, which is better than the reverse, and it may turn out to surprise us further. Like all vintages it will find its place if it is allowed to find its price. When this will be only time will tell. My guess is later rather than sooner. But in the meanwhile here is a progress report, based on a tasting made after the wines had been safely in bottle for a year or more, and before they retire into the shell of adolescence.

THE WEATHER

The winter of 1987/88 was extremely wet. Some 60 per cent more rain than the average fell from November to April, and it continued raining on and off until the first week of July. 'It could hardly have rained more during the first half of the year,' said Gérard Gribelin of Château de Fieuzal in September. Yet, if wet, it was warmer than average. Indeed there was no real winter at all and this stored up potential problems in the form of mildew, black rot and insect depredation, making it necessary to spray, spray and spray again to keep the vegetation and embryonic fruit in a healthy condition. After an April and May which were 1.5 to 2 degrees warmer than normal (and 40 per cent wetter), there was a very cold and stormy end to May followed by a sudden warm period at the beginning of June. This was precisely what had happened in 1984 and there were fears that the disastrous Merlot flowering of four years previously would recur. Thankfully this did not take place. The flowering happened very quickly in the second week of June (*demi-floraison*, 12 June). There was some *coulure* and *millérandage*, and to the Cabernet Sauvignons as well as the Merlots, but this would only serve to increase the concentration of the remaining fruit by reducing the quantity. *Coulure qualitative*, as Alexandre Thienpont of Vieux Château Certan put it. There was also quite a lot of black rot, which further shortened the potential crop, and hail on 29 June which ran through Arsac, Moulis and Listrac and across northern Margaux. Pauillac and the Graves were also touched.

From 5 July onwards the summer was very dry and warm, though seldom hot. July was statistically perfect: almost exactly the equal in temperature and precipitation to the average of the previous 30 years. August was hot and almost totally rainless, 16 millimetres of rain were precipitated against an average of 64, but no one can recall exactly when this occurred. At the beginning of September there was a shower or two, but hardly enough to get to the roots, and after a heatwave between the 4th and the 15th there began to be fears of drought. A lack of moisture actually has the effect of retarding the progress towards maturity, as any gardener will tell you, and though at the time the fruit turned colour (*mi-veraison*, 17 August: similar to 1987 and 1985 but earlier than 1986, 1983 and 1981), a harvest in full swing by Monday, 26 September (for the red wines), had been predicted, growers were now speaking of October.

After 15 September the weather cooled, though there was still no rain, and the white wine harvest began around the 19th. It took place in excellent conditions and the fruit was in an exceptionally healthy state.

The curtains then parted for the red wine harvest. When the growers picked, and precisely how ripe the fruit was to be at the time of collection was, as ever, to prove crucial, as was the amount of grapes collected.

The rain that fell at the end of September seems to have done little harm to the Merlot, certainly in Saint-Emilion and Pomerol, and the grapes, again particularly in the Libournais, were ripe. But the maturity of the Cabernet Sauvignon obstinately refused to progress. The sugar content remained *bloqué* at a potential alcohol level of 10 to 10.5 degrees. Some growers panicked after some heavy rain which fell on the 12 October and rushed straight out to complete the harvest. Others sat it out. Those who waited at least until the weekend of 15/16 October before recommencing did better. The fruit picked between the 21st and the 23rd was better still.

Nevertheless, it soon became apparent that a significant proportion of the crop *had* been picked, not at the beginning or at the end of the month, which would have been ideal, but in the middle. Despite the big gap in optimum maturity between the Merlots and the Cabernets, few properties could afford to leave their pickers standing around idle for a week. The drought particularly affected the Médoc with its well-drained soils. The Cabernet Sauvignon, always the grape that matures the latest, was unwilling to evolve to concentration. Moreover, as one grower pointed out, the *veraison*, when the grapes change from green to black in the middle of August, was slow to complete, and so in October the ripeness within single bunches was uneven. As another told me: 'I waited and waited. And though my tannins did eventually get riper my Cabernets didn't really increase in sugar or decrease in acidity.' In short, the fruit could have been richer. And yet there was one saving grace. There was not a bit of rot.

THE QUANTITY

As important as the climatic conditions and the date of the harvest was the amount of wine produced. The simple global figure hides the real picture. Overall the *appellation contrôlée* red wine *rendement* was 3.64 million hectolitres, the same as 1987 and 25 per cent less than 1986. Yet in Saint-Emilion the harvest was 25 per cent less than 1987! The average yield at *premier grand cru classé* level was 37 hectolitres per hectare. But at Château Latour it was 55 hectolitres per hectare (though less than 50 in the sections which produce the *grand vin*). Nearby at Château Pichon-Longueville, Comtesse de Lalande, the overall figure was 60. In Saint-Julien 'almost everybody' or 'all except one' of the classed growths, according to my sources, applied for the 20 per cent PLC (*plafond limité de classement*) on top of an already generous *rendement annuel* of 48 hectolitres per hectare. And some still had to send surplus wine away for distillation. Of course every single top proprietor will assure you of the remarkable sacrifices they have made in rejecting vats of only marginally inferior wine in the creation of the *grand vin*, and some, such as Prieuré-Lichine and Malescot in Margaux, practised a *saignée de cuve*, draining off some excess liquid before proceeding with the fermentation. Nevertheless one cannot help wondering if their vines would not have yielded more satisfactory fruit in the first place if they had not been so heavily laden.

THE WINES

Nineteen eighty-eight is a vintage where the higher up the hierarchy you progress the better the wines are. The lesser wines, the *bourgeois* growths and minor classed growths of the Graves and Saint-Emilion, and their equivalents, are at best correct, at worst boring and fruitless. What is missing is concentration and richness, heart and soul, personality and depth. Above this level, both in the Libournais and in the Médoc and Graves, particularly in Saint-Emilion and Pomerol, and in Saint-Julien and Pauillac, there is excitement to be found, plenty of consistency and no lack of character. The wines have a good colour, a medium to medium-full weight, good levels of acidity and, at the top levels, plenty of fruit. These wines will need the usual ten-years-after-the-vintage timespan before they will be mature, but will make attractive bottles in the first decade of the 2000s. Overall, judging by the top wines – and there are many – the vintage is superior to 1981 across the board, better than 1983 and 1986 in Saint-Emilion and Pomerol, and firmer but less attractive than the 1985s. There are many better 1982s, 1989s and 1990s, and in the northern Haut-Médoc the 1986s are a great deal more profound. But there is much to enjoy in the years to come.

THE TASTING

The vast majority of the following wines was tasted over a three-day session hosted by Adnams Wine Merchants at The Crown, Southwold in January 1992. There were a few gaps. These I have filled in from similar comprehensive tasting sessions in which I took part in Bordeaux in April 1991, and in the USA the following fall.

	Optimum drinking	Mark out of 20

FRONSAC AND CÔTES-CANON-FRONSAC

Canon 1995–2005 15.5
Good colour. This is very good. Backward, profound nose. Chocolatey. This is serious stuff. Full, concentrated, rich and ample. Almost chocolatey in flavour. Lush, ripe, balanced. Fine for a Fronsac.

Canon-de-Brem Now–1997 13.0
Good. This is firmer and richer, altogether a more serious wine than La Dauphine on the nose. Medium body. A little tannin. Good grip and depth. Not as much style as the other two Canons though. Not bad.

Canon-Moueix Now–1997 14.0
Good colour. Stylish fruit on the nose. Good substance but neither too dense nor too hard. Medium to medium-full. Good tannins. Good grip. This has plenty of well-balanced, rich fruit. Long and rather more stylish than most.

Cassagne-Haut-Canon Now–1997 13.0
Good colour. Plump nose. Not a lot of style but good fruit here. Medium to medium-full. It lacks a little concentration and lushness, and is as much astringent as tannic on the attack. It lacks a little personality as a result, but it's not too coarse. Not bad.

Dalem 1995–2002 14.5
Good colour. Quite a backward nose. But very fruit. Medium-full. Still some tannin. There is concentration here and plenty of depth. Balanced. Long. Complex. Stylish. Very good for a Fronsac.

La Dauphine Drink soon 12.0
Good colour. Merlot nose, but without a great deal of zip or personality. Lightish. A bit raw on the palate. There is an absence of real richness and ripeness here. And a slight lack of style.

Fontenil Now–1999 13.5
Good colour. Good plump rich nose. But a touch hard still. Medium-full. Ripe fruit. A little tannin. A touch bitter on the finish but this is no bad sign. Well-made. Finishes positively.

Moulin-Haut-Laroque Now–1998 13.0
Medium-full colour. Quite dense on the nose but lush fruit underneath if no great style. Medium body. Plump fruit. Lacks zip but quite pleasant.

La Rousselle Now–1997 12.5
Medium-full colour. Lighter, more accessible nose. Higher toned. Medium body. Not a lot of tannin. The fruit is a little bitter and skinny. Unexciting. Lacks zip and fat and elegance.

Vieille-Curé Now–1998 12.5
Good colour. Slightly inky and dense on the nose. Also a little rigid. Medium to medium-full body. A shade rustic on the palate. As much astringent as tannic. Yet it finishes better than it starts. Ripe but lacks style. Not bad.

Villars Now–1998 13.0
Medium to medium-full colour. A little more open on the nose. Medium body. Correct but lacks personality. A bit more richness and a bit of new oak would not have gone amiss. Not bad.

LALANDE DE POMEROL

des Anneraux Drink soon 11.5
Medium colour. A loose-knit, Merlot-based wine on the nose. Medium body. Ripe but a bit superficial. Not bad, but will get attenuated.

De Bel-Air Drink soon 12.0
Medium to medium-full colour. Quite ripe, but a bit tanky on the nose. Reasonable fruit, grip and substance on the palate. This has a positive finish. Quite good. Lacks a bit of style though.

Bertineau-Saint-Vincent
Drink soon 14.0
Medium colour. It is a little overblown on the

nose I find. Not the wood of later vintages. Yet this is evident on the palate. Medium-full, rich, meaty, quite concentrated. Has depth. Good plus. Above all it has style.

Bourseau   Drink soon   10.5
Medium-full colour. Rather dull and tanky on the nose. Medium body. A bit anonymous. Reasonable structure and fruit, even balance. But dull.

Canon-Chaigneau   Drink soon   11.0
Medium colour. Rather dull and tanky on the nose, even more so than the Bourseau. This is a bit rigid and astringent. I can't get excited. Medium body. Will it round off? I doubt it.

La Croix-de-Cheneville
Drink soon   12.5
Medium-full colour. There is not a lot of style here. But there is good fat and grip. Medium body. Ripe fruit. Well-balanced. At least quite good. Just about ready.

La Croix-Saint-André   Drink soon   13.0
Medium-full colour. A meaty, oaky wine. Perhaps a bit rustic, but depth here. Medium to medium-full body. Quite ripe, with grip as well as fruit. Not the greatest of class but better than most. Quite good plus.

Garraud   Drink soon   12.0
Medium colour. This won a gold medal at the 1990 Concours Agricole in Paris. It is less tanky than the Haut-Chaigneau, but nevertheless a bit dumb. Medium body. Some suppleness. Mainly Merlot fruit. Quite good grip but really lacks intensity. Finishes well. Quite good.

Haut-Chaigneau   Drink soon   11.0
Medium-full colour. Silver medal at the Concours Agricole perhaps, but aged all or mainly in tank and a bit rigid as a result. This lacks style and is a bit lumpy. Medium body. Not exciting.

Les Hauts-Conseillants   Now–1998   14.0
Full colour. Quite fat and meaty on the nose. Plump fruit. Good ripeness. A bit of new oak on the nose and palate. Medium to medium-full. Ripe, even rich. This has depth and interest. Good plus.

Moncets   Drink soon   12.5
Medium-full colour. Reasonable fruit on the nose, but could have done with more maturing in wood. Quite ripe and with reasonable grip. Quite good depth. Medium body. Quite good plus.

De Roquebrune   Drink soon   12.0
Medium colour. Plump but essentially a rather loose-knit Merlot on the nose. Reasonable fruit, style and grip though. Medium body. Quite positive. Quite good.

Sergant   Drink up   9.0
Medium colour. Thin, weedy, astringent.

Domaine de Viaud   Drink soon   10.5
Medium colour. Some substance but a bit dry and rustic on the nose. Lightish, some fruit, even a touch of oak. But a bit short. Getting astringent.

Vieux-Chevrol   Drink soon   10.5
Medium colour. A bit too much *cuve*, could have done with a bit of breathing in oak (in fact reared in old *demi-muids*). Pleasantly fruity but little depth and style. Will get attenuated.

SAINT-EMILION GRANDS CRUS

Cartier   Now–1997   13.0
Good colour. Not a lot of body or depth but fruity and charming. Forward. Medium body. Fresh. A little tannin. This has good personality. Well-made. Well-balanced.

La Commanderie   1995–1999   12.5
Good colour. This is a Cordier property, but they didn't make this wine, only reared it. I find it a bit astringent. Good fruit but a lack of grace. A little stewed. Average.

La Fleur   Now–1998   13.5
Medium to medium-full colour. Good middle-of-the-road Merlot on the nose. No great depth but well-made. Medium body. Cheerful, plump, quite forward wine. No pretention but attractively balanced. Finishes positively.

La Fleur-Pourret   Now–2000   13.5
Medium-full colour. This has a very similar nose to Petit Figeac. On the palate a little more flexibility and style. Medium to medium-full. Reasonable fruit and grip. But not that exciting.

Franc-Mayne   Now–1999   14.5
Good colour. This has structure, depth and new oak on the nose. Stylish and balanced. Shows well. Medium body. A little tannin. Round, ample, quite succulent. This is fresh and well-made. Finishes positively.

Haut-Corbin   1995–2004   15.0
Very good colour. Fresh, ripe nose. Good fruit. Medium to medium-full body, good aspect of new oak. Good fat, good grip. This is good for a 1988. The wine is long, stylish and quite complex. Shows well. Plenty of attraction here.

Le Jurat   1995–2002   14.0
Very good colour. Less opulent on the nose than the 1989 but has style and depth. More open. More classic. Medium-full, quite ripe, lacks a bit of grip though. The finish is oaky but not special. Quite good.

Petit-Figeac   Now–1999   13.0
Medium-full colour. Ripe, quite structured nose. Well-made but no great class. Medium-full. A little lumpy. There is substance here but no great finesse.

Saint-André-Corbin Drink soon 12.5

Medium colour. Soft, ripe, cheerful nose. Forward, light, inconsequential. A pleasant wine of good generic standard. But no more.

Le Tertre-Rôteboeuf 1995–2005 16.5

Good colour. Oaky nose, and quite toasted at that. This is very good. Fullish, lush, rich and seductive. Not over-oaked. Quite concentrated. Very ripe. Very well-balanced. A lot of fruit and personality crammed in here. Very good plus.

SAINT EMILION GRANDS CRUS CLASSÉS

L'Angélus Now–2002 14.0

Medium-full colour. Soft, ripe, oaky nose. This has style. Medium body. Not an enormous amount of tannin but this has good balanced fruit, a good oaky base and it finishes well. Needs a bit more class and zip. Quite good.

L'Arrosée 1995–2003 14.5

Medium to medium-full colour. Plump nose but not nearly as oaky as I had expected. Slightly more so on the palate. Medium to medium-full body. Quite rich and lush but not a wine of great concentration.

Balestard-la-Tonnelle Now–1999 13.5

Medium-full colour. Chunky Merlot nose; not a lot of personality. Light to medium body. Reasonable fruit and grip. A bit more class than usual. Less chunky and rustic than on the nose. Not exciting though.

Beau-Séjour-Bécot Now–1997 13.0

Reasonable colour. A bit sweaty on the nose. Rather weak on the palate. This is a bit of a disappointment. It lacks concentration and grip and consequently hasn't much style. Not bad at best. Will get astringent.

Cadet-Piola Now–2004 14.5

Medium-full colour. Ripe, quite voluptuously rich, oaky nose. Medium body. Good ripe tannins. A touch of oak. There is good fruit here, even a touch of concentration. Finishes well. A velvety wine. Good.

Canon-La-Gaffelière 1995–2003 14.0

Medium-full colour. Firm nose, quite closed. Good depth and even concentrated. A touch of oak. Medium body. Some tannin. There is balance and structure here but not a great deal of personality. Finishes positively though. Improved in the glass. Quite good.

Cap-de-Mourlin Drink soon 12.0

Medium-full colour. Less rustic than Balestard (in the same stable) as usual, but I get a curious whiff of old tea on the nose. Lightish. Not much tannin. This is thin and already a bit attenuated. The Balestard is better. This is dreary.

Clos-des-Jacobins Drink now if at all 11.0

Good colour. Cassis jam on the attack. Slightly dense and stalky/lumpy yet oaky underneath. As it developed seemed a bit thin and attenuated. Medium body. Lacks grip. Finishes insipidly. Poor.

Clos-Saint-Martin Now–2000 13.5

Medium-full colour. Quite strongly oaky on the nose, and the oak is more toasted than most. The Merlot is ripe but quite spicy. I miss a bit of style. Medium body. Reasonable balance. Not bad.

La Clotte 1995–2004 15.0

Good colour. Fat, rich but slightly closed and even dense nose. But has depth. Slightly foursquare as yet. Medium-full body, but there is richness here. Good fruit. Good grip. Even quite concentrated. Finishes well.

La Clusière Drink soon 12.5

Medium colour. Pleasant nose, but less personality than the Pavie-Ducasse. On the palate the wine is light, as much astringent as tannic. There is a lack of fruit and personality. Not special.

Corbin Now–2002 14.0

Medium-full colour. Quite firm and rich. A little closed. This has oak and reasonable structure. Some depth. Medium to medium-full. Quite good. Positive finish.

Dassault Now–2002 14.0

Medium-full colour. Good, soft, oaky nose. This is stylish. Medium body. Balanced, ripe and oaky. Yet it lacks just a bit of concentration and personality. A well-made wine though.

La Dominique Now–1998 13.5

Medium-full colour. This is ripe and very Merlot. I don't find the usual oak. Nor is there much concentration. Disappointing it has to be said. A bit better on the palate. Reasonable grip and a bit of oak. But lacks a bit of style. Medium body.

Faurie-de-Souchard Now–1997 13.5

Medium-full colour. A light, forward nose but not without balance and elegance. Well-made. Light to medium body. Not a lot of tannin. Yet harmonious and stylish. But essentially a little slight. Forward.

Fonplégade Now–1998 13.0

Medium colour. Ripe but slightly chunky Merlot on the nose. Not a lot of oak: not a lot of style. Light to medium body. Little tannin. Reasonable acidity but lacks concentration and depth.

Fonroque Now–2002 15.0

Medium-full colour. A little less rich, but slightly more accessible than Moulin-du-Cadet on the nose. There is a slight touch of peppermint here. Just a touch of oak on the palate. Medium body.

Ripe, has personality and grip. Finishes well. Good backbone but not hard. Good. Slightly less to it but more stylish than Moulin-du-Cadet.

Grand-Mayne   Now–2002   14.0
Medium-full colour. Ample, fat, quite oaky nose. On the palate the oak dominates a bit. The wine is only medium-bodied. Reasonable fruit, grip and style. Quite good.

Grand-Pontet   Drink soon   11.5
Medium colour. A bit insipid on the nose and the palate. The wine lacks structure and depth. The dollop of new oak is merely rather cracked make-up which fails to hide the raddled old bag inside. Disappointing.

Guardet-Saint-Julien   Now–2001   14.0
Medium to medium-full colour. This has got some new oak now. But the nose is both soft and a bit rigid. No enormous structure on the palate but ripe and balanced, with a good oaky base, and with stylish fruit. A charming wine.

Haut-Sarpe   Now–1999   13.5
Medium-full colour. Open, slightly jammy-Merlot nose; a bit rustic. Light to medium body. A touch of oak. This is a cheerful, fruity wine with good acidity. A little suave and without much style. Not bad though.

Larcis-Ducasse   Now–1997   12.5
Medium colour. Loose-knit, Merlot nose. Lacks zip and style. Thin on the palate. A lack of selection. Little tannin. Somewhat rustic in character. Unexciting.

Larmande   1995–2005   15.0
Medium-full colour. Quite a firm nose, a touch austere. Quite full but seems to lack a little richness. The tannins are less ripe, but the balance is good and there is no lack of fruit. Medium-full. It will never be as lush or as seductive as the 1989 but this is a good example which will keep well.

Moulin-du-Cadet   Now–2002   15.0
Medium-full colour. Well-made, quite rich, balanced nose. Not a blockbuster and no real depth or class but attractive and harmonious. Medium to medium-full body. Good grip. Good ripe tannins. Long and stylish. Good.

Pavie-Decesse   Now–2000   14.0
Medium to medium-full colour. Ripe, quite classy nose. Good fresh, plummy fruit. Medium body. A little tannin. This is a ripe, pleasantly fruity wine, but it doesn't have enormous length or character. Not bad to quite good.

Pavie-Macquin   Now–2001   14.5
Medium to medium-full colour. Ripe, open, fruity nose. Light to medium body. A bit of new oak. This is by no means a blockbuster but is balanced and stylish and has character. An attractive example with good fruit.

Petit-Faurie-de-Soutard   Drink soon   12.0
Medium-full colour. Merlot nose, rather attenuated; unsophisticated, light, a bit thin, a bit one-dimensional, a bit short. Already a bit attenuated on the finish. Dreary.

La Serre   Now–2000   13.5
Medium-full colour. Quite stylish on the nose but a little raw. Good acidity but lacks real concentration. Medium body. Quite stylish but lacks a bit of structure and zip on the palate. A bit dull.

Soutard   1997–2002   15.5
Medium-full colour. Quite an austere nose, but not too hard. Fullish body. A backward wine. A little tough at first but good fruit and concentration and very good grip underneath. Will need time, but there is quality here. What it lacks is a bit of sex appeal.

La Tour-du-Pin-Figeac (Moueix)   Drink Soon   12.5
Medium-full colour. Soft, ripe nose, very Merlot, not very distinguished. Lightish. Rather blowsy. As much astringent as tannic. Short.

Troplong-Mondot   1996–2006   16.0
Medium-full colour. Good nose; rich, fat, oaky. Good depth here. Medium-full, rich, fat, concentrated and oaky on the palate, with good plummy fruit and good acidity. This is very good. Class as well as character. Needs time; will keep well.

Villemaurine   Drink soon   11.0
Medium colour. Thin attenuated nose. This does not inspire. This has a rather over-evolved nose and is weedy and rustic on the palate. Will fall apart soon.

SAINT-EMILION *PREMIERS GRANDS CRUS CLASSÉS*

Ausone   1998–2020 Plus   18.5
Good colour. Slightly closed. Very classy indeed. Lovely oak base. This has a lot of style indeed. Very lovely silky wine. Not a blockbuster of course. Splendid character and complexity. Medium-full. Very long, very subtle. Very very long and lovely.

Beauséjour-Duffau-Lagarrosse   1998–2015   16.0
Good colour. Full nose. Just a little dense. Medium-full body. Quite a lot of tannin and quite firm still but has grip and depth underneath. It is a touch aggressive but it finishes better than it starts. Very good. Needs time.

Belair   1997–2015   17.0
Medium-full colour. Very classy on the nose. Not a blockbuster but harmonious and subtle. On the palate it is medium to medium-full. Fine acidity. Very elegant. It is a misleading wine at first, but it

has lovely breed and complexity on the finish. Very long and subtle.

Canon 1999–2019 17.5
Medium-full colour. Splendid nose. Closed, rich, old-viney. Less Merlot than most. Marvellous fruit and very good grip. Fullish. Very good tannins. Rich, fat, good oaky base. This has lovely balance. It is backward but very good indeed.

Cheval-Blanc 1999–2019 18.5
Good colour. Splendid nose. This is oaky in a splendidly supportive sense, with lovely rich, fat, concentrated fruit. Real character. Real breed. Less evolved than most. Full, tannic. Quite a lot of oak. Real depth and class but needs time.

Clos-Fourtet 1997–2012 15.5
Good colour. Full rich nose. A touch sturdy but no lack of class. Medium to medium-full. Ample, balanced. Good. It lacks a little subtlety and concentration compared with most, but it is stylish nevertheless.

Figeac 1996–2012 17.0
Medium-full colour. Firm, oaky nose. A little closed and unforthcoming as yet. Medium to medium-full. Ripe, oaky, quite concentrated, certainly stylish. But does it quite have the fat and weight of the best. Very good though light. Best on the finish. This is certainly a success.

La Gaffelière 1997–2012 16.0
Good colour. Quite rich and oaky on the nose. This has depth. Medium to medium-full body. Good balance and good integrated oak. Subtle. Stylish. Good grip. This shows well, but it doesn't quite have the intensity for great. Very good.

Magdelaine 1997–2012 16.0
Medium-full colour. Rich, concentrated Merlot nose. Quite closed but potentially very ample and lush. Medium-full, ripe, rich and plump. Yet I miss a bit of real complexity. Very good but not fine. Lovely balance though. Very seductive.

Pavie 1998–2018 18.0
Good colour. Clean, clear-cut, ripe, rich and classy on the nose. I really do like this very much. Quite full. Excellent ripe tannins. Very concentrated. This is poised, elegant and rich. Long and full of character. Fine.

Trottevieille 1996–2010 15.5
Good colour. Good nose. Fine fruit, balanced, stylish. Not a blockbuster. Medium body. Good integrated oak. Shows well. It is not great but it is stylish and balanced. Cool. Nice. Long.

POMEROL

Beauregard 1997–2012 16.5
Medium-full colour. Firmish, but good fruit on the nose. Nose slightly inflexible. Medium-full. The tannins are a little raw still but it has good oak

and plenty of richness and depth behind it. Long. Very good indeed.

Bonalgue Now–1999 14.0
Medium-full colour. A bit like Prieurs-de-la-Commanderie. Round and ripe but a lack of real personality and class. Slightly less oak. Medium body. Pretty on the attack. Quite accessible. Also quite good. Plump. Ready soon.

Le Bon-Pasteur 1995–2003 15.0
Medium-full colour. Rich and fat and concentrated on the nose. Good oak base. This is better. Medium-full. Ample, quite concentrated. Balanced. Quite lush. Good but lacks the depth and class for any better. Good length. Positive finish.

La Cabanne Now–1997 13.0
Medium-full colour. Quite stylish fruit on the nose. A little too feeble and lacking real grip on the palate though. No more than pretty.

Certan-de-May 1997–2015 18.5
Good colour. This is an exciting 1988. One of the very best. Lovely nose. Very fine concentrated fruit, a lot of depth. Full on the palate. Rich, classic, very classy. A lot of depth and really very fine, complex fruit. High class.

Certan-Giraud Now–2005 15.0
Medium-full colour. Quite a firm nose, but there is good richness here, some new oak. Good attack; amply fruity, gently oaky, medium to medium-full body. Good tannins. Doesn't quite have the intensity and depth for more than 'good', but this is an attractively balanced, stylish wine. An improvement on earlier vintages. Slightly less intense but more elegant than Bon-Pasteur.

Clinet 1997–2010 16.5
Fullish colour. Somewhat herbaceous on the nose. A touch of runner beans. Tannins and long extraction shows. Rich underneath though. Better as it evolved. Fat, fullish, firm, oaky. Good grip. This is surprisingly good. Very good plus.

Clos Du Clocher 1995–2002 14.5
Medium-full colour. Ripe nose. Good substance. A shade raw and four-square. Oaky. Not as rich as Bon-Pasteur. Slightly lumpy. As much astringent as tannic at first. Quite new oaky. A little overwhelmed. Better than most of this flight (of lesser Pomerols) though.

La Conseillante 1995–2008 16.0
Medium-full colour. Soft nose, fragrant, very subtle oak base. Long and lingering and complex. Stylish. Not a blockbuster. Medium to medium-full. Good oak. Lovely fruit. Balanced and complex, but somehow not quite the personality or the intensity for better than very good. Slightly disappointing.

La Croix Now–1996 13.0
Medium to medium-full colour. A bit dense,

even rustic on the nose. Lacks nuance and finesse. Lightish. Short. Boring. One-dimensional. Will get astringent.

La Croix-de-Gay   Now–1999   13.5
Medium-full colour. Somewhat lactic on the nose. This got better on aeration, and one could see reasonable fruit, in a slightly lumpy way, underneath. Medium body. A little astringent. Quite ripe but lacks elegance. A little stewed. Not bad at best.

Clos L'Eglise   1995–2008   16.0
Good colour. Quite a toasted oak, but it doesn't dominate. The wine is fat underneath. This has depth and attraction. Medium-full. Good tannins. This is vigorous, balanced, ripe and full of personality. Good fruit. Very well balanced with acidity. Fresh. Long. Complex. Stylish. Very good.

Domaine de L'Eglise   1995–2005   15.0
Medium-full colour. Quite stylish on the nose. Not too feeble. Medium body. Pretty and certainly not weedy. Balanced and stylish, even quite complex. A little slight but much better than I expected.

L'Eglise-Clinet   1997–2012   17.0
Medium-full colour. Merlot nose. Ample, rich, succulent. But does it lack a little class? Lush though. Yet firm as well as fat and concentration. Medium-full. Rich. Good balance. More class than the nose would suggest. Fat and long and ample on the finish.

L'Enclos   1995–2010   16.5
Medium to medium-full colour. Neatly balanced, stylish nose. Not a blockbuster. Medium to medium-full body. Good grip. It doesn't quite have the concentration and depth of fine but it is balanced and elegant, with a good oaky base. Long and subtle.

L'Evangile   1998–2018   17.5
Medium-full colour. Fine concentration on the nose. Quite backward. This has a lot of depth. But closed. Fullish, very good tannin. Very good subtle oak background. This is fine. Backward. Intense. Balanced. Rich. Masculine for a Pomerol. Very, very long and complex.

Feytit-Clinet   Now–2001   14.0
Medium to medium-full colour. Not a lot of substance here. The nose is vinous but lacks a little personality and depth. Yet good, balanced fruit. Medium body. An attractively balanced if unpretentious bottle. Finishes reasonably long.

La Fleur-de-Gay   Now–2000   14.0
Medium-full colour. This is the 100 per cent new oak *tête de cuvée* of La Croix-de-Gay. On the nose this wood dominates. Good fruit on the attack, and a lot of oak, but underneath there is no concentration. Will always be rather top heavy. If you want to drink oak chippings, this is for you. It is not for me!

La Fleur-Gazin   Now–2001   14.0
Medium-full colour. Riper and more characterful than Feytit-Clinet on the nose. Just a bit more structured. But also a bit denser. I find a little excess *vin de presse* here. Medium body. A bit chewy. Good acidity but not as much charm as the above.

Le Gay   1995–2002   13.0
Medium-full colour. Quite austere on the nose but not too dense. Slightly malic. Quite full. Some tannin. Good grip. But it is a bit lumpy and four-square. It lacks grace, richness and sex appeal. Lacks a smile in fact.

Gazin   1995–2005   15.0
Medium-full colour. Upright, fresh, stylish. Good zip. Good fruit. Medium body. Round and ripe and generous but not quite the concentration and zip and character of the best. Will come forward quite soon. Just a touch one-dimensional.

Gombaud-Guillot   Now–1999   12.0
Medium to medium-full colour. Fruity but a bit rustic on the nose. On the palate yet more rustic. Medium to medium-full. Not short, but has little style.

La Grave-à-Pomerol   1996–2013   16.0
Medium to medium-full colour. Stylish nose. Ripe and balanced. Good zip. Not a blockbuster though. This has good concentration and intensity. Medium to medium-full. Rich, quite fat and ample. Lush fruit and very good grip. Unexpectedly good.

Haut-Maillet   Now–2000   14.0
Medium colour. Plump, attractive nose, if not one of great depth. Medium body, ripe tannins, a touch of oak. Quite succulent fruit. A well-made, *bourgeois* example. A pleasant bottle, without great pretention, for drinking reasonably soon.

Lafleur   1999–2020 plus   18.5
Fine colour. Full, backward, almost dense nose. Full, tannic, solid old viney. This has a really fine intensity of flavour on the follow-through. Concentrated and rich and exciting. Very fine. Very impressive.

Pensées de Lafleur   Now–1997   14.0
Medium to medium-full colour. Light and forward on the nose. A little dilute but gently oaky and quite pleasant. Ditto palate. The oak gives it a bit more personality than some. Positive finish. Forward.

Lafleur-Pétrus   1996–2010   16.5
Medium-full colour. Elegant nose. Good fruit, but it lacks just a bit of intensity. Medium-full. Stylish. But it lacks just a little zip. Round fat and rich. Quite long. Certainly balanced. But no better than very good plus.

Lagrange Now–2003 14.5

Medium-full colour. Rich, quite fat. Fullish and plump but quite open. Medium body. A little tannin. Soft, feminine, elegant, stylish. Good balance. A well-made example, without the depth or personality for great.

Latour-à-Pomerol 1997–2013 17.0

Medium to medium-full colour. Firm, full, rich old viney nose. Intense Merlot fruit. Fullish lush, fat and ripe. It doesn't quite have the intensity or grip of Vieux Château Certan but it is generous and ample and long. Very good indeed.

Mazeyres Now–2000 14.0

Medium to medium-full colour. A little neutral on the nose. Some substance. Good fresh fruit on the palate. Medium body. A bit neutral on the follow-through. Better than Prieurs though.

Montviel

Medium to medium-full colour. This wine won a *médaille d'or* at the Concours Agricole in Paris in 1990. Sadly my bottle was corked and we did not have a duplicate.

Moulinet Now–1998 13.5

Medium to medium-full colour. Medium weight on the nose. Round, plump, quite pleasant, quite accessible. Not bad, but a lack of real richness, weight and personality. Medium body.

Petit-Village 1997–2010 16.0

Medium-full colour. Markedly oaky on the nose and quite a toasted oak at that. A little too much oak perhaps. Medium-full, fat, ample, balanced. But at present I can't see much subtlety and elegance. Very good but no better. Good length.

Pétrus 2000–2025 18.5

Full colour. Quite sturdy, certainly backward on the nose. Very backward on the palate too. Full, tannic, but it doesn't seem to have any more intensity than Lafleur. Fine but not great.

Le Pin 1995–2008 16.0

Good colour. Rich, opulent, oaky nose. On the palate the wine is medium-full. The attack is ripe and opulent, but there is a slight lack of intensity on the follow-through. Fat and rich, balanced and fruity, but not quite the consistency of intensity to be rated better than very good.

La Pointe 1997–2010 15.5

Medium-full colour. Gentle but quite markedly oaky nose. Soft but stylish. Good fruit. Medium body. Ripe tannins. An elegant wine but not a wine of enormous depth or concentration.

Prieurs-de-la-Commanderie
 Now–2000 13.5

Medium-full colour. Round and ripe on the nose but a lack of real personality and class. A touch of oak. Medium body. Quite ripe tannins but a bit boring. Quite good at best.

de Sales Now–2001 14.0

Medium-full colour. Soft and fruity on the nose. Quite elegant but a bit slight. Light to medium body. A better grip than some of the other wines of this size. Good fruit, but no real dimension.

Taillefer Now–1996 13.0

Medium to medium-full colour. A little light on the nose. Lacks grip and class as well as substance. Uninspiring. Weedy, rustic, will get attenuated. Light to medium body. Drink soon.

Trotanoy 1997–2013 17.5

Fullish colour. Lovely nose. Lush, oaky, rich, complete. This has excellent fruit. More generous than Lafleur. Fullish, lush, ample, concentrated. This has breed and voluptuous, potentially silky fruit. No better than Latour-à-Pomerol though.

Vieux-Château-Certan 1998–2020 18.5

Medium-full colour. This is very fine. Lovely concentrated on the nose. Real depth here. Splendid fruit. Even better than the Evangile. Very rich and concentrated on the palate. Really lovely fruit and intensity. Fullish but not sturdy or dense. Splendid fruit. Very, very long and lovely.

GRAVES

Bahans-Haut-Brion Now–2000 14.0

Medium-full colour. The nose has gone back into its shell a little. Medium body. Not a great deal of tannin. This has a reasonable attack. Slightly hard but with plump fruit, but not much of a follow-through. Reasonable finish if without much complexity. Quite good.

Bouscaut 1996–2000 12.5

Medium to medium-full colour. A bit rustic and lacking richness on the nose. Medium body. As much astringent as tannic. No selection here. Somewhat loose and dull. Tailing off at the finish. Unexciting.

Brown Now–1996 12.0

Good colour. Broad nose. Quite ripe but a bit rustic. On the palate medium body. Rather hard and ungenerous. Nothing much to commend it except that it is not short on the palate.

Carbonnieux 1995–2002 13.5

Medium to medium-full colour. Round nose but not much depth and character. Medium body. Not much tannin. Lacks depth and character and also richness and personality. OK but boring.

Les Carmes-Haut-Brion 1996–2005 15.0

Medium colour. Ripe, mulberry nose. Some new oak. Not a blockbuster but stylish. Medium body. This is balanced and stylish. A well-bred wine. Good oak base. Good fruit. Neat. Good. Long.

Domaine de Chevalier 1998–2018 17.5

Medium-full colour. Fine oak, balance, breeding: all on the nose. Typically Chevalier. Medium-full body. Quite pronounced oak on the palate, but this is a support to very stylish, harmonious, complex fruit. This is distinctly classy. Fine.

Du Cruzeau — Now–1997 — 13.0
Good colour. Slightly raw on the nose but reasonable fruit. On the palate medium bodied. Not a lot of class, richness and depth but the fruit is quite ripe and ample. Finish is quite positive. Not bad.

De Fieuzal — 1998–2006 — 13.5
Good colour. Substance here. But a bit sturdy at present. I find this astringent as well as tannic. Inky and bitter. Rather too hard on the attack. Medium to medium-full. Some tannin. Finishes a little better. But unexciting.

Gazin — Now–1997 — 12.5
Medium colour. This wine describes itself as *cuvée vierge blanche*. Plump fruit but not a lot of grip and depth. The fruit seems a bit artificial. medium body. As much astringent as tannic. Unbalanced. Yet the fruit isn't as hard as Brown, for instance.

Domaine de Grandmaison — Drink soon if at all — 11.0
Medium colour. A bit stalky and hard and fruitless on the palate. Lacks generosity. Lightish. Sour. Not much tannin. This is thin and malic.

Haut-Bailly — 1997–2010 — 15.5
Medium-full colour. Quite a solid, confused nose. Yet there is richness underneath. Medium-full. Some oak. Quite backward. There is fruit and grip but not enough concentration and style for more than good plus. Improved on aeration.

Haut-Bergey — Now–1998 — 13.5
Medium colour. Lightish nose. Pleasantly fruity. But not of any great consequence. Medium body. A little tannin. Reasonably ripe and attractive. Good acidity. Quite good.

Haut-Brion — 1998–2020 Plus — 18.5
Full colour. Lovely nose. Concentrated, elegant, subtle. Very good base of oak. Medium-full. As always, a wine of delicacy rather than muscle; intensity rather than power. Very complex, very long, very harmonious. Very fine.

Haut-Gardère — Now–1998 — 14.0
Good colour. Some depth but not a lot of richness on the nose. Medium body. A little tannin. A little firmer than the Haut-Bergey. A little more to it. Reasonable fruit. Good grip. Finishes with reasonable style and length.

Lafargue — Now–1997 — 12.5
Good colour. Ripe, slightly earthy, lacks distinction on the nose. Light to medium body. As much astringent as tannic. No flesh though some fruit. But essentially a bit hard.

Larrivet-Haut-Brion — 1996–2006 — 14.0
Medium-full colour. Pronounced new oak on the nose, and toasted oak at that, but not a wine of great size. Pronounced oak on the palate. Too much so. Too rigid. Not enough concentration and grip in the wine to match it. A pity.

La Louvière — 1997–2005 — 15.0
Medium-full colour. Slightly sweaty nose. Some H2S at first. A bit lumpy. There is depth here, but it is a bit adolescent. Medium to medium-full body. Ripe tannins. Good oak and even quite rich on the finish. I'll give this the benefit of the doubt. Good.

L de Louvière — Now–1996 — 13.5
This is the second wine of La Louvière. Very good colour. Soft, but plump and elegant and quite amply fruity on the nose. No real depth though. A well-made example, which will evolve soon.

Malartic-Lagravière — 1996–2005 — 14.0
Medium to medium-full colour. Slightly inky on the nose. Hard and dense. Medium body. Some substance and depth. Finishes better than it starts. Good grip. But a certain lack of generosity. Quite good.

La Mission-Haut-Brion — 1997–2012 — 18.0
Full colour. Lovely concentrated, blackcurrant fruit. Very classic. Full, good tannin. Classy, rich, concentrated. Very long. Very fine.

Olivier — 1997–2005 — 14.0
Medium-full colour. Clean, not too rustic but somewhat nondescript nose. Slightly dense and raw on the attack. Medium to medium-full. Some tannin. Lacks a bit of richness and personality and new oak at first but finishes better. Quite good.

Le Pape — Now–1997 — 12.5
Good colour. Rather green and herbaceous on the nose. I'm not at all sure that it isn't a bit oxidized as well. There is some fruit here on the palate. Medium body. Lacks style though.

Pape-Clément — 1999–2018 — 17.0
Medium-full colour. Good nose. Fat, rich, oaky, plenty of depth and class. The oak is a touch more obvious than in the Haut-Brion. Fullish, substantial. Complex. Good tannins. This has plenty to commend it. Not quite as subtle as Chevalier.

Pique-Caillou — Now–1997 — 13.5
Good colour. Fresh, fruity, quite stylish nose if no great depth. Light to medium body. Not much tannin. Reasonable fruit. For early drinking. Not bad.

de Rochemorin — Now–1998 — 13.5
Good colour. Not a lot of personality on the nose but clean, ripe, balanced and well-made. Rather more classy than its stable-mate Du Cruzeau. Medium body. Quite round and ripe. Reasonable quality. A bit one-dimensional, though not short.

Le Sartre Now–1998 13.0

Medium colour. Smells a bit papery. Also a touch herbaceous. Medium body. As much astringent as tannic. Yet reasonable fruit underneath. Not short. Not bad.

Smith-Haut-Lafitte Now–1998 13.0

Medium to medium-full colour. A little weak on the nose. Merely pretty. But quite attractive fruit. Lightish. Little tannin. Nothing much here. Forward. What there is has reasonable style and balance.

Domaine de La Solitude
Now–1997 13.0

Medium colour. Light nose. Not much here. Not disagreeable, just anonymous. Lightish. Quite pleasant if not particularly stylish. Forward. A little short.

La Tour-Haut-Brion 1996–2009 15.5

Good colour. Good Cabernet fruit on the nose and the palate. Medium-full. Good grip. And not dense. Positive all the way through. Finishes well.

La Tour-Martillac Now–1997 14.0

Good colour. Soft nose. Pretty but a shade dull and one-dimensional. Lacks depth. Light to medium body. Little tannin. A slight wine, essentially a little lacking in concentration, though not that unstylish.

MÉDOC AND HAUT-MÉDOC

Arnauld Drink soon 12.5

Medium to medium-full colour. Ripe, plump fruit. Clean and stylish if without a great deal of depth. Medium body. Just about ready now. Pleasant but lacks interest on the follow-through. A bit one-dimensional.

Beaumont Now–1998 13.0

Good colour. A more subtle wine than the Arnaud but a little four-square on the nose. Better on the palate. Ripe, plump, plummy wine with a touch of new oak. Good persistence if not much complexity. Not bad.

Belgrave Now–1996 12.5

Medium colour. Nothing much here on the nose. Nor on the palate. This is light, and as much astringent as tannic. Hollow in the middle and not really very stylish on the outside. Disappointing. A lack of a really rigorous selection. Forward.

Du Breuil Drink soon 11.0

Light, forward. One-dimensional. This will get astringent. Unexciting.

Camensac Now–2000 13.5

Medium to medium-full colour. Reasonable nose, though a little anonymous. Medium body. Pleasantly oaky and fruity on the palate but lacks a bit of depth and grip. Correct but not much personality. Not bad.

Caronne-Sainte-Gemme
Now–1998 12.5

Medium to medium-full colour. Quite a solid wine. There is ripeness here. Medium to medium-full. Some tannin. Some fruit, even a bit of concentration but the background is artisanal. Positive finish though. Not bad.

Cissac Now–2000 14.0

Medium-full colour. Not much nose. On the palate this is stylish and well made, with a good oaky background, neat fruit and a positive finish. Not a great wine – not a great vintage – but competent and enjoyable. Quite good.

Citran Now–2003 15.0

Good colour. Interesting, quite high-toned, oaky nose. Good attack. Quite new oaky. Ripe and open with its fruit, almost in a summer-pudding sense. Medium to medium-full. Good grip. Much more positive and elegant than most. Very good for a *bourgeois*. Good length and a long finish.

Coufran Now–1997 12.0

Medium-full colour. Ripe Merlot nose but rather one-dimensional. Not a great deal of weight, nor a great deal of dimension. Not much style to the fruit. Not exactly short but lacks grip.

Hanteillan Now–1999 14.0

Medium to medium-full colour. Good nose. Quite rich, stylish fruit, and a touch of oak. Medium body. Plump and ripe. Good grip. Quite unaggressive and seductive. Ripe and balanced. Good.

La Lagune 1998–2015 16.5

Medium-full colour. Typically rich, ripe, well-made new oaky La Lagune nose. Good. Medium-full. A wine with good concentration of fruit. Good grip and ample and luscious character. Good ripe tannins. Well-integrated oak. Long. Very good plus.

de Lamarque Drink soon 12.0

Medium-full colour. Quite an accessible, open, plump nose, a bit like the Arnauld. Not a great deal of power underneath. Forward. Some fruit. Stylish because it has a hint of oak. But a bit weak and insignificant.

Lanessan Now–1997 12.5

Medium to medium-full colour. Earthy nose. Somewhat lacking character. Medium body. No real class. No real personality. A little tannin. But the wine, essentially, is dull.

Larose-Trintaudon Now–1998 12.0

Medium to medium-full colour. There is fruit and balance here but nevertheless something artisanal on the nose. Rather dull on the palate. Some fruit and reasonable balance but no flair, no excitement.

Liversan   Now–1998   11.5

Medium to medium-full colour. Dull, four-square nose. No excitement here. Medium body. Lacks a bit of class, certainly lacks character and depth.

Malescasse   Now–2000   13.0

Medium colour. Plump, quite classic. Not an enormous amount of depth but has good fruit. Medium body. A gentle, quite stylish wine. A little superficial but balanced and pretty, and it finishes positively. Quite good but lacks a little personality.

du Moulin-Rouge   Now–1997   12.0

Medium to medium-full colour. Plump nose, some Merlot; not bad but without a great deal of style and personality. Pleasant, medium bodied. But a bit dull.

Les Ormes-Sorbet   Now–1997   12.5

Medium-full colour. Attractive oaky element on the nose. Ripe and stylish. Medium body. Quite round already. Not dominated by the oak. This is ripe, with a touch of spice. Good definition. Good fruit.

Patache d'Aux   Now–1997   12.5

Slightly better colour than the La-Tour-de-By. Riper on the nose. This is a well-made *cru bourgeois*. Medium body. Pleasant fruit. The tannin is quite mellow. Attractive and positive. Finishes well.

Plagnac   1995–2002   13.0

Good colour. Good fresh nose and palate. Plump blackberry fruit. No great depth but good acidity. Medium to medium-full. Reasonable balance.

Potensac   1995–2003   13.5

Good colour. The nose is a bit hidden but on the palate this is very good for what it is. Medium-full, quite rich. Very good fruit and balance. In its *bourgeois* way surprisingly stylish if a touch one-dimensional. Well made.

Sénéjac   Now–1998   13.0

Medium to medium-full colour. Some richness and depth on the nose, but a slightly earthy element as well. Medium to medium-full. Good grip. Fresh fruit and some more to offer on the follow-through. Quite good.

Sociando-Mallet   Now–1997   14.0

Good colour. Ripe, gentle, stylish, oaky nose. Medium to medium-full. This is by no means a blockbuster. A bit loose-knit. The attack is good but it tails off a bit at the end. It lacks a bit of zip.

Soudars   Now–1999   13.5

Medium-full colour. Gentle, plump, oaky nose. This has the definition and style the Verdignan lacks. Medium body. Ripe and plump on the palate. Quite good grip. A touch of oak. Reasonable length. Reasonable style. Quite good.

La Tour-de-By   Now–1996   12.0

Medium to medium-full colour. A little hard and fruitless on the nose. Nothing much on the palate. Reasonable grip but no charm or succulence.

La Tour-Carnet   1995–2003   13.5

Medium colour. Soft, fruity nose, quite stylish. Medium body but like with many 1988s, there is a lack of complexity on the follow-through after quite a promising attack. Lacks a bit of concentration and depth but not bad.

Tour-Haut-Caussan   Now–1998   13.0

Good colour. Good blackcurrant, Cabernet fruit on the nose. And a touch of oak. Good depth. Medium to medium-full body. Ripe, even rich. Good structure and balance. Has dimension and style.

La Tour-Haut-Moulin Drink soon   13.5

Medium-full colour. On the nose there is a lack of personality though the fruit has depth and even concentration. On the palate medium to medium-full. Quite rich. There is a little astringent but the net effect is more positive than most. Quite good.

La Tour-de-Mons   Drink soon   11.0

Medium-full colour. Soft and ripe but a shade weak on the nose. A bit astringent on the palate and rather short. A bit loose here.

La Tour-Saint-Bonnet Drink soon   12.0

Medium-full colour. A little blunt on the nose. Light to medium body. Fruity and pleasant but a bit superficial. Ready now.

Verdignan   Now–1997   12.0

Medium-full colour. Rather pedestrian on the nose. No style. A boring Merlot-ish wine. A bit astringent on the palate. No enjoyment to offer.

Vieux Robin, 'Bois de Lumière'
                                 Now–1996   12.5

Good colour. Ripe, touch of oak. Good blackberry fruit on the nose. A little over-extracted on the palate, leaving as much astringency as tannin. Medium body. A touch short. Not bad.

Villegeorge   Now–1998   12.0

Medium colour. Not a lot of weight or interest on the nose and the attack is a bit insipid. There is a lack of depth and concentration, though the wine is not short. Just boring.

LISTRAC AND MOULIS

Chasse-Spleen   1998–2012   14.5

Medium-full colour. More reserved on the nose, more adolescent than Poujeaux. Less new oak. Better as it evolved though it does not show the immediate charm of Poujeaux. Medium-full body. Good and quite rich and balanced underneath. Finishes well. May improve. Today I prefer Poujeaux.

Ducluseau   1996–2000   13.5
Medium-full colour. A little dry on the nose. But there is fruit here. Medium body. As much astringent as tannic, lacks a little grip. Quite clean though. Not bad.

Duplessis   Drink soon   10.5
This is a rather dull, thin wine without much fruit. Rather short and will become astringent.

Fonréaud   Now–1997   11.5
Medium to medium-full colour. Not much personality and style on the nose either. A little more weight, but not much more length or style. A shade astringent on the palate. Boring as well.

Fourcas-Dupré   Now–1998   12.5
Medium to medium-full colour. Ripe, round, reasonable grip on the nose. Medium body. Pleasant, plump, Merlot-ish attack, quite fresh. Lacks a bit of complexity on the follow-through. Not bad.

Lestage   Now–1996   11.5
Medium to medium-full colour. A bit soft, Merlot-y and boring on the nose. Not much here on the palate, and the wine is a bit short. Flat on the finish. Dull.

Maucaillou   Now–2000   13.0
Quite good colour. Fresh nose, without a lot of depth and concentration. The palate substantiates this. Reasonable grip and fruit. But a touch anonymous in the end. Needed to be a bit more concentrated. Not bad.

Moulin-à-Vent   Now–1997   12.5
Medium to medium-full colour. Earthy, *goût de terroir*, but an absence of freshness on the nose. A bit astringent on the palate. There is a lack of grip in most of these Listracs and Moulis. But this is a little riper and more positive than most. Not bad.

Peyredon-Lagravette   Now–1998   12.0
Medium to medium-full colour. Slightly edgy on the nose. A bit astringent on the palate. Dull. Medium body.

Poujeaux   1997–2010   15.5
Medium-full colour. Ripe, oaky, indeed even quite opulent on the nose. Good class. A well-made wine. Medium to medium-full body. Rich oaky balanced and ample. Stylish. Good length.

MARGAUX

d'Angludet   1996–2004   14.5
Medium-full colour. A touch of oak on the nose. Quite sturdy, as usual, but rich underneath on the nose. On the palate, though the elements are there, and the fruit ripe and balanced, it lacks a little richness and excitement. Good though.

Boyd-Cantenac   1998–2006   12.5
Medium-full colour. Full and hard and inky on the nose. As usual this is tannic and rather hard. Lacks suppleness and fruit. No charm.

Brane-Cantenac   Now–1997   13.0
Medium colour. Rather a dry, insipid, papery nose. A little fresher and fruitier on the palate but essentially a rather one-dimensional wine which is somewhat short.

de Candale   Now–1998   13.5
Good colour. Somewhat more austere and tannic on the nose. One can discern the oak. Medium body. The tannins are quite dominant, but the follow-through is rich and plump. This is good for a second wine. Good length. Stylish and positive on the finish. Shows well.

Cantenac-Brown   1995–2000   13.5
Medium-full colour. Some oak, but this is really little more than a mask over a wine with little concentration and style. Medium body. Not much tannin. Lacks grip and real personality. Dull. One-dimensional.

Canuet   Drink soon   11.0
Medium colour. Soft, pleasant nose. A touch of oak, but weak-kneed essentially. Evolves fast in the glass. Got weedy rapidly. Light. Short. Very obviously a second wine. Drink soon.

Dauzac   1995–2000   13.5
Medium-full colour. A lot of oak sitting over a wine which is soft and not nearly concentrated enough to support it. Medium body. Pretty but essentially a bit one-dimensional. Not bad at best.

Desmirail   Now–1998   13.5
Medium colour. A soft but rather four-square wine on the nose. Little oak. Little personality. Medium body. Reasonably fresh and fruity. Not short. It is not too bad, as the finish is positive. But it is a bit dull.

Durfort-Vivens   no Future   11.0
Medium colour. A bit rustic on the nose. Somewhat weak on the palate. There is not really very much here and for a *deuxième cru* it is very disappointing. Lightish, weak, short, will get astringent.

Ferrière   1995–2002   13.5
Medium to medium-full colour. Fresh nose. But not much depth or personality. Medium body. Reasonably well made but dull. Will come forward soon.

Giscours   Drink soon If At All   10.0
Medium to medium-full colour. Poor nose. Very weedy and attenuated. Even worse than the Malescot. Thin, attenuated and distinctly rustic.

La Gurgue   Now–1998   13.5
Good colour. Stylish nose but it lacks a bit of richness and concentration. Medium body. Not a lot of tannin. There isn't a great deal of concentration

here. The wine is well made but a bit one-dimensional. Quite stylish. Quite good.

d'Issan Now–2002 15.0
Good colour. Fresh, ripe, stylish nose. Balanced and charming. On the palate medium bodied, gently oaky, plump and fruity. The attack is good but it doesn't have a lot of depth and dimension behind it. What it lacks is a bit of complexity on the finish. But a good 1988.

Kirwan Now–1997 12.5
Medium-full colour. Smoky, bonfiery nose. Rather light and weedy on the palate. A lack of structure and selection. Dilute and short. Will get astringent and attenuated. A disappointment. Lacks grip.

Labégorce-Zédé Now–2004 15.0
Good colour. A wine of medium weight but with real grace and elegance. Supple fruit. Ripe and balanced. Not a blockbuster but good intensity on the follow-through. Good.

Lascombes 1996–2004 13.5
Medium-full colour. A bit lumpy on the nose. Lacks grace. Not enough selection here. Medium to medium-full body. As much astringent as tannic. Lacks depth as well as class. Dull. One-dimensional.

Malescot Drink soon if at all 11.0
Medium colour. Some *tabac*. Seems a bit weedy and attenuated. Lightish, more astringent than tannic. Weedy on the palate. This is poor.

Margaux 2000–2020 18.0
Fullish colour. Strongly oaky, as usual. But at least this seems to have the weight to support it. Fullish, tannic, ripe, very good grip. Youthful. But a bit rigid at present. I score this highly, but as much giving it the benefit of the doubt as for what reveals itself today.

Marquis d'Alesme-Becker 1996–2004 13.5
Medium to medium-full colour. Quite oaky, but there isn't a great deal underneath. Medium to medium-full. A little forced. A little astringent as if a bit too much *vin de presse* had been added. Some tannin. Lacks grace and real grip. Dull.

Marquis-de-Terme 1996–2006 14.5
Medium-full colour. Quite oaky on the nose. But seems reasonably full and fat as well. Yet more pleasure to be had here than from most. Has balance and length. Not dense, as it has been in the past.

Monbrison 1995–2003 14.5
Medium-full colour. Oaky, stylish, gentle nose. Medium body only. A little tannin. This is quite stylish but there really is not a great deal there. Good fruit and reasonable length though.

Palmer 1995–2005 16.5
Good colour. Soft, fragrant, oaky-cedary nose: lovely fruit. Medium body. Stylish and complex, and elegant on the palate. The fruit is fresh, ripe and quite rich. But it doesn't quite have the intensity and concentration to be rated 'fine'.

Pavillon Rouge du Château Margaux 1995–2005 15.5
Medium-full colour. Good new oaky nose. Ripe and classy. Medium-full. Elegant fruit. Good acidity. Plenty of personality.

Pouget 1995–2002 13.0
Good colour. Slightly better than the Boyd. Rich but slightly bitter blackcurrant nose. Tarry as well. Medium body. The tannins are a bit astringent and the wine is a little short. Some fruit but no real grip and richness. Not bad at best.

Prieuré-Lichine 1996–2005 14.5
Medium to medium-full colour. Not a great deal forthcoming on the nose. Medium to medium-full body. Ripe tannins. This is well balanced but it lacks real richness and concentration. Quite good at best. At least it has some depth and length.

Rausan-Ségla 1995–2008 15.5
Medium-full colour. Stylish, gently oaky nose. Not enough grip and concentration underneath. It is elegant. Medium body and pretty. But it lacks grip and concentration. Good plus at best.

Rauzan-Gassies Now–1997 11.5
Medium colour. Rather inelegant on the nose. A bit astringent on the palate. Medium body. No depth. A lack of grip. Soupy but short.

Segonnes Drink soon 11.0
Medium colour. This is a forward, pleasantly fruity wine with a touch of astringency as much as tannin. A bit weedy on the finish. Forward. Nothing special.

Siran 1995–2002 13.5
Medium to medium-full colour. Not a great deal here. Medium body. As much astringent as tannic. Lacks a bit of grip, as well as class and personality. Not bad at best.

du Tertre 1996–2004 14.5
Good colour. Depth and substance here on the nose. This has good oak if no real breed. Medium-full. Good substance and richness. A well-made example, as often, but what it lacks is real subtlety and class. Reasonably long.

La Tour-de-Mons Now–2002 14.5
Good colour. Soft, quite perfumed nose. There is good fruit here, and good length. A medium-bodied, fresh, charming wine with a good follow-through. Shows well.

SAINT-JULIEN

Beychevelle   1996–2002   15.0
Medium-full colour. The nose lacks depth and personality. By no means a blockbuster. Lack of real selection? Medium body. Only a little tannin. Some fruit but no concentration. Rather flat and one-dimensional. Disappointing.

Branaire   1997–2007   14.0
Medium-full colour. Just a little solid on the nose. Meaty, quite rich. Pedestrian on the palate. Medium body. As much astringent as tannic. Lacks flair and depth.

Ducru-Beaucaillou   1999–2019   17.0
Fullish colour. Hidden nose. Very good fruit underneath. Ripe, classy. Medium-full. It is not as rich or as concentrated as the Léovilles Las-Cases and Barton, but the fruit is very fine and the Ducru breeding is evident. Balanced and lovely.

Duluc   Drink soon   11.0
Medium colour. Plump and cheerful on the nose if not with any great depth. Light and a bit short. Nothing much here. Rather anonymous and will get astringent. Uninspiring.

Les Fiefs de Lagrange   1996–2000   13.0
Medium-full colour. Light, quite forward but quite stylish nose. But a bit one-dimensional. Medium body. A little charmless on the attack. Somewhat neutral. Lacks a bit of flesh.

Gloria   1996–2008   14.5
Medium-full colour. Fragrant Cabernet nose but without a great deal of richness and depth. Pleasant fruit. Medium body. Some tannin. Quite stylish. But lacks a little personality.

Gruaud-Larose   2000–2020   16.5
Medium-full colour. Backward, solid but fleshy nose. Rich. Full bodied. Tannic. A little hard and bitter at present. Yet there is depth and quality here. Needs time.

Lagrange   1998–2012   15.5
Good colour. Good oak. Ripe, quite rich. Certainly stylish. Not a blockbuster though. Medium-full body. Good ripe tannins. Good touch of oak. Balanced and quite concentrated. Not great, but well-made.

Lalande-Borie   1997–2007   14.5
Medium-full colour. A little hard on the nose. Medium body. This has some depth and personality on the palate. Some tannin. Reasonably ripe. Has charm.

Langoa-Barton   1998–2015   16.0
Good colour. Quite closed on the nose. Good Cabernet richness underneath though. Medium body. Good tannins. This has sex appeal and flesh. A ripe wine. Gently oaky. Very good. Finishes long. Good balance and concentration.

Léoville-Barton   2000–2025   18.0
Fullish colour. Marvellous fruit on the nose. Rich, fullish, almost chocolatey. Very good oak base. This is full, has lovely ripe tannins. Ripe and generous. Very long. Very classy and very harmonious. Fine.

Léoville-Las-Cases   2000–2025   18.5
Good colour. Fine nose. A classic. Fullish, concentrated, rich and ripe; with great dignity and poise. Real depth here. This is serious stuff. Concentrated and rich. Fullish. Very good tannins. Firm and classic Cabernet. Very fine.

Léoville-Poyferré   1995–2001   13.5
Reasonable colour. A little lightweight on both nose and palate, as I have noted before, and now the finished article is in bottle one can see that this was not one of Poyferré's greatest successes. The wine lacks concentration. Pretty but forward. A lack of real selection here.

Clos du Marquis   1996–2002   13.5
Medium-full colour. A little forced on the nose. Lacks flair, lacks zip. Medium body. Not a lot of tannin. This is obviously a second wine. The concentration is not there. But the wine has reasonable balance.

Saint-Pierre   1998–2012   15.0
Good colour. Good ripe nose, but without a great deal of depth and concentration, it seems. Medium-full body. Quite rich and concentrated. Some tannin. Just a little four-square. What it lacks is a bit of depth and personality. Reasonable balance.

Talbot   1996–2000   (see note)
Medium-full colour. There is a curious old-tea element on the nose here. I don't remember it like this! Weedy. Vegetal. And not very subtantial. Curious. (To date I've sampled this four times since it was in bottle. On all other occasions I've enjoyed it and given it 15.5.)

Terrey-Gros-Caillou   1994–1998   12.0
Medium-full colour. Lumpy, unstylish nose. A bit stewed. Quite ripe but essentially rather undistiguished. Medium-full body. Reasonable grip. But lacks style.

PAUILLAC

Carruades de Château Lafite   1995–2000   14.0
Medium to medium-full colour. Pleasant, cedary, slightly aromatic nose. Subtle, if not great depth. Good but it nevertheless lacks a bit of grip and dimension. It is stylish but ultimately it is a touch insubstantial.

Clerc-Milon   2000–2020   17.0
Good colour. Quite a bit more concentration than Mouton-Baronne-Philippe. Rich and concentrated. Old-viney even. Similar palate. Fullish.

Good tannins. Rich and potentially opulent.
Good grip. Long. Lovely.

Colombier-Monpelou   Now–1998   12.0
Medium colour. This is rather undistinguished. A
wine with a good dollop of *vin de presse* into a
rather dilute, original wine. Especially weak.
Quite ripe, but a weedy element on the finish.

Cordeillan-Bages   1995–2005   15.5
Good colour. Fullish, earthy nose. Slightly solid.
A good meaty wine on the palate. There is some
old-vine richness here and no lack of depth. Indeed quite concentrated. This shows well. Good
plus. Needs time.

Croizet-Bages   Drink soon   11.0
Medium-full colour. Light nose. Light and sweet
and already as much astringent as tannic on the
palate. Short. Will dry out soon. Unexciting.

Duhart-Milon   2000–2020   16.0
Good colour. Just a little hard on the nose. Solid
and tannic but it lacks a bit of real richness. Full,
plenty of tannin and depth. Not too solid. This
has the richness on the palate. Not quite the flair
of fine but very good.

Fonbadet   Now–1998   12.5
Medium-full colour. Undistinguished, slightly
sweaty nose. A lack of richness on the palate.
Medium-full. Reasonable grip, but neither finesse
nor complexity here. Four-square.

Grand-Puy-Ducasse   Now–2001   14.5
Medium-full colour. This is fresh, balanced and
not without depth. Charming, stylish and balanced. Good length. A wine for the medium
term. Good.

Grand-Puy-Lacoste   1997–2007   14.5
Medium-full colour. This is riper on the nose
than the Haut-Batailley. More personality, more
sex appeal. Medium to medium-full body. Ripe
but a bit superficial for Grand-Puy-Lacoste. Not a
patch on Clerc-Milon. Lacks real grip.

Haut-Bages-Avérous   1997–2005   14.0
Very good colour for a second wine. Quite fleshy
on the nose but lacks a little real richness. Medium
body. A little one-dimensional but good for a second wine. Quite ripe. Quite long.

Haut-Bages-Libéral   Now–2005   15.0
Good colour. This is a good 1988. Ripe blackcurrant nose. Medium-full body. Good tannins. The
attack is quite rich, certainly plump. It has some
drive – more than most – on the palate but a slight
absence of real flair. Good though. More to it
than Grand-Puy-Ducasse.

Haut-Batailley   1996–2002   13.0
Medium-full colour. A little anonymous on the
nose. It lacks concentration and flesh. On the
palate as much astringent as tannic. A bit short.

Lacks real richness and it lacks depth and grip too.
Disappointing.

Lacoste-Borie   1996–2000   12.5
Medium-full colour. A little vegetal and forced on
the nose. Hard and driven. This has a touch of
new oak, but is essentially rather rustic. Lacks
charm. Medium body.

Lafite   2002–2025   18.5
Good colour. Splendid nose. Real breed. Lovely
oaky base. Medium-full body. A subtle, intense
example. Good oak. Good tannin. It is not a great
wine though. An element of real concentration
isn't there. But long, balanced, complex.

Latour   2002–2025   19.0
Good colour. Very Latour. Classically austere.
Firm, Cabernet. Too austere? Quite full, some
tannin. As usual a backward wine with indis-
putable class on the finish. Very fine indeed without a doubt.

Lynch-Bages   1998–2018   17.0
Good colour. Fleshy and ripe. Good new oak.
Not a blockbuster though. Medium-full, ripe and
opulent. This is balanced and generous with a
touch of spice. Good grip. Very good plus. Long.

Mouton-Baronne-Philippe
1998–2008   15.0
Medium-full colour. Good Cabernet on the nose.
Good substance. A little cool though. Not
enough real concentration. Medium to medium-
full body. Good tannin. Quite ripe and balanced.
But it lacks dimension and richness.

Mouton-Rothschild   2000–2018   16.5
Good colour. Opulent, oaky nose, but quite how
much depth is there underneath? Medium-full.
Ripe, but seems strangely uninvolved. The opulence and the concentration are not there. The
least good of the Pauillac first growths.

Pibran   1997–2007   15.0
Medium-full colour. Quite attractive fruit on the
nose but no real weight behind it. Medium body.
Ripe, good tannins. This has charm and even bal-
ance and finesse but is of only *bourgeois* aspiration.
Good though.

Pichon-Longueville-Baron
2002–2025   18.5
Good colour. Quite marked by the new oak on
the nose. But rich, concentrated, fat and successful. Full, tannic, rich and even quite powerful.
This is high class. A true Pauillac. Very concentrated. Very good grip. Long and lovely.

Pichon-Longueville, Comtesse de Lalande
2000–2025   18.5
Good colour. Fleshy, aromatic, very ripe and
concentrated nose. Quite open. Does it have the
grip of Baron? Medium-full. Really very classy

fruit, beautifully balanced. Very, very ripe. This is long and seductive. Plenty of grip indeed. Very complex. Very classy.

Pontet-Canet   Now–2001   14.0
Good colour. Some substance on the nose, though not a lot of style. Medium body. Some tannin. Ripe and fruity though it lacks real concentration. Yet quite well balanced. The finish is positive, but it lacks personality. Quite good at best.

Les Hauts de Pontet   Now–1997   13.0
Quite good colour. There is a certain lack of personality and fruit here, though more substance than the second wine of Lafon-Rochet. Rather anonymous though.

Les Tourelles de Longueville
         Now–1999   13.0
Good colour for a second wine. I don't get a lot on the nose. The palate seems to have a certain extracted, vegetal touch. Medium body. Unexceptional. Future vintages are rather better.

SAINT-ESTÈPHE

Andron-Blanquet   Now–1998   13.0
Good colour. There is something a little rustic and vegetal about the nose. Medium body. Not a lot of backbone and structure. Indeed I wonder if it wouldn't have been better to have bottled it a bit earlier. I find it a touch astringent, and also a little weak-kneed. Fair only.

Calon-Ségur   1995–2000   13.5
Good colour. This is a pretty wine, but it is lighter than I expected and more evolved. Neat, gently oaky, but lacks a bit of grip and dimension. For a Calon, though it has style, it is a bit slight. Not bad.

Chambert-Marbuzet   Now–2001   14.5
Medium colour. A little dense on the nose. Chunky, even. Ripe and chocolatey on the palate. Some oak. Medium body. There is a little bit of astringency on the attack but the follow-through is fat and ample. This is good. A rich wine. Not without concentration – or, indeed, class.

Cos d'Estournel   1999–2020   18.0
Fullish colour. Splendidly rich nose. Very opulent and plump. Quite toasted oak. Medium-full, very ripe tannins. Balanced, rich and sexy. Another lovely seductive wine from Bruno Prats. Very long. Fine.

Cos-Labory   1997–2012   15.5
Medium-full colour. Round nose. Quite charming. Not a blockbuster. Neatly made. Medium

body. Good oak touch to it. Ripe, balanced and attractive. Good length. This has style.

Haut-Marbuzet   1997–2010   15.0
Medium-full colour. Quite an opulent oaky nose. A fleshy wine, markedly oaky. Medium to medium-full body. Ripe, stylish. Lacks a little concentration but balanced and well-made. Good.

Lafon-Rochet   Now–1998   13.5
Medium to medium-full colour. Not a lot of depth on the nose. Medium body. Quite pleasant but a forward wine which essentially lacks grip. Pleasant at best but really a bit short and one-dimensional.

No. 2 de Lafon-Rochet Now–1996   12.0
Quite good colour. A bit empty on both the nose and the palate. Unexceptional. Will evolve soon. Clean and not unstylish though.

De Marbuzet   Now–2000   13.5
Very good colour. Good nose, straight, classic, fresh. Medium body. A little tannin. A pleasant wine with a certain hardness behind it and a lack of really ripe flesh underneath. Quite good but lacks a little personality.

Meyney   1995–2015   15.5
Medium-full colour. Fleshy nose. Quite opulent, just a little four-square. Fullish, plump, tannic. A substantial ample example with good richness and depth. Finishes well. Good grip.

Montrose   2000–2017   15.5
Medium-full colour. Full nose. A little hard. Plenty of substance here. Typically Saint-Estèphe. Medium-full. The tannins lacks a bit of real ripeness. It is a bit typically Montrose. Richness underneath the solidity. But the grip is there. Give it time. A bit austere at present.

Les Ormes-de-Pez   1996–2000   12.5
Medium-full colour. A bit vegetal on the nose. Thin and mean and vegetal. No pleasure here. Rustic.

de Pez   1997–2004   13.0
Medium-full colour. Not a bit closed. But as it evolved in the glass seemed a touch oxidized. Medium body. Not a lot of tannin. Somewhat thin really and it lacks charm. Slightly green touch to it. Uninspiring.

Phélan-Ségur   Now–2000   14.0
Medium-full colour. An ample, plump, brambly-flavoured wine with a slight earthiness and a touch of sulphur. Medium body. A little tannin. Good grip. A stylish, fresh, open-faced wine. Well-made. Good finish. No serious depth but a neat example which finishes well.

1986 CLARET

For climatic reasons which will be later explained, 1986 is a variable claret vintage. At its best – in Saint-Julien, Pauillac and Saint-Estèphe – it is very good indeed; as good, if different, as the best of 1982. Elsewhere the vintage fails to inspire. There is a lot of dross. With a handful of exceptions, the wines of Margaux, the Graves, Saint-Emilion and Pomerol are somewhat dilute, the tannins lack flesh and the wines themselves lack concentration and length on the palate. In the Libournais the 1985 vintage is to be preferred, and the 1982s, 1989s and 1990 are better still. In the southern Médoc and the Graves I would go for the 1983s, or again in the 1982 vintage. As will be made apparent, it was a very large vintage, and the size of the crop is visible in the lack of definition in some of the wines.

THE WEATHER

For three successive seasons – 1987 following 1985 and 1986 – the winter was quite severe in Bordeaux. In 1986 there was no frost damage, as there had been the previous year, but the development of the foliage was retarded, in particular by a very cold April. At the beginning of May the vine was almost a month in arrears. 'We'll be harvesting in October', the locals grumbled to each other, a forecast that was to turn out correct only in part.

May, however, brought the hot, dry spring everyone had missed, and as this weather continued into June the vegetation rapidly began to catch up. The flowering took place only a few days later than the twenty-year average (*mi-floraison* 20 June as against the mean of the 14th) and a large amount of flowers successfully set into embryonic fruit, thus announcing yet again a prolific harvest, particularly in the Merlots.

It continued warm and very dry, producing the driest three months from June to August of the last twenty years. The *veraison* took place at more or less the usual time (*mi-veraison* 19 August) indicating a harvest which would begin about 1 October. As a result of this lack of rain the Cabernet grapes, though abundant, were smaller than usual, and therefore wider apart.

With the instinctive farmers' nose for fatal inevitability the Bordelais waited for the rain to come, hoping it would come sooner than later. On 14 or 15 September it rained evenly over the whole *vignoble*; not too excessively and not too late. The effect was beneficial, aiding rather than deterring the process of ripening and concentration. The damage was done nine days later. On 23 September a violent downpour centred on Bordeaux itself. It was the fact that this time the rain did not fall evenly across the Bordeaux vineyards, coupled with the very high Merlot harvest, which has caused the variation in quality from one commune to another.

The rain fell mainly in Bordeaux itself and to the south and west, that is in the Graves, Entre-Deux-Mers and Libournais. In Bordeaux itself 100 millimetres were recorded: in Pauillac the precipitation was only 20. Thereafter the fine weather returned. It continued warm and sunny, with increasing periods of morning mist, well into October. The red wine harvest took place without a single interruption for rain.

Most of the top properties found themselves starting the harvest by picking the Merlots, and then stopping for a few days until the Cabernets were absolutely *à point*. At Cos d'Estournel Bruno Prats brought in his Merlot between 29 September and 4 October and his Cabernet between 6 and 15 October. The late Mme Villars at Chasse-Spleen began harvesting her Merlot on 6 October and her Cabernet a week later, these dates being almost exactly matched by Alexandre Thienpont at Vieux Château Certan, though others in Saint-Emilion and Pomerol vintaged closer to the rain.

PROBLEMS OF QUANTITY

In 1986 the Gironde produced a total of 6.3 million hectolitres, 4.5 million of which was *ap-*

pellation contrôlée red. This was not only the largest overall crop since 1934 but by some way the largest amount of AC red wine ever: 14.7 per cent more than 1985, the previous record, and 28.7 per cent higher than in 1982. Indeed the figure of *three* million hectolitres of an AC red had only been exceeded four times in recent years: 1979, 1982, 1983 and 1985; though since then it has become commonplace.

In 1986, 87,058 hectares were under AC vines in the Gironde. With a total AC production of 5.62 million hectolitres this gives an average *rendement* of over 64 hectolitres per hectare, beating all previous records. The only other years that 60 had been exceeded were in 1979 and 1985.

Ah, you might say, but surely these sorts of prolific yields occur only in generic Bordeaux *rouge* vineyards, not among the *grands crus*? Well, yes; but only to some extent. At Château Gazin in Pomerol there was no reluctance to admit to a yield of 57 hectolitres per hectare in 1986. Overall in the commune of Saint-Julien, a sector where classed growths and good *bourgeois* so dominate there is hardly a square metre for the *petit vigneron*, the yield was 56 hectolitres per hectare. And these sort of plus-50 yields are now the norm, not the exception.

There are three main ways in which the wine-maker can reduce the effect of what inevitably is a dilution of potential concentration caused by these excess harvests. The first, most important and now almost universal procedure is in the selection of the *cuvées* which will make up the *grand vin*. All the important wine-producers now regularly boast of eliminating a good quarter or even a third. At Château Léoville-Las-Cases only 45 per cent of M. Delon's 1986 harvest, and that solely from vines of twenty-plus years of age, has been named Léoville-Las-Cases. The remainder is Clos du Marquis, the second wine, or Domaine de Bigarnon, the third wine.

The second is what now seems to be called the *vendange verte*, otherwise more prosaically known as crop-thinning. Having been blessed by nature with a successful flowering, the proprietor then orders some of the grapes to be knocked off before the *veraison* in order that the remainder can profit by concentrating further. Christian Mouiex has been doing this at Château Pétrus for a number of years. As a result, he managed to restrict his 1986 harvest to 45 hectolitres per hectare before selection. By 1986 he had been followed by Alexandre Thienpont at Vieux Château Certan, Denis Durantou at L'Eglise-Clinet and Michel Delon, among others. Thienpont culled 35 to 40 per cent of his Merlots and 50 per cent of his small quantity of Malbec on 15 July. His total harvest was 42 hectolitres per hectare. Compare that with Gazin! The grapes were harvested at a natural 12.6 per cent of potential alcohol. In Saint-Julien, by means of this technique, Delon produced 47 hectolitres per hectare in total as against 55 in 1985 and 60 in 1983.

Finally, common in Burgundy, but not, as far as I am aware, widespread in Bordeaux, is the practice of *saignée*, bleeding off some of the excess juice in the must in order to improve the ratio between solids and liquids before vinification. Durantou at L'Eglise-Clinet is an advocate of this.

In comparison with 1985 and other vintages, the 1986 yield varied considerably. In the adjoining communes of Saint-Estèphe, Pauillac and Saint-Julien it was no greater than in 1985, and indeed in Pauillac marginally less. The difference in Pauillac and Saint-Estèphe between 1985 and 1983 was, however, considerable (plus 24 per cent and plus 16 per cent respectively). Margaux shows a 1985/86 increase of 19 per cent, but produced 10 per cent less in 1985 than in 1983. The Graves produced 15 per cent more red wine in 1986 than in 1985, no doubt largely because of the second of the September rains, but again less than in 1982 or 1983. The Libournais figures show the evidence of a large crop of Merlot-based wines: Saint-Emilion is 9 per cent up, but only produced 5 per cent more than in 1982. Pomerol was 23 per cent up; the 1985 figures reduced by frost: Fronsac and Canon-Fronsac almost 10 per cent more. Overall, even here, making allowances for the effects of the cold 1985 weather, the figures in the top regions are not excessively higher than in 1985. They have been high (too high?) for five years.

There is no doubt that despite what may seem like evidence to the contrary, the Cabernet and Merlot vines have difficulty producing wine of high quality once they begin to yield above 50 hectolitres per hectare. We have been spoiled by lucky escapes and superlative *fins de saison* since 1982. We only have to cast our minds back to 1974 and 1973 to remember what can happen when a large crop is further diluted by vintage rain. As Christian Moueix pointed out, the 1986 vintage was very close to disaster; two days more rain in September, so close to the vintage date, and the harvest would have been lost.

THE STYLE OF THE WINE

Broadly, the difference between the quality of the Merlot vats, particularly at those properties which cropped excessively and which vintaged soon after the rain had fallen heavily, and the Cabernet vats, particularly those harvested from old vines in the vineyards which largely escaped the downpour, is enormous. This is a Cabernet year. This is a Médoc vintage.

Overall the wines have a good healthy colour and good fruity aromas. The fruit was in fine sanitary condition when it was brought in and this is reflected in the wine. Acidity levels are not high, if anything in the Graves and the Libournais rather low. Tannin levels are high and even in the Saint-Emilion and Pomerol area are 10 per cent more than in 1985. As a result of the excessively low water-table caused by the early summer drought, you would expect these tannins not to be soft. This is indeed what you find.

In the Libournais the tannins are rather dry and washed out. I felt with some of the wines that the level of *vin de presse* was noticeable and the effect was one of astringency; as if the wines had been deliberately beefed up by the addition of press wine. In the northern Médoc the tannins are a great deal riper and more succulent.

Where the wines differ, and differ greatly from region to region, is in the density of their composition and in the concentration of their fruit. In the Libournais the wines are overall either somewhat limp and anonymous or a little too dense. They lack richness and grip and therefore definition. There are of course exceptions but apart from a few obvious stars (Le Pin, Certan-de-May, Vieux Château Certan, Pavie, Canon) the level is uninspiring. The 1985 vintage is to be preferred.

I also prefer, by some way, the Graves in this earlier vintage. The 1986 Graves range from the frankly weedy and dilute upwards; but not far upwards. The storm has left its mark.

In Margaux and the southern Médoc the effect of the rain is also apparent. There are some very good wines (Labégorce-Zédé and Angludet among the reasonably priced; Rausan-Ségla and Palmer among the more expensive; Château Margaux, of course) but the difference between this half of the region and the rest is distinct.

Further north into the Médoc the change in style and improvement in quality is marked. Here, from Moulis upwards, and particularly so in Pauillac, Saint-Julien and Saint-Estèphe, the wines have a very full colour, huge amounts of tannin – much more than in 1982 – marvellous Cabernet-based concentrated fruit and good levels of acidity. Naturally there are disappointments (though each year one can welcome a few more properties that have turned the corner and are at last making the sort of wine of which they are capable), but overall the quality is very impressive, very impressive indeed.

The quality of these best Médocs is based on this superb, rich, profound Cabernet fruit. In size they resemble the 1982s, and have acidity levels which are similar or better. The Cabernet Sauvignon produces a wine of higher acidity than the Merlot, and in 1986 benefitted from a lower yield. Moreover, in the Médoc the fruit was picked later, and was able to dry out and re-concentrate after the September rains. Many proprietors, having rejected the least good (Merlot) vats, have made a much more Cabernet wine than usual.

The fruit flavours are less cooked and exotic than in 1982, and the spicy elements – grilled nuts, game, chocolate – less obvious. I find the flavours very classic, and the wines full, harmonious, rich, firm and concentrated. As a result I place the quality of the best Médoc 1986s at a very high level indeed. It is a vintage which will take a very long time to mature, and may well turn out better than in 1982, or where 1983 was better than in 1982, than in 1983. This is high praise.

PRICES AND VALUE FOR MONEY

When I first wrote about the 1986s in June 1987, I pointed out that while the 1986s were a little cheaper than the 1985s had been a year previously they were nevertheless expensive. Most proprietors were continuing to ask greedy prices. There was plenty of wine. Not all of it was exciting, by any means. There was no need to buy the 1986s then.

In April 1990, I selected a range of the best wines across the price spectrum: Angludet, Chasse-Spleen, Léoville-Barton, Grand-Puy-Lacoste, Cos d'Estournel, Pichon-Longueville-Lalande and Mouton-Rothschild. I compared the opening offer prices, grossed-up to include duty, shipping and delivery, with the prices current at the time. The overall increase was 21 per cent in the three years which had intervened; which meant that they were no more expensive in real terms than they had been in 1987. Since then, as a result of the recession, prices have remained static. They are now cheaper in real terms than they were *en primeur*. The moral is that while it is desirable for the trade to sell futures, it is not always in the best interests of the consumer.

THE WINES IN 1994

When I began to prepare this book for publication, I thought seriously about making a more up-to-date tasting of the top 1986s. I then began to look at recent notes of the vintage. The word 'adolescent' cropped up with alarming frequency. This is a vintage which has now gone into its shell. It is not showing well. I decided there was nothing to be gained by re-tasting the cream of the 1986s at present. I shall let the following notes speak for themselves and re-taste the vintage in 1996.

THE TASTING

The following clarets were, in the main, tasted at The Crown Hotel, Southwold, in January 1990. A few latecomers were sampled later in London.

	Optimum Drinking	Mark out of 20

CANON-FRONSAC

Canon Drink soon 10.0
Very similar to the Canon-Moueix. The tannins are a bit washed out and there is bitterness and a lack of fruit.

Canon-de-Brem Drink soon 10.5
Medium colour. Somewhat weak on the nose and washed out on the palate. Medium body. Short. Disappointing.

Canon-Moueix Drink soon 10.0
Medium-full colour. Better nose than the above, a little more substance but rather dry and bitter underneath. This is even less exciting.

Mazeris Now if at all 8.0
Weak and astringent. The worst of these Fronsacs.

La Rivière Now–1996 12.0
Medium-full colour. Good new oak on both nose and palate. Some fruit. Reasonable acidity. Medium body. There is some flesh here. But essentially hollow.

SAINT-EMILION

L'Angélus Now–1996 00.0
Medium-full colour. Somewhat stewed and vegetal on the nose. Rather dry and charmless. Medium body. Some fruit but also some astringency. Yet better acidity than the Canon-La-Gaffelière.

L'Arrosée Now–2000 14.0
Medium-full colour. New oaky nose. Quite positive, but nevertheless lacks charm and real richness. Medium body. A little tannin. Better than most. Some fruit. Some concentration and reasonable balance.

Balestard-La-Tonnelle Now–1996 11.0
Medium-full colour. Stewed nose, somewhat bitter. Lacks charm. Medium body.

Beau-Séjour-Bécot Drink soon 12.0
Medium colour. New oaky and quite stylish on the nose. Reasonable attack but rather empty and one-dimensional underneath. Medium body. Finishes short.

Cadet-Piola Now if at all 10.0
Medium-full colour. Curious somewhat dry, spicy nose. Stewed, astringent and short on the palate. Very poor.

Canon-la-Gaffeliere Drink soon 13.0
Medium to medium-full colour. Quite fresh on the nose but somewhat dry. Medium body. A little too much *vin de presse*. Reasonable fruit but also a slightly stewed element.

Cap-de-Mourlin Now–1996 12.0
Medium-full colour. As usual quite a chunky, spicy, robust Merlot-based wine. Lacks style but some substance and reasonable balance.

Chauvin Now–1996 12.0
Medium-full colour. Quite a fat, plump nose. On the palate there is substance but the tannins are a little dry and obtrusive. Not bad.

La Clotte Now–1996 12.5
Medium colour. A bit lumpy on the nose. Stewed on the palate. Rather too much washed out tannin but has reasonable grip.

La Clusière Drink soon 11.5
Medium-full colour. Some substance on the nose but a little anonymous. Medium body. A little fruit but rather one-dimensional and short.

Dassault Drink soon 13.0
Medium-full colour. New oaky nose; quite promising. The oak dominates the palate, which, while quite stylish, is essentially quite light. Not too bad though. At least some finish.

La Dominique Drink soon 11.5
Medium-full colour. Soft, slightly spuriously sweet, new oaky nose. Lightly, short – very short – on the palate. Will get attenuated.

Fonplégade Now–1996 13.5
Medium-full colour on the nose as well as new oak. Similar palate. Not a lot of depth or substance but quite pleasantly balanced.

Fonroque Now if at all 10.0
Medium colour. Weak, anaemic nose. Somewhat unripe. Thin and astringent. Green. Poor.

Grand-Pontet Drink soon 12.0
Medium-full colour. Lightish, somewhat washed-out nose. Reasonable quite sweet fruit on the palate and a touch of new oak. Somewhat assisted. Not bad.

Guardet-Saint-Julien Drink soon 11.0
Medium-full colour. Somewhat dry and very short indeed. Medium body. Edgy.

Haut-Sarpe Drink soon 11.5
Medium-full colour. Somewhat dry and fruitless on the nose. Medium body. Lacks fruit. Short. Boring.

Clos-des-Jacobins Now–1996 11.5
Medium-full colour. Stalky, overheated nose. Stewed and lumpy on the palate. Lacks style. Will get astringent. Uninspiring.

Larcis-Ducasse Now–1996 13.5
Medium-full colour. Stewed, dry and astringent. Very strange vegetal-compost flavour. Definitely dirty. I saw this again in London a fortnight later: medium body, reasonable weight and balance, though with an earthy *goût de terroir*. Not bad.

Larmande Now–1999 14.0
Medium-full colour. Better nose than most but a little stewed and lumpy. Medium-full body. A little tannin. Somewhat rigid on the attack but better on the follow-through. Reasonable grip. Some fruit. A more positive finish than the others.

Clos de L'Oratoire Drink soon 10.5
Medium colour. Weak, scented nose; very curious. Lightish, no tannin. Weak. Spurious.

Pavie-Decesse Now–1196 13.5
Medium-full colour. Less new oak than the L'Arrosée, but better fruit. Medium body. Little tannin. A certain dry bitterness on the finish which will become astringency. Lacks structure and zip but better fruit than most.

Petit-Faurie-de-Soutard
Drink soon 11.0
Medium-full colour. Weedy, Merlot nose. Even lighter and weedier on the palate. Thin. Poor.

Clos Saint-Martin Now–1996 13.0
Medium colour. Quite heavily toasted oak apparent on the nose. Some fruit. New oak a little dominant on the palate but medium bodied. Some tannin. Better than most but a little short.

La Serre Drink soon 11.5
Medium-full colour. Light nose. Lacking fruit and grip. Light-medium body. Short. Uninspiring.

Soutard Now–1997 12.5
Good colour. Firm, solid nose, lacking a bit of flesh underneath. Chunky and tannic on the palate. Somewhat one-dimensional if not a little bitter underneath.

La Tour-Figeac Drink soon 10.0
Medium colour. Lightish, somewhat Merlot-weedy nose. Insipid palate. Astringent finish.

Tournelle-des-Moines Drink soon 9.0
This is the second wine of Beau-Séjour-Bécot.

Medium colour. Weak, rather stretched Merlot nose and palate. Rather an unripe acidity. Lacks charm. Medium body. Uninspiring.

Troplong-Mondot   Now–1997   14.5
Medium-full colour. Much better nose than most. Richness, ripeness, some new oak. Balance and flesh above all. Some tannin but enough grip and depth to balance. This is quite good.

SAINT-EMILION PREMIERS CRUS

Ausone   Now–1998   14.0
Medium colour. No great weight on the nose though some fruit and elegance and reasonable balance. Medium to medium-full. Some oak. I would have expected more concentration than this. There is style but the wine is essentially a bit weak. No complexity and not very long. Uninspiring. The Belair is better.

Beauséjour-Duffau-Lagarrosse   Now–2000   14.0
Medium colour. Rather a dumb nose. Medium body, a little tannin though these tannins are a bit hard. Spicy elements on the palate, slightly sweet, but bitter and resinous. The wine is not weak, but it lacks a bit of breed.

Belair   Now–1997   14.5
Strangely this has a better colour than the Ausone, its stable-mate. Light but elegant nose. Soft, gently oaky on the palate. Little tannin. Fruity, plump and quite attractive but essentially a bit slight, though the wine is not too short.

Canon   Now–2008   17.5
Full colour. This has depth on the nose; even concentration. More backward than most of these Saint-Emilions. Full, rich, ripe attack. Good tannins. It doesn't have the grip or follow-through of the top Médocs but this is a fine result: plenty of fruit, well-balanced, and with depth and finesse. Finishes well. Indeed better and more stylishly than all these top Saint-Emilions.

Cheval-Blanc   Now–2008   17.0
Medium-full colour. Opulent, spicy, exotic, new oaky nose. This is very appealing, indeed seductive wine. Fullish, round, open and sweet; ripely tannic. Much less austere than the Canon, but equally as concentrated, and with perhaps more dimension if not the depth. Fine result though.

Figeac   Now–2006   16.0
Medium to medium-full colour. Somewhat vegetal – in the stemmy sense – on the nose. Medium-full body, some tannin. Good grip here, but as often with Figeac, a more adolescent wine than its peers. Good oak. Better balance than most in Saint-Emilion – the Cabernet Sauvignon has helped – but it doesn't have the concentrated fruit of the Canon or the style of the Pavie.

Clos-Fourtet   Now–1996   14.5
Medium-full colour. Softer than the Canon. Good new oak but not a great deal of weight. Medium body. Ripe, gentle, fruity-oaky attack but then after that it tails off. Attractive though, but a little short.

La Gaffelière   Now–1996   14.0
Medium-full colour. Nothing very much on the nose. Pleasant Merlot attack with some oak. Not a lot of body, and certainly not a great deal of acidity. As much astringency as tannin. Reasonable fruit at first but finishes a bit short. Uninspiring.

Magdelaine   Now–1997   14.5
Medium colour. A little weedy on the nose. The wine is 80 per cent Merlot and the Merlot here lacks a bit of zip. Soft, plump, elegant and forward. Medium-full. An attractive wine which is a little short, and therefore a little dull on the finish.

Pavie   Now–2006   16.5
Fullish colour. Rich, full, oaky nose. A round, ripe, attractive wine which shows the benefit of a severe selection. Medium-full. Good succulent fruit. Ripe tannins and good acidity. A stylish wine which has plenty of depth. Finishes long and positively, and is a fine result for the vintage.

Trottevieille   Drink soon   12.0
Medium-full colour. This is already a little oxidized. Light to medium body. Not tannin. Sweet but weedy. Will get attenuated.

POMEROL

Le Bon-Pasteur   Drink soon   13.5
Medium-full colour. A bit of disappointment. Pleasant fruit. Reasonably balanced but essentially one-dimensional and short.

Bonalgue   Drink soon   13.0
Medium-full colour. Quite plump and fruity on the nose and palate. Round, pleasant. Ready. Well made. Has a positive finish if no real depth.

La Cabanne   Drink soon   12.5
Medium-full colour. Better nose than most. Quite promising fruit on the attack; medium body. But like most a little short.

Certan-de-May   1996–2006   17.0
Good new oak on the nose and certainly has fruit underneath. Medium-full body. Good grip. This has ripe tannins and good concentration. Plenty of fruit and depth. An excellent result.

Clinet   Drink soon   11.5
Medium-full colour. A bit solid on the nose. Too much tannin on the palate. Medium body. Over-balanced. Slightly better on the finish. Will always be too stewed.

Clos-du-Clocher   Now–1998   14.5
Medium colour. Soft, but somewhat one-dimen-

sionally fruity nose. Essentially Merlot. Medium body. A little tannin. Quite pleasant gentle, oaky, fruity attack, but lacks grip. Not bad.

La Conseillante — Now–1998 — 15.5
Medium colour. New oaky nose but not a wine of great substance. Medium body. Not a lot of tannin. A bit more elegant; a bit more positive. Quite good fruit. Lacks real depth and concentration though.

La Croix — Drink soon — 14.0
Medium-full colour. Nose smells of sultanas. A little more substance than the Bonalgue. Also better balanced than most. Plump. Medium body. Finishes positively.

La Croix-de-Casse — Drink soon — 12.0
Medium-full colour. Light nose. Soft on the palate. Light, quite pleasantly fruity attack but tails off on the finish. Short.

La Croix-de-Gay — Drink soon — 13.0
Medium colour. Stewed, *vin de presse*-y nose. Very stewed and astringent on the palate. Essentially unbalanced.

Domaine de L'Eglise — Drink soon — 13.5
Medium colour. Somewhat feeble on the nose. Light to medium body. Little tannin. Quite pleasant. A shade artificially sweet. Not a wine of much depth or consequence.

L'Eglise-Clinet — Now–2000 — 14.5
Medium-full colour. A slightly cooked, spicy element to the fruit here but more to it than most of this group on the nose. Medium-full, somewhat tannic. The attack and the follow-through are quite ample but the wine is a little short.

L'Evangile — 1995–2003 — 16.0
Medium-full colour. More depth on the nose than the Conseillante. Medium-full body. Some tannin. Good rich attack though it tails off a bit on the finish. A lot better than most. Very good.

Feytit-Clinet — Now–2000 — 12.0
Medium colour. Somewhat dry and papery on the nose. One can smell the *vin de presse*. But a forward wine which will get attenuated.

La Fleur-de-Gay — Drink soon — 13.5
Medium-full colour. Soft, but lumpy nose, not entirely clean. Medium-full body. Somewhat astringent. Reasonable (if a sweet/sour) fruit on the attack but tails off on the finish. Lacks finesse.

La Fleur-Tressac — Drink soon — 12.0
Medium-full colour. Smells a little of the filter. A well-made unpretentious wine, somewhat one-dimensional which is ready now. Reasonable fruit. Better balance than most. Ready.

La Grave-Trigant-de-Boisset — Drink soon — 14.0
Medium colour. Soft and fruity on the nose. A

pleasant wine with no great dimension. Medium body. Not much tannin. Pretty but lacks depth. Better made than most.

Lafleur-Petrus — Now–1997 — 15.0
Medium-full colour. Merlot-based, like the Latour, but a little more substance. Medium body. A little astringent because of the addition of *vin de presse*. Good grip. Reasonable fruit.

Latour-à-Pomerol — Now–1996 — 14.5
Medium-full colour. Merlot-based nose. Lacks grip. Medium body. Not much tannin. A pretty wine but lacks grip and backbone. Forward.

Mazeyres — Now if at all — 10.0
Medium to medium-full colour. Weak nose. Very weak and thin on the palate. Really dilute. Tastes like a 1987.

Montviel — Drink soon — 12.0
Medium-full colour. Somewhat rustic on the nose. Medium body. A bit astringent. Short. Lacks fruit.

Moulinet — Drink soon — 11.5
Medium to medium-full colour. This has a bit more substance but lacks fruit. A dull wine which shows dry tannins on the finish.

Petit-Village — 1995–2003 — 16.0
Good colour. Attractive, quite concentrated fruit on the nose; elegant but not a blockbuster. This is a very good result. Medium-full, velvety coffee and chocolate fruit. Ripe round tannins. No fade at the end. Obviously a rigorous selection has been made. Most attractive.

Pétrus — 1997–2015 — 18.0
Fullish colour. Quite a different nose. New oaky, roasted nuts. Full and a lot more concentration, though I do not think it is in any way up with the top Médocs. Ample, slightly opulent, spicy fruit. Long.

Le Pin — Now–2003 — 17.0
Medium colour. New oaky, forward. Round and fruity and a little sweet on the nose. Medium-full body. Quite dominated by the oak on the attack. Good. Concentration underneath and above all good acidity. Shows well.

Prieur-de-La-Commanderie — Drink soon — 12.0
Medium to medium-full colour. Somewhat anaemic Merlot nose. Weak and short on the palate. But quite pleasant fruit if caught now.

Taillefer — Drink soon — 11.5
Medium colour. Pleasant fruit on the nose and attack but really a bit too weak and short. Will get attenuated.

Trotanoy — Now–2002 — 16.0
Medium-full colour. A much more positive nose than the Lafleur-Pétrus. Medium-full body. Some

tannin. Reasonable attack. Some grip but lacks a little freshness and zip on the palate.

Vieux Château Certan   1996–2008   17.5

Medium-full colour. For the first time, a certain amount of real concentration on the nose. Some tannin. Fullish, complete. A wine of real depth and dimension. Good concentration. Good balance. Plump fat finish. Yet a bit tight and unformed at present. Will keep well. High class.

GRAVES

Bahans-Haut-Brion   Now–1996   14.0

Medium-full colour. Light, quite elegant but a little weedy on the nose. Medium body. A pleasant wine with a touch of oak but as much astringency as tannin. Elegant but a bit short on the finish.

Bouscaut   Drink soon   11.5

Medium-full colour. Quite round and fat on the nose. Without great weight. Dilute and short and somewhat synthetic on the palate. The rain shows here. Will get attenuated.

Carbonnieux   Drink soon   12.5

Medium-full colour. Somewhat weedy on the nose. A little washed out and astringent on the palate. Short. No selection. Forward. Banal.

Domaine de Chevalier   Now–2003   16.5

Medium-full colour. Fine elegant oak and delicate fruit on the nose. A very well-made wine. Medium to medium-full body. Good tannins. Fine oak. Grip and breed. Delicate and stylish. Long. An excellent result.

Chicane   Drink soon   10.5

Medium colour. Soft raspberry-flavoured nose. Medium body. The tannins a little washed out. Just about ready. Rather short.

De Fieuzal   Now–2001   15.5

Fullish colour. Slightly cooked on the nose but substance here. Quite full for a Graves. Good ripe, not too diluted tannins. Quite rich and meaty and has grip. Lacks a little real breed but certainly good.

Domaine de Gaillat   Drink soon   11.0

Good colour. Slightly plasticy on the nose. A medium-bodied, soft, quite fruity wine. A little one-dimensional. Ready now.

Haut-Brion   Now–2003   16.0

Medium-full colour. Elegant fruit but not a lot of depth on the nose. Fine oaky background. Medium-full body, this has the most breed but the Chevalier has better length.

Larrivet-Haut-Brion   Now–1998   14.5

Medium-full colour. Good new oak and some concentration, shows well on the nose. Medium-full body. This is quite fat. Some tannin. There is depth here but the tannins are a bit washed out. But a positive, quite rich finish.

La Louvière   Now–2000   14.5

Medium-full colour. Lightish, anonymous nose. A little weedy. Some oak but better on the palate than most of the above. Medium body. A little tannin. Ripe, quite fat. Good if it lacks a bit of elegance and personality.

Malartic-Lagravière   Now–1998   12.0

Medium-full colour. Quite fat, ripe and new oaky on the nose. Better than most. Medium body. More positive. Better balanced. Attractive.

La Mission-Haut-Brion Now–2003   15.5

Fullish colour. Very similar to the Pape-Clément, a little more substance perhaps. Quite astringent as well as the tannin. Certainly more breed though. Medium-full. Good fruit. Reasonable acidity. Somewhat anonymous.

Olivier   Now–1999   14.0

Fullish colour. Somewhat weedy on the nose. Good oak. A lightweight but quite elegant, balanced wine. Forward. Good effort for the vintage.

Pape-Clément   Now–2001   14.0

Medium-full colour. Plump but a little dilute on the nose. Somewhat cooked on the palate. Medium-full, a little tannin but an element of artificial concentration about it.

Smith-Haut-Lafitte   Drink soon   13.0

Medium-full colour. Ripe and pleasant but light on the nose. Medium body. Little tannin. Pleasant but inconsequential. Very forward.

La Tour-Martillac   Drink soon   12.0

Medium-full colour. A little further than the Carbonnieux but only in that it is more stewed. Shorter, more dilute. Disappointing.

MÉDOC AND HAUT-MÉDOC

Cantemerle   1995–2003   15.0

Fullish colour. Stylish but a little weak on the nose. This is not a blockbuster by any means. An elegant wine. Best on the finish. The attack lacks a bit of concentration. But there is balance and above all style here.

Chasse-Spleen   1996–2009   16.0

Fullish colour. Similarly rich and full. But firmer and more concentrated. This has the character and personality the Poujeaux lacks. Full, concentrated, fat and succulent. Rather good.

Cissac   1995–2004   13.5

Medium-full colour. Smoky nose. Somewhat Saint-Estèphey, with a touch of new oak. Medium-full body, some tannin and fruit. But quite pronounced acidity and a lack of real concentration. Lacks charm. Well-balanced though. Finishes better than it starts.

Lachesnaye   Now if at all   10.0

Medium-full colour. Somewhat weedy, vegetal nose. Weak and astringent. Lacks fruit. Dilute.

La Lagune   1995–2005   15.0

Fullish colour. Richly oaky nose. Roasted coffee. Very promising. The oak seems more balanced by concentration than the Poujeaux. But there is an absence of depth and dimension on the follow-through.

Lanessan   Now–2003   14.0

Fullish colour. Quite tannic. Cooked plums nose. Fullish, tannic colour on the palate. There is ripeness but this is quite a structured wine without really the concentration to go with it. Lacks a smile but quite good.

Liversan   Now–1999   13.0

Fullish colour. Merlot-ish nose but without concentration or real grip. Medium to medium-full. Ripe. Balanced. A nice wine without any real pretention. Well made.

Malescasse   Now–1999   12.5

Medium-full colour. Slightly aggressive stalky nose, but has depth underneath. Medium to medium-full body. Lacks real succulence. A young viney taste without fatness. Dull.

Poujeaux   1996–2006   15.0

Fullish colour. Full, rich, succulent, backward nose. A fullish, meaty wine. Ripe tannins. A touch earthy. What it lacks is a bit of personality. Well made. Rich and good.

Sociando-Mallet   1996–2006   15.0

Fullish colour. Strong toasted oak, roast coffee oaky nose. Medium-full, quite oaky and tannic but both are balanced by the fruit and concentration. Good acidity. Not really multidimensional but most attractive and well balanced.

Margaux

d'Angludet   1996–2006   16.0

Fullish colour. Firm, ripe, balanced nose. Style here as well as depth. This has got a bitter grip than most and fine ripe Cabernet fruit. Medium-full body. Balanced. Elegant. Ripe. Finishes longer than most in this flight.

Boyd-Cantenac   1996–2006   15.5

Medium-full colour. Somewhat cooked fruit on the nose. Firm, solid and tannic. Indeed rather good. Certainly better length than the majority of these lesser Margaux.

Brane-Cantenac   Now–1999   14.5

Medium-full colour. Similar nose to the Desmirail, slightly more elegant fruit. A wine of similar weight, slightly better balanced. But essentially a bit dull.

Cantenac-Brown   1996–2006   14.5

Medium-full colour. Quite sturdy but anonymous on the nose. Much better than hitherto on the palate. A little fiery but there is oak, grip and succulence. Quite full. Reasonable finish.

Dauzac   Now–2002   14.5

Medium-full colour. A pretty nose. Quite stylish fruit but no weight behind it. Medium body. Not much tannin. Well made. Balanced and elegant. Not bad at all. Will come forward soon.

Desmirail   Now–1998   14.0

Medium-full colour. Lightish nose, lacks a bit of depth and concentration. Quite light and forward. More astringent than tannic. Pretty fruit but rather one-dimensional.

Du Tertre   1996–2006   16.0

Medium-full colour. Fine new oaky nose, but not dominating. Good ripe concentrated fruit underneath. There is depth and complexity here, as well as breed. Quite full good tannins. Ripe and succulent. This has good grip. Shows well.

Durfort-Vivens   Now–2000   14.5

Medium-full colour. Some weight on the nose; more to it than the Brane-Cantenac but not much finesse or succulence of fruit. Medium body. Ripe but a little dull again. A little tannin. Reasonable finish but doesn't excite.

Ferrière   1995–2002   13.0

Medium-full colour. The nose lacks a bit of personality and concentration. The palate likewise. Medium-full body. A touch stewed. Too much *vin de presse* perhaps. Tannins dominate and the wine lacks dimension. Boring.

Giscours   Now–1999   14.0

Fullish colour. Raisiny nose, lacking grip. Will become attenuated. Quite fat. Cooked medium to medium-full wine. All upfront. Neither grip nor breed behind it. Will be ephemeral. A lack of selection here.

La Gurgue   1995–2003   14.5

Medium-full colour. Fullish, fat, rich, old-viney nose. Good stuff. Fullish, ripe and plump. With some tannin.

d'Issan   Now–2003   15.5

Medium-full colour. Fragrant, perfumed and lightly new oaky on the nose. Medium to medium-full body. Not much tannin. Stylish, ripe and balanced. Good finish. Forward but attractive.

Kirwan   Now–2004   15.5

Medium-full colour. Soft, gently-oaky nose; quite ripe. Medium-full body, some tannin. This has got more concentration than most of these Margaux. Quite fast. Good oak. Positive. Good to very good.

Labégorce-Zédé   1996–2006   15.5

Medium-full colour. Good, fat, rich concentrated nose. Medium-full body. Ripe tannins. Quite structured but the elements are balanced. Good rich fruit and grip. Shows well and is stylish.

Lascombes　　　　1995–2000　　14.0

Fullish colour. Fullish, chunky and slightly cooked on the nose. Does it lack zip? Fullish, tannic, fat but somewhat dominated by the tannins. Yes, it does lack zip.

Malescot-Saint-Exupéry

Now–2004　　15.5

Fullish colour. As always with young Malescot-Saint-Exupéry, it seems on the nose as if it has recently been racked. A softer, succulent more feminine wine on the palate. A real Margaux. Good fruit. A good grip. Elegant balance and delicately oaky. Shows well.

Margaux　　　　1998–2000　　18.0

Fullish colour. Lovely nose. Beautiful oak. Medium-full, quite a lot of oak as well as tannin. But fruit, grip and complexity as well. Clearly the best of the Margaux.

Marquis-d'Alesme-Becker

Now–2004　　13.5

Fullish colour. Rich, fullish, firm nose. Fat and oak here. But how much depth? Medium to medium-full, as much astringence as tannin. Lacks real concentration and an absence of acidity on the palate. Short. Disappointing.

Marquis-de-Terme　　1996–2006　　15.5

Fullish colour. Succulently new oaky on the nose but does it lack a bit of grip? Fullish, meaty, oaky and stylish. Enough grip. This shows well. Good, positive finish.

Monbrison　　　　1995–2004　　15.0

Medium-full colour. Quite a lot of fat and concentration behind it on the nose. Marked new oak on the palate. Stylish and balanced and not overpowerful. Good. Attractive fruit. Finishes well.

Palmer　　　　1996–2006　　16.5

Fullish colour. The nose is still closed. There is concentration here but I do not find much new oak, nor fragrance. Medium-full. Some tannin. I did not find this as exciting as Rausan-Ségla. But it has the usual Palmer breed.

Pavillon Rouge de Margaux

Now–2000　　14.5

Medium-full colour. Good new oak. Fatter than the Issan on the nose. Much less fruit on the palate. A rather hollow wine, dominated by the wood on the attack. The finish is better. But it doesn't really sing.

Pouget　　　　1996–2006　　14.0

Fullish colour. Somewhat cooked and lumpy on the nose. Full but lacks elegance. Quite a lot of tannin but a less solid wine underneath than usual, and not without grip. Lacks a bit of concentration but better than expected.

Prieuré-Lichine　　1995–2005　　15.0

Fullish colour. Some new oak, some fat and concentration but a lack of real breed. There is a *vin de presse* vegetal element here. Medium-full, balanced. Quite ripe tannins. But a lack of real breed. Yet quite fruity and charming.

Rausan-Ségla　　　1996–2006　　16.5

Fullish colour. Not so much new oak but a lot of concentration here on the nose. Fullish in a real Margaux sense. Good concentration. Good oak. Breed here and a lot of depth. This is rather fine.

La Tour-de-Mons　　1995–2002　　13.0

Medium-full colour. Aromatic but slightly sweaty nose. medium body. The tannins dominate a little and the net effect is somewhat astringent. Lacks zip and breed. Unexciting.

SAINT-JULIEN

Beychevelle　　　1995–2003　　14.5

Medium-full colour. Full nose. Good fruit but perhaps a little chunky; a slight lack of nuance. Somewhat stalky and the *vin de presse* shows. Medium-full. Lacks new oak, concentration and elegance. Not a rigorous enough selection.

Branaire　　　　Now–1997　　12.0

Medium-full colour. Fullish on the nose. But closed and does it have depth? It is not absolutely clean. Somewhat weak and astringent on the palate. No selection here: that is quite apparent. Medium body. Poor.

Ducru-Beaucaillou　1995–2008　　See note

Full colour. This too, is a bit of a disappointment on the nose. Somewhat weedy, even. Medium to medium-full only. Lacking concentration and richness. Surely this must be an unrepresentative bottle? On other occasions while not as good as Léoville-Las-Cases it has scored well if not excitingly: 16 say.

Gloria　　　　1995–2005　　14.5

Medium-full colour. Ripe, plump Cabernet on the nose. Not a blockbuster. This is somewhat straightforward. There is a lack of real concentration and grip. Medium-full body. Ripe and balanced. Quite good.

Gruaud-Larose　　1996–2008　　16.0

Fullish colour. Rather richer and more concentrated. Certainly more depth and fatness. Medium-full. Again not a blockbuster. Good rich, fruity attack but lacks a bit of grip so the finish is slightly weak.

Hortevie　　　　Now–2003　　13.5

Medium-full colour. Seems a little richer on the nose. Seems a little chunkier but otherwise very similar. Hortevie is supposed to be a selection of the Terrey-Gros-Caillou vats.

Lagrange   1997–2012   16.5

Fullish colour. Rich, ripe, new oaky nose. Accessible and elegant. There is plenty of extract here. Very stylish. Lovely, long, ripe Cabernet finish.

Lalande-Borie   1995–2003   14.0

Fullish colour. Quite complex, medium-full Cabernet on the nose. Good quality here. Not quite as exciting on the palate. The attack is a bit dominated by the tannin and there is a lack of new oak. Lacks a bit of fruit.

Langoa-Barton   1996–2010   16.5

Fullish colour. Lovely stylish nose. In the same mode as the above. But with more depth and more new oak. As always there is a feminine aspect to this wine. Subtle, complex. Medium-full. Lovely balance. Fine length.

Léoville-Barton   1998–2016   18.0

Full colour. Like the Saint-Pierre the new oak is a bit toasted. Fine quality and complexity. The attack is dominated by the new oak. Rich, concentrated and subtle underneath. Fullish. A wine of balance and breed. Very fine finish. Subtle.

Léoville-Las-Cases   1996–2016   See note

Full colour. Good stylish ripe Cabernet fruit but I don't get the power and the depth on the nose that I am expecting. An elegant wine, but only medium-full. A bad bottle? I've seen this wine elsewhere several times and invariably scored it about 18.5.

Léoville-Poyferré   1996–2006   16.5

Full colour. Slightly solid but firm and chocolatey and plenty of depth. This seems to be a bigger wine than most. Quite full. Good richness and complexity without being quite as exquisite as the Léoville-Barton. Lacks the concentration.

Saint-Pierre   1997–2012   17.0

Fullish colour. Slightly roasted new oak on the nose. Ripeness and depth here as well. Quite full, good tannins. Stylish and concentrated. Rich and meaty, with good grip. Long and fat. Fine. Very long.

Talbot   1995–2003   14.5

Fullish colour. The usual slightly stalky, young Talbot nose, but good richness underneath. Balanced and fresh. Not a blockbuster. Indeed lacks a bit of real concentration. Medium-full body.

Terrey-Gros-Caillou   Now–2003   13.5

Medium-full colour. Cabernet-based but somewhat one-dimensional. Smells a little of filter. Ripe on the palate. Some substance. A little inflexible. A little dull.

PAUILLAC

Batailley   1996–2010   15.5

Medium-full colour. Supple, ripe, stylish nose. Not a blockbuster. Medium-full, some new oak.

Ripe and charming on the attack. And balanced on the finish. Good fruit. Easy to enjoy.

Carruades de Château Lafite

                 1996–2008   16.5

Fullish colour. Stylish nose. Good oak. Quite full, but no second wine. Super-rich but good acidity. Complex on the finish and elegant overall.

Clerc-Milon   1998–2016   17.0

Fullish colour. Firmer nose. Very lovely concentrated Cabernet fruit. Very lovely concentrated Cabernet fruit. This is repeated on the palate. Full, ample, concentrated wine. Fine ripe tannin. Fat and balanced. Classy. Backward. Very fine.

Duhart-Milon   1998–2010   16.0

Fullish colour. Full nose. Somewhat solid and four-square as usual. Rather more accessible than hitherto on the palate. Fullish, meaty. Good oak. Good breed. Now a wine to be reckoned with. Bigger than Carruades but Carruades has more breed and a better finish.

Fonbadet   1996–2006   13.0

Medium-full colour. Slightly lactic and a bit weak on the nose. Attenuated. Medium body. Yet originally good, ripe fruit. Is this a bad bottle?

Grand-Puy-Lacoste   1998–2012   17.5

Fullish colour. Full, rich, concentrated. This has the sort of size and depth one is looking for. Today this is far better than Ducru. Full, rich, concentrated, with very good tannins and fine balancing acidity. Real depth and complexity.

Haut-Bages-Libéral   1996–2006   15.5

Medium-full colour. Firm, full, backward, old-viney nose. Quite full. Good ripe tannins. Perhaps not the real power, depth and concentration of the best but ripe and balanced.

Haut-Batailley   1998–2010   15.0

Fullish colour. Full, solid, but quite powerful nose. And similar on the palate. What it lacks is a bit of breed. There is something a little aggressively firm here. Needs time.

Lafite   1999–2018   19.0

Fullish colour. Closed, backward nose. Good depth. Fine new oak. This is very fine. Quite full, good tannin. Above all balance and elegance. Lovely, ripe, complex fruit. Very long.

Latour   1995–2005   15.5

Fullish colour. Lightish nose, compared with the above. Slightly lactic. Medium-full. Not much tannin. Pretty, elegant, totally atypical of a young Latour. Accessible. Where is the concentration?

Lynch-Bages   Now–1997   13.5

Fullish colour. Rich and ripe on the nose. But does it lack a little power? Fullish, ripe, ample, plump wine. Fine fruit. Good grip. Not quite the blockbuster I expected. Good finish. Fine.

Lynch-Moussas Drink soon 12.5

Medium to medium-full colour. Light nose.
Pleasant but no real depth or concentration. Light
to medium body. Almost ready. Cheerful but of
little consequence.

Mouton-Baronne-Philippe

1998–2006 16.0

Fullish colour. Rich, violet-perfumed nose, like a
masculine Margaux. Fullish body. Good, ripe,
slightly aromatic tannins. Good grip. There is
lovely fruit here. Real charm.

Mouton-Rothschild 2000–2020 20.0

Full colour. Fabulous nose. Extraordinary depth,
concentration and extract. Usual Mouton oaky,
lead-pencilly character. Echoed on the palate.
Very, very rich and concentrated. Real breed and
depth. Excellent. The wine of the vintage.

Pichon-Longueville-Baron

1998–2015 18.5

Good colour. Excellent nose. There is both breed
and concentration here. Lovely balanced Cabernet-based fruit on the palate. Full, rich, oaky and
classic. Excellent ripe succulent tannins. Very
long, very classy. A bigger, more masculine wine
than its neighbour. Quite different in style and
very nearly as good: very complex. The best
Baron for decades.

Pichon-Longueville, Comtesse de Lalande

1998–2015 19.0

Full colour. Fat, opulent in a stylish, feminine
sense – and good new oak on the nose. Powerful,
fat and concentrated. This is very, very fine indeed. Marvellous fruit and extract. Powerful, fat,
concentrated and complex. Splendidly balanced.

Pontet-Canet Now–2000 14.0

Fullish colour. Somewhat neutral on the nose. I
miss the concentration and new oak that was apparent when the wine was in cask. This is missing
on the palate too. Medium body. Lacks personality and selection. A pity after its early promise.

Réserve-de-La-Comtesse

1995–2003 15.0

Fullish colour. Ripe new oaky nose. Medium-full
body. Good fruit. An attractive plump wine. Well
made but lacks the depth and concentration of the
best of the classed growths. Well balanced. Good
finish.

SAINT-ESTÈPHE

Calon-Ségur 1995–2005 16.0

Medium-full colour. Good nose. Ripe, plump,
new oaky, stylish. This is the best Calon for some

years. Has good grip and depth. Fine fruit and
good, ripe acidity. Medium-full body. Complex
follow-through. Long finish.

Cos d'Estournel 1998–2018 18.5

Full colour. Much less accessible and unformed
on the nose than the other Saint-Estèphes. A great
deal more powerful on the palate. Full, backward,
rich and concentrated. There is a lot of depth
here. Very long and multidimensional on the finish. Excellent quality. Distinctly superior.

Cos-Labory 1995–2005 15.0

Fullish colour. Soft but quite concentrated. Ripe
nose with a touch of new oak. Medium-full body.
Stylish, well-made wine. Balanced and long.
Some tannin. By no means a blockbuster but has
depth. Finishes well.

Haut-Marbuzet Now–2003 16.0

Medium-full colour. Quite accessible, opulent,
toasted, roasted-coffee nose. Medium-full body.
Ripe tannins. Not a blockbuster but rich and
plummy and well balanced. Good complexity. A
lot of seductive appeal here. Very good grip and
length.

Lafon-Rochet 1995–2005 15.0

Fullish colour. Firm nose, solid but not aggressive.
A fullish wine with quite a lot of tannin. This
masks the fruit a little. Underneath there is good
grip but not a lot of charm or complexity.

Meyney Now–2001 14.5

Good colour. Rather solid on the nose. A little
coarse and stewed. Quite full. Richer and more
opulent than nose would suggest. Good balance.
More depth than the above.

Montrose 1996–2008 16.0

Fullish colour. Fine ripe blackberry and plum
nose with a touch of new oak. Good concentration here, but Calon is better. Not a blockbuster.
But the wine is not weak. Ripe and chocolatey.

Les Ormes-de-Pez 1995–2005 14.5

Fullish colour. Like the above this is more obviously Saint-Estèphe. A little rustic and stalky.
Medium-full. Good tannins. Again richer than
the nose would suggest. Good grip.

de Pez Now–1999 14.0

Good colour. Again accessible on the nose. Elegant and plump with a touch of new oak. Medium to medium-full body. Slightly chunky tannins. Ripe without being exactly concentrated or
complex. Quite good.

1985 CLARET

Nineteen eighty-five was a very large vintage. The weather was kind. The fruit arrived at the winery in abundance, in a healthy condition and in a satisfactory state of ripeness. Moreover, the entire harvest took place in benign weather. The auguries were promising.

Yet, though extolled at the time, and certainly priced as if it were something exceptional, this is not a great vintage. Very good, yes: great, no. The wines are soft and charming; ripe, succulent and sweet. The fruit element is certainly there and the wines as a result will find many friends. What the vintage lacks – what separates 'very good' from 'great' – is the back-bone, the depth of character, the multidimensional complexity, the concentration, the quantity of tannin and the grip of acidity of a vintage like the best of the 1982, and the best of 1986, 1989 and 1990.

In character the 1985 vintage has much in common with 1970. Both vintages were large; in both years the fruit was very ripe and the wines had a generosity of character. Where it differs from 1970 is in this question of depth and grip. As a result the wines have less definition; they are more diffuse. Now approaching maturity, they are paradoxically too appealing. They lack austerity.

Perhaps this is the way wine is produced today, the Peynaud influence. Wines are certainly much better made than a generation ago. But when discussing the top 100 clarets we are not talking about general wine, we are considering the cream of Bordeaux. Leave the *petits châteaux* to produce their soft, appealing wines for early drinking. At the top we are looking for something more *sérieux*. Could we, should we, have had more serious wines in 1985?

THE WEATHER

The year opened with a spell of really arctic weather throughout France. While the mercury did not completely disappear into the bulb of the thermometer in Bordeaux as it did in Chablis and Champagne, the cold was nevertheless in pockets sufficiently severe to kill off a few young vines, and to restrict severely the potential for the 1985 crop in other locations. Happily, most of the fine wine vineyards emerged unscathed (Domaine de Chevalier, sadly, is an exception, but the wine is brilliant), and with the benefit of a spring and summer free from the usual pests and other depredations the fruit progressed towards maturity without any problem. If it had been only a degree or two colder it would have been a disaster, as in 1956.

March and April were mild but May began cold and wet and ended with hailstorms on the Whitsun weekend, reducing the potential crop in the southern Médoc (particularly, among the top vineyards, at Cantemerle), in the Premières Côtes and in Barsac. June was dry and sunny if a little cooler than average but the flowering nevertheless took place at the normal time and without mishap.

'Thus', to quote Sichel's *Vintage Report*, 'the curtain rose on a summer which was to start well, to improve as it went along, and to finish magnificently.' The 1985 season was characterized by two important and interrelated benefits. It was exceptionally dry, and, from the second half of August onwards, conspicuously and continually warm, without being too hot. With the exception of a weekend of rain at the beginning of October there was an almost total drought from 4 July to 21 October. In August and September only 22 millimetres were recorded, the direst summer since 1929. (Nineteen sixty-one was the only other vintage to register a figure of less than 50.) In contrast, the figures for 1982 and 1983 were 99.8 and 136.6.

Yet there was no heatwave. In July the temperatures were about average; August was decidedly cool – only 1979 and 1963 being cooler since 1959, according to Sichel's records, despite an improvement at the end of the month. September, though, was warmer than average. Only in 1961 and 1964 was it hotter, and it was this balmy end-of-season weather, continuing, after a brief interruption, well into October, which was the making of the 1985 harvest.

In these dry, warm, climatic conditions, the fruit raced towards maturity, both the date of the *veraison*, when the grape begins to change colour, and the date of the harvest being earlier than anticipated, and the picking began on 20th September for the dry white wines and 26th September for the reds, about a week earlier than the date of the flowering would have suggested. The fruit was in magnificent condition. To quote Peter Sichel again, 'It is rare to see Bordeaux vineyards in such exuberant health.'

THE SIZE OF THE HARVEST

If the weather in September 1985, was the making of the harvest, its size was its undoing. We have become used to large crops in recent years: in terms of *appellation contrôlée* wine, 4.5 million hectolitres in 1979 and again in 1982; 4.1 million in 1983. In 1985 the figure was 4.94 million, an average of over 60 hectolitres per hectare. This was a significant two hectolitres per hectare more than in 1982. Moreover, the increase was proportionately more in the red wine vineyards than in the white. If we compare the declarations with 1982 we can see that in Bordeaux Rouge and Bordeaux Supérieur, possibly mainly because of new plantations and the continuing switch from white wine production to red, the rise is over 20 per cent. However, in Pauillac it is a staggering 37 per cent, and in Saint-Estèphe it is 23 per cent. In Saint-Emilion and Pomerol the yield was 6 per cent down. Overall, the AC red wine crop was 12 per cent more than in 1982. With 3.95 million hectolitres, the red wine harvest alone was over half a million hectolitres larger than the total harvest in 1984, white wine and non-AC wine included.

The size of the harvest seems to have caught everyone by surprise. Perhaps because of the January cold, perhaps because the flowering weather was not so obviously magnificent, predictions even immediately prior to the picking were for a crop of 4 million hectolitres overall, hardly significantly higher than in 1984. While the official figure did not appear until March it was already apparent to the proprietors in October that they had a great deal more wine than they had expected.

As the local paper put it, '*On s'est trompé!*, which I translated as 'We boobed!'

Yield Per Hectare – Five-Year Averages

AC Wine	Hectares in Production	Harvest 000 he	Yield he/ha
1951–1955	72,900	2,436	33.4
1956–1960	67,800	1,714	25.3
1961–1965	72,700	2,895	39.8
1966–1970	74,300	3,043	41.0
1971–1975	68,500	2,939	42.9
1976–1980	75,200	3,231	43.0
1981–1985	78,900	3,946	49.5

Recent Large Harvests

AC Wine Production	Red	White	Total (000 he)	Yield (he/ha)
1953	1,226	1,758	2,984	41.7
1955	1,285	1,831	3,116	40.8
1962	1,436	2,305	3,741	44.9
1967	1,513	1,846	3,359	43.7
1970	2,062	1,313	3,375	48.5
1973	2,485	1,290	3,774	44.8

AC Wine Production	Red	White	Total (000 he)	Yield (he/ha)
1974	2,237	1,136	3,373	50.0
1976	2,462	1,059	3,521	49.7
1979	3,308	1,201	4,509	60.7
1982	3,508	1,042	4,550	59.1
1983	3,190	917	4,107	52.7
1985	3,950	990	4,940	61.0

While in 1986 it would be

1986	4,514	1,110	5,624	64.6

THE HARVEST

As I have said, the harvest began for the Merlot grapes on 26th September. Pétrus, which is to all extents and purposes 100 per cent Merlot, was cleared as usual in three afternoons on 2, 3 and 4 October. The Merlot grapes were in splendid condition, yielding (without the aid of chaptalization) musts of 12.5 degrees or more of potential alcohol, with a good acidity, round, ripe tannins and plenty of extract. At this stage, however, the Cabernets were not quite ripe and far from concentrated. These grapes were still at the equivalent of 10.5 degrees, and after heavy overnight dew and morning mists at the end of September, this declined to 9.5. Some proprietors picked part of the vineyard before the rain predicted for the weekend at the beginning of October; others began soon after, when the berries were still to some extent inflated with water, and, equally importantly, when the acidity was temporarily reduced. Thereafter, the fine dry weather returned and those who had courage to wait could harvest a crop with a reasonable potential level of alcohol and at least adequate degrees of acidity and concentration.

THE WINE AND THE IMPORTANCE OF SELECTION

Potentially, therefore, the ingredients for a very good vintage were there. While the harvest would not match 1982, firstly because of its sheer size, secondly, paradoxically, because of the excessive drought (which slows up the ripening) and thirdly, because of the lack of really exceptionally hot, grape-concentrating weather, two fine elements were present: the Merlot wine cropped at the end of September and those Cabernets cropped later in October. Both of these were made from supremely healthy, ripe fruit, and analysis showed good levels of tannin and acidity. Combined, there was no doubt they would make fine wine. The problem was what to do with the vats of weaker wine from the fruit harvested in the middle.

The solution was to reject what was not up to standard into the second or even the third wine. It is heartening to report that it is now *de rigueur* at *cru classé* levels (and even at *bourgeois* levels like at Labégorce-Zédé) to produce a second wine. Some properties, Léoville-Las-Cases for instance, even make a third wine. Others sell off wine unfit for the second wine in bulk.

Yet, easy as it is for us to urge unselfish selection and second and third wines, we must be mindful of what it means in cash terms to the proprietors themselves. A renowned classed growth such as Ducru-Beaucaillou would sell its 1985, ex-château, for about 100 francs. The second wine will make 40. If Jean-Eugène Borie rejects 40 per cent of his harvest from the *grand vin*, as he did in 1985, he is depriving himself in theory of a potential extra 60 francs on the equivalent of 100,000 bottles. Even if, elsewhere, the loss of profit is not as great as 6 million francs it is not hard to recognize that not all proprietors are prepared to be this rigorous. Some, for reasons of '*indivision*' (the shareholding being divided among numerous members of the same family or families), or for other financial pressures, just cannot afford to be.

Nevertheless, selections in general in 1985 were severe. At Haut-Brion, as at Haut-Bailly, only 50 per cent of the crop was declared *grand vin*. Overall, among the best wines, despite the production statistics, only 30 to 40 per cent more than in 1984 was declared as the château wine.

FIRST IMPRESSIONS

My first impression was of wines with a good colour and a most appealing, ripe, almost scented fruit. By and large the wines had a good constitution; they had body, balance, good levels of ripe, round tannin, at least adequate acidity and were positive, accessible and attractive. What the vintage lacked, though of course there were exceptions, was the extra dimension, weight of fruit and concentration, as had the 1982s.

The wines had a lot of charm – the supreme health of the fruit and the ripeness of the Merlot contributed to this – but too often this charm appeared to be all on the surface. One was left looking for the almost bitter austerity underneath the varietal fruit, apparent in a young claret of a great vintage. Moreover, few wines were really as full-bodied as they should be, and some distinctly lacked acidity. Equally, though it was more consistent, the vintage lacked the definition and class of the best of the 1983s.

This was, I said in my original report, a variable vintage. The looser wines, once they had lost their puppy fat, their youthful charm, might go the way of the 1976s – evolve early, age inelegantly. Others with better acidity might turn out like 1979: pleasant but with the lack of complexity of a prolific vintage.

The best wines, however, were quite different. Where the yield had been kept within reasonable bounds, where the average age of the vines was high, and above all, where a rigorous selection had been made, and all, not just some, of the weaker vats rejected, we had wine which, in Jean-Eugène Borie's opinion, 'starts like 1982 and finishes like 1983' or, as Jacques Hébrard of Château Cheval-Blanc put it, a 'a year of finesse, richness and balance'. At this top level the wines were certainly very exciting. Quite a few could be found in the Médoc and Graves, more in Saint-Emilion and especially Pomerol where the vintage was clearly better than 1983 (but then the 1983 vintage in the Libournais was not good as it is in the Médoc).

THE MARKET

As hardly needs to be pointed out any more, the château proprietors had asked high prices for their 1984s. These could in no way be justified on a rational basis but were excused by variously the 'going rate' for the 1982s and 1983s, at the time twice as high as the opening prices, by the poor start to the 1985 viticultural season – before the flowering it was impossible to predict the effect of the January frost – and by the small size of the vintage. Pressure, implicit or not, was put on the *négociants* to purchase 1984s or the 1985s would not be made available to them, and they in turn, attempted to apply the same pressure on some of their customers, some of whom succumbed. This was a ridiculous and potentially dangerous situation, reminiscent of 1972.

It is a fact, whether one considers it desirable or not, that the proprietors of the few most fashionable estates in Bordeaux are – or were in the mid 1980s – in a very powerful position. A seemingly unending queue of buyers beat a path to their door, who will buy irrespective of price or of quality; who will pay 50 per cent more for inferior 1984 than for excellent 1982 or 1983. *Caveat emptor*, perhaps. Yet with power comes, or should come, responsibility. The 1984s should have been left to find their own demand and price levels in their own good time, as happened with the 1980s, where there was no *en primeur* campaign but where the vintage found no shortage of willing applicants three or four years later. With the 1984s, where the powerful led, the others, perforce, followed. This caused a distortion to the market which, as will be seen, was to have repercussions in the 1985 campaign. I blame the powerful and their advisers, the brokers. I blame also the top *négociants* who should equally have counselled prudence, and I was sorry to see British merchants attempting to foist expensive 1984s on to their customers.

Almost immediately the quality of the 1985s became apparent, fears were voiced that the 1985s would open at yet higher prices than the 1984s. Rumours circulated, vigorously denied by Mme de Lencquesaing herself, that Pichon-Lalande would open at 150 francs (1984: 100). Meanwhile the value of the pound sterling, and, particularly, the dollar, had fallen substantially *vis à vis* the franc. With the pound trading at just above 10 francs and the dollar at less than seven, falls of 20 per cent and 35 per cent respectively, it became apparent that even if prices remained at 1984 levels the cost to the customer would be considerably more than he had been invited to pay for the 1982s and the 1983s.

I included the following table in my original report:

Comparative Prices of Château Pichon-Lalande

Year	Price Ex-Château FF Per Bottle	Ex-Negociant FF (Assuming +25%)	Rate of Exchange FF to £ Mid July	Ex-Merchant £ Per Case (Assuming Cost + 40%)
1982	67.00	83.75	11.91	£118.20
1983	85.00	106.25	11.53	£154.80
1984	100.00	125.00	12.25	£171.42
1985	100.00	125.00	10.30	£203.90
	(or if 150, as feared)		(187.50)	(£305.80)

Even if the 1985s sold for the price of the 1984s would the British drinker really pay almost twice as much as he paid for the 1982 vintage, almost a third more than for the 1983? – even if the vintage was quite superb?

Well, 'quite superb' the 1985s were not, however good they might be, and some British merchants began to feel they should take things into their own hands. Robin Kernick of Corney and Barrow wrote to a number of château proprietors and *négociants*, as well as to Pierre Tari of Château Giscours in his capacity as President of the Union des Grands Crus. Restraint was advised, caution was urged, the difficulties of 1973/74 recalled. This was followed up by further, less temperate, more pompous missives from others on this side of the Channel. Meanwhile, the stalwart Mme de Lencquesaing, recently returned from Japan to find rumour rife and alarm ascending about her supposed 1985 prices, was firing off letters to all and sundry which appeared on the one hand to deny she had ever had any intention of so doing while on the other hand giving one of the most convincing demonstrations I have seen yet for justifying such hefty price increases – it was all a question of the comparative ratio between a second growth's prices and those of the firsts over the last century.

Nevertheless, and surprisingly, as far as I was concerned, those in Bordeaux who read the letters from Kernick and others took note of the arguments that were put. As a result a meeting was held – of proprietors, *négociants* and brokers – on 7 February. It was decided that opening prices would be at 1984 levels. Those who bought the 1984 harvest would be offered first option, more extended payment terms and best prices. If there was any left, the rest could follow and pick up the crumbs.

So far, so good. Château Cos d'Estournel, which made a simply splendid wine in 1985, was one of the first big names to appear. Saint-Pierre, Lynch-Bages, La Lagune and others were also among the early arrivals on the market. All these offered a varying proportion of their wines at 1984 levels; in the case of La Lagune, as normal, the totality, but a reduced quantity because of hail damage; in the case of Lynch-Bages, only a portion. By mid-May on the Médoc and Graves side most had played the game. There were two major exceptions. The first growths had maintained their 1982 price throughout the 1983 the 1984 campaigns.

They asked 200–210 francs for their 1985s (1982, 1983 and 1984: 170–180). The other exception was Château Léoville-Las-Cases. Ducru and Pichon-Lalande 1985 appeared on the same day and at the same price (110 francs) M. Delon of Léoville-Las-Cases waited longer and then asked 140 francs, 27 per cent more than his 1984 price and 55.5 per cent more than he had demanded for his 1983. This struck me as ludicrous, good as the wine is. No doubt, however, M. Delon was not short of buyers.

Most Saint-Emilion prices apart from Cheval-Blanc and Ausone, which followed the trend of the Médoc first growths, were steady. Pomerol is another story. Both La Conseillante and L'Evangile have delusions of grandeur and increased their prices to 180 and 185 francs respectively. Vieux Château Certan asked 140.

While most proprietors were doing what they could to keep the market cool, the rest of the trade was losing its reason. Despite all the letters, pompous or not, that had been sent to Bordeaux, merchants were clambering over their telexes trying to acquire stock and, seemingly, paying almost any price for it. It soon became apparent, to the chagrin of those who had bought 1984, that wine was available at no higher price to those who had not, and that instead of, as one might fondly have supposed, being offered say two or three times as much 1985 as one's 1984 purchases, the allocations were considerably reduced – as much as in 1984 but not a drop more. Moreover, while the château owners had kept their side of the bargain, *négociants* in Bordeaux were imposing much higher profit margins than in 1982 and 1983, justifying this by pointing out the losses they would have to take on the 1984s.

As I wrote in 1986, more dangerous, in the long term, was the seeming reluctance or inability of these merchants in Bordeaux to accept orders subject to tasting or, ideally, to reserve stock so that their better customers could make a peaceful and considered evaluation once all the wines were on the market, and when the wines were properly married and tasteable at the end of April or in May. Currently, practically all fine Bordeaux is sold on name, over the telephone or by fax or telex. The days seem to have gone when the British wine-buyer could not buy solely when the quality of the vintage so determined, but also, say, organize a comparative tasting of all the Saint-Julien *crus classés*, with all the prices in front of him, in order dispassionately to decide what to commit himself to. This is more than sad; it is potentially the negation of what being a fine wine-merchant is all about.

As the campaign progressed it became apparent that the market for the 1985s, in western Europe at any rate, extended beyond that of the excitable British wine-merchant. My friends in England reported satisfactory sales. Those in Bordeaux confirmed demand from metropolitan France, Benelux and Scandinavia. The reaction in the USA was more mixed – the dollar had fallen more than the pound, and there was still plenty of 1983 in the pipeline. Yet, nevertheless, business was brisk.

PRICES

Prices to the consumer were substantially up on those of the 1982 and 1983 vintages. Here is a short table taken from the opening offer in each year of Adnams and Co., Southwold:

Price Ex-Cellars Bordeaux

	1982	1983	1985
Labégorce-Zédé	£33.50	£40.00	£67.50
Chasse-Spleen	£49.00	£52.50	£92.50
Haut-Bailly	£72.00	£78.00	£112.75
Palmer	£110.00	£130.00	£221.50
Léoville-Las-Cases	£112.00	£215.00	£290.00
Margaux	£295.00	£295.00	£395.00
Ausone	£320.00	£320.00	£450.00

These increases struck me as excessive. *Caveat emptor*, I said: this was not the vintage for investment, and those who were heavily into 1985 might live to regret it, particularly if 1986 was firstly plentiful and secondly of at least reasonable quality – which in fact it turned out to be. The 1985 clarets were the most expensive Bordeaux vintage in real terms in modern times. Not as ludicrously priced as the 1984s, for it was a better vintage. But the 1985s are not great wines: so to pay double the price of 1982s was in no way justified.

THE WINES NOW

It is generally recognized that this is a very good vintage in the Libournais. The *cuvées* of Merlot were very ripe and round, and this is reflected in the top wines. There is a lot of sweet fruit and a lot of charm. They have more depth and a better grip than the 1983s. The top Pomerols, in particular, are very fine.

Among the lesser right-bank wines, however, there is a certain imbalance. On the one hand there is a richness and succulence, on the other a lack of concentration and grip: the size of the vintage is apparent. Moreover, it is apparent that many wines have been bolstered by the addition of rather too much *vin de presse*. This leaves a certain unripe astringency, almost a bitter inkiness, lurking in the background and masking the fruit and the attraction of many wines; a characteristic that I fear will not be absorbed with time. There are good wines, but in general you will need to go up to *premier cru* level, and its equivalent in Pomerol, to obtain them.

There are one or two oddballs. Figeac 1985 has never really sung to me. I found an odd flavour in the wine at the beginning, and it has continued to be inconsistent. Ausone is not as good as it appeared at the outset. Trotanoy, too, has not lived up to its early promise.

The top wines of the Graves and the Médoc are equally as good as the top wines of Pomerol and Saint-Emilion. Latour has always been a disappointment, and Montrose is somewhat insignificant. Giscours is poor and Issan has developed a bit too fast, but by and large the vintage has developed well. The top wines have personality, elegance and depth even if at lesser levels the wines have proportionally less interest.

In sum, this is a very good vintage. The stellar wines such as Lafleur, La Conseillante and Canon, Domaine de Chevalier and Cos d'Estournel, Lynch-Bages and Léoville-Las-Cases, not to mention Cheval-Blanc and Pétrus and Margaux, the three best first growths, are very exciting. At the top levels there are 1985s to match the best of any of the other vintages in the last decade.

THE TASTING

Most of the following wines were sampled at a session in London organized by Andrew Bruce in May 1993. I have filled in one or two gaps with notes taken in the summer of 1994.

	Optimum Drinking	Mark out of 20

SAINT-EMILION

L'Arrosée — Now–2008 — 16.0

Medium-full colour. Some brown now. Soft, opulent, oaky nose. Sweet and seductive. Medium to medium-full body. Just about ready. An attractive, accessible up-front wine. Well put together. Good balance and long finish. But not the intensity for better than very good. Nor the grip.

Ausone — 1995–2008 — 15.5

Medium-full colour. Just a hint of brown. Ripe on the nose. But rather dumb at present, seems to lack real concentration, richness and depth. Medium-full, the tannins are a little astringent. Ripe if not very rich or structured. The fruit is classy but the wine not of real first growth quality. All a bit mixed up. Less acidity than Belair.

Belair — 1995–2005 — 16.0

Medium-full colour. A little brown. Soft and round and fruity on the nose, but it lacks a bit of zip and real personality. Medium to medium-full body. Fruity, balanced, quite stylish. Lacks real intensity and interest. Very good.

Canon — 1997–2012 — 17.5

Very good colour. Just a hint of brown. Closed, tannic, backward but very very rich and concentrated. Quite marked by new oak. As usual full and tannic but with splendid fruit and depth. Typically Canon. Old viney and very intense. Lovely.

Cheval-Blanc 1997–2015 19.0

Full colour. Just a hint of brown. Fat, rich, opulent, spicy, backward. Very Cheval-Blanc. Fullish. Very good tannins. Sweet, very rich. As usual very voluptuous. Most enjoyable. Very seductive. It really has class, complexity and intensity. Marvellous long finish. Excellent.

Figeac Now–1999 15.0

Fullish colour. Some brown. Opulent, ripe, slightly spicy, certainly quite a lot of new oak in evidence. Ripe and generous. Evolved very fast though. When I came back to taste it again it had collapsed. Fresh but not enough grip.

Clos-Fourtet Now–1998 13.5

Medium-full colour. Slightly sweaty/blowsy on the nose. A bit raw and stewed. Yet thin at the same time. Good acidity but no fat and richness. Unexciting. Just about ready. Not bad plus.

La Gaffelière Now–2000 14.0

Medium to medium-full colour. Some brown. Ripe, essentially Merlot fruit on the nose. Quite evolved. Not really quite enough grip and therefore class. Medium body. Pleasant quite stylish but rather one-dimensional. Lacks zip at the end. Not bad plus.

Magdelaine 1996–2012 17.5

Very good colour. Very fine concentrated ripe Merlot nose. A lot of richness here, plenty of depth. Very fine voluptuous fruit. Medium-full, some tannin. Lovely concentration, good vanilla, new oaky aftertaste. Excellent fruit. Well balanced with ripe acidity. Exciting.

Pavie 1996–2010 17.0

Very good colour. Just a hint of brown. Closed on the nose, a bit adolescent, but plenty of depth and concentration underneath. Old viney fruit. Quite substantial. Fullish. Very good tannins. Lovely fruit. Ripe, elegant, complete. Fine.

Soutard 1997–2010 15.5

Fullish colour. Still youthful. Slightly four-square on the tannins. Lacks a little oxygen. Closed in. Elements of the vat. Good acidity. Better on the palate. Full, rich and meaty. Lacks a little class and generosity but very good. Needs time.

Le Tertre-Rôteboeuf 1996–2010 16.0

Good fullish colour. Now some maturity. A fullish wine, tannins a little raw but rich and opulent and, in the best sense, rustic. This has a good ripe spicy flavour. Good grip. Just the tannins a little untamed. Yet very fine follow-through. Very good.

Troplong-Mondot 1996–2008 14.5

Very good colour. Full, still purple. Elderberries.

Concentrated but a bit dense. Medium-full. Slightly astringent. Yet rich underneath. Lacks a bit of style and balance. Quite good plus.

POMEROL

Beauregard Now–2005 Plus 17.0

Full colour. Still immature. Rich concentrated nose. Good fruit. Some oak. A ripe wine with backbone. Good. Finely poised, elegant, oaky. Fullish. Still tannic. Fine fruit. Good grip. This is long and complex. Very fine for what it is.

Certan-de-May 1996–2010 17.5

Full colour. Quite brown, even old at the rim. Full, meaty, a little adolescent on the nose. Fullish, very ripe. The tannins are better covered. Rich, firm, exotic. Good grip. Finely balanced.

Clinet 1996–2010 15.5

Fullish colour. A little dense, not much sign of maturity. Rich, ripe, meaty nose. Some oak. Good depth. Even concentration. Fullish, still a little tannin. Quite marked by the oak. Rich and meaty. Even sweet. Good grip. This is a little lumpy but very good. Finishes well.

La Conseillante Now–2009 18.5

Medium-full colour. A little mature. Not a blockbuster but lovely fragrant very ripe fruit on the nose. Very complex. A touch of violets. Fullish. Still just a little tannin. Marvellous finesse and delicate balance. Ripe, subtle. Very fine.

Clos L'Eglise Now–2004 13.5

Medium colour. Quite mature nose. Aromatic, evolved Merlot nose, lacks a bit of zip. Medium body. Now just about ready. Quite ample. Not too short, but lacks a little personality and elegance. Quite good. Better in a year.

L'Eglise Clinet 1995–2004 14.0

Good full colour. Youthful. Slightly adolescent on the nose. But substantial. A touch herbaceous at present. Fullish, slightly stewed. Good acidity and reasonable fruit but a bit lumpy. It lacks charm. Quite good only. Too much *vin de presse*.

L'Enclos Now–2003 15.5

Medium-full colour. A little development. Firm nose. Some Cabernet. Still adolescent. But a wine with depth. On the palate it seems a little over-*chambré*d. Medium-full. Best at the finish. Quite good fruit. Some oak. Good acidity. But lacks a bit of real richness again. But an elegant wine which finishes long. Will improve.

L'Evangile 1997–2000 16.0

Full colour, but a little brown. Dense, highish acidity, slightly herbaceous. Lacks a little generosity on the nose. Full, tannic, a bit austere. Yet plenty of richness underneath. Good grip. I think this will always be better with food. Very good but muscular.

Le Gay 1997–2010 16.5

Very full colour. Still very youthful. Big, full, fat, rich nose. Structured, still burly. Better as it evolved in the glass. Full, rich and tannic. A meaty wine with a lot of class and dimension. Good grip. Long. Very good plus.

Lafleur 1998–2020 19.0

Full colour. Just a hint of brown. Backward. Very full, very rich and concentrated. Very full indeed on the nose. This is excellent. Full, tannic, real intensity, very good drive and grip. Hugely concentrated. Exciting. Needs time though.

Lafleur-Pétrus Now–1999 15.5

Medium-full colour. Still youthful. Merlot shows, lush, oaky, broad-flavoured. Seductive. Ripe. A very aromatic wine. Medium body. Slightly more lactic than the others. Finishes well.

Lagrange Now–2003 15.5

Medium-full colour. A little development. An elegant wine, not a blockbuster. Feminine, balanced. Quite oaky. Medium body. Still a bit of tannin. Individual. Slight spice (cinnamon, liquorice). Slightly earthy. Good balance. Long. Good plus. But it lacks just a little real richness.

Pétrus 1995–2010 19.5

Fullish colour. Still youthful. Nose still closed. Good acidity. Still youthful. Full, still some tannin. A masculine wine. Firm, youthful, fine acidity. Has real potential and lovely fruit. Excellent.

La Pointe Now–1997 14.0

Medium colour. Some development. Evolved nose. Now soft, seems quite mature. Pleasant but lacks a bit of strength and depth. Medium body. No tannin. Lacks a bit of richness and concentration. Reasonable acidity though. Quite good.

Trotanoy Now–2005 15.5

Fullish colour. A little brown. Very typical Moueix and Merlot on the nose. Round, very ripe. But lacks a bit of zip. Medium-full. Round, opulent but it lacks a bit of acidity. Fat and fruity, but lacks real dimension. Only good plus.

Vieux Château Certan 1997–2015 17.0

Very good colour. Still very young. Full, a bit adolescent, rich and concentrated and quite oaky. Full, rich concentrated palate. Very ripe. Very good acidity. Still youthful but there is real depth and high class here. Fine plus. Needs time. Very long. Complex finish. But not quite the richness and opulence of Certan-de-May.

GRAVES

Bouscaut Now–1998 13.0

Medium-full colour. Rather dry and undistinguished on the nose. No flesh. No attraction. Medium body. A bit astringent. Just about ready. Lacks charm. Not bad.

Domaine de Chevalier 1998–2018 18.5

Good fullish colour. Little brown. Great subtlety here. Lovely intense but delicate fruit. Very ripe and complex. Raspberries and violets dominate. Closed. Backward. Fullish. Real class. Beautiful integration and subtlety. Lovely. Marvellous fruit. Very, very long. Real breed.

de Fieuzal 1999–2010 14.5

Good fullish colour. Still young. Ample, meaty, fullish mulberry fruity. Graves *goût de terroir* nose. Ripe and substantial but not a lot of class. Medium-full. A little burly, but underneath plenty of fruit. Good balance. But lacks a bit of finesse.

Haut-Bailly 1995–2010 15.0

Medium-full colour. A little brown. Soft and ripe, round, stylish. Less substantial than the other Graves. On the palate medium-full, ripe, seductive. Lacks just a little zip and personality, but finishes well. Long. Good.

Haut-Brion 1997–2015 18.5

Fullish colour. A hint of brown. Slightly adolescent on the nose. Rich, opulent, complex, classy. Mulberry flavours. Very round. Lovely oak integration. This is full and opulent, with splendid fruit and intensity. Very lovely. Very long.

La Mission-Haut-Brion 1998–2020 18.5

Full colour. Still very young. A more refined nose than the La Tour. Very rich, full and concentrated. Very blackcurrant. Good acidity. Youthful but fine. Full, closed, rich, tannic. This has a lot of depth and class. Above all on the finish. Needs time but very fine.

Pape-Clément 1998–2015 17.0

Good fullish colour. Still young. Full, rich, meaty, oaky. Quite Médoc in style. Good depth and class here. Full body. Very good tannins. Lovely oaky background. Good grip. Very good ripe raspberry, blackcurrant fruit. Long. Fine. Lots of dimension here.

La Tour-Haut-Brion 1997–2007 14.0

Good colour. Just a hint of brown. Full nose. Slightly earthy-dense-farmyardy. A bit unyielding. Beefy, slightly over *vin de presse*-d. Astringent. Unexciting. Charmless. One-dimensional and four-square. Yet good acidity. Will improve.

MARGAUX AND THE REST OF THE MÉDOC

Cantemerle Now–2003 14.0

Medium to medium-full colour. Youthful but elegantly fruity nose. Quite complex. On the palate though medium body, ripe and with reasonable grip, it lacks real grip, it certainly lacks depth and fat. Acceptable but unexciting. Thin.

Chasse-Spleen Now–2003 14.0

Youthful colour. Ripe, slightly spicy, opulent,

quite concentrated. Medium full, just a little insufficient in real grip which makes the wine a
touch astringent on the attack. Ripe and quite opulent on the follow-through. But unexciting.

Giscours   Drink up   11.0
Medium-full colour. Rather attenuated on the
nose. No grip. Short. Poor.

d'Issan   Now–2002   13.0
Medium-full colour. Still young. Accessible nose.
Open, aromatic, cedary, gentle and ripe. On the
palate rather overblown. Sweet but lacks acidity
and grip. Ripe but already getting a bit astringent.
A bad bottle?

La Lagune   1996–2010   16.5
Full colour. Still youthful. Full, rich and oaky.
This has good concentration. A very well-made
wine as usual. Full, meaty, oaky, concentrated and
even complex. Very good indeed.

Lascombes   1996–2008   15.0
Full colour. Still youthful. Burly, some reduction
smells. Full but a lack of class on the nose. On the
palate quite meaty, quite stylish fruit. Fullish. A
little burly. But has good grip. Good.

Malescot-Saint-Exupéry   1996–2009   15.5
Medium-full colour. Still young. Still slightly
dense and unforthcoming on the nose. Some SO2
evident still. A meaty wine, slightly dense. Fullish,
good grip. Ripe and fragrant but a little adolescent. This needs time but the finish is promising.

Margaux   1997–2017   19.5
Very full colour. Very young. Splendid nose.
Good oak but not a bit too dominant. Excellent,
multidimensional fruit. Real depth and concentration. Undoubted class. This is brilliant. Marvellous intensity. Excellent concentration of fruit.
Very, very long, complex and full of breed.

Palmer   1996–2014   18.0
Very good full colour. Really classy nose again all
in finesse rather than in power. Great breed, subtle and concentration. Medium-full. Some tannin. So concentrated it is almost sweet. Real class.
Marvellous fruit. Very lovely. Very subtle.

Pavillon Rouge Du Margaux
                   1995–2002   14.0
Very full colour. Very young. Slightly raw, fullish
nose. Some *vin de presse* evidence. A little dense
but good acidity, but lacks generosity. On the
palate slightly astringent. A bit unbalanced. Dull.

Poujeaux   Now–2003   15.0
Medium-full colour. Good nose. Ripe, fleshy,
spicy. You can see the Merlot but fullish and rich.
Medium-full, balanced, stylish. Long. Well-
made. Good.

Prieuré-Lichine   Now–2003 Plus   15.5
Medium-full colour. Good nose. Plump, fresh,

attractive, balanced. Just about ready. Medium
weight, good acidity, long, elegant. Complex.
Finishes well. Good plus.

Rausan-Ségla   1996–2010   17.0
Full colour. Still youthful. A little closed, but un-
derneath there is fruit and concentration. Good
oaky base. Young still. Full, concentrated, classy.
Very good grip. This is complex and intense.
Lovely finish. Fine. Very classic Margaux.

SAINT-JULIEN

Beychevelle   1995–2009   16.0
Fullish colour. A little brown. Soft, round, ripe,
oaky nose. Attractive, even classy. Medium-full,
gentle, easy to enjoy. Good fruit. Quite long and
complex. Not a blockbuster but very good.

Branaire   1995–2005   14.0
Medium to medium-full colour, a little mature. A
little overblown on the nose. Medium body.
Lacks a bit of fat, concentration and real grip.
Reasonable acidity and fruit but one-dimensional.
No depth.

Ducru-Beaucaillou   1998–2015   18.0
Medium-full colour. Just a little hint of brown.
Round, integrated, rich and ripe and with plenty
of class, depth and intensity. Very Ducru. Full,
rich lovely fruit. Very fine tannins. Very good intensity. Round and ripe and very, very complex.
Super sweet on the finish. Multidimensional.

Gruaud-Larose   1998–2012   16.5
Full colour. Still young. A little reduction on the
nose but full, ample, rich and with plenty of dimension. Much better than Talbot. Much more
closed on the palate. Full, tannic, firm, slightly
adolescent. Lots of fruit. But how much class?

Lagrange   1997–2009   15.5
Full colour. Still very young. Slightly raw on the
nose. But good concentrated fruit. Yet has it real-
ly got a lot of class? It seems definitely *arrière côtes*.
Oaky. On the palate fullish, tannic, even rich.
Good plus. Good grip.

Langoa-Barton   1996–2008   15.5
Good colour. Still youthful. Medium full, ripe,
concentrated, classy nose. Youthful. Fullish.
Good acidity. Elegant fruit. This has good intensity if a slight lack of real depth and concentration.

Léoville-Barton   1998–2015   17.5
Very good colour. Still very young. Full, oaky,
closed, but splendid intensity and concentration.
Full, backward. Very good tannins. This is classic
Léoville. Very good grip and classy Cabernet fruit.
Needs time. Super, but not as good as Ducru.

Léoville-Las-Cases   1999–2020   18.5
Full colour. Still very young. The best of the
Saint-Juliens. Lovely fruit. Very classy, very well-
balanced, very complex. Fullish, closed, back-

ward. Splendid fruit. Great intensity. Classic Cabernet. Marvellous balance. Very fine.

Léoville-Poyferré   1999–2012   17.0

Fullish colour. A little dense. Slightly corked on the nose. Fullish, ripe, but a bit four-square. Yet I think this is very good. Fullish, not the backbone of the Barton but ripe, plump, concentrated, balanced and classy.

Saint-Pierre   1997–2010   16.0

Full colour. Just a little hint of brown. A little solid on the nose. Slightly herbaceous. Lacks nuance and a bit of class. Fullish, slightly astringent on the palate. Ripe and rich underneath, but there is a little too much *vin de presse*. Good grip. Finishes well. Very good.

Talbot   1997–2010   15.0

Good colour. Youthful. As usual quite rich but a bit dense and herbaceous on the nose. Medium-full. Good fruit. Not too burly. Balanced and enjoyable if no real class. Ripe and plummy. Good.

PAUILLAC

Batailley   Now–2006   15.5

Medium-full colour. A little mature. Soft, opulent nose. A round wine. Ripe, medium-bodied. Enjoyable now. Reasonable acidity. But no great depth. But balanced and quite classy. Good plus.

Clerc-Milon   1997–2015   17.0

Full colour. Still young. A little more closed than the Mouton-Baronne-Philippe, but has more concentration of fruit. Full, rich, concentrated. Slightly more structure too. Lovely ripeness and even sweetness. Very classy. Lovely.

Duhart-Milon   1997–2012   15.5

Fullish colour. Still young. A little dense on both nose and palate. Very Cabernet. This is fullish and slightly rigid. There is fruit here, even concentrated, even grip. But it is not quite together. But certainly good plus.

Grand-Puy-Lacoste   1997–2015   17.0

Full colour. Still very young. Backward but old viney. Very concentrated, very classic Pauillac on the nose. Full, rich, concentrated and with a lovely old-viney, chocolatey background. Very long and lovely.

Haut-Batailley   1997–2012   16.0

Fullish colour. Closed but good typically Pauillac fruit and depth on the nose. Fullish. Some tannin. Ripe, rich and very Cabernet. This has a four-square aspect but there is fruit and even concentration underneath. Long. Promising. Very good.

Lafite   1997–2009   (16.0–See note)

Full colour. Just a hint of brown. Oak dominates on the nose. Rather astringent. Seems to lack grip. Fresh, not stewed. But nothing much here. Not a typical bottle surely?

Latour   1996–2009   16.0

Medium-full colour. Quite some brown. Rather light for Latour on the nose. Lacks weight and structure. No fatness or concentration. Medium-full body. Not a lot of tannin. Good balance but one-dimensional. Ripe, fresh. Ripe and stylish. But lacks first-growth intensity. Simple in this context.

Les Forts de Latour   Now–2004   15.0

Medium-full colour. Ripe, soft nose. A little dumb. Not too herbaceous though. Medium to medium-full. Soft tannins. Round and pleasant. This is good but not great. Quite forward.

Lynch-Bages   1996–2015   18.5

Full colour. Just a hint of brown. More closed on the nose than Pichon-Lalande. Slight spice but a bigger, fatter, more voluptuous wine. This has splendid fruit. Full and succulent. Rich and very very ripe. But no lack of grip. This is better than Pichon-Lalande. Very, very lovely.

Mouton-Rothschild   1998–2015   18.0

Full colour. Just a hint of brown. Firm, spicy, slightly dense on the nose. This is fullish, ripe, fat and opulent. Oaky and with good grip. But the intensity of great wine is not here. Doesn't have the length of Lynch-Bages.

Mouton-Baronne-Philippe
   1997–2012   16.5

Fullish colour. Still young. Lovely ripe, gently oaky, blackberry nose. On the palate fullish, round, very good tannins. Lovely fruit. This is very good. It has harmony, generosity and complexity. Great charm. Good length.

Pichon-Longueville, Comtesse de Lalande
   1996–2015   17.5

Fullish colour. Still young. Opulent, fat, rich and sweet. Lots of fruit here, raspberry as well as blackberry. Very ripe. Very seductive. Medium-full. Very soft tannins. Stylish, long. Fine. But not great. Doesn't quite have the class or depth.

SAINT-ESTÈPHE

Cos d'Estournel   1998–2015   17.5

Fine colour. Still very youthful. The nose is still a little closed. But splendid concentration underneath. Full and rich and complete. This has splendid concentration and fruit on the palate. Rich and potentially opulent and complex. Very good ir.tensity. Marvellous fruit. Very, very long.

Montrose   1996–2001   15.0

Medium-full colour. Just a hint of brown. On the palate quite fresh, but medium to medium-full and a lack of real intensity. Good but a little boring really. One-dimensional but not short.

1983 CLARET

Now that we can view the decade as a whole, and indeed the 1990 vintage, we can ask ourselves where 1983 lies in the pantheon. It was hailed as a great success at the outset, even by comparison with the previous year, for the wines were held to be more classic. Many wines of the Graves and Margaux were considered superior. If the general view of the Libournais was that they were outclassed by the 1981s, and would be by the 1985s, most of the top Médocs and Graves were deemed very good indeed, and in the southern part of the region would be rated superior to the 1986s.

I must confess to having had a period of doubt, towards the end of the 1980s, over this general view. I had made a comprehensive tasting of the vintage early in 1987, some three years after the harvest and a year or so after the wines had been bottled. I formed then the view expressed in the previous paragraph. Subsequently I saw many of the wines as part of an ongoing series of vertical tastings. Some 1983s disappointed.

Happily, my worries were confounded. Of course there are some disappointments. But these are exceptions, not the rule. And there are some lovely wines: Cheval-Blanc, Pétrus and Pavie; Chavalier, La Mission and Haut-Brion itself; Issan, Palmer and Margaux; Saint-Pierre and Ducru, Las-Cases and Poyferré; Cos d'Estournel; Lafite, Pichon-Lalande, Clerc-Milon and Grand-Puy-Lacoste; all these are great successes. All can be numbered among the best bottles of the 1980s, and all will give much pleasure in the years to come.

THE WEATHER

Nineteen eighty-three had its periods when all looked as if it was going to be catastrophic. As little as a generation ago it probably would have been. From the end of the 1982 harvest to the beginning of June 1983, the Bordeaux weather was cheerless and exceptionally wet. The spring, particularly, was bleak, damp and cold. Summer then arrived with a bang just when the vines were beginning to flower, and they quickly recovered any delay occasioned by the cool April and May. June was very warm, particularly at the beginning of the month, and, as important, very dry, with only 14 millimetres of rain (against an average of over 60) being precipitated during the month. This ensured a successful flowering and guaranteed another large crop, the second in a row.

July was exceptionally hot, with almost half the days registering a maximum temperature over 30°C. The rainfall was average, but intermittent, the result of storms rather than drizzle. There was some hail, particularly on the 17th, which ravaged part of Fronsac, the Côtes de Bourg and Pomerol, but only had a very small and localized effect in the Médoc.

The weather in August, a month in which normally there is little to do in both vineyard and *chai*, and traditionally the weeks when the workers' take their annual leave, could perhaps in earlier times have wrought irreparable damage to the potential crop. The fact that it did not is a tribute to the advances that have been made in treating the vines against cryptogamic diseases such as mildew, oidium and black rot. Overall it was wet; 100 millimetres of rain was the average precipitation against a 30-year mean of 61. However, it was also hotter than normal, and the temperature did not cool off markedly during the night. The result was an almost tropical humidity, and the onset of disease was swift and potentially devastating. It was necessary to spray the vineyards ever more repeatedly, as hardly had one finished one treatment when it would rain again and the chemicals would be washed off the vines.

The first two-thirds of September were warm, but reasonably dry, and the vineyards, having survived the August onslaught, were able to progress evenly towards maturity. Nevertheless, though having flowered and reached *veraison*, at almost exactly the average date for the last 30 years, the ripeness on 20 September was still behind that of 1981, let alone

1982. However, by this time the weather had improved even more. For the rest of the month and well into October – even into November – there was a long succession of hot, sunny days. For the first time in living memory some proprietors brought in their crop without a single interruption of rain. Though it was hot, it was not as hot as 1982, where the temperature reached 32°C during the first couple of days of the harvest. In 1983 it was more like 27°C, but continued at this level for longer. Moreover, the previous year's difficulties had encouraged many to install cooling systems. All the major properties were now well equipped to control the temperatures of fermentation.

The harvest, which had begun on 16 September for the dry white wines, commenced on the 23 for the Merlots and 1 October for Cabernets. The dry weather had shrivelled such grapes as were rotten, and so it was quite easy to eliminate these at the time of cropping, or in the case of whole bunches, to reject them entirely

THE WINE

The quality of the vintage owes much to the splendid weather which set in from 20 September. This permitted the grapes to lose some of their potentially excess acidity and increase correspondingly in sugar and potential alcohol. Indeed, alcohol levels, particularly in the Médoc and in the Cabernet grapes, were as high, if not higher, than in 1982. To have had two such plentiful years in a row, where the grapes achieved well over 12°C without any assistance from chaptalization, is rare. Moreover, not only were the grapes allowed to reach full ripeness, but the continuing fine weather encouraged many growers to retard picking for a few more days, so gaining a concentration of *sur-maturité*. This is particularly noticeable in the wines of the Médoc. First reports indicated wines of good colour, high alcohol and high levels of tannin, with the tannins being harder and more aggressive than those of 1982. Acidity levels were said to be perfectly satisfactory; indeed perhaps rather higher than 1982.

QUANTITY

As I have indicated, 1983 is a large vintage. Overall the declaration of the 1983 red wine *appellation contrôlée* crop was 3.2 million hectolitres as opposed to 3.5 in 1982 and 3.32 in 1979. The six vintages between 1985 and 1990 would be larger – indeed the average over this period was an incredible 4.28 *million* hectolitres. And as all these, bar the 1987s, are at the very least 'good quality', it seems that the Bordelais are capable of producing wines of note on a regular basis even at the very upper end of the yields permitted by the authorities. This says much for the advances made in the last couple of decades in the fields of research into viticulture, vinification and *élevage* techniques.

Three things in particular stand out. Clonal selection has created strains of the local grapes – Cabernet Sauvignon, Cabernet Franc and Merlot – which can be very productive without a concomitant decrease in concentration and extract. Helped by advice from the oenological department of the University of Bordeaux and the local meteorological office, growers know when and what they have to spray to counteract attacks of mildew and oidium and depredations by insects and other pests. They can, if they can afford it, spray the vines to produce grapes which are more resistant to rot. Finally, the more profitable economic position today enjoyed by growers and owners from *bourgeois* level upwards, together with increasing rivalry and competition among these proprietors has led to a position where all – not just the more perfectionistic – are almost duty bound to make a most careful and unselfish selection of only the best vats in the creation of their *grand vin*, and can afford to do so.

Mere statistics of the total harvest, however, tell little about the specific yield among the *crus classés* and their equivalents. The total Bordeaux Rouge average yield may have been quadrupled since the 1950s and doubled since 1970 but it would be ridiculous to assume the same advance among the top growths.

The 1983s in 1984 and 1985

When I first arrived to taste the 1983s in the spring of 1984, I found wines which surprised me by their fruit, and it is this ripeness which is the key to the vintage. Those who harvested late had made the best wine because the grapes were more mature. Those who benifitted most from the glorious autumn made wines which were rich and full, balanced and concentrated, complex and long. In the case of these wines, 1983 is a classic vintage; better than 1981 and 1979; fuller and richer than 1978 and probably as elegant; less overpowered with tannin and more endowed with fruit than 1975. Nineteen eighty-two is stupendous, but the wines are atypical; yet the best 1983s had great finesse; possibly equally good, if quite different.

What was also apparent was that, geographically as well as hierarchically, 1983 was a variable year. Firstly, as with so many recent vintages, the further up the scale from *petit château* to *cru classé* the better, proportionally, as well as the more consistent, the wines became. Secondly, while the Médoc was certainly very successful, the wines of Saint-Emilion were less so, in many cases not as interesting as the 1981s. Yet in the Médoc, particularly in the commune of Margaux, there were wines which were clearly superior to the 1982s, and elsewhere many châteaux had produced a quality which closely approached that of the previous year, though the wines were quite different in style.

A return to Bordeaux in April 1985 confirmed the quality of the 1983s. This was truly, I felt, a classic vintage. There were many excellent wines, and overall, in the Médoc and Graves, I had the impression of more consistency than the 1982 vintage, though as I thought in 1984, the Saint-Emilions and Pomerols were less regular.

The Market

To consider what happened to the market for the 1983s and to the price levels asked for the top wines it is necessary to retrace our steps a year. The 1982 vintage had been a *succès fou*. Demand, fuelled by a cheap franc–dollar ratio, had been unprecedented. For the first time in a wine-merchant's life it was necessary if one wanted to acquire a satisfactory quantity of a fashionable wine to buy a parcel here, a score of cases there, equalize the cost prices, and piece by piece make up a sensibly sized lot for sale.

Those châteaux who came on to the market early, sold their wines, in retrospect, far too cheap. Those who bought the best of these early, in February and March before they had had a chance to taste these wines, acquired bargains. As the campaign progressed, prices rose, leap-frogging each other with relentless rivalry – you could even have said greed except that such was the pressure for wine not even the most excessive prices would dissuade the buyers. It soon became a vintage which was bought more by telex than by careful château-by-château selection at the *négociant* tables in Bordeaux. Since then, incidentally, the market has continued this way, and it is a trend I view with suspicion and regret.

The 1983 campaign opened to find the *négoce* in Bordeaux in a state of some bewilderment. Demand for the 1982s had continued well into the autumn, forcing prices up yet further, and some merchants were unwilling to communicate any enthusiasm for the 1983 vintage to the growers for fear that prices would climb even further above the previous year's very high levels. In many cases the asking price for the 1982s in the spring of 1984 was as much as three times the opening price for the 1981s. The *négoce* was unsure what the reception of the 1983s would be. On the one hand there had been a satisfactory campaign for the 1981s. After 1982 would the trade buy a third vintage in a row? On the other, few had any important stocks of older vintages and everyone needed to keep their place in the queue.

Two things soon became apparent. Initial press reports of the quality of the 1983s had been encouraging and it was clear that the vintage would be widely bought. All who had initiated opening offers of the 1982s had had an unprecedented success, despite many new firms entering this field for the first time. The second was that those properties who had opened early the previous year or those who had sold too cheaply for other reasons were determined to make up for it. Here rises were 33 per cent or more above those opening prices for 1982. Château La Lagune (1982: 36 francs) asked 48 francs. One of the super-seconds had come out at a very reasonable price in 1982, and despite the usual generosity of Peter Sichel was forced to augment its price: Château Palmer (1982: 69 francs) appeared at 85 for its first *tranche* and higher still for the second. At the top levels, however, prices were not far removed, if not with first *tranche* 1982 prices, then with the second offering, and by comparison with the market price for 1982s at the time were not unreasonable. The first growths held their own at 170 francs ex-château (210 to 240 francs to the trade customers of the *négoce*) and the rest of the super-seconds after Palmer were more or less 50 per cent of this level. It would have been foolhardy for, say, Château Ducru-Beaucaillou to appear at its 1982 opening price when the 1982 in April 1984 was being traded at 140 francs.

At the time – and I have continued to hold this view subsequently – the 1983s were not expensive. The dollar was high, as was the pound sterling; the franc cheap. Subsequently the Bordeaux trade – proprietors and *négociants* alike – misjudged the 1984 campaign, imagining everyone would be terrified of missing out if they didn't join the bun-fight, and having little thought for the poor bloody infantry who'd eventually have to open the bottle. And I feel they have been equally greedy and cynical over the 1985s and most of the vintages since, until it came to the 1990. Today the 1983s can be bought for little more, in real terms, than they fetched in 1984. As many are now mature, this means they are cheap.

THE CHARACTER AND BEST BUYS OF THE 1983S

Nineteen eighty-three is a particularly consistent vintage: good to very good within context and aspiration at all levels among the leading wines. Perhaps rarely stunning, especially in comparison with 1982, but certainly highly satisfactory; as good as 1978 if not better; perhaps not as good as 1970; but better, at least in the Médoc and Graves, than 1985.

The wines at this stage seem a little less structured than I had expected after repeated tastings in cask, my usual comprehensive in-bottle tasting three years after the vintage, and a number of smaller tastings since: a good ten-year-after-the-harvest vintage for most of the well-known wines. This may be an illusion. The tannins are rich and ripe, and where the wines have a real grip of acidity they are assured of a good future. One thing that is clear to perceive is excellent fruit. Among the best wines there is an attractive ripeness which sings out of the glass. In some cases I looked for more backbone; elsewhere for more definition; in the Saint-Emilion and Pomerol especially for more concentration and zip. What slightly disturbed me was that there is a lack of acidity not only many of the wines of the Libournais but in some of the left-bank wines as well.

The vintage is uninspired (with one exception) in Saint-Estèphe, fine in the Graves, very good in Saint-Julien and Pauillac, and at its most inconsistent (as always) in the commune of Margaux. It is *supposed* to be at its best in Margaux. Sadly it is not: Palmer and Margaux itself are very good indeed; too many of the rest are uninspiring, and have not lived up to their earlier promise. By and large in Saint-Emilion and Pomerol, though there are a few potentially delicious bottles, the wines are ripe, attractive and stylish, but essentially they lack a little weight and depth, sometimes additionally a little length. Overall it is a very good vintage, however; no one will regret having bought it.

THE TASTING

The following wines were sampled in London in May 1991. My thanks to the wine-merchants who were prepared to pool samples and hunt up missing wines to make this tasting as comprehensive as possible. In particular, a vote to Andrew Bruce who organized the affair.

SAINT-EMILION

L'Angelus Now–1997 15.0

Good colour. Spicy nose. Not much zip or fruit. Better on the palate. This is medium bodied. Quite rich. Has grip. Finishes well. Good.

Ausone Now–1996 14.0

Good colour. A little old tea on the nose. Good richness and fatness on the attack but it lacks a little zip and freshness. Spicy. A touch astringent though. Quite good.

Canon Now–1996 14.0

Good colour. A little dense and attenuated on the nose. Some unresolved tannin now getting a bit astringent on the palate. Yet quite rich as well and, it seems, not short. Fullish. A bit disjointed. Got rather oxidized as it developed. A bad bottle?

Cheval-Blanc Now–2008 18.5

Fullish colour. Rich, ample nose with a touch of mint. Not leafy though. Full, rich, ample and concentrated. Clearly the best Saint-Emilion by a long way. A lush wine with good grip and plenty of depth. Fine. Almost ready. Better than Pétrus.

Clos-Fourtet Drink soon 14.0

Medium-full colour. Ripe, attractive, slightly smoky nose. Surprisingly attractive. Medium body. Fully ready. Starts off with reasonable fruit but finishes a bit short. Stylish though. Not bad.

Figeac Drink soon 13.0

Fullish colour. A bit weak on the nose and short on the palate. Lacks zip and this makes the fruit rather tired. Medium body. Uninspiring.

Magdelaine Now–1997 15.0

Good colour. A little dry on the nose. Richer and meatier on the palate. Fullish, quite concentrated. It lacks a little freshness and style but has concentration and depth. Will still develop. Finishes well though.

Pavie Now–1999 16.0

Good colour. Good ripe nose. Brambles and mulberries. Very good, because it has the acidity. Fullish, ripe, lush and concentrated. A velvety wine. Not great but very good. Second-best Saint-Emilion of this series – and better than Trotanoy.

POMEROL

Certan-de-May Now–1998 15.0

Good colour, some maturity. Fullish, lush, ripe blackberry nose. Good fruit. A touch of new oak. A little dense on the palate. But good fruit and grip. No weakness. Lacks a bit of style but a good example for a 1983 Libournais. Just about ready.

La Conseillante Now–1997 15.0

Good mature colour. Lightish nose. A touch of tabac but some fruit. Medium to medium-full body. Good fruit. This has style and balance. Good blackberry fruit. Ready now.

L'Evangile Now–1999 14.0

Fullish colour, not much sign of maturity. Firm nose. A little dense. A rather sturdier wine than the above. Ample and full with a touch of spice, but also an earthiness. Not as stylish as the Conseillante. A bit lumpy.

La Grave-Trigant-de-Boisset Drink soon 13.5

Good colour. Just a little maturity. Lightish colour. A little attenuation. Medium body. This lacks a little grip and is getting a bit dry. A spicy wine rather than fruity. Not bad.

Lafleur Now–1997 14.0

Good colour. Still immature. Dense, almost rustic nose. Rather dry and stewed. A bit attenuated. A rich but somewhat overblown example. Definite aspects of old tea here. Fullish, a bit dry. Lacks zip.

Pétrus Now–2008 18.0

Very good colour. Still immature. Much more evident new oak than these other Pomerols. Full, still immature and tannic. This has richness and concentration, and above all good grip. Lovely fruit. Fine, long finish.

Trotanoy Now–2002 16.0

Good colour, not much sign of maturity. Lovely ripe blackcurrant nose. Not quite as good on the palate this has richness and depth. Fullish, will still develop. Good.

GRAVES

Domaine de Chevalier Now–2010 18.5

Good colour. Fine, fullish, reserved, classy nose with a touch of new oak. This is very fine indeed. Great complexity and breed. Fullish, still new oaky in a cedary way. Long. Very lovely.

Haut-Bailly Now–1997 14.5

Good colour. Lush, ripe nose perhaps a little overblown. Medium to medium-full. Ripe and plump and quite seductive. But lacks a little zip. Better than the Malartic.

Haut-Brion Now–2013 19.0

Good colour. Classy, balanced nose. Plenty of depth and complexity here. Fullish, still a little unresolved tannin. This is lush, fat, full of fruit and with good concentration and very good grip. A more complete wine than the La Mission. Very fine indeed.

Malartic-Lagravière Now–1996 13.5

Good colour. Slightly dense on the nose. Not enough grip either. Medium to medium-full. A bit attenuated. Starts off quite ripe and plump but short and with suggestions of impending astringency. Not bad.

La Mission-Haut-Brion Now–2009   17.5
Very good colour. Backward nose, quite firm, not dense though, nor too leafy. Full, tannic, backward. Rich and with a touch of liquorice. Very good grip. Long. Still youthful. Quite a powerful wine. Very good indeed.

Pape–Clément   Now–2004   15.5
Good colour. Full and ripe but a little rustic on the nose. Full body. A little tannin. Plenty of old-vine richness. Good grip. Not enough class for better than good plus though. Needs time.

La Tour-Haut-Brion   Now–1998   15.0
Good colour. A bit of H2S on the nose. Fullish, well structured, if a bit earthy. Good grip but lacks a bit of class. Ripe and a touch spicy.

MARGAUX

Boyd-Cantenac   Now–1997   13.0
Very good colour. Dense, dry nose. Fullish, too much *vin de presse* and unresolved tannin to make it an attractive bottle. Will henceforth get astringent.

Brane-Cantenac   Now–1998   15.0
Medium-full colour. Soft tannin, with a touch of spice. This is a pleasant, ripe wine with style and balance. Better freshness than I feared, given its track record recently. Medium body.

Cantemerle   Now–1998   15.0
Good colour. Fine, fragrant, complex, elegant nose. Plump attack, lacks a little grip on the follow-through but a pleasant, ripe, quite fat wine which is by no means short.

Dauzac   Now–1996   14.0
Good colour. A little driven on the nose. Rigid and fruitless. Medium body. Some fruit on the palate and reasonable grip. But a little astringent and it lacks class. Not bad. Just about ready.

Desmirail   Now–1996   13.0
Medium-full colour. The nose smells of old tea – disappointing after the Brane. Slightly better on the palate but lacks style. Medium body. Some fruit. Dull. One-dimensional.

Giscours   Now–1999   15.0
Good colour. A little old tea on the nose. Medium-full body. Quite good, ripe, slightly spicy fruit and reasonable grip. But it lacks a little class and freshness. Good though but a bit dull.

d'Issan   Now–2008   16.5
Medium-full colour. Ripe, soft, elegant nose. Quite an austere wine but good stylish fruit. Medium-full, still needs a year or two. Rich, complex, gently oaky. Long and complex. Very good.

Kirwan   Now–1997   14.0
Good colour. Quite a plump, ripe, even concentrated nose but it lacks a bit of zip on the palate.

Medium to medium-full, spicy but a touch astringent.

La Lagune   Now–2002   16.0
Good colour. Firm, new oaky nose. Quite a high toast. Full, a little tannin still. Rich and lush and ample with good grip and backbone. Classy. Very good.

Lascombes   Now–1998   14.5
Medium-full colour. Ripe, cherry and raspberry nose but without much style. Fullish. Good grip. Lush and fruity, and little tannin still. This is better balanced than some but lacks breed. Just about ready.

Margaux   Now–2014   19.5
Fine colour. Open, rich, high quality, new oaky nose. This still needs time. A brilliant wine. Rich, concentrated and, above all, with balance and breed. Lovely fruit. Great intensity of flavour. The wine of the vintage.

Palmer   Now–2006   18.5
Good colour. The nose doesn't quite sing today but the wine is lovely on the palate. Fullish, ripe, velvety, complex, gently oaky. This has the real Palmer fragrance and subtlety.

Pouget   Now–1998   14.0
Good colour. A similar wine to the Boyd but less rigid, less dense and more fruit apparent. I prefer this. Not bad. Medium body.

Prieuré-Lichine   Now–2002   15.5
Medium-full colour. Rich nose. A plump, lush, fullish, ample, well-made wine. Good grip if no exceptional style. Fat and cedary with a touch of spice.

SAINT-JULIEN

Beychevelle   Now–1997   14.0
Good colour. Broad nose. Lush but lacks a bit of zip. Spicy on the palate. Medium-full. I fear it will get astringent. Lacks style.

Branaire-Ducru   Now–1998   14.5
Medium-full colour. The nose lacks a little freshness. Medium-full body. Quite lush and ripe on the palate. And reasonable grip. It just lacks a little class and zip. Quite good.

Ducru-Beaucaillou   Now–2006   17.0
Medium-full colour. Not as markedly new oaky as the Las-Cases but a wine of lovely ripe fruit on the nose and good concentration on the palate. Just about ready. Good grip. Long complex finish. Fine.

Gruaud-Larose   Now–2003   15.5
Good colour. Slightly dense and earthy on the nose. On the palate full, lush and spicy; still a bit of tannin. An ample wine with good acidity. Yet in the end it doesn't add up to a great deal of interest.

Lagrange   Now–1999   15.0

Medium-full colour. A little dense and rustic on the nose but not too bad. Better on the palate. Rich. Good grip. A balanced wine with a positive finish. Lacks a bit of class.

Langoa-Barton   Now–1996   14.0

Good colour. A little spicy and attenuated on the nose. Medium-full. Ample but lacks grip. Lush but flabby. Unexciting.

Léoville-Barton   Now–2000   15.0

Good colour. Similar to the Langoa on the nose. More grip and style. Still a little unresolved tannin. Good but not exciting. I fear it will get astringent.

Léoville-Las-Cases   Now–2009   17.5

Medium-full colour. Ripe, classy, new oaky nose. Fullish, still needs time. Good grip. A seductive, balanced, classy example. Fine.

Léoville-Poyferré   Now–2006   17.0

Good colour. Fullish, rich, new oaky nose. This has grip and class, concentration and depth. Fullish, ripe, finishes positively. Very good indeed.

Saint-Pierre   Now–2008   16.0

Full colour. Quite a dense nose. This is a backward, firm wine. Rich but a bit leafy. Yet has depth and grip. Not dense. Full. Perhaps not the class of Ducru but very good. Needs time.

PAUILLAC

Clerc-Milon   1993–2008   16.5

Good colour. A little muscular on the nose and palate but rich and with good grip. A touch of unresolved tannin. This has depth and richness. Very good. Better grip but not as classy fruit as the Mouton.

Les Forts de Latour   1994–2004   15.5

Good colour. New oaky and a little dense and leafy on the nose. Very good depth. Still young. Just a touch rigid.

Grand-Puy-Lacoste   Now–2000   16.0

Good colour. Rich, fat, ripe nose. A touch of new oak on the palate. Fullish. Just about ready. Ripe and lush and succulent. Good grip. A fat, ample wine. Very good.

Haut-Batailley   Now–1997   14.5

Good colour. A little weak on the nose and attenuated on the palate. Medium-full. Reasonable grip, and quite lush fruit but the finish is a shade weak. Quite good at best.

Lafite   Now–2009   19.5

Fine colour. Quite disarmingly brilliant and new oaky and very sexy fruit on the nose. Almost too much new oak on the palate. Rich, fullish, concentrated. Good grip. This has a great deal of depth. Very fine indeed.

Latour   Now–2004   16.5

There is not a great deal of difference between this and the Les Forts. This has classier fruit but no more grip or depth. Fullish. Quite long.

Lynch-Bages   Now–2005   16.5

Good colour. Cedary, spicy, new oaky nose. High toast. Fullish, rich, sandalwoody palate. Good grip. This has depth and concentration. Very good plus.

Lynch-Moussas   Now–1995   13.5

Medium colour. Rather weak and dilute on the nose and palate. Not too rustic but now a suspicion of astringency. One-dimensional.

Mouton-Baronne-Philippe
     Now–2004   15.0

Good colour. A bit dull on the nose. Medium-full. Reasonable structure and balance – even fat – but lacks a bit of personality. Good finish though. Needs a year.

Mouton-Rothschild   Now–2003   17.0

Good colour. Ample nose but lacks a little zip. This I find on the palate too. Fullish, rich, ample, but it lacks the follow-through and dimension. Classy fruit though.

Pichon-Longueville-Baron
     Now–1997   13.5

Good colour. Lumpy and dense on the nose and the palate. Yet you can see underlying richness. Lacks zip. Dull. Fullish. Will get astringent.

Pichon-Longueville, Comtesse de Lalande
     Now–2006   17.5

Good colour. Fragrant, complex, new oaky nose. Lovely. Very discreet. Now *à point*. This is a lovely example. Fine fruit. Good acidity. Rich and complex. Medium-full. Very fine finish.

SAINT-ESTÈPHE

Cos d'Estournel   Now–2006   17.0

Good colour. The nose is a bit dumb, like the Palmer, but on the palate a soft, lush, complex wine. Very well-balanced. This is medium-full, cedary and delicious. Fine.

Cos-Labory   Now–1997   14.0

Medium colour. Fruity nose but not much depth. Medium body. Quite ripe and fleshy but a little rustic on the follow-through. Quite good. Reasonable length if no real dimension.

Montrose   Now–1998   14.5

Good colour. Spicy nose but a little overblown. Medium-full body. Quite sweet. This is better than I remember. Not special, but not too short or weedy. Lacks a bit of zip and class though.

de Pez   Drink soon   12.0

Medium-full colour. Smells and tastes a bit of old tea. Astringent on the palate. Uninspiring.

1982 CLARET

Much has already been written about the 1982 Claret vintage. From the outset its quality was extolled from the rooftops with a consistency of hyperbole. 'Not the vintage of the century but the vintage of the millennium,' suggested one well-known château proprietor. Demand, seduced by this relentless enthusiasm, was unprecedented. Greed, fuelled by the demand, was rife. Prices opened high, and as the campaign proceeded they climbed higher still. They have remained on an upswing. Though the 1983s and 1985s were to open higher still, it is the 1982s which fetch much the superior levels whenever they now appear at auction.

I am convinced that as well as risky, and possibly unfair, it is dangerous to attempt this sort of assessment before the wine has completed its *élevage* and is safely in bottle. Bearing in mind that the bottling process is itself fundamentally upsetting to the wine, as is the transportation thereafter, I prefer to postpone making a specific judgement on a particular wine of a claret vintage until three years after the harvest, a year or more after the bottling. I made my first comprehensive survey of the 1982s in bottle in the autumn of 1985. I have since participated in a number of important tastings of the vintage. How do the 1982s show today?

THE 1982s NOW

There is no doubt for some properties and in some regions, 1982 is indeed a vintage of remarkably high quality, and that those who have indicated 1961 as a parallel have not exaggerated. On the other hand, the vintage is not uniform, it is not consistent, and many of the estates which normally produce run-of-the-mill wines have, predictably, again produced dull, unexciting 1982s. The fact that at the top levels the 1982s are indeed stupendous makes the actuality of the average doubly depressing. Only in a year like 1961, it seems, can some châteaux produce a great wine *faute de mieux*. In this respect 1982 is a long way from 1961.

The vintage is at its best in the top echelons of Pomerol and Saint-Emilion, and Saint-Julien and Pauillac. Here the wines are full, fat, rich and concentrated: above all marvellously ripe. The generosity of fruit in the top wines is immensely appealing. In Margaux the 1983s are generally better: and in the Graves this vintage is the equal of its predecessor.

Elsewhere there are some very good wines and a few which are truly excellent, but there are many which have size without definition, density without character, solidity without style. The big names are all very good, and they have been joined by one or two properties like Léoville-Poyferré, hitherto in the doldrums. But there are many wines which are nondescript, particularly in Margaux and the southern Médoc, others which are clumsy and one or two whose *élevage* must be suspect, because when I tasted them in cask in April, 1983, and on three subsequent occasions prior to bottling they were distinctly better. For an explanation of why there is this disparity we must look at the climatic conditions surrounding the vintage.

THE WEATHER

After an unusually mild winter the spring weather prior to the flowering was excellent. April was extremely dry, with less than 6 millimetres of rain being recorded, and it was mild and sunny. There was no frost, and after the good but by no means prolific harvest of 1981 the vines were healthy and able to throw out an encouragingly prolific *sortie* of buds.

The fine weather continued. There was a mini heatwave at the beginning of June which, as Sichel remarked in his *Vintage Report* the following year, 'provided ideal conditions for a successful flowering as well as setting an early date or the vintage'. Not only did the flowering begin about a week earlier than average, but it was uniform and the fruit setting was accomplished very quickly, thus gaining a further week on the norm and ensuring that all the berries would arrive at fruition at the same time. The large amount of flowers developing into embryonic grape bunches meant that a very large vintage was likely to occur.

July was very hot and for the most part dry. Some much-needed rain began at the end of the month and continued on and off during a rather dull August, thus helping the grapes to ripen further and develop toward maturity at an earlier date than normal. By 20 August, the fruit had finished changing colour from green to black and was already showing a promising amount of sugar if not concentration. The skies cleared at the end of the month and ushered in three weeks of exceptional heat, which made the vintage. Temperatures averaged 29°C and the thermometer rose even higher – up to 40 degrees – between the 3 and 5 September and during the ten days after 8 September. In the great heat the grapes galloped not only towards maturity, but towards concentration. This had four important effects:

1. The exceptionally large harvest could ripen fully. As Peter Sichel later pointed out, without this heat there was no way this amount of grapes would have ripened.

2. There was a danger that the grapes would become too ripe before they could be picked and that the resultant acidity would be too weak. This problem was exacerbated by the enormous size of the harvest. Paradoxically the heat was such that in fact the acidity rose during the final few days before the harvest started. The exceptional weather had the effect of concentrating everything – sugar, extract and acidity – as the water evaporated in the berries.

3. During the first week of the harvest the grapes were so warm when they reached the vinification vats that there was a danger of fermentation taking place at too high a temperature. However, many châteaux had made a considerable investment in modern equipment and cooling facilities during the previous decade and were well geared to cope with any excesses.

4. As in 1979, there was a danger that the sheer volume of grapes arriving daily in the *cuverie* would prove an embarrassment: that each batch of new wine would not be able to have enough time to macerate on its skins before the vat was required for a subsequent lot. Few wines appear to have this sort of weakness and fragility; though rumours circulated that there had been difficulties at Château Margaux, where some of the crop had to be decanted from the vats to finish its malolactic fermentation in cask.

The harvest began on 14 September and was in full swing in both the Médoc and Saint-Emilion two days later – one of the earliest on record and a full fortnight before the norm. The Merlots were picked first, super-concentrated by the great heat, and frequently arriving in the winery with potential degrees of 13 and above. Château Pétrus was harvested on the afternoons of 17 and 18 September, and the vats produced alcohol levels of 13.2 to 13.6 degrees, unprecedentedly high. For the first time since 1975 it was quite unnecessary to chaptalize.

After 20 September, the heat was less intense, the Merlots were safely in the vats and collection of the Cabernets commenced. At Château Pichon-Longueville, Comtesse de Lalande and elsewhere, the number of harvesters was doubled in order to bring in the grapes in optimum condition. At Château Mouton-Rothschild they are said to have completed the picking in seven days, an amazing feat for a 75-hectare vineyard. The Petit Verdot, which ripens last of all, and often not completely, was for once fully ripe. Those properties in the Médoc with a high proportion of these grapes are not often rewarded for their perseverance with this variety! There was a weekend of rain during the weekend of the 25/26 September, but this does not appear to have caused any damage.

At the beginning of October, however, there was an abrupt change in the weather. Heavy rain began on the 2nd and hardly ceased throughout the month. Thankfully, as a result of the early start to the vintage, the vast majority of the harvest both of red and dry white wine had been collected. Sadly, the Sauternes châteaux, most of whom had only collected about a third of their crop, were left to suffer.

THE SIZE OF THE CROP

The 1982 harvest produced a record-breaking 3.52 million hectolitres of AC Bordeaux

Rouge. Together with the 1.05 million hectolitres of AC Bordeaux Blanc, this gives an average yield over the 78,000 hectares in production at the time of 58.6 hectolitres per hectare. This statistic by itself would cause one to view the quality with apprehension. To compare it with the previous year, the 1981 crop had produced 2.53 million hectolitres of AC red and 0.78 million hectolitres of AC white. To take a similar prolific year, that of 1970, as a comparison, the overall yield per hectare in 1982 was nearly a quarter more. Coupled with the great heat and consequently accelerated maturation of the grapes in the middle of September, one was entitled to fear that the wines would lack intensity of character.

However, a close look at the production figures for the separate *appellations* revealed that the increase in the size of the crop was most marked at the more everyday level of quality. While the average red wine increase over 1981 was 39 per cent, at the generic Bordeaux Rouge level 45 per cent more wine was produced. In Pauillac, however, the rise was only 25 per cent on 1981, while in Saint-Emilion the crop was less than that of 1973, a previous record. Moreover, it soon became apparent that it was the younger vines which had been particularly prolific. For the older vines, the yield was less prodigious.

At the classed-growth level, production therefore was not excessive. A number of properties had had the courage to knock off a few bunches per vine earlier in the summer once the size of the potential harvest was apparent. At Pétrus, Christian Moueix commanded that one bunch in four should be removed. Fearing that the *vignerons* usually employed would consider this to be sacrilege, he entrusted the task to a few student *stagiaires*. Others severely eliminated between picking and pressing any bunches of grapes which were not well-nigh perfect, and later were even more scrupulous in rejecting all but the very best vats for the final 'château' blend. The yield at the top properties was not unduly high, particularly in terms of what was later declared 'grand vin'. At Château Pichon-Longueville-Lalande less was declared than in 1981, and the quality and concentration of this and other similar wines shows this dedication.

THE CHARACTER OF THE WINE IN CASK

The first thing that was remarkable about the 1982s was the colour. Young wine is always dark and purple, and with modern techniques enabling one to keep the fruit healthy, we have become used to excellent colour, at least initially, in young Bordeaux, year in, year out. The colour of the 1982s however, was truly remarkable. Never had I seen wines with such solidity, such density of colour – a deep, almost black purple, right to the rim of the glass.

The next wonder of the 1982s was the amount of ripe, concentrated fruit. The grapes had been picked with the highest level of natural sugar since 1947. The resulting wines had an almost porty richness, which though enveloped by an equal amount of tannin, was immediately evident on nose and palate. The vintage was big, dense and full, backward and high in alcohol, giving the wines a power which had not been seen in Bordeaux since 1959. On top of this, the tannins were round and sweet. The effect was a fat, perfumed, creamy character, particularly in the top Pomerols and Saint-Emilions. The best wines of the Haut-Médoc, naturally, were more austere, yet had an enormous depth and richness of flavour and fruit. At the top levels the wines were balanced and marvellously long on the palate. Though for long keeping, they were, even at the outset, enormously seductive – if in a mind-bludgeoning way!

Because of their sheer size, tannin and concentration, I found the 1982s an exhausting experience to evaluate. At the end of each day, having tasted perhaps 50 or more wines, my tongue was black and my taste-buds saturated. Yet, despite the power and body of the wines, I did not consider that this would be a vintage which would need *that* long before it was mature. True, the wines were dense, solid and tannic, but they were neither hard nor harsh. The wines were close-textured, but the strands were soft and ripe, silk rather than steel. As Peter Sichel was to point out a year later, commenting on the 1982s after a year in cask, the normally temperate climate of Bordeaux produces wines with a complexity of flavours; after an unusually warm maturation season like 1982 this austere complexity was replaced by a greater generosity and fullness of flavour.

THE MARKET

'Destined to be the most sought-after vintage since 1961,' urged one New York wine-merchant's newsletter – before the merchant in question could have had a chance to taste any of the wines. The statement in fact was not strictly accurate, in the sense that good as they were the 1961s were not sought after *en primeur*: it was only later that demand for this marvellous vintage began to emerge.

Yet the sentiment was accurate. With firms taking pages in the British wine magazine *Decanter* as early as February to advertise wines which no one in the wine trade could have tasted or seen the prices of, and other concerns emerging to broke on the 1982s at first *tranche* prices who had never previously done such a thing, it was soon apparent that something extraordinary was in the air. Worldwide interest in fine Bordeaux had never been higher, and for the first time in a number of years demand for the best wines was strong in all habitual markets; from the USA, which had largely ignored the 1981 vintage, and mainland Europe, as well as from Great Britain. It was in part stimulated by the quality of the vintage and by the hype surrounding it. It was also due to the weakness of the French franc, particularly against the strong dollar. Even in Britain the rate of exchange had moved from 9.40 francs to the pound to 11.50 or more, depending on when one bought. Moreover, there was already evidence that some of the demand was speculative. Many people saw the 1982s as an investment.

OPENING PRICES

Opening prices of the properties which were first to announce reflected the interest in the vintage. It would have been short-sighted to expect them to be at 1981 levels, despite the size of the vintage, yet bearing in mind the quality and French inflation, the increase were not unreasonable. Château La Lagune was one of the first big names to come out, and sold on the export market for 39.75 francs or thereabouts, compared with 35.20 for the 1981. Labégorce-Zédé at 24.55 francs (1981: 22.75), Angludet at 33.00 francs (1981: 29.00), Grand-Puy-Lacoste at 48.96 francs (1981: 40.70), Léoville-Poyferré 51.30 francs (1981: 37.95) were equally reasonable. Overall, those who had put their wine on the market by the end of April could be seen to have raised prices by 20 to 25 per cent over 1981 levels – not the least excessive.

The precedent for more savage rises for the more fashionable wines was set by the first growths. The 1981 price had been 100 to 125 francs (with the exception of Latour); the 1982s came out at 170 francs. Coupled with higher than normal profit margins imposed by the Bordeaux *négoce* it meant that the cost to the overseas buyer was nearly doubled, at around 225 francs. One could have purchased the 1981s for 140.

As far as the 'super-seconds' were concerned greed over prices was complicated by feelings of jealousy and personal rivalry. Mme de Lencquesaing at Château Pichon-Longueville-Lalande is convinced that her wine is as good as Château Ducru-Beaucaillou and Château Léoville-Las-Cases and is determined to sell her wine for as high a price as they. MM. Borie and Delon, meanwhile, were equally determined that she should not. The result was an absurd (and to the overseas buyer intensely irritating) game of 'waiting the other out'; neither side wishing to commit themselves before the other. The result, as the market demand hotted up, was very high prices indeed; Pichon coming out at 67 francs and Ducru and Las-Cases at 70, and all three finding willing buyers at 100 and above. Again, the increase over 1981 was almost two-fold.

To the foreign buyer, the situation was a nightmare. Prices of the important wines refused to emerge, and when they did allocations from one's regular suppliers were pitiful. It became necessary, as one merchant put it, to camp out day and night next to one's telex, in order that as soon as one heard a whisper that a certain property had at last deigned to come on to the market, one could fire off demands in all possible directions so as piece by piece to make up the size of parcel one wished to buy. Customers were not only placing provisional orders but shopping around from merchant to merchant to find out who was prepared to commit themselves to a firm price and a firm order despite the wine not yet being on the market.

By the end of the summer, with all the prices having finally appeared, one might have expected interest in the 1982s temporarily to die down now that initial demands had been satisfied. For a number of reasons this did not happen. Firstly, many merchants oversold, or were forced by the pressure of their demand to sell more than they had originally intended, and were soon back for more. Secondly, the sheer momentum created by the initial hype was in a way self-perpetuating. This had caused prices to open at high levels; it had meant that despite these high levels everything that could possibly be on offer was snapped up as soon as possible; and such was the demand, at the end of the day there were still unfulfilled orders. Prices continued to rise, and by the end of the year first growths were changing hands at 300 francs or more, and super-seconds at as much as half that. The fact that so much of the vintage had been immediately sold on all the way down the chain to the private consumer is noteworthy. It meant that there was no real volume of stock in wine-merchants' hand, and this was going to have two effects. On the one hand, it became apparent that there would be little likelihood of there ever being a slump in the price of 1982s – a slump on the size of 1973/1974 – because this was caused by volume selling, not just by a falling off in demand, and no-one had volumes of 1982s to sell. On the other, it would mean that future auction prices might indeed be very fickle. The fact that so much 1982 was already in private hands might mean that the vintage would always be difficult and expensive to acquire in any quantity. If the trading base was going to be unusually low for an as yet immature vintage in terms of volumes circulating in the market, the arrival of only a few money-is-no-object new buyers would have a marked effect on price levels.

PRICES TODAY

The top 1982s are now like gold dust. I wrote in 1983 that despite seemingly being high at the time, like the 1966s, 1970s, 1975s and 1978s, indeed like any other classic vintage, the opening prices of the 1982s would inevitably seem cheap in retrospect. I did not realize quite how quickly this would be apparent. By 1986/1987 many 1982 prices had doubled or trebled, though they have by and large remained static ever since. A private individual, who might have bought a first growth such as Lafite or Mouton-Rothschild for £300 ex-cellars, or Léoville-Las-Cases or Pichon-Lalande for £110 in 1983, could have sold them three or four years later for £600 (for the Lafite) or £300 (for the Las-Cases). It is interesting to note that the profit on the super-second is higher than that in the *premier cru*. On the one hand, if he had been fortunate enough to have secured a case of Château Pétrus for £470 in bond, British agent Corney & Barrow's original private trade price, he could have sold it three years later for five times as much.

What is remarkable is the relationship between 1982 prices and those of 1983, 1985 and the rest. With the economy in disarray, wine sales at best static, and the value of pound no longer what it was, wine prices are in many cases very much lower in real terms what they were when they were first sold ex-château. Only the 1982s have held their own.

QUALITY NOW

Big, fat, tannic and naturally high in alcohol, the 1982s went into an adolescent, awkward phase in the latter half of the 1980s and are only now, at the top levels, beginning to come out of it. Most, however, are now fully ready. Only one or two of the top Saint-Emilions and Pomerols – Canon, Figeac, Cheval-Blanc, Lafleur and Vieux Château Certan, but not

Pétrus – still need keeping. Naturally the top Médocs and Graves will still improve, but even here there are few wines which will not be *à point* by the time of their thirteenth birthday in 1995. The best, obviously, will keep for a long time; but this is not an austere *millésime de garde*. These are rich and flamboyant wines, opulent and ample, generous and fleshy: certainly fine, but only occasionally truly great. It is a very fine vintage, but few wines have that indefinable extra dimension of character, complexity, grip and above all finesse which elevates them to the pedestal of truly *grand vin*.

If, in the long run, 1982 is not 1961, it is because of the size of the crop. There are those who have argued that the weather pattern in 1982 would have destroyed a harvest of the size of 1961: that the wines would have been hard, baked and unbalanced, even if the vintage had been of normal size. Nevertheless, the perfect weather conditions in the latter part of 1961 coupled with the tiny size of the crop gave a concentration and above all a breed which remains the yardstick.

1982 VERSUS 1989 – AND OTHER VINTAGES

Where one can compare 1982 is, on the one hand, with 1970, and, on the other, with 1986 (in the northern Médoc) and, of course, with 1989. Nineteen seventy was, in its time, a record crop. It was considered at the outset to be one of attractively ripe and fruity wines which would evolve soon: very good, but not, in the last analysis, *sérieux*. Time has proved these critics wrong. The wines had more backbone, more acidity and more potential for ageing than was assessed at the time. As they have matured better than expected, so they have shown more complexity and elegance than anticipated. As a general rule the longer a wine can be kept, and this is determined by its balance, not its sheer size, the more subtlety it acquires. So is 1970 as good as 1982? Probably not. But by a lesser margin than perhaps we thought when we first sampled the 1982s in 1983.

Nineteen eighty-six, splendid in the northern Médoc, is another comparison. These wines are currently in their shells, surly and backward. But in five years' time, I anticipate great things. Good as I find the 1982s from Mouton and Lafite, Las-Cases and Pichon-Longueville-Lalande, I shall not be surprised if I find the 1986s better. The 1986 flavours are more classic, acidity levels are higher. They may be less lusciously fruity, but they may have more breed.

In Saint-Emilion and Pomerol one can draw a distinct parallel between 1982 and 1989. The climatic background was similar. The wines are equally rich and alcoholic, with more (but riper) tannins than usual. And in both, acidity levels are on the low side. Nineteen eighty-nine, at this stage, looks as if it is more consistent. The middle-range wines are better. And of course there has been a distinct improvement at properties such as Beauregard, Clinet, Gazin, Troplong-Mondot and the like. But is the 1982 vintage better at the Cheval-Blanc, Pétrus, Trotanoy, Canon level? Selection is more exigent now. And so, perhaps the 1989s are better. But maybe the 1982s would have been better still if they had been made with that extra bit of perfectionism which pertained seven years later.

THE TASTING

The vast majority of the following wines was sampled over two days at a tasting arranged by John Thorogood of Lay and Wheeler in October 1992. I have added notes on a few other 1982s that came my way in the subsequent six months.

The view shared by a dozen or more respected British palates was one of slight disappointment with the Pomerols which seemed in general to lack grip, but there was greater enthusiasm for the top Saint-Emilions. There was disenchantment with the Margaux, but relief when we came to the top Saint-Juliens and Pauillacs. Mouton-Rothschild, Lafite, Cheval-Blanc, Pichon-Longueville-Lalande, Haut-Brion and Léoville-Las-Cases were singled out as the superstars. I was not the only judge who found Belair superior to Ausone – and better than last time out — though Ausone itself has never lived up to its early promise.

The last time I participated in a big 1982 tasting was in the USA. On that occasion, overall, Cheval-Blanc and Pichon-Longueville-Lalande were preferred to Mouton-Rothschild and Lafite, and Margaux and Trotanoy to Haut-Brion, demonstrating the difference in personal taste between the two countries, perhaps. Pétrus again was not included among the 'greats'.

	Optimum drinking	Mark out of 20

SAINT-EMILION

L'Arrosée 1995–2010 17.0

Medium-full colour. Good nose, meaty and concentrated. Quite firm, new oaky. Less Merlot than most. Fullish, some tannin. Good grip. Backward, very ripe, concentrated, meaty wine. This has very good depth. A sleeper. Very fine. Long, concentrated and complex finish.

Ausone Now–1999 16.0

Medium to medium-full colour. Just about mature. Round, plump, sweet: very Peynaud on the nose. Much more Merlot on the palate than the vineyard's *encépagement* would suggest. Ripe and fleshy. Concentrated and stylish. But not quite enough dimension on the finish for better than very good. The Belair has better balance.

Balestard-La-Tonnelle Now–1998 14.0

Medium-full colour. Soft, plump nose; ripe and Merlot. Quite forward. Not a great deal of acidity. Medium body. No tannin. Rather one-dimensional. Ripe but no great richness. Quite good at best. Reasonable freshness but no depth.

Beau-Séjour-Bécot Now–1997 13.5

Medium to medium-full colour. Now mature. Soft, very Merlot nose. Lacks a little freshness and backbone. Medium body. Quite fruity and attractive, but no complexity or zip.

Belair Now–2005 17.0

Medium-full colour. Still quite young-looking. Round, elegant, balanced nose with a touch of oak. Very stylish fruit here. But not a blockbuster. Medium body. Fully ready. This has great charm and great style. Complex, long, harmonious. A delicious bottle.

Cadet-Piola Now–2004 15.0

Good colour. Sweet, even to the point of being caramelly. Soft, round and ripe. Attractive if on a smaller scale. Less closed than most. Medium body, a little tannin. Good element of new oak. This is another seductive wine. Ripe. Very good but not great. Doesn't have the depth of some.

Canon 1995–2012 17.5

Fullish just about mature. Fat rich and concentrated on the nose. Backward. Quite oaky. Very promising. Full, backward, rather solid attack. Some tannins still unresolved. Rich and concentrated and fat on the follow-through. Very good indeed. Splendid finish.

Cheval-Blanc Now–2024 19.5

Fullish colour. Just about mature. This is clearly in a class of its own over the other Saint-Emilions. Marvellously intense, very oaky, hugely fruity nose. With very good grip and complexity. On the palate full. Very very rich. An abundant, exciting wine. Totally consistent from start to finish.

La Dominique Now–2005 16.0

Medium-full colour. Broad nose, some Merlot. Quite fat but not a great deal of class. Got weightier as it evolved. Medium to medium-full body. Not much tannin. Good class though. Cool and fruity. Balanced and long. Very good indeed.

Figeac Now–2006 16.5

Fullish just about mature. Definite herbaceous elements not in the wines above. Fullish, just about there. Good acidity and style. Good grip and character. Very good plus.

La Gaffelière Now–1996 15.0

Medium-full concentration. Open, plump, fresh nose; but no great concentration. Medium to medium-full body. A little tannin. Lacks a bit of depth and concentration. The middle is a bit watery. Lacks richness and amplitude.

Clos-des-Jacobins Now–2000 13.5

Medium to medium-full colour. Some development. Smoky, rather dry tannic nose; lacks class. Hard, slightly unripe elements. The dry papery element continues on the palate. Medium body. A little tannin, lacks lushness. Uninspiring.

Larcis-Ducasse Now–1997 13.5

Medium-full colour just about mature. Spicy-sweet. Soft Merlot nose. But lacks a little acidity underneath. Medium body. Pleasant but one-dimensional. Lacks grip on the finish.

Laroque Now–1999 14.0

Medium-full colour. Now mature. Fat, rich, cedary nose, with a slight hint of reduction. Medium to medium-full body. Good grip. Attractive, without a great deal of style or depth. Quite good.

Magdelaine Now–2007 17.0

Medium-full colour, just about ready. Elegant, oaky-Merlot, roast-chestnutty nose. Plenty of depth and quality here. Medium-full, just about mature. Ripe and gently. Silky-smooth. Good grip and style. Elegant.

Pavie Now–2009 17.5

Medium-full colour. Just about mature. Rich, fullish and quite substantial on the nose. Good concentration. Good new oak. Medium-full.

This could still do with a year or so. Lovely style. Velvety and crammed with fruit. Has more depth than the Belair. Very good indeed.

Le Prieuré   Now–2004   15.0
Medium to medium-full colour. Now mature. Ripe, fresh nose. Balanced and stylish. A meaty wine. Medium-full. Attractive fruit. Good balance. Finishes well.

La Serre   Now–2008   15.5
Medium-full colour, just about mature. Good richness, ripeness and freshness on the nose. Quite full. Good new oak. Good grip. This has balance and concentration. Lovely fruit. Very good.

Soutard   Now–2004   13.0
Full colour. Just about mature. A little dank on the nose. Fullish, tannic. A bit tough. Slightly bitter. There is substance here but it lacks charm. A bit over-extracted. Not bad at best.

La Tour-Figeac   Drink soon   12.0
Medium-full colour. Now mature. Soft, spicy, Merlot nose. Medium body. Quite evolved if not a little aged. A loose-knit wine, lacking real grip. Now needing drinking soon. Not exciting.

Trottevieille   Drink soon   12.0
Medium-full colour. Fully mature. Somewhat weak and attenuated on the nose. Showing a little astringency. Medium body. Empty in the middle. Merlot-ish in a weak and simple way. No grip.

POMEROL

Beauregard   Now–2000   15.0
Medium-full colour. Little sign of maturity. Good nose. Rich, fat, concentrated, fresh. Good substance here; just a little tough perhaps. On the palate doesn't have a lot of definition and class but is ripe and fleshy, fresh and enjoyable. Good.

Le Bon-Pasteur   1995–2010   16.0
Very good colour. Very rich, meaty, backward nose. Full, solid, meaty and tannic; good richness underneath. More old-fashioned than the Trotanoy. Again a sleeper. Certainly very good.

Canon-Boyer   Drink soon   12.5
Good colour. Fresh nose. A little volatile acidity. A little sweet-sour. Medium body. There is a metallic edge to it and a bit of astringency.

Certan-de-May   1995–2015   17.0
Fullish colour. Little sign of maturity. Firm nose. Rich and concentrated but backward, even dense. Medium-full. Fat on the palate. Lush, concentrated fruit. Still backward, even adolescent.

Clos L'Eglise   Now–1997   14.0
Medium-full colour. Now ready. A bit dense on the nose. A bit rustic in conception. Fullish, chunky, sweet-sour elements. Yet reasonable grip. But it lacks style. A clumsy wine.

La Conseillante   Now–2005   17.0
Medium-full colour. Only a little mature. Soft, ripe, round, blackcurranty nose. Charming and elegant. Medium-full, rich, new oaky, plenty of depth and intensity. Long. Very good indeed.

L'Eglise-Clinet   Now–2005   16.0
Good colour. Firm full, just a little old-fashioned on the nose. Medium-full body, a little tannin. Rich and ripe, good acidity. Quite firm. Good finish. Lacks a *great* deal of concentration and class but at least very good.

L'Enclos   Drink soon   13.5
Medium-full colour. Quite adolescent but a shade rustic on the nose. Medium body, not a lot of tannin. This has less flesh and attraction. Indeed a bit thin in a 1982 Pomerol context. Forward. Dull.

L'Evangile   1995–2008   16.5
Full immature colour. Slightly dense, very oaky nose. A bit solid. Rather tough. Even a bit herbaceous. Full-bodied. Tannic still. A chunky wine. Good acidity and concentration but not enough fat and charm for better than very good plus.

La Fleur-de-Gay   Now–1997   13.0
Medium-full colour. Now ready. Slightly rigid on the nose. Medium to medium-full. This is strangely sweet-sour. Some fruit. Some grip. But a lack of style. An ungainly wine.

Le Gay   Now–2010   15.0
Medium-full colour. Merlot and a shade chunky/coarse. Medium-full, quite tannic. A little old-fashioned. Doesn't quite have the class but has plenty of ripe, ripe fruit. A bit stewed, or does it have too much *vin de presse*?

Gazin   Now–2005   15.0
Fullish mature colour. Ripe nose. A bit chunky. A bit inelegant but there is substance. Medium-full. A bit stewed. Good acidity keeping it fresh. Would be better with food. Finishes well. Good.

La Grave-Trigant-de-Boisset
     Drink soon   14.0
Medium to medium-full colour. Now ready. A soft, typically Moueix, lovely Merlot wine. It lacks just a little zip. Fruity nose. Medium body. Plump, even fat. A little astringent. Not a wine with a great future. More stylish than Nénin.

Junayne   Drink soon   12.5
Medium-full colour. Soft, Merloty nose. Some fruit but not much class. Medium to medium-full body. A little attenuated. Lacking a bit of definition. Unexciting.

Lafleur   (see note)
Medium-full colour. Only a little mature. This bottle has not been well stored. Somewhere, somehow it has become rather weak in acidity and astringent on the palate. Underneath it has lots of fruit. Taste again.

At a Lafleur vertical in Miami in February 1992, I noted as follows: Fine colour. Barely mature. Brilliant nose. Hugely fruity. Full, very very concentrated and chocolatey. Real old-vine flavour. A brilliant example. Very good grip. Massive concentration and fruit. Very fine indeed, even for a 1982. Still needs five years. 18.5–19.0.

Lafleur-Pétrus   Now–1999   15.5
Good colour. Medium-full colour. Not a lot of maturity. Ripe, fleshy, abundantly fruity nose. Agreeable Moueix wine but lacks just a little zip. Medium to medium-full, ample, plump fruit. Quite stylish. But it tails off a little at the end.

Lagrange   Drink soon   14.0
Medium-full colour. Now ready. Quite a chunky wine, judging by the nose. But not one with quite enough grip. Medium-full, fat, but lacks acidity. A pity. There is some concentration here.

Latour-à-Pomerol   Now–2010   17.5
Medium-full colour. Only a little mature. Just a faint hint of austerity on the nose. Fleshier and gamier than Lafleur-Pétrus, and rather better grip. Medium-full, excellently concentrated ripe fruit. Almost sweet. This is much better. Fine in fact. Long and seductive at the end. Just about ready.

Nénin   Now–1996   13.5
Medium colour. Decidedly old. Evolved nose. A bit weak. Already getting a bit dry. Slightly better on the palate. Ripe. Fresher on the nose. Medium body. But the finish is one-dimensional.

Petit-Village   Now–2003 plus   16.0
Medium to medium-full colour. Now just about mature. Looser-knit and higher-toned with an aspect of bonfires. Medium body. Spicy. Good new wood. An attractive, individual wine. But with a slight bitterness on the finish. Just a little tannin still to round off. Positive finish. Very good.

Pétrus   Now–2010   19.0
Medium-full colour. Only a little mature. Rich and concentrated, multidimensional. But not backward. Very accessible. Medium-full. Marvellous fruit. Harmony and style. Quite a lot of new oak. Best of all on the finish, which is multidimensional. Quietly successful – not flamboyant like the Cheval-Blanc.

Le Pin   Now–2008   16.5
Full colour. Good rich nose, though a bit awkward at present. Slightly papery tannins, but there is plenty of fatness and concentration. Full, good, rich, ripe tannins. A lot of extract and fine ripe acidity. Good structure and length. Very good depth. This is high class. But is it all up front with no reserves behind?

Rouget   Drink soon   15.0
Medium-full colour. Some development. Again Merlot, but with a shade of attenuation. Ripe,

medium-full. Some tannin. Lacks a little grip. Good but not great. Elegant but forward.

de Sales   Now–1997   15.0
Medium to medium-full colour. Some development. The nose is a bit undeveloped as yet. Quite Merlot. Medium body, not a great deal of tannin. Lush, ripe, quite forward but balanced and attractive. Reasonably fresh on the finish. A gentle wine with a smile.

Trotanoy   Now–2010   17.5
Medium-full colour. Only a little mature. Ripe, concentrated, abundant nose. Medium-full. Rich and fleshy. Slightly spicy. Old-vine concentration of fruit here. Complex. A sexy harmonious wine. Fine plus. Lovely finish.

Vieux Château Certan   Now–2015   18.5
Medium-full colour. Only a little mature. Fine nose. Balanced, complex, concentrated and fresh. Lovely style. Fullish, oaky – quite markedly so – harmonious and concentrated. Still needs a year or two. A lot of depth. Lovely fruit. Excellent.

GRAVES

Bahans-Haut-Brion   Now–2007   16.0
Medium colour, some development. Soft nose, compared with most of the rest of the Graves. A little forthcoming though. Medium body, a little tannin. Ripe and stylish, if rather more forward than most. Good balance.

Bouscaut   Drink soon   13.5
Medium to medium-full colour. Now ready. Slightly burnt, dry nose. But not objectionable. Medium body. Lacks a bit of bite. But there is some fruit here. Lacks a bit of style but not bad.

Domaine de Chevalier   Now–2004   16.0
Medium-full colour. Not much sign of maturity. A little herbaceous on the nose. It lacks a bit of generosity. Medium to medium-full. Quite a lot of new oak – and very good oak – plus the class of Chevalier shows through. But it lacks the intensity and concentration and sheer class it usually has.

de Fieuzal   Now–2000   14.5
Full colour. Barely mature. Backward but rich and fleshy on the nose. Fullish, some tannin. Ripe, even over-ripe. Good flesh but not quite enough grip. Quite good plus. Just about ready.

Haut-Bailly   Now–2008   15.5
Medium to medium-full colour. Rather more evolved, slightly overblown nose. Lush and cedary. Medium-full body, some tannins. Ripe and meaty and more grip and less attenuation than on the nose. Plump, aromatic. Long. Yet not as classy as the rest.

Haut-Brion   Now–2020   18.5
Fullish colour. Now just about mature. Lovely nose. Super soft red fruit. Cedary and oaky. This is

densely superior to the La Mission. Fullish, just about ready. Ripe, fleshy, abundant, complex. Long. Classy.

La Louvière Drink soon 13.5
Good colour. Now mature. A bit light and even feeble and over-evolved on the nose. Better on the palate. Some fruit. But a touch of astringency too. Medium body. Not bad.

Malartic-Lagravière Now–2010 15.5
Full colour. Little mature. Fullish nose, good ripe fruit, but also the earthy, *goût de terroir* of Graves. Fullish body. Good ripe tannins. Better than Pape-Clément and Fieuzal. Fleshy, abundant. Roast-chestnutty. Good plus. Almost ready.

La Mission-Haut-Brion Now–2014 17.0
Fullish colour. Barely mature. Dense nose. Backward. Unevolved. Still a little raw. Plenty of substance and fruit on the palate but a little too much tannin and extraction for great. Very good plus at best. Yet long and classy on the finish.

Pape-Clément Now–2000 14.0
Full colour. Little mature. Slightly clumsy on the nose. There is substance and flesh here but no elegance. Slightly earthy/rustic elements. Chunky, medium-full. Some tannin. Dull. Perhaps a year or so will improve it. Reasonable grip.

Smith-Haut-Lafitte Drink up 11.0
Medium colour. Now ready. Fruity but a bit slight on the nose. Light on the palate. Old, feeble, no grip. Already faded.

La Tour-Haut-Brion Now–2006 15.0
Full colour, barely mature. Slightly closed and a bit sweaty on the nose. Full, slightly stalky, quite a lot of new wood. Underneath you could see the class, but it lacks balance and charm to be better than 'good'.

MÉDOC

Camensac 1994–2000 13.0
Fullish colour. Just a little brown. Firm but a little unyielding on the nose. Not a lot of class. On the palate medium body only. A lack of depth and intensity here but reasonable balance. Lacks charm. Finishes a bit dry.

Cantemerle Now–2004 15.0
Medium-full colour. Just about mature. Soft, new oaky, cedary nose. Good fruit. Harmonious. Not too structured. Medium body. There is a little astringency here but quite good fruit and elegance. Not great but good. Balanced positive finish.

Chasse-Spleen Now–1998 14.0
Medium-full colour. Just about mature. Rich, full and plummy on the nose. Medium-full, fresh but a little astringency here. There is grip and plump fruit and elegance, but not quite enough acidity. The follow-through lacks fat and intensity.

La Lagune Now–2005 16.0
Good colour. Not much sign of maturity. Rich, harmonious, oaky nose – almost too oaky – because the wine is not that structured. Very new oaky on the palate. But good grip and intensity. Yet most of the wine is now soft and *à point*. Good plus. For those who like oaky wines.

Liversan Now–1998 13.5
Medium-full colour. Mature. Farmyardy nose. But there is reasonable fruit and grip here and some new oak. Lacks grace and charm. But not bad. Medium-full body. Finishes well.

Potensac Now–2000 14.0
Good colour. Not a lot of maturity. Some new oak on the nose. Good Cabernet. Stylish if lacking flesh. But this shows well. Medium to medium-full body. A little astringency but a good follow-through. Well made. Will keep well.

Sociando-Mallet 1995–2010 16.0
Full colour. Still very purple. Dumb nose, closed, but high quality here. Fullish, some tannin. Youthful, subtle, long. Very fine fruit. This has real class for a *bourgeois* wine. Very closed still.

La Tour-de-By Now–1997 14.0
Medium to medium-full colour. Mature. Quite soft on the nose with good style for what it is. Mature, round, soft and fruity. Good grip. This is well made and *à point* now. Shows well.

Villegeorge Now–1997 12.5
Medium-full colour. Mature. Fat and fleshy but somewhat rustic on the nose. On the palate medium-full, rather coarse, but quite substantial and well balanced. Rather a rude wine.

MARGAUX

d'Angludet 1997–2009 15.5
Fullish colour. Little sign of brown. Medium-full, fleshy and oaky on the nose. But a little sweaty as well. Fullish, still tannic. Rich and ample underneath. Good grip. Fat and concentrated. Good.

Boyd-Cantenac Now–2004 14.0
Fullish colour. Little sign of maturity. Firm, solid, fresh nose. Slightly unpolished. Quite full. Underneath here somewhere the fruit is not bad, but the wine is a bit over-macerated. It is full but not concentrated. Better with food.

Brane-Cantenac Now–1998 14.0
Medium-full colour. Mature. Open, fruity nose. But a lack of depth and class. Medium body. Quite fresh, but no depth. Nor finesse. One-dimensional. Lacks grip. Quite good.

Desmirail Now–2000 13.5
Medium-full colour. Just about mature. Soft nose. Reasonable fruit, but not a lot of class. Medium body. Lacks a bit of grip. It tails off on the finish. Lacks class too. One-dimensional.

Durfort-Vivens   Now–1998   15.0

Medium to medium-full colour. Fully ready. Thin nose. Thin palate. This has some new oak and some fruit. Indeed it is better balanced and more classy than Brane-Cantenac. Good. Meaty.

Giscours   Now–2005   14.0

Medium colour. Medium-full, just about mature. Not a lot of personality on the nose. Medium-body. Some new oak. Ripe but one-dimensional. Reasonable grip and follow-through. Rather dull.

d'Issan   Now–2008   15.5

Good colour. Not much sign of maturity. A little rigid, but there is concentration here. A little astringent. Medium to medium-full. A certain dryness to the tannins yet the fruit has concentration and grip and the finish is positive.

Lascombes   Now–2000   14.0

Medium-full colour. Just about ready. Full and fleshy, but slightly sweaty and coarse. Medium-full, fat, ripe. Lacks class but there is some substance here. Quite good at best.

Malescot-Saint-Exupéry Now–1998   13.5

Medium-full colour. Mature. Mixed-up nose. Lacks a bit of class. Lumpy. Medium body. Just about ready. But not much depth, or grip. Disappointing. No class. No structure. No balance.

Margaux   Now–2018   17.5

Full colour. Still very youthful. Very oaky on nose and even more oaky on the palate. Too much so for me. Rich and concentrated but essentially a little rigid. Ripe but not harmonious.

Palmer   Now–1998   15.0

Medium-full colour. Mature. Not much nose. A little too delicate. Disappointing. Soft and fruity, but it lacks intensity and depth. Only 'good'. Elegant though. For Palmer this is disappointing.

Pavillon Rouge du Margaux
    Now–2004   15.5

Fullish colour. Still youthful. Seriously oaky on the nose. Too oaky for the amount of fruit on the palate. Yet the class is here. Medium-full. Will still improve. Balanced and with very good fruit.

Prieuré-Lichine   Now–2008   15.0

Medium-full colour. Mature. Ample, plump and fleshy on the nose. Not the greatest of class but balanced and attractive. Medium to medium-full. Ripe and with good depth and balance. Well-made, but lacks a bit of finesse.

Rausan-Ségla   Drink soon   14.0

Medium-full colour. Fully ready. Oaky. Scented fruit. A bit of sulphur, not enough grip. New oaky but weak on the palate. Tails off. Yet there was class here once. Medium body.

Du Tertre   Now–2004   14.0

Medium-full colour. Mature. A little solid and four-square on the nose. Better on the palate. A little rigid but meaty. Good grip. Lacks class. Medium-full. Quite good.

La Tour-de-Mons   Now–1997   12.0

Medium-full colour. Not much sign of maturity. The nose is a little pinched and the wine is a bit dry. A rather austere, dry wine, a little astringent, with some tannins. No fat, no generosity.

SAINT-JULIEN

Beychevelle   Now–1997   13.5

Medium-full colour. Just a little development. The nose is accessible. It shows fruit but not much new oak or much elegance and even some astringency. *A point.* A lack of real selection evident here. Medium body. Insufficient grip. Slight suggestion of attenuation. Feeble. Disappointing. Lacks depth and freshness and class.

Branaire-Ducru   Now–1998   14.0

Medium-full colour. Some development. Good ripe fruit on the nose. But a little four-square. Medium body. Some astringency. This suffers from lack of grip. So it lacks class and is a bit short.

Connetable de Talbot   Now–2004   13.0

Medium colour. Just about mature. Somewhat four-square on the nose. A bit herbaceous too. On the palate it is ripe and pleasant but a bit over-extracted. Good grip. But a little hard. Not bad. Medium body.

Ducru-Beaucaillou   Now–2020   17.5

Medium-full colour. Still immature. Just beginning to open out on the nose. There is lovely elegant fruit here. Already accessible on the palate. Medium-full. Super fruit but laid back, even delicate. Very long. Very complex. Very classy.

Gloria   Now–2004   15.0

Medium-full colour. Little sign of maturity. Soft plump Cabernet Sauvignon on the nose. Medium to medium-full. Good ripe Cabernet attack. Quite rich. Lacks the definition for better than good. Good balance but not enough personality.

Gruaud-Larose   1996–2016   16.5

Full, backward colour. Rich and concentrated but a little solid on the nose. Full, meaty, tannic but very good tannins. There is Cabernet and a liquorice-like spice here. A lot of depth and concentration. Backward.

Lagrange   Now–2000   14.0

Medium-full colour. Still quite backward. Full and ripe but rustic on the nose. Medium to medium-full. The tannins are a bit common and barnyardy but the follow-through is very rich.

Langoa-Barton   Now–2000   14.0

Medium to medium-full colour. A little hint of brown now. Slightly tanky on the nose. But good if slightly austere Cabernet fruit underneath. On the palate similar. Ripe but a little astringency, as if a bit over-macerated. Better with food. Medium body. Lacks charm. Quite good.

Léoville-Barton Now–1998 14.0
Medium-full colour. Still quite backward. A bit rigid and dense on the nose. Medium to medium-full. Four-square, lacking a bit of grip. It is already astringent. Not better than Langoa.

Léoville-Las-Cases Now–2020 18.5
Full immature colour. Brilliant nose. First growth quality. New oaky. Concentrated and very complex. Lovely depth and definition. Fullish, quite strongly oaky. Ripe, rich and very concentrated. Very classy and very lovely. Needs a year or two.

Léoville-Poyferré Now–2014 16.0
Medium-full colour. Just beginning to turn. Good elegant Cabernet fruit here. Ripe and rich with a touch of oak. Very good. Medium-full, balanced, classy. Lovely ripe concentrated fruit. Good grip. Long and satisfying. Almost ready.

Clos-du-Marquis Now–2004 15.0
Medium-full colour. Still backward. Some new oak. Good class. Very good for a second wine. Medium body. Ripe, oaky, elegant. Ready. This is complex, accessible and very well put together.

Saint-Pierre Now–2014 16.5
Medium-full colour. Little sign of maturity, but a little more than Gloria. More substance than the Gloria on the nose, but a bit driven and herbaceous. Has depth but is a bit hard. Medium-full. Rich and ripe and is concentrated on the palate. A little tannin still. This is old viney and backward. Long and satisfying. Classy. Very good plus.

Sarget de Gruaud-Larose
Now–2007 14.0
Medium-full colour. Little sign of maturity. Quite fat and rich on the nose especially for a second wine. Not a lot of elegance though. This has more depth and richer, more positive fruit. Medium body. Good for a second wine.

Talbot Now–2010 15.5
Fullish backward colour. Ample, fleshy, ripe and rich on the nose. Typically Cordier. Medium to medium-full body. Ripe fruit. Just a little chunky. But sufficiently well balanced to be good plus. Good personality. Still needs a year or two.

PAUILLAC

Batailley Now–2010 15.5
Medium-full colour. Just about mature. Pleasant fruit on the nose. Good balance and style, without having a lot of depth and class. But a very well-made wine. Medium body. Fresh and balanced. Shows well.

Clerc-Milon Now–2007 13.0
Fullish colour, still immature. Good concentra-

tion here on the nose. Some new oak. Still young. Full, quite tannic. Just a little four-square on the attack, but more in a blunt, backward sense, because the finish shows more personality. Round, ripe, oaky. Very good.

Duhart-Milon 1995–2012 14.5
Full colour. Still very immature. Rather dense and herbaceous on the nose. Fullish, a little inflexible. But rich definitely. It just lacks charm and real class. Needs time.

Les Forts de Latour Now–2008 15.0
Full colour. Still youthful. New oak and Cabernet on the nose but not quite enough fat and concentration here. But better than Moulin des Carruades. More structure and personality. Better balance. Good. Medium to medium-full.

Grand-Puy-Ducasse Now–2005 14.0
Very good immature colour. Plump and rich, even velvety, but just a touch sweaty, lacking class. Medium body. Easy to drink, but not fresh or classy enough at the end. A bit concocted.

Grand-Puy-Lacoste Now–2018 17.0
Fullish, immature colour. Rich, ripe and concentrated, but backward on the nose. Fullish, good tannin. Very good fruit. Above all grip and class. Still backward on the attack but long, concentrated and complex on the finish. Very good indeed.

Haut-Bages-Avérous Now–1998 13.0
Good colour for a second wine. Still youthful. Open nose, accessible, plump and plummy. Good fruit but an element of slightly herbaceous tannins. Medium body. Not bad.

Haut-Bages-Libéral Now–2000 12.5
Fullish colour just about on the turn. Slight element of the rustic and astringent on the nose here. On the palate it is also is a little astringent. Lacks class but there is richness. A clumsy wine.

Haut-Batailley 1995–2015 16.0
Good immature colour. Rich Cabernet nose. But a slight lack of personality. Just a little inflexible compared with Grand-Puy-Lacoste. Fullish. Good rich concentrated fruit on the palate. Still backward and tannic, but very good grip. Needs time. Plenty here. Good class too.

Lafite-Rothschild 1995–2030 19.5
Fullish. Still immature. This is very lovely on the nose. Very elegant, very discreet, not too oaky, but with a very good oaky base. Marvellous intensity on the palate. Just a little more structure and tannin than the Pichon-Lalande. Less lush, a touch less acidity. But very fine indeed.

Latour 1995–2012 17.0
Fullish, immature colour. Classy, Cabernet nose. More Latour than 1983. Little cool, austere, but also without the concentration of Lafite or Mouton. Fullish, a touch tannic without the concen-

tration of fruit and real grip to support it. Much less interest. Very good indeed at its best.

Lynch-Bages   Now–2015   16.5

Fullish colour still immature. Opulent and spicy, rich and a little more evolved than Grand-Puy-Lacoste on the nose. Similarly so on the palate. Ample and fullish. Rich and spicy. Good grip. But Grand-Puy-Lacoste has better class.

Lynch-Moussas   Now–1998   14.0

Medium colour. Now some maturity. Open nose. Pretty but rather one-dimensional. Medium body. Pleasant, even quite stylish. And the fruit is ripe and balanced. Quite good. But lacks depth.

Moulin des Carruades   Now–2006   15.0

Medium-full colour. Still youthful. Cedary and damson-mulberry on the nose. Oaky and classy, but not enough concentration. This is confirmed on the palate. Medium body. A bit oak dominated. Balanced but lacks fat and grip. Elegant.

Mouton-Baronne-Philippe Now–2005   14.5

Fullish colour, just a hint of maturity. Good fruit on the nose but not the depth or personality of the Clerc. Medium-full. Some tannin. A bit solid and boring, but there is good fruit and grip.

Mouton-Rothschild   1995–2030   20.0

Full colour. Immature. A little dominated by the oak on the nose. On the palate fullish, very, very rich and concentrated. A totally consistently beautiful wine from start to finish. Great class. Hugely opulent. Very intense. Fat. Very balanced and complex. Brilliant.

Pichon-Longueville-Baron

                 1995–2007   15.0

Medium-full colour. Immature. Solid. Inflexible, a bit tanky on the nose. Lumpy. Fullish. There is tannin. But the tannins are a bit astringent and always will be. But there is also richness and concentration. In three years it will be 'good'.

Pichon-Longueville, Comtesse de Lalande

                 Now–2030   19.0

Medium-full colour. Just showing a hint of maturity. More backward than I had expected on the nose. Lush, rich and concentrated though. Fullish. Very concentrated, marvellous intensity of fruit and real grip. Real depth and complexity here. Very long, very lovely, very special.

Pontet-Canet   Now–2004   13.5

Fullish colour. Still immature. A lack of class and flexibility here on the nose. A bit four-square. A bit over-extracted. There is fruit but not much elegance and structure. Yet underneath possibility. Awkward. No charm.

Reserve-de-la-Comtesse

                 Now–2004   15.5

Fullish colour. Just about there. Gently ample, oaky nose. Very good fruit. Medium to medium-

full body. Ripe, sweet, rich, balanced and classy. Lovely. Very good length.

SAINT-ESTÈPHE

Calon-Ségur   Now–2000   15.5

Medium-full colour. Some maturity. Rather rustic and dry on the nose. Barnyardy. On the palate a bit dried out. Ripe and succulent on the nose, even rich. Medium-full body. Some tannin. Good grip. This is fat and substantial. Finishes well. Plummy and plump. Ample and rich.

Cos d'Estournel   Now–2009   17.0

Good colour. Not much sign of maturity. Rich, concentrated, fat and classy on the nose. Medium-full. This has real depth. It is substantially better than the rest of the Saint-Estèphes. Rich, concentrated, opulent and still backward. Fine complex finish.

Cos-Labory   Now–1997   14.5

Medium to medium-full colour. Some maturity. Light, elegant nose. This has good new oak. Medium body. It is a little deficient in acidity but it is well made, charmingly fruity, and shows class.

Haut-Marbuzet   1995–2010   16.0

Medium-full colour. Sweet, oaky, ripe nose; concentrated, a little roasted nuts aspect. Medium-full, round, opulent, good ripe tannins. Lots of extract. Not the concentration of Château Cos d'Estournel, but very fine and stylish, showing once again what a good wine is made here.

Meyney   Now–2000   14.5

Medium-full colour. Still immature. Rich, fat and meaty. Typically Cordier, typically Saint-Estèphe. Medium-full body. Ripe attack. Balanced, even quite complex on the follow-through. Good fruit. Now ready.

Montrose   Now–2004   15.5

Medium-full colour. Some maturity. A little touch. Not quite enough grace on the nose. Quite good structure. Good freshness. Medium to medium-full. Not a blockbuster. I find this good but not special. But the finish is positive. Showing more elegance than the attack.

Les Ormes-de-Pez   Now–1998   13.5

Medium to medium-full colour. Some maturity. Ripe nose. Softer and more evolved than the Meyney. Medium to medium-full body. Slightly rustic. Reasonable balance but not much excitement.

Prieur de Meyney   Now–1998   12.5

Medium to medium-full colour. Not much brown. Pleasantly plump but a bit nondescript on the nose. Similar on the palate. This isn't bad at all for a second wine though. It has fruit and grip if not much class. Just about ready.

1981 CLARET

The great 1980s decade was ushered in by the 1981. Not with a bang, perhaps, but not with a whimper either. Nineteen eighty-one is one of those eminently satisfactory vintages, neither great nor a disaster: round, soft-centred, early-maturing wines which are very good value. It is now in its prime, and I feel it has not only turned out more satisfactorily than was expected, but better *vis à vis* initial projections than either 1978 or 1979. Like many vintages it is proportionately better at the top of the hierarchy than lower down: there is still plenty of it around; and the best wines of the vintage can offer much pleasure at not too extortionate a cost.

THE WEATHER

After a cold winter an early start to vegetative cycle was precipitated by a very warm spell at the end of March. This encouraged the buds to develop about a fortnight earlier than normal, right at the beginning of April. The *sortie* for the Cabernet Sauvignon was particularly good, though for the Merlot and Cabernet Franc not quite as promising, with some potential bunches too far from the main trunk of the vines (it is best if the bunches are close to the sap). Later in April and throughout May the weather was indifferent, wet but not too cold, though there was some frost damage on the night of 27 to 28 April.

June brought an improvement. The flowering commenced on the 4th (about average), took place in for the most part excellent conditions – there were two rather cold days which led to a bit of *coulure* – and was almost complete in a fortnight. This meant that the bunches would have an even ripeness, obviously a good thing. Having given the vines the opportunity to flower satisfactorily, the sun disappeared at the end of the month. The last week of June and the whole of July was cold, wet and sunless. August, though, was completely the reverse. It was extremely hot – not since 1929 had there been so many days with temperatures over 25°C – and very dry, with a precipitation of only 27 millimetres. The fine weather continued into September: only a few more weeks and 1981 really could be something special.

Sadly, it did not last. Like 1973 and 1976, the elements felt they had to balance the heat and drought of a baking August and from the middle of the month there fell quite a bit of rain. Indeed, between 21 September and 15 October, a total of 118 millimetres was measured at the weather-forecasting station in Bordeaux, giving 1981 one of the wettest ends to vintage since the war. Most of this fell in the last ten days of September.

However, all was not lost. Firstly, unlike in 1976 and 1974, the downpours were not violent. For the most part the rain was gentle, in quantities within the vines' and the soil's capacity to absorb. Secondly, except for a four-day spell at the end of September, the rain was not continuous. The château proprietors were able to call a halt to the picking and wait until the skies had cleared and the fruit had had a chance to dry out. Thirdly, there was no rot; the August heatwave had thickened the grape skins, and this had been aided by the increasingly widespread use of sprays against *pourriture grise*, a technique which had begun to be in common use in the previous vintage. Lastly, by the time the rain commenced, the grapes were more or less ripe. Though rain will inevitably dilute the concentration of the fruit, provided that the fruit is ripe and the rain does not persist, allowing rot to set in, it can do no serious harm. The rain might have dashed hopes of a great vintage, but it certainly did not spell disaster.

THE HARVEST

Contrary to the norm, the red wine vintage started first in the Médoc, on 27 September. Though the Pétrus vineyard was cleared in glorious weather in the last two afternoons of September, the Saint-Emilion/Pomerol harvest did not generally get under way until 3 October. Most of the main properties had finished by 13 October.

It has been suggested by some that those who started the harvest promptly may have produced the best wine. This, I feel, is a moot point. Lafite did not start until 5 October, by which time Latour had finished, yet Lafite currently shows as the best of the Pauillac *premiers crus*. Léoville-Las-Cases, too, was a late starter, yet its wine is the best of the Saint-Juliens. It is all a question of perfectionism, and of being able to wait until the rain had ceased.

Even bunches picked in the rain can make good wine. I was at Las-Cases when a lorry of grapes arrived. Michel Delon ordered the trailer to be raised, but without releasing the tail-flap. A torrent of water, vaguely tinged with pink, ran out. Not until the very last drop had stopped would he allow the contents of the lorry to be tipped into the reception vat.

THE WINE THEN

First reports indicated wines of good colour with a healthy, clean, varietal nose, and low to average acidity, mainly in tartaric – which would mean that despite being on the low side, it would not decrease too dangerously after the malolactic fermentation. Tannin contents were also not too high, but certainly high enough to give the wines adequate substance, particularly those which would be able to enjoy a few months in new oak. The wines were ripe and attractive, and if soft rather than aggressively solid, certainly appeared to have enough backbone and grip to make good and reasonably long-lasting bottles.

QUANTITY

By current standards, the 1981 harvest cannot be considered more than a small average. The total harvest in Bordeaux was 4 million hectolitres of AC wine, about the same as 1978 and 1975, as against over 5 million in 1979 – and even more to come in 1982 and 1983 and later on in the decade. Moreover, the white wine crop had only been smaller since the war in 1977 and had never before represented such a small proportion of the vintage as a whole. However, the quantity of AC red wine produced was 2.5 million hectolitres, substantial by any past standards. Partly this large amount of red wine resulted from an increased area under plantation, partly, of course, it demonstrated the progressive switch by growers in the lesser areas of Bordeaux from white grapes to red. In the 1950s white wine represented two-thirds of the total crop, in the 1980s it was only one-quarter.

While the crop was a quarter as much again as in 1980, the increase was not uniform across the Bordeaux region. The bulk of the rise came from the minor *appellations*. In the top Médoc properties the harvest was 15 to 20 per cent more than in 1980, but in equivalent châteaux in the Graves and Saint-Emilion it was 10 per cent less, and in Pomerol more or less the same. At Château Haut-Brion, for instance, while they declared 145 *tonneaux* in 1979 and 120 in 1980, the 1981 crop was less than 100 *tonneaux*.

PRICES

To appreciate the prices of the 1981s we must first take note of two factors. Opening prices of the 1978s, 1979s and 1980s were similar – though it is uncertain how much 1980 had been sold *en primeur* as demand outside the Bordeaux area was negligible – in the region of 24.00 francs for a well-known *bourgeois* growth like Château Gloria, in the upper 30s for the top second growths and 72.50 for the *premiers crus*. Secondly, and increasingly critical, was the rate of exchange between the franc and the US dollar: 4.20 francs to $1.00 in 1979 (when the 1978s were offered) and 5.40 in 1980. In 1982, the value of the franc had fallen to 6.60, and it was to continue to fall. Moreover, American demand was active. Few buyers anywhere had shown the slightest interest in the 1980 vintage. All were in the market for the 1981s.

Though by comparison with 1982 and 1983 the opening prices of the 1981s now seem reasonable, they appeared to many at the time to be high. Yet, when translated even into pounds sterling, whose rate of exchange had not improved as much as the dollar, they were not unduly excessive. 38.00 francs for Las-Cases 1978, at 8.40 francs to £1.00 equalled £54.28 per dozen; 48.00 francs for Las-Cases 1981 at 10.40 francs worked out at £61.28, an increase of 12.9 per cent, or 4.3 per cent per year.

Yet prices, as I have said, appeared high. The biggest jump, fuelled by US demand, was in the *premiers crus*; from 72.50 francs to between 100.00 (Lafite, Mouton) via 125.00 (Margaux, Haut-Brion, which came out later) to 150.00 (Latour, last of all to come on the market). Moreover, the profits applied on these prices by the Bordeaux *négoce* were also increased. Overall, the increase of prices for the first growths over 1979 was 64 per cent. Lower down the scale, the rises were proportionately less: about 35 to 40 per cent for the top *crus classés*, 16 per cent for the lesser classed growths, while the *petits châteaux* barely moved at all.

THE WINES NOW

Unlike its closest predecessor from the quality point of view, 1981 is not an acid vintage. If the mediocre 1981s are merely empty, low in body and substance, and a little short, most wines are ripe and healthy with a good natural sugar, particularly in the Merlots, but because of the rain, the natural acidity is low, even for those grapes harvested at the beginning, and only the best wines have the substance and real character and length on the palate which will make them bottles to keep until the next century.

However, at classed-growth level, there is plenty of 'best'. Nineteen eighty-one is a vintage like 1978 and 1979 in the sense that there is a wide variation in quality between the hierarchy of classed growths and the *petits châteaux*, but unlike them in that at the top levels the vintage seems more consistent. Among the classed growths of the Haut-Médoc and their equivalents elsewhere in the Bordeaux region, there are few disappointing wines. Nearly all are characterized by a good colour, healthy, attractive fruit, and enough length on the palate to finish them off with style and personality. Most are ready, and will keep well for six or seven years or so. To sum up: this is a consistent, charming, fruity but essentially soft-centred vintage. It will still give a lot of pleasure, and can be bought with confidence.

THE TASTING

The following wines were sampled in London in January 1992.

	Optimum Drinking	Mark out of 20

SAINT-EMILION

Ausone　　Now–2012　　18.0
Fullish, immature colour. The nose is a bit closed at first, and slightly hard. Full, quite tannic; a wine of structure and depth which will still develop. Rich. Good grip. Very fine.

Canon　　Now–2005　　18.0
Fullish colour. Full, rich, old-viney nose. This has substance and depth. Fullish, still the solidity of Canon. Some tannin. Very rich, ripe and concentrated. Lovely fruit. Very good grip. Lovely.

Cheval-Blanc　　Now–2012　　18.5
Fullish colour. Still young. Fine rich nose. Good grip and vigour. Plenty of depth. Full, still tannic. Rich and oaky. More complete, better balanced and richer than the Pétrus. Very fine. Very lovely.

Figeac　　Now–1996　　15.0
Fullish colour. Now mature. Slightly dry and spicy on the nose, compared with the Cheval-Blanc. Medium-full, a touch of astringency. Quite sweet but a bit dry on the palate. A strange mixture of richness and robustness. Good.

Magdelaine　　Now–1996　　16.0
Medium-full colour. Attractive, rich, velvety nose. The attack is rich and opulent but there is a slight lack of freshness at the end. Medium to medium-full. Very good.

Pavie　　Now–2000　　16.0
Medium-full colour. Good nose. Fresh, rich and opulent. Medium body. Good attack. Velvety and full of fruit. Fresh. Well balanced. No enormous depth but very good and very charming.

POMEROL

Certan-de-May　　Now–2000 plus　　16.5
Medium-full colour. Fat nose but with good vigour and grip. Fresh, structured, vigorous, quite Cabernet-flavoured wine. Fullish, still some tan-

nin. A little dense compared with Latour but very good plus.

Feytit-Clinet Now–1996 14.0
Medium to medium-full colour. Soft, Merlot-based nose. Good fruit if no great power. Medium body. No great weight but good grip. Pleasant.

La Grave-Trigant-de-Boisset
Drink soon 13.0
Medium-full colour. A little dry on the nose. Medium body. This is beginning to lose its grip. A little spicy. Lacks zip. Not bad.

Latour-à-Pomerol Now–2000 plus 16.5
Medium-full colour. Fullish, rich nose. This has plenty of grip and concentration. Fullish, quite tannic still. Rich and opulent. Plenty of grip and vigour. Old viney. Very good plus. Will improve.

Pétrus Now–2008 17.5
Full colour. Still immature. Very full, rich, almost dense, noticeably oaky nose. Full, tannic, opulent. Very Merlot, but with no lack of grip. Fine but not overwhelmingly exciting.

de Sales Now–1998 14.0
Medium colour. Mature. Soft Merlot nose. Still a little raw and lacking richness. Medium body, just a little tannin. More generous than the nose would indicate. Plump. Attractive. Good length.

Trotanoy Now–1998 16.5
Medium-full colour. Slight touch of mint on the nose. Quite full. Good structure, but more Merlot and less vigour than Latour-à-Pomerol. Yet individual, with richness and depth. Very good plus.

GRAVES

Domaine de Chevalier Now–2009 18.0
Good colour. Still youthful. Rich, cedary nose. Good grip and depth but elegance above all. Full, rich, oaky, very good grip. Long and complex. Lovely finish. Real style. Fine. Just about ready.

Haut-Bailly Drink soon 15.0
Medium-full, mature colour. Soft but quite opulent nose. Fat and ample, even lush, but lacks a bit of grip. Medium body. Good but not great.

Haut-Brion Now–2006 17.0
Good colour. Still youthful. Lovely nose. Great complexity and real flair and breed. A subtle wine. Medium-full. Very well balanced but the grip isn't as positive. Complex though.

La Mission-Haut-Brion Now–2010 17.0
Full immature colour. Slightly more herbaceous nose than La Tour but fatter and with more substance and backbone. A richer version of the La Tour. Fatter and more complex. Fullish. Fine.

La Tour-Haut-Brion
Now–2000 plus 16.0
Fullish colour. Youthful. A solid nose but not

without depth. Medium-full, good grip. Some tannin. Finishes better than it starts. A lot of personality. Good length. Not too hard. Very good.

MARGAUX

Boyd-Cantenac Now–1996 12.5
Full, immature colour. Dense tannic solid nose. Similar palate. A stewed wine, which lacks suppleness and class. Some grip, but no charm.

Brane-Cantenac Drink soon 14.0
Medium-full colour. Youthful. A little H2S on the nose. Quite soft. Medium body. Some fruit, but a bit one-dimensional. Reasonable balance.

Cantemerle Drink soon 12.0
Medium to medium-full body. Just about mature. Not much nose. A bit lifeless on the palate. Somewhat attenuated. Medium body. A bit astringent. Lacks freshness and class. Uninspiring.

Chasse-Spleen Now–2000 15.0
Good colour. Still youthful. Fresh nose. Good fruit. A well-made wine. Quite full. Quite rich. Good balance. No great class but reasonable depth. Just about ready. Positive finish. Good.

Dauzac Now–1996 13.5
Reasonable colour. Rather anonymous nose. On the palate there is some fruit but a lack of real grip and personality. Yet not too bad. Medium body.

La Lagune Now–2000 15.5
Good fullish colour. Still youthful. Good rich nose with a touch of new oak. Medium-full. Good fruit and even richness on the attack. Some tannin. Longer and more interesting on the finish. Lacks real grip and class. Good plus.

Margaux Now–2015 19.5
Very full immature colour. Strongly oaky. Very young on the nose. Full, rich, quite a lot of tannin. Great class. Great depth. Very good acidity. Long, balanced, classy. Excellent finish. Very fine.

Palmer Now–1997 16.5
Fullish colour just about mature. Lovely nose. Fragrant, with a very delicate camomile touch as well as violets. The attack is delightful, but it tails off just a little in the follow-through. Yet lovely fruit. Soft and very elegant.

Pouget Now–1996 13.0
Medium-full colour. Still youthful. Dense nose. Now a bit attenuated. A bit dense on the palate but not as brutal as the Boyd. I prefer this. Medium-full. Some fruit. Not bad. A bit astringent nevertheless but finishes reasonably.

SAINT-JULIEN

Beychevelle Now–1996 14.0
Good colour. Still youthful. Ripe Cabernet on the nose if no great complexity. Medium to medium-full. It lacks a bit of grip and class. Start-

ing off quite plump and fruity but tailing off. Showing some attenuation. Quite good.

Ducru-Beaucaillou Now–2008 (17.0) see note

Fullish colour. Youthful. A bit oxidized but you can see the class. Medium-full. A very well balanced wine. Surely very good plus if well stored.

Gruaud-Larose Now–2009 15.5

Full colour; still immature, fresh, Cabernet and chocolate but slightly chunky nose. Fullish, still some unresolved tannin, and although beginning to get quite fleshy it lacks suppleness, charm and real finesse. Good plus.

Léoville-Barton Now–2005 15.0

Fullish colour. Still youthful. Slightly austere nose, very Cabernet. Full, quite tannic. Correctly balanced but lacks richness. Yet the finish is better than the start. Good but not great.

Léoville-Las-Cases Now–2011 18.5

Very good colour. Still youthful. Fine nose. Distinctive and oaky, much more so than Ducru. Full, yet not a bit solid. Very intense. Rich fruit. Long, fragrant, complex. Very fine. Almost ready.

Léoville-Poyferré Now–2001 15.5

Good medium-full colour barely mature. A little tough and resinny on the nose. Stalky and one-dimensional. Better on the palate. Fullish, ripe, plump and generous. Good grip. Fine, long, fresh and ample. Slight lack of style compared with Léoville-Las-Cases.

Saint-Pierre Now–2009 16.0

Fullish colour. Still youthful. Structured on the nose if not slightly dense. Good fullish rich palate. Well balanced. Velvety. A big wine but lacks opulence. Not too solid. Very good. Will improve.

Talbot Now–2008 14.5

Fullish colour. Still youthful. The nose is similar to the Saint-Pierre. The maceration shows. Fullish, a bit stalky and tannic. A bit robust. Good grip but lacks charm and class.

PAUILLAC

Grand-Puy-Lacoste Now–1998 15.0

Fullish colour, still young. Opulent nose but it lacks a bit of grip. This is rich but the Haut-Batailley is fresher. Medium-full.

Haut-Bages-Libéral Now–2000 14.0

Medium-full colour, just a little mature. Slightly animal nose, a little solid. Fullish, some tannin. A little stewed, but underneath a certain rich, old vine flavour. Yet a certain bitterness and lack of generosity. Fat though. Good length.

Haut-Batailley Now–2009 16.0

Medium-full colour. Still youthful. Slightly austere on the nose. A true Pauillac. But like Léoville-Barton it lacks a bit of charm. Good balance. Finishes better than it starts. Fullish. Fine Cabernet. Very good. Better in a year.

Lafite Now–2010 plus 19.0

Fullish colour still young. Marvellous nose. New oaky, complex, classy and fragrant. Still young. Even a little raw. Very new oaky on the palate. Medium-full. Fine but the Château Margaux is better. Yet lovely and complex nevertheless.

Latour Now–2010 plus 18.0

Very full immature colour. Austere Cabernet nose. Full, some tannin still. This is a little too unbending. Fine Cabernet fruit. Very good tannins. Long and complex. Better than Mouton but not the flair of Lafite. Lovely finish though.

Lynch-Bages Now–2008 17.0

Medium-full colour. Still youthful. Very good opulent fruit on the nose and palate. Medium-full. Rich but not quite the class of Pichon-Lalande. Yet long. Opulent and fragrant. Very good.

Mouton-Rothschild Now–2008 16.5

Full colour. Immature. This is not a patch on Lafite or Margaux. It is rich and opulent but it lacks real zip and flair. Fullish, just about ready.

Pichon-Longueville-Baron Now–1999 (15.0) see note

Medium-full colour, seems a bit murky. Loose, somewhat dusty and astringent nose. Medium body, now softened. Classy, supple Cabernet fruit, real ripe blackcurrants, but also a coarse element. Good. Second bottle cleaner: 16.0.

Pichon-Longueville, Comtesse De Lalande Now–2011 18.0

Medium-full colour. Still youthful. Lovely fruit on the nose. Silky and rich, even opulent. Very fragrant. Medium to medium-full. A good touch of new oak. Ripe, voluptuous. Great charm. Long and silky. Just about ready.

SAINT-ESTÈPHE

Cos d'Estournel Now–2006 17.0

(Magnum) Medium-full colour just a little mature. Slightly animal nose, a little solid. Fullish, some tannin. A little stewed, but underneath a certain rich, old vine flavour. A certain bitterness and lack of generosity. Fat though. Good length.

Lafon-Rochet Now–1999 13.5

Medium-full colour, just a little mature. Firm Cabernet nose but harder than the Chasse-Spleen. Medium-full. Slightly inky. Lacks suppleness. A bit ungenerous. Not too bad. Lacks real ripeness.

Montrose Now–1997 15.0

Very good colour. Still youthful. Rich, sturdy nose but it lacks a little grip. Fullish. Some tannin, almost sweet. Lacks a bit of real zip and so dimension. Yet good plus.

1979 CLARET

Some vintages, as they develop, perform better than originally anticipated. Others prove disappointing. The 1976 vintage, for instance, so plump and ripe and generously fruity when it first appeared, has matured awkwardly. The wines have aged fast and seem to be losing their fruit; they will not make elegant old bottles. Equally the 1971 vintage, though inherently more stylish than the 1976, has many failures. However, at the top levels the 1979 vintage will not disappoint. The colour is holding up well. Though in most cases not as intense as the 1978, it is fresher and still quite purple, while the 1978s are already showing a hint of maturity at the rim. Moreover, on the palate many wines have both more depth and more flesh than they appeared to possess at first, and the best are ripe, generous, healthy and full of fruit. Above all, perhaps, these have a good acidity, if not the concentration and profundity of the best 1978s. They are certainly worthy of note and with a long life ahead of them.

THE WEATHER

Like 1978, 1979 was a late vintage. Both were years characterized by poor summers, cool rather than wet, after bad weather in the spring. In both cases the development of the vine started late and never really caught up; in both autumns, almost at the last possible minute, the weather brightened up, enabling the fruit finally to attain the correct degree of ripeness.

Following a mild winter, which, as Peter Sichel put it, was wet even by Bordeaux standards, April 1979 was cold. Luckily, the budding was late and the vineyards were spared any damage by frost. It continued wet, the rainfall being almost double the average for each of the months up to May. Sichel observed, 'This has little effect on the vine but is not good for the morale.' Thereafter the summer was one of the coldest on record, but also drier than normal. The vines, however, were able to feed on the amount of water in the soil left over from the previous six months of rain, and the water table showed no signs of descending, as it had done in 1964, to levels where the vine could be harmed through lack of moisture.

The vines flowered in mid-June, in perhaps the only period of extended summer weather the Gironde enjoyed this year, and a very large amount of buds set into fruit. July was average in temperature, and dry; August the coldest for a generation or more, but with only a little rain; and September hardly better, though somewhat less dry.

Overall, some 150 millimetres of rain were recorded in the four months from June to September; equivalent to 1970, and drier than all the vintages of the previous twenty years except 1961, 1962 and 1967. However, unlike most of these vintages such rain as fell did so in August and September rather than in June and July, and similarly, unlike them, these months were also very cold. While the *veraison* was late, but at about the same date as the previous year, the relatively greater amount of rain during the six or seven weeks prior to the harvest meant that maturity was reached a week earlier than 1978, and the picking generally began in the first few days of October. Though an October *vendange* is commonly thought to be late, the current custom of waiting 110 or 120 days rather than 100 between flowering and harvest normally necessitates waiting until the first week in October. Only in exceptional years such as 1982 and 1989, since this practice of what has been pejoratively called 'waiting for *sur-maturité*' will we have harvests which largely take place in September from now on.

Towards the end of the growing season the weather brightened up, there were spells of warm, sunny days, and this continued into October. Though the *vendange* was somewhat interrupted by rain, there was not enough humidity to cause any widespread attack of *pourriture grise*. A record crop of healthy, and, for the most part, ripe grapes was gathered in.

THE SIZE OF THE CROP

The essential difference between 1978 and 1979 is the size of the crop. In both years an

Indian summer enabled the crop to achieve ripeness after a poor summer. However, in 1978, the weather had been bad during the flowering and the crop was short. In 1979, June had produced the one patch of sun in the whole season. Consequently the improvement in the weather had to nourish a much larger amount of grapes that year. This had to have an effect on the concentration of the resulting wine, so the 1979s were to suffer by comparison.

However, in one important aspect the harvest differed from the previous record crop of 1973. In 1973, the size was due to the size of the individual berries, following extensive September rain. As a result the 1973s were weak in colour and had a low fixed acidity. In 1979 the extent of the *récolte* followed the amount of grapes. These were small, as a result of the relative drought, and so the wines would possess a good colour, with a fixed acidity which would be by no means feeble.

The total Bordeaux *rendement* was 6.2 million hectolitres, the highest since 1934 (also a good year for quality). Of this the amount of *appellation contrôlée* wine was a record, and the 3.32 million hectolitres of red AC beat the previous record harvest of 1973 by almost a third as much again. While the total red crop was enormous, much of this could be attributed to new plantations, a move from the production of white to red, and to better husbandry in the lesser Bordeaux areas. Most of the *cru classé* proprietors were at pains to point out that on their estates the harvest was only some 30 per cent more than in 1978, or 20 per cent up on 1976.

THE WINE

Many of the largest châteaux in the Médoc reported yields of well over 400 *tonneaux*. Tasting wines in the early months of 1980 demonstrated the difference from one vat to another, and the extra *puissance* new oak could bring. Some of the wines, even in the best estates, were distinctly thin. A careful selection, selflessly rejecting the unripe and the insubstantial from the *grand vin*, would be necessary to produce an exciting wine.

First reports, dwelling on the size of the crop, indicated at best an average quality vintage, and did not lead one to expect more than soft and pretty wines with a limited amount of richness of fruit for early drinking. My first impression in March 1980, was that the wines were better than that. The colour was good, though at that stage, overall, there did not appear to be a lot of body. In most cases the wines were ripe, fruity and healthy, and had correct levels of acidity. As they had been in 1978, the top wines were proportionately better than the *petits châteaux*. The best of these had finesse and sufficient depth and concentration to make them worth buying, even if one had bought heavily of the 1978s.

THE MARKET

This, however, was part of the problem, as was the growing world recession, high prices, the low level of the rate of exchange between the pound and the franc, and the high cost of money. The 1978 vintage had been very popular and widely bought, certainly at the beginning of the year, but the latter half of 1979 and the beginnings of 1980 were sluggish for exports. Having had their best year since the heady days before the crash of 1973/74, the merchants were short of stock, and ready to buy, provided prices were reasonable.

The merchant and the château proprietor, though, view the word 'reasonable' from opposite points of view. To the former, a large, indeed, record vintage, however good, following a very good one, should be cheaper, particularly in days of high interest rates. Furthermore, it was considered then that it was always difficult successfully to sell two vintages *en primeur* in a row. The Bordeaux *négociants* could see that their customers would not be rushing in to commit themselves, as the latter would feel that they had plenty of time in view of the size of the crop. The merchants expected, or hoped for, a fall in prices from 1978 levels.

But the growers had inflation to contend with; higher prices for wages and materials, and particularly for energy. A large crop was a bonus, but Le Bon Dieu would eventually balance this with a meagre harvest, or one which, despite improved methods of vinification and *élevage*, would be considered too poor to merit widespread attention. They hoped they could obtain 1978 prices. The market was slow to open, but, encouraged by the success of *crus* such as La Lagune, which put all its harvest out to the brokers in one *tranche* and had no difficulty in disposing of it in a couple of days, 1978 prices were what the proprietors deemed their wines would fetch.

Thereafter, fashionable châteaux and first growths sold easily, but lesser wines stuck in Bordeaux. Edmund Penning-Rowsell was told in October of the following year, on his annual vintage pilgrimage, that perhaps half of the classed growths still remained unsold in the *négociants'* hands, though prices of the best wines by then were 20 to 30 per cent up.

Eventually, however, the market for even the lesser 1979s became buoyant. The 1980 vintage was short, and of only fair quality, the 1981s were more expensive, and the 1982 and 1983s were to be more expensive still; considerably so. Meanwhile, demand for any and all good Bordeaux continued to surge, and the quality of the 1979s became more widely recognized. Today, good 1979s are much in demand, and prices are getting high, though still some of the best value on the Bordeaux market.

THE WINES NOW

Nineteen seventy-nine is a variable vintage. Because of the lateness of the harvest, the size of the crop and the interruptions by rain, the state of ripeness and concentration of the fruit when it arrived in the winery varied considerably. Moreover, for some properties, vat space was at a premium. Some *cuvées*, because of the pressure of the amount of grapes daily arriving at the winery, were not given sufficient time to macerate with the skins, and are, as a result, weak and insubstantial. Léoville-Barton is one of these wines. Elsewhere, where the elimination of the lesser quality vats from the *grand vin* had not been courageous enough, the wines are also loose and indefinite. These wines are nearer in character to 1980 than to 1978. There is an inconsistency of quality among the 100 or 200 top wines, as there is in 1978.

The 1979 vintage also varies from district to district and commune to commune. At the outset it was thought most successful in Saint-Emilion and Pomerol, even better there in some cases than in 1978. I have never been convinced of this view, and I feel time has borne me out. Not only is the 1979 vintage equally as good in the Médoc and the Graves, in general, but the 1979 Saint-Emilions and Pomerols are inferior to the 1978, as they may also be to the 1981s. In both these other vintages the harvest was proportionately smaller, and the Merlot grape, predominant in the Libournais, less prolific. The resulting wine, in principle, was hence more concentrated. That said, there are nevertheless many fine bottles among the top estates in these two areas, particularly in Pomerol.

Where the 1979 vintage is at its best, in my view, is at Ausone (better than the 1978), in Pomerol, in the Graves, and in the top estates (Palmer, La Lagune and Margaux itself) of Margaux and the rest of the southern Médoc. Equally, except marginally in the first growths, it is very good in Pauillac, Saint-Julien and Saint-Estèphe. Above all, this is a vintage to buy prudently. Not all the big names, as the tasting notes show, are equally successful.

At best, 1979 is a good vintage. The successful wines are ripe, reasonably full, and have plenty of depth. What particularly appeals to me is the extra zip of acidity – missing in 1976 and to some extent in 1981. This gives them not only length and balance, but an attractive freshness. It will also give them life in the years ahead. All the classed growths are now ready. The more vigorous examples can safely be kept until the year 2000 or so.

THE TASTING

The following tasting was arranged by Farr Vintners, in October 1988.

SAINT-EMILION

L'Angelus   **Drink soon**   **13.5**

Medium-full colour. Broad nose without much oak and a hint of reduction. A medium-bodied, mature, Merlot-based wine. Ripe, fruity and pleasant but without any real depth, class or distinction. Not bad.

Ausone   **Now–2000 plus**   **19.5**

Medium-full colour. Very fine, oaky nose, real depth and distinction here, very elegant fruit. Fullish, some tannin. Good oak and fine, concentrated fruit. Has real breed but still needs a year or two. Splendid, complex finish. Excellent.

Cheval-Blanc   **Now–2000 plus**   **18.0**

Medium-full colour. Ample, rich, ripe nose. A fullish, oaky, opulent wine with plenty of substance and depth, still needing more time before it attains full maturity. Concentrated, ripe fruit together with the usual Cheval-Blanc spice. Classy.

La Dominique   **Now–1997**   **15.5**

Medium-full colour. Good, fat, oaky nose. Medium-full body with a touch of tannin still. This is a well-structured, Pomerol-ish, oaky wine with good grip and a stylish character. Will keep well. Good to very good. Better than I remembered.

Figeac   **Drink soon**

        15.0 (see note)

Was this an unlucky bottle? I have always admired the Figeac 1979 in the past. Today's bottle had a full, rich and a fat, oaky nose, but lacked a bit of punch on the palate. I couldn't get enthused.

La Gaffelière   **Drink soon**   **14.5**

Medium-full colour. An open, fruity, fairly rich but somewhat one-dimensional nose. Medium to medium-full body. Quite stylish on the attack but a certain meanness and astringency on the finish. Lacks depth and grip. Quite good.

Magdelaine   **Now–1997**   **16.0**

Medium-full colour. Rich, concentrated Merlot nose: good ripeness here. Medium-full body with a touch of tannin. Stylish, balanced, plenty of charm but lacks flair or depth. Will keep well.

Pavie   **Drink soon**   **15.0**

Medium-full colour. Soft, cedary nose, but there is something a bit lean, lacking plumpness about it. Medium to medium-full body. Fully ready. Some oak, good fruit and a positive finish but lacks a little generosity. Good though.

POMEROL

Certan-de-May   **Now–2000 plus**   **16.5**

Fullish colour. Less obviously oaky on the nose but quite oaky on the palate. Quite full, some tannin. A ripe, stylish wine with very good grip and old vine concentration, but not a bit dense. Shows very well indeed.

La Grave-Trigant-de-Boisset

        Now–1996   **15.0**

Fullish colour. Ripe, plump, stylish fruit on the nose. Medium-full body, only just ready. Elegant attack and a very enjoyable generous wine. Not enough grip on the finish. Good though.

Lafleur   **Now–2000 plus**   **18.5**

Full colour. Dense nose; old-fashioned long-macerated texture but crammed with fruit and no lack of concentration. Full, tannic, even a little obviously beefed up by *vin de presse*. Needs time to soften but should be splendid if it is not too over-balanced. Finishes very well.

Latour-à-Pomerol   **Drink soon**   **15.0**

Medium-full colour. Slightly spicy on the nose; hints of tobacco. On the palate a little four-square on the attack and some dilution on the follow-through. Good fruit but not enough grip and flesh. An astringency on the finish. Good though.

Pétrus   **Now–2008**   **19.0**

Full colour. Splendid nose: backward, very concentrated. Full on the palate. Rich, ample, beautifully balanced and with heaps and heaps of fruit. Excellent quality. Still needs a couple of years.

Trotanoy   **Now–1997**   **17.0**

Medium-full colour. A most attractive, plump, generous, stylish wine, both on the nose and on the palate. Good oak, good depth. Positive finish. Delicious now.

Vieux Château Certan   **Now–2000**   **16.5**

Fullish colour. Fine, full, rich, cedary nose. Medium-full body, a little more substantial than the above. Ample and plummy fruit on the palate. Good balance. Long, attractive finish. Very good.

GRAVES

Domaine de Chevalier

        Now–2000 plus   **17.5**

Medium-full colour. Very elegant on the nose as always. Lovely, medium-full body, just about ready. Not quite as concentrated on the nose but has very stylish fruit and a soft, complex finish.

de Fieuzal   **Drink soon**   **14.0**

Medium-full colour. A bit nondescript on the nose, lacking a bit of oak and personality. Medium to medium-full body. Quite ripe and plump but a little four-square, a certain amount of *vin de presse* showing and a slightly dry, papery finish.

Haut-Bailly   **Now–1999**   **15.5**

Medium-full colour. Round, ripe, slightly earthy, typically Graves nose. Medium-full body, good mulberry fruit and a touch of spice. Has character and grip. Good length and some, if not enormous, class. Good to very good.

Haut-Brion   Now–2008   18.5

Quite clearly the best wine of the Graves series. Fullish colour. Fine, succulent, complex nose. Good, plump fruit with a lot of depth. Fullish, good ripe tannins. An ample, concentrated, very well-balanced wine which has a lovely long finish and great elegance. Will still improve.

La Mission–Haut-Brion   Now–2005   16.5

Slightly less colour. The nose is less dense. Fullish, a little tannin. Like the La Tour the wine is a bit four-square but the Cabernet-based, somewhat leafy fruit is more positive and there is more oak. Will soften up about the same time and essentially has more personality without being exciting.

Pape-Clément   Drink soon   14.0

Medium colour. Developed nose. Some fruit but no great weight. Medium body. Lacks a bit of class and personality. Quite good but essentially a bit one-dimensional.

Smith-Haut-Lafitte   Drink up   12.0

Lightish colour. Weedy, faded and somewhat attenuated nose. Similar on the palate. Reasonable fruit but somewhat dilute and lacking grip.

La Tour-Haut-Brion   Now–2002   16.0

Full colour. Backward nose; somewhat solid and unforthcoming. Full and tannic. A little dense but has good ripe fruit and no lack of acidity. This is really a good wine, if without quite the depth and concentration to support the size.

MARGAUX AND THE REST OF THE MÉDOC

Brane-Cantenac   Drink soon   12.0

Medium colour. Dull, lean nose, without either generosity or excitement. This is beginning to lighten up. Such charm and fruit as it had is now beginning to dry out. If this is a true bottle this wine has gone downhill rapidly since I last saw it.

Camensac   Drink soon   12.0

Medium colour. Earthy, somewhat tough, rustic nose. Similar on the palate. A bit dense, still with a bit of tannin. Will not improve though.

Cantemerle   Drink up   12.0

Medium colour. Dilute, attenuated nose, lacking ripeness; even mean. Medium body. Quite high but unripe acidity. Hollow. Very undistinguished for a classed growth.

Giscours   Now–1997   15.0

Fullish colour. A full, frank, ripe, toasted nose; there are some rather burnt elements to the oak. Quite full, quite stylish. The roasted aspect persists on the palate. Underneath there is some, but not a great deal of concentration. Good but not great.

La Lagune   Now–2000 plus   16.5

Medium-full colour. Rich and oaky on the nose; full and firm. Shows well. Fullish, some tannin still, oaky. An ample, succulent, balanced wine. Very well made as usual.

Larose-Trintaudon   Drink soon   12.5

Medium colour. Mature, reasonably fruity but somewhat nondescript nose. Medium body. Less rustic than the wine below and with a reasonable finish, but one-dimensional and lacking class.

Lascombes   Now–1996   13.5

Fullish colour. A fullish meaty nose without a great deal of class. Medium-full, some tannin, a little oak. A burly ungenerous wine which still needs to soften but lacks distinction.

Margaux   Now–2008   19.5

Full colour. Full, rich, classy, new oaky nose. This has quality and complexity. Quite clearly the best of this series. Rich and full and ample. Classy, concentrated and subtle. Lovely fruit and excellent balance.

Palmer   Now–2005   18.0

Full colour. The nose is still closed. Fullish on the palate. Good concentration. Very stylish fruit but still a bit adolescent. Yet all the elements are here: balance, depth and class. Very fine.

Rausan-Ségla   Drink up   10.0

Medium colour, fully mature. Soft, somewhat dilute nose, now blowsy, even attenuated. Light and now getting both dirty and astringent. Poor.

SAINT-JULIEN

Beychevelle   Now–2003   15.0

Fullish colour. Full, rich and meaty on the nose, some oak, slight earthiness. Similar on the palate. There is something a bit four-square about this wine. Good but not enough class or richness. It tails off a bit on the finish.

Ducru-Baucaillou   Now–2004   17.5

Medium-full colour. More accessible on the nose. Doesn't quite have the weight, depth and excitement of the above. Yet very elegant though. A fullish, well-balanced wine, once again ripely Cabernet but with less backbone. Fine breed. A very fine bottle.

Gloria   Now–2001   14.0

Medium-full colour. Somewhat young-viney on the nose but quite ample and fruity if not very concentrated. On the palate ripe and fullish, a little four-square. Reasonable acidity. Still needs to soften; may acquire a bit more personality when it does.

Gruaud-Larose   Now–2008   16.0

Fullish colour. Richer and more ample, fuller, more classy and more concentrated than the Talbot. Not surprisingly a wine of similar style. Good grip. Needs tone. Very good but not the class of the two wines below.

Léoville-Las-Cases   Now–2008   18.5

Full colour. Very classy nose; full and oaky, concentrated essentially Cabernet flavour; ripe and complex. Full, still tannic. Backward. A wine of great distinction and real length. Classic Saint-Julien. Lovely.

Léoville-Poyferré   **Drink up**   11.0

Medium-full colour. Dry, papery, rustic nose. Similar on the attack. Attenuated on the finish. Poor.

Saint-Pierre   Now–2008   16.5

Fullish colour. Closed, reserved nose: good fruit, plenty of depth. Full, some tannin. This is rich, concentrated, slightly burly, backward wine. Fine potential though. Old vines here.

Talbot   Now–2005   15.0

Fullish colour. Typical slightly raw and peppery young Cordier nose. Better as it developed. Fulish, meaty, ripe. Good succulent fruit if without enormous breed. Good quality though.

PAUILLAC

Duhart-Milon   Now–1999   13.5

Medium-full colour. Somewhat four-square and rustic. Quite full. Lacks style. Lumpy.

Les Forts de Latour   Now–1996   15.0

Medium-full colour, some maturity. Quite an open, high-toned nose. A reasonably mature, Cabernet-based wine, not too dense, which Les Forts sometimes is. Lacks a bit of essential richness, concentration and charm, but then it is only a second wine. Good nevertheless.

Grand-Puy-Lacoste   Now–1999   15.0

Medium-full colour. Quite a leafy nose, lacking a little richness. Medium-full body, some tannin. Quite fruity but I can't really get enthused. There is an absence of concentration and grip. Still needs a year or so. Good nevertheless, but not quite so good as I remember it.

Haut-Bages-Avérous   **Drink soon**   14.0

Medium-full colour. Quite soft and ripe on the nose but no real definition. Stylish, mellow, pleasant, reasonably fresh and medium-full-bodied. Finishes a little dilute and one-dimensional. Good for a second wine though.

Haut-Batailley   Now–1999   14.0

Full colour. Firm but also a bit dry and hard on the nose. This is a medium-full but rather rigid wine. Is there a bit too much *vin de presse*? May soften but there is a lack of charm at present.

Lafite   Now–2008   18.5

Fullish colour. Round, classy, mulberry-flavoured nose with good oak in evidence. This is a medium-full-bodied, very elegant, very well-balanced wine with none of the diluteness of the vintage and the gentle subtlety typical of Lafite. Very fine.

Latour   —   **See note**

Full colour. Somewhat dilute on the nose for Latour, not absolutely correct and clean neither. On the palate quite full, and still tannic but there is a rather tired, sweaty element to it. I don't think this is a good bottle. Other notes would indicate one of the best wines of the vintage. (Now–2010, ±18.5)

Lynch-Bages   Now–1999   15.5

Fullish colour. Plump, oaky, aromatic nose and attack. Quite full, now ready. More stylish than the Grand-Puy-Lacoste, as well as more positive. Nevertheless not that exciting.

Mouton-Rothschild   Now–2004   16.5

Full colour. Rather unforthcoming on the nose. Quite full and oaky. Certainly has merit but no real *premier cru* quality here. Good length but somewhat four-square, lacking the voluptuous, exciting character Mouton normally shows.

Pichon-Longueville-Baron

            Now–2000   14.5

Full colour. This, too, is a bit unforthcoming on the nose, but it is better on the palate. The usual solid Pichon-Baron character but some fruit as well. Fullish, reasonable grip. Should improve as it softens. Quite good.

SAINT-ESTÈPHE

Cos d'Estournel   Now–2006   17.5

Full colour. Fine, stylish but still immature nose; ripe, concentrated and lovely. Fullish, new oaky and concentrated on the palate. Long, complex and full of both finesse and charm. Best left for a year or two. Will be delicious.

Haut-Marbuzet   Now–2000   16.5

Medium-full colour. Rich, oaky nose and palate. A full, ample, plump wine with good concentration and a fine new oak base. Once again this shows well above its station, though without the class of the Cos. Fine finish.

Meyney   Now–1997   13.5

Fullish colour, mature. Typical slightly burly Cordier-plus-Saint-Estèphe nose. A muscular wine without much style but at least neither weedy nor short of fruit and grip. Not bad.

Montrose   Now–1997   15.5

Medium-colour. Quite an evolved nose. Plump but without great depth. Better on the palate. Medium-full, quite attractive fruit. Good balance and length. Certainly good but a little straightforward.

Les Ormes-de-Pez   **Drink up**   12.5

Medium colour. Slightly dilute on the nose. Not much fruit or grip here. Similar palate. A bit lean and lacking charm. Medium body. Will get attenuated.

1978 CLARET

Nineteen seventy-eight is the third of the serious claret vintages of the 1970s: 1970 itself, 1975 and 1978. Of these my favourite is the 1970, blessed on the counts of both quality and consistency, as well as having a character which can only be described as amicable. The 1975s are troubled by rather austere tannins. There are some wines which are excellent, but you need to pick and choose. And then we have the 1978s. This, as shall be revealed, was a difficult vintage. Up to the end of August the weather was dreary. After that an almost miraculous *fin de saison* rescued the crop from the brink of catastrophe. It was a late vintage, and only those proprietors prepared to sit it out to the end have not made wines with a bitter, green touch of unripe fruit about them somewhere. As a result the quality is uneven. The wines are austere. The best have class and dignity, and will eventually unbend. Others have neither breed nor richness, neither generosity nor charm. In my vintage chart, based on a number of comprehensive in-bottle tastings I have made of the 1978s since they first arrived in this country in 1981, I originally awarded the 1978 vintage 16.5 out of 20 (1966: 16.0; 1970: 17.0; 1975: 15.0). Now the vintage is fifteen years old, and the wines are mature, I think I have been half a point or so too generous. To generalize, 1978 merits 16.0 and not 16.5 – very good but rarely exciting.

THE WEATHER

That the 1978 vintage is a good one has been a point of constant surprise and frequent explanation over the past fifteen years and will continue to be so in the years to come. It was a remarkable vintage. Until mid-August everything went wrong. The ripeness was uneven. Maturity was three weeks behind schedule. Most of the fruit was still green. Growers predicted disaster. One proprietor went on his annual vacation to the West Indies wondering whether to cancel his annual troupe of harvesters and leave the grapes to rot on the vines. However, in the third week of August, the weather changed. Thereafter, it could not have been more perfect. By November some growers were even talking about a *grand millésime*.

The 1978 weather pattern followed that of 1977 and was echoed by both 1979 and 1980 – though not by 1981. The resulting wines are different but one important factor links these four successive harvests. In each, the progress of the vine was severely delayed by poor weather in the spring. Where 1978 differs from the other poor years was in the quality of the weather in late summer and early autumn.

The first shoots appeared on the vines towards the end of March, about normal for Bordeaux and, thankfully, not too early as had happened in the previous year. In 1977, the *débourrement* had started on 5 March. Severe frosts and even snow, a rare occurrence in Bordeaux, at the end of the month and ten days later on the Easter weekend burnt off a lot of the new buds and produced a harvest which was very small indeed. Thankfully, this did not happen in 1978 but the spring was nevertheless cold and wet and the flowering did not start until 10 June, about ten days later than average. The cold, cloudy weather continued, the flowering was prolonged and uneven and the cycle became further retarded. By the time the grapes began to change colour from green to black, it was mid-August. The vine was three weeks behind schedule; worse than the 1972 vintage and as much as a month behind 1976.

It is interesting to compare the three best years of the 1970s.

	First Shoots	Start of Flowering	Start of Ripening	Harvesting
1978	29 March	10 June	12 August	9 October
1975	28 March	2 June	21 July	22 September
1970	28 March	5 June	25 July	21 September

What can be seen is that it requires up to two months and, moreover, two months of fine weather, to bring the grapes from the *veraison* to harvest. Normally, the weather can be expected to be at its best in August and the first half of September and to deteriorate as one gets closer to winter. Most fine vintages are characterized by their dry Augusts and Septembers. Many potentially great vintages are ruined when the heavens open just before the harvest.

In mid-August 1978, then, the outlook was gloomy. It hardly seemed possible that something drinkable would be produced, let alone a wine of quality. French national newspapers, with their talent for prolepsis, announced that the vintage was a catastrophe (normally they proclaim a vintage of the century). At the very last minute, though, the sun began to shine and thereafter conditions could hardly have been more perfect. The rest of August and September was hot and dry but not excessively so. A shower or two during the final stage of ripening is important to keep the juices of the plant flowing, to keep the sap lubricated, so to speak.

Nevertheless, it was one of the driest ends to the growing season on record. The rainfall in August and September was measured at 51.5 millimetres, much the same as 1962 and a figure only bettered in recent years by 1961 and 1985. Moreover, much of this fell in the first two weeks of August. The fine weather continued into October during which only 10 millimetres of rain fell, an unprecedentedly low figure, enabling the vines to complete their maturity without interference and even to catch up on some of the time that had been lost. In the last fortnight, the ripening accelerated, finally removing fears that excessive chaptalization would be required and the harvest began on 9 October and took place in ideal conditions. Curiously, the vintage began at the same time in both the Médoc and in Saint-Emilion – at Palmer and Lafite as well as at Cheval-Blanc – on this or the succeeding day; though at Pétrus and some of the other top Moueix-administered estates in Pomerol they waited a further week.

To digress a little, this question of early or late picking, as well as being conditioned by the *encépagement*, is also dependent on the soil. The Merlot grape ripens early and the micro-climate is marginally warmer on the Dordogne side of the Bordeaux area. This means that, normally, Saint-Emilion and Pomerol start their harvest in advance of the Médoc and Graves. However, once the leaves of the vine begin to turn from green into the liquid and fiery colours of autumn, the sap no longer flows and the grape can no longer be fed internally with nutrient. Once the chlorophyll stops working, the grapes can no longer ripen. You must pick them before they rot whether you like it or not. In addition, where you have a very dry autumn like 1978 and exceptionally well-drained soil as in the gravel of Latour or Lafite, the soil may get so dry that the ripening process decelerates to a snail's pace. Again, any further waiting would be pointless. At Pétrus in 1978, as at other vineyards with a more water-retaining clay-based soil, there was a logic in waiting a few days. Moreover, the size of Pétrus is such that the harvest only takes three afternoons. Unlike larger estates where the harvest must begin a few days before the ideal date in order to avoid it continuing too late beyond it and risking *pourriture grise*, Pétrus could afford to wait for the optimum in maturity.

THE VINTAGE

Though the harvest was late, the grapes were in supremely healthy condition; and they were ripe, particularly in the top properties which had been able to wait longest of all. Elsewhere, as much because of the aspect of the vineyard and the coarser soil as from earlier picking dates and also because the properties could not afford to reject bunches or part bunches which were not fully ripe, the must was higher in acidity and lower in sugar content. In the classed growths, though, the sugar content was good, the acidity was marginally higher than normal – no bad thing for the ageing potential of the wine – and there was no sign of rot. The wines had an excellent colour, not excessively high levels of tannin and, if there was a touch of 'greenness' in some of the wines, others were fully ripe, sufficiently full-bodied and concentrated and were accessible enough from the outset that one could see the elegance and distinction of a fine claret vintage. A greenness, a slight bitterness in a young claret is often a promising thing. In 1978, this occurred because, as Bernard Duten of the shippers Delor explained to me six months later, in the last few weeks before the harvest, both the sugar level and the acidity (expressed in tartaric) concentrated, rather than the acid turning into sugar. No doubt this was a result of the lack of rain.

The size of the crop was almost exactly the mean of the previous ten years, with the Médoc average and Pomerol and the Graves-Saint-Emilion small as a result of the frosts of the year before. At Cos d'Estournel, for example, the amount bottled under the château label was almost identical with 1975. Expressed in overall AC terms for the entire *département*, however, the quantity of red wine, at 2.25 million hectolitres, was unexpectedly large, more than 1970 and equivalent to 1974. The reason for this was the very small amount of non-AC red wine declared and the shift which had occurred from the production of white wine to that of red.

THE MARKET

To appreciate the market for the 1978s we must first go back to the 1977s – that short and generally rather uninspiring, ungenerous vintage. Because of the small crop, stocks had been low but because of a drop in demand, total stock levels had, in fact, improved from 21.6 months' worth to 26 months. Most of this, obviously, was the unwanted 1977 vintage. So when the 1978s arrived, despite what was certainly an adequately sized harvest, it was expected that their prices would be a bit higher than the 1975s and 1976s had been at the outset.

Opening prices, however, were as much as 50 per cent up. Largely this was stimulated by the late Henri Martin, proprietor of Château Gloria, a property he had much enlarged in his lifetime by the acquisition of parcels from classed growths in Saint-Julien. Martin, like Baron Philippe de Rothschild before him, wanted Gloria elevated in the classification hierarchy. This, with more mundane economic reasons, meant that he was very bullish with his prices.

In a well-publicized and early coup, Martin announced that he had sold half his crop to an American importer and the inference was that this had been at 24 francs a bottle – the price at which he offered the remainder. This sold without difficulty, and, as the first 'name' on the market, forced the other proprietors to price their wines accordingly.

Some of the classed-growth proprietors, no doubt recalling the overheated market of half a dozen years previously, were somewhat nervous of this development. But they were in a cleft stick. If they did not follow Gloria and that meant, being a classed growth, at a yet higher price, they might be seen to be admitting to an inferior wine. The reaction, therefore, was at first a bit tentative, with some properties preferring to wait a month or two before they declared and others only putting a few *tonneaux* onto the market.

It soon became apparent, however, that with the exception of the USA, demand was healthy without being excessive and the prices asked were at levels substantially higher than 1975 and 1976 levels. If in 1977, a well-known classed growth was priced ex-château at 18 francs, the same wine's 1978 would be 32 francs. Beychevelle, for instance, opened at this price while its 1976 had been the equivalent of 20 francs (20,000 francs a *tonneau*). The first growths opened at 82,000 and the longer the property waited, the higher the opening price. The price offered to merchants in England for some of the top Graves properties such as Pape-Clément and Domaine de Chevalier, which did not appear until May, was 52 francs. This aspect was watched with interest by Borie of Ducru and Delon of Las-Cases, both of which I bought at under 40 and which had reached a price of 50 francs on *négociants'* lists by the end of the summer.

WHERE ARE THE BEST 1978s?

Nineteen seventy-eight is an inconsistent vintage. It is well to remember that fifteen years ago only a handful of estates were producing a second wine. Rigorous selection – perhaps only 60 per cent of the crop going into the *grand vin* – was by no means prevalent then, even among the top classed growths. It is fair to point out also that profitability was not what it is today. Ex-cellar prices have tripled in the dozen years between 1978 and today. Have costs except for those of marketing risen by 300 per cent? It would be fascinating to compare balance sheets!

For two reasons, selection and the capacity to retard harvesting as late as possible, 1978 is a vintage where the great wines are proportionately better than the lesser wines. We should not forget that the best-exposed sites, which by and large belong to the top properties, have a more favourable microclimate where the fruit can ripen earlier.

The vintage, as so often is the case, is at its best in Saint-Julien and Pauillac. This is not to deny that there are some fine Graves. Domaine de Chevalier and La Mission-Haut-Brion are excellent, though Haut-Brion is a puzzle; I have had too many disappointing if not faulty bottles, and yet again, in the tasting which I report on here, we had an 'off' bottle. The wines of Margaux, always patchy, are even more inconsistent than usual. There is, outside Margaux and normally Palmer (we had an unlucky bottle), an absence of really concentrated fruit, as well as finesse. It is here, and among the lesser Graves, that the lack of real ripeness is at its most evident; the greenness of the vintage most apparent.

By and large the Libournais wines have the succulence but they lack the elegance. Pétrus, Lafleur, Vieux Château Certan, Trotanoy and Certan-de-May in Pomerol, Cheval-Blanc, Ausone, and Canon (possibly Magdelaine also, but not, I regret, Figeac) are the exceptions. Only Cos d'Estournel really excites in Saint-Estèphe.

In Saint-Julien and Pauillac the vintage reaches its peak. Latour and Lafite are the best wines of all. Ducru-Beaucaillou is better than Léoville-Las-Cases. Pichon-Longueville, Comtesse de Lalande, made its first super-second quality wine. Grand-Puy-Lacoste, Lynch-Bages, Clerc-Milon, Mouton-Baronne-Philippe, Duhart-Milon, Pichon-Longueville-Baron, Les Forts de Latour and Haut-Batailley – and even Croizet-Bages! – are 'good' at the very least. So are Saint-Pierre-Sevaistre, Branaire-Ducru and Clos-du-Marquis, though Beychevelle and Léoville-Poyferré are disappointing. Curiously, I have regularly found Talbot more satisfactory than Gruaud-Larose and Langoa to have more charm than Léoville-Barton.

The vintage is characterized by a high level of acidity. This, where it is balanced by plenty of fruit, is no bad thing at all. It means that the wines will stay fresh, long enough for what were not the very ripest of tannins to soften up. Acidity preserves the freshness and elegance of the fruit. It guarantees balance and length on the palate. At its best the 1978 vintage has this. The top wines still need a few more years. But all the successful wines will last at least until the year 2000.

This is a vintage to choose with care. Sadly in addition, it seems to have been more vulnerable to uneven bottlings and bad storage than most. I noticed this when Sotheby's presented a blind tasting of 90 of the top wines in May, 1984. Even bottles from the same box, and direct from the château, varied more than they should have done. In the tasting whose notes follow, we had only a single bottle of each. More than one or two wines did not show as well as they should have done.

THE TASTING

The following range of 1978 claret was sampled in September 1990.

	Optimum Drinking	Mark out of 20

SAINT-EMILION

Ausone — Now–2000 — 16.0

Fullish colour, just about mature. Fine fruit allied with a just slightly too lumpy structure. It's a bit stewed on the palate. Good grip. Full body. Un-

derneath very fine fruit. But will always have a somewhat astringent touch.

Canon — Now–2000 — 15.5

Fullish colour, just about mature. Fat, old-viney, richly perfumed, even scented (in a slightly rustic way) on the nose? Slight lack of acidity. No lack of grip on the palate. It is fullish, a little four-square, but has good fruit and a positive follow-through. Will improve as it mellows further.

Cheval-Blanc Now–2000 16.5
Medium-full colour, just about mature. Fat, firm and spicy on the palate. Fullish, good grip. Plenty of concentration. A lot of wine here but a slight absence of class and intensity.

Figeac Now–2000 15.5
Fullish colour, just about mature. Rather tough and even rustic on the nose. Medium-full. There is structure here but not enough richness. Good acidity but a little skeletal and a slight rustic, lumpy aspect as well. Lacks charm.

Magdelaine Drink soon 14.0
Medium to medium-full mature colour. Soft, mellow, pronounced Merlot nose. Medium body. Rich, fruity attack but it lacks a little grip and finishes a bit attenuated and without enough dimension and class. Only quite good. This doesn't seem to have lived up to original expectations – or have I been unlucky?

POMEROL

Certan-de-May Now–1998 16.5
Medium to medium-full colour. Fully mature. Pronounced, evolved, Merlot nose. Attractive, ripe, complex fruit on the palate and very good grip. Medium body. This has class and intensity. Long on the palate. Very good indeed. Attractive.

La Conseillante Drink soon 15.0
Good full, mature colour. Soft, feminine, quite complex nose. On the palate this lacks a little voluptuousness, and it seems to have lost a bit of richness on the finish. Medium body. Slightly bitter at the end. Good but not great.

La Grave-Trigant-de-Boisset Now–1996 14.5
Medium-full, mature colour. Soft, mellow, Merlot-based nose but with good grip behind it. Medium body, fully ready. A well-balanced wine with attractive fruit but with a slight lack of richness and complexity. Finishes just a little mean. Good length though. Quite good.

Lafleur Now–2004 17.0
Very full, concentrated, little sign of maturity. Firm, strong and slightly inky on the nose, but a lot of richness and depth here. Full, tannic. Tough and masculine. Very fine underneath. Lots of concentration. Not the class for 'great' though.

Lafleur-Pétrus Drink soon 13.5
Medium colour, fully evolved. A little attenuated on the nose and weak on the palate. Some acidity but an absence of concentration and definition.

Latour-à-Pomerol
Fullish colour; barely mature. Corked.

Pétrus Now–2005 18.5
Full colour, now some maturity. Firm, rich, closed, concentrated. A lot of quality here. Not a great deal fuller than the Trotanoy, but not as evolved. Fine acidity. Excellent, complex fruit. Very long and intense on the finish. Will still improve. A lot of depth here but it doesn't have the breed of the top Pauillacs.

Trotanoy Now–2005 18.0
Medium-full colour, mature. Oaky, rich and voluptuous on the nose. Classy and ample. Fully evolved. Medium body. Lovely fruit. Very well balanced. This is seductive, complex, mature. Very lovely. Very classy.

Vieux Château Certan Now–2002 16.5
Medium-full colour. Mature. Fat, plump and rich. Good depth here. New oaky. Quite mature. On the palate it is firmer and less advanced than it seems. Still a bit of tannin. Still a bit closed. Good grip. Rich on the finish, but not quite rich enough. Yet very good nevertheless.

GRAVES

Domaine de Chevalier Now–2005 17.0
Very fine colour. Full, barely mature. Very fine, classy, oaky nose. Full, firm, tannic, slightly austere. Classy, but I don't think it has quite enough richness for great. Good grip but lacks charm. Will still develop though.

Haut-Bailly Now–1996 14.5
Medium-full colour, mature. Soft, mellow nose. Plump and pleasant without riveting excitement. Similar on the palate. Medium body. Fully evolved. Attractive fruit without either the grip or complexity for anything better than good.

Haut-Brion
Fine colour. Full, just about mature. Maderized on the nose. Impossible to judge.

La Mission-Haut-Brion 1996–2016 18.0
Excellent colour. Firm, full, still youthful. Rich, fat, fine. Masculine, closed, a lot of depth. Even some new oak. Lovely complex finish but a slight resinny element. Still needs time.

Pape-Clément Now–2000 14.5
Medium to medium-full colour, mature. Rather four-square and rustic on the nose. An absence of class, indeed real cleanliness. Medium-full, this has more structure and rather better grip than the Haut-Bailly. It is best on the finish, which shows personality but the fruit lacks a bit of style.

La Tour-Haut-Brion Now–2005 16.0
Very fine colour. Full, barely mature. Full nose. Just a little subdued and vegetal. Firm and four-square. Full, ample, firm, good grip. Less vegetal on the palate. Ripe on the finish. Good length.

Margaux and Haut-Médoc

d'Angludet   Now–1996   13.5

Medium-full colour. Just about mature. The nose has now softened and shows the mellowness and slight spice of maturity. This has style. Medium-full. Pleasantly fruity but lacks a bit of complexity and real breed. Quite long though. Not bad.

Cantemerle   Drink soon   14.0

Medium to medium-full colour. Still youthful. Fresh nose but lacking charm and concentration. Medium body. Good acidity. Reasonable fruit and style but lacks richness and generosity. Finishes a little rigid and four-square.

Chasse-Spleen   Now–2000   14.5

Medium-full colour. Still youthful. Firm, quite rich nose with a touch of new oak. Full body, just a little unresolved tannin still. A masculine, slightly sturdy wine. Good depth. Just about ready. Quite rich on the finish. Good.

Cissac   Now–1996   13.0

Medium colour. Only a little sign of maturity. Somewhat unforthcoming on the nose. Ripe and fullish, balanced but without a great deal of style. Little sign of new oak. A little four-square. A good *bourgeois* example though. Slightly bitter and ungenerous on the finish.

Giscours   Drink soon   13.0

Full colour, barely mature. A little lumpy and rustic on the nose. Medium body. Similar on the palate. This lacks length. Has a certain astringency. And has little class.

d'Issan   Now–1996   14.5

Medium-full colour. Just a hint of brown. Quite a fat nose but a little rustic at the same time. Medium to medium-full colour. Similar on the palate. Good grip. Marginally better than the Cantemerle.

La Lagune   Drink soon   15.0

Fullish colour, just a touch of maturity. I don't get much on the nose here. Only a touch of oak. But ripe and succulent fruit. This is good but by no means great. A little more tannin and structure than richness. Medium-full body. Lacks excitement.

Lascombes   Drink soon

                 12.5 (see note)

Medium to medium-full colour, just about mature. Fresh but not very concentrated fruit and now a touch of attenuation. Lumpy and rustic on the palate. Fully evolved and will get coarser from now on. Disappointing. A bad bottle? My memories of it are better than this.

Margaux   Now–2006   18.0

Very full colour. Still immature. Rich, slightly raw and youthful but pronounced new oak on the nose. Medium-full. Even more dominated by new wood on the attack. Yet the fruit and class are there. Yet is it really great? Still needs time.

Palmer   (see note)

                 15.0 (see note)

Fullish colour, just a touch of maturity. Stylish and gently oaky, but not as exciting as Palmer normally is on the nose. Similar on the palate. Good acidity but a lack of concentrated fruit. Lacks dimension and richness. Unexciting. This was an unjust sample. With one exception all my other recent notes have been enthusiastic. (Now–2000 plus, 16.5/17.5)

Saint-Julien

Beychevelle   Drink up

                 11 (see note)

Medium colour, mature. Empty, dilute, slightly astringent nose. Elements of old tea here. Weedy. Empty. Falling apart. Other notes are more encouraging.

Branaire-Ducru   Now–2000   14.5

Medium-full colour, mature. Ample but slightly inky nose. Good acidity. Slight absence of class and real richness. Quite full. Still a bit of unresolved tannin. Somewhat four-square. But has depth and balance. Lacks charm though. I have seen better.

Ducru-Beaucaillou   Now–2004   18.5

Medium-full colour. Still youthful. Not as much new oak as Las-Cases. Slightly less body. But even more class and complexity of fruit. This is fine and verges on great. Medium-full, very harmonious, but while very well balanced, lacks the real concentration of a great vintage. Ultimately it is a little ungenerous. This is the vintage.

Gruaud-Larose   Now–1999   14.5

Full colour, just about mature. Typically Cordier nose. Like the Talbot. Just a little richer and less vegetal. A bit too stewed on the palate though. Lumpy and solid. And I don't think it will ever soften up properly. The Talbot is better.

Langoa-Barton   Now–2000   15.0

Medium to medium-full colour, fully mature. Evolved, pleasant nose but a lack of real richness and concentration. A pretty wine though. Charming. Balanced. Good fruit.

Léoville-Barton   Now–1996   14.0

Medium-full colour, mature. Slightly sweaty nose. A little attenuated. This is very curious. Medium body. Lacks fruit and richness. A bit astringent. Unexciting. I prefer the Langoa. A bad bottle?

Léoville-Las-Cases   Now–2004   18.0

Full colour, still youthful. Fine, closed, classy, new

oaky nose. A lot of quality here. A slightly fuller, fatter, more generous wine than the Ducru. Because of the oak. Not as fine fruit though. Not as concentrated. Not as complex. Very fine though, nevertheless.

Léoville-Poyferré　　　**Drink up**　　10.0

Good full colour. Still youthful. Strange crustaceous nose. Rustic. Very curiously sweet. Concocted. Horrid!

Saint-Pierre-Sevaistre　　**Now–2005**　　16.0

Fullish colour, mature. Masculine, fat, rich and concentrated on the nose. Not the greatest class but very good, old vine fruit. Still needs time. Fullish. Some tannin. A little four-square and even stewed again but good depth and richness. Will develop.

Talbot　　　　　**Now–2002**　　15.0

Fullish colour, fully mature. The usual Cordier nose. Slightly too much *vin de presse*. Ripe, fullish, the tannins are a little solid and earthy but a good example with good grip. Finishes well.

PAUILLAC

Clerc-Milon　　　　**Drink soon**　　14.5

Medium-full colour. Still quite youthful. Quite firm and rich but a slight element of maderization here, a lack of grip. There's a mellow, slightly artificial scented quality here. Lacks style. Medium-full and plump. Not bad. Badly stored?

Les Forts de Latour　　**Now–2002**　　16.0

Full, youthful colour. Slight *herbacé* element on the nose. Typically 1978. Typically Les Forts. Firm but not rich. Slightly unyielding. Similar on the palate. Good class and good fruit though. Finishes well.

Grand-Puy-Lacoste　　**Now–2005**　　17.0

Fullish, youthful colour. Rich, full, concentrated, even fat. Very good. Fullish, firm. Still a bit of tannin. A lot of depth and concentration of fruit here. Fine. Slightly four-square, though, on the finish but will still improve.

Haut-Batailley　　　**Now–1996**　　14.0

Medium to medium-full colour, still quite youthful. A little nondescript on the nose. Some fruit but no concentration or excitement. Four-square. A medium-full wine with reasonable fruit but no depth, concentration or charm.

Lafite　　　　　**Now–2005**　　19.5

Full, immature colour. Soft, complex, harmonious nose. Medium-full body. This is fully ready and quite delicious. Fragrant. Real breed. Medi-

um-full body. Long, subtle. Lovely fruit. Very long indeed. Marginally better than Latour, perhaps.

Latour　　　　　**Now–2008**　　19.5

Full, immature colour. Firm, full, ripe, concentrated nose. Real breed here. Full finesse and concentration of Latour. Very clean. Very complex. Excellent.

Lynch-Bages

Fullish, youthful colour. Oxidized.

Mouton-Baronne-Philippe
　　　　　　　　　Now–2000　　16.0

Medium to medium-full colour, fully mature. Soft, mellow, attractive new oaky nose. Medium to medium-full body. Fresh, ripe, charming and balanced. Good length. I like this.

Château Mouton-Rothschild
　　　　　　　　　Now–2000　　16.0

Very full immature colour. Full but somewhat anonymous nose. A lack of the new-oaky, lead-pencilly Mouton excitement. Medium-full, the tannin is a touch astringent. Doesn't have the concentration and complexity, or the grip of the other two first growths. A bit dull essentially.

Pichon-Longueville, Comtesse de Lalande
　　　　　　Now–2000　　17.0 (see note)

Good colour, still immature. Ripe, ample, oaky-soft nose. Very Pichon. Most attractive on the palate but not great. Mellow, oaky and balanced but neither the concentration nor the class of Ducru. Nor the grip. I have had better bottles.

SAINT ESTÈPHE

Calon-Ségur　　　　**Drink up**　　13.5

Medium to medium-full colour, fully mature. Pronounced Merlot on the nose but a lack of real class, as well as grip. Medium body. A little short. Pleasant but now cracking up.

Cos d'Estournel　　　**Now–2000**　　16.5

Fullish colour. Classy, complex nose. New oak dimension and balance. Medium body. Just about ready. Rich and mellow. Streets ahead of the Montrose and Calon. Balanced. Long. Very good.

Montrose　　　　　**Drink soon**　　15.0

Fullish, mature colour. Firm nose, has dimension here but not a lot of either charm or class. Medium body. A little rigid on the palate. Lacks plumpness and fat. Lacks richness. Yet balanced. Doesn't finish too badly.

1975 CLARET

For a decade or more, pundits have been writing down the 1975 claret vintage: too tannic, too austere, too dry, too tough for its own good. It won't ever come round, soften up, make generous bottles, it was said. Another view is shared by those whose chief interest lies in the wines of the Libournais. Christian Moueix thinks very highly of the Pétrus 1975, and he places it ahead of every vintage in recent years except for the 1982 (and perhaps, I suggest, now that they are in bottle, the 1989 and 1990).

Apart from Christian and his neighbours, almost the only person who has kept faith with the 1975 has been Emile Peynaud. In his *Le Goût du Vin* (1980), he described 1975 as 'one of the greatest years in Bordeaux'. He classed it as high as 1929 and 1947, ahead of 1949, 1953, 1959, 1966 and 1970. In an interview in 1989 he stuck to his guns. The best year between 1961 and 1982 was 1975. In his view it just needed time.

Following a comprehensive tasting set up by the auctioneers Sothebys in May 1984, I expressed my doubts about many of the wines, but my conclusions were positive:

> Many wines are still asleep; they seem rugged and unforthcoming. Some of these currently rough-hewn examples will undoubtedly throw off this cloak of unpenatrability and be rich, full, if enduringly firm bottles by the early 1990s. Others, stubborn now, will continue to be clumsy, and will eventually become astringent.
>
> 'But there is a lot of good wine about. . . . [These] are undeniably rough and dense, for suppleness is not a feature of the 1975 vintage, but underneath is a richness which promises well for those with the patience to bide their time. Choose with care and you will not be disappointed.

Since then I too have had my doubts. In February 1991, however, I sampled 50 of the top wines in the company of a group of experienced tasters. Most of us were prepared for an essentially dispiriting session. We had participated in a comparable tasting of the 1978 vintage some months previously and were expecting to end up deciding that the later vintage was in general the superior. We didn't. We were excited by the quality of most of the top 1975s. Patience has been rewarded. There are some extremely good wines. Peynaud was right.

THE ECONOMIC BACKGROUND

Faced with the success of the wines and the economics of the 1980s in Bordeaux it seems hard to believe that fifteen years ago the whole wine trade was in the throes of a crisis that was as much psychological as financial. Nineteen seventy-three and 1974 had seen two largely indifferent but prolific vintages which no one wanted to buy. There had been a scandal in Bordeaux when one of the oldest and most respected firms had been accused of fraudulent labelling of wine. And all this coincided with an artificially induced oil crisis which was forcing up the price of energy, the cost of loans from the bank and the rate and speed of inflation. After two years of madness, when wine prices quadrupled between the excellent 1970 vintage and the sour unripe 1972s, the bubble burst. Panic buying had changed to panic selling as enormous quantities of very fine wine were unloaded on the market at give-away prices.

In Bordeaux in the spring of 1975 trade was at a standstill and spirits were low. A vintage was needed which would restore confidence as well as improve bank balances. The cure was required to be as much psychological as economic. Luckily, that was precisely what happened.

THE WEATHER

Climatically, 1975 is a curious vintage. On the face of it, it should not be a good vintage at all. The rainfall in August and September measured 216 millimetres, about twice the average, and this should not have augured well. The previous four vintages with rainfalls of over 200 millimetres during this period had been 1969, 1968, 1965 and 1960 – not exactly an inspiring run!

The 1975 season began with a winter which was mild and rather wet, and this encouraged the sap to rise and the growing season to begin rather early. As a result, some of the buds had already begun to burst open by the end of March, and a sudden cold snap inflicted considerable frost damage, though not as bad as it was to be in 1977. This was particularly felt in those parts of the vineyard planted in Merlot, for it is this variety which buds earliest.

Spring and early summer were dry and warm, enabling the flowering to take place without mishap, and this was followed by a long dry spell with some extremely hot days at the end of July and the beginning of August. On 31 July the temperature reached 36.6°C.
In the second week of August the weather broke. There were two immense thunderstorms, on the 7th and the 9th, and thereafter for the next six weeks the days were interrupted with more downpours, though the weather in between continued reasonably warm and sunny.

Nevertheless, the fruit was in excellent condition by the end of September. The skins had been thickened by the dry weather in July, there was no rot and the grapes were ripe. Picking began on 25 September and took place under cloudless skies with the exception of a storm on the 29th, when some extensive hail damage was caused in Listrac, Moulis and Arcins, vineyards in between the classed-growth areas of Margaux and Saint-Julien/Pauillac. The fine weather continued throughout October and for only the second time since 1967 – 1971 was the other vintage – some really good Sauternes were made. The crop was small compared with the excesses of 1973 and 1974: an average of 40 hectolitres per hectare as against 56 in 1973. In all, 1.75 million hectolitres of AC red wine were produced in 1975 in Bordeaux.

THE WINE

The 1975 vintage is a year which demonstrates (unlike most of the other vintages of the 1980s, which were freaks) that quality is inversely proportional to quality. 1973 was similar to 1975 in that a hot July and August was followed by a wet September. However in 1973, as the above yields show, the amount of nutrient from sun and soil was feeding 40 per cent more grapes. Naturally, in 1975 the individual berries would be riper and more concentrated. Indeed they were found to possess the highest degree of natural sugar since 1961.

The resulting wine could immediately be seen to have an impressively deep colour, still a feature of the vintage. Acidity levels were normal, tannin was high and the 'dry extract' content was very good. These were to be wines of considerable body and size, which would take a long time to mature. Initially the wines were difficult to taste, and some fears were expressed that they might lack fatness and fruit, as well as there being doubts that a vintage with so much late summer rainfall could produce good wine.

Nevertheless, the vintage had produced just what Bordeaux had been hoping for: a reasonable quantity after the excesses of 1973 and 1974 (and not disastrously short like 1961) and a quality which was potentially very high, good enough to excite the imagination of the public and to restore interest in red Bordeaux from those merchants who were not still too awash with wines of older vintages.

THE MARKET

Understandably, the market was a little hesitant at the outset. Prices, ex-château, opened at 16 to 18 francs per bottle for well-known growths such as Lynch-Bages, Montrose and La Lagune, a franc or two more for what would become, by 1980, the 'super-seconds', such as Ducru-Beaucaillou, Léoville-Las-Cases, and 45 to 55 francs for the first growths. This meant that prices had returned, more or less, to 1970 levels, though in real terms, with inflation, they were, of course, substantially lower, and significantly less than the prices paid for the 1971s.

Demand was healthy though not excessively enthusiastic. Gone were the big speculators, and many of the larger groups, still recovering from the events of the past few years, sat and watched from the side-lines. Yet the demand was there, and during the year it became sufficiently heavy to move prices upwards. By the time the 1976 vintage was put on the market in the spring of 1977, despite it also being of good quality, and with the added advantage of increased quantity and a potentially earlier development, prices of the 1975s had climbed. A Bordeaux *négociant's* list, dated January 1977, offered Lafite at 73 francs and Léoville-Las-Cases and other similar growths at 27. Dependable if lesser-regarded wines such as Chasse-Spleen, Gloria and Phélan-Ségur could still be bought for 16 or so francs.

PRICES NOW

The vintage provided just the fill the market was looking for. Over the next few years, as prices emerged from the slump, the value of the 1975s rose. There was another surge in 1983/84, reaching a peak in early 1985 when the first growths began to top £500 at auction. After remaining at this level for some time there was a further increase in prices just before the outbreak of the Gulf War though they fell again during the recession which followed. The vintage fetches the same sort of prices as do the 1978s. I would suggest, it is worth more.

THE BEST 1975s

It is fair to say that the 1975 is an uneven vintage and difficult to generalize about. There are many excellent wines, both in the Médoc and in Saint-Emilion/Pomerol, both at classed-growth level and among the *crus bourgeois*. Equally, there are some disappointments, wines which substantiate the original fears that the vintage was too solid and burly for its own good, and would lose fruit before it had had time to soften up. In many ways it has parallels with the 1976 Burgundy vintage. If one were to mark the vintage as a whole on the basis of the successful bottles one would award it 16.0 or 16.5 out of 20; but if one were to assess it on the less exacting wines it would merit no more than 12.0 or 13.0 – perhaps even less.

While there are many less disappointing wines in Saint-Emilion and Pomerol than in the Médoc and the Graves in terms of an imbalance of structure and constituents – the Merlot, on which these wines are based, being an inherently less tannic grape variety – it also has to be said that apart from the very top dozen or so wines, the 1975 Libournais lack elegance. (You could of course argue, when do the ordinary run-of-the-mill Saint-Emilion *grands crus classés* and their Pomerol equivalents ever have elegance?) What they also lack is a little richness and vivacity. Unless I were able to drink wines like Magdelaine, Trotanoy and La Conseillante – La Gaffelière is also very good as is Lafleur – or Cheval-Blanc and Pétrus, I would pass up. Indeed I would go straight to 1982, for the middle of the range 1982 Saint-Emilions and Pomerols are drinking deliciously already.

It is only at the topmost levels that the Graves offers much excitement in the 1975 vintage, and really only La Mission-Haut-Brion is decidedly exciting. The wines of Margaux and the southern Médoc are even more disappointing. Even Palmer, by its admittedly very high standards, is dull. La Lagune and Lascombes are good, Chasse-Spleen is cheaper and better than most. There is little enjoyment to be had elsewhere. And I would not recommend Château Margaux. This vintage took place before the renaissance.

It is in Saint-Julien and Pauillac that the great 1975s are to be found. It is instructive to note that out of nineteen wines we sampled from these two communes only one (Pichon-Longueville-Baron) was less than 'quite good'. Latour and Las-Cases are excellent, second and third to the splendid Pétrus in the entire vintage. Pichon-Lalande is fine, as is Lafite: real breed in both of these. Saint-Pierre has always been surprisingly good (the group as a whole voted it into fourth place). This property made excellent wines in the 1970s. Apart from the underachieving Pichon-Baron, the major disappointment is Mouton. This was not the best of decades for the late Baron Philippe. It is almost as if he relaxed his perfectionist grip after having been promoted to first growth in 1973.

THE TASTING

The following wines were sampled in London at a session organized by Andrew Bruce in February 1991.

SAINT-EMILION

Ausone   Now–2005   16.5

Medium-full, mature colour. Slightly dry on the nose, but undeniably classy. This is a fuller, firmer, more tannic wine than Magdelaine. More austere. Good breed but it is a little tough and charmless on the attack. Rich on the finish though.

Canon   Now–1998   15.5

Medium colour. Mature. Aromatic, earthy nose. This is a bit chunky on the palate, but underneath the solidity there is flesh and fruit. And it is richer than the Figeac. Fully ready. Finishes well.

Cheval-Blanc   Now–2005   18.5

Fullish, mature colour. Fat, rich, spicy nose. Fullish, still a bit of tannin. This is not exactly very elegant. There is a resinny-aromatic element but it is rich and fleshy. Concentrated and well balanced. The best of the Saint-Emilions. Just about ready. An opulent wine.

Figeac   Now–1996   15.0

Medium to medium-full, mature colour. Good, classy nose. Quite reserved. One can discern the Cabernet. Medium to medium-full. Good grip. Attractive fruit if not a great deal of depth and concentration. Quite stylish but lacks richness.

Magdelaine   Now–2000   16.5

Good mature colour. A little dry on the nose but there is some fruit here. Quite rich and concentrated underneath, in fact. Medium-full, a little astringent on the attack but more supple on the follow-through. Good, oaky background. Has fruit and grip and class. Finishes fresh and rich and complex. Very good.

Pavie   Now–1997   15.0

Medium colour, fully mature. Soft, fleshy, roast-chestnutty Merlot on the nose. Medium to medium-full body. Good fruit, an attractively balanced wine. Round. Fully mature. Good.

POMEROL

La Conseillante   Now–2003   17.0

Medium-full colour. Mature. Interesting ripe nose with just a hint of reduction. Medium-full body. This has richness and concentration, and just a little tannin and astringency. Good grip. A complex wine. Very good.

Clos-René   Now–1996   14.5

Medium to medium-full colour, quite vigorous looking. Fat, voluptuous nose. Medium body. There is a certain astringency but fruit and flesh as well. Not a lot of grip and concentration but finishes clean and positively.

L'Evangile   Now–2003   13.5

Fullish colour; some maturity. A slightly stewed element on the nose. Rather hard. Quite a lot of tannin here. A bitter chocolate, austere flavour. Will always be a bit too structured for comfort. Reasonable grip. Too tough.

La Grave-Trigant-de-Boisset   Now–1996   15.0

Medium to medium-full colour. Elegant, fresh nose. No dryness. A slight element of Jerusalem artichokes, curiously. A gentle, soft, slightly oaky wine. Fully ready. This has a lot of charm, if no real depth or concentration. Good though.

Lafleur-Pétrus   Now–2000   14.5

Medium-full colour, mature. Quite a fat nose; if slightly earthy. Good grip. Reasonable fruit if not concentration. Medium to medium-full body. Lacks a little excitement.

La Tour-à-Pomerol   Drink up   12.0

Medium colour; fully mature. Rather over-evolved. Now attenuated and astringent. Yet underneath one can see that there might have been style once. Short.

Petit-Village   Now–1996   14.0

Medium-full colour. Fresh nose, clean and stylish. Good fruit. Medium body. A little one-dimensional on the palate. A little astringent. It also lacks a bit of zip and concentration.

Pétrus   Now–2013   20.0

Fullish colour. Less maturity than most of the Pomerols. High-class nose. Oaky, voluptuous, aromatic, but with more breed than the Cheval-Blanc. Full, tannic, rich and concentrated. Very long and seductive.

Trotanoy   Now–1998   16.0

Medium-full colour, fully mature. A little earthy, a little astringent on the nose. A little loose on the palate. This is ripe and seductive, but doesn't have the grip and concentration of La Conseillante.

Vieux Château Certan   Now–1998   14.5

Medium-full colour, mature. The structure shows a little on the nose. Good attack but tails off a bit on the finish. Lacks a bit of grip and interest. Good but not great.

GRAVES

Domaine de Chevalier   Now–1996   15.0

Medium to medium-full colour. This is looser than the Pessac wines, for instance; it also doesn't

have the depth and richness. Medium body. This
is pleasant but curiously one-dimensional. Very
stylish but a little short.

Haut-Bailly   Drink soon   14.0
Medium colour, fully mature. A little attenuated
on the nose. A bit astringent on the palate.
Medium body. Lacks a bit of class and freshness.

Haut-Brion   Now–1998   16.5
Medium-full colour, a whiff of bonfires on the
nose but a slight absence of real concentration.
This is fully ready. Medium-full. Rich, oaky and
stylish but lacks real concentration and depth – if
judged by *premier cru* standards.

La Mission-Haut-Brion 1995–2005   17.5
Full colour, not much sign of maturity. Fine, rich,
concentrated nose but with an herbal element.
Very typically La Mission. Full, firm and tannic on
the palate. A structured wine. Fine but not great.
It will always lack a little flesh. There is plenty of
richness and concentration, especially on the finish. The tannin will always obtrude.

La Tour-Haut-Brion   Now–2003   15.0
Full colour, not much sign of maturity. Firm nose
a little vegetal and tannic. A little hard and austere.
Fullish and tannic on the palate, but quite rich underneath. Like the La Mission but more so, this is
a bit too structured. Certainly good.

MARGAUX AND HAUT-MÉDOC

Brane-Cantenac   Drink soon   10.0
Medium colour, fully mature. Horrid, dry, attenuated nose. Faded, astringent. Flavours of old
dog-ends. Very poor.

Cantemerle   Now–1996   12.0
Good colour. Little sign of maturity. Hard, austere, somewhat unripe fruit on the nose. No
charm. Medium to medium-full. Rather astringent. No enjoyment.

Cantenac-Brown   Now–1996   12.0
Medium colour, now mature. Lacks concentra-
tion, lacks breed, but not too dry on the nose.
Earthy and vegetal, but not as faded as Brane.
Medium bodied. No richness, no breed.

Chasse-Spleen   Now–2000   14.0
Good colour, fully mature. An earthy nose. No
real breed but has reasonable fruit. Sturdy, tannic.
A little top-heavy but has an element of good old-
vine fruit underneath. And has good grip. Better
than most if no real breed.

Giscours   Now–1998   13.5
Good colour, little sign of maturity. Quite ripe
nose. Some new oak. A sturdy if not slightly
stewed, medium to medium-full wine. There is
richness here but an absence of class and grace.
Yet not too short. Uninspiring though.

La Lagune   Now–2005   16.0
Good colour, just about mature. This is fresh and
has good oak, but has not exactly the breed and
concentration one might have expected. Very
stylish though. Medium-full. This is better than
most but not exactly exciting. There is a lack of
real concentration and depth.

Lascombes   Now–2003   15.0
Medium-full, mature colour. Slightly edgy and
artificially fruity on the nose. Medium-full. A little dry and tannic but there is richness underneath.
Quite fat and concentrated on the finish. Good.

Margaux   Now–1996   14.0
Fullish colour, a little brown. Dumb, heavy-laden
nose. On the palate a curate's egg of a wine. Soft,
slightly sweet and a bit attenuated on the one
hand. Robust, astringent and lumpy on the other.
Yet despite this there is a certain elegance.

Palmer   Now–2002   15.0
Good colour, just about mature. This is fresh and
has good oak, but has not exactly the breed and
concentration one might have expected. Stylish
though. Medium-full. This is better than most but
not exactly exciting. There is a lack of real concentration and depth.

Poujeaux   Drink soon   12.5
Good colour, little sign of maturity. Quite fat, but
an open, ripe nose without much zip or dimension. On the palate lacks fruit and zip. Nothing
much to get excited about here. Short. Lacks class.

Prieuré-Lichine   Drink soon   13.5
Good, mature colour. Soft, aromatic, slightly attenuated nose. Not too dry but lacks a little zip.
Medium to medium-full. Some fruit but has the
dryness of the vintage. Not bad at best.

SAINT-JULIEN

Beychevelle   Now–1999   14.0
Fullish, mature colour. Not too dry on the nose,
but not a lot of concentration either. Medium-full
colour. Lumpy, unstylish, a bit bitter and attenuated on the finish. Finishes a bit astringent.

Ducru-Beaucaillou   Now–2009   17.0
Fullish colour, barely mature. Closed nose, but
good concentration here. This is not as good as
Las-Cases but still very good indeed. Fullish, still
young. A typical 1975, with richness, concentration and breed under the structure. Long.

Gloria   Now–1997   15.0
Good full colour, now mature. Ripe nose.
Medium-full, just a bit of tannin. This is an ample,
fleshy wine with better balance and more charm
than most of the Margaux. Shows well.

Gruaud-Larose   Now–2004   15.0
Medium-full colour, barely mature. Similar nose
to Talbot but richer and oakier. This is still youth-

ful, but too tannic and astringent. Full but not concentrated. Reasonable grip but too solid.

Langoa-Barton   Now–1997   15.0

Medium colour, now mature. This is less tough than the Barton and because it is more supple and accessible I find it very nearly as good. Cabernet, oak, lead-pencil flavour. Medium body. No great depth but stylish and pleasant.

Léoville-Barton   Now–1999   15.5

Fullish colour, just about mature. Very Cabernet. Somewhat inflexible. Medium to medium-full. Strangely one-dimensional. Lacks concentration, lacks interest. A bit four-square. Not as lumpy as Gruaud though.

Léoville-Las-Cases   Now–2014   19.0

Full colour, still immature. Fresh nose. Still youthful. Very Cabernet. Good new wood. This is one of the few wines to have real breed. Full, good oak. Concentrated and balanced. Not too austere. I prefer this to the La Mission. Very well balanced. Complex finish. Very fine.

Léoville-Poyferré   Now–1996   15.5

Fullish colour, mature. A better nose than I expected. This is pleasant. Ripe, good grip. No undue tannin, or rusticity. Quite evolved, showing a little astringency on the palate. Yet reasonably fresh on the finish. Medium body.

Saint-Pierre   Now–2010   17.5

Full colour. Little sign of maturity. Full, rich, closed nose. Old-fashioned, but in the best sense. Rich and fat and old viney. Full but with a lot of depth. There is more to it than the Ducru.

Talbot   Now–2000   15.5

Medium-full colour, barely mature. Firm, full but somewhat four-square on the nose. Tannic on the palate. Fullish. Lacks a bit of personality and dimension. Dull.

PAUILLAC

Clerc-Milon   Now–2000   15.0

Fullish, mature colour. Solid nose, but not too dry. A bit four-square perhaps. Old-fashioned. Fullish, chunky, some tannin. But has good acidity. Lacks a bit of concentration and class but finishes positively. Just about ready.

Les Forts de Latour   Now–2000   16.5

Fullish colour, just about mature. Good style and an element of new oak on the nose. This is well made, but doesn't quite have the zip. Yet not too dry or austere and certainly classy.

Grand-Puy-Lacoste   Now–1996   15.0

Fullish, mature colour. There are faint elements of attenuation. Medium to medium-full. Reasonable attack but a bit astringent on the finish. Good fruit but lacks a bit of concentration and grip. Slightly disappointing.

Lafite   Now–2005   18.0

Medium-full, mature colour. Soft, gentle new oak. Stylish. Not a bit dry. This has class. Medium body. Lovely fruit. Good oaky undertones. Misses a bit of real concentration and intensity but lovely style. Very long and complex. Atypical for a 1975.

Latour   Now–2015   19.5

Full colour, barely mature. Class here, breed, concentration and oak on the nose. Surprisingly intense. Full, rich, concentrated, good backbone. Real breed. Not a bit dry or unduly tannic. Very long. Very fine.

Lynch-Bages   Now–2000   17.0

Fullish, mature colour. Slightly resinny on the nose. Medium-full. This has richness, fatness and a good element of old-vine concentration. Very seductive. Good grip. Stylish. Very good indeed.

Mouton-Rothschild   Now–2000   16.5

Full, mature colour. Ripe, aromatic but not the cedary class of Mouton. Medium-full. Quite rich and balanced. But it misses the usual concentration and breed. For a Mouton this is disappointing.

Pichon-Longueville, Comtesse de Lalande   Now–2010   18.0

Fullish, mature colour. Rich on the nose and quite concentrated, but not as classy as the Las-Cases. Good grip. Full, concentrated, old viney. Rich. This is new oaky. Has good tannin and finishes long. Fine.

Pichon-Longueville-Baron   Now–1997   13.0

Fullish, mature colour. A little rustic on the nose but not too dry. Rather hard on the palate. Lacks concentration, lacks zip. Medium body. A bit lumpy. Finishes astringent.

SAINT-ESTÈPHE

Calon-Ségur   Drink soon   14.5

Medium-full colour, mature. Earthy nose. Not unpleasant, not too dry. But doesn't seem to have that much class. Medium body. Reasonable fruit and balance. Not rustic but doesn't have much depth. Fully evolved and getting a little astringent on the finish.

Cos d'Estournel   Drink soon   14.0

Medium-full colour, mature. Rather a weedy nose. Lacks zip and concentration. On the palate there is ripeness and some style but a lack of grip. It finishes attenuated. Unexciting.

Montrose   Now–2000   15.0

Medium-full colour, mature. Somewhat austere and charmless on the nose. Typically full, muscular and tannic. There is reasonable grip and richness underneath, so the finish is not astringent. But not really much class or generosity.

1971 CLARET

Nineteen seventy-one was a controversial vintage. For a start, it was very expensive; prices were more than double those of the 1970s. Secondly, there was a dispute over its quality. While there were no doubts that it was a successful vintage, some went as far as to cite it above the 1970. Others were less convinced, though conceding that the Saint-Emilions and Pomerols could be awarded parity with their predecessor. Over time, the majority view has shifted from the confident to the sceptic, while the credit of the 1971 vintage has diminished. It was proved to be a vintage of irregular quality, with several wines which have failed to live up to their early promise, and others which are disappointing. This is reflected in the prices the 1971s now fetch at auction. Even the best of the second-growth Médocs – Ducru-Beaucaillou, for example – fetch hardly half that of the 1970. The sole exceptions are those few Pomerols, such as Pétrus and Trotanoy, whose 1971 reputations have achieved superstar status.

THE WEATHER

In 1971 the vines were generally in bud by 16 April, following a fine warm spell in March and early April. The flowering followed in very early June, but the fruit set badly owing to cold rainy weather during the month (at least there were no late frosts, a constant fear in April and May). Suddenly, from July the weather changed to magnificent sunny days, which continued almost to the end of August, with a heatwave between 8 and 17 July. There were some violent storms in the last week of August, followed by another spell of warm sunshine. Then the rain came between 19 and 21 September and the fine spell was broken. As a result the *vendange* began about a week later than forecast. M Jean Lawton, the respected wine-broker, whose family keep a journal of weather conditions, recorded on 7 October that the weather was marvellous; the picking was nearly over and had taken place under ideal conditions.

Those who delayed the picking probably made the best wine, but the losses in June through *coulure* materially affected the crop, especially of the Merlot. The final output was about 40 per cent less than the record-breaking crop of 1970, but only about 10 per cent below the average for the past ten years. It was the areas of Saint-Emilion and Pomerol that bore the brunt of the loss.

This table shows comparative weather conditions between the two years 1970 and 1971:

	June	July	August	September	October
1970	Excellent	Very good	Below average	Superb	Exceptionally good
1971	Very poor	Very good	Below average	Mediocre	Exceptionally good

PRICES

However, when the first *tranche* prices began to appear in the new year, the trade was in for a shock. While the 1970 classed growths, except for the *premiers crus*, had opened at 7,000 to 12,000 francs per *tonneau* (roughly £15 to £18 per dozen in England), the 1971s were twice if not three times as much. Giscours opened in February at 18,000 francs (1970: 6,800 francs), Montrose and Léoville-Las-Cases were 20,000, Brane-Cantenac was 22,000. Second *tranche* prices, and the opening prices of properties later to declare, were even higher. Léoville-Las-Cases' second *tranche* was 30,000 francs, Léoville-Barton opened at 36,000 francs, Figeac was 40,000, Pape-Clément 42,000, Vieux Château Certan 48,000 – all prices hitherto reserved for the first growths.

The first growths, of course, were higher still, though not by so much in relation to the 1970 price. Haut-Brion offered its first *tranche* at 75,000 francs, its second at 110,000 francs; Lafite asked 110,000 and 130,000. Their 1970s had opened at 44,000 and 59,000 respectively.

Some shippers, dazed by these increases, felt they should take a stand against them. Others felt that the price break-through the previous year, when wines not yet in bottle had exchanged hands at ever-escalating levels – leaving the growers angry and feeling foolish that they had sold the wines so cheaply in the first place – justified the 1971 prices. It was, after all, not only a successful vintage, but a short one.

THE MARKET

It was thought that the wines would sell slowly but surely, but in fact sales were extremely good. The high prices encouraged fears of further escalation, and many shippers were short of stock. The Bordeaux trade felt itself compelled to buy, and to buy widely. In retrospect, this was a catastrophic mistake, compounded by some shippers when they continued their buying into the 1972 campaign – a vastly inferior vintage but at the same extravagant prices.

While the Bordeaux trade bought, the foreign merchants were cautious. There was little buying by the UK trade, and the USA and the Benelux countries, traditionally good purchasers of claret, were not enthusiastic. Lafite at 110,000 a *tonneau* for 1971, after 59,000 for 1970, may not have seemed excessive in Bordeaux, but translated into sterling, before it floated, it became £2,090 a hogshead, or £12 a bottle duty paid in London! To put this into context, the 1990 ex-cellars price in francs, twenty years on, was no more than twice this figure.

However, several shippers were on an economic treadmill. They had committed themselves to long-term buying contracts with the growers and at guaranteed prices. When supply was not matched by demand, as was the case from the end of 1973, a serious economic crisis developed and its effects were still to be felt five years later.

THE WINES

The first impression of the 1971 vintage was extremely favourable; the colour was good, the acidity normal, and the grapes healthy, though uneven in ripeness. In the early months of the new year, when the wines were first put on the market, they appeared to have less charm than the 1970s, but had backbone; though the fruit was less intense, the wines showed a concentration and a depth that promised well. Above all, the wines had discretion and elegance.

A number of experienced merchants and brokers as well as château proprietors expected the 1971 to be the better vintage, and the better wines to take longer to mature than the 1970s, though it was accepted that owing to the failure of the Merlot and the uneven ripeness, the quality might be variable.

It is certainly true to say that the vintage is a great deal more uneven than the 1970. Some of the wines, especially from Saint-Emilion and Pomerol, are quite splendid; more, sadly, are disappointing. One is inclined to wonder if some growers, seduced by the short crop, high prices and unprecedented demand, might not have been quite as ruthless as they should have been in excluding from the final blend vats made from young vines or parts of the vineyard badly hit by the weather.

Certainly, too, the original depth of colour was not, as it so often is, a guide to quality. Many wines were really quite brown at the edge after a decade, especially when compared with the 1970s.

The best wines are to be found in Saint-Emilion and Pomerol. Tasting notes follow on most of the leading wines. What is impressive is that even after twenty years there is a surprising amount of vigour in these Libournais, especially now that all but the best Graves and Médocs have dried up. As well as those detailed below, L'Eglise-Clinet, Petit-Village, Latour-à-Pomerol and La Gaffelière are very good. Larmande is also impressive. Lafleur is a bit solid, Clos-Fourtet is not bad, but Figeac has never inspired me. Ausone, though faded, has class, and can be rated at least 'good'.

One might have expected, however, a better result from the Médoc and Graves, traditionally high in Cabernet in their *encépagement*, and therefore less affected by the poor flowering of the Merlot grapes. Equally, as the weather did not really improve until well into September, one might have assumed that the Médoc, always later to harvest than Saint-Emilion, would have produced the better wine, because the grapes are riper.

In fact the Médocs and Graves are inconsistent. Too often there is a lack of ripeness, generosity and warmth in the wines. As they have evolved they have become first skeletal and then astringent. Only a few have the flesh and the fat.

In the Graves there were good results at Domaine de Chevalier, La Mission and at Haut-Brion itself, as one might expect, but also at Pape-Clément, the last vintage here where the wine was as good as it should be until 1984. The remaining *crus classés*, apart from La Tour-Haut-Brion, are uninspiring. All except La Mission now show age. The Margaux wines, as always, were patchy. Palmer is good, though it has never really sung to me (and after all it is normally very good). Prieuré-Lichine, Malescot, Lascombes and Issan can also be considered successes. La Lagune is very competent indeed, perhaps the best wine of the southern Médoc. Apart from this, there isn't really anything to get excited about. Almost all now need finishing up.

Further north there is a little more to applaud. In Saint-Julien, Ducru-Beaucaillou is very good indeed, and still has life. Beychevelle and Gruaud-Larose, Léoville-Barton, Léoville-Las-Cases, Langoa, Gloria and Branaire can all be commended to a lesser degree, but now need drinking.

The Pauillacs and Saint-Estèphes are also showing age, and few were ever really exciting. None of the three first growths are special. Indeed the best wine in the commune is perhaps the Pichon-Longueville, Comtesse de Lalande, and even that is not *that* brilliant. Grand-Puy-Lacoste is quite good; Lynch-Bages a bit rustic; Batailley thin and dried out. Cos is loose and Montrose lacks generosity. All in all, the 1970s are far superior. And all but a handful of the 1971s are at the end of their useful lives.

THE TASTING

The following wines were sampled in London in April and May 1990.

	Optimum Drinking	Mark out of 20

SAINT-EMILION

Canon — Drink soon — 16.5

Medium to medium-full colour. Mature. Fine, graceful, vigorous, complex nose. Fullish on the palate. Some of the Canon chunkiness but rich and concentrated. Balanced and positive to the end. Ripe, a touch of coffee and chocolate. Plenty of life still. Very good plus.

Cheval-Blanc — Now–1998 — 17.5

Medium-full colour. Rich, aromatic, full, plump and concentrated. But the nose is not as exciting as the Mouton-Rothschild — nor is there as much new wood. On the palate medium-full, evolved and spicy — I would have expected a bit more vigour. Ripe and fruity but an absence of real excitement. A little disappointing. Finishes a little flat. Only fine.

Clos-des-Jacobins — Drink up — 13.0

Medium-full colour. Fullish, earthy, ripe and quite robust nose. But beginning to dry up. On

the palate the fruit has begun to dry up a bit. Quite a chunky wine but now soft. Always a little artisanal but not bad.

Magdelaine — Drink soon — 15.0

Medium colour, now fully mature. Minty nose, the fruit now a bit lightweight. A medium-bodied, quite stylish wine which now needs drinking soon. Good acidity. Some richness, but lacks the fat and generosity of the best Pomerols.

Pavie — Drink soon — 15.0

A touch more colour, a shade more vigour. Ripe, soft nose, though not an enormous amount of richness. Stylish though. Medium to medium-full body. There is still interest here. More positive on the palate than on the nose. Ripe and ample still. Good but not great.

Clos-Saint-Martin — Drink up — 14.0

Medium colour. This shows a little age on the nose. The fruit and the elegance have diminished. Originally quite a stylish wine, and still enjoyable, though a little astringency is beginning to show.

More attractive on the palate than the nose. Medium-full. Reasonable finish. Quite good.

POMEROL

La Conseillante   Drink soon   17.5
Good mature colour. Neither as full or as vigorous as the Vieux Certan but a round, ripe, silky wine with plenty of fruit and class. Medium body, mulberry fruit with a hint of sandalwood. Seductive, long and complex on the finish. Fine.

Le Gay   Drink soon   15.0
Fullish colour. Firm, long, macerated, rich nose, with a certain austerity. Still youthful. Very much an austere black-fruit flavour. Fullish, solid, even a little stewed. Yet quite good depth here in its rather dense sort of way. Again the fruit is beginning to dry out a little. Good though.

Lafleur-Pétrus   Drink soon   15.5
Medium-full, mature, vigorous colour. Round, soft, quite sweet, plummy nose. Less vigorous than the Canon but equally elegant and complex. Medium to medium-full body. This is now gently approaching the end of its useful life. It lacks a bit of power at the end. But fragrant and attractive. Good to very good.

Nénin   Now–1996   15.5
Full colour. Quite a full, firm nose. Riper than the Le Gay but a little four-square. Similarly, a chunky wine with a spicy, liquorice touch. Good grip though. This is a bit dense as well but is richer and more generous on the finish. Will still last. Good to very good.

Pétrus   Now–2000 plus   19.0
Full mature colour but showing no sign of age. Ripe, full, vigorous, subtle nose. A lot of quality here. Medium-full, complex. Good grip. Slight chocolate element to the flavour. A reserved wine with a lot of interest, though a slight lack of opulence. Long on the finish. Very fine but not mind-blowing. Still young.

Sales   Drink soon   13.0
Medium-full colour. Quite a plump nose, still fresh if not *that* stylish. A pleasant, ripe, aromatic, quite sweet wine which is holding up well. Good balance but lacks a bit of breed. Seems fuller than the De Sales of more recent vintages. Not bad.

Trotanoy   Now–2000 plus   18.5
Full colour. Splendid nose. Really lovely, ripe, rich, concentrated fruit. Fresh, balanced. Full of character and with a great deal of class. Full, rich, concentrated, quite tannic. Good residual new oak. This has a splendid old-vine, essence of fruit flavour. Great even. Very long, complex finish and still a lot of vigour.

Vieux Château Certan Drink soon   17.5
Good full, mature colour; no undue age.

Interesting nose, with smells of bonfires and aromatic woods. Medium-full, complex, elegant, meaty and vigorous. This has a lot of depth, even concentration still. Chocolate and cigar-boxes. Very stylish. Very long. Fine.

GRAVES

Haut-Brion   Drink soon   18.0
Surprisingly good colour; almost as full as the above. On most occasions when I have tasted this against the La Mission I have preferred the Haut-Brion. It is fatter, spicier, richer and classier. This is still fullish and vigorous, round and aromatic. Long complex finish. Very fine.

La Mission-Haut-Brion Now–1996   17.5
Very good colour. Unmistakably La Mission: the usual rich, quite solid, leafy Cabernet on the nose. Plenty of body and vigour here. Not the class of the Haut-Brion, but has weight, concentration and fruit. But it misses just a bit of lushness. Fine though.

MARGAUX AND HAUT-MÉDOC

La Lagune   Drink soon   17.0
My notes on La Lagune 1971 are consistently high. This has a good vigorous colour, plenty of fruit on the nose, and an ample, generous, full, balanced character with a stylish oaky background. Generous, vigorous and complex. High class.

Margaux   Past its best   12.0
Medium colour, somewhat old looking. There are vestiges of breed and interest, but the wine is now past its best. Light in body, somewhat astringent all the way through, especially on the finish. I don't remember this as ever being very special.

Palmer   Drink soon   15.5
Medium-full colour, fully mature. An elegant wine, in a somewhat austere way. There is a certain Cabernet Franc mintiness on the nose. Medium-full body. Fragrant and mellow, a little dryness, a little lacking generosity. Classy and good to very good quality.

Prieuré-Lichine   Drink soon   15.0
Good colour, not too evolved. Soft, supple nose. This is still aromatic though it now needs drinking. Quite rich, quite classy. Quite full. A good example of the vintage.

SAINT-JULIEN

Gruaud-Larose   Drink soon   14.5
Good colour, a bit dense. Somewhat four-square on the nose but there is some richness underneath. A fullish wine but one which lacks a bit of generosity and excitement. Good grip though. But a bit too chunky. Doesn't have much class.

Léoville–Barton   Drink soon   15.0

This was not as good as a bottle sampled at Langoa
a month previously. Medium-full, mature colour.
A bit dry on the nose and though better on the
palate it was essentially a bit short of charm. Very
Cabernet. And certainly not without class. Only
'good' on this occasion.

Léoville–Las-Cases   Drink soon   15.5

This was one of the better 1971s originally but
doesn't seem to be holding up as well as the
Ducru. Fuller, plumper and more vigorous than
the above, especially on the attack, but the finish
was less positive.

PAUILLAC

Grand-Puy-Lacoste   Drink soon   14.5

Medium-full colour, some age now. A ripe, quite
stylish nose, but it shows signs of lightening up.
Medium body. This is quite a plump, stylish wine,
with some residual richness, but it is beginning to
lose its vigour.

Lafite   Past its best   13.0

This was always the least good of the three first
growths of the commune, and it shows quite a lot
of age. What it lacks is an element of concentration, and even of the breed we associate with
Lafite. An absence of selection in fact. Medium
body. Rather astringent.

Latour   Now–1996   16.0

Like some other 1971s the expression of the tannin and Cabernet comes across in a leafy, almost
minty way. Quite full but rather austere. There is
a lack of sex appeal compared with the Pichon-
Lalande. It has more vigour but it is less attractive.

Lynch-Bages   Drink soon   14.0

A wine at a similar stage of development to the
Grand-Puy-Lacoste, but with less class. Also lightening up, and there is a definite astringency on the
finish. It didn't fade too much in the glass though.
The fruit is still here, if only just. And there is still
some enjoyment to be had.

Mouton-Rothschild   Now–1996   16.0

Full, mature colour. This has a fine nose. Full, rich
and opulent, with a touch of the Mouton lead-
pencils but combined with the austerity of the
vintage. Good quality and depth here. On the
palate not quite so opulent or flamboyant. Rich
but not sweet. Yet plenty of depth and concentration. Fullish. Very good but not great. Still vigorous and long on the finish. But doesn't really excite now.

Pichon-Longueville, Comtesse de Lalande
                  Drink soon   16.5

Like the Las-Cases, this was rather better a decade
ago. The class is still there, the fruit though faded,
still ripe. The wine is soft and seductive and still
quite long on the palate. And at least there is no
astringency. Can still be rated very good indeed.

SAINT-ESTÈPHE

Cos d'Estournel   Drink soon   14.5

Medium-full, mature colour. This is another reasonable but by no means exciting wine. There is
some spicy elegance on the nose but the wine is
losing its grip, and on the palate the fruit has
begun to dry out. The finish is rather pinched.

Montrose   Drink soon   14.0

Slightly more colour. Somewhat rigid on the
nose, without as much charm as the Cos, the fruit
a bit drier. A little more flesh on the palate but also
some astringency. Rather austere. Was rather better from a double magnum in March 1988.

1970 CLARET

I have a very personal interest in the 1970 vintage. It was not only the first vintage I bought as a major professional wine-buyer, it was also the subject of the first article I wrote for *Decanter*. It think it appeared in their third issue in the autumn of 1975.

The first comprehensive tasting of the 1970 vintage I made after the wines were in bottle was in early 1975. I have repeated this at roughly three-yearly intervals ever since. Two things have always struck me. One was that for the first fifteen years of its development the vintage seemed to be more backward as time went on; that is, that one kept putting off further and further into the future the date that the best wines would be at their peak: always a sign of a good vintage. Second, that the wines have always had a sunny disposition. The 1970s have never gone through an awkward adolescent phase like the 1966s and other more recent vintages are doing at the moment; they have always been accessible, generous and welcoming. They also seemed to get better and better. Unlike such as vintages 1971 and 1976, the 1970s developed better than originally predicted.

THE WEATHER

After a late spring, which was probably fortuitous since it lessened the risks of frost, the weather throughout the summer of 1970 and long into the autumn was perfect. From the end of May until the end of July it was warm and sunny. August was indifferent but September was superb with just enough rain in the early part of the month to swell the grapes sufficiently. From then on, throughout the harvest which began late in the month and continued well into October, there was another spell of fine weather. The grapes were gathered in ideal conditions, the berries were large and healthy without a hint of rot anywhere and the crop was large, by far the biggest since the war. The amount of red wine produced was a third as much again as the previous record: 1967.

THE WINE

If the key to the success of vintages in general is the weather, the key to the successful 1970 vintage can be summed up in two words: balance and consistency. The 1970s are beautifully balanced; they have a lot of fruit and they have great style. They are firm – which means that the best will still keep well if properly stored – without being hard. In 1970, the Merlot grape was particularly successful and this has led to a gentle balance of tannin and fruit. In some years when the Merlot fails the resultant wine can be an excess of tannin. These wines can be very hard and austere and will become more and more astringent as they age.

The sheer size of the vintage, coupled with the absence of excessive hardness and tannin, led some to have their doubts about the staying power of the 1970s. Indeed, when they were first sampled in the spring of 1971, they seemed almost too good to be true. They were so agreeable some thought they were too *flatteurs* and would not last. These cynics were quick to point out the size of the harvest (quality being normally inversely proportional to quantity). I have never had such fears. A wine need not have a great deal of tannin and body to keep well; what is required, however, is balance. The 1970s have this in abundance and they have great charm. True, they never had the enormous depth and staying power of the 1961s or 1945s. In character, they most resemble the 1953s – but look how well they turned out! In their consistency they are like the 1961s. From the humblest growth in the Côtes de Bourg or the Premières Côtes, to the roll-call of classed growths in the Médoc, there are few disappointing wines. Those which, now, do not show as well as their peers, have suffered more probably from bad handling and bottling than through any intrinsic fault in the wines themselves.

When I first sampled the wines, I considered that the lesser-classed growths, the good *bourgeois* wines and most Saint-Emilions and Pomerols, would be ready towards the end of the 1970s and that the more substantial Médoc *crus classés* would follow in the early 1980s. As I have said, I have revised my view, postponed my 'optimum drinking' time-spans. Whilst, in 1975, I wrote that all but a few of the really top wines would be ready by 1980, I found in 1985 that there were *still* a few wines which were not yet ready for drinking and many more which, whilst they could be drunk and enjoyed, would still improve.

PRICES

The 1970s are associated with the explosion in wine prices which occurred a few years ago but, although this is certainly valid, it was in 1969 that the absurd increases at source really began. Château Mouton-Rothschild, which had offered its 1966 and 1967 at opening prices at 27,000 francs a *tonneau* (about 27 francs a bottle and about £21 a case at the then rate of exchange), asked 75,000 francs for the 1969. Lafite was not far behind and where these illustrious names led, the rest soon followed. In 1971, Mouton initially even dropped its 1970 price from the 1969 level in an endeavour to keep prices reasonable but, as its great rival Lafite chose to ignore this initiative, reverted to 1969 prices for its second '*tranche*'.

In 1972 the 1971 Mouton price leapt to 120,000 francs, easily five times its 1966 price. Compared with these prices, the opening price of Mouton and Latour 1970, at 36,000 and 40,000 francs respectively, seem quite cheap. The opening prices of other wines – Château Gloria at 6,500 francs, Château Léoville-Las-Cases at 8,700 francs, Château Palmer at 12,000 francs – seem even cheaper.

THE MARKET

In view of these moderate price levels, the much-publicized excellence of the vintage, the poor showing of the two previous vintages and the greatly increased interest in wine in America, it is not surprising that the year 1971 opened with an enormous buying boom in Bordeaux. Several American concerns made some very heavy purchases, closely followed by the wine ends of the British brewery groups. Despite the huge crop, demand was unprecedentedly heavy. Prices began to rise and speculators began to arrive, buyers whose intention was profit, not consumption.

As summer succeeded spring, the hysteria snowballed. Whilst parcels of wine exchanged hands at ever-increasing prices, the châteaux who had announced their second *tranche* prices early watched ruefully as their tardy neighbours got more only a few weeks later and stocks of first-*tranche* wine fetched three or four times their original price. It was this that determined them to fix their prices so high for their 1971s and 1972s.

It was no more comfortable from the buyer's point of view. With prices mounting daily, it was almost impossible to make a cool evaluation of the merits of a number of wines. At the higher levels, the relative qualities of equivalently classed wines were ignored by speculators buying solely on name and this led to a further distortion in prices. Those who bought early were fortunate. Those who bought later or who had to return to the market to replace wine already sold were sucked into in this spiral.

On all sides, grower, *négociant* and buyer, greed overcame reason. While the market was rising, any fool could make a lot of money by buying a name today and selling later. Many firms – and there were a lot of new names which suddenly sprang up from nowhere – did make a lot of money whilst the market continued to rise.

The bubble finally burst and with such savagery that there was hardly a merchant in Britain or France who was not wounded and several who found themselves in acute financial difficulties because they had continued to pay high prices – and, moreover, for the indifferent vintage of 1972 – in anticipation of a further increase in demand which never materialized and were then forced by their accountants and bank managers to de-stock in a great rush.

As a result, there was a time in the mid-1970s when the 1970 and other vintages could be snapped up at little more than original cost despite the fact that they had several years' bottle age, as enormous quantities of classed growth were unloaded on to the market by firms who were forced to release capital or by others frightened that the market would collapse further. This buyer's market lasted until 1977/78. The 1970s, together with the 1966s, became a good currency to acquire because, of all the wine heaped on to the market-place, these were the best vintages obtainable at the lowest prices, being available in the largest quantities.

THE 1970S TODAY

Now well into their third decade, the majority of the 1970s are still holding up well and will last until the end of the 1990s. At the very top level – first growths such as Latour, Mouton-Rothschild and Château Palmer – it can be argued that the 1966s are better. But slightly lower down the scale, particularly in Saint-Emilion and Pomerol, the 1970s are to be preferred.

THE TASTING

Bob Paul, a generous Miami lawyer, hosted the following tasting of 75 1970s in Coral Gables, Florida, in February 1993. I am happy to be able to thank him publicly for sending me an invitation to attend. The vast majority of the wines came from his cellar. This was an impressively comprehensive line-up, and for the most part the wines confirmed my earlier experiences of them. To comment on a few which were not there: Lafleur, Latour-à-Pomerol and Lafleur-Pétrus are very fine, fine and very good respectively; and L'Evangile is also very good. The wine of the vintage is indisputably Château Latour. Many of the wines were served from magnum. Otherwise there were two bottles of each wine circulating. Disconcertingly, given that the bottles were from the same case, and had been lying in Paul's cellar for many, many years, there were more than a few examples of bottle variation. I have commented on both bottles where appropriate.

	Optimum Drinking	Mark out of 20

SAINT-EMILION

L'Arrosée Now–1998 15.5

Good colour. Still vigorous. Fullish. Old viney. A bit old-fashioned. But rich and full and mellow and Merlot-y. Not a wine of real class but there is depth. And fat. Spicy. Still has life. Good plus.

Ausone Drink soon 15.0

Medium to medium-full colour. More evolved than the Belair. Somewhat aged nose, but quite classy. A little more structure and a little more acidity than the Belair but more evolved. Bottled a bit late? Has lost its fruit. Sweeter but older. Getting a little short. Lacks zip.

Beauséjour-Duffau-Lagarrosse
  Drink soon 14.0

Medium to medium-full colour. Fully mature. Slightly hard and vegetal on the nose. A bit austere. Medium-full. A little tannin and a little brutal and solid. The acidity shows. It lacks charm. Quite good. But it will dry out now.

Belair Drink soon 15.0

Medium to medium-full colour. No undue age. Ripe Merlot nose. Lacks a little zip. Medium body. This is beginning to lose its definition and grip. Plump. Round. Quite ample. But getting a little one-dimensional, though not short or astringent yet. Good but not great.

Canon Now–1997 16.0

Medium-full colour. Still plenty of life left. A bit shitty on the nose. Black cherries later. Full, chunky, a little tannin. Good grip and plenty of vigour. Somewhat old-fashioned. Sweet and spicy. Good grip. Very good.

Cheval-Blanc Now–2000 17.5

Fullish vigorous colour. Ripe, ample, rich and oaky on the nose. Fullish, rich and complete. This has much more vigour than the rest of the Saint-Emilion flight. Spicy and plenty of depth and concentration. Long. Fine. Plenty of life still.

Clos-Fourtet Drink soon 14.0

Good colour. Still quite vigorous. Fat, rich and old viney, in a solid sort of way on the nose. On the palate this has lost its sweetness, and dried up a little. But you can see the quality underneath. Cedary. Still finishes reasonably. Quite good. But the fruit is losing sweetness.

La Clusière Drink up 12.0

(Magnum) Medium colour. No undue age. A little thin on the nose and on the palate. Quite fresh but never any real class or depth. Getting a little coarse and mean at the end.

Figeac   **Drink soon**   **15.5**
Medium-full colour. Well matured. This is fading a bit on the nose. One bottle a little better than the other but not a lot of difference. This is a little over the top. Medium to medium-full. Round. Sweet. But loosening up. Only good plus.

Haut-Sarpe   **Drink up**   **12.0**
Medium to medium-full colour. Reasonable vigour. Getting a bit old and dry and shitty on the nose. Chunky but rather astringent on the palate. Quite structured but now past its best. Drying out. Showing its acidity.

Magdelaine   **Now–1996**   **16.5**
Good colour. No undue maturity. Ripe nose. Quite concentrated. Good oaky background. Stylish. This has concentration and depth. Medium to medium-full. *A point.* But not for much longer. Quite rich. Complex. Good breed, good balance and length. Very good plus.

Matras   **Drink soon**   **12.5**
First bottle a bit maderized. Second bottle fresher. Fullish mature colour. A little astringency on the palate. A touch crude, but still fruity, though now needs drinking. The acidity is beginning to show.

Pavie   **Now–1996**   **16.5**
Medium to medium-full colour. Reasonable vigour. Gamey and spicy on the nose, with a hint of astringency. On the palate this is still holding up. Sweet. Medium-full. Ripe and balanced. Long on the palate. Very good plus but not quite as elegant and complete as the Magdelaine.

Simard   **Now–1996**   **13.5**
Medium-full colour. Ripe fleshy nose if without much class. Fresh and vigorous though. On the palate medium body. Soft, round and fruity. A little artisanal but balanced and positive at the end. Not bad plus. Will still hold for a few years.

POMEROL

Clinet   **Now–1997**   **14.5**
Full colour but a little brown at the rim. Burnt caramel on the nose. Fullish, meaty, tannic. But good fruit and grip, even richness on the attack. The finish is a bit more herbaceous and slightly solid. But there is merit here.

La Conseillante   **Now–1999**   **17.0**
Good colour. One bottle a bit denser than the other. The best example was ample and classic. Very well balanced. Rich and full and concentrated. A bigger wine than La Conseillante produces today. Balance and class and very fine harmonious fruit, especially on the finish. Fine.

Le Gay   **Now–1997**   **16.5**
Good full colour. Slightly dense looking. Still

youthful. Well macerated, stalky porty nose. Quite sweet, rich and alcoholic. Old-fashioned, chunky, full and tannic. Plenty of wine here but a touch ungainly. A bit solid. Splendidly rich and sweet. Very good. Still has life. Better with food.

Gazin   **Drink soon**   **14.5**
Good full vigorous colour. Has lost a little of its fruit. Somewhat vegetal and hard. This is a bit sweet/sour and astringent. Medium to medium-full body. Chunky, a bit astringent. Better with food. Good acidity. But a bit artisanal.

La Grave-Trigant-de-Boisset
       Now–1999   **16.5**
Impressive full vigorous colour. Evolved Merlot nose. Old vines. Rich, fat, new oak on the palate. This is concentrated and ample and full of sweet fruit. Unexpectedly good. Still plenty of life. Slightly old-fashioned.

Lafleur-du-Roy   **Drink up**   **12.0**
Medium colour. Well matured colour. Well-matured nose. Sweet and ripe but without a lot of class and grip. Soft, medium body. Has lost a bit of its grip and vigour. It starts ripe but it tails off and gets a bit lean and coarse on the palate. Finishes a little unpleasantly.

Nénin   **Now–1995**   **14.0**
Good colour. Still vigorous. Just a little tanky/old wood/lack of proper aeration on the nose. A bit four-square. Medium-full. Slightly chunky. Some fruit. Reasonable acidity. But a bit coarse at the end. The other bottle rather richer and sweeter.

Pétrus   **Now–2000**   **19.5**
Fullish colour. Solid, spicy and chunky on the nose. Amazingly sweet, chocolaty, oaky and rich. Spicy in a gingerbread sense. Full, ample, fleshy. Seductive. This has plenty of vigour. It seems only just ready. Very long and complex. Streets ahead of the rest of the Pomerol flight. Excellent.

La Pointe   **Now–1998**   **15.5**
Good vigorous colour. Ample rich nose. Merlot but with good grip. Quite structured. More so than the vintages today. Old vines? Medium-full, rich and meaty. Some tannin here but the tannin is now mellow. This has good depth. Still has grip and vigour. Good plus. Finishes well.

Trotanoy   **Now–2000**   **18.0**
Medium-full colour. Still vigorous. Finely concentrated nose. (One bottle rather more alive than the other.) Sweet, full, ripe, excellent grip. Fine concentrated elegant fruit. This is rich and has very fine intensity and vigour. Fine plus. A delight to drink.

Vieux Château Certan   **Now–2000**   **17.5**
Medium-full colour. Still vigorous. Good rich nose. Ample, ripe cedary-sandalwoody. Rich and balanced on nose and palate. This is very well bal-

anced and concentrated. Old vines. Vigorous. Fresh. Long. Fine. Even better than La Conseillante. More vigorous. Marvellous fruit.

GRAVES

Bouscaut　　　　Drink soon　13.5

(Magnum) Good colour. Slightly rigid on the nose. A bit dry and chunky. Medium body. Still holding up well. Fresh. Not very classy or complex. But not bad. Just a bit dull. Quite fresh but drink soon.

Carbonnieux　　　　Drink up　14.0

Good colour. Ripe but beginning to lose its sweetness and generosity. Medium body. Cedary. Losing its grip but still has style. Quite good.

Domaine de Chevalier　Now–1998　18.5

One bottle rather more vigorous than the other. The better wine round, mellow, complex and classy on the nose. Medium-full. This is soft but concentrated and intense. Lots of flavour and complexity. Very long. Very lovely. Plenty of life.

Haut-Brion　　　　Now–1998　16.0

Medium-full colour. Quite a mature nose without real *premier cru* excitement. Medium-full, a touch lactic. I don't find this a great wine by any means. It lacks concentration and intensity.

Malartic-Lagraviére　Now–1998　14.5

Good colour. Full, rich, chunky nose. A touch of H2S but a little astringent. It has got a bit dry and rigid. But underneath the wine has interest. High acidity. Better with food. Fresh. Quite good plus. But lacks nuance and class. Good finish.

La Mission-Haut-Brion　Now–2000　18.0

(Magnum) Slightly less colour than the La Tour. Cleaner nose. Much better than the La Tour. Fullish, rich and concentrated. Plenty of depth and concentration. Lovely ripe blackberry finish. Long. Fine plus.

Pape-Clément　　　　Drink soon　14.0

Medium to medium-full colour. Fully mature. Well-matured nose. Not a lot of character. Medium body. Soft, Graves-earthiness. Reasonable balance but not a lot of nuance. Quite good.

La Tour-Haut-Brion　　Drink up

Good colour. Rich but slightly vegetal. Slightly high volatile acidity on the nose. Medium to medium-full. A little astringency. The volatile acidity apparent almost to point of disagreeability.

MARGAUX AND THE SOUTHERN MÉDOC

Brane-Cantenac　　　Drink soon　13.5

Medium to medium-full colour. Fully mature if not beginning to look old. Spicy and sweet and caramelly on the nose. Medium body. Lightening up. No astringency. Finish is a bit lean. Not bad.

Camensac　　　　Drink soon　12.5/14.0

Medium colour. Lightening up at the rim but not too brown. A little dry and rustic on the nose. Medium body. Rather hard. Even a bit forced. Acidity shows. A little earthy. Not much charm. Not much style. But holding up reasonably well. The second bottle was better: more fruit and charm.

Cantemerle　　　　Now–1996　15.5

Good mature colour. Soft mellow elegant nose. Still alive. Somewhat ethereal but not a bit weak. Nicely complex. Medium to medium-full. Stylish, balanced and with plenty of dimension. Holding up very well. Not quite as rich and sweet as the La Lagune but good plus.

Cantenac-Brown　　　Drink up　12.5

Medium-full mature colour. Somewhat tangy and dry on the nose, lacking charm and style. On the palate medium to medium-full body. A little fruity, but the wine is now drying out and losing what finesse it ever had – which wasn't ever very much.

Chasse-Spleen　　　Now–1996　13.5

Bottle variation here. The better bottle: good colour, still alive and fullish. Quite muscular on the nose. A little artisanal. But in the sense of four-square rather than rustic. Acidity shows. Fullish. A little lumpy, but there is a good fat rich spicy wine underneath.

Giscours　　　　Drink soon　15.0

(Magnum) Very good colour. Full, rich and still very youthful. Plummy nose, just a little dense. Fullish, spicy and chocolatey on the palate. This is now showing a little bitterness and astringency at the end but a good example. Though never one with a great deal of class.

Kirwan　　　　Drink soon　12.5

Medium colour. Fully evolved. Soft nose. Well-matured nose. Lacks a bit of style. Rather dry and barnyardy. Medium body. Now a bit over the top. Reasonable acidity but is losing its fruit and never had much style. But a bit more enjoyment here than in the Pouget.

La Lagune　　　　Now–2000　16.5

(Magnum) Good mature colour. Good nose, mellow, cedary, good spice and complexity. Plenty of depth and richness. Plenty of wine here. Medium-full body. Balanced and integrated and still has plenty of vigour. Good fruit. Positive, rich and long on the finish. Very good plus.

Margaux　　　　Drink soon　15.0

Medium to medium-full colour. Fully mature. A little dried out on the nose. Unfocussed for a *premier cru*. Medium-full body. A little astringent. Good acidity but the fruit lacks real concentration and finesse. Lacking charm and now beginning to dry out. Unexciting. A bit mean at the end.

Palmer Now–2000 18.5

Good fullish mature colour. Splendid nose. This has very lovely fruit, raspberries and violets. Real finesse, real depth, real intensity. Fullish, complete. Harmonious and multidimensional. This has excellent balance and real length and complexity. Beautiful fruit. Very lovely.

Pouget Drink soon 12.0

Medium-full colour still; barely mature. Rather dense and solid, with significant volatile acidity on the nose. Quite full. Quite high acidity. Rather ungenerous and hard. Will begin to get a bit astringent from now on. Never had any charm.

Rausan-Ségla Now–1996 15.5

Good colour. Medium-full, still reasonably fresh. Mellow, plummy nose. Has a velvetiness many of these Margaux never had. Medium to medium-full body. Oaky. Good fruit. Doesn't quite have the grip and concentration of a very good wine but it has elegance, charm and good fruit. Positive finish. Will still keep. Good plus.

Rauzan-Gassies Past its best 10.0

Medium-full colour. Fully mature. Very coarse and dried out on the nose. Vegetal. This is past what was never a very inspiring best. Dry and coarse and a bit acid on the palate. Medium body.

SAINT-JULIEN

Beychevelle Drink soon/Now–1998
14.5/16.0

Medium-full colour. No undue age. A little nondescript. Ripe and fullish. Just a little lumpy. Medium-full. Losing a little of its vigour. It is lightening up and beginning to dry out. The second bottle was better. Richer and more vigorous.

Branaire-Ducru Now–2000 16.5

(Magnum) Medium-full mature colour. Ample nose, fleshy and gamey if no real finesse. Medium-full. Good Saint-Julien second-division flavour and typicity. Has class and balance. Even complexity. Good length. Very good plus.

Ducru-Beaucaillou Now–2000 18.0

Very good colour. Plenty of life here. This is ravishing. Real class and complexity on the nose. Poised and sweet in the best sense. Medium-full. Complex, balanced. Real breed. Fine, long, long finish. Super.

Gruaud-Larose Now–2000 15.5

Good colour. Fullish ripe nose but with more depth than Talbot. Fullish body. Quite muscular. Tannin still evident. Fleshy. Quite rich, but again lacks a bit of roundness and class. Good plus.

Langoa-Barton Now–2000
(this example) 16.5

Good colour. A lovely soft fresh nose with a hint of red fruits as well as black. Good vigour.

Medium-full body. Lively, balanced. Classy. Unexpectedly alive and interesting, but direct from the château. Very good plus.

Lagrange Now–1998 15.0

(Magnum) Good colour. Still vigorous. Fresh Cabernet nose. Clean, surprisingly good, if a bit rigid. Fullish, some tannin. Good acidity. A little solid but there is fruit here and plenty of enjoyment. Better still with food. Good length.

Léoville-Barton Now–1998 16.0

Very good colour. Slightly more *tabac* on the nose than Langoa – but this is not from the château. Medium-full. Just a suggestion it is now beginning to loosen up. Ripe. Quite concentrated. Good finish. Good plus.

Léoville-Las-Cases Now–2000 17.0

(Magnum) Fullish colour. Again a touch of *tabac* on the nose. A full wine. Just a little chunky, especially compared with the velvetiness of the Ducru. Good balance. Very good indeed but not fine. It lacks a little real class. But plenty of vigour. I have had other bottles which were much more evolved.

Léoville-Poyferré Now–1997 14.5

Medium-full colour. A bit dry on the nose. A little astringent on the palate. Yet ripe and sweet, but getting a touch short. Quite good plus but a bit dull.

Talbot Now–2000 15.0

Medium-full mature colour. Fullish, ripe nose. Meaty if without a lot of nuance. Medium-full body. Good acidity. Good fruit. Still has vigour. Good, but lacks generosity and complexity.

PAUILLAC

Batailley Now–1996 14.5

Medium colour. Still quite fresh. Pleasantly fruity if with no great depth, complexity or weight on the nose and on the palate. But still very much alive. Easy to drink. Medium body. Has charm and at least some finesse.

Croizet-Bages Past its best 10.0

Medium colour. Fully matured. Weak and rather faded on the nose. Lightened up and lost its fruit. Not as rustic as Gassies but thin and astringent now. Never a wine of much weight or depth. Over the hill.

Grand-Puy-Lacoste
Drink soon (see note) (16.5)

Good fullish mature colour. No undue age. One bottle a little herbaceous on the nose. A little oxidized. The other much better. Round and rich, concentrated, old viney, spicy. This better bottle is showing a little age – I have had much better still – but fullish, classy, long and complex. In prime condition this would score 17.5.

Haut-Batailley   Now–2000   15.5

Fullish colour. Still very youthful. Rich nose. A little closed perhaps. Quite substantial. Perhaps a little austere. Slightly minty. Fullish, quite structured. Austere at first but sweet fruit on the follow-through. Good grip and length. This has plenty of life ahead of it. Just lacks a little richness and charm and sex appeal.

Lafite-Rothschild   Now–1996   16.0

Very old-looking colour in both bottles. Quite an old nose. Classy but lead-pencilly and a little faded. Yet, undeniably, there is breed here. Medium to medium-full. A little unfocussed but the fruit shows finesse. And despite the colour the wine still has vigour. Very good but a bit thin.

Latour   Now–2005   20.0

Very fine colour. Barely coloured. Firm, full, uncompromising but commandingly authoritative Cabernet nose. Marvellous, aristocratic fruit. Fullish. Cool. Marvellous balance and real amplitude and intensity at the end. This has real depth. Marvellous finish. Barely ready. Very fine indeed.

Lynch-Bages   Now–2000   17.0

Good colour. Full and vigorous. Rich and chocolatey and vigorous on the nose. Good gingerbread spice. Fullish, meaty, concentrated, fat and balanced on the palate. Good rich old-viney fruit here. Good grip. Plenty of life ahead of it. Very good plus. Even fine. Plummier and richer and more spicy but not as classy as Grand-Puy-Lacoste.

Lynch-Moussas   Drink up   12.5

Medium colour. Not too much age. Corked. But quite fresh. Light and fruity. A bit one-dimensional but not too bad.

Mouton-Baron-Philippe   See note

Bottle variation. One was very oxidized – smelled like vegetable soup. The second was also somewhat over the top, but one could see some quite classy fruit underneath. I have good memories of this wine which would score 15 plus if in good condition. Medium to medium-full.

Mouton-Rothschild   Now–1998   17.0

Good fullish colour. The usual cedary lead-pencil opulence of Mouton on the nose. One bottle a bit more attenuated on the nose. The best bottle was full, quite tannic, rich, voluptuous and concentrated on the palate. Good grip. Not quite great but fine.

Pichon-Longueville-Baron
                    Drink soon   13.0

Full colour. Just a little dense perhaps. On the nose, a little dense and inky. On the palate quite full. But rather coarse and the fruit is drying out. Nothing special.

Pichon-Longueville, Comtesse de Lalande
                    Now–1997   16.0

Good colour. Rather chunky and dry on the nose. I have had better than this. I don't think these have been well stored. The second bottle was richer, fuller and altogether better, with concentration and grip if not the richness and opulence of Lynch-Bages. Something a little rustic about this nevertheless.

Pontet-Canet   Drink up   11.5

Medium to medium-full body. Still quite fresh looking. A bit faded and dry on the nose. On the palate a bit dried out and underneath rather a simple one-dimensional wine. Nothing much here. Even a little short. Medium body.

SAINT ESTÈPHE

Beau-Site   Now–1997   14.0

(Magnum) Good mature colour. Slightly chunky nose, but ripe and fleshy underneath. Still vigorous. Medium-full. Saint-Estèphe sturdiness. Slightly earthy. But good balance. Good effort for a *bourgeois*.

Calon-Ségur   Drink soon   13.0

Medium-full colour. A bit dried out and barnyardy on the nose – but it always has been: late bottled. Medium-full body. Merlot in evidence. A certain astringency here. Slightly bitter at the end. Unexciting.

Cos d'Estournel   Now–1999   16.0

Medium-full colour, still vigorous. Ripe and fleshy, but quite chunky. Fullish. Good basis of classy fruit. This has depth and class, but isn't better than very good. A touch dry but still has a future. Merlot in evidence, and a certain feminine softness – in a Saint-Estèphe context, of course.

Lafon-Rochet   Drink soon   13.0

Medium-full colour. A little hard and ungenerous on the nose. Good acidity. Slightly austere Cabernet flavour. But not too tough on the palate. Medium-full. Quite vigorous but a lack of nuance and finesse. Got a bit green-twiggy as it developed.

Montrose   Now–1998   15.0

Big colour. Still very youthful. Vigorous but slightly earthy and tannic Cabernet fruit on the nose. Fullish. More tannic than astringent on the palate. Slightly austere. Better with food. Lacks velvetiness and a bit of charm. Good though.

Phélan-Ségur   Drink up   13.0

Medium to medium-full colour. Cedary nose. Getting a little lean now. But there is style here. Medium body. Mellow, but losing a bit of its fruit. Not astringent. New oaky. Balanced. Elegant. But the sweetness is fading.

1966 CLARET

There is a general agreement that after the classic 1961 the 1966 vintage is the best of the 1960s decade. This is not to say that there were not some very exciting Saint-Emilions and Pomerols in the 1964 vintage or some fine Médocs in 1962, or indeed one or two unexpectedly good and still vigorous wines made in 1967; but for consistency and elegance 1966 was recognized as a very fine vintage from the start. Current auction prices bear out that this view is still held today. First growths make over £1000 a case, as does Château Palmer, and the rest of the super-seconds fetch about half that figure. With many of the very best 1970s still vigorous, and the 1961s almost out of reach – between two and three times more expensive – this would suggest that at the top levels 1966, now more than 25 years old, is *the* fine claret vintage to drink today.

THE WEATHER

Generally, 1966 was a year rather cooler than average, and as far as the summer months were concerned, on the dry side. The *feuillaison*, when the leaves begin to appear on the vines, took place around 15 March, about a week or so earlier than usual, and the flowering began on 25 May, again a little prematurely. So far so good, similar to 1964, but the complete reversal of 1962, when the flowering did not start until 19 June.

The period of the flowering is crucial. Ideally one would like fine, dry weather, so that the setting of the grape can occur quickly, evenly and successfully. Unsettled weather, prolonging this period, and excessive humidity will encourage *coulure*, when the grapes fail to set, and *millérandage*, grape clusters which do not ripen evenly, and which contain some quasi-raisins which remain small, hard and green. Humidity also encourages mildew.

While in 1964 the flowering was over in a fortnight, in 1966 it lasted almost a month, and, though June had been largely fine and warm, July was mixed, sometimes very hot and sometimes rather cool. The *veraison* began on 25 July, a week or so earlier than average. August was unsatisfactory, cool and cloudy, but it remained largely dry. It was not until September that the weather brightened, with almost uninterrupted fine weather right through to the end of the vintage, which began on 20 September.

The following table may be of interest:

	1961	1962	1964	1966
Rainfall: Aug/Sept	36.1 mm	56.1 mm	103.4 mm	75.0 mm
Harvest Date	22 Sept	9 Oct	24 Sept	20 Sept
Size of Harvest	small	very large	large	quite large

THE WINE

Thanks to the fine October, the grapes were in excellent condition when they were picked. A certain amount of *coulure* in June, especially in Pomerol and Saint-Emilion, had reduced the potential size of the harvest, but as often happens, and especially in 1961, this had the effect of enabling the remaining grapes and bunches to ripen more fully. The crop arrived in the press house looking extremely healthy, and the fermentation passed off smoothly.

It was an auspicious start. Right from the beginning the colour was deep and rich. The wines, though they seemed (rather misleadingly) to be on the light side, had elegance, charm and balance. As the Wine Society reported to its members in the spring of 1967, 'Soft, supple wines of deep colour'. And as Peter Sichel said in his customary *Vintage Report*, 'In style they resemble (the 1962s), lighter then 1964 but with sounder balance, more finesse and even more quality'.

THE MARKET

As the new wines began to settle down after the cold winter, and as the buyers began to arrive in Bordeaux, the market for the 1966 Bordeaux began. One might have assumed with two failures out of the last three vintages that demand would be brisk, but there was still plenty of 1964 around, and the 'campaign' opened with some hesitancy. With the exception of the first growths, which returned to 1961 levels, prices opened marginally below those of 1964, that is about 50 per cent above the 1962s. Prices at the time were considered a little high, but in retrospect an ex-cellar opening price for Lafite or Mouton at under £2 a bottle – even if one had paid after the sterling devaluation of November 1967 – seems absurdly cheap.

THE WINES TODAY

The tasting that forms the basis for this article was the fourth occasion I have sampled this vintage in depth since 1977. On the first occasion some wines – Domaine de Chevalier, Brane-Cantenac and especially Palmer – were already delicious; others, particularly the Saint-Julien, Pauillac and Saint-Estèphe Médocs, were still adolescent, hard and ungainly, seemingly a long way off maturity. I reported that the 1966 vintage, in spite of its initial promise, was spending an inordinately long time in the doldrums: seeming to have it all, but not yet coherently together.

Six years on, at another comprehensive survey the overall feeling among those present – a baker's dozen of experienced British professional palates – was one of slight disappointment. Of course, there were some fine wines, and all the big names showed well, but there were others which, though full, seemed to lack a bit of richness, depth and excitement, and some which were definitely showing age and beginning to lose their fruit. Outside Saint-Julien and Pauillac there were few vigorous and exhilarating wines; and those of Saint-Emilion and Pomerol, with one or two exceptions, were largely disappointing and needed drinking soon.

Comparing the individual notes taken then with those I have made subsequently, I find the vintage is continuing to evolve quicker than I have anticipated in 1977, though suggestions of a premature demise across the board in the Libournais now seem a little exaggerated. Judging by the condition of the bottles, and assuming these are representative of others cellared in this country, even the most illustrious are now fully à point, and not many will last beyond the mid-1990s. But, after all, the vintage is now well over 25 years old, and it would be churlish to criticize it solely for not having the capacity for eternal life.

Where there *is* a slight discrepancy is between notes I have made on individual wines in England and those made at the château itself, or on château-stored stock, on occasions where I have made a vertical tasting of a particular property. Naturally a wine not moved since bottling will be more vigorous and concentrated, and therefore at more than 25 years of age showing higher interest, than a bottle which might have changed ownership and been moved several times from one environment to another in the UK. Sometimes the differences are quite marked, though the inherent, 'absolute' quality remains the same. There is a lesson for both commentator and consumer here. On one side people comment on the state of maturity of a 25-year-old wine on the basis of a single sampling occasion. For the consumer it is of paramount importance when purchasing wines like these at auction or elsewhere to get as much information about the *provenance* and appearance of the wine before committing himself. Beware of bad ullages, and, if possible, find someone whose opinion you can rely on who has tasted from that particular lot itself.

THE BEST 1966S – AND THE MOST VIGOROUS

Nineteen sixty-six at its finest in Saint-Julien and Pauillac. There are few wines here which rate less than 'good'. Wines such as Latour and Mouton, Les Forts, Haut-Batailley, Grand-

Puy-Lacoste, Gruaud-Larose, Beychevelle, Talbot, Léoville-Las-Cases, Léoville-Barton, Branaire-Ducru and Ducru-Beaucaillou are all still vigorous, though only Latour, perhaps, can safely be kept. The remainder need drinking, if not straightaway, then soon. Château Grand-Puy-Ducasse, not until recently a name to conjure with, is surprisingly good. Pichon-Lalande is elegant but less vigorous than the wines above.

In Saint-Estèphe, Cos d'Estournel is fine. De Pez and Phélan-Ségur are good too. Calon-Ségur is not without length and personality but is beginning to get a little astringent. Montrose is perhaps a bit tough.

The Margaux wines are now quite evolved. Those that are still vigorous show plenty of class but most now need drinking. Even the delicious Palmer should not be kept for too long. Lascombes, Prieuré-Lichine, D'Issan and Du Tertre are among the other successes.

It was a successful and consistent year in the Graves, and the top wines – Haut-Brion, La Mission, Domaine de Chevalier and Pape-Clément – are still very much alive; rich, harmonious and full of finesse. The remainder need drinking soon.

Most of the Saint-Emilions and Pomerols I have seen recently seem to be showing a little age, and my notes read 'drink soon' or 'drink up' fairly consistently. Cheval-Blanc and Pétrus, Magdelaine, La Gaffelière, Nénin, Lafleur, Petit-Village, La Conseillante, Certan-de-May, Lafleur-Pétrus, Latour-à-Pomerol, Vieux Château Certan and Trotanoy will all still keep well. Figeac and Canon are also good but have less life ahead of them.

THE CHARACTER AND QUALITY OF THE VINTAGE

Nineteen sixty-six is a vintage which in its youth seemed to show all the appearance of a classic claret. It was well-coloured, full in body and had a very fine, indeed slightly austere, balance between the concentration of ripe fruit and the acidity. Compared with 1961, it was, naturally, less rich, less overwhelmingly compact; there was less essence-of-fruit. Compared with 1970 it appeared more reserved, less plump, less generous. Yet the wines were undeniably classy. They had good length, plenty of depth and, above all, finesse.

As they have evolved the best of them have remained fresh, for the acidity level is quite high, yet some of the concentration of the fruit began to loosen up before many of the wines had really begun to soften. This is not to say that they were ever too hard, but more to point out that the vintage never had a lot of 'fat' and not many of the 1966 wines became really velvety. As they aged, many began to show a little excess, unharmonized acidity on the finish, and this has become one of the hallmarks of the vintage.

Nevertheless, at the top levels the vintage is indubitably very fine. Perhaps, overall, it is not as consistent or as appealing as the next great vintage, that of 1970. But perhaps also, at the level of Latour, Palmer, Haut-Brion and La Mission, the top wines are better.

THE TASTING

The majority of the following 1966s were tasted in London at the end of October 1986. I have added a few notes on other wines sampled at two smaller 1966 tastings I attended in the same autumn. The mark indicates how the wine is showing now. In the case of elegant wines which today are showing age, this is perhaps a little unfair. They would have rated higher a decade or so years ago.

	Optimum Drinking	Mark out of 20

SAINT-EMILION

Ausone — Drink up — 15.0

Medium-full colour. Soft, quite elegant Merlot nose. Rather light; the fruit has dried out a bit, but elegance here. A bit over the top but has class.

Cheval-Blanc — Drink soon — 16.0

Very good full mature colour. Full nose, like the Pétrus possibly slightly stewed, yet rich underneath. Full-bodied, chunky, spicy wine, yet also rich and concentrated. Doesn't really sing as far as I'm concerned, but had length and vigour.

La Clotte — —

Good full, mature colour. Stewed, astringent and volatile. Horrid.

Clos-Fourtet   **Drink up**   14.5

Very good full, mature colour. A fat, rich, opulent wine without the usual Fourtet chunkiness and rustic elements. Rather better than expected but fell away in the glass.

Figeac   **Drink up**   15.0

Good colour. Full, chunky nose, but now a hint of attenuation. Medium body. Getting a little mean and bitter. Finishes cedary and quite sweet. Good but losing its class.

La Gaffelière   **Drink soon**   16.0

Good colour. Plenty of fruit and vigour on both nose and palate. Quite full, even a shade solid, but plenty of life ahead of it. Good but not great.

Magdelaine   **Drink soon**   ±17.0 **(see note)**

Good vigorous colour. The sample was corked, but nevertheless a wine with plenty of concentration and vigour. Real depth. Very high class I'm sure.

Pavie   **Drink soon**   14.5

Medium-full colour. Quite a solid wine compared with some Pavies. Ripe, mellow, quite rich. Now showing just a little hint of age; finishing very Merlot and spicy. Quite good.

Soutard   **Drink up**   13.5

Similar colour. Nose is a bit faded and even dirty but the wine is better on the palate. Fullish, ripe and fruity. Quite rich. Evolved quickly in the glass and is now losing such class as it possessed, yet quite good despite this.

POMEROL

La Conseillante   **Drink soon**   17.5

Good full mature colour. Plump, plummy nose. Fully mature but still quite vigorous at first. Medium-full, complex, a wine of real character and depth. Still lovely. Very elegant.

Le Gay   **Drink soon**   15.5

Fullish colour, not that mature looking. Oaky, truffley and roast-chestnuts nose, but earthy and with a hint of farmyard. Fullish, still some tannin, solid – even dense. But plenty of richness. Very good in its old-fashioned way.

Gazin   **Drink soon**   15.0

Medium-full colour, mature but not unduly so. Fullish, slightly earthy nose. Fat, ripe, still vigorous. Fullish body, quite firm, harder than it appears on the nose. At first rich, but lost fruit as it evolved. Good though.

La Grave-Trigant-de-Boisset
                Drink up   13.5

Medium colour, fully mature. Plump, attractive Merlot fruit. Not enormous depth but has style.

Medium body. No great depth or concentration but pretty fruit. Beginning to lighten up and get astringent. Not bad.

Lafleur-Pétrus   **Drink soon**   17.0

Good colour. Fine, complex, aromatic nose. Balanced, ripe, stylish. A little sign of lightening up but still vigorous. Finishes well. Very good.

Latour-à-Pomerol   **Drink up**   16.0

Slightly more colour. Solider, earthier, even a shade robust on the nose. Full and meaty but the fruit seems to be drying up a little. Plenty of wine here nevertheless. Rich and concentrated. Good.

Nénin   **Drink soon**   16.0

Similar colour. Full, firm, ripe and rich. Slightly on the austere side on the palate. More aromatic as it evolved. Good fruit and finishes long.

Pétrus   **Now–1996**   16.0 **(see note)**

This particular sample was ullaged to the high shoulder. Full, firm nose with a bit of mint. A lot of *vin de presse*? Big, firm, tannic but rather dense, if not a touch stewed. Vigorous, long on the palate but lacks a bit of charm. I have seen it better, but 1966 has never been a great Pétrus. The 1967 is better.

La Pointe   **Drink up**   14.5

Medium colour, fully mature. Fully evolved nose. Medium-full body, again a little astringency. Slightly more herby in flavour than the La Grave-Trigant-de-Boisset, and less weak. An elegant wine but beginning to coarsen up. Quite good.

Trotanoy   **Drink soon**   17.5

Similar colour. Lovely nose, plump, full, vigorous, aromatic, complex. Fullish, rich, even fat. Slightly fuller and fatter than the Conseillante. Equally fine.

Vieux Château Certan   **Now–1996**   16.0

Good youthful colour. Nice fresh nose with no hint of age. Ripe, good acidity. Medium body. Attractive blackberry fruit. Good class. Still plenty of life in this sample.

GRAVES

Domaine de Chevalier   **Drink soon**   17.5

Fullish, mature colour. A very elegant, subtle wine. Discreet nose; more power on the palate than nose would indicate. Elegant, richly fruity, ripe. Finishes very well. Good class.

Haut-Bailly   **Drink soon**   15.0

Medium colour, quite a lot of brown. Evolved nose. Some age and now beginning to lighten up. High-toned, aromatic wine, very soft and mellow now.

Haut-Brion   **Now–1996**   19.0

Fullish colour, no undue signs of age. Very lovely, rich, aromatic, complex nose. This is quite magnificent. Real depth and harmony. Cedary and sandalwood flavours and lovely ripe fruit. The best wine of this tasting.

La Louvière   **Drink soon**   14.5

Good colour, little sign of age. Old, mellow nose; slightly artisanal. Fullish, solid but mellow, no astringency. Better than I expected.

La Mission-Haut-Brion   Now–2000   18.0

Very immature colour, still purple. A big, powerful, solid tannic nose. Is it a bit too stewed? On the palate shows better. All the richness and ripeness comes out. Developed in the glass. A claret for Rhône or Californian lovers.

Pape-Clément   Now–1996   16.0

Good full colour. An evolved, quite complex, stylish nose. Has depth, but there is also a touch of austerity about it. Rich, medium-full, classy flavour. Never a blockbuster, but balanced and will still keep. Very good.

LISTRAC

Poujeaux   **Drink up**   14.0

Full colour. Fine, classy, refined, mature Cabernet nose. Elegant and balanced but beginning to show a little age. Medium-full body, still complex, but the fruit is beginning to dry out a little. This was an unexpectedly good wine which would have scored higher five years ago.

SOUTHERN MÉDOC

Cantemerle   **Drink up**   14.0

Medium colour, not too old. Fresh Cabernet fruit; full, four-square, a bit austere. Solid, some tannin. Acidity showing and getting a bit dry on the finish. Lacks charm and a bit of real class.

La Lagune   Drink soon   11.0 (see note)

Very good colour. Slightly dirty on the nose. Rather dried out, and a hint of volatile acidity. Not really very special if this bottle is typical. (Quite good to good, is how I have marked this wine on earlier occasions.)

MARGAUX

Boyd-Cantenac   **Drink up**   13.5

Medium-full colour. Evolved nose, showing some attenuation. High toned, slightly blowsy but not astringent. Ripe, cedary but a little old. Not bad.

Brane-Cantenac   **Drink up**   15.5

Medium-full colour. Mellow, ripe nose, has depth and elegance but now shows age. The class is there but the wine is beginning to shorten and lighten. Nevertheless an attractive wine in the violets and black cherries Margaux style.

Durfort-Vivens   **Drink soon**   14.5

Medium colour, quite a bit of brown. Smoky nose, showing a bit of age, but not inelegant. Medium body, a little astringency, but more fruit

and class than I had expected from my previous experience with this wine.

Giscours   **Drink up**   13.0

Medium colour. Nose shows a wine which has dried out and become a little mean. Medium body, acidity shows as well as astringency. A bit tired now, and was never that remarkable.

Malescot-Saint-Exupéry

                 Drink soon   14.0

Similar colour. Evolved, aromatic, oaky nose; shows a little fade. Medium-full. Some acidity shows. Has fruit and depth nevertheless, and at least some class.

Margaux   **Drink soon**   15.0

Medium colour. Quite a lot of age, if not even oxidation on the nose. Shows much more age than it did at the château in April 1986. Ripe and classy underneath though.

Marquis-de-Terme   **Drink soon**   13.5

Full, mature colour. A solid, earthy, tannic wine, now fully mature but not yet soft. Rather dense and four-square. Not bad.

Palmer   **Drink soon**   17.5 (see note)

Medium-full colour. Full, aromatic nose. Quite solid but ripe, classy with a lot of depth. Quite vigorous, rich, fullish, lovely plump fruit. Cedary. This bottle shows a bit more age than Palmer 1966 usually does. Normally it shows even better.

Prieuré-Lichine   **Drink soon**   15.5

Very good colour, not a lot of brown. At first a bit of liquorice, spice and old tea on the nose rather than plums or blackcurrants but fresher and more interesting as it evolved. Medium-full, ripe, concentrated. This has real style.

Rausan-Ségla   **Drink up**   14.5

Medium colour. The nose shows some quality and depth, but also a little age. Medium body; soft, aromatic and fruity but no real concentration. Quite classy, but a little aged.

SAINT-JULIEN

Beychevelle   Now–1996   16.5

Medium-full colour, fully mature. The nose shows a little acidity and some age, but the wine is rich, fat, full, solid and earthy on the palate. Aromatic Cabernet flavour. Vigorous. Very good.

Branaire-Ducru   Now–1996   17.0

Very good colour, little age. Full, mellow, complex nose. A round, mature voluptuous wine, still vigorous. Fine old-vine fruit. Very Saint-Julien.

Ducru-Beaucaillou   Now–1996   18.0

Good mature colour, a little more so than the above. More open on the nose. Medium-full body, round and rich but still vigorous. This has power and class. A fine wine.

Gruaud-Larose Now–1996 17.5

Medium-full colour, not a lot of development. Good, ripe, rich Cabernet-based nose, with a little acidity underneath. Full, concentrated, attractive wine. Plenty of depth. Long distinguished finish. Very fine.

Langoa-Barton Drink soon 15.0

Medium colour. Round, soft, warm-brick nose. Stylish but evolved, indeed beginning to show a little age. Medium body, gentle, balanced. Charming. An elegant wine, but it now needs drinking.

Léoville-Barton — (see note)

Medium colour, showing a bit of age. Strange nose and flavour, like one of these caramel instant whips, and a sweet-sour finish. Yet not undrinkable. An aberration. It doesn't normally taste like this; usually it has something of the character, if not quite the quality of Las-Cases.

Léoville-Las-Cases Drink soon 17.0

Good colour. Quite rich, cedary nose but seems a bit solid. Better on palate. Full, very Cabernet, rich wine which became more complex as it evolved. Best of all on the finish. Very Las-Cases. Very Saint-Julien.

Saint-Pierre-Sevaistre Drink soon 15.0

Good mature colour. Quite a high-toned, aromatic nose. Medium-full, has fruit and at least some concentration and depth. This is an older and duller bottle than the last I saw. Good but not exciting.

Talbot Now–1996 14.5

Good colour, still vigorous. Firmish nose, a touch dry. Medium-full, has depth and charm. Quite stylish. Finishes a little lean. Quite good.

PAUILLAC

Les Forts de Latour Drink soon 16.0

Good fullish colour. Fullish, fat nose, quite Cabernet, vigorous, even rich. Quite full, some class if not enormous concentration. Good length. Good, just not great.

Grand-Puy-Ducasse Drink soon 16.5

Full colour, barely mature. Good, rich aromatic nose. A wine of unexpected class, size and depth. Full, firm, vigorous. Really quite concentrated. I was most surprised to see what it was when the bottles were uncorked, as on the last occasion it had been farmyardy and astringent.

Grand-Puy-Lacoste Drink soon 17.0

Medium-full, mature colour. A wine of class and depth. Lovely complex, fragrant nose. Medium-full. A lot of character. Will still keep.

Haut-Batailley
Drink soon ± 16.5 (see note)

Medium-full colour; fully mature. Another corked wine sadly, but certainly very fine underneath. Full, concentrated, classy. As good as Grand-Puy-Lacoste?

Lafite Drink soon 16.0

Medium-full colour, fully mature. Fruit is showing some signs of drying out, a taste of wood is beginning to obtrude. Classy nevertheless. Long on the palate.

Latour Now–2000 19.0

Similar colour. Firm nose, a bit closed at first. Evolved to show a wine of considerable class. Good blackberry and cassis flavours. Ripe, fresh, long, rich, very fine distinguished finish. A lovely wine.

Lynch-Bages Drink soon 15.0

Surprisingly full colour; because the wine is quite evolved, almost over-ripe on the nose. More vigorous on the palate. Medium-full body. Some fruit. Good but lacks a little class.

Mouton-Rothschild Now–1996 17.0

Good full colour, just about mature. A big, full, quite tannic wine on both nose and palate. Ripe and rich underneath. Still quite firm. Developed in the glass. Certainly very good but by no means great.

Pichon-Longueville, Comtesse de Lalande
Drink soon 15.0

This is a more evolved bottle than normal. Good colour. Some weakness on the nose, but better on the palate. Ripe, sweet, elegant, fruity but today a little past its best.

SAINT-ESTÈPHE

Cos d'Estournel Drink soon 16.0

Very good colour, little brown. Full, rich, quite concentrated nose if with a little Saint-Estèphe solidity Cos doesn't show today. Ripe, quite chunky, plenty of fruit. Warm generous finish. Shows well.

Montrose Drink soon 15.0

Good colour. Full, mature nose, hints of leather and liquorice. A big, solid wine, very Cabernet, a lot of tannin. A bit overbalanced but there is richness and depth underneath. Will it ever soften?

Phélan-Ségur Drink up 15.0

Medium colour, beginning to lighten up a little. Good, healthy, interesting mature nose. Medium body, elegant – more so than most Saint-Estèphes. Supple and ripe and finishes well, but getting towards the end of its useful life.

1964 CLARET

An irregular decade, the 1960s. One superlative vintage: 1961. Two very good vintages: 1966 and 1962. Three disasters: 1963, 1965 and 1968 – and 1969 was uninspiring in addition. Nineteen sixty was a small but useful vintage; 1967 was large and more useful still. Which leaves us with 1964. The vintage itself was as heterogenous as the decade which contained it. There are some superb wines in Saint-Emilion and Pomerol, indeed in some cases better than the equivalent 1961s. There are some disasters. At the tasting which I describe at the end of this article, Mouton-Rothschild came last but one out of the 44 wines in the average vote of some sixteen tasters. Only Château Margaux scored one point better.

It is now generally recognized that 1964 was the year that the rains came down. A continuous deluge which began on 8 October – and lasted for the rest of the month – effectively ruined the harvest for those who had not collected the majority of their grapes. Those who had completed prior to the 8th made good wine. Saint-Emilion and Pomerol, by beginning their harvest earlier than the Médoc, particularly those who risk an element of 'sur-maturité' in their fruit (some very famous names in Pauillac) were caught and the wines are very poor. This is the accepted view. It is largely true but, of course, it is equally an example of lack of rain at a crucial time leading to a wine's undoing.

THE WEATHER

The beginning was promising: there was no precocious bursting of the vine-buds: no spring frost literally to nip the harvest in the bud. The flowering started fairly early and was in full swing by 9th June. The fruit-setting took place swiftly and smoothly and in ideal conditions. There was no humidity, no sudden drop in temperature which causes the sap to fall and encourages coulure. The potential harvest could already be seen to be large. Then the trouble began – paradoxically, because it did not rain. July was hot; day after day of blue sky but not a drop of rain. There was only a little rain in August; there were no thunderstorms which one would normally expect to punctuate a very hot, dry spell – and it got even hotter.

By this time the vines had begun to suffer. The lack of moisture had retarded the maturity and the veraison was some ten days to a fortnight late, not until the first week of August. The less hardy vines, which means the Merlots and those too young to have an extensive root system, began to show signs of drought. Leaves began to shrivel and with it the plants' capacity to photosynthesize the most out of the sun and soil. This was particularly apparent in those vineyards in sand and gravel soils. The vines in richer, more water-retentive soils, soil with more clay and limestone in it, suffered less.

Though it has been said that 1964 was a more successful year for the Médoc bourgeois wines because these properties tend, or tended then, to harvest before the classified growths, I think there is an additional explanation. A number of the more renowned of these châteaux came from what I call the arrières côtes, the second line of the Médoc which runs behind the four famous villages away from the Gironde; from the hinterland of Saint-Estèphe via Château Cissac, down to Listrac and Moulis, and beyond as far as Arsac. This ridge of the Médoc has a richer soil, with more water-retaining pockets of clay.

I was in Bordeaux myself in the summer of 1964 as a student doing a stage in the cellars of Calvet in the Cours du Médoc and living in the shadow of the Cathedral in the centre of Bordeaux. I well remember the long hot summer and the tan I acquired on the beaches of Porge and Lacanau on the Atlantic coast, less built-up then but still a splendid place to take a holiday or go for a Sunday picnic. I remember also being taken by bus to help with the harvest in some petit château in the Côtes de Bourg or Premières Côtes de Blaye. Today it is almost certainly picked by machine. For three days – all I could stand – I either culled the grapes myself or was the liaison man between the other harvesters and the lorries waiting at the edge of the vineyard. This latter duty entails strapping oneself into a hod which one carries on one's back. You bend down so the pickers can empty their small baskets into your hod. Inevitably, grape juice goes down one's neck. It is sweaty, sticky, hot, itchy and backbreaking. Never, I resolved, will I volunteer myself for the grape harvest again!

THE VINTAGE

The vintage, prematurely claimed in August as a 'vintage of the century' by the Minister of Agriculture, Edgard Pisani, began on 15 September, a little earlier than average, and was generally fully under way about a week later in Saint-Emilion and Pomerol and a week later still in the Médoc. The weather was fine and warm and the initial musts medium-coloured but with low acidity. Some rain fell on the 26th but the grape skins were thick and this did little harm. There was more rain on 1 October for a few days and the humidity mounted; some *pourriture grise* began to appear but the must weights were higher and the colour better. From 5 to 8 October it was sunny but then the heavens opened. It was still raining a fortnight later.

It was, as indicated, a large crop. The red wine *récolte*, at over 1.4 million hectolitres, was only marginally less than 1962 and might have been greater but for some hail in Moulis where Dutruch-Grand-Poujeaux for example lost three-quarters of its crop.

THE MARKET

Prices opened at a high level. Following the appalling 1963s and the successful 1964 flowering, there had been some *sur-souche* buying (trading before the harvest) of the classed growths in the summer, and when the first *tranche* was offered early in 1965 it opened at 1962 levels or higher still. This seemed expensive at the time but was lower than for the 1961s despite three years' inflation and was soon to be eclipsed by the 1966s, not to mention the price explosion of 1969 to 1972. However the market was sluggish, perhaps because some proprietors were following the abominable practice of making a 1964 offer conditional on taking some 1963, and some prices fell by as much as 18 per cent between January and March. In retrospect, The Wine Society's opening price (17s.9d. in 1968) for its own bottling of the excellent Château de Pez seems startlingly cheap.

THE WINES

As I have said, it is a simplification to divide the wines into early and late pickers. It is also misleading to generalize in terms of communes. In Pauillac, they generally picked late but while Lynch-Bages, Mouton and Lafite are disappointing or worse, Pichon-Lalande and Latour are successful wines (but they were not caught by the rain). Calon-Ségur was another late picker and the wine tastes like it, but Cos, Montrose (always an early cropper because of its unique microclimate – they started on 18 September and finished on 1 October) and De Pez are all good as are many other *bourgeois* growths from this commune.

In Saint-Julien the results were generally favourable. Las-Cases is good and Ducru certainly better than most although they harvested late. Beychevelle is another successful wine, as is Gruaud-Larose and Saint-Pierre. Margaux was more variable (although here, most of the crop was in before the deluge), perhaps because of the lightness of the soil. Château Margaux itself is disappointing and Palmer is only medium but Malescot is good, as were Lascombes, Brane-Cantenac and Rausan-Ségla. Generally, though, the Médoc wines were well-coloured and full-bodied but rather sturdy. They lacked acidity, a certain amount of fruit and a crucial element of breeding; four-square wines and unsatisfactorily balanced. Essentially, they were short: generally they were dull.

The best wines on this side of the river undoubtedly come from the Graves. Haut-Brion is excellent, the best left-bank wine. La Mission Haut-Brion, Pape-Clément and Domaine de Chevalier are all successful and I cannot recall a disappointment even among the lesser wines. Most of these, however, like most of the Médoc, are now showing age. They are drying up and losing what breed they once possessed. Drink them up.

But the palm must go in 1964 to the other side of the water. Whilst in other years, 1962 and 1966 for instance, and particularly in poorer years, now long since drunk, like 1958 and 1960, the Médoc is supreme, 1964 belongs to Saint-Emilion and Pomerol. There is absolutely no doubt that the 1964 Saint-Emilions and Pomerols are very fine indeed. Unlike the Médocs, and the Graves to a lesser extent, the Dordogne wines are fat, lush, full of fruit, long on the palate and at the top levels are showing no undue signs of age; in a nutshell, they have correct balance. The best are very fine; finer, indeed, than they are in 1966 let alone in 1962. The very best even rival the 1961s.

THE TASTING

The following splendid range of 1964s were assembled by Jan Paulson, dentist and dealer in rare wines, and sampled in Munich in February 1990. I have added a note on Latour-à-Pomerol which I tasted a week later.

	Optimum Drinking	Mark out of 20

SAINT-EMILION

Ausone — Drink up — 15.0
Medium-full colour. Delicate but complex on the nose. A light wine but has depth, it seems. Like the Belair, a wine of delicacy rather than power but it doesn't have the complexity or the grip. A little short but still enjoyable.

Belair — Drink up — 15.0
Medium-full colour. Mature. This has lightened up a bit on the nose. But there is elegance and cedar underneath. Dried up a little in the glass. This is a bit old and a bit astringent. But there was quality once, quite obviously.

Canon — Drink soon — 16.5
Fullish colour. Mature. Lovely complex fruit on the nose. Real depth and fatness of old vine fruit here. Very complex. On the palate a more meaty, chunky wine. A touch old-fashioned. Rich, good acidity but a little rigid. Yet long and still vigorous. Has a touch of spice.

Canon-La-Gaffelière — Drink soon — 15.0
Medium to medium-full colour. Broad nose. Quite Merlot, quite plump. Medium-full body. Good richness and more grip than was apparent on the nose. Quite classy, with a bit of cedar. Good length. Still sweet. Really still quite fresh.

Cheval-Blanc — Now–1997 — 18.5
Fullish colour. Still vigorous. Fat, rich, buttery with a touch of grilled artichokes. Cedary and oaky. Vigorous. Got a bit smokey/robust as it developed. Better on the palate, though there is a bit of astringency. Ripe, quite muscular. Sweet and ripe. Good grip. Rich and complex. Finishes long. Fine also. But I have had better bottles.

Figeac — Now–1997 — 18.0
Medium-full colour. Mature. Quite an elegant rich nose. There is quality and depth here and no sign of age. Fat, vigorous and oaky. This has concentration and depth, sweet fruit and a good cedary background. Long and complex. Fine.

Clos-Fourtet — Drink soon — 13.0
Good fullish vigorous colour. Fullish, good oak background, and quite toasted oak at that. A little rigid but good depth of fruit. Fullish, rich. Quite chunky. Doesn't have the richness of the Gaffelière but good nevertheless.

La Gaffelière — Now–1997 — 18.0
Good medium-full colour. No undue maturity. Full, rich and vigorous on the nose. Good depth here. Fullish, ripe, sweet and vigorous. This still shows no sign of age. Rich and warm and meaty on the palate, with good concentration and grip. A generous wine. Long. Very good indeed.

Lyonnat — Drink soon — 13.5
Good vigorous, fullish colour. Round, plump, ripe, plenty of depth here. Still vigorous. Full and chunky on the palate. An old-fashioned concentration but there is good richness to balance the rigidity. Finishes vigorously. Good sweetness but somewhat dirty in flavour. Will still last.

Pavie — Drink soon — 15.0
Medium colour. Soft, sweet and cedary on the nose but some age now. Quite a Merlot-based wine. Round and sweet and ripe but a little one-dimensional. Yet it is clearly good.

Vieux-Rivallon — Drink soon — 13.5
Good fullish colour. Mature. A chunky wine. Somewhat inflexible on the nose. Quite high volatile acidity. On the palate a little earthy and old-fashioned but not too bad. Quite full.

POMEROL

La Conseillante   Drink soon   17.0

Medium-full colour. Mature. Quite an old nose.
But fat and quite chunky. Got a bit dry and astringent in the glass. On the palate the wine is round
and sweet. Softer and plumper. Elegant and long
on the palate. Really very good.

Clos L'Eglise   —   (see note)

Medium-full colour. Still quite vigorous. A lot of
volatile acidity on the nose. Out of condition.

Le Gay   Drink soon   17.0

Very fine full vigorous colour. Rich nose. Fat,
youthful, quite muscular, though not exactly
chunky. Full, rich, vigorous, a lot of concentration. This is fine but became rigid as it developed.
Lovely fruit but dried up in the glass fast.

Lafleur   Now–1999   19.0

Fine, fullish vigorous colour. Youthful, slightly
earthy/sooty nose. Good ripe fruit. Fullish, still
some tannin even, it seems. Rich and full. More
mellow and fat. Doesn't quite have the grip or
concentration of Pétrus but excellent.

Lafleur-Pétrus   Drink soon   15.0

Medium-full colour. Fully mature. An elegant
wine but it is showing a little age. Mellow rather
than astringent but getting a little high-toned.
Pleasantly fruity but will get attenuated as it develops. Medium body.

Latour-à-Pomerol   Now–1996   17.0

This is more four-square and old-fashioned. A
roasted caramelly element. Rich and meaty. Fat.
Vigorous. Classy as it evolved.

Pétrus   Now–2005   20.0

Very full mature colour. Full, still seems to be a
little closed. Very rich and concentrated. Very
full, tannic, ripe and vigorous. This is excellent. It
has vigour, complexity, concentration and grip.
Brilliant. Very, very long.

Trotanoy   Drink soon   16.0

Very full colour. Roasted, smoky/bonfire, full,
slightly solid nose. Old-fashioned. Solid, astringent. Tastes like a vine vinified with all its stems
for a long time.

Vieux Château Certan
  Now–2000 plus   19.5

Medium-full colour. Reasonable vigour. This is
vigorous and minty. Quite a lot of fresh oak. Real
depth and class. Ripe, rich, vigorous. Very youthful. A wine with enormous youthful fruit and
concentration. Quite lovely. Very youthful.

GRAVES

Haut-Brion   Now–1996   18.0

Fullish mature colour. Lovely aromatic nose,
chocolate, coffee, fudge and caramel, cooked
black cherries, underpinned with oak. This has

class as well as complexity. Now beginning to
show a little age on the palate. Fullish and still very
complex though. Lovely fragrant fruit and spice.
Long. Delicious.

Malartic-Lagravière   Drink soon   15.0

Medium-full mature colour. Ripe nose, not too
solid. Fullish on the palate. Good fruit. Good grip.
A little rigid but a good result.

La Mission-Haut-Brion
  Drink soon   16.0

Good colour. No undue age, fullish. A little solid
on the nose. Four-square perhaps but not too dry.
It softened up on the nose. It has dried out a little
now. Quite full. Good initial ripe attack. More
lightened up than dried up. But still quite rich and
vigorous in the finish. Very good.

Pape-Clément   Drink soon   16.5

Full mature colour. Another good nose. Rich and
fat, a sort of cross between Montrose and Haut-
Brion. Earthy, quite full. Rich and supple but
without the breed of the Haut-Brion. Yet there is
vigour and fruit. Plenty of depth. Will still keep.

MARGAUX AND HAUT MÉDOC

d'Angludet   Drink soon   14.0

Full colour. Good vigour on the nose. Quite full,
youthful but sturdy. An old-fashioned, long macerated wine. Quite full, a little four-square and astringent but there is still enjoyment here. Dried
out a bit on the palate. But not at all a bad effort.

Cantemerle   Past its best   10.5

Medium colour; fully mature. Stylish nose but
now quite light. Medium body, not much fruit.
Acidity shows. Straight but lacks charm. Too old.

La Lagune   Past its best   13.5

Fullish colour. Round, cedary-oaky nose, initially
good but seems to dry up a bit. Rather tough and
four-square, now a bit dry and brutal. Not much
pleasure to be had now. But not too astringent.

Malescot-Saint-Exupéry
  Drink soon   15.0

Medium-full colour. No undue age. Good nose,
ripe and cedary, youthful, quite sturdy. Good
richness with a touch of caramel and spice.
Medium to medium-full body. There is fruit here
if not a great deal of class. Ripe but now shortening. A sturdy wine. Still some sweetness. Good.

Margaux   Past its best   11.0

Full colour, still vigorous. Stylish nose, though a
little age. A rather weedy wine. But one can see
the echo, especially in the aftertaste, of something.
Good oak, residual sweetness. Not too astringent.
Light/medium body.

Palmer   Drink up   14.0

Medium-full colour. No undue age. Slight element of shit on the nose but there is fruit here. Reasonable fruit and quite supple for a 1964. Medium body. Ripe if not very stylish. But not dry. I think it has *become* a bit dirty rather than was this way in the beginning.

Du Taillan   **Drink up**   13.0

Medium colour; fully mature. Quite an old nose but there is a vestige of class. Medium body, some sweetness of fruit on the attack. Has lightened up a bit on the follow-through and the finish is a little bitter. But no undue astringency. Not bad.

SAINT-JULIEN

Beychevelle   **Drink soon**   15.0

Medium-full mature colour. Fullish nose. A touch of bonfires and something a little robust. But quite rich underneath. Fullish, a little *vin de presse*. Vigorous and rich. But lacks a little distinction. Slightly vegetal.

Ducru-Beaucaillou   **Drink up**   13.5

Good fullish mature colour. Interesting nose. There is fatness, flexibility and depth in a slightly spicy way. Chocolate element. Riper and more flexible than Las-Cases on the nose but a bit less so on the palate and the nose rapidly deteriorated. Fullish, a little four-square. The fruit has dried out a little and the wine is not as clean as it once was.

Gruaud-Larose   **Drink soon**   16.0

Medium-full mature colour. Interesting smoky, slightly compost-heapy nose. Quite flexible. Medium-full. Ripe and spicy. Reasonably plump. Quite attractive fruit and good length on the palate. Spice and bonfire flavours. Very good. Will still keep.

Lagrange   **Past its best**   11.0

Even better colour than Las-Cases. Very full. Only a vestige of brown. Fullish, austere nose. Solid, a bit acidic. The fruit has dried out, which is confirmed on the palate. Not dirty but fruitless.

Léoville-Barton   **Drink soon**   15.5

Medium-full mature colour. This has interest and more class than Gruaud-Larose. It is also more classic. Cabernet and oak. Again some suppleness. But a little austere on the palate. An upright wine with good Cabernet but lacks real richness. Good grip. Reasonable length. Quite full. Still flexible but lacks a bit of generosity. Will still keep.

Léoville-Las-Cases   **Drink soon**   16.5

Very good colour. Fullish and little brown. Rather a solid nose. Full and earthy, but there is at least some richness. This has class. Quite full, very typical Saint-Julien fruit. Good cedary base. No undue age. This has balance, complexity and very good depth. A bottle in vigorous condition.

PAUILLAC

Batailley   **Past its best**   12.0

Medium to medium-full colour. Fully mature. Smells of mint (even peppermint) at first. Medium-full, meaty palate. A curious wine. Now astringent on the finish.

Croizet-Bages   **Past its best**   10.0

Medium colour. Fully mature. Light and dried out on the nose. Dried-up farmyardy flavour. Some sweetness but a little astringent and lacking class. Lightish. Was never very distinguished.

Grand-Puy-Lacoste   **Past its best**   14.0

Medium-full colour. Mature. Rather old on the nose. Soft but feeble. Some quality but light and dried out. Medium body. Elegant old-vine residues.

Lafite   **Drink up**   13.5

Fullish colour. Mature. Rich, full and concentrated on the nose. Quality here. On the palate there is class and depth. A little towards the end of its useful life but a very nice concentration. Very Cabernet I thought.

Latour   **Now–1997**   17.5

Good full vigorous colour. Rich, slightly solid, firm Cabernet on the nose. A little austere and ungenerous. Fullish, rich, concentrated and old viney. This has depth and vigour and is more ample than it appears on the nose. This is fat and it shows very well. It has rather more vigour than even the best of the Saint-Juliens.

Mouton-Rothschild   **Past its best**   10.0

Medium to medium-full colour. Fully mature. Fat nose. Plump, slightly lactic. Collapsed fast on the palate. Dirty, yet there was good wine here once. Soapy flavour now. Astringent and pongy.

SAINT-ESTÈPHE

Cos d'Estournel   **Drink soon**   14.5

Good colour. No undue age. Solid, rigid nose. Quite firm, with some fruit there if not much charm. A bit dried out and astringent now. There is fruit but has the typical 1964 shortness and lack of suppleness. Not bad.

Montrose   **Drink soon**   16.0

Very full colour, vigorous, glowing. Ripe, firm, cedary but austere. There is richness here, as well as depth, but in a rather masculine way. Full, as much tannic as astringent yet on the follow-through is much more supple. Solid. Rich and even concentrated but lacks charm.

de Pez   **Drink soon**   15.0

Full, quite vigorous colour. Full earthy nose. A bit rustic but not unbalanced. Youthful, full, ripe and stylish on the palate. Very good for a *bourgeois* and shows the potential of this estate. Cooked fruit to some extent. A little astringency but a good wine.

1962 CLARET

Arriving as it did after the fabulous 1961 vintage, the 1962s seemed to be the answer to everyone's dream. Here was an abundant crop of wines which were 'good' but, luckily, not *too* good. The vintage appeared as if it would be reasonably quick to develop and the wines were supple, accessible, ripe and fruity. Moreover, prices were reasonable. As a result, the world welcomed the 1962s with open arms. The trade immediately christened the vintage 'commercial' and the wines have been fighting to escape this faint-praise yoke ever since.

After 1961, there are four other vintages in the 1960s decade which are worthy of note. In chronological order: 1962, 1964, 1966 and 1967. The latter, like 1962, was a plentiful year. The wines were pleasant, loose-knit, matured early and had no great pretentions: a 'commercial' vintage. The other two years, though, are generally regarded as superior to the 1962.

I am not sure that I agree. I have for long had a soft spot for the 1962s. I have never warmed to the 1964 Médocs and Graves, and I have found myself being more and more disappointed in the 1966s as they develop. While I am not trying to maintain that the 1962s are quite as good as the 1966s, I do consider that 1962, in the Médoc and Graves at least, is rather better than 1964. The wines are fruitier, better balanced and have lasted better. Indeed, they possess something the 1964s, as a whole, manifestly lack: generosity.

THE WEATHER

Nineteen sixty-two was a late vintage. A wet, cold, miserable spring caused the cycle of the vine to pedal off to a tardy start and, despite later climatic improvement, the vines never really caught up. The start of the budding, as measured by the records of Château Lafite, was three weeks late; flowering did not take place until the middle of June, and the harvest did not commence until the second week of October.

The following table shows the important dates in the life-cycle of the vines at Château Lafite during the period 1961 to 1970:

Vintage	Start of Budding	Start of Flowering	Start of *Veraison*	Start of Harvest
1961	12 March	12 May	22 July	27 September
1962	20 April	9 June	28 July	10 October
1963	16 April	5 June	3 August	10 October
1964	30 March	27 May	17 July	28 September
1965	30 March	12 June	29 July	9 October
1966	25 March	27 May	27 July	6 October
1967	21 March	1 June	25 July	3 October
1968	16 April	8 June	25 July	4 October
1969	14 April	4 June	6 August	6 October
1970	18 April	6 June	28 July	2 October

The ripening of the fruit in 1962 was retarded not so much by poor weather in August and September as by drought. The flowering had taken place under sunny skies and with the barometer high and the fruit-setting had followed successfully, thus ensuring a large crop. Thereafter, the weather had continued fine and, to a large extent, the vines had caught up with the norm when they began to change colour at the end of July. At that point, though it was not unduly hot, the very dry weather commenced. Just 56 millimetres of rain fell in the next two months – a figure only beaten by the 1961, 1978 and 1985 vintages. This delayed the development of the ripening process because the sap in the vine plants tended to dry out. Luckily, however, the dry weather continued into October and so, though late, the crop was ready for the harvest before the autumn rains began. The conditions in October, in fact, were ideal for the development of noble rot on the grapes in the Sauternes and Barsac vine-yards and a large crop of excellent sweet wine – indeed, better than 1961 – was achieved.

FIRST REPORTS

The first reports on the quality of the 1962 harvest were cautious. Allan Sichel reported a lack of maturity because the grapes had been starved of moisture during the summer months. He felt that the vintage would be most successful in the areas where there were the more water-retentive clay and marl soils rather that the quick-to-drain gravel and sand mixtures. He had found the sugar content of the first musts in Saint-Emilion, Saint-Estèphe and Pauillac to be higher than that in Margaux and Graves but there was a lot of variation. A variable year he suggested. On the one hand, well-balanced wines with both colour and flavour; elsewhere, starved, light wines which would need careful vinification to make them palatable.

It was not only the quality of the wine but also its quantity which was deceptive. Sichel speaks of it being rare to see the 'swollen, rounded grapes of a really big vintage'. He reported that the grapes were small if plentiful, but that some were dried up and would not yield much juice. Yet, when the declarations were added up, it was found to be a record year for quantity, with a total of over 1.4 million hectolitres of AC red and 2.3 million of AC white. This was the largest total crop since the war and although in both 1967 and 1970 more AC red would be produced, it would continue to hold the record until the rain-diluted 1973 harvest.

The wines, too, turned out somewhat differently to what Allan Sichel expected. There was no doubt that they were ripe and full of fruit; moreover, there is general agreement that the gravelly soils of the Médoc and the Graves produced more exciting wines than the limestone and clay soils of Saint-Emilion and Pomerol. Equally, I do not consider that the vintage in the Graves and Margaux turned out worse than in Saint-Estèphe or Pauillac. Finally, Allan Sichel's prognosis might suggest a year in which the *crus classés* were more successful as a whole, bear-ing relative prices in mind, than the *petits châteaux*; where the vintage got better, proportion-ately, in quality as one climbed up the hierarchy. This, too, was not so. It was a good year for *petits châteaux* and generic wine despite the late harvest, and it was no more inconsistent, at any level, than were the 1959 or 1966. Indeed, it was a very even vintage in this respect.

THE WINES AS THEY EVOLVED

When the wines were first sampled from cask in the spring of 1963 they were tasted along-side those of 1961. They suffered. Though there was no problem in making a choice over which 1962s to buy – there was plenty of wine; the prices were reasonable; the wines plump and fruity, open and attractive – there did seem to be a slight lack of real depth and defini-tion. Inevitably, they did not shine out like the 1961s. Comparisons were drawn with 1955, a similar year of plenitude, commercial usefulness and medium-weight wines. The 1962s ap-peared medium-bodied, not too excessively tannic, and for the medium term.

As time has gone on, the 1962s appeared both to put on weight and to have a larger po-tential for cellaring than anticipated, like the 1970s would do a decade later. I made my first comprehensive vintage tasting in 1972, when only the *petits châteaux* and lesser *bourgeois* and Libournais wines were ready for drinking. All the classed growths, I found, still needed to be kept. The reason for this, as for the increase in apparent weight and also for the good reten-tion of colour, is the high level of acidity in the 1962s. This has kept the wine fresh, the defi-nition positive and the fruit from dying out. A good acidity level and an abundance of ripe fruit is what will give a claret vintage personality and long life; and even a vintage like 1962, not, apparently, as structured as 1966 or 1959, if it has these attributes, will last just as well.

PRICES

When the 1962s first appeared, prices showed a fall from the very high levels of the year before. Lafite was offered at 16,000 francs a *tonneau* as against 27,500 the year before. Cheval-Blanc sold for 8,500 francs (15,500) and the rest of the *premiers crus* and Mouton filled the gap between. These price levels were some 15 to 20 per cent up on those of 1959 and 1960. Translated into retail terms, this meant that when the 1962s were first listed some three years later, classed growths such as Léoville-Las-Cases and their equivalents across in Saint-Emilion and Pomerol cost 15s (0.75p) to £1, the first growths about double.

THE BEST WINES

Nineteen sixty-two is a Médoc-Graves vintage, the opposite of 1964. Within that general preference, though, it is difficult to pinpoint a commune which is more successful than any other. All produced fine wine. Thirty years on, many of the Margaux and even some of the Saint-Juliens and Saint-Estèphes are showing age, as are the lesser Graves. The best Graves and the top Pauillacs, though, are still vigorous, and these demonstrate a generosity often now apparently lacking in the top 1966s. The feeling of those at both the 1962 tasting and the one held on the 1966s some twelve months earlier was that the 1962s were holding up better.

On this occasion we tasted four of the top Graves, all of which showed very well. The Pape-Clément, in particular, was more alive than I had expected and this makes me feel that Domaine de Chevalier, if well stored, will also be holding up. Haut-Bailly is a classy, mature bottle, surprisingly fine, though not as exquisite as its 1966. The remaining classed growths, apart from those tasted, I would now approach with caution.

Reviewing the Médoc communes from north to south, I have always considered that Saint-Estèphe, which had to some extent missed out in 1961, returned a fine, consistent, all-round performance in 1962 and this was born out by three of the four wines we tasted, one surprise being the Haut-Marbuzet. Again, I would be wary of the remaining growths now.

The flight of nine Pauillacs including not only the second wine of Lafite – Carruades – but the third wine or at least a separate bottling (for Nicolas) of the second wine, Moulin des Carruades, was easily the most successful and most vigorous of the tasting. I rated Mouton and Latour first equal and the Lafite, perceptibly more aged, in third place. Other leading Pauillacs – Grand-Puy-Lacoste, Haut-Batailley and others not present – can still be enjoyed.

The top Saint-Juliens, of which we tasted eight, are also for the most part holding up well. I found the Gruaud better than my memory of it and the Ducru not quite as exciting as at Studley Priory two years previously. A surprise was Beychevelle.

Our flight of Margaux and the Southern Médoc, to include Cantemerle and La Lagune was, with the exception of Château Palmer, somewhat uninspiring. It should be remembered that many estates were in the process of being resurrected from the decay of 1930s and 1940s neglect and these communes' wines evolve much faster than those further north. Most Margaux 1962s need to be avoided now for fear disappointment.

With the exception of Pétrus and Vieux Château Certan and possibly Cheval-Blanc (we had a rogue bottle), the Saint-Emilions and Pomerols now need drinking – up, or at least soon – though elsewhere I have enjoyed bottles of Canon, Latour-à-Pomerol and Lafleur-Pétrus which have all been very much alive. There is in most, though, only the aftermath, the echo of the wines they once were. Nevertheless, despite my pronouncement at the beginning of this section, there were many very good wines on this side of the Bordeaux area.

THE TASTING

The following wines were sampled at The White Horse Inn, Chilgrove, Sussex, in October 1987, at a tasting organized by Farr Vintners. The wines were tasted blind within·the flights concerned. All wines were château-bottled with the exception of the Clos-René. The marks refer to what one might term the 'satisfaction quotient' of the particular bottles in question on the day rather than the absolute quality when they were in their prime.

SAINT-EMILION

l'Angélus   **Drink up**   13.5

Full colour. Plump but attenuated nose. A spicy, four-square wine, which never had a lot of breed. The wine is not dried out but the finish is clumsy.

Ausone   **Past its best**   15.0

Medium colour. A wine which is past its prime but was at least 'good' once. Oak and ripe fruit evident on the nose. Sweet but rather astringent.

Cheval-Blanc   —   —

Medium-full colour. The nose reminds me of sour nettle or sorrel soup. On the palate quite full, sweet and ripe but not a good bottle.

Figeac   **Drink up**   15.5

Medium colour. Soft, cedary nose, now showing a bit of age. Elegant but perhaps never as structured as the above. Oaky, ripe, sweet and stylish. Long, ethereal finish. Has the faded-roses elements of a distinguished but now aged wine.

La Gaffelière   **Drink soon**   16.0

Medium-full colour. Full, rich, even concentrated on the nose. Was quite solid and tannic in its youth and is still holding up well. Good plump fruit and plenty of complexity. Shows well.

Trottevieille   **Drink soon**   16.5

Good, medium-full colour. Rich, fat, plump nose. Full, mellow and cedary on the palate. A wine of some structure and concentration – more than the property produces today. Still quite full and fat. Elegant. A quality wine holding up well.

POMEROL

La Conseillante   **Drink up**   14.0

Medium colour, fully mature. The nose is a bit aged though it improved to some extent in the glass. The fruit has lightened up and the acidity is now a bit dominant, generating bitter elements. Was certainly 'good' once.

Pétrus   **Drink soon**   16.5

Full colour, unforthcoming. Dense nose but fat and rich. Similar on the palate. Ripe and concentrated but perhaps not too well stored. Quite robust and spicy. The bottle in Paris was much more vigorous though I also noted it as 'old-fashioned'.

La Pointe   **Drink up**   13.5

The lightest colour of all these Pomerols. A little attenuated on the nose. Fresh if a little bland and sweet on the palate. Yet reasonable length if a bit dry at the end. Not bad.

Clos-René   **Past its best**   12.0

(London bottled) Medium colour. This is a wine is now a bit old – hence the low mark – but was certainly very elegant in its prime.

Trotanoy   **Drink soon**   16.5

Fullish colour, mature. Full, fat, rich, concentrated nose. At first very fine quality in a rather muscular, earthy sort of way but the fruit dried up fast in the glass. Voted marginally ahead of the Pétrus.

Vieux Château Certan   **Drink soon**   16.5

Medium-full colour, no undue brown. The nose has lightened and dried up a little but is still plump and elegant. Full, ripe, mature, oaky and rich. Good finish. Sweet cedary finish. Very good.

GRAVES

Haut-Brion   **Now–1995**   19.0

Full colour. Good, ripe, complex nose, still vigorous. Quite full. Very classy. Ripe, complex flavours, lovely oaky, mulberry fruit. Real depth. Very fine indeed. Splendid finish. Still bags of life.

La Mission-Haut-Brion   **Drink soon**   16.5

Medium-full colour. Solid, quite structured nose, again a little stewed. Has acidity and earthiness as well as fruit. Big, solid, tannic, rich. Perhaps a bit too structured. Lacks a bit of real class.

Pape-Clément   **Now–1996**   17.0

Medium-colour. Aromatic, harmonious, complex, elegant nose. Fully mature. A classy, medium-bodied, very well-balanced wine. Lovely fruit. Very fine. Still vigorous.

La Tour-Haut-Brion   **Drink soon**   15.5

Medium-full colour. Ripe nose. Not too dense. Quite full, some tannin if not even slightly dense and stewed. Fullish, sweet, has depth but is, at the same time, a little bitter. Good but not great.

MARGAUX AND SOUTHERN MÉDOC

Brane-Cantenac   **Past its best**   14.0

Medium colour. Quite a fresh nose. There is good fruit but it has lost a bit of charm. Medium body. Some age but quite complex. A good wine.

Cantemerle   **Drink soon**   15.5

Medium-full colour. Rich, Cabernet-ish, even a shade solid on the nose. Medium-full body. Has become a bit four-square but is still vigorous. Good acidity. Reasonable length.

Giscours   **Drink up**   13.5

Fullish colour. Broad nose, a little one-dimensional, even a touch attenuated. Medium-full, somewhat sweet and now drying out.

La Lagune   **Drink up**   16.0

Medium colour, quite mature. Rather old on the nose, elements of H2S. Better on the palate. Shows age but is ripe underneath. Medium body. Long, ripe, sweet finish, even complex.

Malescot-Saint-Exupéry

                 Drink soon   15.0

Fullish colour. Blackcurrant nose. Quite a solid,

dense, even gamey flavour. Full, a little astringent but has good acidity. Tough but a good wine.

Margaux **Drink up** 15.0
Medium colour. Slightly old but classy on the nose. Like the Palmer but older, not as sweetly ripe nor as complex but good nevertheless. Typically delicate Margaux but fell away quickly.

Palmer **Drink soon** 18.5
Medium colour. Elegant, plump, violetty, ripe nose. Delicate but concentrated. Distinguished, fragrantly concentrated, real depth, lovely harmony. A delicious wine. Still very long on the palate.

SAINT-JULIEN

Beychevelle **Drink soon** 16.0
Medium-full colour. Backward, 'old-fashioned', slightly austere fruit. Full, rich and concentrated. Softening now. Lacks charm but very good.

Ducru-Beaucaillou **Drink soon** 16.0
Full colour. Rich on the nose, slightly sweeter and not as classy. Seems to be a bigger wine; full and meaty but not the depth nor the acidity of the above. I have seen it classier and better balanced.

Gruaud-Larose **Drink soon** 18.0
Medium-full colour. Good, ripe Cabernet nose. Rich and full if a faint touch of H2S. Fine Saint-Julien fruit. Ripe and concentrated. A generous wine, very well balanced and of high quality.

Léoville-Barton **Drink soon** 17.0
Medium-full colour. Ample, plump. Full, rich, ripe. Cabernet-based wine. Very Saint-Julien. Not quite the class of the Gruaud but very good.

Léoville-Las-Cases - 14.5
Medium colour. Smells of stale tobacco. Dense, solid, slightly rustic, yet ripe underneath. A bad bottle? It has been fine in the past.

Saint-Pierre-Sevaistre **Drink soon** 15.0
Medium-full colour. Somewhat dense and unforthcoming on the nose. Fullish, ripe, a little solid and heavy-footed but good depth and even richness. Will still keep well. Good but not great.

Talbot **Drink up** 13.0
Medium-full colour. Solid but a shade attenuated on the nose and this is echoed on the palate. Thinning at the finish and losing its class.

PAUILLAC

Carruades de Château Lafite
                    Drink soon 16.5
Medium-full colour. Good nose, quite Cabernet in flavour. Cedary, ripe fruit. Medium-full body. Shows very well and more vigorously than the *grand vin*, but lacks the complexity. Very classy.

Croizet-Bages **Drink soon** 14.0
Medium colour. A bit thin and bland on the nose.

Fresher and fruitier on the palate. Quite elegant but lacks weight and complexity. Not bad.

Lafite **Drink soon** 17.0
Medium colour. The nose, though it shows a bit of age, has real breed. Medium body, complex and cedary but dried out rapidly in the glass. Real elegance. A more vigorous bottle might rate 20.

Latour **Now–1997** 19.5
Full colour. Classy, slightly austere, very Cabernet nose. Similar on the palate. Full, rich, vigorous, great style. Essence of Cabernet. Long, complex, real breed. Perhaps superior to the Mouton.

Lynch-Bages **Drink up** 16.5
Full colour. Lovely voluptuous ripe fruit. Concentrated, velvety, medium-full wine. Has depth but aged fast in the glass. Very good.

Moulin Des Carruades **Drink up** 15.0
A little less colour. Soft, elegant nose. Medium body. Interesting flavours though now shows a little age. Good, ripe fruit.

Mouton-Rothschild **Now–1997** 19.5
Full colour. Rich, voluptuous nose. Full, rich, cedary and oaky wine, concentrated and fat. High class! Real depth and excellent balance.

Pichon-Longueville-Baron
                    Drink soon 15.5
Full colour. Slightly older, denser, more Cabernet nose. Good, rich fruit and a noticeable acidity. Fullish, a little solid and four-square yet concentrated underneath. Plenty of wine here and a more vigorous bottle would show better still.

Pichon-Longueville, Comtesse de Lalande
                    Drink soon 17.0
Medium-full colour. Fat, rich and creamy on the nose. Medium body. Complex. Very stylish. Shows a little age yet a lovely ripe wine.

SAINT-ESTÈPHE

Calon-Ségur **Past its best** —
Medium-full colour. Dry, pinched, some volatile acidity on the nose. Dried up on the palate.

Cos d'Estournel **Drink soon** 17.5
Fullish colour. Good nose, a little tough at first but with lots of depth. Big, full, chocolatey-blackberry flavoured. Not a bit dense or tough though. Long, ripe, harmonious finish. Very fine.

Haut-Marbuzet **Drink soon** 16.5
Fullish colour. Unforthcoming on the nose but not aged. Cedary, complex, generous, warm. Fullish, ripe and vigorous. Good fruit. A surprisingly lovely wine.

Montrose **Past its best** 15.0
Medium-full colour. Aromatic nose, some age but has class and complexity. Medium body. Ripe fruit, plenty of character. Just a little past its best.

1961 CLARET

There is little doubt in my mind that 1961 stands supreme among the vintages of the last couple of generations. For me, it demonstrates in a superlative way all that I look for in a fine wine: ripe fruit, elegance, concentration, a 'three-dimensional' quality of flavour and character and, above all, balance. Wine from vintages with balanced, ripe fruit and above all a good acidity keep remarkably well. The 1953s are a case in point. This was not a structured, tannic, blockbuster vintage, yet it has lasted better than others. Too many wines of the vintages of the late 1940s and 1950s were made too large in size. They had too much body and tannin for their fruit and in the end they became astringent before they had softened up. One could even castigate wines in the celebrated 1945 vintage for this. Happily the balance of the 1961s is perfect; the wines were not too dense and were able to demonstrate how excellent they were from the beginning. Unlike other years, they have never been hard to assess or gone through an awkward phase when their quality was difficult to acknowledge. Perhaps this is because though deep in colour, full in body and tannin, they have superbly rich, concentrated fruit.

While always accessible, the 1961s were slow to develop. In 1978 I was invited to a tasting set up by Dr J.D. Taams, a noted Dutch connoisseur. Dr Taams had assembled a cellar of 1961s and managed to produce, from his own stocks, no fewer than 22 classed growths, including all the top wines save Pétrus. At this tasting the vintage still showed itself to be in need of many further years of development despite having had fifteen years in bottle. Most of the top wines, with the possible exceptions of Palmer and Margaux, were not yet *à point* – though already delicious.

Then in April 1983, I attended an even more comprehensive tasting, thanks to the generosity of Keith and Penny Knight of the Houston House Hotel near Edinburgh. Here we tasted 31 top 1961s, including Pétrus, the sole Pomerol representative. By this time, one or two of the minor classed growths were getting to the end of their active life but there were still some bottles – La Mission, Mouton, Latour – which were not yet ready, over twenty years on. Most of the top wines were *à point*. Few would die before the year 2000.

Nineteen sixty-one is a great vintage. It is a vintage that stands continually head and shoulders above all the others in vertical tastings. It should be in every cellar, even at today's extortionate prices.

THE WEATHER

The 1961 vine-cycle began early. The spring was mild after one of the wettest winters on record, and the vine was already in flower on 20 May, about three weeks earlier than normal. Then disaster struck. On the night of 30/31 May, there was a severe frost. Most of the Merlot flowers were 'burnt off', for this variety is always the most precocious. Extensive damage was done to the remainder. Montrose 1961, for example, is, to all intents and purposes, a 100 per cent Cabernet wine.

Thereafter, in contrast, the weather could not have been better. July was evenly warm with some rain at the end of the month. August was hot and practically a drought. September was even hotter with over half the days of the month recording a temperature of 30°C. Again, there was less rain than the norm. In all, the rainfall of the crucial last two months, at 30 millimetres, was the lowest between 1929 and 1985. Only six other years in the last 30 show precipitations of less than 80 millimetres in August and September.

All this drought retarded the harvest which might have been assumed to begin at the beginning of September if not in August. In fact, it did not begin until 22 September, paradoxically later not only than 1959 but also, by a week, than 1960, a vintage which had an unexpectedly early start for an indifferent year.

THE SIZE OF THE HARVEST

The harvest took place in fine weather and an unusually small crop of exceptionally healthy ripe grapes was gathered. When the statistics had been totted up, it was established that the total AC red Bordeaux wine production, at 550,000 hectolitres, was the third smallest since the war. Only 1956, the year of the great February frost, followed by 1957, which suffered equally (for the vine fruits on last year's wood and in 1956 there was so little vegetation that it was inevitable that the successive year would be badly affected) were smaller.

One can further illustrate the short crop by comparing this figure with production figures since. In only one other year (1969) in the 1960s decade was the red-wine production lower than a million hectolitres. In the decade of the 1970s, the average production was 2 million. In the 1980s the mean was well above 3 million. The 1984 harvest, at just under 2 million – four times larger than 1961 – was considered disastrously short.

Right from the start, however, the wine was indisputably of exceptional quality. How much of this was due to the short crop is a matter for conjecture but there is no doubt that the size of the harvest was an important factor. It seems obvious that a finite amount of nutrient from the soil, ripeness from the sun and so on, if spread over a smaller quantity of grape berries, will produce fruit of a higher quality. The weather, however, particularly in August and September, has a greater influence, as is shown by a comparison of the success of the years of low rainfall cited above, all good to very good with the exception of 1977, with the short years of an equivalent period. The small crops, by comparison with the decade average, are 1952, 1954, 1965, 1969, 1971, 1977, 1984 and 1988, not necessarily a series of years to conjure with. Peter Sichel often makes the interesting point in his *Vintage Reports* that it is the years of drought rather than great heat in August and September which produce the finest, most classic claret.

THE MARKET

The 1961s were expensive – exceptionally so – but on both quality and quantity counts one can say, in retrospect, justifiably so. The prices of the top growths varied between 15,500 francs a *tonneau* (Cheval-Blanc) and 27,550 francs (Lafite). To put this in perspective and translating earlier years into what were then still very 'new francs', one should point out that postwar prices – 1945 to 1954 – were fairly static, with the most expensive wine, usually Lafite, asking about 3,000 (new) francs. In 1955 this climbed to 5,000, in 1957 to 7,500 and in 1959 to 11,000, though in this vintage Lafite was a lot more greedy than its rivals. In 1960, despite a larger crop of inferior quality, the Lafite price jumped to 14,000 and Haut-Brion from 7,250 to 12,000. Not surprisingly the 1961 prices, in some cases three times that of 1959, caused many buyers to think again despite the already clearly evident quality.

Prospective purchasers, especially in Britain, had a further reason for being hesitant. The wine trade had bought heavily of the 1959 vintage and had not ignored the 1960s, despite generally higher prices. This meant that purchases of the top 1961s, as far as Britain was concerned, were in token quantity only.

The wines first appeared on the retail market in 1964 at about £1.00 a bottle for a British-bottled classed growth, up to £1.50 for a château-bottled second growth and £3.50 for Lafite and Mouton-Rothschild. By 1968, these had climbed to £1.50, £2.30 and £4.50, and by 1972, primed by the auction boom and speculative buying, prices of over £30.00 a bottle were being realized for the top wines. If £360 a case seemed expensive in 1972 – and at the bottom of the slump which followed you could pick up 1961 first growths for as little as £130 – it was soon to be eclipsed. By 1981, Mouton and Lafite had moved through the £1,000 barrier – two years later they were making over £2,000, and they have continued to climb.

Today, a case of Pétrus 1961 will fetch as much as £10,000 – that's over £150 a glass – and the remaining *premiers crus* well over £2,000, if not £4,000, the same level as La Mission and Palmer. Yet, for under half that, you might pick up the excellent Ducru-Beaucaillou and other impressive wines such as Magdelaine, Vieux Château Certan, Grand-Puy-Lacoste – to mention just a few – for half that again. At these prices, these superlative wines cannot be considered expensive. Indeed, quite the contrary. Assuming the wines have been stored correctly and the levels are good, they are bargains.

THE TASTING

At the end of March 1987, I participated in a tasting of the following 1961 clarets, set up by Steven Browett and Lindsay Hamilton of Farr Vintners, and took place at the White Horse Inn at Chilgrove, Sussex. The wines were tasted blind in communal flights. Bottles of this age can be expected to vary enormously. Marks and state of maturity assessments should be taken therefore as referring to this example only. Where there are low marks, these are far more likely to be due to age of the sample than to any inherent lack of quality.

	Optimum Drinking	Marks out of 20

SAINT-EMILION

Ausone Drink soon 15.0
Medium colour. Quite brown. Rich, full, oaky nose, quite masculine, even firm. Evolved quickly in the glass but there is undoubted quality here. Very good essence of fruit. Very ripe, elegant, even silky though showing age.

Canon Drink up 12.0
Good full colour. The nose is a bit dry and pinched. Quite full, a little tannin and more astringency. This bottle has lost a bit of its fruit. Was better at the château the previous time I saw it.

Cheval-Blanc Now–1997 16.0
Very good colour indeed. Solid, rich, chunky nose. Clearly the product of a long maceration. Tannic, slightly tough Rhônish elements. Ripe and vigorous but lacks a bit of style for greatness.

Clos-Fourtet Drink up 9.5
Very full colour. Some age but rich and caramelly on the nose but with separate aspects of dryness. On the palate, very astringent and a bit stewed, with high acidity and a very dry finish. No longer attractive. Other bottles, I am sure, are better.

Figeac Drink soon 16.0
Medium colour, quite brown at the rim. Full nose, quite evolved. A little Merlot fade beginning to appear as it lightens up. Medium body, elegant and stylish. More vigorous on palate. Not a blockbuster but has finesse and nice ripe fruit. More stylish than the Magdelaine but more age.

La Gaffelière Drink soon 15.5
The first of two bottles was faded and oxidized. The second had a fresher colour. Showed a little astringency but was a good, ripe, concentrated wine with complex, rich fruit. Sturdy for a Saint-Emilion but in an old-vine sort of way. Good.

Magdelaine Drink soon 16.0
(From halves) Good, full colour. Rich, full, meaty nose. Fat and concentrated, with elements of roast chocolate and caramel. No undue age. Ripe, vigorous and opulent. Rich and slightly spicy. Complex. Good quality.

Pavie Drink soon 14.0
Good colour. Fullish, ripe, quite fresh but has lost a little of its zip and begun to coarsen up a little. Good residual ripeness but lacks a little style.

Overall comment: Most wines show a little age; none are of exceptional quality.

POMEROL

Certan-Giraud Drink soon 16.0
Good colour. Fullish nose, with a little H2S. Shows a bit of age and less dimension. Good though. Elegant, not too old-fashioned or sturdy.

La Conseillante Drink soon 16.0
Medium-full colour. Mature, with quite a lot of brown. Evolved, open nose, mellow, a touch of H2S. Medium-bodied. Beginning to lighten up. Good, stylish, ripe fruit nevertheless. Finely balanced and long on the palate.

Lafleur Drink soon 17.0
Very fine colour indeed, full and vigorous. Full, firm, rich nose, still youthful. High class. Lovely silky, concentrated fruit. Full-bodied, rich, some tannin. Ripe. Quite solid. Still plenty of life. Very fine but others are better. This bottle was not up to the quality of that at the New Haven tasting.

Lafleur-Pétrus Drink soon 16.5
Full colour, some brown. A little blunt on the nose. Full and firm but without the nuances of some. Old-fashioned wine-making. Plenty of richness. Lightening up a little but very good.

Latour-à-Pomerol Now–1997 19.0
Very full colour, some age. Lovely blackcurrant nose, not quite as intense as some at first but real solid fruit and a great deal of concentration on the palate. Full, powerful, almost porty. Less age on palate than on the nose. Excellent.

Nénin   Drink soon   17.0

Similar colour. Not as solid as the Trotanoy but again very fine. Delicious soft, mellow, complex nose, really silky. Medium-bodied, velvety, lovely fruit. Long ethereal finish.

Pétrus   Drink soon   19.0

Good colour but not as vigorous as the Nénin, Trotanoy and Vieux Château Certan. On the nose, more evolved, lighter and looser but ripe, concentrated. On the palate medium-bodied, rich, round, sweet, with a touch of spice. Mellow, very complex, real class, multidimensional.

Trotanoy   Drink soon   18.5

Good, full, vigorous colour. Full, quite solid. Rich, meaty nose. Not chunky but a long maceration. Very classy. Full-bodied, rich and tannic but very concentrated and powerful. Lovely rich fruit and real complexity and depth. Excellent.

Vieux Château Certan   Drink soon   17.5

Very good full colour. Another excellent nose, opulent, ample fruit. Profound complexity. Medium-full body, ripe, silky and rich. A little astringency shows on the finish but delicious.

Overall comment: A very fine flight. All wines are still vigorous and none less than very fine.

GRAVES

Domaine de Chevalier   Drink soon   18.0

Very fine colour again. A little more evolved. Mellow, roast-chestnutty nose. Medium-full body, ripe, elegant, even delicate. Very splendid complex finish. Lovely wine.

Haut-Brion   Drink soon   18.0

Good, full, vigorous colour, showing little brown. Firm, slightly porty nose. A bit of vinosity but rich underneath. Full, fresh, complex, lovely soft-red fruit flavours. Bags of interest and class. Very vigorous at first but loosened up a little as it evolved.

La Mission-Haut-Brion
                    Now–2000 plus   17.5

Good, full, vigorous colour. Fullish nose, still seemingly holding back something in reserve. Evolved in the glass. Full, masculine, rich, firm wine. High class and will still improve. Slightly spicy, slightly robust. Very fine but not the tops.

Pape-Clément   Drink soon   14.5

Medium colour, mature but no undue age. The nose is a little pinched. Ripe and sweet but lacks the class and dimension of its neighbours. Medium-full, generous. Didn't hold up very well.

Overall comment: Very classic, very *typé*, fine.

MARGAUX AND SOUTHERN MÉDOC

Brane-Cantenac   Drink soon   15.5

Similar colour. Quite youthful on the nose but lacks a bit of class. Something a little hard somewhere yet rich, vigorous and quite elegant. This has plenty of interest.

Cantemerle   Drink soon   14.5

Medium-full colour. Still vigorous. Quite a chunky nose. Shows a little age and elements of reduction. Evolved, showing a little astringency. Has, or at least had, good class if not very high class. Lacks a bit of mellowness. Not bad.

Giscours   Drink up   12.0

Medium colour. Some age. Four-square on the nose. Acidity shows, not very generous. Medium-full body, rather astringent. Has lost its charm and rather too much of its richness.

La Lagune   Drink soon   15.5

Medium colour, quite a lot of age. Lightening up fast but there is or was class here. Round, ripe, roast-chestnutty flavour. Most attractive. Old but not faded. Not astringent. Curious but good.

Margaux   Drink soon   18.0

Fullish colour but with quite some age. Good, ripe, mellow, complex nose. Very classy. Evolved fast though. Medium-full. A lot of depth. Real breed but beginning to show some age. Delicious.

Palmer   Drink soon   18.5

Full but mature colour. A little age. Quite full on the nose, ripe, rich, almost porty fruit. This has real depth and quality. Fullish, ample wine. This bottle showing little age. Ripe and concentrated. Never a blockbuster but very, very fine.

Overall comment: More vigorous than the Saint-Emilions. Elegant wine as one might expect.

SAINT-JULIEN

Beychevelle   Drink soon   14.0

Medium colour, mature. Evolved nose, ripe and quite classy but more open, less backbone. Somewhat spicy. Medium body but now loosening up and became a little coarse as it evolved. Will get astringent. Quite good.

Branaire   Drink soon   16.5

Good, full colour, not a lot of brown. Soft and ripe on the nose yet with a certain austerity at the same time. Quite full, very Cabernet. Rich and ripe. Good but without quite the concentration, generosity and sheer breed of some.

Ducru-Beaucaillou   Now–1997   19.0

Medium colour. Backward, firm, rich, classy nose. This is very fine indeed! Fuller and more vigorous than the Barton. Very classic Saint-Julien Cabernet. Lovely rich, aristocratic fruit. Tremendous class. Lovely finish. Multidimensional.

Gruaud-Larose   Now–1997   17.0

Good, fullish, mature colour. Firm and at the same time fat and a little spicy. Voluptuous in a slightly overblown sense. Full and rich, ample, still vigorous. Finishes long and finishes well. High-class but not the breed of the above.

Léoville-Barton   Now–1997   17.5

Medium-full colour, not much brown. Not a blockbuster but a good, rich, concentrated nose with lovely Cabernet fruit. Class! Medium-full body. Delicate, complex, real finesse. Very fine.

Léoville-Las-Cases   Drink soon   15.0

Medium-full mature colour. On the nose a bit four-square. Full and solid but lacking generosity and richness. Good and plump but lacking a little extra dimension and nuance for 'great'.

Léoville-Poyférré   Drink soon   16.0

Medium-full colour, quite mature. Soft, ripe, concentrated, classy nose, though more evolved and less rich than the best. Quite full. Good stuff.

Talbot   Drink soon   14.0

Medium-full colour. Not much brown. Quite full nose. Lacks a bit of richness and concentration. Still fresh. Very Cabernet in flavour. Could be warmer and more generous. Lacks complexity. Dried out in the glass. Not bad.

Overall comment: All these are *à point* but most will still keep very well. A good flight of classic Cabernet-Sauvignon-based claret.

PAUILLAC

Carruades de Château Lafite
                                        Drink soon   16.5

Fullish colour, mature but not unduly so. Full, ample nose, possibly slightly overblown but rich and ripe. Good class. Full body, solid, some tannin. Rich, ample and with good concentration.

Grand-Puy-Lacoste   Now–1996   17.5

Very fine colour. Unforthcoming at first. The flavour took a long time to evolve in the glass. When it did, one could see a wine of structure and concentration. Very old-vine, porty-type fruit. Not a bit dense. Velvety. Classic Pauillac.

Lafite   Drink soon   16.0

I have found Lafite 1961 to be very variable indeed. Two bottles out of three are dull, one is superb. This one was dull. Fullish colour. Good nose promising classy fruit but, on the palate, a little astringent. Somewhat four-square and dumb. The magnums are more consistent and high class.

Latour   Now–2010   19.5

The first bottle was oxidized and maderized. A back-up bottle was a bit colder than the remainder of the wines and it made it even more austere than the wine would have shown normally. 'Not yet ready' was the common view. This is classic Latour – aristocratic, reserved, very Cabernet. Full and tannic, obviously immense breed. If it had been at room temperature, I would probably have given it 20.

Lynch-Bages   Drink soon   15.5

Medium-full colour, little sign of maturity. Some age on the nose. Ripe and spicy and voluptuous but seemed to have dried out a little. A little too tough for its own good. A bit four-square. Good and more admired, like the Pichon-Longueville-Baron, by the consensus of the tasters than by me.

Mouton-Baron-Philippe   Now–1996   17.5

Splendid full colour. Firm, rich, quite austere. Very porty fruit and rich concentration. Good but does not have the nuance of other Mouton, yet is in same mould. Unexpectedly good.

Mouton-Rothschild
                                    Now–2000 plus   20.0

Very full colour, little maturity, lovely nose, very fat and rich and voluptuous. Powerful and full but not a bit hard or aggressive. Ample fruit, essence of summer-pudding underpinned with oak. This is simply magnificent!

Pichon-Longueville, Comtesse de Lalande
                                        Now–1997   18.5

Similar colour. Ripe, concentrated, mellow nose, quite full and vigorous. Plenty of lovely classy fruit. Medium-full body, very harmonious, great class. Marvellous balance, real depth. Excellent.

Pichon-Longueville-Baron
                                        Drink soon   14.0

Similar colour. The nose also is similar. Some chunkiness. Ripe fruit and plenty of richness but a little top-heavy, lacking a bit of zip and follow-through. Possibly not very well stored.

Overall comment: the cream of the 1961 crop, and the wines that will keep the longest.

SAINT-ESTÈPHE

Calon Ségur   Drink soon   14.5

Very full colour indeed. Mature. Shades of rubber on the nose. This is another wine which has aged before mellowing. Full, solid, chunky, tannic. Has good ripeness and acidity but is a bit stewed. More alive than the Montrose.

Cos d'Estournel   Drink soon   16.5

Full colour, now mature. Fullish complex nose. Not very generous or forthcoming but seems to have richness and depth. Good if slightly austere and chunky. Full, ripe, good acidity. Vigorous. Good but not outstanding.

Montrose   Drink up   13.5

Full colour. Slightly less brown than the above. Big, full, dense nose. A shade stewed. Now has lightened up and lost some of its fruit without ever having really softened. Some astringency. Medium body. Tails off but not too bad.

Overall comment: These were as one might have expected – all right but not exciting. No 1961 Saint-Estèphe has ever really inspired.

1959 CLARET

In many senses, I began my wine career with the 1959 vintage. After working in Bordeaux, I started work with Hedges and Butler. The latest vintage to be listed – these was the days before *en primeur* selling – was the 1959. Later, the first in-depth tasting I ever made was of the 1959 clarets. This was the subject of the very first article I wrote about wine, for the now defunct *Wine Magazine*, in 1968. I was paid eight guineas, sufficient, in 1968, to buy half a dozen bottles of a good classed-growth 1959 claret. Thus it all began . . .

The 1959 vintage represented a watershed in Bordeaux. It was the last vintage made by old-fashioned, pre-scientific methods – bung it all in and hope for the best – with no temperature control. It marked the end of ridiculously cheap prices on which no wine estate could make a serious profit. And it was the first vintage where what perhaps today would be called media hype – newspaper reports outside the parochial trade press – began, as they increasingly have done since, to talk up the quality and prices of the wines.

For the story behind the 1959s we have first of all to go back to February 1956. This was the month – it happened to a lesser degree in January 1985 – when the mercury almost disappeared into the bulb of the thermometer. Temperatures in Bordeaux descended to levels which even the hardy vine was unable to bear, particularly as, following a warm January, the sap had already begun to rise. The result was widespread devastation; whole vineyards were wiped out, and in the remainder of the *vignoble* the vines which did survive were given such a shock that it took them several years properly to recover. As a result, obviously, the 1956 yield was tiny. The size of the harvest in 1957, 1958 and even 1959 was also severely reduced.

THE WEATHER

By and large 1959 was a fine, hot, dry year. The early spring was particularly fine, with clear skies and high barometer readings, meaning that it was cold at night, crisp in the morning, but, if sheltered from the wind, one could prune in shirtsleeves in the afternoon. April began well but clouded over after Easter, and there were storms at the end of the month. May began indifferently but improved later, ushering in good weather for the flowering at the beginning of June, about a week earlier than normal. July and August are unsettled in Bordeaux, with hail and storms to interrupt the growing cycle of the vine, and with the earlier month frequently colder than June, but in 1959 it was almost entirely warm and sunny, indeed the conditions in July were a real heat-wave. September started hot; there was a lot of rain in the week after the 12th but conditions had improved by the time the picking started on the 25th and continued fine and hot throughout the harvest. Though the rainfall statistics for the two crucial previntage months, at 133 millimetres, bears little resemblance to 1961 and 1985 (both less than 40) and even with 1966 and 1970 (around 75), the rain that fell was almost entirely confined to the week in September mentioned above.

THE WINE AND THE MARKET

It was the first good vintage since 1955, with big, backward, full-bodied, richly coloured, ample wines; full of fruit, full of tannin and full of generosity. The quantity, both because of the residual effects of February, 1956, and as a result of the dry weather, was small, some two-thirds that of the healthily sized 1955 harvest, though as far as the declaration of AC *vin rouge* was concerned, similar to 1952 and 1949. At a mere 700,000 hectolitres, however, the figures are dwarfed by the prolific 3, if not 4, million hectolitre red wine harvests of today.

Because of the shortage, because of the good quality and because of the initial reports of a 'vintage of the century', prices rose, if marginally, on earlier levels. The first growths fetched from 6,500 (Cheval-Blanc) to 11,000 (Lafite) expressed in the then very new 'new francs' (per *tonneau* of 100 cases without bottling and keeping charges), but of these, only Lafite and Mouton were significantly more expensive than the 1957s. Other classed growths also increased slightly. At this level, translated into retail prices to the consumer, a first growth cost 30 shillings (£1.50) a bottle, and a wine like Château Palmer or Gruaud-Larose, almost certainly bottled in Britain, around 12s or 14s (£0.60–£0.70), when the wines were first listed in 1963 or so. It was the 1961 vintage, with an even smaller crop, and with even better wines, which started the forward momentum of ever-higher prices; prices which today, by comparison with those of twenty and more years ago, seem sometimes to be at levels which verge on the ridiculous, and are, for many of us, way out of reach.

Initially, the reputation of the 1959s was very high. If the wines were perhaps over-praised at the start there was certainly plenty to get excited about. They were big and fleshy and old-fashioned in their density and tannin. But, unlike the 1957s, there was a generosity and concentration of fruit; they were fat, not hard; rich, not austere; and had a warmth and spice which made them, especially on the nose, immediately appealing and seductive. A characteristic of this vintage was an almost Rhônish, baked, roasted quality, something I associate with a wine whose fruit has been kept warm during the night by the effect of infra-red heat seeping out of the stones in the vineyard which have soaked up the sun during the day.

Many of the lesser wines have not come my way for several years, and are in any case now over the hill, but my residual memory of the vintage as a whole is of a consistent year, certainly as far as the Médoc and the Graves are concerned, and of a good year for both *petits châteaux* and classed growths. The Saint-Emilions and Pomerols were more uneven, no doubt as a result of the 1956 frosts, but, here again, many fine wines were made.

Today all but the very best now show age. The vintage, if it is to be faulted, suffered from a certain lack of freshness and acidity and this made some of the lesser classed growths and *bourgeois* wines begin to dry out as they advanced towards the middle of their second decade. The grip of concentration began to relax and the wines became rather coarse and astringent as they softened up. Nevertheless, the 1959s have always, and deservedly, been popular, and still now, at the top levels, will give much good drinking in the years ahead.

While it would not be too difficult – it would just take time and be rather expensive – to assemble a large-scale sample of 1959s today, it might also be unfair on some of the wines. Most of the 1959s were bottled by those who bought them, not by the châteaux. With age, even bottles out of the same case can vary enormously, and today a wine may show disappointingly while tomorrow, particularly if of a different provenance, the bottle may be magnificent. What follows is a summary, often based on the tasting notes of a number of bottles, of best wines of the vintage as they have shown themselves to me in the last five or six years.

GRAVES

Nineteen fifty-nine was certainly a very successful year for the Graves: indeed the Graves had a good decade as a whole, for the 1955 vintage has more character than elsewhere and the 1957s were not too hard. Haut-Brion 1959 is one of the stars of the vintage: big in colour, rich, spicy and aromatic, sturdier than the wine is today, a voluptuous bottle which is now well matured and even in magnums should not be kept too long.

La Mission is another star, but can still be kept. The wine has a magnificent colour, the *rôti* character of the vintage coupled with the dense, deep richness of La Mission and heaps and heaps of fruit. Its younger brother La Tour-Haut-Brion is also very good.

I would place Domaine de Chevalier very high in any list of the wines of the 1959 vintage. Elegance is not the first word which would spring to mind in discussing the 1959s but it is the immediate connetation for this lovely mulberry-fruity, supremely stylish example. There is still plenty of life ahead of it. Haut-Bailly is another lovely wine with a very plummy, almost 1961 concentration of old-vine fruit. Carbonnieux is full and oaky, solid but rich; a more substantial wine than it seems to be today. Pape-Clément, in May 1986, was showing a bit more age but this may have been an unlucky bottle. De Fieuzal is a big, solid, rather chunky wine. It should still be alive, if showing a touch of astringency now. Malartic-Lagravière was full, spicy and generous, an impressive bottle.

1961 SAINT-ESTÈPHE

The only Saint-Estèphes I have seen regularly in the past few years have been the top three and of these I would probably rate Montrose the best, though all may now show a little age. Montrose is a wine with great warmth, depth and charm, somehow more generous than the rather austere 1961. Cos d'Estournel produced wines in that period which were less ample and less rich than the wines today. On two separate occasions, when I have participated in a vertical tasting of Cos vintages, it has been overshadowed by a delicious 1962. Calon-Ségur made magnificent wines in the first decade after the war. A château-bottling in April 1985, showed sweetness and fruit but not the depth and quality of earlier vintages. Yet a Hedges and Butler bottling a few months later had plenty of vigour and concentration. I remember Phélan-Ségur from the late 1960s as very good, and was glad to see it again after all these years in such good form.

PAUILLAC

Inevitably, we begin with Pauillac's top three and I would put Latour not only at the head of the list but at the head of the 1959 vintage. Latour is a magnificent wine which is still young and still solid but has real distinction and breed. Very close behind is Mouton (the bottle in Austria in May, 1991, was a sad exception), another very special wine indeed, more voluptuous, richer, cedarwoody; which one prefers is a question of personal taste. The Lafite 1959s I have tasted recently have varied from *à point* and very classy (see below) to decidedly mature, if not over the top; essentially a very complex, subtle, complete wine which, if still fresh, will be simply delicious. This is a splendid trio.

Pichon-Longueville-Baron, as would be expected, is bigger and more masculine than the Comtesse. Pichon-Lalande, in that epoch, was not making the superlative wines it does today but the wine was sweetly fragrant and long on the palate when I sampled it at Pichon in March 1988. Better, in my view, is Grand-Puy-Lacoste – ripe, full, rich and complex, one bottle a little aged, the second still vigorous in May 1985, a third very impressive in March 1988 – and Lynch-Bages, on which I have several excellent notes: full, plump, ripe and spicy. A Wine Society bottling of Croizet-Bages showed unexpectedly well in March 1988. Mouton-Baron-Philippe (as it then was) and Haut-Batailley can also be recommended.

SAINT-JULIEN

Two major properties in Saint-Julien produced better wines in 1959 than they did in 1961: Léoville-Barton and Léoville-Las-Cases. They are similar, very Cabernet Sauvignon wines but with a really rich, warm background and real class. These, I suspect, are the best wines of the commune and are still holding up well today. Poyferré made a good wine in 1959 (after which it declined somewhat) but the examples I have seen recently have shown age. Ducru is also very distinguished indeed (though sadly the bottle we sampled below was uninspiring); beautifully balanced, ripe and complex, but the prodigiously good 1961 is yet better. Gruaud-Larose is full and rich but not quite in the same league though certainly very good. Langoa is round, fragrant, ripe and subtle and was still holding up well last time out. Saint-Pierre (Sevaistre) is another very fine wine: soft, Cabernet-based and with very good fruit. Talbot is smooth and sweet, also very good. Branaire is less exciting but Beychevelle is ripe and stylish.

MARGAUX AND THE SOUTHERN MÉDOC

Superior to Château Margaux itself, which is elegant, refined and fragrant, though now showing a bit of age, is Palmer, another of the stars of the vintage. This is a wine of great finesse and complexity, a lovely subtle, fruity, velvety bottle, which still has a fine future ahead of it. Malescot is big, rich and voluptuous, still very fresh and lively. The property at the time was making superb wines. Brane-Cantenac had class if never a great deal of richness and has now faded. Rauzan-Gassies is rich and ripe, if a bit bulky and lacking in class. Rausan-Ségla is softer and more stylish, still vigorous and fragrant. Lascombes is big, full, rich and meaty and will keep well. Issan, on the one occasion it has come my way, was soft, elegant and fruity but showed a little age. Giscours is good but Kirwan I did not find exciting.

Château Cantemerle I tasted on several occasions when I was working for The Wine Society some 20 to 25 years ago and it was delicious then: complex, refined, delicate and subtle. Judging by the sample below it still is. I have only seen La Lagune once recently. It was somewhat solid and four-square but underneath there was plenty of richness.

SAINT-EMILION AND POMEROL

My experience of Saint-Emilion and Pomerol 1959s is less extensive than that of the wines of the Médoc and Graves. The Libournais were less popular in those days and, as I have said, the wines were found to be more irregular than those on the western side of the Gironde. Cheval-Blanc is very roasted and spicy and I find several references to 'porty' in my notes. Nevertheless, if a little curious in flavour, the wine is good. It was still being shipped in wood in those days and I have notes of bottlings by Dolamore and British Transport Hotels (both successful) in my 'archive'. Ausone hitherto has been decidedly old. The bottle below was a complete surprise. Canon, Clos-Fourtet and Magdelaine are certainly successes, the first two decidedly 'old-fashioned' in their character but all now show a little age. Perhaps Magdelaine had the most finesse. I have also enjoyed Pavie, a bigger wine than today, and on the single occasion I tasted La Gaffelière (then La Gaffelière-Naudes) it was richly fruity, highly concentrated and most enjoyable. Figeac I thought was excellent when I tasted it blind at the château in April, 1985. There had been some mix-up in the presentation (the second wine of the 1959 vintage had been inadvertently substituted – that was very good too) and so the Figeac 1959 was served as the fifteenth bottle in a fourteen-bottle tasting. I took it for a good, late 1940s vintage. A high accolade.

Pétrus I found good but not unmistakably of *premier cru* quality, and I prefered the 1962 at a blind tasting in May 1987. Château Lafleur is very exciting: perhaps the best Pomerol of all. Trotanoy and Latour-à-Pomerol are both excellent, very rich and complex and should still be fine. Lafleur-Pétrus has only come my way recently in Belgian bottlings, rather faded, but earlier was ripe, ample and not too muscular. L'Evangile, in a jeroboam in December 1985, at the Studley Priory Weekend, was a leathery, liquorice-flavoured blockbuster; rich and earthy and intriguing but overshadowed by La Conseillante 1964. La Conseillante 1959 is a lovely, elegant wine, now showing a little age but discreet and aristocratic. Vieux Château Certan is richer and plumper, an excellent bottle which still has a fine future. By and large though, the wines from this side of the river now show age and should not be held for much longer.

THE TASTING

Jan Paulson, a Swedish dentist who practises near Munich and writes his wine notes in English, set up a splendid tasting of 1959 clarets which took place in Linz in Austria in May, 1991. My heartfelt thanks to him for inviting me to attend. The wines are château-bottled except where otherwise stated.

SAINT-EMILION

Ausone   **Drink soon**   16.5

Fullish colour. Smells of celery with a touch of coffee. Ripe and vigorous though. Spicy and tannic. Medium-full body. A bit astringent on the palate but ripe and complex and new oaky. A curious flavour but certainly classy and very good indeed. Finishes long. Still has life.

Canon   **Drink soon**   15.5

Medium-full colour. Evolved nose, but not decayed. Soft and broad. Quite good grip still. Evident Merlot in the *encépagement*. Medium body. Ripe and aromatic in flavour but without great depth. Has charm and sweetness still. Not as stylish as Trottevieille but was holding up better.

Cheval-Blanc   **Now–1998**   18.0

(Bottled by Grafe-Lecocq, Belgium) Fullish colour. Quite strongly minty on the nose but rich and vigorous as well. Spice, honey and candied peel too. Good quality here. Full, ripe, rich and vigorous. This is more elegant than Figeac today, and has more life and depth. Rich and fine. Long and spicy and sweet on the finish.

Cheval-Blanc   **Drink up**   15.0

Medium-full colour. Aromatic nose, a touch lactic. Exotic, a bit overblown. Medium body. A bit maderized. A bit sweet-sour. Not astringent at all but a bizarre wine which doesn't really fit together. Fresh because of the high acidity.

Figeac   **Drink soon**   16.0

Medium-full colour. Full, rich, meaty, old-fashioned nose. Aspects of tar. A bit dense. Full, rich, chunky, a typical old-style wine. Not as dense as a 1950. Good fruit and grip inside, but better with food. Yet still holding up well and finishes positively. Very good quality. I've had better bottles.

Fonroque   **Now–1996**   15.5

Full colour. Still quite vigorous looking. Full, lush, aromatic nose. This is full, rich and concentrated. Still plenty of life. Full body, sweet and ripe and of good quality. A little chunky and astringent but not too much so to detract from the enjoyment. Still long and vigorous. Good plus.

Pavie-Macquin   **Past its best**   —

Medium-full colour. Dirty nose. Not corked, just way past its best and now coarse and decayed. Could have been good once but now finished.

Trottevieille   **Drink up**   14.0

(Bottled by Harveys of Bristol) Fullish colour. Interesting, evolved nose. A touch vegetal/herbal. Rapidly evolved in the glass. Medium body. Still enjoyment to be had here but it is now on the descent. Was fruity and stylish. Not bad, was better.

POMEROL

Beauregard   **Drink soon**   14.0

Medium to medium-full colour. Fragrant nose but quite evolved. High-toned but now fading. A medium-bodied wine with a pleasant, almost boiled-sweety fruit. Doesn't have the class of some but a quite good effort which is still fresh.

Clos René   **Drink soon**   16.0

Full colour. Still vigorous. Ripe, ample, vigorous, rich and voluptuous on the nose. High-toned. Fullish, spicy, fat and old-viney. This is very good. Losing a little of its vigour and became a bit astringent in the glass. Yet still plenty of enjoyment.

Nénin   **Drink up**   14.0

Fullish colour. Little undue maturity. Rich, fat and ample on the nose. A little reduction at first. Somewhat earthy. The fruit seemed to evaporate quickly and the wine got a bit coarse. Medium to medium-full. Not short. Plump and fruity, but the class is beginning to go. Collapsed in the glass. Was good. Not short.

Pétrus   **Past its best**   —

(Bottled by Avits, Belgium) Medium-full colour. The nose has tired a bit. It is spicy but a bit pinched, and there is some oxidation. Medium body. Has lost a lot of its fruit and vigour. I think it had class and balance in its prime though.

Pétrus   **Now–1996**   16.5

Full colour. Still immature looking. A little dense and stewed, the *vin de presse* (or the stalks) showing through, on the nose. Grew muddy and coarse in the glass. On the palate a cedary, rich, voluptuous sort of wine. Sandalwoody. Has sex appeal but lacks a bit of class and grip. Will still keep though.

Latour-à-Pomerol   **Drink soon**   18.0

Fullish colour. A lovely, velvety, rich nose. Old-vine concentration. Very good depth. Full, rich, vigorous and with very concentrated fruit. This is alive and voluptuous. Long and positive. Fine. Still has plenty of life.

Trotanoy   **Drink up**   13.0

(Bottled by Avery's) Medium to medium-full colour. An open nose. A little loose but not pinched or dried out. Not coarse either. Medium body. This has also lost a lot of its fruit. Shows both a little astringency and a little acidity.

GRAVES

Carbonnieux   **Drink soon**   15.0

Good vigorous colour. Very full. Quite austere on the nose. A little dense. Full, quite solid on the palate. There is richness but a little astringency. It lacks generosity. Good though. Will still keep.

Domaine de Chevalier   **Now–1997**   17.5

Fullish, vigorous colour. A lighter nose than the La Mission-Haut-Brion. Good fruit, but it's beginning to dry up. Fine and classy nevertheless. Has depth and length and complexity. Subtle and long. Very lovely. Will still keep well. A more restrained wine than the La Mission. More discreet.

Haut-Brion   Now–1997   18.0
Fullish colour. Somewhat lumpy and dead on the nose. Has lost a bit of its fruit. Touch of bonfires. Got a little less inflexible as it evolved in the glass. Full, rich, fleshy, aromatic and voluptuous. In fact a rich, concentrated, generous wine. Long and spicy on the finish. Fine. Still vigorous.

La Mission-Haut-Brion   Now–1998   19.0
Full, vigorous colour. Rich, fat, complex but full and vigorous nose. This is lovely. Excellent quality here, sweet and ripe. Quite full, balanced and classy. Lovely fruit. Very long and opulent. *Grand vin*! An exuberant example. Plenty of life ahead.

MARGAUX AND SOUTHERN MÉDOC

Cantemerle   Now–1996   16.0
(Bottled by Liggins, Birmingham) Medium colour. A fragrant example on the nose which has now begun to lighten up. Medium body. Soft and gently fruity. Very stylish. No astringency. This is long and classy though without the concentration of great. Very good though. Long and positive on the finish. Will still keep well.

Giscours   Drink soon   15.0
Medium to medium-full colour. Attractive, aromatic, slightly earthy nose. Has lightened up a little now but there is still enjoyment here. Medium-full body. Plump and fruity if just a little four-square. A touch of astringency. Yet quite rich. Certainly good but lacks a little complexity.

Malescot   Drink soon   12.0
Good full colour. Quite a chunky nose. Now showing a bit of age and oxidation. But good ripe fruit as well. Elements of molasses and liquorice now. On the palate the acidity is very apparent, and the wine is a little sour. Medium-full body. No astringency but lacks charm.

Margaux   Drink soon   16.0
Medium-full colour. A little dirty or woody. Possibly corky. Certainly not completely clean. Yet a soft, feminine wine with plenty of class underneath. Cabernet shows. Good acidity. This has finesse. But now needs drinking soon.

Palmer   Drink soon   17.0
Fullish colour. Soft, fragrant, classy nose. Very good fruit. Still plump and vigorous. Beginning to show age but is medium-full, complex and has a lot of finesse and subtlety. Still long, lovely. Fine.

Rauzan-Gassies   Drink up   13.5
(Shipped by Calvet) Fullish colour. A little dry – in a papery sense – on the nose. This has also

began to lose a little of its fruit. Medium-full body. A bit of astringency on the palate. Quite a good wine but now beginning to dry up. I'm not sure it had that much class in its prime.

SAINT-JULIEN

Beychevelle   Drink up   15.5
Medium to medium-full colour. Fragrant nose. Getting soft, but not as yet too astringent. Yet it has lost a bit of its intensity. There is an absence of vigour at the end and also a bit of cleanliness and class. Yet the attack has fruit and good style. Good quality. Was even better. Medium body.

Branaire   Drink soon   15.0
Fullish colour. Quite a sturdy, earthy nose. Yet still has vigour. Not too dense. Full, fat, a touch four-square but rich and muscular and still with life. It has a little astringency but essentially a good, slightly ungainly, structured wine.

Ducru-Beaucaillou   Drink soon   15.0
Good full colour. No undue maturity. Full, rich, aromatic, gamey nose. Still vigorous. Quite a sturdy example. Fullish, rich, meaty, ample. There is still plenty of wine here, though not perhaps a great deal of class. Long though. I've seen better.

Gruaud-Larose   Past its best   —
Medium to medium-full colour. This is now rather old and oxidized on the nose. Minty aspects. High toned. Medium body. Rather too far over the top to offer enjoyment. This was a good wine in its prime. Other bottles recently have still been very good.

Léoville-Barton   Drink soon   16.0
(Bottled by Barton and Guestier, Bordeaux) Medium-full colour. There is a little H2S on the nose and some astringency. It doesn't have the class of the other Léovilles at first. A little pinched. Medium-full. Yet rich and still alive. Very good.

Léoville-Las-Cases   Now–1996   17.5
(Magnum) Medium-full colour. No undue sign of maturity. Fat, rich, concentrated Cabernet nose. There is plenty of depth here. This is very good. Fullish, ripe, vigorous. Very clean and classic. Good grip and still has plenty of life. The finish is rich and ample and positive. Long. Fine.

Léoville-Poyferre   Drink up   15.0
(Bottled by Justerini and Brooks, England) Medium-full colour. Rich, ample, oaky-cedary nose. Good vigour at first. Fine, ripe Cabernet with a lot of depth. Began to oxidize as it developed in the glass though. Fullish, quite structured, still sweet. This has richness and old-vine concentration. I don't find the element of oxidation detracts too much. A little astringent though. Yet finishes well. Didn't hold up in the glass. The oldest of the three Léovilles.

Talbot — —

Medium to medium-full colour. Corked on the nose. Rich and fat and classy on the palate though. And still with life. A pity.

PAUILLAC

Batailley   Drink up   12.5

Medium-full colour. Old nose. Smells a bit of consommé and has a touch of H2S. Somewhat dry on the attack, with the fruit having lost out to the acidity. But not too astringent on the finish. Medium body. Lacks class.

Carruades de Château Lafite

           Drink soon   14.5

Fullish colour. Not a lot of maturity. Sturdy nose. A little dry and lumpy. A good wine but a bit dry and rigid now. Fullish. Yet lacks a bit of fat and dimension on the follow-through. Not too astringent. Not too short.

Grand-Puy-Ducasse   Drink soon   14.0

Good colour. Ripe nose. Lacks a bit of class but reasonable structure and vigour. Medium to medium-full body. Ripe on the palate and has reasonable balance. Quite good fruit but not much depth or style.

Lafite   Now–2000   19.5

Fullish colour. Fat, rich and voluptuous on the nose. Plenty of depth here. This is high quality. Full, tannic, very rich and concentrated. Cedary. Mouton-ish. Lovely wine with fat and crammed with fruit. Very long. Very vigorous. Very classy. Excellent. Lovely finish.

Latour   Now–2000 plus   20.0

Full colour. Classic nose. This is youthful. Has very fine Cabernet fruit. Quite austere but real depth, class and concentration. Classic wine. Full, austere, concentrated and multidimensional. Excellent, totally cool fruit. Very very long and subtle. Quite splendid. *Grand vin*!

Lynch-Bages   Drink up   15.5

Medium-full colour. Minty nose. High-toned. But a little age on the palate. Medium-full. Balanced, stylish, a bit astringent. But a residual class here. Plump and fat. A bit past its best.

Lynch-Moussas   Drink up   13.5

Medium to medium-full colour. A bit old and faded on the nose. Some attenuation. Medium body. A bit astringent. But this had more class than the Pontet-Canet and Batailley. Now a bit past its best yet the finish is reasonably positive.

Mouton-Cadet   Drink soon   15.0

Medium-full colour. Smells of mocha, coffee and chocolate mousse. A full wine. Meaty, rich, concentrated and tannic. This has depth, and still has vigour. Good long finish. Plenty of quality here. Getting a bit astringent as it develops.

Mouton-Rothschild   Drink soon   14.0

Medium to medium-full colour. Soft, herbal nose but lacks a bit of fat and generosity. This shows a bit of age, has become a little coarse. Medium body. Spicy and even a touch of astringency. Never had much depth or concentration. I've had much better bottles.

Pichon-Longueville-Baron

           Drink soon   16.0

Full colour, still no real sign of age. Ripe, rich, youthful, gamey nose. Medium-full, soft, spicy, chocolatey on the palate. Rich and meaty, more structured than Pichon-Lalande, less old-viney too. Plenty of vigour at first but did not hold up very well in the glass. Very good finish. Complex.

Pichon-Longueville, Comtesse de Lalande
Drink soon   16.0

Medium-full colour. There is an aspect of tank about this, and the fruit is now beginning to dry out. Medium body. Not a lot of vigour and depth but well-made. The finish is long and quite complex. Did not fall apart in the glass. Very good.

Pontet-Canet   Drink soon   13.5

(Bottled in Bordeaux by Cruse) Fullish colour. A little dry and lumpy on the nose. A little faded on the palate. Medium body. Somewhat sturdy and old-fashioned with reasonable fruit and grip. Not astringent. But lacks generosity, dimension and class. Not too old though. Not bad.

SAINT ESTÈPHE

Calon-Ségur   Past its best   —

(Bottled by Manoppier-Peyrelongue, Bordeaux) Rather an old-looking colour now. Rather past it on the nose too. One can see on the palate that there was good fruit and style here but it is now well over the hill.

Cos d'Estournel   Drink soon   15.5

Good colour. Aromatic nose. This has good depth, and even style. Ripe, spicy, old-viney. Medium-full body, a bit older than the Phélan-Ségur but also has complexity and good style. Still long and subtle.

Montrose   Now–1996   17.0

Medium-full colour. Rich, full, chunky, earthy nose. It lacks a bit of flexibilty and roundness. On the palate the least spicy and the most vigorous of the four. Cool. Stylish. Has the generosity that seemed lacking on the nose. The best of the four.

Phélan-Ségur   Drink soon   16.0

(Bottled by Justerini and Brooks, England) Full, rich colour. This is full and rich on the nose but there is just a faint whiff of yoghurt. Full body. Quite a tough, tannic wine but rich and fat as well, and although it is a bit astringent there is still plenty of pleasure to be had here. Rich long finish. Ample. Very good.

1955 CLARET

It is remarkable how long correctly stored claret will last. Here is a vintage which was abundant, whose wines were reasonably full but neither *that* concentrated nor *that* high in acidity, which can still offer vigorous wines after more than three decades and a half in bottle. I remember drinking mature 1955 Bordeaux when I was a student in the early 1960s. I recall in particular Cos d'Estournel and Calon-Ségur, Lynch-Bages and the three Léovilles, Palmer and Pape-Clément. They were ripe and attractive then: they are still delicious now. There is an axiom that a wine will remain at its peak – though continuing to evolve, of course – for at least as long as it has taken to get there. The words that need underlining are 'at least'. It seems for good Bordeaux that 'at least' can be, if the vintage is good, safely replaced by 'three or four times'.

THE WEATHER

The climatic pattern presented few problems. After a rainy winter, a brief window of spring in February was followed by a cold and frosty March. April was dry and warm, encouraging an early start to the vegetative cycle. Though it was cooler in May it remained dry, and a successful flowering took place at the usual time at the beginning of June. Thereafter, apart from a rainy week at the end of the month, the weather was almost ideally warm and sunny, indeed at times quite hot, until the beginning of September. There were then some much needed showers, followed by fine conditions throughout the rest of the month and into late October. The run-up to the harvest, which began on 21 September, was one of the driest in the last 45 years, only being surpassed by 1961, 1962, 1978, 1985, 1988 and, often forgotten, 1977.

FIRST REPORTS

It was a plentiful harvest, the biggest of the successful vintages since the war to date: just under 1.3 million hectolitres of red wine and just over 1.8 million hectolitres of white. Nineteen fifty was marginally larger; 1953 just a little smaller. With savage frosts which followed in February 1956, devastating the Bordeaux *vignoble*, it would not be until 1962 that volumes would recover. If the figures seem dwarfed by the 3.5 if not 4 million hectolitre red wine harvests of today, we must remember that in those days Bordeaux was predominantly a white wine producing region. Today over 75 per cent of the harvest is red.

1955 was a consistent vintage across the Gironde *département*; indeed it was a good vintage for white Bordeaux and Sauternes too; but 'good' is about it. Though the wines had body and fruit and reasonable balance they seemed only rarely to shine with that extra spark of excitement which marks a great vintage. The 1952s had been widely bought. The 1955s were too, but by comparison they lacked definition.

Moreover, despite the size of the harvest, they were not cheap. By the time they arrived on the market it was apparent that the 1956 red wine harvest had been almost wiped out – it would yield barely a quarter of its predecessor. Nineteen fifty-five first-growth prices rose from 300,000 to 350,000 (old) francs per *tonneau* to 500,000 to 550,000; an increase which would take them over a £1 per bottle retail for the first time. 'This seemed rather expensive at the time,' says Penning-Rowsell. The second- and third-classed growths I bought in the early 1960s cost me about 15s. (75p), I remember, only about twice as much as the cheapest rot-gut, and less than a bottle of decent sherry. Not having been brought up on the bargain prices which pertained before the war, I did not consider this excessive.

THE BEST WINES

I have always considered the 1955 vintage at its best in the Graves. The top Graves are consistently elegant. Châteaux Haut-Brion, La Mission-Haut-Brion, Pape-Clément and Domaine de Chevalier are all fine. Lesser wines such as Carbonnieux and Haut-Bailly used to be good, but I have not seen them for some while. Malartic-Lagravière is a bit solid, as it usually was in those days. So is La Tour-Martillac.

Some of the wines of Margaux are now past their best. Château Margaux itself is faded, but was still enjoyable from bottles direct from the château recently. The finesse was still there. Palmer is a little more vigorous. At a lower level Rausan-Ségla and Prieuré-Lichine are, if needing drinking, certainly successes. Lascombes is sturdier and still holding up well. Cantemerle, from further south, is soft and fragrant, but towards the end of its useful life. Others are and were always less good. There were a lot of new vines in this conglomerate commune at the time. Indeed some properties in this area were still more or less moribund.

There are many fine 1955 Saint-Juliens. Of the Léovilles, I have always preferred the Barton and the Poyferré to the Las-Cases (I feel it was in 1959 that Las-Cases really began to sing) and Langoa is temptingly seductive too. Gruaud-Larose and to a lesser extent Talbot are rich and full. Beychevelle is subtle and stylish. Ducru-Beaucaillou is good but not exceptional. Lagrange is horrid. To my regret I have never seen Saint-Pierre-Sevaistre: sturdier than most, perhaps a touch too much so, but rich nevertheless, I would think.

Pauillac is another successful commune. Though the Lafite is fading somewhat now, there is plenty of life and plenty of quality in both Latour and Mouton-Rothschild. These are probably the two best 1955s of all. Neither of the Pichons is exceptional, but the Countess was soft and fragrant last time out and the Baron, though chunkier, had no lack of richness (this was the château-bottling, as distinct from the wine which is noted below). Better, I have felt, have been the top fifth growths, in particular Lynch-Bages and Grand-Puy-Lacoste. At a lower level, Batailley, Mouton d'Armailhacq (as Mouton-Baronne-Philippe was then) and Pontet-Canet are all competent.

All three top Saint-Estèphes are fine, Cos better than Calon and Calon superior to Montrose. As far as I know, I have not sampled Cos-Labory or Lafon-Rochet. I do remember a very good De Pez, but that was a long time ago.

There are some good Libournais wines, but in general not as many as there are in the Médoc. The top wines: Pétrus, Cheval-Blanc, Figeac, La Gaffelière, Magdelaine, Canon, Trotanoy, Vieux Château Certan, Lafleur, La Conseillante, Lafleur-Pétrus and Gazin are at least as good as their reputations would indicate, and if recent experiences are anything to go by, not over the hill. Belair and Ausone are gentle and subtle, but fading. There are Belgian bottlings which are as good as the château bottlings.

THE TASTING

Liz and Mike Berry of La Vigneronne held a 1955 claret tasting in March 1990, and another of Belgian bottlings of old Libournais wines in December. At the same time I was on the hunt for other 1955s which I had not seen recently. Here are my notes. The wines are château-bottled unless otherwise stated.

	Optimum Drinking	Mark out of 20

SAINT-EMILION

Cheval-Blanc Now–1996 16.5

(Belgian bottled, Grafe-Lecocq) Fine, full, vigorous colour. A little four-square on the nose. Vinous but otherwise a little characterless. Quite full. Chocolatey but not without fruit. A sturdy wine with unusual structure for a 1955. Good richness. Finishes well. Fine, fat and long. Refined

on the finish. Spicy, even slightly burnt. Still has vigour.

La Dominique Drink up 15.0

(Belgian bottled) Good, mature colour. More Merlot on the nose than Magdelaine. More evolved. Slightly attenuated. Medium body. Quite fat and fruity but has become a bit diffuse. Some touches of astringency. Has character though. And good fruit, which didn't dry out as it evolved. Good.

La Gaffelière-Naudes Drink soon 16.5
(Belgian bottled) Good, mature colour. Still vigorous. Rich but earthy on the nose. Yet more
fruit and depth than Magdelaine if without quite
the class. A full, originally quite tannic wine.
Good old-vine concentration to support it. A bit
old-fashioned. Meaty. Still has life. Very good.
Good finish.

La Gaffelière-Naudes Drink soon 16.5
(Bottled by Corney & Barrow) Good colour.
Firm, concentrated, chocolatey, old-vine nose.
Some age on the palate but stylish and fragrant.
Elegant and originally fullish, if it has not light-
ened up a little. Good fruit. Plenty of depth.
Shows the quality of the wine the estate produced
at the time. Very good.

Magdelaine Drink soon 16.5
(Belgian bottled) Good, vigorous colour. Rich,
plump, elegant nose. Still vigorous on the palate,
though it has perhaps lost a little of its fruit. A
pleasant wine which is beginning to show signs of
shortening and losing elegance on the finish.
Getting a bit diffuse at the end. Very good
though. Especially on the nose.

POMEROL

Clos-du-Commandeur Drink soon 14.0
(Belgian bottled, Vandemeulen) Medium colour.
Soft, ripe nose, slightly spicy but good concentrat-
ed Merlot, well supported by acidity and no fade.
Medium body. A little dry but not astringent.
One bottle which is still most enjoyable and by no
means on its last legs. The other bottle was over
the hill.

Gazin Drink soon 15.5
Good colour, mature. Fat Merlot nose, quite
fresh, though fully mature. Slight touch of age as it
developed. Getting a little pinched. Full, rich,
round, slightly sweet on the palate. Spicy taste.
Plenty of life ahead of it. Finishes well and interestingly.

Pétrus Past its best 16.0
(Belgian bottled by Vandemeulen) Good, full,
mature colour. There is just a touch of maderization on the nose and it appears to be thinning out
a little. But there is still plenty of enjoyment to be
had. Medium body. Ripe and stylish, but getting
a little bitter and astringent. Balanced and plump
but a little past its best. Not short though, nor too
dry on the finish.

Vieux Château Certan Drink soon 16.5
Quite full colour, quite a strong nose. Meaty,
rich, and ample on the nose. Sweet, slightly roasted on the palate. A full, fat, plummy wine which
is still holding up well. No astringency. Good finish. Long and satisfying.

GRAVES

Domaine de Chevalier Drink soon 17.5
(Magnum) Medium-full colour, mature but
youthful for its age. Soft, fragrant nose, now a
touch of lightening up to leave the warm brick,
faded-roses smell of an old Graves. Medium body,
getting a little loose but sweet and ripe, not short
of length. Classy, still vigorous. Proof again of
what a very good vintage 1955 was in the Graves.
Long, fragrant, ripe, even complex. Elegant.

Haut-Brion Drink soon 18.5
Good colour, alive and mature; earthy, slightly
farmyardy nose. Fullish on the palate. Rich and
spicy but again farmyard touches (carthorsey).
Underneath typical Haut-Brion concentration of
cedar and soft fruit and long on the finish.
Complex. Fine old wine. But will go down quite
soon.

La Tour-Martillac Drink up 14.0
Very fine colour, a little maturity. Very fine
cedarwood, warm brick, baked earth and soft
fruit, Graves nose. On the palate this shows some
age, full but a touch drying up. Possibly slightly
inky. Yet it finishes well.

MARGAUX

Margaux Drink up 17.0
Medium colour, mature, certainly shows age; a bit
weak and thin on the nose; medium body. Faded
roses and old tea, yet elegance. Faint chocolate-
toffee residue. Some astringency and age. Yet
quality. Finishes still long if a bit faded.

Prieuré-Lichine Drink soon 15.5
Quite full, slightly fading colour. Lovely, fragrant,
old-vine, concentrated nose. This is gently getting
to the end of its life but still has plenty of fruit. A
lot of elegance. Fine, indeed.

Rausan-Ségla Drink up 15.0
(English bottled ?) Good colour. Quite soft and
aged on the nose, but not dry or mean. Medium
body. The acidity is beginning to show, but underneath the wine is cedary and quite stylish. Still
enjoyable but needs drinking. Got a bit lean as it
evolved in the glass.

SAINT-JULIEN

Beychevelle Drink soon 16.0
Fullish, mature colour. This is holding up well.
Soft, ripe, stylish nose. Medium body. A subtle,
soft wine with lovely fruit. Long and silky. An el-
egant wine. Complex on the finish. Very good.
Still has style and vigour.

Talbot Drink soon 15.0
(Bottled by Corney & Barrow) Some age on the
colour. Ripe but sturdy on the nose. The usual
good workhorse style of Talbot. Slightly sturdy,
slightly sweet, just a vestige of sweet-sour, volatile

acidity. Medium-full, a little astringency. Good but lacks elegance. Still has some life.

PAUILLAC

Grand-Puy-Lacoste   **Drink up**   16.5
Good, full colour, not a lot of maturity. Refined, old Cabernet nose. Lightening up. Medium body. Some age (other bottle quite finished). Looser knit, less fat, more classic Cabernet than Calon-Ségur. Elegant. Not that sturdy. Pretty but very elegant.

Lafite   **Drink up**   17.0
Medium colour, now brown. This is an arsenic and old lace (to borrow Michael Broadbent's expression) sort of wine. Full of old truffle, mushroom, autumn-leaves-after-a-brief-shower sort of spices. Rather older than the wines below. Soft, fragrant. A faded wine but with the charm of a distinguished old gentleman.

Latour   **Now–1997**   19.0
Full colour, less maturity than the Mouton. Austere, restrained, classy nose but no great succulence. This is a little disappointing as the wine seems to have lost a little of its fruit. Fullish, concentrated. Fine but not great. Yet has the breed of Latour. Still plenty of life.

Lynch-Bages   **Drink soon**   14.0
(English bottled) Good, full, vigorous colour. Fading a little on the nose. Lightened but not too lean. Originally ripe and vigorous and with plenty of depth. You can see this on the palate but a certain cloying astringency is now in the way. The other bottle had rather more fruit and life (16.0 plus).

Mouton-Rothschild   **Now–1997**   19.0
Full colour. Opulent, meaty, rich and fat on the nose and palate. Seems riper than the Latour.

More exotic fruit. Fullish, vigorous. Again fine but not great. Plenty of life still.

Pichon-Longueville-Baron
      Past its best   9.0
(English bottled, shipped by Barton & Guestier) Slight muddy colour but still full. Mellow, plump but not exactly elegant on the nose. Excessively acidic and very astringent on the attack, though not too dry on the palate. Too mean for enjoyment though. The other bottle was a bit better but was still rather too lean (12.5).

SAINT-ESTÈPHE

Calon-Ségur   **Drink soon**   16.0
Good, full, mature colour. Interesting, spicy nose, some age but ripe and concentrated. Full, creamy, old-vine taste, fat and rich, shows age and astringency but still has grip on the finish. Warm and round. Good.

Cos d'Estournel   **Drink soon**   16.5
(Magnum) Good, full colour. Now mature. Shows a little age on the nose, just a little astringent and lumpy, it seems. Has dried up quickly in the glass. Yet nevertheless a very complex flavour. Ultimately (or originally) a wine of greater breed than the 1959 I tasted alongside it. Round, harmonious, less bulky. Still very enjoyable.

Montrose   **Drink soon**   15.0
(Bottled by Corney & Barrow) Good, vigorous colour. Good vigorous, black-cherry and chocolate Montrose nose. Fullish, was quite tannic in its youth. This was supported by rich fruit in a typically austere Saint-Estèphe sturdy way. Now the acidity is beginning to show and the fruit is drying up and coarsening. Yet there is still sweetness here.

1952, 1953 CLARET

Adjacent successful claret vintages constantly provide useful opportunities for comparison, enjoyment and discussion over their respective characters, merit and potential for longevity, especially if there are no clear-cut or consistent conclusions to be drawn. Those older than I have deliberated on the relative joys of 1899 and 1900, of 1928 and 1929. I suspect that in the years to come, when the wines are mature, we shall be disputing the superiority of the 1985s over the 1986s, or vice-versa; and making interesting comparisons between the 1989s and the 1990s, with perhaps a 1988 secreted among the range for good measure. After all, any excuse to open a pair of bottles rather than a single example is a good one!

Nineteen fifty-two and 1953 were both very good vintages. The former was firm and tannic, in some cases hard and unyielding, and was particularly fine in the Libournais; the latter was abundant and generous, the epitome of elegance, charm and balance: best in the Médoc and the Graves. They were both in their prime when I first started drinking wine with some discernment in the early 1960s, and I have been enjoying them ever since. Though in my experience some of the 1953s are beginning to show their age – and why not? They are 40 years old, after all – the best are still delicious today.

THE WEATHER

Nineteen fifty-two was a hot year which turned cool as the summer progressed. The development of the vegetation was given an early impetus by a warm spring. June was hot, with the flowering taking place under splendidly clear and sunny skies, and July and most of August were also very warm and dry. Then, abruptly, the summer ended. In the next few weeks a lot of rain was to fall, and even when the downpours intermittently ceased the Bordeaux *vignoble* continued to be covered by grey lowering skies. It was also cold. There is a parallel to be drawn with 1975 here, though in 1975 the precipitation in August and September was even greater (216 millimetres as against 152). In both vintages the grape skins had been toughened by earlier drought and high temperatures. In both vintages the net result in the Médoc, though to a lesser extent in Saint-Emilion and Pomerol, was the creation of wines with somewhat aggressive, unripe tannins which threatened to overwhelm the fruit and which took a long time to mellow. The vintage began reasonably early, on 19 September. The yield was average, larger than 1949 but smaller than 1948; a long way from the abundance of 1947 and 1950, and, as it would turn out, 1953.

Nineteen fifty-three began with an abundant *sortie* of potential bunches of grapes. Spring was early, crisp and dry. It was cold overnight but not sufficiently so to cause any damage. The flowering began a week later than it had done in the previous vintage, and despite some rain at the end took place successfully. July was mixed, August splendid, and September for the most part warm and sunny without being excessively hot. Towards the end of the month there were storms, but despite this the August-September precipitation was only just over half that of 1952, well under the average. The harvest, delayed by this bout of bad weather, was not fully under way until 2 October, but by then the sun had returned. A large crop of healthy, ripe grapes was collected in perfect conditions. The auguries were promising.

THE WINES

If the parallel with 1952 is 1975, the vintage similar to 1953 is 1970. In both years the crop was large, consistent across the Bordeaux area – though at its finest in the Médoc and the Graves – and consistent up and down the hierarchy from *petits châteaux* to first growth. In both vintages the wines initially appeared to have less potential for longevity than in fact was the case. They were round and balanced and full of ripe fruit but did not seem to have much structure. In fact the 1953s lasted exceptionally well, proving once again that it is harmony and not sheer size which ensures a capacity to age.

The 1952s, as I have said, were best in Saint-Emilion and Pomerol. I have three times in recent years had a chance to compare the two Pétrus vintages side by side. On one occasion the 1953 was somewhat over the top and the 1952, though more vigorous, seemed somewhat coarse. On the other occasion both were fine (the 1953 from magnum). The 1952, though, was indisputably better: still a very big wine.

The Trotanoy 1952 has a similar old-fashioned, long-macerated density, showing aspects of leather and coffee and bitter chocolate. It too is not only more vigorous but a finer, more complex wine than the 1953. Vieux Château Certan 1953 is sweet and succulent and seductive, but the 1952 is more vigorous and has more class (if in good condition – the bottle below was not on form). Lafleur I only know from the 1952. This too has the burnt berry taste which seems to be a characteristic of these top Pomerols: a fine wine. It is rather more exciting and positive than the Latour-à-Pomerol though that is still a lovely wine. Lafleur-Pétrus 1953 has come my way more often than the 1952. This 1953 is full, powerful, voluptuous and subtle; an indication that the 1953 is highly successful in the Libournais in those vineyards where the yield was not too excessive. The 1952 below is the only example apart from rather inky Belgian bottlings which I have seen recently: dense but certainly concentrated. Both vintages of La Conseillante are lovely. Petit-Village 1953, in a Belgian bottling, was gentle and attractive, if fading in December 1990. The single recent time I tasted Certande-May 1953 it started off as an ethereal, silky-smooth gem but rapidly fell apart in the glass.

Despite the evidence of the notes in the comparative tasting which follows, the 1952 Cheval-Blanc is superior to the 1953. Twice in previous comparative tastings I have rated it much the better – and the more vigorous. It is a meaty, resiny, complex, powerful wine – what I understand the word 'vinosity' to mean. I have described the Vieux Château Certan 1952 as excellent. In December 1985 I saw VCC and Cheval-Blanc alongside each other. The Cheval-Blanc was in a class of its own. Both vintages of Ausone are rather faded, as we might expect, but elegant none the less. An Avery-bottled 1952 in magnum was the best recent example: long and distinguished and still vigorous in November 1984. But other examples have indicated that both vintages should be approached with caution. I have never seen both Figeacs on form at the same time. In June 1985, at the château, it was the 1953 which was off-form. In December 1989, it was the turn of the 1952. But here it is the 1953 which is the better wine. La Gaffelière (-Naudes, as it was then) is better in the earlier vintage: indeed this is probably the second best Saint-Emilion. Yet the 1953 was still fat, plump and alive in April, 1988. Until recently I had not seen either of the Magdelaines since March 1980. On that occasion the 1952 was very classy; the 1953 disappointing. Canon 1952 was a great deal more vigorous and concentrated last time out than the example below. The 1953 is very good indeed but it does not have the breed of the top Médocs. Belair 1953 was substantial, fruity and very elegant in March 1990. But here I have no experience of the 1952. Pavie 1953 was a gentle, elegant, balanced old gentleman in 1985, a wine with rather more breeding than what must always have been a rather chunky Trottevieille. Again I have no recent experience of the 1952.

It could well be argued that the two vintages are equally successful, if of different character, in the Graves. Back in 1964, when I was undertaking a *stage* in Bordeaux with the firm of Calvet, it was the custom of the family to invite the *stagiaires* to Sunday lunch once a month or so and generously to serve something rather special in order that we could experience what great wine could give. The earlier you implant yardsticks the better! On one occasion the wines were the 1952 and 1953 Haut-Brion. I knew little about wine at the time, but enough to realize that I was in the presence of magic, that I was sampling the rarity of the sublime. The 1952 has come my way rather more often in recent years than the 1953. It is certainly very fine. The 1953, on the other hand, when in good condition, has been sheer nectar. The La Missions of both vintages have been well-liked by such as Penning-Rowsell, Peppercorn and Broadbent but I have found a lack of real breed in both, and they are wines I have seen reasonably often. Chevalier is best in 1953, a lovely bottle, as is the same vintage of Pape-Clément. Malartic-Lagravière 1952 is a generous, less-tough-than-normal bottle. I have not sampled the 1953 recently. La Tour-Haut-Brion 1953 showed well in the tasting which follows, though the Haut-Bailly was faded. But I cannot speak for either 1952. Nor can I speak for De Fieuzal, Carbonnieux and the rest.

It is when we get into the Médoc that the 1952s appear at their toughest and the 1953s at their most perfectly balanced and aristocratic (though this latter remark is not to belittle the Haut-Brion). The reputation of the Lafite 1953 is well known. Bottlings in those days took place barrel by barrel, without prior *égalisage*, and often in the larger properties over a period of months. Wine experiences therefore vary, especially after 30 years or more when the complications of different storage conditions additionally play their part. Happily my encounters with Lafite 1953 have been almost entirely satisfactory, often a glimpse of heaven itself. The beauty of this wine is truly awesome. Margaux at its best is very nearly as exquisite, though now beginning to fade, and the sum of my brushes with 1953s at this level would indicate that both this and the Haut-Brion have the edge over the Mouton despite the results below; though I feel that jockeying wines of this quality into a prosaic pecking order is contempt of court, if not blasphemy. Other 1953s which have given me the sort of pleasure which approaches orgasm include Beychevelle, Ducru, Calon-Ségur, Pichon-Lalande, Léoville-Barton and Palmer (though twice disappointing recently), and perhaps at a slightly lower level Cos d'Estournel, Langoa (a lovely wine – all in finesse), Cantemerle (ditto), Gruaud-Larose, Lynch-Bages, Grand-Puy-Lacoste, Pichon-Baron, Montrose, Talbot, Léoville-Las-Cases, Léoville-Poyferré and Prieuré-Lichine. Some of these are getting a little faded now, but I have rarely had a disappointing Médoc of this vintage.

Many 1952 Médocs began to lose their fruit before they really softened up. There are, nevertheless, bottles which were correctly balanced, if they never had the charm of the subsequent vintage. Mouton and Latour have always seemed to have the edge over the other first growths. Elsewhere Lynch-Bages, both Bartons, Gruaud-Larose and Talbot, Branaire, Beychevelle, Cantemerle, Pichon-Longueville-Baron (better than Lalande in this vintage), Montrose, Calon-Ségur, Cos d'Estournel, Palmer and Ducru-Beaucaillou have stood out. Most, though, are now a little dry and astringent.

THE TASTINGS

In May 1989, I was invited to present the following top 1952s and 1953s to the Jeroboam Club of Bristol.

1953

	Optimum Drinking	Mark out of 20
Cheval-Blanc	Now–1998	18.0

Fullish mature colour. Fine mature nose with a touch of cigar box and caramel. Higher-toned than the 1952. A round, soft, ample medium full bodied wine. Good depth. Fleshy and opulent. Vigorous and most attractive. Will still last well.

Haut-Brion	Drink soon	19.0

Medium-full mature colour. Lighter nose than the La Mission in the sense of less size. But complex, balanced and subtle. Very lovely combination of soft fruit. Definitely first growth. Medium-full. A lovely fragrant, delicate, elegant wine. Very complex. Beginning to show age but such refinement! Lovely. Better than the Margaux today.

Lafite	Now–1997	20.0

Fullish, vigorous colour. Rather better than the 1952. Amazingly vigorous nose. Full, complete, ripe, immaculate. Plump and crammed with fruit. This is an extraordinary wine. Quite full, with enormous concentration (without size) and dimension. Perfect. In amazing condition. Very long. Still very vigorous.

Latour   Now–1998   17.0

Fullish colour, not a lot of maturity. Good fresh Cabernet fruit but not the dimension of the Mouton 1953. Not as big or as masculine as most Latours. Fresh though. Good fruit but not that complex. But not beyond the pale by any means.

Margaux   Drink up   18.5 plus

Medium colour. Fully mature. A little fade on the nose but lovely breed. Gently, subtly fruity. Old roses. Still complex and most enjoyable. Medium body. A ripe, soft, complex wine. Still quite succulent. Very refined. Delicious. But needs drinking soon. Real *premier cru* breed again. Beginning to lighten up.

La Mission-Haut-Brion   Drink soon   16.5

Fullish mature colour. Aromatic, earthy nose with a hint of H2S. Medium-full body. Not – and I don't think it ever was – a blockbuster. Beginning to show a little age. A slight cooked element – treacle tart perhaps. good fleshy spicy fruit. Very good but not really inspiring.

Mouton-Rothschild   Now–1998   19.5

Fullish mature colour. No undue age. Full, round, berry-like fruit on the nose. Ample, fresh, opulent. Very Mouton. Fullish, a generous velvety wine, crammed with fruit. Still vigorous. Lovely.

1952

Cheval-Blanc   Now–1998   17.5

Full mature colour. Full, rich, fat, concentrated nose. Ripe in a slightly cooked plum-tart sense. Full, still tannic. A big, almost dense wine. Old-fashioned, long-macerated wine with a touch of tar and burnt twigs about it. The 1953 has more charm. This has more power. Will still last well.

Haut-Brion   Drink soon   17.5

Fullish mature colour. A little more volatile acidity on the nose than the 1952. Quite chunky. But there is fruit and quality here. Medium-full. A certain astringency but no lack of breed. A gentle wine. Not as magnificent as the 1953 but fine.

Lafite   Drink soon   16.5

Medium-full mature colour. Fragrant nose, but, like the 1952 Margaux, lacking a bit of personality. This is now showing a bit of age. It has lightened up rather than dried out. Yet, like the Margaux there is dimension and breed. Medium-full body. Ripe. Fine quality.

Latour   Now–1997   17.0

Fullish colour, a little more brown than the 1953. Quite a solid nose. Fullish and masculine. Lacks a little grace and sex appeal compared with the Mouton 1952. A solid wine which now shows a bit of its backbone in an astringent way. No better than the 1953 on this occasion. Slightly better on the finish. More age than the 1953. More vigour than the Margaux and the Lafite 1952. I have had better bottles.

Margaux   Drink soon   16.5

Medium-full mature colour. Fine old claret on the nose but without the personality and definition of the 1953. A certain astringency on the palate but a medium to medium-full-bodied, quite classy wine underneath. Better than I had expected. Still enjoyable. Still has first growth class. Older than the Lafite.

La Mission-Haut-Brion   Drink soon   16.0

Fullish mature colour. Full, quite muscular, sturdy nose, but with no lack of flesh. Slightly burnt. Full on the palate. Shows some chunkiness and astringency now. Yet not completely dominated. Again a slight earthy bitterness to the fruit. Beginning to lose its grip. The 1953 is better. Still very good though.

Mouton-Rothschild   Drink soon   18.5

Fine full vigorous mature colour. Rich, opulent, plump, delicious nose, creamy ripe fruit. Still fresh. I find this the most interesting of the 1952s. There is a certain chunky astringency but almost an equal amount of fruit. On palate not as good as the nose but still very fine.

In April 1993 John Avery, Stephen Browett, Lindsay Hamilton and Jan Paulson organized a two-day event. On the first day we sampled, mainly, 1953 Médocs and Graves, on the subsequent afternoon primarily Saint-Emilion and Pomerol 1952s.

1953

Cantemerle   Drink soon   16.0

(Avery's bottling) Mature colour. No undue age. On the nose there is class, but the fruit is drying up now. The wine is medium-bodied. Getting a little astringent but still shows the class and complexity of the vintage. Long and complex still. Very good.

Cantemerle   Drink soon   15.0

This looks as if it has lightened up somewhat. Light on the nose too, though not astringent. Lightish in body, soft, fruity; not dry but has lost its vigour and its complexity. Good, still enjoyable. But not what it was.

Calon-Ségur   Drink quite soon   17.0

Mature colour. No undue age. Refined nose. Soft. No weakness though. But a little dry. Medium body. Classy. Still has plenty of fruit and complexity. Long, subtle with a lot of dimension. Very good indeed. Will still hold up for a while.

Canon   Now–1997   16.5

(Magnum) Medium-full colour mature. Fine, chocolate and cigar boxy. Lovely. Real quality here. Fullish, rich, not a blockbuster, but a wine with lovely fruit. Still holding up. This is complex, fine for a Saint-Emilion. But not the class of the best Médocs.

Domaine de Chevalier Now–1998 17.5
(Magnum) Full colour. Still vigorous. Voluptuous, rich, youthful fruit. This has excellent fruit. At the same time this has great delicacy and intensity. Real class and complexity. It is surprisingly full, surprisingly youthful. Vigorous. At first it seems a bit obvious. But the wine has dimension and class nonetheless. Yet atypical for Chevalier. Usually it is much less voluptuous and much more subtle than this. Fine plus.

Cos d'estournel Drink soon 14.5
Very good colour. Still vigorous. Rich and fat. Fleshy and voluptuous. On the palate a bit four-square and astringent. Medium-full body. There was, I think, always a bit of a hardness about this wine. Yet the finish is long if a little unstylish. Lumpy. Quite good plus.

Gruaud-Larose Now–1997 16.0
(Magnum) Fullish colour. Quite sturdy on the nose and palate. Rich, voluptuous, sweet, earthy in the best sense. Quite a full, solid wine. The sinews show a bit, but still sweet, plenty of enjoyment. Very good but not great. Bigger but not as classy as the Poyferré.

Haut-Bailly Drink up 13.0 (see note)
Light to medium colour. Has lightened up a bit. Light nose. Residue of nuts, but not a lot of fruit. Quite pleasant, but a little hollow in the middle, and has lost a little of its finesse. It is getting a little dirty. Not bad. Was rather better.

Haut-Brion Drink soon 16.0
Excellent full mature colour. Somewhat overblown, a touch of maderization. A bit blowsy. Got a bit dry and dirty as it developed. Open, accessible, high-toned. This has an individual curious flavour. Medium to medium-full. Sweet in a chocolate/coffee *bonbon* sense. I like it but it isn't great. It lacks real class. Will still hold up for a couple of years. Very good.

Lafite Past its best —
Good full colour. Still very vigorous. This is a little oxidized on the nose. But there is still fruit here. And you can still see the finesse. But a bit past its best – or not a good bottle. Very sad. I have had better.

Lafite Drink up 18.0
(Second bottle) Medium-full colour. Mature. A little dry on the nose. The fruit has faded somewhat. On the palate it is a little astringent, a little pinched. The fat has disappeared. Yet the wine has – or had – quality. The finish is still complex. An echo of a *grand vin*.

Langoa-Barton Past its best —
(English bottling) This is brown and old. Old. Oxidized. Finished.

Latour Now–1998 17.0
Very good colour. Still very very youthful. Slightly more four-square on the nose than the others. Rich and fullish, but not as complex. On the palate a bit astringent a bit solid, there is fruit here. Very Cabernet. But it lacks real flexibility and nuance. Very good indeed but not great.

Léoville-Barton Drink soon 17.0
Very good colour. Good vigour. Cedary complex nose. Still vigorous. This has good concentrated fruit. Though at the end it is beginning to show a little age. But it has real depth and old-vine concentration. Now getting towards the end. But still long, classy, multidimensional. A classic. Fine.

Léoville-Las-Cases Drink up 15.0
Good vigorous colour. Round nose. There is an aromatic, sandalwoody element. This is a gentle, classy wine, but it has lost much of its fruit, despite the colour. What is left is ethereally classy, and not short. Still plenty of enjoyment. Good. But not – and never – great.

Léoville-Poyferré Drink soon 17.0
(Magnum) Medium to medium-full colour. Mature. Good nose, but shows a little age on the nose. Yet succulent fruit here nonetheless. Medium-full. Very subtle fruit. Less age on the palate. Classy Cabernet-based fruit. Long. Not quite fine but very good indeed. It doesn't quite have the ripeness and sweetness and intensity.

Lynch-Bages Drink soon 16.5
Fullish, vigorous colour. Very good. Full, rich, old-fashioned nose. Slightly inky, but in the best sense. Malo in bottle here. Even a bit herbaceous. On the palate the wine is meaty, even sweet. It doesn't have quite the grip or complexity or class at the end. I have had it better. But very good plus. Still sweet.

Margaux Drink soon 18.5
Fullish mature colour. Fine, ethereal, super-elegant nose. Sweet. This is medium-full. Rich, silky, perhaps it lacks just a little vigour. But there is still vigour and length and complexity. A lovely example. Really elegant and held up very well in the glass. Fine.

La Mission-Haut-Brion Past its best —
Medium-full, mature colour. A touch dry on the nose. Smells of wet sawdust. Slightly resinous. A little oxidized now. The fruit is faded, the wine a bit short. Past its best. What a pity!

Mouton-Cadet Drink soon 15.5
Mature colour. No undue age. Fullish, aromatic nose. Voluptuous and sexy. Ripe. Medium to medium-full. This is very respectable, if it doesn't

quite have the class and complexity for better than good plus. Still has life.

Mouton-Rothschild   Now–1999   19.0
Full colour. Still immature colour. This is a lovely wine, marvellous succulent but delicate fruity nose. Fabulous fruit. Plump, fullish, ample, very classy. Voluptuous. This has lovely balance. And is still vigorous and very complex. Very nearly *grand vin*. And the best of all today.

Palmer   Drink up   15.5
Mature colour. No undue age. Quite an old nose, but stylish as well as gentle; getting towards the end though. On the palate, though there is residual class, and plenty of it, this is getting a little dry and pinched. Yet the finish is still clean and not really astringent yet. Still agreeable. Medium body. Good plus.

Pape-Clément   Drink up   16.0
Fullish, vigorous colour. Very good but just a bit more age than Lynch-Bages (after which it was served). Ripe, exotic, summer pudding and chocolate. This has a lot of depth and quality – or had at first. But collapsed in the glass. Yet despite the astringency there is class to be seen here. Indeed more class on the finish than the Lynch-Bages.

Pauillac Royale   Past its best   —
(Avery's bottling) Very good colour. Good vigour. There is some volatile acidity and maderization and lactic acid here on the nose. On the palate, despite this, and a little astringency there is plump fruit and some enjoyment. But only for old claret maniacs. Not a good bottle.

Pichon-Longueville, Comtesse de Lalande
**   Now–1998   17.5**
Fullish colour. Still quite youthful, a little cloudy. Ripe, plenty of raspberry-type fruit, but a certain inkiness inside. On the palate fat, plump, very, very ripe and seductive. Fullish, voluptuous. Lovely fruit. Balanced. Long. Fine. Will keep well.

Roc-Saint-Michel   Past Its Best   —
(AC Saint-Emilion) This is very light, though the colour is bright. Somewhat oxidized on the nose. Very dilute on the palate. The fruit is pretty, but the wine is short (though not astringent). Difficult to see what it was really like in its prime.

Talbot   Drink soon   14.5
(English bottled) Good colour. Still looks quite vigorous. Quite sturdy on the nose. A little rigid perhaps. On the palate not too firm. Indeed soft and losing its grip. A bit of a curate's egg. Lacks a bit of real depth, and I wonder if it ever had it. Quite good plus.

La Tour-Haut-Brion   Drink soon   16.0
Good youthful, fullish colour. This is serious wine. Vigour and depth here. This is first growth quality, I wrote at first. Real class. And plenty of life ahead of it. A bit hard though. Got a little inky as it developed. Full, rich, meaty. Ripe and individual. It lacks just a bit of real complexity and fat at the end. But it is certainly very good.

1952

Ausone   Past its best   —
Medium colour. Well matured. Rather thin and pinched now on the nose. Past its best. Rather dried out. The fruit has gone. Not exactly dead, but way over the hill, and not much enjoyment to be had.

Canon   Drink up   14.0
Full colour. Vigorous, youthful. A little fleshy-sweaty on the nose. Has lost a bit of its fruit as well as its elegance. It dried up quickly in the glass. Medium body. A bit mean in the end. A little astringent. This is at the end of its useful life. Quite good at best. Was probably quite a lot better (16–17 or so) five or more years ago.

Cheval-Blanc   Now–2000   19.5
Very full colour. Still very youthful. Full, rich, quite intense. This is balanced, youthful and very concentrated. Fine. Full and opulent on the palate. Still very vigorous. Still lots of ripe, healthy creamy, old-vine concentrated fruit. This is clearly the best of these Saint-Emilions. Lovely rich, spicy aromatic flavour. Excellent. Will last well.

La Conseillante   Now–2000   18.5
Fullish colour. Still vigorous. Lovely rich, aromatic oaky nose. This has concentration, flair and lots of dimension. And a creamy old-vine character as well. Fullish, firm, structured. Very good acidity. Excellent positive fresh fruit. This is long, complex profound and serious. A lovely example. Very fine. Bags of life.

Le Gay   Now–1997   17.0
(Belgian bottled) Good fresh fullish colour. Rich nose, plummy, fat, quite structured, volatile acidity just a touch higher than normal, but this doesn't worry me. On the palate this is fullish, spicy, amply Merlot-y. There is depth here, complexity as well; and also finesse in a slightly earthy sort of way. Long, complex. Still has a few years of life. Very good indeed.

Haut-Brion   Past its best   17.0
Medium-full colour but a little muddy. Slightly old now, but quality there underneath. Not a blockbuster. Medium body. Has lightened up considerably, and also got rather short. It is also not entirely clean now. A bit dry at the end. Not exciting.

Haut-Simard   Drink soon   16.5
Good fullish mature colour. The nose is lightening a little. But there is elegance here. Soft.

Medium body. A ripe wine now showing a little age. But there is quality here. Still some sweetness and still plenty of complexity. Never a blockbuster, I would think. Very good indeed. It tailed off a bit after some time in the glass.

Lafite **Drink up** 15.0

Medium colour. Well matured. Light, slightly faded, but fragrant on the nose. This is now really quite old, though not dried out complexity. But it has lost its sweetness and fat and most of its charm. Yet again one can see the echo of first growth wine. But not as complex as the 1953.

Lafleur **Now–2000** 19.0

Full colour. Vigorous, youthful. Fine, concentrated, very profound nose. This is very special. Full on the palate, mature and complex. Rich, exotic and lovely. The follow-through is vigorous and long and complex. Excellent grip. Quite powerful. Rich and sweet and quite structured. Excellent. Marvellous multidimensional finish. Still has a fine future.

Lafleur-Pétrus **Drink Soon** 18.0

(Not château-bottled) Very full, vigorous, vibrant colour. Still very young. The nose is still a bit closed, it seems, no age, very concentrated indeed. The fruit is still amazingly fresh. Very full, tannic, old-fashioned. There is a certain astringency here but underneath the sheer concentration of the wine comes shining through. Very fine but not as exciting as Lafleur, and it got denser and drier in the glass.

Latour **Now–1997** 17.5

Full colour. Ripe, Cabernet, less rich nose. But fruity and youthful. This is the most vigorous, the most opulent on the palate though, more so than Magdelaine. Good depth, good grip. The most attractive. But not quite as classy and as long at the end.

Magdelaine **Drink soon** 16.0

(Avery's bottling) Good medium-full mature colour. Quite a sturdy nose. Ripe, mellow, rich, aromatic. A fullish wine on the palate, and one which shows a bit of astringency now. This means it doesn't quite have the complexity and dimension for better than very good. The finish is still positive and interesting though.

Magdelaine **Now–1997** 17.5

(Château-bottled) Full mature colour. Still vigorous looking. Rich, a little on the dry side, but elegant and raspberry-flavoured. This is cool and subtle. Not too sturdy. On the palate what was quite a full wine is now mellow and round. Aromatic, spicy, good grip. Plenty of depth. This is fine and complex and still sweet. Finishes very well. Will still keep a bit.

Margaux **Drink soon** 16.0

Medium-full colour. No undue maturity. Plump, vigorous nose. But possibly slightly four-square. This is medium-full. Still quite vigorous. But lacks a bit of depth and nuance. Some depth. Good. But not very exciting. Yet softer and rounder and more fragrant than the Lafite.

Pétrus **Drink up** 15.5

(Belgian bottled) Medium colour. No undue age though. Ripe and still vigorous on the nose. Slightly corky. Clearly predominantly Merlot. Rich and aromatic but a soft round gently intense wine on the palate which is drying up and getting a bit mean at the end now. Not quite what it was, but still enjoyable. Good plus despite the corkiness.

Pétrus **Now–1998** 17.5

Medium-full mature colour. No undue age. Medium-full, fat, plump, concentrated nose. Ample, voluptuous, velvety wine. Fine fruit, seductive and balanced, cedary. This is long and generous and lovely. Sweet and silky. Plenty of life ahead of it. Fine.

Mouton-Rothschild **Now–1996** 18.0

Fullish colour. No undue maturity. Rich plummy nose. This is concentrated and very ample. Fullish, ripe, slightly austere. On the palate the fruit has dried up a bit and lost its generosity. But nevertheless classy, long, complex. Fine. The best at the end of all these.

La Pointe **Drink soon** 16.5

(Château bottled?) Fullish mature colour. This is showing a little age on the nose. It is a little dense and solid, chunky and rather astringent on the palate. But a fullish wine, with good depth: rich and concentrated and oaky. This was rather exciting once, I think, and is still enjoyable. Rich and meaty at the end. Very good plus.

Trotanoy **Drink Soon** 15.5

(Believed 1952, Avery's bottling) Medium to medium-full colour. Mature but no undue age. Light but pleasant, mellow, gently oaky nose. On the palate it is a little dry, but there is fruit and ripe acidity and sweetness here nonetheless. With food it would drink well. The acidity pervades over the finish somewhat. But this is an elegant wine, with good depth. Never a blockbuster. Good plus.

Vieux Château Certan — —

Full colour, but well matured. Oxidized on the nose. This was a bottle I supplied, from an auction job-lot. Full and rich, one could see. But the bottle hadn't been well stored.

1949 CLARET

I have long had a particular admiration for the 1949 Bordeaux vintage. If it lacks the muscular concentration of the 1945s and the sumptuousness of the 1947 vintage, what it possesses in abundance are two elements without which no wine, no vintage can ever be termed great: balance and breed. In this the 1949 has much in common with the Médocs of 1953 – though in this coronation vintage the Saint-Emilions and Pomerols are in general less exciting than they were in 1952. Breed, in the sense of that indefinably aristocratic, harmonious finesse, is the hallmark of the 1949 vintage.

When I first started drinking the top 1949 clarets with any regularity, the vintage was well into its second decade. The very top 1949s were still not yet mature, but the rest were in their prime. I started at the top. Thanks to the generosity of Edmund Penning-Rowsell (who was also to offer Margaux 1953 and Latour 1929 at the same dinner party), one of the first I had the opportunity to enjoy was Mouton-Rothschild. It was fabulous. It remains ensconced as one of the finest clarets I have ever drunk. From my own cellar I remember Léoville-Barton, Gruaud-Larose, Cos d'Estournel, Lynch-Bages, Calon-Ségur and others, the bins long since exhausted, but for some reason few wines from the Libournais. It was to be a decade before I saw Cheval-Blanc, and longer still before I had a chance to sip the fabled Pétrus.

Now the vintage is well over 40 years old. Though I have enjoyed my fair share of the 1949s, it so happens that I had never had the opportunity to indulge in an in-depth comparison of the vintage. Luckily I have friends younger than I. Two of these, Jan Paulson, Swedish by birth, dentist by profession, and dealer in fine and rare wines on the side, and his friend Thomas Dippner, buyer of wines for the Mövenpick group of restaurants in Germany, were both 40 in 1989. This anniversary was celebrated with a tasting of an impressive range of 1949s in Munich in May.

We anticipated that at least some of the wines would be a little faded. It was only to be expected after 40 years. Yet though there were one or two I felt had suffered from poor storage, the vast majority of the twenty wines on the table were not only still in their prime but would still last for another decade yet. The top wine, as far as I was concerned, was clearly Mouton-Rothschild, which I remember the late Baron considered the finest vintage he had ever produced. The group vote placed the Latour second, closely followed by Margaux, Pétrus, La Mission, Cheval-Blanc (though I felt the May bottle did not quite do itself justice), Grand-Puy-Lacoste and Lafite, though in my view this latter example was past its prime. In general the vintage seems remarkably consistent.

THE WEATHER

It was a year of contrasts, of extremes. On 11 July in the Médoc in 1949 the thermometer reached 36 degrees. Yet a month earlier it had been so cold and miserable that Bordeaux experienced one of the worst onsets of *coulure* in recent memory.

January and February were mild and very dry. In March the budding began early, and the vegetation continued to evolve during a soft and pastoral spring until brought to an abrupt halt by cool, rainy, windy weather during the last week of May and the first fortnight in June. Having done its worst and reduced the crop, the weather in the second half of June was fine and warm, progressively getting hotter throughout a record July. This month was extremely dry: August totally rainless. But in early September some much needed water in the form of thunderstorms enabled the ground to avoid totally drying out and prevented the process of maturation from coming to a complete halt. The harvest began in the last week of September, took place under clear skies, with a little rain during one or two nights in the initial week, and it continued fine until the end of October.

THE WINES

It was a small crop. At 734,000 hectolitres (AC Rouge) it was 16 per cent down on that of 1948, 40 per cent less than the abundant 1947 harvest, and only a quarter larger than the tiny 1945 vintage. In part this was the result of the inclement weather conditions during the flowering. The berries themselves were also small.

As a consequence of a summer which was mostly very dry and very hot, one might have expected rather beefy, tannic wines – coarser variations on 1945 perhaps. Thankfully the September rainfall (88 millimetres) occurred at just the right time and was wholly beneficial. The result was wine of immediate attraction, with a good colour, a finely balanced structure, ripe, supple tannins and very stylish, perfumed fruit. While there were some who considered the 1947s to be better across the board – not just in the Libournais – most buyers willingly surrendered to the charms of the 1949. Those who plumped for the 1949 Médocs over those of 1947 have, I think, been proved right.

As far as prices are concerned, a brief glance at the figures might indicate alarming increases over those of 1947: Lafite and Mouton at about 350,000 (1947: 200,000) French francs per *tonneau*; Latour and Margaux about 265,000 (1947: 130,000). But though apparently double in French franc terms one needs to take into account the inflationary state of the national economy and the sinking level of its currency on the world market. Despite the devaluation of the pound in 1949, the British currency bought more francs in 1950 than in 1948, though not enough to make the 1949s cheaper. In dollar terms the two vintages cost the same. Indeed the dollar quadrupled in value against the franc between 1945 and 1950. The 1949s were popular, widely bought, and much in demand. Even after 40 years it remains a glorious vintage, the epitome of claret at its most elegant, as the following notes will amply demonstrate.

THE TASTING

The following wines were tasted in Munich in May 1989. I list them in the order of tasting. I have added a note on Château La Gaffelière, sampled at the château a few days prior to my visit to Germany, and Figeac, sampled in April 1988.

	Maximum Drinking	Mark out of 20
Ausone	Drink soon	16.5

Good colour. Not the greatest structure but soft and plump and classy. Getting towards the end of its useful life. Medium-full body. Fresh and if not that concentrated certainly very classy. Beginning to dry up a little. Soft, sweet, faded-roses character.

Beychevelle	Now–1997	16.0

Medium-full colour. Quite a sturdy nose, but vigorous, good Cabernet. Quite full, coffee and chocolate flavour. Quite substantial. Good fruit. Still quite vigorous on the finish. Very good indeed. Will still last well.

Brane-Cantenac	Drink soon	16.0

Medium-full colour. Slightly faded nose. Ripe but an element of dead leaves. Medium-full body. This is another very classy wine but it is now beginning to dry up a bit. Yet despite a certain astringency on the attack the finish is long, very subtle. Real finesse.

Calon-Ségur	Drink soon	16.5

Medium-full colour. Ripe, voluptuous, fat and rich. Old vines here. Quite full, very ripe fruit. Concentrated and vigorous. Spicy, quite sweet. Saint-Estèphe aspects. Very good but doesn't quite have the breed of the Gruaud.

Cantemerle	Drink soon	15.5

Good colour. Quite an old nose but fragrant and stylish. Medium body. A gentle, complex wine with a feminine, raspberry and violet aspect to the fruit. Now gently fading away but plenty of finesse nevertheless.

Cheval-Blanc	See note	18.0

Good colour. Full, rich nose but now a slight touch of age, even maderization. A ripe wine, medium body. Now a little past its best. Sweet and concentrated on the finish though. Very fine. Badly stored. A bottle sampled the previous October was noted *grand vin*, and still with plenty of life.

Cos d'Estournel	Now–1996	17.0

Medium-full colour. Complex, delicate nose, full of finesse. Very feminine. Might have taken it for a Margaux. Medium-full body. Not quite as vigorous at first because it doesn't have the size of the three above but complex, gentle, very long and lovely. Very classy fruit. Will still keep.

Figeac   Now–1997   17.5

Excellent colour. Really full and rich and dense. Splendid fruit, rich and very, very concentrated, even sweet. Powerful, indeed slightly robust and aggressive but not in a farmyardy sense, just that the structure is very evident. Firm, quite solid, certainly full. Very, very rich. Sumptuous fruit. Sweet; very fine ripe acidity. Very long. Bags of life still.

La Gaffelière-Naudes   Drink soon   17.0

Full colour; mature but no sign of age. Smoky-spicy nose with a touch of caramel and cooked fruit. Fullish, fat, rich and classy on the palate. Good fruit. Freshly balanced. Long and complex. Initially very fine, though a certain amount of underlying decay began to appear as the wine developed in the glass.

Grand-Puy-Lacoste   Now–1996   18.0

Good colour. Marvellous nose. Classic Pauillac breed, old-vine concentration, Cabernet fruit. Fullish, ripe, concentrated, vigorous. Quite an old-fashioned wine in its way. Real class and depth. Very lovely finish. Very high class. Will still keep well.

Gruaud-Larose   Now–1997   17.5

Good colour. Ripe nose with a lot of breed. Very fine and complex. Really classic Saint-Julien breed here. Quite full. This has a touch of astringency about it but essentially a very rich, concentrated wine. Fuller and more vigorous than the Beychevelle and with more depth. Fine. Will still last well.

Haut-Brion   Past its best   17.5

Very good colour. A bit inky on the nose. Fat and rich and honeyed and fruity on the palate. Quite full. Still enjoyable nevertheless. Sweet, raspberry, peachy. I'd like to see a bottle in prime condition. This bottle is past its best.

Lafite   Drink soon   18.0

Medium colour. The nose has lightened up quite a bit but the wine is still fresh and elegant. Light on the palate. An ethereal echo of its original self. Yet good fruit. Fat, rich, originally. No astringency. Indeed a vestigial reminder of new oak on the finish. Good marks for class. Not dead.

Latour   Now–1998   19.0

Good colour. Very elegant nose. Lovely fragrant, classy fruit. Not as full as the above but a nose of great distinction. Real finesse. Real complexity. Brilliant class if not as generous and fabulous as the above. Breed in its Pauillac quintessence. Very long. Very lovely. Will still keep.

Margaux   Drink soon   18.5

Medium colour. More substance and life than the wine below. Fragrant and classy though it shows a little age. First growth breed and complexity. Very ripe fruit on the palate. Honeyed and complex. Great distinction. A lovely wine. Very long. Will still keep.

La Mission-Haut-Brion   Now–1997   18.5

Good colour. Marvellous nose. Velvety and ripe and concentrated. Restrained and classy. Fullish, a slight earthy aspect. This is the only minor distraction. Rich, ripe, concentrated, ample. Lovely distinguished fruit carried right through to the finish. Very classy. Still plenty of life.

Mouton-Rothschild
                   Now–2000 plus   20.0

Good colour. Splendid nose. Aromatic, marvellous, ripe, rich fruit, complex and fat. A wine of real depth and magnificent ripeness and concentration. An exotic element. Very lively though a touch of astringency. A seductive, full, very rich, opulent wine. Tremendous quality. Will still keep.

Pétrus   Now–1998   18.5

Very good colour. Splendid nose. Fat, rich, still vigorous. Real depth and concentration here. Very youthful. This is voluptuous and exotic. Exotic, even like Scheherezade. Very young. Full, rich, vigorous. Will still keep very well.

Peyraud (Saint-Emilion)
                   Drink soon   12.0

Good colour. Rather hard and not entirely clean, yet vigorous. On the nose fullish and still vigorous. Some chunky astringency. Lacks class.

Pichon-Longueville-Baron
                   Now–1996   15.0

Very good colour. Quite a sturdy nose. Just a shade inky. Certainly muscular. Fullish, a little astringency. Quite a ripe wine, but solid. Always a bit old-fashioned in the less good sense. Good but not great. Will still keep well.

Pichon-Longueville, Comtesse de Lalande
                   Drink soon   16.5

Medium-full colour. Good fresh nose but neither the power nor the complexity of some. A medium to medium-full wine. Now showing a little age. Always a very pretty, elegant wine; if not with the greatest power. Yet complex, elegant and classy without a doubt.

Pontet-Canet   Drink soon   15.0

Good colour. Very fine, fragrant nose. Old-vine fruit though more of a mulberry, raspberry fruit than blackcurrants. High toned. Slight extra element of volatile acidity. Medium body. Lovely fruit. Fragrant and still vigorous on the finish. Classy, gentle. Just a curious element of sweet/sour as it evolved.

1947 CLARET

Jan Paulson is a Swedish dentist who works in Waldkirchen somewhere between Munich and the Austrian/Czechoslovak border. He writes his notes in English, having done much of his original studies in England and practising a decade or so ago a stone's throw from Château Coates. His hobby – indeed passion – is wine, and he deals in the fine and rare as a sideline.

Over the past few years Jan has organized some splendid tastings of old wines: 1949, 1959 and 1964 have been some of the highlights. I have reported on all these elsewhere in these pages. The 1992 event was the best yet. The location was Linz. The sponsor was Dr Peter Baumann; and the food was cooked by Gunter W. Hager, owner of several of the best restaurants in the locality. And the vintage, Peter Baumann's as well as the wines', was 1947.

Nineteen forty-seven was the next great vintage after 1945. If 1945 was in general a Médoc and Graves year, 1947 was indisputably the fief of the Libournais, as it would be in 1964 and again in 1982. In each of these three vintages, one of the first words that comes to mind when describing the character of the wines is 'fat'. There is a sumptuous, creamy richness and concentration of fruit in the 1947s, and though they are certainly structured, this structure is hidden behind a covering of very ripe tannins. There is so much velvet glove that the iron fist is barely discernible.

THE WEATHER AND THE CROP

The year had one of those glorious, almost faultless summers that we all remember from our youth and despair of ever getting in the present; when day after day the sun shines with uninterrupted regularity for months on end. No wonder Compton and Edrich could have knocked up over 7,300 runs and 30 centuries between them!

The spring was late in coming after a hard, cold winter but from May onwards the weather was excellent. The flowering in June passed off without mishap, thus ensuring a plentiful harvest. July was fine, August hot and September even hotter. The harvest began on 15 September with temperatures in the high 30s and the grapes were gathered and fermented in a real heatwave. As will be seen, this was the undoing of some.

The fruit was brought into the cellars in a state of ripeness and sugar content that was almost unprecedented. There was so much natural sugar that not all of it was converted into alcohol and in the great heat some wine-makers had difficulty in controlling the fermentations. Some wines had an excess of volatile acidity. Others were simply deficient in fixed acidity and as a result did not live up to their early promise.

It was an abundant vintage: 2.7 million hectolitres, over double that of 1945, with 1.2 hectolitres of AC *rouge* as opposed to 587,000 in the earlier year. The weather continued auspicious long after the red wine harvest and 1947 proved to be another excellent vintage for Sauternes.

The Médoc and Graves are much less consistent than the Libournais as well as being inferior to both 1945 and 1949, and indeed in some cases, to the 1948, a much underrated vintage. Many, even in the mid-1960s when I started drinking the 1947 and other vintages such as these with some regularity, were already somewhat edgy and inky, the fruit having already lost its sweetness and flesh. Some are – or were – very fine though. Calon-Ségur is excellent; both the Bartons are very good. Ducru-Beaucaillou is delicious as are Léoville-Las-Cases and Grand-Puy-Lacoste. Lynch-Bages was certainly good in its prime as was Gruaud-Larose. Further south, Kirwan was splendid and Domaine de Chevalier quite magnificent. In most cases, though, these are now showing age if not past their best.

When I last sampled a range of the top 1947s, in November 1987, the first four wines were Pétrus, Cheval-Blanc, Mouton-Rothschild and Margaux; these were agreed to be well ahead of Lafite, Latour, Haut-Brion and Ausone, though there was nothing seriously to fault in any of these first growths. At the end of the tasting on which I report below, Cheval-Blanc and Lafleur romped home first equal. The château-bottled Pétrus fell apart quickly, which was tragic, as one could see the vestiges of a simply brilliant intensity in the original wine and the Vandemeulen bottling was excellent. Margaux and Mouton were again better than Latour and Lafite. Figeac, Canon, Clos-Fourtet, L'Evangile, Trotanoy and La Mission were also highly praised. From other tastings I can also strongly recommend Vieux Château Certan, Latour-à-Pomerol and Lafleur-Pétrus.

THE TASTING

The following wines were sampled in Linz, Austria, in November 1992. The wines were provided by Dr Peter Baumann, Jan Paulson, Hardy Rodenstock and John Avery. The wines are château-bottled, except where indicated, and the scores refer to these bottles only.

	Optimum Drinking	Mark out of 20

SAINT-EMILION

Ausone Drink soon 17.0

Medium to medium-full colour. Quite some brown. Lightish on the nose, a little lanolin as well as cedar. Breed here but in a delicate way. Lightened up further as it evolved. Sweet and classy on the palate. But it is getting towards its end. Not as complex or as persistent as the Canon but very good indeed. Not astringent. And held up surprisingly well in the glass.

Canon Now–1997 18.5

Medium-full colour. Not too much brown but a little dense. Good nose. Quite delicate but ripe and complex. Still vigorous. Sweet and subtle and classy. Cedary as it evolved and even voluptuous. Lovely palate. Not too old, though well matured. Not a blockbuster. This is medium-full, round, subtle, ripe and positive. It also has a lot of dimension. Good vigour and persistence on the finish. Very fine plus. Lots of dimension here.

Cheval-Blanc Now–2000 20.0

(Magnum) Very good colour. Fullish and still very youthful. Slightly higher-toned than Lafleur and with a hint of reduction at the outset. Later on very classy; lovely definition of fruit. Very complex. Very distinguished. Full, had a lot of tannin in the first place. Old-fashioned. But fat, voluptuous. Old viney. Quite high alcohol. But sweet. Almost porty. Got better and better in the glass. Very fine indeed. *Grand vin* in fact. This is as good as Lafleur.

Cheval-Blanc Now–1995 17.5

(Justerini & Brooks label) Medium-full, vigorous-looking colour. A little inky and clumsy on the nose. A little dry and four-square and lumpy. Slightly old-fashioned and dense but rich, spicy and fat. This is certainly enjoyable. Not too aged. No real astringency. But it lacks the class, concentration and flair of the Vandemeulen bottling. Less finesse but more power than Canon. Better on the palate than on the nose though.

Cheval-Blanc Now–2000 19.5

(Vandemeulen bottling) Full vigorous colour. Much the best of these three non-château bottlings on the nose. This is voluptuous, vigorous, rich and concentrated. Lovely! Up to the standard of the château-bottled. Full, vigorous, super-duper. Very, very concentrated and rich. Porty as it should be. Huge amounts of fruit. Pure essence of wine. Brilliant! Bags of life.

Cheval-Blanc — —

(No capsule. Belgian bottling?) Medium-full, somewhat old-looking colour. Maderized nose. Bought by Paulson as a mixed lot from Sotheby's. Good fill but all the bottles have been bad.

Clos-Fourtet Now–1997 17.0

(Magnum) Very fine full vigorous colour. Rich, full, voluptuous. Lovely damson fruit. Rich, full, earthy; old-fashioned, old-viney meatiness. Tannic once, but ample now with an element of solidity, even astringency as it evolved in the glass. Good acidity. This is fresh. Concentrated. Very good indeed. Long and vigorous at the end. Plenty of life left.

Figeac Now–1995 18.0

(Magnum) The first vintage of Thierry Manoncourt. Very good colour. Fullish. Only just mature. Slightly more evolved than Lafleur and Cheval-Blanc. A little less concentrated, but nicely cool, complex and balanced and multidimensional nonetheless. Medium-full. Ripe, harmonious. Delicious. Beautiful balance. Plenty of vigour. This is fine, and proof of the vigour, freshness and splendid quality of Libournais 1947s. As it evolved it became sweet and spicy even a little burnt. One could see the alcohol. But it held up well in the glass. Classy. Long. Vigorous. Very fine.

Troplong-Mondot Drink up 14.0

Medium-full, mature colour. Still quite vigorous-looking. On the nose fullish but a little dense and old-fashioned. Yet ripe and rich underneath. On the palate the fruit has dried out a bit. Somewhat old-fashioned and lumpy. Rich and fullish but lacks nuance. A bit *bourgeois*.

Trottevieille   Drink soon   16.0

(Magnum) Medium colour now showing a bit of age. On the nose this is a well-matured wine, but it isn't past it. There is interesting fruit here; depth even. On the palate still sweet. Soft and fleshy. Raspberry-jammy. Still fresh at the end. No trace of dryness. Very good but drink soon.

POMEROL

La Conseillante   Now–1995   16.5

(Bottled by Vandermeulen) Fullish colour. Still has vigour. Full fat and caramelly on the nose. But fresh and vigorous underneath. This is promising! Fullish, just a little four-square on the palate. It lacks a little zip and real concentration and class. But still has life. Very good plus but not great. Slight bitterness at the end.

L'Evangile   Now–1997   18.0

(Belgian bottled) Full vigorous colour. Full nose. Meaty, but rich; solid but concentrated. Sweet and caramelly. A little more age than La Conseillante though. Rich, oaky and concentrated on the palate. Old viney. Full-bodied. This is plump, ample and full of ripe fruit. Still has vigour – more than La Conseillante it seems as the wine evolved in the glass. Fine plus. Long. Satisfying.

Lafleur   Now–2000   20.0

(Magnum) Very good colour. Full and barely mature. Lovely nose. Rich voluptuous and concentrated. Crammed with fruit. Very, very fresh. Velvety. Very fat. Heavenly! Very full, very rich, very meaty indeed. Super-duper. Still tannic but not unduly so. Yet still very very vigorous. Porty – very porty. An old-fashioned wine on the palate. Alcohol shows again. Long. Solid. Rich and wonderful. A brilliant wine. Bags of life.

Nénin   Drink up   13.5

(Bordeaux bottled) Fullish colour. No undue maturity. Very minty, almost nettles, at first on the nose. But cat-mint rather than grassy/herbaceous. On the palate a bit dried out. The fruit has just about gone. Not dry but lacking charm. No generosity.

Pétrus   Now–1995   18.5

(Bottled by Vandermeulen) Full vigorous colour. Lovely rich ample concentrated old-viney nose. Full and rich and concentrated but it is not as good as their Cheval-Blanc bottling. There is less vigour and less dimension and less depth. Lovely though. But the palate doesn't quite live up to the nose.

Pétrus   See note

(Château bottled) Good fullish vigorous colour. Very, very concentrated and old viney on the nose. Much more essence of fruit than the

Vandermeulen bottling, but older and denser and a little drier, even a little oxidized. Very quickly became very maderized. This is tragic. Underneath you can see a marvellous concentrated wine of real depth and fabulous intensity. 20/20 if it was in prime condition. Even now one can see and indeed enjoy the possibility.

Rouget   Drink soon   16.5

Fullish colour. No undue maturity. This is corky but you can still see the character and quality of the wine. Not a blockbuster. Fragrant, gentle, stylish, fresh. Medium-full body. Lots of finesse. Very fine fruit. Even with the corkiness this is enjoyable. Mellow sweet. Very good plus. Just a little astringent at the end.

La Tour-à-Pomerol   Past its best

Fullish colour. No undue age. Decayed mushroomy nose. Full and rich but lumpy and four-square. It is difficult to judge this.

Trotanoy   Drink up   17.0

(Nicolas bottling) Medium colour. Well-matured. This is a bit faded and maderized on the nose. On the palate this is still sweet and attractive. Not a blockbuster. Still fresh and plump. Not astringent. Cool and classy. Was fine. Other bottles still may be.

GRAVES

Haut-Brion   Past its best   17.0

Good fullish colour. No undue age. Just slightly dense perhaps. There is just a touch of oxidization and maderization here on the nose but the wine is rich and caramelly and cedary. Still enjoyable. This is getting a little dry but is classy. The fruit is disappearing fast but one can see the class.

La Mission-Haut-Brion   Drink soon   17.0

Good colour. Fullish. No undue age. Firm nose. Slightly austere but good depth. It is getting towards the end of its life but there is good old-viney concentration here, balance and class. Medium-full. Complex, positive. Just a little astringent on the attack, but rather less on the finish. Very good indeed.

Smith-Haut-Lafitte   Drink up   15.0

Medium-full colour. Still quite vigorous. Ripe, vigorous, cedary. Still sweet. Rich and concentrated. Complex and aristocratic. High quality here. On the palate there is a little age but this is soft and mellow. Long and fragrant but now showing on the way down. The palate is not as good as the nose originally indicated. Fell apart in the glass.

La Tour-Haut-Brion   Drink soon   16.5

Good colour. Fullish. No undue age. Soft, well-matured Graves nose. Earthy, warm brick. Mineral. Ripe fruit and good depth though. This dried up quite fast in the glass. Medium body.

Ripe and supple nevertheless. Long. Round, even sweet. This has class and complexity, but not the depth of La Mission. Very good plus.

MARGAUX AND HAUT-MÉDOC

Belgrave   **Past its best**   13.0

Fullish colour originally, but a little age now. Old claret nose: a little dried out. Medium to medium-full. This had good concentration and depth once but is now past its best. The fruit has almost gone. A bit too austere. The acidity shows. Not bad at best.

Boyd–Cantenac   **Now–1996**   15.5

(Magnum) Medium–full colour. Little sign of brown. Full nose. Rich and meaty but a little hard and austere, typically Boyd. But plenty of vigour, if in a muscular sort of way. On the palate full, quite solid. Good grip. Good positive follow-through. Blackcurrant fruit. This is classy and old viney. Has held up well. Good plus but not the complexity and depth of great. Developed in the glass. Plenty of interest. Will still keep.

Cantemerle   **Past its best**   12.0

Medium colour. Now showing age. A little decay on the nose. Mushroomy. On the palate still has a bit of fruit but is also a bit astringent. Medium to medium-full. Dry and bitter and getting coarse.

Chasse-Spleen   **Past its best**   10.0

(Anonymous English bottling) Medium–full colour. Now showing age. Hard, austere and rather fruitless on the nose. Medium body. Very dry and astringent on the palate. I don't think this had much to it in the first place. Over the hill.

Margaux   **Now–1997**   19.0

(Re-corked by the château in 1987) Fullish mature colour. No undue age. Rich, fat, voluptuous. Cedary. Lead-pencilly. Smells like Mouton. Fullish, rich, opulent and sexy. Still vigorous. Concentration and flesh and plenty of life left. This is the best of the first growths today. Very fine indeed.

Palmer   **Past its best**   13.0

Good colour. Still quite vigorous-looking. The nose shows a little age though, but there is evidence of quality here. Medium to medium-full body. A little fruit. Also rather astringent. But this has still a bit of depth and complexity. Over the hill though.

SAINT-JULIEN

Branaire-Ducru   **Drink up**   16.0

Full, rich colour. Plenty of vigour, seemingly. Full, ample, voluptuous oaky nose. Very, very rich and fat. Good concentration and very plump. Fullish, quite tannic. On the palate a little less rich, a bit more dried out. But very good stuff here. A bit dry and ungenerous at the end. Very good. Dried out fast in the glass, sadly.

Gruaud-Larose   **Drink up**   16.5

Medium-full colour. No undue maturity. Cedar and sandalwood. Sweet and aromatic on the nose, with something burnt and smoky lurking in the background. Fullish, rich and concentrated. Meaty but earthy. Yet still has some vigour. Ripe. Interesting. But has lightened up. Very good plus. Still positive at the end.

Léoville-Barton   **Drink up**   16.5

Medium colour. Fully mature. Ripe, sweet, cedary nose with a touch of volatile acidity. At first very good but dried up as it aerated. There is quality here but it is a bit on its last legs. Medium body – has lightened up. Good stylish fruit, almost peachy. Long and subtle. Still has sweetness and it isn't too dry at the end.

Léoville-Las-Cases   **Drink soon**   17.0

Very good colour. Fullish, vigorous, oaky and cedary and coffee and vanilla and ripe and sweet – almost creamy – at first on the nose. This has plenty of vigour still, at first, though it is a touch dry on the attack. Fullish. Cool. Rich and concentrated. Fine quality. Long complex finish. The most vigorous of this flight of Saint-Julien.

Talbot   **Drink up**   16.0

Medium colour. Some age now. New oak on the nose. But a little faded. There is a touch of oxidation and maderization. Medium to medium-full. It has seen better days, but there is sweetness here, and finesse and complexity as well. Very good and still enjoyable. Long and not too astringent.

PAUILLAC

Batailley   **Now–1995**   15.5

(Recorked at the château in 1987) Medium to medium-full colour. No undue age. There is an animal, gamey aspect on the nose here. Quite full and fleshy. Lightened up a bit in the glass but on the palate is medium-full, ripe, ample and full of fruit, and the finish is sweet and plump. Still has life. Good plus but not the finesse for great.

Lafite   **Drink up**   17.5

Medium colour. Quite aged now. Has it lightened up? There is some finesse here, but a lack of vigour. It has lightened and loosened up. Better than Latour. Medium body. Gentle, classy, complex and balanced. A bit over the top but still enjoyment here. Still long and even quite intense at the end. Fine.

Latour   **Past its best**   15.0

Medium colour. Quite bright and clear but aged. This is a bit over the top on the nose. Rather faded, a bit astringent. But not decayed. On the palate the least vigorous of the first growths. A bit dry. A bit faded.

Mouton–Cadet   **Drink soon**   15.5

(Magnum) Medium-full colour. Mature but no undue brown. Ample, soft, fleshy nose. Quite voluptuous. Plenty of ripe fruit here. Medium to medium-full. Good fruit. Showing a little age. Lush and fat and jammy. But a touch astringent at the end. Yet sweet and with plenty of sex appeal. Still vigorous on the finish.

Mouton–Rothschild   **Now–1995**   18.5

Full vigorous colour. Delicate but still fresh. Certainly classy, but this is showing a little age now. Not a blockbuster by any means. Feminine even. Medium body. Persistent, intense, classy, fresh and gentle. But not a muscular wine, even. Second best of the first growths today. Soft, very lovely. Still long and complex on the finish. Still has life. I thought it was a Margaux.

Pichon–Longueville–Baron

Drink up   15.0

(Anonymous English bottling) Medium-full colour. A little old but not unduly brown. A little faded but chocolate and black cherries here on the nose. Sweetness too. Medium body on the palate, has dried up and got a bit coarse. This is also a bit over the top. The finish is a little mean and astringent. But there is quality here. Perhaps originally better than the Lalande.

Pichon–Longueville, Comtesse de Lalande

Now–1997   16.0

Fullish, vigorous colour. Good sweet fruit but a certain lack of nuance on the nose. A bit curate's eggy. It is rich and creamy but a little solid at the same time. On the palate this is a true Pauillac: fullish, quite concentrated, good Cabernet fruit and now getting a little cool and drying but still with finesse and complexity. Dried out in the glass. The acidity is showing. Good length. Fine.

La Rose–Pauillac   **Past its best**   10.0

Fullish colour. No undue age, but looks a bit solid. Strong mushroom aromas. Dry underneath. Difficult to see the fruit. Quite full. Rather astringent and now lumpy. The fruit has dried up. Now rather charmless and austere.

SAINT-ESTÈPHE

Le Bosq   **Drink up**   12.5

Medium-full colour. Fully mature. Slightly austere and hard on the nose. Medium-full. Typically Saint-Estèphe. Muscular, fleshy but a little lacking class and sex-appeal. Old-fashioned wine-making. Long maceration.

Calon–Ségur   **Drink soon**   16.0

Medium colour. A little age. A bit past it on the nose. Slightly sweaty too. Quite a lot of unresolved tannin here now adding to the astringency. Reasonable style and fruit. Medium to medium-full body. Doesn't really sing though. But the finish is positive and not too dried out. Still sweet and became cleaner as it evolved. Very good.

Cos d'Estournel   **Past its best**   —

Medium-full colour but looks a bit old now. Somewhat maderized and vegetable-soupy on the nose. On the palate a bit sweet-sour and dried out. Past its best but a low level (mid-shoulder). I'd like to see the wine with a more reasonable fill for the age before making a judgement.

Montrose   **Drink up**   15.0

Medium to medium-full colour. Still reasonably fresh. Rich and fat and fleshy on the nose. This still has vigour. Medium to medium-full. Beginning to loosen up a bit but there is quite distinguished fruit. But it is drier than the Calon-Ségur.

1945 CLARET

By 1945, France had endured not only six hard years of war, deprivation and occupation, but a fifteen-year run of vintages of almost unparalleled monotony and disappointment. Moreover, the economic depression that also came in the 1930s only served to set the seal on a period of unprofitability and financial misery in the vineyards which had lasted since the Franco-Prussian War and the phylloxera and mildew epidemics of the 1870s and 1880s. For many of the middle-of-the-road classed growths the Second World War was almost the last straw. I calculate that of the 60 or so top Médocs classified in 1855, as many as a quarter were only nominally in existence in the late 1940s. Even those who managed to continue were hardly making money.

It is therefore somewhat ironic that hardly had the dust settled and the troops began to come wearily home, a vintage should arrive which, though minuscule, would be immediately and continually regarded as one of the greatest of all time. For once, the hyperbole was accurate: 1945 was a 'vintage of the century'. It was to be a slow-maturing, long-enduring vintage. Those who drank and can still drink these bottles in their prime may feel themselves long distanced from the austerity of rationing, the threat or the actuality of invasion and the pain of bereavement of the war years. Nevertheless, I have always regarded 1945, not just as the Mouton label proclaims, a vintage which fittingly celebrated the *année de la victoire*, but as a sort of tribute to actual survival; not just in the more limited sense of fine wine and the grand domaines which produce them, but in the broader context of European civilization itself.

THE WEATHER AND THE CROP

It was a tiny crop. After an early bud-break, there was an unusually late and severe frost in May. Further depredation as a result of hail, the lack of chemicals to spray against the various pests and diseases prevalent in the vineyard and the poor condition of the vines themselves after six years of neglect, reduced the size of the crop still further. Moreover, it was a particularly hot, dry summer.

All this led to an early harvest. Picking began on 10 September and was generally under way by the 13th. The weather continued hot throughout the month and well into October producing not only an exceptional red wine vintage but an excellent harvest of Sauternes.

But minuscule in size. In total, some 1.48 million hectolitres of wine were declared, of which 589,000 were AC red and 682,000 AC white. This was the second smallest harvest of the century to date, only 1915 being tinier.

Since then there were smaller crops in 1956 and 1957 as a result of the February frosts in the earlier year. Again in 1961, only 550,000 hectolitres of AC red were produced, the reduction once more being caused by frosts in May, though this time towards the end of the month when the vines were in flower. In contrast, the 1944 vintage had been twice as large as 1945; 1946 was to fall not far short of the 1944 figure, and 1947 would be even larger. Today, a red wine crop more than six times the size is commonplace.

THE WINE

The 1945 red wines were macerated in their skins for a very long time and at high temperatures as a result of the fine weather prevailing during the vintage. This produced wines of a very deep colour and with exceptional levels of tannin: solid, brutal, hard wines which would be slow to develop. Underneath – or perhaps I should say within – the amount of concentration and acidity and the intensity and richness of the fruit were, thankfully, of equal size and proportion to this uncompromising structure. If not, the 1945s, would never have come round satisfactorily. As it was, though at best the 1945s were, and indeed still are, magnificent, some were always a little too massive for their own good. The 1945s took ages to mature. I remember in the early 1960s, when I first entered the wine trade, that even lesser growths seemed to be only just ready and the top wines were still a long way from their peak.

Nineteen forty-five is the earliest vintage of which I can write from any large measure of personal experience. When I first began to take an interest in wine, I was for a time a manager of a small wine-merchants in Pangbourne in Berkshire. Property values being what they were, I found I had made a small profit on moving out of London and installing myself in a house in the neighbourhood. I blew it on wine.

I wrote round to every distinguished wine-merchant I could think of and spent a happy fortnight combing through their lists and deciding how to spend my fortune. What I did was to order one, two or three bottles, depending on the price, of every single classed-growth – or equivalent – claret I could find. I must have amassed about 1,000 different bottles, perhaps 500 different wines, all for an outlay of less than £1,000. With the exception of a handful of prewar wines, the vintages ranged from 1945 – of which I bought over 30 examples – to 1959, of which I had more than 50. It was in drinking these bottles that I began to teach myself something about claret.

I have always been convinced that one of the great 'decades' for red Bordeaux was the eleven-year period between 1945 and 1955. Only 1946 and 1951 were complete disasters. Even in 1954 there were some good examples, if light in structure and short in potential. I can remember many fine clarets from the 1950 vintage and even more from 1948, both years which rather lost out in the plenty which surrounded them. For sheer charm and elegance, the palm might be given to the 1953s. For breed and classicism, the prize could go to the 1949s, but for power, concentration and depth, it is the 1945s which stand out. The best are awe-inspiring and magnificent.

Is 1945 better than 1961? This is a question which is almost impossible to answer because the character of the wines is so different. The 1945s, I believe, give us an idea of the sort of wines which must have been made in the great, almost indestructible years in the golden age prior to the arrival of phylloxera. Nineteen forty-five was made by old-fashioned methods; 1961, on the contrary, looks forward. Modern techniques of vinification under controlled conditions have arrived. It demonstrates the possibilities of the future by indicating what would result today if we had *another* vintage which was so insufficient in quantity but otherwise ripened under perfect conditions. The 1945s are mighty, masculine and austere. The 1961s have an equally immense concentration of fruit but they do not have the same structure. On the other hand, the 1961 vintage is much more consistently successful. I do not think I have ever drunk a 1961 claret, however lowly its aspiration, which was not a conspicuous success within its context. Even 20 or 25 years ago, it was plain that some 1945s were a bit tough and astringent on the finish.

THE BEST WINES

On three separate occasions in the last decade I had the opportunity – indeed, the privilege – of being able to compare the five top left-bank 1945s at the same time. On the first occasion these were tasted 'open' but on the later two, the sessions were blind. In October 1978, the Lafite was unhesitatingly voted top and Margaux came last, there being disagreement about the middle placings of Latour, Mouton and Haut-Brion but my second place going to Latour. At a dinner given by John Avery in March 1983, the bottle of Haut-Brion was slightly oxidized and the order of the rest was: Latour, Lafite, Mouton and Margaux, though I personally preferred the Mouton to what I felt was a somewhat ageing Lafite. Yet, when I compared Latour and Lafite at a special joint vertical in November 1984, the latter was clearly the superior. The third of these occasions was at the home of Daniel and Lori Oliveros in New York in September 1987, and is covered in the tasting notes which follow.

Outside the first growths there are many other magnificent wines. I mention particularly those which have struck me most forcibly in the last fifteen years. I remember both Léoville and Langoa-Barton at the end of a run of superb wines when the late Ronald Barton put up a vertical tasting of both properties for me in March 1979. At the same sort of period and in similar conditions, I enjoyed the 1945s of Montrose and Palmer though both Lynch-Bages and Calon-Ségur proved to be disappointing. Previously, and subsequently, these two have been excellent. Gruaud-Larose is a fine 1945 I have enjoyed on several occasions though Talbot has always seemed a little hard. Grand-Puy-Lacoste, Pontet-Canet, Issan, Kirwan, Malescot, Mouton d'Armailhacq, as it was then, both the Pichons, Cos d'Estournel and Léoville-Poyferré have all been successful bottles in the last decade; and success in 1945 terms means quality at a very high level indeed. Even the *bourgeois* Château Sénéjac made a remarkable wine.

In the Graves, both La Mission and La Tour-Haut-Brion are excellent and are both, as you might expect, exceptionally structured wines, even for the vintage. Domaine de Chevalier was sumptuous on the one occasion I have seen it, but I have not, as I recall, seen any of the remaining Graves recently.

In Saint-Emilion and Pomerol, there are many more splendid wines, though for the most part it is 1947 which is the best of the two vintages. In 1980 compared two different bottlings of the Cheval-Blanc (together with three 1947s, the 1948 and the 1949). The 1945 château-bottling was noted as very fine but not outstanding. La Gaffelière is magnificent, superior to Cheval-Blanc I am sure, and there are some fine Pomerols: La Fleur-Gazin, Lafleur, Vieux Château Certan, Latour-à-Pomerol and Pétrus. Good as these are, they are generally over-shadowed not only by what the region was to produce two years later but by the best of the Médocs and the Graves, though in their time they were more consistent and, certainly during the 1960s, more accessible and generous bottles.

Now, almost 50 years on, only the exceptionally well-stored 1945s outside the first growths can be risked with confidence and it becomes somewhat academic to try and suggest whether a particular wine should be consumed or can still be kept. Of the eight 1945 red wines sampled in New York in September 1987, only the Margaux showed any deterioration in the glass. I do not think we would have been nearly so fortunate if we had a series of lesser growths.

THE TASTING

The following 1945 wines were sampled in New York in September 1987. My deepest thanks to Daniel and Lori Oliveros for their invitation to join them. It was a truly great occasion. It must be stressed that the marks apply solely to the bottles in question.

Haut-Brion — Optimum Drinking: Drink soon — Mark out of 20: **18.5**

Full, mature colour, no undue age. Full, mellow nose, very classy. Hints of sandalwood and roast chestnut. A big wine but delicate in 1945 terms. Classy, ripe fruit; essentially but not exclusively Cabernet. Fragrant, subtle, very long and complex. A mature wine of great breed and finesse. Held up very well in the glass.

Lafite — Drink soon — **18.5**

Medium-full, mature colour. This, again, is perhaps just a little past its best but is a wine of majestic quality and great breed. Round, mellow, fragrant, classy nose. Not as structured as the Margaux but ripe and concentrated. Smooth, sweet, richly fruity. Has lost just a little of its vigour and complexity but certainly a very excellent wine.

Latour — Now–1998 — **17.5**

Full, mature colour. No undue age but there is something a little dead about it. Fullish, quite firm nose, earthy and chocolatey, still some tannin present. Like the Margaux there is a little volatile acidity. Quite full, some tannin. Good better richer in the glass but this bottle lacked a little charm as well as breed.

Léoville–Barton   Now–1998   18.0

Very fine, full mature colour. Rich, meaty,
Cabernet nose. Full-bodied, quite tannic, very
classic Saint-Julien/Pauillac masculine wine.
Austere, concentrated, old-vine fruit, very
Cabernet, with a slight touch of extra spices such
as leather and fine cigars: A structured wine. Rich,
very high class. No sign of old age at all.

Margaux   Past its best   16.0

Very full colour – fuller than the Latour, even.
Rich, aromatic, slightly earthy nose, with a touch
of volatile acidity. At first full, fat, ripe and ample
but quickly became less intense, a little four-
square and a touch astringent. Fine but not great.
Possibly a little past its best now.

Mouton–Rothschild   Now–2000   19.5

The fullest, most majestic colour of all. Splendid
nose, an extraordinary essence of pure blackcurrants. Poised, definitive, brilliant, not a bit dense.
This is a complete wine. Still very strong.
Emphatic, regal quality stamped all the way
through it. Full, very, very rich and concentrated.
Marvellously balanced. The best of the tasting
without a doubt. *Grand vin*!

Pétrus   Now–2000   17.5

Magnificent colour. Very soft, voluptuous, almost
silky nose. Immense ripeness, crammed with fruit.
This is a very seductive bottle without any of the
hard edges and dense structure of its Médoc counterparts. A cornucopia of summer fruits but does-
n't have the power, concentration, complexity
and sheer breed of the Mouton. This is a very
fresh wine still.

Vieux Château Certan   Now–2000   17.5

Very fine colour, dense, almost black right
through to the rim. Intense, voluptuous, perfumed fruit on the nose. Very full, very tannic but
velvety and enormously rich wine. Heaps of old-
vine fruit. Still very young. Excellent.

d'Yquem   Now–2000   20.0

Light amontillado colour, a walnut veneer with a
green rim. This is indisputably *grand vin* from the
moment you come near it. Marvellous intensity
of fruit but no longer full and clenched on the
nose. An explosion of flavours – spice, honey,
peaches, nuts, butterscotch, vanilla and jasmine.
Multidimensional. Marvellously fresh, complex,
vigorous wine. Great complexity, great class. Bags
of life. A truly great bottle.

1934 CLARET

The 1930s were not only a dismal decade for mankind as a whole, but a pretty miserable ten years for wine in Bordeaux. It was a time of economic depression and marginal profitability. And the weather, in contrast to the 1920s, was unkind to the vines. Few vintages stand out; some charming but ephemeral 1933s; some hard and dour 1937s – though the Sauternes are fine and still alive. And the 1934s. That was a huge vintage, but it was a successful one. And the wines, now approaching their sixtieth birthday, can be vigorous if they have been correctly stored.

Despite the huge harvests of recent years, 1934 is still – just – the largest good vintage since modern records began. The harvest measured a gargantuan 6.8 million hectolitres; though it has to be said that the area under vine in 1934 measured approximately 35 per cent more than it does today.

Nevertheless, the wines were by no means vapid and unstructured. If anything they were a bit heavy, a bit too much on the hard and tannic side. And some, like the 1952s a couple of decades later, remained a little bit too muscular throughout their lives, and began to dry out before they had fully softened up.

Given this scenario, one would expect the best of the 1934s to come from Saint-Emilion and Pomerol. Sadly my experience is limited. I have had the Cheval-Blanc twice in recent years: an absolutely splendid bottle at a La Vigneronne tasting in December 1989 (classy, cedary, long and sweet), and a rather older example at a Cheval/Ausone/Figeac back-to-back organized by Bob Feinn in New Haven in the fall of 1990. Ausone has not come my way, but Figeac, a little dense and muscular, but rich and fat nevertheless, was among the range at Bipin Desai's vertical at Taillevent in December 1989. Gaffelière, Canon and one or two lesser wines I also remember well, but I have not sampled them recently.

Only a few Pomerols have passed my lips in recent years. Pétrus twice: but old on both occasions; Vieux Château Certan vigorous, almost porty, very concentrated and complex; Trotanoy three times since 1988, the best example velvety and rich, but solid underneath. But that is just about it.

In the Graves, La Mission and Domaine de Chevalier – supremely elegant – stand out. In my experience the Haut-Brion 1933 is better, though quite different, than the 1934, though this may be because I have for some reason encountered the earlier vintage rather more frequently. Pape-Clément and Malartic-Lagravière were at the very least acceptable on the single occasions I have tasted them in the last decade.

For the Médocs I leave the reader to ponder over the notes below. In addition, I can cite as very good to fine – perhaps no bottles in this decade were ever great, as some were in 1928 and 1929, and would be again in the 1940s – Lynch-Bages, the first of the Cazes vintages, robust and sweet, a little muscular perhaps; Beychevelle, classy, composed, with plenty of ripe fruit; Ducru-Beaucaillou, vigorous, positive, supple and elegant. Las-Cases was complex and gentle, still long but losing its vigour in May 1992; and Léoville-Poyferré, classically Saint-Julien, multidimensional, perhaps the best of the lot. Both the Pichons are also good.

Which is the best of the first growths? Margaux followed by Mouton at the tasting below. But Latour, if in good condition, as it was at the Hewitt tasting in March 1988, would probably be supreme. You would have to be lucky indeed to encounter them all at their best on the same day.

Wine was made differently in those days. The acidity levels at the time the fruit was collected were higher. The maceration was longer. There was less incidence of new oak. Bottling was later. Wines today would be better made, better balanced, cleaner and more consistent. Would they be *better* though? Would they last as long? Without, I hope, setting myself up as a necrophiliac, I do have to say that I like the taste of old wine. There is a complexity there, developed over the decades the wine has carefully rested in bottle; and an absence of the aggressive. The inherent breed of the wine, if there is any, is easier to appreciate and to enjoy. And, of course, it can't be denied, the sheer rarity of being able to open a cobwebbed bottle of history adds to the experience. If the bottles are a bit old, one is prepared to be indulgent. If they are still fine, one is able to experience a brief glimpse of heaven.

THE TASTING

The following wines were sampled over a splendid dinner at the Arlequin restaurant in London in October 1992. All wines are château-bottled, except where stated. The Calon-Ségur appeared by courtesy of Jan Paulson.

Mark out of 20

Calon-Ségur   **15.0**
Good colour. Rich, full but a little four-square on the nose. Attractive attack. Medium body. Still quite fresh. But a lack of real class. Caramelly sweet. But a bit clumsy. Vigorous but earthy.

Cos d'Estournel   **17.5**
(Not château bottled) Medium-full. Slight H2S on the nose but fat and sweet as well. As it evolved got better and better. Real class and depth and complexity here. Lovely. Medium-full body. Fine.

Gruaud-Larose   **16.5**
Full colour. Lovely rich fat nose. Still sweet. Certainly oaky. This still has plenty of life. Rich, full, round and succulent. Sweet on the finish. Fat. Very good indeed but not in class of Cos d'Estournel today.

Lafite   **18.0 (if in good condition)**
Colour a bit cloudy. The nose is a bit dead and astringent. I had better a month ago.

Latour   **18.0 (20.0 if in good condition)**
Full mature colour. Cedary, roast-chestnutty nose. Fat, rich and most attractive. More aged on the palate than on the nose. But there is succulence here. Ripe, but austere, yet in the best sense. Complex at the end. Fullish. Fine. But I have had better bottles.

Léoville-Barton   **16.0**
Full, well-matured colour. Lovely cedary seductive nose. But dried up quickly in the glass. Medium-full. Ripe, sweet and oaky. Not astringent but a bit chewed-lead-pencilly. Like meeting an old friend in a graveyard. Still sweet. Classy. A bit of decay.

Margaux   **19.0**
Medium-full colour. Fully mature. Lovely nose. Fragrant. Very Margaux. Complex, soft, not too aged. On the palate medium-full. Complex, ripe, classy. Very fine. Very lovely. Best of the lot by quite a way.

La Mission-Haut-Brion   **18.0**
Very good colour. Vigorous and intense. Lovely nose. Firm, and rich. It dried out a little in the glass. But rich, meaty, slightly solid, and – in the nicest possible sense – slightly herbaceous. Fine.

Mouton-Rothschild   **18.5**
Full colour. A bit inky on the nose. Rather vegetal. Slight volatile acidity on the nose. Yet on the palate as it developed a wine of richness as well as substance. Full, meaty, voluptuous. A touch late bottled but concentrated. Fine plus.

Palmer   **15.0**
Medium-full colour. A touch dry on the nose. But there is personality and fruit here. As it developed a lot of complexity. On the palate it dried out a little fast and it was not very full bodied. But it was certainly classy. A little over the hill, though.

Rausan-Ségla   **15.0**
(Bottled by Corney & Barrow) Full colour. The nose is a little dense and inky. A little sold but still alive. A bit dry and solid on the palate but there is still a little fruit here. Has interest. Even finesse. Full, sweet but a little astringent. Still good.

Talbot   **15.0**
Fullish colour. Fruity and quite solid on the nose. A firm wine. Rich but a little one-dimensional, a little four-square. But fresher than most. Fullish but lacks a bit of nuance and class. Yet held up better than most.

1928 CLARET

I am not a wine necrophiliac. I see no point in age for age's sake. I get little pleasure save for the satisfaction of a certain idle intellectual curiosity in tasting old bottles which are past their best. Indeed I get irritated when I am offered wines which would have been so much more lovely and seductive a decade or so previously.

On the other hand, well-made, well-balanced wine, if properly stored, can keep for very much longer than anyone would believe. I have had fresh and attractive 25-year-old Beaujolais Villages – and not of very prepossessing vintages either – from Georges Duboeuf's *vinothèque*. In Burgundy in 1988 I mistakenly ordered a twelve-year-old Macon Blanc Villages. It was only when I poured it out and saw the opulent golden colour that I realized it was a 1976 and not a 1986. It was odd but I enjoyed it. At the other extreme, at a Heublein pre-auction tasting which I hosted in Chicago in April, 1982, I sampled *inter alia* a dozen of the oldest wines I had ever seen, including an 1812 Saint-Emilion and an 1825 Hermitage. These were by no means the least vigorous wines of the session. I have had wines of less than a decade's age which were more faded.

Nevertheless, old vintages – and by this I mean anything over twenty years of age in the case of fine claret, less for Burgundy – must be approached with caution. The 1971 red Burgundies, a distinguished vintage in its time, are beginning to show age; so are some of the noble 1966 clarets. It is only the very best wines, or the very curious, which will be better after three decades than they are after two.

A vintage which was both fine and bizarre, monumental but controversial, was the 1928 in Bordeaux. Widely lauded at the outset, the wines subsequently turned out to be much harder and more tannic than originally anticipated, were eclipsed by the softer, exquisitely concentrated and elegant 1929s, and stubbornly refused to come round. Yet come round most eventually did, and of all the vintages ever produced in Bordeaux, save perhaps the fabled 1870s (we will see about 1945 and 1961 in due course), this is the vintage which could be the longest lasting of all, indeed potentially still vigorous and enjoyable – no mere intellectual curiosity – at 60 years of age. When I was invited by my New York friends, Daniel and Lori Oliveros, to put this to the test at a tasting session of no less than twenty examples in September 1988, I accepted with alacrity.

THE 1928 VINTAGE

The years 1928 and 1929 were the last glorious fireworks of a brilliant decade in Bordeaux and were to usher in ten years of not only economic misery and eventual war but of mediocre climatic conditions and uninspiring wines. 'A dreary decade: it seems that bad weather, bad wines and bad times go together,' as Michael Broadbent writes in his *Great Vintage Wine Book*. Both 1928 and 1929 were plentiful vintages. In 1928 it was a very hot summer indeed, especially in August, though not excessively dry, and the harvest took place in fine weather, commencing on 25 September.

Initial reports of the wines in cask were very favourable. These are 'as good as one can hope any young clarets to be', said André Simon. Ian Maxwell Campbell, another wine-trade stalwart, says in his *Wayward Tendrils of the Vine* that at the time he preferred the 1928s to the 1929s: 'They seemed so well-balanced and well-bred, full . . . and at the same time supple . . . . There was a touch of tannin and roughness about them, it is true, but it seemed to me to be counterbalanced by a sufficiency of fruit and sugar.' They were less obviously sweet than the 1929s, but 'I thought to myself, these are fine wines with a sure future . . . Their development, I must confess at once, has been slower than I expected,' he goes on, 'and I must have misjudged the amount of tannin in them.'

Nineteen twenty-eight followed 1925 and 1927, both disappointing vintages, and 1926, a fine year but very short and very expensive. Many merchants had not bought heavily since the 1924 vintage, and took the opportunity to stock up, repeating the exercise with the 1929s. The two years were destined, like 1899 and 1900, to become a famous pair, forever being compared and contrasted with one another.

Nineteen twenty-eight was followed by the gloriously seductive, soft, ripe 1929s, a vintage of charm and breeding, which as the 1928s withdrew into their tannic shells, demonstrated all the attraction and elegant fragrance the former vintage conspicuously seemed to lack. Would the 1928s ever come round? Maxwell Campbell was prepared to continue to give them the benefit of the doubt twenty years later. Later still others were less sanguine. Michael Broadbent remembers Allan Sichel deciding to demote his Latour 1928 to his house wine in the early 1950s and he thought it would never soften in his lifetime. Sadly he was right, says Broadbent. Allan Sichel died in 1965 and the Latour did not reach maturity for another decade.

There are two important 1928s, which were not at the Oliveros tasting and which have dubious reputations: Lafite and Haut-Brion. Penning-Rowsell in his *Wines of Bordeaux* says that the Lafite was pasteurized as a result of the heat, and that the Bordeaux wine-merchants who had bought it *en primeur* subsequently forced the château to take the stock back and re-fund them. Haut-Brion was said to have been pasteurized as well. Broadbent does not like the Lafite but finds the Haut-Brion 'extraordinary and perversely impressive'. I've seen them both recently and have no quarrel with either, though neither is indisputably great. Most au-thorities seem to agree that Latour and Margaux are the best of the first growths, pronounce Léoville-Las-Cases and Léoville-Poyferré equally fine and give honourable mentions to Beychevelle, Palmer, Brane-Cantenac, the Bartons and the Pichons, and Gruaud-Larose-Sarget. The wines of Saint-Emilion and Pomerol were less widely distributed then, and we had few at the Oliveros tasting. I should have thought though, given the climatic conditions, that many were very fine. I would certainly nominate Pétrus as up to the standard of the best of the Médoc. I also remember a beautifully elegant Domaine de Chevalier I was fortunate enough to drink with Claude Ricard at the château in 1981.

THE WINES NOW

The 1928s are still vigorous but they continue to be tough. Out of the twenty wines at the Oliveros tasting only one was over the hill. Otherwise there was no decay, little maderization even after the wines had been left on ullage, and for the most part no undue astringency. They are big and muscular, brutal and hefty nevertheless; the colours are good with no signs of undue maturity. These are wines of size and length; sometimes with tarry or burnt flavours, yet with good ripe tannins and with class, concentration and fruit to balance the structure. It was an impressive range of wines, in remarkable condition given that they had been assembled bit by bit by Daniel Oliveros over the previous few years, and from a variety of sources.

Haut-Brion Blanc   *Mark out of 20* —

Lightish, old-tawny colour. Elements of burnt toffee on the nose, but rich and fat underneath. Concentrated and nutty, with white chocolate truffle undertones. Has lost a little of its fragrance and fruit but is still remarkably alive. I imagine it must have had much of a dry Sauternes character in its infancy.

Malartic-Lagravière   16.5

Full colour; no undue maturity. Burnt nose, with leather but with good rich fruit in a tough sort of way, a characteristic not only of the vintage but of this property. Vigorous, still sweet. Fullish, rich and quite powerful. A spicy, masculine wine, both brutal and fat. Neither astringency nor maderization. Long on the palate. Unexpectedly fine.

Rouget   17.0

Quite full colour; no undue maturity. Nicely mellow and evolved on the nose. This is classy, concentrated and honeyed. Medium structure but very well balanced. Complex and long and lingering on the finish.

Pontet-Canet   15.0

Full colour; no undue maturity. Slight elements of dryness on the nose; it has lightened up but is still clean and classy. Medium-full body. Good ripeness. Finishes better than it starts.

La Tour-Haut-Brion   16.0

Medium-full colour. This has lightened up a bit. There is some spice: coffee, chocolate and prunes. This is showing some age but though there is a little astringency on the finish has ripe tannins. The attack is better than the finish.

Beychevelle   17.5

Very fine, full colour. Firm and rich on the nose, quite solid but not robust, certainly quite tannic and sturdy though. Fullish, very good ripe tannins. No undue solidity. This is very fine. Rich, masculine and multidimensional. It just lacks an element of generosity to be really great.

Léoville-Las-Cases   19.5

Full, mature colour. Excellent quality here. Rich, aromatic, sturdy, spicy and fat. Yet at the same time distinguished and restrained, fragrant, complex and very classy. Mellow, yet austere, in the best claret sense. Marvellous! Still has bags of life.

Léoville-Poyferré   18.5

Medium-full, mature colour. Fine nose, rich coffee and chocolate elements, the concentration overcoming the density. Fullish, ripe and sweet. Splendid fruit. Long and vigorous, though developing a little astringency as it developed. Real breed.

Gruaud-Larose-Sarget   17.5

Full, mature colour. Soft and aromatic and fragrant on the nose (Margaux-ish, I wrote before the labels were revealed). Fullish but now a little age on the palate. A faint hint of volatile acidity developed as well as a little astringency. Good fruit though. Certainly plenty of finesse.

Cos d'Estournel   18.0

Medium-full colour. Aromatic nose, ivy leaves, basil and leather. Medium-full body, good, ripe. Ripe, stylish and fragrant, with more generosity than at first on the nose and neither density nor astringency. Subtle and concentrated. Round, mellow, long on the palate and still fresh and vigorous. High quality!

Pichon-Longueville-Baron   17.5

Medium-full colour. Soft, fragrant nose. Got a bit dense as it evolved but lovely ripe fruit underneath. Medium-full, classy, concentrated and fragrant. Finishes long. Very fine.

Pichon-Longueville, Comtesse de Lalande   15.5

Medium to medium-full colour. Broad nose, quite sweet. Soft, ripe and mellow. Medium body. Fresh but has lightened up a bit. A supple but in this context somewhat uncomplicated wine. Reasonable length.

Canon   —

The sole example which was over the hill. Medium-full, with some age at the rim. Some decay on the nose. Medium body, quite soft. Was round and sweet, at the very least, but now somewhat maderized.

Montrose   16.5

Good fullish colour; still vigorous. Firm, muscular, full, masculine and sweet on the nose. Quite full; it lacks a bit of flexibility but finishes well. Very good but not great.

Vieux Château Certan   15.0

Medium-full colour. This is now on the decline but there is still pleasure to be had. Fullish and plump, finishing positively but a certain combination of oxidation, astringency and volatile acidity as well, particularly as the wine evolved in the glass.

Mouton-Rothschild   18.0

Medium-full colour. Full, ripe, round, stylish nose. This is an elegant, mellow wine, with none of the brutality of the vintage. Medium-full body, very good fruit, fragrant and supple. Vigorous, complex and very fine.

Margaux   20.0

Very fine, full colour, little sign of maturity. Glorious nose; rich, concentrated blackcurrant essence and violets: very complex. This is an amazing wine. Full, vigorous, ripely tannic; with real breed and depth. Very distinguished, very complex, very lovely. The best wine of the tasting.

Latour   18.5

Similarly fine colour. Fullish, spicy, aromatic nose, a shade denser and more woody than the above. This is a big, full, robust wine with all the leather and liquorice flavours of the vintage. One can see the heat of the summer here. There is sweetness but also a certain astringency. Very fine but a brutal wine. Better to drink than to taste.

Palmer   19.0

Full colour. Once again high quality here. More fragrant, more aromatic and mellower than the Margaux. Soft, ripe, sweet, medium-bodied wine with lovely fruit. A lot of breed. Delicious.

As you will see my favourite wine was the Margaux, followed by the Léoville-Las-Cases and the Palmer, the Léoville-Poyferré and the Latour. This was more or less the vote of the group as a whole, except that Las-Cases was voted top, and Poyferré preferred to Palmer, with Mouton coming in with four votes to take sixth spot. A fascinating experience! Thank you, Danny!

POSTSCRIPT

It so happened that a few other 1928s came my way shortly afterwards. Immediately after the Oliveros tasting I had the opportunity to sample both Château La Lagune and Ducru-Beaucaillou. The final three wines come from a tasting of various 1920 clarets I tutored for the Hungerford Wine Company in December 1988. The Cheval-Blanc 1928 was unquestionably the star of that show. Also admired were Châteaux d'Issan 1919, surprisingly more vigorous than a somewhat decayed Margaux 1920, Duhart-Milon 1926 and La Lagune and Gruaud-Larose 1929. The Yquem was served at the end of the Oliveros tasting.

MORE 1928s

Mark out of 20

Chasse-Spleen 13.5

Very fine colour. Could be a 1959. Solid, chunky nose, a little vegetal but not maderized. This has always been a little too tough for its own good. It is now inky and astringent. A bit dead. Not bad though. By no means undrinkable.

Cheval-Blanc 19.5

Splendid colour. This is a lovely wine. Real *premier cru* quality here! Marvellous nose: ripe, rich, concentrated and complex. Not obviously a Libournais wine, though opulent and voluptuous. This has vigour and harmony and great breed and depth. Though not tasted with the other top wines I'm sure it would have give even the best a run for their money. Excellent.

Ducru-Beaucaillou 18.0

Medium-full colour. Good rich, smoky, vigorous nose, somewhat chunky. A full, solid, concentrated wine with an elegant Cabernet character and a positive finish, though with a touch of astringency. Very fine.

Haut-Simard 15.0

Slightly old colour. Ripe, meaty, rich and sweet on the palate nevertheless. Still vigorous. No decay. Finishes long. Most enjoyable.

La Lagune 15.0

(Recorked February 1985) Fullish, mature colour. This is a well-matured wine with an earthy, warm-brick flavour which reminds me of the Graves. Good attack, chocolate and mulberry flavours and no astringency. Finishes less well, the fruit having dissipated leaving a certain sour acidity. Yet fresh. Good but not great.

d'Yquem 18.5

Very dark colour indeed with a green tinge at the edge like an old Madeira. 1928 is said to be a better vintage for Sauternes than the 1929, both in general and for Yquem. This has an interesting old-toffee nose, is rich and caramelly but has high acidity so it not *that* luscious. Full and sweet but not a great deal of *pourriture noble*. Finishes clean but not honeyed. Very fine but not a great Yquem, but perhaps an unlucky bottle.

WHITE GRAVES: RECENT VINTAGES

For as long as I can remember I have had a bee in my bonnet about white Graves. I was brought up on the wines of Bordeaux. My parents rarely drank anything one might term fine wine but they did drink ordinary wine with their evening meal as soon as rationing restrictions were lifted after the war. What they drank was Bordeaux. It came in litres, was bottled in England and the label showed a map of the Gironde indicating the Médoc, Saint-Emilion, Sauternes and so on. It came in two colours: red or pink. At some stage of my youth I must have discovered that Bordeaux also produced white wine. At my insistence, as I recall, a litre of Bordeaux Blanc was produced. It was the first nasty glass of wine I had ever had – sickly and cloying, the sort of 'medium dry' which is really appreciably sweet. It smelled old and dank, it tasted revolting. 'Now you see why we don't drink white wine,' said my father. My mother appropriated the bottle for cooking.

Some years later I was in Bordeaux, a college graduate, working with a major wine-shipper as a *stagiaire*. What this meant was a sort of trainee. You were paid a pittance but you were supernumerary, working a fortnight here and a fortnight there; not so much doing anything useful as watching what went on. I spent some time in the *cuverie blanc* helping to find generic Graves, Sauternes, Entre-Deux-Mers and Bordeaux Blanc with bentonite and rack it off from one tank to another. The whole vat room reeked of sulphur. Every now and then I had to escape into the fresh air to clean my lungs. I spent a fortnight in this miasma and have had a violent aversion to SO2 ever since.

By this time, with my toenail in the wine trade, I had started investigating the white wines of the rest of the world. It had already begun to strike me as singularly inept that the largest quality wine area in France – if not the world – the producer of so many great red wines and so many good, honest red wines (which is perhaps more to the point) should make such a disaster of its whites. Yes – there were the great dry whites: Laville-Haut-Brion, Domaine de Chevalier and Haut-Brion Blanc itself, the equivalents of *grand cru* wines from Puligny and Meursault; but where were the equivalents of Muscadet or Mâcon-Blanc-Villages?

Later still, when I began to visit Bordeaux as a buyer in my own right, I used to ask my suppliers to produce examples of medium-priced dry white Graves. I would also visit the local restaurants to seek out new names and new vintages. This pilgrimage was invariably fruitless. There was nothing but the same old over-sulphured, tank-aged, dead wines. Bordeaux Blanc was still a disaster area. I started making a fuss. I wrote articles criticizing most of the wines. I arrogantly proclaimed that either the proprietors journeyed outside Bordeaux to find out how good white wine should be produced or that they should invite wine-makers from Burgundy, the Loire, Australia and elsewhere to come into their wineries and teach them how to do the thing properly.

Finally, but literally only in the last six or seven years and on a reasonable scale only since the 1988 vintage, improvements have begun to be discernible. I hope I have helped. At last, the Graves is beginning to make 'correct' dry white wine. By comparison with what used to be seen in the bad old days, the improvements have been revolutionary.

This progress has been the result of the amalgamation of a number of ideas, both old and new, and the input of techniques from as far afield as Australia, currently the most progressive part of the world as far as dry white wine is concerned. Briefly, these can be listed as follows: the grapes are picked riper; there is skin contact before pressing; the wines are fermented using specially selected yeasts; fermentations are prolonged at cool temperatures; the wines are often fermented in oak as well as matured in oak; they are kept on their fine lees for several months; often these lees are stirred up, enriching the wine; and they are handled better with less resource to sulphur. Moreover, the Sémillon grape, having long been out of fashion at the expense of the Sauvignon, is now back in favour.

A DEATH OF GOOD WINE

Just over 45 per cent of the annual Graves production of 220,000 hectolitres is white wine. The trend here, as elsewhere in Bordeaux, is from white to red, though it has not been as marked as in the Entre-Deux-Mers and elsewhere. Much of this white wine is uncomplicated generic stuff, Graves or Graves Supérieures. In the northern part of the region, in what is now the Pessac-Léognan *appellation*, only some 32 per cent of the production is white wine but here you will find all the eight classed growths. With the exception of Château Carbonnieux and Château Olivier, most of the classed growths and other leading estates only toy with white wine production, few making more than twenty *tonneaux*. Only one of the classed growths, the divided Château Couhins, solely produces white wine. Some, like Château Haut-Bailly, do not produce any white wine at all.

GRAPE VARIETIES

In this part of the Graves, the dominant white wine grape is Sauvignon Blanc. Château Malartic-Lagravière and Château Smith-Haut-Lafitte, as well as the part of Château Couhins owned by the Lurtons of Château La Louvière (Couhins-Lurton), produce their Graves whites exclusively from this variety. Only at Château Olivier is Sémillon in the ascendant. The 1987 decree outlining the new regulations for the Pessac-Léognan AC stipulated a minimum quantity of 25 per cent Sauvignon Blanc in the vineyards of those properties within the new AC. Personally, I consider this an unnecessary restriction. If growers want to produce wine solely form Sémillon they should be allowed to do so. Sémillon is a higher quality grape variety than Sauvignon. Correctly vinified, the flavours of Sémillon are more subtle and complex, the feel of the wine is richer, more ample and generous, and the wine has a greater capacity for ageing. The combination of Sauvignon and new or newish oak has to be handled with great care lest the oak dominates and the tannins are too blatant. The Sémillon marries better with new wood as all of us who have enjoyed fine Sauternes can substantiate. Further south in Graves, Sémillon is more widely planted. While most of the wines are made for relatively early drinking, the results are increasingly stylish.

A WINE-MAKING REVOLUTION

There are a wide number of different influences involved in this revolution, and these are both domestic and foreign. Firstly, and simply, there was the reaction to criticism and a lack of orders. White Graves had declined in fashion, and rightly so. The proprietors themselves began to consider what was being produced, albeit from other grape varieties, in Burgundy, or from Sémillon and Sauvignon in Australia and California.

Secondly there was the Coste-Dubourdieu effect. Pierre Dubourdieu, proprietor of Château Doisy-Daëne in Barsac, but more interested in dry wine than sweet, had shown that it was possible to produce a dry, Graves-style (being produced in a Barsac vineyard the *appellation* is simply Bordeaux) wine without excessive recourse to sulphur. Oak until recently has played little part in the production of Doisy-Daëne Sec. Dubourdieu makes it, Pierre Coste, *négociant* in Langon, sells it. The two used to jointly own Château Montalivet. Other Dubourdieus own other southern Graves properties. Coste sells other wines from the surrounding area. From the late 1970s the examples were there for all to see. These were the Mâconnais parallels.

There was another Dubourdieu influence; this time in the person of Denis, son of Pierre.

Denis is a professor of oenology at Bordeaux University. Not only has he taught the modern generation of wine-makers how to make stylish white wine, he has written a number of papers with his academic colleagues on such matters as skin contact, fermentation with cultured yeasts, the beneficial effects of leaving a finished wine on its fine lees for several months, *batonnage* (stirring these lees up), and so on. He produces a smashing inexpensive wine at Château Reyon in the Premières Côtes, a really stylish Clos Floridène from vines at Illats in the southern Graves and is now responsible for the white Château Montalivet. Moreover, as consultant or unofficial friendly counsel at a number of top properties – De Fieuzal, La Tour-Martillac, etc. – he has been able directly to influence Graves wine-making for the better. Additionally, there are now a number of Dubourdieu-trained young men making the wine at places such as Carbonnieux.

André Lurton and his son Jacques at Château La Louvière were another influence. Louvière has only recently been vinified in oak. But for more than 25 years, since the Lurtons acquired what was then a sadly neglected property in 1965, Louvière Blanc has shown that white Graves can thrive without being sulphured up to the eyeballs. The Lurton empire has grown inexorably from its base at Château Bonnet in the Entre-Deux-Mers. As well as Louvière, there are Château de Rochemorin and Château du Cruzeau, and of course the sole classed growth exclusively producing white wine, Château Couhins.

Yet another influence was Peter Vinding-Diers. Vinding arrived at Château Rahoul when Len Evans and his colleagues acquired the property in 1978. He continued there until 1988, even after the collapse of the Evans Bordeaux empire in 1982, building up his own small Domaine de la Grave in the neighbourhood. He now also has his own property at Château de Landiras. Vinding, a Dane, is uncontaminated by history. Generations of making wine in the same artisanal manner as one's father do not apply here, nor cloud up his approach. This is empirical, unprejudiced and imaginative. Vinding's contribution has been two-fold. He has firstly shown that it is possible to produce *cru classé* quality wine solely from the Sémillon grape. Secondly he has demonstrated the influence of different yeast cultures. He vinified a barrel or two of his 1985 with cultures from Angludet and Lynch-Bages. A comparison between these and the 'regular' Château Rahoul, vinified with Vinding's own R2 yeast, showed telling differences.

In the early 1980s the penny finally began to drop in the *crus classés* cellars. At Louvière and Couhins they started fermenting in oak in 1982. At Smith-Haut-Lafitte they began vinifying in wood in 1984. At Fieuzal, *directeur technique* Michel Dupuy, prompted by proprietor Gérard Gribelin, vinified half of the 1984 harvest in wood. The results were later blended together with the tank-fermented wine; but the experiment was, even in a lesser vintage, a pronounced success. At Bouscaut, they had even vinified the 1980 entirely in new wood (but had to re-apply for the label of *appellation contrôlée*). Elsewhere, even if they did not ferment, or vinified only partly in wood, the *élevage* was increasingly taking place, in whole or in part, in oak. 1985 was the watershed. From 1988 the properties began to get it right.

As I have said, vinification in new or newish oak, particularly for the Sauvignon, needs to be handled with care. Oak, *per se*, is not a panacea. You only have to taste some California Fumé Blancs, as some proprietors call them, to find an error in the opposite direction: rigid wines with extra tannins extracted from the wood, whose fruit is totally dominated, whose acidity seems artificial. Fieuzal erred in this way to the same extent in 1985.

The treatment of new oak barrels prior to use, their origin (Allier for preference, and with a light toast), the percentage of new barrels employed, and the time the wine remains in them – all these factors are crucial, and they will change with every vintage; the concentration, ripeness and quality of the fruit and pressed must being determinate. Growers have learned by experience: flexibility is all.

The vexed question of skin contact is another moot point in the Pessac-Léognan area. It is argued by some that the extra aromas which result are either alien or will not last. I would certainly myself be more confident in suggesting the technique for a wine which would evolve in the short term than a wine destined for maturing over a ten-year period. Experiments in Burgundy which I was allowed to sample in June 1990, persuaded me that this was not a process which was suitable for Le Montrachet and the like. Moreover, not only must the fruit be spotlessly clean, but the *macération-préfermentaire* has to be done at a cold temperature. If the grapes arrive at 28 degrees, which in these days of end-August harvests is highly probable, they must be cooled, and speedily too, before bacterial infection sets in. If not, you'd have to sulphur the fruit and unpleasant vegetal flavours would be extracted.

Why are people against it? For *macération-préfermentaire* is rarely admitted in the Graves. They employ it at Carbonnieux and La Tour-Martillac but not at Haut-Brion, Chevalier or Fieuzal. As one aficionado put it: because they've mucked it up when they've experimented. It either works or it's a disaster. In this Dubourdieu-inspired view the intensity of flavours realized are highly desirable. Additionally, as the process leads to a diminution in the acidity of the must, the fruit can be picked a couple of days in advance of optimum sugar maturity, and it is at this point that the potential intensity of aroma in the fruit is at its peak. Surely, in this view, we should harvest at the flavour-peak, rather than at the sugar-peak. I would suggest that a couple of percentage points of extra acidity, in all but the meanest vintages, was a positive advantage.

But surely also, as with the equally controversial matter of cold (red grape) maceration before fermentation in Burgundy, skin contact takes place anyway. Just as in Burgundy, in the relative cool of a late September or early October harvest, the grape skins and their juice macerate together before the fermentation gets under way, so in the Graves, skin contact takes place whether the proprietor is aware of it or not. If it takes, as it might, an hour to fill the *pressoir*, and then six hours slowly, carefully and gently to press the grapes, there must necessarily be skin contact.

While the desirability of vinifying at 20 to 22 degrees rather than at rock bottom 'cold temperature' (where the fragrances extracted are too volatile and ephemeral: fine for Entre-Deux-Mers and Bergerac but not for *cru classé* Graves) and of leaving the finished wine on its fine lees for several months after the vintage (extra richness and concentration of flavour, plus the fact that the lees protects the wine: hence less sulphur necessary) has been learned and universally accepted, the technique of *batonnage*, stirring up these lees, is controversial. The same arguments are used: the aromas which result are alien; the wine will not make old bones.

It is, after all, a risk. The lees need to be that bit more clean to avoid tainting the wine. If one barrel is tainted, using the same implement to stir up the lees without cleaning it between casks will impart the taint to the rest. Moreover, it fixes the colour. *Batonné*-ed wines have a deeper colour than the rest.

However it is argued that one does not produce any flavours that are not there anyway. If they seem more exotic it is merely because *batonnage* makes them more volatile. So *batonnage* is a logical development. If keeping the wine on its lees adds fatness and depth, which it does, *batonnage* will add yet more richness and concentration of flavour. Currently, those who use this technique stir up the lees once a week at the start of *élevage*, also eliminating the carbon dioxide. Thereafter the frequency declines to once a month. A typical example, with a wine being held on its fine lees until June, would be sixteen *batonnages* in nine months. Today this technique is employed at Bouscaut, Carbonnieux, Couhins, La Louvière and La Tour-Martillac.

They are only just beginning to make wine correctly on a large scale in the Graves. But the results of the harvests since 1988 are promising. And it is yesteryears' also-rans which are setting the pace. The brothers Kressmann at La Tour-Martillac are making splendid white

Graves today. The Lurton family at La Louvière and François Boutemy at Larrivet-Haut-Brion are making better wine than most of the *crus classés*. Philippe Moureau as wine-maker at Carbonnieux is at long last pushing this largest of white Graves producers into the modern era. Haut-Brion has always, and probably always will, make the finest white Graves. Perhaps here and across the road at Laville and at Domaine de Chevalier we have the only Graves wines with the potential of *grand cru* Burgundy standard. But at least there is no longer just a void lower down the hierarchy.

THE TASTING

The following wines were sampled in Bordeaux in April 1990, and April 1991.

Optimum Drinking   *Mark out of 20*

1990

Bouscaut   Drink soon   13.5
Stylish on the nose. Good oak. A little heavy on the palate. But this is promising. Reasonable depth. Quite good. But starts better than it finishes which is not a very good sign.

Cantelys   Drink soon   14.0
Modern method white Graves. Made by Michel Lurton. Good oak. Good freshness. No enormous depth and not an enormous amount of fruit, but it has got style. Quite good. Finishes well. This has the zip some of the others lack.

Carbonnieux   Now–1999   15.0
Stylish, delicate. Interesting fruit on the nose and attack. Even a bit of richness on the follow-through. Good.

Couhins–Lurton   Now–2000   16.0
I wish they'd plant a bit of Sémillon here. Nevertheless it is impressive – if, as always, a touch rigid. Good fruit, not a bit grassy. Some oak. Good depth. Good grip. Good finish. Good plus.

de Fieuzal   Now–2000   15.5
Lovely fat, rich nose. The attack also is impressive but the follow-through not so special. Ripe, exotic, not over-oaked. Reasonable finish. Good plus.

Doisy-Daëne Sec   Drink soon   16.0
AC Bordeaux. Entirely vinified in wood. This is most attractive. It has a delicious crisp, melony-mango-pineapple flavour. Ripe but not a bit heavy. Long, complex, not a bit over-oaked. Passion fruit is another nuance I find here.

du Cruzeau   Drink soon   13.0
Plump and ripe, but lacks a bit of depth and grip this year. Starts better than it finishes. Not bad.

Haut-Brion Blanc   Now–2005   19.0
Recently racked. Lovely fruit on the nose. A little upset on the palate but a wine of real breed and complexity here. No *batonnage*, they insist. Even when nearly everyone else seems to be doing it.

Haut-Gardère   Drink soon   14.5
This is at least partly oak-fermented. A soft wine with reasonable grip. Quite delicate. Certainly stylish. Like so many it lacks a bit of zip at the end. Well-made though. Quite good plus.

Larrivet-Haut-Brion   Now–1998   15.0
This is more youthful than most. I find it a little heavy and rigid and no more than good this year. Both richness and zip are missing. Yet not short.

Laville-Haut-Brion   Now–2005   19.0
This seems fatter and oakier than the Haut-Brion Blanc. Like it, it has just been racked. Rich, ripe, satisfying. Very good. Better than the Haut-Brion this year, perhaps.

La Louvière   Drink soon   14.5
Good ripe attack, but falls away a bit on the follow-through. Neat and oaky and with reasonable grip and fruit. In fact the finish is positive. This is quite good plus but more forward than the La Tour-Martillac.

La Tour-Martillac   Now–2000   15.5
This hasn't quite the flair of the 1989. There is good fruit and zip. It's a bit richer and more aromatic than the Larrivet. Medium-full. Good length. Good to very good.

Montalivet   Drink soon   15.0
Entirely vinified in oak. Richer and fatter but perhaps not quite as much flair as the Doisy-Daëne Sec. Round and ripe. Will keep well though.

Olivier   Drink soon   14.0
Now vinified in wood but I find this a shade dilute. It lacks a bit of intensity. Neat and clean though. Better on the finish than on the attack, always a good sign. Quite good.

de Rochemorin   Drink soon   14.0
Ripe, quite fragrant. Good acidity. This is a well-made, clean, *bourgeois* example. Good fruit. Positive finish. Quite good. Less fat than the Louvière.

Smith-Haut-Lafitte   Drink soon   15.0
Aromatic, fragrant, quite exotic wine. Gently oaky. This is stylish, and as usual, quite forward. Though the style seems to be evolving into something less ephemeral than hitherto. Good depth. Good.

Domaine de Chevalier   Now–2005   17.0
A subtle, backward wine. Not as upfront as some (no *batonnage* here) but very good depth and richness. This has length and quality. Very good indeed.

Domaine de Grandmaison
Drink soon   14.5
An attractive, plump, balanced, forward example. Good fruit. Touch of oak. This has good grip. It doesn't die away. Well-made. Quite good plus.

Domaine de la Grave   Drink soon   15.0
Soft, aromatic, gently woody. Ripe and delicious. Exotic and gently fruity. This shows the men from the boys. Good.

1989

Baret   Drink soon   13.0
A rather dull, Sauvignonny wine, without grace but reasonably balanced.

Bonnet   Drink soon   14.5
AC Entre-Deux-Mers. A beautifully made, ripe, elegant, essentially Sauvignonny wine of great style. Very good extraction of fruit. Ripe, aromatic. No wood. But within its aspiration an excellent result. *Gouleyant.*

Bouscaut   Now–1996   13.0
Less flair than the 1990. Not as much oak. Reasonable richness and grip but a bit hard.

Cantelys   Drink soon   13.0
This is a well-made, new-style wine. Some depth. Has interest. A bit young-viney, but a good effort. Ripe finish. Not bad.

Carbonnieux   Now–2000   14.5
This has richness and depth. Good fruit. Not quite there, but it shows a promising evolution, finally, at Carbonnieux. Finishes well. This has more to show as it evolves. Quite good.

Domaine de Chevalier   1996–2016   17.5
Currently, like the La Mission, a little adolescent. Nevertheless a wine of real depth and concentration, with a more exotic, tropical flavour than the 1988. Should be fine.

Couhins-Lurton   Now–2005   14.5
A fine, ripe, oaky nose. Very good on the nose. A shade rigid and one-dimensional on the palate (Sémillon needed) because it is 100 per cent Sauvignon. Good depth. Will evolve and improve. Quite good plus.

du Cruzeau   Drink soon   13.0
Round, ripe and stylish if with no great depth. A well-made fruity example. Not bad.

Doisy-Daëne Sec   Drink soon   16.0
This has a more high-toned, flowery nose than the wine below. Just a hint of oak. This is a classic – if individually perfumed – example of modern

white Bordeaux. Round, quite rich, long, harmonious. Quite exotic in its flavours. Ripe and with very good grip. Long and lovely.

Doisy-Daëne, Cuvée Saint-Martin
Drink soon   16.0
AC Bordeaux Blanc. Rich nose but more closed. Less oak apparent on the nose. On the palate altogether more individual. Has taken up less of the wood. Concentrated, rich, very ripe. Quite dry but certainly fat and long on the palate. Still very young. Less spice, less fruit, more flowers though Victoria plums and greengages as well.

de Fieuzal   Now–2005   16.0
This is classy. Good oaky base. Ripe, rich fruit. A masculine, but not rigid example. But it has good backbone and potential for development. Very good.

Clos Floridène   Drink soon   16.0
This doesn't exactly jump out of the glass. But it got better as it evolved. Gently oaky and subtly stylish. Will still develop. Finely, carefully made. Lovely fruit. Long. Very good. Yet is it a bit one dimensional after the 1988?

Domaine de la Grave   Drink soon   15.0
This is clearly superior to Peter Vinding's Château de Landiras. Ripe, rich, amply fruity. Good oak and depth.

Haut-Brion Blanc   Now–2016   20.0
This is honeyed and rich and more oaky than the 1990. I find it very lovely. Very ripe fruit but very well balanced. Long and subtle. Splendid. This is better than the 1990.

Haut-Gardère   Drink soon   13.5
It doesn't have a great deal of nuance but this is a new-wave Graves with ripe fruit. Medium body. Not bad to quite good.

de Landiras   Drink soon   13.5
Good grip. Ripe, Sémillon-y wine. It doesn't have the nuance or depth of flavour of Peter Vinding's Domaine de la Grave, and it is fully ready for drinking. Clean and neat, if a touch simple.

Larrivet-Haut-Brion   Now–2005   16.0
Good oak. The attack is full and still a bit adolescent, but the finish is lush and rich and complex. Fine finish. This is very good. Will still develop. Lovely finish. I rate this better than the Fieuzal.

Laville-Haut-Brion   1996–2016   17.0
Not as lush as the Haut-Brion. Possibly not quite the grip. Good fruit, but not the concentration or richness. A lovely, stylish example but quite accessible already. Very good indeed.

La Louvière   Now–1996   14.5
A rather more forward but plump, stylish example. The fruit is most enjoyable and the wine is balanced and long. Quite good to good.

Olivier   Drink soon   13.0

This is tanky, with some built-in SO2. Improvement evident in 1990 but this 1989 is dull.

Pavillon Blanc du Margaux
                Now–1997   15.0

This is a gentle, pretty, oaky wine, but it doesn't have the depth of the 1988. Ripe, stylish and long. Balanced and elegant. But lacks a bit of concentration and dimension.

de Rochemorin   Drink soon   14.0

This has a delicate touch of oak. Obviously partly fermented in wood. Ripe, stylish and forward. Quite good.

Le Sartre   Drink soon   13.0

No oak here but a clean fruity example. But essentially rather dull.

Smith-Haut-Lafitte   Drink soon   13.5

Almost a bit too oaky and exotic. I get a touch of the overblown and even of astringency. Yet exciting flavours here. But it was bottled a bit late and lacks a bit of zip. I had this bottle two months ago and it was fresher. I don't think this is a representative sample.

La Tour-Martillac   Now–2005   16.5

This is even better. Lovely fruit, a lot of concentration. Fine, fullish wine with real depth and class. Very good intensity. Very good indeed.

1988

Bouscaut   Drink soon   14.0

The oak is a little hidden – indeed the whole wine seems to have gone a bit into its shell. But no SO2. On the palate we have what it in fact is, a blend, and a blend which does not quite fit together. The fruit lacks a bit of concentration, though it is ripe enough. But the tannins stick out. Quite good. But lacks a bit of class and there is a bit of SO2 on the palate.

Carbonnieux   Now–2000   14.0

A lightish, quite forward wine, only very discreetly oaky. Doesn't seem to have enormous depth. The fruit is a little dilute and the wine is not exactly married in with the wood. Better and more elegant than La Louvière though. Quite good.

Domaine de Chevalier   1996–2008   17.0

Another very good nose. Somehow lighter toned. Again complex. Good fresh peachy fruit. This is another fine example. Fresher than the above, with good persistence on the follow-through. Ripe, youthful. Lovely. But lacks the richness and character of the Laville-Haut-Brion at present.

Couhins-Lurton   Now–2000   14.0

Clean and reasonably ripe on the nose but no real depth or pretention. Hard element on the palate. Reasonable fruit but lacks suppleness, depth and charm. Rather a mean, surly wine.

du Cruzeau   Drink soon   13.5

Ripe and pleasant (and clean) but surprisingly evolved on the nose. I would have said it was two years older. Not exactly elegant. Round and plump. Not without depth. Quite fit. Completely clean. Good for what it is.

Doisy-Daëne Sec   Drink soon   15.0

A lighter, less intense, less complex wine than the 1989. Not as rich, or as much depth, and now ready for drinking. Stylish, clean, crisp. Good.

Doisy-Daëne, Cuvée Saint-Martin
                Drink soon   16.5

This is better than the 1989. It is richer and more opulent, spicy and exciting. Fat, long and complex. There is plenty of wine here, and it will still improve in bottle. Delicious.

de Fieuzal   Now–2005   16.0

Ripe nose, a little heavier than the two above. Good fruit/oak blend but it doesn't seem to have quite the flair of the two above. Very good nevertheless. Quite full. Good fruit. Gentle oak support. Very good.

La Garde   Drink up   12.0

A little SO2. High-toned, early-harvested, somewhat raw and rigid on the nose. This is just the sort of thing we have been fighting against. Raw, green and rigid.

Haut-Brion Blanc   Now–2008   18.5

This has gone back to a sort of awkward adolescence. It is ripe and plump, though without the concentration of the 1989. Good fruit but a sort of petrolly aspect at present. This will go.

Haut-Gardere   Drink soon   13.0

This is a little overblown on the nose. Clean, good ample fruit but seems to be ageing far too fast. This has an aspect of wood but seems a bit too evolved. Ripe and plump but shows undue age. Essentially unbalanced.

Larrivet-Haut-Brion   Now–2004   16.0

This has the deepest colour of the last half of the series. Fat, rich, oaky, exotic, ripe and ample on the nose. Immediate attraction. Well-balanced. Lively. This is high class. A lovely concentrated, complex wine with excellent fruit and very stylish, balanced. But it doesn't have the grip or intensity of La Tour-Martillac.

Laville-Haut-Brion   Now–2008   18.5

This has also gone into an adolescent phase, but underneath it is rich and concentrated with a very good grip. This may be better than the Haut-Brion. It is fatter but perhaps not as classy.

La Louvière   Drink soon   13.0

Quite a firm, nutty-resinny nose. Same oak but the flavours and fruit are a bit closed in. On the palate this is a lightweight wine, without a great deal of elegance. There is essentially not enough fat here, and the fruit has been dominated by the structure. Not bad at a generous best.

Malartic-Lagravière   Now–2002   13.0

So much SO2 on the nose it is impossible to discern anything else. On the palate I can't see any oak. Nor much ripeness. A full wine but somewhat malic. Lacks style. Disappointing.

Olivier   Now–1996   13.0

Light colour. A light nose. I don't get much ripeness, oak or depth but I do get some SO2. A little oak but not quite enough. The fruit is quite ripe and succulent though. The *matière première* is here. It just needs working on. Not bad.

Pavillon Blanc du Margaux
Now–2000   15.5

This is less oaky than the 1989 at present, but it has more depth. It is perhaps a touch adolescent but the finish is fat and meaty and rich. Slightly fuller.

de Rochemorin   Drink up   12.0

Ripe, clean, quite fruity. A good standard example but essentially a little dull. On the palate has now softened up and is *à point*. Clean but rather characterless. No depth. No concentration.

Le Sartre   Drink soon (if at all)   10.0

There is quite a bit of free SO2 on the nose. On the palate this is light, fruity, forward and supple. For early drinking. Why inundate it with SO2?

Smith-Haut-Lafitte   Drink soon   14.5

Firm, strongly oaky nose. The wine is ripe and plump but the wood tends to dominate. Sauvignonny. A little SO2. Quite a masculine wine, though not exactly exotic. Yet complex. Good nutty aspects yet not really fat. I would have preferred the succulence of Larrivet. Good though.

La Tour-Martillac   Now–2004   16.5

This has a lovely nose. Discreet, gentle, ripe, supple and complex. Medium body. Ripe, multi-dimensional. A triumphant success. Quietly successful. A wine of depth and intensity of flavour. Beautifully put together. Excellent.

1986

Bouscaut   Drink soon   13.0

I find this a little rigid on the nose. But clean. This is a mixture of ripe but not very concentrated fruit, with some SO2, plus the rigidity of the oak. And it doesn't quite fit together harmoniously. Lumpy. Coarse. Yet there are good elements.

Carbonnieux   Drink soon   13.5

A fullish flavour. Ripe but classically – or should the word be typically – the wet-wool, built-in sulphur flavour of old-style Graves. Unlike the Larrivet the fruit here doesn't really have much depth or class. This is destined always to be dominated by its SO2.

Domaine de Chevalier   Now–2008   18.0

Good depth here on the nose, though a bit of SO2. There is fat and concentration underneath. Fullish. Currently somewhat adolescent. Rich though. Good grip. Quite a masculine sort of wine. Good grip. This has a fine future.

Couhins-Lurton   Drink soon   14.0

Bigger wine, but more rigid. There is oak here, but it is not married in with the fruit. It improved on aeration. A fullish wine. Some fruit but the structure shows, so on the whole this lacks suppleness and generosity. Quite good, and still young but I can't see it really improving.

de Fieuzal   Now–2000   17.0

The oak dominated on the nose but the wine is undeniably attractive. Rich, ripe and opulent. One of the few wines which is definitely a success. Fat, plump, full and rich. Plenty of depth and concentration. Still young, even raw but has plenty of room for development. Fine.

Larrivet-Haut-Brion   Now–1997   15.0

Rather too much SO2 on the nose. But there is a soft, round, supple and fruity wine hiding underneath. The fruit is fine and ripe, indeed balanced and complex but there is no oak and too much SO2. Nevertheless it has the grip to last until the SO2 diminishes, when it will be a nice bottle.

La Louvière   Drink soon   16.0

Soft, gently oaky, stylish, ripe and attractive on the nose. Clean and elegant. This is a great success. Considerable complexity. Has lots of good ripe fruit and a lot of finesse. Just about ready. Well balanced. Very well made. Will last well. This is in quality not that far short of Fieuzal.

Malartic-Lagravière   Now–1998   15.5

Not too dominated by the SO2. Full, rich, ripe and nutty, but the oak is not blended with the fruit and the natural effect is lumpy. Somewhat rigid but the fruit has depth, complexity and interest. I think this will improve in bottle. Good. Could even be very good.

Olivier   Drink soon   13.0

The flavour of this wine has similarities with the Smith (though the *encépagement* is quite different). There is some oak but also a bit of SO2 and a cooked apple flavour. Rather less ripe though. Again they tried even if they didn't succeed. Lacks a bit of ripeness. Not bad though.

de Rochemorin   Drink up   14.0

This is a little riper, cleaner and more interesting than its stable-companion above. Not bad. Indeed has some depth and elegance. A good example of non-oak aged Graves, the parallel of Saint-Vesan. Ripe, balanced. Reasonable depth and style. Good fruit. *A point*.

de Sartre   Drink up   12.5

Dull, tanky nose; not excessively sulphury though but pretty drear. On the palate the attack shows a bit of fruit but the follow-through is dominated by the built-in sulphur. If this had been reduced we might have had a perfectly pleasant – if basic – white wine.

La Tour-Martillac   Drink soon   14.0

This was the year Dubourdieu was called in to advise, but they didn't get their act together immediately. There doesn't seem to be a lot of fruit on the nose and there is a bit of built-in SO2. Wet wool on the palate hiding the fruit. Yet according to Loic Kessmann, the level was 25 (+22 in 87/88). An experimental *cuvée* was held another six months in wood. This has less SO2, seems richer, but is more rigid. Interesting oak/apricot flavours. Good acidity, good ripeness. Good.

Please note: neither Haut-Brion Blanc nor Laville-Haut-Brion were declared in the 1986 vintage.

1985

Bouscaut   Drink soon   13.0

This is more anonymous than the 1986 because it has a touch of built-in SO2. The fruit is better, because it is fatter, despite the sulphur elements, and the oak is less obtrusive. Not exactly elegant though. And not enough concentration.

Carbonnieux   Drink soon   15.0

This is fatter and richer than the 1986, but somewhat dominated by SO2 nevertheless. Yet it may have the depth to last until the sulphur has diminished enough. Quite fat and rich. A reasonable example of old-style Graves.

Domaine De Chevalier   Now–2010   18.0

There is a little more So2 on the nose than in the 1986, and the fruit seems less intense. Soft, plump, ripe and fruity. As usual very subtle and classy. The flavour is a bit subdued by the SO2 at present, but nevertheless there is concentration, complexity and breed here. Very fine indeed.

Couhins-Lurton   Drink soon   14.0

Quite firm and full on the nose. Some oak, some structure but rather less fruit evident. Though this has oak (and no SO2, it goes without saying), it has much less interesting fruit and the fruit that it has is beginning to dry out. Not bad. Quite good.

de Fieuzal   Now–2000   16.0

Fat, rich, oaky nose. Good ripe honeyed fruit. But the oak tends to dominate. A fine ripe masculine wine with plenty of depth. It lacks a little flexibility and it doesn't quite have the class it seemed to have at the outset. But a fine example. A lot more muscle than the 1986 but perhaps not as elegant.

Haut-Brion Blanc   Now–2015   20.0

This is less adolescent than the Laville. A really beautiful, distinguished example. Fullish, marvellously balanced. Really long and complex – and more elegant. Flavours of peaches, flowers such as *citronelle*, freesia and camomile, and residual flavours of roasted nuts. Lovely.

Larrivet-Haut-Brion   Drink soon   13.5

Like the 1986 the first thing you get is SO2 but unlike it I don't get the plumpness of fruit behind it. More to it but also more SO2. This is rather dead. The 1986 is better.

Laville-Haut-Brion   Now–2010   19.0

A full rich oaky wine, more opulent but marginally less racy and flowery than the Haut-Brion. A fascinating foil to it. Fat and concentrated, potentially honeyed (but dry of course) and opulent.

La Louvière   Drink soon   13.5

I don't get any oak on the nose and the wine doesn't seem to be as crisp and therefore as fruity as the Rochemorin. On the palate it is softer but more subtle. Has plenty of fruit, is fatter and more concentrated but not quite the grip.

Malartic-Lagravière   Now–2000   16.0

Little SO2. This has depth. Rich and concentrated, this has quite an individual flavour. Quite sturdy, indeed four-square. Rich, full and oaky. Fat, ripe and concentrated. This is currently a bit adolescent but there is depth here and the power and grip to keep it alive. Very good.

Olivier   Drink up   11.0

Somewhat evolved on the nose. Still dominated by its sulphur. This will never make it. Far too much SO2. Weak and insipid. Poor.

de Rochemorin   Drink soon   14.0

A pleasant, ripe wine on the nose. No oak but clean and fruity, and with no undue signs of age. Like the 1986 this is a great deal more enjoyable than most. Good fruit. Good balance, good depth. Quite rich and ripe even on the finish. *A point*, but will keep. Better than the 1986.

de Sartre   Drink up   11.0

Old, tanky and sulphury on the nose. I wouldn't drink this. Mean and old and coarse and now getting astringent on the palate. A cheap brew.

Smith-Haut-Lafitte   Drink up   13.0

Quite a pleasant lightish but quite plump and fruity wine. No SO2. No oak. But a little tanky and anonymous perhaps. A little bit of SO2 on the palate. A light wine whose fruit is now drying out.

La Tour-Martillac   Drink soon   13.0

Old-style Graves on the nose. No oak, a bit of SO2, but a ripe fullish wine underneath nevertheless. Plump, ripe, even honeyed on the palate. Not bad. Has the depth to endure until the SO2 diminishes.

1990, 1989 AND 1988 SAUTERNES

When I first began to travel extensively in the area in the early 1970s, Sauternes was the most backward, the most depressing of all the Bordeaux regions. Apart from Château d'Yquem the *appellation* was in disarray. One felt the medieval bastion of Yquem not only majestically dominated the surrounding vineyards but that its aloof magnificence intimidated the neighbouring proprietors.

The mood was sad and listless. A succession of mostly indifferent vintages following that of 1962 was to continue for twenty years, relieved only by 1967, 1971, 1975 and 1976. But even these were not as fine as they should have been. Such was the nadir of profitability the growers were caught in a vicious circle. No money meant few *passages* through the vines to collect the fruit at its optimum of ripeness and noble rot. No money meant no new oak and no selection. No noble rot, no selection and no new oak, so unexciting wine – which no-one was very interested in anyway. It is interesting to note, given that it costs, say, three times as much to harvest a Sauternes property than one in the Médoc, and that you only collect one-third the amount, that while in 1947 a wine like Château Rieussec would sell for as much as Château Latour – about 130,000 (old) francs a *tonneau* – Rieussec 1971 could only command one-tenth the price of the first growths, 10,800 (new) francs against 110,000 to 120,000.

In short, making Sauternes was uneconomic. One proprietor, M. Pontac of Château de Myrat, first of the second growths in the 1855 Classification, even went as far as ripping out his vines and letting his land go fallow. Others just sold up. In 1971 alone four properties changed hands.

It is partly fate, partly a change in fashion, perhaps largely the arrival of a succession of fine vintages in the 1980s, but Sauternes is once again in demand and commands high prices. The production of fine sweet wine is once again an economic proposition. The 1983 vintage gave us both quality and abundance and sold for high prices. Even if not all the wines are quite as good as they might have been, at least all the estates made a profit; a profit which has been re-invested back in the wine. This meant that when the equally successful (though softer) 1986 vintage came along, all were in a position to capitalise on its delights. This has been followed by three potentially magnificent vintages in 1988, 1989 and 1990. The wines are very exciting indeed.

The mood has changed dramatically. Today the growers have a confidence in their product where a decade or more ago they could only communicate a feeling of futility. Today the atmosphere is one of optimism and perfectionism. Today there is an abundance of new oak. There is a rigorous elimination of lesser *cuvées* in the creation of the *grand vin*. Cooling equipment has been installed for the precipitation of yeasts, tartrates and the rest, thus producing a cleaner wine which does not have to be so highly sulphured to keep it stable. Even the lesser vintages have improved significantly in quality. There is a consistent level of high quality across the board.

1990

To have had two fine vintages (1989 and 1988) in a row was almost unprecedented. For this to be followed by a third is unique. I have records going back to the eighteenth century. Never before has a hat-trick been achieved.

The climatic conditions were quite different from the rest of the region, in the main that there was a thunderstorm on 13 August, which released 50 millimetres of rain to keep the maturation cycle ticking over, followed by a further 23 millimetres on the 22nd and 23rd of the month, ideal to kick-start the incidence of botrytisation. The result was that the grapes were already physiologically ripe before the noble rot set in, and when it did it did so with a rapidity and uniformity that meant a swift collection without the necessity to pick over the same row of vines more than a couple of times. Incredibly the harvest began – on 11 September – even before some of the red wine châteaux had started their collection. From 8 September a very hot southerly wind intensified the concentration of the fruit, and potential alcohol levels in excess of 25 degrees in some pressings were announced by some astonished growers. The harvest was finished by 16 October, well before the weather broke. At Guiraud it was over by 29 September.

Nineteen ninety is the richest, in terms of its sugar and alcohol levels, of all the three recent vintages. It is also a plentiful crop. Which of the three is the best is difficult to generalize. Compared with the 1989s the wines are more backward than one year's difference would suggest. They are fuller too. Some are richer and better. In other cases the alcohol shows and I prefer the greater finesse of the 1989s. In general the lighter wines— the less Barsacs for instance – are better in 1989. In the rest of the region the position may be the reverse.

The Tasting: 1990 Sauternes

I sampled the following wines at Château Suduiraut in September 1994. Château d'Yquem and de Fargues were not yet available for tasting (the Yquem team, when pushed, declare a preference for 1989). Not shown were Châteaux Bastor-Lamontagne (quite good in the spring of 1992; the last time I made a tasting of these three vintages). Broustet (very good), Doisy-Daëne (very good), Doisy-Dubroca (very good indeed) and Rabaud-Promis (quite good).

	Optimum Drinking	Mark out of 20
Caillou	1999–2009	13.0

Mid-gold colour. Youthful, sweet nose. Ripe but not much nuance and not much grip. Rather four-square and inelegant. And a touch of sulphur to boot. Better on the palate. Plenty of body and sweetness and no lack of concentration. But the overall effect is lumpy, and the finish is a little coarse. Not bad at best.

Climens	2000–2025	19.5

Mid-gold colour. Full and oaky, fat and accessible on the nose. And good botrytis. This is a composed wine. There is not a hair out of place. It is not a blockbuster but it is really intense, very harmonious, and has splendid fruit. Very very long. Quite lovely. And with all the elegance of a 1989. Even better than the Climens 1989. Brilliant.

Clos-Haut-Peyraguey	1998–2012	16.0

Mid-gold colour. Backward, closed, concentrated but unforthcoming on the nose. There is a little sulphur here. On the palate an ample plump, medium-full wine; but not one with the greatest of depth and personality. Very good but not great.

Coutet	2002–2025	18.5

Mid-gold colour. Closed nose, but concentrated and classy. Very good depth and breed. This is very, very lovely. Round, fullish, intense and composed. Very complex fruit. Very elegant. Very long on the palate. Very fine. Close, but not quite as exciting as the 1989.

Doisy-Vedrines	1999–2019	18.5

Light, golden colour. Good nose. Delicate, flowery. Has grip. Good *pourriture noble*. Good elegance. Medium-full body. Lovely crisp flowery-fruity style. Racy. Archetypal Barsac. This is very well-balanced. It has very good intensity. And it shows real breed. Another excellent example of what is today a really high-flying cru. Indisputably first growth quality. But not quite as fine as the 1989.

Filhot	1997–2008	14.5

Light, golden colour. Youthful nose. But not the greatest of excitement. As usual it is clean and elegant. But there isn't mich botrytis here and so a lack of real concentration and intensity. Medium body. One and a half dimensions only. Yet well made, and certainly harmonious. Quite good plus.

Guiraud	1999–2019	16.5

Fullish golden colour. Not too evolved though. Honeyed, high-toned, flowery nose. Good acidity. Very elegant, I thought at first, but when I came back to it it had lost some of its finesse. Medium full, slight alcohol burn. Reasonable grip. Very good but not quite intense or elegant enough for fine. Yet long, youthful; more ample and better balanced and more stylish than the 1989.

Lafaurie-Peyraguey	2002–2025	18.5

Mid-gold colour. Soft, elegant flowery-rich nose. Good botrytis and good style. Fullish, very intense, beautifully balanced. A very well-put-to-gether wine with real intensity, Lovely fruit. A lot of *pourriture noble*. Very long. Very elegant. High class. But not as complex as the 1989. Yet more adolescent. In fact there is not much to chose between them.

Lamothe (Despujols) 1998–2007 13.0

Mid-gold colour. Quite fat on the nose. Some honey but not much elegance. Not much evidence of *pourriture noble* either. On the palate it is a little burnt and heavy. The alcohol shows at the end. Fullish, sweet, but rather coarse.

Lamothe-Guignard 1997–2010 15.0

Mid-gold colour. A little more developed than most. Rather over-evolved on the nose. Lacks grip. Fat and rich and honeyed on the palate. Not unclean. Not coarse. But it is a bit diffuse. Medium-full. Lacks a bit of nuance on the follow-through. The 1989 is far better. Good, merely.

De Malle 1998–2010 15.0

Mid-gold colour. A little more developed than most. More evolved on the nose. Certainly no lack of pourriture noble. But not a blockbuster. Is it a little blowsy? More grip in evidence as it developed. Fullish, ripe, spicy. Just a little heavy and unbalanced. This is a richer fuller wine than the 1989, but it is not as elegant. The alcohol shows at the end. Good but not great.

Nairac 2000–2015 16.0

Light, golden colour. Honey, toffee and botrytis here. But not the greatest of finesse. Yet it improved on aeration, and on the palate it showed better. Medium to medium-full. Good acidity. Still youthful. A touch of oak. The finish is the best part. This is a bit adolescent. But it is long and it has depth. Very good, but the 1989 is more elegant.

Rayne-Vigneau 2000–2020 18.0

Mid-gold colour. Full and concentrated, backward, a lemon marmalade aspect on the nose. A slight lack of zip and nuance though. Fullish, gentle, oaky, honeyed. Good grip. But it doesn't quite add up. Yet it is adolescent. At present there is slight alcohol burn. The finish is fine. Meaty, concentrated, long. Surely fine quality at the very least. Needs time. Perhaps even better than the 1989.

Rieussec 2002–2020 17.0

Mid-gold colour. A bit of sulphur here on the nose. But good weight and richness. Full, fat, ample, ripe and some botrytis. Still quite youthful. At first this was good plus, even very good on the attack: a backward wine with more to show for itself. The finish is better still: rich, concentrated, quite powerful. A true Sauternes. Very good indeed. But not quite elegant enough for great. The 1989 is better.

Romer-Du-Hayot 1988–2007 13.0

Light, golden colour. Somewhat flat on the nose. Lacks finesse; a little sulphur. Quite evolved. Medium to medium-full body. Sweet but one dimensional. Not too short but it doesn't have much finesse. Unexciting.

Sigalas-Rabaud 2002–2025 18.5

Mid-gold colour. Real concentration here, splendid botrytis. Lovely honeyed fruit. Real depth on the nose. Class too. Fullish, fat and rich and honeyed. A concentrated wine with very good grip and an exciting example. Youthful. Intense. Potentially very fine. Richer and more concentrated than the 1989.

Suau 1998–2008 14.0

Mid-gold colour. Backward nose. Quite concentrated and full. On the palate a slightly heavy wine. There is plenty of *matière* here: fullish, reasonable grip, reasonable concentration, reasonable fruit. But lacks a bit of zip and real intensity and class. And there isn't the greatest amount of botrytis. Quite good. But better than Suau usually is: better than the 1989.

Suduiraut 1998–2002 15.0

More than a mid-gold colour. Rather evolved. Good – and quite fresh – botrytis and sweetness on the nose. But it lacks the grip of most of the *premiers crus*. Medium to medium-full. Soft and barley-sugar honeyed. Reasonable acidity. But a lack of real zip and elegance. This will turn out like the 1976. Good but not great. But I think this is better than the 1989.

La Tour-Blanche 2002–2025 18.5

Mid-gold colour. The nose is still hidden. But there is good richness and depth underneath. Fullish. Not really a blockbuster but real intensity and concentration. Good vanilla aspects from the oak. Still very young. But a splendid example. Very very lovely concentration. Sweet fruit. Very good grip. An infant. But very fine potential here. Excellent quality. This is clearly better than the La Tour Blanche 1989.

1989

The vintage began around 18 September, and lasted until the final days of October. The grapes were exceptionally rich, a full degree of potential sugar above that of 1988. This has produced very powerful concentrated, *liquoreux* wines which are more burnt in taste – toffees rather than fruit salad – than those of the previous year, and which will take rather longer than the 1988s to mature. Perhaps some have been harvested a little early, and lack real botrytis character. The best though, and this must at this stage remain a tentative judgement, look to combine the finesse of the 1988s with the structure and richness of the 1990s. Perhaps at the topmost levels, therefore, the best vintage of the three. Despite some hail damage it was once again a plentiful crop.

THE TASTING: 1989 SAUTERNES

I sampled most of the following wines (De Fargues and Yquem were tasted separately) at Château Suduiraut in September 1994. Not shown were Châteaux Bastor-Lamontagne (good in April 1992), Broustet (fair), Coutet Cuvée Madame (brilliant), Doisy-Daëne (very good indeed), Doisy-Dubroca (very good indeed) and Rabaud-Promis (very good indeed).

	Optimum Drinking	Mark out of 20

Caillou   1997–2007   13.0
Light golden colour. Rather coarse and four-square on the nose. A bit of SO2. Slightly better on the palate. Quite full, reasonable grip. Quite honeyed. Rather edgy. This has little finesse. It is all rather four-square. Not bad at best.

Climens   2000–2030   18.5
Lemon gold colour. Full, youthful nose. Plenty of depth and plenty of *pourriture noble*. Quite accessible. Plump and ample and fruity on the palate. A medium-full weight very complex elegant wine. Not a blockbuster. But a wine of lovely style, and one which finishes very very long and complex. High class. Very subtle. Real dimension.

Coutet   2000–2030   19.0
Mid-gold colour. Rich concentrated and youthful on the nose. Good touch of oak. This has a lot of depth. Good *pourriture noble*. Full, quite firm. Very ripe and concentrated. This is fat and honeyed and very plump. Lovely fruit. Very good grip. Very fine quality. Especially long and lovely at the end. Very classy indeed.

Clos-Haut-Peyraguey   1999–2015   15.0
Light, golden colour. Delicate, very stylish, balanced nose. Perhaps a bit lightweight. This is a lighter wine and with less grip and dimension than its 1988. Pleasant but rather one-dimensional. Slightly coarse elements at the end. Has elegance though. And not short. Good.

Doisy-Vedrines   2000–2025   19.0
Mid-gold colour. Rich, concentrated, ripe and oaky on the nose. This is full and crammed with fruit. Most impressive. A very, very lovely wine on the palate. Quite full, absolutely delicious ripe, balanced fruit, *crème brûlée* background. Real breed and depth here. Very fresh and long and elegant. Very lovely indeed. A brilliant wine.

De Fargues   2000–2025   18.0
Light gold colour. Honeyed nose with splendid acidity. Youthful and vibrant. Beeswaxy honeyed, but allied to marvellous fruit. Fat, medium-full, sweet and rich. Very harmonious. This is intense, concentrated and has a lot of depth. Very fine. Very youthful.

Filhot   1998–2009   14.0
Light golden colour. Ripe and honeyed, even concentrated on the nose. But there is a herbal element. Lacks grace. Slightly four-square. Over-ripe melons said my companion, and I can see the decay she referred to. Sweet on the palate. Quite full, but little to support it. Only one and a half dimensions, and unstylish at that. Unbalanced too. Not very long. Quite good at best. But at least clean. Youthful.

Guiraud   1998–2012   15.0
Mid-gold colour. Good nose. Still youthful. Not as much weight or dimension as some though. On the palate medium-full weight, plump and spicy, showing a touch of oak. But there is a little alcohol on the follow-through. Quite fat. Reasonable grip. But it lacks a little finesse. Good, merely.

Lafaurie-Peyraguey   2000–2030   18.5
Mid-gold colour. Full, rich and ample on the nose. Plenty of depth here. A full, oaky, concentrated wine. Lots of botrytis. Still very youthful. It is even quite firm on the palate. Very good grip and concentration though. And lovely honeyed fruit. Backward but very fine.

Lamothe (Despujols)   1998–2004   12.0
Straw-gold colour. Flat and coarse on the nose. Some sulphur, little *pourriture noble*. Medium full, quite honeyed, but far too sulphury. Sweet in a *fondant* sense. No finesse. Poor.

Lamothe-Guignard   1999–2019   17.0
Mid-gold colour. Lovely nose. Honey and nougat, very flowery, plus peaches and cream. This is a very good example. Fat and rich, fullish, ample, plump and generous. Plenty of botrytis. Good grip. Honeyed, spicy finish. Fine. Very good indeed.

De Malle   1998–2015   16.5
Light golden colour. Fine herbal nose. Acacia, citronelle; very well balanced and full of interest. A delicate wine though. Not a blockbuster but a

stylishly put together, complex wine on the lean, fresh, Barsac side. Good intensity. Very harmonious. Fine finish. Plenty of depth. Very good plus.

Nairac   2000–2020   16.5
Mid-gold colour. Full, ample oaky nose. Firm and backward. Fat, rich, stylish and really quite oaky on the palate. Good grip. This is still very youthful. But it is going a long way. Firm finish. Plenty of wine here. Very good plus.

Rayne-Vigneau   2000–2020   17.5
Mid-gold colour. Firm, backward nose. Plenty of depth though. Slightly more accessible on the palate. Round and ripe, fat and plump. Fullish. Good intensity and plenty of *pourriture noble* especially on the follow-through. The finish is concentrated; the wine very good indeed, even fine. The fruit is very elegant. Very long. Needs time.

Rieussec   2000–2030   18.5
Mid-gold colour. Firm, youthful, oaky nose. Big, firm and backward on the palate. Currently adolescent. But lots and lots of wine here. At present it is almost top heavy. But very very long and rich and concentrated. Certainly fine plus at last. Needs time.

Romer-Du-Hayot   1999–2009   14.0
Light golden colour. Some *pourriture noble* here but a bit of sulphur too. This is better than the 1988. Ample and honeyed with reasonable grip. Quite full. Some depth. But it lacks a little grace. Quite good though.

Sigalas-Rabaud   1996–2008   16.5
Quite an evolved golden colour. Medium-full,

plump, quite oaky nose. But it is quite evolved already and it doesn't have the backbone or depth of some. Medium body. Honeyed and aromatic. A slight lack of structure and firmness compared with the longer living wines.

Suau   1998–2006   13.5
Mid-gold colour. Sweet, nutty nose, but not a lot of botyrtis or grip. Medium-full body. Reasonable quality. A little oak. Rather better than most Suaus. But it is a little lumpy for all that. Currently a bit adolescent. Not bad plus.

Suduiraut   1999–2015   15.0
Mid-gold colour. Medium weight nose. Not a blockbuster. Plenty of botrytis. Some development. Ripe and ample. Fullish, not as backward as some, but still a bit raw. On the palate it lacks a little thrust and fat. Better than the 1988 though. But it could have been a bit more elegant. Good.

La Tour-Blanche   2000–2020 plus   18.0
Mid-gold colour. Youthful, nobly-rotten nose. Good fruit and depth here. Spicy. Very good intensity. Perfumed fruit. Fullish, very concentrated without being a blockbuster. Plenty of botrytis. Very stylish and balanced. Very very long and youthful. Fine very ripe finish. Fine plus.

d'Yquem   2010–2050   20.0
Light golden colour. More concentrated, more fat, more honeyed than the 1988. Very lovely harmony, and real underlying power. On the palate the power is much more obvious. This is twice the wine of Fargues. Still very young. Very very long. Brilliant!

The Tasting: 1988 Sauternes

I sampled most of the following wines (De Fargues and Yquem were tasted separately) at Château Suduiraut in September 1994. Not shown were Château Bastor-Lamontagne (quite good in April 1992), Broustet (quite good), Coutet (very good), Doisy-Daëne (very good), Doisy-Dubroca (very good indeed) and Rabaud-Promis (good).

	Optimum Drinking	Mark out of 20

Caillou   1996–2006   14.0
Lemon gold colour. Sweet nose but it lacks a bit of grip and intensity. Medium body on the palate. Quite sweet and certainly fresh and clean and balanced. But forward and one-dimensional. No depth or grip. But not short, and the finish is quite elegant. Quite good.

Climens   1999–2025   17.5
Green-gold colour. A hint of reduction on the nose but fullish rich, good botrytis, proper Sauternes. Fullish, fat, rich and honeyed. Real barley sugar on the follow-through. A concentrated wine. Still young. Very sweet. This is fine, but it doesn't quite have the intensity for great.

Clos-Haut-Peyraguey   1999–2025   17.5
Lemon gold colour. Full, concentrated, intense, masculine nose. Fullish on the palate, with very good grip. Quite oaky. This has a lot of depth and intensity, and good class and length. The best Clos-Haut-Peyraguey in years! Fine.

Doisy-Vedrines   1997–2020   18.0
Light gold colour. Closed but concentrated. This has depth and quality. Very promising nose. Quite full. Totally clean. Very stylish. Beautifully balanced. This is a lovely wine. The fruit is subtle, the whole thing splendidly integrated. The finish very long and complex. Fine plus.

De Fargues   1988–2015   16.0
Light gold colour. A broader nose than the 1989. Not as obvious an acidity. A touch of SO2. This

has about the same weight as the 1989, and is of fine quality: balanced, rich and honeyed. But the 1989 seems to have a little more intensity and complexity at the end.

Filhot   1995–2005   14.5

Light green gold colour. Fragrant and flowery on the nose. Ripe, sweet and charming. But not a wine of great weight or power. Barsac in structure. But nicely fat and honeyed. Medium body. Just a little *pourriture noble*. Slightly adolescent. But the finish is more expansive. Balanced but it lacks depth and intensity. One and a half dimensions only. Quite good plus.

Guiraud   1995–2007   15.5

Lemon gold colour. Luscious, spicy, honey and nuts on the nose. Medium to medium-full body. Fresh and balanced. Good botrytis. The attack is fruity, but it lacks a little dimension on the follow-through. Good plus. Yet a most attractive wine, nevertheless. Quite forward.

Lafaurie-Peyraguey   2000–2025   18.0

Light golden colour. Fat, rich, opulent, plenty of noble rot. Fullish, honeyed, luscious, very ripe, very generous. A fat, rich oaky example. What it lacks is just a little grip. But it is seductive and expansive and very long on the palate. Fine plus.

Lamothe-Guignard   1995–2005   15.0

Mid-gold colour. Evolved nose. Loose-knit. Sweet with good acidity, but without the usual strength of Sauternes. Indeed there is a German/Austrian weight here. A typical, but good intensity. Very fruit salady. Curious. Yet not unstylish. Good.

De Malle   1997–2015   17.5

Lemon gold colour. Not a blockbuster but ripe, balanced, very fruity, very stylish. Medium body. Honeyed. Good noble rot flavours. This is intense and concentrated, though Barsac-like in style and weight. Splendid follow-through. Lots of depth here. Still very young. Fine.

Nairac   1995–2007   15.5

Light golden colour. Medium weight, honeyed, vanilla custard-y nose. But good acidity here. Lovely ripe fruit. Medium body. A touch of oak. Quite evolved. A balanced, attractive wine with good depth and length, but not quite the concentration and dimension for great. Good plus.

Rayne-Vigneau   1998–2020   18.5

Lemon gold colour. Lightish but intense and flowery on the nose. This has great breed. A fullish wine, though not a blockbuster, but very concentrated and intense, and splendid balance and complexity on the finish. Very lovely and flowery. Very fine.

Rieussec   2000–2020 plus   18.0 (see note)

Half-bottle. Mid-gold colour. Rather a flat nose, with plenty of SO_2. Underneath fat and rich and oaky but the built-in sulphur kills it and the wine lacks grip. Surely a bad example! Later I sampled a full bottle. This was quite different: very youthful and intense, slightly adolescent, but very honeyed and concentrated and with a great deal of depth. Certainly fine plus. Needs time.

Romer-Du-Hayot   1996–2006   13.0

Light green gold colour. Quite fat and sweet on the nose. Lacks a little grip and style though. There is a touch of SO_2 and it is a bit heavy. Better on the palate though. Medium-full. Honeyed. Reasonable acidity. Yet there are some oily, hard aspects to this wine on the follow-through. Not bad at best.

Sigalas-Rabaud   1998–2018   17.0

Light, golden colour. Full, firm, backward nose. A touch of SO_2. New oak as well. True Sauternes here. Sweet, vanilla and toffee. Lovely balanced fruit-salady flavours. Very ripe. Fullish, ample, generous. Very good indeed. Lacks just a sparkle of acidity for really fine.

Suduiraut   1996–2006   14.0

Light, golden colour. Soft, gentle, ripe nose. But not a great deal of depth or strength. Forward. Medium sweet. Medium body. A ripe, reasonably balanced, elegant wine. But it tails off. There is a lack of grip and intensity here. Quite forward. Quite good at best.

La Tour-Blanche   1997–2012   16.0

Mid-gold colour. Strange, perfumed nose. Sweet but not Sauternish. Medium to medium-full. This is very ripe and fruity and not lacking intensity and grip by any means. But it doesn't have the fat and honey-toffee-vanilla character one expects. Very good but lacks a bit of breed.

d'Yquem   2005–2025   19.5

Light golden colour. An aspect of angelica and herbs on the nose. Honeyed, delicate. Subtle. Sweet rather than really fat and luscious. Splendid flowery overtones and real breed. Balanced finish. long, complex. Excellent.

1986 SAUTERNES

If 1983 was the vintage which finally broke the cycle of unprofitability, bad vintages and declining quality, 1986 was the year when the region was able to demonstrate that it had been injected with a new elixir of life. In short: in 1983 the properties made money; this money was re-invested in the domaines; in 1986 the climatic conditions produced a large vintage of splendidly botrytized fruit; the estates had the confidence to make the most of this good fortune; and for the first time for a generation, perhaps for the first time ever, the quality was high and consistent across the board. What is particularly encouraging is that the top wines include not only Climens and Rieussec, well-known and reliable, but wines like Rabaud-Promis and Rayne-Vigneau which had hitherto been decidedly uninspiring.

It is this consistency which is perhaps of greater long-term significance than the success of the vintage itself. Even by comparison with years as recent as 1983, there has been a considerable improvement in the wine-making and the *élevage*. Less and less does one come across Sauternes without any *pourriture noble* or new oak. Everywhere investment is being made to promote the standard of the wine. There is a new mood in the air: a confidence, a pride.

There are two main reasons for this change. The first, quite simply, is profitability. First growth 1986 Sauternes such as Rieussec, Suduiraut and Guiraud opened at 85 francs upwards ex-chateâu. The 1983s sold *en primeur* for around 50 francs; the 1979s for 27; whilst the 1975s and the 1976s fetched only 20. If one bears in mind that the Sauternes *rendement* is a third that of the Médoc, that it costs three or four times as much to collect the harvest and, moreover, that successful, much-in-demand vintages are few and far between, the 1986 prices, still less, mind you, than a super-second claret, cannot be considered excessive.

The second reason, which really goes hand in hand with the first, is that the locals can see a future for the wine, and this is encouraging them to invest in equipment, such as cold-stabilization tanks, new oak, cryo-extraction facilities and the like; expenditure which can only be amortized over a number of years. It is also providing them with a rationale to produce a second wine, thus inevitably increasing the quality of the *grand vin*. The Sauternais courage has been rewarded. After 1986 would come 1988, 1989 and 1990, an unprecedented trio of successful vintages.

THE WEATHER

A wet spring was followed by a very dry early summer. June, July and the first half of August saw hardly a cloud in the skies. A successful flowering had produced a potentially large crop. September would be wetter than the norm, however, but October, especially the first fortnight of it, would be drier: ideal conditions for the development of noble rot.

Surprisingly, the botrytis seems to have arrived first of all in the higher ground of Sauternes itself rather than nearer the River Garonne in Barsac. By 18 September, there was already some sign of *pourriture noble* and by the last week of the month or the first week of October, most of the top growths had made their first *passage* through the vineyards. Guiraud and Yquem were among the first to start picking. Further rain in the last week of September followed by warm dry days in the first half of October produced a rapid and widespread onset of noble rot across the region. More rain in the middle of the month, plus the usual morning mists, continued its development.

The incidence of noble rot was plentiful and even – 'The most botrytis I have ever seen in 25 years in Sauternes,' said Pierre Meslier, the now-retired *régisseur* of Yquem. Essentially, the difference between 1983 and 1986 is that in 1983 there was a very high degree of physiological ripeness before the botrytis arrived. In 1986, this final element of over-ripeness developed at the same time as the spread of noble rot.

Hamilton Narby at Château Guiraud had completed his harvest by 20 October, an early date for a Sauternes. Most others continued into November but by this time the weather had broken, the *pourriture noble* had begun to lose its aristocracy and the acidity of the must had become a bit feeble. The last third of the harvest at Rieussec, which continued until 10 November, and the last two *tris* at Yquem did not go into the *grand vin*. The difference in the picking dates – and the results therefrom at Nairac in 'lower' Barsac shows the importance of the microclimate in this part of the world. Heeter made four *tris* from 13 to 16 October, 22 to 27 October, 3 to 6 November and 12 to 13 November. There was no deterioration in the quality of the wine produced in the later *passages*. The grapes for the third *cuvée* were collected in freezing weather and only pressed once. The result was like a botrytized ice-wine.

THE CHARACTER OF THE WINES

1986 is a vintage of honeyed, sweet, rich wines with plenty of depth and a good balancing acidity. But it has a soft centre. The wines have less structure than the 1983s or the 1988s and 1989s and will evolve a little sooner. Ample, plump and opulent, with a peachy fruit rather than a marmaladey spice: Bommes and Barsac rather than Fargues and Sauternes. These are the characteristics, but it will certainly keep well. 1983, at its best – Climens, Yquem – has produced bigger, more intense and powerful wine; 1988 yet more consistency and high quality. But there is plenty of good wine in 1986. It is a landmark vintage.

THE TASTING

I sampled the following wines in Sauternes in January 1991.

	Optimum Drinking	Mark out of 20

d'Arche Now–2008 15.5

Lightish colour. Elegant, flowery and gently oaky but honeyed and fruity on the nose. This is a very stylish, balanced, medium-weight wine. Richer and more concentrated on the finish than the attack suggests. Finishes well. Promising.

Bastor-Lamontagne Now–1999 14.0

Light green-gold colour. The nose is high-toned, but less rich and intense but there is *pourriture noble* here. Lacks a bit of grip. Lighter, rather more forward, than the 1988. Quite stylish. Quite good.

Broustet Now–2004 15.0

Mid-gold colour. Rich, fat and concentrated and honeyed on the nose. Good but a touch overblown. Evolved on the palate. Medium body. Lacks a bit of lusciousness. Good acidity. Peachy. Attractive, but it lacks a bit of depth and class.

Caillou Now–2002 13.0

Lightish colour. Youthful. Slightly rigid nose. A little ungainly. Not great depth or style. SO2 shows. A bit heavy. Uninspiring. Medium body.

Climens 1996–2016 18.5

Lightish colour. Closed, sweet, fat, opulent nose. Good *pourriture noble*. There is a bit of SO2 but the wine is full and rich, with a good base of oak. Slightly solid. Fat, quite intense. Long and stylish but doesn't quite have the dimension until it developed in the glass. Still youthful, indeed adolescent. Potentially excellent.

Coutet 1995–2005 14.0

Light colour. Medium weight, fat nose. Some depth and style but a little four-square. On the palate I find it has less class. Ample and fullish but has a bit of SO2 and lacks a bit of zip and elegance. A bit heavy and boring. Medium-full.

Coutet, Cuvée Madame 1996–2020 19.0

Light colour. Reserved, intense, very sweet and concentrated on the nose. This is luscious and new oaky and unexpectedly structured. Good grip and a lot of depth. Brilliant it has to be said.

Doisy-Daëne 1995–2009 15.5

Lightish colour. Gentle, delicate, stylish nose. Honeyed, some *pourriture noble*. Not a blockbuster though. Fullish, ample, fat and gently oaky. A plump wine but it lacks a little intensity and drive. Very stylish. Certainly good. The oak dominates just a little at the end.

Doisy-Dubroca 1995–2011 16.0

Lightish colour. Closed, oaky, quite concentrated nose. Very Barsac. Very elegant. Lovely peachy fruit. Very good acidity. A balanced, fragrant example with a complex finish. Very good.

Doisy-Védrines 1995–2015 18.0

Lightish colour. Very good nose. Rich, concentrated, stylish and honeyed. Good *pourriture noble*. Very good indeed. Good intensity here, better than the Filhot. Full, rich, gently oaky. This has depth. Still backward. Plenty of dimension. Youthful but fine. Very fine grip. Lovely.

de Fargues 1996–2015 17.5

Light-golden colour. Oak and apricots and hazel-nuts on the nose. A broad-flavoured, stylish, intense wine. Fat and quite powerful. Sweet and rich, and certainly very oaky. Very seductive.

Filhot 1995–2015 16.0

Lightish colour. This is very good. Clean, stylish, concentrated nose. Good *pourriture noble*. This has depth. Medium-full. Elegant with lovely fruit. Good intensity. A racy wine with depth and dimension. Very good. Long and complex.

Guiraud 1995–2015 16.0

Mid-gold colour. Backward, concentrated. Good *pourriture noble*. A touch of new oak. A touch of marmalade. Exotic. Sweet, quite intense and luscious. Good intensity. A complex wine. Medium-full. Individual.

Clos-Haut-Peyraguey Now–2009 16.0

Lightish colour. Plump, sweet, fragrant nose. A touch deadened by sulphur. Youthful, broad, luscious palate. No lack of noble rot. This has depth but lacks a bit of definition. Very good though.

Lafaurie-Peyraguey 1995–2010 17.0

Lightish colour. Slightly oxidized, slightly petrolly. Quite evolved. Rich and fat without much class or depth. Very ripe and honeyed. Some new oak. Lacks a bit of zip, yet plenty of *pourriture noble*. Adolescent. Certainly very good.

Lamothe (Despujols) Now–2002 14.5

Medium colour. Quite a full, fat wine but a lack of zip and class. There is certainly noble rot here and plenty of plummy fruit. Quite supple and forward. Medium body. A reasonable example.

Lamothe-Guignard 1996–2009 16.0

Lightish colour. Open, evolved, fat, *citronelle* nose. Some depth and concentration. Flowery. A medium weight, sweetish, marmaladey wine. Good grip and intensity. The Muscadelle shows. Youthful. Very good. Sweet and concentrated.

de Malle Now–2006 15.0

Lightish colour. This is stylish and concentrated. A touch of marmalade and peaches on the nose. Clean. Has depth. But quite evolved. An exotic wine on the palate. Medium body. Flowery and sweet. Some *pourriture noble*. Good grip but it lacks a little real class and concentration. Good though. Fresh and lovely and attractive.

Nairac 1995–2010 16.0

Lightish colour. Racy. Some oak. Concentrated. Very Barsac. Reserved and stylish; honeyed and backward. Very good but not the depth of Doisy-Védrines. Fullish, intense, concentrated, but almost too oaky on the palate. Very good.

Rabaud-Promis 1995–2012 17.5

Lightish colour. Flowery but ripe concentrated nose. No lack of *pourriture noble*. Similar but more

concentrated than La Tour-Blanche. As it evolved it became more blunt. Yet on the palate sweet, ripe and concentrated. Fruity and generous and ample, if adolescent and fat on the finish.

Raymond-Lafon 1995–2005 14.0

Medium colour. A little sulphur on the nose but certainly some *pourriture noble*. Backward. A little four-square. There is richness and sweetness here but not really a lot of class or zip. Fair at best.

Rayne-Vigneau 1997–2020 19.0

Lightish colour. Fat, rich, youthful nose. Weight, depth and quality here. Good oak. This is very fine indeed. A fullish, very concentrated, youthful wine with a lot of depth and a good oaky base. Rich but racy. A lot of *pourriture noble*. Very, very long. Great intensity of flavour. Quite lovely.

Rieussec 1997–2020 19.0

Mid-gold colour. Closed and concentrated. Fat and rich. A backward wine with a lot of depth and potential. Full, rich, fat, intense, luscious, backward. There is a lot of depth here. New oaky. Yquem-ish. Youthful but very fine indeed. Needs a lot of time. Very long.

Romer-du-Hayot 1995–2009 15.0

Lightish colour. Quite a fat nose. A touch of SO2. Quite rich. Medium-full. Stylish, balanced, honeyed. Some oak. Good *pourriture noble*. Good. Lacks just a little zip.

Sigalas-Rabaud 1996–2015 17.0

Slightly fuller colour than the above. Backward, honeyed, marmaladey nose. Fat, closed, full and rich. A proper Sauternes. There is concentration here. Ungainly but potentially very good indeed.

Suau Now–1997 13.0

Quite an evolved colour. Not a great deal of style and little noble rot on the nose. This is a bit coarse. Some SO2. On the palate it is fullish and sweet, and reasonably fresh. But there is a heavy edge to it as well. A curious sweet-sour mixture. A bit lumpy. Uninspiring.

Suduiraut Now–1998 13.0

Lightish colour. The nose is a bit coarse. Lacks style and concentration and *pourriture noble*. Thin and disappointing. Medium sweet. Insipid. Poor.

La Tour-Blanche Now–2005 14.0

Lightish colour. A flowery, stylish nose, more accessible than most of the Sauternes. Honeyed. Some *pourriture noble*. There is a herbal element here. Medium weight. Quite luscious but slightly oily. Lacks a little class. Quite rich. Quite good.

d'Yquem 2000–2030 Plus 20.0

Unmistakable as Yquem because of the sheer power and intensity. Very backward and concentrated. Yet not a bit ungainly. Sweet and rich, a lot of *pourriture noble*. Luscious, oaky, honeyed and potentially very delicious. In a class of its own.

1985 SAUTERNES

Nineteen eighty-five was a difficult vintage because it was too dry. The botrytis was slow to develop. In an area where, contrary to normal agricultural practice, the grower is actively encouraging the fruit to rot, hoping for the combined efforts of early morning mist and balmy afternoons to produce the right sort of decay known as noble rot, which will realize the spicy taste we recognize in the top wines of Sauternes and Barsac, the autumn was reluctant to create the humidity essential to this phenomenon. It was a vintage where courage was required. For those who had the patience, 1985 has produced a more than 'acceptable' vintage.

THE WEATHER

In August and September only 22 millimetres of rain was precipitated, the driest end to the summer since 1929. Nineteen eighty-five is a Sauternes vintage where a lot of courage was required, but where patience eventually was amply rewarded. Throughout October the botrytis failed to appear and there were fears for another 1978. Nevertheless in the final few days of the month it began belatedly to occur. Those who delayed and who harvested the bulk of their crop in November have made good wine. At Yquem, the harvest did not finish until five days before Christmas. It was not a large crop, not only because a severe selection was required but because of hail and frost damage. Hail on the Whitsun weekend particularly hit parts of Preignac and Barsac. At both Nairac and De Malle the yield was severely reduced.

SELECTION

1985 has shown the importance of selection. Much of what was picked during the first half of October must have produced wine similar to that of 1978, another vintage where the autumn was fine, but paradoxically too dry for the formation of *pourriture noble*.

These wines are full and sweet, but somewhat lumpy and four-square, without the spice or the acidity of the noble rot. It is a reflection of the dedication now prevalent in Sauternes – Hamilton Narby at Guiraud, for instance, rejected 47 per cent of his harvest – that this 1978 flavour is rarely apparent in the top wines. Indeed, given the difficulties, the quantity of botrytis in the wines is surprising. So is the consistency. It is not a great vintage and there were more exciting things to come in 1986, let alone in 1988, 1989 and 1990, but there are some good things in 1985. It is not a year to overlook.

THE TASTING

I sampled most of the following wines at a tasting organized by Liz and Mike Berry in London in May 1988. Subsequently I tasted a further selection in September. At the time the wines of Yquem and Fargues had not yet been released.

	Optimum Drinking	Mark out of 20
d'Arche	Now–2004	15.5

Stylish, peachy nose. An attractive, plump, medium-bodied wine; slightly less honeyed, slightly firmer than the above. Good new oak background and no lack of botrytis.

Climens	Now–2010	18.5

Fine, concentrated nose: unmistakeable noble rot. This is full, very rich, luscious, concentrated wine. It does not have the oaky structure of Nairac but there is certainly plenty of new wood. Powerful,

closed, a lot of depth. Apricot flavours on the finish. Very fine indeed.

Coutet	Now–2000	14.5

Light, flowery nose. Medium body, clean and elegant, quite honeyed but not a lot of botrytis. It lacks the weight of the above and the dimension of the wine below. Nevertheless balanced and stylish. Reasonably forward.

Filhot	Drink soon	11.0

Powerful, alcoholic nose. Lacks sufficient grip to balance it. Closed in, coarse-flavoured, sweet but diffuse; an oily, fiery wine with little or no sign of botrytis. Finishes a little better than it starts. Poor quality. I'm not surprised this wine doesn't appear on any of the retail lists I have to hand.

Guiraud   Now–2008   17.0

Less fat and opulent but with more obvious new oak: the higher proportion of Sauvignon is evident. Good noble rot though and stylish, concentrated flowery fruit. Not quite as good as the Rieussec but certainly very fine.

Clos-Haut-Peyraguey   Now–2003   15.5

This is a wine of similar style and intensity to the wines above. It is not quite as oaky as the Lafaurie, nor as backward as the La Tour-Blanche, but has a good botrytis flavour, crisp balance and plump fruit. An attractive wine. Reasonably forward.

Lafaurie-Peyraguey   Now–2005   16.0

Fine, rich, full, opulent, oaky nose. Quality and noble rot here! Medium-full body, quite firm and rich on the attack. Flavours of orange, grapefruit and candied peel. Generous and attractive. Perhaps it lacks just a bit of intensity and concentration on the follow-through. Slightly less *pourriture noble* than the above.

Lamothe-Guignard   Now–2002   15.0

Soft, honeyed nose. A medium-bodied wine with good citrussy-peachy fruit. Not that powerful or intense but well-balanced and satisfactory noble rot flavours. Finishes well.

Nairac   1995–2010   16.5

Full, closed nose. Later-bottled than some and so just a whiff of sulphur which will soon pass. Firm and very oaky, deceptively somewhat hiding the *pourriture noble*. Rich and balanced. Full, fragrant, flowery, honey-and-vanilla flavour with a touch of *citronelle*. Intensely flavoured. A *vin de garde*. Classy as usual. (La Vigneronne £12.95 and halves.)

Rabaud-Promis   Now–2003   15.5

Rabaud-Promis is another property where great strides have been made in recent years. A fullish, rich, sweet wine with a good oaky background and satisfactory noble rot flavours. Slightly more four-square than the Haut-Peyraguey and shows a touch of sulphur.

Rayne-Vigneau   Now–2005   16.0

Fresh, flowery, honeyed and oaky nose. Good botrytis for the vintage. A medium-full, balanced accessible wine which shows the progress that has been made at the property in recent years.

Rieussec   1996–2013   17.5

Slightly deeper colour than the rest, though not as much as earlier vintages of this wine have commonly shown. Big, fat, closed, nutty nose. An opulent wine underneath. Rich and full but with rather more sulphur in it than the rest. Luscious and honeyed though. Fine potential.

Sigalas-Rabaud   Now–2003   15.0

A little sulphur-dioxide is currently blunting the flavour of this wine. On the nose it seems a little adolescent, but on the palate, if not showing as much *pourriture noble* as the Rayne-Vigneau, it is stylish, honeyed and oaky. Medium-full body. Certainly good. Sigalas is not often seen abroad. Most of the production is sold through an exclusivity with the Savour Club on the domestic market.

Suduiraut   Now–1999   14.0

Lightish, flowery nose; doesn't seem to have as much weight or depth of flavour, or as much botrytis as most of the above. Medium-body, sweet. Reasonable grip but a certain lack of dimension and zip.

La Tour-Blanche   Now–2010   16.0

Good nose. Quite full and intense with a touch of mint, camomile and greengages. Some oak. Some botrytis. Quite full and plump. Good grip. A fat, citrussy wine, rich and long on the palate. Quite reserved. Shows very well.

1983 SAUTERNES

Whereas it is the September weather which makes or breaks the quality of the red or dry white wine vintage, it is the climate and micro-climate in October which is crucial to the character and concentration of the sweet wines, for the Sauternais often do not begin to harvest until the other growers have finished and frequently, in the top properties, continue picking until November even December.

Sauternes is made not merely from over-ripe grapes but grapes which have been attacked by a fungus – the *Botrytis cinerea*. The advent of this fungus – the product of morning mists and balmy afternoons – causes the grapes to split and rot; the water inside the grape evaporates, the sugar and extract therein concentrates and the rot, not the grey or *grise* rot of a wet autumn but the noble rot or *pourriture noble*, imparts a particular spicy *liquoreux* flavour.

One of the risk factors in the harvesting of Sauternes is that the noble rot does not arrive evenly. It takes time to spread not only from one part of the vineyard to another but over a single bunch. As a result, the pickers, experienced locals rather than itinerants or students, comb each row of vines several times over, selecting just the best bunches, parts of bunches or, at its most perfectionistic, at Yquem, even single grapes. These *tris* or *passages* may number as many as a dozen in a single vintage.

Each vine may be visited a dozen times. It is a process both expensive and hazardous. We are playing poker with the elements, one grower once told me. The Sauternes proprietor will anxiously watch the sky and listen to the weather forecast. Will the summer break and the autumn rains arrive? Once they do, if it turns continually wet (cold is not so much of a problem), the rot will quickly turn from *noble* to *grise* and the remaining fruit will be lost. At Yquem, in and out of the rain in 1974, they made eleven *passages*. Not a single bottle of *grand vin* was produced however. None of the *cuvées* was good enough.

It is only rarely that the weather is sufficiently dry and warm but misty in the morning throughout October and great Sauternes can be made. 1983 was one of those vintages. The top wines have great depth and concentration and, particularly, balance. In the last great pair of vintages, 1975 and 1976, some wines in the earlier year were insufficiently botrytized while some of the later vintage were too fat and heavy and have aged coarsely. What characterizes the best 1983s is the sheer harmony of the wines and the beauty of their fruit. Because of the excellence of the balance, the vintage can be drunk now. Some will not be at their best, however, until later this decade. The cream of the crop will be vigorous as much as twenty years later still.

THE WEATHER

In the locality for a long weekend at the beginning of October, I was able to experience the ideal Sauternes micro-climate for myself. Separating Barsac from the remaining four communes to the south is a stream of clear, cold, spring-fed water called the Ciron and the warmer River Garonne which produces the district's morning mists. In the first few days of October, 1983, the skies above the gloom were cloudless but it was not until lunchtime that the sun broke through.

Until midday headlights were necessary. It was like driving in a semi-permanent fog. Wandering through the vineyards in the afternoon one could perceive the grapes glistening in the sun. Minute droplets of water clung to each berry. The fruit was marvellously ripe but, at this stage, few berries had begun to take on the almost purple-brown hue of over-ripeness. Fewer still were in any way rotten.

The *pourriture noble* was slow to arrive. Throughout October, rainfall was minimal and the weather marvellously hot. After a *tri de nettoyage*, a *passage* through the vines to eliminate rotten dried-out bunches caused by the almost tropically humid weather in August, the growers had to sit back and wait. By the middle of the month most properties had made a first *passage*. By this time, the grapes were abundantly over-ripe though there was still little widespread botrytis. This juice would give wines of high alcohol and high acidity but low or lowish residual sugar and not the real *pourriture noble* flavour. The reverse was true at the end of the harvest, though in general terms there was less variation between different *lots* at one end of the harvest and the other in 1983 than normal.

The botrytis did not begin to arrive in earnest until the end of October and the beginning of November. Suduiraut, always an early picker, had finished by the 7th, Yquem continued until the 18th. Pierre Dubourdieu at Château Doisy-Daëne did not even start until most of the rest had finished. He then fermented his Sauternes on the lees of his dry wine in order to preserve a racy acidity and so add elegance to the fruit.

A NADIR IN THE FORTUNES OF SAUTERNES

There were however some who, for various reasons, were not so patient. There are those who are less ambitious, less perfectionist, less willing or able to afford the reduction in crop and the expense of collection over a month or more which a proper Sauternes harvest requires. In addition in 1983 there was another factor. 1982 had been a precocious crop, the noble rot already present by the end of September. But the weather broke in early October. Most had only managed to collect a third or a half of their grapes. The remainder quickly attracted grey rot in the teeming weeks between 3 October and the end of the month. This part of the crop was a write-off. Quite understandably, some growers were unwilling to risk this sort of debacle twice in a row.

And there was another more important factor. For the previous decade and a half, Sauternes had been in the doldrums. Interest was slight; prices were low; profitability was negligible. As a result investment – in new oak and cooling equipment in the cellar, as well as in risk – had all but disappeared except in the top half-dozen estates. There was little in the way of selection. Unlike in the red wine estates, there was, as yet, no concept of a second wine.

This is therefore an 'if only' vintage. The top few wines are brilliant. But if only all the classed growths had been able to approach their Sauternes wine-making in this same perfectionist manner . . . ! Potentially, judging by Château d'Yquem, 1983 could have been the greatest vintage of the decade. Instead one is forced to cite 1986, 1988, 1989 and 1990 as preferable, for the simple reason that they are very much more consistent. But at least the growers made a profit on the 1983 vintage which they were able to plough back into the image of the wine. And thankfully this courage was blessed in the succession of fine vintages which followed later in the decade.

THE WINES

Thanks to the splendid weather which began at the beginning of September and continued almost to Christmas, the basic fruit from which the 1983 Sauternes was produced was in an exceptional condition. It was already abundantly ripe, if not over-ripe, before the botrytis arrived. It is this splendid physiological maturity, underlying a high degree of botrytis in the grapes harvested in November, which forms the base for the exceptional quality of the top 1983s. In 1976 the botrytis arrived in eight days; its incidence was overwhelming but the fruit was not in such a perfect condition. Moreover, like in 1982, there was rain, though happily not in such excessive quantity. The best 1976s are voluptuous but almost over-luscious. The very best 1975s – a vintage where like 1983 the botrytis was slow to appear – have less incidence of noble rot than 1983 but, in contrast to the 1976s, are firm and have good acidity.

The top 1983s combine the beauties of both. There is, above all, an intensity of fruit which in the case of Yquem is breathtaking in its perfection. There is weight, there is power, there is grip and there is finesse. Indeed, there was the ripest acidity that I had ever seen in a Sauternes vintage in its infancy.

Thus there were at least two good fairies at the christening of the 1983 Sauternes. One gave it attraction and elegance, the other a long and healthy life. If some growers lacked the expertise and finance or a perfectionist attitude, and others, because of 1982, made a 1983 rather over-egged with *cuvées* picked before the botrytis had really arrived; and if these vines are not quite as good as they might have been; there is, nevertheless, a high overall standard. And the best are simply sublime.

THE TASTING

The following wines were sampled in London in September 1991.

	Optimum Drinking	Mark out of 20

Bastor-Lamontagne   Drink soon   12.5

Marginally lighter colour than the Chartreuse. Quite a lot of sulphur on the nose. Medium body. Sweet but fairly nasty. Rather too much sulphur. Not maderized though, but rather mean on the finish: even bitter.

Broustet   Drink soon   12.5

Mid-gold colour. Dryish, rather full nose with a little sulphur. No botrytis. A little better on the palate. Reasonably clean but it lacks grip and richness. Thinning out at the end. A bit coarse.

de la Chartreuse (Saint-Amand)
   Now–2010   15.5

Mid-gold colour. Clean, ripe nose. Good *pourriture noble* here. Stylish, crisp and plump on the palate. This has balance and ripe flowery fruit. Medium body. Gently honeyed. Very good, especially for a non-classified growth.

Climens   Now–2020   18.0

Light golden colour. Some sulphur but rich, concentrated and closed. Quality here. Some evidence of new oak. This is very fine. Rich, full, balanced and stylish on the palate. A lot of depth. Honeyed, gently oaky, long, complex and with plenty of *pourriture noble* but crisply harmonious.

Coutet   Drink soon   13.0

Light golden colour. Just a little sulphur but quite good concentration here. Yet a bit coarse. On the palate this is rather insipid. Medium body. Lacks a bit of grip and fat. Uninspiring, and now finishing a bit short.

Doisy-Daëne   Drink soon   14.5

Light golden colour. Curious nose. Not really very sweet at all. Not *pourriture noble* but a touch of marmalade. Fresh on the palate. Sweet, crisp and flowery. Good length. Very competent but it lacks glycerine and botrytis.

Doisy-Dubroca   Now–2009   15.0

Great gold colour. Quite a fat nose, still youthful and closed, but a bit of sulphur. Quite full body.

Some botrytis. Ripe but lacks a little elegance. Certainly good though. Will still improve. The finish is the best bit.

Doisy-Védrines   Now–2000   15.0

Light golden colour. Light, gentle nose, sweet but not very intensely botrytized nose. Surprisingly, this is very similar to the Daëne; just a little fatter and more intense. Little botrytis.

de Fargues   Now–2014   16.5

Quite a deep colour. Closed, concentrated but flowery nose. A very fresh and fruity wine with good grip and quite a pronounced touch of new oak. Rich. Fullish. Racy. Very good but not as concentrated or as honeyed as the Rieussec.

Filhot   Now–1999   12.0

Deep golden colour. Dry overblown nose. Hardly even a hint of *pourriture noble*. Sweet on the palate but rather one-dimensional and a bit short. Quite full, but bland and slightly insipid. Finishes a bit astringent.

Guiraud   Drink soon   14.0

Mid-gold colour. Curious herbal elements on the nose. Aniseed, even liquorice. Quite clean and sweet not exactly a fat or intensely-flavoured wine. Slightly metallic finish but not short. Odd.

Lafaurie-Peyraguey   Now–2020   18.0

Deepish golden colour. Rich, very concentrated nose. Oaky and citrussy. Clean and spicy and vanillary. Still closed. This is fine. Rich, full and not too oaky. Good grip. Still very young. Honeyed and fat with a goodly amount of botrytis. Very fine. Will still improve.

Lamothe-Guignard   Now–2005   16.0

Mid-gold colour. Good citrussy concentration on the nose. Plenty of botrytis and fat here. Not a wine of the greatest weight but quite concentrated, plenty of noble rot. Good fat, slightly spicy flavour. Balanced. Long. Very good.

Liot   Now–2005   14.0

Lightish colour. Fat, quite sweet nose but a bit of built-in sulphur. Less sulphur on the palate. Medium-full, ripe, honeyed, some *pourriture noble*. This is a well-made wine; better than many classed growths, but it lacks depth and finesse. Ready.

de Malle   do Not Drink   9.0

Very light colour. Nasty nose. Free as well as built-in sulphur. So overladen it is undrinkable.

Nairac   Now–2005   15.5

Light golden colour. Rich, opulent but very new oaky nose. Good botrytis though. Was there too much new wood here? Full, very oaky, vanillary and buttery. This is an individual, intriguing wine but it is no longer exactly rich. Will it dry out?

Rabaud-Promis   Now–2005   15.0

Mid-gold colour. A fat nose with some botrytis and some sulphur. There is substance here but not much style. Cleaner on the palate. Quite full and rich. Reasonable balance. Good *pourriture noble*. But slightly lumpy. Good though.

Raymond-Lafon   Now–1997   11.5

Mid-gold colour. Rather overblown on the nose. Rather a coarse, full wine with a strange metallic edge to it. Some botrytis. Some built-in sulphur. Heavy footed. A second bottle was a maderized, oxidized version of the first. A lot of the UK shipments suffered from fermentation in bottle. Yet the colour doesn't show much difference from the original sample.

Rayne-Vigneau   Now–1999   14.5

Mid-gold colour. Slightly watery on the nose but not too much built-in sulphur. Not much noble rot but quite fresh and fruity and reasonably elegant. Medium body.

Rieussec   Now–2009   17.5

Deep gold colour – almost bronzed. Rich, fat, vanillary nose. Opulent. Spicy. Plenty of *pourriture noble*. Voluptuous, alcoholic. Full but open. It doesn't quite have the style of the Climens or the concentration of the Lafaurie-Peyraguey but it is rich and balanced, ample and long on the palate. Very good indeed.

Sigalas-Rabaud   Now–1997   14.5

Mid-gold colour. Slightly heavy on the nose but rich and fat as well. Good *pourriture noble*. Not quite as fat and as concentrated as I thought from the nose. Yet balanced and with a little less sulphur than Rabaud. But it is getting a bit thin at the end.

Suduiraut   Now–1999   14.0

Light golden colour. Soft nose. A little SO2. Lacks zip. Essentially this is rather bland. A wine with no selection. Lacks noble rot and concentration. Medium body. Pretty but of little consequence. Reasonable length.

La Tour-Blanche   Now–2005   14.5

Lightish green-gold colour. Sulphur on the nose and a strange herbal element. This could have been good with a little less sulphur, because there is good acidity here and some new oak. And this wine is quite rich and concentrated. But the sulphur kills it. May improve.

d'Yquem   1999–2039   20.0

Deep golden colour. Very closed on the nose. Youthful, concentrated and new oaky. Twice as youthful, twice as concentrated as the rest. This is still a long way from being ready for drinking. Intensely flavoured. Very classy. Very fresh. Brilliant.

1975 AND 1976
SAUTERNES

Together with the 1971 vintage, 1975 and 1976 are the most successful Sauternes vintages of the decade. There are good wines in both vintages, though they are somewhat of a contrast to one another, and the best of these, now nearly twenty years on, are holding up well. The 1976s are lush and fat, with plenty of noble rot, but in some cases not enough acidity and class. The 1975s are firmer, if less luscious, but often better balanced and with more finesse. In the case of Château d'Yquem, not noted below (but see page 000) I prefer the 1975, as I do for the Coutet, but in other cases – Climens, for example – the 1976 is the better vintage. Sauternes, by its very nature, is less uniform than the Médoc or Saint-Emilion, and it was even more so in the less profitable, less fashionable days of the 1970s.

THE WEATHER:1976

1976 was a long, hot summer. From June onwards the sun raged its scorching way across the heavens. Throughout Europe man sweltered, and couldn't wait for the weekend to escape the city into the relative freshness of the countryside. I remember a performance of Don Giovanni at Covent Garden. As I had not only been to a suitably well-lubricated farewell lunch to mark the retirement of a well-known wine-trade personality but then gone on to a wedding reception, I was in no fit state to sit through Don Giovanni's long acts in an amphitheatre temperature of over 100°F. As has been said elsewhere in another context, I made my excuses and left. And I hope Mozart forgives me if ever I should encounter him in the hereafter.

June was not only hot but extremely dry. July was hot with average rainfall and August hot and humid, with above average rainfall. In September the weather broke. Some 68 millimetres of rain – a month's average – fell between 11 and 15 September, and in all 170 millimetres were precipitated in the two months. Luckily the weather improved in October, and those who delayed the completion of the harvest, which had begun for the sweet wines on 21 September, were able to harvest fruit which showed plenty of signs of the noble rot.

The incidence of attack of *pourriture noble* was speedy in 1976. As a result of the mid-September rains and showers thereafter, the fungus spread rapidly once it had occurred, and as a result, even those whose policy is to get the harvest over as soon as possible made wine with the true taste of Sauternes. Fermentations were not easy, however. Some of the fruit had been bruised by the earlier storms. This led to premature oxidation resulting in some cases in wines of rather alarmingly deep colour, even in their infancy. Others who picked early made wine from fruit still engorged by the rain, and as a consequence wines with low acidity which became blowsy in due course. The wines therefore, while normally full, rich, sweet and with the taste of noble rot, vary between those with grip and backbone, and therefore depth and concentration, to those which are loose and lack finesse. Those in the former category are still vigorous, and will keep another twenty years. Those in the latter have evolved quickly and need drinking soon.

THE WEATHER: 1975

In 1975, in contrast, the harvest was small owing to frost damage in the spring. This particularly affected the crop in Barsac, as it always does, for the land is lower. Thereafter, the spring and the early part of the summer was dry and warm, with a period of intense heat – temperatures within a whisker of blood heat – at the end of July and beginning of August.

For the next six weeks it alternated between being wet and miserable and warm and sunny. The weather was extremely changeable, and hardly had one brief fine spell dried up the vegetation when the skies would darken again and another bout of rain would threaten. Nevertheless the fruit remained healthy and just before the harvest was due to begin for the red and dry white wines the weather cleared. Throughout October the skies remained clear, the temperatures warm, and the Sauternes grapes were able to gradually acquire noble rot without any fears that it might suddenly change to being 'ignoble'.

These properties who dared to delay the harvest and make several *passages* in the vineyard were able so to do, and while the incidence of botrytis was not complete it was nevertheless higher than in both 1971 and 1970. The musts had good acidity, the fruit flavours were rich and clean and the levels of potential alcohol were high. Nearly everyone profited by that very fine *fin de saison*, except for those who in retrospect harvested too early.

THE BEST WINES

As can be seen from the notes below, the best wines of the 1975 vintage include Climens, Lafaurie-Peyraguey, Nairac, Sigalas-Rabaud and Doisy-Daëne. Of those not present Coutet, as I have said, is very good, though now needing drinking soon, and, like Rieussec, better in this vintage than in 1976. Château d'Yquem is glorious, still young; and Château de Fargues is very good. Doisy-Védrines is also a success. Clos-Haut-Peyraguey, D'Arche and Broustet are quite good. Rayne-Vigneau, Rabaud-Promis, De Malle and Guiraud, of those not noted below, are not to be recommended.

In 1976 the stars are Climens, even better than the 1975, Sigalas-Rabaud (ditto), Nairac, Doisy-Dubroca and Doisy-Daëne, with an honourable mention for Château Filhot, unexpectedly. Château d'Yquem is of course very fine, but I prefer the 1975. De Fargues is very good, Rieussec very luscious, but variable – it can be impressive; Coutet and Clos-Haut-Peyraguey are quite good, but fading. Guiraud, Rabaud-Promis and Rayne-Vigneau, among those not tasted below, are undistinguished. Lafaurie-Peyraguey, last time out, was acceptable, but not up to the standard of the 1975.

THE TASTING

I sampled the following wines in Sauternes in September 1993.

	Optimum Drinking	Mark out of 20

1976

Caillou Now–1997 13.0
Light gold colour. Some botrytis, but a little oily and cardboardy. Some built-in sulphur. Medium body. Quite high volatile acidity. Slightly petrolly on the finish. Some sweetness, some botrytis. But little class and not much lusciousness.

Climens Now–2010 Plus 19.0
Mid-gold colour. Still closed on the nose. A little sulphur. Full powerful, rich, and with plenty of botrytis. Very youthful. Medium-full. Rich, fat, no SO2 on the palate. Creamy and mature. More botrytis than the 1975, and even better complexity and dimension. Marvellous balance. Lovely.

Doisy-Daëne Now–2000 16.0
Light, fresh, golden colour. Some botrytis on the nose. Plenty of intensity. Good fruit and grip. Clean and stylish. Medium body. Fresh, clean and balanced. Never a blockbuster, and never very fat and luscious, though more so than the 1975. But it is vigorous, intense and complex. Long and classy. Very good. But an atypical 1976.

Doisy-Dubroca Now–2000 Plus 16.5
Mid-gold colour. Quite rich. A little dominated by sulphur on the nose. On the palate it is a little better. Medium weight. Slightly fatter than Daëne. A bit more botrytis. Good intensity. Very Barsac. Rich and composed on the finish. Very good plus.

Filhot Now–1999 15.0
Gently bronzed gold colour. Fat and sweet on the nose, but lacks the concentration and grip of a really botrytized wine. Medium body, fresh and sweet and quite honeyed and persistent. But neither fat nor luscious. Some botrytis though. Quite long. Good.

Lafaurie-Peyraguey — —
Quite a deep bronzed gold colour. This has now

become a bit aged. Rather oily and petrolly on the nose. Bitter too. On the palate the wine is way past its best. And it is difficult to see what the best was. The second bottle was identical.

Nairac   Now–2005   17.0
(Magnum) Full rich gold colour. Youthful, fresh, concentrated nose. This has a lot of complexity and class. Plenty of *pourriture noble* as well. Like the 1975 the wood gives it a bit of a hard edge and hides the fruit. But medium-full, fresh, very vigorous and with plenty of depth. Bags of life. Very good indeed.

Sigalas-Rabaud   Now–2000 Plus   17.5
Gently bronzed gold colour. Closed nose, but good class and intensity. Complex fruit here and good botrytis. Medium-full. Gently luscious. Fat. Persistent. Lovely soft honeyed fruit. Rich and round. Voluptuous yet very Bommes, not Sauternes. Classy. Fine.

Suduiraut   Drink soon   13.0
Fully golden colour. The nose, once sweeter and richer than the 1975, has lost intensity and became a little coarse. On the palate the attack is sweet and honeyed, showing some botrytis but then it tails off. Unexciting.

La Tour-Blanche   Now–2000 Plus   14.5
Medium-gold colour. Broad nose. Quite sweet and honeyed. But a lack of grip. Has lost intensity. A little coarse. Medium-full. Rich and fat but rather sulphury. Good originally, but the sulphur was laid on with far too heavy a hand. A pity. The finish is fresh, vigorous and long. Even intense. Quite good plus.

1975

Caillou   Now–1997   13.0
Light golden colour. Slightly heavy on the nose. Fat but fresh. Not much botrytis. A little dead sulphur. Quite fresh and peachy-sweet on the palate. Medium body. Good acidity. But not very stylish. Holding up quite well. Not bad.

Climens   Now–2010   18.5
Mid-gold colour. Fine nose. Full, *liquoreux*, rich, concentrated. A lovely example. Honeyed, vigorous, complex, fullish. Some *pourriture noble*. Very good grip. Expansive luscious classy finish. Lots of future still. Very fine quality.

Doisy-Daëne   Now–1999   15.5
Light, fresh, golden colour. Elegant, youthful, flowery nose. Good intensity, lovely harmony. A

lightish wine. No real concentration and no botrytis. But fresh and balanced. Complex and long on the palate. Good plus.

Doisy-Dubroca   Drink soon   14.5
Mid-gold colour. Sweet, quite concentrated nose. Slightly burnt. Medium weight. Quite fresh and classy. But a little one-dimensional. Only a modicum of botrytis. Pleasantly sweet and honeyed, but for drinking soon. Quite good plus.

Filhot   Now–1997   13.5
Mid-gold colour. Beeswaxy nose. Quite sweet. Not very intense. Medium weight. Not a lot of botrytis. Medium body. Merely sweet and never a wine of any great fat or complexity. Quite fresh still but rather anonymous. Not bad plus.

Lafaurie-Peyraguey   Now–2005   18.0
Gently bronzed gold colour. Fat, rich, concentrated nose. Botrytis here, new oak too. Plenty of depth and style. Full, oaky, caramelly and concentrated on the palate. Vanilla and cream. Fat and voluptuous but with very good grip. Not quite as classy as Climens but certainly fine.

Nairac   Now–2000   16.0
Rich gold colour. Quite a lot of oak on the nose, rather dominating the fruit. But there is richness and botrytis underneath. On the palate there is good intensity but not much fat. It is just a little rigid. But it is classy and complex. Very good.

Sigalas-Rabaud   Now–1998   15.5
Mid-gold colour. The nose is a little pinched, as it evolved it became gently marmaladey. Interesting and stylish. On the palate this is medium-bodied but gently fat and luscious. Sweet and quite intense, but the flavours are a little burnt. Yet the finish is long and clean. Good plus.

Suduiraut   Drink soon   13.0
Quite a deep gold colour. Broad nose. A little blowsy. Gently sweet. But not much grip. A little built-in sulphur. On the palate light-medium body. Some sweetness but no botrytis. It is a bit flabby and the finish is a little astringent now. Getting thin and insipid.

La Tour-Blanche   Now–1997   13.0
(Half-bottle) Deep gold colour. A little coarse on the nose. Some built-in sulphur. All you can discern underneath is a bit of sweetness. On the palate it is fullish, sweet and quite fat, and still reasonably vigorous, but the sulphur dominates. No botrytis. Rather coarse.

1962 SAUTERNES

When I look back over the succession of Sauternes vintages since the war I am reminded of the harvests in the Old Testament. There are lean years and there are years of plenty. Success and failure seems to be cyclical. Of late, with four fine vintages: 1986, 1988, 1989 and 1990 following 1983 we have enjoyed a period of plenty. And for this, as we say before we sit down to dinner, may the Lord make us truly thankful.

But prior to 1983 there was a long sequence of famine. The decades of the 1960s and 1970s produced few successful Sauternes vintages, and because of the vicious circle of a declining demand, a lack of profit and a dearth of investment, even when the weather was auspicious, few could take advantage and the results were consequently uneven.

The previous cycle of plenty, which itself followed the lean and depressing 1930s, started in 1945 and continued until 1962. Of the fine vintages of the late 1940s, 1949 is perhaps the most glorious of all, though I have sampled some sumptuous 1947s. 1950 and 1953 are very good, and I have tasted a few good 1952s, though the Yquem crop was lost as a result of hail. 1955 is another delicious vintage; elegant and fruity and almost delicate, in conspicuous contrast to the luscious, almost muscular concentration of the 1959s. There are some surprisingly good 1958s, rather better than the red wines, though the 1961 sweet wine harvest is the reverse; good rather than superb. The last of this fine run is the 1962 vintage, and it is that which is the subject of this article.

THE WEATHER

Following a cold, wet spring, the flowering of the vine was retarded until the latter half of June, but passed off successfully. The summer that followed was hot, though not unduly dry, and a mixture of sun, warmth and showers in September unusually brought the Sauternes vines to the brink of harvest at the same time as the reds further north. Picking started at Château d'Yquem on 2 October. A fine Indian summer continued throughout the month and a large sweet wine harvest was brought in under ideal conditions.

THE WINE

The 1962s are consistent – indeed it would have been hard not to have made good sweet wine in the weather conditions which prevailed – and characterized by a plump, soft fruit and a fine, ripe acidity. The vintage is in the mould of 1955 rather than 1959. Balance and elegance rather than concentration and power are the key notes, though there is no lack of intensity and depth in the top wines. Perhaps the wines would have been bigger had the harvest been not quite so plentiful.

All Sauternes are delicious young, none more so than a 'feminine' vintage like 1962, and I remember sampling a whole series out of cask when I was in the area during a *stage* in the summer of 1964. Sauternes was bottled later in those days than it is today, and nearly all the classed growths left the wine in wood for a good two years after the vintage. I spent two long, hot days travelling round the Sauternais with one of the buyers for Calvet, culminating, appropriately, with my first visit to Yquem. Of course we did not taste the 1962 Yquem, but the newly arrived *régisseur*, Pierre Meslier, did open a bottle of the 1959. It was the first time I had ever tasted an Yquem, and I was so amazed by the wine I could not bear to spit it out. I don't think that M. Meslier approved.

My next sight of the 1962s was when they began to arrive in this country in 1966 or so. I remember a number of Barsacs, wines like Climens and Coutet, the Doisys Daëne and Védrines, both English – and château-bottled. They sold for 15 shillings (75 pence) to £1.00. Even Yquem was only £2.50 or so.

Today the vintage is over 30 years old, but the wines are still reasonably fresh and vigorous. They are fine but rare, only Yquem being a relatively common sight on the auction stage. For Yquem you will have to pay £200 or so, for the best of the rest £50 or more. If you can find a good bottle of Climens for £50 – no more than the current vintage of a *de luxe* Champagne after all – I suggest you snap it up. If you find a case, I'll go halves with you!

THE BEST WINES

Château d'Yquem is the only 1962 Sauternes I have seen in recent years with any degree of regularity, and my notes show consistent approval at a very high level. Château Guiraud was a wine I sold at the Malmaison Wine Club. It was very fine a decade ago and in all my notes since, save for one of the two bottles at the Studley Priory Wine Weekend in December, 1987. Suduiraut, not tasted below, is very fine as is La Tour-Blanche; Sigalas-Rabaud was more vigorous last time out, and I have good notes on Rabaud-Promis, Rayne-Vigneau and Caillou in recent years.

THE TASTING

The following wines were sampled in December 1989, at a tasting organized by La Réserve.

	Optimum Drinking	Mark out of 20
Climens	Now–2000	18.5

Golden colour. Rich, succulent, concentrated, complex and honeyed on the nose. Full, fat, rich and oaky on the palate. Simply lovely fruit. Very good vigour. This is a lovely wine which will last and last. Sumptuous and very elegant indeed.

Coutet	Drink soon	17.5

Medium golden colour; good *pourriture noble* on the nose, an elegant wine now fully mature if not showing a little age. Does not show the fat, weight and lusciousness of Climens. Ripe, quite full, plump, peachy. Honeyed, flowery and classy. Long and complex. Very typical Coutet at its best. Long, fragrant. Will still keep well.

Doisy-Védrines	Drink soon	16.0

Fresh golden colour. Very lovely balanced, elegant flowery-marmalady nose. Still fresh. Fullish, luscious, ripe, intensely sweet. Good grip on the palate but not quite as much as the nose indicated. It could do with a little more and it probably had this originally. Is fat and long on the palate though. Very good.

Gillette	Drink up	11.0

Light, golden colour. Dumb on the nose. Sugar here but neither botrytis nor suppleness. I find something rather chemical about this wine. One-dimensional, no class, no *pourriture noble*. Not really very fresh either.

Guiraud	Drink up	14.5

Quite a deep colour, almost a little old. An old nose, slightly resinny. Now lacks class. Sweet, some *pourriture noble* but has not lost grip and intensity.

Rieussec	Past its best	–

Medium golden colour. The nose has lightened up a bit and slightly coarsened. On the palate only the echo remains. Somewhat bitter, even, a little unclean and petrolly.

Sigalas-Rabaud	Drink up	15.0

Fresh golden colour. Fuller, richer and fatter on the nose than Doisy-Daëne but does not have the delicacy, nor the freshness, nor the elegance. Less intense. Quite full, the sugar has diminished a bit leaving a sweet toffee-spice aspect but a slight bitterness at the end. A bit past its best. Good.

d'Yquem	Now–2000	18.5

Deep golden colour. The nose is still very closed. Immensely rich, fat, almost heavy, luscious and concentrated, oaky and honeyed, but not quite as lovely as I had expected. Full and fat, very rich and sweet, fine *pourriture noble*. A lot of concentration. Delicious and still very fresh but not quite the fragrance and complexity and breed I anticipated, and therefore the intensity and grip. I've had even better bottles.

1949 SAUTERNES

Let us go back into history. Wine is a beverage as old as water. Whether it evolved by accident or design or a mixture of the two (which seems most likely), wine is unique. Grape juice is the one liquid that you can obtain from ripe fruit which possesses enough inherent sugar to ferment out on its own. It also happens to taste delicious, is very good for the metabolism, the heart, the soul and the digestion; and it is a great deal cleaner and freer from bacterial infection than water. But wine – dry wine – is a beverage. It was part of the everyday diet of that part of mankind fortunate enough to live in the sort of temperate, Mediterranean climate where the vine would grow successfully.

Sweet wine, on the other hand, was an indulgence. Sweet wine was something special, reserved for the rich; confined to high days and holidays; something to be sipped and savoured rather than quaffed to quench the thirst; something to be offered to honoured guests; something to save up for. Moreover sweet wines kept better than dry ones.

Long before the discovery of botrytized wines – again by accident or design or a combination of the two we do not know – sweet wines were a separate glory: a celebration which was a greater part of the art of good living than ordinary dry wines. Naturally those in a position to do so indulged themselves with sweet wine as often as they could. A mark of a person's standing could be measured by his consumption of sweet wines. And the visual proof of this was his girth. Fashions change, and sexual fashions as much as any, but throughout history until the modern era fat was beautiful, because fat meant prosperous and healthy. You only have to look at medieval pictures. Even what we would consider today to be the disfiguring results of an indulgence in sugar were considered attractive. Queen Elizabeth I of England was admired for her black teeth. It showed that her diet had no lack of sugar.

In those days all the great white wines were sweet. Probably the oldest wine anybody alive today has ever drunk was a bottle of *Steinwein* opened in London in 1961. The vintage was 1540. It was a freak vintage. The weather was so hot that the Rhine dried up. You could walk across. At the end of the summer some extraordinary wine was made from dried-out, over-ripe, shrivelled-up grapes. As was the custom, this celebrated vintage was commemorated by building a special, decorated cask. You can still see this one in the Residenz of the Prince-Bishops of Wurzburg. The wine in it must have been remarkable. It was not bottled until very late in the seventeenth century, 150 years later (no doubt it was to some extent topped up with similar wine of later vintages), and the last remaining bottles were kept in the cellar of King Ludwig of Bavaria in the nineteenth century, from which, via the auction house, a final bottle was opened in 1961. Sadly, nobody thought to invite me, but I am told that the wine was, albeit briefly, still alive, 421 years later.

The Rhineland was not the only place were sweet wines were revered, where viticulture's object was to produce a wine as sweet as possible and where the richer the wine, the higher the price it fetched. Let us take that romantic, misty and arcane part of eastern Hungary, hardly a midnight's carriage drive from Count Dracula's Transylvanian castle: Tokay.

It was in Tokay, legend has it, and in the mid seventeenth century – 100 or more years before it was discovered in Germany – that the noble fungus, *Botrytis cinerea*, first made its appearance. (In fact, Austrian scholars would dispute this. In 1526, three years before the first Turkish invasion, there was a famous vintage, made from nobly rotten grapes in the Burgenland. But, of course, the Burgenland was then part of Hungary, not Austria.) Tokay's most fabulous wine was its Essencia, notable for its properties both as an aphrodisiac and as an elixir of life. There are countless tales, and not all of them merely apocryphal, of the seemingly inert corpses of notables being restored to life by the administering of a tablespoonful of this magic golden liquid. And one Habsburg Count, indeed, bed-ridden and apparently well into his dotage, is said to have fathered a family of six when he was in his nineties, thanks to the restorative – or should I say invigorative – powers of this unique syrup.

France came late to the realization of the glories of botrytis-affected wine: not until the last half of the eighteenth century. But almost as soon as the Sauternais realized that botrytized wine was even better than merely over-ripe sweet wine, which they had been producing for centuries, the wines of the top properties such as Château d'Yquem began to command extravagant prices. In 1859, Duke Constantine, brother to the Czar of Russia, paid the incredible price of 20,000 francs for a cask of Yquem 1847, approximately four times the price of any other wine in France.

But it was not just today's recognized sweet white wine areas which produced honeyed ripe wine. All of France produced rich wines when weather permitted. Savennières was sweet as well as Vouvray and the Coteaux du Layon; Condrieu and Château Grillet and the small amount of white Châteauneuf-du-Pape were all sweet Rhône wines. So was nearly all champagne, until fashions changed in the 1870s. Even, as I found out when I sampled some venerable wines in Beaune a couple of years ago, Le Montrachet was a sweet wine in the finest of nineteenth century vintages. The great white wines were sweet wines.

Sweet wines continued to be admired and appreciated – and high prices paid for them – until the 1960s when a crisis of confidence set in which lasted until the mid-1980s. In 1922 and 1924, the second growth Sauternes, Château Broustet, fetched as much as a *premier cru* claret. Climens was half as much again. Yquem double that. As late as 1949 Château Rieussec sold for the same price as Château Margaux. Wine lists of the time show that the *Auslesen* and *Beerenauslesen* of Germany were no less highly prized. Both in the 1920s, and in the fifteen or so years after the Second World War, the succession of successful sweet wine vintages, in France as well as in Germany, was as regular as that of the red wines.

THE 1949 VINTAGE

One of the greatest of these vintages, fine for sweet wines as well as for reds, was 1949. After a fine summer and a very dry August, the beginning of September was stormy. As the harvest approached the weather improved though, and October was to turn out excellent. Down in the Sauternes area there were a few showers followed by clear sunny skies, enabling a satisfactory amount of botrytis to set in, facilitating the picking, which began in the last few days of the month, and resulting in a plentiful crop of must with high sugar readings and good acidity. Judging by the Yquems – the only Sauternes which I have been able to sample side by side on a regular basis – the 1949s are not as powerful as the 1945s, nor quite as luscious as the 1947s, but they are splendidly balanced: honeyed and rich, with undertones of apricot and peach. They have breed, they are opulent, and they have a flowery peachiness that makes one think of the 1962s, or the 1988s, closer to home. There is certainly plenty of life left in the top wines, even at more than 40 years of age.

THE TASTING

Some years ago Jeffrey Benson invited me to speak to a range of 1949s for the Wine and Dine Society. The star of the tasting was the Suduiraut, with Rabaud-Promis and Doisy-Védrines also showing well. The line-up below was rather more prestigious. The wines were tasted in October 1992.

Mark out of 20

d'Arche-Lafaurie — 15.0

Light golden colour. Fresh for the vintage. Medium-full, fat, lively. Caramelly on the finish. Good length.

Climens — 18.5

Golden colour. Full, concentrated nose. Fat and voluptuous. Concentrated and slightly burnt-caramelly. Rich, very good grip. This is long and complex and vigorous. Very fine.

Coutet 16.5

Very light amontillado colour. A concentrated nose with quite a bit of botrytis but loosening up. But elegant and classy. Still fresh. Barley-sugar rather than honey. On the palate a slight lack of grip. Very good indeed but not great.

Doisy-Daëne 17.5

Light golden colour. Lovely ripe, concentrated nose. Really classy. Medium-full. Rich, concentrated and fat. Very good grip. Intense and vigorous. Fine.

Filhot 14.5

Mid-gold colour. Good nose. Not as concentrated or as classy as the Doisy-Daëne but ripe and fleshy. But not as intense. Ripe but slightly blowsy and one-dimensional.

Gillette, *Tête de Cuvée* 12.5

Light amontillado colour. Full, slightly clumsy, barley-sugar nose. Melted barley-sugar flavour. Little acidity.

Guiraud 16.5

Mid-deep-gold colour. Oaky, fleshy, fat and rich. Some grip but not a lot of class. Luscious on the palate. Long and intense. This is surprisingly good. Complex even. Very good indeed.

Lafaurie-Peyraguey (See note)

Golden colour. This is corked but rich, fat and concentrated. Yet on the palate there is a slight hollowness. I have had better bottles. This property produced lovely wines in these days.

Rieussec 18.0

Golden colour. This is lovely and round and rich and soft. Very ripe and luscious. But gentle and intense. Fat, balanced, concentrated and delicious. Sweet and creamy. Very fine. Seductive.

d'Yquem 20.0

Light golden nose. Intense and concentrated but not a blockbuster on the nose. Full. Very, very concentrated. Still youthful. Marvellous, soft, very intensely sweet but concentrated fruit. Beautiful balance. *Grand vin.* Bags of life.

1947 SAUTERNES

The following wines were sampled at the Jan Paulson/Peter Baumann tasting in Linz, Austria, in November 1992. I have added a note on Château Bronstet sampled in May 1994.

	Optimum Drinking	Mark out of 20
Bronstet	Drink up	16.0

Light amantillado colour. Honeyed caramel and a touch of dill mustard – as in gravlax. Fresh. Medium body. Creamy. It is beginning to lose its fat and elegance. But still plenty of fruit and enjoyment and sweetness. Very good.

Caillou, *Crème de Tête*

Drink soon 15.0

Mid-gold colour. Strange nose. Somewhat sweaty, even corky. Sweetish. Has lightened up. I don't see much botrytis. A little cleaner and more positive on the palate. A gentle wine. Peachy fruit. But is beginning to show its age. Pity about the nose. Good length.

Climens Drink up 14.0

Light bronzed gold colour. This is the least vigorous of these last three wines. The fruit has dried up a little. On the palate there is style and depth, but it has lost its grip and fat and the finish is a touch bitter. Was fine. Now needs drinking. As it evolved even got a little dirty.

Coutet Now–2000 18.0

Light; mid-bronzed gold colour. This is fine. Full, very, very rich and concentrated on the nose. Fresh, new oak in evidence. Concentrated, fat and vigorous. This is a little more loose-knit than the Yquem but has lovely complex fruit. Flowery and peachy. Very good acidity. Positive finish – more so than Rabaud. Very fine.

Gillette Now–1997 14.5

Light gold colour. Fresh for the age. A little four-square on the nose. Rich full and sweet but not very stylish. Not a lot of noble rot. Medium-full on the palate. Some honey. Reasonable grip. But not much class. Good, just. But still has life. Lumpy, essentially.

Rabaud (Réuni) Now–2000 17.0

(Sigalas-Rabaud and Rabaud-Promis) Bronzed gold colour. Fat, slightly *crème brûlée* on the nose. Plenty of *pourriture noble.* Full, rich, sweet. On the palate the wine is ample, honeyed and well-balanced. Even concentrated. This is complex, rich and fine. Proper Sauternes. Fat. Long, vigorous, subtle finish. Lovely. Bags of life still.

d'Yquem Now–2000 Plus 19.0

Light to mid bronzed gold colour. Sweet nose, but without the fat of a 'real' Sauternes. Quite firm, good vigour. Concentrated and with plenty of depth nevertheless. Full and rich and honeyed on the palate. Fine quality. Concentrated. Very good grip. Long complex, vigorous finish. Very lovely balance. Powerful even. Lots of intensity. Still bags of life. More to it than the nose would indicate. Brilliant.

GLOSSARY

acetic The sweet/sour smell of vinegar given by a wine which has been affected by vinegar bacteria.

acid, acidity Essential constituent of a wine (though not in excess!). Gives zip and freshness and contributes to the balance and length on the palate.

aftertaste The residual taste-impression left in the mouth and memory after the wine has been swallowed or spat out.

alios Hard sandstone rock. A primary subsoil in the Bordeaux area.

amateur French for lover, in the sense of wine-lover.

à point Ready for drinking.

Appellation Contrôlée (AC) French legislative term referring to the top category of quality wines and the controls surrounding their production.

argile French for clay.

aroma The smell or 'nose' of a wine.

aromatic Flavours/constituents of smell: more than just the grape variety.

astringent Dry taste and finish of a wine which has lost some of its fruit.

austere Restrained, 'shy' taste – of a Médoc as opposed to the more open, accessible taste of a Saint-Emilion.

backbone Structure, implying body and grip.

baked Slightly burnt flavour resulting from a very hot dry vintage.

balance The harmony of a wine; its balance between body, fruit, alcohol and acidity.

batonnage Stirring up of the lees in a cask.

bead The 'tears' formed by a ripe, full wine on the side of the glass.

Belleyme Detailed map of the Bordeaux area produced in 1770s and 1780s.

Bien national Term given to estates sequestered and then sold by the state at the time of the French Revolution.

bitter Self-explanatory, but if not in excess, not necessarily a bad thing in an immature claret.

blackcurrants Said to be the characteristic fruit taste of Cabernet Sauvignon.

blowsy Fat but without enough zip, or acidity.

body The 'stuffing' or weight of a wine.

boisé Excess of a woody taste, resulting from a prolonged use of new oak.

bouquet The smell or 'nose' of a wine. A term used for mature rather than immature wine.

Bourgeois Denoting a wine of lower than 'classed growth' status. Applies particularly to properties in the Médoc and Haut-Médoc.

Bourgeois supérieur The best of the above; applies to Haut-Médoc properties.

breed Finesse, distinction.

Cabernet Sauvignon One of the classic – if not *the* classic – grapes of Bordeaux: see introduction.

caillou French for pebble.

calcaire French for limestone.

cépage French for vine variety.

chai(s) Outbuildings, cellars, where wine is made and matured.

chapeau The 'cap' of accumulation of grape skins etc., which tends to rise to the top of the must during fermentation.

chaptalisation Addition of sugar to the must with a view to increasing the eventual alcoholic content of the wine.

character Self-explanatory: the depth or complexity.

château The country house or villa on a Bordeaux wine estate.

coarse Lacking finesse and possibly not very well made.

Cocks and Féret Authors of the 'Bible of Bordeaux'. *Bordeaux et Ses Vins* lists all the main properties and other information. Has been republished in a number of editions since first appearing in 1850.

commune French for parish.

corked, corky An off, oxidized and dirty smell owing to a defective or diseased cork.

coulure Failure of a vine's flowers to set into grapes. Results from poor, humid weather during the flowering.

courtier French for wine broker – the 'middle-man' between the grower and the négociant.

creamy A richness and concentration in a wine's character and flavour as a result of old vines.

croupe French term for a gravel ridge or mound. Highly suitable soil for vines, particularly in the Médoc.

cru French term for 'growth', or vineyard and the vines thereof.

cru classé Officially classed growth: see introduction.

cuvaison The (length of) time a red wine must macerates with the skins.

cuve French term for wine vat.

cuvée The contents of a wine vat: used to denote a blend or particular parcel of wine.

cuvier, cuverie French for the vat house or part of the cellar where the vinification takes place.

cébourbage Term for the process of allowing must to settle and deposit soil particles and other sediment before fermentation is allowed to commence.

débourrement French term for 'bud-break'.

delicate Charm and balance in a wine of light style.

demi-muids A cask of capacity, larger than a hogshead.

département French for county.

depth Subtlety, 'dimensions' of flavour.

deuxième marque/vin Second wine: hence the produce of the less good vats or less mature wines.

domaine Estate

dry Opposite of sweet. Sometimes, when used of a wine, indicates a lack of ripe fruit.

dull Boring, uninteresting, absence of character and complexity.

dumb Used for an immature wine which has character but is still undeveloped.

earthy Character deriving from the nature of the soil. Not necessarily be a pejorative expression.

eclaircissage Crop-thinning by removal of buds or embryonic grape bunches.

ecoulage French term for the process of draining wine off the residual skins, pips etc. after cuvaison is completed.

égrappage à la main Hand de-stalking.

égrappoir Machine which de-stalks.

elegant Style, finesse.

elevage Literally the 'rearing'. In wine used to denote the length of time and processes undergone between vinification and bottling.

en fermage Tenant farming.

en primeur Sale of the young wine within the first few months of the harvest.

encépagement Proportion of grape varieties.

fat Full in the sense of high in glycerine, ripeness and extract.

feuillaison Coming into leaf.

finesse Style, breed, distinction.

finish The 'conclusion' of the taste of a wine.

first growth The top wines in a classification. Traditionally used for the four wines: Lafite, Latour, Margaux and Haut-Brion, so classed in 1855.

flat Dull, lacking in zip of acidity.

floraison Flowering of the vine.

foudre Large oak vat.

fouloir-égrappoir Crushing and de-stalking machine.

four-square Somewhat solid and heavy and as a result lacking zip and finesse.

Franck, Wilhelm Author of *Traité sur les Vins du Médoc*, etc., etc. First published in 1824, and revised several times during the next generation, this was one of the first works comprehensively to cover the wines of the Bordeaux area.

full (bodied) Ample body. High in extract and (probably) alcohol and tannin.

gelée French for frost.

goût de terroir Earthy, though not necessarily in a pejorative sense. Denoting literally a 'taste of soil'.

grand cru 'Great Growth': without the qualification *classé* need not necessarily mean anything.

grand cru classé 'Classed great growth': a term used in the official classifications of the Graves and Saint-Emilion.

grand vin The first wine, i.e. product or blend which will eventually be bottled under the château name. Can also be used, of course, simply in its literal, complimentary sense.

graves French for gravel.

green Used to describe an unripe flavour, possibly also denotes the produce of immature vines.

green harvest Removal of excess bunches of grapes before veraison.

grêle French for hail.

grip Opposite to flat or flabby. Satisfactory acidity level which 'finishes' the taste-impression off well. Applies particularly to wines with a level of youth in them.

guyot Eponymous system of long-cane pruning.

hard Firmness of an immature wine normally denoting plenty of body, tannin and acidity as yet unmellowed.

harsh As above, but in a fiery way, i.e. perhaps to excess.

heavy Denoting a full, alcoholic wine; could be used where it is rather too full-bodied, perhaps out of balance and 'stewed'.

hectare International measure of area; equivalent to 2.471 acres.

hectolitre International measure of capacity; 100 litres equivalent to 11 cases of wine or 22 Imperial gallons.

hogshead English name for the traditional Bordeaux barrel, holding 49.5 Imperial gallons or 225 litres.

horizontal tasting Tasting of a group of wines of the same vintage.

INAO Institut National Des Appellations D'origine. french Government Body Which Legislates vine-growing and wine-making controls.

Indivision Joint possession (of a property between a large number of heirs).

inky A rather stewed, metallic taste.

lees Sediment or deposit of dead yeast cells, tartrate crystals etc. which settles out of a wine.

lieu-dit Place-name.

long (on the palate) Finish continues for some time and has complexity and interest.

maderized Combination of oxidized and volatile acidity flavour in a wine which has been badly stored or is over the hill.

Maître de chai Cellar-master or manager.

Malbec One of the main grapes of the Bordeaux area: see introduction.

Marne Marl, a clay-limestone soil.

meaty Full, rich, fat wine, normally used of a wine still young, with a tannic grip – almost a chewable quality.

mellow Round, soft, mature – no longer hard, firm or harsh.

Merlot One of the most important grapes of the Bordeaux area, particularly in Saint-Emilion and Pomerol: see introduction.

mildew A cryptogamic or fungus disease of the vine. Counteracted by the application of copper-sulphate solution. Also known as 'downy' mildew.

Millérandage Shot berries. As a result of poor flowering some of the berries fail to develop.

millésime Vintage year.

Muscadet a subsiduary white wine variety

must Grape juice which has not yet fully fermented out and become wine.

négoce Collective term for the wine trade or merchants in Bordeaux or elsewhere.

négociant A wine-merchant.

neutral Self-explanatory: absence of character but without any positive defect save that.

noble Top quality, breed, distinction.

oenology Science of wine and wine-making.

off-taste An alien smell or flavour.

oïdium Or 'powdery' mildew. A cryptogamic or fungus disease of the vine. Counteracted by the application of sulphur.

ouillage Literally ullage: applied to the *élevage* of wine it means the regular topping up of the barrels to replace wine lost through evaporation.

oxidized Flat, tired taint in a wine which has at some time had excessive exposure to air.

palus Alluvial land closest to the Gironde estuary. Not suitable for the production of fine wine.

petit verdot Late-maturing grape givin good acidity, backbone and colour. Rarely seen outside the top Médoc estates.

phylloxera A parasitic disease of the vine caused by a member of the aphid family. The problem is held at bay by grafting European vines on to phylloxera-resistant American root-stock.

Pijassou, René Professor René Pijassou of Bordeaux University has done an immense amount of pioneering research into the history of wine and the major estates in Bordeaux. His thesis, *Le Médoc*, was published in 1980.

PLC Plafond Limité de Classement. Percentage which can be added to the yearly authorized yield, subject to tasting.

porte-greffe Rootstock.

pourriture grise 'Grey rot' caused by the same fungus that is responsible for 'noble' rot in Sauternes and elsewhere, but occurring in wet, humid weather. The grape skins can now to some extent rendered resistant to rot by sprays.

premier cru (classé) First (classed) growth.

président à mortier A vice-president of the Bordeaux *parlement*, so-called after the mortar-board headgear.

puissance Literally power, but when used of wine it means more than that, more the kinetic energy of a youngish wine.

rack(ing) To pump out or empty off and separate the clear wine in a cask from its lees.

récolte Harvest.

régisseur Bailiff, estate manager.

rendement Quantitative harvest, the yield.

réserve du château Specially selected superior *cuvée* created by some Bordeaux properties.

resinous Not, in the case of Bordeaux, used literally! Indicating a suggestion of resin.

rich For red wines, doesn't indicate sweetness, more a combination of fullness of body, abundance of ripe fruit, extract and probably alcohol.

ripe The result and a confirmation of healthy fruit picked in a ripe condition, giving richness and fullness of flavour to a wine.

robust Full not round, slightly tough, hard and perhaps earthy; possibly also a bit coarse.

rootstock The American base on to which European vines have been grafted since the phylloxera epidemic.

round Soft and mellow, a characteristic of a mature wine.

Sauvignon Important grape variety, especially for dry wines: see introduction

Sémillon *The* Sauternes grape; equally important for dry white wines: see introduction.

severe Hard, austere, unforthcoming. A characteristic of an immature wine.

sharp An excessive, normally youthful, acidity, possibly sour.

silky Soft yet rich-textured, implying ripeness and fullness.

smoky A self-explanatory description of particular aromas.

smooth Round, no hard edges, even silky.

soft Looser-textured than the above, round, mellow, normally mature.

sous-sol French for subsoil.

soutirage French for racking.

spicy Richly aromatic, strong-flavoured.

stage Colloquial French word for a period of time worked as a student with a French *négociant* or grower.

stalky A 'green', rather raw, possibly stewed flavour particularly noticeable in young wine. Can derive from over-long maceration with the stalks.

style/stylish Breed, finesse, character.

superficial Lacking depth and complexity.

supple Absence of hard edges, round, yet not without vigour and grip.

sur souche Purchase (and sale) of wine in advance of the harvests.

sur-maturité An optimum ripeness, which may be associated with a marginal deficiency of acidity.

Syrah Classic grape variety of the northern Rhône, planted in the Gironde up to the first half of the nineteenth century, but no longer authorized.

tannin An essential constituent of young red wine. An acid deriving from the skins of the grape which leaves an astringent, chewy taste in the mouth. Adds to the weight of the wine. Broken down and mellowed by ageing.

tartaric acid Natural acid in grapes, and the base by which the acidity is measured.

terrier The manifest of an estate.

thin Deficient in body and substance, watery.

tonneau Measure of the production of a Bordeaux estate; equivalent to four hogsheads or 1,000 dozen.

tonnellerie Part of the *chai* where hogsheads are made and mended.

tough Full-bodied, hard, tannic, perhaps robust; if young, may soften when mature: also used of over-balanced older wines.

tranche Literally 'slice'; a portion of the yield.

tri, triage The sorting through of the fruit to eliminate the substandard.

velvety Silky, opulent, rich, smooth.

vendange Harvest.

vendange verte Removal of excess bunches of grapes before veraison.

veraison The point at which the ripening grapes begin to turn into their mature colour, i.e. from green to black in the case of a red wine estate.

vertical tasting Tasting of a number of vintages of the same property.

vignoble Vineyard area.

vigorous Lively, balanced flavour with grip and some element of youth.

vin de presse Wine produced from pressing the skins, pips etc., after the free-run juice has been tapped off. Usually high in tannin and acidity, the incorporation of a judicious amount of *vin de presse* can add backbone to the blend.

viniculture All that is involved in the production of the wine.

vinification The process of wine-making.

vinothèque Library or collection of wine bottles.

vintage The year of the harvest.

viticulture All that is involved in the rearing of the vines and the production of its fruit.

volatile (acidity) Present in all wine; yet when used refers to an excess, a whiff of sweet-sour vinegar.

well balanced Harmonious, the constituents of the wine.

woody Normally used in a pejorative sense not so much referring to an excess of oak-ageing (new or old) as to an off-taste due to a faulty stave.

BIBLIOGRAPHY

ALLEN, H. Warner
The Wines of France, 1924 (London)
The Romance of Wine, 1931 (London)
Natural Red Wines, 1951 (London)
Through the Wine Glass, 1954 (London)
A History of Wine, 1961 (London)
AUSSEL, Pierre
La Gironde à Vol d'Oiseau, 1865 (Bordeaux)
BARTON, Anthony and Petit-Castelli, Claude
La Saga des Bartons, 1991 (Paris)
BAUREIN, Abbé J.
Variétés Bordelaises (originally published in 6 volumes) 1784–86. (Bordeaux) 2nd edition G. Meron, 1876 (4 volumes)
BENSON, Jeffrey and Mackenzie, Alastair
Sauternes, 1979 (London)
The Wines of Saint-Emilion and Pomerol, 1983 (London)
BERRY, Charles Walter
Viniana, 1929 (London)
A Miscellany of Wine, 1932 (London)
In Search of Wine, 1935 (London)
BERT, Pierre
In Vino Veritas: L'Affaire des Vins de Bordeaux, 1975 (Paris)
BERTALL (real name ARNOUX)
La Vigne: Voyage Autour des Vins de France, 1878 (Paris)
BOLTER, William
The Red Wines of Bordeaux, 1988 (London)
The White Wines of Bordeaux, 1988 (London)
BRIGGS, Asa
Haut-Brion, 1994 (London)
BROADBENT, J. Michael
The Great Vintage Wine Book, 1980 (London)
The Great Vintage Wine Book II, 1992 (London)
BROOK, Stephen
Liquid Gold, 1987 (London)
BUTEL, P.
'Grand Propriétaires et Production des Vins du Médoc au XVIIIe Siècle', article in *Le Médoc*, 1964.
CAMPBELL, Ian Maxwell
Wayward Tendrils of the Vine, 1947 (London)
Reminiscences of a Vintner, 1951 (London)
CASSAGNAC, Paul de
French Wines, translated by Guy Knowles, 1930 (London)
COATES, Clive
Claret, 1982 (London)
The Wines of France, 1991 (London)
COCKS, Charles   *Bordeaux, Its Wines and the Claret Country*, 1846 (London)
COCKS, Charles and Féret, Edouard
Bordeaux et Ses Vins, various editions in English and French, 1850–1991 (Bordeaux)
CRESTIN-BILLET, Frédérique
Les Châteaux du Médoc, 1988 (France)
Les Châteaux de Saint Emilion, 1989 (France)
Les Châteaux de Sauternes et Graves, 1990 (France)
D'ARMAILHACQ, Armand
De la Culture des Vignes, de la Vinification et des Vins dans le Médoc, various editions, 1855–1867 (Bordeaux)

DANFLOU, Alfred
Les Grands Crus Bordelais, 1867 (Bordeaux)
DION, Roger
Histoire de la Vigne et du Vin en France des Origines au XIXème Siècle, 1959 (Paris)
DOUFRELANT, Pierre-Marie
Les Bons Vins et les Autres, 1976 (Paris)
DOVAZ, Michel
Encyclopédie des Crus Classés du Bordelais, 1981 (France)
The Good Wines of Bordeaux, 1980 (London)
DUIJKER, Hubrecht
The Great Wine Châteaux of Bordeaux, 1975 (London)
ENJALBERT, Henri
Comment Naissent les Grands Crus, Annales ESC 1953
(ed) *Les Grands Vins de Saint-Emilion, Pomerol et Fronsac*, 1985 (Paris)
EYRES, Harry
Wine Dynasties of Europe, 1990 (London)
FAITH, Nicolas
The Winemakers, 1978 (London)
Château Margaux, 1980 (London)
Victorian Vineyard, 1983 (London)
Château Latour, 1992 (London)
Château Beychevelle, 1991 (France)
FÉRET, Edouard
Saint-Emilion et Ses Vins, 1893 (Bordeaux)
FORSTER, Robert
'The Noble Wine Producers of the Bordelais in the Eighteenth Century', article in the *Economic History Review*, 1961
FRANCIS, A.D.
The Wine Trade, 1972 (London)
FRANCK, Wilhelm
Traité sur les Vins du Médoc et les Autres Rouges du Département de la Gironde, various editions, 1824–1871 (Bordeaux)
GALET, P.
Cépages et Vignobles de France, 1958 (Montpellier)
GINESTET, Bernard
La Bouille Bordelaise, 1975 (Paris)
Margaux, 1984 (Paris)
Saint-Julien, 1984 (Paris)
Pauillac, 1985 (Paris)
Saint-Estèphe, 1985 (Paris)
Médoc, 1989 (Paris)
Saint-Emilion, 1986 (Paris)
Pomerol, 1984 (Paris)
Barsac, Sauternes, 1987 (Paris)
GUILLON, Edouard
Les Châteaux Historiques et Vignobles de la Gironde, 4 volumes, 1867–1870
HEALY, Maurice
Claret and the White Wines of Bordeaux, 1934 (London)
Stay with Me Flagons, 1940 (London)
HENDERSON, Alexander
The History of Ancient and Modern Wines, 1824 (London)

HIGOUNET, Charles
   (Ed.) *Histoire de Bordeaux*, 6 volumes, 1962–1969 (Bordeaux)
   La Seigneurie et le Vignoble de Château Latour, 2 volumes, 1974 (Bordeaux)
HYAMS, Edward
   Dionysus: A Social History of the Vine, 1965 (London)
JAMES, Marjory
   Studies in the Medieval Wine Trade, 1971 (Oxford)
JOHNSON, Hugh
   The World Atlas of Wine, revised edition, 1985 (London)
   The Story of Wine, 1989 (London)
JULIEN, André
   Topographie de Tous les Vignobles Connus, various editions 1832 (Paris)
JULLIAN, Camille
   Histoire de Bordeaux (2 vols), 1985 (Paris)
KAY, Billy and Maclean, Cailean
   Knee Deep in Claret, 1983 (Edinburgh)
KRESSMANN, Edouard
   Le Guide des Vins et des Vignobles de France, 1975 (Paris-Bruxelles)
'G.A.K.'
   Clarets and Sauternes, 1920 (London)
LACHIVER, Marcel
   Vins, Vignes et Vignerons, Histoire du Vignoble Français, 1988 (Paris)
LAFFORGUE, Germain
   Le Vignoble Girondin, 1947 (Paris)
LAWRENCE, R.de Treville, Sr
   (Ed.) *Jefferson and Wine*, 1973 (Virginia, USA)
LICHINE, Alexis
   Guide to the Wines and Vineyards of France, revised edition 1987 (London)
   Encyclopeadia of Wines and Spirits, revised edition 1985 (London)
LITTLEWOOD, Joan
   Mouton-Baronne-Philippe, 1982 (London)
   Milady Vine, 1984 (London)
LORBAC, Charles (real name CABROL)
   Les Richesses Gastronomiques de la France: Les Vins de Bordeaux, 1867 (Strasbourg)
MALVESIN, Franz
   Histoire de la Vigne et du Vin en Aquitaine, 1919 (Bordeaux)
MALVESIN, T. and Féret, E.
   Le Médoc et Ses Vins, 1876 (Bordeaux)
MALVESIN, Théodore
   Histoire du Commerce de Bordeaux, 1892 (Bordeaux)
MARCHIOU, Gaston
   Bordeaux sous le Règne de la Vigne, 1947 (Bordeaux)
MONSEIGNEUR LE VIN (Georges Montorgueil)
   Le Vin de Bordeaux, volume 2, 1925 (Paris)
MOTHE, Florence
   Graves de Bordeaux, 1965 (Paris)
OLNEY, Richard
   Yquem, 1985 (Paris)
ORDISH, George
   The Great Wine Blight, 1972 (London)
PAGUIERRE, M.
   Classification et Description des Vins de Bordeaux et des Cépages Particuliers au Département de la Gironde: Mode de Culture, 1828 facsimile edition, 1977 (Bordeaux)
PARKER, Robert
   Bordeaux, 1986 (London), 2nd edition, 1992
   The Wine Advocate (no. 64)

PENNING-ROWSELL, Edmund
   The Wines of Bordeaux, 6th edition, 1989 (London)
   Latour, 1994 (London)
PEPPERCORN, David
   The Mitchell Beazley Guide to the Wines of Bordeaux, 1986 (London)
   Bordeaux, 2nd edition, 1991, (London)
PEYNAUD, Prof. Emile
   Le Goût du Vin, 1980 (Paris)
   Connaissance et Travail du Vin, 1981 (Paris) (The photograph on the cover is of Léon Thienpont in his *chais* at Vieux Château Certan)
PIJASSOU, René
   'Un Château du Médoc: Palmer', 1964 (Bordeaux, published in the journal *Le Médoc*)
   Le Médoc, 2 volumes, 1980 (Paris)
PLUMB, J.H.
   Men and Places, Chapter 12: 'Mr. Walpole's Wine', 1966 (London)
   Lafite, 1968 (London)
   Fide et Fortudine, The Story of a Vineyard, 1971 (London)
RAY, Cyril
   Mouton Rothschild, 1974 (London)
REDDING, Cyrus
   A History and Description of Modern Wines, 1833 (London)
RHODES, Anthony
   Princes of the Grape, 1975 (London)
RIBADIEU, Henri
   L'Histoire des Châteaux de la Gironde, 1856
   Histoire de Bordeaux pendant le Règne de Louis XVI, 1853 (Bordeaux)
ROBINSON, Jancis
   Vines, Grapes and Wines, 1986 (London)
ROGER, Prof. I.R.
   The Wines of Bordeaux, English edition, 1960 (London)
ROTHSCHILD, Philippe de
   Vivre la Vigne, 1981 (Paris)
SAINTSBURY, George
   Notes in a Cellar Book, 1920 (London)
SEELY, James
   Great Bordeaux Wines, 1986 (London)
SHAND, P. Morton
   A Book of French Wines, 1928 (London)
   Revised edition by Cyril Ray, 1964 (London)
SHAW, Thomas George
   Wine, The Vine and the Cellar, 1863 (London)
SICHEL, Allan and Peter
   Yearly Vintage Reports (1961–1994)
SIMON, André L.
   History of the Wine Trade in England, facsimile edition, 1964 (London)
   Bottlescrew Days, 1926 (London)
   Vintagewise, 1945 (London)
TERS, Didier
   Haut-Médoc, 1985 (Paris)
   Moulis et Listrac, 1990 (Paris)
VANDYKE PRICE, Pamela
   Guide to the Wines of Bordeaux, 1977 (London)
   French Vintage, 1986 (London)
   The Wines of the Graves, 1988 (London)
YOUNGER, William
   Gods, Men and Wine, 1966 (London)

INDEX

Estate and commune names refer to wines unless otherwise stated. For purposes of alphabetical order, 'de', 'le' etc. are ignored except where they are capitalized at the start of a name. Names which are sometimes divided into two words, such as 'Latour' and 'La Tour', are listed together. Abbreviations: Ch. = Château; com. = commune; est. = estate; fam. = family.

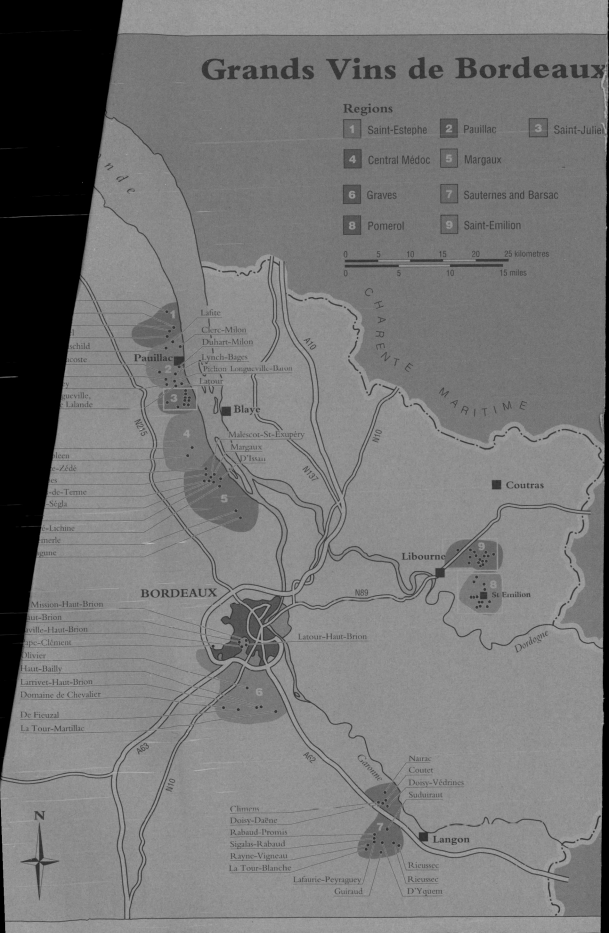

Grands Vins de Bordeaux

Regions

1 Saint-Estephe   **2** Pauillac   **3** Saint-Julie[n]

4 Central Médoc   **5** Margaux

6 Graves   **7** Sauternes and Barsac

8 Pomerol   **9** Saint-Emilion

0   5   10   15   20   25 kilometres

0   5   10   15 miles

CHARENTE MARITIME

Lafite
Clerc-Milon
Duhart-Milon
Lynch-Bages
Pichon Longueville-Baron
Latour

Pauillac

Blaye

Malescot-St-Exupéry
Margaux
D'Issan

Coutras

Libourne

St Emilion

BORDEAUX

Mission-Haut-Brion
Haut-Brion
aville-Haut-Brion
Pape-Clément
Olivier
Haut-Bailly
Larrivet-Haut-Brion
Domaine de Chevalier

De Fieuzal
La Tour-Martillac

Latour-Haut-Brion

Dordogne

N89

N215

N10

N137

A10

A63

A62

Garonne

Nairac
Coutet
Doisy-Védrines
Suduiraut

Climens
Doisy-Daëne
Rabaud-Promis
Sigalas-Rabaud
Rayne-Vigneau
La Tour-Blanche

Rieussec
Rieussec
D'Yquem

Lafaurie-Peyraguey
Guiraud

Langon

en
re-Zédé
es
-de-Terme
-Ségla

é-Lichine
rmerle
gune

N

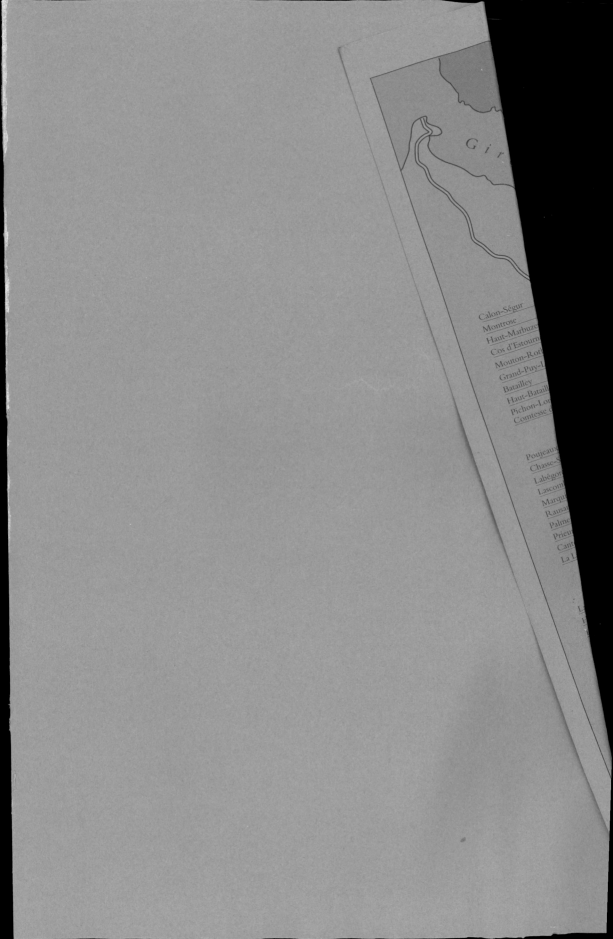

Gir*onde*

Calon-Ségur
Montrose
Haut-Marbuze
Cos d'Estourn
Mouton-Rot
Grand-Puy-
Batailley
Haut-Batail
Pichon-Lo
Comtesse

Poujeaux
Chasse-S
Labégor
Lascom
Marqui
Rausar
Palme
Prieu
Cant
La L